Principles of Multimedia

Principles of Multimedia introduces and explains the theoretical concepts related to the representation, storage, compression, transmission and processing of various multimedia components, including text, image, graphics, audio, video and animation, as well as their use across various applications. The book provides the necessary programming tools and analysis technique concepts to perform practical processing tasks in software labs and to solve numerical problems at the postgraduate level. For this new third edition, every chapter has been updated and the book has been carefully streamlined throughout.

Chapter 1 provides an overview of multimedia technology, including the definition, major characteristics, hardware, software, standards, technologies and relevant theorems with mathematical formulations. Chapter 2 covers text, including digital text representations, text editing and processing tools, text application areas and text file formats. Chapter 3 explores digital image input and output systems, image editing and processing tools, image application areas, image color management and image file formats. Chapter 4 discusses 2D and 3D graphics algorithms, transformation matrices, splines, fractals, vectors, projection application areas and graphics file formats. Chapter 5 covers audio, including digital audio input and output systems, audio editing and processing tools, audio application areas and audio file formats. Chapter 6 looks at video, including digital video input and output systems, video editing and processing tools, video application areas and video file formats. Chapter 7 focuses on animation, covering 2D and 3D animation algorithms, interpolations, modeling, texture mapping, lights, illumination models, camera, rendering, application areas and animation file formats. Finally, Chapter 8 covers compression, including lossless and lossy compression techniques, and various algorithms related to text image audio and video compression. Every chapter includes solved numerical problems, coding examples and references for further reading.

Including theoretical explanations, mathematical formulations, solved numerical problems and coding examples throughout, ***Principles of Multimedia*** is an ideal textbook for graduate and postgraduate students studying courses on image processing, speech and language processing, signal processing, video object detection and tracking, graphic design and modeling and related multimedia technologies.

Principles of Multimedia

Third Edition

Ranjan Parekh

CRC Press
Taylor & Francis Group
Boca Raton New York London

CRC Press is an imprint of the
Taylor & Francis Group, an informa business

Designed cover image: Ranjan Parekh

Third edition published 2025
by CRC Press
2385 NW Executive Center Drive, Suite 320, Boca Raton FL 33431

and by CRC Press
4 Park Square, Milton Park, Abingdon, Oxon, OX14 4RN

CRC Press is an imprint of Taylor & Francis Group, LLC

First edition published by McGraw-Hill 2006

British Library Cataloguing-in-Publication Data
A catalogue record for this book is available from the British Library

Library of Congress Cataloging-in-Publication Data
Names: Parekh, Ranjan, author.
Title: Principles of multimedia / Ranjan Parekh.
Description: 3rd edition. | Boca Raton ; London : CRC Press, 2025. |
Includes bibliographical references and index. | Contents: Text – Image – Graphics – Audio – Video – Animation – Compression. |
Identifiers: LCCN 2024029165 | ISBN 9781032643328 (hardback) | ISBN 9781032642949 (paperback) | ISBN 9781032643342 (ebook)
Subjects: LCSH: Multimedia systems. | Digital video. | Image processing–Digital techniques. | Sound–Recording and reproducing–Digital techniques. | MATLAB.
Classification: LCC QA76.575 .P345 2025 | DDC 006.7–dc23/eng/20240910
LC record available at https://lccn.loc.gov/2024029165

ISBN: 978-1-032-96109-5 (hbk)
ISBN: 978-1-032-96110-1 (pbk)
ISBN: 978-1-003-58803-0 (ebk)

DOI: 10.1201/9781003588030

Typeset in Palatino
by SPi Technologies India Pvt Ltd (Straive)

Dedicated to the Loving memory of my mother Uma Parekh (1936–2023)

Contents

Preface

I am pleased to bring out the 3rd edition of the *Principles of Multimedia* after a gap of ten years. In this edition attempts have been made to include the latest updates and standards that have come up over the past decade in the field of multimedia and at the same time reduce or remove concepts and applications that have become obsolete. Each chapter begins with a list of major key terms to give the reader a feel of a snapshot of the important ideas discussed in the chapter. These terms are expanded in the remaining sections of the chapter in their proper contexts. This edition comprises eight chapters, six for the media components and one each for the overview and compression technologies. Each chapter now contains a section on legal and ethical considerations, and another on the challenges and emerging trends. Numerical problems and MATLAB® coding are now discussed in dedicated sections at the end of the chapters. Also each chapter now contains its own reference section.

The new topics and sections added in this edition are outlined below:

Chapter 1: Multimedia – An Overview

Historical evolution of multimedia, hardware and software related to AR and VR, standalone and Web-based editing and authoring tools, APIs and libraries, standards and standards organizations, expanded lists of JPEG and MPEG standards, multimedia frontend and backend technologies, multimedia platforms, transport mechanisms, multimedia games and interactivity, multimedia content creation workflow, discrete wavelet transforms, legal and ethical considerations for multimedia products, challenges and emerging trends.

Chapter 2: Text

Historical evolution of digital text editing, details on Unicode character set, text extraction and transformation, text enhancement and effects, typography and fonts, Web-based design and applications including HTML, CSS, JavaScript, DHTML and SVG, text-to-speech (TTS) and speech-to-text (STT) applications, text localization and text internationalization, text in AR and VR applications, legal and ethical considerations in text processing, challenges and emerging trends.

Chapter 3: Image

Historical evolution of digital image processing and image processing applications like enhancement restoration segmentation, object detection in images, image analysis recognition and classification, legal and ethical considerations in image processing, challenges and emerging trends.

Chapter 4: Graphics

Historical evolution of 2D and 3D graphics, spline properties like length area and centroid, 3D rotation parallel to primary axes, 2D and 3D vectors, homogeneous vector equations, foreshortening factors, isometric diametric and trimetric projections, cavalier and cabinet projections, legal and ethical considerations in graphics production, challenges and emerging trends.

Chapter 5: Audio

Historical evolution of digital audio processing, progressive waves, key features of MIDI 2.0, audio segmentation, noise gate, dynamic range compression, legal and ethical considerations in audio production, challenges and emerging trends.

Chapter 6: Video

Historical evolution of digital video processing, video-based applications like blob detection, human detection, face detection and motion tracking, legal and ethical considerations in video production, challenges and emerging trends.

Chapter 7: Animation

Historical evolution of 2D and 3D animation, 3D surface equations, surface color and texture mapping, lights and illumination models, legal and ethical considerations in animation production, challenges and emerging trends.

Chapter 8: Compression

Historical evolution of compression techniques, LZ77, LZ78, LZW, quadtree segmentation, fractal compression, H.265 / HEVC.

In general, the book, like its previous editions, explains the concepts and principles of multimedia information processing and its applications, and, at the same time, provides hands-on techniques for solving numerical problems and writing program codes. The book has been written for graduate and postgraduate students studying courses on image, audio and video processing as well as 2D and 3D graphics modeling and animation. Objectives of the book include providing overviews of hardware and software technologies related to multimedia processing together with steps for problem-solving and practical implementations using data analysis and visualization tools.

As in previous editions, MATLAB has been used to illustrate the coding examples, primarily because of the extensive libraries of functions and toolkits supported by MATLAB which helps to decrease coding time and improve efficiency. A second reason is the benefit of the advanced visualization tools offered by MATLAB in the form of various types of 2D and 3D graphs, plots and figures for displaying image, graphics and video media components as well as playback of sample-based audio and MIDI notes. The number of MATLAB functions discussed has been increased significantly in this edition to more than 200 and a one-line description for each has been added where the functions are introduced for the first time as well as in the Appendix.

The book contains more than 90 solved numerical problems and more than 130 coding examples in MATLAB for hands-on practice in order to gain a deeper understanding of the subject matter and improve trouble shooting skills. More than 300 figures, illustrations, graphs and plots have been included to provide adequate pictorial representations and visualization aids to help understand the core concepts, especially those involving 3D environments. More than 170 references have been included for providing the sources of the information included in the book as well as for providing further reading materials to the interested reader. Wherever possible, website addresses have been mentioned to enable further studies and exploration regarding the latest updates and state-of-the-art advancements in the field. Queries and feedback can be addressed to the author via the e-mail ID author.principlesofmultimedia@yahoo.com, as well as to obtain a softcopy of the MATLAB codes on production of proof of purchase of the book.

Ranjan Parekh, PhD
Former Professor
Jadavpur University
Calcutta, India
2024

Author Biography

Dr. Ranjan Parekh, PhD (Engineering), is Former Professor, School of Education Technology, Jadavpur University, Calcutta, India. He teaches courses related to graphics and multimedia at postgraduate and doctorate levels, and his research interests include multimedia information processing, pattern recognition and computer vision.

He is also the author of the following books :

Fundamentals of Graphics using MATLAB (CRC Press, 2020) [https://www.routledge.com/Fundamentals-of-Graphics-Using-MATLAB/Parekh/p/book/9780367184827]

Fundamentals of Image Audio and Video Processing using MATLAB with Applications to Pattern Recognition (CRC Press, 2021) [https://www.routledge.com/Fundamentals-of-Image-Audio-and-Video-Processing-Using-MATLAB-With/Parekh/p/book/9780367895242]

1

Multimedia: An Overview

1.1 Multimedia Fundamentals

1.1.1 Key Terms

Hello Readers! We begin the book with a snapshot of the important terms relevant to multimedia technology, to present the contents of the entire chapter in a nutshell. These terms will be expanded in the following sections of the chapter in their proper contexts.

AR: Augmented reality (AR) is a technology that overlays digital information, such as images, text, or 3D models, onto the real-world environment, enhancing the user's perception and interaction with their surroundings. AR integrates computer-generated content seamlessly into the user's physical environment, offering an immersive and interactive experience that blurs the line between the digital and real worlds.

Artifacts: Unintended and undesirable alterations or distortions in digital images caused by compression, manipulations or other factors. These can include visual anomalies like blurriness, pixelation or color distortions, introduced during various types of signal processing.

CDN: A Content Delivery Network (CDN) is a network of distributed servers strategically positioned to deliver Web content, such as images, videos and scripts, to users based on their geographical locations. By caching and serving content from servers closer to the end-users, CDNs enhance website performance, reduce latency and improve overall user experience.

CMS: A Content Management System (CMS) is a software application that enables users to create, manage and modify digital content on a website without requiring specialized technical knowledge. CMS platforms provide a user-friendly interface for content creation, editing and organization, facilitating efficient website management for individuals and organizations.

CSS: Cascading Style Sheets (CSS) is a stylesheet language used to describe the presentation and formatting of a document written in HTML or XML. It enables Web developers to control the layout, design and appearance of Web pages by defining styles for elements such as fonts, colors, spacing and positioning.

DAM: Digital Asset Management (DAM) is a system that organizes, stores and retrieves digital assets such as images, videos and documents in a centralized and efficient manner. DAM solutions streamline the management and distribution of digital content, providing tools for version control, metadata tagging and collaborative workflows to enhance the overall accessibility and usability of digital assets within an organization.

DASH: Dynamic Adaptive Streaming over HTTP (DASH) is a standard for delivering multimedia content, such as videos, over the internet by dynamically adjusting the quality of the content based on the viewer's network conditions. DASH enables a smoother streaming experience by allowing the client device to adaptively switch between different quality levels of the video, optimizing playback for varying bandwidth and device capabilities.

DBMS: A Database Management System (DBMS) is software that facilitates the creation, organization, retrieval and management of data in a database. It provides an interface for users and applications to interact with the database, ensuring data integrity, security and efficient data handling operations.

DCT: Discrete Cosine Transform (DCT) is a mathematical operation commonly used in signal processing and image compression to transform spatial data into frequency components. It's widely employed in various multimedia applications, such as JPEG compression for images and MPEG compression for videos, helping reduce data redundancy and achieve more efficient storage or transmission.

DFT: The Discrete Fourier Transform (DFT) is a mathematical operation used to analyze

DOI: 10.1201/9781003588030-1

the frequency content of discrete signals or sequences. By converting a sequence of time-domain data points into its equivalent frequency-domain representation, the DFT is a fundamental process in fields like signal processing and telecommunications for analyzing and manipulating signals in the frequency domain.

DMCA: The Digital Millennium Copyright Act (DMCA) is a U.S. law enacted to address copyright challenges arising from digital technologies. It provides a framework for copyright holders to protect their content online and outlines procedures for service providers to respond to claims of copyright infringement.

DRM: Digital Rights Management (DRM) is a technology used to protect and control access to digital content, such as music, videos and e-books, by imposing restrictions on copying, sharing and modifying the content. DRM systems aim to prevent unauthorized distribution and ensure that users comply with licensing agreements, often through encryption and access control mechanisms.

DWT: The Discrete Wavelet Transform (DWT) is a mathematical operation to transform and analyze signals or images into different frequency components using small wave-like oscillations called wavelets as basis functions. DWT is used in signal processing and image compression and represents visual data in multiple resolutions by capturing both high and low-frequency information.

Euler Formula: Euler's formula on complex numbers is a mathematical identity that relates the exponential function, the imaginary unit (*i*), Euler's number (e), and the mathematical constant pi (π). The theorem is given by the formula: $e^{i\pi}+1=0$, expressing a profound connection between fundamental mathematical constants and complex numbers on the complex plane.

Fourier Theorem: Fourier's theorem states that any periodic function can be represented as the sum of sinusoidal functions (sine and cosine) with different frequencies and amplitudes. This mathematical concept is fundamental in signal processing, allowing complex waveforms to be analyzed and synthesized using simpler sinusoidal components.

HLS: HTTP Live Streaming (HLS) is a streaming protocol developed by Apple for delivering live and on-demand multimedia content over the internet. It uses standard HTTP protocols, allowing adaptive streaming of media content, dynamically adjusting the quality based on the viewer's network conditions for a smoother viewing experience.

HTML5: HTML5 is the latest version of the Hyper Text Markup Language, widely used for structuring and presenting content on the World Wide Web. It introduces new features and improvements, such as native support for audio and video embedding, canvas elements for graphics rendering, and enhanced semantic tags, contributing to a more dynamic and interactive Web experience.

Interactivity: Interactivity in multimedia refers to the capability of engaging the user through dynamic and responsive elements, allowing them to actively participate and influence the content. This can include interactive features such as clickable buttons, animations, quizzes or user-controlled navigation, enhancing the user experience and enabling a more engaging and personalized interaction with multimedia content.

JPEG 1: JPEG (Joint Photographic Experts Group) is a widely used image compression standard that employs lossy compression techniques to reduce the file size of digital images. JPEG 1, the initial version of the standard, was introduced in 1992, defining the baseline compression algorithm using DCT-based methods and encoding method for storing photographic images with good compression efficiency.

JPEG 2000: JPEG 2000 is an image compression standard introduced by the Joint Photographic Experts Group (JPEG) in the year 2000 which employs more advanced DWT-based compression techniques compared to the original JPEG which uses DCT. It enables signals to be represented using multiples resolutions and finds extensive applications in image compression and noise reduction.

MPEG 1: MPEG (Moving Picture Experts Group) 1 is an audio/video compression standard developed to provide VHS-quality video and CD-quality audio for digital storage and transmission. Introduced in 1991, MPEG-1 is widely known for its role in creating the popular MPEG-1 Audio Layer III format, commonly known as MP3, which revolutionized digital audio compression and distribution.

MPEG 2: MPEG-2 is a video compression standard designed for higher quality digital video transmission and storage. Introduced in 1995, MPEG-2 is widely used in DVDs, digital television broadcasting, and video streaming, providing improved video quality and support for interlaced video compared to its predecessor, MPEG-1.

MPEG 4: MPEG-4 is a versatile video compression standard that supports a wide range of multimedia applications, including streaming, broadcasting and interactive media. Introduced in 1999, MPEG-4 provides efficient compression while allowing for advanced features such as object-based coding, content-based interactivity and support for various multimedia formats, making it widely utilized in online video, mobile devices, and multimedia streaming.

MPEG 7: MPEG-7 is a multimedia content description standard that focuses on providing a standardized set of descriptors to describe multimedia content for search and retrieval purposes. Introduced in 2001, MPEG-7 aims to enable efficient indexing and searching of multimedia content, offering a standardized way to describe the visual, auditory and multimedia aspects of the data.

MPEG 21: MPEG-21 is a multimedia framework standard designed to enable transparent and augmented use of multimedia resources across various networks and devices. Introduced in 2001, MPEG-21 provides a comprehensive set of tools and standards to address content creation, delivery, consumption and protection, supporting a wide range of applications in the evolving landscape of multimedia technologies.

Non-Linearity: Non-linearity in multimedia refers to the ability for users to navigate and interact with content in a customized fashion, rather than viewing it linearly from begin to end. It allows them to choose different navigational paths and experiences within the multimedia content, enabling interactive storytelling, user-controlled exploration, simulations and feedback schemes.

Nyquist Theorem: Nyquist's theorem, also known as the Nyquist-Shannon sampling theorem, states that to accurately reconstruct a continuous signal, it must be sampled at a rate that is at least twice the highest frequency present in the signal, during digitization. This theorem is fundamental in digital signal processing and ensures that sampled signals can be faithfully reconstructed without loss of information.

SNR: Signal-to-Noise Ratio (SNR) is a measure used in signal processing to quantify the ratio of the strength of a signal to the level of background noise present. A higher SNR indicates a clearer and more reliable signal, while a lower SNR implies that the signal may be more challenging to discern from the surrounding noise.

SVG: Scalable Vector Graphics (SVG) is an XML-based file format used for describing vector graphics, which can be scaled to different sizes without losing quality. SVG is widely used on the Web for creating interactive and resolution-independent graphics, offering a versatile and lightweight format for displaying diagrams, figures and illustrations.

VR: Virtual Reality (VR) is a computer-generated simulation of an immersive environment that can be interacted with and explored by users. It typically involves the use of specialized hardware, such as headsets and controllers, to provide a sensory-rich experience that can simulate real or imaginary worlds.

WebGL: WebGL (Web Graphics Library) is a JavaScript API that enables rendering 3D and 2D graphics within Web browsers without the need for plug-ins. It allows developers to leverage the GPU (Graphics Processing Unit) to create high-performance interactive graphics directly in the browser, facilitating the development of sophisticated Web-based visualizations and games.

WebRTC: WebRTC (Web Real-Time Communication) is a free, open-source project that provides real-time communication capabilities directly in Web browsers through simple application programming interfaces (APIs). It allows for peer-to-peer communication, including audio and video calling, as well as data sharing, without the need for plug-ins or additional software installations.

WebVR: WebVR (Web Virtual Reality) is an API that allows developers to create virtual reality experiences that can be accessed directly through Web browsers. It enables users to explore VR content on compatible devices, fostering accessibility and ease of use for virtual reality applications on the Web.

WebXR: WebXR (Web Extended Reality) is an API that expands on WebVR to support a broader range of immersive technologies, including augmented reality (AR) and mixed reality (MR) experiences in addition to virtual reality (VR). It enables developers to create cross-platform, immersive Web-based experiences that can be accessed on various devices, from VR headsets to AR-enabled smartphones.

1.1.2 Definitions

The word "multimedia" comes from the Latin words "multus", which means numerous, and "media", which means middle or center. More recently, the word "media" (singular "medium") started to convey the sense "intermediary." "Multimedia" therefore means "multiple intermediaries" or "multiple means." The word "multimedia" may be used as a noun (e.g., multimedia is a new technological field) and as an adjective (e.g., a multimedia document). Multimedia, in the general sense, therefore, means "multiple intermediaries" between the source and sink of information or "multiple means" by which information is stored, transmitted, presented or perceived. In modern times we use six different means to convey information: text (e.g., book chapter, newspaper article), image (e.g., photograph, scanned document), graphics (e.g., sketch, drawing), sound (e.g., speech, music), video (e.g., TV program, movie clip), animation (e.g., cartoon, simulation).

Here are some definitions from extant literature:

> Multimedia refers to the integration of various media types, such as text, images, audio, video, and interactive elements, to convey information or entertainment through digital platforms.
>
> **(Valdez, 2006)**

> Multimedia is a technology that combines different forms of media content, enabling the presentation of information in a rich, interactive format, often delivered via computer systems.
>
> **(Sharda et al., 2018)**

> Multimedia encompasses the use of multiple communication channels, including visual, auditory, and interactive elements, to engage and inform audiences, often through digital media and technology.
>
> **(Steinmetz & Nahrstedt, 1995)**

> Multimedia involves the seamless integration of text, graphics, audio, video, and interactivity to create a dynamic, immersive user experience, commonly facilitated by computers and the internet.
>
> **(Vaughan, 2014)**

> Multimedia denotes the convergence of diverse media forms, allowing the simultaneous presentation of visual, auditory, and interactive content to convey messages, educate, entertain, or enhance user experiences in digital environments.
>
> **(Moreno, 2007)**

From the above we can summarize as follows: the term "multimedia" refers to an integrated multidisciplinary field which combines various media elements including text, image, graphics, audio, video, animation and interactivity to convey information.

1.1.3 Historical Evolution

The historical evolution of multimedia spans over several decades marked by significant technological advancements and innovations. Some of the key milestones are listed below:

1960s: The foundation for multimedia was laid with the development of early computer systems and graphical user interfaces. Ivan Sutherland's Sketchpad (Sutherland, 1963) is considered one of the earliest examples of interactive computer graphics.

1970s: Witnessed the emergence of computer-based interactive multimedia with the advent of laser discs and the development of text-based computer games. The first arcade video game, "Pong", was released in 1972, introducing interactive audio-visual entertainment. Alan Kay's work on the Dynabook concept laid the groundwork for portable, multimedia-enabled computing.

1980s: Marked the rise of personal computers, which brought multimedia capabilities to homes and offices. In 1984, Apple introduced the Macintosh, which featured a graphical user interface and could handle multimedia applications. The introduction of CD-ROMs (Compact Disc-Read Only Memory) allowed for the storage and distribution of multimedia content, including encyclopedias and educational software. MIDI (Musical Instrument Digital Interface) technology facilitated digital music composition and playback.

1990s: Turning point for multimedia, with the proliferation of multimedia software, games and educational CD-ROMs. The World Wide Web was born in 1991 (Berners-Lee, 1999) bringing multimedia to the internet. HTML (Hyper Text Markup Language) allowed for the integration of text, images and hyperlinks. The release of Adobe Flash in 1996 revolutionized Web multimedia, enabling animations, games and interactive content. Digital image and video compression standards, such as JPEG and MPEG, made it possible to view photographic images and videos online.

2000s: Witnessed the convergence of multimedia technologies on mobile devices, such as smartphones and tablets. YouTube, founded in 2005, became a platform for sharing and consuming multimedia content, including videos and music. High-definition (HD) and Blu-ray Disc technology provided superior multimedia experiences, with sharper images and better sound quality.

2010s: Saw the rise of streaming platforms like Netflix and Spotify, which delivered multimedia content over the internet, leading to the decline of physical media. Virtual reality (VR) and augmented reality (AR) gained momentum, offering immersive multimedia experiences. The development of 4K and 8K video resolutions enhanced the quality of multimedia content. Interactive storytelling and narrative-driven video games reached new heights.

2020s: Continue to see the evolution of multimedia with advancements in AI-driven content creation, 5G connectivity for seamless streaming and the growth of live streaming platforms.

1.1.4 Main Characteristics

To create a successful multimedia production it is important to incorporate some of the main characteristics as discussed below.

1.1.4.1 Multiple Media

The first characteristic of a multimedia presentation is, of course, the use of multiple media. Text has been the main mode of communication for many years during the pre-multimedia era, and still continues to be one, but it is now more and more supplemented by other media, which often prove more effective. Everybody has heard the phrase: "A picture is worth a thousand words." Going along those lines, a video must be worth a million. As computer technology progressed, in addition to text, pictures sound video and animation also started being used to communicate ideas. Pictures were subdivided into two types: the real-world pictures captured by a camera, called images, and the hand-drawn pictures like sketches, diagrams and portraits, called graphics. Text, images and graphics are together referred to as static elements, as they do not change over time. The usage of dynamic or time-varying elements like audio, video and animation began with further improvement in technology. Audio requires speakers to be played back and can comprise music, human speech or other environmental sounds like laughter, applause, horns, thunder and so on. Videos are combinations of images and sound; instead of a single image, a video is composed of a series of images shown one after another at a certain speed, while the sound is played together in the background in a synchronized manner with the visual content. Videos are referred to as motion picture, when they are recorded on film/celluloid and as motion video when recorded on electro-magnetic media. Animation is a combination of graphics and sound, a series of graphic pictures shown in a specific sequence along with the added sound. According to general convention a legitimate multimedia presentation should contain at least one static media, like text, image or graphics, and at least one dynamic media, like audio, video or animation, along with some form of interactivity and non-linearity. Different types of information might warrant the use of different types of media. For example, to show the exterior shape, size and color of a car, one would use photographic images; to show the internal parts of its combustion engine, one would prefer graphics with specific parts highlighted or detailed out if required; to depict how the pistons of its engine move or how the gearing system works, one would prefer animation; to exhibit the quality of its music system, one would use audio; and to give a sense of its pickup and braking systems, one would use video. In general, one should use static media like images and graphics if they are sufficient for explaining relevant concepts, (e.g., for depicting size, shape, color of objects) and use video only when images are not sufficient for the purpose, as video takes up a lot of space and their use should be justified (e.g., when explaining dynamic processes or moving parts). Animation is used in situations where capturing video is not practicable, e.g., when the objects are too small to be photographed (e.g., motions of sub-atomic particles), or too large (e.g., planetary bodies), or something difficult to photograph (e.g., electromagnetic waves). Text is usually used as bulleted points to highlight main concepts, while other media are used as supplementary information for better cognition.

1.1.4.2 Non-Linearity

Non-linearity indicates the capability of navigating from one point within a presentation to another point without appreciable delay. TV shows and motion pictures are considered linear presentations because the user has to watch the information being displayed, in a pre-defined sequential manner as determined by the producer or creator of the show. The sequence of frames or the timing between them cannot be changed if desired. Devices like the video cassette player allows some flexibility during playback of a recorded video cassette by enabling forward, backward, start, stop or pause operations; however, these cannot be done instantly as the tape has to rotate forward or backward to skip intermediate frames, which causes delays in displaying non-contiguous portions. In a multimedia presentation, the user is able to instantly navigate to different parts of the presentation without appreciable delays; however, such navigation is not arbitrary but only along the pathways defined by the author or developer. The author needs to ensure that the presentation behaves in a consistent manner irrespective of the sequence or order in which it is viewed.

1.1.4.3 Interactivity

To make non-linearity a possibility, a user needs to interact with a presentation. A linear presentation is usually watched passively without changing the order or sequence in which it is displayed. For a non-linear presentation, a user will have to specify the manner of non-linear navigation, e.g., directly navigate to an area of interest instead of watching something from the beginning. Such interaction is made possible through a set of interactivity elements embedded within the presentation like buttons, menu items or hyperlinks. To enable interactivity, a presentation should be able to accept user inputs and allow changing the sequence of information to be displayed. Interaction is not only limited to changing the order of display, a user can also interact to start/stop individual media elements within a presentation, e.g., click a button to start a video sequence within the presentation or pause the background music. Interactivity is a powerful tool and has potentials to achieve much more than simply switching on/off media elements: it allows one to get involved with the presentation content, like provide feedback, answer questions in a quiz, simulate an experiment and so on. This is considered very useful for applications like training and learning. It has been observed that human beings tend to remember only 20% of what they read, 40% of what they see and hear over an extended period of time, and 80% of what they do or experience. Multimedia-based education programs like CBTs (computer-based training) and CAIs (computer-aided instructions) try to exploit this property to create effective training and learning modules with better retentivity. On one hand, these use several media components to explain a subject matter more thoroughly from various aspects, and to create a more profound influence on the human mind; on the other hand, the modules are designed so as to provide ample scopes for interactivity like practice sessions, drills and tutorials to get the learner more involved. Interactivity is considered to be one of the salient features on which the new generation e-learning tools are expected to rely for greater effectiveness.

1.1.4.4 Digital Representation

Audio and video cassette players use media recorded on magnetic tapes in analog format. Magnetic tapes are called sequential access storage devices, wherein data is recorded sequentially along the length of the tape. When a specific portion of the data is required to be played back, the portion before it needs to be skipped. This creates a delay in accessing the arbitrary portions of the data which is unsuitable for requirements like teaching and learning. Multimedia productions provide instant access to different portions of the presentation using digital computers and random access devices like flash memory, hard disks and compact discs. Multimedia presentations are therefore produced and played back using digital representations. Each of the media types, like text, image, audio and video needs to be expressed in the digital form before it can be utilized within a multimedia presentation. Digital representation has other advantages too, like software-based programs that can be used to edit the digitized media in various ways to improve their quality and compress file sizes to increase performance efficiency (Steinmetz & Nahrstedt, 2004). Digitization of the media components requires specialized hardware, software, compression schemes and file formats.

1.1.4.5 Integrity

One would tend to believe that any set of media files played on a computer would comprise a multimedia presentation. For example, we can edit a text document in a word processor, play a video clip in the Media Player and listen to an Audio-CD using the CD-Player. All these applications collectively, however, would not constitute a multimedia presentation. To clarify that, we introduce another important characteristic of a multimedia presentation called integrity. It implies that although there may be several media types present and playing simultaneously, they need to be integrated or be part of a single entity, which is the presentation. We should not be able to separate out the various media and control them independently; rather they should be controlled from within the framework of the presentation. Moreover, the presentation should decide how the individual elements can be controlled. For example, it might or might not be possible to turn off the background audio depending on whether the developer has allowed it from within the presentation.

1.1.4.6 Narrative and Storytelling

A compelling narrative or storyline is often at the heart of a multimedia presentation. Stories create a logical flow and help the audience connect with the content on an emotional level. From interactive e-books and multimedia-rich documentaries to video games and virtual reality experiences, multimedia provides a versatile canvas for crafting compelling stories. It enables creators to engage their audiences on multiple sensory levels, enhancing emotional resonance and understanding. Multimedia also offers opportunities for user interaction and personalization, allowing consumers to actively participate in the unfolding narrative. Whether in entertainment, education, or marketing, the capacity to blend various media types results in storytelling that is not only informative and entertaining but also emotionally impactful, leaving a lasting impression on audiences (Nunes et al., 2017).

1.1.4.7 Informational Value

Multimedia presentations need to be informative and convey a message or share knowledge. Content should be accurate, well researched and relevant to the audience's needs or interests. Overloading the presentation with unnecessary media should be avoided. Through a seamless fusion of text, images, audio, video and interactive elements, multimedia presents information in a comprehensive and accessible manner. This convergence of media types enables content creators to provide context, depth and clarity to their messages, catering to diverse learning and communication styles. Since information needs of audiences differ, frequently a multimedia presentation would list out the pre-requisites of the target audience for which it has been designed and the objectives it is expected to fulfill in terms of learning out comes.

1.1.4.8 Adaptability and Compatibility

Multimedia presentations should be designed to work across various devices and platforms, including computers, tablets, and smartphones. Compatibility ensures that the audience can access the content easily. Multimedia presentations should be scalable to accommodate different screen sizes and resolutions. This ensures that the content remains visually appealing and functional on various devices. Additionally, multimedia files are often encoded in standard and open formats that are compatible with various software and hardware configurations, promoting interoperability. This ensures that presentation can be easily shared, integrated into different applications and enjoyed by a broad audience without the constraints of proprietary systems.

1.1.4.9 Engagement and User Experience

An effective multimedia presentation is designed with the user in mind. It aims to engage the audience and create a positive user experience through intuitive navigation and well-structured content. Multimedia content leverages the power of visuals, audio, and interactivity to immerse users in compelling experiences. From interactive storytelling to visually rich presentations and video games, multimedia heightens engagement by appealing to multiple senses and emotions. By catering to diverse learning styles and preferences, multimedia not only educates and entertains but also enhances retention and understanding. Its capacity to evoke emotions, deliver information effectively and offer interactive elements ensures that users remain deeply engaged and invested in the content, making it an invaluable tool for communication, entertainment, and education.

1.1.4.10 Feedback and Assessment

Interactive elements can include quizzes, surveys, or feedback forms to gather information from the audience or assess their understanding. Feedback mechanisms enhance the learning process. Use of analytics tools to track audience engagement and gather insights into how users interact with the presentation can lead to improvements for future presentations. In other interactive applications, multimedia allows users to make informed decisions, play games and explore virtual environments while receiving instant feedback on their actions. By facilitating this feedback loop, it opens up scopes for future improvements that cater more closely to user needs.

1.1.4.11 Accessibility and Consistency

Accessibility ensures that content can be enjoyed and understood by a diverse audience, including individuals with disabilities. Multimedia technologies offer various tools and features, such as closed captions, screen readers and alternative text for images, to make content accessible to individuals with visual or hearing impairments. In multimedia design, consistency involves maintaining uniformity in the presentation of elements, including layout, color schemes, fonts, navigation, and user interface components. Consistency ensures that users can predict how to interact with multimedia content, making it intuitive and easy to navigate. Whether in websites, mobile apps or educational materials, a consistent design fosters a sense of familiarity, reducing cognitive load and enhancing usability. It also reinforces the brand identity and message, making content more recognizable and memorable.

1.1.4.12 Legal and Ethical Considerations

In a digital landscape where multimedia content is prevalent, issues surrounding intellectual property, copyright and fair use come to the forefront. Content creators must be mindful of using licensed materials and respecting the rights of others. Furthermore, the rise of deep-fakes and misinformation underscores the importance of ethical practices in multimedia production and distribution. Users, on the other hand, need to be discerning consumers of multimedia, understanding the potential for misinformation and respecting privacy rights.

1.2 Application Areas

Multimedia has found extensive application in various and varied fields. Text, image, graphics, audio, video and animation can be integrated together to provide a wealth of resources and multisensory user experiences in home entertainment and gaming, education and learning, business and industry, advertising and marketing, communication and marketing, engineering and manufacturing, medicine and healthcare along with a host of other application areas. In recent years, AR (augmented reality) and VR (virtual reality) have revolutionized how we perceive and interact with the digital world. AR enhances our real-world environment by overlaying digital information and objects, making it invaluable in areas like gaming, navigation and industrial training. On the other hand, VR immerses users in entirely virtual environments, offering unparalleled experiences in fields such as gaming, education and therapy (Chen & Fragomeni, 2020). Some of the major applications include, but not limited to, the following.

1.2.1 Home Entertainment

Application of multimedia technology related to home entertainment includes computer-based games, interactive encyclopedias, storytelling, cartoons, movies and other immersive experiences. Through high-definition displays, surround sound systems and streaming services people can enjoy all the above experiences from the comfort of their homes. Audio/video-on-demand systems employing multimedia technologies enable users to specify the content they would like to watch, not simply by their names, but by a host of other criteria like creator, music, genre, year of release, and awards. Smart TVs integrate multimedia content with internet connectivity offering access to a vast array of streaming platforms and online content. Additionally virtual reality headsets bring a new dimension to home entertainment and games, allowing users to experience immersive games and immersive storytelling (Steinkuehler et al., 2012).

1.2.2 Education and Learning

Multimedia technology enhances education by providing dynamic and engaging learning experiences. Education-based multimedia applications include learning packages, CBTs (computer-based training), CAIs (computer-aided instructions) and simulation of lab experiments (especially those which cannot be easily performed in practice). Different aspects of the course curriculum which cannot be explained or grasped easily through simple text and images (as offered by the books) could be presented through video clips, animation, 3D modeling and audio annotations, AR and VR for making them easily understandable. Interactive whiteboards, educational videos and online courses offer students access to a wealth of resources that cater to diverse learning styles. Moreover, expertise of the best instructors could be used to create these online content and distribute them to students all over the globe as part of "distance education" or "e-learning" programs. The multisensory perceptions of such study material is expected to provide a good grasp of the subject matter and interactivity elements to provide for better retention (Clark & Mayer, 2016).

1.2.3 Business and Industry

Multimedia technology has revolutionized various aspects of operations and communication in the business and industry sector. Through multimedia presentations and virtual demonstrations companies can effectively showcase products and services to clients and stakeholders, which facilitate business transactions and marketing endeavors. Computer-based learning and training packages for employees, both technical and marketing, enable organizations to maintain a high level of staff training and development. Many people can use each of these courses when imparted using networked environments and do not need to spend time away from office. Also people can learn at their own paces without the need to hire full time instructors. Because the best instructors could be used to make these materials, they could be of a high quality, to provide hands-on learning experiences enhancing skill development and safety protocols. Additionally multimedia technology enables remote collaboration through video conferencing and virtual meetings facilitating seamless communication among team members regardless of geographical location (Jong & Sarti, 2012). Business houses utilize multimedia technology to display items difficult to stock like glassware, chemicals and industrial equipment to prospective customers. Real-estate agents can display interior and exterior of buildings along with necessary information like dimension and price. In electronic commerce, customers can compare different products in relation to their quality, price and appearance without leaving their homes and offices. Once they decide on purchasing an item, hyperlinks could connect them directly to an online store where they could place their orders. The benefits include saving on space, inventory and distribution (Milutinovic, 2013).

1.2.4 Advertising and Marketing

Multimedia is a driving force in advertising and marketing. Interactive multimedia advertisements, video commercials and social media campaigns use graphics, video and sound to capture the audience's attention. Advertisers employ multimedia techniques to create immersive brand experiences. Multimedia advertising encompasses a wide range of formats, including video commercials, interactive banners, social media campaigns and multimedia-rich websites. Video content, in particular, has become a cornerstone of advertising strategies, providing a compelling medium to convey brand messages and showcase products or services, especially in online platforms like YouTube, which in turn provide incentives to create quality content. Interactive multimedia elements, such as clickable ads and immersive experiences, enable brands to create memorable and engaging campaigns. Online catalogs can also server as expert systems, which could take a list of criteria from customers and provide a list of products which satisfy them. This would serve to guide the customers into choosing the appropriate items they want. Such systems can also be useful in providing after-sales services by taking in a list of symptoms from a user and suggesting to them the possible actions to be taken including troubleshooting or subscribing to on-call services. Multimedia also facilitates cross-platform advertising, allowing seamless integration across television, online platforms and social media. With the widespread adoption of smartphones and tablets, multimedia technology is extensively used in mobile advertising campaign (Hua, 2010).

1.2.5 Communications and Information

Multimedia technologies facilitate creation of engaging and informative digital content for websites, blogs, social media, e-books and other digital publications. These applications allow real-time interactions between people who need to work together but cannot be in the same place at the same time. In order to cater to these needs, many public and private networks support services like voice-mail and teleconferencing. Voice-mail enhances the effectiveness of normal e-mail by allowing messages to be composed and sent using audio instead of text, while teleconferencing is used where the parties need to communicate in real time. Internet Telephony involves establishing long distance telephone calls by logging into a local server and using the Internet to connect to a remote server. Other similar uses include groupware/whiteboard applications in intranets, e-learning applications in virtual classrooms. In an information kiosk, information is accessed through a touch screen and viewed on a monitor. A wide range of information, products and services, like for example, sales product catalogs, transport timetables, way finding assistance, news updates, event schedules, ticket purchases, bill payments and so on. Links to payment systems and distribution channels would enable the kiosks to accept orders and promote e-commerce practices. Kiosks can also be used to capture statistical data for an in-depth market research to be carried out on consumer trends. Multimedia elements can be employed to convey information dynamically based on user requirements, often with audio cues, step by step instructions, customizable fonts and subtitles to cater to a wide range of users (Tatipamula & Khashnabish, 1998).

1.2.6 Engineering and Manufacturing

In computer-aided design (CAD) and manufacturing (CAM) multimedia elements such as 3D modeling, animations and simulations play a crucial role in visualizing complex structures and systems. Engineers use multimedia presentations to communicate design concepts, project proposals and technical documentation effectively. Virtual reality (VR) and augmented reality (AR) technologies, which heavily rely on multimedia, are increasingly employed in engineering for immersive design reviews and training simulations.

Multimedia presentations aid in the analysis of data from simulations, experiments and sensor networks, providing engineers with a comprehensive understanding of performance metrics. Product lifecycle management (PLM) systems utilize multimedia technology to manage and coordinate entire lifecycle of engineering products from conception and design to manufacturing maintenance and disposal. Multimedia technology enhances engineering education and training through virtual laboratories and simulation-based training modules, and facilitates visualization and analysis of sensor data and simulation results. Collaborative tools like video-conferencing and interactive whiteboards promote teamwork and project completion (Chen & Shyu, 2013).

1.2.7 Medicine and Healthcare

Multimedia technology has revolutionized the way medical information is communicated, medical procedures are conducted and patient care is administered. High-quality images, video, animation, virtual reality has led to advancements of medical education, patient communication, diagnostic tools and therapeutic interventions. Medical students and professionals can access a wealth of visual resources, including 3D anatomical models, surgical procedure simulations and interactive case studies. Virtual dissections, medical animations and multimedia presentations enhance understanding, making complex medical concepts more accessible and memorable. Modalities such as magnetic resonance imaging (MRI), computed tomography (CT) and ultrasound generate detailed visual representations of internal structures. The integration of multimedia in telemedicine facilitates remote consultations and enhances the quality of virtual healthcare interactions. Video conferencing, multimedia-rich medical records and interactive patient portals allow healthcare professionals to remotely assess patients, discuss treatment plans, and provide visual explanations of medical conditions, fostering a more personalized and accessible healthcare experience. Archives of X-ray images, CT scans and ultrasonography scans enable doctors to provide better consultations, and serve as an expert system. Transmission of these images over geographical boundaries can help in the growth of telemedicine and medical repositories. The DICOM (Digital Imaging and Communications in Medicine) standard is a foundational framework in the field of medical imaging and healthcare informatics, which not only standardizes the structure and format of medical images but also the communication and networking protocols required for seamless data exchange within healthcare facilities (Tyagi et al., 2021).

1.2.8 Travel and Tourism

Multimedia technology enables creation of virtual tours and destination marketing campaigns that showcase tourist attractions, hotels, resorts and landmarks. Virtual reality, 360° videos and interactive content provide potential customers with immersive experiences allowing them to virtually explore destinations before making travel decisions. Hotel owners can utilize the technology to display details of facilities offered at various hotels at different locations. Museums and art galleries may provide digital versions of their specimens for public viewing, exhibition, auction, etc. A multimedia system implementing intelligent travel agent software would enable the users to specify their travel needs and budgets, and then make the system list out possible destinations that meet these criteria and create multimedia presentations about one or more of these. Travels apps incorporate multimedia elements such as maps, GPS, travel reviews, destination guides to offer personalized travel itineraries. Airlines and hospitality provides can provide passengers with personalized entertainment options and enhance on-board comfort. Museums, heritage sites and cultural centers can use audio guide, digital storytelling and interactive exhibits to engage visitors about local cultures traditions and history (Pirolli, 2018).

1.2.9 News and Journalism

Multimedia technologies have allowed news organizations to present stories in more engaging and informative ways. News websites incorporate images, videos and interactive graphics to provide comprehensive coverage and context. Live streams and social media posts enable real-time reporting of events as they unfold. Multimedia also offers new avenues for citizen journalism, where individuals can capture and share news through their smartphones and social media platforms. The integration of multimedia in journalism has made news more accessible and engaging for audiences, enhancing understanding and awareness of global events. Live streaming, live blogs and social media platforms enable journalists to report news in real time providing audiences with immediate access to headlines, live updates and eyewitness accounts. Data journalism enables journalists to analyze, interpret and visualize complex datasets to uncover insights, trends and patterns in data. Mobile journalism is a growing trend, which empower journalists to capture, edit and share news content on the go (Hernandez & Rue, 2015).

1.2.10 Design and Architecture

Architects, interior designers and urban planners employ multimedia to create virtual 3D models, walk-throughs, and flyovers, offering clients a realistic and immersive understanding of proposed projects. Multimedia also facilitates collaborative design processes, allowing teams to share ideas and visualize concepts in real time, regardless of geographical distances. Furthermore, multimedia enhances architectural presentations and marketing materials, enabling professionals to showcase their work through visually stunning renderings, animations and interactive portfolios. Augmented and virtual reality technologies enable architects to immerse stakeholders in virtual environments, enhancing the understanding of the proposed designs.

1.2.11 Museums and Exhibits

Multimedia technologies have enabled museums to create dynamic and interactive exhibits that captivate audiences of all ages. Interactive touchscreens, immersive virtual reality experiences and multimedia guides have become integral to modern museums, providing deeper insights into art, history and science. Visitors can explore artifacts and artworks in greater detail, access contextual information and even participate in hands-on simulations. Additionally, multimedia has expanded the reach of museums, allowing them to create virtual exhibits and online collections accessible to a global audience (Vatsky, 2023).

1.2.12 Government and Public Services

Government agencies use multimedia to communicate policies, health information, emergency alerts and civic engagement initiatives effectively. Multimedia elements, such as video conferences and webinars, facilitate remote collaboration and public participation in government meetings and decision-making processes. The application of multimedia in government also extends to e-learning platforms for employee training and public education (Mehta & Gaie, 2023).

1.2.13 Farming and Agriculture

Multimedia technologies offer farmers valuable resources, from online tutorials and interactive applications to informative videos and webinars. These resources cover a wide range of topics, including crop management, pest control, livestock care, and sustainable farming practices. Multimedia also plays a role in precision agriculture, utilizing sensors and data visualization to improve crop yield and resource management. Moreover, multimedia assists in sharing vital agricultural knowledge and research, aiding farmers in adapting to changing environmental conditions and emerging challenges (Bansal & Uddin, 2022).

1.2.14 Social Media and Content Creation

Social media platforms like Facebook, Instagram, Twitter(X) and YouTube are powered by a diverse mix of multimedia elements, from images, videos and GIFs to audio clips and interactive posts. Content creators, influencers and individuals use multimedia to craft compelling narratives, share their experiences and connect with global audiences. Multimedia content spans a wide spectrum, including vlogs, podcasts, visually engaging info-graphics and live streaming, all fostering vibrant online communities (Adornato, 2021).

1.2.15 Sports and Athletics

High-definition video broadcasts, slow-motion replays and interactive graphics provide viewers with immersive and engaging coverage. In addition, multimedia analysis tools have become essential for coaches and athletes, enabling in-depth performance assessments, injury prevention and tactical strategies. Multimedia-driven sports journalism has also become integral, offering fans in-depth insights through podcasts, videos and interactive articles. In these platforms, multimedia fuels user-generated content, shaping trends, sparking discussions and amplifying digital voices

1.2.16 Environment and Conservation

Multimedia technologies enable researchers and environmentalists to capture and share stunning visuals of ecosystems, wildlife and natural phenomena, conveying the urgency of conservation efforts. Educational institutions and environmental organizations use multimedia resources, such as documentaries, interactive websites and virtual tours, to inform the public about critical environmental issues. These tools encourage advocacy, support sustainable practices and foster appreciation for the natural world. Additionally, GIS (Geographic Information System) mapping, which relies on multimedia data, aids in ecological research, land management and conservation planning (Gadsden & Artz, 2023).

1.2.17 Pattern Recognition and Deep Learning

In recent years multimedia technologies have played crucial roles in enhancing algorithms of pattern recognition, computer vision and Content Based Storage and Retrieval (CBSR) systems. Traditionally, data-searching activities have been performed on textual databases by string matching. As large repositories of media elements like images, audio and video are growing up all over the world, efficient methods of searching non-textual media are being developed. Machine learning algorithms trained on multimedia datasets are utilized to detect and recognize faces, fingerprints, signature, speech, speaker and other patterns in data. Deep learning models trained on large-scale datasets utilize convolutional neural networks (CNN) to classify multimedia data into predefined categories. Interpretation of hand gestures, body movement and facial expressions, have led to the development of human computer interface (HCI) systems. Biometric systems identify and verify individuals based on their facial features, fingerprints, iris patterns, voice patterns and other biometric characteristics. Video analysis and recognition systems interpret motion patterns and events in video streams to enable automated classification of sports videos, crowd management from drone videos, and scene understanding of surveillance videos. Voice activated systems recognize speech and speaker patterns from audio streams in security and authentication systems. Medical diagnosis systems use CBSR techniques for detecting diagnosing and monitoring medical conditions and diseases. Semantic segmentation algorithms use deep learning models to partition images and videos into meaningful regions like foreground objects and background areas to enable robotic systems and automated vehicular systems to function properly (Marquis & Furht, 2012).

1.3 Multimedia Hardware

To make multimedia work requires an array of hardware devices and instruments of varying functionalities. These range from input devices like cameras, scanners, microphones to processing units like CPU, GPU, DSP to storage devices like HDD, SSD, NAS to output devices like monitors, tablets, printers to network devices like hubs, routers, switches to specialized hardware like capture cards, head mounted displays and haptic gloves.

1.3.1 Input Devices

Input devices are essential for capturing and digitizing multimedia content for enabling users to interact with digital platforms. They include a wide range of devices tailored for specific tasks ranging from scanners for documents, to cameras for images and video, and microphones for audio.

1.3.1.1 Cameras

Digital Cameras: Digital cameras come in various types, including compact point-and-shoot cameras, DSLRs (digital single-lens reflex) and mirror-less cameras. They offer a wide range of features and capabilities, making them suitable for different applications. DSLRs and mirror-less cameras are favored by professional photographers and videographers for their advanced settings, interchangeable lenses and high-quality image sensors.

Camcorders: Camcorders are dedicated video cameras designed for recording high-quality video. They come with features like image stabilization and versatile zoom lenses. Professional camcorders offer advanced settings for cinematographers and videographers.

Action Cameras: Action cameras are compact, rugged cameras designed for capturing extreme sports and outdoor activities. They are known for their durability and wide-angle lenses, which provide a unique perspective for action shots and video recording.

1.3.1.2 Scanners

Flatbed Scanners: Flatbed scanners are the most common type and are suitable for scanning flat and single-sheet documents, photographs and images. They offer high-resolution scanning and color accuracy, making them ideal for archiving and digitizing printed media.

Sheet-Fed Scanners: Sheet-fed scanners are designed for scanning multiple sheets of documents quickly. They are commonly used in office environments for digitizing large volumes of documents, such as contracts, invoices and forms.

Film Scanners: Film scanners are specialized devices for digitizing photographic film, including negatives and slides. They provide high-resolution scans and color accuracy, making them a valuable tool for photographers and archivists.

1.3.1.3 Microphones

Condenser Microphones: Condenser microphones are highly sensitive and deliver exceptional audio quality. They are commonly used in studios for recording vocals, musical instruments and podcasts. Condenser microphones require external power, typically provided through a USB connection or an audio interface.

Dynamic Microphones: Dynamic microphones are robust and less sensitive to sound variations. They are ideal for live performances, broadcasting and recording instruments like drums and electric guitars. Dynamic microphones do not require external power and are known for their durability.

Lavalier Microphones: Lavalier microphones, often referred to as lapel or clip-on microphones, are small and unobtrusive. They are commonly used in broadcasting, presentations and interviews, as they can be discreetly attached to clothing for clear audio capture.

1.3.1.4 MIDI Controllers

MIDI (Musical Instrument Digital Interface) controllers are used by musicians and music producers to create, record and perform music electronically, including controlling virtual instruments and synthesizers in digital audio workstations (DAWs). MIDI controllers come in various forms, including MIDI keyboards with velocity-sensitive keys and MIDI pad controllers with pressure-sensitive pads for drum programming and performance. Many MIDI controllers feature knobs and faders that can be assigned to control parameters in music software, offering tactile and real-time manipulation of sound.

1.3.2 Digitizing Devices

Specialized hardware plays a crucial role in converting analog data to digital format to be used as input to multimedia processing systems.

1.3.2.1 Graphics Tablets

Graphics tablets, also known as pen tablets or drawing tablets, are used by graphic designers, digital artists, and illustrators for precise and natural input when creating digital artwork, graphics, and animations. Graphics tablets come with a stylus pen that offers pressure sensitivity, allowing artists to control line thickness and opacity by adjusting the pressure they apply, akin to traditional drawing and painting. Many graphics tablets feature shortcut buttons on the stylus or the tablet surface, providing quick access to frequently used functions and tools in graphic design software.

1.3.2.2 Audio Capture Cards

Audio capture cards or sound cards are essential for recording, digitizing and playback of audio in digital computers. These offer input ports for microphones and audio players, for capturing clean and clear audio signals. They provide low-latency monitoring via bundled software, allowing musicians and audio professionals to hear themselves in real time while recording, without audio delays. They also have multiple output ports for routing audio to various speakers, headphones and audio storage devices.

1.3.2.3 Video Capture Cards

Video capture cards are used to capture video from external sources like cameras, gaming consoles and video players for use in video production, live streaming and content creation. These cards offer inputs compatible with HDMI and SDI, ensuring compatibility with a wide range of video sources. Video capture cards can capture video in real time, enabling live streaming and recording without delay. Many capture cards come with built-in streaming support, allowing users to broadcast live video content directly to online platforms.

1.3.3 Processing Units

Multimedia content often requires significant processing power for tasks such as editing, rendering and real-time effects. Processing units are responsible for executing these operations, and they include a variety of components tailored for specific functions:

1.3.3.1 Central Processing Unit (CPU)

The CPU is the central processing unit of a computer and plays a crucial role in multimedia content creation and manipulation. Many CPUs feature multiple cores, allowing them to execute multiple tasks simultaneously. This is particularly valuable for multimedia applications, which often involve running complex operations in parallel. The clock speed, measured in gigahertz (GHz), determines how quickly a CPU can execute instructions. High clock speeds are beneficial for tasks that require rapid processing, such as real-time rendering and video encoding. Hyper-threading is a technology that enables each CPU core to handle multiple threads simultaneously. This feature enhances multitasking and can improve the performance of multimedia applications. Enthusiasts and professionals may overclock their CPUs to increase their clock speeds beyond the manufacturer's specifications. Overclocking can provide additional processing power for resource-intensive multimedia tasks.

1.3.3.2 Graphics Processing Unit (GPU)

GPUs are specialized processors primarily responsible for rendering graphics, but they also contribute significantly to multimedia production. GPUs excel in parallel processing, making them suitable for tasks like video rendering, 3D modeling and real-time effects. They can handle multiple operations simultaneously, resulting in faster multimedia processing. Many modern GPUs support technologies like CUDA (Compute Unified Device Architecture) for NVIDIA GPUs [www.developer.nvidia.com/cuda-zone] and OpenCL (Open Computing Language) [www.khronos.org/opencl], enabling them to accelerate multimedia and scientific applications through parallel computing. Video RAM (VRAM) is dedicated memory on a GPU used to store textures, frame buffers and other graphics-related data. A larger VRAM capacity is advantageous for rendering high-resolution textures and complex 3D scenes.

1.3.3.3 Digital Signal Processor (DSP)

DSPs are specialized processors designed for efficient audio signal processing and real-time audio effects. DSPs are commonly used in audio equipment, such as digital audio workstations (DAWs) and effects processors, to apply effects like reverb, equalization and compression to audio signals in real time. DSPs offer low-latency audio processing, making them ideal for live audio applications, including recording, mixing, and live sound reinforcement. They are optimized for specific audio tasks and are often found in audio interfaces, hardware synthesizers and effects units. They offload audio processing from the CPU, ensuring smooth real-time performance.

1.3.4 Storage Devices

Efficient storage devices are essential for preserving and managing multimedia content. A variety of storage options are available, each with specific characteristics and use cases.

1.3.4.1 Hard Disk Drives (HDD)

HDDs offer a range of storage capacities, from gigabytes to multiple terabytes, making them suitable for archiving and storing vast amounts of multimedia data, including photos, videos, and audio recordings. They are robust and can withstand regular use, making them reliable for long-term storage and less susceptible to physical damage. HDDs are cost-effective in terms of storage capacity, and provide a larger storage-to-cost ratio, making them a practical choice for multimedia professionals with substantial storage needs. HDDs contain spinning magnetic platters and read/write heads and are widely used for media libraries, backups and content archiving due to their affordability and durability. They are also used as external drives for archives.

1.3.4.2 Solid-State Drives (SSD)

SSDs are significantly faster than HDDs in terms of data access and transfer speeds. This speed advantage is critical for multimedia applications that require rapid data retrieval, such as video editing and gaming. Also SSDs do not have any moving parts, which make them less prone to physical damage and failure. Usually SSDs are robust and can withstand shocks, vibrations and temperature variations, making them suitable for portable multimedia production environments. SSDs can come in various form factors, allowing them to fit in a range of devices such as laptops, desktops and external enclosures.

1.3.4.3 Network Attached Storage (NAS)

NAS devices provide a centralized storage solution that can be accessed and shared by multiple users over a network. They are particularly valuable for collaborative multimedia projects and remote access to multimedia files. Many NAS systems support redundancy through RAID (Redundant Array of Independent Disks) configurations, which ensures data integrity and availability, even in the event of drive failure. NAS devices come with features for remote access, allowing multimedia professionals to access their content from anywhere with an internet connection. NAS systems can function as media servers, enabling the streaming of multimedia content to various devices, including smart TVs, gaming consoles and mobile devices. NAS devices often provide backup and synchronization solutions, which are crucial for preserving multimedia content and ensuring data security.

1.3.4.4 Optical Drives

Optical drives, such as CD/DVD/Blu-ray drives, are used for reading and writing optical media. They are still relevant for distributing multimedia content on physical media and archival purposes. Different types of optical discs, including CD-ROM, DVD-R and Blu-ray discs, offer varying storage capacities; Blu-ray discs, for example, can store high-definition video content. Optical media is often used for long-term archival of multimedia content, providing a physical backup of critical data. They are popular for playback and distribution of multimedia content such as movies, music albums and software installations. One advantage of optical drives over magnetic storage is that they are unaffected by strong magnetic and electric fields in the vicinity, hence they are preferred when such situations are encountered.

1.3.5 Output Devices

Output devices are essential for presenting and delivering multimedia content to the audience in various forms. They encompass a range of devices tailored for specific multimedia applications:

1.3.5.1 Visual Display Units (VDU)

Monitors: Monitors come in various sizes and resolutions to cater to different multimedia needs. High-resolution displays are crucial for tasks like video editing, graphic design and professional content creation. Professional-grade monitors often feature accurate color reproduction, making them suitable for work like photo and video editing. Some monitors offer high refresh rates, which are particularly important for gaming and video playback. High refresh rates ensure smoother motion and reduced motion blur. There are different panel types, such as CRT (cathode ray tube). LCD (liquid crystal display), LED (light emitting diode) and PDP (plasma display panel), each with unique characteristics that impact factors like color accuracy, response time and viewing angles.

Touchscreen Displays: Touchscreen displays are used in interactive multimedia applications and kiosks, allowing users to engage directly with multimedia content like product information, transport timetables, tourist guides and stock exchange fluctuations.

Projectors: Projectors are used to display multimedia content on a larger scale. They are valuable for presentations, home theaters and events. High-end projectors offer features like 4K resolution and 3D support.

1.3.5.2 Printers

Inkjet Printers: Inkjet printers are versatile and suitable for printing high-quality color images and graphics. They are often used for photo printing and graphic design projects.

LASER Printers: Laser printers offer fast and efficient printing of text documents and are commonly used in offices. Color laser printers are used for producing marketing materials and graphics.

Large-Format Printers: Large-format printers are designed for printing posters, banners and high-resolution graphics in sizes larger than standard letter or A4 paper.

3D Printers: 3D printers are used for creating three-dimensional objects from digital designs. They have applications in product prototyping, modeling and even custom multimedia accessories.

1.3.5.3 Speakers and Headphones

High-quality speakers are essential for playing audio content with fidelity. They come in various configurations, including 2.0 (stereo), 2.1 (stereo with a subwoofer), and 5.1/7.1 (surround sound) setups. Headphones are critical for tasks like audio editing, sound design and music production. Open-back headphones are favored for their natural sound reproduction, while closed-back headphones provide sound isolation in noisy environments. Soundbars are compact speaker systems designed for home theater setups and provide improved audio quality for multimedia content consumption. Wireless audio systems enable the streaming of audio content to speakers or headphones via Bluetooth or Wi-Fi, offering convenience and mobility. Virtual surround sound technologies create a spatial audio experience through headphones, simulating a multi-speaker setup.

1.3.6 Network Infrastructure

Network infrastructure plays an important role in multimedia content distribution, streaming, collaboration and real-time communication. It encompasses a variety of components and technologies.

1.3.6.1 Routers and Switches

Home routers are the central networking devices in residential environments, which connect multiple devices to the internet and each other, allowing multimedia content sharing and streaming within a home network. In business and large-scale multimedia production environments, enterprise-grade routers are employed to manage network traffic, ensure security and provide high-speed connectivity.

Ethernet switches are used to connect multiple devices within a local area network (LAN) and facilitate high-speed data transfer between multimedia workstations, servers and storage devices, enhancing collaboration and data sharing. In professional multimedia production settings, managed switches offer greater control over network traffic, including the ability to prioritize multimedia data to ensure uninterrupted streaming and real-time collaboration.

1.3.6.2 Wireless Access Points (WAPs)

Wireless access points provide Wi-Fi connectivity, allowing multimedia professionals to work wirelessly with their devices. This is particularly valuable in collaborative environments, studios and locations where wired connections are impractical. Wi-Fi standards, like 802.11ax/Wi-Fi 6, offer high-speed wireless connections suitable for multimedia applications and enhanced performance, especially in crowded areas. WAPs work by broadcasting wireless signals within a specific range allowing devices to connect to the network seamlessly. Additionally WAPs can support technologies like MIMO (multiple input multiple output) and beamforming (focusing transmitted signal directly to intended receiver) to enhance signal strength and coverage.

1.3.6.3 CDN and QoS

Content Delivery Network (CDN) is a critical part of network infrastructure for online multimedia content delivery and distribution of multimedia content to servers strategically located around the world, reducing latency and ensuring fast delivery to users regardless of their geographical location. CDNs employ load balancing to distribute traffic efficiently, ensuring multimedia content can handle sudden surges in demand, cache content in servers, optimize bandwidth usage and reduce network congestion. Moreover, CDNs often include security features to protect multimedia content from unauthorized access. CDNs improve Quality of Service (QoS) by reducing latency, increasing throughput and enhancing reliability for end users. QoS is a network technology that prioritizes certain types of data traffic to ensure a consistent and high-quality experience for multimedia applications. QoS ensures that video conferences and real-time collaboration tools receive priority, resulting in reduced lag and smooth communication. Streaming media, such as high-definition video and audio, benefits from QoS to prevent buffering and maintain playback quality. Voice over Internet Protocol (VoIP) calls and multimedia content with voice components are less prone to interruptions and delays with QoS.

1.3.7 AR and VR Hardware

1.3.7.1 AR (Augmented Reality) Hardware

Smart Glasses: AR smart glasses, like Microsoft HoloLens and Google Glass, overlay digital information onto the user's view of the real world. Key features include:

Smartphone AR: Many smartphones are equipped with AR capabilities, enabling users to experience AR through their phone's camera and screen. ARKit for iOS [developer.apple.com/augmented-reality/arkit] and ARCore for Android [developers.google.com/ar/develop] are software frameworks that support AR on mobile devices.

Wearable AR: Some AR wearable, like the Magic Leap [www.magicleap.com], are designed for more immersive AR experiences by integrating sensors, cameras, and spatial audio.

Industrial and Medical AR: AR hardware is used in industrial settings for remote assistance and training. In the medical field, AR glasses can display patient data and surgical guidance to healthcare professionals.

Immersive AR: Immersive AR experiences are delivered through headsets that offer a wide field of view and realistic 3D interactions, blurring the line between AR and VR.

1.3.7.2 VR (Virtual Reality) Hardware

Head-Mounted Displays (HMDs): VR HMDs are the primary hardware for VR experiences. They are designed to be worn on the head and cover the user's field of vision with stereoscopic displays.

Controllers: VR controllers are handheld devices that allow users to interact with the virtual environment. They may include buttons, triggers and motion sensors for precise tracking and manipulation.

Room-Scale Tracking: Room-scale tracking systems use external sensors or cameras to track the user's movement in physical space, allowing for more natural and immersive interactions in VR.

PC-Based VR: PC-based VR systems, such as the Oculus Rift [www.oculus.com/rift-s] and HTC Vive [www.vive.com/us], require powerful computers with dedicated GPUs to run high-fidelity VR content.

Stand-alone VR: Stand-alone VR headsets, like the Meta Quest [www.meta.com/quest], do not require a PC or console and are self-contained, making them more accessible and portable.

Wireless VR: Wireless VR adapters eliminate the need for tethering the HMD to a computer, offering greater freedom of movement.

Eye Tracking: Eye-tracking technology is being incorporated into VR HMDs for more realistic rendering, which reduces GPU load by rendering only the part of the scene the user is currently looking at.

Haptic Gloves: Haptic devices provide tactile feedback to users, allowing them to feel the virtual or augmented environment, enhancing the sense of immersion. Haptic gloves are designed with sensors and actuators to provide realistic feedback to users' hands. This allows users to touch and manipulate virtual objects, making it crucial for applications like VR training simulations and virtual surgeries.

Haptic Vests and Suits: These wearable haptic devices cover the user's body with multiple haptic points, enabling sensations like impact, pressure and vibration. They are used in gaming, training and medical simulations to simulate various physical interactions.

Force Feedback Devices: Force feedback steering wheels and joysticks provide resistance and vibration during virtual driving and flying experiences, improving the sensation of control and interaction.

Haptic Sound Systems: These systems use sound waves to create physical sensations. Ultrasonic haptic speakers can make users feel vibrations in the air, which is particularly useful for VR experiences.

Bone Conduction Headphones: Bone conduction headphones transmit audio vibrations through the bones in the user's skull, allowing them to hear sounds while maintaining spatial awareness in AR applications.

1.4 Multimedia Software

Multimedia production relies heavily on a wide array of application software that facilitates content creation, editing and enhancement. Editing software is used to create and edit specific media components like image, graphics, audio, video, animation while authoring software is required to combine all edited media into a single integrated presentation, typically a runtime format either stand-alone like .EXE or a Web-based format like.SWF. As Web-based content creation developed, languages like HTML5, CSS, JavaScript as well as multimedia APIs and libraries were extensively used to create rich and interactive content that can be accessed by a global audience.

1.4.1 Editing Software

1.4.1.1 Text Editing

Text is a fundamental component of multimedia, and its effective integration into multimedia content requires specialized tools. These tools provide features for text editing, formatting and layout design. Major text editing tools include the following:

Word Processors: Word processing software, such as Microsoft Word [microsoft.com/en-us/microsoft-365/word] and Google Docs [www.google.com/docs], offers features for creating, formatting and editing text. They are essential for developing scripts, articles and textual content in multimedia projects.

Desktop Publishing Software: Desktop publishing software like Adobe InDesign [www.adobe.com/products/indesign] is employed for designing visually appealing documents and layouts. It is valuable for multimedia projects that involve brochures, magazines and print materials.

1.4.1.2 Image Editing

Images are a crucial component in multimedia production. Image editing software empowers creators to manipulate, enhance and optimize images for various applications. Prominent image editing tools include the following:

Adobe Photoshop: Adobe Photoshop [www.adobe.com/products/photoshop] is a versatile image editing software that enables advanced image manipulation, retouching, and creative design. It is widely used in multimedia projects for image enhancement and compositing.

GIMP: The GNU Image Manipulation Program (GIMP) [www.gimp.org] is an open-source alternative to Adobe Photoshop. It provides many of the same features for image editing and is favored by many multimedia professionals.

1.4.1.3 Audio Editing

Audio is integral to multimedia content, and dedicated software is used for audio recording, editing and production. These tools enable sound engineers, musicians and content creators to craft audio components. Major audio editing tools include the following:

Adobe Audition: Adobe Audition [www.adobe.com/products/audition] is a professional audio editing software that offers a comprehensive set of tools for recording, editing and mixing audio content, including features like waveform editing, spectral frequency display, and a robust multi-track environment. It provides advanced audio restoration capabilities, real-time effects and seamless integration with other Adobe Creative Cloud applications, making it a versatile choice for audio professionals and content creators.

Audacity: Audacity [www.audacityteam.org] is a free and open-source audio editing software known for its simplicity and versatility, offering features like multi-track editing, audio recording and precise waveform editing. It supports a wide range of audio formats, includes built-in effects and tools for noise reduction, and is accessible for users across different skill levels, making it a popular choice for various audio editing needs.

1.4.1.4 Video Editing

Video is a dynamic multimedia format, and video editing software is essential for creating, editing and refining video content. Leading video editing tools include the following:

Adobe Premiere Pro: Adobe Premiere Pro [www.adobe.com/products/premiere] is a professional video editing software with a range of powerful features, including a seamless workflow for editing, color grading, audio processing and visual effects in a single application. It offers an intuitive interface, advanced timeline editing, support for various video formats, and integration with other Adobe Creative Cloud applications, making it a popular choice for filmmakers, video editors and content creators.

Apple Final Cut Pro X: Final Cut Pro X [www.apple.com/final-cut-pro] is a professional video editing software known for its optimized performance on macOS, featuring a timeline for intuitive editing, advanced color grading tools, and a range of powerful audio editing capabilities. With a focus on speed and efficiency, it also offers features like multi-cam editing, 360-degree video editing and seamless integration with other Apple devices, making it a preferred choice for many filmmakers and video editors.

Avid Media Composer: Avid Media Composer [www.avid.com/media-composer] is a leading professional video editing software widely used in the film and television industry, offering robust tools for precise editing, color correction and audio post-production. Known for its reliable media management capabilities and collaborative workflow features, it provides a comprehensive solution for large-scale video projects.

Corel VideoStudio: Corel VideoStudio [www.videostudiopro.com] is designed for enthusiasts and beginners, offering an intuitive interface with drag-and-drop functionality, as well as a wide range of creative tools for editing, enhancing and sharing videos. With features like multi-camera editing, 3D title creation and built-in templates, it provides a versatile and accessible platform for individuals looking to create polished and engaging video content.

1.4.1.5 Graphics and Animation

2D and 3D graphics and animation tools enable creation, editing and publishing of 2D and 3D vector graphics and animation content. Usually incorporate a run-time software to render the graphics during playback.

Adobe Animate: Adobe Animate [www.adobe.com/products/animate.html] is a 2D animation tool known for its robust features in creating interactive and animated content for various platforms, including Web and mobile applications. With support for vector graphics, a timeline-based interface and the ability to publish content in multiple formats, Adobe Animate is widely used for designing engaging animations, interactive games and dynamic Web content.

Autodesk 3d Studio Max: Autodesk 3ds Max [www.autodesk.com/products/3ds-max] is a powerful 3D modeling and animation software widely utilized in the fields of architecture, gaming and visual effects production.

With a comprehensive set of modeling tools, advanced rendering capabilities and support for complex animations, it enables artists and designers to create realistic 3D content for various industries.

Autodesk Maya: Autodesk Maya [www.autodesk.com/products/maya] is a 3D animation and modeling software known for its versatile tools and capabilities, catering to industries such as film, television and game development. With advanced features like character rigging, dynamic simulations and a robust rendering engine, Maya empowers artists and animators to create highly realistic and visually stunning 3D content for a wide range of applications.

1.4.2 Authoring Software

Multimedia integration or authoring tools are essential components of the content creation process, enabling the seamless amalgamation of various multimedia elements such as text, images, audio, video and animation. These tools come in both stand-alone and Web-based formats, offering diverse capabilities to cater to the specific requirements of multimedia projects.

1.4.2.1 Stand-alone Authoring

Stand-alone multimedia integration software is installed on a local computer, providing a dedicated environment for content creators to compile, edit and synchronize multimedia components. The output file is usually published as an executable with its own run-time engine, for distribution on various platforms, including CD-ROMs, the Web using plug-ins and stand-alone applications for PCs. Some well-known stand-alone multimedia integration tools include the following.

Macromedia/Adobe Director: Adobe Director [www.adobe.com/support/director/downloads.html], initially developed by Macromedia and later acquired by Adobe, was a powerful multimedia authoring platform used for creating interactive multimedia applications. It allowed content creators to combine text, images, audio, video and animations into cohesive presentations or games. Its integrated scripting language Lingo was used for creating interactive and engaging multimedia content. However, it has been succeeded by Adobe Animate in more recent years. In 2017, Adobe officially announced the discontinuation of Adobe Director.

Macromedia Authorware/Adobe Captivate: Macromedia Authorware, also developed by Macromedia, now Adobe Captivate [www.adobe.com/products/captivate], is renowned for its capability to create e-learning and training applications. It employs a flowchart-based visual authoring environment that enabled content creators to integrate multimedia elements, quizzes and interactive simulations. Macromedia Authorware was particularly valuable for educational multimedia. Macromedia Authorware was officially discontinued by Adobe in the year 2007.

Adobe Flash: Adobe Flash [www.adobe.com/products/flashruntimes.html], while no longer actively developed by Adobe, played an important role in multimedia content creation, especially on the Web. Flash enabled the creation of interactive animations, games and multimedia-rich websites. Its integrated scripting language called ActionScript was used to add interactivity and animations to content. With the rise of HTML5 and Web standards, Adobe phased out Flash, and Web browsers discontinued support, rendering it obsolete.

Asymetrix Toolbook: Asymetrix Toolbook was a multimedia authoring tool and development environment that gained popularity in the 1990s and early 2000s. Toolbook, created by Asymetrix, now Sum Total Systems [www.sumtotalsystems.com], allowed developers to create interactive multimedia content for various purposes, including e-learning courses, multimedia presentations, simulations and interactive applications. Toolbook featured a visual, drag-and-drop interface that made it accessible to users with varying levels of technical expertise. Its integrated scripting language called OpenScript was used for adding interactivity and functionality to multimedia projects. OpenScript allowed developers to create custom behaviors and interactions within their content.

1.4.2.2 Web-Based Authoring

As Web technologies evolved, the demand for CD-ROM-based multimedia content also diminished. Director's strengths in creating interactive CD-ROMs and stand-alone applications were less relevant in a world dominated by Web-based content, mobile apps and responsive design. This shift in Web standards, combined with the rise of HTML5 and JavaScript, made it increasingly challenging for these tools to remain relevant. Web-based multimedia authoring software is accessible through Web browsers and allows collaboration from different locations. These tools are often preferred for their ease of access and collaborative features. Notable Web-based multimedia authoring tools include the following:

Canva: Canva [www.canva.com] is a user-friendly graphic design platform that offers a wide range of features for creating visually appealing content. With an extensive library of templates, customizable design elements and a drag-and-drop interface, it enables users to effortlessly design social media graphics, presentations, posters and more.

Prezi: Prezi [www.prezi.com] is a dynamic presentation software that distinguishes itself from traditional slideshows by offering a zoomable canvas, allowing users to create non-linear and engaging presentations. With features like motion paths, interactive elements and the ability to present ideas in a visually compelling way, it promotes a more dynamic and memorable presentation experience.

Crello: Crello [www.appsumo.com/products/crello] is a Web-based graphic design tool that allows users to create static and animated designs for social media, advertising and presentations. It provides access to a vast library of templates and design elements.

Kapwing: Kapwing [www.kapwing.com] is a Web-based video editing platform that simplifies video creation and editing. It offers a range of tools for trimming, adding text, memes, collages and creating engaging video content for social media.

Articulate Storyline: Articulate Storyline [www.articulate.com/360/storyline] is a robust e-learning authoring tool known for its powerful features in creating interactive and engaging online courses. Its major features include a user-friendly interface, drag-and-drop functionality and a vast library of customizable templates for building multimedia-rich content, with support for branching scenarios, quizzes and responsive design.

H5P: H5P [www.h5p.org] is an open-source platform for creating and sharing interactive HTML5 content. It's a versatile tool for building interactive multimedia content, including presentations, quizzes and games.

Tumult Hype: Tumult Hype [www.tumult.com/hype] is known for its focus on creating interactive and engaging HTML5 content. It provides a user-friendly interface for designing animations, presentations and interactive Web content without requiring extensive coding knowledge.

Vyond (formerly GoAnimate): Vyond [www.vyond.com] enables users to create animated videos without the need for extensive coding skills. Its user-friendly interface allows individuals, educators and businesses to produce professional-looking animations using a drag-and-drop approach.

Genially: Genially [www.genial.ly] is a versatile online tool designed for creating interactive and visually appealing content such as presentations, info-graphics and educational materials. It offers a variety of templates across different categories, making it convenient for users to start their projects with pre-designed structures.

Adobe Spark: Adobe Spark [express.adobe.com/page/9bPqZ] offers a suite of Web-based tools for creating social media graphics, Web pages and short videos. It simplifies graphic design for users without extensive design skills, offering an intuitive platform to create visually appealing graphics, Web pages and short videos.

Ceros: Ceros [www.ceros.com] is a cloud-based interactive content creation platform, supporting real-time collaboration, allowing teams to work together seamlessly on projects. It is designed for marketers and content creators to build interactive Web experiences, including info-graphics, microsites and digital magazines.

Wix: Wix [www.wix.com] is a website builder that offers a range of multimedia and interactive features. It enables users to create visually appealing websites with multimedia elements, including videos, animations and interactive forms.

1.4.3 Multimedia APIs and Libraries

Multimedia is a rich and diverse field encompassing a wide range of content types, including images, audio, video, and interactive applications. As Web-based multimedia content creation gained momentum, developers relied on multimedia Application Programming Interfaces (APIs) and libraries, to provide the building blocks necessary to harness the power of Web-based multimedia. Developers could integrate multimedia APIs and libraries into their applications by including the necessary libraries, linking them to their code and leveraging their functions and classes. Programming languages such as C++, Python, Java and JavaScript can also interact with multimedia APIs. Specific libraries may have language bindings or wrappers to facilitate integration. These APIs and libraries provide methods and functions to perform operations like resizing images, applying filters, converting media formats, extracting metadata and more. They also enable multimedia streaming, live broadcasting and playback functionality, making them essential for applications like video conferencing, online media streaming and gaming.

Image Processing: Libraries like OpenCV [www.opencv.ai] and Pillow (PIL) [www.python-pillow.org] offer extensive image processing capabilities, enabling tasks such as image editing, manipulation, filtering and computer vision applications. OpenCV (Open Source Computer Vision) library is a powerful open-source library designed for computer vision and machine learning applications with a comprehensive set of tools and functions that allow developers to build and implement computer vision algorithms, image and video processing, and object detection. Pillow, a Python Imaging Library (PIL) fork, is a comprehensive image processing library, designed to be cross-platform and works seamlessly on different operating systems, including Windows, macOS and Linux.

Audio Processing: Libraries like Libsndfile [libsndfile.github.io/libsndfile] and PyDub [www.pypi.org/project/pydub] provide tools for audio file format conversion, processing, editing and streaming. Libsndfile is a C library that provides functionalities for reading and writing audio files in various formats, and supports multi-channel audio, allowing developers to work with stereo, surround sound, and other multi-channel configurations. PyDub is a Python library that simplifies audio processing tasks by providing a high-level interface for common audio operations, allowing users to manipulate audio files, including tasks such as cutting, concatenating and applying various effects, all with a straightforward syntax.

Video Processing: FFmpeg [www.ffmpeg.org] is a powerful multimedia framework that encompasses a vast set of tools and libraries for handling audio and video processing tasks. Its major feature lies in its ability to decode, encode, transcode, multiplex, de-multiplex, stream and filter multimedia content.

Graphics and 2D/3D Rendering: APIs like OpenGL [www.opengl.org], Vulkan [www.vulkan.org] and DirectX [learn.microsoft.com/en-us/windows/win32/directx] are used for creating and rendering graphics and 3D models in interactive applications, including games and simulations. OpenGL is an open-source graphics API that facilitates cross-platform rendering of 2D and 3D graphics by taking advantage of hardware acceleration and utilizing the capabilities of graphics processing units (GPUs). DirectX is a collection of APIs developed by Microsoft, primarily designed for multimedia and gaming applications on the Windows platform and includes components like Direct3D, DirectSound and DirectShow for graphics, audio and playback systems. Vulkan is a low-level, cross-platform graphics API designed for high-performance graphics rendering across different operating systems with explicit control over the GPU, enabling more efficient use of hardware resources and allowing for advanced graphics rendering techniques.

Multimedia Playback: Libraries such as VLC [www.videolan.org/vlc] and GStreamer [gstreamer.freedesktop.org] allow developers to integrate multimedia playback into their applications. VLC (VideoLAN Client) is a free and open-source versatile and widely used media player known for its cross-platform compatibility, supporting various operating systems including Windows, macOS, Linux, Android and iOS and its ability to play a vast array of multimedia file formats. GStreamer is an open-source multimedia framework designed for building multimedia applications across different platforms supporting a modular architecture, and offering a pipeline-based model that enables developers to create complex multimedia workflows.

User Interface Development: Frameworks like Qt [www.qt.io], GTK [www.gtk.org] and JavaFX [openjfx.io] enable the creation of multimedia-rich user interfaces with features like multimedia playback, image rendering and animations. Qt is a powerful cross-platform application development framework that enables developers to create applications that run seamlessly on various operating systems, including Windows, macOS, Linux, Android and iOS and provides an extensive set of tools and libraries for creating graphical user interfaces (GUIs) with a wide range of widgets and styles. GTK (GIMP Toolkit) is a cross-platform widget toolkit used for creating graphical user interfaces (GUIs) and provides an extensive set of widgets and tools for creating modern and responsive user interfaces. JavaFX is a Java library for creating rich GUIs with a diverse set of built-in UI components, including a comprehensive collection of customizable UI elements, such as charts, tables and multimedia support.

Web-Based Multimedia: Web technologies like HTML5, CSS3, and JavaScript offer powerful capabilities for embedding multimedia content within Web applications, allowing for audio and video playback, animations, and interactive multimedia elements. HTML5 introduces native support for multimedia elements such as audio and video, eliminating the need for third-party plugins like Flash, which enables developers to embed and control multimedia content directly within Web pages. CSS3 introduces a wide range of new styling features, including gradients, shadows, and flexible box layouts, providing developers with more versatile and expressive tools for designing modern Web layouts. JavaScript14 introduces new set of functions for manipulating, searching and sorting arrays.

1.5 Multimedia Standards

Multimedia standards are essential in the world of digital content creation, storage, transmission and playback. They define the technical specifications, formats and protocols that ensure consistency and interoperability across various multimedia devices and platforms. These standards help in the seamless exchange and playback of multimedia content, as well as collaborative ventures in content creation.

CODEC Standards: Multimedia CODECs (coder-decoder) play a crucial role in encoding and decoding image, audio and video data. Popular codec standards include JPEG2000 [jpeg.org/jpeg2000] for image, H.264 [itu.int/rec/T-REC-H.264] for video and AAC [mpeg.chiariglione.org/standards/mpeg-4/audio] for audio, while emerging standards like H.265 (or HEVC – High Efficiency Video Coding) [itu.int/rec/T-REC-H.265] and AV1 [aomedia.org/av1-features] aim to improve compression efficiency.

Streaming Protocols: Standards like HTTP Live Streaming (HLS) [developer.apple.com/streaming], Dynamic Adaptive Streaming over HTTP (DASH) [mpeg.chiariglione.org/standards/mpeg-dash] and Real-Time Messaging Protocol (RTMP) [helpx.adobe.com/adobe-media-server/dev/stream-on-demand-media-rtmp.html] govern the delivery of multimedia content over the internet, ensuring adaptive streaming for various bandwidth conditions.

Image Standards: Image formats like JPEG [jpeg.org], PNG [libpng.org/pub/png], GIF [w3.org/Graphics/GIF/spec-gif89a.txt] and WebP [developers.google.com/speed/webp] are standardized for still images, offering varying levels of compression, quality and support for transparency.

Audio Standards: Audio standards include formats like MP3 [mpeg.chiariglione.org/standards/mpeg-1/audio] [iso.org/standard/22412.html], WAV [learn.microsoft.com/en-us/windows/win32/multimedia/waveform-audio] and FLAC [xiph.org/flac] for audio encoding and playback. The development of spatial audio standards like Dolby Atmos [dolby.com/technologies/dolby-atmos] and DTS:X [dts.com/dtsx] has transformed the audio experience.

Video Container Formats: Container formats, such as MP4 [mpeg.chiariglione.org/standards/mpeg-4/video], MKV [matroska.org], and AVI [learn.microsoft.com/en-us/windows/win32/directshow/avi-file-format], wrap multimedia content, including video, audio, subtitles and metadata, into a single file. These formats are standardized to ensure compatibility across various devices and players.

Metadata Standards: Metadata standards like Exif [cipa.jp/e/std/std-sec] for images and ID3 [mpgedit.org/mpgedit/mpeg_format/mpeghdr.htm#mpegtag] for audio allow multimedia content to carry information such as date, location, artist, album and copyright details.

Color Management Standards: Standards like sRGB [webstore.iec.ch/publication/6169], AdobeRGB [color.org/chardata/rgb/adobergb.xalter] and ProPhoto/ROMM RGB (reference output medium metric) [iso.org/standard/56591.html] define color spaces, ensuring consistent color reproduction across devices and platforms.

Captioning and Subtitle Standards: Formats like WebVTT (Web Video Text Track) [w3.org/TR/webvtt] and TTML (Timed Text Markup Language) [w3.org/TR/ttml] are used to create captions and subtitles for multimedia content, making it accessible to a broader audience. WebVTT is a standard designed for adding captions, subtitles and other text tracks to HTML5 videos, TTML is a standard for representing timed text, such as captions and subtitles, in online media content.

Medical imaging standard: The DICOM (Digital Imaging and Communications in Medicine) standard [dicomstandard.org] provides a foundational framework for medical imaging and healthcare informatics by defining a structure and format of medical images as also the communication and networking protocols required for seamless data exchange within healthcare facilities.

1.5.1 JPEG Overview

JPEG (Joint Photographic Experts Group) [jpeg.org] is a standard for lossy compression for digital photographic images.

1.5.1.1 JPEG 1

The original JPEG specification, called JPEG 1 [jpeg.org/jpeg], published in 1992, implements processes from various earlier research papers and patents cited by the CCITT (now ITU-T) and Joint Photographic Experts Group. The standard specifies the CODEC (coder/decoder) used to compress and decompress the image while the Exif and JFIF standards define the file format. The degree of compression can be adjusted by selecting a parameter for controlling image quality, but typically it achieves a 10:1 compression ratio with acceptable quality. The MIME type for JPEG is "image/jpeg" and a filename extension of ".jpg" or ".jpeg". The JPEG committee has as one of its explicit goals that their standards, especially their baseline methods, be implementable without payment of license fees. The original JPEG standard was adopted by ITU-T as Recommendation T.81 and by ISO as standard ISO/IEC 10918-1 [www.iso.org/standard/18902.html]. The standard consists of the following parts:

- Part 1: ISO/IEC 10918-1:1994 – Requirements and guidelines
- Part 2: ISO/IEC 10918-2:1995 – Compliance testing
- Part 3: ISO/IEC 10918-3:1997 –Extensions
- Part 4: ISO/IEC 10918-4:1999 – Registration authorities
- Part 5: ISO/IEC 10918-5:2013 – File Interchange Format
- Part 6: ISO/IEC 10918-6:2013 –Application to Printing Systems
- Part 7: ISO/IEC 10918-7:2023 –Reference Software

1.5.1.2 JPEG 2000

JPEG 2000 [jpeg.org/jpeg2000], formally ISO/IEC 15444 [www.iso.org/standard/78321.html], offered a number of benefits over the original JPEG format, namely, multiple resolutions of the same image, progressive decoding, choice of lossy or lossless modes, error resilience, flexible file format, HDR support, support for transparency and alpha channels. It consists of the following parts:

- Part 1: ISO/IEC 15444-1:2000 – Core coding system
- Part 2: ISO/IEC 15444-2:2004 – Extensions
- Part 3: ISO/IEC 15444-3:2002 – Motion JPEG 2000 (MJ2 or MJP2)
- Part 4: ISO/IEC 15444-4:2002 – Conformance testing
- Part 5: ISO/IEC 15444-5:2003 – Reference Software
- Part 6: ISO/IEC 15444-6:2003 – Compound image file format
- Part 7: abandoned
- Part 8: ISO/IEC 15444-8:2007 – Secure JPEG 2000
- Part 9: ISO/IEC 15444-9:2005 – Interactivity tools, APIs and protocols
- Part 10: ISO/IEC 15444-10:2008 – Extensions for three dimensional data (JP3D)
- Part 11: ISO/IEC 15444-11:2007 – Wireless (JPWL)

- Part 12: ISO/IEC 15444-12:2004 –Base media file format
- Part 13: ISO/IEC 15444-13:2008 –Entry level encoder
- Part 14: ISO/IEC 15444-14:2013 – XML representation (JPXML)
- Part 15: ISO/IEC 15444-15:2019 – High throughput format
- Part 16: ISO/IEC 15444-16:2019 – High efficiency file format

1.5.1.3 JPEG AI

JPEG AI [jpeg.org/jpegai], formally ISO/IEC CD 6048 [www.iso.org/standard/81984.html], is designed for creation of a learning-based image coding standard offering a single-stream, compact compressed domain representation, targeting both human visualization, with significant compression efficiency improvement over image coding standards in common use at equivalent subjective quality, and effective performance for image processing and computer vision tasks, with the goal of supporting a royalty-free baseline. It consists of the following parts:

- Part 1: ISO/IEC 6048-1 – Core coding system
- Part 2: ISO/IEC 6048-2 – Profiling
- Part 3: ISO/IEC 6048-3 – Reference software
- Part 4: ISO/IEC 6048-4 – Conformance

1.5.1.4 JPEG AIC

JPEG Advanced Image Coding and Evaluations [jpeg.org/aic], formally ISO/IEC 29170 [www.iso.org/standard/66094.html], is designed to locate and evaluate new scientific developments and advancements in image coding research. Relevant topics include new compression methodologies and quality evaluation methodologies and procedures. It consists of the following parts:

- Part 1: ISO/IEC 29170-1 – Guidelines for image coding system evaluation
- Part 2: ISO/IEC 29170-2 – Evaluation procedure for nearly lossless coding

1.5.1.5 JPEG Pleno

JPEG Pleno [jpeg.org/jpegpleno], formally ISO/IEC 21794 [www.iso.org/standard/74531.html], aims to provide a standard framework for representing new imaging modalities, such as texture-plus-depth, light field, point cloud, and holographic imaging. Such imaging should be understood as light representations inspired by the plenoptic function, which describe intensity of light rays as functions of visual angle, wavelength, time and visual angle. It consists of the following parts:

- Part 1: ISO/IEC 21794-1 – Framework
- Part 2: ISO/IEC 21794-2 – Light field coding
- Part 3: ISO/IEC 21794-3 – Conformance testing
- Part 4: ISO/IEC 21794-4 – Reference software

1.5.1.6 JPEG Systems

JPEG Systems [jpeg.org/jpegsystems], formally ISO/IEC 19566 [www.iso.org/standard/81643.html], is a suite of standards developed by the JPEG Committee that extend JPEG coding standards with wider system aspects and extensions. It describes file formats, transport mechanism, adds metadata and additional functionalities that are necessary to support applications beyond purely coded image data. It consists of the following parts:

- Part 1: ISO/IEC 19566-1 – Packaging of information using codestreams and file formats
- Part 2: ISO/IEC 19566-2 – Transport mechanisms and packaging
- Part 4: ISO/IEC 19566-4 – Privacy and security
- Part 5: ISO/IEC 19566-5 – JPEG universal metadata box format (JUMBF)
- Part 6: ISO/IEC 19566-6 – JPEG 360
- Part 7: ISO/IEC 19566-7 – JPEG linked media format (JLINK)
- Part 8: ISO/IEC 19566-8 – JPEG Snack

1.5.1.7 JPEG Trust

JPEG Trust [jpeg.org/jpegtrust] defines a framework for establishing trust in media. It addresses aspects of authenticity, provenance and integrity through secure and reliable annotation of media assets throughout their life cycle to address problems related to AI-based synthetic media such as deepfakes. The new standard is expected to be published in 2024.

1.5.1.8 JPEG XL

JPEG XL [jpeg.org/jpegxl], formally ISO/IEC 18181 [www.iso.org/standard/77977.html], is designed to meet the needs of image delivery on the Web and professional photography. It supports wide color gamut as well as high dynamic range and high bit depth images. JPEG XL further includes features such as animation, alpha channels, layers, thumbnails, lossless and progressive coding to support a wide range of use cases, including, but not limited to, photo galleries, e-commerce, social media, user interfaces and cloud storage. To enable novel applications, it also adds support for 360 degree images, image bursts, large panoramas/mosaics and printing. It consists of the following parts:

- Part 1: ISO/IEC 18181-1:2022 – Core coding system
- Part 2: ISO/IEC 18181-2:2021 – File format
- Part 3: ISO/IEC 18181-3:2022 – Conformance testing
- Part 4: ISO/IEC 18181-4:2022 – Reference software

1.5.1.9 JPEG XR

JPEG XR [jpeg.org/jpegxr], formally ISO/IEC 29199 [www.iso.org/standard/79414.html], provides a practical coding technology for a broad range of applications with excellent compression capability and important additional functionalities. The primary intended application of JPEG XR is the representation of continuous-tone still images such as photographic images. It consists of the following parts:

- Part 1: ISO/IEC 29199-1 – System architecture
- Part 2: ISO/IEC 29199-2 – Image coding specification
- Part 3: ISO/IEC 29199-3 – Motion JPEG XR
- Part 4: ISO/IEC 29199-4 – Conformance testing
- Part 5: ISO/IEC 29199-5 – Reference software

1.5.1.10 JPEG XS

JPEG XS [jpeg.org/jpegxs], formally ISO/IEC 21122 [www.iso.org/standard/81551.html], is an extension for visually lossless, low-latency and lightweight files, designed for applications like virtual reality, drones and self-driving cars. It consists of the following parts:

- Part 1: ISO/IEC 21122-1 – Core coding system
- Part 2: ISO/IEC 21122-2 – Profiles and buffer models
- Part 3: ISO/IEC 21122-3 – Transport and container formats
- Part 4: ISO/IEC 21122-4 – Conformance testing
- Part 5: ISO/IEC 21122-5 – Reference software

1.5.1.11 JPEG XT

JPEG XT [jpeg.org/jpegxt], formally ISO/IEC 18477 [www.iso.org/standard/79103.html], is a backward compatible extension to the legacy JPEG standard with additional support for higher integer bit depths, HDR imaging, lossless coding, alpha channel coding and extensible file format. It consists of the following parts:

- Part 1: ISO/IEC 18477-1 – Core coding system
- Part 2: ISO/IEC 18477-2 – HDR (High dynamic range) imaging
- Part 3: ISO/IEC 18477-3 – File format
- Part 4: ISO/IEC 18477-4 – Conformance testing
- Part 5: ISO/IEC 18477-5 – Reference software
- Part 6: ISO/IEC 18477-6 – IDR Integer coding
- Part 7: ISO/IEC 18477-7 – HDR Floating-Point Coding
- Part 8: ISO/IEC 18477-8 – Lossless and Near-lossless Coding
- Part 9: ISO/IEC 18477-9 – Alpha channel Coding

1.5.1.12 JPEG LS

JPEG LS [jpeg.org/jpegls], formally ISO/IEC 14495 [www.iso.org/standard/22397.html], was defined to address the need for effective lossless and near-lossless compression of continuous-tone still images. JPEG LS is especially suited for low-complexity hardware implementations of very moderate complexity, while at the same time providing state-of-the-art lossless compression performance. It consists of the following parts:

- Part 1: ISO/IEC 14495-1 – Baseline
- Part 2: ISO/IEC 14495-2 – Extensions

1.5.1.13 JPSearch

JPSearch [jpeg.org/jpsearch], formally ISO/IEC 24800 [www.iso.org/standard/78323.html], is designed to address interoperability in image search and retrieval systems. For this purpose, JPSearch puts forward an abstract image search and retrieval framework. Interfaces and protocols for data exchange between the components of this architecture are standardized. It consists of the following parts:

- Part 1: ISO/IEC 24800-1 – System framework and components
- Part 2: ISO/IEC 24800-2 – Registration, identification and management of schema and ontology

- Part 3: ISO/IEC 24800-3 – Query format
- Part 4: ISO/IEC 24800-4 – File format
- Part 5: ISO/IEC 24800-5 – Data interchange format
- Part 6: ISO/IEC 24800-6 – Reference software

1.5.1.14 JBIG

JBIG1 [jpeg.org/jbig] is an early lossless image compression standard for binary images released by the Joint Bi-level Image Experts Group, in 1993 as standard ISO/IEC 11544 [www.iso.org/standard/19498.html], and widely used in fax machines, Later in 2000, an improved version JBIG2 with better coding efficiency was released as standard ISO/IEC 14492 [www.iso.org/standard/75396.html]. It consists of the following parts:

- ISO/IEC 11544:1993 – Coded representation of picture and audio information
- ISO/IEC 14492:2019 – Lossy/lossless coding of bi-level images

1.5.2 MPEG Overview

The Motion Pictures Expert Group (MPEG) [mpeg.chiariglione.org] is a working group under ISO/IEC (International Standards Organization/International Electrotechnical Commission) set up to formulate a set of standards relating to a range of multimedia application involving audio and video primarily. Since its first meeting in 1988, MPEG has grown to include approximately 350 members from the industry and academia. MPEG's official designation is ISO/IEC JCT1/SC29 WG11 [www.iso.org/committee/45316.html]. This section contains an overview of the various standards developed.

1.5.2.1 MPEG-1

The International Standards Organization (ISO) and the International Electro-technical Commission (IEC) formed the Moving Pictures Experts Group (MPEG) in 1988 to devise compression techniques for audio and video. This group has developed a number of highly successful standards. It first devised the ISO/IEC International Standard 11172 for reduced data-rate coding of video and audio signals. The standard was finalized in November 1992 and is commonly known as MPEG-1 [mpeg.chiariglione.org/standards/mpeg-1]. It was later used as a standard for Video CD and includes the popular MP3 audio format. It is defined in a series of documents all subsets of ISO/IEC Recommendation 11172. It consists of the following parts:

- Part 1: ISO/IEC 11172-1:1993 – Systems
- Part 2: ISO/IEC 11172-2:1993 – Video
- Part 3: ISO/IEC 11172-3:1993 – Audio
- Part 4: ISO/IEC 11172-4:1995 – Compliance Testing
- Part 5: ISO/IEC 11172-5:1998 – Software Simulation

1.5.2.2 MPEG-2

MPEG-2 [mpeg.chiariglione.org/standards/mpeg-2], formally ISO/IEC 13818, is a video and audio storage and transmission standards for broadcast quality television. It is used for digital TV transmission, digital satellite TV services, digital cable TV signals and for DVD applications. It is defined in a series of documents which are all subsets of ISO Recommendations 13818. The standard currently has nine parts: the first three have reached international standard status, while the others are at different levels of completion; one has been withdrawn. It consists of the following parts:

- Part 1: ISO/IEC 13818-1:2000 – Systems
- Part 2: ISO/IEC 13818-2:2000 – Video
- Part 3: ISO/IEC 13818-3:1998 – Audio
- Part 4: ISO/IEC 13818-4:1998 – Conformance Testing
- Part 5: ISO/IEC 13818-5:1997 – Software Simulation S
- Part 6: ISO/IEC 13818-6:1998 – Extensions for DSM-CC (Digital Storage Media Command and Control)
- Part 7: ISO/IEC 13818-7:1997 – Advanced Audio Coding AAC
- Part 8: ISO/IEC 13818-8:1997 – abandoned
- Part 9: ISO/IEC 13818-9:1996 – Extensions for Real-time Interface for System Decoders
- Part 10: ISO/IEC 13818-10:1999 – Conformance Extensions for DSM-CC

1.5.2.3 MPEG-4

MPEG-4 [mpeg.chiariglione.org/standards/mpeg-4], formally ISO/IEC 14496, introduced in late 1998, is the designation for a group of standards for coding of audio visual objects and related technology agreed upon by the ISO/IEC Moving Picture Experts Group (MPEG). The primary uses for the MPEG-4 standard are Web (streaming media) and CD distribution, conversational (videophone), and broadcast television. MPEG-4 absorbs many of the features of MPEG-1 and MPEG-2 and other related standards, adding new features such as (extended) VRML support for 3D rendering, object-oriented composite files (including audio, video, and VRML (Virtual Reality Modeling Language objects), support for externally specified Digital Rights Management and various types of interactivity. Most of the features included in MPEG-4 are left to individual developers to decide whether to implement them. This means that there are probably no complete implementations of the entire MPEG-4 set of standards. To deal with this, the standard includes the concept of profiles and levels, allowing a specific set of capabilities to be defined in a manner appropriate for a subset of applications. It consists of the following parts:

- Part 1: ISO/IEC 14496-1 – Systems
- Part 2: ISO/IEC 14496-2 – Visual
- Part 3: ISO/IEC 14496-3 – Audio
- Part 4: ISO/IEC 14496-4 – Conformance
- Part 5: ISO/IEC 14496-5 – Reference Software
- Part 6: ISO/IEC 14496-6 – Delivery Multimedia Integration Framework (DMIF)
- Part 7: ISO/IEC 14496-7 – Optimized Reference Software
- Part 8: ISO/IEC 14496-8 – Carriage on IP Networks
- Part 9: ISO/IEC 14496-9 – Reference Hardware
- Part 10: ISO/IEC 14496-10 – Advanced Video Coding (AVC)
- Part 11: ISO/IEC 14496-11 – Scene Description and Application Engine
- Part 12: ISO/IEC 14496-12 – ISO Base Media File Format
- Part 13: ISO/IEC 14496-13 – Intellectual Property Management and Protection (IPMP) Extensions
- Part 14: ISO/IEC 14496-14 – MPEG-4 File Format
- Part 15: ISO/IEC 14496-15 – Advanced Video Coding (AVC) File Format
- Part 16: ISO/IEC 14496-16 – Animation Framework eXtension (AFX)
- Part 17: ISO/IEC 14496-17 – Timed Text Subtitle Format
- Part 18: ISO/IEC 14496-18 – Font Compression and Streaming.
- Part 19: ISO/IEC 14496-19 – Synthesized Texture Stream
- Part 20: ISO/IEC 14496-20 – Lightweight Application Scene Representation (LASeR)
- Part 21: ISO/IEC 14496-21 – MPEG-J Graphics Framework eXtensions (GFX)
- Part 22: ISO/IEC 14496-22 – Open Font Format
- Part 23: ISO/IEC 14496-23 – Symbolic Music Representation (SMR)
- Part 24: ISO/IEC 14496-24 – Audio and Systems Interaction
- Part 25: ISO/IEC 14496-25 – 3D Graphics Compression Format
- Part 26: ISO/IEC 14496-26 – Audio Conformance
- Part 27: (ISO/IEC 14496-27) 3D Graphics Conformance

1.5.2.4 MPEG-5

MPEG-5 [mpeg.chiariglione.org/standards/mpeg-5], formally ISO/IEC 23094, is an evolution of MPEG-4 aiming to improve compression efficiency and support emerging technologies like 3D video and ultra-high definition. It introduces new tools for coding efficiency and provides enhanced features for video coding. MPEG-5 builds upon the foundations of MPEG-4 but incorporates advancements to deliver better video coding performance and accommodate evolving industry needs. It consists of the following parts:

- Part 1: ISO/IEC 23094-1 – Essential Video Coding (EVC)
- Part 2: ISO/IEC 23094-2 – Low Complexity Enhancement Video Coding (LCEVC)
- Part 3: ISO/IEC 23094-3 – Attribute value coding for ISO base file format

1.5.2.5 MPEG-7

MPEG-7 [mpeg.chiariglione.org/standards/mpeg-7], formally ISO/IEC 15938, is a suite of standards for description and search of audio, visual and multimedia content, referred to as Multimedia content description interface. It consists of the following parts:

- Part 1: ISO/IEC 15938-1 – Systems
- Part 2: ISO/IEC 15938-2 – Description Definition Language
- Part 3: ISO/IEC 15938-3 – Visual
- Part 4: ISO/IEC 15938-4 – Audio

- Part 5: ISO/IEC 15938-5 – Multimedia Description Schemes
- Part 6: ISO/IEC 15938-6 – Reference Software
- Part 7: ISO/IEC 15938-7 – Conformance Testing
- Part 8: ISO/IEC 15938-8 – Extraction and use of MPEG-7 descriptions
- Part 9: ISO/IEC 15938-9 – Profiles and Levels
- Part 10: ISO/IEC 15938-10 – Schema Definitions
- Part 11: ISO/IEC 15938-11 – Profile Schemas
- Part 12: ISO/IEC 15938-12 – Query format
- Part 13: ISO/IEC 15938-13 – Compact Descriptors for Visual Search (CDVS)
- Part 14: ISO/IEC 15938-14 – Reference software, conformance and usage guidelines for CDVS
- Part 15: ISO/IEC 15938-15 – Compact descriptors for video analysis (CDVA)
- Part 16: ISO/IEC 15938-16 – Conformance and Reference Software for CDVA
- Part 17: ISO/IEC 15938-17 – Compression of neural networks for multimedia content description and analysis

1.5.2.6 MPEG-21

MPEG-21 [mpeg.chiariglione.org/standards/mpeg-21], formally ISO/IEC 21000, is a suite of standard that define a normative open framework for end-to-end multimedia creation, delivery and consumption that provides content creators, producers, distributors and service providers with equal opportunities in the MPEG-21 enabled open market, and also be to the benefit of the content consumers providing them access to a large variety of content in an interoperable manner. It consists of the following parts:

- Part 1: ISO/IEC 21000-1 – Vision, Technologies and Strategy
- Part 2: ISO/IEC 21000-2 – Digital Item Declaration
- Part 3: ISO/IEC 21000-3 – Digital Item Identification
- Part 4: ISO/IEC 21000-4 – IPMP (Intellectual Property Management and Protection) Components
- Part 5: ISO/IEC 21000-5 – Rights Expression Language
- Part 6: ISO/IEC 21000-6 – Rights Data Dictionary
- Part 7: ISO/IEC 21000-7 – Digital Item Adaptation
- Part 8: ISO/IEC 21000-8 – Reference Software
- Part 9: ISO/IEC 21000-9 – File Format
- Part 10: ISO/IEC 21000-10 – Digital Item Processing
- Part 11: ISO/IEC 21000-11 – Evaluation Tools for Persistent Association
- Part 12: ISO/IEC 21000-12 – Test Bed for MPEG-21 Resource Delivery
- Part 13: ISO/IEC 21000-13 – void
- Part 14: ISO/IEC 21000-14 – Conformance
- Part 15: ISO/IEC 21000-15 – Event reporting
- Part 16: ISO/IEC 21000-16 – Binary format
- Part 17: ISO/IEC 21000-17 – Fragment Identification
- Part 18: ISO/IEC 21000-18 – Digital Item Streaming
- Part 19: ISO/IEC 21000-19 – White paper on MPEG IPR Ontologies
- Part 20: ISO/IEC 21000-20 – Contract Expression Language
- Part 21: ISO/IEC 21000-21 – Media Contract Ontology
- Part 22: ISO/IEC 21000-22 – User Description

1.5.2.7 MPEG-A

MPEG-A [mpeg.chiariglione.org/standards/mpeg-a], formally ISO/IEC 23000, is a group of standards for composing MPEG systems referred to as Multimedia Application Format. It consists of the following parts:

- Part 1: ISO/IEC 23000-1 – Purpose for multimedia application formats
- Part 2: ISO/IEC 23000-2 – MPEG music player application format
- Part 3: ISO/IEC 23000-3 – MPEG photo player application format
- Part 4: ISO/IEC 23000-4 – Musical slide show application format
- Part 5: ISO/IEC 23000-5 – Media streaming application format
- Part 6: ISO/IEC 23000-6 – Professional archival application format
- Part 7: ISO/IEC 23000-7 – Open access application format

- Part 8: ISO/IEC 23000-8 – Portable video application format
- Part 9: ISO/IEC 23000-9 – Digital Multimedia Broadcasting application format
- Part 10: ISO/IEC 23000-10 – Surveillance application format
- Part 11: ISO/IEC 23000-11 – Stereoscopic video application format
- Part 12: ISO/IEC 23000-12 – Interactive music application format
- Part 13: ISO/IEC 23000-13 – Augmented reality application format
- Part 14: ISO/IEC 23000-14 – Closed (was Mixed and Augmented Reality Reference Model)
- Part 15: ISO/IEC 23000-15 – Multimedia Preservation Application Format
- Part 16: ISO/IEC 23000-16 – Publish/Subscribe Application Format
- Part 17: ISO/IEC 23000-17 – Multisensory Effects Application Format
- Part 18: ISO/IEC 23000-18 – Media Linking Application Format
- Part 19: ISO/IEC 23000-19 – Common Media Application Format
- Part 20: ISO/IEC 23000-20 – Visual Identity Application Format

1.5.2.8 MPEG-B

MPEG-B [mpeg.chiariglione.org/standards/mpeg-b], formally ISO/IEC 23001, is a suite of standards for systems technologies that do not fall in other well-established MPEG standards. It consists of the following parts:

- Part 1: ISO/IEC 23001-1 – Binary MPEG format for XML
- Part 2: ISO/IEC 23002-2 – Fragment Request Unit
- Part 3: ISO/IEC 23003-3 – XML Representation of IPMP-X messages
- Part 4: ISO/IEC 23001-4 – Codec Configuration Representation
- Part 5: ISO/IEC 23001-5 – Bitstream Syntax Description Language
- Part 6: ISO/IEC 23001-6 – void (to MPEG-DASH part 1)
- Part 7: ISO/IEC 23001-7 – Common Encryption for ISO Base Media File Format Files
- Part 8: ISO/IEC 23001-8 – Common Encryption for MPEG-2 Transport Stream
- Part 9: ISO/IEC 23001-9 – Carriage of Timed Metadata Metrics of Media in ISO Base Media File Format
- Part 10: ISO/IEC 23001-10 – Green Metadata
- Part 11: ISO/IEC 23001-11 – Sample Variants in the ISO Base Media File Format
- Part 12: ISO/IEC 23001-12 – White paper on Media Orchestration
- Part 13: ISO/IEC 23001-13 – Media orchestration
- Part 14: ISO/IEC 23001-14 – Partial File Format
- Part 15: ISO/IEC 23001-15 – Carriage of Web Resource in ISOBMFF

1.5.2.9 MPEG-C

MPEG-C [mpeg.chiariglione.org/standards/mpeg-c], formally, ISO/IEC 23002, is a suite of video standards that do not fall in other well-established MPEG video standards. It consists of the following parts:

- Part 1: ISO/IEC 23002-1 – Accuracy specification for implementation of integer-output IDCT
- Part 2: ISO/IEC 23002-2 – Fixed point 8x8 DCT/IDCT
- Part 3: ISO/IEC 23002-3 – Auxiliary Video Data Representation
- Part 4: ISO/IEC 23002-4 – Video Tool Library
- Part 5: ISO/IEC 23002-5 – Reconfigurable Media Coding Conformance and Reference Software
- Part 6: ISO/IEC 23002-6 – Tools for reconfigurable media coding implementations
- Part 7: ISO/IEC 23002-7 – Supplemental enhancement information messages for coded video bit-streams

1.5.2.10 MPEG-D

MPEG-D [mpeg.chiariglione.org/standards/mpeg-d], formally ISO/IEC 23003, is a suite of audio standards that do not fall in other well-established MPEG audio standards. It consists of the following parts:

- Part 1: ISO/IEC 23003-1 – MPEG Surround
- Part 2: ISO/IEC 23003-2 – Spatial Audio Object Coding
- Part 3: ISO/IEC 23003-3 – Unified Speech and Audio Coding

- Part 4: ISO/IEC 23003-4 – Audio Dynamic Range Control
- Part 5: ISO/IEC 23003-5 – Uncompressed Audio in MP4 FF

1.5.2.11 MPEG-E

MPEG-E [mpeg.chiariglione.org/standards/mpeg-e], formally ISO/IEC 23004, is a standard for an Application Programming Interface (API) of Multimedia Middleware (M3W) that can be used to provide a uniform view to an interoperable multimedia middleware platform. It consists of the following parts:

- Part 1: ISO/IEC 23004-1 – Architecture
- Part 2: ISO/IEC 23004-2 – Multimedia API
- Part 3: ISO/IEC 23004-3 – Component Model
- Part 4: ISO/IEC 23004-4 – Resource and Quality Management
- Part 5: ISO/IEC 23004-5 – Component Download Framework
- Part 6: ISO/IEC 23004-6 – Fault Management Framework
- Part 7: ISO/IEC 23004-7 – Integrity Management Framework
- Part 8: ISO/IEC 23004-8 – Reference Software and Conformance

1.5.2.12 MPEG-G

MPEG-G [mpeg.chiariglione.org/standards/mpeg-g], formally ISO/IEC 23092, is a suite of standards to provide new effective and interoperable solutions for genomic information processing applications. It consists of the following parts:

- Part 1: ISO/IEC 23092-1 – Transport and Storage of Genomic Information
- Part 2: ISO/IEC 23092-2 – Genomic Information Representation
- Part 3: ISO/IEC 23092-3 – API for Genomic Information Representation
- Part 4: ISO/IEC 23092-4 – Reference Software
- Part 5: ISO/IEC 23092-5 – Conformance
- Part 6: ISO/IEC 23092-6 – Genomic Annotation Representation

1.5.2.13 MPEG-H

MPEG-H [mpeg.chiariglione.org/standards/mpeg-h], formally ISO/IEC 23008, is a suite of standards for heterogeneous environment delivery of audio-visual information compressed with high efficiency. It consists of the following parts:

- Part 1: ISO/IEC 23008-1 – MPEG Media Transport (MMT)
- Part 2: ISO/IEC 23008-2 – High Efficiency Video Coding
- Part 3: ISO/IEC 23008-3 – 3D Audio
- Part 4: ISO/IEC 23008-4 – MMT Reference Software
- Part 5: ISO/IEC 23008-5 – HEVC Reference Software
- Part 6: ISO/IEC 23008-6 – 3D Audio Reference Software
- Part 7: ISO/IEC 23008-7 – MMT Conformance testing
- Part 8: ISO/IEC 23008-8 – HEVC Conformance testing
- Part 9: ISO/IEC 23008-9 – 3D Audio conformance testing
- Part 10: ISO/IEC 23008-10 – MPEG Media Transport FEC Codes
- Part 11: ISO/IEC 23008-11 – MPEG Composition Information
- Part 12: ISO/IEC 23008-12 – Image File Format
- Part 13: ISO/IEC 23008-13 – MMT Implementation Guidelines
- Part 14: ISO/IEC 23008-14 – Conversion and coding practices for high-dynamic-range and wide-colour-gamut video
- Part 15: ISO/IEC 23008-15 – Signaling, backward compatibility and display adaptation for HDR/WCG video

1.5.2.14 MPEG-I

MPEG-I [mpeg.chiariglione.org/standards/mpeg-i], formally ISO/IEC 23090, is a collection of standards to digitally represent immersive media. It consists of the following parts:

- Part 1: ISO/IEC 23090-1 – Immersive Media Architectures
- Part 2: ISO/IEC 23090-2 – Omnidirectional Media Format
- Part 3: ISO/IEC 23090-3 – Versatile Video Coding
- Part 4: ISO/IEC 23090-4 – Immersive Audio Coding

- Part 5: ISO/IEC 23090-5 – Point Cloud Compression
- Part 6: ISO/IEC 23090-6 – Immersive Media Metrics
- Part 7: ISO/IEC 23090-7 – Immersive Media Metadata
- Part 8: ISO/IEC 23090-8 – Network Based Media Processing
- Part 9: ISO/IEC 23090-9 – Geometry-based Point Cloud Compression
- Part 10: ISO/IEC 23090-10 – Carriage of Point Cloud Data
- Part 11: ISO/IEC 23090-11 – Implementation Guidelines for Network-based Media Processing
- Part 12: ISO/IEC 23090-12 – Immersive Video

1.5.2.15 MPEG-M

MPEG-M [mpeg.chiariglione.org/standards/mpeg-m], formally ISO/IEC 23006, is a suite of standards to enable the easy design and implementation of media-handling value chains whose devices interoperate because they are all based on the same set of technologies, especially MPEG technologies accessible from the middleware and multimedia services, also known as MPEG eXtensible Middleware (MXM). It consists of the following parts:

- Part 1: ISO/IEC 23006-1 – Architecture
- Part 2: ISO/IEC 23006-2 – MPEG Extensible Middleware API
- Part 3: ISO/IEC 23006-3 – Reference Software and Conformance
- Part 4: ISO/IEC 23006-4 – Elementary Services
- Part 5: ISO/IEC 23006-5 – Service aggregation

1.5.2.16 MPEG-U

MPEG-U [mpeg.chiariglione.org/standards/mpeg-u], formally ISO/IEC 23007, is a set of specifications of the exchange, the display, the control and the communication of widgets with other entities and for data format for advanced user interaction (AUI) interfaces to support various advanced user interaction devices. It provides a general-purpose technology with innovative functionality that enables its use in heterogeneous scenarios such as broadcast, mobile, home network and Web domains. It consists of the following parts:

- Part 1: ISO/IEC 23007-1 – Widgets
- Part 2: ISO/IEC 23007-2 – Advanced User Interaction Interface
- Part 3: ISO/IEC 23007-3 – Reference Software and Conformance

1.5.2.17 MPEG-V

MPEG-V [mpeg.chiariglione.org/standards/mpeg-v], formally ISO/IEC 23005, outlines an architecture and specifies associated information representations to enable interoperability between virtual worlds (e.g., digital content provider of a virtual world, gaming, simulation), and between real and virtual worlds (e.g., sensors, actuators, vision and rendering, robotics). It consists of the following parts:

- Part 1: ISO/IEC 23005-1 – Architecture
- Part 2: ISO/IEC 23005-2 – Control Information
- Part 3: ISO/IEC 23005-3 – Sensory Information
- Part 4: ISO/IEC 23005-4 – Virtual World Object Characteristics
- Part 5: ISO/IEC 23005-5 – Data Formats for Interaction
- Part 6: ISO/IEC 23005-6 – Common Types and Tools
- Part 7: ISO/IEC 23005-7 – Reference Software and Conformance

1.5.2.18 MPEG-DASH

MPEG-DASH [mpeg.chiariglione.org/standards/mpeg-dash], formally ISO/IEC 23009, is a suite of standards providing a solution for the efficient and easy streaming of multimedia using existing available HTTP infrastructure (particularly servers and CDNs, but also proxies, caches, etc.), i.e., dynamic adaptive streaming over HTTP. It consists of the following parts:

- Part 1: ISO/IEC 23009-1 – Media presentation description and segment formats
- Part 2: ISO/IEC 23009-2 – Reference software and conformance
- Part 3: ISO/IEC 23009-3 – Implementation guidelines
- Part 4: ISO/IEC 23009-4 – Format Independent Segment encryption and authentication
- Part 5: ISO/IEC 23009-5 – Server and network assisted DASH (SAND)
- Part 6: ISO/IEC 23009-6 – DASH with Server Push and WebSockets

- Part 7: ISO/IEC 23009-7 – Delivery of CMAF (Common Media Application Format) content with DASH
- Part 8: ISO/IEC 23009-8 – Reference Software and Conformance

1.5.2.19 MPEG-IoMT

MPEG-IoMT [mpeg.chiariglione.org/standards/mpeg-iomt], formally ISO/IEC 23093, is a set of APIs for communicating media devices (called Media Things), i.e., Internet of Media Things. It consists of the following parts:

- Part 1: ISO/IEC 23093-1 – IoMT Architecture
- Part 2: ISO/IEC 23093-2 – IoMT Discovery and Communication API
- Part 3: ISO/IEC 23093-3 – Media data formats and API
- Part 4: ISO/IEC 23093-4 – IoMT Reference Software and Conformance

1.5.2.20 MPEG-CICP

MPEG-CICP [mpeg.chiariglione.org/standards/mpeg-cicp], formally ISO/IEC 23091, is a suite of standards to specify code points for non-standard specific media formats. It consists of the following parts:

- Part 1: ISO/IEC 23091-1 – Systems
- Part 2: ISO/IEC 23091-2 – Video
- Part 3: ISO/IEC 23091-3 – Audio
- Part 4: ISO/IEC 23091-4 – Usage of video signal type code points

1.5.2.21 MPEG-MAR

MPEG-MAR [mpeg.chiariglione.org/standards/mpeg-mar], formally ISO/IEC 18039, is a Mixed and Augmented Reality Reference Model developed jointly with SC 24/WG 9. It consists of the following part:

- Part 1: ISO/IEC 18039-1 – Mixed and Augmented Reality Reference Model

1.5.3 Standards Organizations

Several organizations are responsible for developing and maintaining multimedia standards. These organizations bring together experts from various industries to develop and maintain standards that cover a wide range of multimedia aspects, including audio, video, graphics and interactive content. These bodies work collaboratively to define technical standards, file formats, compression algorithms and protocols that facilitate the creation, distribution and playback of multimedia content across diverse platforms and devices. Some of the well-known organizations, along with their activities, are discussed below.

1.5.3.1 Audio Engineering Society (AES)

The AES [aes.org] has been involved in setting technical standards for audio since 1977. The AES Standards Committee (AESSC), through a consensus system, develops and publishes a number of standards on the subject of analog and digital audio recording, transmission and/or reproduction. Notable standards include: (1) AES3 (also commonly known as AES/EBU) for digital audio interconnection (2) AES10 (also commonly known as MADI) for multichannel digital audio interconnection (3) AES11 for digital audio synchronization (4) AES31 file exchange format (5) AES53 for sending AES3 digital audio data over Asynchronous Transfer Mode networks (6) AES67 for audio over IP interoperability.

1.5.3.2 Advanced Television Systems Committee (ATSC)

The Advanced Television Systems Committee (ATSC) [aes.org] is an important organization in the field of digital television broadcasting standards, established in 1982. The ATSC is renowned for its work in shaping the digital television landscape and ensuring the seamless transition from analog to digital television. The ATSC develops and maintains a set of standards that encompass various aspects of digital television, including transmission, video coding, audio coding, and interactive television. The ATSC standards have played a critical role in enhancing the quality and efficiency of television broadcasting, leading to innovations such as high-definition television (HDTV), 4K ultra-high-definition television (UHDTV), and the advanced broadcast capabilities used for over-the-air, cable, satellite and internet-based TV services. Notable standards include: (1) A/52, Digital Audio Compression (AC-3), (2) A/53, Digital TV standard, (3) A/70, Conditional access system for terrestrial broadcast, (4) A/72, AVC video, (5) A/81, DTH satellite broadcast standard, (6) A/90, ATSC data broadcast system and (7) A/153, Mobile DTV standard.

1.5.3.3 International Commission on Illumination (CIE)

The International Commission on Illumination (CIE) [cie.co.at], established in 1913, is the global authority on the science and art of light and lighting.

This international organization, often referred to as the CIE from its French name "Commission Internationale de l'Éclairage," is dedicated to promoting the understanding and application of light and color. Headquartered at Vienna, Austria, the CIE develops and publishes standards, recommendations, and reports that encompass various aspects of light and lighting, including photometry, colorimetry, and the effects of light on human well-being. It plays a vital role in fields such as architecture, lighting design, automotive lighting and display technology. The CIE's work ensures that lighting is not only functional but also safe, energy-efficient, and conducive to human comfort and productivity. The organization's contributions extend to diverse domains, including healthcare, transportation, and environmental sustainability. Notable contributions include: (1) formalization of the CIE 1931 XYZ color space, (2) definitions of the 1931 CIE 2° standard observer, (3) definitions of the 1964 10° CIE standard observer, (4) development of the CIELAB and CIELUV color spaces.

1.5.3.4 Digital Imaging and Communications in Medicine Systems Committee (DICOM)

The DICOM Systems Committee [dicomstandard.org] is a vital component of the healthcare and medical imaging industry, responsible for developing and maintaining the DICOM standard. DICOM, short for Digital Imaging and Communications in Medicine, is a standardized protocol and file format used for the exchange and management of medical imaging data and associated information. This standard ensures that medical imaging devices, systems and software from different manufacturers can seamlessly communicate and share medical images and related data. The DICOM Standard Committee is responsible for: (1) Developing proposed standards within the scope of the committee, (2) Voting to approve proposed standards within its scope, (3) Maintaining the committee's standard by reaffirming, revising or withdrawing the standard within five years of its approval.

1.5.3.5 European Broadcasting Union (EBU)

The European Broadcasting Union (EBU) [ebu.ch] is a leading alliance of public service media organizations in Europe, founded in 1950. Headquartered in Geneva, Switzerland, the EBU represents over 100 member broadcasters across the European continent and beyond. The organization plays a crucial role in promoting and advocating for public service broadcasting, which aims to provide high-quality, diverse and impartial content for the public's benefit. The EBU serves as a platform for collaboration among its member organizations, facilitating the exchange of content, technology and best practices. Furthermore, the EBU actively engages in addressing technological and regulatory challenges in the broadcasting industry, emphasizing issues like spectrum management, digital transition and innovation in media content production and delivery. Notable contributions include: (1) The AES/EBU digital audio interface, formally known as AES3, (2) Serial and parallel interfaces for digital video (ITU-R Recommendations 601 and 656), (3) RDS – the radio data system used on FM broadcasting, (4) Digital radio (DAB) through Eureka Project 147 (5) DVB (Digital Video Broadcasting).

1.5.3.6 European Computer Manufacturers Association (ECMA)

The European Computer Manufacturers Association (ECMA) [ecma-international.org] is an international standards organization founded in 1961, headquartered in Geneva, Switzerland. ECMA plays a vital role in the development and standardization of information and communication technology (ICT) standards. Its primary mission is to foster innovation, interoperability and competitiveness in the ICT sector. ECMA is particularly known for its work in developing standards for various technologies, including computer programming languages, file formats and optical storage media. Notable contributions include: (1) ECMA -6, 7-bit coded character set, (2) ECMA-107 – FAT12/FAT16 file system, (3) ECMA-119 – CD-ROM volume and file-structure (later known as ISO 9660), (4) ECMA-130 – CD-ROM "Yellow Book" format, (5) ECMA-262 – ECMAScript Language Specification (based on JavaScript), (6) ECMA-334 – C# Language Specification, (7) ECMA-335 – Common Language Infrastructure (CLI), (8) ECMA-372 – C++/CLI Language Specification, (9) ECMA-376 – Office Open XML (10) ECMA-404 – JSON.

1.5.3.7 International Color Consortium (ICC)

The International Color Consortium (ICC) [color.org] is a global organization formed in 1993 that focuses on developing and promoting open, vendor-neutral color management standards. The ICC plays a critical role in ensuring consistent and accurate color reproduction across different devices, applications and media. Its primary goal is to create a standard framework for translating and preserving color information, which is essential in industries like graphic design, printing, photography and digital imaging. The ICC defines color profiles, such as International Color Consortium Profile (ICC profile), which provides detailed information about a device's color capabilities enabling color sensitive software to render and reproduce colors consistently. These profiles are used to maintain color fidelity from the creation of an image to its final output, be it on a computer monitor, in print or on other display devices.

1.5.3.8 International Electrotechnical Commission (IEC)

The International Electro-technical Commission (IEC) [iec.ch] is a prominent global organization dedicated to standardizing and promoting international standards in the field of electro-technology. Founded in 1906, the IEC plays an important role in advancing safety, efficiency and interoperability in electrical and electronic devices, systems, and technologies. Its broad scope encompasses a wide array of subjects, including electrical standards for appliances, power generation, renewable energy and telecommunications, among others. The IEC's comprehensive standardization work ensures that products and systems are safe to use, energy-efficient, and compatible with global markets. The IEC cooperates closely with the International Organization for Standardization (ISO) and the International Telecommunication Union (ITU). In addition, it works with several major standards development organizations, including the IEEE. Standards developed jointly with ISO, carry the acronym of both organizations. The use of the ISO/IEC prefix covers publications from ISO/IEC Joint Technical Committee 1 – Information Technology. Some notable contributions include: (1) IEC 60065 Audio, video and similar electronic apparatus – Safety requirements, (2) IEC 60118 Electro-acoustics – Hearing aids, (3) IEC 60461 Time and control code, (4) IEC 60500 Underwater acoustics – Hydrophones, (5) IEC 60558 Type C helical video tape recorders, (6) IEC 60601 Medical electrical equipment, (7) IEC 60617 Graphical symbols for diagrams, (8) IEC 60757 Color codes in electronic components, (9) IEC 60794 Optical fiber cables, (10) IEC 60908 Audio recording – Compact disc digital audio system, (11) IEC 60958 Digital audio interface, (12) IEC 61747 Liquid crystal display devices,(13) IEC 61988 Plasma display panels, (14) IEC 62272 Digital radio mondiale (DRM), (15) IEC 62680 Universal Serial Bus (USB) interfaces.

1.5.3.9 Institute of Electrical and Electronics Engineers (IEEE)

The Institute of Electrical and Electronics Engineers (IEEE) [ieee.org] is a renowned and globally influential professional organization dedicated to the advancement of technology and innovation in the fields of electrical engineering, electronics and computer science. Established in 1963 through the merger of the American Institute of Electrical Engineers (AIEE) and the Institute of Radio Engineers (IRE), IEEE has grown to become the world's largest technical professional organization. It provides a wide array of resources, services and opportunities for its members, who include engineers, scientists and technologists. IEEE's core mission involves the development and promotion of industry standards, publications, conferences and educational programs, with a particular focus on areas such as telecommunications, electronics, power and energy, and computing. The IEEE Standards Association (IEEE SA) [standards.ieee.org] is an operating unit within IEEE that develops global standards in a broad range of industries, including power and energy, artificial intelligence systems, internet of things, consumer technology and consumer electronics, biomedical and health care, learning technology, information technology and robotics, telecommunication, automotive, transportation, home automation, nanotechnology, information assurance and emerging technologies. Notable contributions include: (1) IEEE 802.3 Ethernet Standards for Carrier Sense Multiple Access with Collision Detection (CSMA/CD), (2) IEEE 802.11 Wireless Networking – "WiFi", (3) IEEE 802.8 Fiber-optic connection, (4) IEEE P1363 Public key cryptography, (5) IEEE 1394 Serial bus – "FireWire", (6) IEEE 2413 Standard for an Architectural Framework for the Internet of Things (IoT).

1.5.3.10 Internet Engineering Task Force (IETF)

The Internet Engineering Task Force (IETF) [ietf.org] is an important and highly influential open international community of network designers, operators, vendors and researchers. Founded in 1986, the IETF plays a central role in shaping the architecture, protocols and standards of the Internet. It operates under the auspices of the Internet Society (ISOC) and supervised by the Internet Society's Internet Architecture Board (IAB). It provides a collaborative and open forum for the development and evolution of internet-related technologies. The IETF's work is driven by a commitment to openness, innovation and the principle of "rough consensus." It encompasses a wide array of technical areas, including internet protocols, routing, security, privacy and internet governance. The documents that specify and discuss current and developing standards for the Internet are called Requests for Comments, or RFCs. Notable contributions include: (1) Development of protocols and architectures related to communications like HTTP, FTP, URI schemes, MIME types, authentication mechanisms, data formats, metrics, and codecs. (2) Development of Internet protocols like IP versions 4 and 6, DNS, DHCP, host and router configuration, VPNs, etc. (3) Development of network management protocols like NETCONF, SNMP, RADIUS, Diameter, and CAPWAP. (4) Development of routing and signaling protocols such as OSPF, IS-IS, BGP, RSVP-TE and LDP. (5) Development of architecture and protocols for IoT.

1.5.3.11 International Organization for Standardization (ISO)

The International Organization for Standardization (ISO) [iso.org] is a globally recognized and influential entity that develops and publishes international standards aimed at promoting quality, safety, efficiency and innovation in various industries and sectors. Founded in 1947, ISO is a nongovernmental organization comprising representatives from over 160 member countries. It collaboratively creates and maintains standards that cover a wide spectrum of domains, including technology, manufacturing, healthcare and environmental management. ISO standards offer a common language and framework for businesses, organizations, and governments worldwide, facilitating international trade, interoperability and the delivery of safe and high-quality products and services. The ISO certification process is widely used to demonstrate compliance with these standards, signaling a commitment to excellence and best practices in fields ranging from quality management (ISO 9001) to environmental management (ISO 14001). It has published over 24,500 international standards covering almost all aspects of technology and manufacturing. The organization develops and publishes standardization in all technical and nontechnical fields other than electrical and electronic engineering, which is handled by the IEC. ISO has a joint technical committee (JTC) with the International Electrotechnical Commission (IEC) to develop standards relating to information technology (IT). Known as JTC 1 and entitled "Information technology," it was created in 1987 and its mission is "to develop worldwide Information and Communication Technology (ICT) standards for business and consumer applications." Some popular standards include: (1) ISO 9000 family – Quality management (2) ISO/IEC 27000 family – Information security management (3) ISO 45001 and related standards – Occupational health and safety (4) ISO 8601 – Date and time format (5) ISO 13485 – Medical devices (6) ISO 31000 – Risk management (7) ISO 50001 – Energy management (8) ISO 9660 – ISO images for computer files in CD (9) ISO 14000 family – Environmental management (10) ISO 22000 – Food safety management (11) ISO 4217 – Currency codes (12) ISO 3166 – Country Codes.

1.5.3.12 International Telecommunication Union (ITU)

The International Telecommunication Union (ITU) [itu.int] is a specialized agency of the United Nations dedicated to the field of information and communication technologies (ICTs). Established in 1865, the ITU has played an important role in facilitating global communication and connectivity. It develops and manages international standards, regulations and policies for telecommunications and radiocommunications, ensuring that networks and technologies can interoperate seamlessly across borders. The ITU encompasses three sectors: the Radiocommunication Sector (ITU-R), which deals with spectrum management and satellite communications; the Telecommunication Standardization Sector (ITU-T), responsible for developing technical standards; and the Telecommunication Development Sector (ITU-D), which focuses on bridging the digital divide and extending access to ICTs in underserved regions. The ITU's work is fundamental in enabling the global telecommunications ecosystem, including the development of new technologies, broadband connectivity, and emerging innovations such as 5G and the Internet of Things (IoT). The ITU-T recommendations are divided into categories, namely, G: Transmission systems and media, H: Audio-visual and multimedia systems, I: Integrated services digital network (ISDN), J: transmission of multimedia signals, V: Data communication over the telephone, X: Data networks, open system communications, Notable ITU-T recommendations include: (1) G.657: single mode optical fiber cable, (2) G.711: PCM (pulse code modulation) of audio signals, (3) G.726: ADPCM speech codec, (4) G.992.5: ADSL (asynchronous digital subscriber line) broadband Internet access, (5) H.261: video compression standard, (6) H.262: video coding format or MPEG-2 part 2, (7) H.264: AVC (advanced video coding) or MPEG-4 part 10, (8) H.265: high efficiency video coding or MPEG-H part 2, (9) H.331: standards for video conferencing, (10) T.38: fax over IP network, (11) X.25: packet switched data communicated in WAN (12) X.400: message handling system (MHS).

1.5.3.13 Joint Photographic Experts Group (JPEG)

The Joint Photographic Experts Group (JPEG) [jpeg.org] is a renowned and pivotal organization in the field of digital image compression and encoding. Established in 1986, JPEG is known for its work in developing and maintaining international standards for image compression and the storage of digital images. The JPEG format, which is one of the most widely used image compression standards, has revolutionized the way images are stored and transmitted across various digital media. JPEG's standards are integral to the efficient compression and decompression of digital images, significantly reducing file sizes while preserving image quality. The organization has also developed several JPEG-related standards, including JPEG 2000 and JPEG XR, which offer enhanced compression capabilities and image quality. JPEG's work is instrumental in applications ranging from digital photography and Web graphics to medical imaging and satellite imagery, contributing to faster data transfer and the widespread sharing of images across digital platforms.

1.5.3.14 MIDI Manufacturers Association (MMA)

The MIDI Manufacturers Association (MMA) [midi.org] is a significant organization in the realm of music and audio technology, primarily known for its work in the development and promotion of the Musical Instrument Digital Interface (MIDI) standard. Established in 1984, the MMA serves as a collaborative forum for manufacturers, developers and professionals in the music industry to create and maintain MIDI standards. MIDI is a crucial protocol that allows electronic musical instruments, computers and software to communicate and synchronize with one another. It has revolutionized music production and performance, enabling musicians and composers to connect a wide range of devices, from synthesizers to digital audio workstations, and control them in a standardized way. The MMA's standards ensure that MIDI remains an adaptable and versatile tool for musicians and producers, promoting compatibility and interoperability across various hardware and software platforms. MIDI has not only had a profound impact on music creation but also extended to other applications like lighting control, video production and interactive installations.

1.5.3.15 Moving Picture Experts Group (MPEG)

The Moving Picture Experts Group (MPEG) [mpeg.chiariglione.org] and [www.mpeg.org] is a renowned and influential entity in the domain of audio and video compression and coding standards. Established in 1988, MPEG operates under the International Organization for Standardization (ISO) and the International Electrotechnical Commission (IEC). Its primary mission is to develop and maintain international standards for the compression, decompression, processing and transmission of digital audio and video content. These standards significantly impact various industries, including digital television, streaming media, multimedia applications, and digital cinema. Some of the most well-known MPEG standards include MPEG-1, responsible for the development of formats like MP3 for audio compression, and MPEG-2, widely used in DVDs and digital broadcasting. MPEG-4 and its successors have contributed to the growth of multimedia applications, including video conferencing and internet streaming. The latest standards, such as High Efficiency Video Coding (HEVC) and Versatile Video Coding (VVC), are pivotal in enabling high-quality video compression for applications like 4K and 8K video streaming. MPEG's work continues to shape the digital media landscape, enabling efficient data transmission and multimedia experiences across various platforms and devices.

1.5.3.16 National Television Systems Committee (NTSC)

The National Television Systems Committee (NTSC) [ntsc-tv.com] is a historically significant organization in the United States that played a fundamental role in the development and standardization of analog television broadcasting systems. Established in 1940, the NTSC was responsible for defining the analog broadcast television standards that shaped the American television landscape for decades. One of its most notable contributions is the creation of the NTSC color television standard, which introduced color television broadcasts in the United States. The NTSC color standard, adopted in 1953, became the foundation for color television broadcasting in North America and several other countries. This innovation revolutionized the way people experienced television, offering a richer and more immersive viewing experience. Over time, the NTSC standards became the basis for broadcasting worldwide, with minor variations and adaptations in different regions. However, as technology advanced and the transition to digital broadcasting began, the NTSC analog system was gradually phased out, and digital television standards, such as ATSC (Advanced Television Systems Committee) standards, took its place. The NTSC's work not only marked a significant milestone in the history of television but also demonstrated the importance of establishing standardized systems to ensure a consistent and high-quality viewing experience for audiences. While the NTSC's analog standards are no longer in use, its legacy remains in the form of digital television standards and the principles of standardization that continue to shape the broadcast industry today.

1.5.3.17 Open Archives Initiative (OAI)

The Open Archives Initiative (OAI) [openarchives.org] is a vital initiative in the field of digital information sharing and open access to scholarly and cultural resources. Established in 1999, OAI aims to facilitate interoperability and efficient sharing of digital content, particularly in the academic and research domains. At the core of the OAI is the development and promotion of protocols and standards that enable repositories, such as digital libraries and archives, to make their content openly accessible and discoverable on the internet. The most well-known standard developed by OAI is the OAI Protocol for Metadata Harvesting (OAI-PMH), which allows repositories to expose their metadata to others, making it easier for services and search engines to index and retrieve scholarly and cultural resources. OAI has significantly contributed to the open-access movement, ensuring that research, educational materials and cultural heritage resources are readily available to a global audience. It has also played a crucial role in fostering collaboration among institutions and organizations committed to open-access principles, ultimately promoting the dissemination of knowledge and cultural heritage in the digital age.

1.5.3.18 Radio Corporation of America (RCA)

The Radio Corporation of America (RCA) [rca.com] was one of the most influential and pioneering electronics companies in the 20th century. Established in 1919, RCA was a key player in the development of radio and television technology and a major contributor to the early days of the American broadcasting industry. The corporation's founder, David Sarnoff, played a visionary role in advocating for the widespread adoption of radio and television. RCA made several ground-breaking contributions to the world of electronics, including the development of the National Broadcasting Company (NBC), one of the major television networks in the United States. RCA also played a significant role in the development of color television, introducing the NTSC color television standard in the 1950s. RCA's inventions and innovations extended to the production of electronic equipment and components. The company was a leader in the manufacturing of radios, televisions and a wide range of electronic products. Over time, RCA evolved into a diversified conglomerate with interests in various industries, including defense electronics, aerospace and semiconductor manufacturing. The corporation's research and development efforts made substantial contributions to the advancement of electronics and telecommunications technology.

1.5.3.19 Society of Motion Picture and Television Engineers (SMPTE)

The Society of Motion Picture and Television Engineers (SMPTE) [smpte.org] is a highly respected and influential organization in the world of film, television and motion-imaging technology. Established in 1916, SMPTE has been at the forefront of the motion-imaging industry, playing an important role in standardization, innovation, and the development of technologies that have shaped the way we create, deliver, and experience motion pictures and television content. SMPTE is renowned for its work in establishing standards for the film and television industries, including frame rates, aspect ratios, color spaces, and digital cinema. Its standards have ensured consistency and compatibility in the production, distribution and display of content, and have been integral to the transition from analog to digital technology in the industry. SMPTE has also played a vital role in the development of high-definition television (HDTV) and ultra-high-definition television (UHDTV), and it continues to address emerging technologies like high dynamic range (HDR) and immersive audio. As the industry continues to evolve with innovations in areas like virtual reality, augmented reality and streaming media, SMPTE remains an essential organization in the ongoing development and standardization of technologies that enrich the world of motion pictures and television.

1.5.3.20 Unicode Consortium (UC)

The Unicode Consortium [unicode.org/consortium] is a pioneering and essential organization that has revolutionized text encoding and character standards in the digital world. Founded in 1987, the consortium is a collective effort of major technology companies, software developers, linguists and experts from around the globe. Its primary mission is to develop and maintain the Unicode Standard, a comprehensive character encoding system that has become the backbone of multilingual text representation in computing. This standard provides a consistent and universal framework for encoding and processing text in different languages, scripts and writing systems, ensuring seamless interoperability across digital platforms, devices, and applications. The Unicode Standard supports an extensive range of characters, including alphabets, ideographs, symbols, emojis and more.

It also provides guidelines for text layout, line-breaking and bidirectional text support, making it possible to handle complex scripts and diverse languages with precision.

1.5.3.21 World Wide Web Consortium (W3C)

The World Wide Web Consortium (W3C) [w3.org], founded in 1994 by internet pioneers such as Tim Berners-Lee (Berners-Lee, 1990), is a globally recognized organization dedicated to the development and standardization of Web technologies. W3C plays an important role in ensuring the interoperability and accessibility of the World Wide Web. It develops open, vendor-neutral standards and recommendations that define the building blocks of the Web, including HTML, CSS and Web accessibility guidelines. These standards are crucial in ensuring that Web content can be created, presented and accessed consistently across different platforms, browsers, and devices. Furthermore, the W3C focuses on Web security, privacy, and emerging technologies like the Web of Things (WoT) and WebAssembly. Its commitment to Web accessibility promotes an inclusive digital environment, allowing all users, regardless of abilities or disabilities, to access and engage with Web content. W3C's impact extends to Web development, design, and user experience, as well as applications like e-commerce, social media and e-learning. As the steward of Web standards, the W3C continues to foster innovation and maintain the fundamental principles of an open, accessible and universally usable World Wide Web.

1.5.3.22 Web Hypertext Application Technology Working Group (WHATWG)

The Web Hypertext Application Technology Working Group (WHATWG) [whatwg.org] is a standards body with representations from Apple, Mozilla, Google, Opera and Microsoft, responsible for maintaining multiple Web-related technical standards, including the specifications for the Hyper Text Markup Language (HTML) and the Document Object Model (DOM). The WHATWG was formed in response to the slow development of World Wide Web Consortium (W3C) Web standards and W3C's decision to abandon HTML in favor of XML-based technologies. In 2019, the W3C and WHATWG agreed to a memorandum of understanding where development of HTML and DOM specifications would be done principally in the WHATWG. The HTML specification has been designated a living document, which implies a document which is continually edited and updated.

1.6 Multimedia Technologies and Platforms

1.6.1 Frontend Technologies

Frontend technologies for multimedia production primarily involve the tools and frameworks used to create, display and interact with multimedia content on the user's side. These technologies encompass various aspects, from Web and mobile development to user interfaces and user experience design. Major frontend technologies and components for multimedia production include the following.

HTML5: HTML5 [html.spec.whatwg.org/multipage] is the standard markup language for structuring and presenting content on the Web. It includes elements and attributes for embedding multimedia content such as audio and video using the "audio" and "video" tags.

CSS3: Cascading Style Sheets (CSS) [www.w3.org/TR/CSS] is used for styling and formatting multimedia content. CSS3 introduces advanced styling features, animations and transitions that enhance the visual appeal of multimedia elements.

JavaScript: JavaScript [ecma-international.org/publications-and-standards/standards/ecma-262] is a critical programming language for multimedia interactivity and user experience enhancement. Libraries and frameworks like jQuery [jquery.com], Three.js (for 3D graphics) [threejs.org] and PixiJS (for 2D graphics) [pixijs.com] are commonly used for multimedia applications.

WebRTC: Web Real-Time Communication (WebRTC) [webrtc.org] technology enables real-time communication, including video and audio conferencing, screen sharing and peer-to-peer multimedia streaming directly in Web browsers.

Media Player Libraries: Various JavaScript libraries and frameworks provide customizable media players for Web applications. Examples include Video.js [videojs.com], Plyr [plyr.io], and JW Player [jwplayer.com].

Canvas and WebGL: The HTML5 "canvas" element and WebGL [khronos.org/webgl] are used for rendering 2D and 3D graphics, making them suitable for interactive multimedia experiences and games.

Web Audio API: The Web Audio API [w3.org/TR/webaudio] is used to create, manipulate and process audio content in real time, making it ideal for multimedia applications that involve sound generation and processing.

Responsive Design: Responsive Web design techniques and frameworks like Bootstrap [getbootstrap.com] and Foundation [get.foundation] are crucial for ensuring multimedia content displays properly on various screen sizes and devices.

UI/UX Frameworks: User interface (UI) and user experience (UX) frameworks like React [react.dev], Angular [angular.dev] and Vue.js [vuejs.org] are used for building interactive multimedia applications and providing a seamless user experience.

Mobile App Development: Technologies such as React Native [reactnative.dev] and Flutter [flutter.dev] are used for creating cross-platform mobile applications that can incorporate multimedia elements.

Augmented Reality (AR) and Virtual Reality (VR): AR and VR technologies often rely on frontend frameworks and libraries like A-Frame [aframe.io] and AR.js [ar-js-org.github.io/AR.js-Docs] for building immersive multimedia experiences.

SVG (Scalable Vector Graphics): SVG [w3.org/Graphics/SVG] is used for creating vector-based graphics and animations that can be scaled without loss of quality, making it suitable for multimedia applications.

Animation Libraries: Animation libraries like GreenSock (GSAP) [gsap.com] and Anime.js [animejs.com] are used to create dynamic and interactive animations within multimedia content. GreenSock Animation Platform (GSAP) is a robust JavaScript animation library known for its versatility and performance, including advanced features like Bezier curves, physics-based motion and precise control over timelines. Anime.js is a lightweight JavaScript animation library designed for simplicity and flexibility, and supports a variety of animation properties, easing functions and call-backs.

Font and Icon Libraries: Libraries like Google Fonts [fonts.google.com] and Font Awesome [fontawesome.com] are used to enhance the visual aspects of multimedia content by providing a wide range of fonts and icons.

UI Design and Prototyping Tools: Design and prototyping tools such as Adobe XD [adobe.com/xd], Sketch [sketch.com] and Figma [figma.com] help designers create multimedia interfaces and test user interactions. Adobe XD is a powerful design and prototyping tool tailored for user experience (UX) and user interface (UI) designers with features like responsive resizing, shared design components and collaborative design capabilities. Figma is a cloud-based design and collaboration platform that stands out for its real-time collaboration features allowing instant collaboration with team members. Sketch is a vector-based design tool tailored for macOS, widely used by UI and UX designers, known for its extensive plugin ecosystem, offering additional functionalities and integrations.

WebVR and WebXR: WebVR [webvr.info] and WebXR [w3.org/TR/webxr] technologies allow the creation of VR and AR experiences directly within Web browsers, enabling immersive multimedia content.

These frontend technologies are essential for creating engaging and interactive multimedia content for the Web and mobile platforms. They provide the tools and frameworks necessary to design, develop and deliver multimedia applications and experiences to users.

1.6.2 Backend Technologies

In multimedia production, backend technologies play a crucial role in managing, processing and delivering multimedia content efficiently. Some major backend technologies and components commonly used in multimedia production are discussed below.

Media Servers: Media servers are essential for streaming audio and video content. They handle tasks such as content delivery, load balancing, and real-time transcoding. Popular media server software includes Wowza Streaming Engine [wowza.com/streaming-engine], Adobe Media Server [business.adobe.com/products/primetime/adobe-media-server.html] and Red5 [red5server.com].

Content Management Systems (CMS): CMS platforms are used to organize, store, and manage multimedia assets. They provide tools for content creation, version control, metadata management and asset organization. Examples include WordPress [wordpress.org], Adobe Experience Manager [business.adobe.com/products/experience-manager/adobe-experience-manager] and Drupal [drupal.org].

Media Encoding and Transcoding: Media encoding and transcoding tools are used to convert multimedia content from one format to another, ensuring compatibility and optimizing file size for various devices and platforms. FFmpeg [ffmpeg.org] and HandBrake [handbrake.fr] are widely used tools for this purpose.

Database Management Systems (DBMS): DBMS is used to store metadata, organize content libraries, and manage user access rights. Popular DBMS options include MySQL [mysql.com], PostgreSQL [postgresql.org], MongoDB [mongodb.com] and Microsoft SQL Server [microsoft.com/en-us/sql-server].

Digital Asset Management (DAM) Systems: DAM systems focus on organizing and distributing multimedia assets. They provide features for asset metadata, version control, access control and asset distribution. Examples include Adobe Experience Manager [business.adobe.com/products/experience-manager/adobe-experience-manager], Widen Collective [acquia.com/products/acquia-dam] and Bynder [bynder.com].

Content Delivery Networks (CDNs): CDNs are used for efficient content distribution by replicating multimedia content across geographically distributed servers. CDN providers include Akamai [akamai.com], Cloudflare [cloudflare.com] and Amazon CloudFront [aws.amazon.com/cloudfront].

Video and Audio Editing Tools: Backend servers may integrate video and audio editing tools for post-production tasks, including editing, transcoding and rendering. Adobe Premiere Pro [adobe.com/products/premiere], Final Cut Pro [apple.com/final-cut-pro] and Avid Media Composer [avid.com/media-composer] are examples of video editing software.

Machine Learning and AI: Backend technologies leverage machine learning and artificial intelligence for content analysis, automatic tagging, facial recognition and content recommendation. TensorFlow [tensorflow.org], PyTorch [ai.meta.com/tools/pytorch] and OpenCV [opencv.ai] are commonly used libraries for AI and ML in multimedia production.

Cloud Computing Services: Cloud platforms such as Amazon Web Services (AWS) [aws.amazon.com], Microsoft Azure [azure.microsoft.com] and Google Cloud [cloud.google.com] offer a wide range of tools and services for multimedia processing, storage, and delivery.

Security and Rights Management: Solutions for digital rights management (DRM) like Fasoo [en.fasoo.com/strategies/enterprise-drm] and encryption are used to protect multimedia content from piracy and unauthorized access. Fasoo provides data security solutions, with advanced tools to protect, manage and control sensitive digital assets, using a file-centric security model, ensuring that security measures are embedded directly within the files themselves.

Content Analytics: Backend technologies for multimedia production often include analytics tools that track user engagement, content performance and audience behavior. Google Analytics [analytics.google.com], Adobe Analytics [business.adobe.com/products/analytics] and custom analytics solutions are used for this purpose. Google Analytics enables the tracking of a wide array of metrics related to website and app performance, from visitor traffic and user engagement to conversion rates and e-commerce transactions, the platform provides a comprehensive overview of how users interact with online content. Adobe Analytics excels in providing a unified view of customer interactions across multiple channels, including websites, mobile apps, social media and more; by aggregating data from various touch-points, businesses gain a comprehensive understanding of the customer journey.

These backend technologies, work in tandem to facilitate the creation, management, and distribution of multimedia content, ensuring it reaches the intended audience while maintaining quality, security and efficiency.

1.6.3 Multimedia Platforms

Multimedia platforms are integral to the creation, distribution and consumption of multimedia content. These platforms encompass a wide range of technologies, applications and services that enable the seamless integration of multimedia elements, such as images, audio, video, animations and interactive experiences, into various digital environments. From social media networks and streaming services to interactive Web applications and virtual reality experiences, multimedia platforms are the driving force behind engaging and immersive content delivery.

Social Media Networks: Platforms like Facebook [facebook.com], Instagram [instagram.com], Twitter/X [twitter.com] and TikTok [tiktok.com] enable users to create and share multimedia content, fostering social interactions through images, videos, live streams and stories.

Streaming Services: Platforms like YouTube [youtube.com], Netflix [netflix.com], Spotify [open.spotify.com] and Twitch [twitch.tv] provide on-demand access to multimedia content, including videos, music, podcasts and live broadcasts, enhancing user entertainment options.

E-commerce Platforms: Platforms like Amazon [amazon.com], Shopify [shopify.com] and WooCommerce [woo.com] incorporate multimedia features to showcase products through images, videos and 360-degree views, enhancing the shopping experience. They leverage high-quality product imagery and videos to provide customers with a detailed and immersive view of the products, typically a gallery of images from various angles, zoom capabilities and sometimes product demonstration videos.

Gaming Consoles and Engines: Platforms like PlayStation [www.playstation.com], Xbox [www.xbox.com], Steam [store.steampowered.com], Unity [unity.com] and Unreal Engine [www.unrealengine.com] offer multimedia capabilities for gaming, including immersive 3D graphics, spatial audio and streaming services.

Augmented Reality (AR) and Virtual Reality (VR): AR and VR platforms such as ARKit [developer.apple.com/augmented-reality/arkit], Oculus [www.oculus.com] and HTC Vive [www.vive.com] create immersive multimedia experiences with 3D audio, video and interactive elements.

1.6.4 Transport Mechanisms

Multimedia content delivery over networks is a crucial aspect of the multimedia landscape, enabling the seamless distribution of multimedia content to users around the world.

1.6.4.1 Communication Protocols

Hypertext Transfer Protocol (HTTP): HTTP [httpwg.org/specs] is the foundation of the World Wide Web and is widely used for delivering multimedia content over the internet. HTTP is essential for accessing Web pages and multimedia files, making it one of the most common protocols for content delivery.

Hypertext Transfer Protocol Secure (HTTPS): HTTPS is the secure version of HTTP, using encryption to protect the integrity and confidentiality of multimedia content during transmission. It is especially crucial for e-commerce, online streaming and secure communication.

File Transfer Protocol (FTP): FTP [datatracker.ietf.org/doc/html/rfc114] is an older protocol used for transferring multimedia files between a client and a server. While less commonly used for Web content delivery, FTP remains relevant for managing large multimedia files and server-to-server transfers.

Real-Time Transport Protocol (RTP): RTP [datatracker.ietf.org/doc/html/rfc3550] is specifically designed for real-time multimedia data transmission, making it vital for video and audio streaming, video conferencing and online gaming. RTP is often used in combination with Real-Time Control Protocol (RTCP) [datatracker.ietf.org/doc/html/rfc5760] to monitor data delivery and quality.

Internet Protocol (IP) and Transmission Control Protocol (TCP): IP [datatracker.ietf.org/doc/html/rfc791] and TCP [datatracker.ietf.org/doc/html/rfc9293] are fundamental to internet communication. IP handles routing and addressing, while TCP ensures reliable data delivery. These protocols are essential for multimedia content delivery, ensuring that data packets reach their destination accurately.

1.6.4.2 Streaming Protocols

HTTP-based streaming, using protocols like HTTP Live Streaming (HLS) [developer.apple.com/streaming/] and Dynamic Adaptive Streaming over HTTP (DASH) [www.iso.org/standard/83314.html], is a widely used method for delivering multimedia content. It allows adaptive streaming, optimizing quality based on the viewer's internet connection.

Real-Time Streaming Protocol (RTSP): RTSP [https://datatracker.ietf.org/doc/html/rfc2326] is designed for real-time streaming and controlling the delivery of multimedia content. It is commonly used for video surveillance systems, video conferencing and real-time applications.

Peer-to-Peer (P2P) Streaming: P2P streaming leverages the resources of viewers, distributing multimedia content efficiently. This technology is used in applications like live streaming, where multiple users share the streaming load.

Progressive Download: Progressive download allows multimedia content to start playing as soon as a portion of the file is downloaded. It is often used for Web video players, making content accessible even before the entire file is received.

WebRTC (Web Real-Time Communication): WebRTC [https://www.w3.org/TR/webrtc/] enables real-time communication directly between Web browsers. It is commonly used for video conferencing, live streaming and interactive multimedia applications.

Content Delivery Networks (CDNs): CDNs are networks of servers distributed globally to deliver multimedia content efficiently. They optimize content delivery by caching data closer to end-users, reducing latency and bandwidth usage.

VoIP (Voice over Internet Protocol): VoIP technology supports real-time voice communication over the internet. It is used in multimedia applications like online calls, video conferencing and voice chat in online gaming.

Real-Time Messaging Protocols: Real-time messaging protocols, such as MQTT [mqtt.org] and XMPP [xmpp.org], enable real-time communication for messaging and presence information. These protocols are essential for chat applications and multimedia messaging.

1.7 Multimedia and Games

Multimedia and games are deeply intertwined, as multimedia elements play a fundamental role in creating engaging, interactive and immersive gaming experiences. The integration of multimedia elements, such as graphics, audio, video and animations, is essential for enhancing the visual and auditory aspects of games and immersing players in virtual worlds (Gazaway, 2021).

1.7.1 Role of Multimedia in Games

Graphics: High-quality graphics are a cornerstone of modern games. Graphics encompass 2D and 3D visuals, character models, environments, textures and special effects. Multimedia elements, such as images and videos, are used to create captivating in-game visuals that range from realistic to stylized art.

Audio: Audio is crucial for setting the mood and creating an immersive gaming experience. Sound effects, background music, voice acting and spatial audio contribute to a game's atmosphere and storytelling.

Video: Video sequences, including cut-scenes and cinematics, help convey the game's narrative and add cinematic flair. Videos can be pre-rendered or displayed in real time within the game engine.

Animation: Animations breathe life into characters and objects within the game. Multimedia elements, such as animated sprites and character models, enable fluid movements and realistic interactions.

UI/UX Design: User interfaces (UI) in games benefit from multimedia elements, incorporating images, icons, animations and video to create intuitive and engaging menus and HUDs (Heads-Up Displays).

Storytelling: Multimedia elements, such as voice-overs and visual narratives, facilitate storytelling and character development within games.

1.7.2 Impact on Player Engagement

Immersive Experience: High-quality graphics and audio contribute to a more immersive gaming experience, drawing players into the game world.

Emotional Connection: Multimedia elements can evoke emotions, making players more invested in the game's characters and storyline.

Interactivity: Games utilize multimedia to create interactive environments where players can explore, solve puzzles and make choices.

Atmosphere: Soundtracks and audio effects set the tone for different game situations, from tense battles to tranquil exploration.

Feedback: Visual and auditory cues provide feedback to players, helping them understand the game's mechanics and progress.

1.7.3 Technologies

Game Engines: Game engines like Unity [unity.com], Unreal Engine [unrealengine.com] and Godot [godotengine.org] provide a framework for creating games with integrated multimedia elements. They offer tools for graphics, audio, animations and scripting. Unity is a powerful and versatile game development engine that has evolved into a comprehensive platform for creating a wide range of digital experiences, from video games to augmented reality (AR), virtual reality (VR) and simulations with extensive support for cross-platform compatibility. Unreal Engine is a leading game development framework renowned for its cutting-edge graphics, robust features with advanced rendering capabilities, including real-time global illumination, dynamic lighting and sophisticated texture mapping. Godot Engine, an open-source game development framework, has gained prominence for its versatility, ease of use and collaborative community-driven approach which includes a visual scripting system that allows developers to create game logic through a node-based interface without writing traditional code.

3D Modeling and Animation Software: Tools like Blender [www.blender.org], Maya [www.autodesk.in/products/maya] and 3ds Max [www.autodesk.com/products/3ds-max] are used to create 3D models, characters and animations.

Sound Design Software: Audio professionals use software like Adobe Audition [www.adobe.com/products/audition], Pro Tools [www.avid.com/pro-tools] and Audacity [www.audacityteam.org] to create and edit sound effects and music for games.

Video Editing Software: Video sequences and cut-scenes are often created and edited using software like Adobe Premiere Pro [www.adobe.com/products/premiere], Final Cut Pro [www.apple.com/final-cut-pro] and Sony Vegas [www.vegascreativesoftware.com/us/vegas-pro].

Texture and Image Editing Software: Tools like Adobe Photoshop [www.adobe.com/products/photoshop] and GIMP [www.gimp.org] are used to create and edit textures and visual assets for games.

Interactive Storytelling Tools: Game development platforms like Twine [twinery.org] and Ren'Py [www.renpy.org] facilitate the creation of interactive narratives in games. Twine is an open-source tool that has gained popularity for its simplicity and effectiveness in creating interactive stories and text-based games, through decision trees, enabling writers to create multiple paths and outcomes based on user choices. Ren'Py is a free and open-source visual novel engine designed to facilitate the creation of interactive storytelling experiences using a scripting language to define characters, dialogue, choices and branching narratives.

1.7.4 Mobile Gaming

Mobile phone games have become an integral part of the modern digital entertainment offering diverse genres and experiences to players of all ages. One of the key strengths of mobile phone games lies in their accessibility – since nearly everyone owns a smartphone, gaming is no longer restricted to dedicated gaming consoles or PCs. Players can enjoy games anytime, anywhere, making mobile gaming a convenient and versatile form of entertainment. An extensive variety of game genres and gameplay styles ensure that players can find experiences that align with their interests and preferences. Many mobile games operate on a freemium model, allowing players to download and play for free while offering in-app purchases for additional content, virtual items or premium features. This model has proven successful, enabling developers to reach a broad audience and monetize their games through various strategies. In addition to in-app purchases, advertising, sponsorships and subscription services contribute to the monetization scenario of mobile games. Moreover, mobile games often incorporate social and multiplayer features, fostering a sense of community and interaction among players. Integration with social media platforms further allows players to share achievements, scores, and experiences, creating a connected gaming community. In recent times augmented reality (AR) and virtual reality (VR) technologies are also making their way into mobile gaming, promising new dimensions of immersive gameplay.

1.8 Multimedia and Interactivity

Multimedia and interactivity are intertwined in various digital experiences, from websites and applications to e-learning modules and entertainment content. Interactivity refers to the ability of users to engage with digital content, while multimedia encompasses visual, audio and interactive elements (Isaias & Blashki, 2014).

1.8.1 User Engagement

Visual Engagement: Multimedia elements, such as images, videos, animations and graphics, capture users' attention and convey information more effectively than text alone.

Audio Enhancement: Sound and music enrich the user experience, setting the mood, conveying emotions and providing auditory feedback.

Interaction: Interactivity allows users to participate actively rather than passively consume content. It can take the form of clickable buttons, interactive widgets, drag-and-drop actions and more.

Feedback Mechanism: Interactivity enables real-time feedback. Users receive responses to their actions, such as confirmation messages, error alerts or dynamic content updates.

Personalization: Interactive multimedia can adapt to users' preferences and behaviors, creating a more personalized and engaging experience.

1.8.2 Role of Interactivity

Enhanced Learning: In e-learning, interactive multimedia engages learners, making the learning process more effective and enjoyable.

Storytelling: Multimedia and interactivity bring narratives to life, making storytelling in video games, virtual reality experiences and interactive websites more immersive.

Engaging Presentations: Interactive multimedia presentations are more compelling and memorable, making them effective in business, education and entertainment.

Gamification: Gamification elements in multimedia content enhance user engagement by introducing game-like features, such as points, rewards and challenges.

1.8.3 Technologies

JavaScript: JavaScript is a versatile language for creating interactive multimedia elements on websites, such as image sliders, video players and interactive forms.

HTML5: HTML5 offers native support for multimedia elements like video and audio, making it easier to integrate and control interactive multimedia.

CSS Animations: CSS animations and transitions bring interactivity to Web design, allowing for hover effects, smooth transitions and interactive buttons.

WebGL: WebGL enables 3D graphics and interactivity in Web applications, leading to more immersive experiences.

e-Learning Authoring Tools: Tools like Articulate Storyline, Adobe Captivate and Moodle [moodle.org] enable the creation of interactive e-learning modules with multimedia components.

Game Engines: Game engines like Unity [unity.com] and Unreal Engine [www.unrealengine.com] provide the foundation for creating highly interactive multimedia-rich video games.

1.8.4 Interactive Elements

Buttons and Hyperlinks: Buttons and hyperlinks are fundamental interactive elements in multimedia. Users can click or tap on them to navigate between different sections of the content or access additional information. They are commonly used in websites, e-books and presentations.

Forms and Input Fields: Forms with input fields allow users to submit data, such as text, numbers or selections, into the multimedia application. These are frequently used for user registrations, surveys and e-commerce transactions.

Sliders and Scrollers: Sliders and scrollers enable users to interact with multimedia content by adjusting values or scrolling through information. They are used in settings like audio and video players, interactive info-graphics and product galleries.

Interactive Images: Images can become interactive by incorporating hotspots or clickable areas that reveal additional information or trigger actions when selected. Interactive images are valuable for educational content, product catalogs and storytelling.

Animations and Transitions: Multimedia elements like animations, transitions and animated characters respond to user input or time-based triggers. These enhance storytelling, user engagement and interactive learning experiences.

Games and Simulations: Interactive multimedia elements are prominently featured in gaming and simulation applications. Users can control characters, make decisions, and influence outcomes, resulting in immersive gaming and training experiences.

Interactive Video: Interactive video allows users to make choices within the video, leading to different storylines or outcomes. This is commonly used in interactive movies, training videos and marketing campaigns.

1.8.5 Application Areas

E-Learning and Education: Interactive multimedia elements play a vital role in e-learning platforms, where they facilitate quizzes, simulations and personalized learning experiences. They cater to diverse learning styles and engage students effectively.

Entertainment and Gaming: Games and entertainment applications heavily rely on interactive multimedia elements to create immersive experiences. Gamers can control characters, solve puzzles and explore virtual worlds, fostering engagement and enjoyment.

Marketing and Advertising: Interactive multimedia elements are used in marketing campaigns and advertisements to encourage user participation. Interactive banners and product configurators enable users to interact with brands and products.

Museums and Exhibitions: In cultural institutions and exhibitions, interactive multimedia elements enhance visitor experiences. Touchscreen kiosks, augmented reality displays, and interactive installations provide in-depth information and engagement.

Healthcare and Simulations: Healthcare training and simulations use interactive multimedia elements to simulate medical procedures, patient scenarios and surgical training. These elements ensure realistic and hands-on learning experiences.

1.8.6 Challenges and Considerations

Usability and Accessibility: Designing interactive multimedia elements that are user-friendly and accessible to a broad audience is a challenge. Ensuring that elements are intuitive and comply with accessibility standards is essential.

Performance Optimization: Interactive multimedia elements can be resource-intensive. Optimizing performance to ensure smooth user experiences, particularly on mobile devices and Web applications, requires careful consideration.

Content Integration: Seamlessly integrating various interactive elements within multimedia applications while maintaining a coherent user experience can be complex. Synchronization, data formats and content presentation are critical considerations.

Cross-Platform Compatibility: Ensuring that interactive multimedia elements function consistently across different devices and platforms requires extensive testing and adaptation.

1.9 Multimedia Content Creation

Multimedia content creation typically follows a structured workflow. While specific workflows may vary depending on the project and organization, a general outline includes the following stages of content design, implementation and delivery (Assuncao & Gotchev, 2019).

1.9.1 Workflow

Concept and Planning: The process begins with the conceptualization of the multimedia project. This stage involves defining objectives, target audiences, and the overall content strategy. Creators establish a clear vision and outline the scope of the project, and also specify the objectives of the project, usually in terms of learning outcomes.

Story, Scriptwriting and Storyboarding: For multimedia projects a story outlines the entire content to be represented within the presentation. The story is designed keeping in mind the target audience and the objectives expected to be fulfilled. A well-crafted script outlines the narrative, dialogue and structure. It specifies which media element is used to represent which portions of the story, and how text image audio video should be synchronized with each other to deliver an integrated presentation. Storyboarding is a visual representation of the script, helping to plan the visual elements, layout, placements and orientations. It breaks up the content into individual screens and specifies how each screen should look like.

Content Creation: This stage focuses on the actual creation of multimedia assets. Depending on the project, this can involve writing text, capturing images, recording audio, shooting video or creating animations. Content creators use various tools and techniques specific to their medium.

Editing and Post-Production: Editing is a fundamental step for multimedia content refinement. For video and audio, post-production involves tasks like trimming, adding transitions, color correction and sound mixing. In image and animation projects, post-production entails image manipulation and compositing.

Integration: Multimedia content integration is the process of combining text, images, audio, video and animations into a cohesive final product. It involves careful synchronization and alignment of multimedia elements to achieve the desired user experience.

Quality Assurance and Testing: Before publishing or sharing multimedia content, it undergoes quality assurance and testing. This phase includes checking for errors, broken links and ensuring that the content performs as intended across various devices and platforms.

Distribution and Delivery: The final stage involves distributing multimedia content to the intended audience. This may involve uploading content to websites, streaming platforms, or packaging content for various mediums like CDs, DVDs or digital downloads.

1.9.2 Implementation Techniques

The techniques employed for creating multimedia content vary based on the medium. Here are some key techniques for text, image, audio, video and animation:

1.9.2.1 Text

Copywriting: Effective copywriting techniques are crucial for crafting engaging text content. This involves using persuasive language, storytelling and maintaining clarity and conciseness.

Typography: Proper selection of fonts, font sizes, line spacing and text formatting is vital for text readability and aesthetics.

1.9.2.2 Image

Photography: Techniques for capturing high-quality images include understanding lighting, composition and camera settings.

Editing: Techniques for image editing include tonal correction, color correction, sharpening, resizing and cropping, removing noise and applying filters using software like Adobe Photoshop.

1.9.2.3 Graphics

Illustration: Digital illustration techniques using software like Adobe Illustrator and Adobe Animate enable the creation of custom graphics and vector images.

1.9.2.4 Audio

Recording: Audio recording techniques encompass microphone selection, positioning, and sound treatment to capture clean and clear audio.

Editing: Techniques for audio editing include noise reduction, equalization and audio effects processing using software like Adobe Audition or Audacity.

1.9.2.5 Video

Filmmaking: Understanding camera operation, shot composition, lighting and framing are key to creating compelling video content.

Editing: Techniques for video editing involve timeline management, transitions, color grading and special effects using software like Adobe Premiere Pro or Final Cut Pro.

1.9.2.6 Animation

Keyframing: Animation techniques often involve keyframing, where key poses or states are defined, and the software interpolates between them to create smooth animations.

Rigging: In 3D animation, rigging is the process of creating skeletons and controls for characters, enabling realistic movement.

1.10 Theorems and Mathematical Formulations

1.10.1 Nyquist's Sampling Theorem

An important theorem frequently used in digital signal processing is the Nyquist Sampling Theorem named after Swedish-American engineer and physicist Harry Nyquist (1889–1976) who proposed it while investigating the bandwidth requirements for transmitting information through a telegraph channel (Nyquist, 1928). Sampling is a step for converting a continuous analog signal to a discrete set of values by examining the magnitude of the signal at specific points in time or space. The number of times sampling is done per second is called the sampling frequency. The theorem states that "When converting an analog signal into digital form, the sampling frequency used must be at least twice the bandwidth of the input signal in order to be able to reconstruct the original signal accurately from the sampled version." For a baseband signal, the bandwidth is the same as the highest frequency component, and so the theorem is often stated as the sampling frequency needs to be twice the highest frequency on the input signal. This condition is often referred to as the Nyquist criterion. If the sampling frequency falls below this threshold, then the reconstruction of the signal exhibits imperfections or artifacts, which are referred to as aliasing defects.

Thus, if f be the frequency of the analog wave and F be the sampling frequency required to digitize it, we need to have

$$F \geq 2f$$

The following figure illustrates the Nyquist's theorem by progressively sampling a sinusoidal waveform at low frequencies to generate a staircase waveform. The first figure in the top row shows the original waveform, and the second row depicts the waveform after sampling more than ten times per cycle. The third row depicts the limiting condition when the original waveform is sampled at exactly twice the frequency, i.e., two times per cycle at $\pi/2, 3\pi/2, 5\pi/2, 7\pi/2, 9\pi/2,$ and $11\pi/2$ over a period of three cycles or 6π. This plot shows that since the sampling is done once in the positive half and once in the negative half of each cycle, the generated staircase waveform has at least some information to represent the two halves, i.e., their approximate durations and approximate values. The fourth row depicts the case when sampling rate is equal to the frequency of the wave; i.e., sampling is done once in each cycle. The resulting wave is a low-frequency wave which contains no information of the original wave cycles. This distortion is referred to as aliasing and occurs when the sampling rate falls below twice the wave frequency, which illustrates the Nyquist theorem (Figure 1.1)

The sampling rate and bit-depth together decide the quality of the output signal. As the sampling rate is increased, more information about the analog wave is obtained, which correspondingly increases its quality. However, more information also implies more storage space is required and powerful processors are needed to deal with them, which increases the cost. To determine a set of digitization parameters like sampling rate and bit-depth, one is required to strike a balance between the quality required and the cost which can be afforded. If a high sample rate and low bit-depth is used, then it will not be possible to represent all the sample values, hence the advantage of using a higher sampling rate will be lost. On the other hand, if a high bit-depth and low sample rate is used then there will be provisions for representing a large number of samples but actually only a fraction of it will be used, because the low sampling rate will not typically generate enough samples to fill up all the empty slots, hence, the advantage of using a higher bit-depth will be lost. Thus, in conclusion, it could be stated that sampling rate and bit-depth are independent of each other because each could be adjusted without affecting the other; however, both of them play a combined role in deciding the final quality of the digital output.

During the digitization process, a lot of approximations are used at various stages. Initially, during sampling, values of the wave only at discrete points of time are considered, again during the quantization stage, sample values are rounded off to limited number of levels, hence, errors are introduced between the digital output and analog input. Specifically, the error introduced at the quantization stage is referred to as the quantization error. The maximum error is measured as being equal to one step size of the digital output and this distortion effect is referred to as noise, since the error will randomly vary from sample to sample (in electrical circuits any signal whose amplitude varies randomly with time is referred to as "noise"). To eliminate noise fully during digitization, it must sampled at an infinite rate which is impossible in practice, hence, because of the quantization error, digitization always leads to a degradation of the original analog signal. This degradation is usually compensated at a later stage through the use of editing software.

Signal-to-Noise Ratio (SNR) is a measure of the quality of a signal and is closely related to quantization

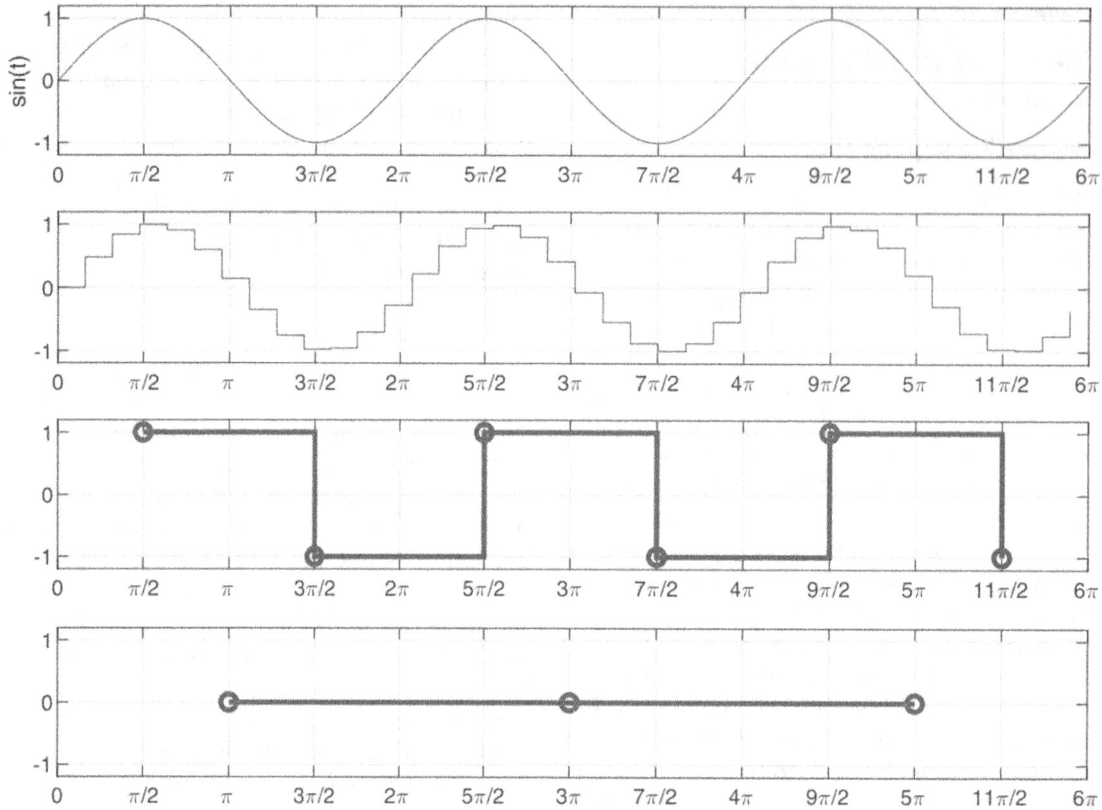

FIGURE 1.1
Illustration of Nyquist theorem.

error. SNR quantifies the ratio of amplitude of the signal of interest (A_{signal}) to the amplitude of the noise (A_{noise}) during the digitization process.

$$\text{SNR} = \frac{A_{\text{signal}}}{A_{\text{noise}}}$$

If n be the bit-depth then number of steps is 2^n. If S be peak-to-peak height of the wave, then height of each step is $S/2^n$ which is a measure of the quantization error e.

$$\text{SNR} = \frac{S}{e} = 2^n$$

Because for many signals, there is a wide difference between these two power values, SNR is often expressed in a logarithmic scale and the unit of SNR is called decibel (dB).

$$\text{SNR}_{dB} = 20\log_{10}\left(A_{\text{signal}} / A_{\text{noise}}\right)$$

$$\text{SNR}_{dB} = 20\log_{10}\left(2^n\right) = 20n(0.3) = 6n$$

The above implies that that if bit-depth is increased by 1 during digitization, the signal-to-noise ratio increases by 6 dB.

1.10.2 Euler's Theorem

Leonhard Euler (1707–1783) was a Swiss mathematician, physicist and engineer who made significant contributions to various fields of mathematics. Euler's theorem can be expressed as:

$$e^{i\pi} + 1 = 0$$

where e is the base of the natural logarithm (approximately 2.71828), i is the imaginary unit $\sqrt{-1}$, π represents the mathematical constant pi (approximately 3.14159) (Euler, 1748),

Rewriting we get:

$$e^{i\pi} = -1 = -1 + i(0) = \cos\pi + i.\sin\pi$$

Generalizing:

$$e^{ix} = \cos x + i.\sin x$$

Alternatively, from Taylor series expansion we have:

$$e^x = \sum_{n=0}^{\infty} \frac{x^n}{n!} = 1 + x + \frac{x^2}{2!} + \frac{x^3}{3!} + \ldots$$

$$\sin x = \sum_{n=0}^{\infty} x - \frac{x^3}{3!} + \frac{x^5}{5!} - \ldots$$

$$\cos x = \sum_{n=0}^{\infty} 1 - \frac{x^2}{2!} + \frac{x^4}{4!} - \ldots$$

Now,

$$e^{ix} = 1 + ix + \frac{(ix)^2}{2!} + \frac{(ix)^3}{3!} + \ldots$$

Substituting $i^2 = -1, i^3 = -i, i^4 = 1$ and so on, we get,

$$e^{ix} = 1 + ix - \frac{(x)^2}{2!} - \frac{i(x)^3}{3!} + \frac{(x)^4}{4!} + \frac{i(x)^5}{5!} \ldots$$

$$e^{ix.} = \left(1 - \frac{x^2}{2!} + \frac{x^4}{4!} - \ldots\right) + i\left(x - \frac{x^3}{3!} + \frac{x^5}{5!} - \ldots\right)$$

$$e^{ix} = \cos x + i.\sin x$$

1.10.3 Fourier Theorem

The Fourier theorem and Fourier series are fundamental mathematical tools in the fields of mathematics, engineering, physics and signal processing. They are named after the French mathematician and physicist Jean-Baptiste Joseph Fourier (1768–1830), who made significant contributions to the understanding of these concepts. The Fourier Theorem states, that any complex waveform, whether continuous or discrete, can be represented as a sum of sinusoidal (sine and cosine) functions with different frequencies and amplitudes (Fourier, 1822). The Fourier Transform is a mathematical operation, which allows us to decompose a signal into its constituent frequency components, providing insights into its frequency content and enabling various applications in science and engineering. The Fourier Transform is widely used in various fields, including signal processing, audio analysis, image processing, communication systems and quantum mechanics. It is used for tasks such as filtering, modulation, spectrum analysis and data compression. The Fourier Theorem facilitates the transformation of a signal from the time domain (original signal) into the frequency domain (representation in terms of sinusoidal components). In the time domain, a signal is described by its amplitude as a function of time. In the frequency domain, the signal is described by the amplitudes of various frequency components.

The Continuous Fourier Transform (CFT) represents a continuous analog signal as a sum of sinusoidal components with different frequencies. The amplitude of each component represents its contribution to the original signal. The phase of each component determines its alignment within the signal. For continuous-time signals, the forward Fourier Transform is used. It is represented by the equation:

$$X(f) = \int x(t).e^{-j2\pi ft}dt$$

where $X(f)$ is the complex amplitude spectrum in the frequency domain, $x(t)$ is the continuous-time signal in the time domain, f is the frequency variable, j is the imaginary unit $\sqrt{-1}$, $\int$ denotes integration over all sample values.

The inverse Fourier Transform is used to recover a continuous-time signal $x(t)$ from its complex frequency-domain representation $X(f)$. It is defined mathematically as follows:

$$x(t) = \int X(f).e^{j2\pi ft}df$$

where $x(t)$ is the original continuous-time signal, $X(f)$ is the complex frequency-domain representation of the signal, f is the frequency variable, j is the imaginary unit $\sqrt{-1}$, $\int$ denotes integration over all frequencies. This integral represents the sum of all frequency components weighted by their complex amplitudes in the frequency domain.

1.10.4 Discrete Fourier Transform (DFT)

1.10.4.1 Forward DFT

For discrete-time signals, the Discrete Fourier Transform (DFT) or Fast Fourier Transform (FFT) is used. The forward DFT is represented as:

$$X(k) = \sum_{i=0}^{N-1} x(i).e^{-j.\frac{2\pi ki}{N}}$$

where $X(k)$is the complex amplitude spectrum in the frequency domain, $x(i)$ is the discrete-time signal in the time domain, $k$is the discrete frequency variable, N is the total number of samples, Σ denotes summation over all components $(N-1)$, j is the imaginary operator $\sqrt{-1}$.

The above operation might be represented symbolically as below, where $\mathcal{F}$ denotes the DFT operator.

$$X(k) = \mathcal{F}\{x(i)\}$$

1.10.4.2 DFT Coefficients

The term $X(k)$ is called DFT Coefficient and is in general a complex number; i.e., it consists of real and imaginary parts. To separate out these terms we represent the forward DFT expression in terms of sinusoidal components by utilizing the Euler's formula: $e^{jx} = \cos(x) + j.\sin(x)$.

$$X(k) = \sum_{i=0}^{N-1} x(i).\left(\cos\frac{2\pi ki}{N} - j.\sin\frac{2\pi ki}{N}\right)$$

Separating out the real and imaginary parts:

$$X(k) = \mathrm{Re}\{X(k)\} - j.Im\{X(k)\}$$

$$X(k) = \sum_{i=0}^{N-1} x(i).\left(\cos\frac{2\pi ki}{N}\right) - j.\sum_{i=0}^{N-1} x(i).\left(\sin\frac{2\pi ki}{N}\right)$$

$$X(k) = A(k) - j.B(k)$$

A is called the real part of the coefficient, where

$$A(k) = \mathrm{Re}\{X(k)\} = \sum_{i=0}^{N-1} x(i).\cos\frac{2\pi ki}{N}$$

B is called the imaginary part of the coefficient, where

$$B(k) = Im\{X(k)\} = \sum_{i=0}^{N-1} x(i).\sin\frac{2\pi ki}{N}$$

Angular arguments are in radians. Since k ranges from 0 to $N-1$ collecting all the A and B terms together:

$$A = \{A(0), A(1), A(2), \ldots, A(N-1)\} = \bigcup_{k=0}^{N-1} A(k)$$

$$B = \{B(0), B(1), B(2), \ldots, B(N-1)\} = \bigcup_{k=0}^{N-1} B(k)$$

The U (union) symbol indicates collection of individual terms into a vector. The first term is:

$$X(0) = A(0) - j.B(0)$$

$$X(0) = \sum_{i=0}^{N-1} x(i).(\cos 0) - j.\sum_{i=0}^{N-1} x(i).(\sin 0) = \sum_{i=0}^{N-1} x(i)$$

This is proportional to the average of all the sample values of the time domain signal, and is devoid of any sinusoidal terms. This term is, therefore, referred to as the DC coefficient. All the other terms contain sinusoidal components and therefore referred to as AC coefficients.

The frequency domain term can now be expressed as: $X = A - j.B$ in which the absolute value indicates the magnitude and phase angle indicates the direction

$$|X(k)| = \sqrt{\{A(k)\}^2 + \{B(k)\}^2}$$

$$\varphi(k) = \tan^{-1}\left\{\frac{B(k)}{A(k)}\right\}$$

1.10.4.3 DFT Basis Functions

The output of the forward DFT is a set of coefficients that are to be used as scaling factors for a set of sinusoidal waves. The sine and cosine waves are called basis functions and have a fixed amplitude of 1 (unity) and a set of pre-defined frequencies. The basis functions are, thus, independent of the actual time-domain values. These are to be multiplied by the coefficients to produce a set of scaled sine and cosine waves, which when added up form the original time-domain signal. The k-th basis function is given by:

$$\omega(k) = e^{j.\frac{2\pi ki}{N}}$$

Separating into sinusoidal components:

$$C(k) = \bigcup_{i=0}^{N} \cos\frac{2\pi ki}{N} = \cos(0), \cos\left(\frac{2\pi k}{N}\right), \cos\left(\frac{4\pi k}{N}\right)\ldots$$

$$S(k) = \bigcup_{i=0}^{N} \sin\frac{2\pi ki}{N} = \sin(0), \sin\left(\frac{2\pi k}{N}\right), \sin\left(\frac{4\pi k}{N}\right)\ldots$$

Here $C(k)$ is the k-th cosine wave and $S(k)$ is the k-the sine wave. $C(0)$ is a cosine wave of zero frequency that has a constant value of 1 while $S(0)$ is a sine wave of zero frequency that has a constant value of 0. $C(1)$ and $S(1)$ each make one complete cycle over Nsample values, $C(2)$ and $S(2)$ each make two complete cycles and so on towards higher frequency values.

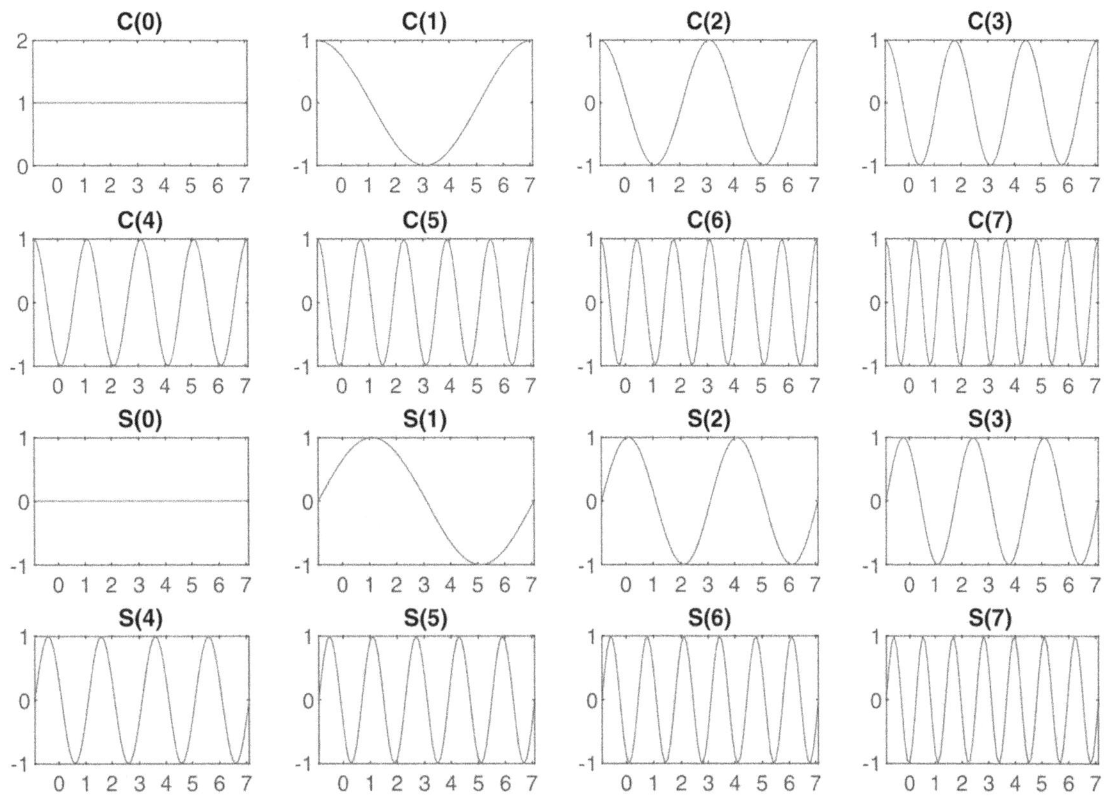

FIGURE 1.2
DFT basis functions.

A property of these basis functions is that they are orthogonal. This implies that multiplication of any waveform with another waveform followed by a summation leads to a zero scalar value. Another property of basis function is that they are independent of the original time domain signal and only depend on the number of samples N. Below are shown cosine and sine basis functions for $N = 8$ (Figure 1.2).

The complete time-domain signal can be obtained by multiplying the coefficients with the basis functions before adding them up.

1.10.4.4 Inverse DFT

The inverse DFT (IDFT) is used to recover a discrete-time signal $x(i)$ from its complex frequency-domain representation $X(k)$. It is defined mathematically as follows, where the symbols have the same meanings as before.

$$x(i) = \frac{1}{N}\sum_{k=0}^{N-1} X(k).e^{j.\frac{2\pi ki}{N}}$$

The above operation might be expressed symbolically as below, where $\mathcal{F}$ denotes the DFT operator.

$$x(i) = \mathcal{F}^{-1}\{X(k)\}$$

This equation represents the weighted sum of all frequency components in the frequency domain, each multiplied by a complex exponential term. Expanding the above expression by utilizing Euler's formula:

$$x(i) = \frac{1}{N}\sum_{k=0}^{N-1} X(k).\left(\cos\frac{2\pi ki}{N} + j.\sin\frac{2\pi ki}{N}\right)$$

$$x(i) = \frac{1}{N}\sum_{k=0}^{N-1} \mathrm{Re}\{X(k)\}.\left(\cos\frac{2\pi ki}{N}\right) + \frac{1}{N}\sum_{k=0}^{N-1} Im\{X(k)\}.\left(\sin\frac{2\pi ki}{N}\right)$$

$$x(i) = \frac{1}{N}\{a(i) + j.b(i)\}$$

Here:

$$a(i)=\sum_{k=0}^{N-1}A(k).\left(\cos\frac{2\pi ki}{N}\right)$$

$$b(i)=\sum_{k=0}^{N-1}B(k).\left(\sin\frac{2\pi ki}{N}\right)$$

1.10.4.5 Forward 2D DFT

The Forward 2D DFT is used to transform a two-dimensional discrete signal, typically an image, into its frequency-domain representation. It is defined mathematically as follows:

$$F(u,v)=\sum_{x=0}^{M-1}\sum_{y=0}^{N-1}f(x,y).\exp\left\{-j.2\pi\left(\frac{ux}{M}+\frac{vy}{N}\right)\right\}$$

where: $F(u,v)$ represents the complex frequency-domain representation at coordinates (u,v). $f(x,y)$ is the pixel value at coordinates (x,y) in the 2D input signal, M and N are the dimensions (width and height) of the input signal, u and v are the frequency indices, ranging from 0 to $M-1$ and 0 to $N-1$ for respectively, j is the imaginary unit ($\sqrt{-1}$). Σ denotes summation over all pixel coordinates (x,y) and angular arguments are in radians. This equation computes the sum of all pixel values in the input signal, each weighted by a complex exponential term. The result is the complex frequency-domain representation of the image.

1.10.4.6 Inverse 2D DFT

The Inverse 2D DFT (IDFT) is used to reconstruct the original two-dimensional discrete signal from its complex frequency-domain representation. It is defined mathematically as follows, where the symbols have the same meanings as before.

$$f(x,y)=\frac{1}{MN}\sum_{u=0}^{M-1}\sum_{v=0}^{N-1}F(u,v).\exp\left\{j.2\pi\left(\frac{ux}{M}+\frac{vy}{N}\right)\right\}$$

This equation calculates the weighted sum of all frequency components in the frequency domain, each multiplied by a complex exponential term, to reconstruct the original image. The above operations might be represented symbolically as below, where $\mathcal{F}$ denotes the DFT operator.

$$F(u,v)=\mathcal{F}\{f(x,y)\}$$

$$f(x,y)=\mathcal{F}^{-1}\{F(u,v)\}$$

In practical applications, the 2D DFT and IDFT are widely used in image processing, data compression, and various other fields where analyzing and manipulating two-dimensional signals is essential. These transformations allow for operations such as filtering, image enhancement and feature extraction in the frequency domain.

1.10.5 Discrete Cosine Transform (DCT)

We have already seen that a DFT transforms a time-domain signal into real and imaginary components in the frequency domain, represented by cosine and sine functions respectively. To reduce computational complexities, we can approximate the frequency-domain representation by considering only the real part (the cosine components) and discarding the imaginary part (the sine components). Such a transform is called a Discrete Cosine Transform (DCT). The DCT is also known for its energy compaction property; i.e., it concentrates the signal energy in a smaller number of coefficients, making it suitable for data compression and image coding. Although the DCT has several variants, the most popular and commonly used variant (type II) is discussed below. DCT II has better energy compaction properties, does not duplicate any information in the transform domain and its basis functions are orthogonal, due to which it is mostly used compared to the other variants DCT I and DCT III.

1.10.5.1 Forward DCT

The Forward DCT transforms a sequence of data from the spatial domain to the frequency domain. For an input sequence $x(i)$ of length N, the Forward DCT is defined as follows:

$$X(k)=\alpha(k).\sum_{i=0}^{N-1}x(i).\cos\left\{\frac{(2i+1)\pi k}{2N}\right\}$$

where: $X(k)$ is the DCT coefficient at frequency index k, $x(i)$ is the input sequence, N is the length of the sequence, k is the frequency index, ranging from 0 to $N-1$, angular arguments are in radians. $\alpha(k)$ is a scaling factor: $\alpha(0)=\sqrt{\frac{1}{N}}$ and $\alpha(k)=\sqrt{\frac{2}{N}}$ for $k>0$.

1.10.5.2 Inverse DCT

The 1D Inverse DCT reconstructs the original sequence from its DCT coefficients. It is defined as follows, where the symbols have the same meanings as before.

$$x(i)=\sum_{k=0}^{N-1}\alpha(k).X(k).\cos\left\{\frac{(2i+1)\pi k}{2N}\right\}$$

1.10.5.3 DCT Basis Functions

As with DFT, the basis functions are independent of the original signal and only depend on the number of the samples N. However unlike DFT, here since the frequency representation only consists of the real part, hence basis functions only consists of the cosine components. The k-th basis function is given by:

$$C(k)=\bigcup_{i=0}^{N-1}\cos\left\{\frac{(2i+1)\pi k}{2N}\right\}$$

These when multiplied by the coefficients produce a set of scaled cosine waves, which when added up form the original time-domain signal.

1.10.5.4 Forward 2D DCT

The 2D Forward DCT extends the 1D DCT to two dimensions, typically used for image compression. For an input image $f(x,y)$ of size $M\times N$, the Forward 2D DCT is defined as follows:

$$F(u,v)=\alpha_u.\alpha_v.\sum_{x=0}^{M-1}\sum_{y=0}^{N-1}f(x,y).\cos\left\{\frac{(2x+1)\pi u}{2M}\right\}.\cos\left\{\frac{(2y+1)\pi v}{2N}\right\}$$

where: $F(u,v)$ is the DCT coefficient at frequency indices (u,v), $f(x,y)$ is the pixel value of the input image at coordinates (x,y), M and N are the dimensions of the image, u and v are the frequency indices, ranging from 0 to M-1 and 0 to N-1 respectively, angular arguments are in radians, and $\alpha_u=\sqrt{\frac{1}{M}} for\, u=0$, $\alpha_u=\sqrt{\frac{2}{N}} for\, u\neq 0, \alpha_v=\sqrt{\frac{1}{N}} for\, v=0, \alpha_v=\sqrt{\frac{2}{N}} for\, v\neq 0.$

1.10.5.5 Inverse 2D DCT

The 2D Inverse DCT reconstructs the original image from its DCT coefficients. It is defined as follows, where the symbols have the same meanings as before.

$$f(x,y)=\sum_{u=0}^{M-1}\sum_{v=0}^{N-1}\alpha_u.\alpha_v.F(u,v).\cos\left\{\frac{(2x+1)\pi u}{2M}\right\}.\cos\left\{\frac{(2y+1)\pi v}{2N}\right\}$$

The DCT and IDCT are used extensively in image and video compression standards like JPEG and MPEG. They enable efficient coding of image and video data by representing information in the frequency domain while discarding less significant coefficients, thereby achieving compression with minimal loss of quality.

1.10.5.6 DCT vs. DFT

The Discrete Fourier Transform (DFT) and the Discrete Cosine Transform (DCT) are both mathematical techniques used for analyzing and transforming signals in the context of signal processing and image compression. They share some similarities but also have key differences. Important differences between DFT and DCT are discussed below.

Basis Functions: The basis functions of the DFT are complex sinusoids (sine and cosine functions), which oscillate at different frequencies. The DFT represents a signal in terms of both magnitude and phase information, making it suitable for a wide range of applications, including spectral analysis. The basis functions of the DCT are only cosine functions. Unlike the DFT, the DCT does not represent phase information but focuses solely on magnitude information. This characteristic makes it particularly suitable for applications where phase information is less critical, such as image and audio compression.

Energy Concentration: The DFT spreads the signal's energy across all frequency components, including both low and high frequencies. As a result, DFT coefficients can have significant values even for signals with limited spectral content, which can lead to inefficiencies in compression. The DCT has the property of energy compaction; it tends to concentrate most of the signal's energy into a smaller number of coefficients, making it well suited for compression applications. High-frequency components often have smaller DCT coefficients, which can be quantized and discarded without a significant loss in quality.

Applications: The DFT is commonly used in applications where both magnitude and phase information are critical, such as audio processing, spectral analysis and communications. It is valuable for tasks like filtering, modulation and feature extraction. The DCT is widely used in image and video compression, including popular formats like JPEG and MPEG and also used in audio compression (e.g., MP3). The DCT's energy compaction property makes it ideal for these applications because it allows for efficient coding by focusing on the most important coefficients.

Compression: The DFT is not typically used for compression directly, it can be used as a pre-processing step for feature extraction, but it does not provide the energy compaction property necessary for efficient compression. The DCT is specifically designed for compression tasks, its ability to concentrate signal energy into fewer coefficients simplifies quantization and encoding processes, reducing file sizes while preserving visual or auditory quality.

Lossless vs. Lossy: The DFT is inherently a lossless transform. It preserves all information in the original signal. The DCT is often used in lossy compression, where some information is intentionally discarded to achieve higher compression ratios. However, it can also be used in lossless compression, although this is less common.

1.10.6 Discrete Wavelet Transform (DWT)

The concept of "wavelet" meaning "small wave" was developed to address some of the limitations of Fourier Transform (Mallat, 1989). As we have seen, the Fourier Transform (FT) provides information about magnitudes of frequency components of a signal but does not tell us at what points in time these frequency components occur. So FT is ideal for stationary signals whose frequencies do not change over time, but cannot represent non-stationary signals accurately. Moreover FT also cannot represent abrupt changes and transients in the signal efficiently as it uses smooth sinusoidal basis functions which are not localized in time or space. For non-stationary signals, the Short Time Fourier Transform (STFT) was developed to provide a time-frequency representation of the signal, by assuming that some portion of the non-stationary signal is stationary. FT of each stationary portion is computed separately and then added up, by using a rectangular window function of fixed length which is slided along the signal from start to end. At each position of the window the signal is multiplied by the window function after which FT is calculated, assuming that frequency of the signal within the window remains constant. Mathematically the STFT can be represented as:

$$X(f,\tau) = \int x(t).w(t-\tau).e^{-j2\pi ft}dt$$

Here w is a window function which can be translated through time using a translation parameter. So the STFT is said to provide some time localization in addition to frequency information, i.e., because the window width is fixed, it can be inferred over which time ranges which frequencies are occurring but not accurately at an exact instant of time. The STFT therefore provides limited time and frequency resolutions. However, real world applications require a high frequency resolution for low frequency components and a high time resolution for high frequency components. The wavelet transform addresses this issue by analyzing a signal into different frequencies at different resolutions, instead of a fixed resolution for STFT, and this is referred to as multi-resolution analysis. Mathematically the wavelet transform can be represented as follows:

$$X(s,\tau) = \frac{1}{\sqrt{|s|}} \int x(t).\psi\left(\frac{t-\tau}{s}\right)dt$$

Essentially the transform represents the original signal in terms of wavelets, which are finite duration wave like oscillatory functions with zero mean, as the new basis functions instead of the sinusoidal functions as in the case of FT. Here ψ is called a wavelet function, $s > 0$ is called a scale parameter, which is inverse of frequency, and τ is the translation or shift parameter. A larger scale parameter results in a stretched wave which corresponds to a lower frequency, while a lower scale parameter results in a shrunken wavelet which corresponds to a higher frequency. The wavelets behave as window functions as for STFT, but instead of fixed width, the s parameter can be used to change the frequency and width of the wavelet. Expanded wavelets can be used to find low frequency components of the signal with good frequency resolution while compressed wavelets can be used to find high frequency components of the signal with good time resolution. The τ parameter is used to shift the wavelet so as to cover the entire width of the signal. When the frequency of the wavelet matches part of the signal with similar frequencies, a high output is produced, the output being referred to as the wavelet coefficient. The original function $\psi(t)$ is called the mother wavelet while shifted and scaled versions of it are called daughter wavelets. Also a scaling function $\varphi(t)$ is also used to actually scale the wavelet and this is sometimes called the father wavelet.

Computing wavelet coefficients at every possible scale and every possible location generates a large amount of data. This can be reduced by choosing discrete values of s and τ. The discrete wavelet transform (DWT) can be represented as follows:

$$X(a,b) = \frac{1}{\sqrt{b}} \sum_{i=0}^{N-1} x(i).\psi\left(\frac{i-a}{b}\right)$$

If s and τ are based on powers of two, called dyadic, then analysis becomes more efficient and accurate. For dyadic representation, $a = k.2^{-j}$ and $b = 2^{-j}$ where j is the scale index and k is the shift index.

1.10.6.1 1D DWT

The wavelet transform can be efficiently computed by passing the signal through a set of high-pass and low-pass filters, known as filter bank decomposition. If $x(n)$ be the 1D input signal where n is the discrete time index then the analysis (decomposition) equation is written as follows:

$$a_{j+1}(n) = \sum_k h(k).x(2n-k)$$

$$d_{j+1}(n) = \sum_k g(k).x(2n-k)$$

The first equation represents low-pass filtering and $a_{j+1}(n)$ is called the approximation (low-pass) coefficient at level j, the second equation represents high-pass filtering and $d_{j+1}(n)$ is called the detail (high-pass) coefficient at level j, $h(k)$ and $g(k)$ are the coefficients of the low-pass (L) and high-pass (H) filters and k represents the index of the filter coefficients. The inverse wavelet transform can be used to get back the original signal from approximation and detail components and this is referred to as the synthesis (reconstruction) equation as shown below:

$$x(n) = \sum_k h(-k).a_{j+1}(2n-k) + \sum_k g(-k).d_{j+1}(2n-k)$$

The factor 2 in the expression $2n-k$ is related to a down-sampling operation. During the filtering operations, since half of the frequencies of the signal are being considered, half of the samples can be discarded according to Nyquist's rule and the frequency is effectively doubled. The DWT is typically performed in a recursive manner, where the approximation coefficients from one scale j become the input for the next scale $j+1$. This allows for a multi-resolution analysis of the signal, with each level of decomposition capturing different frequency components.

The actual filter coefficient values would depend on the type of wavelets used. There are a large variety of wavelets possible, each suitable for specific applications. Each wavelet type or family is associated with a scaling function φ associated with the low-pass coefficients and a wavelet function ψ associated with the high-pass coefficients. The simplest called the Haar wavelet consist of square waveforms with a scaling function $\varphi(t)$ and wavelet function $\psi(t)$ given as follows:

$$\varphi(t) = \begin{cases} 1, & 0 \le t < 1 \\ 0, & \text{otherwise} \end{cases}$$

$$\psi(t) = \begin{cases} 1, & 0 \le t < 0.5 \\ -1, & 0.5 \le t < 1 \\ 0, & \text{otherwise} \end{cases}$$

The Haar filter coefficients are $h = \left(\frac{1}{\sqrt{2}}, \frac{1}{\sqrt{2}}\right)$ and $g = \left(\frac{1}{\sqrt{2}}, -\frac{1}{\sqrt{2}}\right)$. The Daubechies 2 wavelet scaling and wavelet functions are shown below and the filter coefficients are $h = (-0.129, 0.224, 0.836, 0.482)$, $g = (-0.482, 0.836, -0.224, -0.129)$. The Coiflets1 filter coefficients are $h = (-0.015, -0.073, 0.385, 0.852, 0.338, -0.073)$ and $g = (0.073, 0.338, -0.853, 0.385, 0.073 - 0.015)$. The Biorthogonal 2.2 (bior2.2) coefficients are $h = (0, -0.177, 0.353, 1.060, 0.353, -0.177)$ and $g = (0, 0.353, -0.707, 0.353, 0, 0)$. These values ensure that the energy (or sum of squares) of the coefficients is 1, to preserve the signal energy during the transform (Figure 1.3).

1.10.6.2 2D DWT

The 2D wavelet transform is an extension of the 1D transform and is performed in two ways: first, by applying 2D low-pass and high-pass filters $h(k,l)$ and $g(k,l)$, and second, by applying 1D filters $h(k)$ and $g(k)$ separately along each dimension. For the first case, called the non-separable approach, the analysis or decomposition equations are depicted below, where A and D are the approximation and detail coefficients for a specific level j, $x(m,n)$ is the input signal, m and n are the sample indices along the horizontal and vertical directions, and k and l are the indices of the filter coefficients along these two directions.

$$A_{j+1}(m,n) = \sum_{k,l} h(k,l).x(2m-k, 2n-l)$$

$$D_{j+1}(m,n) = \sum_{k,l} g(k,l).x(2m-k, 2n-l)$$

The synthesis or reconstruction equation specify how the original 2D signal is obtained from the filter coefficients, where $h(-k,-l)$ and $g(-k,-l)$ represents the time reversed coefficients of the filters.

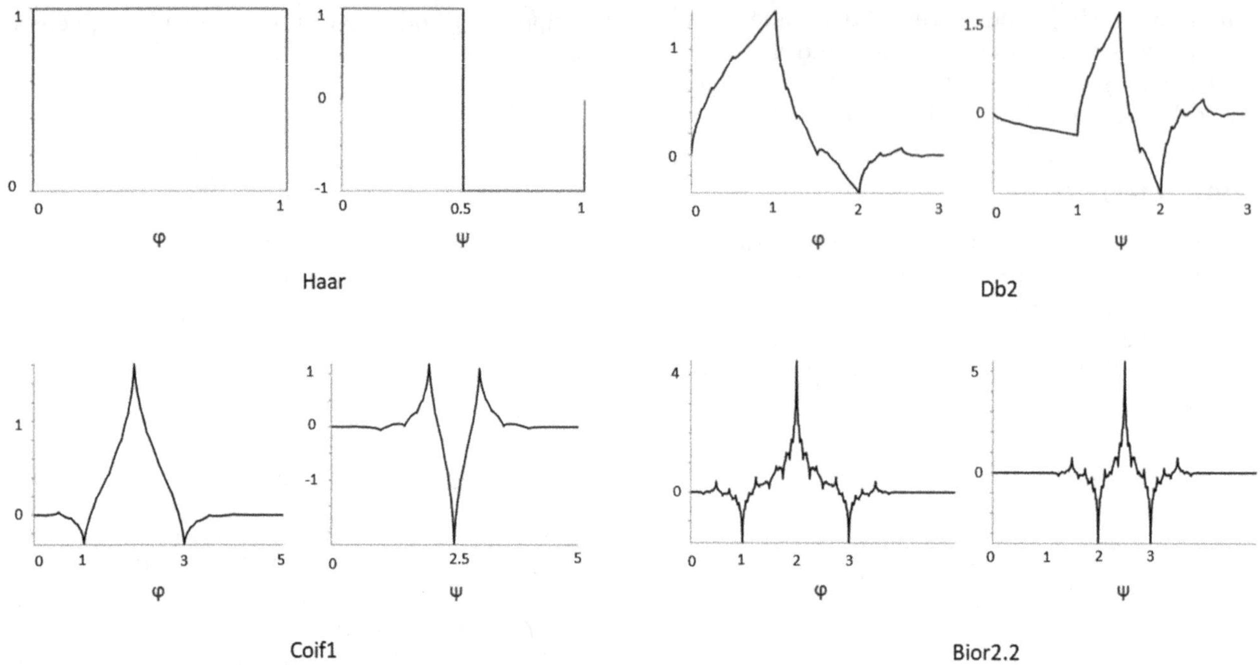

FIGURE 1.3
Scaling and wavelet functions of (row1) Haar, Db2, (row2) Coif1, Bior2.2 wavelets.

$$x(m,n)=\sum_{k,l}h(-k,-l).A_{j+1}(2m+k,2n+l)+\sum_{k,l}g(-k,-l).D_{j+1}(2m+k,2n+l)$$

Alternatively, it is also possible to apply two 1D filters first along one dimension (horizontal) and then along the other dimension (vertical), which is called the separable approach. For this case the analysis equations are depicted below which indicate four coefficients, where k is the index along the horizontal direction (along rows i.e. across columns) and l is the index along the vertical direction (along columns i.e. across rows).

$$A_{j+1}(m,n)=\sum_k\sum_l h(k).h(l).x(2m-k,2n-l)$$

$$H_{j+1}(m,n)=\sum_k\sum_l h(k).g(l).x(2m-k,2n-l)$$

$$V_{j+1}(m,n)=\sum_k\sum_l g(k).h(l).x(2m-k,2n-l)$$

$$D_{j+1}(m,n)=\sum_k\sum_l g(k).g(l).x(2m-k,2n-l)$$

In the first stage, rows of two-dimensional signals are convolved with h (low-pass) and g (high-pass) filters and then columns are down-sampled by 2 (i.e. only even indexed columns are kept). In the next stage, columns are convolved with the filters h and g and then rows are down-sampled by 2 (i.e. only even indexed rows are kept). In other words, an $N \times N$ signal is transformed into two $N \times (N/2)$ signals after first stage and four $(N/2) \times (N/2)$ signals after the second stage. The above steps are collectively referred to as decomposition or analysis step. This generates one approximation coefficient (A) using the combination hh (low-low), and three detail coefficients, named as horizontal coefficient (H) using hg (low-high), vertical coefficient (V) using gh (high-low) and diagonal coefficient (D) using gg (high-high) (Figure 1.4). The approximation and detail components can be combined together to reconstruct the original image by again passing through low-pass and high-pass filters, which is called the reconstruction or synthesis step in accordance with the following equation:

$$\begin{aligned}x(m,n)=&\sum_k\sum_l h(-k).h(-l).A_{j+1}(2m+k,2n+l)\\&+\sum_k\sum_l h(-k).g(-l).H_{j+1}(2m+k,2n+l)\\&+\sum_k\sum_l g(-k).h(-l).V_{j+1}(2m+k,2n+l)\\&+\sum_k\sum_l g(-k).g(-l).D_{j+1}(2m+k,2n+l)\end{aligned}$$

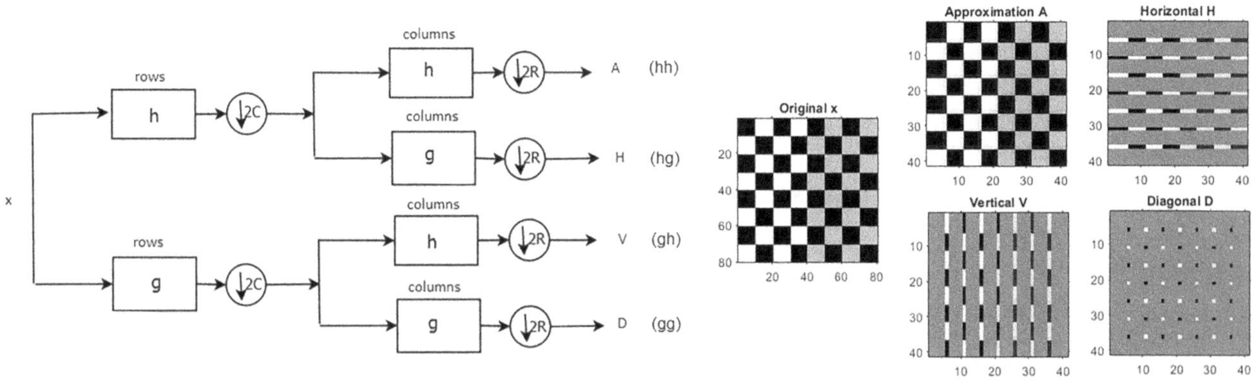

FIGURE 1.4
2D wavelet decomposition.

1.10.7 Using Transformation Matrices

Both the DFT and DCT transform a sequence of N data points into another sequence of N values representing the amplitude and phase of frequency components of the original data. Hence both DFT and DCT can be represented as transformation matrices, which when multiplied with the original space/time domain values generates the frequency domain values. Unlike the DCT transformation matrix which contains of only real values, the DFT matrix can contain both real and imaginary values.

1.10.7.1 DFT Transformation Matrix

The DFT coefficients can also be calculated using a transformation matrix W of size $N \times N$, where N is the length of the sequence, such that: $X = W.x$

$$W = \begin{pmatrix} 1 & 1 & 1 & \cdots & 1 \\ 1 & D & D^2 & \cdots & D^{N-1} \\ 1 & D^2 & D^4 & \cdots & D^{2(N-1)} \\ \vdots & \vdots & \vdots & \vdots & \vdots \\ 1 & D^{N-1} & D^{2(N-1)} & \cdots & D^{(N-1)(N-1)} \end{pmatrix}$$

where: $D = e^{-j.\frac{2\pi}{N}}$. Also it can be shown that $x = \left(\frac{1}{N}\right)W^{*}.X$, where W^{*} is the complex conjugate of W.

1.10.7.2 DCT Transformation Matrix

To calculate DCT coefficients, the DCT transformation matrix T of size $N \times N$ can be used, where N is the length of the sequence, such that $X = T.x$.

In this case, the (p,q)–th term of the matrix T is given by:

$T(p,q) = \sqrt{1/N}$, for $p = 0, 0 \le q \le N-1$
$T(p,q) = \sqrt{2/N}.\cos\{p(2q+1)\pi/(2N)\}$, for $1 \le p \le N-1, 0 \le q \le N-1$

$$T = \begin{pmatrix} \frac{1}{\sqrt{N}} & \frac{1}{\sqrt{N}} & \cdots & \frac{1}{\sqrt{N}} \\ \sqrt{\frac{2}{N}}\cos\frac{\pi}{2N} & \sqrt{\frac{2}{N}}\cos\frac{3\pi}{2N} & \cdots & \sqrt{\frac{2}{N}}\cos\frac{\{2(N-1)+1\}\pi}{2N} \\ \vdots & \vdots & \vdots & \vdots \\ \sqrt{\frac{2}{N}}\cos\frac{(N-1)\pi}{2N} & \sqrt{\frac{2}{N}}\cos\frac{3(N-1)\pi}{2N} & \cdots & \sqrt{\frac{2}{N}}\cos\frac{\{(N-1)(N-1)+1\}\pi}{2N} \end{pmatrix}$$

Also, it can be shown that $x = T'.X$, where T' is the transpose of T.

These matrix-based calculations allow efficient computations of DFT and DCT coefficients from input sequences.

1.11 Legal and Ethical Considerations

Legal and ethical considerations for multimedia content involve ensuring compliance with copyright laws to protect intellectual property, obtaining proper permissions for the use of third party materials and respecting privacy and consent. Additionally adherence to community standards and cultural sensitivities is crucial to avoid offensive or harmful content. Content creators are required to prioritize transparency providing accurate content and avoid deceptive practices to uphold ethical standards (Mhiripiri & Chari, 2017).

1.11.1 Copyright

Understanding Copyright: Copyright is a legal concept that grants creators exclusive rights to their original works. In the context of multimedia, copyright applies to various elements, including text, images, audio, video, software code and interactive content. Creators automatically hold copyright to their works as soon as they are created and fixed in a tangible medium.

Fair Use: Fair use is an exception to copyright law that allows limited use of copyrighted material without permission from the rights holder. It is intended for purposes such as criticism, commentary, news reporting and education. Determining fair use can be subjective and often requires a case-by-case analysis.

Public Domain: Works in the public domain are not protected by copyright and can be freely used by the public. This status can result from the expiration of copyright or when creators intentionally release their work into the public domain.

1.11.2 Licensing and Permissions

Types of Licenses: Multimedia creators can choose to license their works under various licensing models. Common licenses include:

Creative Commons Licenses: These licenses offer a range of permissions, allowing creators to specify how their work can be used, modified and shared. Open Source Licenses: Open source software licenses, such as the GPL (General Public License), dictate how software can be used, modified and distributed. Proprietary Licenses: Proprietary software licenses are more restrictive and may limit how the software is used or shared.

Obtaining Permissions: When using copyrighted material in multimedia projects, obtaining proper permissions is essential. This may involve seeking explicit consent from the copyright holder, licensing content under a suitable license or complying with terms specified in open-source or creative commons licenses.

1.11.3 Legal Considerations

Digital Millennium Copyright Act (DMCA): The DMCA is a U.S. law that addresses copyright issues in the digital realm. It establishes rules for takedown notices in response to copyright infringement and provides safe harbor protections for online service providers.

Software Licensing: Software used in multimedia development often comes with specific licensing terms. Creators must ensure that they comply with these terms and respect software licenses, whether open-source or proprietary.

International Copyright Treaties: Multimedia creators should be aware of international copyright treaties and agreements, such as the Berne Convention. These treaties establish a framework for copyright protection across countries and may affect how copyrights are enforced globally.

1.11.4 Ethical Considerations

Plagiarism and Attribution: Ethical multimedia creation involves giving credit to the original creators. Plagiarism, which involves presenting someone else's work as your own, is considered unethical. Proper attribution and citation are crucial in ethical multimedia production.

Privacy and Consent: Respecting individuals' privacy rights and obtaining consent for the use of personal information or images in multimedia projects is an ethical responsibility. Failure to do so may result in privacy violations and legal issues.

Representation and Stereotypes: Multimedia creators should be mindful of their responsibility to depict people and communities accurately and without promoting stereotypes, bias or discrimination. Ethical multimedia seeks to reflect diversity and inclusivity.

1.11.5 Integrity and Authenticity

Misinformation and Deepfakes: Misleading content and deepfake technology pose ethical challenges. Creators should be committed to producing truthful and authentic content, and viewers should be critical consumers of multimedia information.

Credible Sources: Creators should rely on credible and reliable sources of information to ensure the accuracy and credibility of their content. Misinformation can have severe consequences, including damage to one's reputation and legal liability.

1.11.6 Digital Rights Management (DRM)

Digital Rights Management (DRM) is a set of technologies and practices aimed at protecting digital content from unauthorized access, distribution and use. In the context of various digital media, including music, movies, e-books, and software, DRM plays a crucial role in preserving the intellectual property rights of content creators and distributors.

One of the primary features of DRM is the implementation of robust encryption mechanisms to safeguard digital content. Through encryption, DRM ensures that files remain unreadable and inaccessible without proper authorization. This prevents unauthorized users from copying, sharing or modifying digital assets, mitigating the risk of piracy and unauthorized distribution

Secondly, DRM employs licensing models to regulate the usage of digital content. Content distributors issue licenses to users, specifying the terms of use, such as the number of devices on which the content can be accessed and the duration of access. Access control mechanisms embedded in DRM systems enforce these terms, allowing only authorized users with valid licenses to consume the content.

1.12 Challenges and Emerging Trends

Challenges in multimedia include the demand for efficient compression techniques to handle the increasing size of multimedia files, addressing issues of interoperability across diverse devices and platforms, and mitigating concerns related to digital rights management and piracy. Emerging trends in multimedia involve the integration of artificial intelligence for content analysis and personalized recommendations, the rise of immersive technologies like virtual and augmented reality, and the continuous evolution of interactive and user-generated content, shaping new avenues for engagement and storytelling in the multimedia landscape (Solanki et al., 2019).

1.12.1 Challenges

Bandwidth and Data Consumption: As multimedia content becomes richer and more high-definition, bandwidth and data consumption remain significant challenges, especially in areas with limited internet connectivity. Balancing quality with accessibility is an ongoing struggle.

Cross-Platform Compatibility: Ensuring consistent performance and user experience across various devices, operating systems and screen sizes is a challenge. Adapting multimedia applications to different platforms requires thorough testing and optimization.

Privacy and Security: Multimedia applications often handle sensitive user data, making privacy and security paramount concerns. Data breaches, unauthorized access and the potential for malicious multimedia content present risks.

Accessibility: Creating multimedia content that is accessible to all users, including those with disabilities, is both a legal requirement and an ethical consideration. Designing multimedia that accommodates various accessibility needs is a continuous challenge.

Content Piracy and Copyright Infringement: The ease of copying and sharing multimedia content has led to issues of copyright infringement and content piracy. Protecting intellectual property, while allowing for fair use, is an ongoing legal challenge.

1.12.2 Emerging Trends

360-Degree and Virtual Reality (VR) Content: Immersive experiences, including 360-degree videos and virtual reality applications, are gaining popularity. These technologies offer new ways to engage users in storytelling, gaming and education.

Augmented Reality (AR) Integration: AR is transforming how users interact with multimedia content. Applications that overlay digital elements on the real world are used in fields like retail, healthcare and education.

AI and Machine Learning: AI and machine learning are enhancing multimedia applications in various ways. This includes content recommendation, image and speech recognition, and automated video editing.

5G Connectivity: The rollout of 5G networks has revolutionized multimedia streaming and real-time communication. The increased speed and reduced latency enable high-quality multimedia experiences on mobile devices.

Interactive Live Streaming: Interactive live streaming platforms, where users can actively participate in live content, are gaining popularity. Gamers, educators and content creators use these platforms to engage with their audiences.

The field of multimedia technology is continually evolving, driven by both challenges and emerging trends. As the industry continues to evolve, multimedia professionals must stay informed and adapt to new challenges and opportunities, ultimately shaping the multimedia landscape of the future.

1.13 Numerical Problems

1.13.1 Discrete Fourier Transform (DFT)

PROBLEM 1.1

Compute the DFT representation of the discrete signal with four sample values $x = \{9,7,3,5\}$.

Here, $x = [3,5,7,9]$, number of terms $N = 4$.

Let X be the corresponding frequency domain representation.

$$X = Re(X) - jIm(X) = A - jB$$

$$\text{Here, } A = \bigcup_{i=0}^{N} A(k) \text{ and } A(k) = \sum_{i=0}^{N-1} x(i).\cos\left(\frac{2\pi ki}{N}\right)$$

$$B = \bigcup_{i=0}^{N} B(k) \text{ and } B(k) = \sum_{i=0}^{N-1} x(i).\sin\left(\frac{2\pi ki}{N}\right)$$

$$\text{In this case, } A(k) = \sum_{i=0}^{3} x(i).\cos\left(\frac{2\pi ki}{4}\right)$$

$$A(0) = \sum_{i=0}^{3} x(i).\cos(0) = 9(1) + 7(1) + 3(1) + 5(1) = 24$$

$$A(1) = \sum_{i=0}^{3} x(i).\cos\left(\frac{2\pi i}{4}\right) = x(0)\cos 0 + x(1)\cos\left(\frac{\pi}{2}\right) + x(2)\cos\left(\frac{2\pi}{2}\right) + x(3)\cos\left(\frac{3\pi}{2}\right) = 9(1) + 7(0) + 3(-1) + 5(0) = 6$$

$$A(2) = \sum_{i=0}^{3} x(i).\cos\left(\frac{4\pi i}{4}\right) = x(0)\cos 0 + x(1)\cos(\pi) + x(2)\cos(2\pi) + x(3)\cos(3\pi) = 9(1) + 7(-1) + 3(1) + 5(-1) = 0$$

$$A(3) = \sum_{i=0}^{3} x(i).\cos\left(\frac{6\pi i}{4}\right) = x(0)\cos 0 + x(1)\cos\left(\frac{3\pi}{2}\right) + x(2)\cos\left(\frac{6\pi}{2}\right) + x(3)\cos\left(\frac{9\pi}{2}\right) = 9(1) + 7(0) + 3(-1) + 5(0) = 6$$

$$A = Re(X) = [24,6,0,6]$$

$$\text{Again, } B(k) = \sum_{i=0}^{3} x(i).\sin\left(\frac{2\pi ki}{4}\right)$$

$$B(0) = \sum_{i=0}^{3} x(i).\sin(0) = 9(0) + 7(0) + 3(0) + 5(0) = 0$$

$$B(1) = \sum_{i=0}^{3} x(i).\sin\left(\frac{2\pi i}{4}\right) = x(0)\sin 0 + x(1)\sin\left(\frac{\pi}{2}\right) + x(2)\sin\left(\frac{2\pi}{2}\right) + x(3)\sin\left(\frac{3\pi}{2}\right) = 9(0) + 7(1) + 3(0) + 5(-1) = 6$$

$$B(2) = \sum_{i=0}^{3} x(i).\sin\left(\frac{4\pi i}{4}\right) = x(0)\sin 0 + x(1)\sin(\pi) + x(2)\sin(2\pi) + x(3)\sin(3\pi) = 9(0) + 7(0) + 3(0) + 5(0) = 0$$

$$B(3)=\sum_{i=0}^{3}x(i).\sin\left(\frac{6\pi i}{4}\right)=x(0)\sin 0+x(1)\sin\left(\frac{3\pi}{2}\right)$$
$$+x(2)\sin\left(\frac{6\pi}{2}\right)+x(3)\sin\left(\frac{9\pi}{2}\right)$$
$$=9(0)+7(-1)+3(0)+5(1)=-2$$

$$B=Im(X)=[0,2,0,-2]$$

Combining:

$$X=Re(X)-j.Im(X)=[24,6-2j,0,6+2j]$$

PROBLEM 1.2

For the previous example, convert the DFT coefficients back to original signal values.

Here $X=[24,6-2j,0,6+2j]=A-j.B$, number of terms $N=4$.

Here $A=[24,6,0,6]$ and $B=[0,2,0,-2]$.

Let x be the corresponding time domain representation, then $x=(1/N)(a+j.b)$.

$$a(i)=\sum_{k=0}^{3}A(k).\cos\left(\frac{2\pi ki}{4}\right)$$

$$a(0)=\sum_{k=0}^{3}A(k).\cos(0)=24(1)+6(1)+0(1)+6(1)=36$$

$$a(1)=\sum_{k=0}^{3}A(k).\cos\left(\frac{2\pi k}{4}\right)=A(0)\cos 0+A(1)\cos\left(\frac{2\pi}{4}\right)$$
$$+A(2)\cos\left(\frac{4\pi}{4}\right)+A(3)\cos\left(\frac{6\pi}{4}\right)$$
$$=24(1)+6(0)+0(-1)+6(0)=24$$

$$a(2)=\sum_{k=0}^{3}A(k).\cos\left(\frac{4\pi k}{4}\right)=A(0)\cos 0+A(1)\cos\left(\frac{4\pi}{4}\right)$$
$$+A(2)\cos\left(\frac{8\pi}{4}\right)+A(3)\cos\left(\frac{12\pi}{4}\right)$$
$$=24(1)+6(-1)+0(1)+6(-1)=12$$

$$a(3)=\sum_{k=0}^{3}A(k).\cos\left(\frac{6\pi k}{4}\right)=A(0)\cos 0+A(1)\cos\left(\frac{6\pi}{4}\right)$$
$$+A(2)\cos\left(\frac{12\pi}{4}\right)+A(3)\cos\left(\frac{18\pi}{4}\right)$$
$$=24(1)+6(0)+0(-1)+6(0)=24$$

Thus, $a=[36,24,12,24]$

$$b(i)=\sum_{k=0}^{3}B(k).\sin\left(\frac{2\pi ki}{4}\right)$$

$$b(0)=\sum_{k=0}^{3}B(k).\sin(0)=0(0)+2(0)+0(0)+(-2)(0)=0$$

$$b(1)=\sum_{k=0}^{3}B(k).\sin\left(\frac{2\pi k}{4}\right)=B(0)\sin 0+B(1)\sin\left(\frac{2\pi}{4}\right)$$
$$+B(2)\sin\left(\frac{4\pi}{4}\right)+B(3)\sin\left(\frac{6\pi}{4}\right)$$
$$=0(0)+2(1)+0(0)+(-2)(-1)=4$$

$$b(2)=\sum_{k=0}^{3}B(k).\sin\left(\frac{4\pi k}{4}\right)=B(0)\sin 0+B(1)\sin\left(\frac{4\pi}{4}\right)$$
$$+B(2)\sin\left(\frac{8\pi}{4}\right)+B(3)\sin\left(\frac{12\pi}{4}\right)$$
$$=0(0)+2(0)+0(0)+(-2)(0)=0$$

$$b(3)=\sum_{k=0}^{3}B(k).\sin\left(\frac{6\pi k}{4}\right)=B(0)\sin 0+B(1)\sin\left(\frac{6\pi}{4}\right)$$
$$+B(2)\sin\left(\frac{12\pi}{4}\right)+B(3)\sin\left(\frac{18\pi}{4}\right)$$
$$=0(0)+2(-1)+0(0)+(-2)(1)=-4$$

Thus, $b=[0,4,0,-4]$

$$\text{Combining, } x=(1/N)(a+jb)$$
$$=(1/4)[(36+0),(24+4),(12+0),(24-4)]$$
$$=[9,7,3,5]$$

PROBLEM 1.3

For the previous problem, compute the basis functions. Hence, show that the original signal can be represented as a combination of DFT coefficients and basis functions.

Here $A=[24,6,0,6], B=[0,2,0,-2]$

Basis functions $C(k)=\bigcup_{i=0}^{N}\cos\left(\frac{2\pi ki}{N}\right)$ and $S(k)=\bigcup_{i=0}^{N}\sin\left(\frac{2\pi ki}{N}\right)$

Computing components,

$$C(0)=\bigcup_{i=0}^{N}\cos(0)=[1,1,1,1]$$

$$S(0)=\bigcup_{i=0}^{N}\sin(0)=[0,0,0,0]$$

$$C(1)=\bigcup_{i=0}^{N}\cos\left(\frac{2\pi i}{4}\right)=\left[1,\cos\frac{2\pi}{4},\cos\frac{4\pi}{4},\cos\frac{6\pi}{4}\right]$$
$$=[1,0,-1,0]$$

$$S(1)=\bigcup_{i=0}^{N}\sin\left(\frac{2\pi i}{4}\right)=\left[1,\sin\frac{2\pi}{4},\sin\frac{4\pi}{4},\sin\frac{6\pi}{4}\right]$$
$$=[0,1,0,-1]$$

$$C(2)=\bigcup_{i=0}^{N}\cos\left(\frac{4\pi i}{4}\right)=\left[1,\cos\frac{4\pi}{4},\cos\frac{8\pi}{4},\cos\frac{12\pi}{4}\right]$$
$$=[1,-1,1,-1]$$

$$S(2)=\bigcup_{i=0}^{N}\sin\left(\frac{4\pi i}{4}\right)=\left[1,\sin\frac{4\pi}{4},\sin\frac{8\pi}{4},\sin\frac{12\pi}{4}\right]$$
$$=[0,0,0,0]$$

$$C(3)=\bigcup_{i=0}^{N}\cos\left(\frac{6\pi i}{4}\right)=\left[1,\cos\frac{6\pi}{4},\cos\frac{12\pi}{4},\cos\frac{18\pi}{4}\right]$$
$$=[1,0,-1,0]$$

$$S(3)=\bigcup_{i=0}^{N}\sin\left(\frac{6\pi i}{4}\right)=\left[1,\sin\frac{6\pi}{4},\sin\frac{12\pi}{4},\sin\frac{18\pi}{4}\right]$$
$$=[1,-1,0,1]$$

$$xr=(1/N).A.C'=(1/4).\left[A(0)C(0)+A(1)C(1)+A(2)C(2)+A(3)C(3)\right]$$

$$(24/4)*[1,1,1,1]+(6/4)*[1,0,-1,0]+(0/4)*[1,-1,1,-1]+(6/4)*[1,0,-1,0]$$

$$[6,6,6,6]+[1.5,0,-1.5,0]+[0,0,0,0]+[1.5,0,-1.5,0]$$

$$[9,6,3,6]$$

$$xi=(1/N).B.S'=(1/4).\left[B(0)S(0)+B(1)S(1)+B(2)S(2)+B(3)S(3)\right]$$

$$(0/4)*[0,0,0,0]+(2/4)*[0,1,0,-1]+(0/4)*[0,0,0,0]+(-2/4)*[0,-1,0,1]$$

$$[0,0,0,0]+[0,0.5,0,-0.5]+[0,0,0,0]+[0,0.5,0,-0.5]=[0,1,0,-1]$$

$$x=xr+xi=[9,6,3,6]+[0,1,0,-1]=[9,7,3,5]$$

1.13.2 Discrete Cosine Transform (DCT)

PROBLEM 1.4

Compute the DCT representation of the discrete signal $x = \{9,7,3,5\}$.

$$X(k)=\alpha(k).\sum_{i=0}^{N-1}x(i).\cos\left\{\frac{(2i+1)\pi k}{2N}\right\}$$

where $\alpha(0)=\sqrt{\frac{1}{N}}$ and $\alpha(k)=\sqrt{\frac{2}{N}}$ for $k>0$

Here, $X(k)=\alpha(k).\sum_{i=0}^{3}x(i).\cos\left\{\frac{(2i+1)\pi k}{8}\right\}$

$$X(0)=\alpha(0).\sum_{i=0}^{3}x(i).\cos(0)$$
$$=\sqrt{\frac{1}{4}}\left[x(0)+x(1)+x(2)+x(3)\right]=\frac{24}{2}=12$$

$$X(1)=\alpha(1).\sum_{i=0}^{3}x(i).\cos\left\{\frac{(2i+1)\pi}{8}\right\}=\sqrt{\frac{2}{4}}\left[x(0)\cos\frac{\pi}{8}+x(1)\cos\frac{3\pi}{8}+x(2)\cos\frac{5\pi}{8}+x(3)\cos\frac{7\pi}{8}\right]=3.695$$

$$X(2)=\alpha(2).\sum_{i=0}^{3}x(i).\cos\left\{\frac{2(2i+1)\pi}{8}\right\}=\sqrt{\frac{2}{4}}\left[x(0)\cos\frac{\pi}{4}+x(1)\cos\frac{3\pi}{4}+x(2)\cos\frac{5\pi}{4}+x(3)\cos\frac{7\pi}{4}\right]=2$$

$$X(3)=\alpha(3).\sum_{i=0}^{3}x(i).\cos\left\{\frac{3(2i+1)\pi}{8}\right\}=\sqrt{\frac{2}{4}}\left[x(0)\cos\frac{3\pi}{8}+x(1)\cos\frac{9\pi}{8}+x(2)\cos\frac{15\pi}{8}+x(3)\cos\frac{21\pi}{8}\right]=-1.5307$$

Thus $X=[12,3.6956,2,-1.5307]$

PROBLEM 1.5

For the previous problem, revert back the original signal values from its DCT representation.

Here, $X = [12, 3.6956, 2, -1.5307]$, number of terms $N = 4$

$$x(i) = \sum_{k=0}^{N-1} \alpha(k).X(k).\cos\left\{\frac{(2i+1)\pi k}{2N}\right\}$$

where $\alpha(0) = \sqrt{\frac{1}{N}}$ and $\alpha(k) = \sqrt{\frac{2}{N}}$ for k > 0

$$\text{Here}, x(i) = \sum_{k=0}^{3} \alpha(k).X(k).\cos\left\{\frac{(2i+1)\pi k}{8}\right\}$$

$$x(0) = \sum_{k=0}^{3} \alpha(k).X(k).\cos\left\{\frac{\pi k}{8}\right\}$$

$$= \alpha(0).X(0).\cos 0 + \alpha(1).X(1).\cos\frac{\pi}{8} + \alpha(2).X(2).\cos\frac{2\pi}{8} + \alpha(3).X(3).\cos\frac{3\pi}{8} = 9$$

$$x(1) = \sum_{k=0}^{3} \alpha(k).X(k).\cos\left\{\frac{3\pi k}{8}\right\}$$

$$= \alpha(0).X(0).\cos 0 + \alpha(1).X(1).\cos\frac{3\pi}{8} + \alpha(2).X(2).\cos\frac{6\pi}{8} + \alpha(3).X(3).\cos\frac{9\pi}{8} = 7$$

$$x(2) = \sum_{k=0}^{3} \alpha(k).X(k).\cos\left\{\frac{5\pi k}{8}\right\}$$

$$= \alpha(0).X(0).\cos 0 + \alpha(1).X(1).\cos\frac{5\pi}{8} + \alpha(2).X(2).\cos\frac{6\pi}{8} + \alpha(3).X(3).\cos\frac{9\pi}{8} = 7$$

$$x(3) = \sum_{k=0}^{3} \alpha(k).X(k).\cos\left\{\frac{7\pi k}{8}\right\}$$

$$= \alpha(0).X(0).\cos 0 + \alpha(1).X(1).\cos\frac{7\pi}{8} + \alpha(2).X(2).\cos\frac{14\pi}{8} + \alpha(3).X(3).\cos\frac{21\pi}{8} = 5$$

Hence $x = [9, 7, 3, 5]$

PROBLEM 1.6

For the previous problem, show that the original signal can be represented as a combination of DCT coefficients and basis functions.

Basis functions: $C(k) = \bigcup_{i=0}^{N} \cos\left\{\frac{(2i+1)\pi k}{2N}\right\}$

$$\text{Here}, C(k) = \bigcup_{i=0}^{3} \cos\left\{\frac{(2i+1)\pi k}{8}\right\}$$

$$C(0) = \bigcup_{i=0}^{N} \cos(0) = [1, 1, 1, 1]$$

$$C(1) = \bigcup_{i=0}^{N} \cos\left\{\frac{(2i+1)\pi}{8}\right\} = [0.9239, 0.3827, -0.3827, -0.9239]$$

$$C(2) = \bigcup_{i=0}^{N} \cos\left\{\frac{2(2i+1)\pi}{8}\right\} = [0.7071, -0.7071, -0.7071, 0.7071]$$

$$C(3) = \bigcup_{i=0}^{N} \cos\left\{\frac{3(2i+1)\pi}{8}\right\} = [0.3827, -0.9239, 0.9239, -0.3827]$$

$$x = a.X.C' = [a(0)X(0)C(0) + a(1)X(1)C(1) + a(2)X(2)C(2) + a(3)X(3)C(3)]$$

$$x = \left\{\begin{array}{l} \sqrt{\frac{1}{4}}(12)[1, 1, 1, 1] \\ +\sqrt{\frac{2}{4}}(3.69)[0.9239, 0.3827, -0.3827, -0.9239] \\ +\sqrt{\frac{2}{4}}(2)[0.7071, -0.7071, -0.7071, 0.7071] \\ +\sqrt{\frac{2}{4}}(-1.53)[0.3827, -0.9239, 0.9239, -0.3827] \end{array}\right\}$$

$$x = [6, 6, 6, 6] + [2.414, 1, -1, -2.414] + [1, -1, -1, 1] + [-0.414, 1, -1, 0.414]$$

$$x = [9, 7, 3, 5]$$

1.13.3 Transformation Matrix

PROBLEM 1.7

Compute DFT and IDFT of the sequence x = {9, 7, 3, 5} using transformation matrices.

Forward DFT:

$$W=\begin{pmatrix}1&1&1&1\\1&D&D^2&D^3\\1&D^2&D^4&D^6\\1&D^3&D^6&D^9\end{pmatrix}$$

Here $D=e^{-j.\frac{2\pi}{N}}=e^{-j.\frac{2\pi}{4}}=e^{-j.\frac{\pi}{2}}=\cos\frac{\pi}{2}-j.\sin\frac{\pi}{2}=-j$

$$D^2=D.D=(-j)(-j)=-1$$

$$D^3=D.D^2=(-j)(-1)=j$$

$$D^4=D.D^3=(-j)(j)=1$$

$$D^6=D^2.D^4=(-1)(1)=-1$$

$$D^9=D^3.D^6=(j)(-1)=-j$$

$$W=\begin{pmatrix}1&1&1&1\\1&D&D^2&D^3\\1&D^2&D^4&D^6\\1&D^3&D^6&D^9\end{pmatrix}=\begin{pmatrix}1&1&1&1\\1&-j&-1&j\\1&-1&1&-1\\1&j&-1&-j\end{pmatrix}$$

$$X=W.x=\begin{pmatrix}1&1&1&1\\1&-j&-1&j\\1&-1&1&-1\\1&j&-1&-j\end{pmatrix}\begin{pmatrix}9\\7\\3\\5\end{pmatrix}=\begin{pmatrix}24\\6-2j\\0\\6+2j\end{pmatrix}$$

Inverse DFT:

$$x=\left(\frac{1}{N}\right)W^{*}.X$$

where W^{*} = complex conjugate of W = [1,1,1,1 ; 1,j,–1,–j ; 1,–1,1,–1 ; 1,–j,–1,j]

$$x=\left(\frac{1}{4}\right)\begin{pmatrix}1&1&1&1\\1&j&-1&-j\\1&-1&1&-1\\1&-j&-1&j\end{pmatrix}.\begin{pmatrix}24\\6-2j\\0\\6+2j\end{pmatrix}=\begin{pmatrix}9\\7\\3\\5\end{pmatrix}$$

PROBLEM 1.8

Compute DCT and IDCT of the sequence x = {9, 7, 3, 5} using transformation matrices.

Forward DCT:

$T(p,q)=\sqrt{1/N}$, for $p=0, 0\le q\le N-1$

$T(p,q)=\sqrt{2/N}.\cos\{p(2q+1)\pi/2N\}$, for $1\le p\le N-1, 0\le q\le N-1$

$$T=\begin{pmatrix}\frac{1}{\sqrt{N}}&\frac{1}{\sqrt{N}}&\frac{1}{\sqrt{N}}&\frac{1}{\sqrt{N}}\\ \sqrt{\frac{2}{N}}\cos\frac{\pi}{2N}&\sqrt{\frac{2}{N}}\cos\frac{3\pi}{2N}&\sqrt{\frac{2}{N}}\cos\frac{5\pi}{2N}&\sqrt{\frac{2}{N}}\cos\frac{7\pi}{2N}\\ \sqrt{\frac{2}{N}}\cos\frac{2\pi}{2N}&\sqrt{\frac{2}{N}}\cos\frac{6\pi}{2N}&\sqrt{\frac{2}{N}}\cos\frac{10\pi}{2N}&\sqrt{\frac{2}{N}}\cos\frac{14\pi}{2N}\\ \sqrt{\frac{2}{N}}\cos\frac{3\pi}{2N}&\sqrt{\frac{2}{N}}\cos\frac{9\pi}{2N}&\sqrt{\frac{2}{N}}\cos\frac{15\pi}{2N}&\sqrt{\frac{2}{N}}\cos\frac{21\pi}{2N}\end{pmatrix}$$

$$T=\begin{pmatrix}\frac{1}{\sqrt{4}}&\frac{1}{\sqrt{4}}&\frac{1}{\sqrt{4}}&\frac{1}{\sqrt{4}}\\ \sqrt{\frac{2}{4}}\cos\frac{\pi}{8}&\sqrt{\frac{2}{4}}\cos\frac{3\pi}{8}&\sqrt{\frac{2}{4}}\cos\frac{5\pi}{8}&\sqrt{\frac{2}{4}}\cos\frac{7\pi}{8}\\ \sqrt{\frac{2}{4}}\cos\frac{2\pi}{2N}&\sqrt{\frac{2}{4}}\cos\frac{6\pi}{2N}&\sqrt{\frac{2}{4}}\cos\frac{10\pi}{8}&\sqrt{\frac{2}{4}}\cos\frac{14\pi}{8}\\ \sqrt{\frac{2}{4}}\cos\frac{3\pi}{2N}&\sqrt{\frac{2}{4}}\cos\frac{9\pi}{8}&\sqrt{\frac{2}{4}}\cos\frac{15\pi}{8}&\sqrt{\frac{2}{4}}\cos\frac{21\pi}{8}\end{pmatrix}$$

$$T=\begin{pmatrix}0.5&0.5&0.5&0.5\\0.653&0.270&-0.270&-0.653\\0.5&-0.5&0.5&0.5\\0.270&-0.653&0.653&-0.270\end{pmatrix}$$

$$X=T.x=\begin{pmatrix}0.5&0.5&0.5&0.5\\0.653&0.270&-0.270&-0.653\\0.5&-0.5&0.5&0.5\\0.270&-0.653&0.653&-0.270\end{pmatrix}\begin{pmatrix}9\\7\\3\\5\end{pmatrix}$$

$$=\begin{pmatrix}12\\3.69\\2\\-1.53\end{pmatrix}$$

Inverse DCT:

$$T'=\begin{pmatrix}0.5&0.653&0.5&0.270\\0.5&0.270&-0.5&-0.653\\0.5&-0.270&-0.5&0.653\\0.5&-0.653&0.5&-0.270\end{pmatrix}$$

$$x = T'.X = \begin{pmatrix} 0.5 & 0.653 & 0.5 & 0.270 \\ 0.5 & 0.270 & -0.5 & -0.653 \\ 0.5 & -0.270 & -0.5 & 0.653 \\ 0.5 & -0.653 & 0.5 & -0.270 \end{pmatrix} \begin{pmatrix} 12 \\ 3.69 \\ 2 \\ -1.53 \end{pmatrix}$$

$$= \begin{pmatrix} 9 \\ 7 \\ 3 \\ 5 \end{pmatrix}$$

1.14 Coding Examples using MATLAB®

1.14.1 Discrete Fourier Transform

The following example performs a DFT operation on a 1D discrete signal with four sample values followed by an IDFT to revert back the original values. The functions "fft" and "ifft" are used to compute the forward and inverse DFT of a 1D signal, "clear" clears items from workspace memory and "clc" clears the command window of previous text.

EXAMPLE 1.1 EXAMPLE TO COMPUTE DFT AND IDFT

```
clear; clc;
x = [9,7,3,5];
X = fft(x)
y = ifft(X)
```

The following example performs a DFT operation on a 1D step signal and plots the magnitude and phase of the spectrum. The function "fftshift" is used to shift the zero-frequency component to the center of the plot, "real" and "imag" return the real and imaginary

EXAMPLE 1.2 EXAMPLE TO PLOT SPECTRUM OF A 1-D FUNCTION

```
clear; clc;
a = zeros(1,1024);
a(1:10) = 1;
b = fft(a);
c = fftshift(b);
M = abs(b);
N = abs(c);
R = real(c); I = imag(c); P =
   atan(I./R);
figure,
subplot(221), plot(a); axis tight;
   title('Input Signal')
subplot(222), plot(M); axis tight;
   title('Spectrum')
subplot(223), plot(N); axis tight;
   title('Shifted Spectrum')
subplot(224), plot(P); axis tight;
   title('Phase')
```

portions of complex values, 'zeros' creates an array of specified size and fills it with all zeros, "atan" computes the arctan or inverse tan, "figure" generates a new figure window, 'plot' function generates a 2D line plot with a specified title, "axis" sets axis limits and aspect ratio of the plot, 'subplot' generates an array of multiple plots within a single figure window. The "." in the "atan" argument signifies element wise operation; i.e., each element of I is divided by corresponding element of R, both of which must be of the same dimensions (Figure 1.5).

The following example performs a DFT operation on a 2D step signal and plots the magnitude and phase of the spectrum. The function "fft2" is used to apply 2D Fourier transform to a two-dimensional signal, "ifft2" calculates the inverse 2D DFT and returns the spatial domain signal from its spectrum, "size" returns the array size (Figure 1.6).

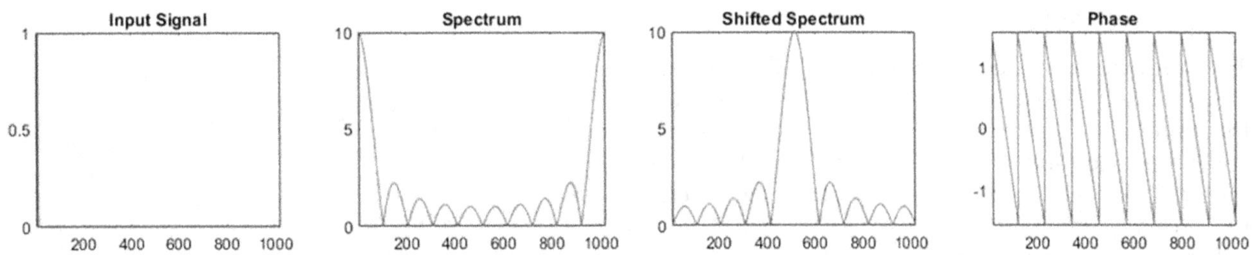

FIGURE 1.5
Output of Example 1.2.

EXAMPLE 1.3 EXAMPLE TO COMPUTE DFT AND IDFT OF A 2-D SIGNAL

```
clear clc;
dim = 30; f = zeros(dim, dim);
h = size(f,1); w = size(f,2);
f(h/3:2*h/3, w/3:2*w/3) = 1;
F = fft2(f);
F1 = fft2(f, 200, 200);
F2 = fftshift(F1);
F3 = log(1+abs(F2));
g = ifft2(F);
figure,
subplot(231), imshow(f); title('f');
subplot(232), imshow(abs(F), []); title('|F|');
subplot(233), imshow(abs(F1), []); title('|F1|');
subplot(234), imshow(abs(F2), []); title('|F2|');
subplot(235), imshow(F3, []); title('F3');
subplot(236), imshow(g, []); title('g');
```

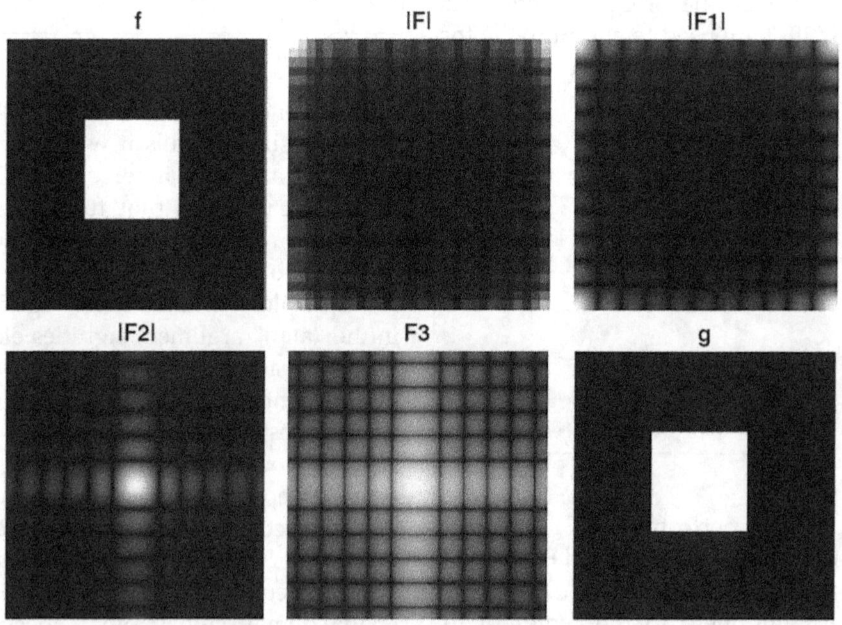

FIGURE 1.6
Output of Example 1.3.

1.14.2 Discrete Cosine Transform (DCT)

The following example 1.4 performs a DCT operation on a 1D discrete signal with four sample values. The function "dct" computes the DCT from a 1D signal and returns an output array of coefficients the same size as the input array, "idct" computes the inverse DCT from the coefficients.

The following example 1.5 converts a one dimensional signal to frequency domain using DCT and then inverts it back with a subset of the coefficients

EXAMPLE 1.4 EXAMPLE TO COMPUTE DCT AND IDCT OF A 1-D SIGNAL

```
x = [9,7,3,5];
X = dct(x)
y = idct(X)
```

EXAMPLE 1.5 EXAMPLE TO COMPUTE IDCT USING A SUBSET OF THE COEFFICIENTS

```
clear; clc;
x = zeros(1,1024);
x(1:100) = 1;
X = dct(x);
[val, idx] = sort(abs(X),'descend');
i = 1;
while norm(X(idx(1:i)))/norm(X) < 0.99
   i = i + 1;
end
n = i; % no. of coefficients for 99%
   of energy
perc = n*100/numel(X) % percentage of
   coefficients
val(idx(n+1:end)) = 0;
xx = idct(val);
y = idct(X);
figure,
subplot(131), plot(x);
   title('Original'); axis tight;
   axis square;
subplot(132), plot(xx); axis tight;
   axis square;
title({'Reconstructed with', '99%
   energy'});
subplot(133), plot(y); axis tight;
   axis square;
title({'Reconstructed with', '100%
   energy'});
```

EXAMPLE 1.6 EXAMPLE TO COMPUTE 2D IDCT USING A

```
% subset of the coefficients for
an image
clear; clc;
I = imread('coins.png');
J = dct2(I);
JL = log(abs(J));
J(abs(J) < 10) = 0; % remove
coefficients less than 10
J1 = log(abs(J));
K1 = idct2(J);
J(abs(J) < 50) = 0; % remove
coefficients less than 50
J2 = log(abs(J));
K2 = idct2(J);
figure
subplot(231), imshow(I); title('I');
subplot(232), imshow(JL, []);
   title('JL');
subplot(233), imshow(J1, []);
   title('J1');
subplot(234), imshow(K1, []);
   title('K1');
subplot(235), imshow(J2, []);
   title('J2');
subplot(236), imshow(K2, []);
   title('K2');
```

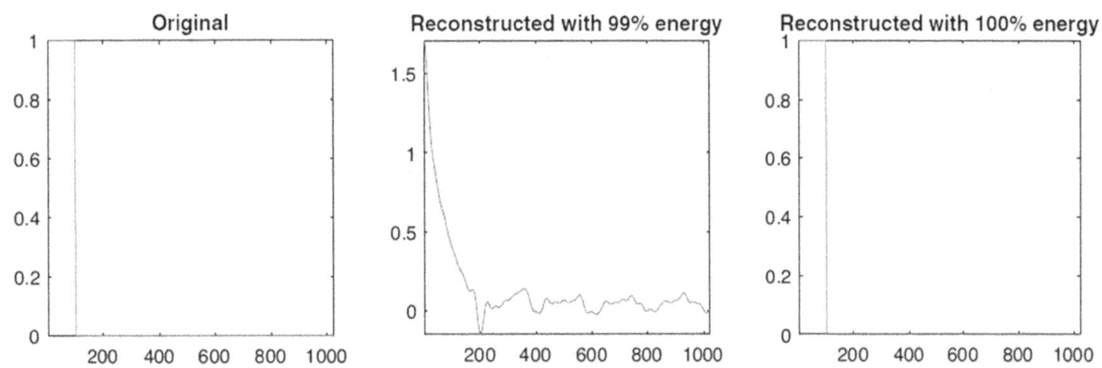

FIGURE 1.7
Output of Example 1.5.

sufficient to represent 99% of the energy of the signal. The function "sort" sorts array elements into ascending or descending orders, "norm" returns the magnitude of a vector, "numel" returns the number of array elements (Figure 1.7).

The following example 1.6 computes 2D IDCT using a subset of the coefficients, which provides the basis of compression. In the first case all coefficients with absolute values less than 10 are converted to 0 and the remaining are used to generate back the image. In the second case all coefficients with values less than 50 are converted to 0 which leads to a greater compression and hence more degradation in image quality (Figure 1.8).

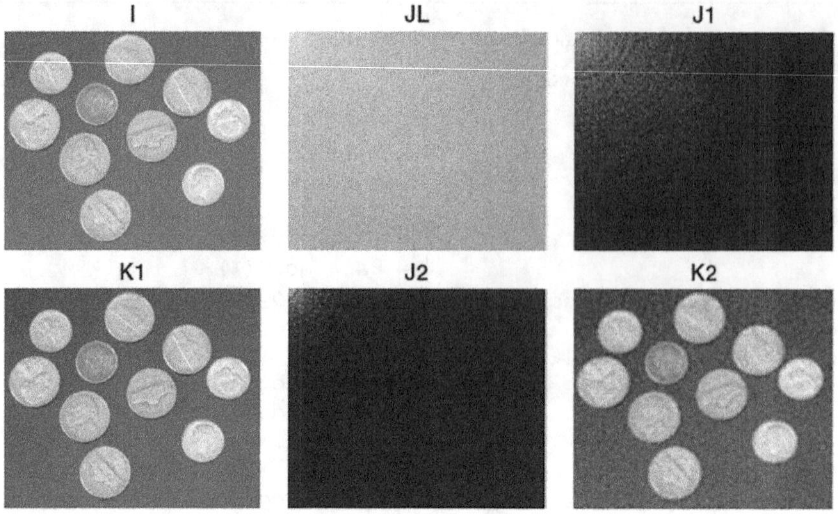

FIGURE 1.8
Output of Example 1.6.

1.14.3 Discrete Wavelet Transform (DWT)

In the following example 1.7, a single-level DWT is computed and the approximation and detail coefficients are displayed. The function "dwt2" computes a single-level 2D wavelet transform using a specified wavelet name and returns the approximation, horizontal, vertical and diagonal coefficients, "idwt2" performs the inverse wavelet transform by reconstructing the original image from the coefficients, "imagesc" displays a scaled image from an array, "checkerboard" creates a checkerboard pattern of alternate white and black squares, "colormap" specifies a set of colors to use when displaying an array as an image. The option "sym4" specifies the type of wavelet, i.e., symlet order 4 (Figure 1.9).

EXAMPLE 1.7 EXAMPLE TO DEMONSTRATE DWT AND IDWT FOR AN IMAGE

```
clear; clc;
X = checkerboard(10);
wname = 'sym4';
[cA, cH, cV, cD] = dwt2(X, wname);
subplot(2,2,1), imagesc(cA); colormap gray; title('Approximation')
subplot(2,2,2), imagesc(cH); colormap gray; title('Horizontal')
subplot(2,2,3), imagesc(cV); colormap gray; title('Vertical')
subplot(2,2,4), imagesc(cD); colormap gray; title('Diagonal')
A0 = idwt2(cA, cH, cV, cD, wname, size(X));
figure
subplot(121), imshow(X); title('original');
subplot(122), imshow(A0); title('reconstructed');
max(max(abs(X-A0)))
```

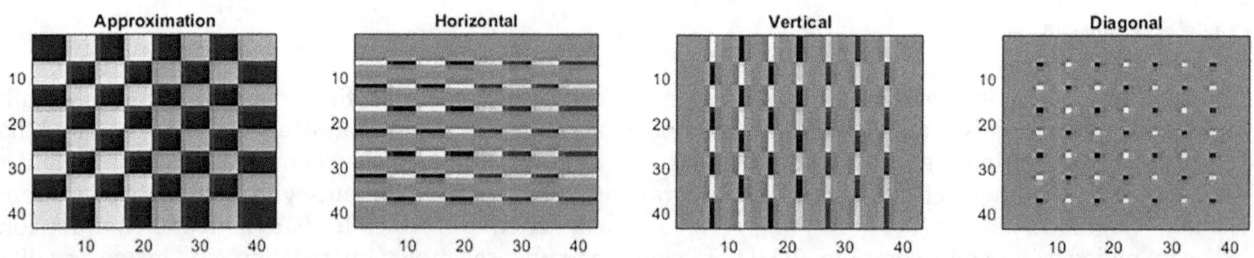

FIGURE 1.9
Output of Example 1.7.

The function 'wavedec2' can be used to perform multi-level decomposition. The following example 1.8 shows a two-level decomposition and displays the approximation and detail components of both the levels. The function "appcoef2" computes the approximation coefficients at the specified level, "detcoef2" computes the detail coefficients at the specified level. The eight coefficients of both the levels are subsequently displayed according to the following scheme (Figure 1.10):

```
C = [A2 | H2 | V2 | D2 | H1 | V1 | D1]
S = [A2(1), A2(2)]
[H2(1), H2(2)]
[H1(1), H1(2)]
[X(1), X(2)]
```

EXAMPLE 1.8 EXAMPLE TO DEMONSTRATE MULTI-LEVEL WAVELET DECOMPOSITION

```
clear; clc;
X = checkerboard(10);
[C, S] = wavedec2(X,2,'db2');
A1 = appcoef2(C, S, 'db2', 1);
[H1, V1, D1] = detcoef2('all',
   C, S, 1);
A2 = appcoef2(C, S, 'db2', 2);
[H2, V2, D2] = detcoef2('all',
   C, S, 2);
subplot(4,2,1),
imagesc(A1); colormap gray;
   title('Approximation Coef. of
   Level 1');
subplot(4,2,2),
imagesc(H1); colormap gray;
   title('Horizontal detail Coef. of
   Level 1');
subplot(4,2,3),
imagesc(V1); colormap gray;
   title('Vertical detail Coef. of
   Level 1');
subplot(4,2,4),
imagesc(D1); colormap gray;
   title('Diagonal detail Coef. of
   Level 1');
subplot(4,2,5),
imagesc(A2); colormap gray;
   title('Approximation Coef. of
   Level 2');
subplot(4,2,6),
imagesc(H2); colormap gray;
   title('Horizontal detail Coef. of
   Level 2');
subplot(4,2,7),
imagesc(V2); colormap gray,
   title('Vertical detail Coef. of
   Level 2');
subplot(4,2,8),
imagesc(D2); colormap gray;
   title('Diagonal detail Coef. of
   Level 2');
```

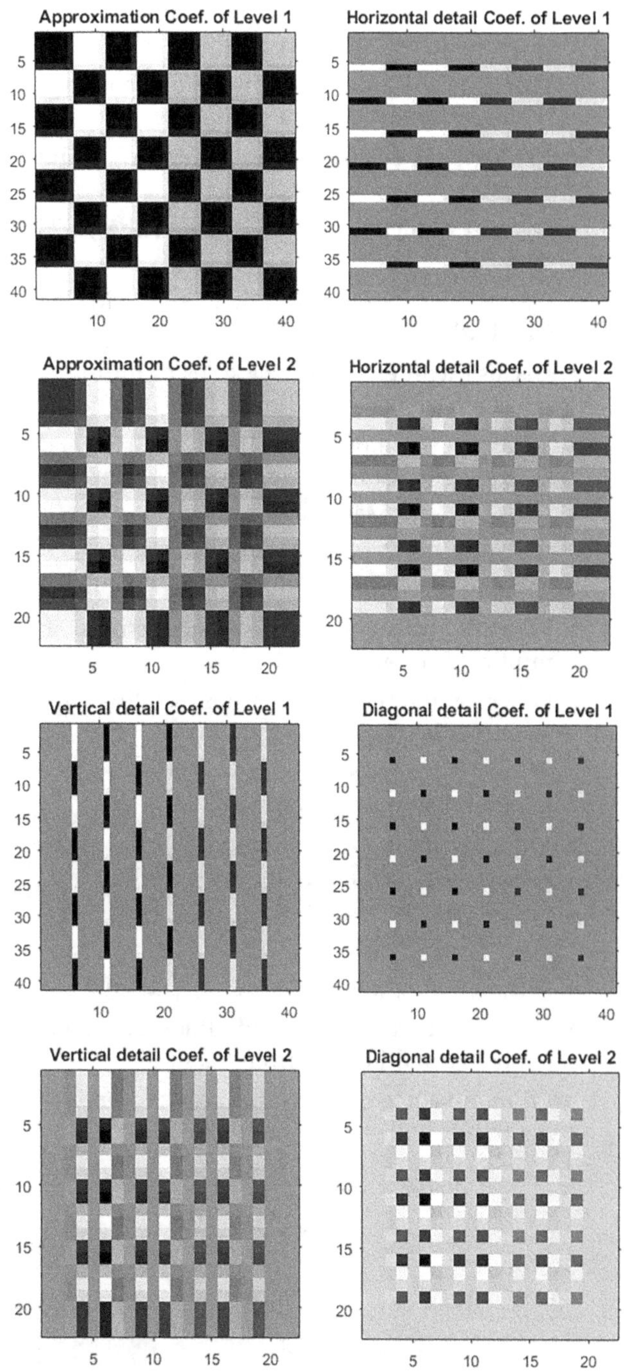

FIGURE 1.10
Output of Example 1.8.

Review Questions

- What is a multimedia presentation, and what are its main characteristics?
- What is meant by the terms "non-linearity" and "interactivity"?
- Discuss some of the major applications of multimedia technology.
- What are the main hardware components required for multimedia production?
- Discuss the functionalities of software required for multimedia production.
- Explain the roles of multimedia APIs and libraries.
- Discuss the features of variants of the JPEG standard.
- Discuss the features of variants of the MPEG standard.
- Discuss with examples the roles of multimedia standards organizations.
- What are some of the frontend and backend technologies for multimedia production?
- Discuss some of the prevalent platforms and transport protocols used for multimedia.
- Discuss in brief role of multimedia in games.
- What is the significance of interactivity in multimedia content?
- Describe the workflow steps required for multimedia content creation.
- What is Nyquist's theorem and its relevance in quality of multimedia content?
- What are the basic concepts of Fourier theorem in multimedia signal processing?
- What are DFT coefficients and DFT basis functions?
- Differentiate between DFT, DCT and DWT.
- Discuss the major legal and ethical considerations for multimedia production.
- What are some of the challenges and emerging trends in the field of multimedia?

References

Adornato, A., *Mobile and social media journalism: a practical guide for multimedia journalism*, Routledge, 2021.

Assuncao, P. A., A. Gotchev, *3D visual content creation, coding and delivery*, Springer Nature Switzerland AG, 2019

Bansal, J. C., M. S. Uddin, *Computer vision and machine learning in agriculture*, Springer, 2022.

Berners-Lee, T. & M. Fischetti, *Weaving the Web : The original design and ultimate destiny of the World Wide Web by its inventor*, Harper Collins, 1999 https://www.w3.org/People/Berners-Lee/Weaving/Overview.html

Chen, J. Y. C., G. Fragomeni (eds), *12th International conference on virtual, augmented and mixed reality design and interaction*, Springer, 2020.

Chen, S.-C., M.-L. Shyu, *Multimedia data engineering: applications and processing*, Idea Group US, 2013.

Clark, R. C., R. E. Mayer (eds), *E-Learning and the science of instruction: proven guidelines for consumers and designers of multimedia learning*, Wiley, 2016.

Euler, L. *Introductio in analysin infinitorum*, Marcum-Michaelem Bousquet, vol. 1, pp. 1–320, 1748.

Fourier, J. B. J., *Theorie analytique de la chaleur*, Chez Firmin Didot, 1822.

Gadsden, D., M. Artz, *Preserving our planet: GIS for conservation*, ESRI Press, 2023.

Gazaway, D., *Introduction to game systems design* Pearson Education (US), 2021

Hernandez, R. K., J. Rue, *Principles of multimedia journalism: Packaging digital news*, Routledge, 2015.

Hua, X.-S., *Online multimedia advertising techniques and technologies*, IGI Global, 2010.

Isaias, P., Blashki, K., *Human computer interfaces and interactivity*, Idea Group US, 2014.

Jong, T., L. Sarti (ed), *Design and production of multimedia and simulation based learning material*, Springer, 2012.

Mallat, S. G., A theory for multi-resolution signal decomposition: the wavelet representation, *IEEE Pattern Recognition and Machine Intelligence*, vol. 11, no. 7, pp. 674–693, 1989.

Marquis, O., B. Furht, *Content-based image and video retrieval*, Springer, 2012.

Mehta, M., C. Gaie (eds), *Recent advances in data and algorithms for e-Government*, Springer, 2023.

Mhiripiri, N. A., T. Chari, *Media law, ethics and policy in the digital age*, IGI Global, 2017.

Milutinovic, V., *Infrastructure for electronic business on the Internet*, Springer, 2013.

Moreno, R., Optimising learning from animations by minimising cognitive load: Cognitive and affective consequences of signalling and segmentation methods", *Applied Cognitive Psychology*, vol. 21, no. 6, pp. 765–781, 2007.

Nunes, N., I. Oakley & V. Nisi (eds), *10th international conference on interactive digital storytelling (ICIDS)*, Springer, 2017.

Nyquist, H., Certain topics in telegraph transmission theory, *Transactions of American Institute of Electrical Engineers (AIEE)*, vol. 47, no. 2, pp. 617–644, 1928.

Pirolli, B., *Travel journalism: informing tourists in the digital age*, Routledge, 2018.

Sharda, R., D. Delen & E. Turban, *Business intelligence and analytics: systems for decision support*, Pearson, 2018.

Solanki, A., S. Kumar & A. Nayyar, *Handbook of research on emerging trends and applications of machine learning*, IGI Global, 2019.

Steinkuehler, C., K. Squire & S. Barab, *Games, learning, and society: learning and meaning in the digital age*, Cambridge University Press, 2012.

Steinmetz, R. & K. Nahrstedt, 'Multimedia computing: Prologue and overview, *Communications of the ACM*, vol. 38, no. 11, pp. 20–30, 1995.

Steinmetz, R. & K. Nahrstedt, *Multimedia fundamentals: Media coding and content processing*. Prentice Hall, 2004.

Sutherland, Ivan E., *Sketchpad : A man-machine graphical communication system*, Technical Report UCAM-CL-TR-574, University of Cambridge, 1963 https://www.cl.cam.ac.uk/techreports/UCAM-CL-TR-574.html

Tatipamula, M., B. Khashnabish, *Multimedia communications networks: technologies and services*, Artech Publishers, 1998.

Tyagi, A. K., A. Abraham & A. Kaklauskas (eds), *Intelligent interactive multimedia systems for e-healthcare applications*, Springer, 2021

Valdez, G. *Multimedia in education: designing complex systems for learning*, IGI Global, 2006.

Vatsky, S., *Interactive museum tours: a guide to in person and virtual experiences*, Rowman and Littlefield, 2023

Vaughan, T. *Multimedia: Making it work*, McGraw-Hill Education, 2014

2

Text

2.1 Text Fundamentals

2.1.1 Key Terms

We begin with a snapshot of the important terms relevant to the field of digital text processing, to present the entire chapter in a nutshell. These terms will be expanded in the subsequent sections of the chapter in their proper contexts.

ASCII: ASCII (American Standard Code for Information Interchange) is a character encoding standard that represents text using integers. In ASCII, each character is assigned a unique numerical value, allowing computers to store and exchange textual information using a standardized encoding scheme.

CSS 3: CSS3 is the latest version of the Cascading Style Sheets (CSS) language, introducing new features and enhancements for Web page styling. It includes capabilities such as advanced selectors, transitions, animations and flexible box layouts, providing Web developers with more tools to create visually appealing and responsive designs.

Dynamic HTML: Dynamic HTML (DHTML) refers to a combination of technologies, including HTML, CSS and JavaScript, that allows Web content to be manipulated and updated in real time without requiring a page reload. DHTML enables interactive and dynamic Web pages by allowing developers to change the content and appearance of elements dynamically based on user interactions or other events.

Fonts: Fonts refer to a set of typefaces or designs for characters that share a consistent and distinguishable style. In digital design and typography, fonts play a crucial role in conveying the visual identity and tone of written content on various media, ranging from websites and documents to graphic designs.

HTML5: HTML5 is the latest version of the Hypertext Markup Language, widely used for structuring and presenting content on the World Wide Web. It introduces new features and improvements, such as native support for audio and video embedding, canvas elements for graphics rendering and enhanced semantic tags, contributing to a more dynamic and interactive Web experience.

JavaScript: JavaScript is a versatile scripting language primarily used for Web development to create dynamic and interactive content on Websites. As a client-side programming language it is executed inside Web browsers and allows Web developers to capture and respond to user interactions, generate update and remove HTML pages in real time, and add feature-rich multimedia content to Web pages like image-sliders, audio/video players, games and more.

OCR: Optical Character Recognition (OCR) is a technology that converts different types of documents, such as scanned paper documents, PDFs or images captured by a camera, into editable and searchable data. OCR software analyzes the shapes and patterns of text characters in an image to recognize and convert them into machine-encoded text.

SVG: Scalable Vector Graphics (SVG) is an XML-based file format used for describing two-dimensional vector graphics. It is widely employed on the Web for creating interactive and resolution-independent graphics, as it allows images to be scaled without loss of quality.

SMIL: Synchronized Multimedia Integration Language (SMIL) is an XML-based markup language that enables the integration and synchronization of various multimedia elements, such as audio, video and animations, in a Web presentation. SMIL facilitates the creation of interactive and time-based multimedia content, defining how different media components should be displayed and coordinated for a cohesive user experience.

STT: Speech-to-Text (STT) is a technology that converts spoken language into written text. Utilizing advanced algorithms and machine learning, STT systems analyze audio input, recognize spoken words and transcribe them

DOI: 10.1201/9781003588030-2

into text, serving applications ranging from transcription services to voice-activated assistants.

Text extraction: Text extraction is the process of automatically identifying and extracting textual information from documents, images or other sources of unstructured data. It often involves using techniques such as Optical Character Recognition (OCR) to convert text from images or PDFs into machine-readable formats for further analysis or indexing.

Text transformation: Text transformation involves altering the structure or presentation of text to achieve a desired format or representation. This can include tasks like converting uppercase to lowercase, changing the encoding or rearranging the layout of text to suit specific requirements in data processing or document formatting.

Text enhancement: Text enhancement refers to the process of improving the legibility, clarity or overall quality of text in a document or image. This can involve techniques such as contrast adjustment, sharpening or anti-aliasing to make the text more visually appealing and readable.

Text file formats: Text file formats are standardized structures for encoding and organizing plain text data, often used for storing and exchanging information in a human-readable form. Common examples include CSV (Comma-Separated Values), TXT (Plain Text) and JSON (JavaScript Object Notation), each serving specific purposes in data storage and interchange.

Text Internationalization: Text internationalization is the process of designing and preparing software or content to be easily adaptable and culturally sensitive for users from different linguistic and cultural backgrounds. It involves using techniques such as encoding, language support and formatting to ensure that text-based elements can be translated and displayed appropriately for diverse global audiences.

Text Localization: Text localization is the process of identifying and adapting text in images or documents to a specific language or regional context. It involves techniques such as language detection, character recognition and translation to make text content more relevant and understandable for a target audience.

TTS: Text-to-Speech (TTS) is a technology that converts written text into spoken words, generating synthetic speech output. TTS systems use natural language processing and voice synthesis techniques to provide audible content, making it accessible for various applications such as assistive technology, navigation systems and voice interfaces.

Typography: Typography is the art and technique of arranging and designing written text in a visually appealing and readable manner. It involves selecting fonts, adjusting spacing and organizing text elements to enhance the overall aesthetic and communicative qualities of written content.

Unicode: Unicode is a standardized character encoding system that assigns unique codes to characters from nearly all writing systems, allowing consistent representation of text across different platforms and languages. It supports a vast range of characters, including letters, numerals, symbols and emojis, providing a universal encoding for text in diverse scripts.

XML: XML (eXtensible Markup Language) is a versatile and extensible markup language designed to store and transport structured data in a human-readable format. It uses tags to define elements and attributes, providing a platform-independent way to exchange information between different systems and applications.

2.1.2 Historical Evolution

1800s–1900s: The origins of text processing can be traced back to the era of punch cards and early mechanical computing devices in the 19th and early 20th centuries. Punched cards were used to input and process textual information in a rudimentary form.

1950s–1960s: With the advent of mainframe computers in the 1950s, the field of text processing witnessed a leap forward. Batch processing systems allowed for the automated handling of large volumes of textual data, laying the groundwork for early word processing applications.

1970s: The 1970s marked the emergence of dedicated word processors. Systems like IBM's Magnetic Tape/Selectric Typewriter (MT/ST) and Wang Laboratories' Wang 1200 Word Processor introduced users to interactive text editing, enabling more dynamic and efficient document creation.

1980s: The widespread adoption of personal computers in the 1980s brought text processing capabilities to individual users. Text editors like Microsoft Word and WordPerfect became popular, providing a range of features for document creation, editing and formatting.

1980s–1990s: The advent of desktop publishing in the late 1980s transformed how text was processed for print. Software such as Adobe PageMaker and QuarkXPress allowed users to create visually appealing documents, combining text and graphics seamlessly.

1990s: Optical Character Recognition (OCR) technology gained prominence in the 1990s, enabling computers to recognize and convert printed or handwritten text into digital formats. This technology played a crucial role in digitizing large volumes of textual content.

1990s–Present: The rise of the Internet brought about new challenges and opportunities for text processing. Search engines, Web browsers and content management systems revolutionized how users interacted with textual information online.

2000s–Present: The 21st century saw significant advancements in Natural Language Processing (NLP), a branch of artificial intelligence focused on enabling computers to understand, interpret and generate human language. NLP technologies power virtual assistants, language translation tools, sentiment analysis and more.

2010s–Present: The integration of machine learning algorithms into text processing has allowed for more sophisticated analysis and interpretation of textual data. Sentiment analysis tools, powered by machine learning, can gauge the sentiment expressed in written content, providing valuable insights for businesses and researchers.

2015–Present: In recent years, the development of chatbots and conversational interfaces has leveraged advanced text processing capabilities. These systems use natural language understanding to engage in conversations with users, providing customer support, information retrieval and more.

The historical evolution of digital text processing reflects a continual quest for more efficient, interactive and intelligent ways to handle textual information. From punch cards to advanced natural language processing, digital text processing has played an important role in shaping the way people interact with textual content. As technology continues to advance, the future holds promises for even more sophisticated text processing applications across various domains.

2.1.3 Basic Concepts

Text is a versatile and indispensable element in multimedia content, serving various vital functions. Text processing enhances search ability by enabling efficient indexing and retrieval of relevant information. It facilitates language-based analysis, allowing for sentiment analysis, topic modeling and contextual understanding, thereby improving content categorization and organization. Additionally, text processing enables the creation of interactive transcripts, supporting accessibility features and enhancing user engagement with multimedia content (Chaudhuri, 2007).

2.1.3.1 Role of Text

Communication and Information: Text is an important means of conveying information and ideas, with key roles in communication and information. Text is used to provide essential information, explanations and narratives in various media formats, such as articles, reports, e-books and news segments. In multimedia, text often forms the backbone of storytelling, whether through written narratives, subtitles in films or captions in photo essays. Text is used to present data, statistics and facts, often accompanied by visual aids like charts and graphs. In user interfaces and Web applications, text-based buttons, menus and forms enable users to interact with digital content. User comments, reviews and discussions in multimedia platforms are textual contributions that foster engagement and interaction. In real-world multimedia applications, such as museums or public spaces, text is used to provide directions, historical context and information about exhibits or displays.

Enhancement and Emphasis: Text plays a vital role in enhancing multimedia content and guiding the user's attention. Text can be styled to draw attention, such as through the use of bold, italics or color. It is employed to emphasize key points and highlight important information. Text is used to provide context and explanations for visuals, ensuring that the audience comprehends the content fully. This is common in art exhibitions, museums and documentaries. In multimedia presentations, text often acts as navigation aids. Menus, labels and headings guide users through interactive content and ensure they can access various sections or features.

User Guidance and Instruction: Text is an essential element for guiding users and providing clear instructions. Multimedia often includes textual instructions in the form of tutorials and how-to guides to help users understand how to operate software, assemble products or complete tasks. Textual user manuals accompany a wide range of products and software, providing step-by-step guidance on usage and troubleshooting.

Accessibility and Inclusivity: Text also plays a vital role in making multimedia content accessible to a wide range of audiences. Text is the basis for screen readers used by individuals with visual impairments to access multimedia content. Proper text descriptions and alternative text for images are crucial for this audience. In video content, subtitles and closed captions provide textual support for individuals who are deaf or hard of hearing.

Branding and Identity: Text contributes to branding and identity through specific visual representations. The choice of fonts, typography and the design of textual logos are crucial for establishing a brand's visual identity in multimedia. Short and memorable textual elements, such as slogans and taglines, help reinforce brand messaging.

2.1.3.2 Digital Revolution

The transition to the digital age ushered in a new era for multimedia, and the incorporation of text became more dynamic, allowing for interactive and multimedia-rich content. The concept of hypertext, introduced the ability to link text to other forms of media, creating a Web of interconnected information. The development of the World Wide Web in the early 1990s made this concept accessible to the masses, leading to the proliferation of multimedia content on the internet. Educational software, encyclopedias and interactive games utilized text to deliver content and instructions. The 21st century witnessed the rise of e-books and digital publishing platforms. The emergence of Web 2.0 and social media platforms encouraged user-generated content, with text playing a central role in communication and expression. Blogs and social networking sites relied heavily on textual content. The proliferation of mobile devices introduced new challenges and opportunities for text in multimedia. Responsive design became essential for ensuring that text and multimedia elements adapt to different screen sizes and orientations. As digital multimedia evolved, there was a growing emphasis on accessibility and inclusivity. Ensuring that text-based content is accessible to individuals with disabilities, including those with visual impairments, became a priority. Screen readers, alternative text for images and other technologies were introduced to enhance the user experience.

2.1.3.3 Multimodal Nature of Text

Text is often thought of as a unimodal form of communication, primarily involving the visual representation of words on a page or screen. However, text can be a gateway to a multimodal experience that goes beyond the written word. Combining visual, auditory and interactive elements with text allows for more comprehensive and engaging communication, as it accommodates different learning and engagement preferences. A multimodal approach ensures that content is accessible to individuals with varying abilities, including those with visual or auditory impairments. Educational materials that integrate text with visuals, audio and interactivity often result in more effective and engaging learning experiences (Danielsson & Selander, 2021).

Visual Multimodality: The integration of images and icons alongside text enriches the visual experience. These visual elements can provide context, enhance understanding and convey emotions or concepts. The use of color for text, background and highlighting, as well as styling elements such as bold, italics and underlining, adds visual depth and emphasis to textual content. In technical and informational texts, graphs and charts are often used to present data visually, aiding comprehension and analysis.

Auditory Multimodality: Text-to-speech (TTS) technology allows text to be converted into spoken words, offering an auditory dimension to written content. This is especially valuable for individuals with visual impairments. In digital books and e-learning materials, audio files may complement text, providing explanations, music or sound effects to enhance the overall experience. In PDF readers the "read-aloud" mode provides functionalities to convert the written text to audible speech.

Interactive Multimodality: Links embedded in text lead to further content or resources, enabling readers to explore related information, enhancing the interactive aspect of text.

Text can be a gateway to multimedia elements, such as videos, animations and interactive info-graphics, providing a holistic and engaging experience. In digital spaces, text is often accompanied by user-generated content in the form of comments, reviews and discussions. This adds an interactive and social layer to textual communication.

2.1.3.4 Text Rendering

Text rendering is the process of converting digital character data into legible and visually pleasing text for display on screens, in print or within digital content. It encompasses a range of techniques and technologies aimed at ensuring that text appears crisp, well designed and readable (White, 2012).

The choice of fonts and typefaces significantly influences the visual style of text. It's essential to select appropriate fonts that align with the intended design and readability goals. Anti-aliasing is a technique used to smooth the jagged edges of characters, making text appear more visually pleasing. It works by blending the edges of characters with the background pixels, resulting in a smoother appearance. Kerning deals with the spacing between specific pairs of characters to improve the overall visual consistency of text. Tracking involves adjusting the overall character spacing. Both factors impact the readability and aesthetics of text. Ligatures are special characters that combine two or more individual characters into a single glyph. They are used to improve the appearance of specific character combinations and are often found in script and calligraphic fonts. The color of text and its contrast with the background are essential for readability. Proper color selection ensures that text stands out and is easily distinguishable. Line spacing, often referred to as leading, defines the vertical space between lines of text. Appropriate line spacing is crucial for readability and the overall aesthetics of text blocks. Text justification determines how text is aligned on a line. It can be left-aligned, right-aligned, centered or justified (aligned on both left and right edges). Proper justification enhances the visual flow of text.

Effective text rendering is fundamental for ensuring that text is legible and easy to read. It directly impacts the user experience, whether in print materials, websites or user interfaces. Well-rendered text enhances the overall visual appeal of content. It contributes to the design and aesthetics of various media, from books and posters to websites and mobile apps. In user interface design, text rendering is critical for creating clear and attractive layouts that guide users and communicate information effectively. Text rendering considerations are essential for making content accessible to individuals with visual impairments. Proper rendering ensures compatibility with screen readers and other assistive technologies. In the digital publishing industry, text rendering is vital for e-books, Web content and digital magazines, where text must be displayed consistently across various devices and screen sizes.

2.2 Digital Text Representation

Digital text representation is the art and science of encoding written language into a format that computers and digital devices can interpret, manipulate and display. Character encoding is the process of mapping characters, symbols and control codes to numerical values or "code points." It serves as the bridge between human-readable text and the binary data that computers work with.

ASCII: ASCII (American Standard Code for Information Interchange), developed in the early days of computing, was one of the first character encoding standards. It used 7 bits to represent 128 characters, of which 95 are printable, including letters, digits and control characters.

Extended ASCII: To accommodate additional characters and symbols, extended ASCII uses 8 bits, providing room for 256 characters. Various extended ASCII tables were created for different languages and regions.

Unicode: As the limitations of ASCII and Extended ASCII became apparent for supporting a wide range of languages and characters, Unicode emerged as a comprehensive character encoding standard. It's designed to encompass characters from virtually all writing systems and symbol sets used worldwide.

UTF-8, UTF-16 and UTF-32: Unicode defines several encoding schemes. UTF-8, UTF-16 and UTF-32 are the most commonly used. UTF-8 is backward-compatible with the 8-bit format of ASCII, while UTF-16 and UTF-32 use 16 and 32 bits, respectively, to represent characters.

2.2.1 ASCII

The American Standard Code for Information Interchange (ASCII) [www.iso.org/standard/4777.html] is one of the earliest and simplest character encoding standards used for representing text in digital form. Developed in the early days of computing as ISO/IEC 646, ASCII has been a foundational element in digital communication, text processing and data storage (Godse & Godse, 2020).

2.2.1.1 Basic ASCII

ASCII is a character encoding standard that assigns unique numeric values (code points) to a limited set of characters and control codes, covering English alphabet letters, digits, punctuation marks and various control characters. ASCII uses 7 bits to represent characters, allowing for a total of 2^7 or 128 possible characters, including control codes. Out of these 95 are printable characters including digits 0 to 9, lowercase letters a to z, uppercase letters A to Z and punctuation symbols. The remaining 33 are control characters, like carriage return and line feed. Special symbols like the dollar sign ($) and the at symbol (@) are also included within the set. This compact encoding was suitable for early computer systems with limited storage and processing capabilities. Other international standards like ISO 646 (1967) are nearly identical to the ASCII set with extensions for outside the English language and symbols outside the US. Different countries developed adapted versions of ASCII suitable for their needs, like the UK's pound (£) symbol and Japan's Yen (¥) symbol as well as non-English alphabets like Russian and Greek characters.

ASCII was first published in 1963 as a standard to ensure compatibility among various computer systems, enabling data exchange and text communication. ASCII was essential in the early days of computing, where text-based interfaces and data exchange were prevalent. Its simplicity allowed different computers and systems to communicate and share data reliably, creating a common ground for text representation. It remains a fundamental format for storing text in files and databases, even in modern computing. ASCII characters are extensively used in programming languages to define variable names, operators and other textual elements (Figure 2.1).

Dec	Hex	Character	Dec	Hex	Character	Dec	Hex	Character	Dec	Hex	Character
0	0	NUL (null)	32	20	Space	64	40	@	96	60	`
1	1	SOH (start of heading)	33	21	!	65	41	A	97	61	a
2	2	STX (start of text)	34	22	"	66	42	B	98	62	b
3	3	ETX (end of text)	35	23	#	67	43	C	99	63	c
4	4	EOT (end of transmission)	36	24	$	68	44	D	100	64	d
5	5	ENQ (enquiry)	37	25	%	69	45	E	101	65	e
6	6	ACK (acknowledge)	38	26	&	70	46	F	102	66	f
7	7	BEL (bell)	39	27	'	71	47	G	103	67	g
8	8	BS (backspace)	40	28	(	72	48	H	104	68	h
9	9	TAB (horizontal tab)	41	29	)	73	49	I	105	69	i
10	A	LF (NL line feed, new line)	42	2A	*	74	4A	J	106	6A	j
11	B	VT (vertical tab)	43	2B	+	75	4B	K	107	6B	k
12	C	FF (NP form feed, new page)	44	2C	,	76	4C	L	108	6C	l
13	D	CR (carriage return)	45	2D	-	77	4D	M	109	6D	m
14	E	SO (shift out)	46	2E	.	78	4E	N	110	6E	n
15	F	SI (shift in)	47	2F	/	79	4F	O	111	6F	o
16	10	DLE (data link escape)	48	30	0	80	50	P	112	70	p
17	11	DC1 (device control 1)	49	31	1	81	51	Q	113	71	q
18	12	DC2 (device control 2)	50	32	2	82	52	R	114	72	r
19	13	DC3 (device control 3)	51	33	3	83	53	S	115	73	s
20	14	DC4 (device control 4)	52	34	4	84	54	T	116	74	t
21	15	NAK (negative acknowledge)	53	35	5	85	55	U	117	75	u
22	16	SYN (synchronous idle)	54	36	6	86	56	V	118	76	v
23	17	ETB (end of trans. block)	55	37	7	87	57	W	119	77	w
24	18	CAN (cancel)	56	38	8	88	58	X	120	78	x
25	19	EM (end of medium)	57	39	9	89	59	Y	121	79	y
26	1A	SUB (substitute)	58	3A	:	90	5A	Z	122	7A	z
27	1B	ESC (escape)	59	3B	;	91	5B	[	123	7B	{
28	1C	FS (file separator)	60	3C	<	92	5C	\	124	7C	|
29	1D	GS (group separator)	61	3D	=	93	5D	]	125	7D	}
30	1E	RS (record separator)	62	3E	>	94	5E	^	126	7E	~
31	1F	US (unit separator)	63	3F	?	95	5F	_	127	7F	DEL

FIGURE 2.1
Basic ASCII set.

2.2.1.2 Extended ASCII

While ASCII was sufficient for representing English text and basic control characters, it posed challenges for representing non-English languages, special symbols and characters from various writing systems. It also lacked support for diacritics and characters with accent marks. As a result, the 7-bit ASCII was extended to the 8-bit format to formulate the ISO/IEC 8859 standard [www.iso.org/standard/28245.html], which provides additional characters and symbols. The standard only define printable characters, although they explicitly set apart the some byte ranges as combinations that do not represent graphic characters (i.e., which are reserved for use as control characters). The standard is divided into a number of parts to cater to different languages. Part 1 is the most widely used covering most of Western European languages, part 2 covers central and eastern European languages, part 3 covers south European areas, part 4 covers north European areas, part 5 covers Slavic languages that use a Cyrillic alphabet, part 6 covers Arabic, part 7 Greek, part 8 Hebrew, part 9 Turkish, part 10 Nordic and part 11 Thai. Part 12 was designed for Devanagari characters but later abandoned in preference of Unicode. Part 13 contains characters of Baltic languages, part 14 covers Celtic areas, part 15 covers French areas and part 16 covers South-Eastern European languages. Each part of ISO/IEC 8859 is designed to support languages that often borrow from each other, so the characters needed by each language are usually accommodated by a single part.

Today, ASCII is still present in various aspects of computing and data communication, though its role has evolved. It is often used as a foundational building block in more complex character encodings, and many programming languages and systems continue to rely on ASCII-compatible character sets. In conclusion, ASCII is a historic and foundational character encoding standard that has played a crucial role in the early development of computing and digital text representation. While it is limited in terms of character coverage, it remains relevant and is a part of the larger landscape of character encoding standards used in modern computing and communication (Figure 2.2).

2.2.2 Unicode Character Set

Unicode [home.unicode.org] is a standardized system for digital text representation that has superseded ASCII and plays a fundamental role in enabling the use of diverse writing systems, characters and symbols in the digital world. It provides a unified encoding for text across different languages, making it possible to display, exchange and process text accurately and consistently on various digital platforms (Gillam, 2003).

Dec	Char	Dec	Char	Dec	Char	Dec	Char	Dec	Char	Dec	Char	D Dec	Char	Dec	Char
128	Ç	144	É	160	á	176	░	193	┴	209	╤	225	ß	241	±
129	ü	145	æ	161	í	177	▒	194	┬	210	╥	226	Γ	242	≥
130	é	146	Æ	162	ó	178	▓	195	├	211	╙	227	π	243	≤
131	â	147	ô	163	ú	179	│	196	─	212	╘	228	Σ	244	⌠
132	ä	148	ö	164	ñ	180	┤	197	┼	213	╒	229	σ	245	⌡
133	à	149	ò	165	Ñ	181	╡	198	╞	214	╓	230	µ	246	÷
134	å	150	û	166	ª	182	╢	199	╟	215	╫	231	τ	247	≈
135	ç	151	ù	167	º	183	╖	200	╚	216	╪	232	Φ	248	°
136	ê	152	_	168	¿	184	╕	201	╔	217	┘	233	Θ	249	·
137	ë	153	Ö	169	_	185	╣	202	╩	218	┌	234	Ω	250	·
138	è	154	Ü	170	¬	186	║	203	╦	219	█	235	δ	251	√
139	ï	156	£	171	½	187	╗	204	╠	220	▄	236	∞	252	_
140	î	157	¥	172	¼	188	╝	205	═	221	▌	237	φ	253	²
141	ì	158	_	173	¡	189	╜	206	╬	222	▐	238	ε	254	■
142	Ä	159	ƒ	174	«	190	╛	207	╧	223	▀	239	∩	255	
143	Å	192	└	175	»	191	┐	208	╨	224	α	240	≡		

FIGURE 2.2
Extended ASCII set.

Unicode is a character encoding standard that assigns unique numeric values (code points) to virtually every character and symbol used in written languages and scripts. Its primary goals are to: (1) Unify Writing Systems: Unicode brings together the world's writing systems, from Latin and Cyrillic scripts to ideographic languages like Chinese and Japanese (2) Facilitate Multilingual Text: It allows the mixing of characters from different languages in a single text, enabling multilingual communication and content creation. (3) Ensure Cross-Platform Compatibility: Unicode ensures that text can be displayed consistently on different devices, operating systems and software applications (4) Search and Text Analysis: Unicode enables powerful search and text analysis tools that work across languages, benefiting information retrieval and data processing. Currently there are 1112064 Unicode code points which requires 21 bits to be encoded.

The Unicode Consortium based in California overlooks the development of the standard. Members include major software and hardware vendors like Apple, Adobe, IBM, Microsoft, HP, etc. The Consortium first published the Unicode Standard 1.0 in 1991, covering around 25 languages across the globe, including Arabic, Bengali, Cyrillic, Devanagari, Greek, Gujarati, Gurmukhi, Hebrew, Kannada, Latin, Malayalam, Odia, Tamil, Telugu, Thai and Tibetan. Version 2.0 was released in 1996 where Hangul syllables were added. Version 3.0 was released in 1999 with the addition of another set of around 15 languages, including Cherokee, Khmer, Mongolian, Burmese, Sinhala, Syriac, Thaana and braille patterns. Version 4.0 was released in 2003 and includes Limbu, Osmanya, Shavian, Tail Le, Hexagram symbols; version 5.0 in 2006 and includes, among others, NKo and Phoenician symbols; version 6.0 in 2010 and includes among others Batak, Brahmi, Mandaic and other symbols like playing cards, emoticons and Indian rupee sign. Version 7.0 in 2014 included, among others, Bassa Va, Caucasian, Grantha, Kojki and dingbats. Version 8.0 in 2015 added scripts like hieroglyphs and sign-writing. Version 9.0 in 2016 added scripts like Adlam and Newa; version 10.0 in 2017 added scripts like Zanzabar and Soyombo. The current version is 15.1 released in September 2023 and defines around 150,000 characters and 160 scripts, with a capability of encoding more than 1 million characters.

The character set [symbl.cc/en/unicode] is organized into several categories with hex codes ranging from 00 to FF.

Cat	Languages included
00	Basic Latin (0000 – 007F), Latin-1 Supplement (0008 – 00FF)
01	Latin Extended A (0100 – 017F), Latin Extended B (0180 – 024F)
02	IPA Extensions (0250 – 02AF), Spacing Modifier Letters (02B0 – 02FF)
03	Diacritical Marks (0300 – 036F), Greek (0370 – 03FF)
04	Cyrillic (0400 – 04FF)
05	Cyrillic supplement (0500 – 052F), Armenian (0530 – 058F), Hebrew (0590 – 05FF)
06	Arabic (0600 – 06FF)
07	Syriac (0700 – 074F), Arabic supplement (0750 – 077F), Thaana (0780 – 07BF), NKo (07C0 – 07FF)
08	Samaritan (0800 – 083F), Mandaic (0840 – 085F), Syriac supplement (0860 – 086F), Arabic extended B (0870 – 089F), Arabic extended A (08A0 – 08FF)
09	Devanagari (0900 – 097F), Bengali (0980 – 09FF)
0A	Gurmukhi (0A00 – 0A7F), Gujarati (0A80 – 0AFF)
0B	Oriya (0B00 – 0B7F), Tamil (0B80 – 0BFF)
0C	Telugu (0C00 – 0C7F), Kannada (0C80 – 0CFF)
0D	Malayalam (0D00 – 0D7F), Sinhala (0D80 – 0DFF)
0E	Thai (0E00 – 0E7F), Lao (0E80 – 0EFF)
0F	Tibetan (0F00 – 0FFF)
10	Myanmar (1000 – 109F), Georgian (10A0 – 10FF)
11	Hangul Jamo (1100 – 11FF)
12	Ethiopic (1200 – 12FF)
13	Ethiopic (1300 – 137F), Ethiopic Supplement (1380 – 139F), Cherokee (13A0 – 13FF)
14-16	Canadian Aboriginal (1400 – 167F)
16	Ogham (1680 – 169F),Runic (16A0 – 16FF)
17	Tagalog (1700 – 171F), Hanunoo (1720 – 173F), Buhid (1740 – 175F), Tagbanwa (1760 – 177F), Khmer (1780 – 17FF)
18	Mongolian (1800 – 18AF), Canadian aboriginal (18B0 – 18FF)
19	Limbu (1900 – 194F), Tai Le (1950 – 197F), Tai Lue (1980 – 19DF), Khmer symbols (19E0 – 19FF)
1A	Buginese (1A00 – 1A1F), Tai Tham (1A20 – 1AAF), Diacritical marks extended (1AB0 – 1AFF)
1B	Balinese (1B00 – 1B7F), Sundanese (1B80 – 1B7F), Batak (1B80 – 1BFF)
1C	Lepcha (1C00 – 1C4F), Ol Chiki (1C50 – 1C7F), Cyrillic extended (1C80 – 1C8F), Georgian extended (1C90 – 1CBF), Sundanese aupplement (1CC0 – 1CCF), Vedic extensions (1CD0 – 1CFF)
1D	Phonetic extensions (1D00 – 1D7F), Phonetic extensions supplements (1D80 – 1DBF), Diacritical marks supplements (1DC0 – 1DFF)
1E	Latin extended additional (1E00 – 1EFF)
1F	Greek extended (1F00 – 1FFF)
20	General punctuation (2000 – 206F), Superscripts and subscripts (2070 – 209F), Currency symbols (20A0 – 20CF), Diacritical marks for symbols (20D0 – 20FF)
21	Letterlike symbols (2100 – 214F), Number forms (2150 – 218F), Arrows (2190 – 21FF)
22	Mathematical symbols (2200 – 22FF)
23	Miscellaneous technical (2300 – 23FF)

Cat	Languages included
24	Control pictures (2400 – 243F), OCR (2440 – 245F), Enclosed alphanumerics (2460 – 24FF)
25	Box drawings (2500 – 257F), Block elements (2380 – 239F), Geometric shapes (23A0 – 23FF)
26	Miscellaneous symbols (2600 – 26FF)
27	Dingbats (2700 – 27BF), Miscellaneous mathematical symbols A (27C0 – 27EF), Supplemental arrows A (27F0 – 27FF)
28	Braille patterns (2800 – 28FF)
29	Supplemental arrows B (2900 – 297F), Miscellaneous mathematical symbols B (2980 – 29FF)
2A	Supplemental mathematical operators (2A00 – 2AFF)
2B	Miscellaneous symbols & arrows (2B00 – 2BFF)
2C	Glagolitic (2C00 – 2C5F), Latin extended C (2C60 – 2C7F), Coptic (2C80 – 2CFF)
2D	Georgian supplement (2D00 – 2D2F), Tifinagh (2D30 – 2D7F), Ethiopic extended (2D80 – 2DDF), Cyrillic extended A (2DE0 – 2DFF)
2E	Supplemental punctuation (2E00 – 2E7F), CJK radicals supplement (2E80 – 2EFF)
2F	Kangxi radicals (2F00 – 2FDF), Not defined (2FE0 – 2FEF), Ideograph description characters (2FF0 – 2FFF)
30	CJK symbols and punctuation (3000 – 303F), Hiragana (3040 – 309F), Katakana (30A0 – 30FF)
31	Bopomofo (3100 – 312F), Hangul compatibility Jamo (3130 – 318F), Kanbun (3190 – 319F), Bopomofo extended (31A0 – 31BF), CJK strokes (31C0 – 31EF), Katakana phonetic extensions (31F0 – 31FF)
32	CJK letters and months (3200 – 32FF)
33	CJK compatibility (3300 – 33FF)
34 – 4D	CJK unified ideographs extension A (3400 – 4DBF)
4D	Yijing hexagram symbols (4DC0 – 4DFF)
4E – 9F	CJK unified ideographs (4E00 – 9FFF)
A0 – A4	Yi Syllables (A000 – A4BF)
A4	Yi radicals (A490 – A4CF), Lisu (A4D0 – A4FF)
A5	Vai (A500 – A63F)
A6	Cyrillic extended B (A640 – A69F), Bamum (A6A0 – A6FF)
A7	Modifier tone letters (A700 - A71F), Latin extended D (A720 - A7FF)
A8	Syloti Nagri (A800 – A82F), Common Indic number forms (A830 – A83F), Phags-Pa (A840 – A87F), Saurashtra (A880 - A8DF), Devanagari extended (A8E0 - A8FF)
A9	Kayah Li (A900 – A92F), Rejang (A930 – A95F), Hangul Jamo extended A (A960 – A97F), Javanese (A980 – A9DF), Myanmar extended B (A9E0 – A9FF)
AA	Cham (AA00 – AA5F), Myanmar extended A (AA60 – AA7F), Tai Viet (AA80 – AADF), Meetei Mayek extensions (AAE0 – AAFF)
AB	Ethiopic extended A (AB00 – AB2F), Latin extended E (AB30 – AB6F), Cherokee supplement (AB70 – ABBF), Meetei Mayek (ABC0 – ABFF)
AC – D7	Hangul syllables (AC00 – D7AF)
D7	Hangul Jamo extended B (D7B0 – D7FF)
D8 – DB	High surrogates (D800 – DB7F)
DB	High private use surrogates (DB80 – DBFF)
DC – DF	Low surrogates (DC00 – DFFF)
E0 – F8	Private use area (E000 – F8FF)
F9 – FA	CJK compatibility Ideographs (F900 – FAFF)
FB – FD	Alphabetic presentation forms (FB00 – FB4F), Arabic presentation forms A (FB50 – FDFF)
FE	Variation selectors (FE00 – FE0F), Vertical forms (FE10 – FE1F), Half marks (FE20 – FE25), CJK compatibility forms (FE30 – FE4F), Small form variants (FE50 – FE6f), Arabic presentations form B (FE70 – FEFF)
FF	Halfwidth and fullwidth forms (FF00 – FFEF), Specials (FFF0 – FFFF)

A sample of visual representations of some of the characters is given in Figure 2.3.

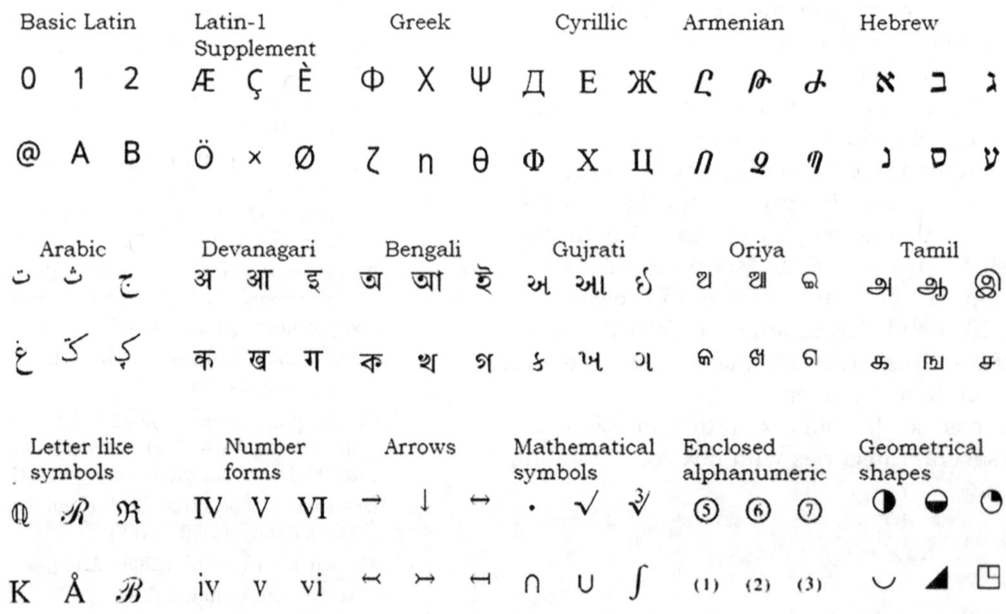

FIGURE 2.3
Samples of unicode set.

2.2.3 Unicode Transformation Formats (UTF)

Several methods have been suggested to implement Unicode based on variations in storage space and compatibility. The mapping methods are called Unicode Transformation Formats (UTF) and Universal Character Set (UCS). Some of the major mapping methods are the following:

2.2.3.1 UTF-32

The UTF-32 scheme uses 32 bits for each character. The simplest scheme, as it consists of fixed length encoding, is not efficient with regard to storage space and memory usage, and therefore rarely used. The main advantage of UTF-32 is that the Unicode code points can be directly indexed as each value represents exactly the numerical value of that code point, however the main disadvantage is that it is space inefficient using 32 bits for all code points out of which 11 bits are always zero since Unicode code points actually need 21 bits to be encoded.

2.2.3.2 UTF-16

The UTF-16 scheme uses 16 bits for each character [datatracker.ietf.org/doc/html/rfc2781.html]. In its native format it can encode code points up to FFFF in hex format, i.e., as xxxxxxxx xxxxxxxx. For coding beyond this, the original code point is expressed as a combination of two 16-bit numbers. These two 16-bit numbers are chosen from a surrogate range D800 to DFFF which are not assigned to normal characters. Hence a UTF-16 code can either consist of a single number within the ranges 0000 – D7FF and E000 – FFFF, or using a combination of two numbers using the surrogate range D800 – DFFF, the latter being applicable for numbers greater than FFFF within the range 10000 to 10FFFF. This follows a three step process as follows, where all numbers are expressed in hexadecimal format: (1) 10000 is subtracted from the original number leaving a 20-bit number in the range 0000 – FFFFF (2) the high 10-bits are added to D800 to generate the first 16-bit number called the high surrogate (3) the low 10 bits are added to DC00 to generate the second 16-bit number called the low surrogate. Accordingly the range D800 – DBFF is called the high surrogate range and the range DC00 – DFFF is called the low surrogate range. Thus if U be the original Unicode number then the following steps are executed: (1) subtract 10000 from U to generate 20-bit number aaaaaaaaaabbbbbbbbbb (2) add D800 to aaaaaaaaaa to generate the high surrogate S1 = 110110aaaaaaaaaa (3) add DC00 to bbbbbbbbbb to generate the low surrogate S2 = 110111bbbbbbbbbb.

2.2.3.3 UTF-8

UTF-8 is a variable-width encoding method where characters are represented using 8, 16, 24 or 32 bits. It is widely used in Web content and is space-efficient for text primarily in the Latin script. It was designed for backward compatibility with ASCII with the first 128 characters being identical in both sets. The encoding process is as follows: (1) code points within the range 0000 – 007F having 7 bits uses a one-byte representation: 0xxxxxxx (2) range 0080 – 07FF having 11 bits uses a two-byte representation: 110xxxxx 10xxxxxx (3) range 0800 – FFFF having 16 bits uses a three-byte representation: 1110xxxx 10xxxxxx 10xxxxxx (4) range 010000 – 10FFFF having 21 bits uses a four-byte representation: 11110xxx 10xxxxxx 10xxxxxx 10xxxxxx.

In conclusion, Unicode is a foundational technology for digital text representation, providing a unified and standardized approach to encoding characters from all languages and scripts. It fosters global communication, supports cross-platform compatibility and is essential for modern software and content creation in the multilingual digital landscape. It should be noted that both ASCII and Unicode provides only an internal digital representation of the alpha-numeric and special characters which determine how they are stored inside a digital computer and do not in any way deal with the visual representation of the characters when displayed on screen or printed. The visual representation of the characters, called glyph, is determined by fonts and the rendering process, as discussed in the next section.

2.3 Text Editing and Processing

Digital text editing and processing offer advanced formatting options, allowing users to manipulate font styles, sizes and colors with ease. Collaborative features enable multiple users to edit and comment on documents in real time, fostering efficient teamwork. Additionally, version control ensures the tracking and management of document revisions, providing a structured approach to document editing and preventing data loss (Deegan & Sutherland, 2016).

2.3.1 Word Processing

Word processing software and desktop text editors are widely used for creating and editing documents, reports and other textual content. Users can format text by adjusting fonts, sizes, styles and colors. They can also apply paragraph formatting, headers, footers and page layouts. Built-in spell checkers and grammar checkers help users detect and correct errors in their text. The ability to copy and paste text allows for efficient content reuse within the same document or across different applications. Users can also search for specific words or phrases and replace them with other text, making it easier to revise documents. Word processing software often includes templates and predefined styles to maintain consistency in document formatting. Collaborative editing features allow multiple users to make edits while tracking changes, comments and suggestions.

Text editing is fundamental for programmers and developers working with code. Code editors highlight syntax elements with distinct colors to improve code readability. Code suggestions and auto-completion features help programmers write code more efficiently. Integration with version control systems like Git [git-scm.com] allows developers to manage and track code changes. Code editors can also identify and highlight syntax errors, helping developers identify and correct issues. Developers often work on multiple files simultaneously, requiring features like tabbed interfaces and split views. Many code editors support extensions and plugins that enhance functionality and support various programming languages.

Content management systems (CMS) and website builders often include text editors for creating and editing Web content. WYSIWYG (What You See Is What You Get) editors provide a visual representation of the Web page, allowing users to edit content without coding knowledge. Some CMS platforms offer SEO (search engine optimization) features to improve the discoverability of Web content. Editors allow users to insert images, videos and other multimedia elements directly into Web pages. Scheduling features enable users to plan and publish content at specific times. CMS systems often support multiple users collaborating on content creation and editing.

2.3.2 Text Extraction

Text extraction is the process of capturing, parsing and converting textual content from various digital documents and files into a structured format that can be analyzed, searched or repurposed. Text extraction is crucial in today's digital age because it enables organizations and individuals to harness the vast amount of unstructured data found in documents. Text extraction allows access to information trapped in various document formats, making it searchable and usable. Automating text extraction reduces manual data entry efforts and errors. Extracted text can be processed and analyzed, providing insights and trends within the data, a concept referred to as text mining.

Text extraction techniques vary depending on the source document's format. Optical Character Recognition (OCR) software recognizes printed or handwritten text from scanned documents, images or PDFs. It converts text into editable and searchable text. Document parsing algorithms analyze the structure and content of documents, extracting text, headings, tables and other elements. Web scraping tools extract text from websites and online content, allowing organizations to gather data for various purposes, such as price monitoring, sentiment analysis or content aggregation. Natural Language Processing (NLP) techniques process text data, extracting entities, keywords and sentiment, which are used for information retrieval and analysis.

Text extraction finds applications across numerous domains, each reaping its benefits. Text extraction simplifies the organization of digital documents, making them searchable and sortable. Document management systems use text extraction to categorize, tag and index documents. Researchers, businesses and institutions leverage text extraction to analyze textual data, extracting insights from sources such as surveys, social media and customer reviews. Legal professionals use text extraction to identify and collect relevant information from electronic documents for litigation and investigations. Search engines and information retrieval systems rely on text extraction to index and retrieve information from the Web. News websites, blogs and content aggregators extract and repurpose information from various sources for publication. Libraries, archives and historical societies use text extraction to digitize and preserve historical documents and manuscripts.

Despite its benefits, text extraction presents challenges. Extracted text may contain errors, especially when dealing with handwritten or damaged documents. Maintaining the original document's formatting during extraction can be challenging. Handling text in multiple languages and character sets requires robust language support. Extracting and processing personal or sensitive data must adhere to privacy regulations and security measures.

2.3.3 Text Transformation

Text transformation is a process that involves modifying, reformatting or enhancing textual content to meet specific needs, improve readability or adapt for different media or platforms. Text transformation plays a critical role in making content more accessible, engaging and adaptable. Its significance is evident in various aspects of digital communication. Text transformation allows content to be repurposed for different platforms, devices and languages, ensuring a consistent user experience. Transforming text can enhance accessibility for individuals with disabilities, making content more inclusive and compliant with accessibility standards. Search Engine Optimization (SEO) often involves text transformation to improve content visibility and ranking on search engines. Text transformation can enrich content by adding multimedia elements, interactive features and links, making it more engaging and informative. Transforming text may also involve translating content to make it accessible to a global audience, overcoming language barriers.

Text transformation techniques encompass a range of processes to tailor and optimize textual content. Adjusting fonts, styles, sizes and colors to enhance readability and visual appeal is particularly important in typography and Web design. Creating concise summaries of longer text provides readers with a quick overview of content. Converting text from one language to another while preserving the original meaning and context caters to a global audience. Adapting content for different media and devices, such as converting print content to Web formats or mobile-friendly versions, promotes device adaptability. Adding multimedia elements, such as images, videos and interactive features provides content augmentation. Transforming text into audio to enable auditory consumption, benefits individuals with visual impairments. Modifying content to align with cultural norms, regional preferences in different regions, provides language localization. Text Encryption to protect sensitive information, making it unreadable without the proper decryption key, provides an additional layer of security.

2.3.4 Text Enhancement

Text enhancement is the practice of refining and improving textual content to maximize its readability, visual appeal and effectiveness in conveying information. Text enhancement is important in digital communication as it serves multiple crucial roles. Enhanced text ensures that content is easily readable, comprehensible and accessible, benefiting all readers, including those with visual impairments. Visually appealing and well-structured text captures and retains the reader's attention, leading to better engagement with the content. Search engine optimization (SEO) relies on well-optimized text to improve search rankings and visibility. Text enhancement also maintains brand consistency by using specific fonts, styles and colors, reinforcing brand identity. Moreover, enhanced text adheres to accessibility standards, making content inclusive and usable by a wider audience.

Various techniques are employed to enhance text, making it more effective and engaging. Selection of appropriate fonts, font sizes, styles (e.g., bold, italics) and line spacing is followed to improve readability and aesthetics. Consistent and well-structured formatting, including headings, subheadings, bullet points and numbered lists are hallmarks of enhanced text. Careful use of text colors is done to ensure contrast, readability and visual appeal. Strategic use of white space around text prevents clutter and improves visual clarity. Clear and descriptive hyperlinks provide better navigation and user experience. Integration of relevant images, videos and info-graphics can be done to supplement and enhance textual content. Creation of visual aids, such as charts and graphs, can be done to illustrate complex concepts. Inclusion of alternative text for images and multimedia ensures accessibility and understanding for those using screen readers. Tailoring language for the target audience can be done by avoiding jargon and employing plain language principles. Offering text-to-speech functionality to cater to visually impaired readers provides an additional mode of content consumption.

2.3.5 Typography and Fonts

Typography and fonts are at the heart of digital text design, influencing how written content is presented and perceived in the digital realm. Typography is the art and technique of arranging type to make written language visually appealing and readable. It involves selecting typefaces, determining font sizes, line spacing and overall layout to convey a specific message or evoke a particular aesthetic. The careful consideration of typography is crucial in graphic design, publishing and Web development, as it significantly influences the way information is perceived and understood by the audience (Boss & Teague, 2017).

Typography is the art and technique of arranging type to make language visible. A typeface is a set of characters with a consistent design, which includes letters, numerals, punctuation marks and symbols. The choice of typeface sets the tone and style of the text. Typography also establishes a visual hierarchy in text, guiding readers to prioritize the most important information through variations in font size, weight and style. Text alignment, whether left, right, centered or justified, impacts the visual flow of content and overall readability. Proper leading, which refers to the vertical space between lines of text, ensures text is readable and visually appealing. Kerning adjusts the space between individual characters, while tracking adjusts the overall character spacing. The length and width of lines of text play a role in readability and aesthetics, with longer lines potentially being harder to read. Contrast, achieved through variations in type color (lightness or darkness), affects text legibility, while text color relative to the background is essential for readability. The arrangement of type elements, such as headings, subheadings, body text and captions, is key to creating a harmonious typographic layout.

Fonts and typefaces are often used interchangeably, but they have distinct meanings. A typeface is the design or style of a set of characters, and may encompass various font styles within the same design, such as bold, italic and regular. A font on the other hand, is a specific instance of a typeface at a particular size and style, such as "Arial Regular 12pt" or "Times New Roman Italic 18pt". Fonts can be categorized into different classifications: (1) Serif Fonts: These fonts have small decorative lines (serifs) at the ends of characters. They are often associated with tradition and readability in printed material (2) Sans-serif Fonts: These fonts lack serifs and offer a clean, modern and often more readable appearance. They are commonly used on digital screens (3) Script Fonts: Script fonts mimic cursive or handwriting and are often used for decorative or personalized purposes (4) Display Fonts: These fonts are designed for headlines and titles, offering unique and eye-catching designs (5) Mono-spaced Fonts: In mono-spaced fonts, each character takes up the same horizontal space, providing a uniform appearance often used in coding and typewriter-like text.

Digital typography has unique considerations which need to be adhered to for improving the way written content is presented and perceived on digital devices. Text may appear differently on screens compared to print, and requires adjustments in font choice and size. Typography must adapt to various screen sizes and orientations in responsive Web design. Ensuring readability and legibility is crucial for users with visual impairments, making accessible typography practices vital. Challenges in digital typography include cross-browser and cross-platform compatibility, as well as the need for responsive typography in an era of varied screen sizes. Advancements involve the use of variable fonts, which allow greater flexibility in font styles, and the use of AI for font recognition and generation.

Font rendering, also known as type rendering, is the process of converting digital font data into on-screen or printed text. Fonts are typically vector-based, but digital displays consist of pixels. Rasterization converts vector fonts into pixel-based representations, ensuring that characters are displayed clearly and accurately. Anti-aliasing techniques smooth the edges of characters to reduce the appearance of jagged lines, resulting in more visually appealing text. Hinting is the process of adjusting the position of individual character pixels to improve legibility, especially at small font sizes. Sub-pixel rendering takes advantage of the RGB sub-pixels in modern displays to enhance font rendering quality and clarity. Font rendering also considers the color and contrast of text to ensure readability, especially against various backgrounds.

Text layout involves arranging characters and words to form coherent and aesthetically pleasing text. Determining where to break lines of text is crucial for readability and page layout. Text layout algorithms ensure that lines are broken logically, minimizing awkward line breaks. Kerning adjusts the spacing between specific character pairs, while tracking deals with overall character spacing. Proper kerning and tracking enhance the appearance of text. Text can be left-aligned, right-aligned, centered or justified. Justified text is aligned both on the left and right, creating a clean and organized look. Line spacing, also known as leading, defines the vertical space between lines of text. Proper line spacing is essential for readability and aesthetics. Languages that are written from right to left, such as Arabic and Hebrew, require special handling to ensure correct layout and rendering.

2.3.6 Text Effects

Text effects are creative design techniques applied to textual content to make it visually striking, engaging and memorable. Text effects play a vital role in digital communication as they can offer several utilities. Eye-catching text effects immediately draw the viewer's attention to the content, making it stand out in a visually cluttered environment. Text effects can convey emotions, moods and themes effectively, making the content more relatable to the audience. Consistent use of specific text effects can reinforce brand identity and recognition. Text effects can help establish a visual hierarchy in the content, guiding the viewer's focus to key information. Visually appealing and creatively designed text encourages user engagement and shares in digital marketing.

Various techniques are employed to create visually appealing and engaging text effects. Techniques include custom fonts, font size variations, font color gradients and text warping. Adding shadows to text creates depth and dimension, making it appear raised or recessed. Applying gradient colors to text, allows for smooth transitions from one color to another. Embossed text provides a raised or engraved appearance to create a 3D effect. Placing an image or pattern within the text, allows for creative background effects through text masking. Creating a glowing effect around text is often used for neon signs and futuristic designs. Adding textures or patterns to text makes it visually interesting and tactile. Employing layer styles like bevel, stroke and inner shadow can be done to enhance text appearance. Applying animation effects to text, such as fade-ins, typewriter effects or kinetic typography enhances user engagements is dynamic environments.

Text effects are widely applied in various communication contexts, enhancing content in different ways. Text effects are used to create attention-grabbing headlines, call-to-action buttons and interactive menus on websites. Graphic designers use text effects to create posters, flyers, banners and advertisements that resonate with viewers. Text effects are employed in video introductions, credits, transitions and to add visual appeal. Engaging text effects in digital marketing campaigns boost user engagement and conversion rates. Creative text effects on social media posts and stories capture the audience's attention and drive engagement. In presentations, text effects emphasize key points and make content more engaging. Text effects are a staple in digital art and illustration, creating expressive and imaginative text designs. Text gradients involve transitioning between colors to create visually appealing and dynamic text effects. Gradients can be linear, radial or angular, and designers can control gradient direction and color stops. 3D extrusion gives text a three-dimensional appearance, making it appear as if it's rising from the screen. This effect involves depth, lighting and shading to create a realistic 3D look.

2.3.7 Text Animation

Text animation is a dynamic design technique that involves moving, transforming or sequencing text to create engaging and visually appealing digital content. Animated text captures and sustains viewer attention, making content more interactive and memorable. Dynamic text animations can clarify complex concepts, processes and data through visual storytelling. Consistent use of specific text animations can reinforce brand recognition and identity. Animations add an element of visual interest and creativity to digital media, making it more compelling and enjoyable. In user interfaces, subtle text animations can guide users and improve the overall experience.

Various techniques are employed to create captivating text animations. Animated transitions include fades, slides or zooms to introduce or remove text elements. Kinetic typography sequences text elements to synchronize with voice-overs or music, enhancing storytelling. Various text effects can be animated, such as glow, neon, pulsing and flickering. Keyframing allows precise control over text movement, rotation and scaling over time. Text can also follow predefined paths, curves or patterns, creating unique motion effects. Concealing and revealing text through animation can add an element of surprise and engagement. Background animations can complement text by providing context or setting the mood. User interactions, such as hovering or clicking, can trigger text animations, creating engaging user experiences.

Text animation finds applications in diverse communication contexts, enhancing content in various ways. Text animations are commonly used in video intros, titles, lower thirds and kinetic typography in explainer videos. Motion graphics designers use text animation to create visually appealing animated logos, info-graphics and product advertisements. Animated text elements in Web design capture user attention, guiding them through the user interface. Text animations in presentations make content more engaging and help convey complex information effectively. Dynamic text in digital advertising banners and videos can boost click-through rates and conversion. Animated text aids in creating interactive and engaging educational content, enhancing the learning experience. In app and Web design, subtle text animations can guide users, provide feedback and improve navigation. Interactive multimedia often incorporates user-triggered text animations. JavaScript can be used to create interactive effects, responding to user actions like clicks or hovers (Flanagan, 2017).

2.4 Text Applications

2.4.1 Web Design

Text is the cornerstone of Web design, serving as the primary medium for conveying information, engaging users and creating a seamless online experience. Text is the primary vehicle for communicating information, providing context and conveying messages to users. Well-crafted text, along with appealing visuals, enhances user engagement by telling a compelling story and guiding users through the website. Text content ensures that websites are accessible to a wide range of users, including those with disabilities who rely on screen readers. Search engines rely on text to index and rank websites, making text critical for search engine optimization (SEO) and discoverability. Consistent use of specific fonts, styles and colors in text contributes to brand recognition and identity (Robbins, 2012).

2.4.1.1 CSS (Cascading Style Sheets)

Cascading Style Sheets (CSS) [w3.org/Style/CSS] is an effort by W3C and Web-browser vendors to allow for sophisticated sizing, positioning and other appearance, related manipulations of Web page contents. Advanced text styling with CSS is pivotal in Web design for several compelling reasons (Duckett, 2014).

CSS allows designers to apply a wide range of styles, making text more visually appealing and engaging. Creative and unique text styles using CSS capture user attention and encourage interaction, ultimately enhancing the user experience. CSS-driven text styling ensures consistent and brand-specific typography, reinforcing brand recognition and identity. CSS enables designers to establish clear text hierarchies, guiding users to key information and actions on the website. While offering creative freedom, website developers need to prioritize readability and accessibility to ensure content is easily consumed and comprehensible by all users. Some techniques for incorporating text styling with CSS are discussed below (Figure 2.4).

Background color and image effects: Background colors and images can be applied to specific elements like words and paragraphs instead of the whole page. Moreover, the starting position of the image can be specified as well as direction in which it should repeat.

```
.bkg-col {background-color: #FFFF66}
.bkg-img {background-image:
   url(image1.jpg); background-
   position: center right;
   background-repeat: repeat-y}
```

Borders: An element like an image can have its own border optionally with a padding space in between.

```
.bor {border-style: solid; border-
   width: 10; padding: 10; border-
   color: green}
```

Text Effects: Text effects like shadows, outlines and strokes can be applied.

```
.txt-shd {text-shadow: 2px 2px 4px
   rgba(0, 0, 0, 0.5)}
```

Absolute and relative positioning: Elements can be positioned accurately on a Web page by mentioning absolute distances from left and top margins of the browser window or relative distances from another element.

```
.pos-abs {position: absolute; left:
   100px; top: 10px}
.pos-rel {position: relative; left:
   20px; top: 20px}
```

Layering: Vertical ordering or layering of elements can be specified by a z-index value: a low z-index value makes elements appear below elements having a higher z-index value.

```
.A {position: absolute; z-index: 3}
.B {position: absolute; z-index: 4;
   font-size: 50; left: 30; top: 50}
.C {position: absolute; z-index: 1;
   left: 50; top: 10}
```

Font variations and cursors: Different types of font sizes, variants and cursors may be specified.

```
.A {font-family: arial; font-style:
   italic; cursor: crosshair}
.B {font-size: 30px; cursor: help}
.C {font-variant: small-caps;
   cursor: hand}
.D {font-weight: 900; cursor: wait}
```

Animations: Dynamic text effects can be created.

```
<style>
    @keyframes slide
     {
         0% { transform:
            translateX(-100%); }
         100% { transform:
            translateX(0); }
     }
     .animated-text {animation: slide
        2s ease infinite;}
</style>
  <p class="animated-text">Animated
     Text</p>
```

Color Gradients: Color gradients can be applied to background and text.

```
.gradient-text {
    background: linear-
   gradient(45deg, #ff8a00,
   #e52e71);
    -webkit-background-clip: text;
    color: transparent;
}
```

2.4.1.2 JavaScript

Interactive text elements powered by JavaScript [developer.mozilla.org/en-US/docs/Web/JavaScript] add a layer of dynamism and engagement to websites (Flanagan, 2017). Interactive elements such as tooltips, interactive forms and real-time updates keep users engaged and encourage exploration. Interactive text responds to user actions, making websites more intuitive and user-friendly. Interactive

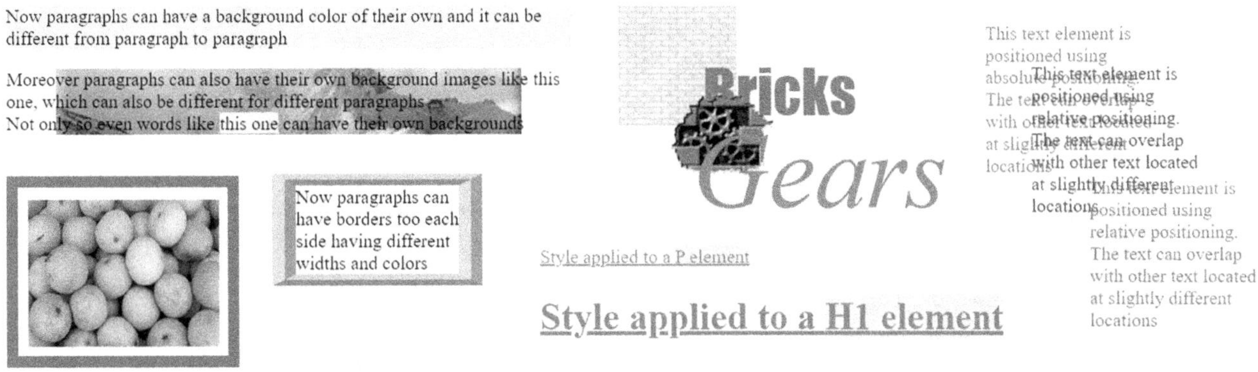

FIGURE 2.4
Examples of CSS output.

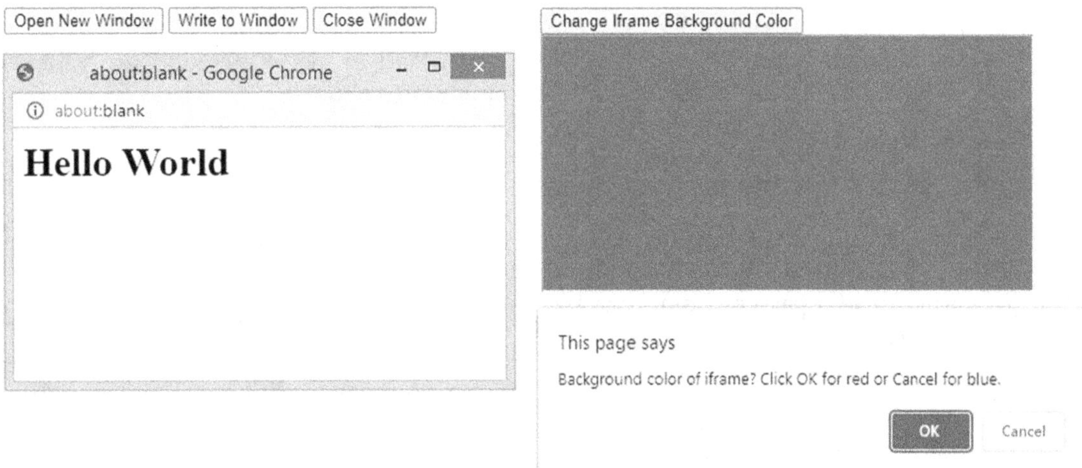

FIGURE 2.5
Examples of JavaScript output.

charts, graphs and info-graphics powered by JavaScript enhance data presentation and user understanding. JavaScript-driven interactive text can be tailored to individual user preferences, creating a personalized browsing experience. Some techniques for incorporating interactive elements with JavaScript are discussed below (Figure 2.5).

Dedicated windows: New windows can be generated in real time having customized appearances, specified content can be written to them and then the windows can be closed.

```
<script>
var newWindow; // Declare newWindow
   variable globally
function openNewWindow() {
  // Open a new window
  newWindow = window.
     open('', '_blank',
     'width=400,height=200');
}

function writeToWindow() {
  // Check if the new window
    is opened
  if (newWindow) {
    // Write "hello world" to the
   new window
    newWindow.document.
       write("<h1>Hello World</h1");
  } else {
    alert("Please open a new window
       first.");
  }
}

function closeWindow() {
  // Check if the new window
     is opened
  if (newWindow) {
    // Close the new window
    newWindow.close();
  } else {
    alert("Please open a new window
   first.");
```

```
    }
  }
  </script>

  <body>
  <button onclick="openNewWindow()">
     Open New Window</button>
  <button onclick="writeToWindow()">
     Write to Window</button>
  <button onclick="closeWindow()">
     Close Window</button>
  </body>
```

Read user input and generate alert boxes: Customized messages can be generated based on input from the user.

```
function readName()
        {
                var name =
                   prompt("Enter
                   your name");
                alert('Hello
                   '+ name);
        }
```

Read user decisions via buttons: Changes in a page, like the background color of a page or frame, can be done based on user feedback.

```
<script>
// Declare iframe variable globally
   to access it from different
   functions
var iframe;

function changeIframeColor() {
  if (!iframe) {
    // Create an iframe element if
       it doesn't exist
    iframe = document.
       createElement("iframe");
    // Set attributes for the iframe
    iframe.width = "400";
    iframe.height = "200";
    iframe.src = "about:blank";
       // Set a blank URL for
       the iframe
    // Append the iframe to the
       document body
    document.body.
       appendChild(iframe);
  }

  // Ask the user for input
  var userResponse =
     confirm("Background color of
     iframe? Click OK for red or
     Cancel for blue.");

  // Change the background color of
     the iframe based on user input
  if (userResponse) {
    iframe.style.backgroundColor
   = "red";
  } else {
    iframe.style.backgroundColor
   = "blue";
  }
}
</script>

<body>
<button onclick="changeIframe
    Color()">Change Iframe
    Background Color</button>
<div id="iframeContainer"></div>
</body>
```

Dates and arrays: Dates and array items can be manipulated about.

```
var myDate = new Date();
alert(myDate.getHours());
var myArray = new Array("One",
   "Two", "Three", "Four");
alert(myArray.reverse());
```

Rollover elements: Rollover images and buttons can be created for changing its content whenever the mouse moves over a link.

```
<IMG SRC = "image1.gif" NAME =
   "an_image">
<A HREF = "" onMouseOver =
   "document.an_image.src = "image2.
   gif;">Change</A>
```

2.4.1.3 Dynamic HTML

Dynamic HTML (DHTML) is a term used to imply a collection of technologies used to create animated web sites using a combination of markup language like HTML, flexible element positioning using CSS and client-side scripting languages like JavaScript for interactive elements, along with an underlying Document Object Model (DOM) (Goodman, 2007). A Document Object Model (DOM) is an underlying platform to enable manipulation of Web objects in a language independent manner within a browser and is used by languages like JavaScript to change content of a page dynamically. The public interface of a DOM is specified in its Application Programming Interface (API). The requirement for a standardized DOM was recommended by W3C that defines the DOM as a platform- and language-neutral interface that allows programs and scripts to dynamically access and update the content, structure and style of a document. The basic concepts of DOM designed by W3C are discussed below. Firstly, each HTML object that needs to be identified by an unique ID. For example,

```
<P ID="one"> This is the first
  paragraph </P>
```

The concerned element is accessed by passing the ID as an attribute value to a method of the Document object, known as getElementById. For example,

```
document.getElementById('one')
```

DHTML allows the use of variables and programming constructs like branching and looping to change the appearances of Web pages during the viewing process after they are loaded. Hence, the term "dynamic" really refers to the change in appearance rather than the change in content. Shown below is an example where DHTML changes the appearance of an image by clicking a button. The image object is accessed by its "getElementById" method and using its style, border property, a border is inserted around it and its background color is changed. The return false statement prevents reloading the Web page (Figure 2.6).

```
<img id = "b" src="a.gif">

<input type = "button" value =
   "Decorate Image"
       Onclick = "document.
          getElementById('b').
          style.border = '10px
          ridge skyblue';
          getElementById('b').
          style.backgroundColor
          = 'yellow'; return
          false;"> 

<input type = "button" value =
   "Reset Image"
       Onclick = "document.
          getElementById('b').
          style.border = '0';
          getElementById('b').style.
          backgroundColor = 'white';
          return false;">
```

2.4.1.4 HTML5

HTML5, [html.spec.whatwg.org/multipage/] the latest revision of the Hypertext Markup Language, has brought significant enhancements to multimedia on the Web. It introduces native support for multimedia elements, making it easier for Web developers to integrate and control multimedia content seamlessly. HTML5 introduces some primary elements for embedding multimedia content as discussed below (Frain, 2022).

The "video" element allows the seamless integration of video content on Web pages. It supports multiple video formats and codecs, making it possible to provide videos that are compatible with various browsers. Web developers can control video playback, add captions and enable responsive design.

```
<video controls>
    <source src="video.mp4"
       type="video/mp4" width=100>
</video>
```

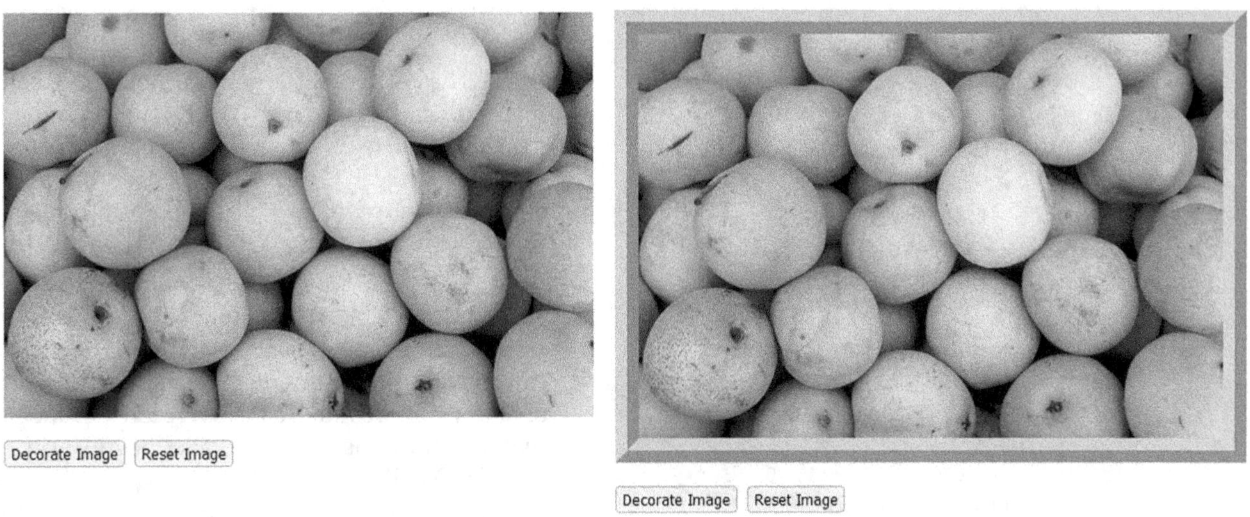

FIGURE 2.6
Examples of dynamic HTML output.

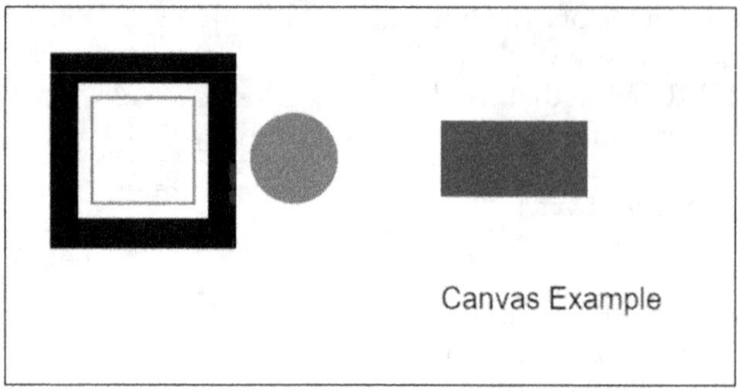

FIGURE 2.7
Example of HTML5 output.

The "audio" element serves a similar purpose to the "video" element but is tailored for audio content. It allows Web developers to embed audio files, control playback and provide alternative formats for cross-browser compatibility.

```
<audio controls>
    <source src="audio.mp3"
       type="audio/mpeg">
</audio>
```

The "canvas" element is primarily used for graphics and animations. The following example depicts drawing of graphical figures and text at specific locations with specific dimensions (Figure 2.7).

```
<style>
    canvas {border: 1px
       solid black;}
</style>

<canvas id="myCanvas" width="500"
   height="250"></canvas>
<script>
    // Get the canvas element
       var canvas = document.
         getElementById("myCanvas");

    // Get the 2D drawing context
       var ctx = canvas.
          getContext("2d");

    // Draw a rectangle
       ctx.fillStyle = "blue"; //
          Set fill color
       ctx.fillRect(300, 75, 100,
          50); // Draw rectangle

    // Draw a circle
       ctx.beginPath();
       ctx.arc(200, 100, 30, 0, 2 *
          Math.PI); // Draw circle
       ctx.fillStyle = "red"; //
          Set fill color
       ctx.fill(); // Fill circle

    // Draw text
       ctx.font = "20px Arial";
       ctx.fillStyle = "black";
       ctx.fillText("Canvas
          Example", 300, 200);

    // Draw stroked rectangle
     ctx.fillRect(30,30,130,130);
     ctx.clearRect(50,50,90,90);
     ctx.strokeRect(60,60,70,70);

</script>
```

WebRTC: WebRTC (Web Real-Time Communication) [webrtc.org] enables real-time audio and video communication within Web applications that works on top of an open standard. It supports video, audio and generic data to be sent between peers. It is available on all modern browsers as well as native clients like Android and iOS applications. The technologies behind WebRTC are implemented as an open Web standard and available as regular JavaScript APIs. The WebRTC project is open sourced and supported by Apple, Google, Microsoft and Mozilla among others.

Media Capture: The media capture API [w3.org/TR/html-media-capture] allows Web applications to access streams from multimedia capture devices like cameras and microphones, enabling features such as video recording and live streaming using the JavaScript function "getUserMedia()".

WebGL: Web Graphics Library (WebGL) [khronos.org/webgl] is a JavaScript API for rendering 2D and 3D graphics within a compatible Web browser without the use of plug-ins. One of its major features is the ability to interact with the GPU, leveraging hardware acceleration for complex graphical tasks.

2.4.1.5 XML (Extensible Markup Language)

XML is a W3C standard [w3.org/XML] since 1998. XML is not a replacement for HTML; they have been designed with different objectives. While HTML is concerned with the formatting and appearance of data, and focuses on how the content on a page is displayed to the user, XML is concerned with how to structure and store the data so that it can be subsequently searched for and possibly transported from one place to another. Essentially XML does not do anything, it is just information wrapped in tags. The name "extensible" comes from the fact that newer tags can be incorporated within the document without modifying the earlier tags and the earlier application will continue to work. An XML document must be validated against a DTD (document type definition) which specifies the rules about the correct syntax and structure.

```
<note id="101010">
        <date>
                <day>10</day>
               <month>October</month>
                <year>2010</year>
        </date>
</note>
```

2.4.1.6 SVG (Scalable Vector Graphics)

Scalable Vector Graphics (SVG) [w3.org/Graphics/SVG] is a set of XML based specifications for describing 2D vector graphics. SVG has been under development by W3C since 1999 its current version is 2 as of 2023. The advantages of SVG include the fact that being a vector format the graphics do not suffer from pixelation due to zooming (Royds et al., 2018). Being XML they can be edited using a text editor and can be indexed and searched for. They have compact file sizes and that the standard is an open standard. Two profiles called SVG Tiny (SVGT) and SVG Basic (SVGB) which are subsets of the full SVG standard are defined for mobile devices like cellphones and handheld devices. SVG files must be saved using the.SVG extension (Figure 2.8).

```
<svg id="d1" height=200
    xmls="http://www.
    w3.org/2000/svg">
<circle cx=60 cy=60 r=50
    stroke="black" stroke-width=2
    fill="red"/>
</svg>
```

SVG also defines other pre-defined shape elements like rectangle (RECT), ellipse (ELLIPSE), line (LINE), polyline (POLYLINE) and polygon (POLYGON). CSS attributes like opacity can be applied with SVG elements to change their appearances.

```
<svg>
<circle cx=60 cy=60 r=50
     style="fill:green;stroke:
        orange;stroke-width:5;
        opacity:0.5"/>
</svg>
```

The PATH element is used to define a path which can be straight or curved. For example the following code draws a red triangle.

```
<svg width="100" height="100" xmlns
    = "http://www.w3.org/2000/svg">
     <path d = "M 50, 10 L 90, 90 L
        10, 90 Z" fill="red"/>
</svg>
```

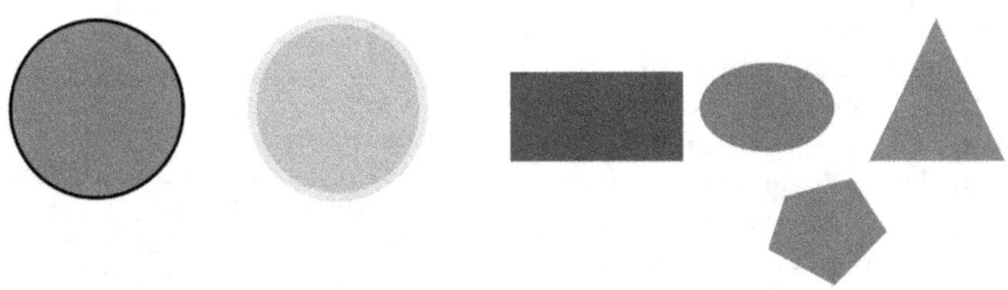

FIGURE 2.8
Examples of SVG output.

2.4.1.7 SMIL (Synchronized Multimedia Integration Language)

Synchronized Multimedia Integration Language (SMIL) (pronounced "smile") [w3.org/TR/SMIL3] is an XML based W3C recommendation for describing multimedia presentations. It defines markup elements for timing, layout, animations and transitions. SMIL 1.0 was first published in 1998 and SMIL 2.0 in 2001, the latter introducing a modular language structure which facilitated its integration with XML-based languages. A SMIL document must be enclosed within the <smil> and </smil> tags. Within it, there can be a head section for storing metadata and a body section for displaying content. SMIL allows Web developers to synchronize multimedia elements, such as audio, video, text and animations, ensuring that they play in harmony and in response to user interactions. SMIL also supports user interactions by defining events and triggers, enabling actions like clicking, hovering or keyboard input to affect the playback and behavior of multimedia elements The "seq" element specifies a sequence of elements to be displayed in a predefined order, and "par" element defines parallel elements that play simultaneously.

2.4.1.8 PHP (Hypertext Preprocessor)

PHP [php.net] is primarily designed for server-side scripting, enabling the execution of code on the Web server to generate dynamic Web pages. It is an open-source language, which means its source code is freely available, allowing developers to modify and distribute it according to their needs. PHP is cross-platform, making it compatible with various operating systems like Windows, Linux and macOS, ensuring flexibility in Web application development. PHP code can be seamlessly embedded within HTML code, allowing developers to mix dynamic and static content in a single file, simplifying the creation of dynamic Web pages. PHP has a vast collection of libraries and extensions that facilitate a wide range of functionalities, from database access to image processing, making development more efficient. PHP supports integration with numerous databases, with native support for MySQL and compatibility with other databases like PostgreSQL, Oracle and Microsoft SQL Server. PHP is highly scalable, making it suitable for both small websites and large, complex applications, allowing developers to scale their projects as needed. With a large and active community, PHP benefits from continuous development, bug fixes and the sharing of best practices among developers worldwide.

2.4.1.9 JSON (JavaScript Object Notation)

JSON [json.org] is a data interchange format designed for efficient data transmission between Web servers and clients. It is a text based format using a simple syntax resembling key-value pairs and supports a nested hierarchical structure. It supports several data types which allow developers to represent a variety of data structures in a standardized format, and can be easily parsed and generated by a wide variety of programming languages. JSON supports Unicode, allowing the representation of a wide range of characters and facilitating the exchange of data in multiple languages and closely resembles JavaScript object notation which makes it straightforward for Web applications, written in JavaScript, to work with JSON data seamlessly (Prettyman, 2016).

2.4.1.10 Web Color Names

Textual names can be used to represent around 148 colors that can be used for Web design and supported by all major browsers although the exact shade of color rendered on screen can differ slightly [www.w3.org/TR/css-color-3]. The following is a list of major color names sorted by their RGB color values in hexadecimal numbers where the first two values are for red, the next two values for green and last two values for blue:

```
black (000000), navy (000080), darkblue
  (00008B), mediumblue (0000CD),
  blue (0000FF), darkgreen (006400),
  green (008000), teal (008080),
  darkcyan (008B8B), deepskyblue
  (00BFFF), darkturquoise (00CED1),
  mediumspringgreen (00FA9A), lime
  (00FF00), springgreen (00FF7F), cyan/
  aqua (00FFFF), midnightblue (191970),
  dodgerblue (1E90FF), lightseagreen
  (20B2AA), forestgreen (228B22),
  seagreen (2E8B57), darkslategray
  (2F4F4F), limegreen (32CD32),
  mediumseagreen (3CB371), turquoise
  (40E0D0), royalblue (4169E1), steelblue
  (4682B4), darkslateblue (483D8B),
  mediumturqoise (48D1CC), indigo
  (4B0082), darkolivegreen (556B2F),
  cadetblue (5F9EA0), cornflowerblue
  (6495ED), rebeccapurple (663399),
  mediumaquamarine (66CDAA), dimgray
  (696969), slateblue (6A5ACD),
  olivedrab (6B8E23), slategray
  (708090), lightslategray (778899),
  mediumslateblue (7B68EE), lawngreen
  (7CFC00), chartreuse (7FFF00),
  aquamarine (7FFFD4), maroon
  (800000),  purple (800080), olive
```

`(808000), gray (808080), skyblue (87CEEB), lightskyblue (87CEFA), blueviolet (8A2BE2), darkred (8B0000), darkmagenta (8B008B), saddlebrown (8B4513), darkseagreen (8FBC8F), lightgreen (90EE90), mediumpurple (9370DB), darkviolet (9400D3), palegreen (98FB98), darkorchid (9932CC), yellowgreen (9ACD32), sienna (A0522D), brown (A52A2A), darkgray (A9A9A9), lightblue (ADD8E6), greenyellow (ADFF2F), paleturquoise (AFEEEE), lightsteelblue (B0C4DE), powderblue (B0E0D6), firebrick (B22222), darkgoldenrod (B8860B), mediumorchid (BA55D3), rosybrown (BC8F8F), darkkhaki (BDB76B), silver (C0C0C0), mediumvioletred (C71585), indianred (CD5C5C), peru (CD853F), chocolate (D2691E), tan (D2B48C), lightgray (D3D3D3), thistle (D8BFD8), orchid (DA70D6), goldenrod (DAA520), palevioletred (DB7093), crimson (DC143C), gainsboro (DCDCDC), plum (DDA0DD), burlywood (DEB887), lightcyan (E0FFFF), lavender (E6E6FA), darksalmon (E9967A), violet (EE82EE), palegoldenrod (EEE8AA), lightcoral (F08080), khaki (F0E68C), aliceblue (F0F8FF), honeydew (F0FFF0), azure (F0FFFF), sandybrown (F4A460), wheat (F5DEB3), beige (F5F5DC), whitesmoke (F5F5F5), mintcream (F5FFFA), ghostwhite (F8F8FF), salmon (FA8072), antiquewhite (FAEBD7), linen (FAF0E6), lightgoldenrodyellow (FAFAD2), oldlace (FDF5E6), red (FF0000), fuchsia (FF00FF), magenta (FF00FF), deeppink (FF1493), orangered (FF4500), tomato (FF6347), hotpink (FF69B4), coral (FF7F50), darkorange (FF8C00), lightsalmon (FFA07A), orange (FFA500), lightpink (FFB6C1), pink (FFC0CB), gold (FFD700), peachpuff (FFDAB9), navajowhite (FFDEAD), moccasin (FFE4B5), bisque (FFE4C4), mistyrose (FFE4E1), blanchedalmond (FFEBCD), papayawhip (FFEFD5), lavenderblush (FFF0F5), seashell (FFF5EE), cornsilk (FFF8DC), lemonchiffon (FFFACD), floralwhite (FFFAF0), snow (FFFAFA), yellow (FFFF00), lightyellow (FFFFE0), ivory (FFFFF0), white (FFFFFF).`

2.4.2 Text-to-Speech (TTS)

TTS involves the process of converting written text into spoken language, including synthesis methods and prosody modeling which are the patterns of stress and intonation. It offers support for multiple languages and dialects, enabling a diverse range of users to access content in their preferred language. TTS applications often provide customization features, allowing users to adjust the speed, pitch and voice characteristics to enhance the listening experience and cater to individual preferences (Dutoit, 2013).

TTS technology relies on several key components. The TTS engine analyzes the input text, breaking it down into individual words, sentences and phonetic components. The engine converts text into phonemes, the smallest units of sound in a language. TTS uses pre-recorded human voices or synthetic voices generated through speech synthesis algorithms to produce spoken language. TTS considers prosody, including pitch, volume and speech rate, to create natural-sounding speech.

TTS enables individuals with visual impairments to access digital content, including websites, e-books and documents. TTS assists language learners in improving pronunciation and comprehension by providing correct pronunciation models. TTS is integrated into assistive technology devices and software to help individuals with disabilities access and interact with digital content. TTS is also a core technology for voice-activated virtual assistants like Siri, Google Assistant and Alexa. It is used to convert written content into spoken form for audiobook and podcast production. TTS can instantly convert text into spoken language in various languages, enabling global communication and information dissemination. It is used in voice-activated systems, making it possible to interact with devices, applications and websites through speech commands. TTS is commonly used for audiobooks, podcast narration and other forms of spoken content.

2.4.3 Speech-to-Text (STT)

STT technology converts spoken words and phrases into written text, providing a convenient and efficient way for users to transcribe spoken content. Speech-to-text solutions often support multiple languages and dialects, making them versatile tools for users across diverse linguistic backgrounds. Often these systems offer real-time recognition capabilities, allowing users to see the transcribed text as they speak. This feature is beneficial for live transcription, dictation and accessibility applications. STT functionality is frequently integrated into various applications, such as voice assistants, transcription services and accessibility tools, enhancing user interactions and enabling hands-free or voice-activated commands (Jurafsky & Martin, 2013).

STT technology involves several key steps. The STT system receives an audio input, typically in the form of spoken language. The system pre-processes the audio, which may involve noise reduction and audio enhancement to improve accuracy. STT technology analyzes the audio to identify phonetic components, words and sentences, after which language models are employed to understand and interpret the spoken language, considering grammar, syntax and context. The technology produces a textual representation of the spoken content, which can be used for various purposes.

STT technology makes spoken content accessible to individuals with hearing impairments by providing real-time captions. STT automates transcription, saving time for professionals, researchers and content creators. STT is a core component of virtual assistants like Siri, Google Assistant and Alexa, enabling voice interaction. STT provides live captions for events, broadcasts and presentations, enhancing accessibility.

2.4.4 Natural Language Processing (NLP)

NLP is a field of artificial intelligence that focuses on the interaction between computers and human language. NLP has traditionally been associated with text data. However, as the volume of multimedia data (text, images, audio and video) continues to grow, the integration of NLP techniques into multimedia analysis has become increasingly important. For example, combining the transcript (text) of a video with its visual content (frames) and audio (speech) can aid in content summarization or indexing (Eisenstein, 2019).

NLP is integral to various applications in the digital age. It enhances human-computer and human-human communication by enabling language understanding and generation. NLP automates the analysis of vast textual data, deriving insights, sentiment analysis and knowledge extraction. It is fundamental to search engines, enabling users to find relevant information through keyword searches. It powers chatbots and virtual assistants, facilitating natural and interactive interactions.

Breaking text into individual words or tokens is a fundamental step for text analysis, called tokenization. In the next step comes stemming where words are reduced to their base forms by stripping affixes. Next grammatical tags are assigned to words to understand their roles in sentences. This is followed by named entity recognition (NER) which is identifying and categorizing named entities such as names, locations and organizations. Parsing sentences to understand their structure and relationships between words is called syntax analysis while extracting meaning from text, including sentiment, intent and context is called semantic analysis. Finally machine learning algorithms are used to build models for text classification, translation, summarization and more.

NLP in multimedia has a wide range of applications, including content-based retrieval, where using text, audio or image queries are used to retrieve multimedia content from large databases. Sentiment analysis in videos involves analyzing spoken or text data in videos to detect sentiment or emotions, commonly used for product reviews and social media monitoring. Automated image captioning involves generating descriptive captions for images without human intervention. Other applications include building chatbots that can understand and respond to text and voice input, automatically translating text between languages, enabling global communication, creating concise summaries of long texts, saving time for readers, developing systems that can understand and answer questions based on text input, and categorizing documents into predefined classes for information retrieval.

2.4.5 Text Localization (L10n)

Text localization, often abbreviated as L10n (where "10" represents the number of letters omitted between "L" and "n"), is a crucial process in the realm of digital content that involves adapting products, services or applications to meet the linguistic, cultural and functional expectations of a specific locale or target audience, and in the process, encompassing a holistic adaptation that considers language cultural contexts, and regional preferences. On the other hand, text internationalization, often denoted by the abbreviation I18n (where "18" represents the number of letters omitted between "I" and "n"), is a foundational step that focuses on designing and building applications to be culturally and linguistically adaptable for diverse global audiences. Unlike localization (L10n), which involves adapting a product for a specific locale, internationalization is about creating a framework that supports seamless adaptation to various languages and cultural contexts [w3.org/International/questions/qa-i18n.en.html].

Effective localization significantly improves the user experience by making digital content more accessible and relatable to a diverse audience. Users are more likely to engage with content that feels familiar and aligns with their cultural expectations. For businesses and organizations expanding into international markets, localization is instrumental in breaking down language barriers and making products or services appealing to a broader customer base. It facilitates market penetration by establishing a connection with local consumers. By adapting branding elements and messaging to align with local norms, organizations can ensure that their brand is perceived consistently and positively. Localization also ensures that digital content complies with local laws and regulations. This is crucial for avoiding legal issues and building trust with users in different regions. Internationalizing content ensures that it can be readily adapted to various languages and regions, broadening its global reach. Internationalization involves removing cultural and language-specific elements, making content culturally neutral and adaptable. Additionally, internationalized content streamlines the localization process, reducing duplication of effort and cost. By internationalizing content upfront, it becomes easier to localize it for specific markets or regions.

At the core of localization is language translation. However, it's not a straightforward one-to-one conversion; it involves understanding idioms, expressions and linguistic nuances specific to the target audience. Skilled translators play a pivotal role in ensuring the accuracy and cultural relevance of the content. Localization extends beyond language to include cultural elements. This encompasses the adaptation of visuals, symbols, colors and even the overall design to resonate with the cultural preferences of the target audience. Different regions follow distinct date and time formats. Localization involves adapting these formats to align with local conventions, ensuring that dates, times and other temporal references are presented in a familiar and understandable manner. Numeric conventions, such as the representation of decimal points and thousands separators, vary across cultures. Localization ensures that numerical data is formatted according to the preferences of the target audience. Localization also takes into account legal and regulatory requirements specific to a particular region. This includes compliance with privacy laws, data protection regulations and other legal considerations that may vary from one locale to another.

2.4.6 Text Internationalization (I18n)

For internationalization, the first step might be to utilize Unicode for text encoding which allows content to represent various languages and scripts. Also involves ensuring that dates, times and calendars can be adjusted for different regions and cultures, as well as adapting numerical formats, such as currency, measurement units and numerical symbols, for specific locales. Implementing language detection mechanisms help to serve content in the user's preferred language or region, for example implementing support for bidirectional text when dealing with languages that are written from right to left, such as Arabic or Hebrew ensures proper rendering and readability. Other considerations include designing the application to dynamically load content based on the user's language preference, and ensuring cultural sensitivity by avoiding images symbols or idiomatic expressions that may be inappropriate or offensive in certain cultural contexts.

2.4.7 Text in AR and VR

Text in AR (augmented reality) delivers information, and seamlessly integrating digital content with the real world. AR text provides real-time information and context that enhances the understanding of the physical environment. It enables interaction with digital content in the real world, blurring the lines between physical and digital experiences. AR text can guide users, offering instructions, explanations and navigation cues in a user-friendly manner and provide valuable tools for education, training and skill development in a wide range of fields. VR (virtual reality) text allows users to communicate with each other and interact with the virtual environment. It conveys information, instructions and context that enrich the virtual experience. VR text is also a valuable tool for learning, training and skill development in diverse fields. Moreover, it provides an essential component of narrative and storytelling in VR content and games (Doerner et al., 2022).

AR devices, such as smart glasses or mobile apps, display text in the user's field of view, ensuring it's seamlessly integrated with the real world. AR technology recognizes the physical environment, allowing text to be anchored to specific locations or objects. It can provide dynamic information, such as live translations, real-time data or context-aware instructions. Users can often interact with AR text, either through touch or voice commands, enhancing user engagement. AR often combines text with other sensory inputs, such as audio or haptic feedback, for a more immersive experience.

VR environments incorporate text elements within the digital landscape, providing information, labels and messages. VR text can appear as part of the virtual world or as overlays on a user's display. Users may interact with VR text through gaze, gesture or controllers, enabling actions like selecting, typing or scrolling. Audio cues and text-to-speech technology enhance the immersive experience and assist in reading text content. VR text can be dynamic, responding to user input, context or real-time data.

2.5 Legal and Ethical Considerations

The rapid advancements in digital text processing technologies bring about a host of legal and ethical considerations that demand careful attention. As these tools become integral parts of various industries, from healthcare to finance and beyond, it is crucial to navigate the complex landscape of legal frameworks and ethical guidelines to ensure responsible and accountable use (Iglezakis & Synodinou, 2010).

2.5.1 Legal Considerations

Data Privacy and Compliance: Digital text processing often involves the analysis of large volumes of textual data, potentially containing sensitive information. Adherence to data protection regulations, such as the General Data Protection Regulation (GDPR) [eur-lex.europa.eu] in the European Union, is essential. Ensuring proper consent and secure storage are critical components of compliance.

Intellectual Property Rights: Textual data often includes copyrighted material. Digital text processing systems must respect intellectual property rights, avoiding unauthorized use or reproduction of copyrighted content. NLP applications should be designed to comply with copyright laws and fair use principles.

Liability and Accountability: As automated text processing systems make decisions or provide insights, questions of liability arise. Determining responsibility in cases of errors, biases or adverse outcomes becomes a legal challenge. Establishing clear guidelines and accountability frameworks is crucial to mitigate legal risks.

Regulatory Compliance in Specific Industries: Different industries may have specific regulations governing the use of digital text processing technologies. For instance, healthcare applications need to comply with regulations of the U.S. Department of Health and Human Services [hhs.gov], while financial applications must adhere to guidelines set by financial regulatory bodies, like the U.S. Securities and Exchange Commission [www.sec.gov]. Understanding and conforming to industry-specific regulations is imperative.

2.5.2 Ethical Considerations

Bias and Fairness: Digital text processing models can inadvertently perpetuate biases present in training data. Ensuring fairness and equity in the outcomes of these systems is a significant ethical concern. Developers must actively work to identify and mitigate biases in both training data and algorithms.

Transparency and Explainability: The opacity of complex text processing models raises ethical questions about transparency. Users and stakeholders may demand explanations for decisions made by these systems. Striving for transparency and developing interpretable models can enhance trust and accountability.

Informed Consent: Users should be adequately informed about how their textual data is being processed and for what purposes. Obtaining informed consent is not only a legal requirement in many jurisdictions but also an ethical principle that respects individuals' autonomy and privacy.

Social and Cultural Sensitivity: Digital text processing systems need to be culturally and socially sensitive. Language nuances, cultural contexts and regional variations must be considered to avoid perpetuating stereotypes or unintentionally causing offence. Ethical guidelines should incorporate considerations for diverse audiences.

Security and Misuse Prevention: Ensuring the security of textual data and preventing misuse are ethical imperatives. Safeguarding against malicious use, such as the generation of fake news or manipulation of information, is crucial to maintaining the integrity of digital text processing applications.

In navigating the legal and ethical landscape of digital text processing, a proactive and multidisciplinary approach is essential. Collaboration between technologists, legal experts, ethicists and stakeholders can contribute to the development and implementation of responsible and ethical practices in the use of these powerful technologies.

2.6 Challenges and Emerging Trends

Digital text processing, involves the manipulation, analysis and understanding of textual data using computational methods, and has witnessed remarkable advancements in recent years. However, along with these advancements come several challenges that researchers and practitioners need to address. Additionally, emerging trends are shaping the landscape of digital text processing, paving the way for novel applications and improved methodologies (Zaramenskikh & Fedorova, 2020).

2.6.1 Challenges

Ambiguity and Contextual Understanding: Ambiguity in natural language poses a significant challenge for digital text processing systems. Words often have multiple meanings based on context, making it difficult for algorithms to accurately interpret and process the intended message.

Lack of Annotated Data: Building robust machine learning models for text processing relies heavily on annotated datasets. The scarcity of high-quality, domain-specific labeled data hinders the development of accurate and generalizable models.

Cross-Lingual Processing: Processing text across multiple languages remains a challenging task. Differences in syntax, semantics and cultural nuances make it difficult to create universally applicable models, requiring sophisticated techniques for cross-lingual understanding.

Ethical and Bias Concerns: Biases present in training data can be perpetuated by text processing models, leading to biased outcomes. Ensuring fairness and mitigating biases in natural language processing systems is an ongoing challenge that demands attention to ethical considerations.

Dynamic Nature of Language: Language evolves over time, introducing new words, phrases and meanings. Digital text processing systems must adapt to these changes to maintain relevance and accuracy, which poses a constant challenge for model developers.

2.6.2 Emerging Trends

Explainability and Interpretability: As text processing models become more complex, there is a growing emphasis on making them interpretable and explainable. Understanding the decision-making process of models is crucial, especially in sensitive applications like healthcare and finance.

Transformative Power of Pre-trained Models: Pre-trained language models, such as BERT (Bidirectional Encoder Representations from Transformers) and GPT (Generative Pre-trained Transformers), have demonstrated remarkable capabilities in various text processing tasks. Fine-tuning these models on domain-specific data allows for efficient transfer learning, reducing the need for extensive labeled datasets.

Advancements in Multimodal Processing: Integrating text with other modalities, such as images and videos, is an emerging trend. Multimodal models enable a more comprehensive understanding of content, opening avenues for applications in areas like content recommendation and sentiment analysis.

Zero-shot and Few-shot Learning: Efforts are being made to develop models that can perform tasks with minimal or no task-specific training examples. Zero-shot and few-shot learning approaches are gaining traction, allowing models to generalize across a broader range of tasks.

Focus on User-Centric Applications: The field is increasingly moving toward applications that prioritize user experience. Sentiment analysis, chatbots and personalized content recommendations showcase the shift toward tailoring digital text processing solutions to meet individual user needs.

In conclusion, while digital text processing has made significant strides, overcoming challenges related to language ambiguity, bias and cross-lingual processing remains at the forefront. The field's future lies in addressing these challenges while embracing emerging trends that contribute to more interpretable, adaptable and user-centric text processing systems.

2.7 Text File Formats

2.7.1 TXT

Plain Text (.txt): A plain text file format, often denoted by the file extension ".txt", is a simple file format that contains only unformatted text. In a plain text file, each line of text is terminated by a newline character, and there are no special formatting or styling elements such as fonts, colors or images. Plain text files are commonly used for storing textual data that does not require any formatting, such as program source code, configuration files, log files and simple documents. They are supported by virtually all text editors and word processors, making them widely accessible and easy to work with across different platforms and applications.

2.7.2 CSV

Comma-Separated Values (.csv): CSV is a simple and widely used file format for storing tabular data in plain text. In a CSV file, each line represents a record, and fields within each record are separated by commas or other delimiter characters, such as semicolons or tabs. CSV files are easy to create, read and edit using simple text editors or spreadsheet software and they can be imported and exported by most spreadsheet applications, database systems and programming languages. CSV files support various delimiters (not limited to commas) and can include special characters, making them versatile for different data formats and requirements.

2.7.3 DOC, DOCX

Microsoft Word Document (.doc, .docx): DOC and DOCX are file formats used for documents created by Microsoft Word, a popular word processing application [www.microsoft.com/en-us/microsoft-365/word]. The .doc extension is associated with the DOC format, which was the default file format used by earlier versions of Microsoft Word, up to Word 2003. DOC files are binary files containing formatted text, images, tables and other elements. The.docx extension is associated with the DOCX format, which is the default file format used by Microsoft Word since Word 2007. DOCX files are based on the Open XML standard and are essentially ZIP archives containing XML files, media files and other resources. They use XML to store document content, formatting and structure, making them more interoperable and compatible with other software applications. DOCX files are more efficient in terms of file size and offer improved data recovery capabilities compared to the older DOC format. Additionally, DOCX files support features such as document encryption, content controls and compatibility modes for earlier versions of Word.

2.7.4 PDF

Portable Document Format (.pdf): PDF is a file format developed by Adobe [pdfa.org/resource/pdf-specification-archive] that preserves the layout, formatting, fonts and images of a document, regardless of the software or operating system used to view it. PDF files can be viewed and printed on any device or operating system without requiring the original software used to create the document. This platform independence makes PDFs widely accessible and ensures consistent display across different devices and platforms. PDF files maintain a fixed layout, preserving the exact positioning of text, images and other elements as they appear in the original document, which ensures that the document's visual appearance remains consistent, regardless of the device or screen size. PDF files support interactive features such as hyperlinks, bookmarks, form fields, multimedia elements (audio and video) and annotations, makes them suitable for a wide range of applications, including forms, presentations and e-books. The files can be encrypted and password-protected to restrict access, prevent unauthorized copying or modification and ensure document security. Encryption options include password protection, certificate-based security and digital signatures, providing robust security features for sensitive documents. The files support various compression methods to reduce file size without compromising the quality of the content. Compression techniques such as image compression (e.g., JPEG and ZIP compression) and font embedding help optimize PDF files for efficient storage, transmission and distribution. It is an open standard maintained by ISO [www.iso.org/standard/75839.html], ensuring its compatibility and interoperability with a wide range of software applications and devices.

2.7.5 DJVU

DjVu (.djvu): DJVU [www.djvuzone.org] is a file format primarily used for storing scanned documents, especially those containing a combination of text, line drawings, indexed color images and photographs. Developed by AT&T Labs, DJVU files are designed to provide high-quality document compression while maintaining readability and image quality. DJVU files use advanced compression techniques, including wavelet-based compression algorithms to achieve high levels of compression without significant loss of quality. This makes DJVU files suitable for storing large volumes of scanned documents efficiently. The files typically consist of multiple layers, including a background layer containing the main document content (usually text), foreground layers containing high-resolution images or photographs, and optional mask layers for enhancing image quality and compression. One of the key features of DJVU files is the ability to separate the text layer from the image layer. This allows for text to be stored separately and rendered at different resolutions, enabling efficient text searching, copying and extraction from DJVU documents. It is an open file format, and its specifications are publicly available, which allows for interoperability between different software applications and platforms, ensuring compatibility and accessibility. While DJVU files can be viewed using specialized viewers, such as DjVuLibre [djvu.sourceforge.net], they can also be viewed using Web browsers with appropriate plug-ins installed. DJVU files are commonly used for storing scanned documents, ebooks, academic papers, technical manuals and other types of documents that require high-quality compression and efficient storage.

2.7.6 RTF

Rich Text Format (.rtf): RTF is a document file format developed by Microsoft in the 1980s for cross-platform document interchange. They are plain text files that can contain some formatting information and are human-readable and editable using any text editor as they consist of ASCII text with embedded formatting commands. A variety of formatting information is supported, including font styles (e.g., bold, italic), font sizes, font colors, paragraph alignment, line spacing and text attributes (e.g., superscript, subscript). RTF files can contain metadata, such as document properties (e.g., title, author, subject), creation date, modification date and document version information. The files are compatible with a wide range of word processing software, including Microsoft Word, LibreOffice Writer and Google Docs.

2.7.7 ODF

Open Document Format (.odf): An open standard XML-based file format for office documents, maintained by OASIS (Organization for Advancement of Structured Information Standards) [www.oasis-open.org/committees/office]. ODF documents are based on a modular structure, with each type of document (text, spreadsheet, presentation, etc.) represented as a collection of XML files within a ZIP archive. This modular approach allows for efficient storage, management and manipulation of document content and metadata. ODF files can be created, edited and viewed using a wide range of office productivity software, including LibreOffice, Apache OpenOffice, Calligra Suite and Microsoft Office (with compatibility plugins) and can be exchanged and accessed across different operating systems, including Windows-, macOS-, Linux- and Unix-based systems. They can contain text, graphics, formulas, charts, tables and other elements and can be converted into alternative formats, such as HTML or plain text. ODF also supports encryption and digital signatures, allowing users to protect sensitive document content and verify document authenticity and integrity. The format has been standardized as ISO/IEC 26300 [www.iso.org/standard/66363.html].

2.7.8 EPUB

Electronic Publication (.epub): Developed by the International Digital Publishing Forum (IDPF) [www.idpf.org], EPUB is based on open Web standards and is designed to provide a flexible and accessible format for distributing electronic books across different devices and platforms. EPUB documents contain reflowable text, which means that text and images can adapt to different screen sizes and orientations, which allows readers to adjust font sizes, margins and line spacing according to their preferences, enhancing readability and accessibility on various devices, including e-readers, tablets and smartphones. EPUB documents are based on HTML, CSS and XML technologies and can include interactive elements, such as hyperlinks, multimedia content (audio, video) and scripting capabilities (JavaScript), allowing for enhanced reading experiences and interactivity in digital publications. It also supports DRM (Digital Rights Management) solutions for protecting copyright and controlling access to digital publications. EPUB version 3 has been declared as a standard by W3C [www.w3.org/publishing/epub3].

2.8 Coding Examples Using MATLAB®

The function `text' inserts text descriptions in graphical plots at specified locations, as shown in Example 2.1. Arguments can be used to specify font and size (Figure 2.9).

EXAMPLE 2.1 MATLAB EXAMPLE TO DISPLAY TEXT IN DIFFERENT SIZES AND FONTS

```
figure; axis;
text(0.1, 0.6, 'Normal Text',
   'FontSize', 12);
text(0.1, 0.4, 'Larger Text',
   'FontSize', 16);
text(0.5, 0.5, 'Arial', 'FontName',
   'Arial', 'FontSize', 20);
text(0.5, 0.3, 'Times New Roman',
   'FontName', 'Times New Roman',
   'FontSize', 20);
```

```
text(0.8, 0.2, 'Script', 'FontName',
   'Brush Script MT Italic',
   'FontSize', 20);
text(0.7, 0.1, '\fontname{Courier}
   \fontsize{15} Courier');
```

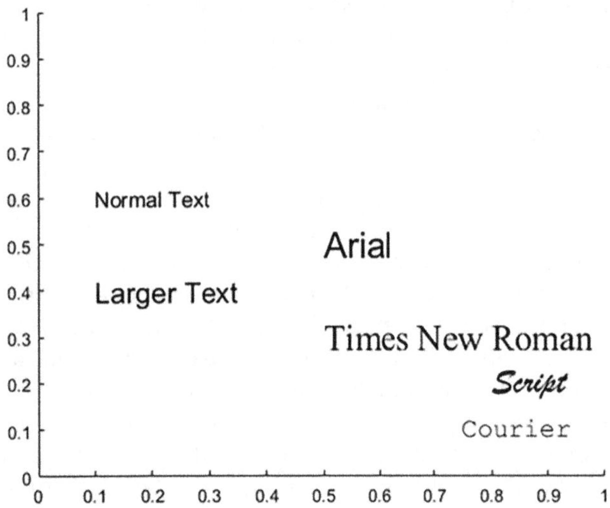

FIGURE 2.9
Output of Example 2.1.

Different styles like bold, italics, superscript, subscript can be specified as arguments to the 'text' function, as shown in Example 2.2 (Figure 2.10).

Text color can be specified either using a color name or using RGB triplets, as shown in Example 2.3 (Figure 2.11).

EXAMPLE 2.2 MATLAB EXAMPLE TO DISPLAY TEXT IN DIFFERENT STYLES

```
figure; axis;
text(0.1, 0.6, 'Normal Text',
   'FontSize', 20);
text(0.2, 0.5, 'Bold Text', 'FontSize',
   20, 'FontWeight', 'bold');
text(0.3, 0.4, 'Italic Text',
   'FontSize', 20, 'FontAngle',
   'italic');
text(0.6, 0.6, 'Text^{superscript}',
   'FontSize', 20);
text(0.6, 0.5, 'Text_{subscript}',
   'FontSize', 20);
text(0.6, 0.4, '\bf Bold Text',
   'FontSize', 20);
text(0.6, 0.3, '\it Italic Text',
   'FontSize', 20);
```

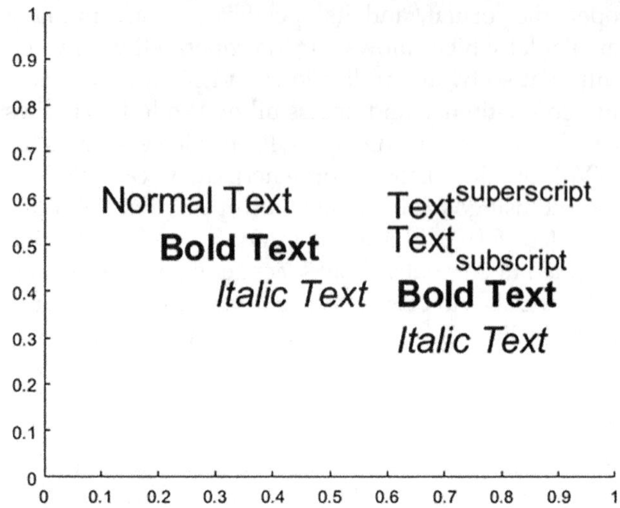

FIGURE 2.10
Output of Example 2.2.

EXAMPLE 2.3 MATLAB EXAMPLE TO DISPLAY TEXT IN DIFFERENT COLORS

```
figure; axis;
text(0.1, 0.6, 'Normal Text',
   'FontSize', 20);
text(0.2, 0.5, 'Red Text', 'FontSize',
   20, 'Color', 'red');
text(0.3, 0.4, 'Magenta Text',
   'FontSize', 20, 'Color', [1 0 1]);
text(0.4, 0.3, '\color{cyan} \
   fontsize{15} Cyan Color Size 15');
text(0.5, 0.2, '\color[rgb]{0.8500
   0.3250 0.0980} Brown text
   default size');
```

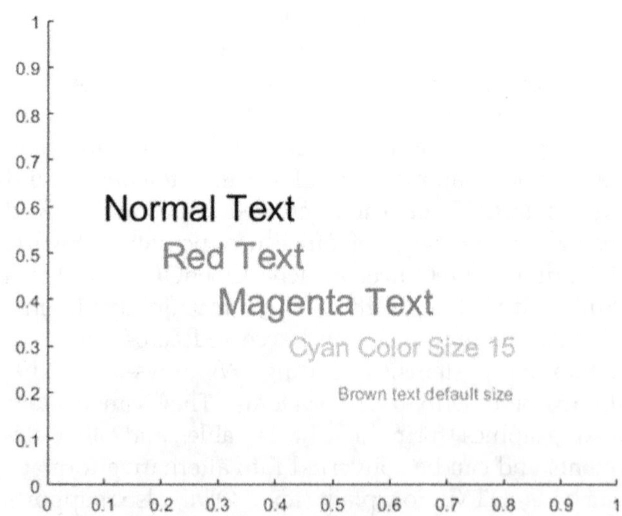

FIGURE 2.11
Output of Example 2.3.

Greek alphabets and mathematical symbols can be specified using a backslash followed by reserved keywords, as shown in Example 2.4 (Figure 2.12).

EXAMPLE 2.4 MATLAB EXAMPLE TO DISPLAY GREEK LETTERS AND MATHEMATICAL SYMBOLS

```
figure; axis;
text(0.1, 0.7, '\alpha',
   'FontSize', 20);
text(0.1, 0.6, '\beta',
   'FontSize', 20);
text(0.1, 0.5, '\gamma',
   'FontSize', 20);
text(0.1, 0.4, '\delta',
   'FontSize', 20);
text(0.1, 0.3, '\theta',
   'FontSize', 20);
text(0.1, 0.2, '\sigma',
   'FontSize', 20);
text(0.1, 0.1, '\pi', 'FontSize', 20);
text(0.3, 0.7, '\Phi', 'FontSize', 20);
text(0.3, 0.6, '\Omega',
   'FontSize', 20);
text(0.3, 0.5, '\Gamma',
   'FontSize', 20);
text(0.3, 0.4, '\Delta',
   'FontSize', 20);
text(0.3, 0.3, '\Theta',
   'FontSize', 20);
text(0.3, 0.2, '\Sigma',
   'FontSize', 20);
text(0.3, 0.1, '\Pi', 'FontSize', 20);
text(0.5, 0.7, '\forall',
   'FontSize', 20);
text(0.5, 0.6, '\cong',
   'FontSize', 20);
text(0.5, 0.5, '\approx',
   'FontSize', 20);
text(0.5, 0.4, '\Re', 'FontSize', 20);
text(0.5, 0.3, '\oplus',
   'FontSize', 20);
text(0.5, 0.2, '\surd',
   'FontSize', 20);
text(0.5, 0.1, '\leq', 'FontSize', 20);
text(0.7, 0.7, '\infty',
   'FontSize', 20);
text(0.7, 0.6, '\leftarrow',
   'FontSize', 20);
text(0.7, 0.5, '\rightarrow',
   'FontSize', 20);
text(0.7, 0.4, '\Rightarrow',
   'FontSize', 20);
text(0.7, 0.3, '\pm', 'FontSize', 20);
text(0.7, 0.2, '\partial',
   'FontSize', 20);
text(0.7, 0.1, '\propto',
   'FontSize', 20);
text(0.7, 0.9, '\int_1^{20} x^2 dx',
   'FontName', 'Times New Roman',
   'FontSize', 20);
```

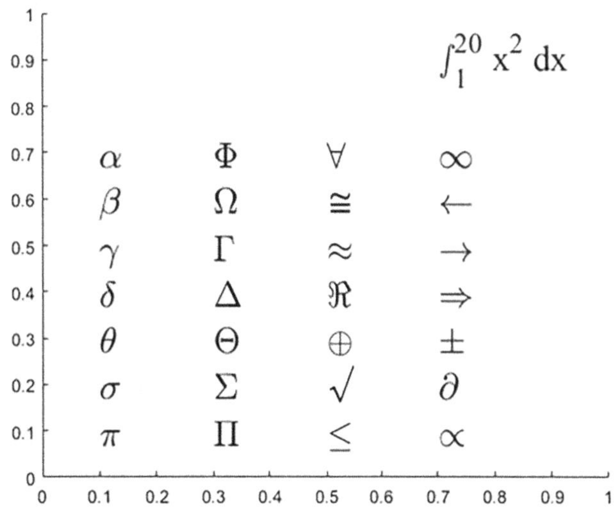

FIGURE 2.12
Output of Example 2.4.

The functions 'imread' reads an image from a file into the system, 'ocr' recognizes text using optical character recognition (OCR), 'msgbox' creates a message box to display textual messages, as illustrated in Example 2.5 (Figure 2.13).

EXAMPLE 2.5 MATLAB EXAMPLE TO READ TEXT FROM IMAGE USING OCR

```
I = imread('businessCard.png');
textFromImage = ocr(I);
msgbox(textFromImage.Text);
```

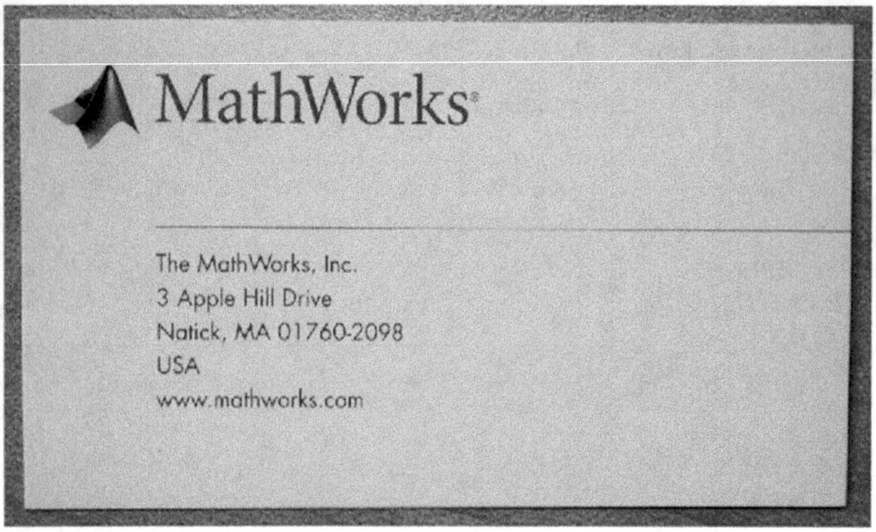

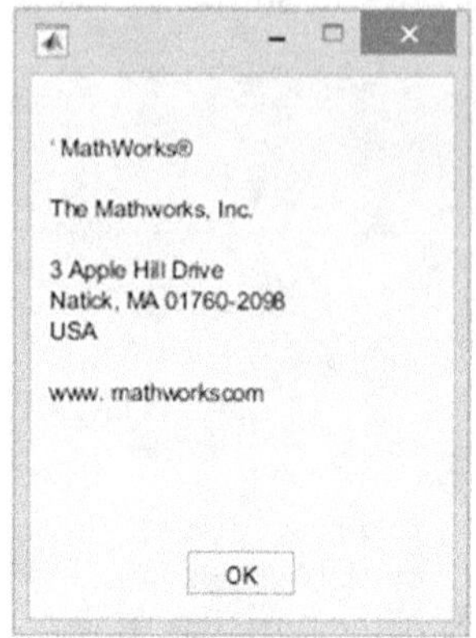

FIGURE 2.13
Output of Example 2.5.

The function 'datetime' displays date and time for specific locales around the world and in specific formats, as shown in Example 2.6

EXAMPLE 2.6 MATLAB EXAMPLE TO DISPLAY DATE AND TIME FOR VARIOUS LOCALES

```
clear; clc; format compact;
disp('local');
t = datetime('now','TimeZone','local','
   Format','d-MMM-y HH:mm:ss Z')
disp('Africa/Johannesburg');
t = datetime('now','TimeZone','Afr
   ica/Johannesburg','Format','d-MMM-y
   HH:mm:ss Z')
disp('America/Chicago');
t = datetime('now','TimeZone','Ame
   rica/Chicago','Format','d-MMM-y
   HH:mm:ss Z')
disp('America/New_York');
t = datetime('now','TimeZone','Ame
   rica/New_York','Format','d-MMM-y
   HH:mm:ss Z')
disp('Asia/Kolkata');
t = datetime('now','TimeZone','Asia/
   Kolkata','Format','d-MMM-y
   HH:mm:ss Z')
disp('Australia/Sydney');
t = datetime('now','TimeZone','Aus
   tralia/Sydney','Format','d-MMM-y
   HH:mm:ss Z')
disp('Europe/London');
t = datetime('now','TimeZone','Eu
   rope/London','Format','d-MMM-y
   HH:mm:ss Z')
```

The following example 2.7 positions and orients a text string in a 3D environment. The functions "xlabel", "ylabel", "zlabel" label the x-axis, y-axis and z-axis of a graphical plot. The function "view" sets the viewing parameters, azimuth and elevation, for viewing a 3D plot from a specific viewpoint, "grid" displays grid lines in a plot (Figure 2.14).

EXAMPLE 2.7 MATLAB EXAMPLE TO POSITION AND ORIENT TEXT IN A 3D ENVIRONMENT

```
clear; clc;
position = [.5, .5, 1]; % X, Y, Z
   coordinates
xlabel('x'); ylabel('y'); zlabel('z');
axis square; view(-10, 30); grid;
textObj = text('Position', position, ...
    'Rotation', 60, 'String',
      'Hello, VR', ...
    'EdgeColor', 'r',
      'BackgroundColor', 'y', ...
    'LineStyle', '--', 'LineWidth',
      1.5, ...
    'FontSize', 12, 'FontWeight',
      'bold');
```

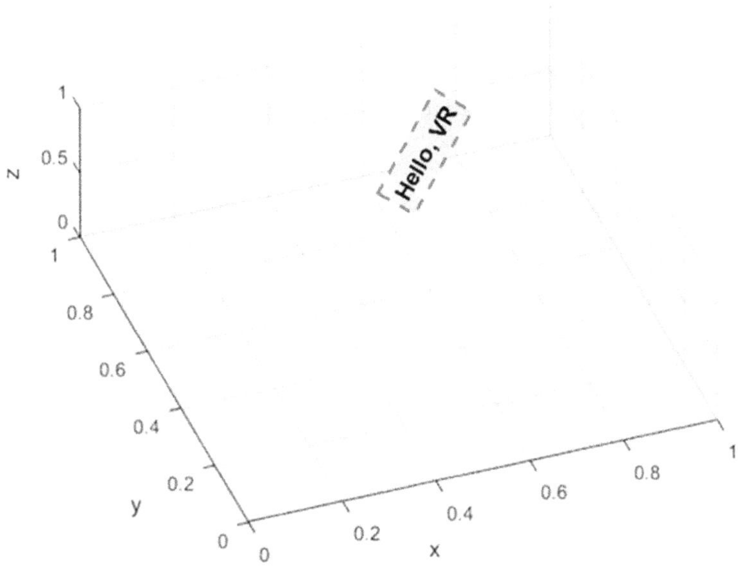

FIGURE 2.14
Output of Example 2.7.

The following example 2.8 demonstrates printing of a word cloud. The function "wordcloud" creates a word cloud chart with sizes of the words proportional to their counts, i.e., the number of times they occur.

> **EXAMPLE 2.8 MATLAB EXAMPLE TO CREATE WORD CLOUD**
>
> ```
> clear; clc;
> load sonnetsTable
> tbl
> wordcloud(tbl,'Word','Count');
> ```

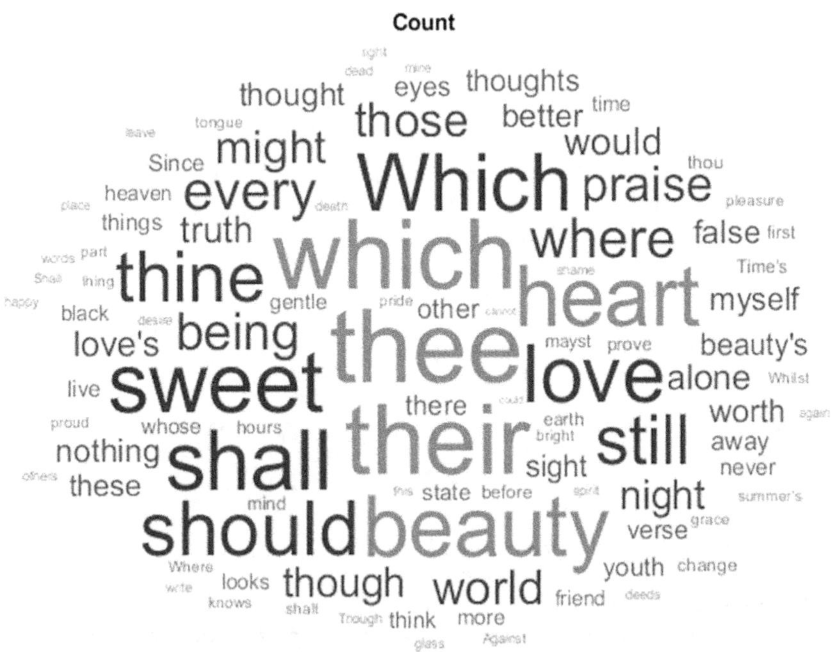

FIGURE 2.15
Output of Example 2.8.

The following example 2.9 demonstrates text processing by reading a paragraph of text, counting the number of words and displaying them in descending order of frequencies. The functions "extractBefore" extracts a portion of a text before a specified string, "lower" converts to lowercase, "split" splits text using whitespace characters, "replace" replaces text strings, "containers.Map" creates a data structure to store the words and their counts.

EXAMPLE 2.9 MATLAB EXAMPLE TO COUNT WORDS IN A PARAGRAPH

```
clear; clc;

%read input text file
textData = string(fileread('sonnets.txt'));
textData = extractBefore(textData,"II")

% Convert text to lowercase
textData = lower(textData)

% Tokenization: Split text into words
words = split(textData)

% Remove punctuation marks
punctuationCharacters = ["." "?" "!" "," ";" ":"];
textData = replace(textData,punctuationCharacters,'')

% Create a map to store word frequencies
word_map = containers.Map;

% Count the frequency of each word
for i = 1:numel(words)
    word = words{i};
    if isKey(word_map, word)
        word_map(word) = word_map(word) + 1;
    else
        word_map(word) = 1;
    end
end

% Display the word frequencies
fprintf('\nSorted in alphabetical order ...\n');
fprintf('Word\t\tFrequency\n');
fprintf('-----------------------\n');
keys = word_map.keys;
values = word_map.values;
for i = 1:numel(keys)
    fprintf('%s\t\t%d\n', keys{i}, values{i});
end

fprintf('\nSorted in descending order of frequencies ...\n');
fprintf('Word\t\tFrequency\n');
fprintf('-----------------------\n');

[word_frequencies_sorted, idx] = sort(cell2mat(word_map.values), 'descend');
words_sorted = keys(idx);
for i=1:1:numel(words_sorted)
    fprintf('%s\t\t%d\n', words_sorted{i}, word_frequencies_sorted(i));
end
```

```
Sorted in alphabetical order ...          Sorted in descending order of frequencies ...
Word          Frequency                    Word            Frequency
------------------------                   ------------------------
                  1                        the                7
a                 1                        thy                5
abundance         1                        to                 4
and               3                        and                3
art               1                        by                 3
as                1                        but                2
be                1                        his                2
bear              1                        might              2
beauty's          1                        own                2
bright            1                        self               2
bud               1                        tender             2
buriest           1                        that               2
but               2                        thine              2
by                3
```

FIGURE 2.16
Output of Example 2.9.

The following example 2.10 demonstrates removing some common stop words from the text paragraph before counting the frequencies of words. The functions "regexprep" replace text using regular expression, "strsplit" splits strings using whitespace characters, "setdiff" returns values in the first argument that are not in the second argument. Here "regexprep" removes all strings not starting with alphanumeric characters and followed by a white space, i.e., all punctuation marks, and "setdiff" returns the original text after removing the stop words and all repetitions.

EXAMPLE 2.10 MATLAB EXAMPLE TO REMOVE COMMON WORDS

```
clear; clc;
sonnets = string(fileread('sonnets.txt'));
file_contents = extractBefore(sonnets,"III");

% Convert to lowercase to ensure case-insensitive counting
file_contents = lower(file_contents);

% Remove punctuation marks
file_contents = regexprep(file_contents, '[^\w\s]', '');

% Split the text into words
words = strsplit(file_contents);
numel(words)

% Remove stop words (common words that do not carry much meaning)
stopWords = {'the', 'and', 'is', 'are', 'in', 'on', 'at', 'to', 'for', 'of',
'a', 'an'};
cleanedWords = setdiff(words, stopWords);

numel(cleanedWords)
```

Review Questions

- Trace the historical evolution of text processing highlighting landmark events.
- Mention the utilities of text as an element in multimedia content.
- Explain the multimodal nature of text.
- What are the techniques of text rendering?
- Discuss how digital text is represented by ASCII character set.
- What are the main features and benefits of Unicode character set?
- What are the benefits of digital text editing?
- What the benefits and techniques of text extraction?
- What is text transformation, and what are the techniques for implementing it?
- What is text enhancement, and what are the techniques for implementing it?
- What is the importance of typography and font in digital text design?
- Mention some of the techniques of text effects used in digital communication.
- How can text animation be implemented to make content visually engaging?
- Describe with examples role of HTML, CSS and JavaScript in Web design.
- How can SVG be used to create graphical content on the Web?
- Specify techniques and advantages of TTS and STT applications.
- What are the methods and applications of NLP?
- Differentiate between text localization and text internationalization.
- How is text incorporated in AR and VR environments?
- What are the legal and ethical considerations for text content?
- Mention some of the challenges and emerging trends related to textual content.
- Describe features of important text file formats.

References

Boss, S., J. C. Teague, *The new Web typography*, CRC Press, 2017

Chaudhuri, B. B., *Digital document processing: Major directions and recent advances*, Springer London, 2007.

Danielsson, K., S. Selander, *Multimodal texts in disciplinary education: A comprehensive framework*, Springer Switzerland, 2021.

Deegan, M., K. Sutherland, *Text editing, print and the digital world*, Routledge, 2016.

Doerner, R., W. Broll, P. Grimm & B. Jung (eds), *Virtual and augmented reality (VR/AR)*, Springer Nature Switzerland, 2022.

Duckett, J., *HTML and CSS: Design and build websites*, John Wiley & Sons, 2014

Dutoit, T., *An introduction to text to speech synthesis*, Springer Netherlands, 2013.

Eisenstein, J., *Introduction to natural language processing*, MIT Press, 2019

Flanagan, D., *JavaScript: the definitive guide*, O'Reilly Media, 2017.

Frain, B., *Responsive Web design with HTML5 and CSS*, Packt Publishing Ltd., 2022.

Gillam, R., *Unicode demystified: A practical programmer's guide to the encoding standard*, Addison-Wesley Professional, 2003.

Godse, A. P., D A Godse, *Multimedia technologies"*, Technical Publications, 2020.

Goodman, D., *Dynamic HTML – the definitive reference*, O'Reilly Media, 2007

Iglezakis, I., T.-E. Synodinou (eds), *E-publishing and digital libraries: Legal and organizational issues*, IGI Global, 2010.

Jurafsky, D., J. H. Martin, *Speech and language processing*, Pearson Education India, 2013.

Prettyman, S., *Learn PHP 7: object oriented modular programming using HTML5, CSS3, JavaScript, XML, JSON and MySQL*, Apress, 2016.

Robbins, J. N., *Learning Web design: A beginner's guide to HTML, CSS, JavScript and Web graphics*, O'Reilly Media, 2012.

Royds, A. B., K. Cagle & D. Storey, *Using SVG with CSS3 and HTML5*, O'Reilly Media, 2018.

White, B., *HTML and the art of authoring for the World Wide Web*, Springer US, 2012.

Zaramenskikh, E., A. Fedorova, *Digital transformation and new challenges*, Springer Nature Switzerland, 2020.

3

Image

3.1 Image Fundamentals

3.1.1 Key Terms

We begin with a snapshot of the important terms relevant to the field of digital imaging, to present the entire chapter in a nutshell. These terms will be expanded in the subsequent sections of the chapter in their proper contexts.

2D Coordinate system: A 2D Cartesian coordinate system, named after the French mathematician Rene Descartes, is used to measure the location of a point with respect to a reference point known as the origin. The location is represented as a pair of offsets measured along two orthogonal directions, the x-axis or the horizontal direction and the y-axis or the vertical direction. The distances from the two axes, known as the primary axes, are written as an ordered pair of numbers within parenthesis as (x, y) coordinates.

Accelerated Graphics Port (AGP): An older interface standard designed for connecting graphics cards to a computer's motherboard, providing a dedicated high-speed pathway for graphics data. AGP significantly increased the bandwidth available for graphics data, allowing for faster data transfers between the CPU and GPU.

Active Matrix LCD: A type of liquid crystal display (LCD) which employs a matrix of thin-film transistors (TFTs) to individually control each pixel, providing faster response times and higher image quality compared to passive matrix LCDs.

Affine transformation: A type of composite geometrical transformation of images involving a combination of translation, rotation, scaling, Reflection and shear such that parallel lines remain parallel, equal distances remain equal and a rectangle in general is converted to a parallelogram.

Aliasing and Anti-Aliasing: Aliasing occurs when an image is displayed or sampled at a lower resolution than its original resolution, causing jagged or stair-step patterns. Anti-aliasing techniques are used to reduce or eliminate these artifacts, often by smoothing or blurring the edges of objects to create gradual transitions between contrasting colors.

Arithmetical Operations: Arithmetical operations on images involve manipulating pixel values through addition, subtraction, multiplication, division and linear combinations, to create new images or modify existing ones.

Aspect Ratio: The aspect ratio of an image is the ratio of its width to its height. Common aspect ratios include 4:3 (standard definition), 16:9 (widescreen and HDTV) and 1:1 (square, often used in social media profile pictures). Maintaining the correct aspect ratio is important to prevent distortion when resizing or displaying images.

BMP (Bitmap): A widely used raster image format developed by Microsoft. It stores graphical information as an uncompressed bitmap, offering simple and direct pixel-by-pixel representation without any loss of quality, but resulting in larger file sizes compared to compressed formats.

Bit Depth: Refers to the number of bits used to represent each pixel's color. A higher bit depth allows for a more extensive range of colors and greater color accuracy. Common bit depths include 8-bit (256 colors), 24-bit (true color: 16.7 million colors) and 32-bit (true color with an additional alpha channel for transparency).

Binary images: A type of image where the pixel values are represented using a single bit, 0 or 1, and hence capable of displaying only two colors, black and white.

Canny Operator: A type of edge detector which computes the local gradient magnitude and direction at each point of a digital image to locate and highlight the edges of objects in the image. Edges are identified by a change in local intensity around each pixel.

DOI: 10.1201/9781003588030-3

Cathode Ray Tube (CRT): A type of monitor display unit based on the principle of electron emissions. By controlling a beam of electrons falling on phosphor coated screens, specific areas of the screen is illuminated to enable display of visual data like text, images, graphics and video.

CMY(K) Color Model: A subtractive color model which represents colors by subtracting percentages of Cyan (C), Magenta (M), Yellow (Y), and, optionally, Key/Black (K), from white light. Works on the principle of color absorption and determines how colored inks appear on printing systems.

Color depth: Refers to the number of distinct colors that can be displayed or represented in an image. It is typically measured in bits per pixel (bpp), with a higher color depth allowing for a larger and more varied palette, resulting in more realistic and detailed visual representations.

Color Image: A type of image where the pixel values represent different colors. Divided into 8 bits for each primary color red, green, blue, color images are capable of displaying 2^8 or 256 colors for diagrams and illustrations, 2^16 or 65K colors (high color) and 2^24 or 16.7M colors (true color).

Color Look Up Table (CLUT): A table containing indexed color values stored in memory which is used to display colors in a type of image called indexed image. Also called a colormap, the indexed values in the table are used to specify pixel colors when the image is displayed on screen.

Color Model: A mathematical model representing colors as tuples of numbers, allowing for the precise specification of various colors in a standardized way. Common color models, such as RGB (Red, Green, Blue) and CMYK (Cyan, Magenta, Yellow, Black), define colors based on specific combinations of primary color components, facilitating consistent color reproduction across different devices and applications.

Color Space: A specific instance or subset of a color model that defines a range of colors supported by a specific device or application. Examples like sRGB and AdobeRGB ensure consistent color representations on the Web and consumer electronics.

Color Calibration: Process of adjusting and standardizing the colors displayed or reproduced by a device to ensure consistency and accuracy across different systems. A set of procedures involving adjustment and correction of colors across various devices like scanners, monitors and printers, to achieve a standardized and perceptually uniform representation of colors.

Color Profiles: A set of data that characterizes the color properties of a device, ensuring consistency in color representation across various devices and applications. Often referred to as ICC profiles, standardized by the International Color Consortium (ICC) are used to maintain consistent colors across different devices, such as monitors, printers and scanners.

Compression: A process of reducing the size of a digital file by using encoding techniques that discard or represent redundant data more efficiently. This reduction in file size allows for faster transmission, efficient storage and quicker loading times in digital applications while aiming to maintain an acceptable level of image quality.

Contrast Stretching: An image enhancement technique used in digital image processing to improve the visibility of details by expanding the range of intensity values of pixels. It involves linearly scaling the pixel values of an image to cover a wider range, effectively increasing the contrast between different elements in the image.

Convolution: A mathematical operation applied in image processing and signal processing, involving the combination of an input signal with a filter or kernel to produce an output. It systematically processes data by multiplying and summing the elements of the input and filter, allowing for tasks like blurring, sharpening or edge detection in images.

Digital Image Processing: Involves the application of various techniques and algorithms to manipulate and enhance images and includes operations like resizing, cropping, color correction, filtering and object recognition, among many others. The processing operations also include image enhancement, filtering and restoration, for various applications.

Deconvolution: A mathematical operation in image processing aimed at undoing the effects of convolution, essentially recovering the original signal or image from the convoluted data. It involves reversing the convolution process using methods like inverse filtering to restore details or features that may have been blurred or altered.

Dots Per Inch (DPI): A measure of printing resolution or the number of dots that can be printed in a linear inch. For printers, scanners and other printing devices, DPI indicates how finely the printer can reproduce detail, while in the context of monitors and digital displays, DPI is often used to describe the pixel density or the number of pixels within one inch of the display.

Dynamic Range: Refers to the range of intensity levels in an image, spanning from the darkest to the brightest areas. A high dynamic range (HDR) indicates that the image can represent a wide range of tones, providing greater detail in both shadows and highlights.

Edge Detection: A set of procedures involving kernel-based convolutions, to identify edges of regions in an image. Edges are identified by looking at change in image intensities along the horizontal and vertical directions.

Erosion: A type of morphological operation, involving kernel-based convolutions, which shrinks the boundaries of foreground (white) pixels. Usually applied on binary images, it particularly useful for tasks such as image segmentation, noise removal and feature extraction.

Extended Graphics Array (XGA): A graphics display resolution introduced by IBM, commonly associated with a resolution of 1024 × 768 pixels. It became widely used in the late 1980s and 1990s, offering enhanced visual clarity and detail compared to the previous standard VGA (Video Graphics Array).

Gamma Adjustments: Procedures for adjusting pixel intensities of an image using input-output transfer functions involving power curves where the output value is proportional to the input value raised to an index value called gamma. By applying a power-law function to the pixel values, it enhances or compresses image contrast, playing a crucial role in optimizing visual representation and maintaining perceptual consistency.

Gaussian filter: A kernel where the coefficient values represent a 2D Gaussian distribution, frequently used as a noise filter to improve or enhance image quality corrupted by small white dots. It applies a weighted average to each pixel, with the weights determined by the Gaussian function, resulting in a smoother image while preserving important features.

Grayscale image: A type of image where the pixel values are represented using 8 bits and represent different shades of gray. Starting with 0 to denote black at one extreme and 255 to denote white at the other extreme, there are 254 levels of gray shades possible in between, taking the total number of values possible to 256.

Gray-Level Co-occurrence Matrix (GLCM): A type of 2D matrix used to represent the statistical variation of gray shades over an image. Frequently used for texture analysis of an image for applications like image recognition and content-based retrieval.

Histogram: A 2D plot of the number of pixels against their intensities in an image. Frequently used for tonal correction of an image involving enhancement of the brightness and contrast through a process called histogram equalization.

Horizontal Scan Rate: In a monitor, especially a CRT, depicts the number of horizontal lines generated by second. It determines the maximum frequency at which the monitor can display horizontal lines and is a crucial factor in ensuring stable and flicker-free visual output.

HSV Color Model: Represents colors using three components: Hue, which denotes the type of color; Saturation, indicating the intensity or vividness of the color; and Value, representing the brightness or lightness of the color. This model is particularly useful for color manipulation tasks, allowing intuitive adjustments such as changing the shade or intensity of a color while maintaining perceptual uniformity.

Image Acquisition: Process of capturing visual information from the real world using devices such as cameras or scanners and converting it into a digital format. This involves the conversion of optical information into a digital signal, enabling further processing, analysis or storage of the captured image.

Image Enhancement: A set of procedures which involves manipulating an image to improve its visual quality, emphasizing certain features or reducing undesired effects. It includes a set of diverse techniques like tonal correction, color corrections and edge sharpening.

Image Restoration: Involves techniques for recovering the original, undistorted version of an image by mitigating degradations introduced during image acquisition or transmission like de-blurring and nose reduction.

Image File Formats: Standardized structures that dictate how digital images are stored and encoded. They define how image data is compressed, organized and represented in a file, allowing for compatibility and efficient sharing of images across different software applications and platforms.

Image Transforms: Refers to the mathematical conversion of the pixel values from the spatial domain (i.e., intensity values) to some other domain, usually the frequency domain (i.e., rate of change of intensity values). Such conversion is done in order to study details about the frequency components within the image typically for applications like compression.

Indexed Images: An image where the pixel values do not contain the actual color information but only index numbers. The index numbers are converted to color values by looking up a colormap or a table in memory with a set of rows and four columns, called the color look up table (CLUT).

Inkjet Printer: A type of printer which uses droplets of chemical ink onto paper to create text, graphics and images, making them ideal choices for a range of applications like photo printing, graphic design and marketing materials.

Intensity Transformations: Involve modifying the pixel intensity values to enhance or adjust the visual appearance of the image. These transformations, such as gamma adjustments, contrast stretching or histogram equalization, are applied to improve visibility, highlight features or adapt the overall brightness and contrast of the image.

JPEG file: A JPEG (Joint Photographic Experts Group) file is a widely used image compression format that employs lossy compression techniques to reduce file size. It is particularly suitable for photographs and complex images, providing a good balance between compression efficiency and acceptable image quality for various digital applications.

LASER Printer: A type of printer which uses electrostatic charges on a photoconductor drum and powered toner to produce high-quality prints on paper. A LASER beam generates a charge image on the drum to which the toner particles stick. These are subsequently fused to the paper using heat and pressure.

Liquid Crystal Display (LCD): A type of monitor display which use liquid crystal display material and light polarizing filters to generate images on a flat panel screen. Thin film transistors (TFT) are usually used as switching elements to switch each LCD cell on or off to control each pixel on screen.

Lossless compression: A compression procedure where data in a file is simply rearranged to reduce file size and not deleted. Since no data is discarded, the original data can be recovered during decompression and there is no degradation in quality.

Lossy compression: A compression procedure where data in a file is actually deleted to reduce file size. This data cannot be recovered during decompression and hence there is a permanent degradation in quality, however the amount of compression is much more than for lossless compression techniques.

Median filter: A type of noise filter which replaces pixel values by the median of the neighboring pixels under the kernel during convolution. Media filters are especially useful in reducing noise generated by black and white dots called salt and pepper noise

Monitor Specifications: A set of parameters defining the structural and functional characteristics of a monitor which play decisive roles in determining picture quality. Examples include its size, horizontal and vertical scan rates, resolution, pixel density, dot pitch, aspect ratio.

Passive Matrix LCD: A type of liquid crystal display (LCD) which does not allow precise controlling of each pixel on the panel. Pixels are activated sequentially by switching on each row and column and thus leads to contrast and brightness problems since each row remains active for a very small duration.

Pixels: At the core of every digital image are pixels, short for "picture elements." A pixel is the smallest discrete unit of an image and is essentially a square or rectangular area that can be assigned a specific color or shade. The arrangement and combination of pixels create the visual representation of an image. Pixels are the structural units of a digital image similar to molecules making up real-world objects. Each pixel is identified with two parameters: its location and value.

Plasma Display Panel (PDP): A type of flat-panel display technology that uses small cells containing electrically charged ionized gases to produce images. The ionized gas emits ultraviolet (UV) radiation that strikes the red, green or blue phosphors on the cell, causing them to emit visible light.

RGB Color Model: A color model which specifies colors to be made up of three primary components red, green and blue mixed in varying proportions. The model is applicable for colored lights and used to describe behavior of TV screen, computer monitor and glow signs.

Resolution: Resolution refers to the number of pixels displayed on the screen and is typically measured in terms of horizontal and vertical pixel dimensions (e.g., 1920 × 1080 for Full HD). Higher-resolution images have more pixels per unit area, resulting in greater detail and clarity; however, higher-resolution images also consume more storage space and processing power.

TWAIN: An interface standard that acts as an intermediary, enabling seamless communication between software applications and a variety of image capture devices, including scanners, cameras and digital photocopiers.

Visual Display Systems: A visual display system enables the image to be displayed using colored lights emitted from monitor pixels in accordance with the RGB color model. These include various technologies like CRT, LCD, LED and PDP each designed to meet specific needs and preferences.

Vector vs. Raster: Images are also referred to as bitmaps or raster-based which indicate they are composed of a grid of pixels and suitable for photographs, color shading and continuous tones. An alternate form called vector-based graphics represents content within the image as points, lines, curves and polygons by their mathematical equations, which are suitable for diagrams, logos, charts, maps with typically limited number of colors.

3.1.2 Historical Evolution

The history of digital imaging traces back to the mid-20th century when researchers and engineers began exploring ways to represent visual information in digital form.

1940s–1960s: The roots of digital image processing can be traced back to the 1940s and 1950s when early digital computers were developed. Researchers explored the potential of using computers to process and analyze images. The development of rudimentary image processing techniques began in the 1960s with the advent of computers capable of handling digital data.

1970s: In the 1970s, the introduction of charge-coupled devices (CCDs) and other image sensors marked a significant leap in digital image acquisition. These sensors allowed for the direct conversion of light into electronic signals, replacing traditional film-based photography and providing a foundation for digital imaging.

1970s–1980s: During this period, researchers and engineers developed foundational image processing algorithms. Techniques such as image filtering, edge detection and noise reduction were explored. The field expanded with the introduction of dedicated image processing hardware and software, paving the way for applications in medical imaging, satellite imagery analysis and industrial quality control.

1980s–1990s: The 1980s saw a significant application of digital image processing in the field of medicine. Digital imaging modalities, including computed tomography (CT), magnetic resonance imaging (MRI) and digital radiography, became standard. This era witnessed the transformative impact of digital image processing on medical diagnostics and visualization.

1990s: The 1990s brought advancements in image compression techniques and the establishment of standards such as JPEG (Joint Photographic Experts Group) for efficient storage and transmission of digital images. These developments played a crucial role in the proliferation of digital photography and the emergence of the World Wide Web.

2000s: The 2000s witnessed a convergence of digital image processing with computer vision and pattern recognition. These interdisciplinary fields contributed to the development of sophisticated algorithms for object recognition, image segmentation and scene understanding. Applications expanded to include facial recognition, autonomous vehicles and augmented reality.

2010s–Present: The last decade has seen a paradigm shift with the advent of deep learning and convolutional neural networks (CNNs).

Deep learning approaches have demonstrated remarkable success in tasks such as image classification, object detection and image synthesis. CNNs, in particular, have become the backbone of many state-of-the-art image processing applications.

Present-Future: In the present era, computational photography has emerged as a focal point, leveraging advanced algorithms and sensor technologies to enhance imaging capabilities. Techniques such as high dynamic range (HDR) imaging, multi-frame image processing and computational image editing are transforming the way images are captured and manipulated.

The historical evolution of digital image processing showcases a progression from foundational algorithms and hardware to the era of deep learning and computational photography. As technology continues to evolve, the field holds promises of more sophisticated image analysis techniques, real-time processing applications and innovations that will shape the future of digital imaging.

3.1.3 Basic Concepts

3.1.3.1 Pixel

A digital image is a 2-dimensional (2D) array of points each associated with a value. The arrangement can be represented by a function $f(x,y)$, where (x,y) are the coordinates of a point in an image and the function f denotes the value of a specified point. The point is referred to as a pixel and the value is the intensity level of the pixel, i.e., a measure of how bright the point is. Analog images in the real world (e.g., a painting on paper, a conventional photograph on film) are continuous entities (at least at distance scales used in our daily lives), but their digital representations are a collection of discrete points, each specified by a pair of coordinate values and an intensity value. Hence, we say that an image is made up of a finite collection of pixels, so the pixels are considered to be the structural units or building blocks of an image (similar to molecules making up of a real-world object). Pictorially, an image is represented as a grid of square blocks, where each block represents one pixel. Each pixel P has a specific value V and location L. The pixel value V is usually depicted by an integer or a floating-point number, and physically represents the brightness or color of the image at that point. The location L is represented as a pair of integer valued coordinates, measured with respect to an origin O located at the top-left corner, the x-axis from left to right and the y-axis from top to bottom (Figure 3.1).

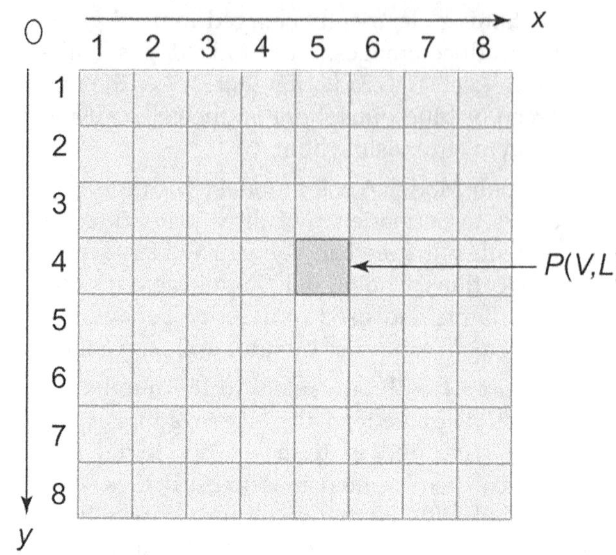

FIGURE 3.1
Pixel and 2D coordinate system.

3.1.3.2 Color

The phenomenon of seeing color is dependent on a triad of factors: the nature of light, the physiology of human vision and the interaction of light with matter. Each factor plays a vital part and the absence of any one would make seeing color impossible. Light is a form of energy known as electromagnetic radiation. Electromagnetic radiation consists of a large number of waves with varying frequencies and wavelengths. At one extreme are the radio waves having the longest wavelengths (in meters) and at the other extreme are the gamma rays with the shortest wavelengths (in nanometers). Out of the total electromagnetic spectrum a small range of waves cause sensations of light in our eyes, ranging from around 400 nm to 700 nm in wavelength. This is called the visible spectrum of waves.

The second part of the color triad is human vision. The retina is the light-sensitive part of the eye and its surface is composed of photoreceptors. There are three types of photoreceptors in the retina, known as cone cells, which respond to three different colors — red, green and blue. A fourth type of cell, called the rod cell, respond to the brightness of light. These cells receive light and pass the stimulus through the optic nerve to the brain. The different frequencies of light gives rise to the different color sensations in our eyes. Within the visible range, shorter wavelengths gives rise to colors like violet, blue and green, while longer wavelengths produce yellow, orange and red. All the colors together combine to produce white light. White light can be split into the component colors by passing it through an optical splitter like a prism.

The third factor is the interaction of light with matter. Whenever light waves strike an object, part of the light energy gets absorbed, part transmitted, part scattered and part reflected to our eyes. If most of the light is transmitted, the object is called transparent, if some light gets absorbed and the remaining transmitted the object is called translucent. If most of the light gets absorbed, scattered and reflected the object is called opaque. If most of the light gets absorbed the object looks dark, while if most of the light gets reflected the object looks bright. The wavelengths present in the reflected light impart a specific color to the object from which the light is reflected. For example, a red ball looks red because it absorbs all the other wavelengths in white light and reflects back only those wavelengths, which produce a red color sensation in our eyes. If a large percentage of the light gets scattered the object looks rough, otherwise if scattering is small the body look shiny and polished.

3.1.3.3 Primary Colors

When dealing with human vision for colored lights, it has been observed that all colors seen by the human eye can be represented as a combination of three primary colors namely, red green and blue, in short referred to as RGB. Proportion of each primary color, specified by their intensities, determines the resultant color. An arbitrary color, say, orange, can be specified as 100% red, 65% green and 0% blue. All three primaries combining at their full 100% intensities produce white, and with lower intensities a shade of gray will be produced. Colors at 100% intensities are called saturated while those having lower intensities are called unsaturated.

When working with digital systems, it is customary to represent each primary color using 8 bits of information. This means that each primary color has a range of values from 0 to 255. Since any arbitrary color is expressed as RGB triplets, specifying a color requires 24 bits of information, the first 8 bits representing amount of red, the next 8 bits representing amount of green and the last 8 bits representing amount of blue. A 24-bit representation allows a total of 16.7 million colors to be displayed (2^24 = 16777216) which is thought to be sufficient for true representations of all colors in our everyday life. The proportions expressed in percentage values can now be represented as integers within the range [0, 255]. Thus, the color orange having composition 100% R, 65% G, 0% B can now be written as (255, 165, 0) since 100% of 255 = 255, 65% of 255 = 165 and 0% of 255 = 0. A more compact representation can also be used by writing the numbers using hexadecimal notation, in this case, #FFA500, the hash symbol denotes the following numbers are in hex. A limited number of colors, around 148, can also be denoted by standardized names on a Web page. See Chapter 2 for a list of Web Color Names. A sample of some composite colors along with their primary R, G, B components is shown below to illustrate the concept (Figure 3.2).

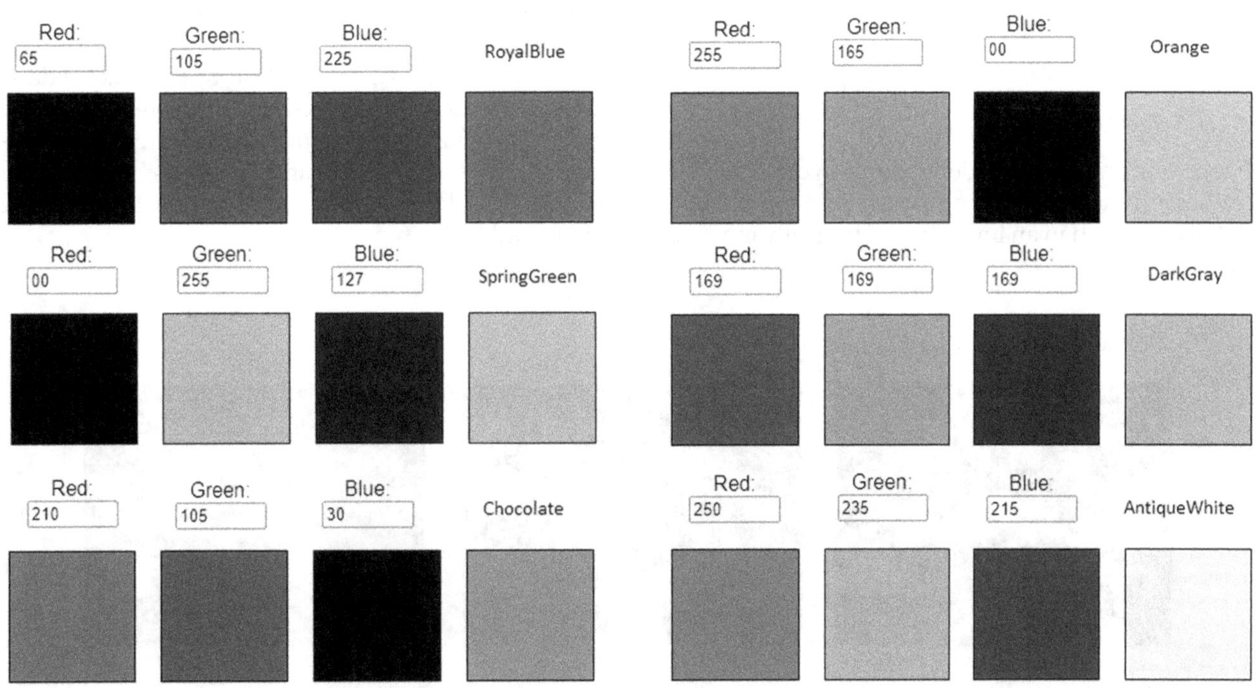

FIGURE 3.2
Sample of web colors with primary components.

3.1.3.4 Image Types

A digital image can be broadly classified into three types depending on the range of values a pixel can take.

Binary image: If the pixel values are represented using a single binary digit, i.e., either 0 or 1, then such images are called "binary" images. Such images can have only two colors, either black or white. Pixels having value 0 indicate black color, while those having value 1 indicate white color.

Grayscale image: If the pixel values are represented using 8 bits, then such types of images are called "grayscale" as these values are used to indicate different shades of gray. Starting with 00000000 to denote black at one extreme and 11111111 to denote white at the other extreme, there are 254 levels of gray shades possible in between, taking the total number of values possible to 256.

Color image: If the pixel value is represented using 24 bits, then such images are called "color" images as they are capable of displaying 2^24 or 16.7 million colors. All these colors are generated from a combination of three primary colors: red (R), green (G), blue (B). Out of the 24 bits, the first 8 bits are used to the represent various intensities of red, the next 8 bits for green and the last 8 bits for blue (Figure 3.3).

3.1.3.5 Image Quality

Image quality primarily depends on two factors: resolution and bit depth. Resolution refers to the level of details captured in an image and is typically measured in pixels per inch (ppi) or dots per inch (dpi). Higher-resolution images have more pixels per unit length, resulting in sharper images with more details, which provides more clarity when displayed as more pixels imply more information content within the image. While resolution is associated with the number of pixels, bit depth measures how many different colors can be displayed by the image. Real world photographs need to have a bit depth of 24 bits which means the image can represent a total of 2^24 or 16.7 million colors which is thought to be sufficient for true representations of all colors in our everyday life, as perceived by human vision.

3.1.3.6 Aspect Ratio

The aspect ratio of an image is the ratio of its width to its height. Common aspect ratios include 4:3 (standard definition), 16:9 (widescreen) and 3:2 (common in photography). Aspect ratio affects the shape and composition of an image and is an important consideration for printing and display on different devices like computer monitors and mobile phones.

3.1.3.7 Image Compression

When digital images are stored in storage devices they usually undergo a process of compression before they are saved. Compression is done by modifying the pixel values so that they take up less space to ensure efficient utilization of storage space. Compression can either be lossless, where the pixel data is changed temporarily and can be reverted back to their original values, or be lossy, where a portion of the pixel data is deleted permanently to reduce space requirements, and the original values cannot be reverted back. The choice between lossless and lossy compression is determined by the applications in which the image will be utilized.

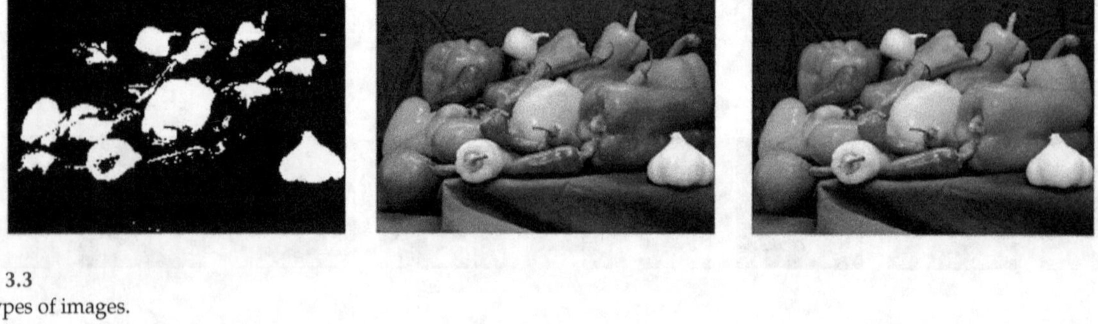

FIGURE 3.3
Three types of images.

3.2 Image I/O

Image acquisition involves capturing visual data and converting it into a digital format. At its core, this process relies on several fundamental elements:

Image Sensors: Image sensors are electronic devices that convert light into an electrical signal. They are classified into two main types: charge-coupled devices (CCD) and complementary metal-oxide-semiconductor (CMOS) sensors. Both have their advantages and are widely used in various imaging devices (Sinha, 2012). CCD sensors are known for their high-quality image output, making them suitable for applications like professional photography and scientific imaging. CMOS sensors are widely used in consumer cameras, smartphones and other portable devices due to their lower power consumption and faster data readout.

Optics: Optical systems, including lenses and apertures, play a crucial role in image formation. They control factors such as focus, depth of field and light gathering, influencing image quality.

Light Sources: Light sources, such as natural light or artificial illumination, provide the necessary illumination for image capture. Understanding lighting conditions is vital for achieving desired image outcomes.

In general there are two popular categories of image capture acquisition: scanner and digital camera.

3.2.1 Scanner

Scanners are input devices that have played a transformative role in the digitization of physical documents, images and objects. These devices capture analog information and convert it into digital form, enabling the storage, manipulation and sharing of a wide array of content. Scanners are widely used in various industries and applications, including document management, graphic design, medical imaging, archaeology and more. The ability to convert physical content into digital format with high precision and detail has made scanners indispensable in the modern age, facilitating the transition to a paperless, digital world while preserving valuable historical and artistic records. One of the key advantages of scanners is their versatility. They can scan a wide range of materials, including single or multiple sheets of paper, photos, book pages, 3D objects and even transparent items such as film negatives or slides. This flexibility makes them invaluable for various applications, from document digitization and image archiving to graphic design and art reproduction.

3.2.1.1 Image Digitization

As the scan head moves from left to right and top to bottom, the light is reflected from all parts of the document and falls on an array of electronic sensors like CCD or CMOS. The sensors convert the light from the document into electrical signals with amplitudes proportional to the intensity of light. The electrical signals are then fed to an analog-to-digital converter (ADC), which in turn converts these to digital data. The original document is sampled at regular intervals typically in a grid pattern to capture the intensity of light at each point to generate a grid of pixels whose values depend on the intensity of the reflected light. The resolution of the digital image is determined by the spacing between the samples measured in dots per inch or dpi (sometime referred as pixels per inch, or ppi). The color of the samples is determined by the bit depth or color depth of the scanner and is typically 24 bits to capture the true color of the original source. To reduce file size and storage requirements the digital image is usually compressed using either lossless or lossy techniques and then saved using a specific file format. The digital image is now ready for further editing, printing or transmission over a network (Figure 3.4).

3.2.1.2 Scanner Software

A software interface is used to specify parameters associated with digitization, namely, the spacing between pixels called the image resolution, measured in dots per inch (dps), and the number of bits for representing the pixel values called bit depth. Scanner software plays a crucial role in converting physical documents into digital formats, facilitating efficient document management and storage. High-quality image capture is a fundamental feature, allowing the software to acquire clear and detailed scans of documents. Advanced image enhancement features, such as color correction, auto-cropping and de-skewing, contribute to improved scan quality. OCR technology enables the conversion of scanned images into editable and searchable text, vital for digitizing text-heavy documents and making them accessible for text-based searches. Scanner software typically supports a variety of file formats for saving scanned documents, including PDF, TIFF, JPEG and PNG, which ensures compatibility with various applications and systems. Efficient organization and management of scanned

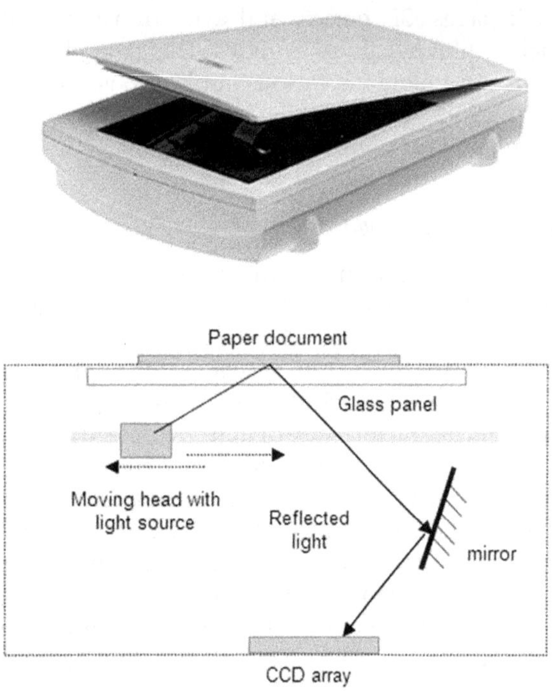

FIGURE 3.4
Scanner.

documents are facilitated through features like batch processing, file naming conventions and the ability to create folders or categories. Integration with document management systems and cloud storage platforms allows seamless storage and retrieval. Robust security features, including user authentication and access control, safeguard sensitive information. Encryption protocols ensure that scanned documents remain secure during transmission and storage. Users can customize scanning parameters such as resolution, color mode and compression settings based on their specific requirements. Profile creation allows users to save and easily apply preferred scanning configurations for different types of documents. Automation features enable users to streamline repetitive scanning tasks by setting up predefined workflows and automating processes such as file naming, destination selection and post-scan actions. Batch processing capabilities facilitate the scanning of multiple documents in a single operation, enhancing efficiency.

3.2.1.3 Scanner Types

Flatbed scanners are one of the most common types of scanner, consisting of a glass panel on which the document is placed face down and a scan head below it containing a source of white light. It uses an optical system comprising of lenses, mirrors and sensors to capture the image of the document. Light from a source like a LED is reflected from the document onto the sensors. The resolution is typically from 600 dpi (dots per inch) to 4800 dpi or higher. In most cases the color depth supported is 24 bits and the interface to the computer is via USB.

Sheet-fed scanners are designed for high-speed, high-volume document scanning. They excel at processing multiple pages quickly, making them ideal for businesses and offices where document digitization and management are essential.

Handheld and portable scanners provide flexibility and mobility, allowing users to scan items on the go. They are useful for fieldwork, inventory management and capturing content from various locations.

Film scanners are specialized devices designed for digitizing photographic film, such as slides and negatives. They offer high resolution and color depth, making them valuable for photographers and archivists.

Drum scanners are renowned for their exceptional scanning quality and are often used for high-end graphic and prepress work.

3.2.2 Digital Camera

Digital cameras have revolutionized photography and visual storytelling in the digital age. These compact devices capture images and videos as digital files, making it easy to store, edit and share visual content (Kallen, 2014). The transition from film to digital technology marked a significant turning point in the history of photography. Digital cameras use image sensors, such as CCD or CMOS, to convert light into electronic data, producing digital images with remarkable clarity and color accuracy. They offer a wide range of features and capabilities, from point-and-shoot models for casual photographers to professional-grade DSLRs and mirror-less cameras. Key advantages of digital cameras include instant feedback, as photographers can view and assess their shots immediately, and the ability to take a large number of photos without the cost of film and development. Furthermore, the flexibility of digital image editing software allows photographers to enhance and manipulate their photos creatively. The widespread integration of digital cameras into smartphones has made high-quality photography and videography accessible to a broader audience, influencing various fields, from journalism and social media to art and science. Digital cameras continue to evolve, introducing new features like 4K video recording, advanced image stabilization and wireless connectivity, ensuring they remain a powerful tool for capturing and expressing the visual world.

Light enters through the camera's lens which focuses it onto the camera's sensor grid. The lens controls aspects such as focus, aperture and exposure. The CCD or CMOS sensor grid captures the incoming light and converts it to electrical signals, which are subsequently fed to an ADC to quantize the signals and generate discrete values called pixels. The resolution of the resulting digital image is determined by the number of pixels generated and the quality of the sensors, determine the bit depth, using which the pixels are stored. The generated digital image usually undergoes some processing within the camera like color correction and noise reduction, before it is stored in storage memory using a standard file format like JPEG. The digitized image can be viewed on the camera's LCD screen and then transferred to a computer for further editing or storage via USB or Wi-Fi interfaces. From the computer it can be displayed on a monitor, printer on a printer or transmitted over a network (Figure 3.5).

Digital cameras, in their various forms, have become an integral part of modern life, offering a host of features and capabilities that have reshaped the way we capture and share visual content. Point-and-shoot digital cameras are known for their user-friendliness and compact designs, making them ideal for everyday photography. They often feature automatic modes for convenience and are equipped with zoom lenses, image stabilization and face detection technology. These cameras are favored by casual photographers for their simplicity and portability.

Digital Single-Lens Reflex (DSLR) and mirror-less cameras are the choice of professionals and enthusiasts alike. They provide good image quality, manual control and the ability to interchange lenses for various photographic purposes. DSLRs use a mirror mechanism to direct light to an optical viewfinder, while mirror-less cameras employ electronic viewfinders or LCD screens. Both offer exceptional image quality and creative control, making them popular for portrait, landscape and action photography.

The advent of smartphones with high-quality built-in cameras has put the power of photography into the hands of billions. Mobile phones offer convenience and the ability to instantly share photos and videos through social media. The integration of advanced features like multiple lenses, computational photography and AI-driven enhancements has elevated smartphone photography to new heights. In addition to still photography, digital cameras have greatly advanced video recording capabilities. Many cameras, especially mirror-less models, offer 4K and even 8K video recording facilities, for high-quality video production for amateurs and professionals.

Digital cameras have also found applications in various industries beyond photography, such as medical imaging, security and surveillance, and scientific research. They have even been integrated into drones, contributing to aerial photography and videography. As digital camera technology continues to evolve, we can expect further innovations in image sensors, image processing and connectivity features. Digital cameras remain a versatile and indispensable tool for capturing, preserving and sharing visual experiences in our rapidly advancing digital age.

3.2.3 Image Quality

The quality of a digital image is often determined by two important parameters: resolution and bit depth. The resolution is specified by the sample rate and provides a measure of the pixel density, i.e., how many pixels are generated per unit length of the image. High-resolution scans contain a large number of dots per inch and hence encapsulate more information. This is reflected in the overall clarity and finer details in the image. The bit depth is determined by the quantization levels and provides a measure of the number

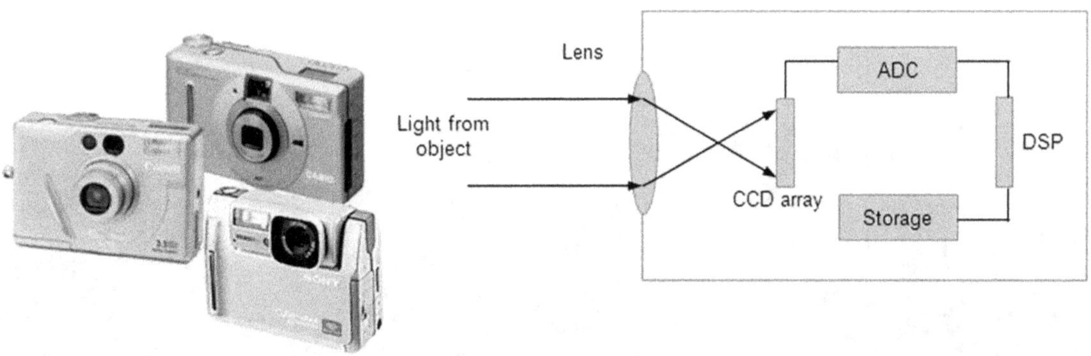

FIGURE 3.5
Digital camera.

of colors the image can contain. Higher color depth enables representation of a larger number of colors which can truly capture the real life shades. The image sensor type (CMOS, CCD) and its physical dimensions impact image quality. Larger sensors generally capture more light and provide better performance, especially in low-light conditions. Resolution, measured in megapixels, determines the level of detail in an image. Higher megapixel counts allow for larger prints while maintaining quality. Dynamic range measures the ability of a camera to capture details in both bright highlights and dark shadows. Higher dynamic range results in more balanced exposures. The quality of the lens, including the number and arrangement of optical elements, influences factors like sharpness, distortion and chromatic aberration. The maximum aperture (represented by f-stop) affects the depth of field and the amount of light entering the lens. The autofocus system's speed and accuracy are crucial for capturing sharp images, especially in dynamic or fast-paced situations. Image stabilization reduces the impact of camera shake, leading to sharper images, particularly at slower shutter speeds. White balance settings ensure accurate color representation under different lighting conditions. Controlled sharpening enhances image clarity without introducing artifacts. Cameras with robust in-camera editing capabilities offer greater control over post-processing and image refinement. Higher frames-per-second (fps) rates and efficient buffer systems allow for capturing fast-action sequences. High-quality video recording capabilities contribute to the camera's overall versatility. High-speed data transfer options, such as USB, Wi-Fi and Bluetooth, facilitate efficient file transfer and remote control capabilities (Figure 3.6).

3.2.4 Interface Standards

Interface standards for image capture devices, notably TWAIN and ISIS, play a pivotal role in ensuring efficient and consistent integration between software applications and a diverse range of image capture hardware. By adhering to these standards, organizations can ensure that their chosen image capture devices, whether it's a flatbed scanner or a high-speed document scanner, can effortlessly integrate into their software systems. This compatibility and consistency are essential in various professional applications, where image acquisition is a fundamental component.

TWAIN (Technology Without An Interesting Name): TWAIN [www.twain.org] is a widely adopted standard in the realm of image acquisition. It acts as an intermediary, enabling seamless communication between software applications and a variety of image capture devices, including scanners, cameras and digital photocopiers. TWAIN's architecture offers a versatile and open framework, empowering software developers to effortlessly integrate scanning and imaging functionalities into their applications. The standard defines a set of well-documented commands and data formats that enable applications to control scanning parameters, retrieve image data and maintain consistent communication with hardware. Its user-friendly approach has made it prevalent in several industries, such as healthcare (for medical imaging), graphic design and office document management.

ISIS (Image and Scanner Interface Specification): ISIS [https://help.accusoft.com/ImageGear/v19.1/Windows/DLL/ISIS_Scanning.html] serves as a specialized standard geared toward high-speed, high-volume document scanning applications. Its primary focus is on optimizing the efficiency and reliability of document capture workflows, where rapid and precise scanning is paramount. ISIS standardizes image processing techniques, including features like text enhancement, image restorations and advanced data compression. These optimizations are vital for industries such as banking, insurance and government agencies, where large volumes of documents need to be swiftly digitized and managed with the utmost precision.

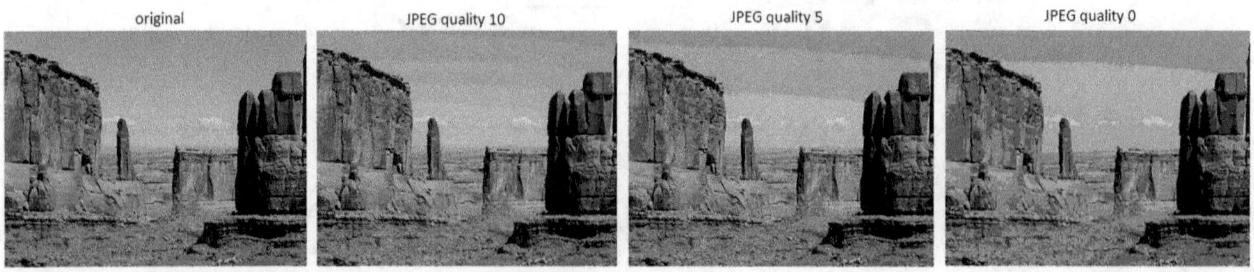

FIGURE 3.6
Image quality in JPEG.

3.2.5 Visual Display Systems

The image after the processing and editing stages and appropriate color calibration procedures are completed proceeds to the output stage via a visual display system or a printer (Kriss, 2015). A visual display system enables the image to be displayed using colored lights emitted from monitor pixels in accordance with the RGB color model. These systems encompass a wide array of devices and technologies, each designed to meet specific needs and preferences. Major types of visual systems include the following:

Television Displays: Television sets have evolved significantly, moving from bulky cathode-ray tube (CRT) displays to sleek and energy-efficient LED, OLED and AMQLED screens. They are the primary source of home entertainment, delivering high-definition and even 4K and 8K resolution content.

Computer Monitors: Computer monitors come in various sizes and technologies, including CRT, LCD, LED and gaming-specific displays. They are essential for productivity, gaming and content creation.

Projectors: Projectors are used to display large-scale images and presentations on screens or walls. They find applications in home theatres, classrooms, conference rooms and theatres.

Virtual Reality (VR) and Augmented Reality (AR) Displays: VR headsets and AR glasses provide immersive experiences by placing digital content within the user's field of view. They are used in gaming, education, training and various industrial applications.

Billboards and Public Displays: Large outdoor LED and PDP displays and digital billboards are used for advertising, public information and outdoor events. They offer high brightness and weather-resistant designs.

Medical Displays: Specialized displays are used in healthcare for tasks like medical imaging and patient monitoring. They are calibrated for precise color reproduction and clarity.

Automotive Displays: Modern vehicles come equipped with various displays for infotainment, navigation and driver information. These displays enhance the driving experience and safety.

Aviation and Military Displays: Aircraft and military vehicles use ruggedized displays that can withstand harsh conditions and provide critical information to pilots and personnel.

3.2.5.1 CRT (Cathode-Ray Tube) Display

Monochrome CRT displays were once widely used in older computer monitors and televisions and work based on the following principles. A cathode-ray tube contains an electron gun, which emits a stream of electrons when heated. These electrons are focused into a narrow beam. Magnetic coils and an electron gun are used to control the direction of the electron beam. By adjusting the intensity and position of the beam, specific areas of the screen are illuminated. The front of the CRT is covered with a phosphorescent screen that emits light when struck by the electron beam. The intensity of the emitted light varies based on the strength of the electron beam. The electron beam is rapidly scanned across the screen horizontally and then moves down to the next row in a systematic pattern, creating a series of lines (raster) that form the images.

Color CRT displays use the same principles as monochrome CRT displays, but they incorporate color technology through a shadow mask or aperture grille. These displays create color by combining the primary colors (red, green and blue) using tiny phosphorescent dots. By varying the intensity of each primary color, a wide range of colors is achieved. Three electron beams falling on the corresponding sub-pixel dots in proper intensity proportions were able to produce large number of colors in accordance with RGB principles (Figure 3.7).

Interlacing is a technique used in some display technologies, particularly in older CRT displays. It involves dividing each frame into two fields, with odd and even rows of pixels updated alternately. For example, in "360i" or "480i", the "*i*" stands for "interlaced." This technique was common in older standard-definition TVs, such as those with 480i resolution. However, it could result in flickering and reduced image quality compared to progressive scanning. Progressive scanning is denoted by "p" in resolutions like "360p" or "1080p." In progressive scanning, the entire frame is displayed at once, providing smoother and higher-quality images. Modern high-definition displays predominantly use progressive scanning.

3.2.5.2 LCD (Liquid Crystal Display)

An LCD monitor is a common and versatile display technology used in various applications, from computer monitors to televisions. LCD monitors function on the principle of manipulating the properties of liquid crystals to control the passage of light and create images. The core element of an LCD monitor is the liquid crystal. Liquid crystals are organic compounds that have properties of both liquids and solid crystals. In their natural state, liquid crystals are in a twisted or

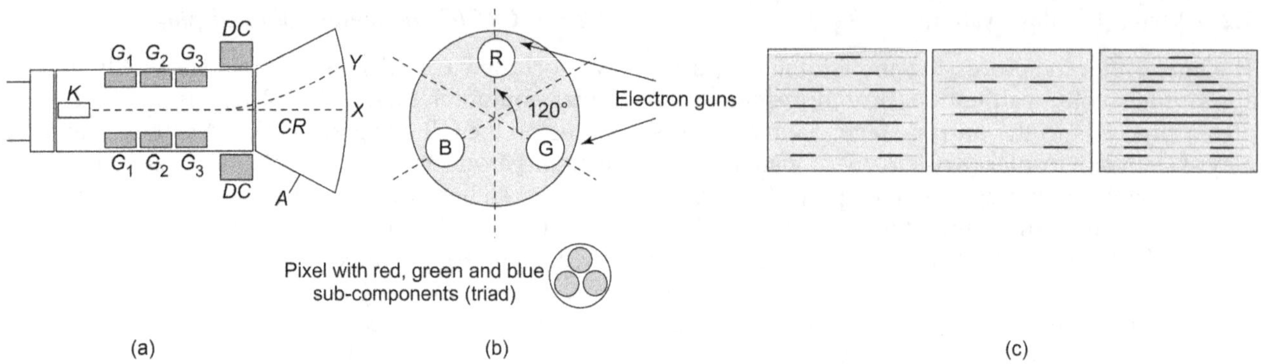

FIGURE 3.7
CRT and electron guns (a) CRT (b) electron guns (c) interlacing.

helical structure, allowing light to pass through. However, they don't have a preferred direction of alignment. An LCD monitor consists of two sheets of polarized glass placed parallel to each other. The front glass panel (closest to the user) has a layer that contains vertical polarizing filters, meaning it only allows light waves oscillating vertically to pass through. Between the two polarized glass panels, a layer of liquid crystals is present. These liquid crystals are aligned in a specific way depending on the electrical charge applied to them. When an electrical current is applied to a specific pixel on the LCD panel, it aligns the liquid crystals within that pixel. Behind the layer of liquid crystals, there is a grid of thin-film transistors (TFTs). These transistors act as switches, allowing the individual pixels to be turned on or off. The aligned liquid crystals in a pixel twist the light waves as they pass through. The light then moves through a horizontal polarizing filter on the rear glass panel, which is oriented perpendicular to the front panel's filter. If the liquid crystals are unaligned (no electrical current), they block the passage of light because their twisted structure disrupts the polarization of light, and it cannot pass through the rear filter. If the liquid crystals are aligned (electrical current applied), they untwist, allowing the light to pass through the rear filter. To generate colors, most LCD monitors use a combination of red, green and blue subpixels. These subpixels are individually controlled to create a full spectrum of colors. The LCD monitor consists of a vast grid of pixels. Each pixel contains red, green and blue subpixels. By varying the alignment of the liquid crystals in each subpixel, the monitor can create a wide range of colors and shades. To illuminate the screen, LCD monitors typically use a backlight source. This can be a cold cathode fluorescent lamp (CCFL) or more commonly, light-emitting diodes (LEDs) in modern monitors. The backlight source emits white light, and the liquid crystals control how this light is filtered and displayed as colors on the screen. By turning specific pixels on or off and adjusting the alignment of liquid crystals in each subpixel, the LCD monitor creates images on the screen. Images are formed by combining thousands or millions of individual pixels, each capable of displaying a specific color and intensity (Figure 3.8).

There are two major categories of LCD devices: the passive matrix and the active matrix.

PMD (Passive Matrix Display) technology has played a significant role in the evolution of flat-panel displays. It represents an earlier generation of LCDs and is distinguished by its simpler construction and lower cost. A PMD relies on a grid of conductive lines

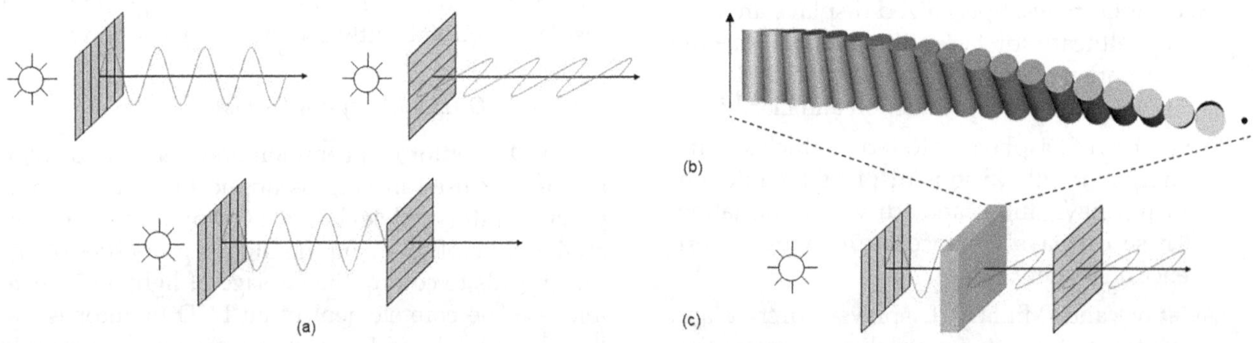

FIGURE 3.8
LCD and polarization (a) Polarizing filters (b) Liquid crystal molecules (c) Twisting of light rays.

(usually made of Indium Tin Oxide ITO) both horizontally (row electrodes) and vertically (column electrodes). Liquid crystals are sandwiched between two layers of glass, and the intersections of the row and column electrodes control the individual pixels. The application of a voltage to a specific intersection alters the orientation of liquid crystals, modulating the passage of light and creating the display. This sequential addressing method results in a slower refresh rate, however PMDs are generally more economical to manufacture and tend to consume less power compared. These are used in applications where cost and power consumption were primary concerns, such as small handheld devices, simple calculators and certain types of information displays.

AMD (Active Matrix Display) uses separate electrodes for each LCD element that can be independently controlled. This allows precise controlling of each cell and minimizes refresh problems, leading to overall improved brightness and contrast features, although it also leads to an increase in cost. Modern-day laptop screens are usually of the active-matrix type. Each element is associated with a Thin Film Transistor (TFT) for storing the electrical state of each pixel while the other pixels are being updated. Furthermore, because of the thin film transistor's ability to hold a charge, the pixel remains active until the next refresh. AMDs therefore allow for precise control of each pixel independently, which results in improved response times and enables the display of high-resolution and high-quality images.

3.2.5.3 LED Displays

Light-emitting diode (LED) displays utilize a grid of light emitting diodes, each representing a pixel on the screen, and the light they emit combines to form images. LED displays are widely used in various applications and can be of different types.

OLED (Organic Light-Emitting Diode) use organic materials that emit light when an electric current is applied. These organic compounds are sandwiched between two conductive layers. Each pixel in an OLED display is made up of red, green and blue sub-components. When a voltage is applied, the organic materials emit light directly, creating self-emissive pixels. This eliminates the need for a separate backlight, resulting in deep blacks and vibrant colors. OLED displays can be made flexible, allowing for curved and foldable screens. However the disadvantage of OLED is being organic hydrocarbons they tend to degrade when exposed to air and also create burn-in images when exposed to white light for long durations.

QLED (Quantum Dot Light-Emitting Diode) displays are a variation of LED displays, and incorporate quantum dots to enhance color and brightness. These displays use a layer of quantum dots in front of the LED backlight, which, instead of blocking the backlight, they themselves emit light of specific colors, to produce more vibrant and accurate colors.

AMOLED (Active Matrix Organic Light-Emitting Diode) Displays are similar to OLED displays but use an active matrix backplane to control each individual pixel. This means that each pixel consists of an array of red green blue LED lights which can be individually controlled. This allows for faster response times, improved color accuracy and much thinner panels as there is no separate layer for conducting current or blocking light; some AMOLED displays can even be transparent. AMOLED displays are commonly used in smartphones and high-end TVs.

WOLED (White OLED) is an OLED panel that emits white light. In a WOLED screen the white light is transmitted through color filters, similar to LCD screens, and in contrast to the AMOLED screens which use direct emission of RGB lights. In addition to RGB color filters, WOLED panels contain a fourth filter which passes the white light of the back-panel.

An upcoming panel technology is microLED where a grid of hundreds or thousands of microscopic LEDs make up each individual pixel. MicroLEDs have much lower energy consumptions compared to LCD panels, together with better constant and response times. The inorganic nature of the microLEDs (indium gallium nitride InGaN) implies longer lifetimes than OLED whose organic materials tend to degrade faster, and also minimizes screen burn-in issues. The faster response times of the order of nanoseconds makes microLEDs suitable for 3D and VR applications.

3.2.5.4 Plasma Display Panel (PDP)

A Plasma Display Panel (PDP) is a type of flat-panel display technology that uses small cells containing electrically charged ionized gases to produce images. PDPs were once popular for large-screen televisions and commercial displays but have been largely replaced by LCD and OLED technologies. However, understanding how PDPs work provides insights into the development of modern display technologies. PDPs are made up of thousands or even millions of tiny cells filled with neon and xenon gases. These cells are arranged in a grid, forming the display. Each cell has two electrodes: an address electrode and a sustain electrode. These electrodes are positioned on the front and rear of the cell. A dielectric layer separates the two electrodes in each cell. This layer helps control the discharge of electrical current within the cell. The cells are coated with red, green and blue phosphors. When excited by the gas discharge, these phosphors emit visible light. To create an image on the PDP, an addressing electrode generates an electrical pulse in a specific cell. This pulse ionizes the gas in the cell, creating a small plasma discharge. The ionized gas emits ultraviolet (UV) radiation. The UV radiation strikes the red, green or blue phosphors on the cell, causing them to emit visible light. PDPs use sub-pixel control, with each cell containing red, green and blue phosphors. By varying the intensity and duration of the discharges in these cells, the PDP can create a full range of colors and brightness levels.

Major advantages of the PDPs include excellent contrast ratios, resulting in deep blacks and vibrant colors, as well as wide viewing angles without significant color distortion, making them suitable for larger displays often viewed from various angles. Limitations include large power consumption as well as significant heat generation during operation, which may require cooling systems. Also PDPs are relatively heavy and thicker than modern flat-panel displays, limiting their use in slim and lightweight devices.

3.2.6 Video Adapter Card

Video adapters, also known as graphics cards or display adapters, are essential components in a computer system responsible for rendering and transmitting visual data to a display device. They play a pivotal role in determining the quality of images and videos that users see on their screens. Video adapters house a Graphics Processing Unit (GPU), a specialized chip designed for rendering and accelerating graphics. Modern GPUs are highly advanced and capable of handling complex 3D graphics, video playback and more. Video adapters also include dedicated video memory (VRAM) that stores image data, textures and frame buffers. Sufficient VRAM is crucial for smooth gaming and video editing. Video adapters feature various output ports such as HDMI, DisplayPort, DVI and VGA, allowing them to connect to different display devices. These ports support specific resolutions and refresh rates. Some video adapters support multiple displays, enabling users to extend or duplicate their desktop across multiple monitors. This is particularly useful for productivity and gaming. Video adapters require drivers to communicate with the operating system and applications. Manufacturers regularly update drivers to optimize performance and compatibility.

3.2.6.1 Accelerated Graphics Port (AGP)

Accelerated Graphics Port (AGP) was a high-speed point-to-point channel for attaching a graphics card to a computer's motherboard. It played a crucial role in improving graphics performance during the late 1990s and early 2000s. AGP provided a dedicated connection for the graphics card, ensuring that the GPU could communicate directly with the CPU without going through the system bus. AGP significantly increased the bandwidth available for graphics data, allowing for faster data transfers between the CPU and GPU. This resulted in improved graphics rendering and gaming performance. AGP came in various versions, including AGP 1x, 2x, 4x and 8x, with each version offering higher data transfer rates. AGP was widely used in the late 1990s and early 2000s. However, it has been largely replaced by PCI Express (PCIe) as the standard interface for connecting graphics cards to motherboards.

3.2.6.2 PCI Express (PCIe)

PCI Express (PCIe) introduced in 2004, is a high-speed serial interface that replaced both AGP and the standard PCI bus. It was designed to address the growing demand for more bandwidth, especially in the context of modern graphics cards. PCIe offers greater scalability and flexibility compared to AGP. It comes in various versions, such as PCIe 1.0, 2.0, 3.0, 4.0 and 5.0, with each version providing increased bandwidth. PCIe 5.0, for example, has a maximum theoretical bandwidth of 32 GB/s, significantly surpassing AGP. PCIe utilizes a lane-based system, with each lane providing a specific amount of bandwidth. Graphics cards can be configured with different lane counts, typically x16, x8, x4 or x1, depending on the motherboard and graphics card compatibility. PCIe also allows for multiple graphics cards to be connected in parallel using technologies like SLI (Scalable Link Interface) and CrossFire.

3.2.6.3 Cables and Connectors

Video cables and connectors: Video cables and connectors are essential for transmitting video and audio signals from a source device (such as a computer or gaming console) to a display device (like a monitor, TV or projector). The choice of cable and connector depends on the devices involved and the desired resolution and features. Common Video Cables and Connectors include the following.

HDMI: HDMI (High-Definition Multimedia Interface) [hdmi.org] cables and connectors are prevalent for connecting devices like TVs, monitors and projectors to sources such as gaming consoles, Blu-ray players and computers. HDMI supports high-definition video and audio in a single cable.

DisplayPort: DisplayPort [displayport.org] is a versatile digital video and audio interface used for connecting computers and displays. It supports high resolutions, multiple monitors and can even carry audio signals.

Thunderbolt: Thunderbolt [thunderbolttechnology.net] is a hardware interface developed by Intel in collaboration with Apple. It combines PCI Express and DisplayPort into two serial signals using a multiplex scheme. The latest version uses a USB-C port and supports a speed of 40 GB/sec.

3.2.6.4 Monitor Specifications

The following important monitor specifications play decisive roles in determining picture quality.

Refresh Rate (or Vertical Scan Rate): This is defined as the number of frames displayed by a monitor in one second and measured in a unit called hertz (Hz). Typical values lie within the range 60–70 Hz. A monitor having a refresh rate of 60 Hz is capable of generating 60 frames per second.

Horizontal Scan Rate: This is defined as the number of horizontal lines displayed by the monitor in one second. It is measured as the product of the refresh rate and the number of horizontal lines on the screen, and expressed in hertz (Hz). For a monitor having a refresh rate of 60 Hz and 600 horizontal lines on the screen, the horizontal scan rate equals 36 kHz.

Dot Pitch: This is defined as the shortest distance between two neighboring pixels (for monochrome monitors) or triads (for color monitors). It is usually of the order of 0.25 mm to 0.4 mm.

Pixel Resolutions: It is defined as the total number of pixels that can be addressed on the screen. It is measured by the product of number of horizontal pixel rows and the number of pixels per row. Modern monitors have pixel resolutions of 640 x 480 or 800 x 600 or higher.

Aspect Ratio: This is defined as the ratio of the horizontal number of pixels (number of pixels along a horizontal row) to the vertical number of pixels (number of horizontal rows of pixels). For a computer monitor or a TV screen, the ratio is fixed and equals 4:3. For certain display media like movie theatres and High Definition TVs, the ratio is 16:9. The aspect ratio represents the proportional relationship between the width and height of the screen. Common aspect ratios include 16:9 (widescreen) and 4:3 (traditional).

Monitor Size: The size of the monitor is defined as the longest diagonal length of the monitor. Standard computer monitors are usually between 15 inches to 20 inches in size.

Pixel Density (PPI): Pixel density is the number of pixels per inch on the screen. Higher pixel density results in sharper images, as the increased number of pixels are capable of storing more details in the image. Standard monitors usually have resolutions of 72 to 96 dpi. By comparison, printers typically have pixel densities of 300 to 600 dpi while scanners have pixel densities of 600–1200 dpi. Images scanned at higher densities when display on monitors with lower densities, look larger in size as the additional number of pixels take up additional space.

Resolution: This is defined as the total number of pixels per unit length of the monitor in the horizontal direction. It is expressed in a unit called dots per inch (dpi). Introduction: The resolution of a monitor is a critical specification that defines the number of pixels displayed on the screen, influencing the clarity, detail and overall visual experience. In this technical section, we explore the key aspects of monitor resolution, including the definition, types and considerations when choosing an appropriate resolution for specific applications. Definition of Resolution: Monitor resolution is expressed as the number of pixels arranged in a grid, typically denoted by two values representing the horizontal and vertical dimensions. For example, a resolution of 1920 × 1080 indicates 1920 pixels in width and 1080 pixels in height. The total number of pixels (resolution) directly impacts the amount of visual information the monitor can display. Common Resolutions: HD (High Definition): 720p: 1280 × 720 pixels. 1080p (Full HD): 1920 × 1080 pixels. Quad HD (QHD) or 2K: 1440p: 2560 × 1440 pixels. 4K Ultra HD: 2160p: 3840 × 2160 pixels. True 4K: 4096 × 2160 pixels. 5K and 8K: 5K: Typically 5120 × 2880 pixels. 8K: Typically 7680 × 4320 pixels.

Color Depth: This is a measure of the total number of colors that can be displayed on a monitor and depends on the total number of varying intensities of the electron beam of a

CRT. Modern color monitors usually have a color depth of 24 bits implying that they can display up to 2^24 or 16.7 million colors.

Some mathematical formulations associated with monitor specifications are discussed below:

If w be the width and h the height of the monitor in pixels ($w > h$) then total number of pixels P is given by: $P = w.h$

Let b be the bit depth or color-depth supported by the monitor, in bits. Then total number of colors C that can be displayed is given by: $C = 2^b$

The memory M in bits, required to store one screen of information of the monitor, is given by: $M = w.h.b = P.b$

Let W and H be the width and height of the monitor in inches. Then its size D, i.e., length of its diagonal, is given according to properties of right-angled triangles as $D = \sqrt{W^2 + H^2}$

The resolution R in dots per inch (dpi) is the number of pixels per unit width or height of the monitor. In most cases, these are assumed to be equal unless specified otherwise. $R = w / W = h / H$

If $m : n$ be the aspect ratio of the monitor ($m > n$) then we have $w / h = m / n$

Let d be the dot-pitch of the pixels. Since R is the number of pixels in one inch, the distance between each pair of pixels is given by: $d = \frac{1}{R}$

3.2.6.5 Display Resolutions

Display resolutions are a key aspect of visual display systems, defining the number of pixels that make up an image. Different resolutions offer varying levels of detail and clarity.

- VGA (Video Graphics Array): VGA was one of the earliest widely used display resolutions, featuring a resolution of 640 × 480 pixels. It became a standard for computer monitors and displays, offering basic color capabilities and facilitating the transition from text-based to graphical interfaces.
- SVGA (Super Video Graphics Array): SVGA improved upon VGA with a resolution of 800 × 600 pixels. This allowed for crisper visuals and better support for graphics and multimedia applications.
- XGA (Extended Graphics Array): XGA pushed the boundaries further with a resolution of 1024 × 768 pixels. It offered enhanced image quality and became a common standard for many computer monitors.
- WXGA (Wide Extended Graphics Array): WXGA maintains a 16:9 aspect ratio and typically has a resolution of 1280 × 720 or 1366 × 768 pixels. It is prevalent in modern laptops, LCD TVs and projectors, providing widescreen viewing.
- SXGA (Super Extended Graphics Array): SXGA offers a resolution of 1280 × 1024 pixels, providing high detail for professional and industrial applications, as well as older CRT monitors.
- UXGA (Ultra Extended Graphics Array): UXGA has a resolution of 1600 × 1200 pixels and is suitable for tasks requiring precise detail, such as medical imaging and design work.

Each of these resolutions has played a significant role in the evolution of display technology, catering to various needs, from basic computing to professional tasks. Today, higher resolutions like Full HD (1920 × 1080), 4K (3840 × 2160) and 8K (7680 × 4320) have become increasingly common, delivering stunning visual experiences across a wide range of devices, from monitors to televisions.

A summary of the various approximate resolutions used in the industry along with their approximate megapixel counts is given in Table 3.1, although exact specifications might vary slightly over different manufacturers.

Visual display systems continue to evolve, with ongoing advancements in technologies like OLED, microLED and quantum dot displays, providing brighter, more vibrant and energy-efficient options. These systems are instrumental in enriching our visual experiences and facilitating communication, entertainment, education and numerous other applications in the digital age.

3.2.7 Printing Systems

Printing systems are essential components in the world of document reproduction, facilitating the transformation of digital data into tangible hard copies. A printing system produces a hardcopy of an image using colored chemical inks or powdered toners on paper in accordance with the CMYK color model. Two types of printers are popularly used for multimedia-based outputs: the Laser printer and the inkjet printer (Kriss, 2015).

3.2.7.1 Laser Printers

Laser printers are a staple of modern office environments and personal use, offering efficient,

TABLE 3.1
Common Display Resolutions

Code	Name	Aspect ratio	Width	Height	Mega-pixels
QCIF	Quarter CIF	11:9	176	144	0.025
SIF	Source Input Format	13:9	352	240	0.08
CIF	Common Intermediate Format	11:9	352	288	0.1
VGA	Video Graphics Array	4:3	640	480	0.3
SVGA	Super VGA	4:3	800	600	0.5
XGA	eXtended Graphics Array	4:3	1024	768	0.8
WXGA	Wide XGA (720p)	8:5	1280	800	1.0
SXGA	Super XGA	5:4	1280	1024	1.3
UXGA	Ultra XGA	4:3	1600	1200	1.9
FHD	Full HD (1080p)	16:9	1920	1080	2
WUXGA	Wide Ultra XGA (1080p)	16:9	1920	1200	2.3
QXGA	Quad XGA (4 * XGA)	4:3	2048	1536	3.1
WQXGA	Wide Quad XGA	8:5	2560	1600	4.1
SQXGA	Super Quad XGA	5:4	2560	2048	5.2
QUXGA	Quad ultra XGA	4:3	3200	2400	7.7
UHD 4K	4K or Ultra high definition	16:9	3840	2160	8
WQUXGA	Wide quad ultra XGA	16:10	3840	2400	9
UW5K	Ultra wide 5K	21:9	5120	2160	11
UHD 5K	Ultra-high definition 5K	16:9	5120	2880	15
HXGA	Hex XGA	4:3	4096	3072	12.5
WHXGA	Wide hex XGA	16:10	5120	3200	16
HSXGA	Hex super XGA	5:4	5120	4096	21
UW8K	8K or Ultra wide	12:5	7680	3200	25
WHSXGA	Wide hex super XGA	25:16	6400	4096	26
UHD 8K	Ultra-high definition 8K	16:9	7680	4320	33
16K	16K resolution	16:9	15360	8640	132
32K	32K resolution	16:9	30720	17280	530

high-quality document and image printing. They operate on the principle of electrophotography, commonly known as xerography, which involves creating a charged image on a photosensitive drum, transferring it to paper, and then fusing the toner onto the paper using heat. Laser printers are known for their remarkable speed and precision, making them a preferred choice for large-scale printing tasks. One of the standout features of laser printers is their ability to produce sharp, consistent and professional-quality text and graphics. The use of a laser beam for precise scanning and the uniform distribution of toner create clear, smudge-free prints, whether for text documents or high-resolution images. Additionally, laser printers are cost-effective over time, as they produce a large number of prints per toner cartridge, resulting in a lower cost per page compared to inkjet printers (Figure 3.9).

3.2.7.2 Inkjet Printers

Inkjet printers have become a ubiquitous and versatile tool in the world of home and office printing. These printers operate by propelling tiny droplets of ink onto paper to create text, graphics and images. They offer several key advantages, making them a popular choice for a wide range of applications. One of the standout features of inkjet printers is their ability to produce high-quality color prints with exceptional detail and vibrant colors. This makes them ideal for tasks such as photo printing, graphic design and marketing materials. Many inkjet printers are equipped with multiple ink cartridges, including dedicated ones for photo-quality output, enhancing their versatility and enabling accurate color representation.

Inkjet printers come in various types, with thermal inkjet printers and piezoelectric inkjet printers being the most common. Thermal inkjet printers use a heating element located in each ink nozzle to vaporize the ink, creating small air bubbles. These bubbles quickly expand and force ink droplets onto the paper. This process is precise and rapid, allowing for sharp and detailed prints, making thermal inkjet printers well suited for high-resolution photo printing and general document printing. Piezoelectric inkjet printers, on the other hand, employ piezoelectric crystals located

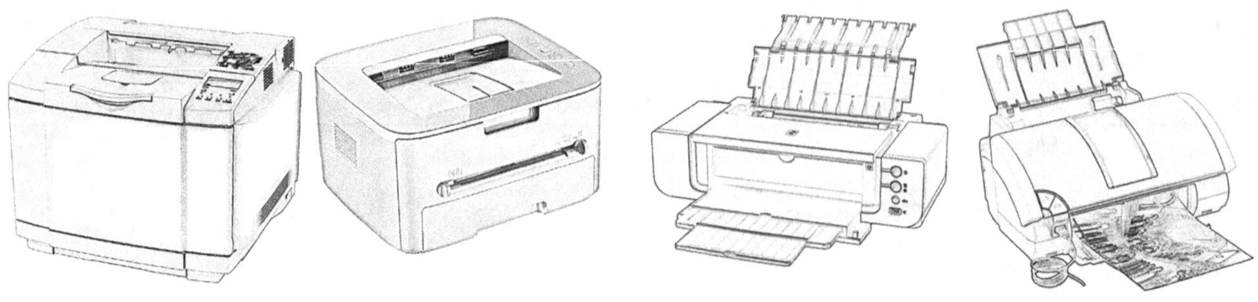

(a) (b)

FIGURE 3.9
LASER and inkjet printers (a) LASER and (b) ink-jet printers.

behind each ink nozzle. When an electric current is applied, these crystals deform, causing a pressure wave that expels ink droplets onto the paper. Piezoelectric printers are known for their ability to handle a wider range of ink types, including pigment-based inks that offer increased durability and longevity. They are often favored for their versatility, especially in applications where a variety of media and ink types are required.

In recent years, inkjet technology has seen significant advancements, with the introduction of eco-friendly, high-speed and wide-format models. Some inkjet printers offer wireless connectivity and mobile printing options, further enhancing their usability in today's digital world. While laser printers excel in high-volume and text-focused printing, inkjet printers remain the go-to option for those who require high-quality color printing, image reproduction and versatility in a compact and affordable package. They have continued to adapt to changing printing needs and technologies, ensuring their relevance in the ever-evolving landscape of home and office printing.

3.2.7.3 Printer Software

Printer software is a critical component that bridges the gap between digital content and tangible hard copies. It plays a pivotal role in managing print jobs, optimizing print quality and ensuring seamless communication between computers and printing devices. Print queue management features allow users to monitor, prioritize and cancel print jobs. Advanced print job scheduling enables users to set up printing tasks at specific times, optimizing resource utilization. Printer software includes settings for optimizing print quality, allowing users to adjust parameters such as resolution, color profiles and print mode (e.g., draft, normal, high quality). Color management features ensure accurate reproduction of colors, especially important in graphics and photo printing. Configuration options for paper size, type and orientation enable users to match printing parameters with the physical characteristics of the media being used. Duplex printing settings facilitate automatic double-sided printing when supported by the printer. Printer software incorporates security measures, which allow users to send sensitive documents to the printer and release them only upon authentication at the device. Support for network printing protocols, such as TCP/IP and SNMP, ensures seamless integration with local and enterprise-wide networks. Cloud printing capabilities enable users to print documents from remote locations or mobile devices. Real-time monitoring of printer status, consumable levels and error notifications provide insights into print usage, helping organizations optimize their printing resources and costs.

3.2.8 Digital Image Representation

Digital image representation involves encoding visual information in images into a format that can be stored, processed and transmitted by computers. The process starts with digitizing devices like scanner and digital camera, in which light from the image or object is focused using lenses and mirrors, on an array of electronic sensors like CCD or CMOS. The sensors work by converting the light energy into electrical energy, the amplitude of the electrical signal generated from each sensor in the array being proportional to the intensity of incident light on that sensor at a particular instant of time. This process continues until all the light from the image has been converted, after which the electrical pulses are sent to an ADC which converts the analog signal into discrete digital value, each value being represented as a pixel. The resolution of the image measures how many pixels are created within the image which in turn depends on the number of sensors in the sensor array, high-resolution images having more clarity and able to capture more details, a typical value being 1920 (width) × 1080 (height) for Full HD, but result in larger file sizes.

The color depth of the digitizing system determines how accurately each sensor has captured the light intensities which in turn determines how many colors can be represented in the image, typical values being 8-bit (256 colors), 16-bit (65K colors) and 24-bit (16.7M colors). Higher bit depth allows for greater color precision and smoother gradients but result in larger file sizes. Hence quality of digital images is seen to depend on both resolution and bit depth (or color depth), good quality images being able to capture more information through higher resolution and higher bit depth, and therefore requiring more storage space and more computing resources to edit and process. Based on the size and resolution, images can be classified into several categories, ranging from 640 × 480 (VGA), 1280 × 1024 (SVGA), 1920 × 1080 (full HD), 3840 × 2160 (4K), 7680 × 3200 (8K), 15360 × 8640 (16K) and so on, while based on the color depth images are typically categorized as binary (1-bit), grayscale (8-bit) and color (24-bit). The color in digital images can be represented using a small number of primary colors which when combined in specific proportions give rise to all other colors. Accordingly various color models like RGB, CMYK, HSV and L*a*b* have been defined based on what primaries they use, what specific applications the image will be used in and how color is quantified in numeric terms. For colored light applicable for visual displays like monitor, TV, projectors and glow signs, the RGB color model is the most prevalent where the colors red, green and blue are chosen as the primary colors each quantified into 256 levels (8-bit) and are mixed into different proportions to reproduce other colors. For images used in printing applications using chemical inks, the CMYK color model is more appropriate where cyan, magenta, yellow and black are chosen as primaries, each quantified into 100 levels (in percent) and mixed to produce other colors. Other models are based on the how the human retina perceives color using rod and cone cells, like HSV which represents color as luminance and chrominance, using hue (light wavelengths), saturation (purity) and brightness as the primary components, and L*a*b* which uses lightness, red-green axis, blue-yellow axis as the primary components. In other application systems, like TV transmission standards, the YCbCr color model is primarily used where Y denotes the luminosity and Cb, Cr denotes the color difference components. For efficient storage and transmission digital images need to be compressed using either lossless or lossy compression schemes. Lossless methods preserve all image information without any loss in quality, and includes algorithms like RLE, Huffman coding and LZW dictionary-based coding, while lossy methods reduce file size by discarding high-frequency image data resulting in a slight loss of quality, and includes algorithms like DCT and quantization, which are part of the JPEG standard. Digital images can contain metadata, which provides additional information about the image, like Exif (Exchangeable Image Format) which includes details like camera settings, exposure and GPS coordinates, while IPTC (International Press Telecommunications Council) metadata contains editorial information like captions and copyright. The file size of an image can be calculated by multiplying the number of pixels with the bit depth: if "w" and "h" be the width and height of the image in pixels and "b" be the bit depth, then the file size is ($w \times h \times b$) in bits. The aspect ratio "a" is the ratio of width by height: $a = w/h$, common aspect ratio values being 4:3 and 16:9. The compression ratio "r" of an image is the ratio of its uncompressed file size "u" to the compressed file size "c": $r = u/c$. If "b" be the bit depth, then the maximum number of colors that can be contained within the image is 2^b. If the pixel density in the image be "d" in pixels per inch (*ppi*), then the printed dimensions W and H of the image in inches will be $W = w/R$ and $H = h/R$.

3.3 Image Editing and Processing

Image editing and processing are fundamental processes in computer vision, graphics and multimedia, playing a crucial role in enhancing, analyzing and presenting visual data. They encompass a range of operations that modify the appearance of images for specific objectives. These objectives include improving visual aesthetics, preparing images for analysis and adapting images for various applications like medical imaging or advertisements. The first step of image processing is to read the pixel values of an image and store them in memory. The image can now be viewed in an on-screen window and information about the image like its dimensions, file size, file format and bit depth can be displayed. It is also possible to write an image back to the disk after editing operations. Editing operations involve changing the pixel locations or values or both, with the objective of bringing about some kind of enhancement in its quality. These can be categorized into geometric transformations which typically change pixel locations and intensity/color transformations which change pixel values. Pixel values can either be changed in an isolated manner using an input-output transfer function, or using kernel-based filters which can change each pixel value in a manner dependent on its neighboring pixels (Gonzalez & Woods, 2008; Jain, 1989).

3.3.1 Geometric Transformations

Precise image processing tasks are usually carried out using programming environments professional applications like diagnostics and research. Geometric transformations alter the spatial relationships between pixels, facilitating tasks such as image registration, alignment and correction. Common geometric transformations include translation, rotation, scaling, shearing and cropping crucial for adjusting images to a desired configuration.

3.3.1.1 *Translation*

Translation can be done by moving segments or the entire image on a 2D plane by specifying translation amounts along the $x-$ and $y-$ directions. If the translation amounts are positive, then the image segments move from left to right and top to bottom, i.e., along the positive directions of the $x-$ and $y-$ axes, if they are negative, then the movements are in the opposite direction (Figure 3.10). For images translation can be followed by increasing the size of the canvas if the entire image needs to be viewed or a portion of the image can be cropped if the canvas needs to be maintained at its original size. A pixel with coordinates P(x_1, y_1) when translated by amounts (t_x, t_y) has new coordinates Q(x_2, y_2) given by:

$$x_2 = x_1 + t_x$$

$$y_2 = y_1 + t_y$$

3.3.1.2 *Rotation*

Rotation implies moving the pixels of an image along the circumference of a circle with the origin of the coordinate system as the pivot point. Counter-clockwise (CCW) rotations are considered positive while clockwise (CW) rotations are negative. Like translation, rotation can be followed by increasing the size of the canvas if the entire image needs to be viewed or a portion of the image can be cropped if the canvas needs to be maintained at its original size. A pixel P(x_1, y_1) when rotated by angle θ about the origin, has new coordinates Q(x_2, y_2) given by (Figure 3.11):

$$x_2 = x_1.\cos(\theta) - y_1.\sin(\theta)$$

$$y_2 = x_1.\sin(\theta) + y_1.\cos(\theta)$$

3.3.1.3 *Scaling*

Scaling occurs when the dimensions of an image are multiplied by constants, which are known as scaling factors. There are two scaling factors one for the height and the other for the width. If both the factors are equal, then the scaling is called uniform, as the ratio of the height to width (aspect ratio) remains the same. If the factors are unequal, then the scaling is non-uniform which usually results in distortion of the image. If the factors are greater than 1, then it leads to an increase in the image size, if less than 1 then it reduces the image size. A pixel P(x_1, y_1) when scaled by amounts (s_x, s_y) has new coordinates Q(x_2, y_2) given by (Figure 3.12):

$$x_2 = x_1.s_x$$

$$y_2 = y_1.s_y$$

3.3.1.4 *Reflection*

A refection operation about an axis reverses the sign of the coordinate of the pixels which are perpendicular to the axis. A refection about the y-axis reverses the

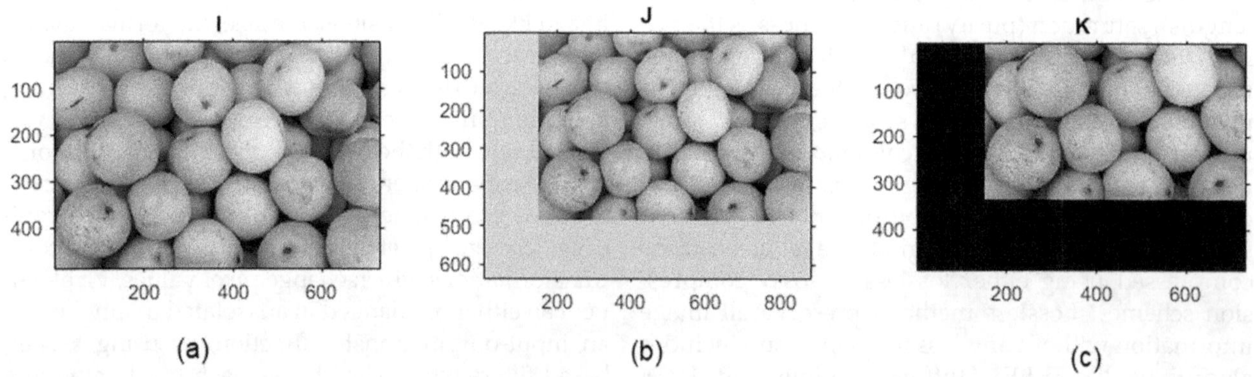

FIGURE 3.10
Translation (a) original image (b) with increase in canvas size (c) with cropping.

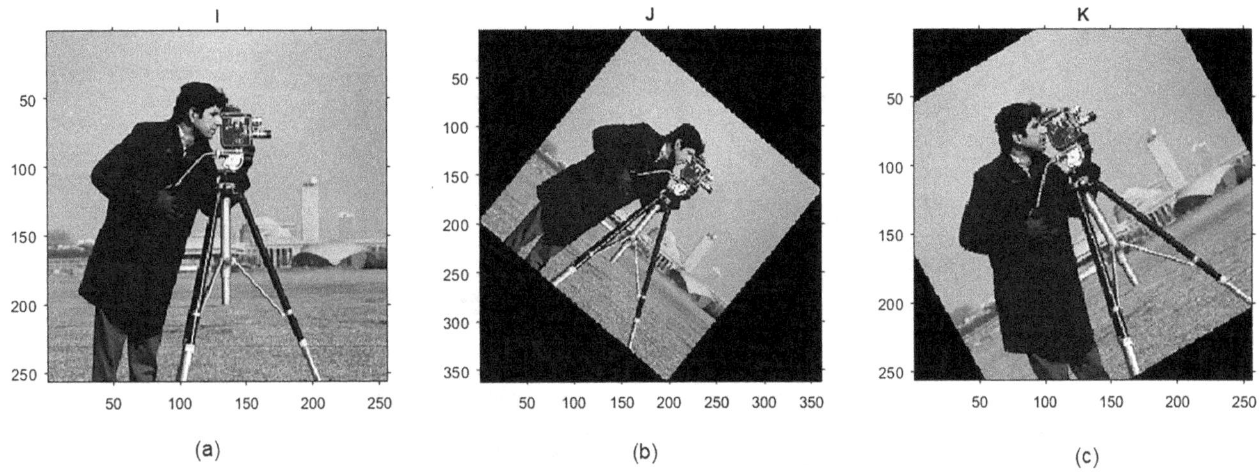

FIGURE 3.11
Rotation (a) original image (b) with increase in canvas size (c) with cropping.

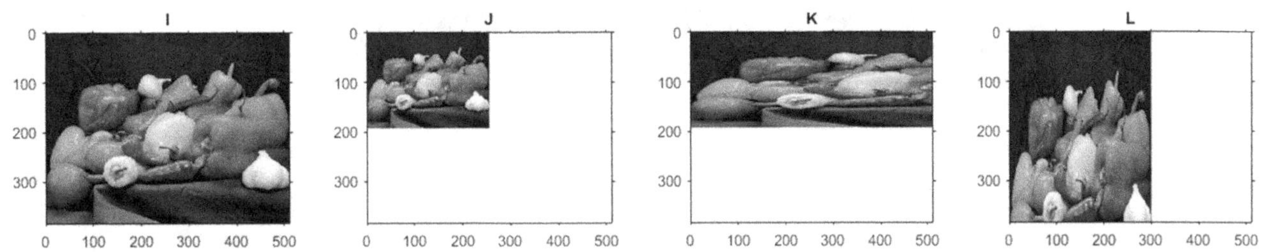

FIGURE 3.12
Scaling : original image (I), with uniform scaling (J), with non-uniform scaling (K and L)

x-coordinates of the image pixels while a refection about the x-axis reverses the y-axis coordinates. The concerned axis behaves like a mirror, and the reflected image behaves as a flipped mirror image of the original. A refection can also take place about the origin in which case both x- and y-coordinates are reversed. A pixel $P(x_1, y_1)$ when subjected to y-axis refection has new coordinates $Q(x_2, y_2)$ given by (Figure 3.13):

$$x_2 = -x_1$$

$$y_2 = y_1$$

When subjected to x-axis refection the y-coordinates reverse in sign:

$$x_2 = x_1$$

$$y_2 = -y_1$$

When subjected to refection about the origin both coordinates reverse in sign:

$$x_2 = -x_1$$

$$y_2 = -y_1$$

3.3.1.5 Shear

Shear occurs when one coordinate changes in a way proportional to the other coordinate. For an x-direction shear, the x-coordinates of a point is shifted by an amount proportional to its y-coordinate, while the actual y-coordinate remains unchanged (Figure 3.14).

$$x_2 = x_1 + h_x.y_1$$

$$y_2 = y_1$$

For a y-direction shear, the y-coordinates of a point is shifted by an amount proportional to its x-coordinate, while the actual x-coordinate remains unchanged.

$$y_2 = y_1 + h_y.x_1$$

$$x_2 = x_1$$

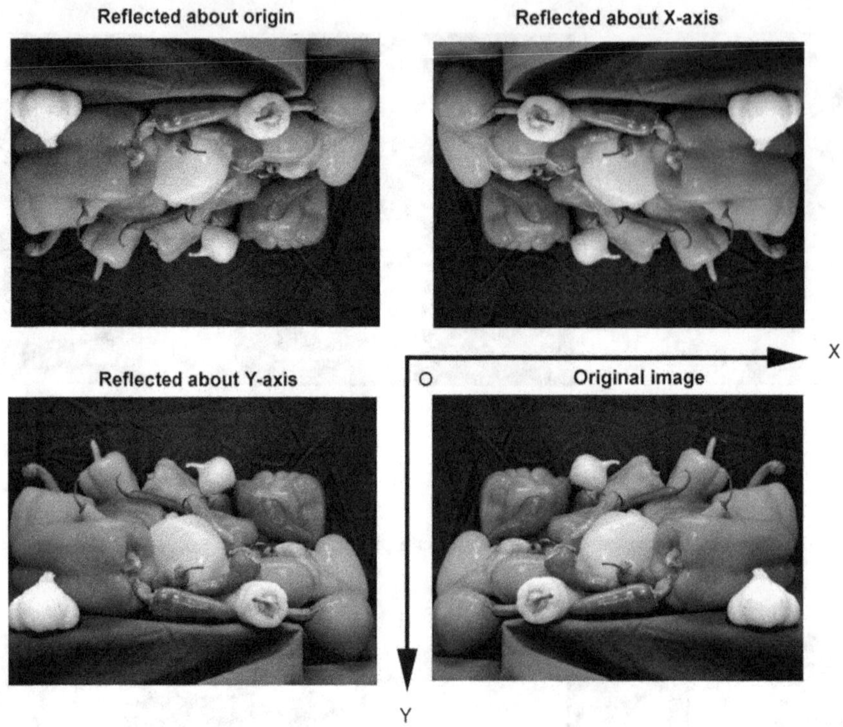

FIGURE 3.13
Reflection.

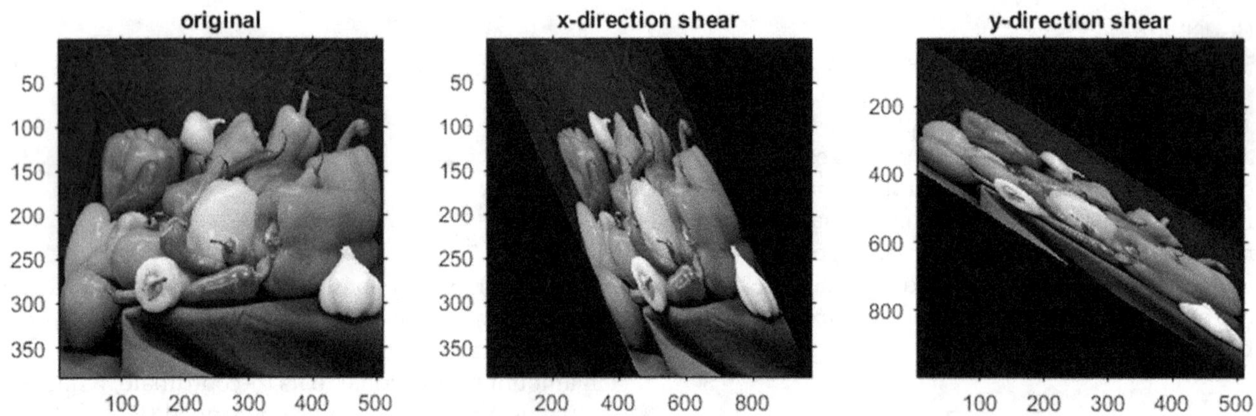

FIGURE 3.14
Shear.

3.3.1.6 Affine and Perspective Transformations

Geometric Transformations can in turn either be affine or be non-affine. A composite transformation involving a combination of translation, rotation, scaling and shear is referred to as affine transformation. In affine transformation, parallel lines remain parallel, equal distances remain equal and a rectangle in general will be converted to a parallelogram. Under affine transformation, the transformed coordinates of a point are given by (Figure 3.15):

$$x_2 = ax_1 + by_1 + c$$

$$y_2 = dx_1 + ey_1 + f$$

In non-affine transformations, like perspective transformations, parallel lines converge with distance

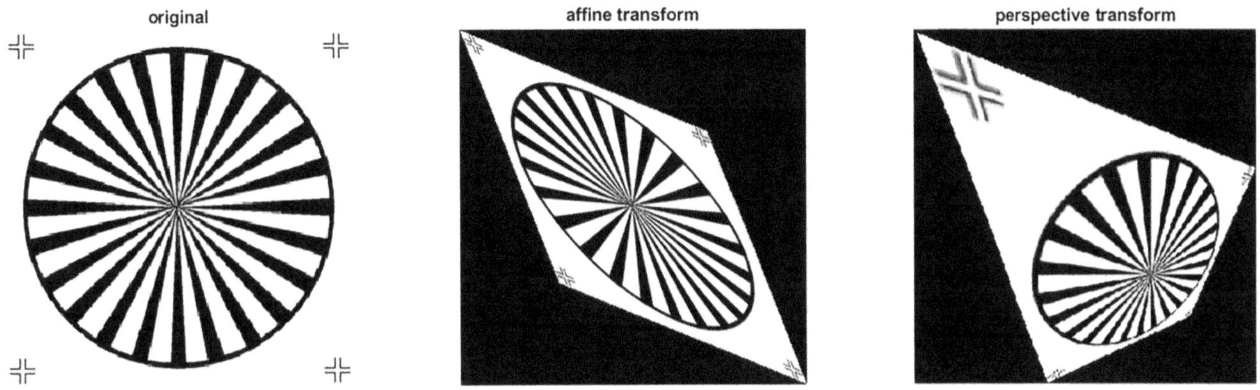

FIGURE 3.15
Affine and perspective transformations.

and introduce distortions that mimic real-world viewing conditions. A rectangle in general will be converted to a parallelogram as equal distances of opposite sides are not maintained. Under non-affine transformation, the transformed coordinates of a point are given by:

$$x_2 = \frac{ax_1 + by_1 + c}{gx_1 + hy_1 + 1}$$

$$y_2 = \frac{dx_1 + ey_1 + f}{gx_1 + hy_1 + 1}$$

3.3.2 Intensity Transformations

These operations modify the pixel values using certain rule-based techniques. Based on the rules employed there can be several approaches. Major techniques include gamma adjustments, histogram equalizations and kernel-based operations, as well as numerical methods like arithmetical and logical operations (Sundararajan, 2017).

3.3.2.1 Gamma Adjustments

Gamma adjustments or corrections adjust the brightness and contrast of an image using input-output transfer functions. These are written as $s = T(r)$, where r denotes the input pixel values, s denotes the output pixel values and T denotes the transfer function. For gamma adjustments the transfer function typically takes the form of power curves defined as:

$$s = c.r^{\gamma}$$

Here c is a constant and the index γ (gamma) determines how the output changes with respect to the input. These curves are referred to as "gamma curves". A plot of r vs. s curves for various ranges of γ values is shown below (Figure 3.16).

For $\gamma < 1$, a narrow range of input values are mapped to a broad range of output values, which increases the brightness of the image. For $\gamma > 1$, a broad range of input values are mapped to a narrow range of output values, which decreases the brightness of the image. An image is called inverted if all gray levels are replaced by their opposite values, i.e., $s = 255 - r$.

3.3.2.2 Contrast Stretching

Contrast stretching, also known as normalization or contrast enhancement, is a fundamental image processing technique employed to improve the visibility of features in an image by expanding the range of intensity values. This process aims to stretch the pixel values of an image across a wider dynamic range, thereby enhancing the contrast and making details more distinguishable. Often this is done by combining both of the gamma ranges into a single S shaped curve to expand both the lower and upper gray levels. For computational convenience, a piecewise linear version of the combined curve may be used for linearly stretching the intensity of a smaller range of input values from r_1 to r_2 to a wider set of output values from s_1 to s_2 while keeping values below r_1 and those above r_2 to their original values (Figure 3.17). Consider for example a range of input values from $r_1 = s_1 = 100$ to $r_2 = s_2 = 200$, having a contrast of 100, to be stretched to new output values from 50 to 225 having contrast of 175, i.e., $r_1 = 100, s_1' = 50, r_2 = 200, s_2' = 225$. The transfer function is the equation of the line through points (100, 50) and (200, 225) which is $y = 1.75(x - 100) + 50$ whose gradient has increased from 1 to 1.75 to reflect an increase of contrast. This formula ensures that each pixel value is proportionally stretched to fit within the desired intensity range. The new value of an existing pixel, say, $x = 150$, can now be obtained by plugging it

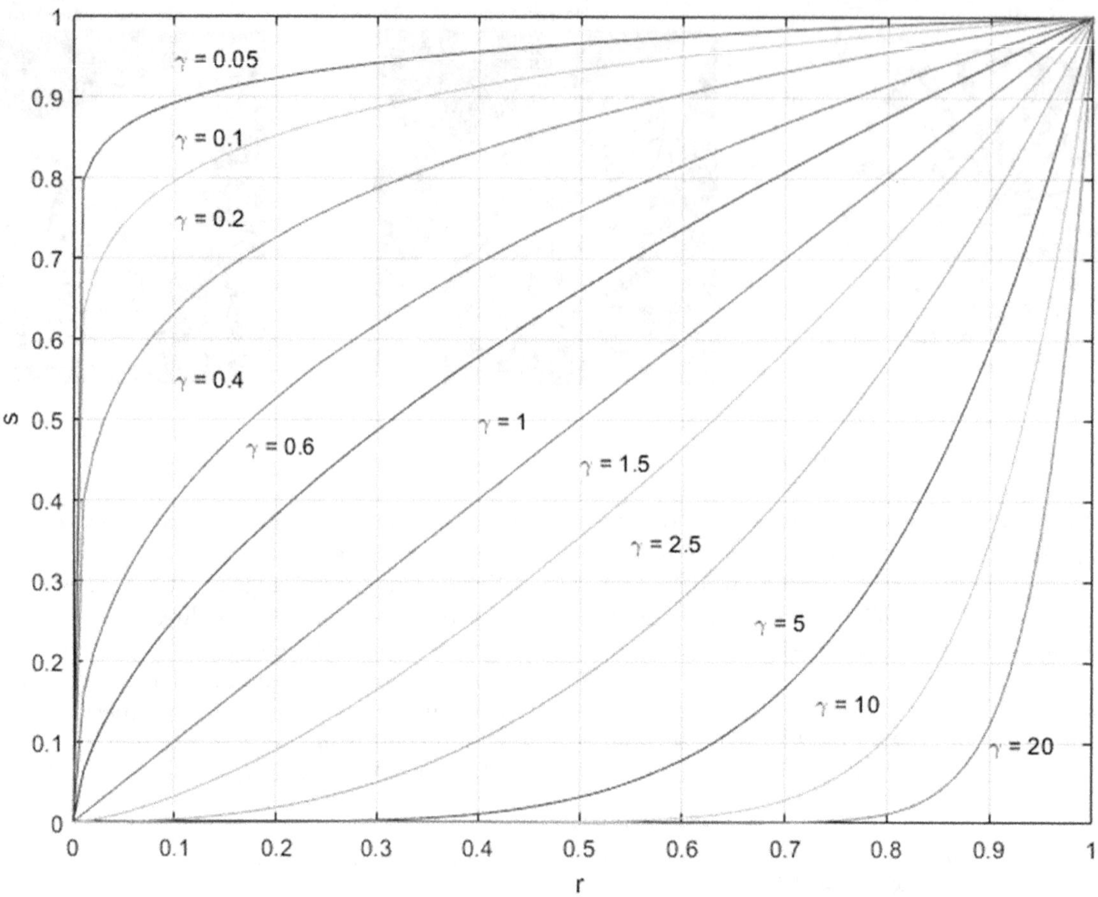

FIGURE 3.16
Gamma curves.

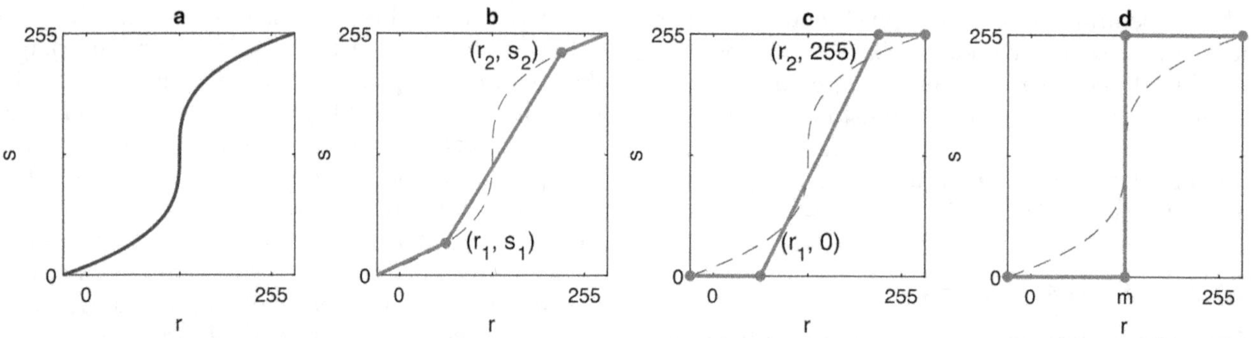

FIGURE 3.17
Contrast stretching and thresholding.

in the above equation to be $y = 1.75(150 - 100) + 50$ or approximately 138.

In some cases the stretching is done to force the values below r_1 to 0 and those above r_2 to 255, i.e., to cover the entire range of 0 to 255 in which case $s_1' = 0$ and $s_2' = 255$. The transfer function is now the equation of the line through points (100, 0) and (200, 255) which is $y = 2.55(x - 100)$ whose gradient has increased from 1 to 2.55.

By redistributing pixel values over a broader range, subtle details in the image become more distinguishable. Contrast stretching is particularly useful in medical imaging, satellite imagery and various scientific applications, where enhancing the visibility of features can aid interpretation. While contrast stretching is beneficial for many images, it should be applied judiciously to avoid saturating extreme pixel values, which could lead to loss of information. In cases where

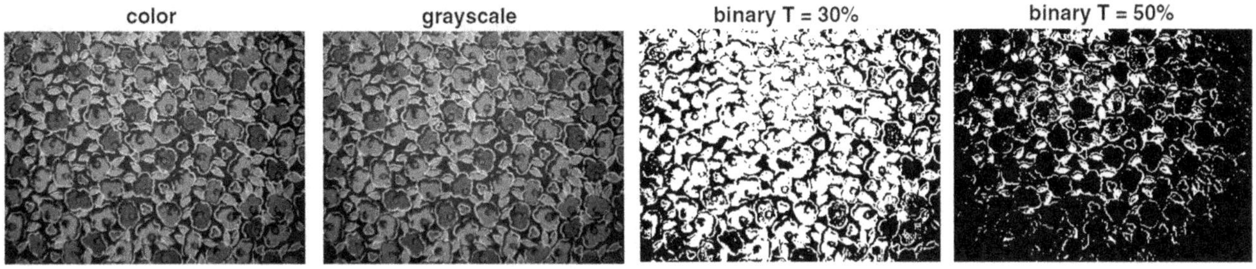

FIGURE 3.18
Different thresholds for binarization.

an image contains noise, contrast stretching may amplify the noise along with the useful signal.

3.3.2.3 Thresholding

In the previous section, if $r_1 = r_2 = m$, then it becomes a binarization operation as all values below the threshold m become 0 and all values above m become 255, and the operation is referred to as thresholding. When a grayscale image is converted to a binary image, all pixel values must be categorized either as 1 or as 0. The decision as to which pixel should be 1 and which should be 0 depends on the threshold m. Depending on the threshold itself, the same grayscale image can give rise to different binary images (Figure 3.18). Using smaller thresholds results in brighter images as a larger percentage of pixels become white. Conversely, using larger thresholds results in darker images. Since different thresholds generate different images, the question of a best or optimum threshold arises. Nobuyuki Otsu proposed a method (Otsu, 1979) henceforth referred to as Otsu's method, to automatically calculate the threshold from grayscale images which minimizes the intra-class variance of black and white pixels from image histograms. If t be the threshold intensity level and σ_1 and σ_2 be the standard deviation of the histogram values on either side of the threshold, then the Otsu's method fixes the threshold at a point where the weighted sum of the variances ($q_1 . \sigma_1^2 + q_2 . \sigma_2^2$) is minimum. Here q_1 and q_2 are the weights, and if $p(i)$ be the pixel count at the i-th intensity level, and L be the total number of intensity levels, then:

$$q_1 = \sum_{i=1}^{t} [p(i)]$$

$$q_2 = \sum_{i=t+1}^{L} [p(i)]$$

The class means are defined as follows:

$$\mu_1 = \sum_{i=1}^{t} [i.p(i) / q_1]$$

$$\mu_2 = \sum_{i=t+1}^{L} [i.p(i) / q_2]$$

The class variances are defined as follows:

$$\sigma_1^2 = \sum_{i=1}^{t} \left[(i - \mu_1)^2 . p(i) / q_1 \right]$$

$$\sigma_2^2 = \sum_{i=t+1}^{L} \left[(i - \mu_2)^2 . p(i) / q_2 \right]$$

Apart from single thresholds which leads to a binary image, multiple thresholds can also be computed which generates an image with two or three gray levels.

3.3.2.4 Histogram Equalization

Histogram equalization enhances the contrast of an image by redistributing pixel intensities, particularly useful in improving the visibility of features in images with uneven lighting. An image histogram is a 2D plot of the number of pixels against their intensities. The horizontal axis depicts pixel intensities from 0 to 255 which the vertical axis depicts the number of pixels belonging to each gray level. Ideally the histogram of an image should be evenly spread out over the entire range of gray levels. If, however, the image is excessively dark then the histogram will be clustered to the left toward the low intensity values, while if the image is excessively bright then the histogram will be clustered to the right toward the high intensity values. If an image has low contrast, then the histogram is

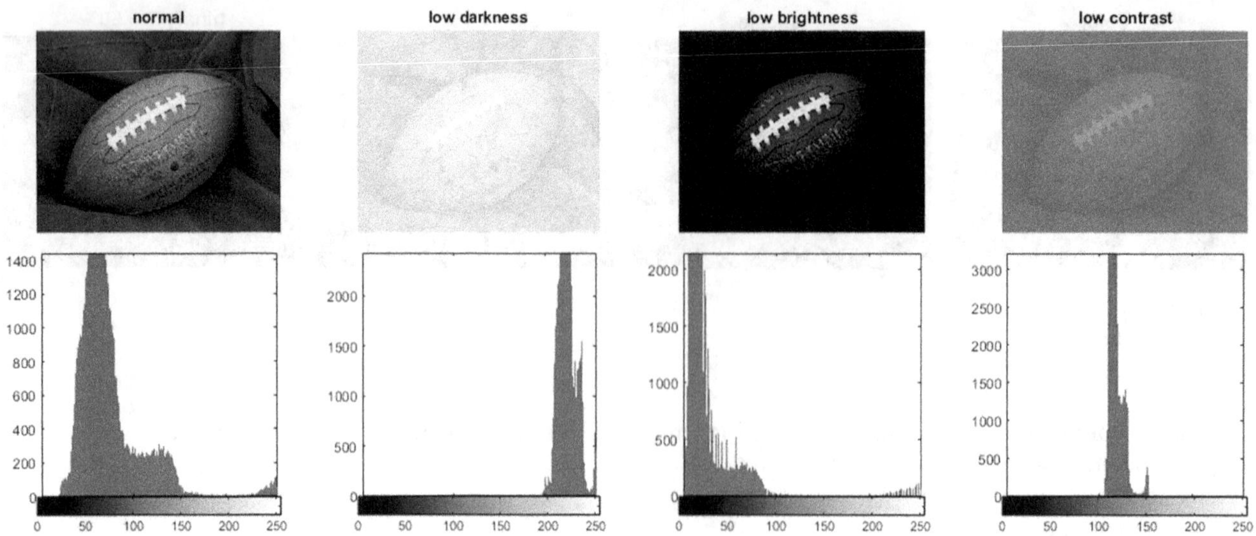

FIGURE 3.19
Images and their histograms.

clustered toward the middle signifying absence of both pure black and pure white shades (Figure 3.19).

In such cases the tonal correction of the images can be done by histogram equalization which is a process of stretching the histogram so that it covers the entire range from 0 to 255. If L be the total number of gray levels and k be a specific intensity level, then the histogram value $h(k)$ required for equalization is given by the following relation:

$$h(k) = round\left[\frac{CDF(k) - CDF(\min)}{N - CDF(\min)}\right] \times (L-1)$$

Here CDF is the cumulative distribution frequency which counts the total number of pixels upto level k, and N is the total number of pixels in the image (Figure 3.20).

3.3.3 Arithmetical Operations

Arithmetical operations on images involve manipulating pixel values to create new images or modify existing ones. These operations are fundamental in image processing and play a crucial role in tasks such as contrast adjustment, blending and combining multiple images.

3.3.3.1 Addition and Multiplication

For addition operation, corresponding pixel values of two images are added together, or, a scalar value is added to all pixels of a single image. For multiplication operation, either pixel values of two images are multiplied together or a scalar value is multiplied to each pixel of a single image. The general purpose is to increase the value of the pixels and hence improve the brightness of the image. However, it needs to be noted that a pixel value cannot exceed the maximum value of 255.

$$(P_1 + P_2) \leq 255$$

$$(P_1 + k) \leq 255$$

$$(P_1 \times P_2) \leq 255$$

$$(P_1 \times k) \leq 255$$

3.3.3.2 Subtraction and Division

For subtraction operation, corresponding pixel values of two images are subtracted one from the other, or, a scalar value is subtracted from all pixels of a single image. For division operation, either pixel values of one image are divided by those of the other or each pixel of a single image is divided by a scalar value. The general purpose is to decrease the value of the pixels and hence reduce the brightness of the image. However, it needs to be noted that a pixel value cannot reduce below the minimum value of 0.

$$(P_1 - P_2) \geq 0$$

$$(P_1 - k) \geq 0$$

$$(P_1 / P_2) \geq 0$$

$$(P_1 / k) \geq 0$$

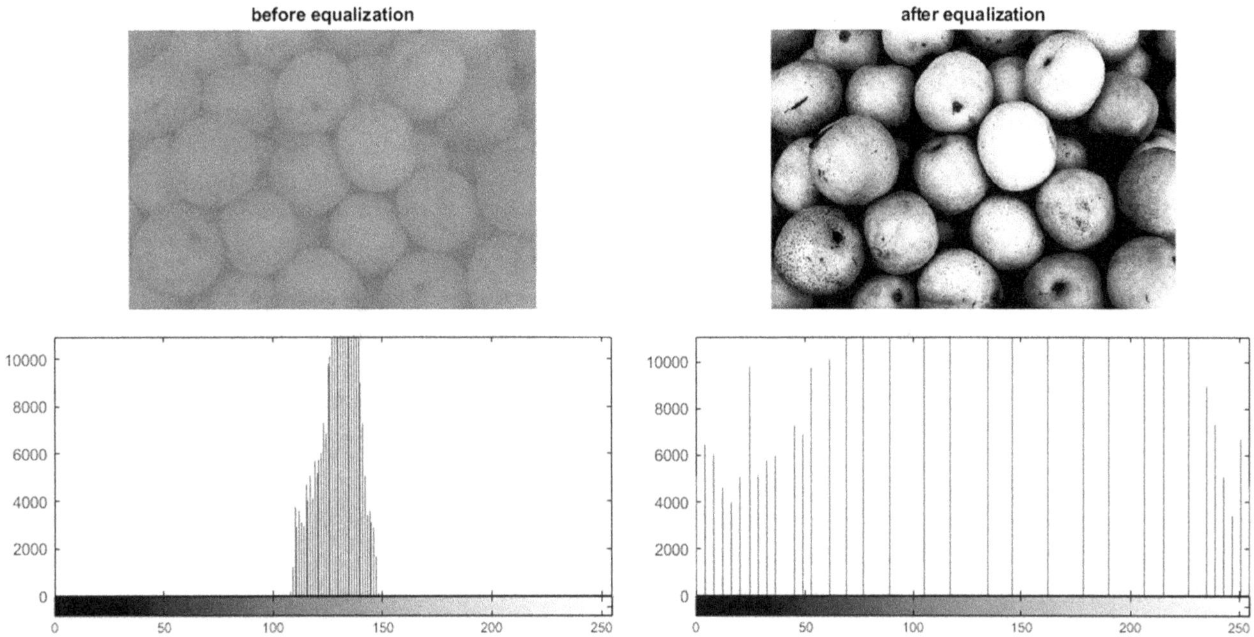

FIGURE 3.20
Histogram equalization.

3.3.3.3 Linear Combinations

This involves combining two images with a weighted sum. If P_1 and P_3 be the corresponding pixel values from two images, then a linear combination is defined as: $\alpha \times P_1 + (1 - \alpha) \times P_2$ where $0 \leq \alpha \leq 1$. Different values of α can produce different visual effects on the combination image (Figure 3.21). Here, d = a – b.

3.3.3.4 Blending Modes

Predefined blending modes inbuilt into image processing software can be used to produce customized effects. If P_1 and P_2 be the corresponding pixel values from two images, then the following blending modes are defined as follows:

- Multiply: $(P_1 \times P_2)/255$. This will always produce a darker image as either pixel is multiplied by a factor less than 1.

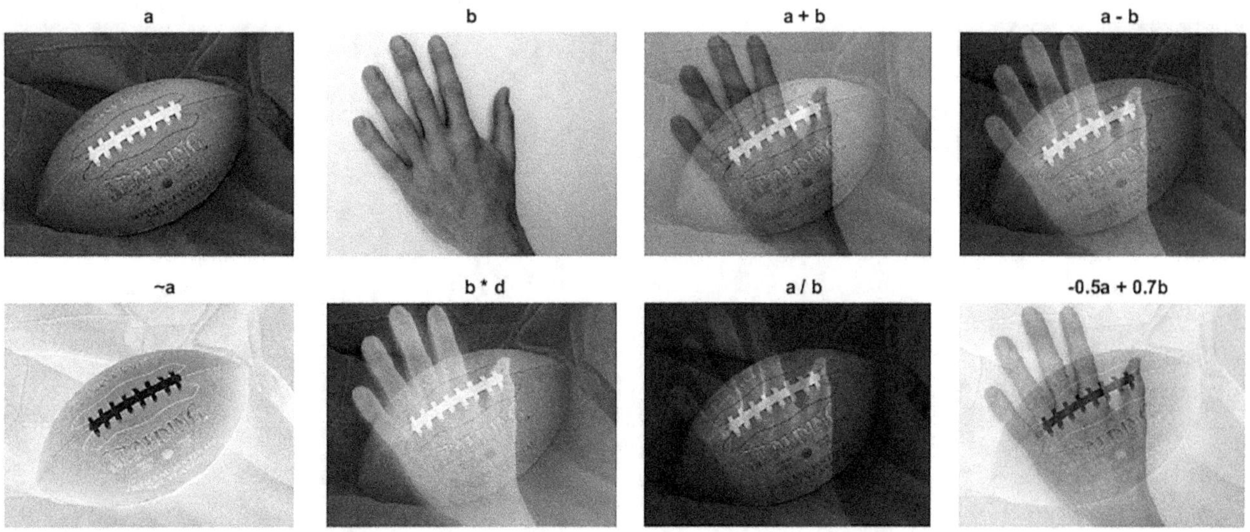

FIGURE 3.21
Arithmetic operations.

- Screen: 255 – [(255 – P_1)(255 – P_2)/255]. This will always produce a lighter image as a darker image is subtracted from 255.
- Difference: $|P_1 - P_2|$
- Darken: min(P_1, P_2)
- Lighten: max(P_1, P_2)

3.3.4 Logical Operations

Logical operations AND, OR, XOR, NOT are performed at the bit level between corresponding pixels. Bitwise operations are employed in image masking, region of interest extraction and compression. The results of the logical operators are defined in the same way as dictated by the truth tables of standard logic gates. For each pixel-pair *A* and *B* of two images *I* and *J*, the output value of any logical operations on them are determined by the right-hand sides of the above relations (Figure 3.22).

- A AND B = a.b = min(A,B)
- A OR B = a + b = max(A, B)
- NOT A = a′ = 1 – A
- NOT B = b′ = 1 – B
- A XOR B = a.b′ + a′.b

3.3.5 Kernel-Based Operations

Kernel-based operations modify the value of a pixel, not in an isolated manner but in a manner dependent on the values of the neighboring pixels. A kernel or mask or template is a small array, typically of size 3 × 3 or 5 × 5, and contains some coefficient values. Starting from the top-left corner of the image the kernel is slided over the image left to right and top to bottom until it reaches the bottom-right corner of the image. At each position of the kernel, the coefficients of the kernel are multiplied with the pixel value just below it and all such products are summed up (Figure 3.23). The sum is now made to replace the pixel value just under the center of the kernel. For a kernel of size 3 × 3, if the coefficients range from $w(-1,-1)$ through $w(0,0)$ to $w(1,1)$ and the pixel values below the kernel range from $f(x-1,y-1)$ through $f(x,y)$ to $f(x+1,y+1)$, then the sum is:

$$S = \sum_{a=-1}^{1}\sum_{b=-1}^{1} w(a,b).f(x+a,y+b)$$

This operation is repeated for all positions of the kernel, and the entire operation is called correlation. The same operation is referred to as convolution if the kernel is first rotated by 180° before carrying out the process. If the values of the coefficients of the kernel are equal, the kernel is called an average kernel. To prevent the pixel values from exceeding 255, the average kernel is divided by the sum of the coefficients, hence the name.

The effect of correlation or convolution is image blurring, the amount of blur depending on the size of the kernel, the larger the kernel greater is the blurring. The blurring is a result of the fact that each pixel of the input image is replaced by a weighted average of the neighboring pixels, due to which the operation behaves like a low-pass filter.

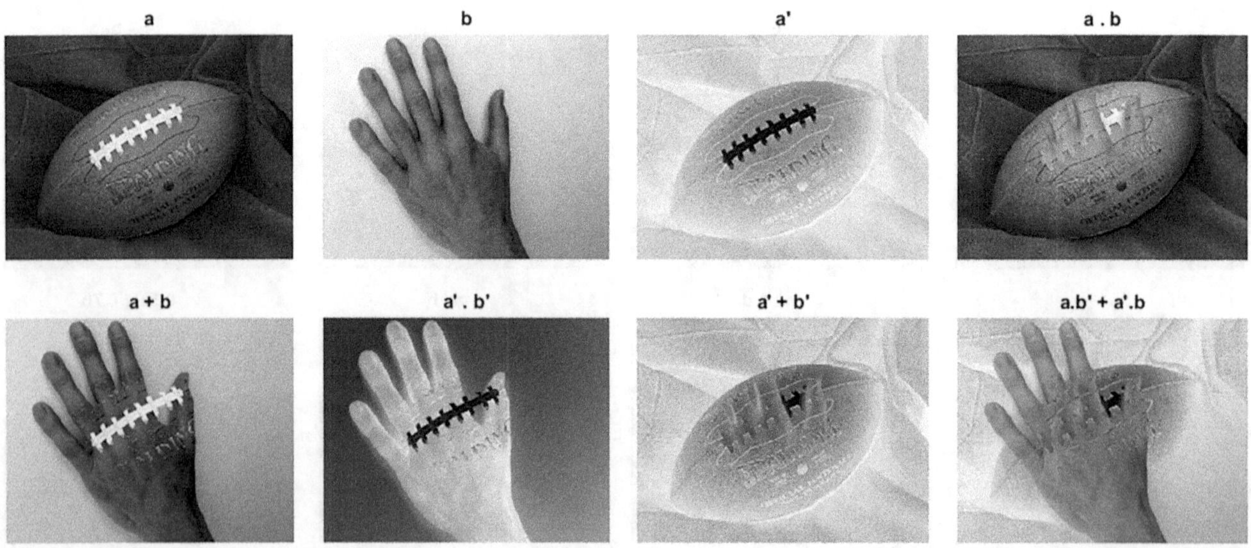

FIGURE 3.22
Logical operations.

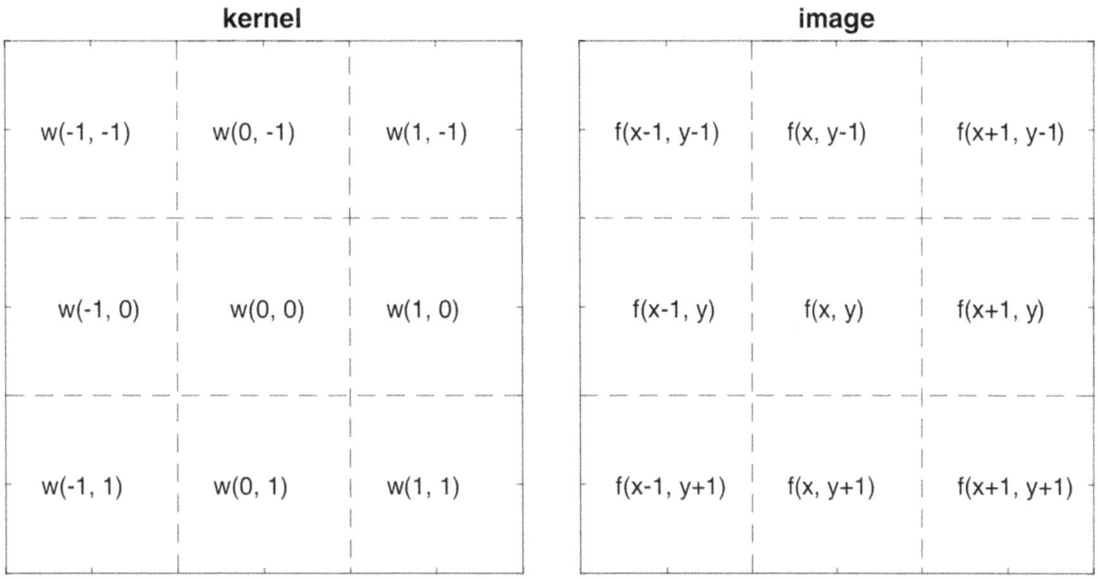

FIGURE 3.23
Kernel coefficients and image pixels.

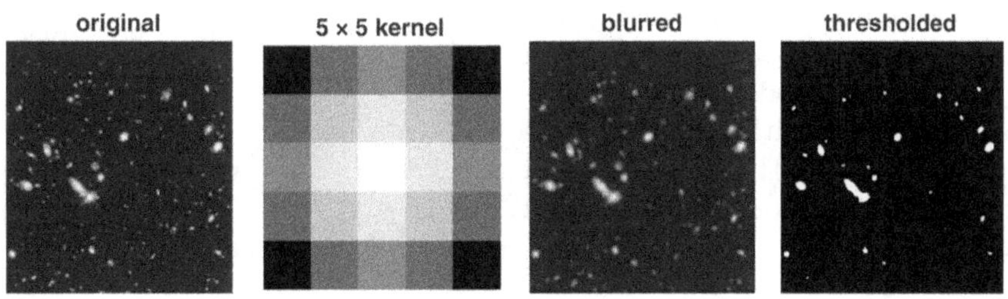

FIGURE 3.24
Noise filtering.

3.3.6 Noise Filtering

A major application of convolution is to reduce the effect of noise in an image, as noise is frequently represented as small dots in the background and blurring can effectively reduce this effect to some extent. The blurred image can subsequently be binarized with an appropriate threshold to eliminate the smaller dots. Applied this way, the kernel is referred to as a noise filter. Usually, the kernel is a Gaussian kernel, where the coefficient values represent a 2D Gaussian distribution.

$$G(x,y) = \exp\left(-\frac{x^2+y^2}{2\sigma^2}\right)$$

A Gaussian kernel is frequently used as a noise filter to improve or enhance image quality corrupted by small white dots. On blurring the smaller spots is reduced in the intensities due to the convolution with the black background. On thresholding, the smaller dots are effectively removed leaving on the larger spots in the image (Figure 3.24). Another type of noise consisting of both white and black dots is called salt-and-pepper noise. Such noise can more effectively be removed by a median filter. A median filter replaces the central pixel value by the median of the pixel values under the kernel. Other similar filters include the min-filter and max-filter, where the minimum and maximum of the pixel values under the kernel is used to replace the central pixel value. The min-filter can remove bright spots from an image while the max-filter can remove dark spots.

3.3.7 Edge Detection

A second major application of convolution is edge detection. Converse to image blurring which uses low-pass or integral filters, image sharpening is implemented using high-pass filters which are differential filters based on derivatives of the image. Their effect is to highlight the high-frequency components like edges and corners. Edge detection is an important step in pattern recognition whereby foreground objects are separated from the background by highlighting their contours or edges. Three of the most frequently used edge detection kernels are the Roberts operator (Rx, Ry), Sobel operator (Sx, Sy) and Prewitt operator (Px, Py). Each of these actually consists of two kernels one for horizontal edges and one for vertical edges. The final result is a combination of both the outputs.

$$Rx = \begin{bmatrix} -1 & 0 \\ 0 & +1 \end{bmatrix} ; \; Ry = \begin{bmatrix} 0 & -1 \\ +1 & 0 \end{bmatrix}$$

$$Sx = \begin{bmatrix} -1 & 0 & +1 \\ -2 & 0 & +2 \\ -1 & 0 & +1 \end{bmatrix} ; \; Sy = \begin{bmatrix} -1 & -2 & -1 \\ 0 & 0 & 0 \\ +1 & +2 & +1 \end{bmatrix}$$

$$Px = \begin{bmatrix} -1 & 0 & +1 \\ -1 & 0 & +1 \\ -1 & 0 & +1 \end{bmatrix} ; \; Py = \begin{bmatrix} -1 & -1 & -1 \\ 0 & 0 & 0 \\ +1 & +1 & +1 \end{bmatrix}$$

An edge detector is essentially a differential filter; i.e., it detects edges by calculating difference between pixel values along the same row and column. It calculates the derivative of a signal which for digital images is approximated by the difference. This is also referred to as the gradient of the image along the horizontal and vertical directions.

$$g_x = \frac{\partial f(x,y)}{\partial x} = \{f(x+1,y) - f(x-1,y)\}$$

$$g_y = \frac{\partial f(x,y)}{\partial y} = \{f(x,y+1) - f(x,y-1)\}$$

Two slightly more complex edge detectors are the LoG and Canny operators. The Canny edge detector first smoothens the image using a Gaussian filter and then computes the local gradient magnitude and direction at each point of the resulting image. The gradient magnitude is $g = \sqrt{g_x^2 + g_y^2}$ and gradient direction is $\theta = \arctan(g_y / g_x)$. The third step involves a process called non-maximum suppression which retains those edges which have the maximum gradient magnitude along the maximum gradient direction (Figure 3.25).

The Laplacian of Gaussian (LoG) edge detector first implements a Gaussian filter to blur the image for removing noise and then applies the Laplacian operator to the resulting image. The Laplacian operator is computed by adding the second derivatives of pixel intensities along the $x-$ and $y-$ directions, i.e.,

$$\nabla^2 f(x,y) = \frac{\partial^2 f(x,y)}{\partial x^2} + \frac{\partial^2 f(x,y)}{\partial y^2}$$

Expressed as a kernel the Laplacian mask is:

$$L = \begin{bmatrix} 0 & 1 & 0 \\ 1 & -4 & 1 \\ 0 & 1 & 0 \end{bmatrix}$$

3.3.8 Morphological Operations

Morphological operations are fundamental techniques in image processing that focus on the shape and structure of objects within an image. These operations are particularly useful for tasks such as image

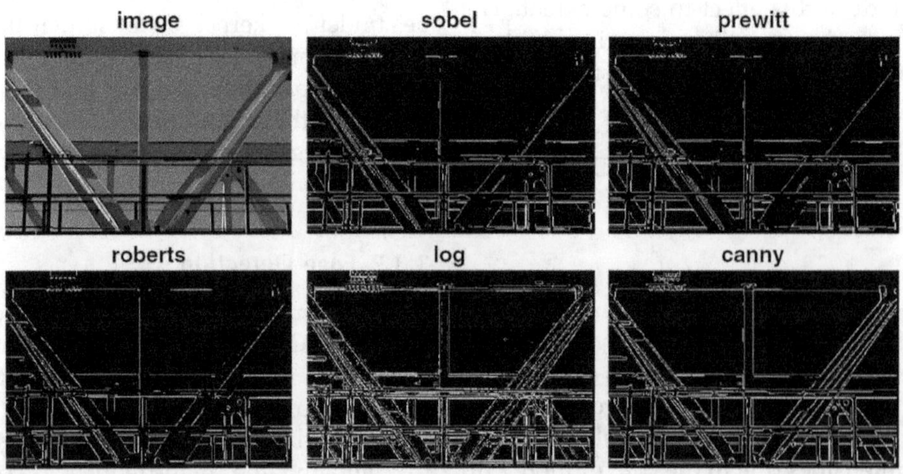

FIGURE 3.25
Edge detection.

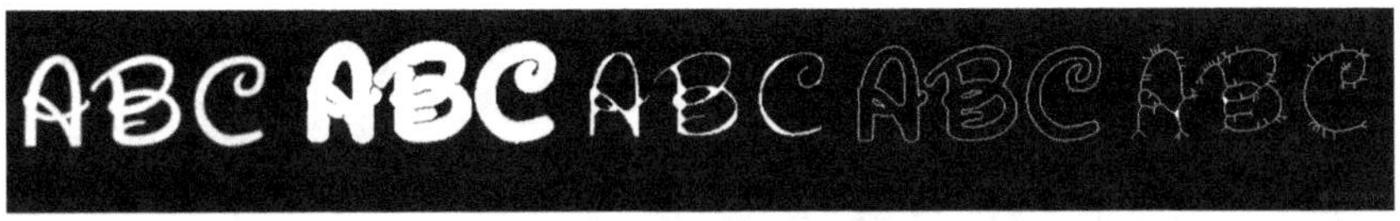

FIGURE 3.26
Morphological operations: Original image and effects of dilation, erosion, edge detection and skeletonization.

segmentation, noise removal and feature extraction. These operations involve the interaction of an image with a kernel called the structuring element or mask. There can be several types as discussed below (Figure 3.26).

Dilation: The dilation operator enlarges the boundaries of foreground (white) pixels. At each position of the kernel, if a 1 on the kernel coincides with a 1 on the image beneath then the input image pixel beneath the center of the kernel is set to 1, if not already so. This results in thickening of lines.

Erosion: The erosion operator works opposite to dilation; i.e., it shrinks the boundaries of foreground (white) pixels. At each position of the kernel, if a 1 on the kernel coincides with a 1 on the image beneath, then the input image pixel beneath the center of the kernel is set to 0, if not already so. This results in thinning of lines.

Opening: Erosion followed by dilation. Effect is somewhat similar to erosion but less pronounced.

Closing: Dilation followed by erosion. Effect is somewhat similar to dilation but less pronounced (Figure 3.26).

Thickening: Similar to dilation and closing and results in thickening of lines, but the process is stopped when doing so would result in previously unconnected objects being connected.

Thinning: Similar to erosion and opening and results in thinning of lines, but the process is stopped when doing so would result in previously connected objects being unconnected.

Remove: Removes interior pixels by setting a pixel to 0 if all its connected neighbours on four sides are 1, leaving only the boundary pixels on. This is similar to edge detection.

Skeletonization: Removes foreground pixels but does not allow objects to break apart thereby arriving at a skeletal remnant of a shape.

3.3.9 Frequency Transformations

Until now all the filtering operations performed have been performed in the spatial domain, i.e., the $xy-$ plane of the image. An alternative form of processing is called the frequency domain processing, where the image is transformed from the spatial domain to the frequency domain using the Discrete Fourier Transform (DFT), Discrete Cosine Transform (DCT) and Discrete Wavelet Transform (DWT). In all these cases, the image is expressed as a weighted sum of predefined frequency components which define how fast the pixel intensities are varying spatially. The frequency components are called basis functions while the weights are called coefficients. The abovementioned transforms differ in their choice of basis functions (Burger & Burge, 2013).

3.3.9.1 Discrete Fourier Transform (DFT)

The Discrete Fourier Transform (DFT) is used to represent the image in terms of basis functions which take the form of spatially varying sine and cosine waves. If the image has M columns and N rows, then the forward and inverse 2D DFT are given by:

$$F(u,v) = \sum_{x=0}^{M-1}\sum_{y=0}^{N-1} f(x,y).\exp\left\{-j.2\pi\left(\frac{ux}{M}+\frac{vy}{N}\right)\right\}$$

$$f(x,y) = \frac{1}{MN}\sum_{u=0}^{M-1}\sum_{v=0}^{N-1} F(u,v).\exp\left\{j.2\pi\left(\frac{ux}{M}+\frac{vy}{N}\right)\right\}$$

where $F(u,v)$ represents the complex frequency-domain representation at values (u,v), $f(x,y)$ is the pixel value at coordinates (x,y) in the 2D input signal, M and N are the dimensions (width and height) of the input signal, u and v are the frequency indices, ranging from 0 to $M-1$ for u and 0 to $N-1$ for v, j is the imaginary unit $\sqrt{-1}$, Σ denotes summation over all values of (x,y) or (u,v). The Fourier Transform of a 2D image is also displayed as an image itself, since it is a 2D matrix of coefficients. However since the values are complex in nature we calculate its absolute value $|F|$. The zero frequency components are shifted to the center of the plot for better visualization. The DFT coefficients usually span over a large range of values of the order of 10^6. To display these values in the form of an image they need to be compressed to within the range 0 to 255. This is achieved by using the log function (Figure 3.27). To avoid possibility of a 0 value, 1 is added to it before calculating logarithm, i.e., $\log(1+|F|)$.

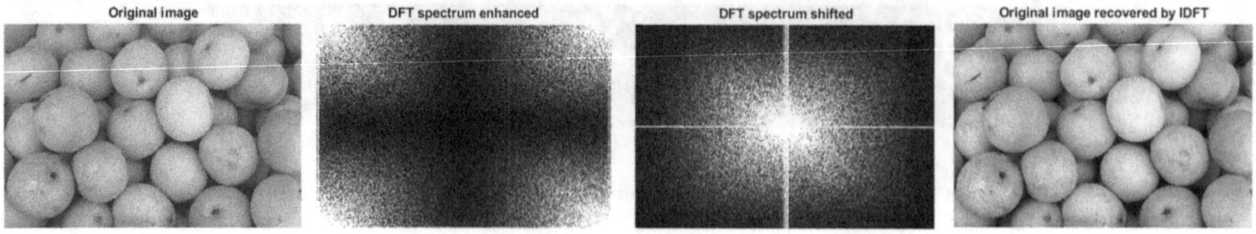

FIGURE 3.27
DFT output of an image.

3.3.9.2 Discrete Cosine Transform (DCT)

The Discrete Cosine Transform (DCT) is an alternative to the DFT using which the signal can be transformed into the frequency domain using only real components and thereby avoid complex arithmetic. The forward and inverse 2D DCT are given by:

$$F(u,v) = \alpha_u.\alpha_v.\sum_{x=0}^{M-1}\sum_{y=0}^{N-1} f(x,y)$$

$$.\cos\left\{\frac{(2x+1)\pi u}{2M}\right\}.\cos\left\{\frac{(2y+1)\pi v}{2N}\right\}$$

$$f(x,y) = \sum_{u=0}^{M-1}\sum_{v=0}^{N-1} \alpha_u.\alpha_v.F(u,v)$$

$$.\cos\left\{\frac{(2x+1)\pi u}{2M}\right\}.\cos\left\{\frac{(2y+1)\pi v}{2N}\right\}$$

where $F(u,v)$ represents the complex frequency-domain representation at coordinates (u,v), $f(x,y)$ is the pixel value at coordinates (x,y) in the 2D input signal, M and N are the dimensions (width and height) of the input signal, u and v are the frequency indices, ranging from 0 to $M-1$ for u and 0 to $N-1$ for v, j is the imaginary unit ($\sqrt{-1}$), Σ denotes summation over all values of (x,y) or (u,v),

$$\alpha_u = \sqrt{\frac{1}{M}}\ for\, u = 0 \ \ and\ \ \alpha_u = \sqrt{\frac{2}{N}}\ for\, u \neq 0,$$

$$\alpha_v = \sqrt{\frac{1}{N}}\ for\, v = 0 \ \ and\ \ \alpha_v = \sqrt{\frac{2}{N}}\ for\, v \neq 0$$

As for DFT, the DCT of an image is a 2D array of values and can be displayed as an image itself. Usually, the DCT coefficients are displayed using a logarithmic scale to compress the large range of values within the display range of 0 to 255 (Figure 3.28).

3.3.9.3 Discrete Wavelet Transform (DWT)

The forward 2D DWT involves applying two 1D filters, a low pass (L) filter h and a high pass (H) filter g along the rows (k) and columns (l) of the 2D signal. If A (hh), H (hg), V (gh), D (gg) denote the approximation, horizontal detail, vertical detail and diagonal detail coefficients respectively (Mallat, 1989), then we have:

$$A_{LL}(n,m) = \sum_k\sum_l h(k).h(l).x(2m-k, 2n-l)$$

$$H_{LH}(n,m) = \sum_k\sum_l h(k).g(l).x(2m-k, 2n-l)$$

$$V_{HL}(n,m) = \sum_k\sum_l g(k).h(l).x(2m-k, 2n-l)$$

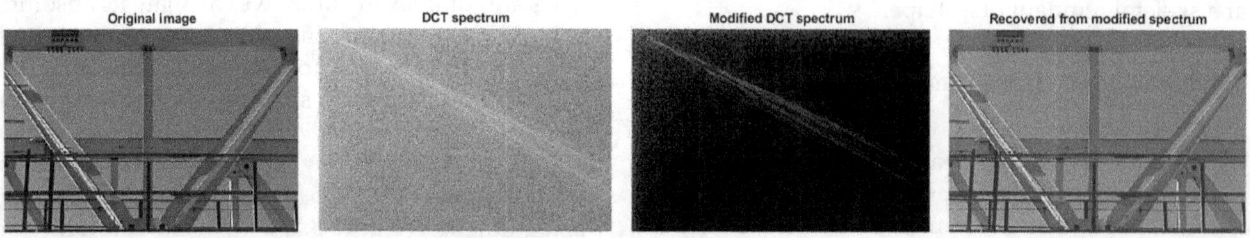

FIGURE 3.28
DCT output of an image.

$$D_{HH}(n,m) = \sum_k \sum_l g(k).g(l).x(2m-k, 2n-l)$$

When applied to a 2D signal like an image I, a 2D wavelet transform operation can be represented by the following scheme, which is called a 1-level or single-level decomposition, where W is the 2D wavelet transform matrix:

$$W * I * W^T \rightarrow \begin{bmatrix} LL & LH \\ HL & HH \end{bmatrix} \rightarrow \begin{bmatrix} A & H \\ V & D \end{bmatrix}$$

Here, LL indicates low-pass filtering along both the rows (width) and columns (height) of the input image, generating the approximation coefficient A which is a copy of the original image but scaled by half (averaging) along both width and height. LH indicates low-pass filtering along the rows and high-pass filtering along the columns, generating the horizontal coefficient H which is an image produced by averaging along the width and differencing along the height and so able to identify horizontal edges. HL indicates high-pass filtering along the rows and low pass filtering along the columns, generating the vertical coefficient V which is an image produced by averaging along the height and differencing along the width and so able to identify vertical edges. HH indicates high-pass filtering along both the rows and columns, generating the diagonal coefficient D which is an image produced by differencing along both the width and height and so able to identify diagonal edges. The above steps are collectively referred to as decomposition or analysis step. The approximation and detail components can be combined together to reconstruct the original image which is called the reconstruction or synthesis step. Multi-level decomposition can also be done by using the approximation image of the previous level as the starting image for the next level (Figure 3.29).

The inverse 2D DWT involves applying the 1D IDWT along the columns and rows of the transformed signal.

For Haar wavelets (Haar, 1910), $h = \frac{1}{\sqrt{2}}(1 \quad 1)$ and $g = \frac{1}{\sqrt{2}}(1 \quad -1)$

3.3.10 De-Convolution

De-convolution is a mathematical process used to reverse the blurring effects introduced during image acquisition. By modeling the degradation process, de-convolution algorithms can estimate and restore the original image. For example, in astronomical imaging, de-convolution is employed to enhance the clarity of celestial objects by compensating for atmospheric distortions and telescope imperfections.

According to the degradation-restoration model, an original image $f(x,y)$ is assumed to be degraded in two steps: blurring and additive noise. In the first step, a point spread function (PSF) is thought to blur an image by causing lack of focus, usually arising from imperfections of the camera and/or motion of the object with respect to the camera. In the second step, a random noise from the environment, arising due to factors like electrical interference or low lighting conditions, is added to the blurred image.

If $g(x,y)$ be the degraded image, then the original image $f(x,y)$ is converted to it as part of the degradation process, by first convolving it with a PSF function $h(x,y)$ causing a blurring effect and then by addition of a random noise function $n(x,y)$. Combining both effects the degradation process can be mathematically represented as below, where $\otimes$ is the convolution operator:

$$g(x,y) = f(x,y) \otimes h(x,y) + n(x,y)$$

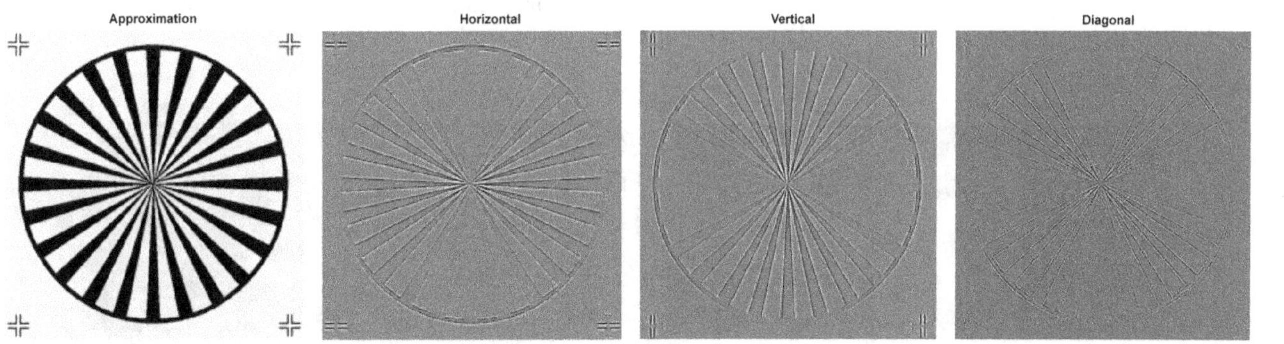

FIGURE 3.29
DWT output of an image.

The purpose of image restoration is starting from $g(x,y)$ to get back an estimated image $e(x,y)$ which will not in general be identical to the original image $f(x,y)$ but a close estimate of it. This is because the actual degradation function h may not exactly be known, and the noise n being a random process cannot be accurately modeled either. Taking Fourier Transform on either side and using the Convolution Theorem we can rewrite the above as follows:

$$G(u,v) = F(u,v).H(u,v) + N(u,v)$$

The Convolution Theorem states that a convolution operation in the spatial domain is equivalent to a multiplication operation in the frequency domain and vice versa. In the absence of noise, a deconvolution operation can reverse the effects of convolution. In this case, if $N(u,v) = 0$:

$$G(u,v) = F(u,v).H(u,v)$$

$$F(u,v) = G(u,v) / H(u,v)$$

This implies in the frequency domain, deconvolution is equivalent to multiplying the degraded image with the reciprocal of the PSF and hence it is also called inverse filtering.

$$F = \left(\frac{1}{H}\right).G$$

If both degradation and noise is present, then an inverse filtering is not sufficient. One of the filters used in such cases is the Wiener filter, proposed by Norbert Wiener (Wiener, 1949). The estimate image $E(u,v)$ is given by:

$$E = \left(\frac{H^*}{H^2 + k}\right).G$$

Here $H^*(u,v)$ is the complex conjugate of $H(u,v)$ and k is a factor which depends on the power spectrum of the noise and the original image, both of which needs to be estimated. If noise is absent, k becomes zero and the Wiener filter reduces to an inverse filter (Figure 3.30).

While Wiener deconvolution is a non-iterative frequency domain process and can be applied when both PSF and noise are known or can be estimated, an alternative method called Lucy-Richardson deconvolution (L-R), is an iterative process in the spatial domain which can be applied only when the PSF and not the noise is known. The method is named after Leon Lucy (Lucy, 1974) and William Richardson (Richardson, 1972) who described the method independently. In order to estimate E given the observed image G and the PSF H an iterative procedure is followed in which the estimate of W for iteration number r is expressed as follows:

$$E_{i,r+1} = E_{i,r} \sum_k \frac{H_{i,k}.G_k}{\sum_j H_{j,k}.E_{j,r}}$$

Here E_i, G_k and H_j denote the i-th, k-th and j-th elements. It can be shown that this equation converges to the maximum likelihood solution for E.

3.3.11 Common Editing Tasks

Some of the most common image editing tasks that can be done using a GUI-based image editing software like Photoshop [www.adobe.com/products/photoshop], GIMP [www.gimp.org] and Canva [www.canva.com] are listed below (Figure 3.31):

Cropping and Resizing: Use cropping to eliminate unnecessary elements and resize to meet specific width and height requirements for specific applications.

Tonal correction: Adjust gray tones by using brightness, contrast and histogram-based

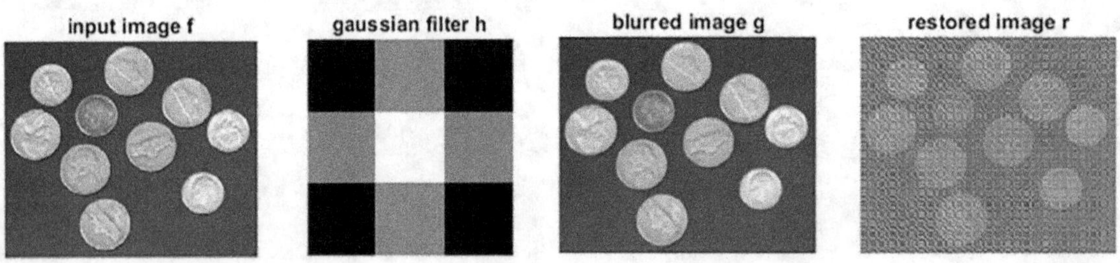

FIGURE 3.30
De-convolution and inverse filtering.

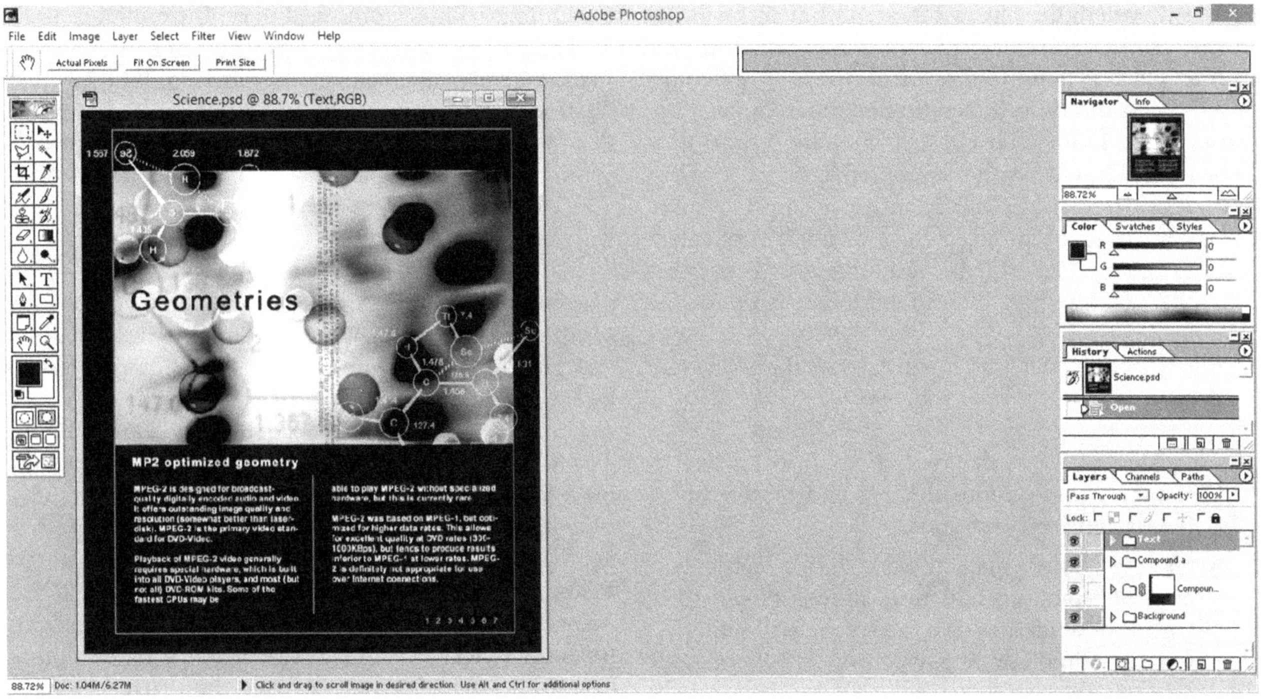

FIGURE 3.31
Typical GUI-based image editor interface.

adjustments to rectify excessively dark or bright images.

Color Correction and Adjustment: Enhance or modify the color balance, brightness, contrast and saturation of an image, by typically adjusting sliders. Additional facilities to select the color channels on which to make the changes, allow fine tuning of the adjustments.

Retouching: Remove imperfections, blemishes or unwanted elements from an image, by using brushes, clone stamps and fill tools.

Sharpening and Blurring: Enhance or soften the focus of an image, to emphasize details or create depth, typically along edges of image objects.

Background Removal and Replacement: Isolate subjects or remove distracting backgrounds, by using selection tools, masks and layers.

Adding Text and Graphics: Incorporate text, logos or graphic elements into an image, by using appropriate fonts, colors, positions and styles. Text parameters like leading and kerning can be modified and visual effects like drop shadow and emboss can be used to adhere to specific styles, for example, in logo design.

Filters and Effects: Apply creative filters and effects to apply artistic effects, or add subtle enhancements like vignettes and glows.

Collage and Composition: Combine multiple images into a cohesive composition or create a photo collage, by using layers and masking features.

Image Compression and Optimization: Reduce file size for efficient Web and digital media distribution, by choosing appropriate file formats, adjust compression settings and balance quality with file size for optimized images.

HDR Imaging: Combine multiple exposures to create high dynamic range images, by using specialized software like Photomatix or HDR features in certain image editing applications.

3.4 Image Color Management

The phenomenon of color perception depends on three factors: nature of light, physiology of human vision and interaction of light with matter. Out of the total range of electromagnetic spectrum, a small part called visible spectrum, spanning around 400–700 nm in the wavelength, causes the sensation of vision in our eyes. The photoreceptors in the retina of the human eyes respond to three different types of colors – red, green and blue, depending on the frequencies of light. When light strikes an opaque object, part of it gets absorbed and part of it gets reflected back to our eyes. The frequencies present in the reflected light, impart the color of the object from which it is reflected. Studies have revealed that the human eye is capable of distinguishing more than 16 million different colors (Young, 1802).

Color management in images is vital for several reasons:

Consistency: It ensures that colors appear consistent across various devices and under different lighting conditions.

Accuracy: Color management helps achieve accurate color reproduction, allowing users to trust that what they see on a screen will match what is printed or displayed on other devices.

Brand Identity: In graphic design and branding, color consistency is crucial to maintain a brand's identity across different media.

Visual Appeal: In photography and design, color management enhances the visual appeal of images, making them more engaging and professional.

Color management is a complex process that involves understanding color spaces, profiles, calibration and rendering intents.

3.4.1 Color Models

A color model is a mathematical abstraction that defines a way to represent colors as numerical values. These models are used to describe how colors are created, mixed and displayed. Essentially color models enable us to represent and communicate information regarding color in a meaningful and computer recognizable way. All colors that we see around us can be derived by mixing a few elementary colors in different proportions, called primary colors. Primary colors mixed together gives rise to composite colors, while two primary colors mixed in equal proportions generate secondary colors. The total range of primary, secondary and composite colors is defined by the color space of the model (Guild, 1931; Wright, 1929). A number of color models have been developed over the years, and formulae for conversion between the color spaces defined by these models have been standardized by global standards bodies like International Color Consortium (ICC) and International Commission on Illumination (CIE) and documented in their specifications. These specifications are technically identical to ISO 15076-1: 2010 standard [www.iso.org/standard/54754.html]. A few of these models and inter-relations between them are discussed below (Hunt & Wright, 2014).

3.4.1.1 RGB

The RGB (Red, Green, Blue) color model is used to represent all colors produced by mixing red (R), green (G) and blue (B) primaries. Each primary color is quantized to 256 levels so that the total number of colors in the RGB model is 256 × 256 × 256 or 16.7 million. The RGB color model is applicable for emission of colored lights such as those emitted from monitors, display panels and glow signs, and is additive in nature; i.e., the intensities increase when primary colors are mixed. When all three primaries are added in full intensities, the resultant color is white (255, 255, 255), whereas black (0, 0, 0) is the absence of all colors. Equal amounts of primary colors when mixed together produce secondary colors: red and blue produce magenta, blue and green produce cyan, green and red produce yellow. The visual representation of the RGB model takes the form of a color cube, comprising of three orthogonal axes R, G, B along which the red, green, blue components are plotted in the range 0 to 255. A color having value 255 is present in its full intensity and is referred to as saturated, if the intensity is less than 255 then it is called unsaturated. Three corners of the color cube are occupied by saturated primaries red, green, blue, three other corners by saturated secondaries magenta, cyan, yellow and other two corners by white and black. Any point inside the cube represents a specific color determined by its coordinates. For example the coordinates of color orange made up of 96% red, 40% green, 14% blue is (245, 102, 36) [0.96*255 = 245, 0.40*255 = 102, 0.14*255 = 36] (Figure 3.32).

3.4.1.2 CMY

The CMY (Cyan, Magenta, Yellow, Key/Black) color model is used to represent all colors produced by cyan (C), magenta (M) and yellow (Y) primaries. Each primary color is expressed in percentage values and quantized to 100 levels so that the total number of colors in the CMY model is 100 × 100 × 100 or 1 million. The CMY model also takes the visual form of a color cube, where cyan, magenta and yellow are plotted along three orthogonal axes C, M, Y in the range 0 to 100. The CMY color model is applicable for colored inks printed on paper and is based on absorption of light instead of emission. The model is therefore

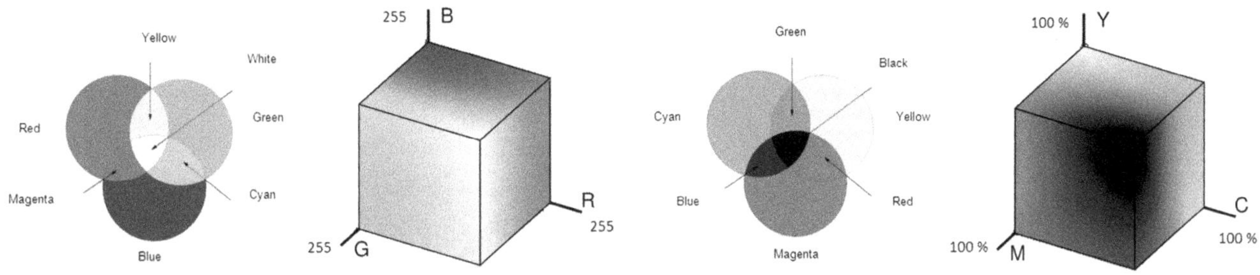

FIGURE 3.32
Visual representation of RGB and CMY color spaces.

subtractive in nature; i.e., the intensities decrease when primary colors are mixed due to absorption. Since magenta is formed by mixing red and blue, and cyan is formed from blue and green, when magenta is mixed in equal amounts to cyan, blue is obtained as a secondary color, the other components of red and green being absorbed. Similarly cyan mixed with yellow produces green, and yellow mixed with magenta produces red. When all three primaries are mixed in equal proportions, the resultant color is theoretically black (0%, 0%, 0%). However, since chemical inks cannot be absolutely pure in their composition, the color actually obtained is usually dark brown, thus a fourth component of pure black (K) ink is added along with the three primaries to generate the CMYK model. Any point inside the cube therefore represents a specific color. Three vertices of the cube are occupied by saturated primaries magenta, cyan, yellow, three other vertices are occupied by saturated secondaries red, green, blue, the remaining two vertices black and no color (produced by absence of any ink). The conversion relations between CMY and CMYK are as follows:

$$K = \min(C, M, Y)$$

$$C = (C - K)/(1 - K)$$

$$M = (M - K)/(1 - K)$$

$$Y = (Y - K)/(1 - K)$$

3.4.1.3 HSV

The HSV (Hue, Saturation, Value) color space takes the form of an inverted cone, the base of the cone being referred to as the color wheel (Tondreau, 2012). "Hue" defines the color itself represented by the dominant wavelength of light and is measured along the circumference of the color wheel in degrees. By convention, red is assigned an angle of 0° which increases to 120° for green and 240° for blue. Intermediate colors like yellow, cyan and magenta are located in between the primary colors. "Saturation" is a measure of the purity/vividness of the color and indicates the amount of gray added to the hue, specified as percentage value between 0 and 100. If no gray is added, then the color is called pure or saturated color and has a saturation of 100%. As more and more gray is added to the color, its saturation decreases until at 0% the actual color is fully converted to gray. On the color wheel, saturation decreases radially from periphery of the circle toward the center. The third parameter "value" indicates the brightness or level of illumination of the color. Colors on the color wheel have a value (brightness) of 100% which however decreases in a perpendicular direction toward the apex of the cone, where all colors become black with a value of 0. The pictorial representation of the color wheel can be derived by looking at the RGB color cube from the white vertex toward the black vertex along the gray diagonal. The primary and secondary colors are at the six vertices of a hexagon which has been smoothed into a circle (Figure 3.33).

A variation of the HSV model is called HSL (hue saturation lightness) is also used in some applications which is similar to HSV with some differences. Instead of an inverted cone for HSV, the pictorial representation of the HSL space is thought to be a double cone. The brightness parameter V ranges from $V = 0$ for black to $V = 1$ for the brightest (saturated) colors in HSV, but in HSL, the lightness parameter L ranges from $L = 0$ for black to $L = 1$ for white and is $L = 0.5$ for the brightest colors. The saturation parameter S ranges from 1 for brightest colors to 0 for white in HSV, but in HSL, the parameter S ranges from 1 for brightest colors to 0 for gray. Conceptually, the HSL model is thought to be more improved than HSV as it is symmetrical with respect to saturation and lightness. Typically, reducing saturation is a color image reduces it to a grayscale image, so minimum saturation should correspond to gray (as in HSL) rather than white (as in HSV). Moreover lightness or brightness starts from black and should proceed to the other extreme white

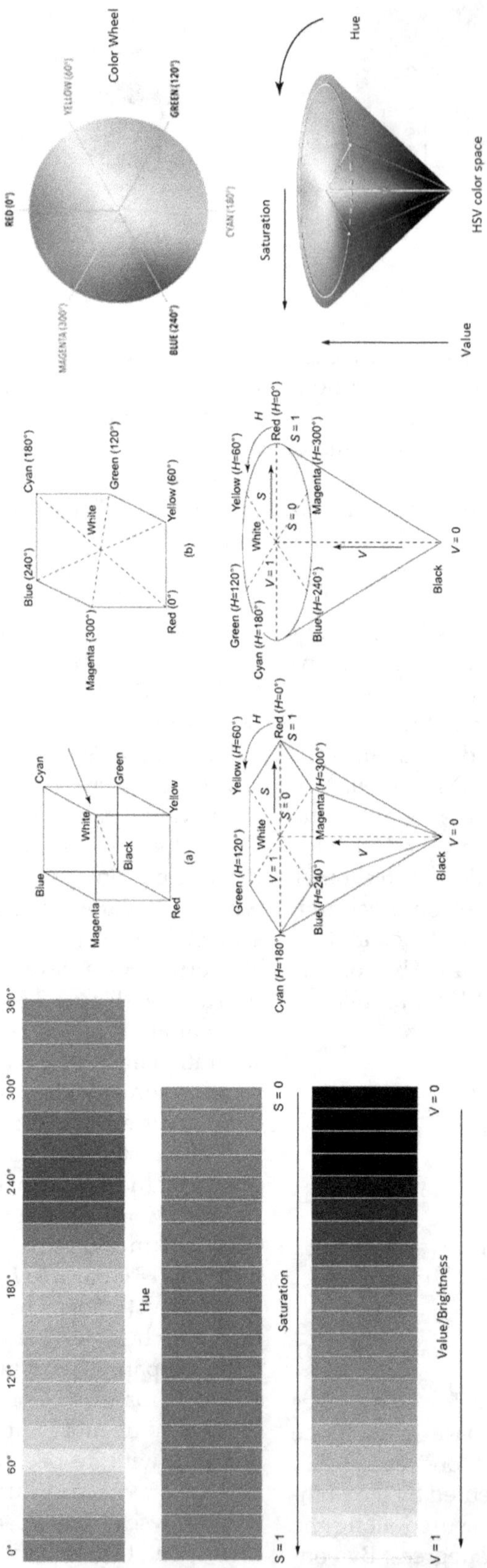

FIGURE 3.33
Visual representation of HSV color space.

(as in HSL) rather than be truncated at the brightest colors (as in HSV). So, HSL is usually preferred to HSV because of its more intuitive symmetry.

3.4.1.4 *L*a*b**

The CIE *L*a*b** model has been derived in 1976 from the CIE *XYZ* model to design a more perceptually uniform color space, which means that equal changes in color values produce equal changes in color as perceived by the human visual system [www.cie.co.at/publications/colorimetry-part-4-cie-1976-lab-colour-space-1]. It expresses color as a set of three values: L* for lightness or brightness ranging from black (0) to white (100), a* for color ranging from green (−128) to red (+127), and b* for color ranging from blue (−128) to yellow (+127); the color values being represented as signed 8-bit integers. Thus, when the color channels need to be displayed on the screen, the values need to be mapped to the range [0, 255] by adding 128 to them. With respect to a given white point, like D50 or D65, the *L*a*b** model is device-independent; i.e., it defines colors as they are perceived by the human vision irrespective of how they are created by devices. The asterisk (*) after the letters were inserted to distinguish them from another similar color space called Hunter Lab defined by Richard Hunter in 1948 (Hunter, 1948). The figure below depicts the visual representations of the color axis and the individual channels, where *L** depicts brighter regions for yellow/green and darker regions for red/blue as per the luminance relation, *a** depicts brighter regions for red and darker regions for green, *b** depicts brighter regions for yellow and darker regions for blue (Figure 3.34).

3.4.2 Chromaticity

Both the RGB and CMY color models have one similarity – they are device-dependent models. This means that the actual colors produced are dependent on the physical characteristics of the devices using which the colors are displayed. RGB-based colors depend on the LED/CRT properties of the monitors and CMY colors depend on the chemical properties of the printing inks. The colors therefore are not absolute or constant and would tend to vary from device to device.

To define device-independent color models, the global standards body International Commission on Illumination (CIE) defined the CIE XYZ color model in 1931. The human eye had photoreceptors called cone cells, which had peak sensitivities at wavelengths around 700 nm for red, 550 nm for green and 440 nm for blue (Wright, 1929; Guild, 1931). These parameters are called tri-stimulus values, and they describe a color sensation [www.cie.co.at/publications/colorimetry-part-3-cie-tristimulus-values-2]. To model the color sensation, the CIE proposed a color model based on the tri-stimulus values denoted as *X, Y, Z* and the color space was henceforth known as the CIE *XYZ* color space.

Due to the nature of distribution of the cone cells within the human eye, the *XYZ* values depend on the observer's angular field of view. To standardize this, CIE in 1931 defined the standard angular view as 2°. Since colors look different under various lighting conditions, two standard white point illuminant specifications were used: (1) D50 which has a color temperature of 5003 K and (2) D65 which has a color temperature of 6504 K. The letter "D" indicates daylight, meaning that the standard illuminants were proposed to simulate daylight conditions.

Chromaticity values x, y, z were defined as proportions of tri-stimulus values as follows:

$$x = X / (X + Y + Z)$$

$$y = Y / (X + Y + Z)$$

$$z = Z / (X + Y + Z)$$

Since $z = 1 - x - y$, only two parameters x and y were sufficient to define a specific color which can now be plotted on a planar surface. By plotting x and y for all

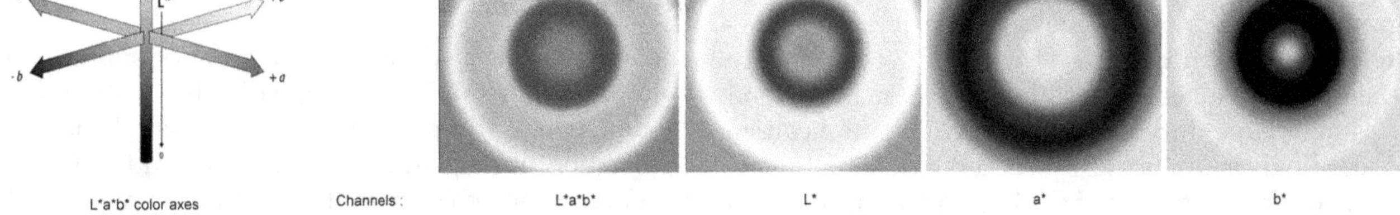

FIGURE 3.34
Visual representation of *L*a*b** color space.

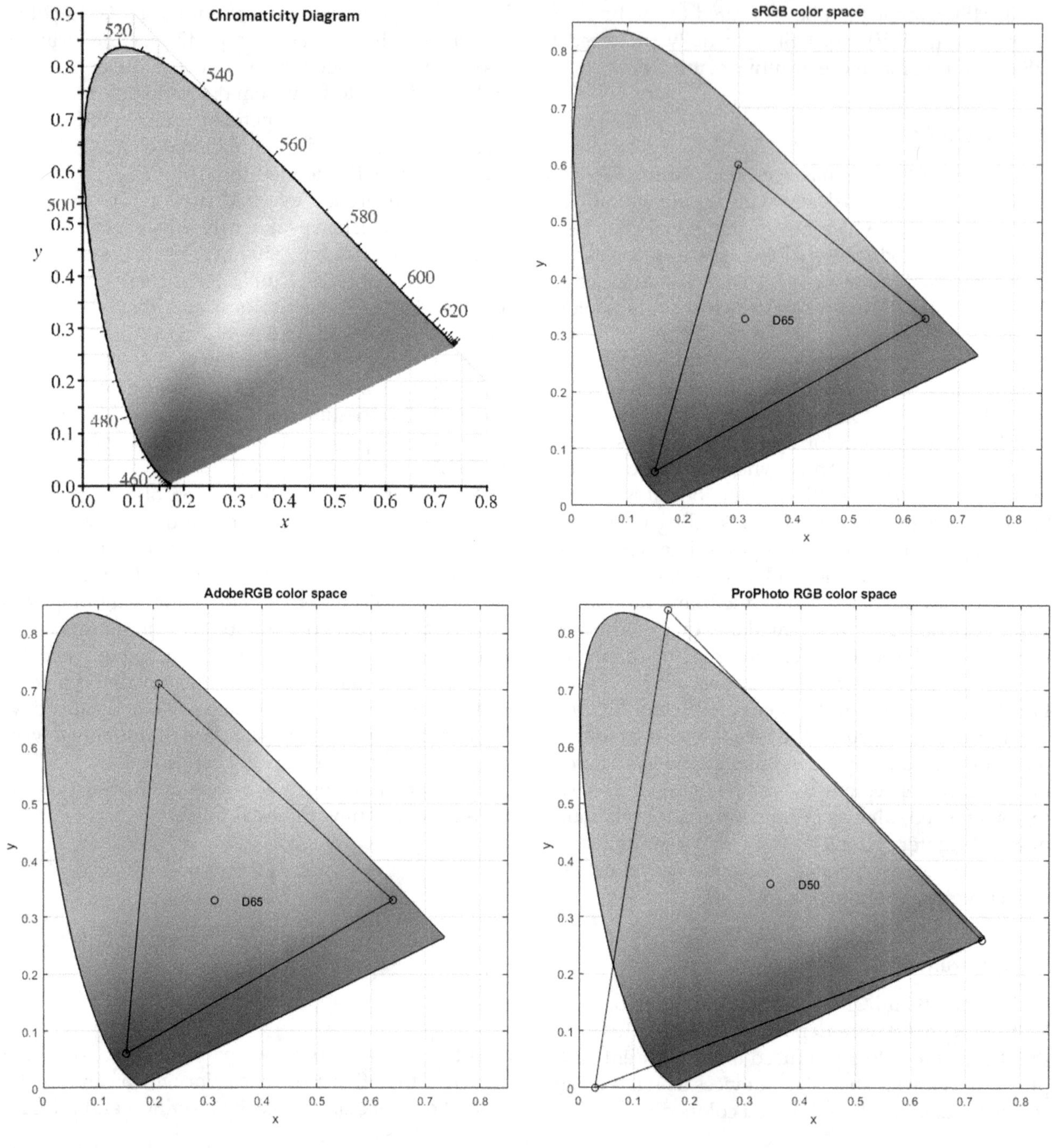

FIGURE 3.35
Chromaticity diagram and sRGB and AdobeRGB color spaces.

visible colors, we obtain the CIE chromaticity diagram. The values around the periphery indicate wavelengths in nanometers. The XYZ color space encompassed all colors visible to the human eye and was too large for a single device or application. Accordingly, subsets like sRGB and AdobeRGB were defined for specific sets of devices and applications in the form of triangles within the chromaticity diagram by specifying the three vertices and a white point in the middle (Figure 3.35).

3.4.3 Color Spaces

A color space is a specific instantiation or subset of a color model that defines a range of colors within that model, usually applicable for a specific device or application. It maps the abstract mathematical representation of the color model to real-world colors that can be displayed or printed. Since a color model generally defines a very large number of colors, a color space for a particular device or application is usually a subset of those colors chosen in accordance with its requirements. Color spaces play a crucial role in ensuring color consistency and accuracy. One of the objectives of the color calibration process is to maintain uniformity across different color spaces as far as possible. For doing that it makes use of ICC profile files which contain the color space specifications of a device like monitor, scanner or printer. Some popular color spaces are discussed below.

3.4.3.1 sRGB

sRGB (standard RGB) is an RGB color space designed to ensure consistent color representation across different devices, particularly on the Web and consumer electronics like computer and mobile screens [www.iso.org/standard/33293.html]. Proposed by Hewlett-Packard and Microsoft, it uses color primaries defined in the ITU-T Rec. 709 [www.itu.int/rec/R--REC-BT.709/en]. sRGB is widely used for Web content and digital media due to its consistent appearance on a wide range of devices. The primary colors of sRGB defined in terms of CIE chromaticities [www.color.org/chardata/rgb/srgb.xalter] are shown below, which specify the boundaries of a triangle encompassing approximately 35% of the total CIE color space.

Chromaticity	Red	Green	Blue	White (D65)
x	0.64	0.30	0.15	0.3127
y	0.33	0.6	0.06	0.3290

3.4.3.2 AdobeRGB

AdobeRGB is another RGB color space originally developed by Adobe Systems, which offers a wider color gamut than sRGB, making it suitable for professional photography and design work [www.iso.org/standard/45115.html]. AdobeRGB is often preferred when maintaining a larger color range is essential, but it requires careful color management to ensure accurate reproduction on devices that support it. The primary colors of AdobeRGB defined in terms of CIE chromaticities are shown below, which specify the boundaries of a triangle encompassing approximately 50.6% of the total CIE color space.

Chromaticity	Red	Green	Blue	White (D65)
x	0.64	0.21	0.15	0.3127
y	0.33	0.71	0.06	0.3290

3.4.3.3 ProPhoto RGB

The ProPhoto RGB color space is a wide-gamut RGB color space used primarily in advanced imaging applications, especially in the world of high-quality photography and professional graphic design [www.iso.org/standard/56591.html]. ProPhoto RGB is known for its exceptionally wide gamut, which encompasses an extensive range of colors that are beyond the capabilities of most devices and media, including computer monitors, printers and photographic papers. This expansive gamut makes it an ideal choice for preserving and editing the broadest possible spectrum of colors, ensuring that the full range of colors captured by high-end cameras can be retained and manipulated without loss of data. The primary colors of ProPhotoRGB defined in terms of CIE chromaticities are shown below, which specify the boundaries of a triangle encompassing more than 90% of the total color space.

Chromaticity	Red	Green	Blue	White (D65)
x	0.73	0.16	0.03	0.3127
y	0.26	0.84	0.00	0.3290

In summary, a color model provides a theoretical framework for understanding color, while a color space is a practical realization of that model that defines the actual colors within a specific context, device or application. Color spaces help ensure that colors are displayed or printed accurately and consistently, making them a fundamental concept in color management. The concept of chromaticity diagram described next will further help to distinguish color models from color spaces.

3.4.3.4 Rec. 601

Rec. 601/BT 601/CCIR 601 [www.itu.int/rec/R--REC-BT.601] refers to a standard issued by ITU-R (formerly CCIR) in 1982 which defines rules for encoding analog video signals for the standard definition (SD) televisions: 525-line NTSC and 625-line PAL. The standard defined a color space with chromaticity values for the primaries as given below:

Chromaticity	Red	Green	Blue	White (D65)	SD TV standard
x	0.64	0.29	0.15	0.3127	PAL (625-lines)
y	0.33	0.6	0.06	0.3290	
x	0.63	0.31	0.155	0.3127	NTSC
y	0.34	0.595	0.07	0.3290	(525-lines)

3.4.3.5 Rec. 709

Rec. 709/BT 709/CCIR 709 [www.itu.int/rec/R--REC-BT.709] refers to a standard issued by ITU-R (formerly CCIR) in 1993 which defines rules for encoding digital video signals for high definition (HD) TV, with a widescreen aspect ratio of 16:9, 1080 active lines per frame and 1920 pixels per line. The color specification is as follows:

Chromaticity	Red	Green	Blue	White (D65)
x	0.64	0.3	0.15	0.3127
y	0.33	0.6	0.06	0.3290

3.4.3.6 Rec. 2020

Rec. 2020/BT 2020 [www.itu.int/rec/R-REC-BT.2020] refers to a standard issued by ITU-R in 2012 which defines rules for encoding digital video signals for ultra-high-definition (UHD) TV, using standard dynamic range (SDR) and wide color gamut (WCG). It specifies two image formats: 4K (3840 × 2160) and 8K (7680 × 4320) both with aspect ratio 16:9. The color specification is as follows:

Chromaticity	Red	Green	Blue	White (D65)
x	0.708	0.170	0.131	0.3127
y	0.292	0.797	0.046	0.3290

3.4.3.7 Rec. 2021

Rec. 2021/BT 2021 [www.itu.int/rec/R-REC-BT.2021] refers to a standard issued by ITU-R in 2015 which defines rules for encoding digital video signals for ultra-high-definition (UHD) TV, using high dynamic range (HDR) and wide color gamut (WCG). In this specification the Adobe color space was also included with the Rec. 2020 to constitute the wide color gamut.

3.4.4 Color Conversions

Now that it is clear that each device and application has its own dedicated color space, the next step is to investigate how color space conversions can be done to ensure proper reproduction of color across devices and applications. This process is called color calibration. Below we discuss the protocols and mathematical formulations for conversion between major color models. These have been collectively defined by Poynton [poynton.ca/PDFs/coloureq.pdf][www.poynton.ca/PDFs/ColorFAQ.pdf] (Poynton, 1995), CIE [http://cie.co.at/publications/cie-collection-colour-and-vision], W3C [www.w3.org/Graphics/Color/sRGB], ICC [www.color.org/icc_specs2.xalter], ISO [www.iso.org/standard/68761.html] as well as others. Note that the standard color space associated with the RGB color model is sRGB.

3.4.4.1 RGB to CMY

To convert from RGB to CMY, the following relations can be used, where RGB values are in the range [0, 255] and CMY values are in the range [0, 1]:

$$C = 1 - (R/255)$$

$$M = 1 - (G/255)$$

$$Y = 1 - (B/255)$$

3.4.4.2 CMY to RGB

To convert from CMY to RGB, the following relations can be used, where RGB values are in the range [0, 255] and CMY values are in the range [0, 1]:

$$R = 255(1 - C)$$

$$G = 255(1 - M)$$

$$B = 255(1 - Y)$$

3.4.4.3 RGB to HSV

To convert from RGB to HSV, you can use the following formula:

// Step 1: Compute m, n, d

$m = \max(R, G, B)$

$n = \min(R, G, B)$

$d = m - n$

// Step 2: Compute S and V based on m and d

$$V = (m/255) * 100$$

if $m = 0$

$$S = 0$$

else

$$S = (d/m) * 100$$

// Step 3: Compute H based on m and d

if $d = 0$

$$H = 0$$

else if $m = R$

$$H = \left\{60\left(\frac{G-B}{d}\right)+360\right\}\%360$$

else if $m = G$

$$H = \left\{60\left(\frac{B-R}{d}\right)+120\right\}\%360$$

else if $m = B$

$$H = \left\{60\left(\frac{R-G}{d}\right)+240\right\}\%360$$

3.4.4.4 HSV to RGB

// Step 1: Compute C, k, m

If S and V are in percentage, normalize by dividing by 100

$S = S\%/100, V = V\%/100$

$C = V.S$

$$k = C.\left(1 - abs\left(\left(\frac{H}{60}\right)\%2 - 1\right)\right)$$

$m = V - C$

// Step 2: Compute R, G, B based on value of H

$$\begin{aligned}
&\text{If } 0 \le H < 60 \quad then \quad (R,G,B) = (C+m, k+m, m)\\
&\text{If } 60 \le H < 120 \quad then \quad (R,G,B) = (k+m, C+m, m)\\
&\text{If } 120 \le H < 180 \quad then \quad (R,G,B) = (m, C+m, k+m)\\
&\text{If } 180 \le H < 240 \quad then \quad (R,G,B) = (m, k+m, C+m)\\
&\text{If } 240 \le H < 300 \quad then \quad (R,G,B) = (k+m, m, C+m)\\
&\text{If } 300 \le H < 360 \quad then \quad (R,G,B) = (C+m, m, k+m)
\end{aligned}$$

// Step 3: Calculate round off values

$$R = round(255R)$$
$$G = round(255G)$$
$$B = round(255B)$$

3.4.4.5 RGB to XYZ

// Step 1: Normalize RGB values to the range [0, 1]

$$R' = R/255$$
$$G' = G/255$$
$$B' = B/255$$

// Step 2: Do if less than 0.04045

if $R', G', B' \le 0.04045$

$$R'' = \frac{R'}{12.92}$$
$$G'' = \frac{G'}{12.92}$$
$$B'' = \frac{B'}{12.92}$$

// Step 3: Do if more than 0.04045

if $R', G', B' > 0.04045$

$$R'' = \left\{\frac{R'+0.055}{1.055}\right\}^{2.4}$$
$$G'' = \left\{\frac{G'+0.055}{1.055}\right\}^{2.4}$$
$$B'' = \left\{\frac{B'+0.055}{1.055}\right\}^{2.4}$$

// Step 4: Compute linear combinations

$$X = 0.4212R'' + 0.3576G'' + 0.1805B''$$
$$Y = 0.2126R'' + 0.7152G'' + 0.0722B''$$
$$Z = 0.0193R'' + 0.1192G'' + 0.9505B''$$

3.4.4.6 XYZ to RGB

// Step 1: Compute R', G', B'

$$R' = 3.2406X - 1.5372Y - 0.4986Z$$
$$G' = -0.9689X + 1.8758Y + 0.0415Z$$
$$B' = 0.0557X - 0.2040Y + 1.0570Z$$

// Step 2: Do if less than 0.0031308

if $R', G', B' \le 0.0031308$

$$R = 12.92R'$$
$$G = 12.92G'$$
$$B = 12.92B'$$

// Step 3: Do if more than 0.0031308

if $R', G', B' > 0.0031308$

$$R'' = 1.055 * (R')^{\frac{1}{2.4}} - 0.055$$
$$G'' = 1.055 * (G')^{\frac{1}{2.4}} - 0.055$$
$$B'' = 1.055 * (B')^{\frac{1}{2.4}} - 0.055$$

// Step 4: Calculate round off values

$$R = round(255R'')$$
$$G = round(255G'')$$
$$B = round(255B'')$$

*3.4.4.7 RGB to L*a*b**

// Step 1: Convert *RGB* to *XYZ*

// Step 2: Define reference white point (D65)

$$X_w = 0.950456$$
$$Y_w = 1.000000$$
$$Z_w = 1.088754$$

// Step 3: Compute X', Y', Z'

$$X' = X / X_w$$
$$Y' = Y / Y_w$$
$$Z' = Z / Z_w$$

// Step 4: Do if more than $\left(\frac{6}{29}\right)^3$

If $X', Y', Z' > \left(\frac{6}{29}\right)^3$

$$X'' = (X')^{\frac{1}{3}}$$
$$Y'' = (Y')^{\frac{1}{3}}$$
$$Z'' = (Z')^{\frac{1}{3}}$$

// Step 5: Do if less than $\left(\frac{6}{29}\right)^3$

If $X', Y', Z' \leq \left(\frac{6}{29}\right)^3$

$$X'' = \frac{1}{3}\left(\frac{29}{6}\right)^2 X' + \frac{4}{29}$$
$$Y'' = \frac{1}{3}\left(\frac{29}{6}\right)^2 Y' + \frac{4}{29}$$
$$Z'' = \frac{1}{3}\left(\frac{29}{6}\right)^2 Z' + \frac{4}{29}$$

// Step 6: Compute L^*, a^*, b^*

$$L^* = 116 * Y'' - 16$$
$$a^* = 500 * (X'' - Y'')$$
$$b^* = 200 * (Y'' - Z'')$$

*3.4.4.8 L*a*b to RGB*

// Step 1: Compute $X', Y' Z'$

$$Y' = \frac{L + 16}{116}$$
$$X' = \frac{a}{500} + Y'$$
$$Z' = \frac{-b}{200} + Y'$$

// Step 2: Do if more than 6/29:

If $X', Y', Z' > \frac{6}{29}$

$$X'' = (X')^3$$
$$Y'' = (Y')^3$$
$$Z'' = (Z')3$$

// Step 3: Do if less than 6/29:

If $X', Y', Z' \leq \frac{6}{29}$

$$X'' = 3\left(\frac{6}{29}\right)^2 \left(X' - \frac{16}{116}\right)$$
$$Y'' = 3\left(\frac{6}{29}\right)^2 \left(Y' - \frac{16}{116}\right)$$
$$Z'' = 3\left(\frac{6}{29}\right)^2 \left(Z' - \frac{16}{116}\right)$$

// Step 4: Define reference white point (D65)

$$X_w = 0.950456$$
$$Y_w = 1.000000$$
$$Z_w = 1.088754$$

// Step 5: Compute X, Y, Z

$$X = X''.X_w$$
$$Y = Y''.Y_w$$
$$Z = Z''.Z_w$$

// Step 6: Compute *XYZ* to *RGB*

3.4.5 Color Calibration

Color calibration involves compensating for sensor imperfections, lens distortions and lighting variations to produce accurate and high-quality images. Color calibration systems use ICC profiles, a color management module and a device independent color space (Michael, 2015).

ICC Profiles: ICC (International Color Consortium) profiles are files that describe the color behavior of a device or the device color space. They enable software and devices to interpret and translate colors accurately. ICC profiles are crucial for achieving consistent color rendering across different devices.

Color Management Module: A Color Management Module (CMM) would read multiple device profiles, analyze the difference between them and adjust the image colors accordingly so that perceptually the color appears same or very similar in all devices. The CMS never guarantees that the adjustment will be 100% effective but attempts to minimize the difference.

Device-independent Color Space: For translating from one device color space to another, the CMM needs to map the first color space to a device– independent color space and then maps it again to the second color space. A device-independent color space is one where the set of displayable colors is independent of any specific device but rather is based on the human perception of color. In most cases the *L*a*b* color space is used for this purpose. In a sense, each device speaks its own color language, which it cannot communicate well to another device. What is needed is an interpreter and CMM acts as the interpreter between two device color spaces, each characterized by their ICC profiles.

Monitor Calibration: Calibrating computer monitors involves adjusting settings like brightness, contrast, gamma and color temperature to ensure accurate color display. Calibration hardware and software tools are used for this purpose. Regular monitor calibration is essential to maintain color accuracy over time. After the calibration the device characteristics are written to an ICC device profile file.

Printer Calibration: Printers require calibration to produce accurate colors. This involves adjusting ink levels, color settings and other parameters to match the intended output. Printer calibration ensures that printed materials, such as photographs and graphics, faithfully reproduce the intended colors. After the calibration the device characteristics are written to an ICC device profile file.

Color Proofing: Color proofing involves creating accurate previews of how colors will appear in print. Designers use color proofs to identify and correct color issues before sending their designs to print. It ensures that the final printed materials match the intended colors and appearance.

Pantone Matching System (PMS): Pantone [www.pantone.com] is a widely adopted color matching system that provides a standardized way to identify and reproduce colors accurately. Designers use Pantone colors to ensure consistency in print and packaging materials. Each Pantone color has a unique code, simplifying communication between designers and printers. Pantone was created to solve the problem of inconsistent color reproduction in the design and printing industry. With PMS, each color is assigned a unique alphanumeric code, which eliminates the ambiguity associated with color names and ensures that the intended color remains consistent across different media and materials. Color guides and swatch books, such as the Pantone Formula Guide and Pantone Color Bridge, provide physical references for designers and printers to match colors accurately.

3.4.6 Indexed Image and CLUT

An indexed image is a color image, where the pixel values do not contain the actual color information but only index numbers. The index numbers are converted to color values by looking up a colormap or a table in memory with a set of rows and four columns, called the color look up table (CLUT). The first column contains the index number of the row in a sequential manner, while the other three columns contain the RGB values for each index number. When the image is to be displayed, the index numbers from the image are converted to color values using the table, and corresponding pixels are generated. To display an indexed image, the corresponding colormap needs to be specified. The colormap usually contains 64 or 128 or 256 colors, but a smaller subset of colors can also be used to display an approximate version of the image. When an image is displayed using a CLUT containing a smaller number of colors than the original, then a process called dithering is used to approximate the colors absent in the CLUT. Dithering is a process which mixes available colors to produce new colors. It varies the distribution of the existing colors to simulate colors not present in the color table, in a way similar to how distribution of black dots can be varied to simulate shades of gray, usually seen in the print medium. An indexed image can be displayed using a colormap different from the original containing a different number of colors. If the number of colors is more in the new map, then the original set of colors are displayed in the image. If the number of colors is less in the new map, the image is displayed using a subset of the original colors. Dithering can be used to improve the quality of image by simulating colors not present in the new map (Figure 3.36). A color RGB image can be converted to an indexed image. The pixel values are replaced by index values of the CLUT, and the color table is created in memory to reference

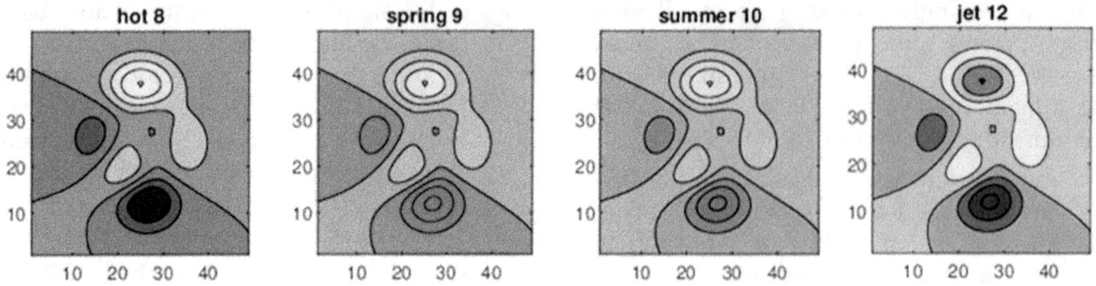

FIGURE 3.36
Index image with different colormaps.

those values. The CLUT contains as many entries as there are colors in the image and each entry contains the *R*, *G*, *B* components of the corresponding color. The process of conversion from RGB to indexed format can also be reversed by specifying an indexed color image and a map to transform it back to *RGB* format. In this case, the index values in the image are replaced by actual RGB pixel values read from the colormap (Fortner & Meyer, 1997).

3.5 Image Applications

3.5.1 Image Enhancement

Image enhancement involves manipulating an image to improve its visual quality, emphasizing certain features or reducing undesired effects (Rajput et al., 2022). Image enhancement techniques are diverse and versatile, addressing a wide range of visual challenges to improve the overall quality and interpretability of digital images. Each technique targets specific aspects such as contrast, brightness and color balance, contributing to the enhancement of visual information for various applications. In satellite imagery, for example, enhancement techniques can bring out specific details on the Earth's surface.

Histogram equalization is a widely used technique that enhances the contrast of an image by redistributing pixel intensities. This process aims to ensure a more uniform distribution of pixel values, making it particularly effective in scenarios where images suffer from poor contrast. In aerial imaging, histogram equalization can reveal details in satellite images, aiding in land cover classification. Adaptive Histogram Equalization (AHE) extends the concept of histogram equalization by dividing an image into smaller regions and applying histogram equalization independently to each region. AHE can be effective in scenarios where different parts of an image have varying illumination conditions.

Contrast stretching expands the range of pixel intensities in an image, effectively increasing the contrast between the darkest and lightest areas. This technique is valuable in scenarios where images exhibit low contrast, such as in medical imaging. In X-ray images, contrast stretching can highlight subtle anatomical details for more accurate diagnosis.

Spatial filtering involves applying convolution masks to an image, emphasizing or de-emphasizing certain features. Filters, such as edge detection filters, can enhance specific characteristics in images. In automotive applications, spatial filtering can be employed to detect and enhance the edges of objects in images, contributing to object recognition in autonomous vehicles.

Color correction adjusts the color balance of an image, ensuring that it accurately reflects the true colors of the scene. This technique is crucial in fields such as satellite imaging, where accurate representation of land cover types is essential. Color correction helps in producing images that facilitate precise environmental monitoring and analysis.

Wavelet transforms decompose an image into different frequency components, allowing for selective enhancement. This technique is particularly powerful in handling images with both low- and high-frequency details. In art restoration, wavelet transform can be applied to restore and enhance aged paintings by revealing fine details without amplifying noise.

Gamma correction adjusts the intensity of an image to account for the non-linear relationship between pixel values and the actual scene radiance. This correction is crucial in scenarios where the display device has a different gamma value than the image acquisition device. In multimedia applications, gamma correction ensures consistent and accurate display of images and videos on different screens.

Image sharpening techniques enhance the edges and fine details in an image, making it visually clearer. This is beneficial in scenarios where images have undergone blurring during acquisition. In microscopy, image sharpening can improve the visibility of cellular structures in microscopic images for better analysis.

3.5.2 Image Restoration

Image restoration techniques are essential for recovering the original, undistorted version of an image by mitigating degradations introduced during image acquisition or transmission (Gunturk & Li, 2018). These techniques aim to improve the visual quality, clarity and interpretability of images, making them valuable in various fields such as medical imaging, surveillance and cultural heritage preservation.

In accordance with the degradation-restoration model, in the absence of noise, image restoration can be done using a deconvolution operation to reverse the effects of convolution. In the frequency domain, deconvolution is equivalent to multiplying the blurred image with the reciprocal of the PSF and hence it is also called inverse filtering. In astronomical imaging, deconvolution is employed to enhance the clarity of celestial objects by compensating for atmospheric distortions and telescope imperfections.

If both degradation and noise is present, then an inverse filtering is not sufficient. In such cases is the Wiener deconvolution can be used to recover a close approximation of the original image using an estimated noise to signal ratio, in the frequency domain or the Lucy-Richardson deconvolution can be used as an iterative process in the spatial domain.

Super-resolution techniques aim to generate high-resolution images from low-resolution counterparts. By utilizing information from neighboring pixels, these techniques enhance image details and improve clarity. In satellite imaging, super-resolution is crucial for obtaining high-quality images that facilitate accurate land cover mapping and environmental monitoring.

Inpainting is the process of filling in missing or damaged parts of an image. Algorithms analyze the surrounding image content to intelligently reconstruct missing details. In cultural heritage preservation, inpainting is applied to restore damaged artworks or historical photographs by recreating missing sections.

Total variation regularization is a technique used to restore images while preserving sharp edges. By minimizing the total variation of pixel intensities, this method removes noise without excessively smoothing image details. In industrial inspection, total variation regularization can enhance the detection of defects in manufactured products by maintaining edge sharpness.

Deep Learning–based Restoration often utilizes convolutional neural networks (CNNs), Models like the Deep Image Prior and DnCNN learn complex mappings from noisy or degraded images to clean ones. In medical imaging, deep learning–based restoration enhances the accuracy of diagnostic scans by reducing artifacts.

Wavelet-based restoration techniques leverage the multi-resolution properties of wavelet transforms to selectively enhance or reduce noise in different frequency bands. In underwater exploration, wavelet-based restoration can improve the visibility of underwater scenes by reducing noise and enhancing important features.

Generative Adversarial Networks (GANs) have gained prominence in image restoration tasks by generating realistic details and textures. In art restoration, GANs can be applied to restore and enhance aged paintings by creating missing details that align with the artistic style.

3.5.3 Image Segmentation

Image segmentation involves partitioning images into meaningful segments and identifying objects within them. An image is divided into distinct regions based on certain criteria, such as color, intensity or texture. This process is crucial for understanding the structure and context of an image. Image segmentation techniques span from traditional methods to cutting-edge deep learning approaches. Each method has its strengths and is suited to specific applications, providing a diverse toolkit for addressing various challenges in segmenting images (Lei & Nandi, 2022).

3.5.3.1 Thresholding

Thresholding is a simple, yet effective, segmentation technique that separates an image into regions based on intensity values. Pixels with intensities above a certain threshold are classified as foreground, while those below the threshold are considered background. This method is particularly useful for images with distinct intensity differences between objects and the background. For instance, in medical imaging, thresholding can be employed to segment bones based on their intensity in X-ray images.

Global thresholding involves selecting a single intensity value to divide the image into foreground and background. This method assumes a consistent intensity distribution throughout the image. The choice of the threshold can be determined manually or through automated algorithms, such as Otsu's method, which maximizes the inter-class variance.

Adaptive thresholding is employed in cases where the lighting conditions vary across different regions of an image. This technique calculates different thresholds for different regions, taking into account the local characteristics of the image. Adaptive thresholding is particularly useful in handling uneven illumination and shadows.

Multi-level Thresholding involves dividing the image into more than two intensity levels. This is suitable for images with multiple objects or regions of interest that exhibit different intensity characteristics. The challenge lies in determining the optimal thresholds, which can be achieved through iterative methods or clustering approaches.

3.5.3.2 Region-Based Segmentation

Region-based segmentation is a category of image segmentation techniques that groups pixels into regions based on certain criteria such as color, texture or intensity homogeneity. Unlike simple thresholding methods that classify individual pixels as foreground or background, region-based segmentation aims to form coherent and meaningful regions within an image. This approach is particularly effective for images with complex structures and varying intensity distributions.

Region growing is an iterative technique that starts with a seed pixel or set of seed pixels and grows a region by incorporating neighboring pixels that satisfy a similarity criterion. The criterion is often based on the similarity of pixel intensities. Pixels are added to the region if their intensity values are within a specified threshold of the seed pixel. This process continues until no more pixels meet the criteria. In satellite imagery, region growing can be used to identify contiguous areas of vegetation. The quality of seed selection influences the success of the segmentation; well-chosen seeds should be representative of the regions to be segmented.

Region Splitting and Merging is a hierarchical image segmentation technique that combines the processes of dividing large regions (splitting) and joining (merging) smaller regions based on certain criteria. This approach aims to achieve a balance between local homogeneity and global consistency in the resulting regions. The algorithm begins with the entire image considered as one large region. A homogeneity test is performed on this region based on a specified criterion, e.g., color similarity. If the test fails, indicating that the region is not homogeneous, the region is split into sub-regions. The splitting process is applied recursively to each of the sub-regions that fail the homogeneity test. This recursive splitting continues until all resulting sub-regions satisfy the homogeneity criterion. After the splitting phase, the algorithm examines neighboring regions to determine whether they should be merged based on another set of criteria. Merging criteria may include measures of similarity between adjacent regions. If the merging criteria are met, the algorithm recursively merges the neighboring regions. This merging process continues until no further merging is possible, and the segmentation is considered complete.

3.5.3.3 Edge-Based Segmentation

Edge-based segmentation is a technique that focuses on identifying and delineating boundaries, or edges, within an image. Edges represent abrupt changes in intensity, color or texture and often correspond to object boundaries. This segmentation approach leverages edge detection methods to locate these transitions and subsequently separates regions based on the detected edges.

Edge Detection involves convolution-based operators like Sobel, Prewitt and Roberts that calculates the gradient of the image intensity along the horizontal and vertical directions, highlighting edges by emphasizing changes in intensity along these directions. The Canny edge detector is a multi-stage algorithm that includes smoothing, gradient computation, non-maximum suppression and edge tracking by hysteresis.

Edge Linking and Thresholding involve steps for processing the edge map to achieve segmentation. Thresholding the edge map involves setting a threshold value to distinguish between strong and weak edges. Pixels with edge strengths above the threshold are considered part of the segmented region. Edge linking involves connecting adjacent edge pixels to form continuous contours. This process helps overcome gaps in the edges detected by considering neighboring pixels that may collectively represent a meaningful edge.

3.5.3.4 Clustering-Based Segmentation

Clustering algorithms are a category of unsupervised machine learning techniques that group similar data points into clusters, with the goal of maximizing intra-cluster similarity and minimizing inter-cluster similarity. In the context of image segmentation, clustering is often applied to group pixels or regions based on certain feature similarities. Various clustering algorithms have been developed, each with its own strengths and suitability for different types of data.

K-Means Clustering is a partitioning algorithm that divides the dataset into a predefined number (k) of clusters. It iteratively assigns each data point to the nearest centroid and updates the centroids based on the mean of the assigned points (MacQueen, 1967).

Hierarchical Clustering builds a tree-like hierarchy of clusters. It can be agglomerative (bottom-up) or divisive (top-down). The algorithm iteratively merges or splits clusters-based on proximity until a hierarchy is formed.

DBSCAN (Density-Based Spatial Clustering of Applications with Noise) groups data points based on their density. It defines clusters as areas of high density separated by areas of low density. Data points in lowdensity regions are considered noise (Ester, 1996).

GMM (Gaussian Mixture Model) represents the data as a mixture of Gaussian distributions. It models the probability that each data point belongs to a particular cluster and estimates the parameters of the Gaussians.

Fuzzy C-Means Clustering extends the traditional K-Means algorithm by allowing data points to belong to multiple clusters with varying degrees of membership. It introduces fuzziness into the assignment of data points to clusters.

3.5.3.5 Deep Learning–Based Segmentation

Deep learning–based segmentation has emerged as a powerful and effective approach to image segmentation, leveraging the capabilities of deep neural networks to automatically learn hierarchical representations from data. Convolutional Neural Networks (CNNs) are particularly well suited for this task due to their ability to capture spatial hierarchies and local patterns in images. Several architectures have been developed specifically for image segmentation, and they have shown remarkable success in various applications.

U-Net Architecture [arxiv.org/abs/1807.10165] is widely used for biomedical image segmentation and other tasks. It consists of a contracting path to capture context and a symmetric expanding path to achieve precise localization. Skip connections between corresponding layers facilitate the transfer of fine-grained information (Zhou et al., 2018).

Fully Convolutional Network (FCN) [arxiv.org/abs/1411.4038] is designed for end-to-end segmentation without the need for fully connected layers. It utilizes transposed convolutions to upsample feature maps, enabling pixel-wise predictions. Skip connections from lower layers aid in preserving spatial information (Long et al., 2015).

DeepLab [arxiv.org/abs/1606.00915] utilizes atrous (dilated) convolutions to capture multi-scale contextual information without downsampling the spatial resolution. It employs a deep convolutional backbone, typically based on ResNet or MobileNet and includes atrous spatial pyramid pooling (Chen e tal., 2017).

Mask R-CNN [arxiv.org/abs/1703.06870] extends the Faster R-CNN architecture by adding a branch for predicting segmentation masks alongside object detection. It introduces a Region of Interest (RoI) Align layer to accurately extract features from irregularly shaped regions (He et al., 2018).

Attention Mechanisms [arxiv.org/abs/2204.13154], such as the self-attention mechanism in the Transformer architecture, have been incorporated into segmentation networks to enhance the model's focus on relevant image regions. This helps capture long-range dependencies (Soydaner, 2022).

3.5.3.6 Graph-Based Segmentation

Graph-based segmentation is an approach that models an image as a graph, where pixels or image regions are represented as nodes, and edges encode relationships between them. The goal is to partition the graph into meaningful and coherent segments, making it a valuable technique for image segmentation tasks. Graph-based methods leverage principles from graph theory to identify optimal partitions based on certain criteria.

Graph Cut methods model image segmentation as an energy minimization problem. Pixels are represented as nodes, and edges are assigned weights based on the dissimilarity between pixel values. The algorithm seeks to find the cut that minimizes the total energy, separating the image into distinct segments.

Minimum Spanning Tree (MST) Segmentation [arxiv.org/abs/2302.12029] constructs a minimum spanning tree of the image graph, where edges represent the most similar connections. Segmentation is then performed by iteratively removing edges with the highest weights until a predefined number of segments is achieved (Berg et al., 2023).

Watershed Transform [arxiv.org/abs/1611.08303] is often associated with morphological operations; it can also be viewed as a graph-based segmentation technique. The image gradient is used to create a topographic surface, and the watershed algorithm simulates flooding to identify catchment basins, representing segmented regions (Bai & Urtasun, 2017).

Random Walks algorithm [arxiv.org/abs/2008.03639] models segmentation as a random walk on a graph, where each pixel acts as a node and edge weights represent pairwise affinities. The algorithm assigns probabilities to pixels belonging to different segments and iteratively adjusts these probabilities based on random walks (Xia et al., 2020).

Active Contour Models [arxiv.org/abs/2403.07570], commonly called "snakes", are a family of deformable models used for image segmentation and object tracking. These models are particularly effective in scenarios where the shape of the object of interest is not well defined or when the object exhibits irregular boundaries. Snakes operate by evolving a parametric curve or contour to align with the desired object boundary in an image.

3.5.4 Object Detection

Object detection is a fundamental task in computer vision that involves identifying and locating objects within an image or video frame. Various techniques have been developed to tackle the challenges associated with object detection, each with its strengths and limitations. Here, we'll explore some key techniques in object detection within the realm of computer vision. Object detection is a key component in the perception systems of autonomous vehicles. It allows the vehicle to identify and track pedestrians, vehicles and obstacles in real time, ensuring safe navigation. Object detection is extensively used in surveillance systems for identifying and tracking individuals or objects of interest (Cyganek, 2013).

3.5.4.1 Traditional Approaches

Computer vision–based methods relied on handcrafted features such as edges, corners and textures. Algorithms like Haar cascades and Histogram of Oriented Gradients (HOG) are examples of feature-based approaches. Sliding Window technique involves sliding a window of varying sizes across an image and classifying each window as containing an object or not. While intuitive, this method can be computationally expensive.

3.5.4.2 Machine Learning–Based Approaches

Supervised Learning techniques are where models are trained on annotated datasets. Common models include Convolutional Neural Networks (CNNs), which have shown remarkable success in image classification and localization tasks.

Region-based CNNs (R-CNNs) [arxiv.org/abs/2404.16633] propose regions of interest and classify each region independently. The Fast R-CNN subsequent models, such as Fast R-CNN and Faster R-CNN, improved efficiency by introducing a Region Proposal Network (RPN) that shared convolutional layers with the detection network. This is useful in applications like content-based image retrieval, where users search for images based on the objects they contain (Girshick et al., 2015).

You Only Look Once (YOLO) [arxiv.org/abs/2404.08979] is a real-time object detection system that divides an image into a grid and predicts bounding boxes and class probabilities for each grid cell simultaneously. YOLO models, particularly YOLOv3, offer high accuracy with impressive processing speed. This makes them suitable for applications requiring real-time responses, such as video surveillance.

Single Shot MultiBox Detector (SSD) [arxiv.org/abs/1512.02325] is an efficient object detection algorithm that utilizes a set of default bounding boxes with varying aspect ratios at each feature map location. It predicts multiple bounding boxes and class probabilities in a single pass, achieving a balance between speed and accuracy. SSD is well suited for applications like pedestrian detection in crowded scenes (Liu et al., 2016).

Region Proposal Networks (RPNs) [arxiv.org/abs/1506.01497] are stand-alone modules introduced in Faster R-CNN to generate region proposals. They operate on the convolutional feature map of an image, proposing potential regions for object presence. In aerial imagery analysis, RPNs assist in identifying specific structures, like buildings or vehicles.

RetinaNet [developers.arcgis.com/python/guide/how-retinanet-works] addresses the issue of class imbalance in object detection by incorporating a focal loss function. This allows the model to focus more on hard-to-detect objects. In retail settings, RetinaNet can accurately detect and classify products on store shelves.

EfficientDet [arxiv.org/abs/1911.09070] introduces compound scaling, optimizing model efficiency by scaling up the depth, width and resolution simultaneously. This approach achieves better accuracy while maintaining computational efficiency. Feature Pyramid Network (FPN) is integrated into EfficientDet to capture multiscale features effectively, enhancing the model's ability to detect objects at different scales (Tan et al., 2020).

Cascade R-CNN [arxiv.org/abs/1712.00726] improves detection accuracy by employing a cascaded structure, where multiple detectors are applied in sequence, each focusing on refining the results of the previous one. In industrial quality control, Cascade R-CNN can enhance the identification of defects in manufactured products (Cai & Vasconcelos, 2017).

3.5.5 Image Analysis and Recognition

Image analysis and recognition is the process of identifying and detecting objects, patterns or entities within visual data. For instance, in autonomous v

ehicles, image recognition enables the identification of pedestrians, vehicles and road signs to ensure safe navigation. Traditional feature-based methods include shape analysis, texture analysis, SIFT, SURF, Bag-of-Visual-Words, which have now been largely superseded by CNNs.

3.5.5.1 Shape Analysis

Shape analysis techniques aim to extract and characterize the shape or contour of objects in images. These techniques are widely used in object detection, recognition and classification tasks in computer vision.

Various methods exist for analyzing shape, few of which are discussed below (Lancaric, 1998; Dryden & Mardia, 2016).

Contour detection: Contour detection is the process of identifying the boundary or outline of objects in an image. Techniques include edge detection methods, gradient-based methods and region growing methods. Edge Detection methods like the Canny edge detector, Sobel operator and Prewitt operator are commonly used to detect edges in images, which highlight significant changes in intensity that correspond to object boundaries. Gradient-based methods compute the gradient magnitude and direction at each pixel in the image, high gradient magnitudes indicating potential edge locations, which can be connected to form contours. Region growing methods start with seed points and iteratively grow regions by including neighboring pixels that satisfy certain criteria (e.g., similar intensity values or gradients).

Shape descriptors: Shape descriptors are numerical representations that capture various geometric properties of object contours. Some common shape descriptors include area, perimeter, compactness, eccentricity, aspect ratio, centroid, radius, bounding box, major axis length, minor axis length, moments. The area is the total number of pixels enclosed by the contour, which provides a measure of the size of the object. The perimeter is the total length of the contour, which indicates the extent of the object boundary. The aspect ratio is the ratio of the width to the height of the bounding box around the shape, which provides information about the elongation or stretching of the object. The bounding box is the smallest rectangle containing the shape. The centroid is the coordinates of the center of mass of the shape. The major axis length is the length in pixels of the major axis of the ellipse that has the same normalized second central moments as the shape. The minor axis length is the length in pixels of the minor axis of the ellipse that has the same normalized second central moments as the shape. The compactness measures how closely a shape's area approaches that of a circle with the same perimeter and is measured as the ratio of the area of the shape to the area of a circle with the same perimeter. Eccentricity refers to a measure of how elongated or stretched a shape is compared to a perfect circle and is measured as the ratio of the distance between the foci of the shape's elliptical boundary to the length of its major axis.

Contour matching: Contour matching techniques compare the contours of objects in an image to predefined templates or models to determine object presence and identity. Common contour matching methods include shape similarity, distance transforms and dynamic programming techniques. Shape similarity techniques involve matching contours based on measures of shape similarity, such as the Hausdorff distance which quantifies the similarity between two shapes by measuring the maximum and minimum distances between points on the contours. Distance transforms work by transforming the image contour into a distance map, where each pixel value represents the distance to the nearest point on the contour. Dynamic programming algorithms can be used to find optimal correspondences between points on different contours by minimizing a cost function based on local shape similarity measures

Shape context: Shape context methods use descriptor that captures the spatial relationships between points on a shape's contour. Key aspects of shape context include point distribution, histogram representation and matching techniques. Point distribution involves dividing the contour into a set of discrete points and representing each point based on its relative distances and angles to other points on the contour. Histogram representation works by constructing a histogram of relative distances and angles for each point, which encodes the shape's local structure and spatial layout. Matching techniques compare shape contexts between different contours using methods like nearest neighbor search, graph matching or kernel methods to determine shape similarity and correspondence.

3.5.5.2 Texture Analysis

Texture analysis techniques aim to characterize spatial arrangement of pixel intensities in an image region. Textures are patterns of local variations in intensities or color that repeat over space that often provide discriminative information about object appearance and identity, giving rise to visual perceptions like rough, smooth, coarse and fine. Major texture analysis includes statistical methods, co-occurrence matrices, Gabor filters and local binary patterns (LBP) (Hung et al., 2019).

Statistical methods: Statistical texture analysis methods compute statistical measures from pixel intensity distributions within image regions. These statistical measures can be computed at various spatial scales and orientations to capture texture variations. Common statistical measures include: mean, the average pixel intensity value; variance, the measure of dispersion of pixel intensity values; skewness, the measure of asymmetry in the intensity distribution indicating whether values are skewed to the left or right; kurtosis, the measure of the peakedness or flatness of the intensity distribution.

Gabor filters: Gabor filters are a family of bandpass filters tuned to different frequencies and orientations. They are commonly used for texture analysis due to their ability to capture both spatial and frequency information. Gabor filter responses provide multi-scale and multi-orientation representations of texture patterns in images.

Local Binary Patterns (LBP): LBPs are descriptors that encode local texture patterns based on the binary comparison of pixel intensities with neighboring pixels. LBP operators compute binary codes for each pixel by comparing its intensity with the intensities of its neighbors. Texture features are extracted from LBP histograms, which represent the frequency of different texture patterns in the image.

Co-occurrence matrices: Co-occurrence matrices quantify the spatial relationships between pairs of pixel intensities within an image region. They capture information about texture patterns such as smoothness, roughness and regularity. Common texture features derived from co-occurrence matrices include: contrast, the measure of intensity differences between neighboring pixels; energy, the measure of texture uniformity or homogeneity; correlation, the measure of linear dependency between pixel intensities; entropy, the measure of randomness or disorder in the intensity distribution. One of the important methods in texture analysis is the Gray Level Co-occurrence Matrix (GLCM) proposed by Haralick et al. (1973). GLCM defines the probability of gray level i occurring in the neighborhood of gray-level j at an offset distance d and angle:

$$G = P(i, j|d, \theta)$$

GLCMs can be considered at various angles by varying θ: horizontal (0° and 180°), vertical (90° and 270°), right-diagonal (45° and 225°), left-diagonal (135° and 315°). GLCMs for a specific direction, is the transpose of the GLCM for the opposite direction. The transpose is added to the original matrix to make it symmetrical to take both the directions into account. To make the GLCM independent of the image size it is normalized by dividing by the sum of all elements to obtain a set of symmetrical normalized directional GLCMs.

The dimensions of a GLCM depend on the total number of gray levels in the image. Since for a typical grayscale image total number of gray levels can be upto 256, the GLCM becomes a high dimensional matrix which cannot be directly incorporated within applications efficiently. It is therefore conventional to calculate some scalar statistical properties from a GLCM and incorporate these into calculations instead of the GLCM itself. Typical features include contrast, correlation, energy, homogeneity. If $G(i,j)$ represents the (i,j)-th element of a directional normalized symmetrical GLCM and N denotes the number of gray levels, then the features Contrast C, Homogeneity H, Energy E and Correlation R are defined as follows:

$$C = \sum_{i=1}^{N}\sum_{j=1}^{N} G(i,j).(i-j)^2$$

$$H = \sum_{i=1}^{N}\sum_{j=1}^{N} \frac{G(i,j)}{1+|i-j|}$$

$$E = \sum_{i=1}^{N}\sum_{j=1}^{N} \{G(i,j)\}^2$$

$$R = \sum_{i=1}^{N}\sum_{j=1}^{N} G(i,j).\frac{(i-\mu_i)(j-\mu_j)}{\sigma_i.\sigma_j}$$

Here, the μ and σ terms denote the mean and standard deviations, respectively, along specific directions indicated (Armi & Fekri-Ershad, 2019).

3.5.5.3 SIFT and SURF

SIFT (Scale-Invariant Feature Transform) (Lowe, 2004) and SURF (Speeded-Up Robust Features) (Bay et al., 2008) methods detect and describe distinctive features in images, making them invariant to scale and rotation. They are widely used in image matching and recognition tasks. SIFT starts by building a scale space representation of the input image which involves creating a series of blurred and down-sampled images at different scales. At each scale the algorithm identifies key-points where the Difference of Gaussian (DoG) function has a local extrema in multiple scales at the same location in space. Once potential key-points are detected the algorithm performs precise localization by fitting a quadratic function to nearby samples in scale space. Each key-point is assigned one or more orientations based on local image gradient directions. A histogram of gradient orientations is constructed, and the peak(s) in this histogram indicate the dominant orientations of the key-point. SIFT generates a descriptor for each key-point to represent its local appearance. The descriptor captures information about the gradient magnitudes and orientations in a region around the key-point. After descriptors are computed for key-points in multiple images, SIFT matches key-points between different images based on the similarity of their descriptors. SURF identifies interest points in the image by convolving the image with a series of box filters at different scales and orientations. These box filters are approximations of Gaussian filters and are computationally efficient to apply. Interest points are detected at locations where the response to the box filters is maximum across scales and orientations. After interest points are detected, SURF assigns orientations to each interest point. Unlike SIFT, which uses gradients for orientation assignment, SURF uses Haar wavelet responses for speed and efficiency. Once orientations are assigned, SURF constructs descriptors for each interest point to represent its local appearance. SURF descriptors are based on a grid of square regions around each interest point. Within each region, SURF computes the sum of Haar wavelet responses in horizontal and vertical directions. SURF descriptors from different images are compared for feature matching. SURF is designed to be computationally faster than SIFT, making it suitable for real-time applications and large-scale image processing tasks. Similar to SIFT, SURF is invariant to changes in scale and rotation, making it robust to geometric transformations. While SURF provides good performance in many scenarios, it may not be as robust as SIFT in highly challenging or cluttered environments.

3.5.5.4 Bag-of-Visual-Words (BoVW)

The Bag-of-Visual-Words (BoVW) representation treats images as collections of local features, similar to how documents are treated as collections of words in text analysis. BoVW begins with the extraction of local features from images. Common local feature detectors and descriptors include SIFT, SURF, ORB and HOG. These local features capture distinctive information about key-points or regions in the image, such as gradients, texture patterns or color histograms. The extracted local features are clustered into a set of visual words or codebook using clustering algorithms like K-means clustering. The codebook represents a vocabulary of visual patterns present in the dataset. Each cluster centroid serves as a representative visual word. Each local feature is assigned to the nearest visual word in the codebook. This process is known as feature quantization or vector quantization. The assignment of local features to visual words creates a histogram representation of the image, where each bin corresponds to the frequency of a visual word in the image. The histogram representations of images are used as feature vectors for classification or object detection tasks. Various classifiers or machine learning algorithms, such as Support Vector Machines (SVM), Random Forests or Neural Networks, can be trained on these feature vectors for tasks like image classification, object recognition or scene categorization. BoVW is robust to variations in scale, rotation and viewpoint, as it captures local information from images and can handle large datasets efficiently, as it reduces the dimensionality of feature representations. However BoVW does not capture spatial relationships between visual words, which may limit its performance in tasks requiring precise localization or spatial reasoning. Also the size of the codebook can affect the performance of BoVW, with larger codebooks potentially leading to higher accuracy but also increased computational complexity (Csurka et al., 2004).

3.5.5.5 PCA and LDA

Principal Component Analysis (PCA) and Linear Discriminant Analysis (LDA) are techniques used to reduce the dimensionality of image data and feature extraction. PCA is a technique used for dimensionality reduction by transforming the original data into a new set of variables, called principal components, that are linear combinations of the original variables. In image analysis, PCA can be applied to reduce the dimensionality of high-dimensional image data while preserving as much variance as possible. Images are usually represented as high-dimensional vectors, where each pixel corresponds to a feature. Before applying PCA, it's common to preprocess the images by standardizing their pixel values (mean centering and scaling). PCA calculates the covariance matrix of the standardized image data, which represents the relationships between pixel intensities across all images. The covariance matrix is then decomposed into its eigenvectors and eigenvalues. The eigenvectors represent the principal components, and the corresponding eigenvalues indicate the amount of variance explained by each principal component. Principal components are ranked in descending order of their corresponding eigenvalues. The top k eigenvectors (principal components) are selected to retain the most significant variance in the data. The original image data is projected onto the selected principal components, resulting in a lower-dimensional representation of the images. This reduces the dimensionality of the data while preserving the most important features.

LDA is a supervised dimensionality reduction technique that aims to maximize the separation between classes in the data. In image analysis, LDA can be used for feature extraction and classification by finding a linear transformation that maximizes the between-class scatter while minimizing the within-class scatter. Similar to PCA, image data is preprocessed by standardizing pixel values. LDA calculates the mean vector for each class (or category) in the dataset. LDA computes the within-class scatter matrix, which represents the variance within each class, as also the between-class scatter matrix, which represents the variance between class means. LDA seeks to find a transformation matrix that maximizes the ratio of between-class scatter to within-class scatter. Finally, the original image data is projected onto the optimal transformation matrix, resulting in a lower-dimensional representation that maximizes class separability.

PCA is useful for reducing the dimensionality of image data while retaining the most important information. It is widely used in tasks such as image compression, denoising and visualization. LDA goes beyond dimensionality reduction and aims to find discriminative features that maximize class separability. It is commonly used for feature extraction and classification in tasks such as face recognition, object recognition and image retrieval.

3.5.5.6 Convolutional Neural Networks (CNNs)

CNNs, a breakthrough in image recognition, excel at automatically learning hierarchical features from images. They consist of convolutional layers that scan the input for local patterns, pooling layers that downsample the spatial dimensions, and fully connected layers for high-level abstraction. LeNet [medium.com/@siddheshb008/lenet-5-architecture-explained-3b559cb2d52b], AlexNet, [arxiv.org/abs/2404.07395] and VGGNet [viso.ai/deep-learning/vgg-very-deep-convolutional-networks] are early CNN architectures. For instance, in object recognition applications, CNNs can distinguish between various objects in a scene by learning complex hierarchical features.

3.5.5.7 Transfer Learning

Transfer learning leverages knowledge gained from pre-training on large datasets and applies it to a specific task. Pre-trained models like ResNet [ieeexplore.ieee.org/document/7780459] or Inception [cloud.google.com/tpu/docs/inception-v3-advanced], trained on vast image datasets like ImageNet [www.image-net.org], can be fine-tuned for custom tasks with limited labeled data. In medical image classification, a pre-trained CNN can be adapted to identify specific diseases based on a smaller dataset, enhancing performance.

3.5.5.8 Ensemble Methods

Ensemble methods combine predictions from multiple models to improve accuracy and generalization. Bagging (Bootstrap Aggregating) [www.ibm.com/topics/bagging] and boosting are common techniques. In image classification, an ensemble of CNNs with diverse architectures or trained on different subsets of data can enhance overall performance, reducing over-fitting.

3.5.5.9 Spatial Transformer Networks

Spatial Transformer Networks (STN) [arxiv.org/abs/1506.02025] dynamically transform input images to improve spatial alignment. STNs can be embedded within CNNs, allowing the network to learn transformations such as rotation, scaling and cropping. In facial recognition, STNs can aid in aligning faces for improved feature extraction.

3.5.5.10 Attention Mechanisms

Attention mechanisms [arxiv.org/abs/2404.17254] focus on relevant parts of an image during processing, allowing models to concentrate on specific regions. Transformer models, initially designed for natural language processing, have been adapted to computer vision tasks. In image captioning, attention mechanisms enable the model to describe specific objects or regions of interest in images. Facial recognition applications benefit from attention mechanisms, allowing the model to focus on key facial features.

3.5.5.11 Capsule Networks

Capsule Networks [arxiv.org/abs/2404.15445] aim to overcome limitations in traditional pooling layers by preserving hierarchical relationships between features. Capsules represent spatial hierarchies and pose information, enabling better generalization. In medical image diagnosis, Capsule Networks may capture intricate structures, improving diagnostic accuracy.

3.5.5.12 Recurrent Neural Networks (RNNs)

RNNs [arxiv.org/abs/2404.12745] are a class of artificial neural networks designed to handle sequential data and capture dependencies over time. Unlike traditional neural networks, RNNs have connections that form directed cycles, allowing them to maintain a memory of previous inputs. This is achieved through recurrent connections, where the output of a neuron is fed back as an input to the same or other neurons in the network. This unique architecture makes RNNs well suited for tasks involving sequences, such as natural language processing, speech recognition and time-series analysis.

3.5.6 Image Classification

Image classification is a specific aspect of image recognition that involves assigning predefined labels or categories to images based on their content. In medical imaging, classification helps in diagnosing diseases by categorizing images into different pathological conditions. Different classifiers employ distinct working principles, and their effectiveness depends on the nature of the data and the underlying assumptions of the model (Das, 2020).

3.5.6.1 Support Vector Machines (SVM)

SVM [arxiv.org/abs/2404.16724] aims to find a hyperplane that best separates data into different classes while maximizing the margin, i.e., the distance between the hyperplane and the nearest data points (support vectors). SVM can handle non-linearly separable data by mapping the input features into a higher-dimensional space using a kernel function (e.g., polynomial or radial basis function). This is referred to as the "kernel trick". In this space, a hyperplane can effectively separate the data (Christianini & Shawe-Taylor, 2000).

3.5.6.2 k-Nearest Neighbors (k-NN)

k-NN [arxiv.org/abs/2403.12792] classifies a data point by considering the class labels of its k nearest neighbors in the feature space. The class with the majority among these neighbors becomes the predicted class for the query point. The choice of distance metric (e.g., Euclidean distance or Manhattan distance) influences the neighbor selection process. The choice of the parameter k also influences the decision boundaries: smaller values of k result are more complex boundaries, while larger values of k lead to smoother boundaries (Roussopoulos et al., 1995).

3.5.6.3 Decision Tree and Random Forest

Decision trees recursively split the feature space into regions based on the most informative feature at each node. Each leaf node corresponds to a class label. The choice of splitting criteria, guides the decision tree in selecting the most discriminative features (Coppersmith et al., 1999). Random forests [arxiv.org/abs/2404.15392] are an ensemble of decision trees. Multiple decision trees are trained on different subsets of the data, and their predictions are aggregated to improve overall accuracy and robustness. Random forests use bootstrapping to create diverse datasets for training each tree, and bagging to combine the predictions of individual trees. Bootstrapping is a statistical technique that involves creating multiple random samples (with replacement) from the original dataset (Breiman, 2001).

3.5.6.4 Naive Bayes

Naive Bayes [arxiv.org/abs/2403.14069] is based on Bayes's theorem and assumes that features are conditionally independent given the class label. It calculates the probability of each class given the input features and selects the class with the highest probability. Despite the "naive" assumption of feature independence, Naive Bayes often performs well in practice, especially with text data (Hastie et al., 2008).

3.5.6.5 Logistic Regression

Logistic regression models [arxiv.org/abs/2404.17482] the probability that a given input belongs to a particular class (Strano & Colosimo, 2006). It uses the logistic function to transform a linear combination of input features into a probability score, which is then thresholded to make a binary classification decision. Essentially it minimizes a loss function to optimize model parameters and maximize the likelihood of correct class predictions. It uses a sigmoid activation function to map the output of a linear combination of features to a probability score between 0 and 1, making logistic regression suitable for binary classification.

3.5.6.6 Neural Networks

Neural networks (NN), also known as multi-layer perceptrons (MLP), consist of interconnected layers of neurons that transform input data through weighted connections and activation functions (Haykin, 2009). NNs consist of an input layer, one or more hidden layer and an output layer. Non-linear activation functions (e.g., ReLU, sigmoid, tanh) are applied to the output of each neuron to introduce non-linearity and enable the network to approximate complex functions. They are trained using backpropagation, an optimization algorithm that adjusts the network's weights iteratively to minimize a loss function between predicted and true labels. NNs require tuning of various parameters, including the number of layers, the number of neurons per layer, learning rate and regularization strength.

3.5.6.7 Deep Neural Network Architectures

Architectures like Convolutional Neural Networks (CNNs) and Recurrent Neural Networks (RNNs) leverage specialized layers (e.g., convolutional layers, recurrent layers) to capture hierarchical features in images or sequences. Convolutional layers apply convolutional filters to extract spatial features while pooling layers downsample feature maps to reduce spatial dimensions and improve invariance to transformations. Pre-training on large datasets, such as ImageNet, and fine-tuning on specific tasks is a common strategy. In manufacturing, traditional methods combined with CNNs can identify and classify defects in products (Bengio, 2009).

3.6 Legal and Ethical Considerations

3.6.1 Legal Considerations

Legal considerations are crucial when working with digital imaging to ensure compliance with intellectual property laws, privacy regulations and other legal standards (Reed, 2015). Here are key legal considerations for digital imaging:

Copyright and Intellectual Property: Respect copyright laws when using digital images. Ensure that you have the right to use and manipulate images and respect the intellectual property rights of photographers, artists or other content creators.

Licensing Agreements: Adhere to the terms and conditions specified in licensing agreements associated with digital images. Licensing agreements may dictate how the images can be used, whether for personal or commercial purposes.

Public Domain and Creative Commons: Be aware of the licensing status of digital images. Some images may be in the public domain, while others may be available under Creative Commons licenses. Understand the terms of these licenses and comply with them.

Fair Use: Understand the concept of fair use, which allows the use of copyrighted material under certain circumstances, such as for purposes of criticism, commentary, news reporting, education and research. However, fair use is a nuanced legal concept, and its application can vary.

Model Releases: If your digital images include recognizable individuals, ensure that you have obtained the necessary model releases. Model releases grant permission to use the likeness of individuals, particularly for commercial purposes.

Property Releases: Obtain property releases for digital images that feature private property, especially if the images are intended for commercial use. Property releases help protect against legal claims related to property rights.

Privacy Laws: Be aware of privacy laws that may apply to the capture and use of digital images, especially when individuals are involved. Respect privacy rights and obtain consent when required by law.

Digital Forensics and Authentication: Understand the legal implications of digital forensics and image authentication. Misuse of these techniques, such as creating misleading deepfakes, may have legal consequences, including potential liability for defamation or harm.

Commercial Use and Endorsements: Exercise caution when using digital images for commercial purposes. Be aware of laws related to false advertising and endorsements, and ensure that you have the right to use images featuring recognizable products or brands.

Child Protection Laws: Take extra care when working with digital images that involve minors. Child protection laws may impose additional requirements for obtaining consent and protecting the privacy of minors in images.

Digital Watermarks: Understand the legal implications of digital watermarks. While watermarks can help protect the copyright of images, their use should comply with relevant laws, and removing watermarks without permission may constitute a violation of copyright.

Jurisdictional Differences: Be mindful of the legal landscape in different jurisdictions. Laws related to intellectual property, privacy and other considerations can vary, and it's important to understand and comply with the relevant laws in the locations where your work is distributed or used.

3.6.2 Ethical Considerations

Ethical considerations in digital imaging are essential to ensure responsible and respectful practices. These considerations encompass issues such as representation, authenticity, privacy and the impact of digital manipulations (Andina & Dreier, 2022).

Authenticity and Truthfulness: Maintain the authenticity of digital images. Avoid misleading manipulations that could alter the context or meaning of the image. Clearly disclose any modifications made to the original content.

Informed Consent: Obtain informed consent when capturing or using images that involve individuals, especially in contexts where privacy or sensitive topics are concerned. Clearly communicate how the images will be used.

Representation and Diversity: Promote diversity and inclusivity in digital imaging. Be conscious of the representation of different cultures, genders and ethnicities. Avoid reinforcing stereotypes or biased narratives.

Cultural Sensitivity: Exercise cultural sensitivity when creating or using digital images, particularly when representing rituals, symbols or practices associated with specific cultures. Be respectful and avoid appropriation.

Privacy: Respect the privacy of individuals featured in digital images. Avoid capturing or sharing images that intrude on private moments, and be mindful of the potential impact of your work on the subjects' lives.

Avoiding Harm: Consider the potential impact of your digital imaging work on individuals, communities or society at large. Avoid creating or sharing content that may cause harm, offense or distress.

Context and Intent: Be mindful of the context and intent of your digital images. Ensure that the images are used in a way that aligns with their original purpose and does not mislead or manipulate viewers.

Child Protection: Exercise special care when working with images featuring minors. Respect child protection laws, obtain necessary permissions and avoid using images in ways that may exploit or harm children.

Environmental Impact: Consider the environmental impact of digital imaging practices. Minimize resource consumption, use sustainable practices and be conscious of the environmental footprint associated with storing and processing digital images.

Digital Manipulation Disclosure: Clearly disclose any digital manipulations or alterations made to images, especially if they could affect the viewer's interpretation. Transparency about the creation process builds trust and avoids misleading audiences.

Educational Use: When using digital imaging in educational contexts, provide context and critical analysis. Encourage learners to think critically about the images they encounter, considering issues of bias, representation and authenticity.

Credibility and Trust: Uphold the credibility of digital imaging work. Misleading or deceptive practices erode trust and can have negative consequences for both creators and viewers.

3.7 Challenges and Emerging Trends

3.7.1 Challenges

Digital imaging technologies have witnessed rapid advancements, transforming how we capture, process and interact with visual information. However, alongside these innovations come challenges that require thoughtful solutions. Additionally, emerging trends are shaping the future of digital imaging. This section explores both the current challenges and the exciting trends on the horizon (Liu & Ramakrishnan, 2020).

Data Overload: The increasing resolution and capabilities of imaging devices result in vast amounts of data, posing challenges in storage, processing and transmission. Handling this data efficiently is crucial for real-time applications and large-scale imaging projects.

Privacy Concerns: Advanced imaging technologies, such as facial recognition and high-resolution surveillance cameras, raise concerns about privacy and the ethical use of visual data. Striking a balance between technological innovation and privacy rights is an ongoing challenge.

Computational Complexity: The implementation of complex algorithms for image processing and analysis, including machine learning models, can be computationally intensive. This poses challenges in terms of energy consumption, especially in resource-constrained environments.

Standardization and Interoperability: The diversity of imaging devices and formats creates challenges in standardization and interoperability. Achieving seamless integration across different platforms and devices remains an ongoing challenge for the imaging industry.

Ethical Use of AI: As artificial intelligence (AI) plays a greater role in image analysis, ensuring ethical use and preventing biases in AI algorithms become critical challenges. The responsible development and deployment of AI in imaging applications require careful consideration.

3.7.2 Emerging Trends

Computational Photography: Computational photography involves using advanced algorithms and AI to enhance and manipulate images. This trend includes features like enhanced low-light photography, depth mapping and the ability to refocus images after capture.

Immersive Imaging: The future of imaging includes technologies that provide immersive experiences [dl.acm.org/doi/abs/10.1145/3394171.3418550]. This encompasses virtual reality (VR), augmented reality (AR) and 360-degree imaging, enabling users to engage with visual content in more immersive and interactive ways.

Multispectral and Hyperspectral Imaging: Beyond visible light, multispectral and hyperspectral imaging [arxiv.org/abs/2404.15781] capture information across a broader range of the electromagnetic spectrum. This has applications in fields like agriculture, environmental monitoring and medical diagnostics.

AI-driven Image Enhancement: AI algorithms will play a significant role in automatically enhancing and optimizing images [arxiv.org/abs/2404.13784]. This includes features like upscaling, denoising and intelligent image editing, where AI assists in creating visually appealing and high-quality images.

Edge Computing for Imaging Devices: Edge computing involves processing data closer to the source rather than relying solely on centralized servers. In imaging, this trend enables devices to perform real-time image analysis locally, reducing latency and improving responsiveness.

Explainable AI in Imaging: As AI becomes more prevalent in image analysis, the need for explainable AI grows [arxiv.org/abs/2404.17350]. Ensuring that AI algorithms provide transparent and understandable results is crucial, particularly in fields like healthcare and criminal justice.

3D Imaging and LiDAR Technology: The integration of 3D imaging and LiDAR technology [arxiv.org/abs/2207.01452] is gaining momentum. This has applications in areas such as autonomous vehicles, robotics and augmented reality, where accurate depth perception is essential.

Quantum Imaging: Quantum imaging [arxiv.org/abs/quant-ph/0203046] explores the application of quantum mechanics principles to capture and process images. While still in the early stages, quantum imaging holds potential for advancements in sensitivity and precision beyond classical imaging methods.

Dynamic Imaging in Medicine: Advances in medical imaging include dynamic imaging [www.dynamicimaging.com/] techniques that capture real-time physiological processes. This trend enhances diagnostic capabilities and contributes to personalized healthcare.

3.8 Image File Formats

Images may be stored in a variety of file formats. Each file format is characterized by a specific compression type and color depth. The choice of file formats would depend on the requirements of the application which the image will be utilized. Some of the major file formats are discussed below:

3.8.1 BMP

The BMP (Bitmap) file format, developed by Microsoft [learn.microsoft.com/en-us/windows/win32/gdi/bitmaps], is a widely used raster graphics format known for its simplicity and versatility. BMP files store images as a series of pixels in a grid, providing uncompressed or minimally compressed data. BMP supports various color depths, including 1-bit (monochrome), 8-bit (grayscale), 24-bit (true color), 32-bit (with alpha channel). The color information is typically stored in the order of Blue, Green and Red, with an optional Alpha channel for transparency. While BMP files are often uncompressed, they can also support basic compression methods like RLE (Run-Length Encoding), to reduce file size. A BMP file consists of a file header, an optional color palette, an information header and image data. The file header contains information about file type and size, the color palette contains entries for color values used in the image stored as RGB triplets, the information header contains details about the image like dimension color depth and file size, the image data contains the pixel values of the image.

3.8.2 JPEG

JPEG (Joint Photographers Experts Group) [jpeg.org] format is commonly used to display photographs and other continuous-tone images in HTML documents over the World Wide Web and other online services. JPEG format supports CMYK, RGB, YCbCr and

Grayscale color modes, but does not support alpha channels. JPEG uses a 24-bit format and, therefore, retains all color information in an RGB image but compresses file size by selectively discarding data using a method based on the discrete cosine transform. However, JPEG also supports a lossless mode. A higher level of compression results in lower image quality, and transparent pixels usually show up as white. A JPEG file structure consists of segments each with its own marker, for example, start of image, metadata, quantization table, Huffman table and so on. JPEG compression algorithm involves several stages: converts RGB color space to YCbCr, chrominance components are sub-sampled, pixels are grouped into 8 × 8 blocks, DCT is applied on each block to convert spatial data into frequency domain coefficients, which are subsequently quantized using quantization tables allowing for lossy compression, the DCT coefficients are finally entropy coded using Huffman coding.

3.8.3 GIF

GIF (Graphics Interchange Format) [www.w3.org/Graphics/GIF/spec-gif89a.txt] is the file format commonly used to display indexed-color graphics and images in hypertext markup language (HTML) documents over the World Wide Web and other online services. GIF format preserves transparency in indexed-color images; however, it does not support alpha channels. The GIF format uses 8-bit color and efficiently compresses solid areas of color while preserving sharp detail, such as that in line art, logos or illustrations with type. The GIF format can also be used to create animated images by combining multiple images (frames) into a single animated GIF file. GIF is supported by most browsers. Since GIF can represent at most 256 colors, for images of higher color depth, e.g., 24-bit, the 256 most representative colors are chosen. This is done by using a Color Look-Up Table (CLUT).

3.8.4 PNG

PNG (Portable Network Graphics) [www.w3.org/TR/png] format, developed as a patent-free alternative to GIF, is used for lossless compression and for display of images on the World Wide Web. Unlike GIF, PNG supports 24-bit images and produces background transparency without jagged edges. PNG format supports RGB, indexed-color, grayscale and Bitmap-mode images without alpha channels. PNG preserves transparency in grayscale and RGB images. A PNG file consists of a signature, a series of chunks containing image data and metadata and an end of file marker. The signature identifies a PNG file; the chunks contain information about the image such as height, width, color depth, textual metadata, compressed data and CRC (cyclic redundancy check) checksum for data integrity. PNG uses lossless compression to preserve image quality that uses a combination of LZ77 (Lempel Ziv) and Huffman coding. It supports alpha channels allowing for transparent regions that makes it suitable for logos and icons. Unlike GIF, PNG does not support animation, for which the Animated PNG alternative is used.

3.8.5 TIFF

TIFF (Tagged-Image File Format) designed by Aldus Corporation (now part of Adobe Systems Inc.) [developer.adobe.com/content/dam/udp/en/open/standards/tiff/TIFF6.pdf] in 1987, is used to exchange files between applications and computer platforms. TIFF is a flexible bitmap image format supported by virtually all paint, image-editing and page-layout applications. Also, virtually all desktop scanners can produce TIFF images. Although 8 bits/channel is the most common color depth in which TIFF images are processed, the format also supports color depths of 16 bits/channel. Moreover, it can be stored in a number of different color models including CMYK, RGB, Lab, indexed-color and grayscale images with alpha channels and bitmap-mode images without alpha channels. This is why the acronym is sometimes jokingly referred to as "Thousands of Incompatible File Formats". It optionally uses the lossless LZW compression method and hence, is an appropriate format for archiving master copies and printing purposes. The latest version of the TIFF specification TIFF6.0 was published in 1992. TIFF files are limited in size to 2^32 bytes or about 4.2 GB.

3.8.6 JPEG2000

The original JPEG standard created in 1992 uses the DCT to convert the spatial domain to frequency domain. JPEG2000 [jpeg.org/jpeg2000], created in 2000, uses the same basic principle of conversion to frequency domain and removal of redundant frequency components to reduce the file size, but instead of DCT it uses another techniques known as Discrete Wavelet Transform (DWT). The specification is named ISO/IEC 15444-2 (www.iso.orf/standard/84573.html) and standardizes a filename extension of .JP2. The image can be coded using multiple resolutions, which means that different scaled-down representations of the original image can be derived and each representation can be compressed separately. As per the requirements of the application, the appropriate version can be retrieved and decompressed for viewing. Superior compression ratios are achieved with better quality output where artifacts are less visible. Also support for progressive coding implies that the image might be decoded partially and a low-quality version can be viewed while the remaining data is downloaded in the background. The standard also supports storing different parts of the image, called Regions-Of-Interest (ROI), at different levels of quality or granularity, and further supports for transparency and alpha channels.

3.8.7 WebP

WebP (Web Picture) [developers.google.com/speed/webp] is a modern image format developed by Google that aims to provide high-quality image compression with smaller file sizes, making it suitable for Web content. It supports both lossy and lossless compression, and its features include improved compression efficiency, transparency support and animation capabilities. WebP supports both lossy and lossless compression modes, allowing users to choose between smaller file sizes with a certain loss of image quality or maintaining higher quality without compression artifacts. It employs advanced compression techniques, such as predictive coding and entropy encoding, to achieve smaller file sizes without significant loss of quality. It supports both fully opaque and semi-transparent pixels, making it suitable for images with alpha (transparency) channels. This support is crucial for creating visually appealing graphics and images on the Web. In addition to static images, WebP also supports animation as it can store multiple frames in a single file, making it suitable for creating animated images with smaller file sizes compared to traditional formats like GIF. A WebP file consists of a WebP file header followed by one or more image data chunks. The image data includes compressed image data, alpha channel data (if applicable) and other metadata. Lossy compression in WebP allows users to adjust parameters such as quality and target size, providing a balance between file size and image quality. The lossless compression mode in WebP achieves competitive compression ratios with other lossless formats while supporting transparency. WebP has gained popularity for web developers and designers aiming to optimize website performance; its support for transparency, animation and efficient compression makes it a versatile choice for various types of Web content.

3.9 Numerical Problems

3.9.1 Image Fundamentals

PROBLEM 3.1

A GIF image occupies a rectangular area of A inch by B inch on a monitor screen. The resolution of the monitor is C *dpi*. What is the file size of the image in *KB*?

Width $W = A$ and height $H = B$

Let width and height in pixels be w and h respectively. Resolution $R = C\ dpi$

Now $w = W * R = AC$ and $h = H * R = BC$

Total number of pixels in image $= w.h = ABC^2$

A GIF image has a color depth of 8 bits

Hence size of image $S = w.h.b = 8ABC^2$bits

$$= 8ABC^2 / (8*1024)KB$$

$$= ABC^2 / 1024KB$$

PROBLEM 3.2

An image of dimensions 1024 × 768 has a color depth of 24 bits. If the image is to be transmitted along a 1 Mbps line from a Web server, how long would it take to display the entire image on screen?

Size of image $S = w.h.b = 1024 * 768 * 24 = 18874368$ bits

To be transmitted along a 1 Mbps line would take $(18874368/1000000) = 18.87$ seconds

PROBLEM 3.3

An image has an aspect ratio of m:n and a bit depth b. The longest diagonal within the image has a size d pixels. Compute the file size of the image in terms of m, n, b and d.

Let width and height of the image be mx and nx respectively.

Length of diagonal $d = \sqrt{(mx)^2 + (nx)^2} = x\sqrt{m^2 + n^2}$

Solving for x: $= \dfrac{d}{\sqrt{m^2 + n^2}}$. Hence width of image $w = mx = \dfrac{md}{\sqrt{m^2 + n^2}}$ and height $h = nx = \dfrac{nd}{\sqrt{m^2 + n^2}}$

Size of image $S = w.h.b = \dfrac{bmnd^2}{m^2 + n^2}$ bits

3.9.2 Visual Display Units

PROBLEM 3.4

A 15-inch monitor with an aspect ratio of 4:3 can address 800 × 600 pixels. Calculate its pixel density and dot-pitch.

Let W and H the width and height of the monitor be $4x$ and $3x$ respectively

Size of diagonal $D = 15 = \sqrt{(3x)^2 + (4x)^2}$

Solving: $x = 3$. Hence width $W = 4x = 12$ inch.

Pixel density: (number of pixels along width)/ (width in inches) = 800/12 = 66.67 *dpi*

Dot pitch = 1/66.67 = 0.015 inch

PROBLEM 3.5

A monitor of aspect ratio 4:3 with 900 dots along a vertical column needs to display images with 32768 colors. Calculate the minimum amount of display memory required in its adapter card.

Height of monitor in pixels h = 900. Aspect ratio $m{:}n = 4{:}3$.

Hence width in pixels $w = (4/3)*900 = 1200$ pixels

Let bit depth be b. Since number of colors is 32768 we must have $2^b = 32768$, i.e., $b = 15$

Memory required $M = w.h.b$ = 1200*900*15 bits ≈ 2 MB

PROBLEM 3.6

A 15 inch monitor having aspect ratio 9:5 has 1080 pixels along a row and refresh rate of 60 Hz. What is the horizontal scan rate?

Pixels along a column is: (1080/9)*5 = 600

Thus 600 lines are scanned in 1/60 – th of a second

Hence horizontal scan rate is 600*60 = 36000 Hz = 36 kHz

PROBLEM 3.7

A monitor with aspect ratio $m{:}n$ ($m > n$) has a refresh rate R and horizontal scan rate H. Find its width in pixels. Also find its pixel density if its size is S.

Let no. of horizontal lines in a screen = h

Horizontal scan rate = refresh rate * h, i.e., $H = R.h$. Thus $h = H / R$

Let w be the width of monitor in pixels. Since $w / h = m / n$, we have $w = mh / n = (m / n)(H / R)$

Let r be the pixel density in dpi of the monitor. Thus $r = w / W$, where W is the width in inches

Let physical width $W = mx$ and physical height $H = nx$

Since size is S, $S = \sqrt{(mx)^2 + (nx)^2}$. Hence $x = \dfrac{S}{\sqrt{m^2 + n^2}}$

Thus physical width $W = mx = \dfrac{mS}{\sqrt{m^2 + n^2}}$

Also pixel density $r = w / W = \left(\dfrac{mH}{nR}\right) / \left[\dfrac{mS}{\sqrt{m^2 + n^2}}\right]$ $= \dfrac{H\sqrt{m^2 + n^2}}{nRS}$

3.9.3 Geometrical Transformation

PROBLEM 3.8

For an image with r rows and c columns, $Q1$ and $Q3$ are swapped and $Q2$ and $Q4$ are swapped. Find translation amounts.

Translation of $Q1$: $\Delta x = +c / 2, \Delta y = +r / 2$

Translation of $Q3$: $\Delta x = -c / 2, \Delta y = -r / 2$

Translation of $Q2$: $\Delta x = -c / 2, \Delta y = +r / 2$

Translation of $Q4$: $\Delta x = +c / 2, \Delta y = -r / 2$

PROBLEM 3.9

For image of width w height h, consider origin at center of image, and top-left corner $A(-w/2, h/2)$. Find its new location after CCW and CW rotations of 90°.

CCW rotation implies θ = 90°. Let $A'(x_2, y_2)$ be the new location of the vertex A.

$$\text{Then } x_2 = \left(-\frac{w}{2}\right).(\cos 90) - \left(\frac{h}{2}\right).(\sin 90) = -\frac{h}{2}$$

$$\text{Also } y_2 = \left(-\frac{w}{2}\right).(\sin 90) + \left(\frac{h}{2}\right).(\cos 90) = -\frac{w}{2}$$

$\therefore$ New location is: $A'\left(-\dfrac{h}{2}, -\dfrac{w}{2}\right)$

CW rotation implies θ = –90°. Let $A''(x_3, y_3)$ be the new location of the vertex A.

$$\text{Then } x_3 = \left(-\frac{w}{2}\right).(\cos 90) + \left(\frac{h}{2}\right).(\sin 90) = \frac{h}{2}$$

$$\text{Also } y_3 = -\left(-\frac{w}{2}\right).(\sin 90) + \left(\frac{h}{2}\right).(\cos 90) = \frac{w}{2}$$

$\therefore$ New location is: $A''\left(\dfrac{h}{2}, \dfrac{w}{2}\right)$

PROBLEM 3.10

For image of width w height h, consider origin at center of image, and top-left corner A $(-w/2, h/2)$. Find its new location after being scaled down by 30% along X-axis and scaled up by 40% along Y-axis directions.

Let scaling factors be sx and sy along x and y directions. In this case $sx = 0.7$ and $sy = 1.4$

In matrix form:

$$\begin{pmatrix} x_2 \\ y_2 \end{pmatrix} = \begin{pmatrix} s_x & 0 \\ 0 & s_y \end{pmatrix} \begin{pmatrix} x_1 \\ y_1 \end{pmatrix}$$

$$= \begin{pmatrix} 0.7 & 0 \\ 0 & 1.4 \end{pmatrix} \begin{pmatrix} -w/2 \\ h/2 \end{pmatrix} = \begin{pmatrix} -0.35w \\ 0.7h \end{pmatrix}$$

New coordinates of A: $(-0.35w, 0.7h)$

3.9.4 Intensity Transformation

PROBLEM 3.11

A 400 × 400 square image contains a smaller square 200 × 200 at the center. The smaller square is filled with gray level 127, while 50% of the remaining area is filled with gray level 63 and the other half with gray level 191. Represent a 3-bin histogram of the image as a normalized vector in format value@level.

Outer square has area 160000 and inner square has area 40000

If N be the total number of pixels, then $N/4$ pixels has level 127

The remaining area has $3N/4$ pixels

Out of this $3N/8$ pixels have level 63 and $3N/8$ pixels have level 191

Histogram normalized vector:

$$H = \left[\frac{3}{8}@63, \frac{1}{4}@127, \frac{3}{8}@191\right]$$

PROBLEM 3.12

An image segment is divided into four equal sized quadrants having intensity values 0, 50, 100, 150. Perform histogram equalization and find new intensity values.

Index k: 0 1 2 3

Level r: 0, 50, 100, 150

Freq f: $N/4, N/4, N/4, N/4,$

CDF: $N/4, N/2, 3N/4, N$

Here, CDF (min) = $N/4$, $L = 256$

For histogram equalization: h(k) = round[{CDF(k) – CDF_min}/{N – CDF_min}] × (L – 1)

$h(0) = [(N/4 - N/4)/(N - N/4)] \times 255 = 0$

$h(1) = [(2N/4 - N/4)/(N - N/4)] \times 255 = (1/3)\times 255 = 85$

$h(2) = [(3N/4 - N/4)/(N - N/4)] \times 255 = (2/3)\times 255 = 170$

$h(3) = [(4N/4 - N/4)/(N - N/4)] \times 255 = (1)\times 255 = 255$

New intensity values: 0, 85, 170, 255

PROBLEM 3.13

Let an image section be represented by the following matrix: [3, 2, 4, 5 ; 7, 7, 8, 2 ; 3, 2, 2, 3 ; 5, 4, 6, 7]. Perform a histogram equalization and calculate new values if the total range of values is from 0 to 20.

index: 0, 1, 2, 3, 4, 5, 6

pixel values: 2, 3, 4, 5, 6, 7, 8

no. of pixels: 4, 3, 2, 2, 1, 3, 1

CDF: 4, 7, 9, 11, 12, 15, 16

We know: $h(k)$ = round [{CDF(k) – CDF(min)} / {N – CDF(min)}] * L

Here $L = 20$, CDF(min)=4 and $N = 16$.

$h(0)$ = CDF(0) – CDF(min) = 4 – 4 = 0

$h(1)$ = round [{CDF(1) – CDF(min)} / {N – CDF(min)}] * L = round [{7 – 4} / {16 – 4}] * 20 = 3*20/12 = 5

$h(2)$ = round [{CDF(2) – CDF(min)} / {N – CDF(min)}] * L = round [{9 – 4} / {16 – 4}] * 20 = 5*20/12 = 8.33 ≈ 9

$h(3)$ = round [{CDF(3) – CDF(min)} / {N – CDF(min)}] * L = round [{11 – 4} / {16 – 4}] * 20 = 7*20/12 = 11.67 ≈ 12

$h(4)$ = round [{CDF(4) – CDF(min)} / {N – CDF(min)}] * L = round [{12 – 4} / {16 – 4}] * 20 = 8*20/12 = 13.33 ≈ 14

$h(5)$ = round [{CDF(5) – CDF(min)} / {N – CDF(min)}] * L = round [{15 – 4} / {16 – 4}] * 20 = 11*20/12 = 18.33 ≈ 19

$h(6)$ = round [{CDF(6) – CDF(min)} / {N – CDF(min)}] * L = round [{16 – 4} / {16 – 4}] * 20 = 12*20/12 = 20

Mapping of values: 2 --> 0, 3 --> 5, 4 --> 9, 5 --> 12, 6 --> 14, 7 --> 19, 8 --> 20

3.9.5 Color Management

PROBLEM 3.14

The sRGB chromaticity values for green are (x = 0.3, y = 0.6, z = 0.1) (a) Derive these values using the sRGB to *XYZ* conversion relation(b) Convert the chromacity values back to RGB using *XYZ* to sRGB conversion relations.

(a) Using sRGB to XYZ conversion relations:

For green : $R = 0, G = 255, B = 0$

$$R' = \frac{R}{255} = 0, G' = \frac{G}{255} = 1, B' = \frac{B}{255} = 0$$

Since $R', B' \le 0.04045, R'' = \frac{R'}{12.92} = 0$ and $B'' = \frac{B'}{12.92} = 0$

Since $G' > 0.04045$, $G'' = \left\{\frac{G' + 0.055}{1.055}\right\}^{2.4} = 1$

$$X = 0.4212R'' + 0.3576G'' + 0.1805B'' = 0.3576$$

$$Y = 0.2126R'' + 0.7152G'' + 0.0722B'' = 0.7152$$

$$Z = 0.0193R'' + 0.1192G'' + 0.9505B'' = 0.1192$$

$$x = \frac{X}{X+Y+Z} = \frac{0.3576}{1.192} = 0.3$$

$$y = \frac{Y}{X+Y+Z} = \frac{0.7152}{1.192} = 0.6$$

$$z = \frac{Z}{X+Y+Z} = \frac{0.1192}{1.192} = 0.1$$

(b) Using XYZ to sRGB conversion relations:

For green, $X = 0.3576,\ Y = 0.7152,\ Z = 0.1192$

$$R' = 3.2406X - 1.5372Y - 0.4986Z = 0$$

$$G' = -0.9689X + 1.8758Y + 0.0415Z = 1$$

$$B' = 0.0557X - 0.2040Y + 1.0570Z = 0$$

Since, $R', B' \le 0.0031308, R = 12.92R' = 0$ and $B = 12.92B' = 0$

Since, $G' > 0.0031308, G'' = 1.055 * (G')^{\frac{1}{2.4}} - 0.055 = 1$

$$R = round(255R'') = 0, G = round(255G'') = 1,$$
$$B = round(255B'') = 0$$

PROBLEM 3.15

Convert the *XYZ* values of green in previous example to *L*a*b values using D65 white point illuminant.**

For green, $X = 0.3576,\ Y = 0.7152,\ Z = 0.1192$

For white, $R = G = B = 255$. Using sRGB to XYZ relations:

$$R' = R/255 = 1, G' = G/255 = 1, B' = B/255 = 1$$

Since $R', G', B' > 0.04045$

$$R'' = \left\{\frac{R' + 0.055}{1.055}\right\}^{2.4} = 1$$

$$G'' = \left\{\frac{G' + 0.055}{1.055}\right\}^{2.4} = 1$$

$$B'' = \left\{\frac{B' + 0.055}{1.055}\right\}^{2.4} = 1$$

$$X_w = 0.4212R'' + 0.3576G'' + 0.1805B'' = 0.9505$$

$$Y_w = 0.2126R'' + 0.7152G'' + 0.0722B'' = 1$$

$$Z_w = 0.0193R'' + 0.1192G'' + 0.9505B'' = 1.089$$

These are the reference tri-stimulus values for white point.

From sRGB to $L^*a^*b^*$ conversion relations:

$$X' = \frac{X}{X_w} = \frac{0.3576}{0.9505} = 0.3762$$

$$Y' = \frac{Y}{Y_w} = \frac{0.7152}{1} = 0.7152$$

$$Z' = \frac{Z}{Z_w} = \frac{0.1192}{1.089} = 0.1095$$

Since $X', Y', Z' > \left(\frac{6}{29}\right)^3 = 0.0089$,

$$X'' = (0.3762)^{\frac{1}{3}} = 0.7219$$

$$Y'' = (0.7152)^{\frac{1}{3}} = 0.8943$$

$$Z'' = (0.1095)^{\frac{1}{3}} = 0.4784$$

$$L = 116 * Y'' - 16 = 87.7388$$

$$a = 500 * (X'' - Y'') = -86.2$$

$$b = 200 * (Y'' - Z'') = 83.18$$

PROBLEM 3.16

Convert *RGB* magenta to *HSV* (b) Convert back from *HSV* to *RGB*.

(a) For magenta, $R = 255, G = 0, B = 255$

Using *RGB* to *HSV* conversion relations:

$$m = \max(R, G, B) = 255$$
$$n = \min(R, G, B) = 0$$
$$d = m - n = 255$$

$$V = \left(\frac{m}{255}\right) * 100 = 100\%$$

Since, $m \ne 0$, $S = \left(\frac{d}{m}\right) * 100 = 100\%$

Since, $m = R$,

$$H = \left\{60\left(\frac{G-B}{d}\right) + 360\right\}\%360$$
$$= \left\{60\left(\frac{0-255}{255}\right) + 360\right\}\%360 = 300^\circ$$

(b)

$$S = \frac{100}{100} = 1, V = \frac{100}{100} = 1$$

$$C = V.S = 1$$

$$k = C.\left(1 - abs\left(\left(\frac{H}{60}\right)2 - 1\right)\right)$$

$$= 1\left(1 - abs\left(\left(\frac{300}{60}\right)2 - 1\right)\right)$$

$$= \left(1 - abs(1 - 1)\right) = 1$$

$$m = V - C = 1 - 1 = 0$$

Since $300 \leq H < 360, (R,G,B) = (C+m, m, k+m) = (1,0,1)$

$$R = \text{round}(255R) = 255$$

$$G = \text{round}(255G) = 0$$

$$B = \text{round}(255B) = 255$$

3.10 Coding Examples Using MATLAB

3.10.1 Introduction

Once an image is represented in digital form, i.e., as a collection of pixels, editing and programming software tools can be used to change the pixel values and hence modify the image in a variety of ways. A collective term used to denote all these various operations for modifying images is called image processing. Image processing operations can be categorized into a number of categories: Import Export and Conversions, Display and Exploration, Transformation and Registration, Filtering and Enhancement, and Segmentation and Analysis.

MATLAB® functions for image processing can be divided into two broad categories: basic functions and toolbox functions. Basic MATLAB (BM) functions provide a set of supporting functionalities to the core media processing tasks like *I/O* operations, matrix manipulations and plotting routines. The toolbox functions provide a set of more advanced features for specialized processing tasks like geometrical transformations, filtering, enhancement and segmentation. For image processing tasks, the main toolbox is the Image Processing Toolbox (IPT) which provides a comprehensive set of reference standard algorithms and workflow apps for image processing, analysis, visualization and algorithm development. The image file formats supported by MATLAB include BMP (Windows Bitmap), GIF (Graphics Interchange Format), ICO (Icon File), JPEG (Joint Photographic Experts Group), JPEG 2000, PBM (Portable Bitmap), PCX (Windows Paintbrush), PGM (Portable Graymap), PNG (Portable Network Graphics), PPM (Portable Pixmap), RAS (Sun Raster) and TIFF (Tagged Image File Format). Most of the images used in the examples are included in the MATLAB package and do not need to be supplied externally. The image samples are available in the following folder: (matlab-root)/toolbox/images/imdata/.

3.10.2 Import Export and Conversions

The following example 3.1 demonstrates reading and writing of images. The function "imread" is used to read data from an image and the data is stored using a variable name. The image is displayed in a figure window by referring to the variable name using the function "imshow". The function "whos" displays the height and width of the image in pixels along with the number of channels, the byte size of the file, and the data type. The string "uint8" indicates unsigned integer 8 bits, which means that the pixels are represented using 1 byte each and hence can range in value from 0 to 255. The function "imfinfo" displays information about the image file like the file path, file modification date, file format and bit depth. The function "imwrite" allows us to save an image in the clipboard onto a file. The file format used is JPEG which being a lossy format, a quality factor can be specified during saving. The smaller the quality value, the more degraded the image becomes and smaller is its file size. The function "figure" creates a new figure window to display the images, while the function "subplot" partitions a single figure window into partitions or cells by specifying the number of rows and columns for displaying multiple images. The function "title" displays a title on top of the individual cells (Figure 3.37).

The following example 3.2 demonstrates display of *R*, *G*, *B* color channels. The ":" (colon) operator signifies the range of values from start to end, for each channel. The colon only by itself indicates all current values. After the three-dimensional color image is read and stored in a variable, a value of 1 for the third dimension indicates the *R* channel, a value of 2 indicates the G channel and a value of 3 indicates the *B* channel. The "%" (percent) symbol indicates comments (Figure 3.38).

EXAMPLE 3.1 EXAMPLE TO READ, WRITE AND DISPLAY AN IMAGE ALONG WITH SOME IMAGE INFORMATION

```
clear; clc;
a = imread('peppers.png');
whos
imfinfo('peppers.png')
imwrite(a, 'p10.jpg', 'quality', 10);
imwrite(a, 'p5.jpg', 'quality', 5);
imwrite(a, 'p0.jpg', 'quality', 0);
b = imread('p10.jpg');
c = imread('p5.jpg');
d = imread('p0.jpg');
figure,
subplot(221), imshow(a);
   title('original PNG');
subplot(222), imshow(b); title('JPG
   quality 10');
subplot(223), imshow(c); title('JPG
   quality 5');
subplot(224), imshow(d); title('JPG
   quality 0');
```

EXAMPLE 3.2 EXAMPLE TO READ AN RGB COLOR IMAGE AND DISPLAY ITS COLOR CHANNELS

```
clear; clc;
a = imread('peppers.png');
ar = a(:,:,1); % red channel
ag = a(:,:,2); % green channel
ab = a(:,:,3); % blue channel
subplot(221), imshow(a); title('RGB');
subplot(222), imshow(ar); title('R');
subplot(223), imshow(ag); title('G');
subplot(224), imshow(ab); title('B');
```

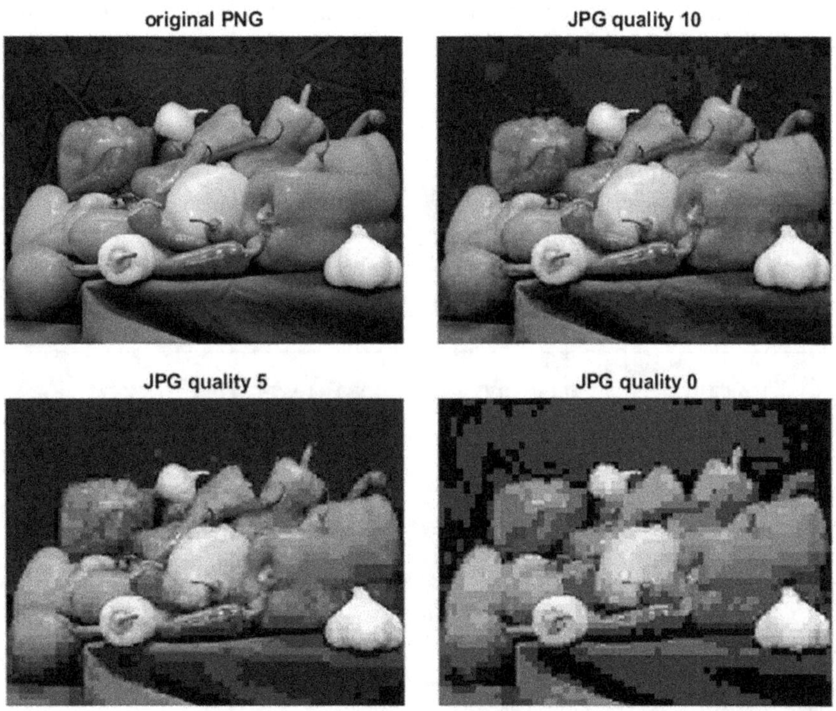

FIGURE 3.37
Output of Example 3.1.

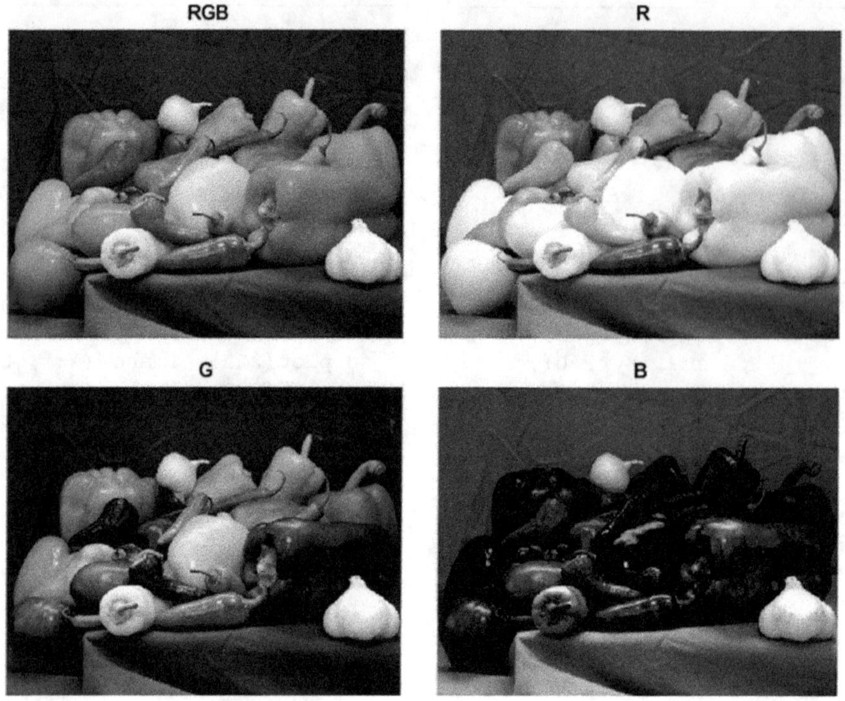

FIGURE 3.38
Output of Example 3.2.

The following example 3.3 demonstrates type conversion in images. The function "rgb2gray" converts an *RGB* color image to grayscale intensity image using the above equation, "imbinarize" is used to convert the grayscale image to binary image by specifying a threshold value (*T*). In the following example, two different threshold values $T = 0.3$ and $T = 0.5$ are used. In the first case, all pixel values from 0 to $0.3 \times 255 = 76$ are converted to black and all values from 77 to 255 are converted to white. In the second case, all values from 0 to 127 are converted to black and values from 128 to 255 are displayed as white (Figure 3.39).

The following example 3.4 show how color can be used to fill shapes. The functions "rectangle" and "polyshape" can be used in conjunction with the function "fill" to color polygonal areas. Circular shapes can be created by specifying a "Curvature" parameter. For primary colors the letters "*r*", "*g*" and "*b*" can be used for red, green, blue, custom colors can also be defined using the normalized *RGB* triplets, i.e., values within the range 0–1. The function "fprintf" prints out strings and values using formatting options and "hex2dec" converts values from hexadecimal to decimal (Figure 3.40).

EXAMPLE 3.3 EXAMPLE TO CONVERT A COLOR IMAGE TO GRAYSCALE AND BINARY

```
clear; clc;
a = imread('peppers.png');
b = rgb2gray(a);
c = imbinarize(b, 0.3);
d = imbinarize(b, 0.5);
figure,
subplot(221), imshow(a); title('color');
subplot(222), imshow(b); title('grayscale');
subplot(223), imshow(c); title('binary T = 30');
subplot(224), imshow(d); title('binary T = 50');
```

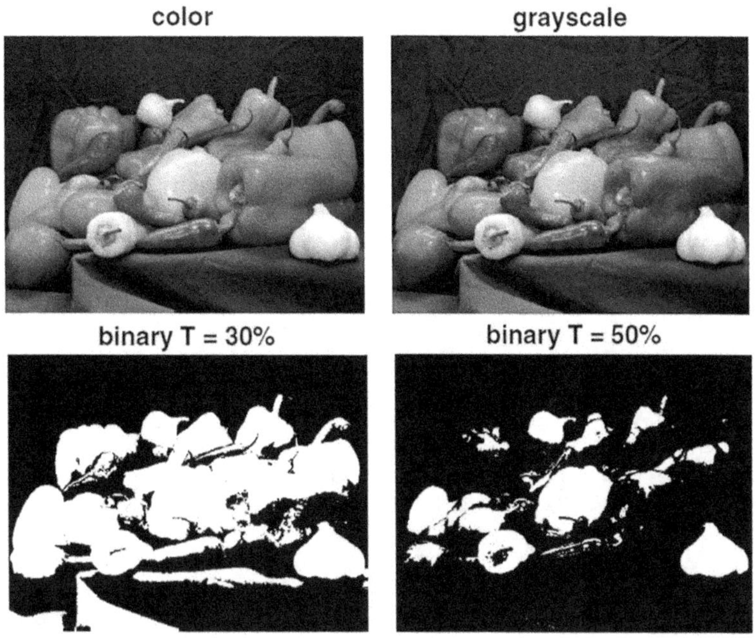

FIGURE 3.39
Output of Example 3.3.

EXAMPLE 3.4 EXAMPLE TO DRAW SOME CLOSED SHAPES AND FILL THESE WITH SPECIFIC COLORS

```
aquamarine = [0.4980, 1, 0.8314];
subplot(131),
rectangle('Position',[1,2,5,10],'FaceColor',aquamarine, 'LineStyle', '--');
axis square;
subplot(132),
pgon = polyshape([0 0 1 3], [0 3 3 0]);
plot(pgon);
fill([0 0 1 3], [0 3 3 0], 'b'); axis square;
subplot(133),
tomato = [hex2dec('ff'), hex2dec('63'), hex2dec('47')]/255;
orange = [245, 102, 36]/255;
axis square;
rectangle('Curvature',[0.5 1], 'FaceColor', tomato, ...
    'LineWidth',4, 'EdgeColor', orange-0.1);
```

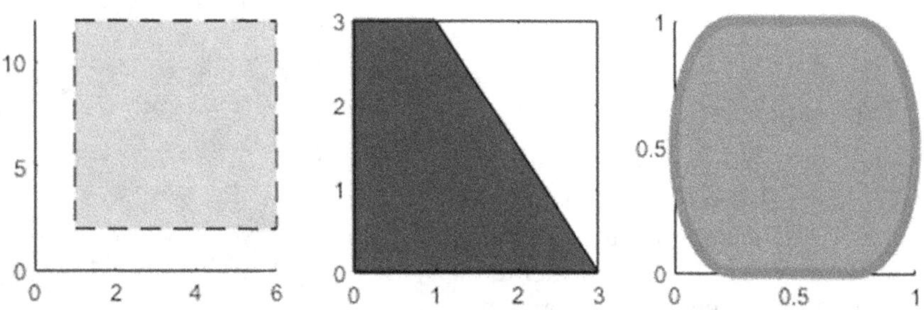

FIGURE 3.40
Output of Example 3.4.

The following examples 3.5 and 3.6 demonstrate color conversion. The function "rgb2xyz" converts color values from RGB space to XYZ chromaticity values while "xyz2rgb" reverts back the values (Examples 3.5 and 3.6).

EXAMPLE 3.5 EXAMPLE TO CONVERT FROM RGB TO XYZ VALUES

```
fprintf('sRGB Green D65 : \n');
XYZ = rgb2xyz([0 1
   0],'WhitePoint','d65',
   'ColorSpace','srgb')
X = XYZ(1); Y = XYZ(2); Z = XYZ(3);
xyz = [X/(X+Y+Z), Y/(X+Y+Z), Z/(X+Y+Z)]
RGB = xyz2rgb([X Y Z],'WhitePoint','d65
   ','ColorSpace','srgb')
fprintf('\n')
```

The functions "rgb2hsv" and "rgb2lab" convert color values from the RGB color space to HSV and L*a*b* color spaces respectively.

EXAMPLE 3.6 EXAMPLE TO CONVERT RGB TO HSV AND L*A*B* VALUES

```
clear; clc;
rgb1 = imread('peppers.png');
r = rgb1(:,:,1);
g = rgb1(:,:,2);
b = rgb1(:,:,3);

hsv = rgb2hsv(rgb1);
h = hsv(:,:,1);
s = hsv(:,:,2);
v = hsv(:,:,3);

lab = rgb2lab(rgb1);
l = lab(:,:,1);
a = lab(:,:,2);
b = lab(:,:,3);
```

3.10.3 Display and Exploration

The following example 3.7 demonstrates contrast stretching in grayscale images. The function "imshow" can stretch the range covering existing minimum and maximum values to the entire range [0, 255] by including a pair of empty square brackets "[]", a concept called contrast stretching. In the following example, the empty square values [] map the existing minimum

EXAMPLE 3.7 EXAMPLE TO DEMONSTRATE CONTRAST STRETCHING IN A GRAYSCALE IMAGE

```
clear; clc;
I = imread('pout.tif');
title('grayscale image');
Imin = min(min(I)); Imax = max(max(I));
subplot(121), imshow(I);
   title('Original');
subplot(122), imshow(I, []);
   title('Corrected');
```

(74) and maximum (224) gray values of the image to 0 and 255, respectively (Figure 3.41).

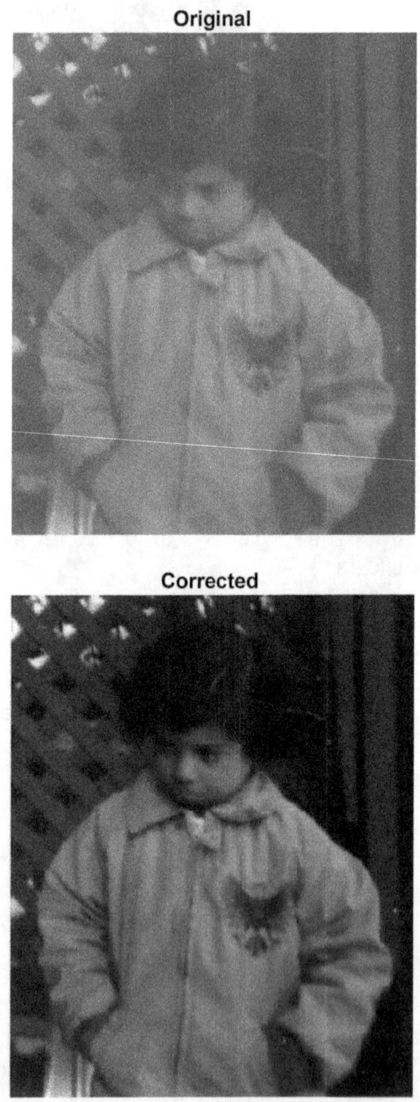

FIGURE 3.41
Output of Example 3.7.

The following example 3.8 demonstrates displaying images side by side. The function "subplot" can be used for multiple plots as we have seen previously. Alternatively, the function "imshowpair" can be used to display two images in a number of ways. Using the option "montage" places them side by side in the same image, while using the option "blend" overlays the two images on each other using alpha blending. The function "edge" finds edges in grayscale images using the algorithm specified in the argument, in this case the "Canny" edge detector (Figure 3.42).

The following example 3.9 demonstrates interactive image exploration. The function "imtool" provides an integrated environment called Image Viewer for displaying images and performing some common image processing tasks. Apart from basic display capabilities it provides additional tools for displaying pixel values, specifying magnification factors, adjusting contrast and color, measuring distances between points, cropping the image and so on. The "Pixel Region" tool displays a selected region of pixels along with pixel values, the "Image Information" tool displays information about the image and file metadata, the "Measure Distance" tool measures distances from one point to another point within the image, the "Crop Image" tool is used for defining a crop region on the image and cropping the image. These tools can also be invoked using appropriate function calls, for example, the "impixelregion" invokes the "Pixel Region" tool (Figure 3.43).

EXAMPLE 3.8 EXAMPLE TO DISPLAY TWO IMAGES SIDE BY SIDE USING MONTAGE AND BLEND EFFECTS

```
clear; clc;
a = imread('cameraman.tif');
b = edge(a, 'canny');
figure, imshowpair(a, b, 'montage');
figure, imshowpair(a, b, 'blend');
```

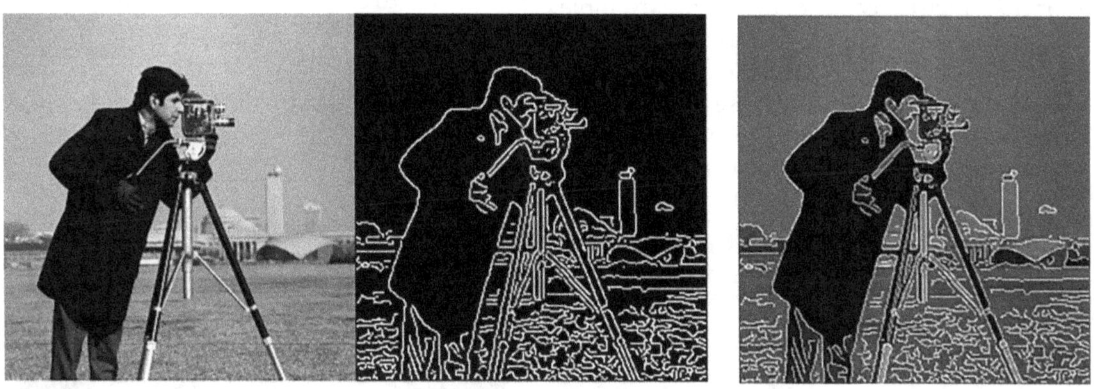

FIGURE 3.42
Output of Example 3.8.

EXAMPLE 3.9 EXAMPLE TO DISPLAY AN IMAGE ALONG WITH PIXEL VALUES FOR A SELECTED REGION

```
clear; clc;
h = imtool ('peppers.png');
impixelregion(h)
```

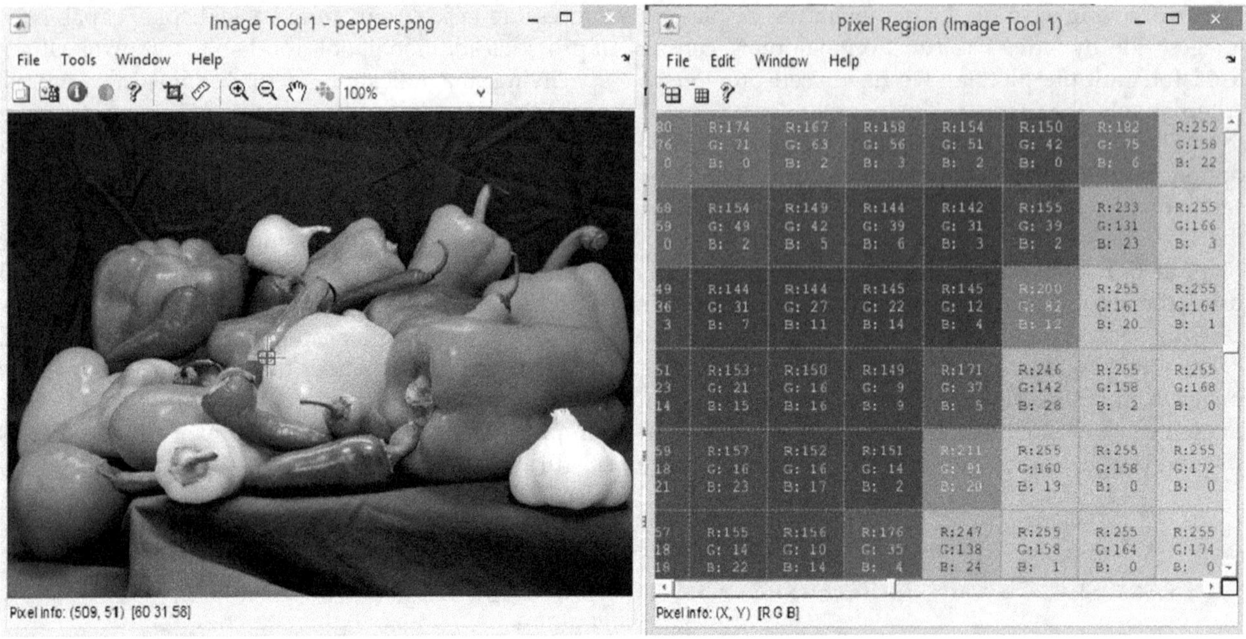

FIGURE 3.43
Output of Example 3.9.

3.10.4 Geometric Transformation

The following example 3.10 demonstrates cropping an image. The function "imcrop" is used for cropping an image. The crop rectangle can be specified either interactively or parametrically. The following example illustrates interactive cropping. The user is asked to draw the cropping rectangle over the image in the figure window, right-click on it and choose option "Crop Image" from the pop-up menu. The portion of the image within the rectangle is retained and displayed beside the original image (Figure 3.44).

EXAMPLE 3.10 EXAMPLE TO DEMONSTRATE CROPPING

```
clear; clc;
I = imread('cameraman.tif');
[J, rect] = imcrop(I);
imshowpair(I, J, 'montage');
```

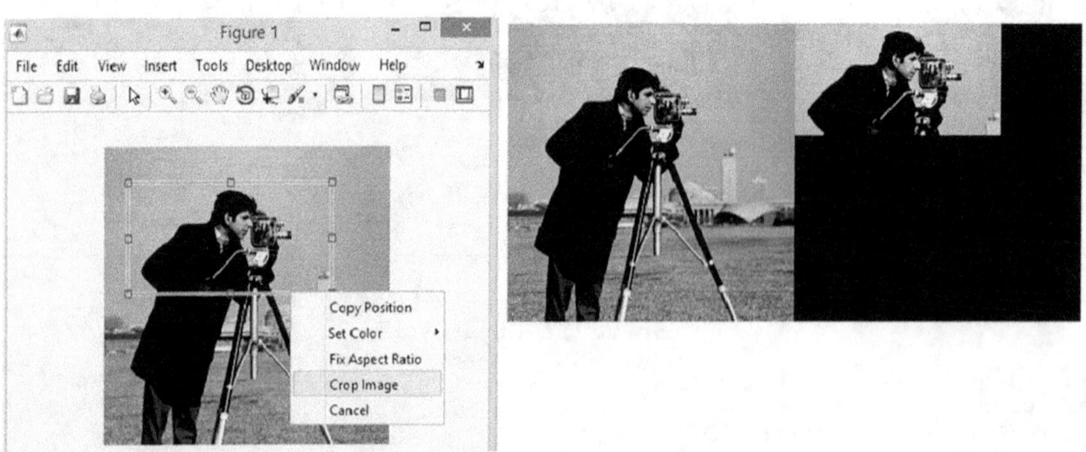

FIGURE 3.44
Output of Example 3.10.

The following example 3.11 demonstrates translation of an image. The function "imtranslate" is used to translate an image by specifying a translation vector (tx, ty), i.e., x and y values by which the image should be moved. In the following example, the "FillValues" option is used to fill the region outside the image by a gray-level intensity between 0 and 255. The "OutputView" option is used to specify whether the translated image will be viewed as cropped or full. In case of a full view, the image canvas area is increased to accommodate the image and the extra portion by which the image has moved. In case of a cropped view, the image canvas remains at its original size so that the cropped portion of the image is viewed along with the extra portion by which the image has moved. In the following example, a translated image is viewed using the full and cropped option (Figure 3.45).

The following example 3.12 demonstrates rotation of an image. The function "imrotate" is used to rotate an image by specifying the angle in degrees. The "crop" option makes the output image size same as the input image cropping the additional portions of the image, while the "loose" option makes the image canvas large enough to view the entire image. The following example displays a rotated image using both options (Figure 3.46).

EXAMPLE 3.11 EXAMPLE TO DEMONSTRATE TRANSLATION

```
clear; clc;
I = imread('coins.png');
J = imtranslate(I, [25, -20],
   'FillValues', 200, 'OutputView',
   'full');
K = imtranslate(I, [-50.5, 60.6],
   'FillValues', 0, 'OutputView',
   'same');
subplot(131), imshow(I); title('I');
   axis on;
subplot(132), imshow(J); title('J');
   axis on; % full view
subplot(133), imshow(K); title('K');
   axis on; % cropped view
```

EXAMPLE 3.12 EXAMPLE TO DEMONSTRATE ROTATION

```
clear; clc;
I = imread('saturn.png');
J = imrotate(I, 30, 'crop');
K = imrotate(I, -40, 'loose');
figure,
subplot(131), imshow(I); title('I');
subplot(132), imshow(J); title('J');
   % crop option
subplot(133), imshow(K); title('K');
   % loose option
```

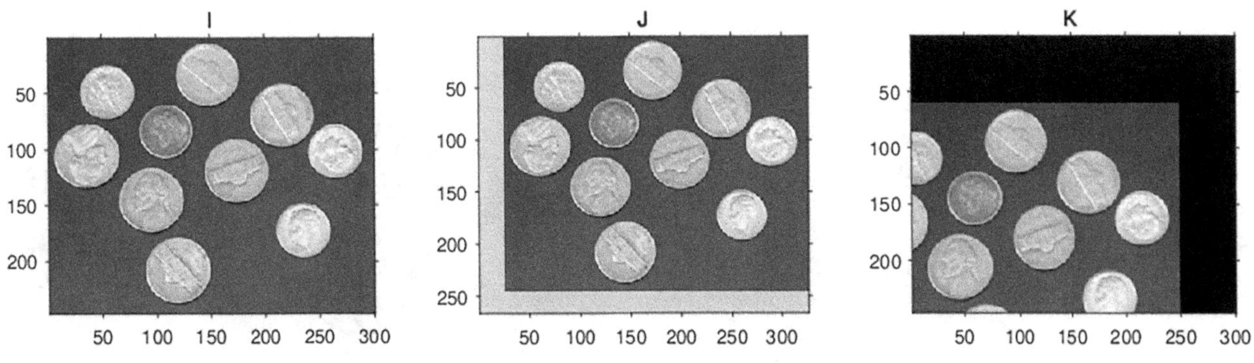

FIGURE 3.45
Output of Example 3.11.

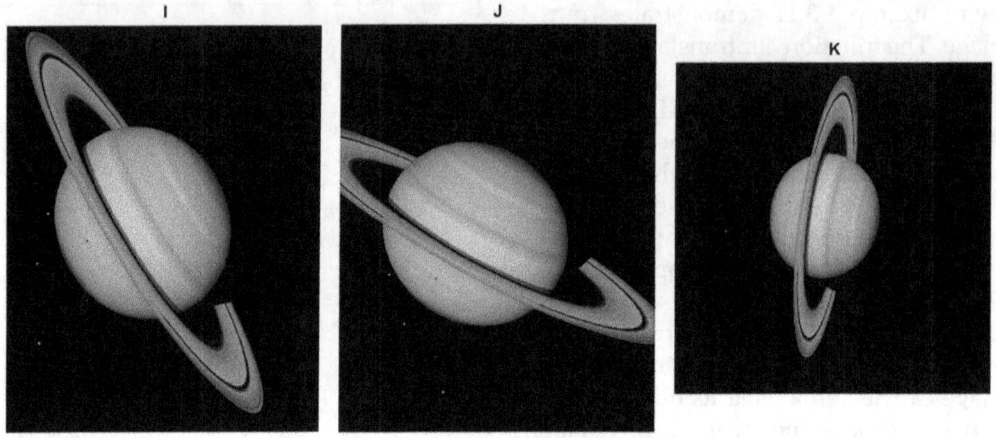

FIGURE 3.46
Output of Example 3.12.

The following example 3.13 demonstrates scaling of an image. The function "imresize" is used to resize the image dimensions with one or two following arguments indicating the scaling factors. The following example illustrates the various ways in which scaling parameters can be specified. If there is a single argument, it indicates the scaling factor by which both the height and width are to be scaled. If there are two arguments, it indicates the number of rows and number of columns, respectively. If one of the arguments is a number and the other argument is set as "NaN" (not a number), then both the dimensions are set to the single value (Figure 3.47).

EXAMPLE 3.13 EXAMPLE TO DEMONSTRATE UNIFORM AND NON-UNIFORM SCALING

```
clear; clc;
I = imread('testpat1.png');
h = size(I, 1); w = size(I, 2);
J = imresize(I, 0.5);
K = imresize(I, [h/1.3, 1.5*w]);
L = imresize(I, [500, 300]);
M = imresize(I, [400, NaN]);
subplot(151), imshow(I); title('I');
   axis on; axis ([0 w 0 h]);
subplot(152), imshow(J); title('J');
   axis on; axis ([0 w 0 h]);
subplot(153), imshow(K); title('K');
   axis on;
subplot(154), imshow(L); title('L');
   axis on;
subplot(155), imshow(M); title('M');
   axis on; axis ([0 w 0 h]);
```

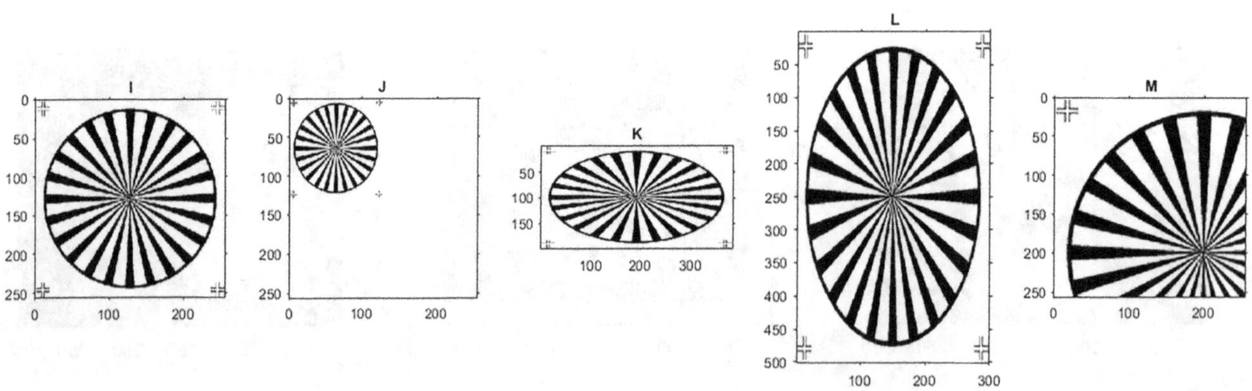

FIGURE 3.47
Output of Example 3.13.

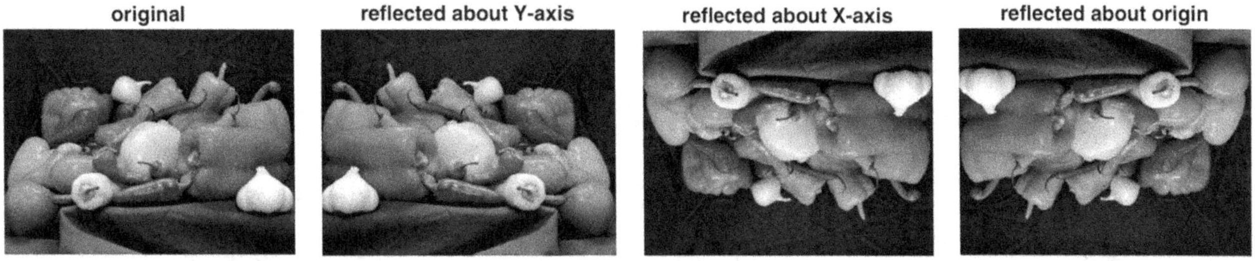

FIGURE 3.48
Output of Example 3.14.

The following example 3.14 demonstrates reflection of an image. The function "fliplr" is used to flip an image left to right which is equivalent to a y-axis reflection, while "flipud" flips an image up to down which is equivalent to an x-axis reflection. Reflection about the origin combines both the above two types together. The following example illustrates the three types of refection (Figure 3.48).

The following example 3.15 demonstrates shear of an image along the horizontal and vertical directions. The function "affne2d" creates an affne transformation object using a mapping between the initial and final position of a pixel given a specified transformation matrix, while the function "imwarp" applies the transformation object to a specified image (Figure 3.49).

EXAMPLE 3.14 EXAMPLE TO DEMONSTRATE REFLECTION

```
clear; clc;
I = imread('peppers.png');
J = fliplr(I); % Reflection
   about Y-axis
K = flipud(I); % Reflection
   about X-axis
L = flipud(J); % Reflection
   about origin
subplot(221), imshow(I); title('I');
subplot(222), imshow(J); title('J');
subplot(223), imshow(K); title('K');
subplot(224), imshow(L); title('L');
```

EXAMPLE 3.15 EXAMPLE TO DEMONSTRATE SHEAR

```
clear; clc;
C = imread('gantrycrane.png');
hx = 1.2; hy = 1.2;
Hx = [1, hx, 0 ; 0, 1, 0 ; 0, 0, 1];
Hy = [1, 0, 0 ; hy, 1, 0 ; 0, 0, 1];
A1 = affine2d(Hx');
I1 = imwarp(C, A1);
A2 = affine2d(Hy');
I2 = imwarp(C, A2);

subplot(131),imshow(C); axis on; title('original'); axis square;
subplot(132),imshow(I1); axis on; title('x-direction shear');axis square;
subplot(133),imshow(I2); axis on; title('y-direction shear');axis square;
```

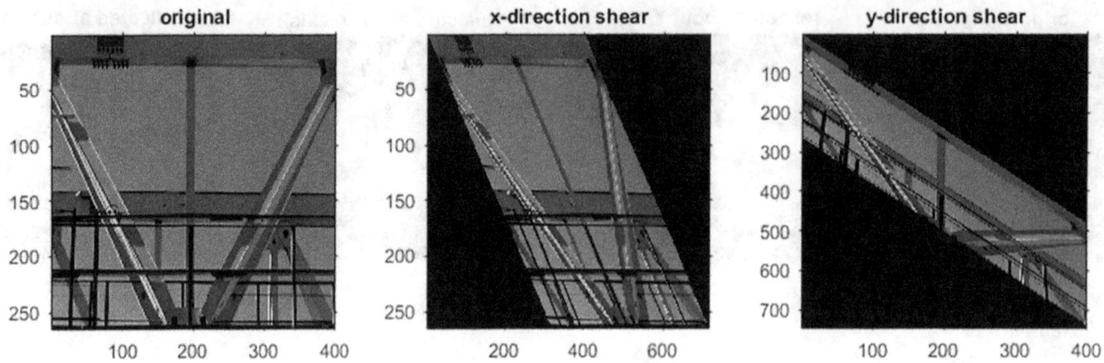

FIGURE 3.49
Output of Example 3.15.

The following example 3.16 demonstrates affine and projective transformations of an image. The function "affine2d" creates an affine transformation object using a mapping between the initial and final position of a pixel given a specified transformation matrix *M*, while "imwarp" applies the transformation object to a specified image. The function "projective2d" creates a projective transformation object using a mapping between the initial and final position of a pixel given a specified transformation matrix *M* (Figure 3.50).

EXAMPLE 3.16 EXAMPLE TO DEMONSTRATE AFFINE

```
clear; clc;
C = checkerboard(10);
M = [5 2 5 ; 2 5 5 ; 0 0 1];
A = affine2d(M'); I = imwarp(C, A);
M = [5 2 5 ; 2 5 5 ; 0.01 0.01 1];
B = projective2d(M'); J = imwarp(C, B);
figure,
subplot(131), imshow(C);
   title('original');
subplot(132), imshow(I); title('affine
   transform');
subplot(133), imshow(J);
   title('perspective transform');
```

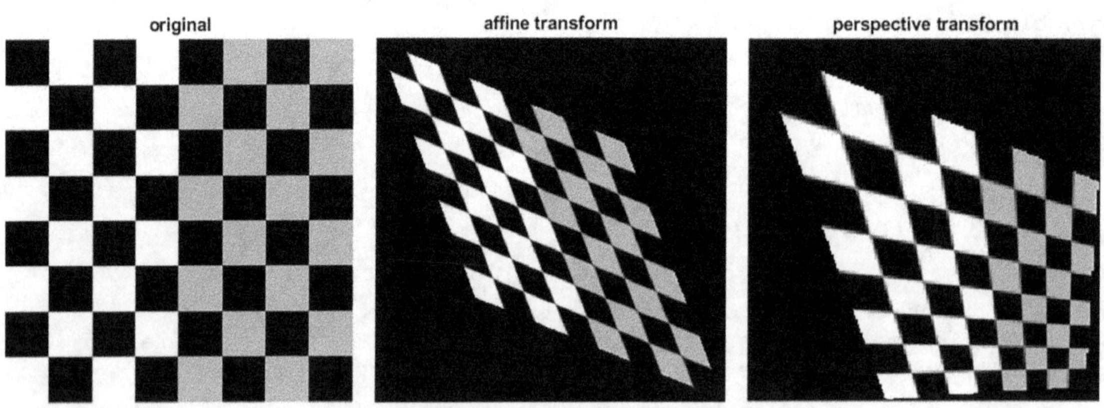

FIGURE 3.50
Output of Example 3.16.

3.10.5 Filtering and Enhancement

The following example 3.17 demonstrates filtering of an image. The function "imfilter" is used to filter a data matrix using a specified kernel. In the following example, the data matrix A is filtered using the kernel H once using correlation, specified using the "corr" option and once using convolution, specified using the "conv" option (Figure 3.51).

The following example 3.18 demonstrates creating customized kernels. The function "fspecial" is used to create a customized 2D kernel of the specified type and size. The option "average" creates a averaging filter, "disk" creates a circular averaging filter, "gaussian" creates a Gaussian filter of the specified standard deviation, "motion" creates a motion blur filter (Figure 3.52).

EXAMPLE 3.17 EXAMPLE TO DEMONSTRATE FILTERING

```
clear; clc;
A =     [       0, 0, 1, 1, 0, 0, 0 ;
                0, 0, 0, 1, 0, 0, 0 ;
                0, 0, 0, 1, 0, 0, 0 ;
                0, 0, 1, 0, 1, 0, 0 ;
                0, 0, 1, 0, 1, 0, 0 ;
                0, 1, 1, 1, 1, 1, 0 ;
                0, 1, 0, 0, 0, 1, 0 ;
                0, 1, 0, 0, 0, 1, 0 ;
                1, 1, 1, 0, 1, 1, 1 ];

H = [0 0.3 0.7; 0 0.3 0.7; 0 0.3 0.7];
B = imfilter(A, H, 'corr');
C = imfilter(A, H, 'conv');
subplot(221), imshow(A, []);
  title('A');
subplot(222), imshow(H); title('H');
subplot(223), imshow(B, []);
  title('B');
subplot(224), imshow(C, []);
  title('C');
```

EXAMPLE 3.18 EXAMPLE TO DEMONSTRATE CUSTOMIZED KERNELS

```
clear; clc;
a = imread('cameraman.tif');
k1 = fspecial('average', 10);
k2 = fspecial('disk', 10);
k3 = fspecial('gaussian', 10,10);
k4 = fspecial('motion', 10, 45);
b1 = imfilter(a, k1, 'conv');
b2 = imfilter(a, k2, 'conv');
b3 = imfilter(a, k3, 'conv');
b4 = imfilter(a, k4, 'conv');
figure
subplot(241), imshow(k1, []);
  title('k1');
subplot(242), imshow(b1, []);
  title('b1');
subplot(243), imshow(k2, []);
  title('k2');
subplot(244), imshow(b2, []);
  title('b2');
subplot(245), imshow(k3, []);
  title('k3');
subplot(246), imshow(b3, []);
  title('b3');
subplot(247), imshow(k4, []);
  title('k4');
subplot(248), imshow(b4, []);
  title('b4');
```

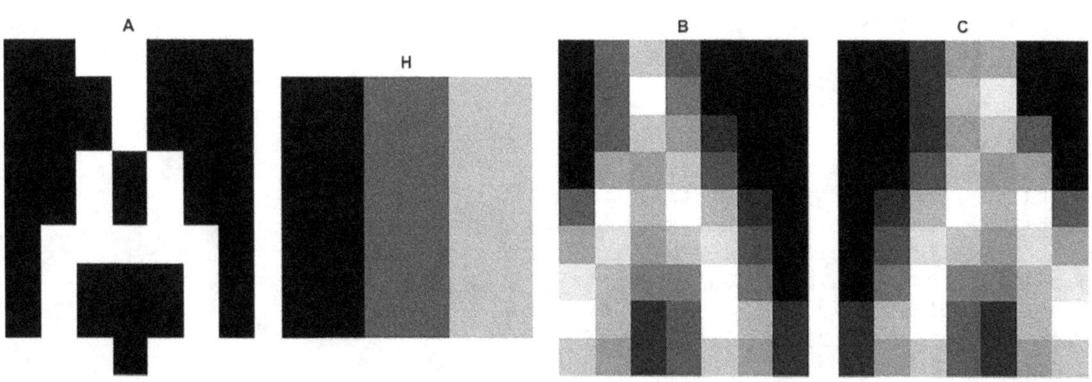

FIGURE 3.51
Output of Example 3.17.

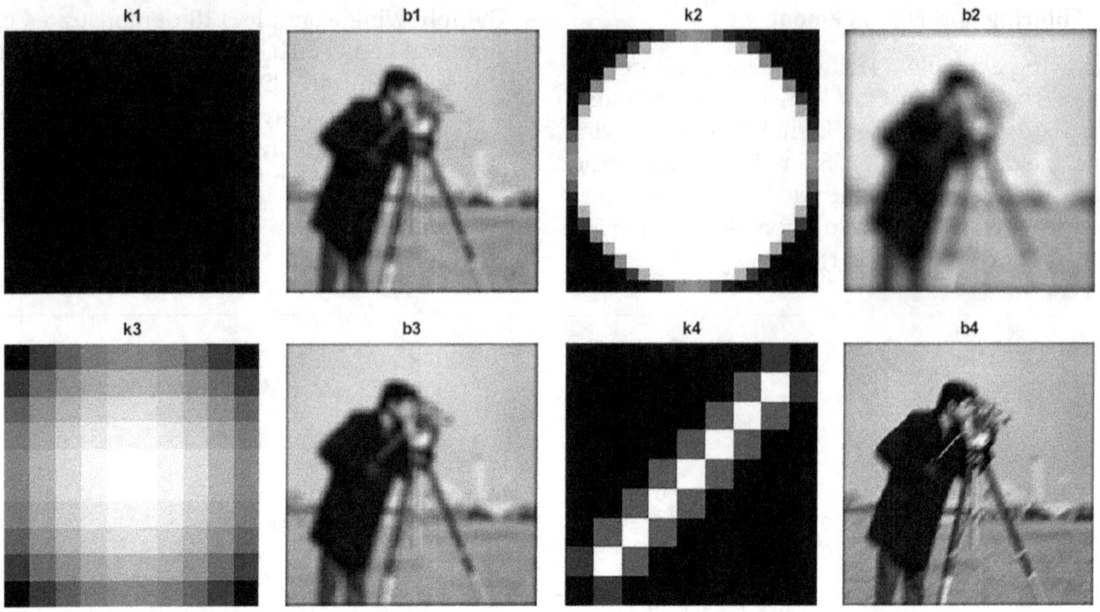

FIGURE 3.52
Output of Example 3.18.

The following example 3.19 demonstrates noise filtering in an image. An image is filtered using a 5 × 5 and a 10 × 10 Gaussian kernel and then converted to binary using a specific threshold. The effect of the kernel is to blur the image, the larger the size of the kernel the more pronounced the blurring effect. On blurring the smaller spots have their intensities reduced due to the convolution with the black background. On thresholding, the smaller dots are effectively removed leaving the larger spots in the image, thereby effectively producing a noise filtering effect. This illustrates that using different sizes of the kernel can produce different effects. The function "im2bw" converts an image into a binary format using a specified threshold (Figure 3.53).

EXAMPLE 3.19 EXAMPLE TO DEMONSTRATE NOISE FILTERING

```
clear; clc;
a = imread('sky.png');
k1 = fspecial('gaussian', 5, 5);
k2 = fspecial('gaussian', 10, 10);
b1 = imfilter(a, k1, 'conv');
b2 = imfilter(a, k2, 'conv');
c1 = im2bw(b1, 0.5);
c2 = im2bw(b2, 0.5);
subplot(241), imshow(a); title('original');
subplot(242), imshow(k1, []); title('5 x 5 kernel');
subplot(243), imshow(b1); title('blurred');
subplot(244), imshow(c1); title('thresholded');
subplot(245), imshow(a); title('original');
subplot(246), imshow(k2, []); title('10 x 10 kernel');
subplot(247), imshow(b2); title('blurred');
subplot(248), imshow(c2); title('thresholded');
```

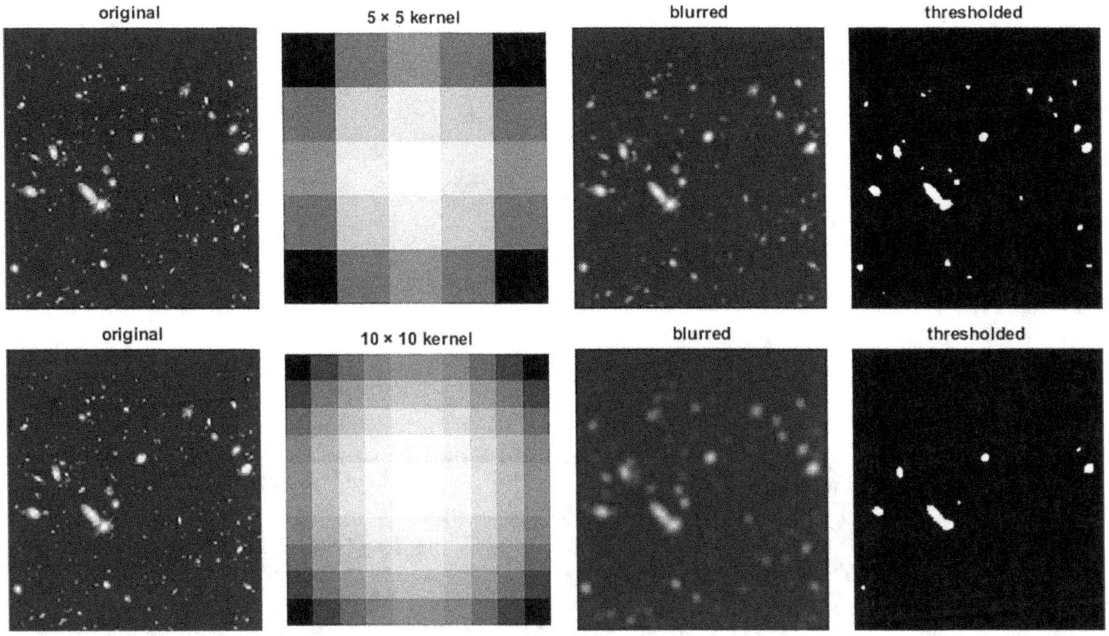

FIGURE 3.53
Output of Example 3.19.

The following example 3.20 demonstrates use of a median filter. A 2D median filter can be implemented using the function "medflt2". In the following example an image is first corrupted by adding salt-and-pepper noise using the function "imnoise" and then a median filter is used to remove the noise (Figure 3.54).

EXAMPLE 3.20 EXAMPLE TO DEMONSTRATE MEDIAN FILTER

```
clear; clc;
a = imread('peppers.png'); a =
rgb2gray(a);
b = imnoise(a, 'salt & pepper', 0.1);
% add salt-&-pepper noise
c = medfilt2(b);
subplot(131), imshow(a); title('a');
subplot(132), imshow(b); title('b');
subplot(133), imshow(c); title('c');
```

The following example 3.21 and 3.22 demonstrate edge detection in an image. The function "edge" is used to detect edge pixels in an image using the specified kernels. The options "sobel", "prewitt" and "roberts" incorporate the corresponding Sobel, Prewitt and Roberts masks (Figure 3.55).

EXAMPLE 3.21 EXAMPLE TO DEMONSTRATE EDGE DETECTION

```
clear; clc;
a = imread('cameraman.tif');
b = im2bw(a, 0.5);
c = edge(b, 'sobel');
d = edge(b, 'prewitt');
e = edge(b, 'roberts');
subplot(221), imshow(a);
   title('image');
subplot(222), imshow(c);
   title('sobel');
subplot(223), imshow(d);
   title('prewitt');
subplot(224), imshow(e);
   title('roberts');
```

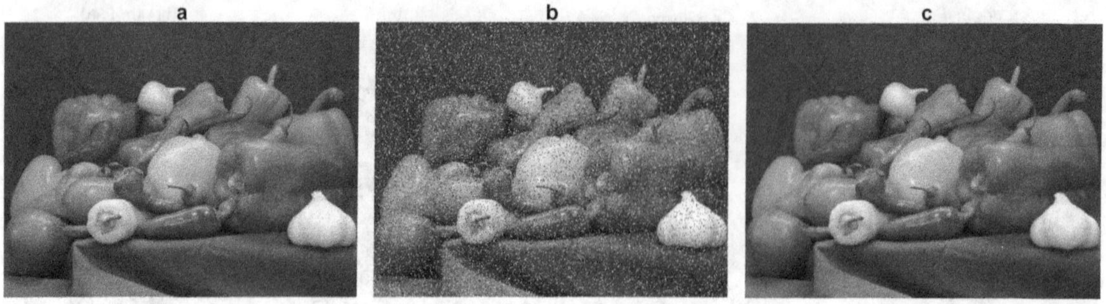

FIGURE 3.54
Output of Example 3.20.

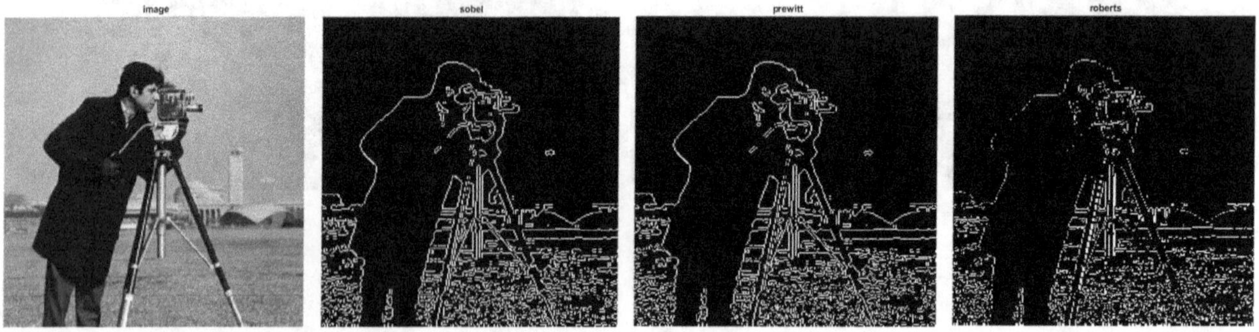

FIGURE 3.55
Output of Example 3.21.

The arguments "log" and "canny" specified with the "edge" function can be used to implement the LoG and Canny edge detectors (Figure 3.56).

EXAMPLE 3.22 EXAMPLE TO DEMONSTRATE LOG AND CANNY EDGE DETECTORS

```
clear; clc;
a = imread('gantrycrane.png');
b = rgb2gray(a);
th = 0.1; % threshold
sigma = 0.5; % standard deviation
b = edge(b, 'log', th, sigma);
c = edge(b, 'canny', th, sigma);
subplot(131), imshow(a);
  title('image');
subplot(132), imshow(b); title('log');
subplot(133), imshow(c);
  title('canny');
```

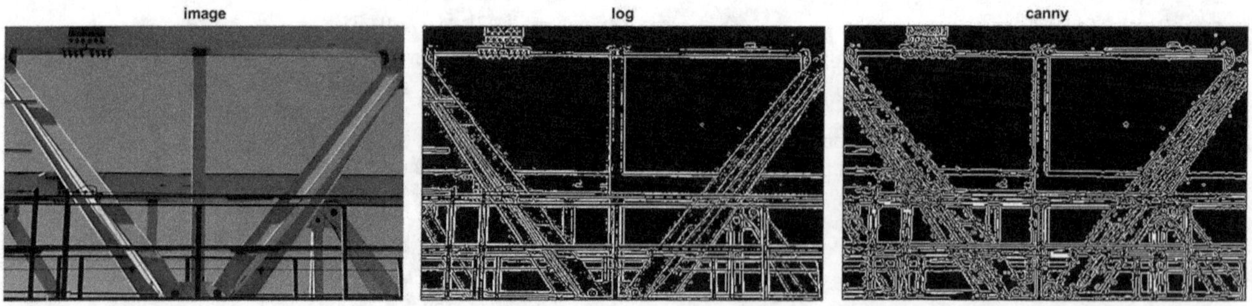

FIGURE 3.56
Output of Example 3.22.

The following example 3.23 demonstrates gamma adjustments in an image. The function "imadjust" is used to implement gamma adjustment by specifying three arguments, namely, range of input values, range of output values and the gamma index, as normalized values, i.e., [0, 255] is represented as [0, 1]. A set of empty braces [] implies all existing values in the input image and all possible values in the output image, i.e., [0 1]. For image "*b*", all existing gray values of "*a*" are mapped to the range [0, 255] and the mapping takes place along the curve for gamma = 0.5. For image "*c*", the mapping takes place along gamma = 3. For image "*d*", all values in range [0.4, 0.6] are linearly mapped to values in range [0,1], i.e., values between 0.4 × 255 = 102 to 0.6 × 255 = 153 are mapped to 0–255 along gamma = 1. For image "*e*" all values in the range [0.2, 0.8] are linearly mapped to the range [0.4, 0.6]. Image "*f*" illustrates image inversion, i.e., [0, 1] is mapped to [1, 0], which means that any value x in the input image gets converted to value $255 - x$ in the output image (Figure 3.57).

EXAMPLE 3.23 EXAMPLE TO DEMONSTRATE GAMMA ADJUSTMENTS

```
clear; clc;
a = imread('peppers.png'); a = rgb2gray(a);

% syntax: g = imadjust(f, [low_in high_in], [low_out high_out], gamma);
b = imadjust(a, [ ], [ ], 0.5);
c = imadjust(a, [ ], [ ], 3);
d = imadjust(a, [0.4 0.6], [0 1]);
e = imadjust(a, [0.2 0.8], [0.4 0.6]);
f = imadjust(a, [0 1], [1 0]);

figure,
subplot(231), imshow(a); title('a: Original');
subplot(232), imshow(b); title('b: \gamma = 0.5');
subplot(233), imshow(c); title('c: \gamma = 3');
subplot(234), imshow(d); title('d: [0.4, 0.6] to [0, 1]');
subplot(235), imshow(e); title('e: [0.2, 0.8] to [0.4, 0.6]');
subplot(236), imshow(f); title('f: Inversion');
```

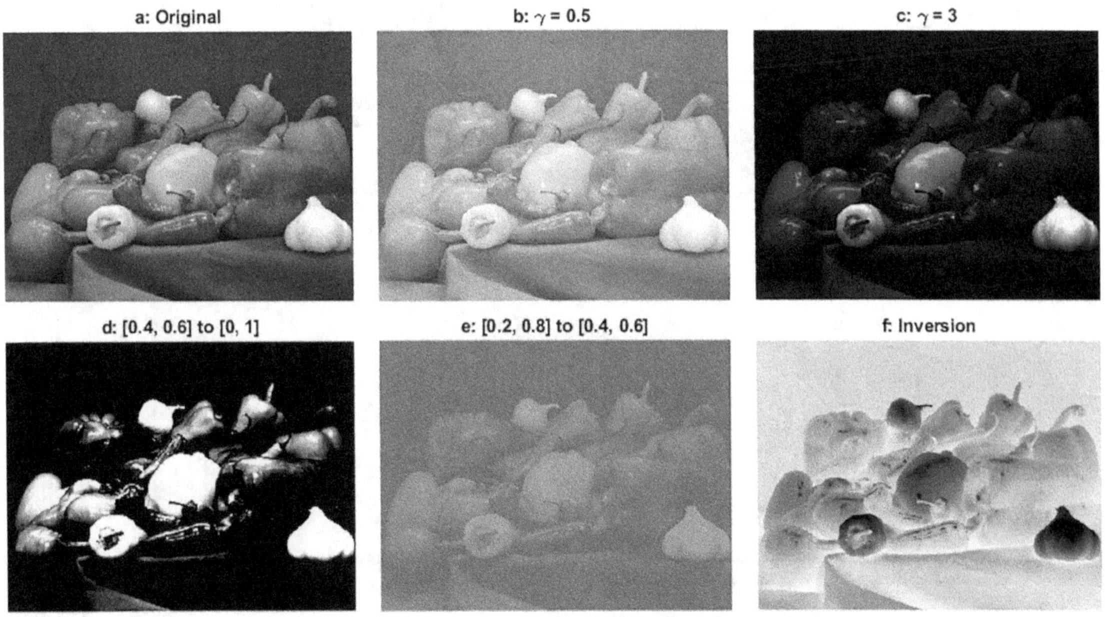

FIGURE 3.57
Output of Example 3.23.

The following example 3.24 demonstrates histogram equalization in an image. The function "imhist" displays the histogram of an image, where the horizontal axis denotes the range of gray-level intensities 0–255, while the vertical axis denotes the number of pixels belonging to each gray-level intensity. The function "histeq" equalizes a histogram by stretching it so that it covers the entire intensity range of 0–255. In the following example, a low-contrast image is converted to a bright image using histogram equalization to stretch the histogram and this is reflected by the tonal improvement (Figure 3.58).

EXAMPLE 3.24 EXAMPLE TO DEMONSTRATE HISTOGRAM EQUALIZATION

```
clear; clc;
a = imread('peppers.png'); a = rgb2gray(a);
b = imadjust(a, [0 1], [0.4 0.6]); % creates low-contrast image
c = histeq(b); % performs histogram equalization
subplot(221), imshow(b); title('before equalization');
subplot(222), imshow(c); title('after equalization');
subplot(223), imhist(b);
subplot(224), imhist(c);
```

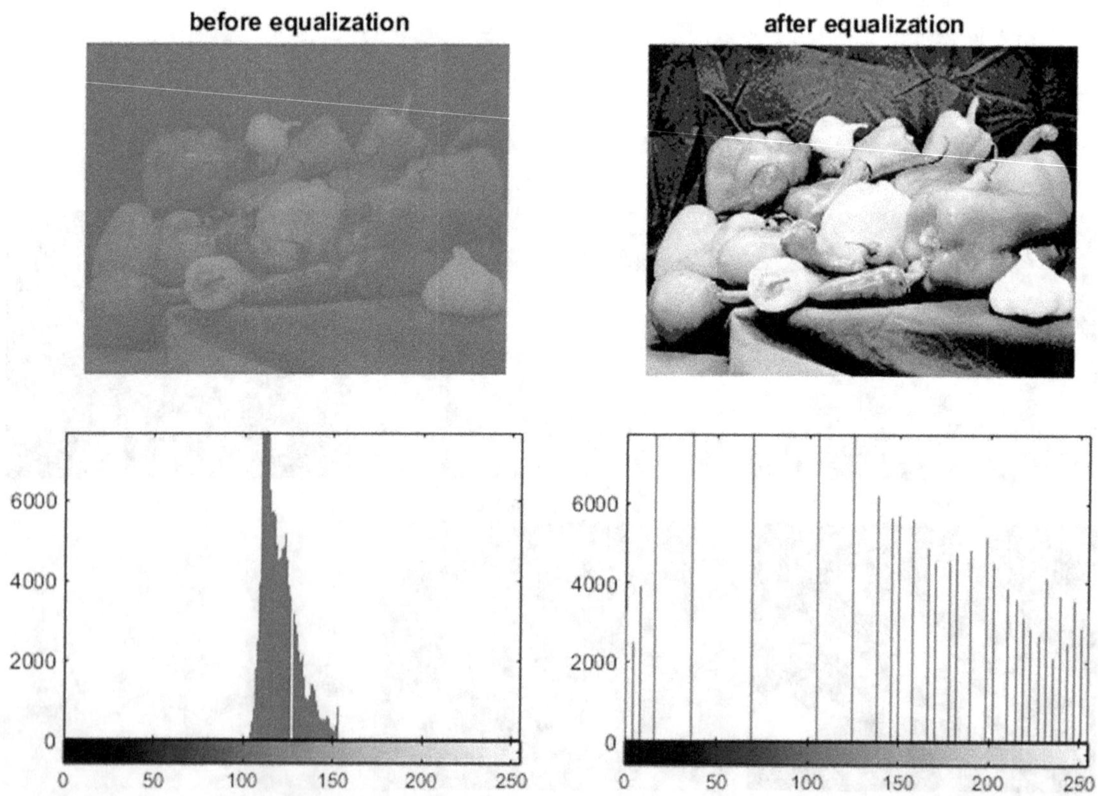

FIGURE 3.58
Output of Example 3.24.

The following example 3.25 demonstrates morphological operations. The function "bwmorph" is used to perform morphological operations using a kernel which is a 3 × 3 matrix of all 1s. The option used along with the function, define the type of operation. The number of times the operation is to be repeated can be specified. If the repetition value is set to "Inf", the operation is repeated until the image no longer changes (Figure 3.59).

The following example 3.26 demonstrates block processing in an image. The function "roiflt2" is used to apply a filter within a region of interest (ROI) specified by the coordinates of a rectangle over the image, "roipoly" is used to create a polygonal mask over a specific region, in this case a rectangle having one-third the image dimensions over the middle of the image. The function "imrect" is used to specify the location and size of the mask. An edge detection Laplacian filter is applied over the image through the region allowed by the mask. The height of the mask is arbitrarily specified as one-third the height of the image and its width as one-third the width of the image (Figure 3.60).

EXAMPLE 3.25 EXAMPLE TO DEMONSTRATE MORPHOLOGICAL OPERATIONS

```
clear; clc;
a = imread('circles.png');
h = bwmorph(a, 'thick', 10);
c = bwmorph(a, 'close', Inf);
d = bwmorph(a, 'dilate', 10);
e = bwmorph(a, 'erode', 10);
n = bwmorph(a, 'thin', 10);
r = bwmorph(a,'remove');
s = bwmorph(a,'skel',15);
figure
subplot(241), imshow(a);
   title('original');
subplot(242), imshow(h);
   title('thick');
subplot(243), imshow(d);
   title('dilate');
subplot(244), imshow(c);
   title('close');
subplot(245), imshow(e);
   title('erode');
subplot(246), imshow(r); title('rem');
subplot(247), imshow(s); title('skel');
subplot(248), imshow(n); title('thin');
```

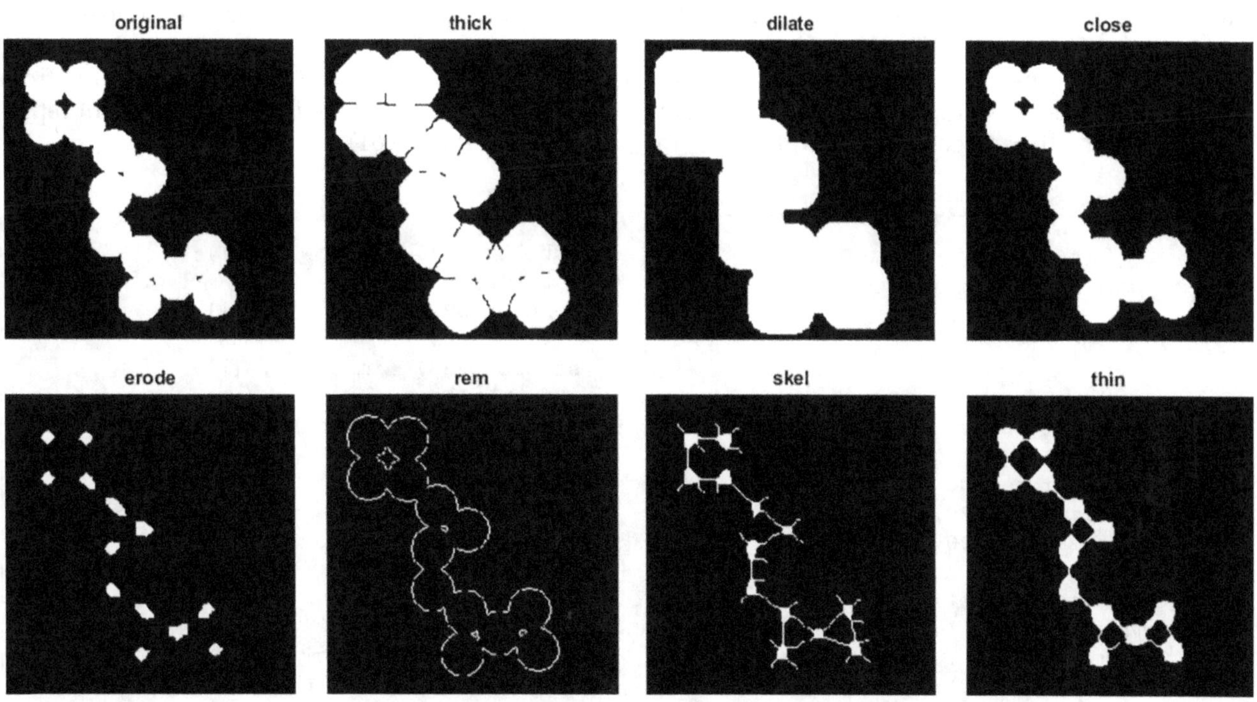

FIGURE 3.59
Output of Example 3.25.

EXAMPLE 3.26 EXAMPLE TO DEMONSTRATE REGION-OF-INTEREST (ROI)

```
I = imread('coins.png');
h = size(I,1); w = size(I,2);
c = [w/3 2*w/3 2*w/3 w/3]; r = [h/3 h/3 2*h/3 2*h/3 ];
BW = roipoly(I, c, r); % binary mask
H = fspecial('laplacian'); % edge detection filter
J = roifilt2(H, I, BW); % filter on image through mask
figure, imshowpair(I, J, 'montage')
imrect(imgca, [w/3, h/3, w/3, h/3]);
```

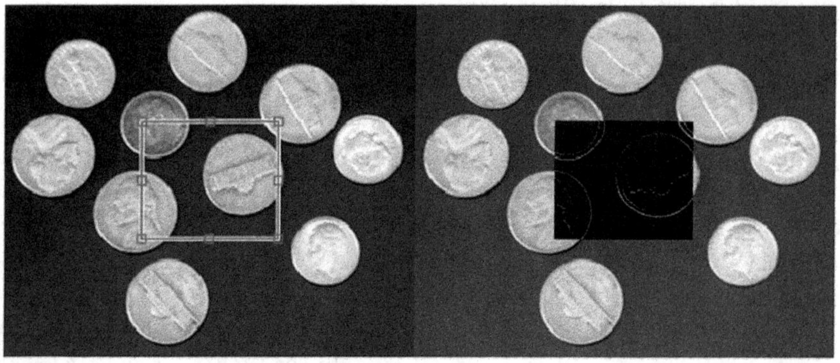

FIGURE 3.60
Output of Example 3.26.

The following example 3.27 demonstrates arithmetical operations. The functions "imadd", "imsubtract", "imabsdiff", "imcomplement", "immultiply", "imdivide" and "imlincomb" are used to implement the arithmetic operations addition, subtraction, absolute difference, complement, multiplication, division and linear combination. Before the operations are performed, the data types of the images are converted to double precision from an unsigned integer 8-bit so that a larger number of values can be represented without truncation. The function "double" converts a numerical value from 8-bit to 64-bit double-precision floating-point representation (Figure 3.61).

EXAMPLE 3.27 EXAMPLE TO DEMONSTRATE ARITHMETICAL OPERATIONS

```
clear; clc;
a = imread('threads.png'); a =
  double(a);
b = imread('rice.png'); b = double(b);
a = imresize(a, [300, 400]);
b = imresize(b, [300, 400]);
c = imadd(a, b, 'uint16');
d = imsubtract(a, b);
e = imabsdiff(a, b);
f = imcomplement(a);
g = immultiply(b, d);
h = imdivide(a, b);
i = imlincomb(0.7,f,0.3,e);
subplot(331), imshow(a, []);
   title('a');
subplot(332), imshow(b, []);
   title('b');
subplot(333), imshow(c, []);
   title('c=a+b');
subplot(334), imshow(d, []);
   title('d=a-b');
subplot(335), imshow(e, []);
   title('e=|a-b|');
subplot(336), imshow(f, []);
   title('f=~a');
subplot(337), imshow(g, []);
   title('g=b*d');
subplot(338), imshow(h, []);
   title('h=a/b');
subplot(339), imshow(i, []);
   title('i=0.5f+0.8e');
```

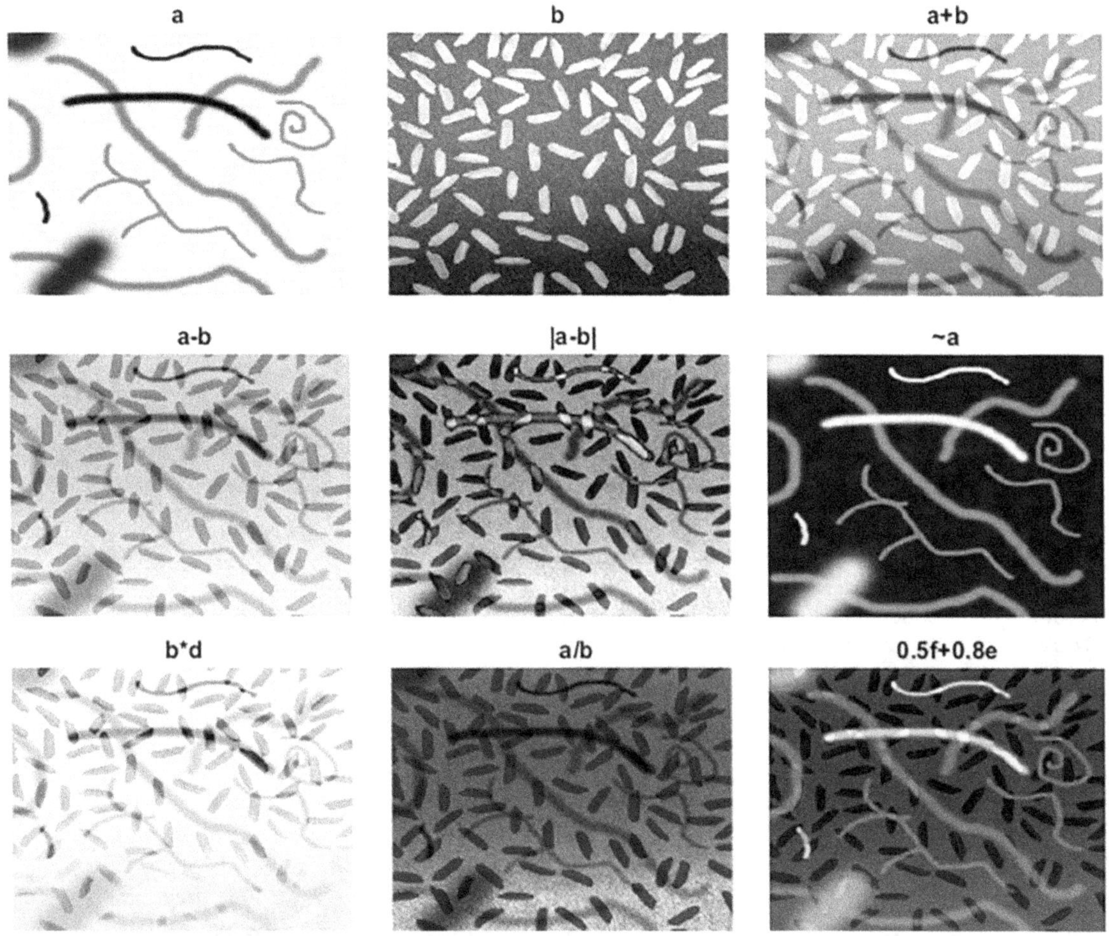

FIGURE 3.61
Output of Example 3.27.

The following example 3.28 demonstrates logical operations. The AND operation between two pixels is defined as the minimum of their values. The OR operation similarly is the maximum of their values. The NOT operation on a pixel returns the complement of its value.

A AND B = min(A, B) = A.B
A OR B = max(A, B) = A+B
NOT A = 255 – A = A'

The basic logical operations can be combined to form extended operations, for example XOR operation: A XOR B = A.B' + A'.B. In the following example, the functions "min" and "max" are used to simulate the logical operators. The function "double" converts the image pixel values from unsigned 8-bit integer to floating-point double precision values, so that subsequent numerical operations do not result in loss of information (Figure 3.62).

EXAMPLE 3.28 EXAMPLE TO DEMONSTRATE LOGICAL OPERATIONS

```
clear; clc;
a = imread('toyobjects.png'); a = double(a);
b = imread('coins.png'); b = double(b);
a = imresize(a, [300, 400]);
b = imresize(b, [300, 400]);
c = min(a,b);
d = max(a,b);
na = 255-a; nb = 255-b;
c1 = min(a,nb); c2 = min(na,b);
d1 = max(a, nb); d2 = max(na, b);
subplot(331), imshow(a, []); title('a');
subplot(332), imshow(b, []); title('b');
subplot(333), imshow(na, []); title('a''');
subplot(334), imshow(c, []); title('a.b');
subplot(335), imshow(d, []); title('a + b');
subplot(336), imshow(min(na,nb), []); title('a''.b''');
subplot(337), imshow(max(na,nb), []); title('a''+b''');
subplot(338), imshow(max(c1, c2), []); title('a.b'' + a''.b');
subplot(339), imshow(min(d1, d2), []); title('(a+b'').(a''+b)');
```

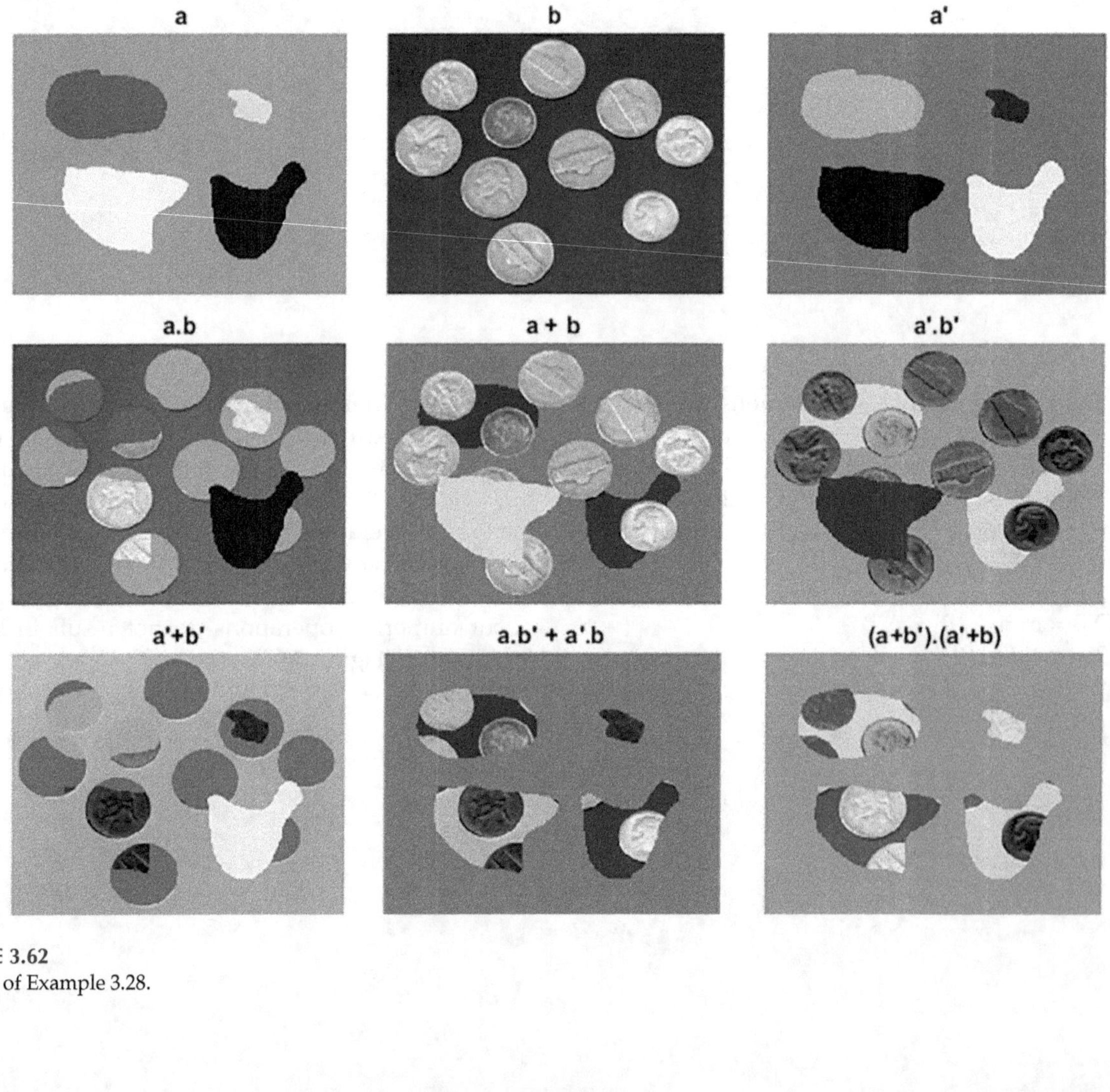

FIGURE 3.62
Output of Example 3.28.

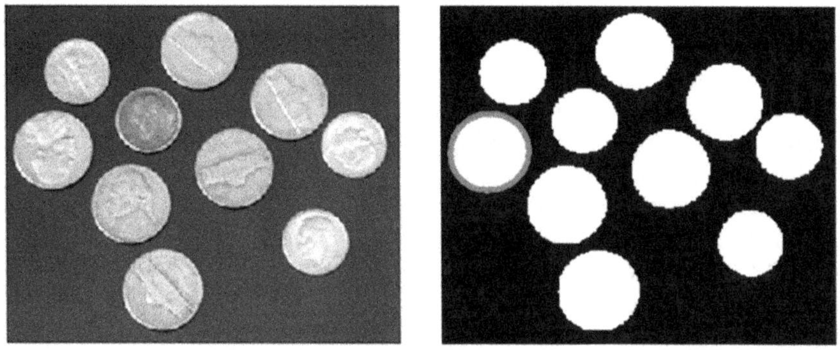

FIGURE 3.63
Output of Example 3.29.

3.10.6 Image Segmentation and Analysis

The following example 3.29 demonstrates image segmentation. The function "bwboundaries" traces region boundaries in a binary image. It returns a cell array of boundary pixel locations (B), a label matrix (L) and the number of objects found (N). In the following example, out of the ten objects found, the boundary of the first object from the left-hand boundary is traced out. The "hold" function holds on to the image of the label matrix L while its boundary is plotted using the pixel locations in B (Figure 3.63).

EXAMPLE 3.29 EXAMPLE TO DEMONSTRATE SEGMENTATION

```
clear; clc;
D = imread('coins.png');
I = imbinarize(D, 0.4);
[B, L, N] = bwboundaries(I);
N % return number of objects
b = B{1}; % consider the first object
y = b(:,1); x = b(:,2); % boundary
   coordinates
figure,
subplot(121), imshow(D); title('D');
subplot(122), imshow(L); title('L');
hold on; plot(x,y, 'm','LineWidth', 2);
   hold off;
```

The following example 3.30 demonstrates object analysis in an image. The function "imfindcircles" finds circles in an image belonging to a specified range of radii lengths and returns the actual centers and radii found. In the following example, the function is used to find all circles with radius between 15 and 25 in the input image (Figure 3.64).

EXAMPLE 3.30 EXAMPLE TO DEMONSTRATE OBJECT ANALYSIS

```
clear; clc;
A = imread('coins.png');
[centers, radii] = imfindcircles(A,
   [15 25]);
figure, imshow(A); hold on;
plot(centers(:,1), centers(:,2), 'r*');
```

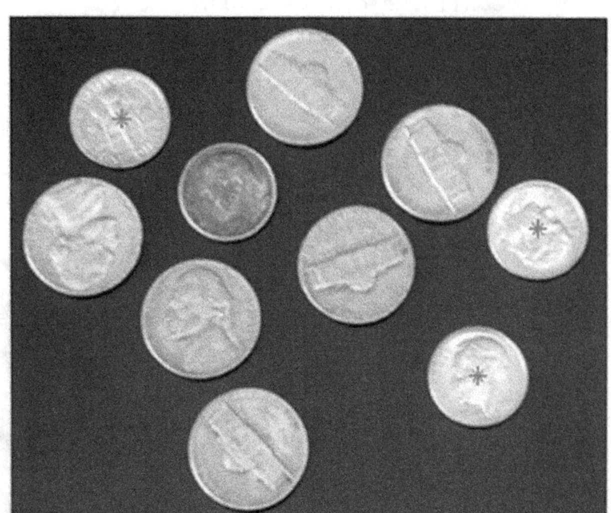

FIGURE 3.64
Output of Example 3.30.

The following example 3.31 and 3.32 demonstrate measuring region and image properties. The function "regionprops" measures properties of objects in a binary image like area, centroid, major axis length, minor axis length, bounding box, eccentricity, orientation and convex hull. In the following example, objects with intensity less than 100 (dark objects) are first extracted and their boundaries are traced using their center and radius information. Secondly, objects with intensity more than 200 (bright objects) are likewise extracted and their boundaries traced out. The function "viscircles" draws circles using the extracted center and radius (Figure 3.65).

EXAMPLE 3.31 EXAMPLE TO DEMONSTRATE REGION PROPERTIES

```
clear; clc;
I = imread('circlesBrightDark.png');
figure,
subplot(131), imshow(I);
BW = I < 100; % detect regions of low
   intensity
s = regionprops('table',BW, 'all');
c = s.Centroid;
d = mean([s.MajorAxisLength
   s.MinorAxisLength],2); r = d/2;
subplot(132), imshow(BW); title ('dark
   objects');
hold on;
viscircles(c,r, 'Color', [0.7 0.4 0]);
hold off;
BW = I > 200; % detect regions of high
   intensity
s = regionprops('table',BW, 'all');
   title ('bright objects');
c = s.Centroid;
d = mean([s.MajorAxisLength
   s.MinorAxisLength],2); r = d/2;
subplot(133), imshow(BW);
hold on;
viscircles(c,r, 'Color', [0 0.5 0]);
hold off;
```

EXAMPLE 3.32 EXAMPLE TO DEMONSTRATE AREA AND PERIMETER CALCULATIONS

```
I = imread('circlesBrightDark.png');
b1 = im2bw(I, 0.5);
a1 = bwarea(b1);
p1 = bwperim(b1);
e1 = bweuler(b1);
b2 = im2bw(I, 0.7);
a2 = bwarea(b2);
p2 = bwperim(b2);
e2 = bweuler(b2);
subplot(151), imshow(I); title('I');
subplot(152), imshow(b1);
title(strcat('b1 : area =',num2str(a1),
', e =', num2str(e1)));
subplot(153), imshow(p1);
title('perimeter of b1');
subplot(154), imshow(b2);
title(strcat('b2 : area =',num2str(a2),
', e =', num2str(e2)));
subplot(155), imshow(p2);
title('perimeter of b2');
```

The function "bwarea" estimates the area of objects in a binary image, "bwperim" returns a binary image containing the perimeter of the objects in the image, "bweuler" returns the Euler number of the binary image. The Euler number is the total number of objects in the image minus the total number of holes in those objects. In the following example, for the binary image b1, the white portion is considered as the object and the three black circles are considered as holes, and the Euler number is computed as $1 - 3 = -2$. For the second binary image b2, the three white areas are considered as objects which do not contain any holes, and so the Euler number is computed as $3 - 0 = 3$. The perimeters of the detected regions are also traced out (Figure 3.66).

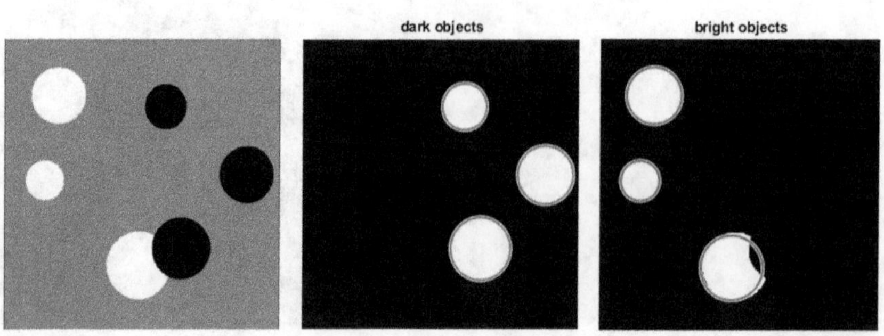

FIGURE 3.65
Output of Example 3.31.

The following example 3.33 demonstrates texture analysis in an image. The function "graycomatrix" is used to calculate GLCMs given the data matrix, offset distance, number of gray levels and the minimum and maximum gray intensities. The following example illustrates how the symmetrical GLCMs are computed along four directions (Figure 3.67).

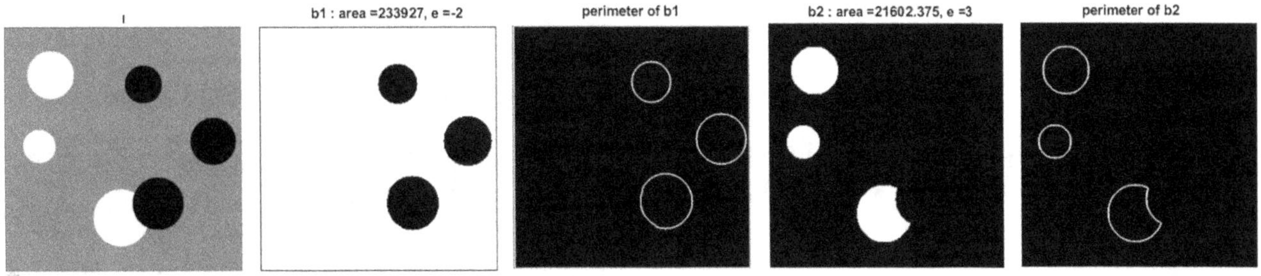

FIGURE 3.66
Output of Example 3.32.

EXAMPLE 3.33 EXAMPLE TO DEMONSTRATE TEXTURE ANALYSIS USING GLCMS

```
clear; clc;
I = [0 0 1 1; 0 0 1 1; 0 2 2 2; 2 2 3 3];
d = 1; lev = 4;
minI = min(min(I)); maxI = max(max(I));
glcm0 = graycomatrix(I, 'Offset',[0 d], 'NumLevels', lev, ...
'Symmetric', true, 'GrayLimits', [minI, maxI]);
glcm45 = graycomatrix(I, 'Offset',[-d d], 'NumLevels', lev, ...
'Symmetric', true, 'GrayLimits', [minI, maxI]);
glcm90 = graycomatrix(I, 'Offset',[-d 0], 'NumLevels', lev, ...
'Symmetric', true, 'GrayLimits', [minI, maxI]);
glcm135 = graycomatrix(I, 'Offset',[-d -d], 'NumLevels', lev, ...
'Symmetric', true, 'GrayLimits', [minI, maxI]);
subplot(231), imshow(I,[]); title('I');
subplot(233), imshow(glcm0,[]); title('G0');
subplot(234), imshow(glcm45,[]); title('G45');
subplot(235), imshow(glcm90,[]); title('G90');
subplot(236), imshow(glcm135,[]); title('G135');
```

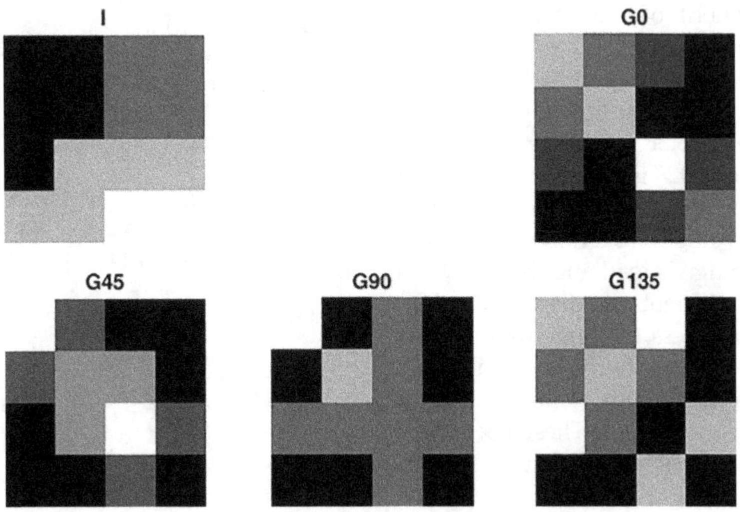

FIGURE 3.67
Output of Example 3.33

The function "graycoprops" calculates the statistical properties contrast, energy homogeneity and correlation from a GLCM. The following example 3.34 illustrates calculation of features for the 0 degree GLCM of the previous example. (Example 3.33).

EXAMPLE 3.34 EXAMPLE TO CALCULATE STATISTICAL PROPERTIES OF TEXTURES

```
clear; clc;
G = glcm0;
s = graycoprops(G);
C = s.Contrast
E = s.Energy
H = s.Homogeneity
R = s.Correlation
```

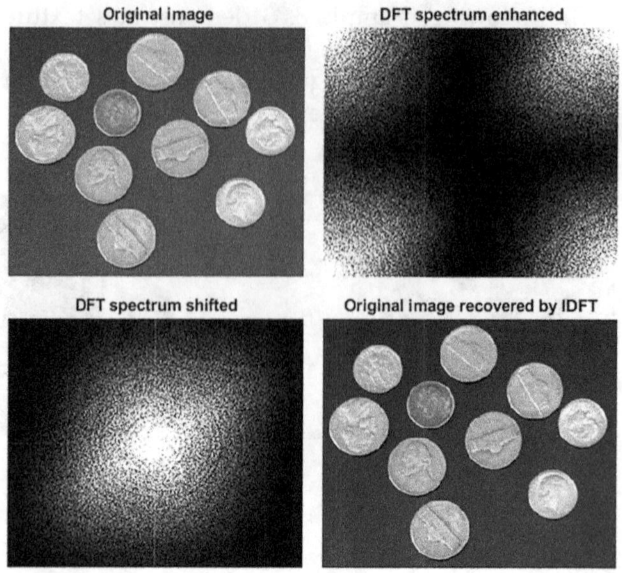

FIGURE 3.68
Output of Example 3.35.

3.10.7 Image Transforms

The following example 3.35 demonstrates DFT of an image. The function "fft2" is used to apply 2D Fourier Transform to the image and the absolute values of the coefficients are calculated to avoid the need for handling imaginary values. The function "ifft2" calculates the inverse DFT and returns the spatial domain image from its spectrum. The following example shows a 2D step input signal and the logarithm value of its shifted spectrum. The spectrum is also transformed back to the spatial domain using the inverse DFT. Since the original matrix is only of size 30 × 30, the size of the coefficients matrix is increased to 200 × 200 by padding with zeros for better visualization. By default the zero-frequency component of the spectrum is displayed at the left corner of the plot. It is customary to shift this to the center of the plot for better viewing. The function "fftshift" is used for this (Figure 3.68).

The following example 3.36 demonstrates DCT of an image. The function "dct2" is used to return the 2D DCT of an input data matrix, and the function "idct2" is used to return the inverse 2D DCT. In the following example, a grayscale image is read and the 2D DCT is computed. The DCT coefficients are displayed using a logarithmic scale to compress the large range of values within the display range of 0–255. Now, all coefficients with values less than 10 are removed, and the resulting DCT matrix is displayed. These coefficients are converted back to the spatial domain, and the resulting image is displayed. The result shows some degradation due to the missing coefficients (Figure 3.69).

EXAMPLE 3.35 EXAMPLE TO DEMONSTRATE DFT AND IDFT

```
clear; clc;
a = imread('coins.png');
b = fft2(a);
c = abs(b*0.0001);
d = fftshift(c);
e = abs(d*0.0001);
f = ifft2(b);
figure,
subplot(221), imshow(a);
   title('Original image')
subplot(222), imshow(c); title('DFT
   spectrum enhanced')
subplot(223), imshow(d); title('DFT
   spectrum shifted')
subplot(224), imshow(f,[]);
   title('Original image recovered
   by IDFT')
```

EXAMPLE 3.36 EXAMPLE TO DEMONSTRATE DCT AND IDCT

```
clear; clc;
a = imread('coins.png');
b = dct2(a);
c = log(abs(b));
b(abs(b) < 10) = 0 ;
d = log(abs(b));
e = idct2(b);
figure,
subplot(221), imshow(a); title('Original image')
subplot(222), imshow(c,[]); title('DCT spectrum')
subplot(223), imshow(d,[]); title('Modified DCT spectrum')
subplot(224), imshow(e,[]); title('Recovered from modified spectrum')
```

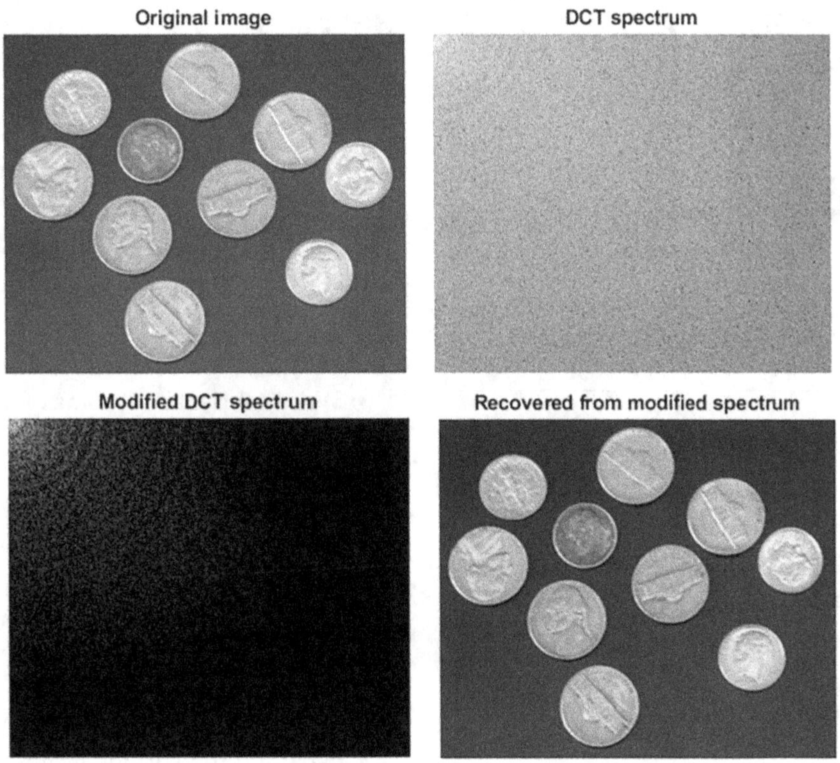

FIGURE 3.69
Output of Example 3.36.

The following example 3.37 demonstrates de-blurring of an image. In the following example, a 2D step function is first convolved with a Gaussian kernel to create blurring. To de-blur it, both the image and the kernel are converted to frequency domain using 2D DFT after which the degraded image spectrum is multiplied by the reciprocal of the kernel spectrum to implement an inverse filtering. The resulting spectrum is converted back to spatial domain using a 2D IDFT to derive the de-blurred image (Figure 3.70).

EXAMPLE 3.37 EXAMPLE TO DEMONSTRATE DE-BLURRING

```
clear; clc;
f = zeros(30,30);
f(10:20,10:20) = 1;
h = fspecial('gaussian', 5, 5);
g = imfilter(f, h, 'conv');
 [rows, cols] = size(f);
H = fft2(h, rows, cols);
G = fft2(g, rows, cols);
R = G./H;
r = ifft2(R);
subplot(141), imshow(f); title('input image f');
subplot(142), imshow(h, []); title('gaussian filter h');
subplot(143), imshow(g); title('blurred image g');
subplot(144), imshow(r, []); title('restored image r');
```

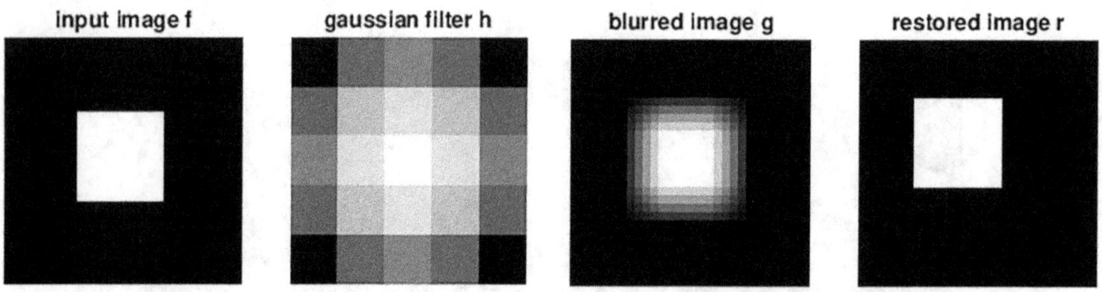

FIGURE 3.70
Output of Example 3.37.

Review Questions

- Trace the historical evolution of digital image processing highlighting landmark events.
- What is a pixel and what parameters are used to represent it?
- What are the factors responsible for display of colors?
- Mention characteristics of different image types.
- What are the major devices used for image acquisition?
- Differentiate between the working principles of a scanner and digital camera.
- On what factors does image quality depend?
- What are the interface standards for connecting image acquisition devices?
- Differentiate between the working principles of the CRT, LCD and LED.
- Discuss about the major components of a display card and its interface standards.
- Write in brief about some of the major specifications of display monitors.
- Discuss some the display resolutions in use today.
- Differentiate between the working principles of the LASER printer and inkjet printer.
- Name some of the common image editing tasks offered by a GUI-based software.
- What are the characteristics of different types of geometrical transformations?
- What are the various techniques of intensity transformations in an image?
- Define an image histogram and discuss methods of histogram equalization.
- How can arithmetical and logical operations implemented on images?
- What is an image kernel and what is meant by convolution operation?
- How can kernel-based methods be used for noise reduction and edge detection?
- What is meant by morphological operations on images?

- What is a frequency-based transformation, and how it is done using DFT?
- Differentiate between DFT, DCT and DWT.
- How can de-convolution be used to restore a degraded image?
- Mention characteristics of major color models.
- What is a chromaticity diagram, and what information does it depict?
- Discuss the steps of color conversion from RGB to CMY, HSV and L*a*b*.
- How does color calibration ensure consistent color reproduction over various devices?
- What is an indexed image and how is it related to a color lookup table?
- Discuss about various techniques of image enhancement and image restoration.
- What is image segmentation, and what are the different techniques to implement it?
- What are the various approaches for object detection in images?
- Discuss about different methods of image analysis and recognition.
- Discuss about various classifiers that can be used for image classification.
- Discuss about legal and ethical issues in the domain of digital imaging.
- What are the current challenges and emerging trends in digital imaging?
- Discuss about characteristics of major image file formats.

References

Andina, T., T. Dreier (eds), *Digital ethics: The issue of images*, Nomos, 2022.

Armi, L., S. Fekri-Ershad, *Texture Image Analysis and Texture Classification Methods: A review"*, 2019. https://arxiv.org/ftp/arxiv/papers/1904/1904.06554.pdf

Bai, M., R. Urtasun, *Deep Watershed Transform for Instance Segmentation*, 2017

Bay, H., T. Tuytelaars & L.V. Gool, SURF: Speeded up robust features, *Computer Vision and Image Understanding*, vol. 110, no. 3, pp. 346–359, 2008.

Bengio, Y., Learning deep architectures for AI, *Foundations and Trends in Machine Learning*, vol. 2, no. 1, pp. 1–127, 2009.

Berg, M., J. Boyar, L. M. Favrholdt & K. M. Larsen, Online minimum spanning trees with weight predictions, 2023. https://arxiv.org/abs/2302.12029

Breiman, L., Random forests, *Machine Learning*, vol. 45, no. 1, pp. 5–32, 2001.

Burger, W., M. J. Burge, *Principles of digital image processing: Advanced methods*, Springer Verlag, 2013.

Cai, Z., N. Vasconcelos, Cascade R-CNN: Delving into high quality object detection, 2017. https://arxiv.org/abs/1712.00726

Chen, L.-C., G. Papandreou, K. Murphy & A. L. Yuille, *DeepLab: Semantic image segmentation with deep convolutional nets, atrous convolution and fully connected CRFs*, 2017. https://arxiv.org/abs/1606.00915

Christianini, N., & J. C. Shawe-Taylor, *An introduction to support vector machines and other kernel based learning methods*, Cambridge University Press, 2000.

Coppersmith, D., S. J. Hong & J. R. M. Hosking, Partitioning nominal attributes in decision trees, *Data Mining and Knowledge Discovery*, vol. 3, pp. 197–217, 1999.

Csurka, G., C. R. Dance, L. Fan, J. Williamowski & C. Bray, *Visual categorization with bags of key-points, Proceedings of ECCV International Workshop on Statistical Learning in Computer Vision*, 2004.

Cyganek, B., *Object detection and recognition in digital images*, Wiley, 2013.

Das, R., *Content-based image classification*, CRC Press, 2020.

Dryden, I. L., K. V. Mardia, *Statistical shape analysis*, Wiley, 2016.

Ester, M, Kriegel, H.-P., Sander, J., Xu, X., Simoudis, E., Han, J. & Fayyad, U. M. (eds.). A density-based algorithm for discovering clusters in large spatial databases with noise. *Proceedings of the Second International Conference on Knowledge Discovery and Data Mining (KDD-96)*, AAAI Press. pp. 226–231, 1996.

Fortner, B., T. E. Meyer, *Number by colors*, Springer, 1997.

Girshick, R., J. Donahue, T. Darrell & J. Malik, Region based convolutional networks for accurate object detection and segmentation, *IEEE Transactions of Pattern Analysis and Machine Intelligence*, 2015.

Gonzalez, R. C., R. E. Woods, *Digital image processing*, Prentice Hall, 2008.

Guild, J., The colorimetric properties of the spectrum, *Pholosophical Transactions*, vol. 230, no. 685, pp. 149–187, 1931.

Gunturk, B. K., X. Li (eds), *Image restoration: fundamentals and advances*, CRC Press, 2018.

Haar, A., "Zur Theorie der orthogonalen Funktionensysteme", *Mathematische Annalen*, vol. 69, pp. 331–371, 1910.

Haralick, R.M., K. Shanmugan & I. Dinstein, Textural features for image classification, *IEEE Transactions on Systems, Man, and Cybernetics*, vol. SMC-3, pp. 610–621, 1973.

Hastie, T., R. Tibshirani, & J. Friedman, *The elements of statistical learning*, Second edition. Springer, 2008.

Haykin, S., *Neural networks and learning machines*, Third edition, Prentice Hall, 2009.

He, K., G. Gkioxari, P. Dollar & R. Girshick, *Mask R-CNN*, 2018. https://arxiv.org/abs/1703.06870

Hung C-C, E. Song, Y. Lan, *Image texture analysis: Foundations, models and algorithms*, Springer, 2019.

Hunt, R. W. G., D. Wright, in Luo, R. (ed.), *Encyclopedia of color science and technology*, Springer, 2014.

Hunter, R., Photoelectric color-difference meter, *Journal of Optical Society of America*, vol. 38, no. 7, p. 661, 1948.

Jain, A. K., *Fundamentals of digital image processing*, Prentice Hall, p. 439, 1989.

Kallen, S. A., *Digital cameras and camcorders*, Lucent Books USA, 2014.

Kriss M (ed.), *Handbook of digital imaging*, Wiley, 2015.

Lancaric, S., A survey of shape analysis techniques, *Pattern Recognition*, vol. 31, no. 8, pp. 983–1001, 1998.

Lei, T., A. K. Nandi, *Image segmentation: principles techniques and applications*, Wiley, 2022.

Liu, C. Z., S. Ramakrishnan, *Image recognition: Progress trends and challenges*, Nova Science Publishers, 2020.

Liu, W., et al., SSD: Single shot multibox detector, 2016.

Long, J., E. Shelhamer, T. Darrell, Fully convolutional networks for semantic segmentation, 2015. https://arxiv.org/abs/1605.06211

Lowe, D. G., Distinctive image features from scale-invariant key-points, *International Journal of Computer Vision*, vol. 60, no. 2, pp. 91–110, 2004.

Lucy, L.B., "An iterative technique for the rectification of observed distributions", *Astronomical Journal*, vol. 79, no. 1, pp. 745–754, 1974.

MacQueen, J. B. Some methods for classification and analysis of multivariate observations, *Proceedings of 5th Berkeley Symposium on Mathematical Statistics and Probability*, vol. 1. University of California Press. pp. 281–297, 1967. https://projecteuclid.org/euclid.bsmsp/1200512992

Mallat, S. G., A theory for multiresolution signal decomposition: The wavelet representation, *IEEE Transactions on Pattern Analysis and Machine Intelligence*, vol. 11, no. 7, pp. 674–693, July 1989.

Michael, W., *Color calibration techniques for true color measurement*, Lap Lambert Academic, 2015.

Otsu, N., A threshold selection method from gray-level histograms, *IEEE Transactions on Systems, Man, and Cybernetics*, vol. 9, no. 1, pp. 62–66, 1979.

Poynton, C., A guided tour of color space, *Proceedings of the SMPTE Advanced Television and Electronic Imaging Conference*, pp. 167–180, 1995.

Rajput, S. S., N. U. Khan, A. K. Singh & K. V. Arya (eds.), *Digital image enhancement and reconstruction*, Elsevier Science, 2022.

Reed, C. S., *Copyright workflow for photographers*, Peachpit Press, 2015.

Richardson, W., Bayesian based iterative method of image restoration, *Journal of the Optical Society of America (JOSA)*, vol. 62, no. 1, pp. 55–59, 1972.

Roussopoulos, N., S. Kelley, F.D.R. Vincent, "Nearest neighbor queries", *Proceedings of 1995 ACMSIGMOD International Conference on Management of Data – SIGMOD '95*, p. 71, 1995.

Sinha, P. K., *Image acquisition and preprocessing for machine vision systems*, SPIE, 2012.

Soydaner D, Attention mechanisms in neural networks: Where it comes and where it goes, 2022. https://arxiv.org/abs/2204.13154

Strano, M., B. M. Colosimo, Logistic regression analysis for experimental determination of forming limit diagrams, *International Journal of Machine Tools and Manufacture*, vol. 46, no. 6, pp. 673–682, 2006.

Sundararajan, D., *Digital image processing: a signal processing and algorithmic approach*, Springer Nature Singapore, 2017.

Tan, M, R. Pang, Q. V. Le, EfficientDet: scalable and efficient object detection, 2020. https://arxiv.org/abs/1911.09070

Wiener, N., *Extrapolation interpolation and smoothing of stationary time series*, John Wiley & Sons Inc., 1949.

Wright, W. D., A re-determination of the trichromatic coefficients of the spectral colours, *Transactions of the Optical Society*, vol. 30, no. 4, pp. 141–164, 1929

Xia, F., J. Liu, H. Nie, Y. Fu, L. Wan & X. Kong, *Random walks, a review of algorithms and applications*, 2020. https://arxiv.org/abs/2008.03639

Young, T., On the theory of light and colors, *Philosophical Transactions of the Royal Society of London*, vol. 92, pp. 12–48, 1802.

Zhou, Z., M. R. Siddiquee Md, N. Tajbakhsh, & J. Liang, *UNet++: A nested U-net architecture for medical image segmentation*, 2018. https://arxiv.org/abs/1807.10165

4

Graphics

4.1 Graphics Fundamentals

4.1.1 Key Terms

We begin with a snapshot of the important terms relevant to the field of 2D and 3D graphics, to present the entire chapter in a nutshell. These terms will be expanded in the subsequent sections of the chapter in their proper contexts.

3D Coordinate System: A normal 2D Cartesian coordinate system with the addition of the third dimension (z-axis) to accurately represent objects in 3D space. Here, the location of a point is represented by three coordinates measured along three axes x-axis, y-axis and z-axis mutually at right angles or 90°.

2D Graphics: 2D graphics involve two-dimensional graphical entities, created on a flat plane, using only the X and Y coordinates. They are commonly found in user interfaces, logos, icons, typography and vector illustrations.

3D Graphics: In addition to 2D graphics, it introduces an additional dimension, the Z-axis, allowing for depth and perspective. This dimensionality gives a sense of realism and depth perception, making them suitable for immersive experiences.

Affine transformation: A mathematical mapping that preserves parallel lines and ratios of distances, commonly used in computer graphics to perform various geometric manipulations on objects such as translation, rotation, scaling and skewing. It is a linear transformation that can be represented by a matrix and typically transforms a rectangle to a parallelogram.

Approximating spline: An approximating spline is a type of spline that aims to approximate a set of given points with a smooth curve while minimizing the deviation from those points. It is commonly used in computer graphics, CAD and other applications where a smooth and continuous curve is desired to represent or interpolate a series of specified data points.

Axonometric projection: Axonometric projection is a type of orthographic projection used in technical and architectural drawing where objects are represented without perspective distortion. It preserves the relative sizes of objects along each axis, making it useful for visualizing three-dimensional objects in a clear and undistorted manner.

B-spline: A B-spline, or basis spline, is a piecewise-defined polynomial function commonly used in computer graphics and computer-aided design to represent smooth curves and surfaces. It is defined by a set of control points and a set of basis functions that determine the shape and flexibility of the spline.

Bezier spline: A Bezier spline is a type of curve defined by control points that determine its shape and characteristics. Widely used in computer graphics and design, Bezier splines provide a smooth and intuitive way to create curves and surfaces by manipulating the positions of control points.

Blending functions: Blending functions define the weight or influence of control points on the shape of the spline curve. They determine how the contributions of individual control points are combined to produce the final curve, allowing for fine control over the curve's behavior and smoothness.

Bresenham's Circle Algorithm: A method used in computer graphics to efficiently approximate the points along the circumference of a circle using integer arithmetic. Developed by Jack E. Bresenham, it minimizes computational complexity by avoiding floating-point operations, making it well suited for implementation in digital systems and displays.

Bresenham's Line Algorithm: A method used to draw a straight line between two points with integer coordinates. Developed by Jack E. Bresenham, the algorithm optimally determines the pixels to be illuminated, utilizing integer arithmetic for efficiency and simplicity in drawing lines on pixel-based displays.

DOI: 10.1201/9781003588030-4

Circle drawing algorithm: Circle drawing algorithms are mathematical techniques used in computer graphics to generate the points that define a circle on a pixel-based display. Common algorithms include Bresenham's Circle Algorithm, which efficiently determines the points to be plotted for a circle by utilizing integer arithmetic, making it suitable for implementation in digital systems.

Clipping algorithm: A clipping algorithm is a computer graphics technique used to selectively display or remove portions of an object or scene that fall outside a specified region, known as the clipping window. Various algorithms, such as the Cohen-Sutherland and Liang-Barsky algorithms, efficiently determine which parts of graphical elements lie within the viewport, optimizing rendering and improving overall performance.

Cox de Boor algorithm: The Cox-de Boor algorithm is a method used in computer graphics and computer-aided design for evaluating B-spline basis functions. It efficiently calculates the weights associated with control points to define the shape of a B-spline curve or surface, playing a crucial role in creating smooth and flexible representations of complex shapes.

Critical points: Refer to locations on a spline curve or surface where changes in its characteristics, such as maxima, minima, concavity or inflection, occur. Identifying these points is crucial for understanding the behavior of the spline and can help optimize its design or control its visual appearance in applications like computer-aided design and computer graphics.

Cross product: The cross product is a mathematical operation that combines two vectors to produce a third vector perpendicular to the plane containing the original vectors. It is used in geometry and physics to calculate vectors that are orthogonal to the given vectors, providing a useful tool for determining orientation and generating normal vectors in three-dimensional space.

Cubic spline: curve formed by joining together cubic polynomials, typically used in computer graphics and interpolation. It provides a smooth and continuous representation through a set of control points, allowing for flexible curve design and approximation.

Dimetric projection: Dimetric projection is a type of axonometric projection used in technical and architectural drawing where three-dimensional objects are represented with a combination of two different angles for depth, typically using one horizontal and two vertical axes. It maintains parallel lines and shows all three dimensions with unequal foreshortening, offering a visually balanced representation of objects in an isometric-like style.

Dot product: The dot product, also known as the scalar product, is a mathematical operation that takes two equal-length sequences of numbers and returns a single number. It is calculated by multiplying corresponding components of the two sequences and then summing up the results, providing a measure of similarity or projection between the vectors.

Extrusion: Extrusion in 3D modeling is a technique where a 2D shape is extended in a third dimension to create a three-dimensional object. It involves pushing or pulling the shape along a specified axis, resulting in the formation of a solid object with depth.

Filling algorithm: A filling algorithm in computer graphics is a method used to determine the interior color or shading of closed regions in a digital image. Common algorithms include scanline fill and flood fill, which efficiently determine and apply colors to the pixels enclosed by a closed boundary in the image.

Foreshortening factors: Foreshortening factors refer to adjustments made in a two-dimensional representation to account for the distortion of objects that are viewed at an angle in three-dimensional space. These factors help accurately depict the apparent size and shape of objects when their dimensions are altered due to perspective, as observed in drawings or computer graphics.

Graphics file formats: Vector graphics file formats store images using mathematical equations to define shapes and lines, allowing for scalability without loss of quality. Examples include SVG (Scalable Vector Graphics) and AI (Adobe Illustrator), which are commonly used for logos, illustrations and other graphics where precision and scalability are important.

Homogeneous coordinates: Homogeneous coordinates are an extension of Cartesian coordinates used in computer graphics and projective geometry, introducing an additional coordinate to represent points in space. This extra coordinate simplifies operations like translations and perspective transformations, making them more efficient to perform mathematically.

Hybrid spline: A hybrid spline is a mathematical curve that combines different types of splines, such as interpolating and approximating splines, to achieve specific characteristics. These splines interpolate through a subset of its control points while the remaining characteristics are usually derived from predefined blending functions.

Illumination model: An illumination model is a mathematical representation that simulates how light interacts with surfaces to determine their appearance. It takes into account factors such as light sources, material properties and the viewer's perspective to calculate the color and brightness of each pixel in a rendered image, contributing to the realistic portrayal of 3D scenes.

Implicit surfaces: Implicit surfaces are mathematical representations of surfaces defined by an implicit equation that relates the coordinates of points on the surface. These surfaces are characterized by points where the implicit equation equals zero, providing a compact and versatile way to describe complex shapes in computer graphics and modeling.

Interpolating spline: An interpolating spline is a type of spline that passes through a specified set of control points, ensuring that the curve interpolates those points. This property makes it particularly useful for accurately representing a curve that must pass through predefined positions in applications such as computer-aided design and computer graphics.

Isometric projection: Isometric projection is a method of representing three-dimensional objects in two dimensions, preserving the relative proportions of the object's sides and ensuring that all three spatial axes make equal angles with the plane of projection. It provides a visually clear and balanced representation of objects, often used in technical and architectural drawings.

Knot vector: In B-spline representation, the knot vector is a sequence of values that determine the positions of the knots, influencing the shape and continuity of the spline curve or surface. The arrangement of knots in the vector defines the control over the blending functions, allowing for flexible control of the B-spline's geometry.

Lathing: Lathing in 3D modeling is a technique where a two-dimensional profile is rotated around an axis to generate a three-dimensional object. This process creates symmetrical shapes and is commonly used in computer-aided design to produce objects like cylindrical or conical forms.

Lights: n 3D modeling, lights are virtual sources that simulate illumination, affecting the appearance of objects in a scene. They contribute to the realistic rendering of 3D environments by casting shadows, highlighting surfaces and influencing the overall visual quality of the rendered image or animation.

Line drawing algorithm: A line drawing algorithm is a set of procedures used in computer graphics to determine which pixels to illuminate in order to represent a straight line on a digital display. Common algorithms, such as Bresenham's Line Algorithm, efficiently calculate the points along the line using integer arithmetic, making them suitable for implementation in digital systems.

Linear spline: A spline generated using a polynomial equation of degree 1, i.e., $y = a + bx$. Visually a linear spline takes the form of a straight line and can be determined it two points along its path are known.

Lofting: Lofting in 3D modeling is a technique where two or more profiles or shapes are used to create a smooth transition or blend between them, generating a complex and continuous surface.

Modifiers: Geometric modifiers are tools or operations in 3D modeling software that alter the shape, position or characteristics of geometric objects within a scene. These modifiers can include transformations like scaling, rotation and deformation, providing a means to manipulate and refine the appearance of 3D models.

Oblique projection: Oblique projection is a type of projection used in technical and architectural drawing where three-dimensional objects are represented with one axis at an angle to the plane of projection. It maintains parallel lines along the chosen axis while showing the other two axes with foreshortened lines, providing a distorted but visually informative representation of objects.

Orthographic projection: Orthographic projection is a method of representing three-dimensional objects in two dimensions, using parallel projectors to create a set of two-dimensional views without any perspective distortion. It provides a standardized and detailed representation of objects, commonly used in technical and engineering drawings for accurate depiction of shapes and measurements.

Parametric equations: Parametric equations are mathematical expressions that describe the coordinates of a point in terms of one or more independent parameters.

Parametric surfaces: Parametric surfaces are mathematical representations of surfaces in three-dimensional space using parametric equations. These equations define the coordinates of points on the surface in terms of two or more parameters, allowing for the creation of complex and varied shapes used extensively in computer graphics and geometric modeling.

Perspective projection: Perspective projection is a method of representing three-dimensional objects on a two-dimensional surface with the application of depth and distance cues, mimicking how the human eye perceives spatial relationships. It involves projecting points from the three-dimensional space onto a two-dimensional plane, considering the diminishing size of objects as they recede into the distance.

Perspective transformation: A mathematical mapping that in general do not preserve parallel lines and ratios of distances. It is a linear transformation that can be represented by a matrix and typically transforms a rectangle to a quadrilateral.

Polynomial: A polynomial is a mathematical expression consisting of variables raised to non-negative integer powers, multiplied by coefficients. Polynomials are widely used in various mathematical fields and applications, representing functions that can describe curves, shapes and other mathematical relationships.

Primitives: Geometrical primitives are basic shapes or elements used in computer graphics and modeling to construct more complex objects. Common examples include points, lines and polygons, which serve as the fundamental building blocks for creating detailed and intricate 3D scenes in virtual environments.

Quadratic spline: A curve formed by joining together quadratic polynomials, typically used in computer graphics and interpolation. It provides a smooth and continuous representation through a set of control points, allowing for flexible curve design and approximation.

Spline: A spline is a smooth curve or mathematical function defined by multiple control points, allowing for the creation of complex and smooth shapes in computer graphics and design. It is often used in graphics software and computer-aided design to create curves that interpolate between specified points, providing flexibility and precision in shape representation.

Surface of revolution: A surface of revolution is created by rotating a two-dimensional curve around an axis in three-dimensional space. This rotational symmetry results in a three-dimensional surface that resembles the original curve's shape, forming a shape similar to that of a spun object.

Surface texture: Surface texture refers to the visual and tactile characteristics of a surface, including its roughness, smoothness, pattern or grain. In computer graphics and 3D modeling, surface texture is often simulated using texture mapping techniques to enhance the realism of rendered objects by applying images or patterns to their surfaces.

Reflection: Reflection in computer graphics refers to the simulation of how light interacts with surfaces, causing some of it to bounce off and reach the viewer's eye. Accurate rendering of Reflections adds realism to images, and techniques like ray tracing or Reflection mapping are commonly used to achieve this effect in computer-generated scenes.

Rotation: Rotation in computer graphics involves transforming an object by changing its orientation around a specific axis or point in three-dimensional space. This transformation is often used to animate objects, simulate motion or manipulate their orientation for visual effects in digital environments.

Scaling: Scaling in computer graphics involves resizing an object or an image, changing its dimensions along one or more axes. It is a geometric transformation that can either enlarge or shrink the size of an object, affecting its overall appearance in a graphical representation.

Shear: Shear in computer graphics is a transformation that distorts the shape of an object by shifting its parts in a specified direction and by a specified amount. It is commonly used to create slanted or skewed effects in 2D and 3D graphics, altering the proportions of the object along one or more axes.

Spline: A spline is a flexible and smooth curve that passes through a set of control points, used in computer graphics, computer-aided design and mathematical modeling. It provides a versatile way to represent complex curves and surfaces, allowing for precise control over the shape and characteristics of the interpolated curve.

Translation: Translation in computer graphics involves moving an object or an image from one location to another in two-dimensional or three-dimensional space. This transformation is commonly applied to simulate motion, reposition objects or animate scenes in digital environments.

Trimetric projection: Trimetric projection is a type of axonometric projection used in technical and artistic drawing, presenting three-dimensional objects with three mutually inclined axes. Unlike isometric projection, trimetric projection allows for different foreshortening along each axis, providing a more realistic representation of objects in three-dimensional space.

Vectors: In computer graphics, vectors are mathematical entities used to represent various geometric elements such as points, directions and transformations in a three-dimensional space. They play a fundamental role in defining and manipulating graphical objects, enabling precise representation and manipulation of shapes and positions in digital environments.

4.1.2 Historical Evolution

4.1.2.1 2D Graphics

The historical evolution of 2D graphics creation spans several decades, witnessing significant milestones in the development of tools and techniques that have shaped the visual communication and artistic expression of our digital world.

1950s–1960s: The roots of 2D graphics creation can be traced back to the early days of computer graphics in the 1950s and 1960s. Researchers and artists explored ways to create visual representations using early mainframe computers. Basic line drawings and primitive shapes were among the earliest forms of computer-generated graphics.

1960s–1970s: The concept of vector graphics, based on mathematical equations to define shapes, emerged in the 1960s. The development of systems like Sketchpad by Ivan Sutherland in 1963 allowed users to create scalable 2D graphics. Vector graphics laid the foundation for precise and scalable graphic design.

1970s–1980s: The 1970s and 1980s marked the rise of bitmap graphics, where images were represented as grids of pixels. The advent of personal computers and graphical user interfaces (GUIs) brought bitmap-based paint programs and drawing tools to a broader audience. Software like MacPaint on the Apple Macintosh (1984) introduced intuitive interfaces for creating 2D graphics.

1980s–1990s: The desktop publishing revolution in the 1980s, facilitated by software like Adobe Illustrator and Aldus PageMaker, empowered designers to create professional-quality layouts and illustrations. Scalable Vector Graphics (SVG) formats gained prominence, allowing for high-quality graphics that could be resized without loss of detail.

1980s–Present: The graphical user interface (GUI) became a defining feature of personal computers in the 1980s. This era saw the rise of icon design for GUIs, shaping the visual language of digital interfaces. Icons, designed in 2D, became integral to user experience in operating systems and applications. The gaming industry has been a driving force in pushing the boundaries of 2D graphics. From pixel art in early arcade games to the sophisticated 2D graphics of modern games, the medium continues to showcase the creative potential of 2D visual storytelling.

1990s–Present: The 1990s witnessed the proliferation of powerful graphic design software such as Adobe Photoshop and CorelDRAW. These applications provided a comprehensive set of tools for creating and manipulating 2D graphics. Digital artists embraced these tools for illustrations, photo editing and digital painting. With the advent of the World Wide Web in the 1990s, 2D graphics played a crucial role in Web design. Formats like GIF and JPEG became standard for Web images. The evolution of Web standards and the introduction of scalable vector graphics (SVG) contributed to more dynamic and responsive Web graphics.

2000s–Present: The rise of smartphones and mobile apps in the 2000s brought new challenges and opportunities for 2D graphics creation. App icons, user interfaces and interactive elements on mobile devices rely heavily on well-designed 2D graphics. The emphasis on responsive design and high pixel density further influenced the evolution of mobile graphics.

4.1.2.2 3D Graphics

The evolution of 3D graphics creation is a fascinating journey that has transformed visual storytelling, video games, simulations and various industries. A glimpse into the historical development of 3D graphics is given below.

1960s–1970s: The foundations of 3D graphics were laid in the 1960s and 1970s as researchers explored computer-generated imagery. Ivan Sutherland's "Sketchpad" (1963) introduced the concept of interactive computer graphics. Wireframe models, consisting of simple lines and vertices, marked the early attempts at creating three-dimensional visualizations.

1970s–1980s: The 1970s witnessed the development of 3D wireframe modeling techniques. The Utah Teapot, a famous computer graphics model created in 1975 by Martin Newell at the University of Utah, became an iconic symbol of early 3D graphics. Researchers began exploring algorithms for rendering wireframe models, setting the stage for more advanced 3D rendering methods. The 1980s saw advancements in solid modeling techniques, enabling the creation of more realistic 3D objects. Ray-tracing algorithms, developed in 1986, started to simulate the behavior of light, enhancing the realism of rendered scenes.

1980s–1990s: Computer-aided design (CAD) systems played a crucial role in the evolution of 3D graphics during the 1980s and 1990s. These systems were employed for architectural design, industrial modeling and engineering simulations, providing professionals with powerful tools for 3D visualization and analysis. Texture mapping, a technique to apply images or patterns to 3D surfaces, gained popularity which significantly enhanced the visual quality of 3D graphics by adding surface details and realism to rendered objects. The 1990s marked the widespread adoption of polygonal modeling techniques. 3D artists began creating complex models using polygons, and rendering engines evolved to handle more intricate scenes. Video games, in particular, embraced polygonal graphics, leading to the 3D gaming revolution.

1990s–Present: The late 1990s and early 2000s saw the emergence of virtual reality (VR) technologies. 3D graphics played a central role in creating immersive virtual environments for applications ranging from gaming to architectural visualization. The entertainment industry witnessed a significant impact from 3D graphics in the creation of special effects for movies. Blockbusters like "Jurassic Park" (1993) showcased the potential of computer-generated imagery (CGI).

2000s–Present: The 2000s marked a paradigm shift with the widespread adoption of real-time 3D graphics in gaming. Advanced graphics processing units (GPUs) and game engines enabled developers to create visually stunning and immersive gaming experiences.

2010s–Present: The present era is characterized by advancements in global illumination techniques and real-time ray tracing. These technologies enhance the realism of lighting and reflections in 3D scenes, contributing to the cinematic quality of modern video games and visualizations.

4.1.3 Basic Concepts

4.1.3.1 Role of Graphics

The term "graphics", indicates a pictorial representation of some notion or ideas, in the form of a diagram, drawing or portrait. A fundamental characteristic of graphics is that it is a synthetic portrayal, either drawn using pen and paper, or using computer software. This is in contrast with the concept of "image" which is a snapshot of the real world taken using a capture device like a camera. Popular examples of graphics would include diagrams, drawings, sketches, charts, logos, maps, paintings, portraits. It can be either monochrome like pencil sketches or color like maps. However even if color is present, it is usually limited in number, typically less than 50, without too many varying shades, unlike a photograph. These properties enable graphics to be represented inside a computer in a different way compared to images, as we shall presently see (Godse & Godse, 2021).

Graphics is a fundamental element in multimedia, serving several critical roles:

Enhancing communication: Graphics help convey complex information more effectively than text alone. They can simplify concepts, highlight key points and engage the audience.

Visual appeal: High-quality graphics improve the visual appeal of multimedia content, making it more attractive and engaging to users.

Emotion and atmosphere: Graphics can evoke emotions and create specific atmospheres. For example, vibrant colors and lively animations can convey excitement, while muted tones may evoke calmness.

Interactivity: Graphics enable user interaction in multimedia applications, such as video games and interactive simulations.

4.1.3.2 Raster Versus Vector Graphics

Graphics can be categorized into two main types: raster (or bitmap) graphics and vector graphics.

Raster graphics: These are composed of pixels or dots arranged in a grid, just like images. Raster graphics are created when a drawing using conventional media like pen, paper, ink and paint, is subsequently digitized using a scanner or digital camera and stored as a file in a computer. Although it is actually a synthetic drawing, nevertheless it is stored digitally as a collection of pixels, just as a photographic image would be. The file formats used are same as those for images, e.g., BMP, JPG, PNG, GIF. Structurally it is same as an image although content-wise it is artificial or synthetic in contrast to an image which is real.

Vector graphics: The term graphics by default usually indicates an alternative form of graphics called vector graphics which is generated and stored inside a computer using mathematical equations in the form of a collection of points, lines and curves, instead of a collection of pixels. The drawings are not represented as pixel grids but they are broken down to their component lines and curves, which are in turn represented by their equations and stored internally as arrays of numbers. In fact the term vector in mathematics refers to a one-dimensional array of values. File formats like SVG (Scalable Vector Graphics) AI (Adobe Illustrator) and EPS (Encapsulated PostScript) are used to store such numeric arrays. Such representation has advantages compared to images as they can be compact in size and can be scaled to any size without degradation in quality. However the disadvantage is that complex image like photographs cannot be stored effectively, relatively simple drawings using a limited number of colors are ideal for graphics.

4.1.3.3 Components of a Graphics System

Graphics Processing Unit (GPU): The GPU is the workhorse of the graphics system. It specializes in parallel processing, making it well-suited for rendering complex visuals and animations. Modern GPUs are highly specialized and optimized for graphics tasks, offering immense computational power for tasks like shading, rendering and image processing. They often consist of thousands of cores that work in parallel.

Central Processing Unit (CPU): While the GPU handles the heavy lifting in graphics processing, the CPU is responsible for managing the overall system, running applications and initiating rendering tasks. It communicates with the GPU, sending instructions and data for rendering. Effective coordination between the CPU and GPU is essential for smooth graphics performance.

Memory: Graphics systems require significant memory capacity. System RAM stores data related to the application, textures, models and various other graphical assets. The GPU also has its dedicated memory, known as VRAM, where it stores the immediate data required for rendering. Efficient memory management is critical to maintaining high-performance graphics.

Display Device: The display device, such as a computer monitor, projector or head-mounted display, presents the final visual output to the user. The quality and capabilities of the display device significantly influence the overall graphics experience, including factors like resolution, refresh rate, color accuracy and 3D capabilities.

Input Devices: Graphics systems interact with users through various input devices. These can include keyboards, mice, game controllers, touchscreens and stylus pens. Specialized input devices are used in applications like 3D modeling and virtual reality, where precise control is essential.

Software Components: Graphics software components encompass graphics libraries and APIs (Application Programming Interfaces). These libraries, such as OpenGL, DirectX and Vulkan, provide developers with a set of functions and tools to create and manipulate graphics. They abstract the complexity of interacting with hardware, enabling cross-platform compatibility and simplifying the development process. A graphical user interface (GUI) is often part of the graphics system, providing users with a way to interact with the application or system. Effective UI design and integration are essential for user-friendly experiences.

Graphics Drivers: These software components act as intermediaries between the hardware and the operating system. Graphics drivers are essential for proper communication between the operating system, GPU and software applications. They translate high-level instructions from the graphics API into low-level instructions that the GPU can execute.

Rendering Programs: As vector graphics is stored internally as mathematical arrays and values, rendering programs are required to convert these to visual objects, which can then be displayed on a monitor screen. This is called rasterization which means generating the required number of pixels to display the points, lines and curves maintaining their smoothness. Shaders are small programs to control various aspects of the rendering pipeline, such as vertex, fragment and geometry. These programs define how materials, lighting and visual effects are applied to objects in the scene. Shading languages like GLSL (OpenGL Shading Language) and HLSL (High-Level Shading Language) enable developers create intricate patterns of colors and textures. GLSL provides developers with a high-level language for programming shaders, which are small programs executed on the GPU (Graphics Processing Unit) to handle tasks related to lighting, materials and more. HLSL, developed by Microsoft, serves a similar purpose as GLSL but is tailored for integration with the DirectX graphics API, commonly used in Windows-based applications and gaming consoles. Vulkan, introduced by the Khronos Group, stands out as a powerful low-level graphics API designed to provide developers with greater control and performance. Vulkan is often referred to as a low-level graphics API, distinguishing it from higher-level alternatives like OpenGL and DirectX. This low-level nature grants developers a more direct and fine-grained control over the GPU, enabling them to optimize performance for specific hardware configurations. Vulkan hands developers explicit control over GPU resources, such as memory and synchronization, allowing for more efficient management and utilization. Vulkan embraces a multi-threading design, enabling parallel command buffer recording and submission. The rendering pipeline is a series of stages through which graphics data is processed. It includes geometry processing, rasterization, shading and texturing, among others. Understanding and optimizing this pipeline is crucial for achieving efficient and visually appealing graphics (Wong, 2017).

4.1.3.4 2D Graphics Versus 3D Graphics

2D graphics as the name suggests, is two-dimensional; i.e., it is created on a flat plane, using only x and y coordinates. 2D graphics is inherently simpler because it lacks the added dimension of depth, which makes it well-suited for creating straightforward and easy-to-understand visual content. It is commonly found in user interfaces, logos, icons, typography and vector illustrations, and often used in print media, websites and mobile apps, and is ideal for conveying information, brand identity and artistic expression. They can be displayed on a wider range of devices, including older and less powerful hardware, because computationally it is less demanding than 3D graphics.

3D graphics, on the other hand, adds depth to the visual representation, allowing objects to occupy space, as it incorporates an additional dimension, the z-axis, allowing for depth and perspective. This dimensionality provides a sense of realism and depth perception, making it suitable for immersive experiences. 3D graphics excel at creating realistic environments, objects and characters, essential in video games, movies, architectural simulations, product design and scientific visualizations. Creating 3D graphics is significantly more complex than 2D graphics, as it involves modeling, texturing, lighting, camera movements and often complex physics simulations. As a result, 3D graphics demands more advanced software and hardware and is computationally more demanding than 2D graphics. To render 3D graphics in real time, powerful hardware, including dedicated graphics cards (GPUs) and high-performance CPUs are necessary. 3D graphics is the choice for interactive multimedia, as it enables users to explore virtual worlds, manipulate objects and experience simulations in a highly immersive manner.

4.1.3.5 Coordinate Systems

The 2D Cartesian coordinate system, with its x and y axes, known as the primary axes, is fundamental to 2D graphics. It defines points in a plane and enables precise positioning of objects. In a right-handed coordinate system, the thumb of the right hand denotes the positive x-axis and the forefinger the positive y-axis. The angle of rotation around a primary axis is considered positive when in counter-clockwise (CCW) direction when seen from the tip of the axis toward the origin. The two axes divide the plane into four parts called quadrants such that in the first quadrant (Q1) both x and y are positive, in the second quadrant (Q2), x is negative, in the third quadrant (Q3) both are negative, and in the fourth quadrant (Q4), y is negative (Figure 4.1).

The 3D Cartesian coordinate system introduces the third dimension (z-axis) to accurately represent

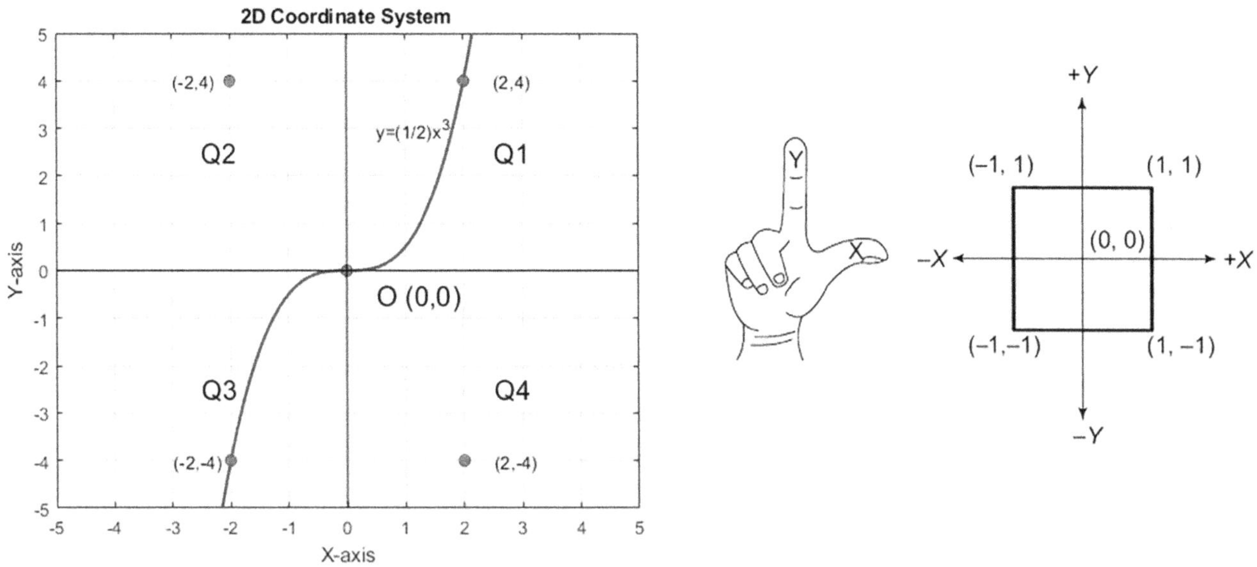

FIGURE 4.1
Right-handed 2D coordinate system.

objects in 3D space. Here, the location of a point is represented by three coordinates measured along three axes x-axis, y-axis and z-axis mutually at right angles or 90°. The three primary axes and the three primary planes meet at the origin O (0, 0, 0). This system is pivotal for defining the position and orientation of objects. The positive directions of the axes are defined using the right-handed rule, which states that if the thumb, the fore-finger and the middle-finger of the right-hand are stretched so that they are mutually at right angles to each other, then the thumb indicates the positive direction of the x-axis, the fore-finger indicates the positive direction of the y-axis and the middle-finger indicates the positive direction of the z-axis. Angles are considered positive when measured in the counter-clockwise (CCW) direction observed from the tip of a primary axis and negative in the clockwise (CW) direction. Along with the three primary axes, there are three primary planes which together divide the coordinate space into eight octants. The $x-y$ plane is located at $z=0$ and divides the space into top and bottom segments, the $y-z$ plane is located at $x=0$ and divides the space into left and right segments, the $x-z$ plane is located at $y=0$ and divides the space into front and rear segments (O'Rourke, 2003) (Figure 4.2).

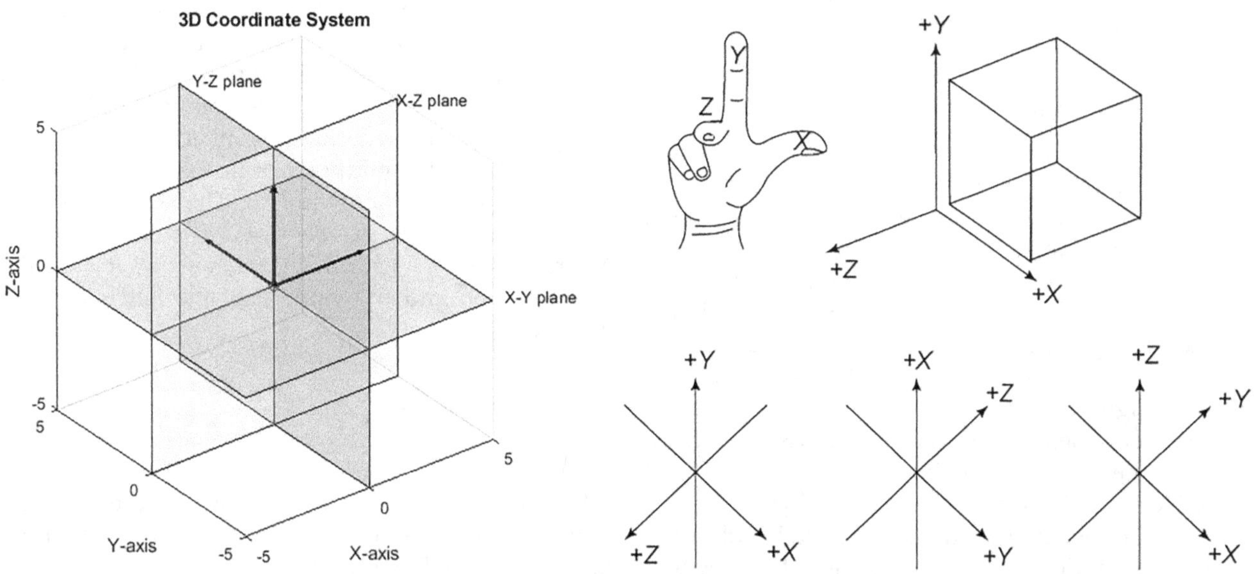

FIGURE 4.2
Right-handed 3D coordinate system.

4.2 2D Graphics

4.2.1 Basic Structures

A point is the most basic geometrical structure in graphics which indicates simply a position without any dimensions. If a point is moved along one direction then the trace is called a straight line, which has a single dimension length and is essentially a series of dots joined together. When a line moves perpendicular to itself a two-dimensional structure called plane is generated which has length and width, and which represents a series of lines joined together. Alternatively a plane can be formed by joining three different non co-linear points, in the form of a triangle, each point being called a vertex. Triangles can be joined together along edges to form polygons. A grid of polygons defines a mesh. The topology of a mesh determines the number of edges and vertices. In graphics, these basic structures are represented by their equations and matrix of values, and sometimes referred to as primitives as they can be combined together to form more complex structures.

A point is displayed on a visual display system by switching on/off a monitor pixel. To display a line or circle however needs certain amount of computations. As mentioned previously, before being displayed on the screen, the graphics system needs to convert the mathematical entities into a collection of pixels. For this it needs to execute certain algorithms to decide which dots need to be generated in which locations. The situation is complicated by the fact that since the screen pixels form a rectangular grid, a dot cannot be placed anywhere but has to comply with the grid structure. The algorithms discussed below attempt to find out the optimum locations of generating dots for specific figure line lines, circles etc.

4.2.2 Drawing Algorithms

A fundamental aspect of computer graphics is the precise representation of geometric shapes and the efficient rendering of these shapes on a display screen. Line drawing algorithms are the foundations of many applications responsible for rendering straight lines between given points. Circle drawing algorithms extend these principles for creation of smooth circular shapes, especially required for the fields of computer aided design and manufacturing. Filling algorithms are required when the internal area of a defined shape needs to be filled with colors. Clipping algorithms optimize graphics display on screen by selectively rendering only those portions which fall within the visible boundaries of the screens (Foley et al., 1990).

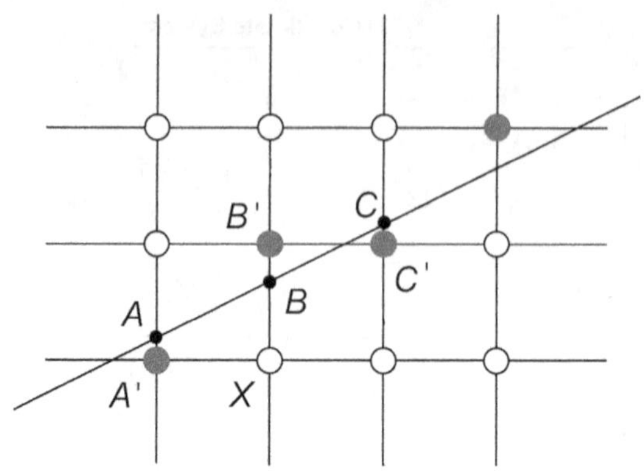

FIGURE 4.3
Incremental line algorithm.

4.2.2.1 *Incremental Line Algorithm*

The method uses the line equation $y = mx + c$ where m is the slope and c the intercept. The drawing process starts from an initial point (x_0, y_0) and computes the next point (x_1, y_1) as a function of the previous point.

$$y_1 = mx_1 + c = m(x_0 + \Delta x) + c = y_0 + m.\Delta x$$

If $\Delta x = 1$, then $y_1 = y_0 + m$. This value is rounded to the nearest integer to correspond to the rectangular pixel grid. This process is repeated until all the pixels have been drawn (Figure 4.3).

4.2.2.2 *Bresenham's Line Algorithm*

A drawback of the incremental line algorithm is the need for rounding off which makes the process slow. The midpoint algorithm by Bresenham uses only integer arithmetic thereby avoiding the rounding off operation. In this case the routine is initiated from a starting point (x_0, y_0) and the next point (x_1, y_1) is to be computed. From the figure possible candidates are A or B. Let M be the midpoint of line AB and N be the intersection of the line with AB. The equation of the line is expressed as: $ax + by + c = 0$. The coordinates of M are $(x_0 + 1, y_0 + 0.5)$ which are substituted into the line equation and the value P of the left hand side computed, i.e.,

$$P = a(x_0 + 1) + b\left(y_0 + \frac{1}{2}\right) + c$$

If $P < 0$, then the line passes below M and the nearest point is A. If $P > 0$, the line passes above M, and the nearest point is B (Figure 4.4).

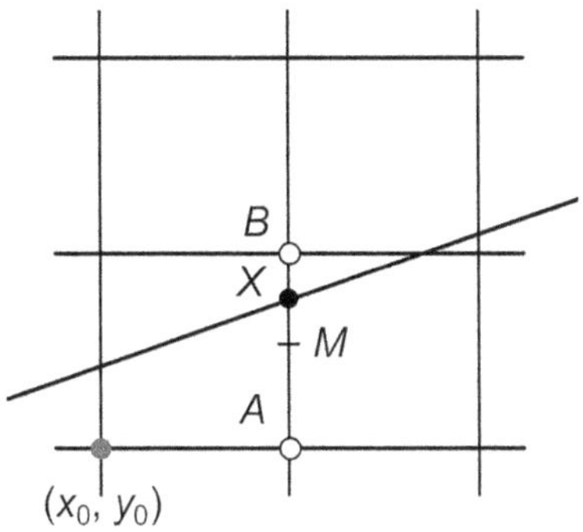

FIGURE 4.4
Bresenham's line algorithm.

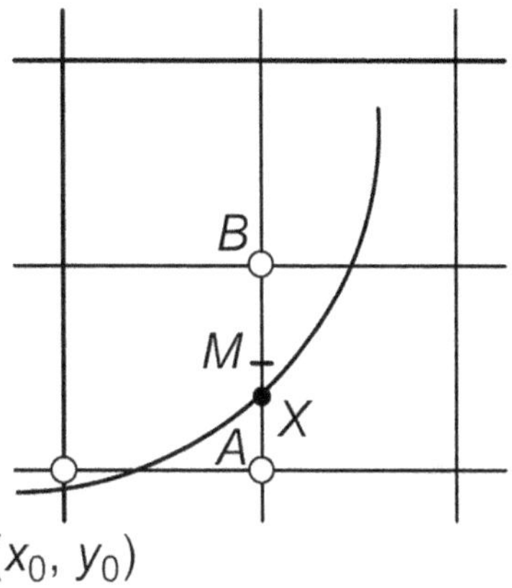

FIGURE 4.6
Midpoint circle algorithm.

4.2.2.3 *Eight-Point Circle Algorithms*

If (a,b) is a point on a circle $x^2 + y^2 = r^2$, with center at the origin, then 7 other points on the circle can be computed trivially, namely, $(a,-b),(-a,b),(-a,-b),(b,a)$, $(b,-a),(-b,a),(-b,-a)$. This process can be repeated for all points on a quarter segment of the circle whereupon all points on the circle will be obtained. Circles not centered on the origin can be translated to the origin (Figure 4.5).

4.2.2.4 *Midpoint Circle Algorithm*

Similar to the midpoint line algorithm, the strategy is to select which of the two pixels is closer to the circle by evaluating a function at the midpoint between the two pixels. Given the center of the circle at coordinates (x_c, y_c) and its radius 'r', we start at the top-most point on the circle, which is $(x_c, y_c + r)$. This is the initial point to be plotted. If (x_0, y_0) is a point already chosen on the circle it is required to find out which of the two A or B should be the next point. If M $(x_0 + 1, y_0 + 0.5)$ be the midpoint of the line segment AB then the strategy is to test the value of the expression $P = (x_0 + 1)^2 + (y_0 + 0.5)^2 - r^2$. If $P < 0$ it implies M is inside the circle and so A should be the nearest point. If $P > 0$ it implies M is outside the circle and so B should be the nearest point (Figure 4.6).

4.2.2.5 *Filling Algorithms*

Filling algorithms are used to paint or render the interior of regions efficiently. Several well-known filling algorithms include the flood fill, boundary fill and scanline fill algorithms. The Flood Fill algorithm, for example, starts by selecting a seed point within the closed area to be filled and recursively "floods" the neighboring pixels with the chosen color until a boundary is reached. The Boundary Fill algorithm, in contrast, fills an area between specified boundaries. The Scanline Fill algorithm divides the polygon into horizontal lines and fills each line individually by determining the intersections of the scanline with polygon edges using the odd parity rule. Starting with an initial even parity, as each edge is encountered parity is reversed. The rule is to draw when parity is odd and inhibit drawing when parity is even (Figure 4.7).

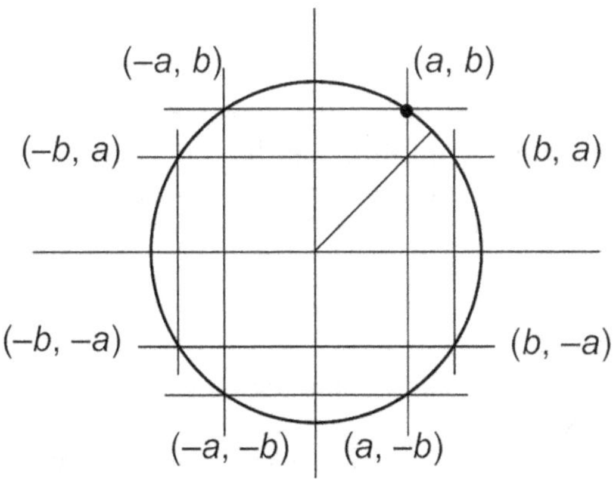

FIGURE 4.5
Eight point circle algorithm.

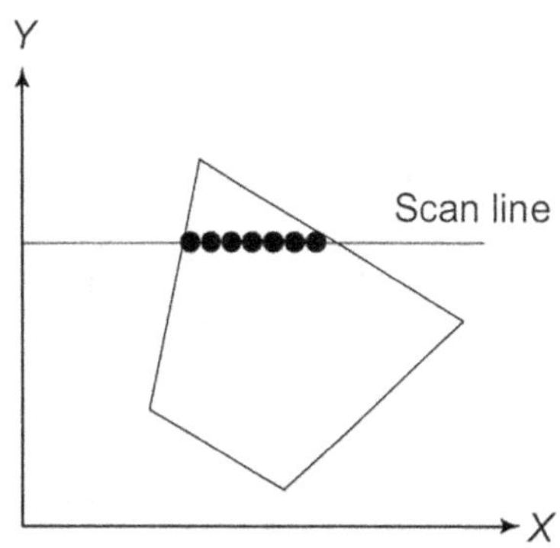

FIGURE 4.7
Filling algorithm.

4.2.2.6 *Clipping Algorithms*

Clipping algorithms are fundamental tools used to determine which parts of an object or scene should be displayed on a screen or in a rendering, discarding portions that fall outside a specified region or viewport. These algorithms enable the efficient culling of objects or parts of objects that are not visible, thereby saving computational resources (Hearn & Baker, 1996). The basic strategy is to define a rectangular viewport or clipping window that represents the visible portion of the graphics display. This window is typically specified by two diagonal corner points, (x_{min}, y_{min}) and (x_{max}, y_{max}).

The Cohen-Sutherland algorithm is a widely used and efficient method for clipping lines against a rectangular viewing window or viewport. It classifies line segments and quickly identifies and discards those entirely outside the viewport, greatly optimizing the rendering process. For a point (x, y) to be inside the clip rectangle, the following four inequalities should be satisfied:

$$x_{min} \leq x \leq x_{max}$$

$$y_{min} \leq y \leq y_{max}$$

If any of the four inequalities does not hold, the point is outside the rectangle. If both endpoints of a line lie inside the clip rectangle, the entire line can be trivially accepted to be lying inside the rectangle. If one endpoint lies inside and the other lies outside the rectangle, we must compute the intersection point. If both endpoints are outside, the line may or may not intersect with the rectangle, and we need to perform further calculations to determine whether there are any intersections (Figure 4.8).

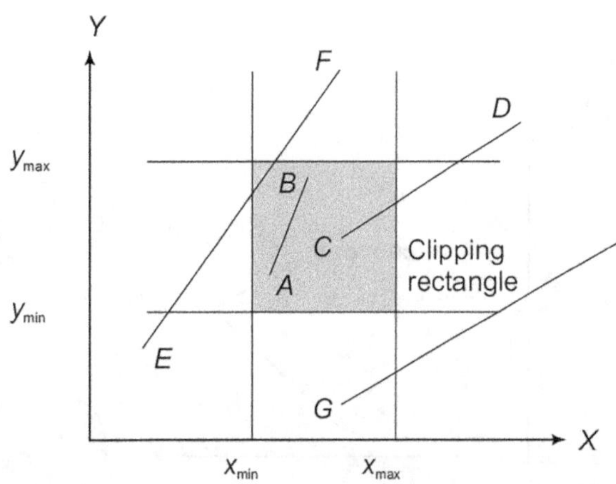

FIGURE 4.8
Clipping algorithm.

4.2.3 2D Transformations

Changing the location, orientation and size of graphic objects is called transformations. These involve changing the coordinates of a set of points on a 2D plane in accordance with certain specified relations which define the type of transformation as translation, rotation, scaling, reflection or shear or a combination of some or all of these operations. Below we discuss mathematical principles and transformation matrices used to implement these within algorithms (Hearn & Baker, 1996).

4.2.3.1 *Translation*

Translation involves moving objects from one location to another in the 2D plane. A point $P(x_1, y_1)$ can be moved to a new point $Q(x_2, y_2)$ by adding offsets $t_x = x_2 - x_1$ and $t_y = y_2 - y_1$ to its coordinates. If an offset is positive, then the movement is toward the positive direction of the axis; likewise, if an offset is negative, then the movement is toward the negative direction of the axis. The new coordinates (x_2, y_2) can be derived from the original coordinates (x_1, y_1) as below:

$$x_2 = x_1 + t_x$$

$$y_2 = y_1 + t_y$$

4.2.3.2 *Rotation*

Rotation involves changing the orientation of points. Let point $P(x_1, y_1)$ can be rotated by angle θ about the origin in the counter-clockwise direction to a new point $Q(x_2, y_2)$. The new coordinates (x_2, y_2) can be derived from the original coordinates (x_1, y_1) as below:

$$x_2 = x_1.\cos\theta - y_1.\sin\theta$$

$$y_2 = x_1.\sin\theta + y_1.\cos\theta$$

4.2.3.3 *Scaling*

Scaling involves changing the size of a graphic object. This is done by multiplying the coordinates of points by a scalar quantity. If s_x and s_y be the scaling multipliers along the x and y directions then:

$$x_2 = s_x.x_1$$

$$y_2 = s_y.y_1$$

If $s_x = s_y$ then the scaling is called uniform, otherwise non-uniform. If their values are greater than 1, then it results in increase in size, if the values are less than 1 then it results in decrease in size.

4.2.3.4 Reflection

Reflection transforms objects by flipping them across a mirror line. It reverses the sign of the coordinate perpendicular to the mirror while keeping the other coordinate unchanged. If reflection is about the x-axis then the y-coordinate is reversed as shown below:

$$x_2 = x_1$$

$$y_2 = -y_1$$

If reflection is about the y-axis then the x-coordinate is reversed:

$$x_2 = -x_1$$

$$y_2 = y_1$$

A reflection can also take place about the origin in which case both the $x-$ and $y-$ coordinates gets reversed.

$$x_2 = -x_1$$

$$y_2 = -y_1$$

4.2.3.5 Shear

A shear operation distorts a graphic object by changing one set of coordinates proportional to the other coordinate and keeping other values constant (Chakraborty, 2010). A shear can be along either x or y direction. For an x-direction shear, the x-coordinates of a point is shifted by an amount proportional to its y -coordinate, while the actual y-coordinate remains unchanged, as shown below, where h_x is a constant of proportionality:

$$x_2 = x_1 + h_x.y_1$$

$$y_2 = y_1$$

For a y-direction shear, the y-coordinates of a point is shifted by an amount proportional to its x-coordinate, while the actual x-coordinate remains unchanged, as shown below, where h_y is a constant of proportionality (Figure 4.9):

$$y_2 = y_1 + h_y.x_1$$

$$x_2 = x_1$$

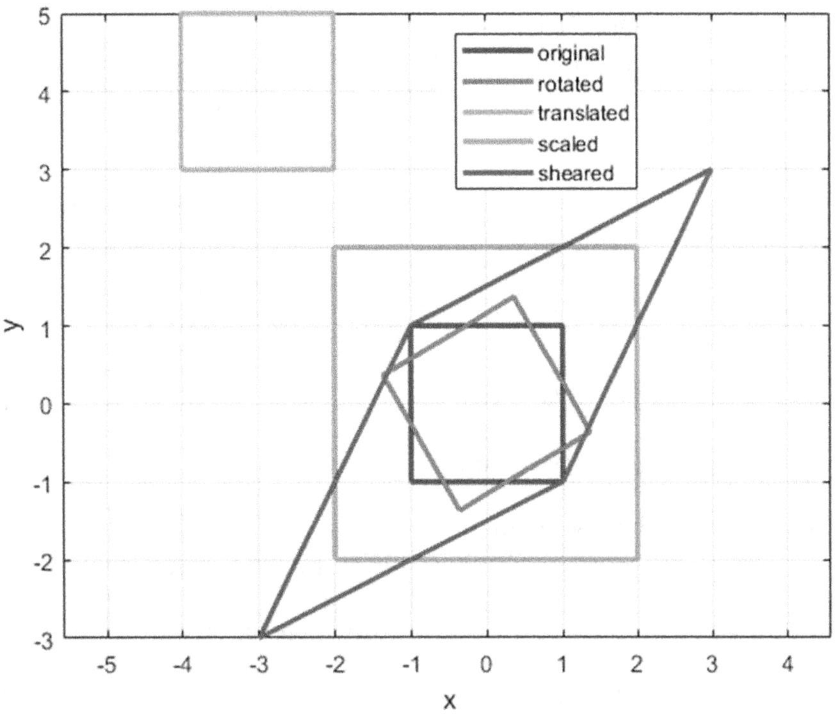

FIGURE 4.9
2D transformations: translation, scaling, rotation.

4.2.3.6 *Homogeneous Coordinates*

When multiple transformation operations are to be performed one after another, then a different form of the transformation equations are more convenient. This is called homogeneous coordinates, and its advantage is that it provides us with a multiplicative form of a transformation matrix for all operations. This allows individual matrices to be multiplied with each other arriving at the final result in one step instead of calculating intermediate results at each step. Another advantage is that a reverse transformation can be calculated by calculating the inverse of the transformation matrix. Homogeneous coordinates of (x, y, h) implies Cartesian coordinates of $(x/h, y/h)$. In most cases $h = 1$, so the values are equal, but in some cases if $h \neq 1$, then a conversion from one system to another will be necessary.

The homogeneous transformation matrix for the translation operation is shown below, where the third row is included to generate a square matrix and is typically ignored after the new coordinates are calculated.

$$\begin{pmatrix} x_2 \\ y_2 \\ 1 \end{pmatrix} = \begin{pmatrix} 1 & 0 & t_x \\ 0 & 1 & t_y \\ 0 & 0 & 1 \end{pmatrix} \begin{pmatrix} x_1 \\ y_1 \\ 1 \end{pmatrix}$$

Symbolically, if $T(t_x, t_y)$ denotes the homogeneous forward translation matrix, then

$Q(x_2, y_2) = T(t_x, t_y).P(x_1, y_1)$ or simply $Q = T.P$

If $T' = inv(T)$ or T^{-1} denote the inverse translation, it can be shown that:

$$T' = T(-t_x, -t_y)$$

The matrix notation for the rotation operation is:

$$\begin{pmatrix} x_2 \\ y_2 \\ 1 \end{pmatrix} = \begin{pmatrix} \cos\theta & -\sin\theta & 0 \\ \sin\theta & \cos\theta & 0 \\ 0 & 0 & 1 \end{pmatrix} \begin{pmatrix} x_1 \\ y_1 \\ 1 \end{pmatrix}$$

Symbolically, $Q(x_2, y_2) = R(\theta).P(x_1, y_1)$ or simply $Q = R.P$

If $R' = inv(R)$ or R^{-1} denote the inverse rotation, it can be shown that:

$$R' = R(-\theta)$$

The matrix notation for the scaling operation is:

$$\begin{pmatrix} x_2 \\ y_2 \\ 1 \end{pmatrix} = \begin{pmatrix} s_x & 0 & 0 \\ 0 & s_y & 0 \\ 0 & 0 & 1 \end{pmatrix} \begin{pmatrix} x_1 \\ y_1 \\ 1 \end{pmatrix}$$

Symbolically, $Q(x_2, y_2) = S(s_x, s_y).P(x_1, y_1)$ or simply $Q = S.P$

If $S' = inv(S)$ or S^{-1} denotes the inverse scaling then it can be shown that:

$$S' = S(1/s_x, 1/s_y)$$

Similarly the transformation matrixes for reflection across the x-axis and y-axis and about the origin are respectively:

$$F_x = \begin{pmatrix} 1 & 0 & 0 \\ 0 & -1 & 0 \\ 0 & 0 & 1 \end{pmatrix}$$

$$F_y = \begin{pmatrix} -1 & 0 & 0 \\ 0 & 1 & 0 \\ 0 & 0 & 1 \end{pmatrix}$$

$$F_o = \begin{pmatrix} -1 & 0 & 0 \\ 0 & -1 & 0 \\ 0 & 0 & 1 \end{pmatrix}$$

Also the transformation matrixes for shear along the x-axis and y-axis are respectively:

$$H_x = \begin{pmatrix} 1 & h_x & 0 \\ 0 & 1 & 0 \\ 0 & 0 & 1 \end{pmatrix}$$

$$H_y = \begin{pmatrix} 1 & 0 & 0 \\ h_y & 1 & 0 \\ 0 & 0 & 1 \end{pmatrix}$$

4.2.3.7 *Fixed Point Rotation*

A fixed point rotation is where rotation occurs about an arbitrary fixed point $F(x_f, y_f)$ instead of the origin. In this case the steps to be followed are:

(1) Apply translation so that the fixed point moves to the origin i.e. : $T_1 = T(0 - x_f, 0 - y_f)$

(2) Apply rotation about the origin i.e. $R(\theta)$

(3) Apply reverse translation to move the fixed point back to its original location i.e $T(x_f - 0, y_f - 0)$

(4) Compute composite transformation : $M = T(x_f, y_f).R(\theta).T(-x_f, -y_f)$

4.2.3.8 Fixed Point Scaling

A fixed point scaling is where scaling occurs about an arbitrary fixed point $F(x_f, y_f)$ instead of the origin. In this case the steps to be followed are:

(1) Apply translation so that the fixed point moves to the origin i.e. $T(0 - x_f, 0 - y_f)$

(2) Apply scaling about the origin i.e. $S(s_x, s_y)$

(3) Apply reverse translation to move the fixed point back to its original location i.e $T(x_f - 0, y_f - 0)$

(4) Compute composite transformation : $M = T(x_f, y_f).S(s_x, s_y).T(-x_f, -y_f)$

4.2.3.9 Fixed Line Reflection

A fixed line reflection is where reflection takes place across an arbitrary fixed line with equation $y = mx + c$ instead of a primary axis. The steps to compute the transformation matrix of reflection are (Figure 4.10):

(1) Intercept point of line with y–axis is $(0, c)$. Translate point to origin: $T(0, -c)$

(2) Rotate line about origin by angle $-\theta$ where θ = arctan (m): $R(-\theta)$

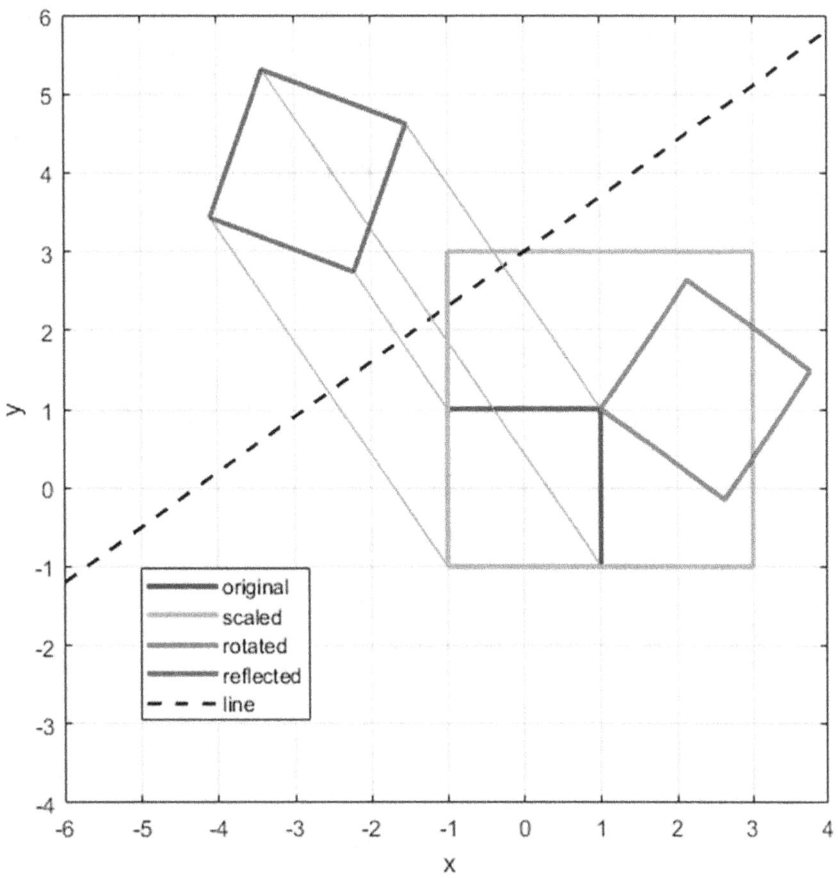

FIGURE 4.10
Fixed point scaling, rotation and fixed line reflection.

(3) Apply Reflection across x –axis: F_x
(4) Reverse rotate around x –axis: $R(\theta)$
(5) Reverse translate to intercept point to original location: $T(0,c)$
(6) Calculate composite transformation: $M = T(0,c).R(\theta).F_x.R(-\theta).T(0,-c)$

4.2.3.10 Affine vs. Perspective Transformations

A composite transformation involving a combination of translation, rotation, scaling and shear is referred to as affine transformation (Hearn & Baker, 1996; Shirley, 2002). An affine transformation preserves the following property: if P was an arbitrary point located on the line segment joining endpoints A and B before the transformation, then after the transformation the transformed point P' will still be located on the line segment joining the transformed endpoints A' and B'. In general, a rectangle under affine transformation will be converted to a parallelogram. Composite transformation is calculated as follows:

$$M = T.S.R.H = \begin{pmatrix} a & b & c \\ d & e & f \\ 0 & 0 & 1 \end{pmatrix}$$

Under affine transformation, the transformed coordinates x', y' of a point are related to the original coordinates x, y by the general relation of the form:

$$\begin{pmatrix} x' \\ y' \\ 1 \end{pmatrix} = \begin{pmatrix} a & b & c \\ d & e & f \\ 0 & 0 & 1 \end{pmatrix} \begin{pmatrix} x \\ y \\ 1 \end{pmatrix}$$

This implies:

$$x' = ax + by + c$$

$$y' = dx + ey + f$$

Reflection can also be added to the set of transformations, which will simply change the sign of some of the coefficients depending on the type of reflection. During this transformation, a set of constraints are applied, which converts a rectangle into a parallelogram.

However if the constraints are not applied, then a rectangle will be converted to an arbitrary quadrilateral and the corresponding transformation does not remain affine any more (Rovenski, 2010). The new transformation is called a perspective (or projective) transformation and is described by the transformation matrix shown below (Figure 4.11):

$$\begin{pmatrix} x' \\ y' \\ w \end{pmatrix} = \begin{pmatrix} a & b & c \\ d & e & f \\ g & h & 1 \end{pmatrix} \begin{pmatrix} x \\ y \\ 1 \end{pmatrix}$$

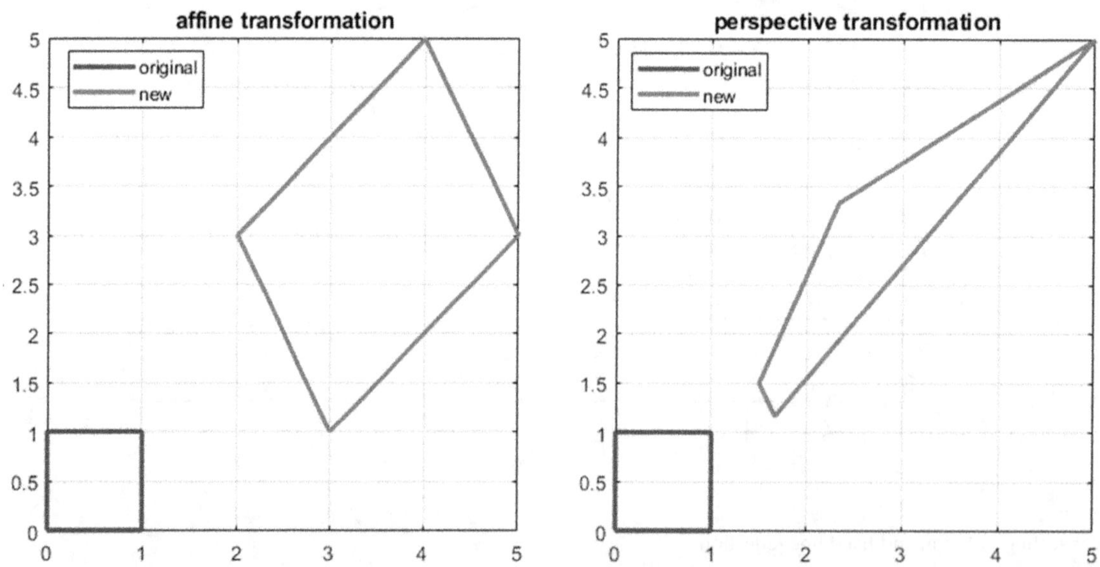

FIGURE 4.11
Affine and perspective transformations.

Here x' and y' are in homogeneous coordinates. The Cartesian coordinates are:

$$X = \frac{x'}{w} = \frac{ax + by + c}{gx + hy + 1}$$

$$Y = \frac{y'}{w} = \frac{dx + ey + f}{gx + hy + 1}$$

4.2.4 Overview of Splines

While lines, circles, ellipses have regular shapes, in major cases curves need to be generated which have irregular shapes, e.g., to indicate a shape or path of a moving object. Based on the coordinates of some of the points on the curves, or slopes of lines along the curves, the graphics system needs to calculate a mathematical representation of these curves. The term "spline" has been derived from the ship building industry where it is used to refer to wooden planks bent between wooden posts for building the curved hull of ships. The location of the fixed posts controls the shape of the plank. In graphics, specific points along the spline curve are used to control the shape of the spline and hence they are aptly referred to as "control points" shortened as CPs. Depending on the relationship between the CPs and the actual curves, the splines can be broadly categorized into three types: (1) interpolating splines, where the spline actually goes through the CPs; (2) approximating splines, where the spline goes near the CPs but not actually through them; and (3) hybrid splines, where the spline goes through some of the CPs but not through all (O'Rourke, 2003; Hearn & Baker, 1996) (Figure 4.12).

Splines are mathematically modeled using polynomials. Polynomials are expressions constructed from variables and constants, and involve addition, subtraction, multiplication and non-negative integer exponents. A polynomial can be 0 (zero) or a sum of non-zero terms. Each term consists of a constant, called coefficient, multiplied by a variable. The exponent of the variable is called its degree. The general n-th degree polynomial is shown below:

$$a_n x^n + a_{n-1} x^{n-1} + \ldots + a_1 x + a_0$$

Each term consists of a constant, called the coefficient, multiplied by a variable, which may be raised to a non-negative integer exponent, called the degree of the variable.

A polynomial equation is: written when one polynomial is set equal to another. It can either be in explicit form, e.g., $y = f(x)$ when either side of the equation contains variables of explicit type, [e.g. $y = x^2$] or it can be in implicit form, e.g., $f(x,y) = 0$ where multiple types of variables can be on the same side [e.g. $x^2 + y^2 - 5xy = 0$]. Polynomial equations can also be represented in parametric form where the variables are expressed as functions of another variable t, e.g., $x = f(t), y = g(t)$. As a convention, the value of t is

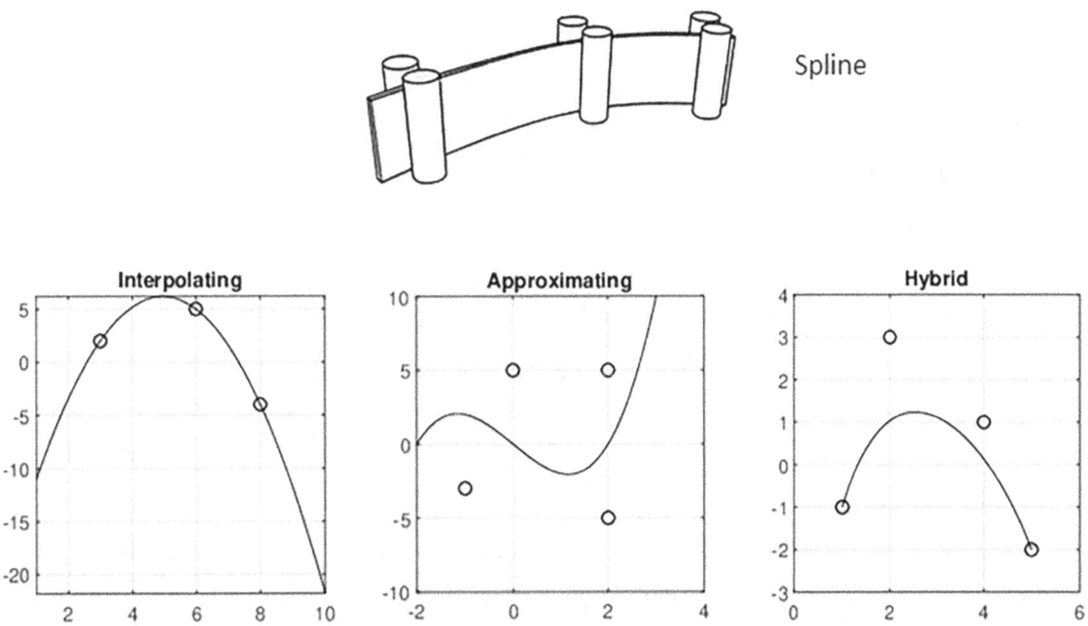

FIGURE 4.12
Types of splines.

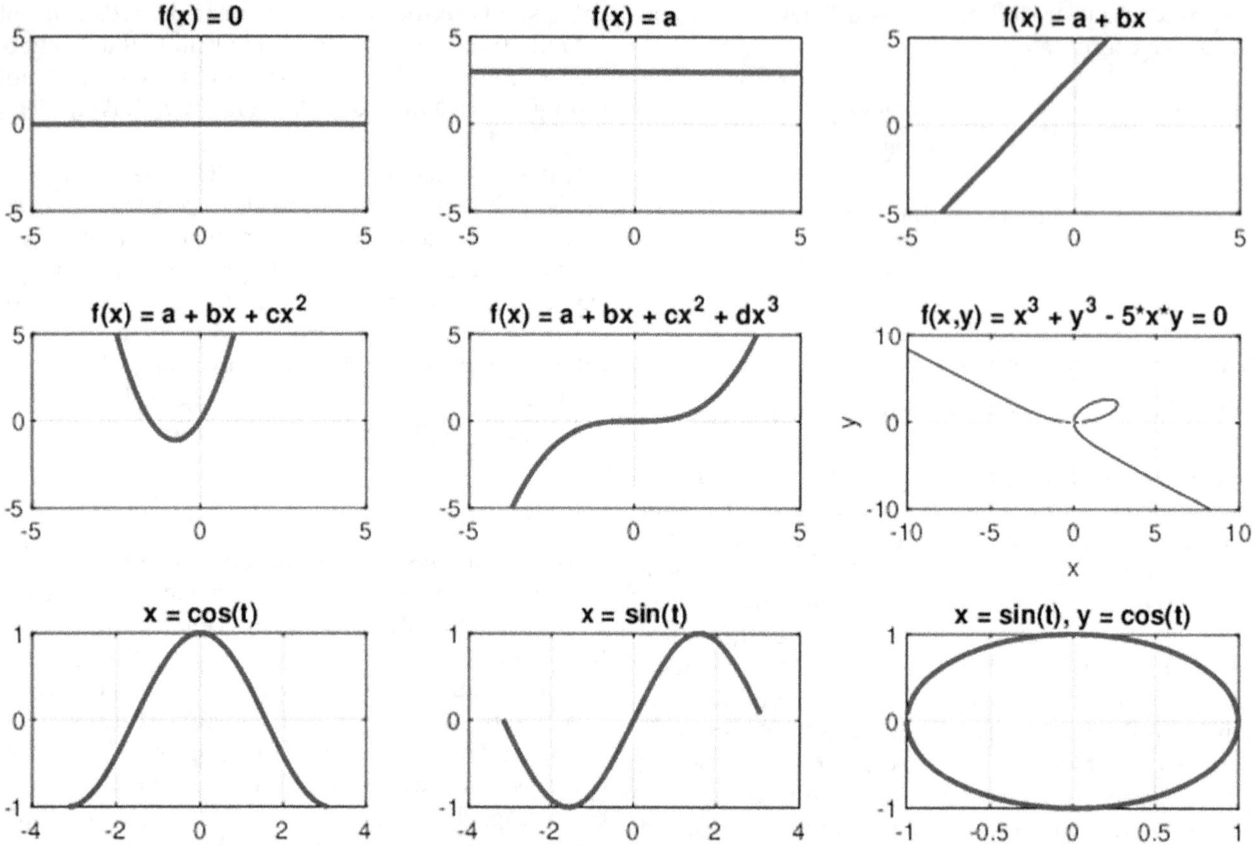

FIGURE 4.13
Graphs of polynomials.

usually taken to lie between 0 and 1 unless otherwise specified. The value of $t = 0$ corresponds to the start point and $t = 1$ to the end point of the spline curve. As an example the parametric equation of a circle with radius r is: $x = r.\sin t, y = r.\cos t$ (Figure 4.13).

4.2.5 Interpolating Spline

4.2.5.1 *Linear Interpolating Spline*

A linear spline is a straight line represented by a first-degree polynomial and can be generated given two points are known along it. Standard form of a linear spline implies the spline equation is: computed in the spatial domain, i.e., the $x - y$ plane. Let the given points be P_1 (x_1, y_1) and P_2 (x_2, y_2). Choosing a starting linear equation and writing it in matrix form we have:

$$y = a + bx = \begin{pmatrix} 1 & x \end{pmatrix} \begin{pmatrix} a \\ b \end{pmatrix} = X.A$$

Substituting the given points, we get a matrix equation of the form $Y = C.A$, where C is called the constraint matrix and A is called the coefficient matrix:

$$\begin{pmatrix} y_1 \\ y_2 \end{pmatrix} = \begin{pmatrix} 1 & x_1 \\ 1 & x_2 \end{pmatrix} \begin{pmatrix} a \\ b \end{pmatrix}$$

The equations are solved to find the unknown coefficients, namely, $A = inv(C) * Y$:

$$\begin{pmatrix} a \\ b \end{pmatrix} = \begin{pmatrix} 1 & x_1 \\ 1 & x_2 \end{pmatrix}^{-1} \begin{pmatrix} y_1 \\ y_2 \end{pmatrix}$$

The values of the coefficients are substituted in the starting equation to arrive at the equation of the spline (Figure 4.14).

$$y = \begin{pmatrix} 1 & x \end{pmatrix} \begin{pmatrix} 1 & x_1 \\ 1 & x_2 \end{pmatrix}^{-1} \begin{pmatrix} y_1 \\ y_2 \end{pmatrix}$$

4.2.5.2 *Quadratic Interpolating Spline*

A quadratic spline is a parabolic curve represented by a second-degree polynomial equation and can be generated if at least three points are known along the

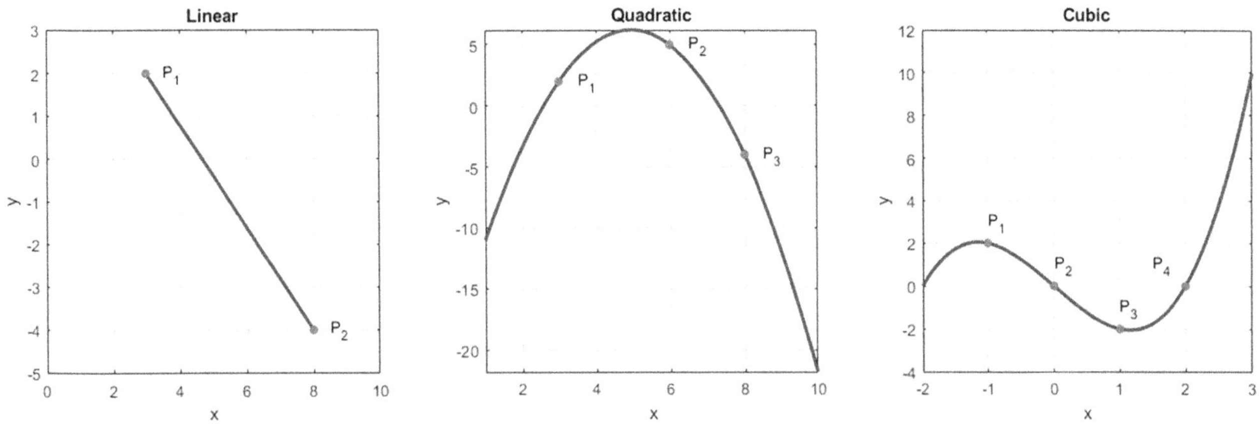

FIGURE 4.14
Interpolating splines: linear, quadratic, cubic.

curve. Let the three known points be P_1 (x_1, y_1), P_2 (x_2, y_2) and P_3 (x_3, y_3). Choosing a starting quadratic equation and writing it in matrix form we have:

$$y = a + bx + cx^2 = \begin{pmatrix} 1 & x & x^2 \end{pmatrix} \begin{pmatrix} a \\ b \\ c \end{pmatrix}$$

As before the three equations can be written in matrix form $Y = C.A$

$$\begin{pmatrix} y_1 \\ y_2 \\ y_3 \end{pmatrix} = \begin{pmatrix} 1 & x_1 & x_1^2 \\ 1 & x_2 & x_2^2 \\ 1 & x_3 & x_3^2 \end{pmatrix} \begin{pmatrix} a \\ b \\ c \end{pmatrix}$$

The equations are solved to find the values of the coefficients: $A = inv(C) * Y$

$$\begin{pmatrix} a \\ b \\ c \end{pmatrix} = \begin{pmatrix} 1 & x_1 & x_1^2 \\ 1 & x_2 & x_2^2 \\ 1 & x_3 & x_3^2 \end{pmatrix}^{-1} \begin{pmatrix} y_1 \\ y_2 \\ y_3 \end{pmatrix}$$

Substituting the coefficients in the starting equation we arrive at the equation of the spline

$$y = \begin{pmatrix} 1 & x & x^2 \end{pmatrix} \begin{pmatrix} 1 & x_1 & x_1^2 \\ 1 & x_2 & x_2^2 \\ 1 & x_3 & x_3^2 \end{pmatrix}^{-1} \begin{pmatrix} y_1 \\ y_2 \\ y_3 \end{pmatrix}$$

4.2.5.3 Cubic Interpolating Spline

A cubic spline is an S-shaped curve represented by a third-degree polynomial equation and can be generated if at least four points are known along the curve. Let the four known points be P_1 (x_1, y_1), P_2 (x_2, y_2), P_3 (x_3, y_3) and P_4 (x_4, y_4). Choosing a starting cubic equation and writing it in matrix form we have:

$$y = a + bx + cx^2 + dx^3 = \begin{pmatrix} 1 & x & x^2 & x^3 \end{pmatrix} \begin{pmatrix} a \\ b \\ c \\ d \end{pmatrix}$$

As before the four equations can be written in matrix form: $Y = C.A$

$$\begin{pmatrix} y_1 \\ y_2 \\ y_3 \\ y_4 \end{pmatrix} = \begin{pmatrix} 1 & x_1 & x_1^2 & x_1^3 \\ 1 & x_2 & x_2^2 & x_2^3 \\ 1 & x_3 & x_3^2 & x_3^3 \\ 1 & x_4 & x_4^2 & x_4^3 \end{pmatrix} \begin{pmatrix} a \\ b \\ c \\ d \end{pmatrix}$$

The equations are solved to find the values of the coefficients: $A = inv(C) * Y$

$$\begin{pmatrix} a \\ b \\ c \\ d \end{pmatrix} = \begin{pmatrix} 1 & x_1 & x_1^2 & x_1^3 \\ 1 & x_2 & x_2^2 & x_2^3 \\ 1 & x_3 & x_3^2 & x_3^3 \\ 1 & x_4 & x_4^2 & x_4^3 \end{pmatrix}^{-1} \begin{pmatrix} y_1 \\ y_2 \\ y_3 \\ y_4 \end{pmatrix}$$

Substituting the coefficients in the starting equation we arrive at the equation of the spline:

$$y = \begin{pmatrix} 1 & x & x^2 & x^3 \end{pmatrix} \begin{pmatrix} 1 & x_1 & x_1^2 & x_1^3 \\ 1 & x_2 & x_2^2 & x_2^3 \\ 1 & x_3 & x_3^2 & x_3^3 \\ 1 & x_4 & x_4^2 & x_4^3 \end{pmatrix}^{-1} \begin{pmatrix} y_1 \\ y_2 \\ y_3 \\ y_4 \end{pmatrix}$$

4.2.5.4 Parametric Form of Representation

Any spline can also be represented using parametric equation of the form $P(t)$ shown below. To derive the parametric equation of a cubic spline, let it pass through four known points P_0 (x_0, y_0), P_1 (x_1, y_1), P_2 (x_2, y_2), P_3 (x_3, y_3). As per conventions mentioned before, the first point corresponds to the point where $t = 0$ and the last point corresponds to $t = 1$, i.e., $P_0 \equiv P(0)$ and $P_3 \equiv P(1)$. To determine the curve uniquely two additional pieces of information are required regarding the value of parameter t at the middle points P_1 and P_2. Let these values of t be m and n, where $0 \le m, n \le 1$, i.e., $P_1 \equiv P(m)$ and $P_2 \equiv P(n)$. Different values of m and n will give rise to curves with the same start and end points but having different shapes.

Choose starting cubic parametric equation written in matrix form

$$P(t) = a + bt + ct^2 + dt^3 = \begin{pmatrix} 1 & t & t^2 & t^3 \end{pmatrix} \begin{pmatrix} a \\ b \\ c \\ d \end{pmatrix} = T.A$$

Substitute the given points in the starting equation by choosing $t = 0$ at start, $t = m, n$ at the middle points, and $t = 1$ at end. Combine the four equations into matrix form $G = C.A$ where G is called the geometry matrix.

$$\begin{pmatrix} P_0 \\ P_1 \\ P_2 \\ P_2 \end{pmatrix} = \begin{pmatrix} 1 & 0 & 0 & 0 \\ 1 & m & m^2 & m^3 \\ 1 & n & n^2 & n^3 \\ 1 & 1 & 1 & 1 \end{pmatrix} \begin{pmatrix} a \\ b \\ c \\ d \end{pmatrix}$$

Solving for A: $A = inv(C).G = B.G$ where B is called the basis matrix.

$$\begin{pmatrix} a \\ b \\ c \\ d \end{pmatrix} = \begin{pmatrix} 1 & 0 & 0 & 0 \\ 1 & m & m^2 & m^3 \\ 1 & n & n^2 & n^3 \\ 1 & 1 & 1 & 1 \end{pmatrix}^{-1} \begin{pmatrix} P_0 \\ P_1 \\ P_2 \\ P_3 \end{pmatrix}$$

Substitute the coefficient values in the starting equation.

$$P(t) = \begin{pmatrix} 1 & t & t^2 & t^3 \end{pmatrix} \begin{pmatrix} 1 & 0 & 0 & 0 \\ 1 & m & m^2 & m^3 \\ 1 & n & n^2 & n^3 \\ 1 & 1 & 1 & 1 \end{pmatrix}^{-1} \begin{pmatrix} P_0 \\ P_1 \\ P_2 \\ P_3 \end{pmatrix}$$

Finally, separate out the x and y components of the equation keeping in mind that P_0 (x_0, y_0), P_1 (x_1, y_1) and so on (Figure 4.15).

$$x(t) = \begin{pmatrix} 1 & t & t^2 & t^3 \end{pmatrix} \begin{pmatrix} 1 & 0 & 0 & 0 \\ 1 & m & m^2 & m^3 \\ 1 & n & n^2 & n^3 \\ 1 & 1 & 1 & 1 \end{pmatrix}^{-1} \begin{pmatrix} x_0 \\ x_1 \\ x_2 \\ x_3 \end{pmatrix}$$

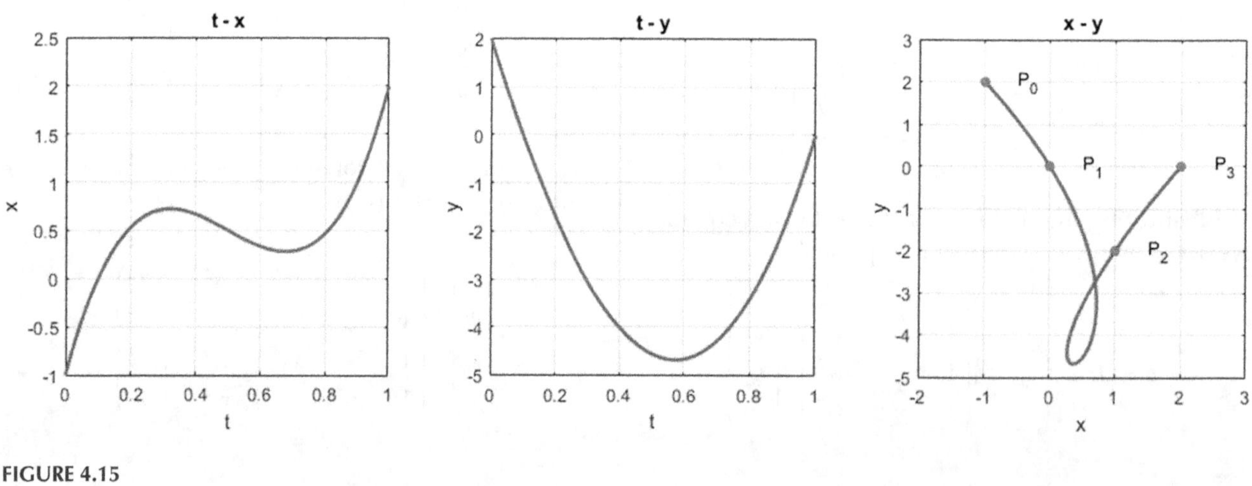

FIGURE 4.15
Cubic interpolating spline in parametric form.

$$y(t) = \begin{pmatrix} 1 & t & t^2 & t^3 \end{pmatrix} \begin{pmatrix} 1 & 0 & 0 & 0 \\ 1 & m & m^2 & m^3 \\ 1 & n & n^2 & n^3 \\ 1 & 1 & 1 & 1 \end{pmatrix}^{-1} \begin{pmatrix} y_0 \\ y_1 \\ y_2 \\ y_3 \end{pmatrix}$$

4.2.6 Hybrid Spline

4.2.6.1 Blending Functions

A hybrid spline, in contrast to an interpolating spline, does not pass through all its control points but typically a subset of them. The concept of blending functions was proposed as a means for calculating equations of curves, which are non-interpolating; i.e., they do not pass through some or all of the CPs (Hearn & Baker, 1996). For interpolating curves, the coordinates of the CPs are substituted in the starting equations to solve for the unknown coefficients. However, if the curve does not pass through the CPs, then this method does not work and a new approach is required to determine the trajectory of a point on the curve with respect to the CPs.

Consider a spline curve whose CPs are at locations P_0, P_1, P_2, P_3. In general, none of the CPs are actually located on the curve but would be around it somewhere in the neighborhood. Let us assume that four masses L_0, L_1, L_2, L_3 are located on the CPs P_0, P_1, P_2, P_3, which exert gravitational pull on the spline. Then the center of mass is located at P given by (Figure 4.16)

$$P = \frac{L_0P_0 + L_1P_1 + L_2P_2 + L_3P_3}{L_0 + L_1 + L_2 + L_3}$$

Now, consider that the masses are not constant but change their values as a function of the parametric variable $t\,(0 \le t \le 1)$, i.e., $L_i = f(t)$. The center of mass P will also shift to different points with different values of t. If all these points are joined together as t takes on various values from 0 to 1, then the locus of P would indicate the actual spline we are interested in. The function $L_i = f(t)$ is known as blending function (BF). It is obvious that the total number of BFs would be equal to the total number of masses, which in turn would be equal to the total number of CPs. Thus, for a cubic curve there are in general four BFs.

To reduce complexity of computations, an additional constraint is applied: $\sum L_i = 1$, i.e., $L_0 + L_1 + L_2 + L_3 = 1$. This reduces the denominator of the above equation to 1 and gives us

$$P = L_0P_0 + L_1P_1 + L_2P_2 + L_3P_3$$

Writing the above in matrix form we get

$$P = \begin{pmatrix} L_0 & L_1 & L_2 & L_3 \end{pmatrix} \begin{pmatrix} P_0 \\ P_1 \\ P_2 \\ P_3 \end{pmatrix} = L.G$$

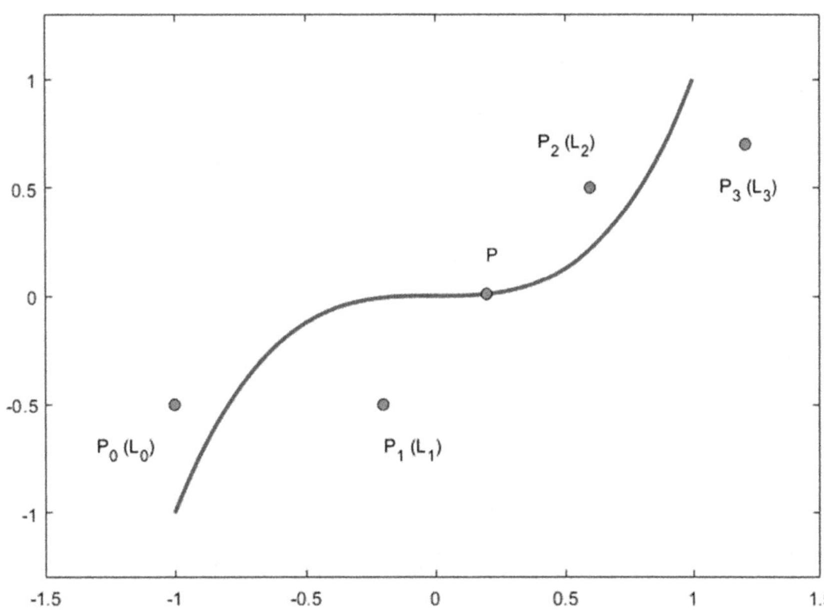

FIGURE 4.16
Concept of blending function.

The matrix L, known as the blending function matrix, provides us with a characterization of any point P on the spline independent of the CPs located in matrix G, known as the geometry matrix.

From previous discussions we know that for a parametric cubic curve

$$P(t) = T.A = T.(B.G) = (T.B).G = L.G$$

where A is the coefficient matrix, B is the basis matrix, T is the parametric matrix, G is the geometry matrix and L is the BF matrix. The above expression shows us that $L = T.B$; i.e., the BF matrix L is nothing but the product of the parametric matrix T and the basis matrix B.

Below we summarize all the relevant relations,

$$G = C.A$$

$$B = inv(C)$$

$$A = B.G$$

$$P = L.G$$

$$L = T.B$$

$$P = T.A$$

4.2.6.2 Quadratic Bezier Spline

Bezier spline, named after French engineer Pierre Bezier, is a popular type of hybrid splines, which satisfies the following characteristics: (a) it passes through the first and last CPs, (b) line joining the first CP and the second CP is tangential to the curve, (c) line joining the last CP and the previous CP is tangential to the curve.

To satisfy the above conditions the BFs of a Bezier spline is generated by Bernstein polynomials (Hearn & Baker, 1996), named after the Russian mathematician Sergei Bernstein. Bernstein polynomials of degree n are depicted below:

$$L_k = {}^nC_k.(1-t)^{n-k}.t^k.P_k$$

Here ${}^nC_k = \dfrac{n!}{k!(n-k)!}$ denotes the combination of k items out of n and $0 \le t \le 1$. Equation of the curve is $P = L.G$, where P_k denotes the control points:

$$P(t) = \sum_{k=0}^{n} L_k P_k = \sum_{k=0}^{n} {}^nC_k.(1-t)^{n-k}.t^k.P_k$$

For a quadratic curve putting $n = 2$ we get

$$P(t) = (1-t)^2.P_0 + 2(1-t).t.P_1 + t^2.P_2$$

Separating out the component BFs we get

$$L_0 = (1-t)^2 = 1 - 2t + t^2$$

$$L_1 = 2(1-t).t = 2t - 2t^2$$

$$L_2 = t^2$$

Since $L = T.B$ the basis matrix can also be computed trivially (Figure 4.17)

$$B = \begin{pmatrix} 1 & 0 & 0 \\ -2 & 2 & 0 \\ 1 & -2 & 1 \end{pmatrix}$$

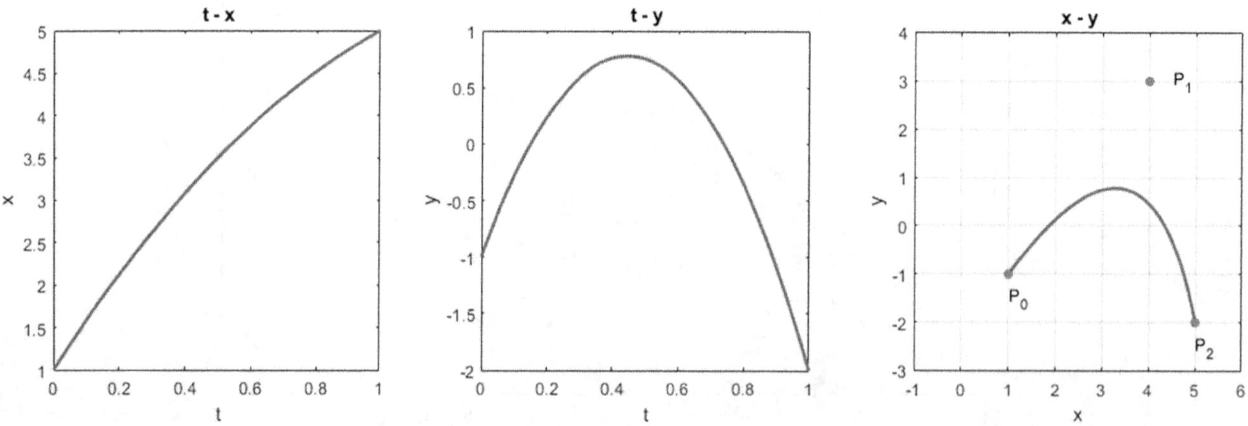

FIGURE 4.17
Quadratic Bezier spline.

4.2.6.3 Cubic Bezier Spline

As discussed earlier, equation of a Bezier curve of degree n is:

$$P(t) = \sum_{k=0}^{n} {}^{n}C_k.(1-t)^{n-k}.t^k.P_k$$

Putting $n = 3$ we get

$$P(t) = (1-t)^3.P_0 + 3.(1-t)^2.t.P_1 + 3.(1-t).t^2.P_2 + t^3.P_3$$

Separating out the component BFs we get

$$L_0 = (1-t)^3 = 1 - 3t + 3t^2 - t^3$$

$$L_1 = 3(1-t)^2.t = 3t - 6t^2 + 3t^3$$

$$L_2 = 3(1-t).t^2 = 3t^2 - 3t^3$$

$$L_3 = t^3$$

The basis matrix can be computed as before (Figure 4.18):

$$B = \begin{pmatrix} 1 & 0 & 0 & 0 \\ -3 & 3 & 0 & 0 \\ 3 & -6 & 3 & 0 \\ -1 & 3 & -3 & 1 \end{pmatrix}$$

4.2.7 Approximating Spline

4.2.7.1 B-Spline

In the previous sections, we have discussed how interpolating splines and hybrid splines are characterized using control points (CPs) and blending functions (BFs). Bezier splines in particular are quite popular and extensively used tools in graphics packages for modeling splines. However, Bezier splines have two major drawbacks, which have been the motivation for designing approximating splines. The first drawback is that the number of CPs is dependent on the degree of the curve; i.e., it is not possible to increase the number of CPs for smoother control without increasing the degree of the polynomial and hence computational complexity. The second drawback is that there is no provision of local control, i.e., shifting the location of a single CP will change the shape of the entire spline instead of a local portion of the spline. In graphics local, control is usually desirable since it enables small adjustments in the spline to be made Hearn & Baker, 1996.

To overcome, these drawbacks a new type of spline called B-spline has been proposed. B-spline stands for "basis spline" and these are truly approximating, i.e., in general they do not go through any of the CPs but under special conditions they may be forced to do so. Essentially, B-splines consist of multiple curve segments with continuity at join points. This enables local control, i.e., when a CP is moved only a set of local curve segments are changed instead of the entire curve. Values of the parametric variable t at the join points are stored in a vector called the "knot vector" (KV). If the knot values are equally spaced, then the resulting spline is called uniform B-spline; otherwise, it is referred to as non-uniform. B-splines are called open uniform when KV values are repeated.

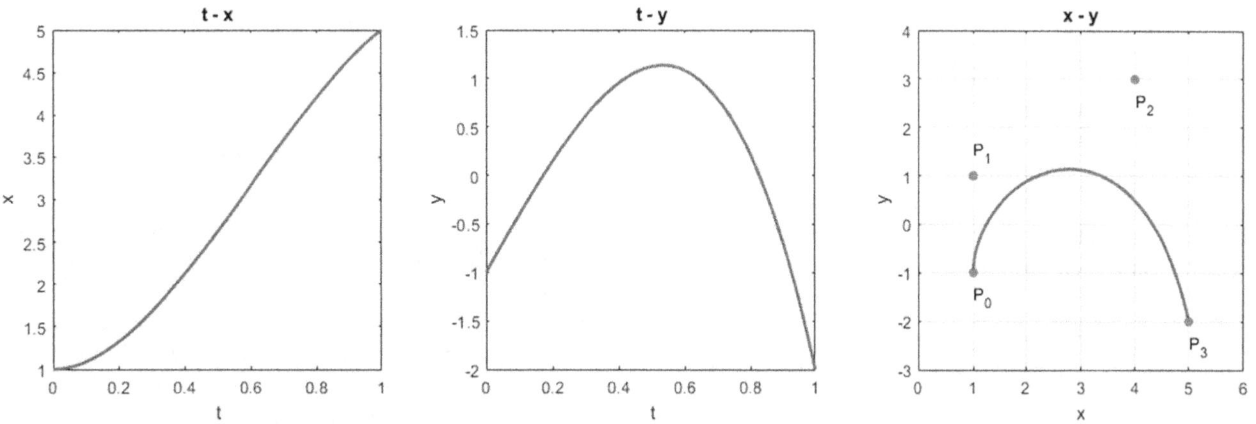

FIGURE 4.18
Cubic Bezier spline.

The BFs and equation of B-splines are not single entities but a collection of expressions for each segment. For example, if there are four segments, designated as A,B,C and D then each blending function L has four sub-components: L^A, L^B, L^C and L^D and represented as a collection in a vector $L=\{L^A, L^B, L^C, L^D\}$. If there are, say, three control points P_0,P_1,P_2, then there would be three blending functions L_0,L_1,L_2 each with four sub-components, i.e., L_0^A,L_0^B,L_0^C,L_0^D, $L_1^A,L_1^B,L_1^C,L_1^D,L_2^A,L_2^B,L_2^C,L_2^D$. Usually the BFs are represented one per line as:

$$L_0=\left\{L_0^A,L_0^B,L_0^C,L_0^D\right\}$$

$$L_1=\left\{L_1^A,L_1^B,L_1^C,L_1^D\right\}$$

$$L_2=\left\{L_2^A,L_2^B,L_2^C,L_2^D\right\}$$

Similarly, the curve equation P also would have four sub-components $P=\{P^A, P^B, P^C, P^D\}$. We have seen before that equation of a curve can be expressed as products of CPs and BFs, hence the sub-components can be written as:

$$P^A=P_0.L_0^A+P_1.L_1^A+P_2.L_2^A$$

$$P^B=P_0.L_0^B+P_1.L_1^B+P_2.L_2^B$$

$$P^C=P_0.L_0^C+P_1.L_1^C+P_2.L_2^C$$

$$P^D=P_0.L_0^D+P_1.L_1^D+P_2.L_2^D$$

Note that the sub-components are valid for different ranges of t and hence cannot be added up but needs to be represented as a matrix of values. In a typical scenario, segment A is valid over the range $0 \le t < 1$, B over range $1 \le t < 2$ and so on.

4.2.7.2 Cox de Boor algorithm

The expressions for BFs are calculated using an algorithm known as Cox de Boor algorithm, named after the German mathematician Carl-Wilhelm Reinhold de Boor (Boor, 1971) which is represented below. The blending functions are represented in the form $L_{k,d}$ where d is related to the degree of the curve, and k is related to the knot vector.

$$L_{k,1}=1, if\ t_k \le t < t_{k+1}, \text{else } 0$$

$$L_{k,d}=\left(\frac{t-t_k}{t_{k+d-1}-t_k}\right).L_{k,d-1}+\left(\frac{t_{k+d}-t}{t_{k+d}-t_{k+1}}\right).L_{k+1,d-1}$$

The first line states that the first order terms ($d=1$), of the blending functions, are equal to 1 if value of t for a particular segment lies within a specific range, else 0. The second line dictates how the higher-order terms ($d>1$) are calculated based on lower-order terms ($d-1$). The algorithm is therefore recursive in nature as the higher-order terms, pertaining to degree d, are calculated based on the lower-order terms, pertaining to degree $d-1$. Thus, even though the equation of the curve requires only highest-order terms $L_{k,d}$ the lower-order terms $L_{k,d-1},\ldots,L_{k,1}$ would need to be computed initially. Let us illustrate the algorithm by computing the blending functions and equation of a uniform quadratic B-spline.

4.2.7.3 Uniform Quadratic B-Spline

A B-spline has two defining parameters: d which is related to the degree of the spline, and n which is related to the number of control points. The degree of the spline is actually $(d-1)$ and the number of CPs is $(n+1)$. The other related parameters are derived as explained below.

For generating a quadratic B-spline, we need to start with $d=3$ and $n=2$, since the degree of a quadratic spline is 2 and for a curve of degree we need to have (degree + 1) number of control points to specify it uniquely.

Then, degree of the curve: $d-1=2$

Number of CPs: $n+1=3$

Number of BFs: $n+1=3$

Number of curve segments: $d+n=5$

Number of elements in the KV: $d+n+1=6$

Let the curve segments be A,B,C,D,E and CPs be P_0,P_1,P_2

Let the KV be $T=\{t_k\}$ for $k=\{0,1,2,3,4,5,\}$. In this case, $T=[t_0,t_1,t_2,t_3,t_4,t_5]$.

Let the BFs be L_0,L_1,L_2 and equation of the curve be

$$P=L_0P_0+L_1P_1+L_2P_2$$

Using the notation $L_{k,d}$ we re-write as:

$$P=L_{0,3}P_0+L_{1,3}P_1+L_{2,3}P_2$$

Let us make a simplifying assumption that KV values are as follows: $t_k=k$, i.e., $t_0=0$, $t_1=1, t_2=2, t_3=3$ and so on. Thus the KV becomes $T=[0,1,2,3,4,5]$. This is a valid assumption, and later we will justify it. Here, the value of k will range from 0 to 5 and d will range from 1 to 3. Based on this assumption, the representation of the algorithm becomes

$$L_{k,1}=1, if\ k \le t < k+1, \text{else } 0$$

$$L_{k,d} = \left(\frac{t-k}{d-1}\right).L_{k,d-1} + \left(\frac{k+d-t}{d-1}\right).L_{k+1,d-1}$$

From the second line of the algorithm we get the following,

For $d = 2$ and $k = 0$, $L_{0,2} = \left(\frac{t-0}{2-1}\right)L_{0,1} + \left(\frac{2-t}{2-1}\right)L_{1,1} = (t-0)L_{0,1} + (2-t)L_{1,1}$

For $d = 2$ and $k = 1$, $L_{1,2} = \left(\frac{t-1}{2-1}\right).L_{1,1} + \left(\frac{3-t}{2-1}\right).L_{2,1} = (t-1).L_{1,1} + (3-t).L_{2,1}$

For $d = 2$ and $k = 2$, $L_{2,2} = \left(\frac{t-2}{2-1}\right).L_{2,1} + \left(\frac{4-t}{2-1}\right).L_{3,1} = (t-2).L_{2,1} + (4-t).L_{3,1}$

For $d = 2$ and $k = 3$, $L_{3,2} = (t-3).L_{3,1} + (5-t).L_{4,1}$

For $d = 3$ and $k = 0$, $L_{0,3} = \left(\frac{t-0}{3-1}\right)L_{0,2} + \left(\frac{3-t}{3-1}\right)L_{1,2} = \left(\frac{t-0}{2}\right)L_{0,2} + \left(\frac{3-t}{2}\right)L_{1,2}$

For $d = 3$ and $k = 1$, $L_{1,3} = \left(\frac{t-1}{3-1}\right).L_{1,2} + \left(\frac{4-t}{3-1}\right).L_{2,2} = \left(\frac{t-1}{2}\right).L_{1,2} + \left(\frac{4-t}{2}\right).L_{2,2}$

For $d = 3$ and $k = 2$, $L_{2,3} = \left(\frac{t-2}{3-1}\right).L_{2,2} + \left(\frac{5-t}{3-1}\right).L_{3,2} = \left(\frac{t-2}{2}\right).L_{2,2} + \left(\frac{5-t}{2}\right).L_{3,2}$

Thus equation of the curve is:

$$P = L_{0,3}P_0 + L_{1,3}P_1 + L_{2,3}P_2 = \left[\left(\frac{t-0}{2}\right)L_{0,2} + \left(\frac{3-t}{2}\right)L_{1,2}\right]P_0 + \left[\left(\frac{t-1}{2}\right).L_{1,2} + \left(\frac{4-t}{2}\right).L_{2,2}\right]P_1 + \left[\left(\frac{t-2}{2}\right).L_{2,2} + \left(\frac{5-t}{2}\right).L_{3,2}\right]P_3$$

$$\begin{aligned} P &= L_{0,3}P_0 + L_{1,3}P_1 + L_{2,3}P_2 \\ &= \left[\left(\frac{t-0}{2}\right).\{(t-0).L_{0,1} + (2-t).L_{1,1}\} + \left(\frac{3-t}{2}\right).\{(t-1).L_{1,1} + (3-t).L_{2,1}\}\right]P_0 \\ &+ \left[\left(\frac{t-1}{2}\right).\{(t-1).L_{1,1} + (3-t).L_{2,1}\} + \left(\frac{4-t}{2}\right).\{(t-2).L_{2,1} + (4-t).L_{3,1}\}\right]P_1 \\ &+ \left[\left(\frac{t-2}{2}\right).\{(t-2).L_{2,1} + (4-t).L_{3,1}\} + \left(\frac{5-t}{2}\right).\{(t-3).L_{3,1} + (5-t).L_{4,1}\}\right]P_3 \end{aligned}$$

To find the actual expression, the first line of the Cox de Boor algorithm needs to be applied to each segment separately.

Segment A: $t_0 \le t < t_1$, i.e., $0 \le t < 1$

k	$L_{k,1}$	$L_{0,3}$	$L_{1,3}$	$L_{2,3}$
$k=0$	$L_{0,1}=1$	$\frac{(t-0)^2}{2}$	0	0
$k=1$	$L_{1,1}=0$			
$k=2$	$L_{2,1}=0$			
$k=3$	$L_{3,1}=0$			
$k=4$	$L_{4,1}=0$			

Segment B: $t_1 \le t < t_2$, i.e., $1 \le t < 2$

k	$L_{k,1}$	$L_{0,3}$	$L_{1,3}$	$L_{2,3}$
$k=0$	$L_{0,1}=0$	$\frac{(t-0)(2-t)}{2}+\frac{(t-1)(3-t)}{2}$	$\frac{(t-1)^2}{2}$	0
$k=1$	$L_{1,1}=1$			
$k=2$	$L_{2,1}=0$			
$k=3$	$L_{3,1}=0$			
$k=4$	$L_{4,1}=0$			

Segment C: $t_2 \le t < t_3$, i.e., $2 \le t < 3$

k	$L_{k,1}$	$L_{0,3}$	$L_{1,3}$	$L_{2,3}$
$k=0$	$L_{0,1}=0$	$\frac{(3-t)^2}{2}$	$\frac{(t-1)(3-t)}{2}+\frac{(t-2)(4-t)}{2}$	$\frac{(t-2)^2}{2}$
$k=1$	$L_{1,1}=0$			
$k=2$	$L_{2,1}=1$			
$k=3$	$L_{3,1}=0$			
$k=4$	$L_{4,1}=0$			

Segment D: $t_3 \le t < t_4$, i.e. $3 \le t < 4$

k	$L_{k,1}$	$L_{0,3}$	$L_{1,3}$	$L_{2,3}$
$k=0$	$L_{0,1}=0$	0	$\frac{(4-t)^2}{2}$	$\frac{(t-2)(4-t)}{2}+\frac{(t-3)(5-t)}{2}$
$k=1$	$L_{1,1}=0$			
$k=2$	$L_{2,1}=0$			
$k=3$	$L_{3,1}=1$			
$k=4$	$L_{4,1}=0$			

Segment E: $t_4 \le t < t_5$, i.e. $4 \le t < 5$

k	$L_{k,1}$	$L_{0,3}$	$L_{1,3}$	$L_{2,3}$
$k=0$	$L_{0,1}=0$	0	0	$\frac{(5-t)^2}{2}$
$k=1$	$L_{1,1}=0$			
$k=2$	$L_{2,1}=0$			
$k=3$	$L_{3,1}=0$			
$k=4$	$L_{4,1}=1$			

The blending functions are:

$$L_{0,3} = \begin{cases} L_{0,3}^{A} \\ L_{0,3}^{B} \\ L_{0,3}^{C} \end{cases} = \begin{cases} \dfrac{(t-0)^2}{2}, 0 \le t < 1 \\ \dfrac{(t-0)(2-t)}{2} + \dfrac{(t-1)(3-t)}{2}, 1 \le t < 2 \\ \dfrac{(3-t)^2}{2}, 2 \le t < 3 \end{cases}$$

$$L_{1,3} = \begin{cases} L_{1,3}^{B} \\ L_{1,3}^{C} \\ L_{1,3}^{D} \end{cases} = \begin{cases} \dfrac{(t-1)^2}{2}, 1 \le t < 2 \\ \dfrac{(t-1)(3-t)}{2} + \dfrac{(t-2)(4-t)}{2}, 2 \le t < 3 \\ \dfrac{(4-t)^2}{2}, 3 \le t < 4 \end{cases}$$

$$L_{2,3} = \begin{cases} L_{2,3}^{C} \\ L_{2,3}^{D} \\ L_{2,3}^{E} \end{cases} = \begin{cases} \dfrac{(t-2)^2}{2}, 2 \le t < 3 \\ \dfrac{(t-2)(4-t)}{2} + \dfrac{(t-3)(5-t)}{2}, 3 \le t < 4 \\ \dfrac{(5-t)^2}{2}, 4 \le t < 5 \end{cases}$$

In the above expression only the non-zero terms have been shown. The above equations imply that the first BF $L_{0,3}$ influences the first three segments *A*, B, C, the second BF $L_{1,3}$ influences the segments B, C, D and the third BF $L_{2,3}$ influences the segments C, D, E. This provides local control, which implies that changing one control point does not change the entire curve but only a portion of it, which is influenced by it. A plot of the blending functions is shown below, $L_{0,3}$ in blue $L_{1,3}$ in red $L_{2,3}$ in black (Figure 4.19).

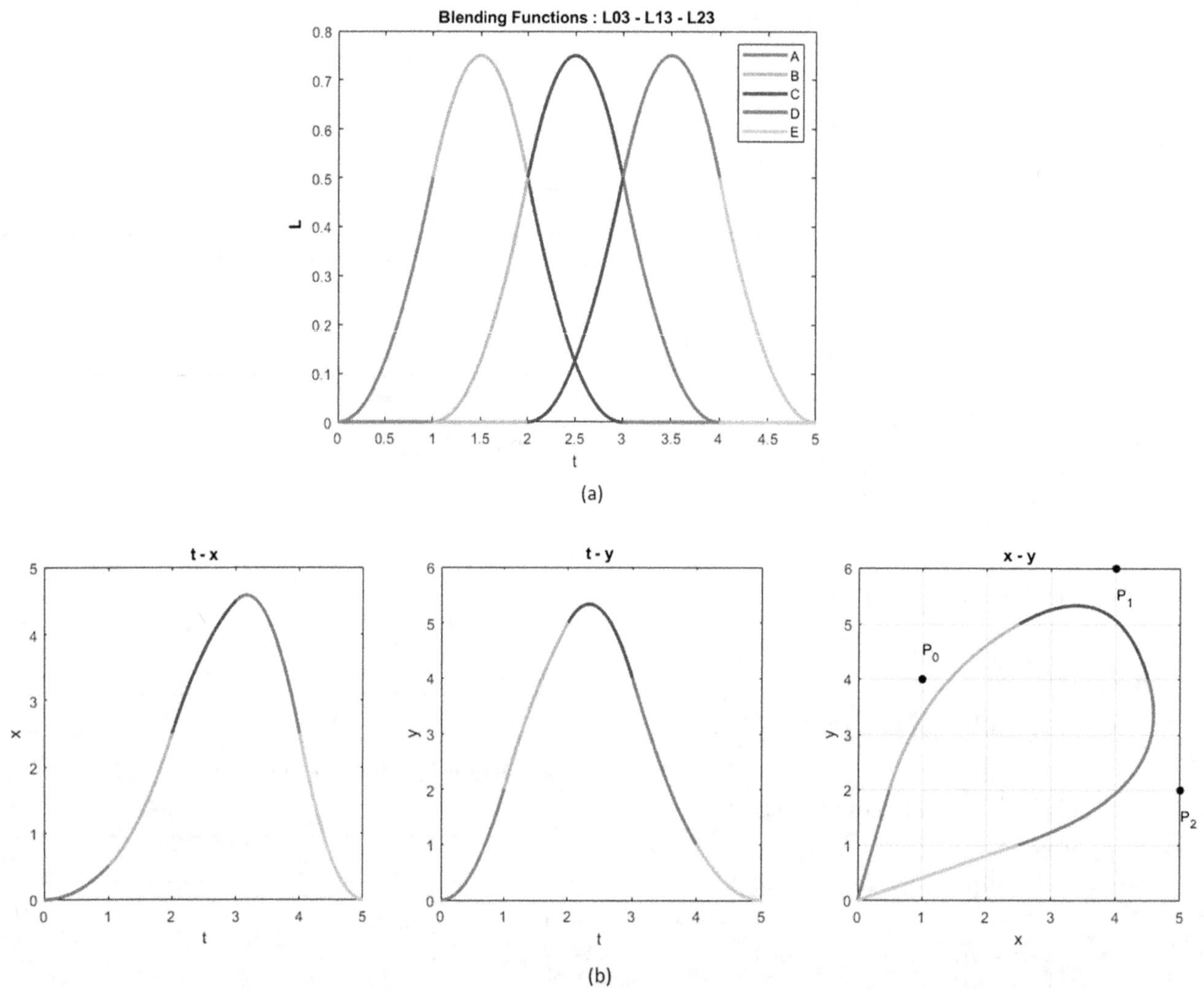

FIGURE 4.19
Uniform quadratic B-spline.

Collecting all the BF terms the equation of the curve can be written as below:

$$P(t)=\begin{cases} P_0.L_{0,3}^A \\ P_0.L_{0,3}^B+P_1.L_{1,3}^B \\ P_0.L_{0,3}^C+P_1.L_{1,3}^C+P_2.L_{2,3}^C \\ P_1.L_{1,3}^D+P_2.L_{2,3}^D \\ P_2.L_{2,3}^E \end{cases}=\begin{cases} P_0.\left[\frac{(t-0)^2}{2}\right] \\ P_0.\left[\frac{(t-0)(2-t)}{2}+\frac{(t-1)(3-t)}{2}\right]+P_1.\left[\frac{(t-1)^2}{2}\right] \\ P_0.\left[\frac{(3-t)^2}{2}\right]+P_1.\left[\frac{(t-1)(3-t)}{2}+\frac{(t-2)(4-t)}{2}\right]+P_2.\left[\frac{(t-2)^2}{2}\right] \\ P_1.\left[\frac{(4-t)^2}{2}\right]+P_2.\left[\frac{(t-2)(4-t)}{2}+\frac{(t-3)(5-t)}{2}\right] \\ P_2.\left[\frac{(5-t)^2}{2}\right] \end{cases}$$

The plot of the curve is shown below taking arbitrary control points. In the above expression only the non-zero terms have been shown.

4.2.7.4 Justification for Knot-Vector Values

Here we provide a justification for choosing KV values of $T = [0, 1, 2, 3, 4, 5]$. For a uniform B-spline we have seen previously the expressions for the BFs are as follows:

$$L_{0,3}^A=\frac{(t-0)^2}{2},$$

$$L_{0,3}^B=\frac{(t-0)(2-t)}{2}+\frac{(t-1)(3-t)}{2},$$

$$L_{0,3}^C=\frac{(3-t)^2}{2},L_{1,3}^B=\frac{(t-1)^2}{2},$$

$$\ldots$$

and so on. Let us now choose some other set of values and observe what difference in result we get. Let us assume that for a uniform quadratic B-spline the KV is changed to We can choose arbitrarily any set of values, thev only constraint being that gaps between the values should be uniform for a uniform B-spline. We proceed along the previous steps and compute the expressions for the BFs. In this case the BFs come out as follows:

$$L_{0,3}^A=\frac{(t/5-0)^2}{2},$$

$$L_{0,3}^B=\frac{(t/5-0)(2-t/5)}{2}+\frac{(t/5-1)(3-t/5)}{2},$$

$$L_{0,3}^C=\frac{(3-t/5)^2}{2},L_{1,3}^B=\frac{(t/5-1)^2}{2},$$

$$\ldots$$

It is evident that in the second case t has been replaced by $t/5$. On plugging in the scaled t values we see that the $x(t)$ and $y(t)$ are likewise scaled and their graphs are similarly affected, i.e., to get the same values of x and y as before, requires the t values to be 5 times larger than previously. However, since the x and y values have remained unchanged, the $x-y$ plot remains exactly the same as before as it is unaffected by any change in t values so long as it affects the x and y values uniformly by the same amount. Obviously, this is true for any scaling factor by which t is changed. This leads us to conclude that the actual curve in the spatial domain is independent of the KV values since it does not depend on the scaling factor of the t values. Hence, it is customary to choose the smallest t values, namely, 0, 1, 2, etc. to reduce the complexity of the equations but in reality, we can choose any values for the KV and would get the same result (Figure 4.20).

4.2.7.5 Adding Control Points

It has been mentioned previously that B-splines have been designed to overcome two limitations of Bezier splines, namely, local control and independence of control points over the degree of the curve. It has been discussed before that since each control point influences a portion instead of the entire curve, local control is implicitly provided for. To demonstrate the independence of number of control points on the degree this section discusses the resulting equations

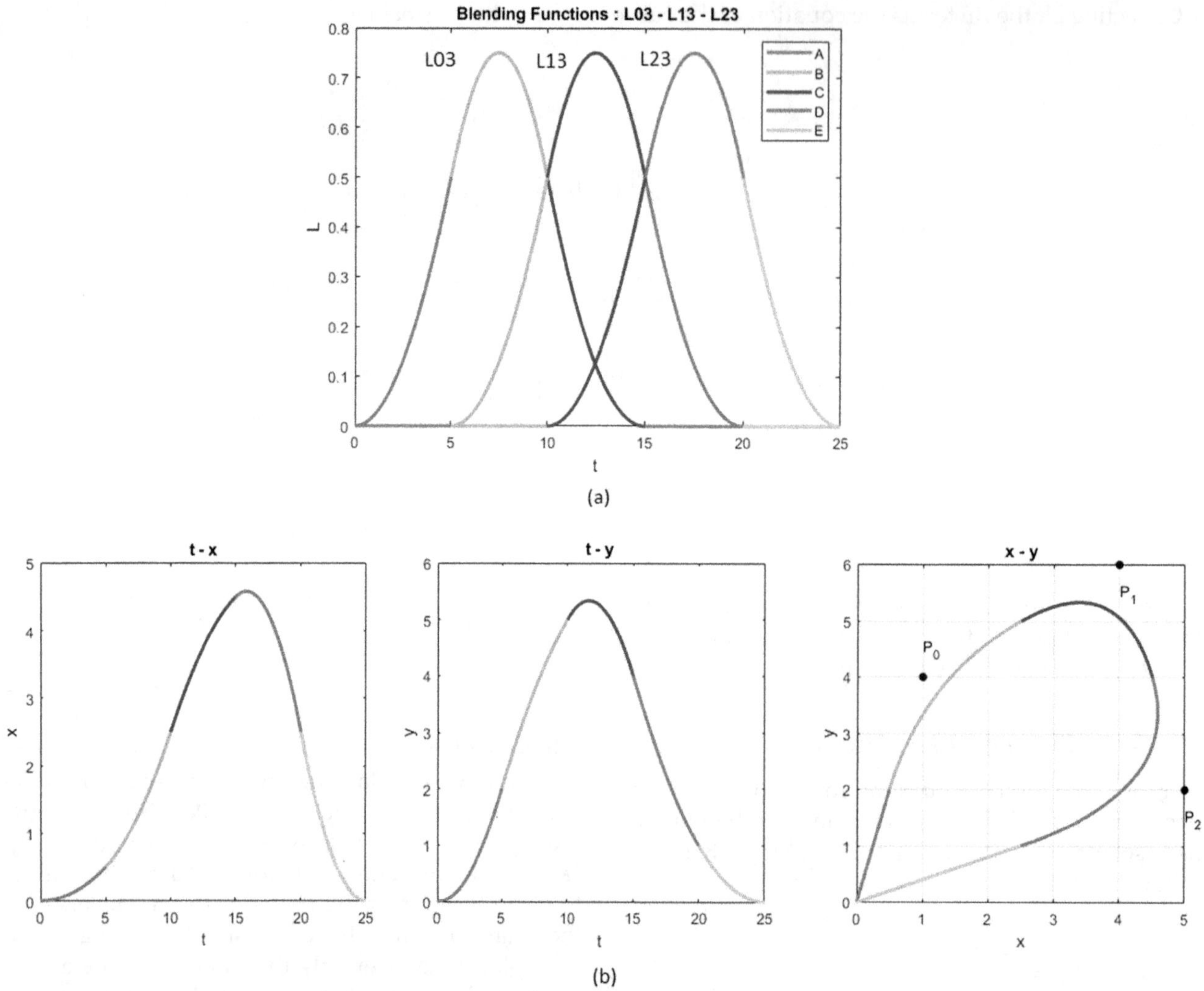

FIGURE 4.20
Effect of changing the knot vector gaps.

TABLE 4.1
Blending Functions for a Uniform Quadratic B-spline with 4 CPs

Seg	$L_{k,1}$	$L_{0,3}$	$L_{1,3}$	$L_{2,3}$	$L_{3,3}$
A	$L_{0,1}=1$	$\frac{(t-0)^2}{2}$	0	0	0
B	$L_{1,1}=1$	$\frac{(t-0)(2-t)}{2}+\frac{(t-1)(3-t)}{2}$	$\frac{(t-1)^2}{2}$	0	0
C	$L_{2,1}=1$	$\frac{(3-t)^2}{2}$	$\frac{(t-1)(3-t)}{2}+\frac{(t-2)(4-t)}{2}$	$\frac{(t-2)^2}{2}$	0
D	$L_{3,1}=1$	0	$\frac{(4-t)^2}{2}$	$\frac{(t-2)(4-t)}{2}+\frac{(t-3)(5-t)}{2}$	$\frac{(t-3)^2}{2}$
E	$L_{4,1}=1$	0	0	$\frac{(5-t)^2}{2}$	$\frac{(t-3)(5-t)}{2}+\frac{(t-4)(6-t)}{2}$
F	$L_{5,1}=1$	0	0	0	$\frac{(6-t)^2}{2}$

when an additional control point is added to the previously discussed curve. So here the process is started with $d = 3$ and $n = 3$, in which case number of control points as well as the number of blending functions is 4, number of curve segments is 6 (A to F) and number of elements in KV is 7. Let the CPs be P_0, P_1, P_2, P_3. As before, we consider $T = [0,1,2,3,4,5,6,7]$. Let the BFs be L_0, L_1, L_2, L_3 and equation of the curve becomes:

$$P = L_{0,3}P_0 + L_{1,3}P_1 + L_{2,3}P_2 + L_{3,3}P_3$$

Following the procedures outlined previously we get:

$$\begin{aligned}P &= L_{0,3}P_0 + L_{1,3}P_1 + L_{2,3}P_2 + L_{3,3}P_3 \\ &= \begin{bmatrix}\left(\frac{t-0}{2}\right).\{(t-0).L_{0,1} + (2-t).L_{1,1}\} + \\ \left(\frac{3-t}{2}\right).\{(t-1).L_{1,1} + (3-t).L_{2,1}\}\end{bmatrix} P_0 \\ &+ \begin{bmatrix}\left(\frac{t-1}{2}\right).\{(t-1).L_{1,1} + (3-t).L_{2,1}\} \\ +\left(\frac{4-t}{2}\right).\{(t-2).L_{2,1} + (4-t).L_{3,1}\}\end{bmatrix} P_1 \\ &+ \begin{bmatrix}\left(\frac{t-2}{2}\right).\{(t-2).L_{2,1} + (4-t).L_{3,1}\} \\ +\left(\frac{5-t}{2}\right).\{(t-3).L_{3,1} + (5-t).L_{4,1}\}\end{bmatrix} P_2 \\ &+ \begin{bmatrix}\left(\frac{t-3}{2}\right).\{(t-3).L_{3,1} + (5-t).L_{4,1}\} \\ +\left(\frac{6-t}{2}\right).\{(t-4).L_{4,1} + (6-t).L_{5,1}\}\end{bmatrix} P_3\end{aligned}$$

The blending functions will be same as before with an additional term:

$$L_{3,3} = \begin{cases} L_{3,3}^D \\ L_{3,3}^E \\ L_{3,3}^F \end{cases} = \begin{cases} \dfrac{(t-3)^2}{2}, 3 \le t < 4 \\ \dfrac{(t-3)(5-t)}{2} + \dfrac{(t-4)(6-t)}{2}, 4 \le t < 5 \\ \dfrac{(6-t)^2}{2}, 5 \le t < 6 \end{cases}$$

Equation of the spline:

$$P(t) = \begin{cases} P_0.L_{0,3}^A \\ P_0.L_{0,3}^B + P_1.L_{1,3}^B \\ P_0.L_{0,3}^C + P_1.L_{1,3}^C + P_2.L_{2,3}^C \\ P_1.L_{1,3}^D + P_2.L_{2,3}^D + P_3.L_{3,3}^D \\ P_2.L_{2,3}^E + P_3.L_{3,3}^E \\ P_3.L_{3,3}^F \end{cases}$$

$$= \begin{cases} P_0.\left[\dfrac{(t-0)^2}{2}\right] \\ P_0.\left[\dfrac{(t-0)(2-t)}{2} + \dfrac{(t-1)(3-t)}{2}\right] + P_1.\left[\dfrac{(t-1)^2}{2}\right] \\ P_0.\left[\dfrac{(3-t)^2}{2}\right] + P_1.\left[\dfrac{(t-1)(3-t)}{2} + \dfrac{(t-2)(4-t)}{2}\right] + P_2.\left[\dfrac{(t-2)^2}{2}\right] \\ P_1.\left[\dfrac{(4-t)^2}{2}\right] + P_2.\left[\dfrac{(t-2)(4-t)}{2} + \dfrac{(t-3)(5-t)}{2}\right] + P_3.\left[\dfrac{(t-3)^2}{2}\right] \\ P_2.\left[\dfrac{(5-t)^2}{2}\right] + P_3.\left[\dfrac{(t-3)(5-t)}{2} + \dfrac{(t-4)(6-t)}{2}\right] \\ P_3.\left[\dfrac{(6-t)^2}{2}\right] \end{cases}$$

Thus, it is observed that it is indeed possible to form a valid equation of the spline by adding control points but without increasing the degree of the curve. Conversely it is also possible to increase the degree of the curve without increasing the number of control points. It is left for the reader as an exercise to form equations of a cubic uniform B-spline with four control points by extending the procedure outlined above.

4.2.7.6 Non-Uniform Quadratic B-Spline

In a non-uniform spline, the KV is not uniform; i.e., the gaps between the knot elements are different. This makes the BFs un-symmetric and they tend to cluster together where the gaps are smaller. This has the effect of drawing the curve toward the corresponding CPs. Figure below shows the BFs of a non-uniform quadratic *B*-spline with four control points. The amount of non-symmetry would depend upon the gaps in the KV (Figure 4.21).

4.2.7.7 Open-Uniform Quadratic B-Spline

In an open uniform spline, the KV is uniform except at the ends where it is repeated d times where $(d-1)$ is the degree of the curve. Repeated values are referred to as multiplicity. Multiplicity implies that denominators of the Cox de Boor terms become zero in many cases. Hence, an important assumption needs to be made here: division by zero is treated as zero. Consider an open-uniform quadratic B-spline with $d = 3$ and $n = 2$. Let the KV be chosen as $T = \{1,1,1,2,2,2\}$. As before, performing a segment-wise analysis the blending functions and the actual curve obtained are shown below. It can be observed that the BFs pertaining to the segments C are present while others are zero. The spline also contains only segment C with other

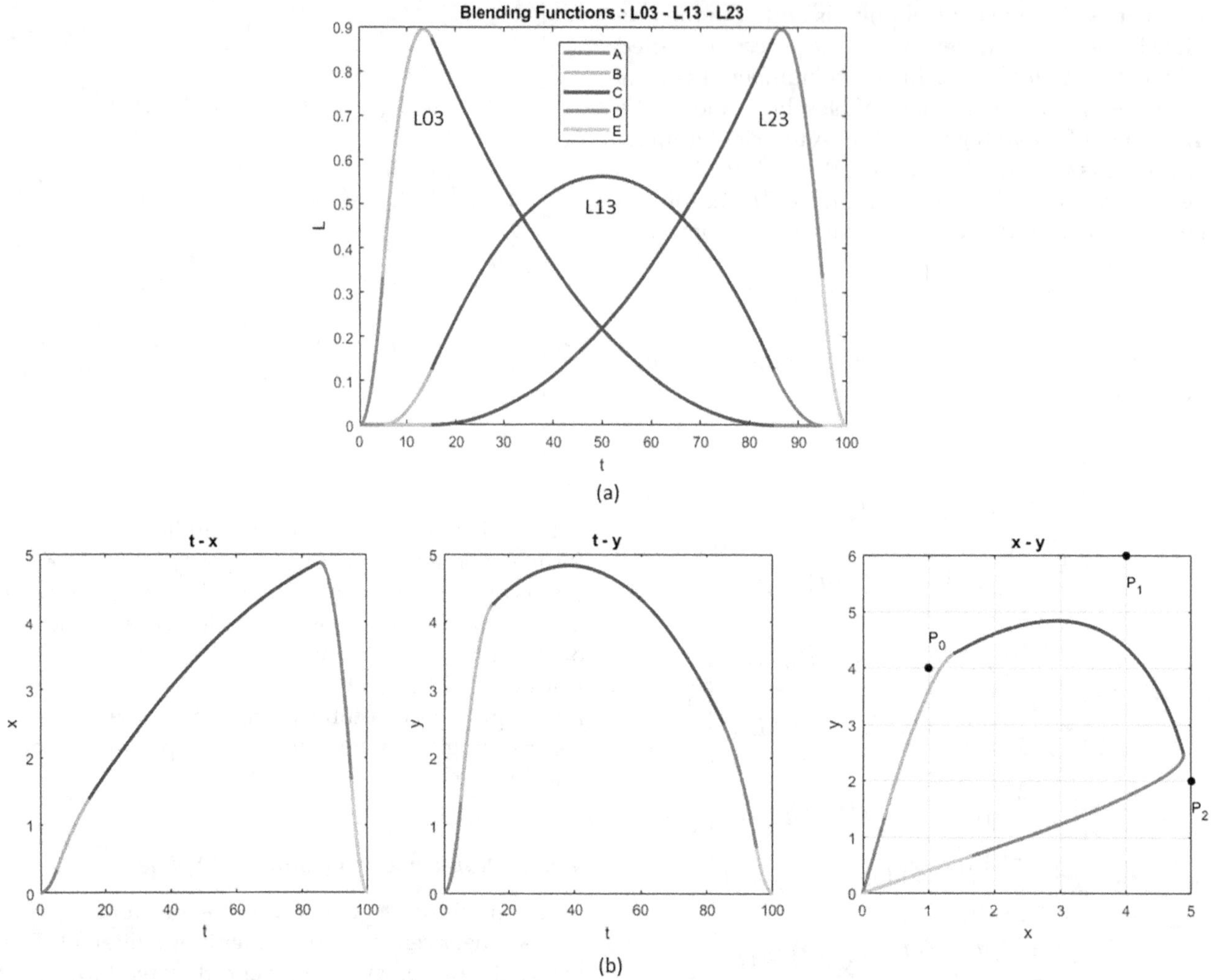

FIGURE 4.21
Non-uniform quadratic B-spline.

segments non-existent. The effect of multiplicity has forced the spline to actually go through the first and last control points behaving more like an interpolating spline than an approximating spline (Figure 4.22).

4.2.7.8 Uniform Cubic B-Spline

To generate a cubic uniform B-spline with four control points the starting parameters need to be $d = 4$ and $n = 3$. Number of curve segments would be $d + n = 7(A\,to\,G)$, number of elements in the knot vector would be $d + n + 1 = 8$. In this case the equation of the curve would be:

$$P = L_{0,4}P_0 + L_{1,4}P_1 + L_{2,4}P_2 + L_{3,4}P_3$$

It is left as an exercise for the reader to compute the blending functions and curve equations by following the procedures outlined above.

4.2.8 Spline Conversions

A spline of one type can be expressed as a spline of another type. Since the spline physically remains the same, its equation is: unaltered. However, the basis matrix and CPs change (Hearn & Baker, 1996).

Suppose a spline of type 1 specified by its basis matrix B1 and CPs in geometry matrix G1 needs to be converted to a spline of type 2 with basis matrix B2 and geometry matrix G2. Then equation of the first spline is $P(t) = T.B_1.G_1$ and equation of the second spline is $P(t) = T.B_2.G_2$. Note, however, that the actual spline physically remains the same and it is only

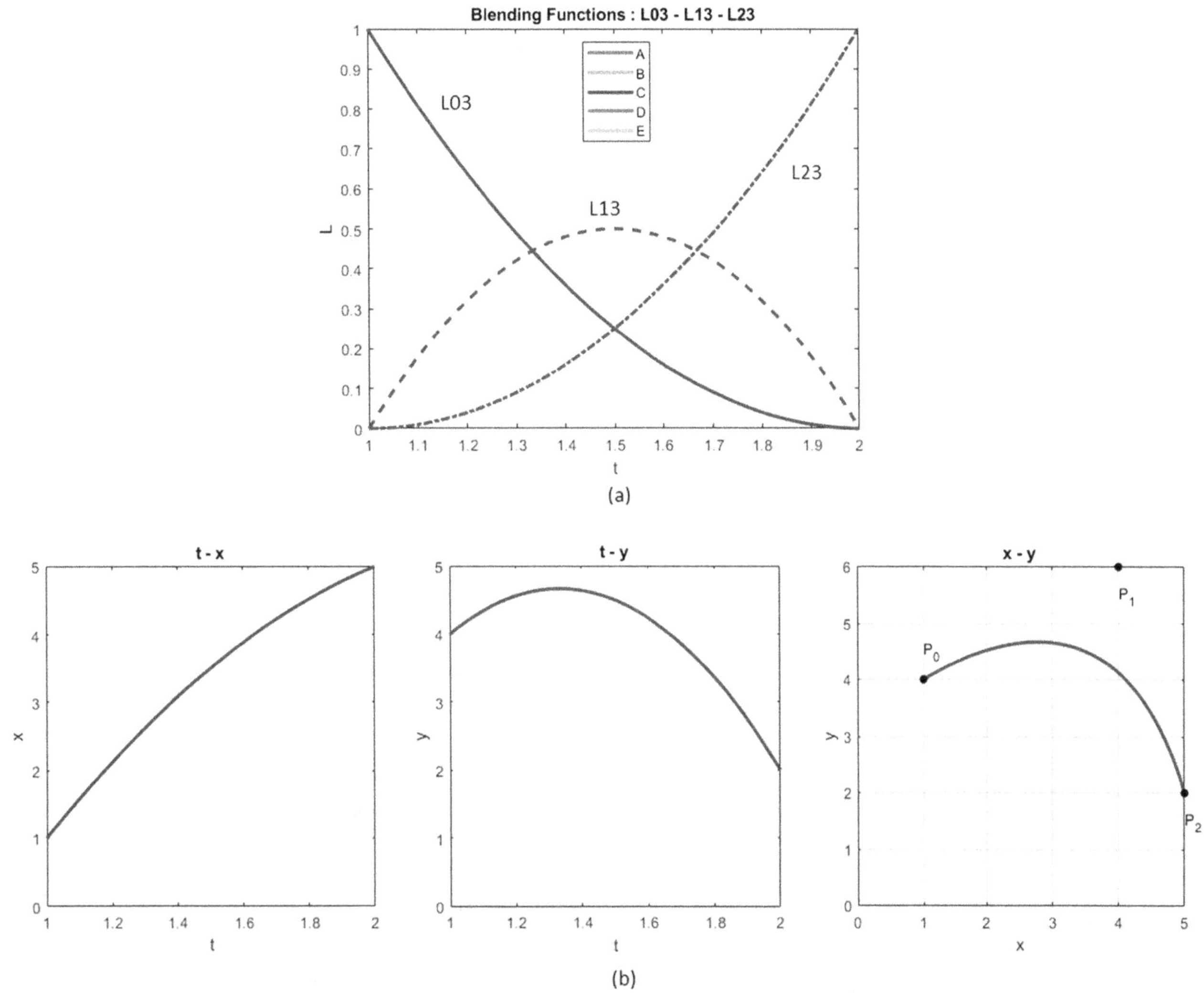

FIGURE 4.22
Open uniform quadratic B-spline.

represented in two different manners. The two equations are therefore equivalent, and can be equated:

$$P(t) = T.B_1.G_1 = T.B_2.G_2$$

Basis matrices of both splines are known as they are characteristic of the spline type. CPs of the first spline should also be known. CPs of the second spline are found out by solving the following:

$$G_2 = B_2^{-1}.B_1.G_1$$

Even if for the first curve the CPs are not specifically known but the curve can be expressed in the parametric form $P(t) = T.B_1.G_1$, then for a quadratic or cubic curve since T is known, the product $B_1.G_1$ can be extracted and plugged in the equation above to determine G_2 (Figure 4.23).

4.2.9 Properties of Splines

The following section discusses calculation of various properties of splines like length of a curve between two points, area enclosed between the curve and primary axes, centroid of the enclosed area, maxima and minima of the curve and the POI (point of inflection) where the curvature changes (Mathews & Fink, 2004).

4.2.9.1 Length of Curve

A section of a spline curve $y = f(x)$ between points $x = a$ and $x = b$ can be approximated by a number of small line segments. For such a small line segment if δx be the horizontal distance and δy be the vertical distance, then the length of the segment can be approximated by:

$$\delta r = \sqrt{(\delta x)^2 + (\delta y)^2}$$

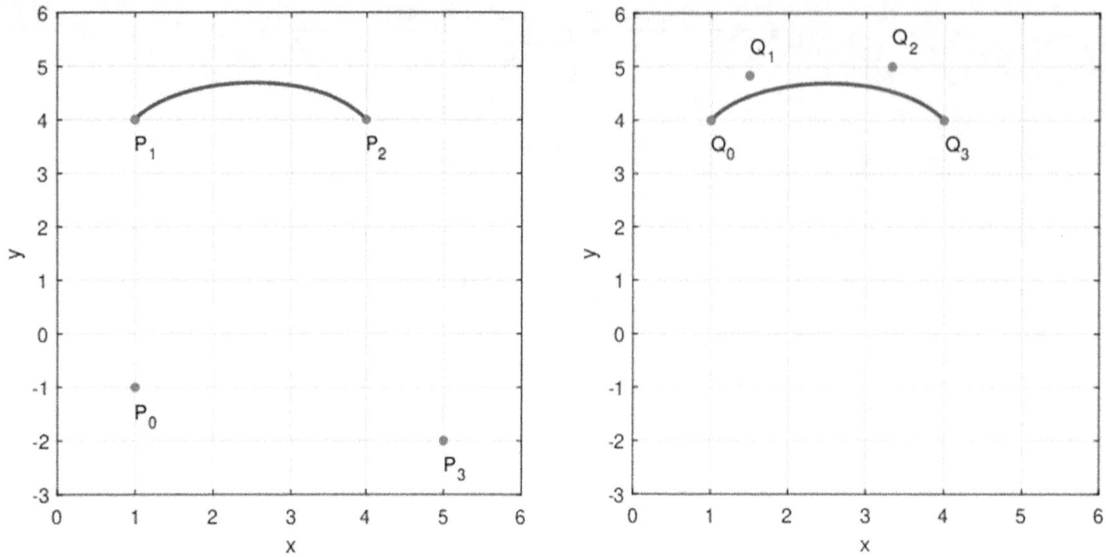

FIGURE 4.23
Spline conversion.

The length of the entire curve is the sum of these small segment distances between $x = a$ and $x = b$ (Figure 4.24). Integrating:

$$L = \int_a^b \sqrt{(dx)^2 + (dy)^2}$$

Simplifying:

$$L = \int_a^b \sqrt{1 + \left(\frac{dy}{dx}\right)^2}\, dx$$

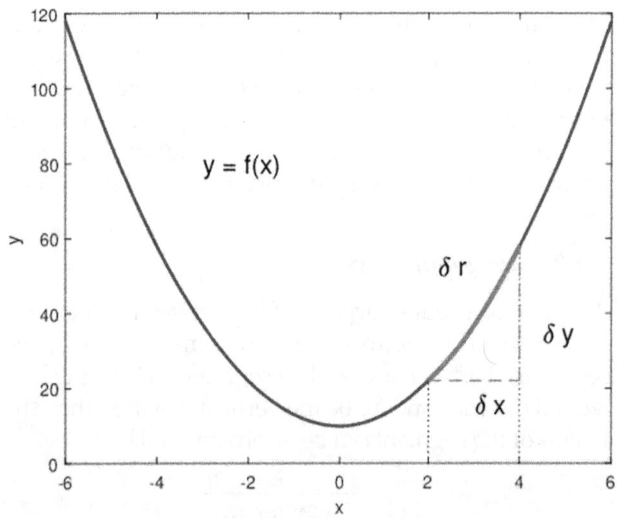

FIGURE 4.24
Determining length of a curve.

If the equation of the curve is in parametric form then we have (Figure 4.24):

$$L = \int_a^b \sqrt{\left(\frac{dx}{dt}\right)^2 + \left(\frac{dy}{dt}\right)^2}\, dt$$

4.2.9.2 *Area under Curve*

Area below a curve $y = f(x)$ between $x = a$ and $x = b$ is computed by considering a very small rectangular area of width dx and height $y = f(x)$. The area of this rectangular area is $f(x).dx$. To find the entire area, we integrate the small rectangular area over the specified limits (Figure 4.25).

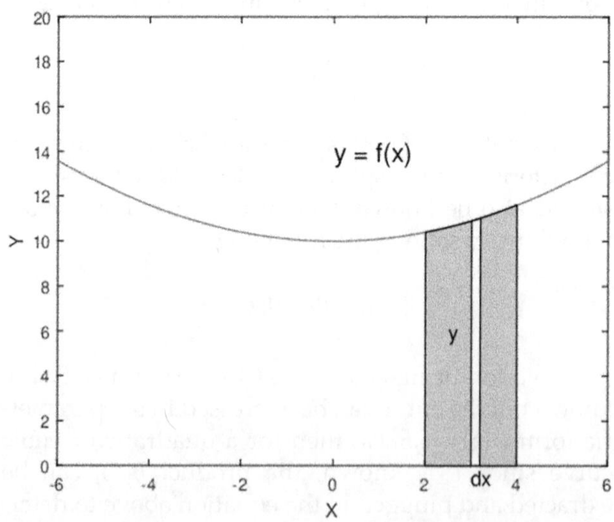

FIGURE 4.25
Determining area under a curve.

$$A = \int_a^b f(x)dx$$

The above area computed is actually the area between the curve $f(x)$ and the x-axis. However, if the curve itself lies below the x-axis then the area computed by the above formula comes out as negative. In such cases, we need to take the absolute value of the area.

If the area is required between a curve and the y-axis, then by an extension of earlier ideas we first express the curve in the form $x = f(y)$ and then by drawing a series of small rectangle of width dy and height $x = f(y)$, we integrate over the specified limits c to d. In this case:

$$A = \int_c^d f(y)dy$$

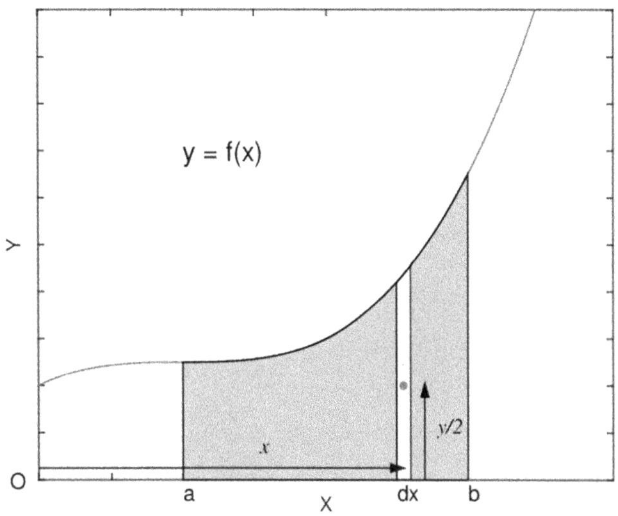

FIGURE 4.26
Determining centroid of an area.

4.2.9.3 Centroid of Area

Centroid of an area under the curve $y = f(x)$ bounded on the other three sides by the x-axis, and the lines $x = a$ and $x = b$, can be formulated from the general rule that the centroid of an area is equal to the sum of the moments of its component parts divided by the whole area. Consider a very thin strip of width dx at a distance of x from the y-axis and of height $y = f(x)$ so that the area of the strip is $y.dx$. Moment of the strip along x-direction is thus $(y.dx).x$ and moment of the strip along y-direction is $(y.dx).(y/2)$ since the center of the strip is exactly at the middle along the height of the strip. Equating the moments of all such strips within the area and dividing by the area itself we obtain the centroid $(\overline{x}, \overline{y})$ of the area as below, where the area is $A = \int_a^b f(x).dx$ (Figure 4.26).

$$\overline{x} = \frac{\int_a^b x.f(x).dx}{A}$$

$$\overline{y} = \frac{\int_a^b \{f(x)\}^2.dx}{2A}$$

4.2.9.4 Maxima, Minima and POI

For both minimum and maximum points, the slope of the curve is zero as the line is horizontal. Both points of the curve $y = f(x)$ can be found by computing roots of the equation $f'(x) = 0$. Let r be a root of the equation $f'(x) = 0$. To determine whether the root corresponds to a minimum or maximum, consider that for a minimum point as we move from left to right the slope changes from negative to positive; i.e., the rate of change of slope is positive. This implies that for a minimum point:

$$f'(r) = 0 \text{ and } f''(r) > 0$$

Alternatively, for a maximum point as we move from left to right the slope changes from positive to negative, i.e., the rate of change of slope is negative. This implies that for a maximum point:

$$f'(r) = 0 \text{ and } f''(r) < 0$$

A POI or Point of Inflection exists only for splines with degree 3 or more. A POI is where curvature changes from positive (convex) to negative (concave) or vice versa. The necessary conditions to be satisfied are that the curvature should be zero at the POI and the sign of curvature on either side should be opposite. Let r be the root of the equation $f''(x) = 0$. Consider a small displacement δ to the left and right of r. Thus conditions necessary for a POI to exist are (Figure 4.27):

$$f''(r) = 0 \text{ and}$$

$$sign\left[f''(r-\delta)\right] \neq sign\left[f''(r+\delta)\right]$$

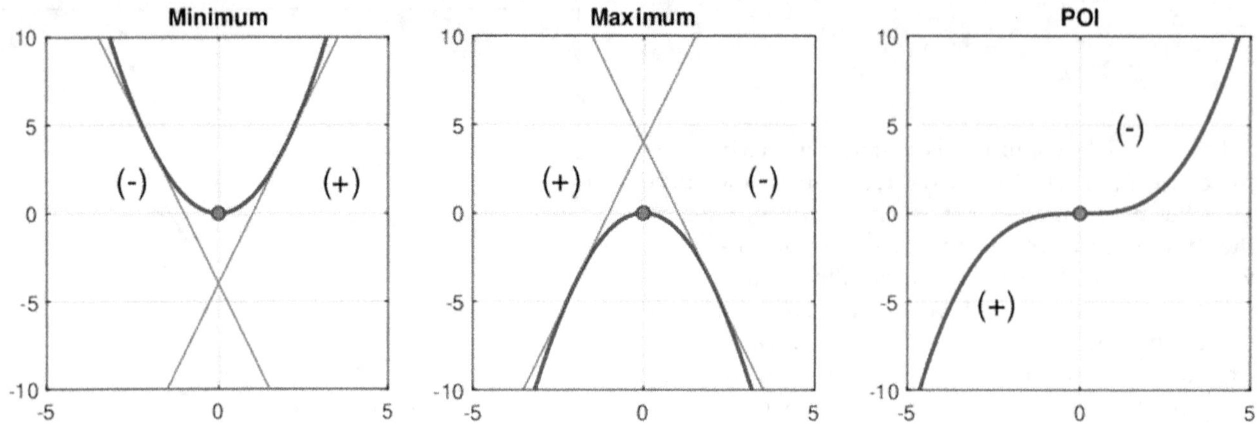

FIGURE 4.27
Maxima minima and POI of a curve.

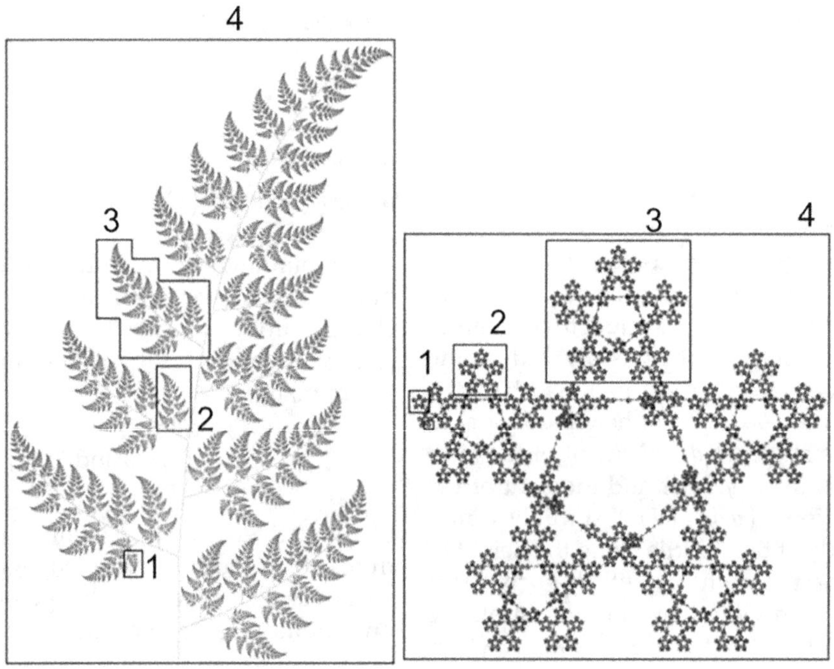

FIGURE 4.28
Fractals: fern leaf and snowflake, show self-replicating structures 1,2,3,4.

4.2.10 Fractals

Fractal geometry was invented by the French mathematician Benolt Mandelbrot in the 1970s, who laid down its principles in his famous book *The Fractal Geometry of Nature* (Mandelbrot, 1982). This turned out to be extremely rich in possibilities for computer graphics. He termed the new branch of mathematics as fractal because it involved the possibility of writing mathematical equations for geometries of fractional dimensionality. The images that result when fractal equations are plotted produce some very intricate, unexpected and beautiful results. Most interestingly they found that graphs of fractal equations produce imagery that captures some of the characteristics of natural phenomena, e.g., structure of snowflakes, ferns, electric charge patterns within an acrylic block (Figure 4.28). These images are characterized by self-replicating structures at different scales.

4.2.10.1 Koch Curve

Fractal imagery often has an irregularity and unpredictability that is reminiscent of forms found in nature. One of the most important characteristics of fractals is that at any level of detail you can see similarities in the forms. The forms at the most minute levels look similar to the forms at higher levels. This characteristic called self-similarity also belongs to nature as well. To see how self-similarity works in a fractal image, consider a simple and common example called the Koch curve, named after the Swedish mathematician Helge von Koch. You start generating this fractal curve with a simple equilateral triangle. Next you break the straight line comprising each side into a pattern consisting of two equilateral line segments forming a bump. Breaking each of the straight lines that make up the generator into yet smaller versions of the generator pattern yields a new pattern consisting of multiple occurrences of the generator. Subdividing each straight line of that pattern into the generator pattern yields the "next generation" of that curve. This process can be repeated indefinitely creating ever more detailed and refined repetition of the generator pattern. Notice that each new generation of the Koch curve is defined in terms of the previous Koch curve. The process of defining something in terms of itself is called recursion and the process is said to be recursive (Figure 4.29).

4.2.10.2 Generating Fractals

To generalize the fractal drawing procedure, we start with an initiator and a generator and replace the initiator with the generator at each successive step. This is illustrated for the Koch curve. The initiator is a straight-line segment, while the generator consist of 4 line segments each one-third the length of the initiator. At every step, each line segment is replaced by four line segments whose total length is 4/3 times the line segment they are replacing. Thus, at every step, the length of the Koch curve increases, and if we continue this process indefinitely, the length of the resulting curve becomes infinite (Figure 4.30).

4.2.10.3 Calculating Fractal Dimensions

The term "fractals" also imply the fact that the images have fractional dimensions. The following rule is used to calculate dimensions of graphical figures. A line is broken or split into four smaller pieces each similar to the original but at one-fourth the original scale. Also, four smaller lines are required to build up the original line. So we define the scale $s = 1/4$ and the total number of smaller items required as $N = 4$. Then, dimension D of the line is computed according to the following formula:

$$N = (1/s)^D$$

$$D = \frac{\log N}{\log 1/s}$$

For the straight line putting $s = (1/4)$ and $N = 4$, we get $D = \log(4)/\log(4) = 1$ which agrees with our notion that a line is a single-dimensional figure. Considering a square, if each side is split into 4 parts, then it takes 16 smaller squares to build up the original square. Hence, in this case, $s = 1/4$ and $N = 16$. Putting these values we get $D = \log(16)/\log(4) = 2$ which also agrees with our notion that a square is a two-dimensional figure. For a cube, if each side is split into 4 parts then it takes 64 smaller cubes to build up the original cube.

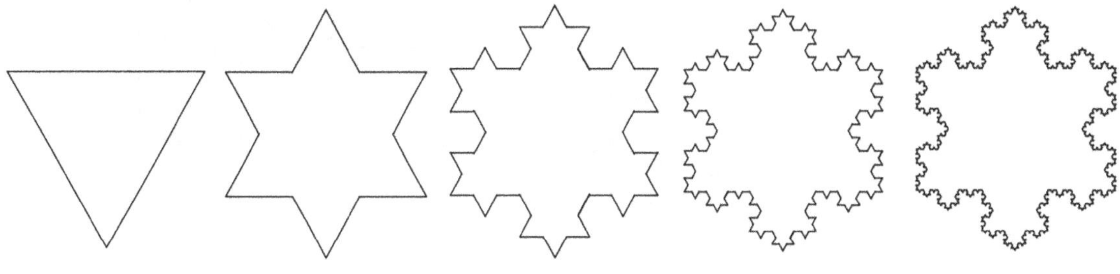

FIGURE 4.29
Generating a fractal Koch curve.

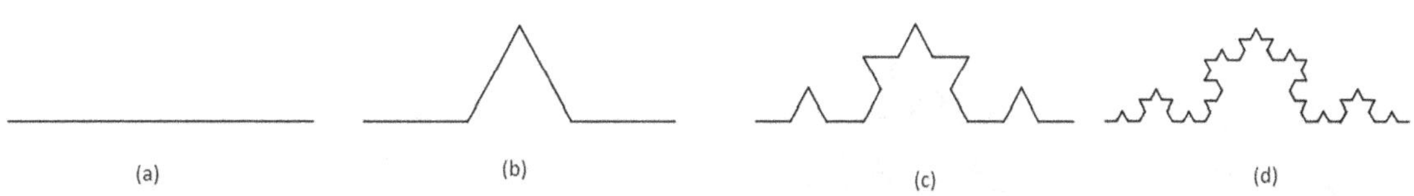

FIGURE 4.30
Initiator and generator for fractals.

Hence, in this case $s = 1/4$ and $N = 64$. Putting these values we get $D = \log(64)/\log(4) = 3$ which too agrees with our notion that a cube is a three-dimensional figure.

We apply the same concept to calculate dimensions of fractal images. For a Koch curve, the initiator is split into three parts which implies that scale $s = 1/3$, but the generator uses 4 lines to replace the original figure, which makes $N = 4$. Hence, dimension $D = \log(4)/\log(3) = 1.26$, which reiterates the fact that fractals have fractional dimensions (Figure 4.31).

4.2.10.4 Sierpinski Triangle

The Sierpinski triangle is another famous fractal. To generate it, start with an equilateral triangle. In each iteration, each side of a triangle is subdivided into two equal parts resulting in the construction of three smaller triangles that are then used to replace the original bigger triangle. Here, the initiator is split into two parts, which implies that scale $s = ½$, but the generator uses three triangles to replace the original figure, which makes $N = 3$. Hence, dimension $D = \log(3)/\log(2) = 1.585$ (Figure 4.32).

4.2.10.5 Cantor Dust

Cantor dust is a fractal formed by repeatedly removing segments from a line. To generate, start with a line segment, in each iteration, the line segment is subdivided into three equal parts out of which two smaller lines are used to replace the original bigger line. Here, the initiator is split into three parts, which implies that scale $s = 1/3$, but the generator uses 2 lines to replace the original figure, which makes $N = 2$. Hence, dimension $D = \log(2)/\log(3) = 0.63$

4.2.10.6 Vicsek Fractal

Here a square is decomposed into nine smaller squares in the 3-by-3 grid. The four squares at the corners and the center square are left, the other squares being removed. In an alternative variation, the corner squares are removed and the middle squares are kept. The process is repeated recursively for each of the five remaining subsquares. Here, $N = 5$ and $s = 1/3$, so dimension $D = \log(5)/\log(3) = 1.465$ (Figure 4.33).

4.2.10.7 Menger Sponge

This is a 3D fractal. Start with a cube as the initial shape. Each face is decomposed into nine smaller squares in the 3-by-3 grid, producing a total of 27 smaller cubes. Then each middle cube of each face and the central cube, i.e., a total of 7 smaller cubes are removed leaving in place a total of 20 cubes. Here, $N = 20$ and $s = 1/3$ so that dimension $D = \log(20)/\log(3) = 2.726$.

4.2.11 Common Editing Tasks

Some of the most common 2D graphics editing tasks that can be done using a GUI-based image editing

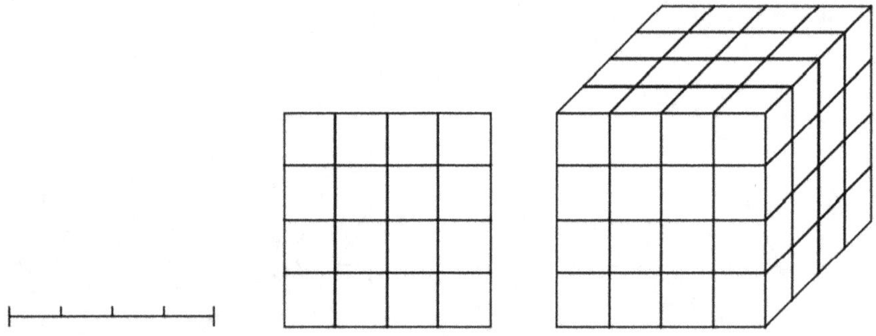

FIGURE 4.31
Calculating dimensions.

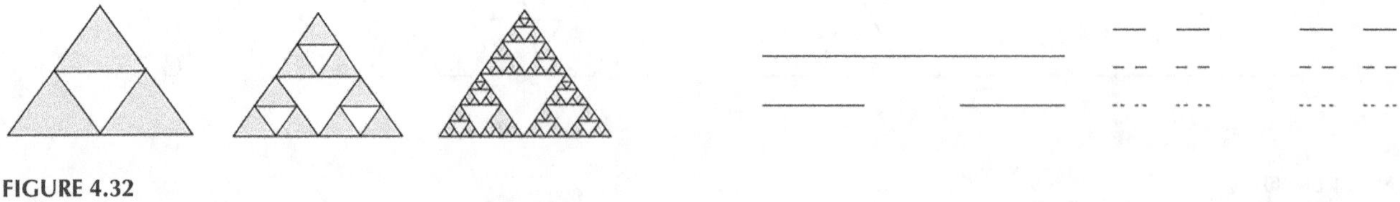

FIGURE 4.32
Sierpinski triangle and Cantor dust.

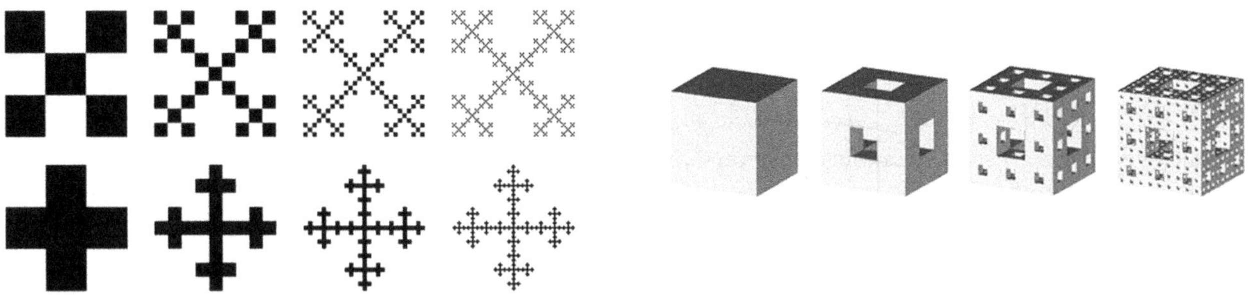

FIGURE 4.33
Vicsek fractal and Menger sponge.

software like Adobe Flash or Adobe Animate are listed below:

Drawing and Coloring: A tool palette containing a variety of drawing, selection and transform tools enables creation of geometrical and irregular vector shapes on a canvas or stage, filling them with colors selected from a color palette, selection of one or more of these shapes and transforming them by moving rotating and scaling them. A color mixer allows for modification of colors as well as choosing alpha (transparency) values and specifying gradient effects. A gradient tool allows for filling objects with linear and radial gradients.

Aligning and Positioning: Rulers and grids help in positioning and aligning objects precisely. Several objects can be grouped together to handle them together. Multiple objects can be aligned together horizontally or vertically or distributed over the stage.

Vertical layering: Graphical objects can be vertically ordered on top of each other using layers. Each layer can contain one or more objects and can have turned on or off to view or hide objects.

Viewing: A zoom tool can be used to magnify content on stage. Due to the vector nature of the contents, there is no degradation associated with zooming. A hand tool can be used to pan content outside the viewing range (Figure 4.34).

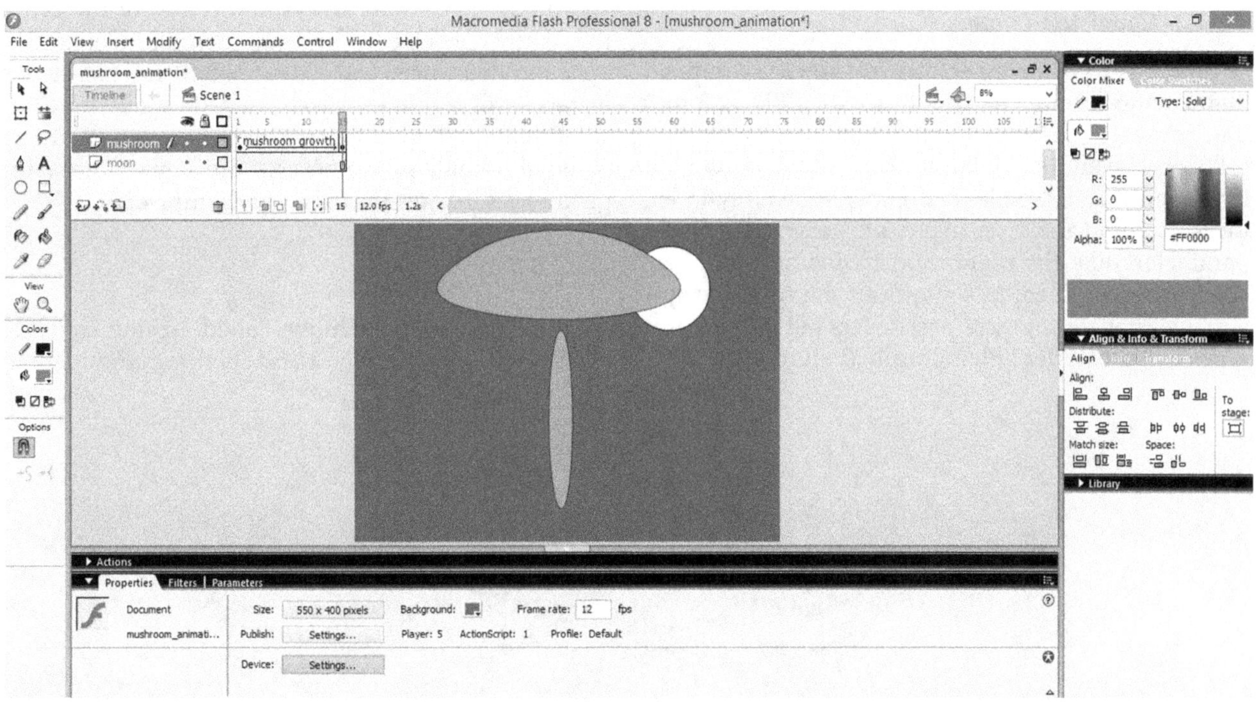

FIGURE 4.34
Typical GUI-based 2D graphics editor interface.

4.3 3D Graphics

4.3.1 3D Modeling

Modeling a 3D graphics object implies how you define it so that the computer system may be able to display it on screen, often from a number of different viewpoints. This involves specifying its structure, shape and orientation in 3D space. The modeling techniques can very broadly be divided into two categories: (1) starting from an existing 3D object and applying modifications to it, and (2) starting from an existing 2D shape and converting it to a 3D object. The first class of techniques are usually a bit simpler and include combining geometric primitives in various combinations using arrays, Boolean operations and modifiers like bend, twist and taper. The second class of techniques involve moving or rotating the 2D shape in specified ways to generate 3D envelopes and includes extrusion, lathing and lofting. A 3D model by default is usually depicted as a wireframe model where only the vertices and edges are shown without surfaces. On one hand, it helps to visualize the underlying structure of a 3D model; and on the other hand, since the surfaces and associated texture and color are not shown, it helps in faster processing of the structure when such objects are animated. For a real-world look, surface textures are added to the wireframe model before final rendering.

4.3.1.1 Geometric Primitives

Certain basic geometric shapes are so easily defined mathematically and so widely used in 3D graphics that software packages handle them separately as a set of special entities. These shapes are called geometric primitives. Examples are cube, sphere, cylinder, torus, pyramid and cone. In order to generate a sphere, parameters like the center and radius of the sphere need to be specified. In some cases the software system does not ask for these parameters but instead provides default values automatically (Figure 4.35).

4.3.1.2 Geometric Modifiers

After a 3D object is formed, its properties can be changed by applying geometric modifiers like bend, twist, bulge and taper. A Boolean operation allows you produce a single piece of geometry by compositing several existing objects. There are three distinct Boolean operators. The first is the addition or union of two objects to form a third object. The overlap – the volume occupied by both cubes – has been modified so that a single object occupies that space. The opposite of a Boolean addition is a Boolean subtraction or difference. It takes away from an object the space occupied by another object. The third operator is the intersection operator. It finds those parts that are shared by both objects and produces a new object consisting of only the shared portions. For systems based solely on splines and patches, there is a function called trimming, which consists of cutting some pattern into a surface patch. The first technique for creating a trim on a patch is to draw a curve in space and project it onto the surface to be trimmed; the second method is to use two objects intersecting one another in order to calculate the curve of intersection. A trim operation is not the same as Boolean subtraction. A trim simply cuts the surface; it does not add geometry to a surface, whereas a Boolean subtraction does generate new surface area. Multiple copies or instances of 3D objects can be drawn using linear and circular arrays. For linear arrays, parameters like the count of objects along each axis and the distance between them need to be specified; for circular arrays, the center of the array, the count of objects and the angular separation between them need to be specified. If the objects are instances of a single object, then they all share the same geometry with only the transformation matrices being different. If the objects are copies, then the geometries can also be different (Figure 4.36).

4.3.1.3 Lathing

A wood working technique called lathing involves clamping a piece of wood and then rotating it about

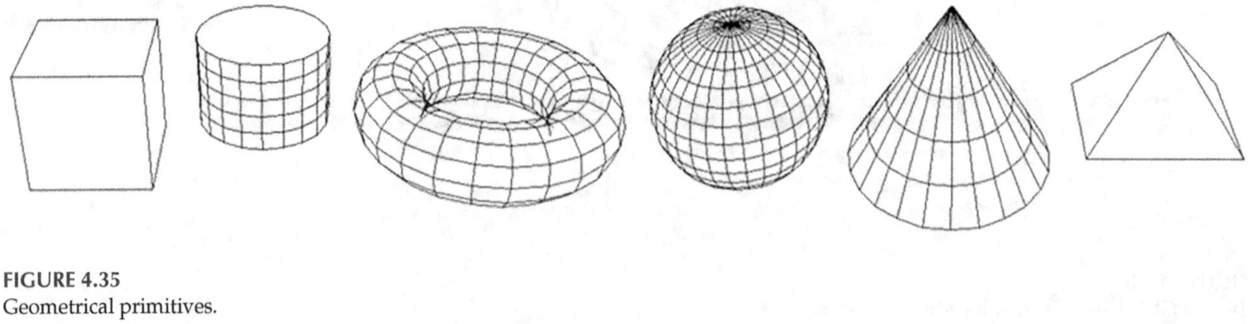

FIGURE 4.35
Geometrical primitives.

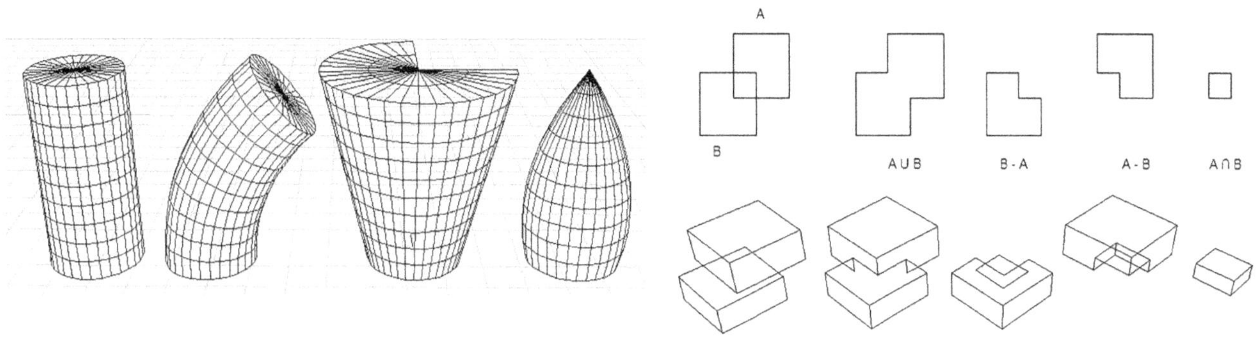

FIGURE 4.36
Geometrical modifiers and Boolean operators.

the long axis. As the wood rotates, the wood worker holds a chisel to the wood cutting it symmetrically about its axis of rotation. With computer graphics, a lathed surface is generated by drawing a 2D curve in space and rotating it around some axis. The trace left by the curve as it rotates around the axis becomes the generated surface. A surface produced in this way is also called a surface of revolution. Two important factors determine the object produced: direction of axis of rotation, and distance of the shape from the axis. The same shapes if rotated about different axes produce different surfaces. Moreover, which point of the shape touches the axis (minimum, center or maximum) or how far from the axis the shape is located also determines the final shape of the surface (Figure 4.37).

4.3.1.4 Extrusion

A common technique called extrusion involves the generating curve being pushed straight back in space along a direction perpendicular to its plane. The trace left by the curve when it is extruded through space generates a surface that corresponds only to the sides of the object; there is no front or back to the extruded surface. Most modeling systems address this problem by extruding a flat surface instead of a curve, generating surface produces the front and back of the final extrusion.

4.3.1.5 Lofting

Many systems extend the concept of extrusion by enabling the generating curve to be pushed in a

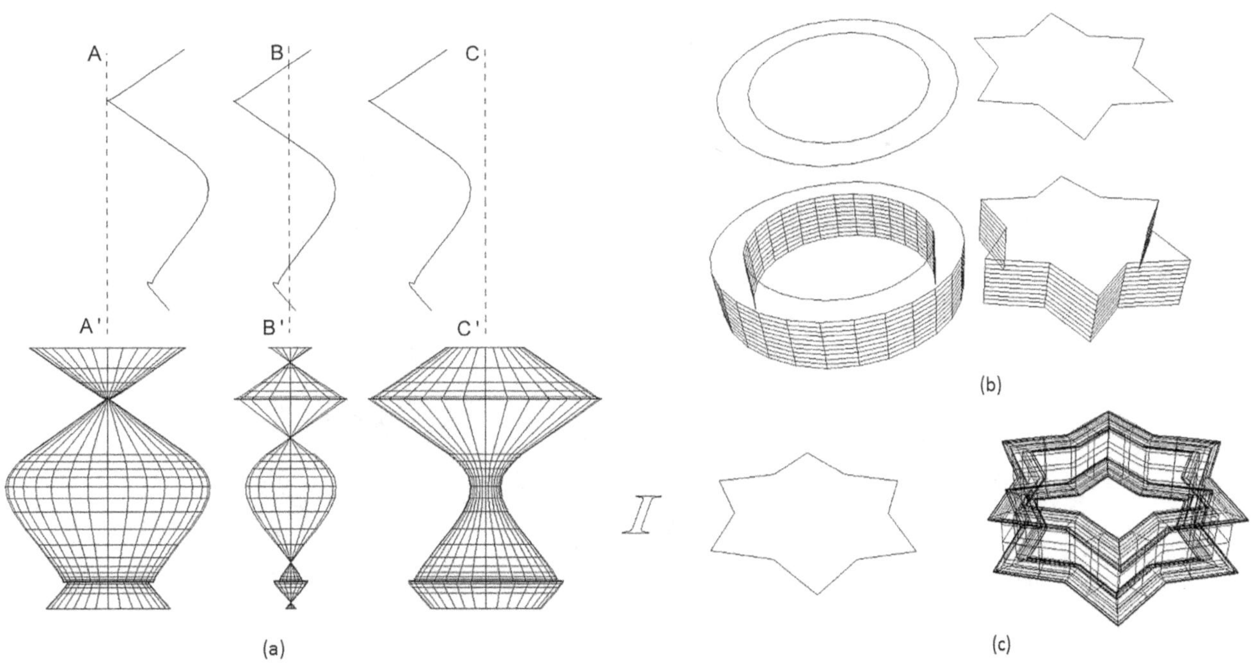

FIGURE 4.37
Lathing, extrusion and lofting.

direction other than a straight line. A circle extruded along a curved path forms a pipeline surface. This process is called lofting. The curve that is pushed is called the shape, while the trajectory along which it is pushed is called the path. Figure shows an example of the lofted object created when an I-section is moved along the periphery of a star shape. The extrusion technique can be extended further if the generating curve is transformed at the same time that it moves along the extrusion path. For example, if the curve is scaled at the same time that it is pushed back in space, the resulting surface will be wider at the back than at the front.

4.3.1.6 *Arrays*

Multiple copies or instances of 3D objects can be drawn using linear and circular arrays. For linear arrays, parameters like the count of objects along each axis and the distance between them need to be specified. For circular arrays, the center of the array, the count of objects and the angular separation between them need to be specified. If the objects are instances of a single object, then they all share the same geometry with only the transformation matrices being different; however, if the objects are copies, then the geometries can also be different (Figure 4.38).

4.3.2 3D Transformations

Three-dimensional transformations enable changing the location, orientation and shapes of splines in 3D space. These transformations are translation, rotation, scaling, reflection and shear applied individually or in combination of two or more. Given known coordinates of a point, each of these transformations can be represented by a transformation matrix which when multiplied to the original coordinates generate a new set of coordinates. Similar to the case of 2D transformations, homogeneous coordinates can be used to derive transformation matrices. Coordinates of points are measured using a right-handed 3D coordinate system where the location of each point is measured by three numbers representing coordinates along an $x-, y-$ and $z-$axes mutually at right angles or 90°. Angles are considered positive when measured in the counter-clockwise (CCW) direction observed from the tip of a primary axis and negative in the clockwise (CW) direction (O'Rourke, 2003).

4.3.2.1 *Translation*

Extending the concept of 2D translation, 3D translation involves moving objects in 3D space, whose initial and final positions can be calculated using homogeneous coordinates. A point $P(x_1, y_1, z_1)$ can be

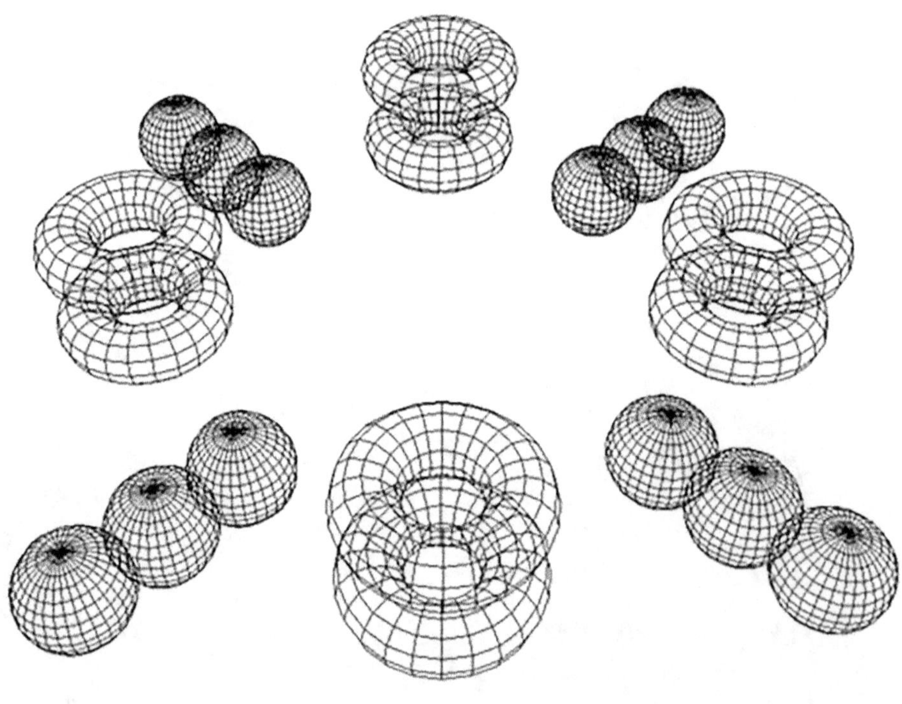

FIGURE 4.38
Arrays.

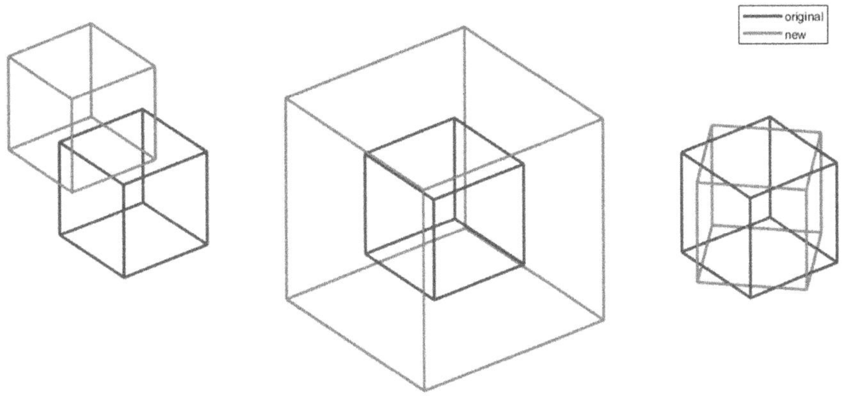

(a) (b) (c)

FIGURE 4.39
3D transformations: (a) translation, (b) scaling and (c) rotation.

moved to a new point $Q(x_2, y_2, z_2)$ by adding offsets $t_x = x_2 - x_1, t_y = y_2 - y_1$ and $t_z = z_2 - z_1$ to its coordinates. If an offset is positive, then the movement is toward the positive direction of the axis; likewise, if an offset is negative, then the movement is toward the negative direction of the axis. The new coordinates can be derived from the original coordinates using a homogeneous translation matrix (Figure 4.39):

$$\begin{pmatrix} x_2 \\ y_2 \\ z_2 \\ 1 \end{pmatrix} = \begin{pmatrix} 1 & 0 & 0 & t_x \\ 0 & 1 & 0 & t_y \\ 0 & 0 & 1 & t_z \\ 0 & 0 & 0 & 1 \end{pmatrix} \begin{pmatrix} x_1 \\ y_1 \\ z_1 \\ 1 \end{pmatrix}$$

Symbolically if $T(t_x, t_y, t_z)$ denotes translation, then

$$Q = T.P$$

If $T' = inv(T)$ or T^{-1} denote the inverse translation, it can be shown that

$$T' = T(-t_x, -t_y, -t_z)$$

4.3.2.2 Scaling

The homogeneous matrix notation for the scaling operation is:

$$\begin{pmatrix} x_2 \\ y_2 \\ z_2 \\ 1 \end{pmatrix} = \begin{pmatrix} s_x & 0 & 0 & 0 \\ 0 & s_y & 0 & 0 \\ 0 & 0 & s_z & 0 \\ 0 & 0 & 0 & 1 \end{pmatrix} \begin{pmatrix} x_1 \\ y_1 \\ z_1 \\ 1 \end{pmatrix}$$

Symbolically if $S(s_x, s_y, s_z)$ denotes the scaling matrix, then

$$Q = S.P$$

If $S' = inv(S)$ or S^{-1} denote the inverse scaling, it can be shown that

$$S' = S\left(\frac{1}{s_x}, \frac{1}{s_y}, \frac{1}{s_z}\right)$$

4.3.2.3 Rotation

A rotation operation moves a point along the circumference of a circle centered at the origin and radius equal to the distance of the point from the origin. Unlike the 2D case where there is a single rotation matrix, for 3D, there are three different rotation matrices depending on which of the three primary axes is the axis of rotation (Shirley, 2002).

Rotation about x-axis:

$$R_x(\theta) = \begin{pmatrix} 1 & 0 & 0 & 0 \\ 0 & \cos\theta & -\sin\theta & 0 \\ 0 & \sin\theta & \cos\theta & 0 \\ 0 & 0 & 0 & 1 \end{pmatrix}$$

Rotation about y-axis:

$$R_y(\theta) = \begin{pmatrix} \cos\theta & 0 & \sin\theta & 0 \\ 0 & 1 & 0 & 0 \\ -\sin\theta & 0 & \cos\theta & 0 \\ 0 & 0 & 0 & 1 \end{pmatrix}$$

Rotation about z-axis:

$$R_z(\theta) = \begin{pmatrix} \cos\theta & -\sin\theta & 0 & 0 \\ \sin\theta & \cos\theta & 0 & 0 \\ 0 & 0 & 1 & 0 \\ 0 & 0 & 0 & 1 \end{pmatrix}$$

Rotation by default is always with respect to the origin around any of the three primary axes.

If $R' = inv(R)$ or R^{-1} denote the inverse rotation, it can be shown that:

$$R' = R(-\theta)$$

4.3.2.4 Fixed Point Rotation

As mentioned previously, a rotation operation is by default with respect to the origin. For a general rotation operation with respect to a fixed point $F(x_f, y_f, z_f)$, the following steps are required:

- Apply translation to move F to origin: $T(-x_f, -y_f, -z_f)$
- Rotate about origin around specified primary axis, say, x-axis: $R_x(\theta)$
- Reverse translate to original location of F: $T(x_f, y_f, z_f)$
- Compute composite transformation matrix: $M = T(x_f, y_f, z_f).R_x(\theta).T(-x_f, -y_f, -z_f)$

4.3.2.5 Fixed Point Scaling

As mentioned previously, a scaling operation is by default with respect to the origin. For a general scaling operation with respect to a fixed point $F(x_f, y_f, z_f)$, the following steps are required (Figure 4.40):

- Apply translation to move F to origin: $T(-x_f, -y_f, -z_f)$
- Scale about origin: $S(s_x, s_y, s_z)$
- Reverse translate to original location of F: $T(x_f, y_f, z_f)$
- Compute composite transformation matrix $M = T(x_f, y_f, z_f).S(s_x, s_y, s_z).T(-x_f, -y_f, -z_f)$

4.3.2.6 Rotation about a Line Parallel to Primary Axes

Consider a straight line parallel to the y-axis joining points $P(a,b,c)$ and $Q(a,0,c)$. To derive the matrix for rotation by angle θ in the CCW direction about this line, the following steps are taken:

- Translate line such that Q coincides with origin: $T(-a,0,-c)$
- Rotate about origin around y-axis by angle θ: $R_y(\theta)$
- Reverse translate back to original location: $T(a,0,c)$
- Composite transformation: $M = T(a,0,c).R_y(\theta).T(-a,0,-c)$

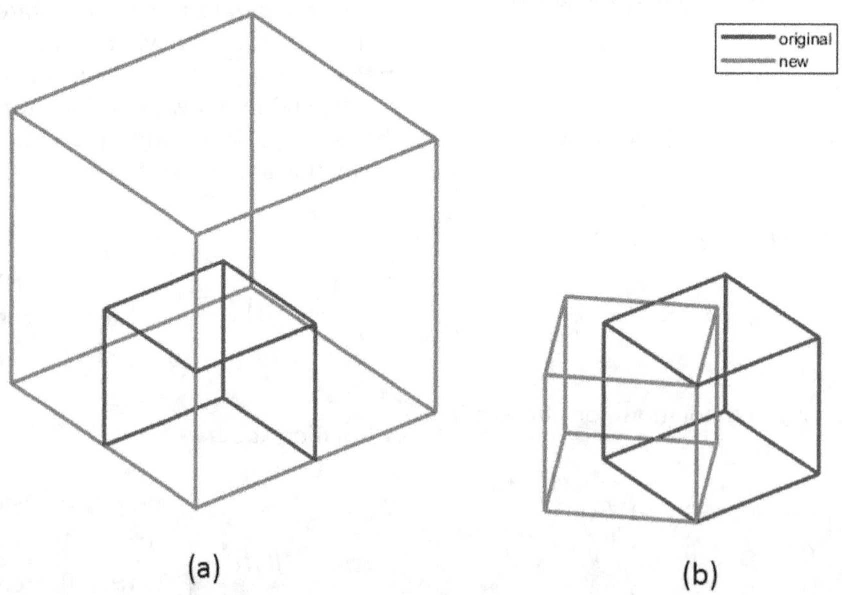

FIGURE 4.40
Fixed point scaling and rotation.

Next consider a straight line parallel to the z-axis joining points $P(a,b,c)$ and $Q(a,b,0)$. To derive the matrix for rotation by angle θ in the CCW direction about this line, the following steps are taken:

- Translate line such that Q coincides with origin: $T(-a,-b,0)$
- Rotate about origin around z-axis by angle θ: $R_z(\theta)$
- Reverse translate back to original location: $T(a,b,0)$
- Composite transformation: $M = T(a,b,0).R_z(\theta).T(-a,-b,0)$

Finally, consider a straight line parallel to the x-axis joining points $P(a,b,c)$ and $Q(0,b,c)$. To derive the matrix for rotation by angle θ in the CCW direction about this line, the following steps are taken (Figure 4.41):

- Translate line such that Q coincides with origin: $T(0,-b,-c)$
- Rotate about origin around x-axis by angle θ: $R_x(\theta)$
- Reverse translate back to original location: $T(0,b,c)$
- Composite transformation: $M = T(0,b,c).R_x(\theta).T(0,-b,-c)$

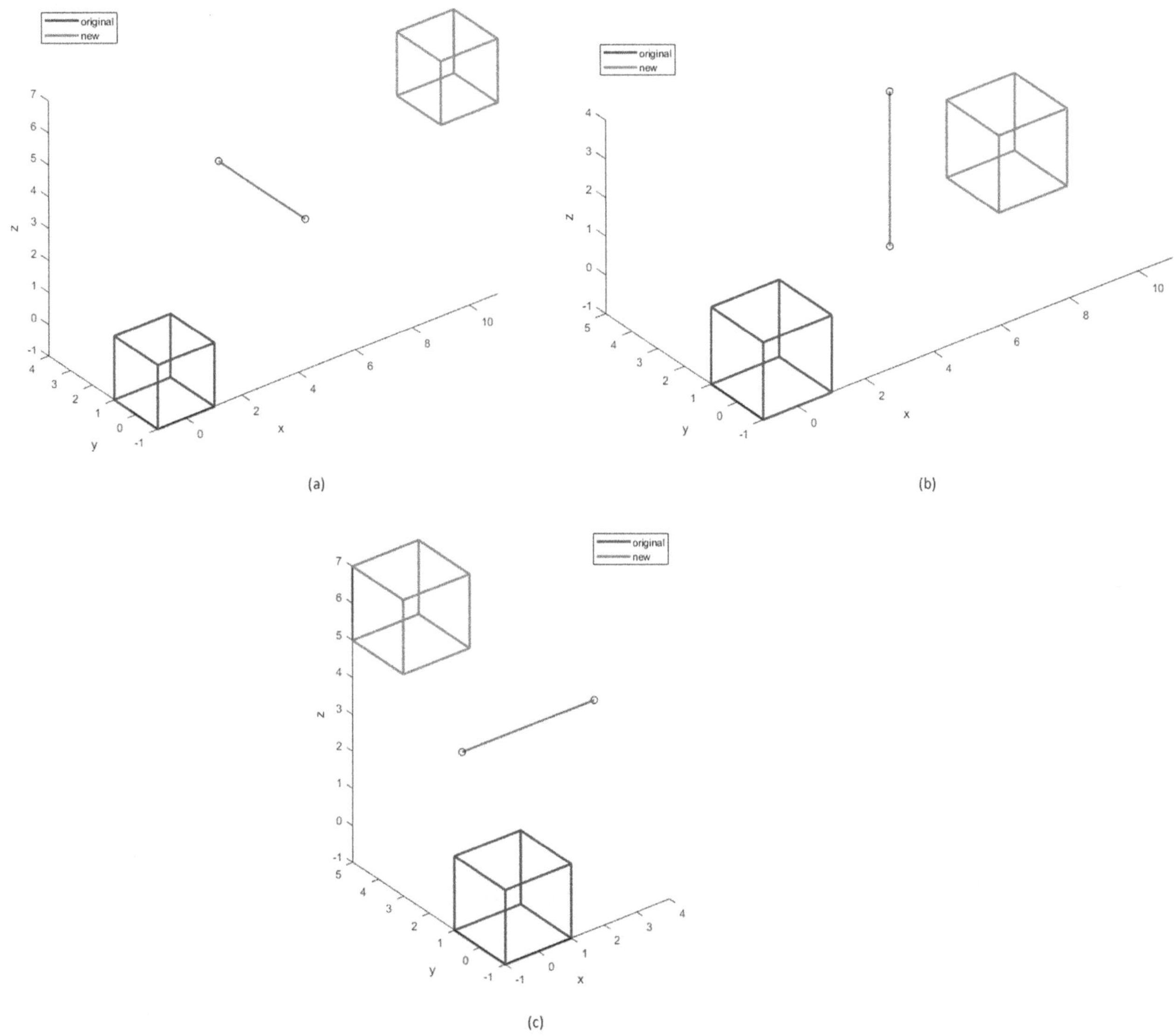

FIGURE 4.41
Rotation parallel to (a) y-axis (b) z-axis (c) x-axis.

4.3.2.7 Reflection

Reflection about a primary plane reverses the coordinate value along an axis perpendicular to the plane (Hearn & Baker, 1996). Reflection along x-axis is equivalent to reflection about yz-plane and reverses the x-coordinate of a point. The corresponding matrix is given by:

$$F_x = \begin{pmatrix} -1 & 0 & 0 & 0 \\ 0 & 1 & 0 & 0 \\ 0 & 0 & 1 & 0 \\ 0 & 0 & 0 & 1 \end{pmatrix}$$

Similarly, reflection along y-axis is equivalent to reflection about xz-plane and reverses the y-coordinate of a point. The corresponding matrix is given by

$$F_y = \begin{pmatrix} 1 & 0 & 0 & 0 \\ 0 & -1 & 0 & 0 \\ 0 & 0 & 1 & 0 \\ 0 & 0 & 0 & 1 \end{pmatrix}$$

Reflection along z-axis is equivalent to reflection about xy-plane and reverse the z-coordinate of a point. The corresponding matrix is given by:

$$F_z = \begin{pmatrix} 1 & 0 & 0 & 0 \\ 0 & 1 & 0 & 0 \\ 0 & 0 & -1 & 0 \\ 0 & 0 & 0 & 1 \end{pmatrix}$$

If the plane of reflection is not a primary plane then it is first made to coincide with one of the primary planes and then the above relations can are applied (Figure 4.42).

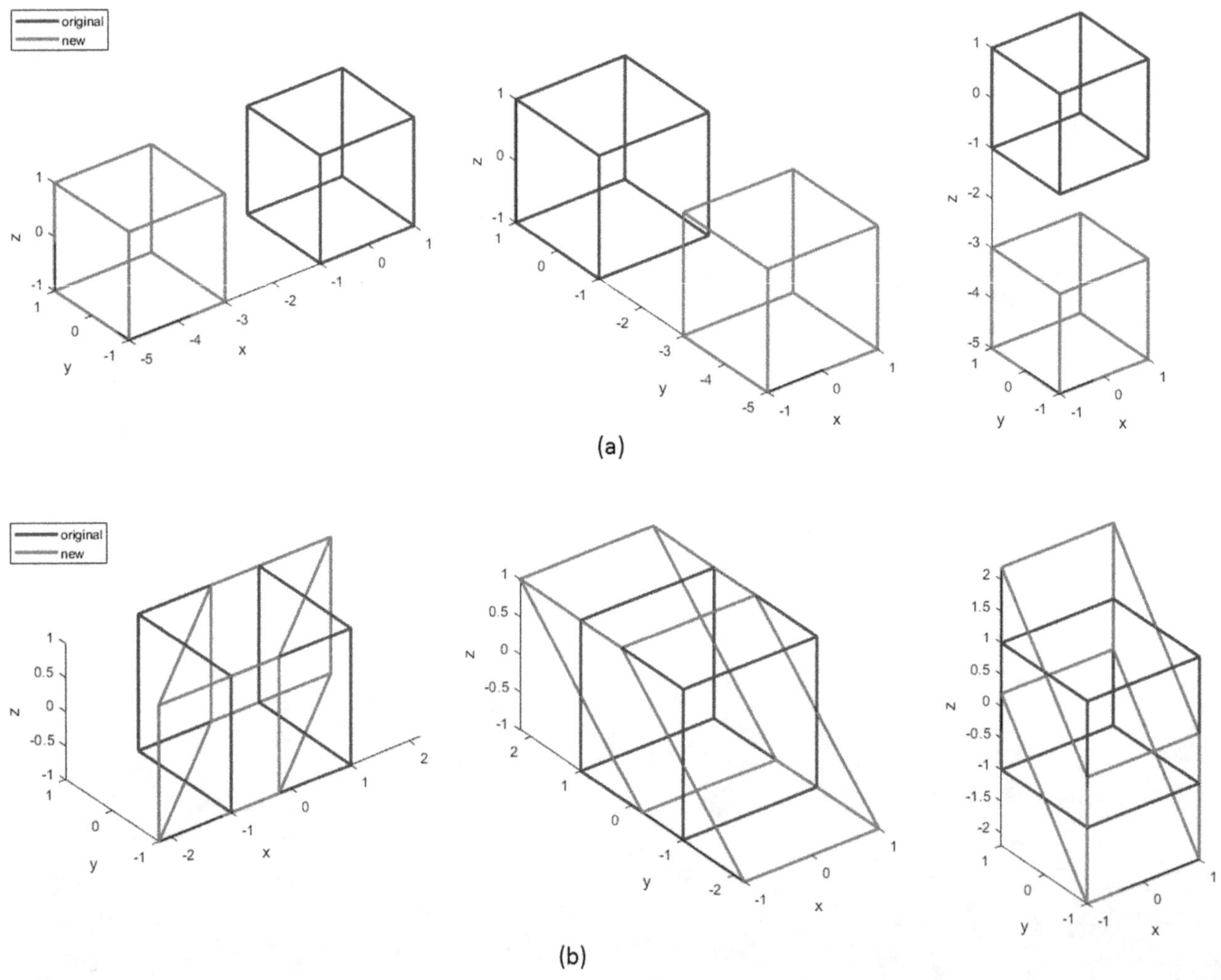

FIGURE 4.42
(a) 3D reflection along x-, y- and z-axis (b) 3D shear along x-, y- and z-axis.

4.3.2.8 Shear

Shear involves changing coordinate values along one axis by adding an amount proportional to coordinate values along another axis (Hearn & Baker, 1996). Shear along each axis can be of two types:

Shear along x-axis can be parallel to $y = 0$ plane (front and back faces) governed by the relation $x_2 = x_1 + h.y$, where h is the constant of proportionality. The corresponding transformation matrix is:

$$H_{xy} = \begin{pmatrix} 1 & h & 0 & 0 \\ 0 & 1 & 0 & 0 \\ 0 & 0 & 1 & 0 \\ 0 & 0 & 0 & 1 \end{pmatrix}$$

Shear along x-axis can also be parallel to $z = 0$ plane (top and bottom faces) governed by the relation $x_2 = x_1 + h.z$. The corresponding transformation matrix is:

$$H_{xz} = \begin{pmatrix} 1 & 0 & h & 0 \\ 0 & 1 & 0 & 0 \\ 0 & 0 & 1 & 0 \\ 0 & 0 & 0 & 1 \end{pmatrix}$$

If both the above shears occur simultaneously then the transformation matrix becomes:

$$H_x = \begin{pmatrix} 1 & h_1 & h_2 & 0 \\ 0 & 1 & 0 & 0 \\ 0 & 0 & 1 & 0 \\ 0 & 0 & 0 & 1 \end{pmatrix}$$

In a likewise manner, shear along y-axis can be along $x = 0$ plane and $z = 0$ plane. The general transformation matrix is of the form:

$$H_y = \begin{pmatrix} 1 & 0 & 0 & 0 \\ h_1 & 1 & h_2 & 0 \\ 0 & 0 & 1 & 0 \\ 0 & 0 & 0 & 1 \end{pmatrix}$$

Shear along z-axis can be along $x = 0$ plane and $y = 0$ plane. The general transformation matrix is of the form:

$$H_z = \begin{pmatrix} 1 & 0 & 0 & 0 \\ 0 & 1 & 0 & 0 \\ h_1 & h_2 & 1 & 0 \\ 0 & 0 & 0 & 1 \end{pmatrix}$$

4.3.3 Common Editing Tasks

Some of the most common 3D graphics editing tasks that can be done using a GUI-based image editing software like Autodesk 3D Studio or Autodesk Maya are listed below:

Modeling: A wide variety of modeling tools and geometric primitives enables creation of graphical objects usually by specifying associated parameters like radius, length, height and location.

Positioning: Positioning tools allow precise positioning and aligning of objects using top, left and front views and the result is viewed on the perspective viewport.

Modifiers: Modifiers like taper, twist, bend and deform can be used to change the appearances of the objects.

Viewing: A universal plane and four viewports are used to display the top, left, front and perspective views of the objects in the scene. A zoom tool and pan tool can be used for zooming and panning the scenes.

Arrays: A number of different types of arrays which may be one, two or three dimensions, as well as linear, circular or spiral can be created using appropriate tools.

Surfaces: 3D surfaces of various types can be created from 2D shapes using operations like extrusion, lathing and lofting. 3D surfaces can also be created from existing 3D objects using various transformation tools like translation, rotation, scaling, slicing, arrays and Boolean operations.

Surface Texture: Surface texture can be applied on modeled surfaces by choosing a multitude of materials like wood, stone, concrete and bricks from a materials library.

Effects: Transparent and reflective materials like glass and metal can be applied on surfaces along with parameters for controlling amounts of reflection, refraction and transparency.

Lights: A number of different light types like point light, spot light and ambient light can be placed at various points on the 3D scene, in accordance to which shading and shadows on 3D surfaces can be computed based on the distance, direction, intensity and color of the lights..

Rendering: Rendering algorithms can be used to transform 3D models into 2D raster images on screen to view the final outputs with respect to the surface models, texture maps, lighting and effects (Figure 4.43).

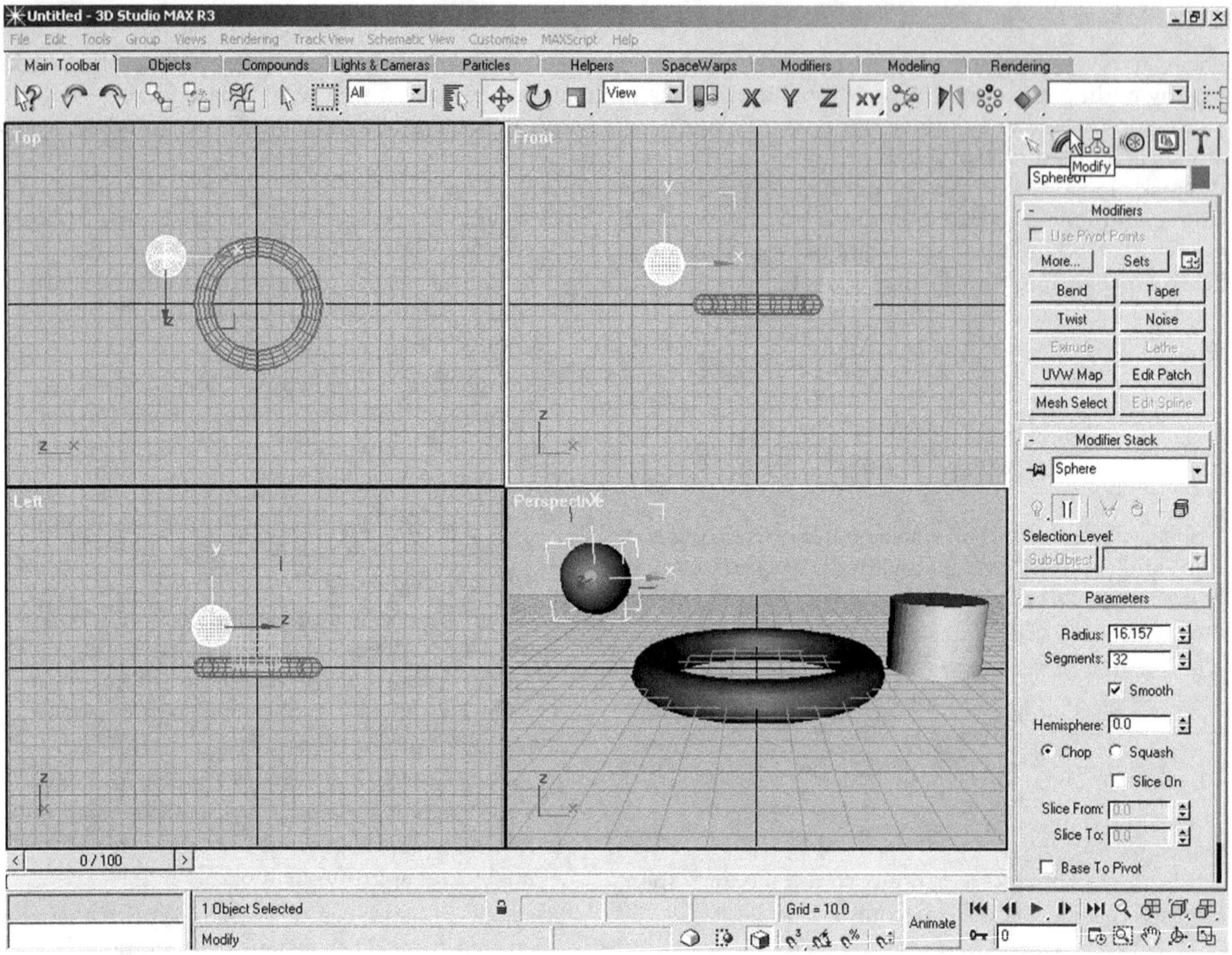

FIGURE 4.43
Typical GUI-based 3D graphics editor interface.

4.4 Vectors

4.4.1 Introduction

Vectors involve both magnitude and direction. Two vectors are equal if they have the same magnitude and direction. Vectors a and b are not equal even if they have same magnitude. Vector $-c$ is defined as having same magnitude but reverse direction as c. Multiplying a vector by a scalar changes its magnitude but keeps direction same, e.g., $2a$. By default vectors are "free", i.e., parallel shifting does not change their magnitude or direction. Vectors can also be "bound", i.e., cannot be shifted, e.g., position vector of point P with respect to origin O (Olive, 2003; Shirley, 2002).

Vector addition implies finding the resultant of two vectors. There are two methods to do this, both of which are essentially equivalent. The triangle rule states that, if p and q represents two sides of a triangle, then $p+q$ is given by the third side. The parallelogram rule states that if P and Q be two adjacent sides of a parallelogram, $P+Q$ is given by its diagonal. If there are more than two vectors, then we use the polygon rule, which says that addition of any number of vectors is obtained by arranging them end to end and closing the final side of resulting polygon, i.e., $r=a+b+c+d$. For 3D vectors, they are to be joined end to end in 3D space (Figure 4.44).

Vectors are represented in two forms: (1) using components, namely, $r=ai+bj+ck$ where a,b,c are scaling factors multiplied to unit vectors i,j,k along $x-,y-$ and $z-$ directions respectively (2) as coordinates in vector space, namely, (a,b,c) with respect to unit vectors $(1,0,0),(0,1,0)$ and $(0,0,1)$ along $x-,y-$ and $z-$ directions respectively. The magnitude of $r=ai+bj+ck$ or $r=(a,b,c)$ is $|r|=\sqrt{(a^2+b^2+c^2)}$ and unit vector along direction of r is: $u=r/|r|$

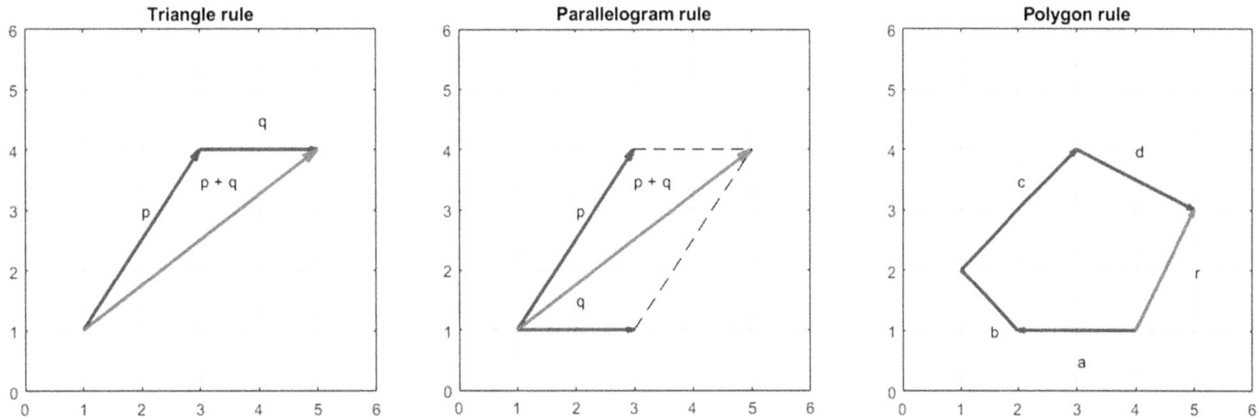

FIGURE 4.44
Vector addition.

4.4.2 Dot Product

Dot product of two vectors $A = ai + bj + ck$ and $P = pi + qj + rk$ with angle θ between them is given by:

$$A \bullet P = |A||P|\cos(\theta)$$

It follows that angle between them is:

$$\cos(\theta) = (A \bullet P)/(|A||P|)$$

Even though it is a product of two vector quantities, the product itself is a scalar number. This is because:

$$A \bullet P = (ai + bj + ck) \bullet (pi + qj + rk)$$

$$A \bullet P = ap + bq + cr$$

The above expression is: true because $i \bullet i = j \bullet j = k \bullet k = 1$ as each has a magnitude of 1 and angle between them is 0. Also $i \bullet j = j \bullet k = k \bullet i = 0$ as angle between each pair is 90°.

Corollary 1: If vectors are parallel, then $\theta = 0^\circ$ hence $A \bullet P = |A||P|$

Corollary 2: If vectors are perpendicular, then $\theta = 90^\circ$ hence $A \bullet P = 0$

4.4.3 Cross Product

Cross product of two vectors $A = ai + bj + ck$ and $P = pi + qj + rk$ with angle θ between them is given by:

$$A \times P = \{|A||P|\sin\theta\}.n$$

The resultant is a vector in the direction of the unit vector n, which is a vector perpendicular to both A and P. The positive direction of n is governed by the right-handed corkscrew rule, which says that if a right-handed corkscrew is rotated from A to P, then the positive direction of n will be that along which the corkscrew advances. The magnitude of the resultant is $|A||P|\sin\theta$.

Substituting the vector components in the above expression we get:

$$A \times P = (ai + bj + ck) \times (pi + qj + rk)$$

$$A \times P = (br - cq)i + (cp - ar)j + (aq - bp)k$$

The above expression is: true because $i \times i = j \times j = k \times k = 0$ as angle between each pair is 0°. Also $i \times j = k, j \times k = i, k \times i = j$ as angle between each pair is 90° and the resultant is orthogonal to each of the components.

4.4.4 2D Vector Alignment

A position vector $P = ai + bj$ can be aligned with a primary axis along positive or negative directions by rotating through the appropriate angle $\theta = \arctan(b/a)$. Depending on the orientation of the original vector and the primary axis along which it is to be aligned, the angle of rotation can be either positive or negative.

If the angle of orientation with respect to $+x$ axis, of vector $(ai + bj)$ be θ, then angle of orientation of vector $(-ai + bj)$ is $(180 - \theta)$, angle of orientation of vector $(-ai - bj)$ is $(180 + \theta)$, and angle of orientation of vector $(ai - bj)$ is $-\theta$.

Angles are positive measured along counter-clockwise (CCW) direction and negative along the clockwise (CW) direction. The rotation angles for aligning these vectors with the $+x$ axis will be just the negative of these angles of orientation, i.e.,$-\theta$, $-(180-\theta)$, $-(180+\theta)$ and $+\theta$ respectively. The rotation matrix is calculated based on these latter set of values, e.g., for $(ai+bj)$ the rotation matrix is $R(-\theta)$, for $(-ai+bj)$ the rotation matrix is $R\left[-(180-\theta)\right]$.

Apart from the $+x$ axis angles of orientation can also be calculated with respect to the other primary axes. If θ be the angle with the $+x$ axis, then angle with $+y$ axis will be $(90-\theta)$, angle with the $-x$ axis will be $(180-\theta)$, and angle with the $-$y axis will be $(90+\theta)$. The signs are calculated by observing whether we are moving in the CW or CCW direction. For example, for vector $(ai+bj)$ which is in quadrant $Q1$ quadrant, when angle is measured from $+x$ axis we are moving in CCW direction hence $+\theta$, when measuring from $-x$ axis we are moving in CW direction hence $-(180-\theta)$, when measuring from $+y$ axis we are moving in CW direction hence $-(90-\theta)$, when measuring from $-y$ axis we are moving in CCW direction hence $+(90+\theta)$ (Figure 4.45). Table 4.2 lists out all the possibilities.

TABLE 4.2
Angle between Vectors and Primary Axes

Vector	Quadrant	$+x$–axis	$-x$–axis	$+y$–axis	$-y$–axis
$ai+bj$	Q_1	$+\theta$	$-(180-\theta)$	$-(90-\theta)$	$+(90+\theta)$
$-ai+bj$	Q_2	$+(180-\theta)$	$-\theta$	$+(90-\theta)$	$-(90+\theta)$
$-ai-bj$	Q_3	$+(180+\theta)$	$+\theta$	$+(90+\theta)$	$-(90-\theta)$
$ai-bj$	Q_4	$-\theta$	$+(180-\theta)$	$-(90+\theta)$	$+(90-\theta)$

4.4.5 3D Vector Alignment

Consider a position vector $P=(a,b,c)$ from origin O to point P, which needs to be aligned along the z-axis. To derive the transformation matrix, the following steps are taken (Chakraborty, 2010):

- Step 1: Rotate vector OP by angle α CCW around x –axis to lie on $x-z$ plane at OQ: $R_x(\alpha)$
- Step 2: Rotate vector OQ by angle ϕ CW around y –axis to coincide with z –axis at R: $R_y(-\varphi)$

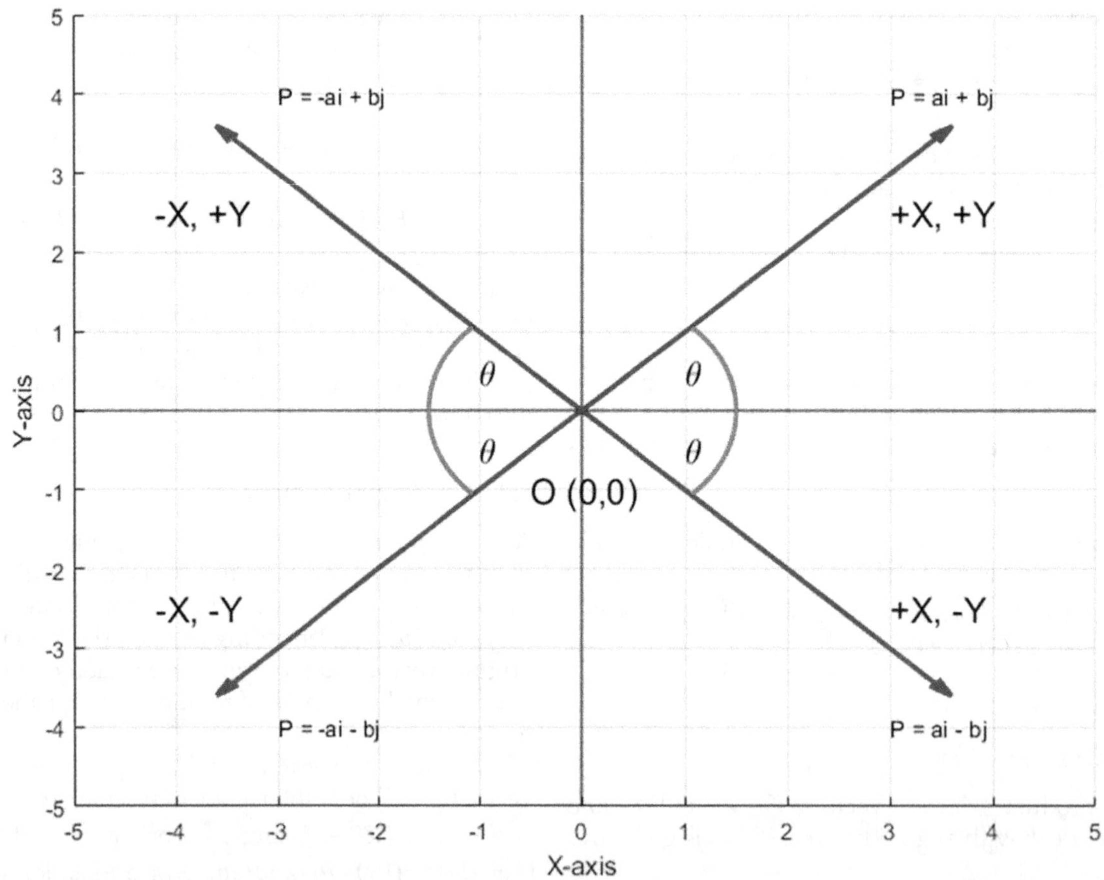

FIGURE 4.45
2D Vector alignments.

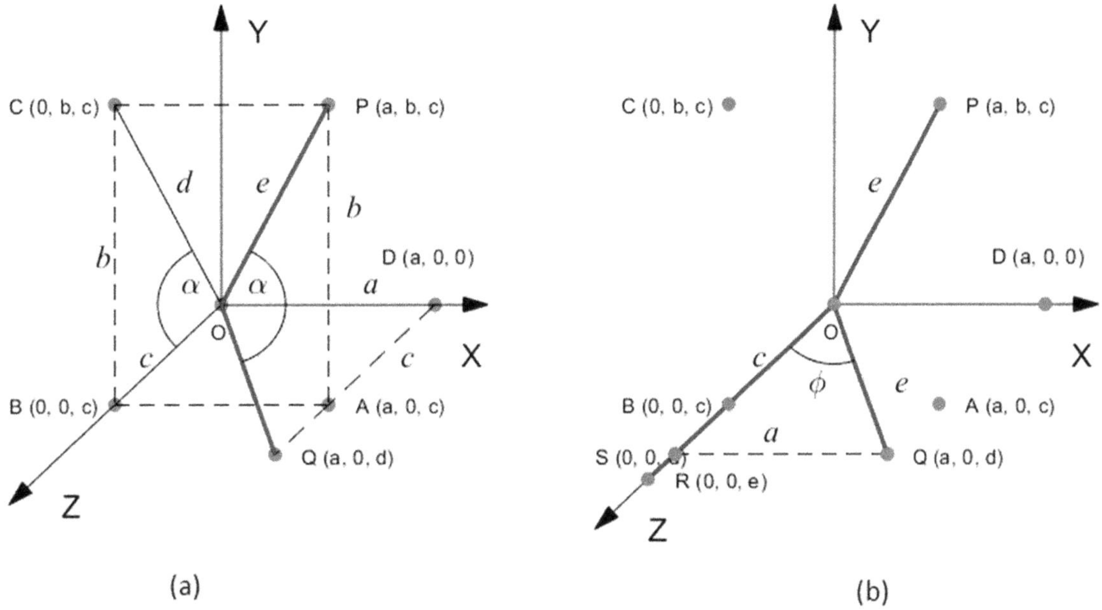

FIGURE 4.46
3D vector alignments : (a) step 1 (b) step 2.

Step 1:
To represent α and ϕ in terms of a, b, c the following set of constructions are performed:

- Project $P(a,b,c)$ onto $x-z$ plane at $A(a,0,c)$
- Project $A(a,0,c)$ along $x-z$ plane onto Z-axis at $B(0,0,c)$
- Project $P(a,b,c)$ onto $y-z$ plane at $C(0,b,c)$
- Join BC and OC

We now observe the following (Figure 4.46):

$$\angle POQ = \alpha = \angle BOC$$

Since, C has coordinates $(0,b,c)$ and B has coordinates $(0,0,c)$, length BC equals b. Also since B has coordinates $(0,0,c)$, length OB equals c. Let length OC be $d = \sqrt{b^2+c^2}$

Then in $\Delta OBC, \cos(\alpha) = OB/OC = c/d$ and $\sin(\alpha) = BC/OC = b/d$. Thus,

$$R_x(\alpha) = \begin{pmatrix} 1 & 0 & 0 & 0 \\ 0 & \cos\alpha & -\sin\alpha & 0 \\ 0 & \sin\alpha & \cos\alpha & 0 \\ 0 & 0 & 0 & 1 \end{pmatrix}$$
$$= \begin{pmatrix} 1 & 0 & 0 & 0 \\ 0 & c/d & -b/d & 0 \\ 0 & b/d & c/d & 0 \\ 0 & 0 & 0 & 1 \end{pmatrix}$$

Coordinates of Q:

$$R_x(\alpha).P = \begin{pmatrix} 1 & 0 & 0 & 0 \\ 0 & c/d & -b/d & 0 \\ 0 & b/d & c/d & 0 \\ 0 & 0 & 0 & 1 \end{pmatrix} \begin{pmatrix} a \\ b \\ c \\ 1 \end{pmatrix} = \begin{pmatrix} a \\ 0 \\ d \\ 1 \end{pmatrix} \text{i.e}(a,0,d)$$

Step 2:
To find the value of ϕ in terms of a, b, c the following set of constructions are done.

- Project $Q(a,0,d)$ along $x-z$ plane onto $z-$ axis at $S(0,0,d)$

Let length(OP) = length(OQ) = length(OR) = $e = \sqrt{a^2+b^2+c^2}$. Since coordinates of Q are $(a,0,d)$, length QS equals a. Since coordinates of S are $(0,0,d)$, length OS equals d. In triangle OQS, angle QOS equals φ. Thus, $\sin(\varphi) = a/e$, $\cos(\varphi) = d/e$. Hence

$$R_y(-\varphi) = \begin{pmatrix} \cos(-\varphi) & 0 & \sin(-\varphi) & 0 \\ 0 & 1 & 0 & 0 \\ -\sin(-\varphi) & 0 & \cos(-\varphi) & 0 \\ 0 & 0 & 0 & 1 \end{pmatrix}$$
$$= \begin{pmatrix} d/e & 0 & -a/e & 0 \\ 0 & 1 & 0 & 0 \\ a/e & 0 & d/e & 0 \\ 0 & 0 & 0 & 1 \end{pmatrix}$$

TABLE 4.3

Alignment of Vector $ai+bj+ck$ with Primary Axes $\left(e=\sqrt{a^2+b^2+c^2}\right)$

Primary Axis	d	$\cos\alpha$	$\sin\alpha$	$\cos\varphi$	$\sin\varphi$	M
z-axis	$d=\sqrt{b^2+c^2}$	c/d	b/d	d/e	a/e	$R_y(-\varphi).R_x(\alpha)$
x-axis	$d=\sqrt{b^2+c^2}$	c/d	b/d	a/e	d/e	$R_y(\varphi).R_x(\alpha)$
y-axis	$d=\sqrt{a^2+c^2}$	a/d	c/d	b/e	d/e	$R_z(\varphi).R_y(\alpha)$

Coordinates of

$$\mathrm{R}=R_y(-\varphi).Q=\begin{pmatrix} d/e & 0 & -a/e & 0 \\ 0 & 1 & 0 & 0 \\ a/e & 0 & d/e & 0 \\ 0 & 0 & 0 & 1 \end{pmatrix}\begin{pmatrix} a \\ 0 \\ d \\ 1 \end{pmatrix}=\begin{pmatrix} 0 \\ 0 \\ e \\ 1 \end{pmatrix},$$

i.e., $(0,0,e)$

This matches our expectation since the length of vector OP is $\sqrt{a^2+b^2+c^2}=e$; hence, when it is aligned along the z-axis, the tip of the vector should have coordinates $(0,0,e)$. Composite transformation: $M=R_y(-\varphi).R_x(\alpha)$.

In a similar fashion alignment with the x- and y-axes can be likewise analyzed. These are left for the reader as exercises. The final results are summarized in Table 4.3.

4.4.6 Rotation Around 3D Vector

The transformation matrix for rotation around a vector $P=ai+bj+ck$ by a specified angle, θ, is derived by the following steps:

- Step 1: Align the vector along a primary axis: $R_y(-\varphi).R_x(\alpha)$
- Step 2: Rotate around that primary axis by the specified angle: $R_z(\theta)$
- Step 3: Reverse align vector to its original location: $R_y(\varphi).R_x(-\alpha)$
- Step 4: Compute transformation matrix: $M=R_y(\varphi).R_x(-\alpha).R_z(\theta).R_y(-\varphi).R_x(\alpha)$

4.4.7 Rotation Around 3D Line

The transformation matrix for rotation around an arbitrary line joining P and Q in the CCW direction by an angle θ along a plane perpendicular to the line is derived by the following steps:

- Step 1: Translate line so that one end coincides with origin: $T(t_x,t_y,t_z)$
- Step 2: Align the resulting vector along a primary axis: $R_y(-\varphi).R_x(\alpha)$
- Step 3: Rotate around that primary axis by the given amount: $R_z(\theta)$
- Step 4: Reverse align vector to its original location: $R_y(\varphi).R_x(-\alpha)$
- Step 5: Reverse translate line to original location: $T(-t_x,-t_y,-t_z)$
- Step 6: Compute transformation matrix: $M=A.B$ where $A=T(-t_x,-t_y,-t_z).R_y(\varphi).R_x(-\alpha).R_z(\theta)$ and $B=R_y(-\varphi).R_x(\alpha).T(t_x,t_y,t_z)$

4.5 Projection

4.5.1 Types of Projection

Projection is used to map a higher-dimensional object to a lower-dimensional view. For a 2D to 1D projection, points on a plane are projected onto a line, called a view-line, for a 3D to 2D projection, points on an object are projected onto a plane, called the view-plane. Projection is of two types: parallel and perspective. In parallel projection, projection lines are parallel to each other and all things near and far appear at their true sizes. In perspective projective projection lines appear to converge at a point or diverge from a point called the PRP (projection reference point) or VP (view point) or COP (center of projection) and sizes of the objects reduce with distance. Parallel projection can again be of two types: orthographic and oblique. In parallel orthographic projection, the projection lines are perpendicular to the view plane. In parallel oblique projection, the projection lines can be oriented at any arbitrary angles to the view plane. Usually for 3D projection, parallel orthographic projection can also be subdivided into two types: multi-view and axonometric. In multi-view projection, the projection occurs on the primary planes, i.e., $xy-$, $yz-$ or $zx-$ planes. Such views are called top, side and front views, and display only one face of the object. In axonometric projection, the projection occurs on an arbitrary plane other than primary planes (Figure 4.47). In this case more than one face of the object can be viewed (Hearn & Baker, 1996).

4.5.2 Homogeneous Vector Equations

In homogeneous vector equations (Marsh, 2005), both points and lines are treated as vectors and relations are derived based on their intersections. Cartesian equation of a line is $ax+by+c=0$ and can be expressed in the form $L=(a,b,c)$. Let $P(X,Y,W)$ be the

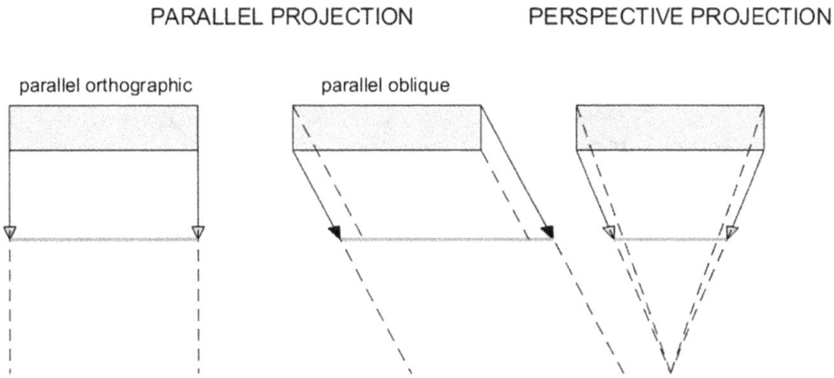

FIGURE 4.47
Types of projection.

homogeneous coordinates of a point (x,y), i.e., $x=\frac{X}{W}, y=\frac{Y}{W}$. For line L passing through point P we must have $aX+bY+cW=0$, i.e., $L \bullet P=0$.

For line L passing through two points P_1 and P_2, we must have $L \bullet P_1 = 0$ and $L \bullet P_2 = 0$. Thus vector L is perpendicular to both P_1 and P_2, i.e., $L = P_1 \times P_2$. This is the condition to be satisfied for determining whether a line passes through two given points or not.

Again, the intersection P of two lines L_1 and L_2 implies $L_1 \bullet P = 0$ and $L_2 \bullet P = 0$. Thus vector P is perpendicular to both L_1 and L_2, i.e., $P = L_1 \times L_2$. This is the condition to be satisfied for determining whether two given lines intersect at a point or not (Figure 4.48).

4.5.3 2D Projection

Let P be a point on a plane projected on the view-line L projected along VP at Q, where V is the projection reference point. Let the line VPQ be K. Since line K passes through two points V and P we have $K = V \times P$. Also point Q passes through two lines L and K, so we have $Q = L \times K = L \times (V \times P)$.

To find the projected point coordinates we make use of the vector identity, where A' and B' denote the transpose of the corresponding matrices, "•" denotes the dot product and I is the identity matrix of appropriate dimensions (Marsh, 2005):

$$A \times (B \times C) = (C \bullet A).B - (A \bullet B).C = \left[B'.A - (B.A').I\right].C$$

In the current scenario we have:

$$Q = L \times (V \times P) = \left[V'.L - (V.L').I\right].P = M.P$$

Here M is the perspective projection matrix of point P onto view-line L along direction V and V' and L' notations indicate transpose (Marsh, 2005). Note that the points and lines are represented using homogeneous vector notations with $L=(a,b,c)$ and $V=(v_1,v_2,1)$. For parallel projection V can be thought to be located at infinity so in this case $V=(v_1,v_2,0)$. For a 2D projection the identity matrix is of dimensions 3 × 3, i.e., $I = \begin{pmatrix} 1 & 0 & 0 \\ 0 & 1 & 0 \\ 0 & 0 & 1 \end{pmatrix}$ (Figure 4.49).

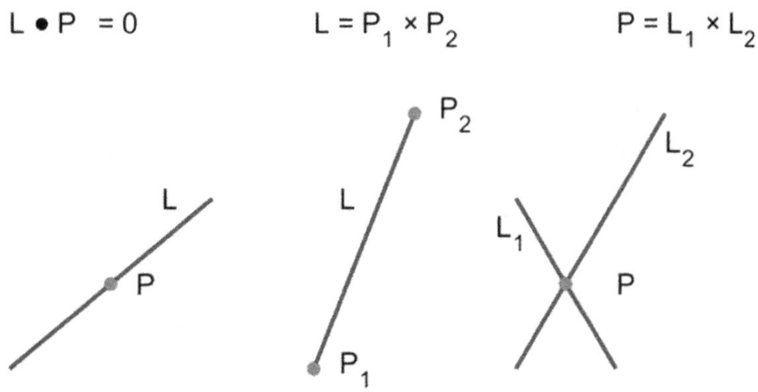

FIGURE 4.48
Deriving homogeneous vector equations.

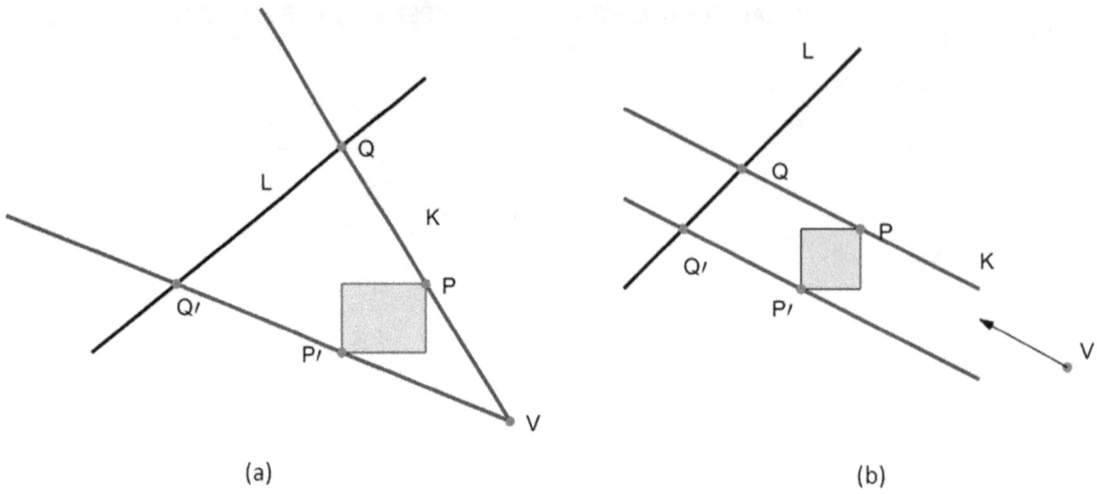

FIGURE 4.49
3D projections : (a) perspective and (b) parallel.

4.5.4 3D Orthographic P rojection

In a likewise manner, for a 3D to 2D projection, it can be shown that the projection Q of a point P in 3D space along direction V onto view-plane with normal N is given by the following, where V' and N' indicate transpose (Marsh, 2005) (Figure 4.50). In this case the coefficients of the Cartesian equation of a plane are proportional to the components of the normal vector of the plane, I is the 4×4 identity matrix: $\begin{pmatrix} 1 & 0 & 0 & 0 \\ 0 & 1 & 0 & 0 \\ 0 & 0 & 1 & 0 \\ 0 & 0 & 0 & 1 \end{pmatrix}$.

$$Q = L \times (V \times P) = [V'.N - (V.N').I].P = M.P$$

4.5.4.1 *Multi-View Projections*

These are a type of parallel orthographic projections where the view-planes are the primary planes or planes parallel to them. Such views are called top, front and side views and display only one face of the object (Foley et al., 1990). If view plane coincides with primary planes, then projection matrices are as shown below, where the subscripts indicate projection on the $x-y$, $x-z$ and $y-z$ planes (Figure 4.51).

$$P_{xy} = \begin{pmatrix} 1 & 0 & 0 & 0 \\ 0 & 1 & 0 & 0 \\ 0 & 0 & 0 & 0 \\ 0 & 0 & 0 & 1 \end{pmatrix}$$

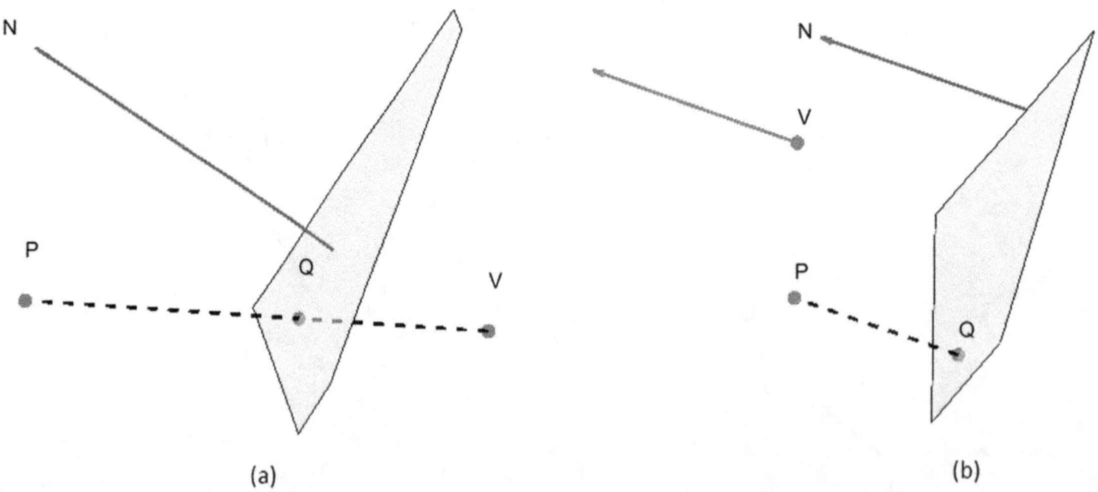

FIGURE 4.50
3D projections : (a) perspective and (b) parallel.

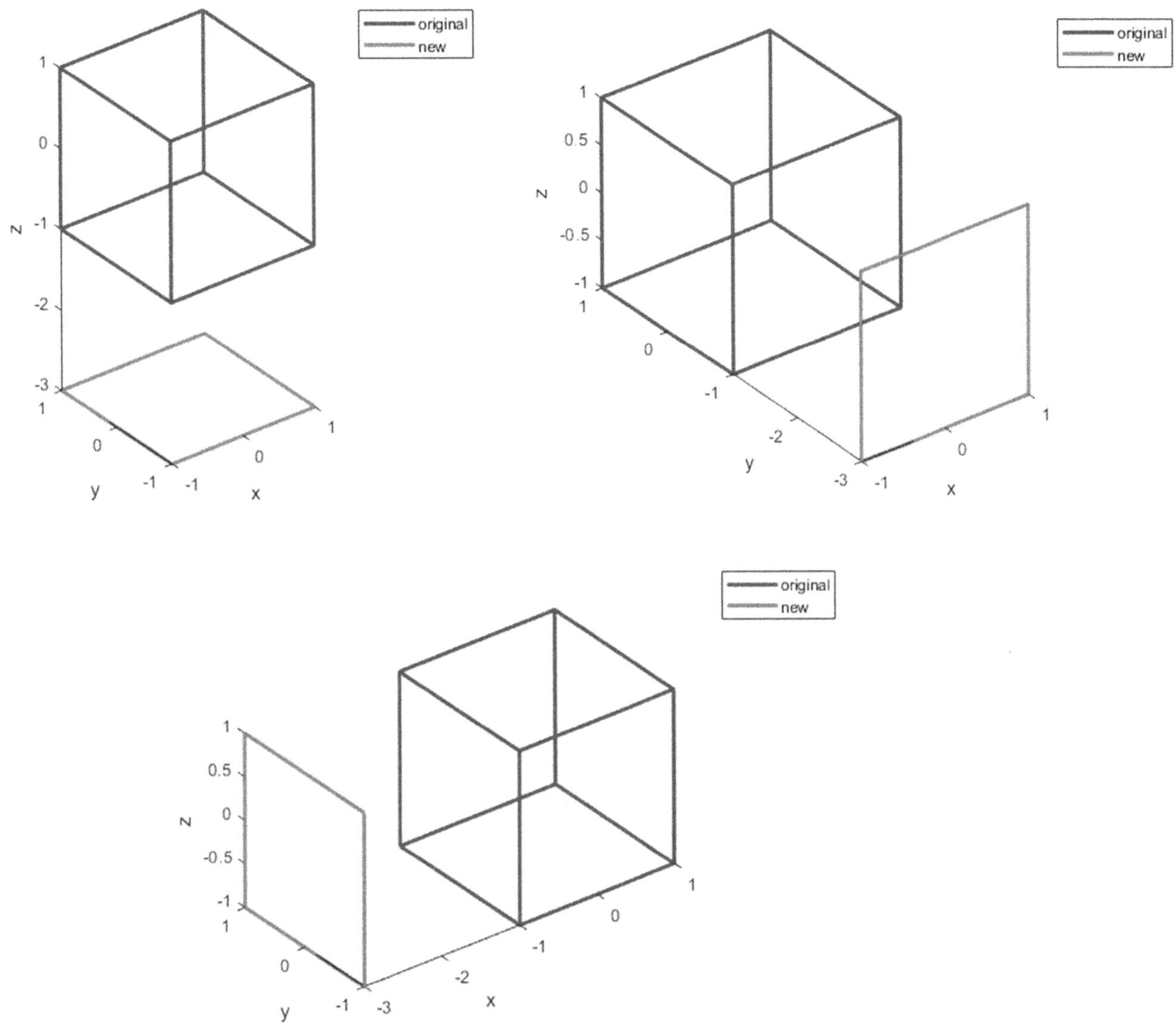

FIGURE 4.51
Multiview projections on planes parallel to (a) $x-y$ (b) $x-z$ (c) $y-z$.

$$P_{xz} = \begin{pmatrix} 1 & 0 & 0 & 0 \\ 0 & 0 & 0 & 0 \\ 0 & 0 & 1 & 0 \\ 0 & 0 & 0 & 1 \end{pmatrix}$$

$$P_{yz} = \begin{pmatrix} 0 & 0 & 0 & 0 \\ 0 & 1 & 0 & 0 \\ 0 & 0 & 1 & 0 \\ 0 & 0 & 0 & 1 \end{pmatrix}$$

4.5.4.2 Axonometric Projections

Here the projection lines are parallel to each other and perpendicular to the viewplane, but the view-plane does not coincide with the primary planes (Chakraborty, 2010). For example, consider an axonometric plane with normal along $i+j+k$ and passing through the point $(0,0,p)$. In this case equation of the viewplane is $(x-0)+(y-0)+(z-p)=0$. Thus, $N=(1,1,1,-p)$. Also since the projection is parallel and orthographic the projection lines are along the normal to the plane and the viewpoint is located at infinity (Figure 4.52). Thus, $V=(1,1,1,0)$. Projection matrix is:

$$\begin{pmatrix} 1 \\ 1 \\ 1 \\ 0 \end{pmatrix} \begin{pmatrix} 1 & 1 & 1 & -p \end{pmatrix} - \begin{pmatrix} 1 & 1 & 1 & 0 \end{pmatrix} \begin{pmatrix} 1 \\ 1 \\ 1 \\ -p \end{pmatrix} \begin{pmatrix} 1 & 0 & 0 & 0 \\ 0 & 1 & 0 & 0 \\ 0 & 0 & 1 & 0 \\ 0 & 0 & 0 & 1 \end{pmatrix}$$

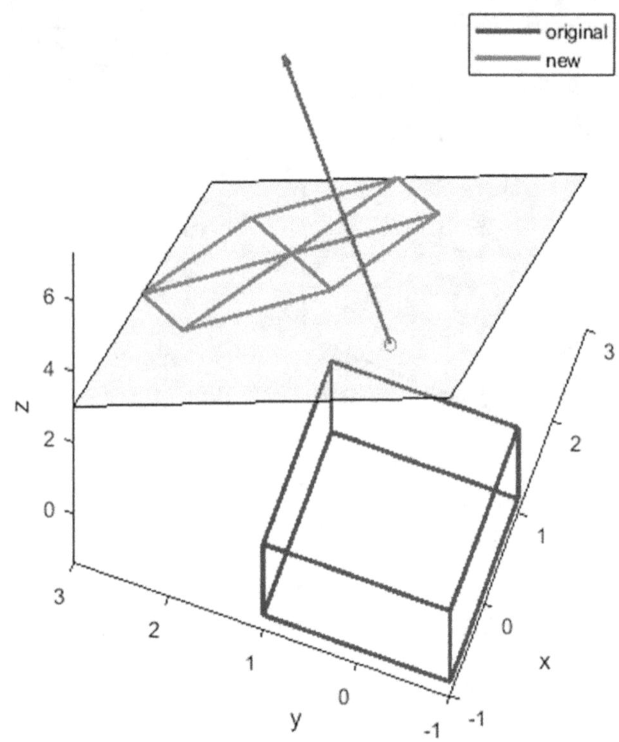

FIGURE 4.52
Axonometric projection.

4.5.4.3 Foreshortening Factors

Foreshortening factors are ratios of the projected lengths to the original lengths of components of a vector along the three principle axes. Let a line *PQ* on a plane be projected on the xy-plane at *pq*. Then the ratio of length (*pq*) to the ratio of length (*PQ*) is referred to as the foreshortening scaling factor and defines how much the original line has been scaled due to projection (Marsh, 2005). It turns out that this ratio is same for all lines on the plane and does not depend on the actual coordinates of the line (Figure 4.53).

Consider an axonometric plane with normal $N = ai + bj + ck$. For aligning the normal to a primary axis, say, z-axis, it has to be first rotated by angle α to place it on a plane containing the primary axis, and then rotated by angle φ along the plane to align it to the required primary axis. Finally, project on the xy-plane along the z-axis. The combined transformation matrix is: $M = P_{xy}.R_y(-\varphi).R_x(\alpha)$. Expanding, we get:

$$M = \begin{pmatrix} \cos\varphi & -\sin\alpha.\sin\varphi & -\cos\alpha.\sin\varphi & 0 \\ 0 & \cos\alpha & -\sin\alpha & 0 \\ 0 & 0 & 0 & 0 \\ 0 & 0 & 0 & 1 \end{pmatrix}$$

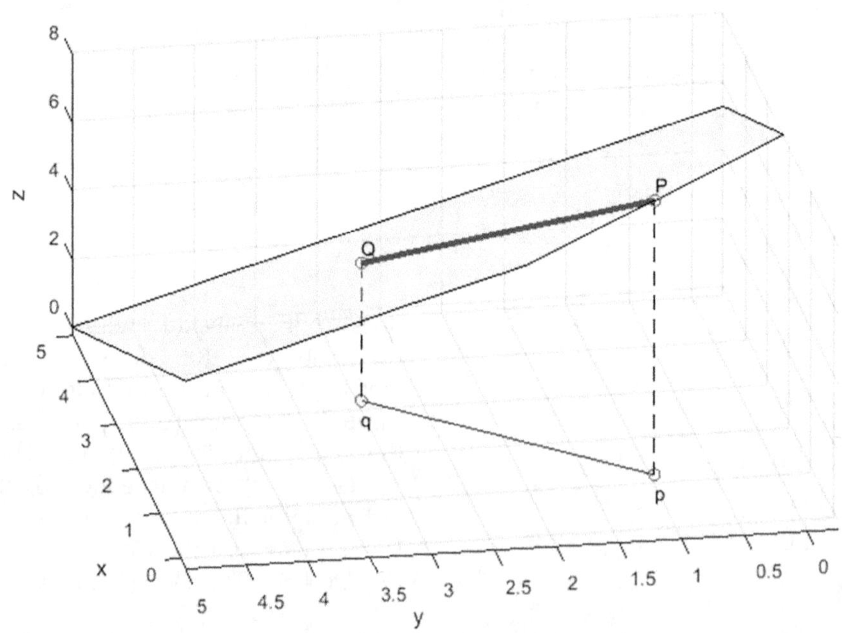

FIGURE 4.53
Determining foreshortening factors.

Now consider a vector $P = Ai + Bj + Ck$. Its component vectors along the three principle axes are given by $P_x = (A,0,0), P_y = (0,B,0), P_z = (0,0,C)$. The length of the vectors along the primary axes is:

$$L(P_x) = A, L(P_y) = B, L(P_z) = C$$

The projected components of P onto the primary axes are calculated as follows:

$$Q_x = M.P_x, Q_y = M.P_y, Q_z = M.P_z$$

If $Q = (q_1, q_2, q_3)$ then the projected length is $L(Q) = \sqrt{(q_1)^2 + (q_2)^2 + (q_3)^2}$. In this case the projected lengths are $L(Q_x), L(Q_y), L(Q_z)$. It can be shown that the foreshortening factors are representable in terms of these two angles as shown below:

$$ff_x = \frac{L(Q_x)}{L(P_x)} = \cos\varphi$$

$$ff_y = \frac{L(Q_y)}{L(P_y)} = \sqrt{(\cos\alpha)^2 + (\sin\alpha.\sin\varphi)^2}$$

$$ff_z = \frac{L(Q_z)}{L(P_z)} = \sqrt{(\sin\alpha)^2 + (\cos\alpha.\sin\varphi)^2}$$

It can be observed from the above relations that foreshortening factors are independent of vector components A, B, C and only depend on the angles of vertical rotation α and horizontal rotation φ. This independence also holds for projections on the other two primary planes, i.e., the yz –plane and zx –plane.

4.5.4.4 *Isometric, Dimetric and Trimetric Projections*

Consider an axonometric plane with normal $N = ai + bj + ck$. Expressions for foreshortening factors have been shown in the previous section.

If all three factors ff_x, ff_y, ff_z are unequal, then it is referred to as trimetric projection, which occurs when $|a|, |b|, |c|$ are all different (March, 2005).

If two of the factors are equal to each other then it is referred to as dimetric projection. This occurs when α, $\varphi = \pm 45°$ or $\pm 90°$ or $\pm 135°$, which in turn occurs when either $|a| = |b|$ or $|b| = |c|$ or $|c| = |a|$.

If all three factors are equal then it is referred to as isometric projection (Figure 4.54). This occurs when $\alpha = \pm 45°$ and $\varphi = \pm 35.264°$, which in turn occurs when $|a| = |b| = |c|$.

4.5.5 3D Oblique Projections

When the direction of parallel projection on the viewplane is not perpendicular, then it is called an oblique projection. When the viewing direction makes an angle of 45° with the viewplane, then the projection obtained is called cavalier projection (Marsh, 2005). If $V = (v_1, v_2, v_3)$ be the viewpoint vector, then a cavalier projection satisfies the condition:

$$v_3^2 = v_1^2 + v_2^2$$

Here, the image of the projected object looks much thicker than in reality as the foreshortening factor for faces perpendicular to the viewing plane is 1. To reduce the thickness, a projection type called cabinet projection can be used, which reduces this factor to 0.5. This is possible when the viewpoint vector makes

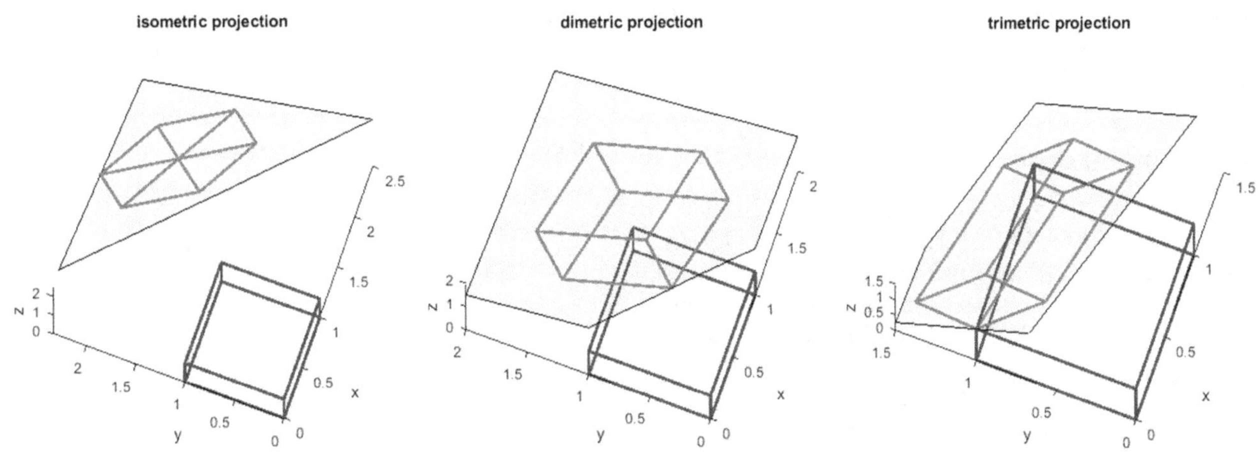

FIGURE 4.54
Isometric, dimetric and trimetric projections.

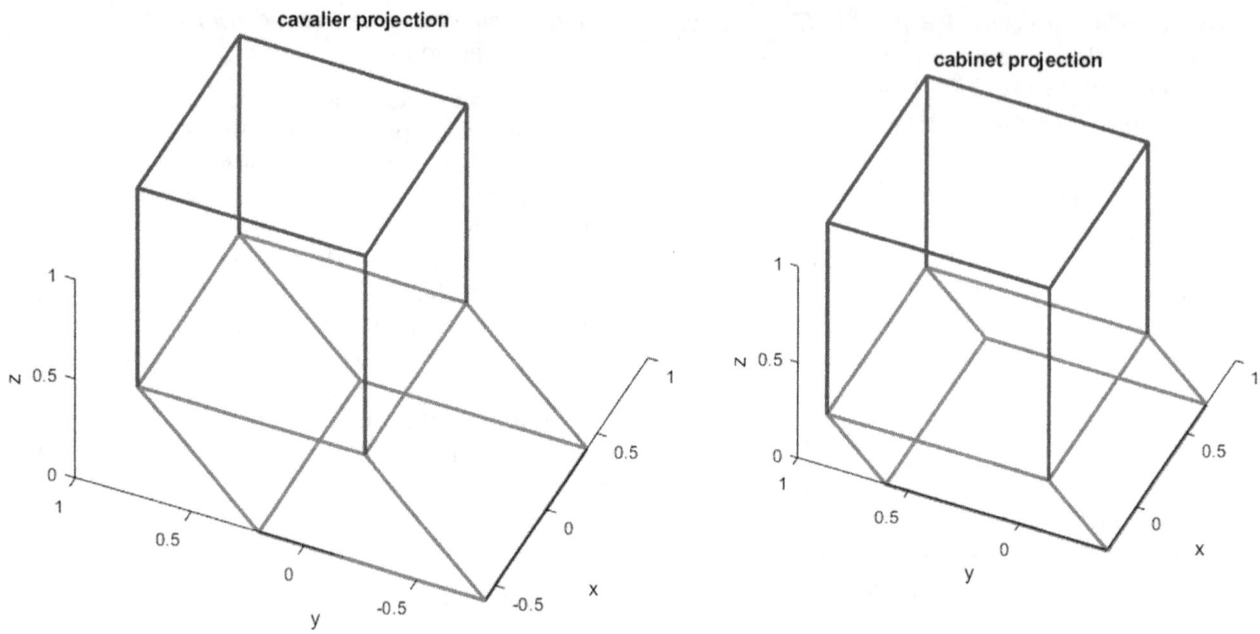

FIGURE 4.55
Cavalier and cabinet projections.

an angle of 63.4° with the viewplane. A cabinet projection satisfies the condition (Figure 4.55):

$$v_3^2 = 4\left(v_1^2 + v_2^2\right)$$

4.5.6 3D Perspective Projections

Under perspective projection images of parallel lines in space appear to converge to a point called PRP (projection reference point). Let the point $A(x, y, z)$ be projected on a view-plane coinciding with $x-y$ plane, at $P(x_p, y_p, 0)$. Let $R(0,0,r)$ be the PRP along z-axis and let O be the origin. It is required to find the values of x_p and y_p in terms of x, y, z, r. Two cases can arise (1) when A and R are on opposite sides of viewplane (2) when A and R are on the same side of viewplane (Foley et al., 1990).

4.5.6.1 *Type 1: Opposite Side of View-plane*

From similar triangles RCB and ROQ, CB/OQ = CR/OR (Figure 4.56a) Here $CB = x$, $OQ = x_p$, $CR = r + z$, $OR = r$ Substituting: $x / x_p = (r+z)/r$, i.e., $x_p = \{r/(r+z)\}.x$ From similar triangles ARB and PRQ, AB/PQ = BR/QR Here AB = y, $PQ = y_p$, $\text{BR} = \sqrt{(r+z)^2 + x^2}$, $\text{QR} = \sqrt{r^2 + x_p{}^2}$

Substituting: $y / y_p = \sqrt{(r+z)^2 + x^2} / \sqrt{r^2 + x_p{}^2}$, i.e., $y_p = \{r/(r+z)\}.y$

Note: Since C is on the negative side of the z-axis, we substitute z with $-z$ to obtain the length of CR.

Thus, $x_p = \{r/(r-z)\}.x$ and $y_p = \{r/(r-z)\}.y$

4.5.6.2 *Type 2: Same Side of View-plane*

From similar triangles OQR and CBR, CB/OQ = CR/OR (Figure 4.56b)

Here $OQ = x_p$, $CB = x$, $\text{OR} = r$, $CR = r - z$

Substituting: $x / x_p = (r-z)/r$, i.e., $x_p = \{r/(r-z)\}.x$

From similar triangles PQR and ABR, AB/PQ = BR/QR

Here $PQ = y_p$, $AB = y$, $QR = \sqrt{r^2 + x_p{}^2}$, $BR = \sqrt{(r-z)^2 + x^2}$

Substituting: $y / y_p = \sqrt{(r-z)^2 + x^2} / \sqrt{r^2 + x_p{}^2}$, i.e., $y_p = \{r/(r-z)\}.y$

In each case

$$x_p = \left(\frac{r}{r-z}\right).x = x \bigg/ \left(1 - \frac{z}{r}\right)$$

$$y_p = \left(\frac{r}{r-z}\right).y = y \bigg/ \left(1 - \frac{z}{r}\right)$$

$$z_p = 0$$

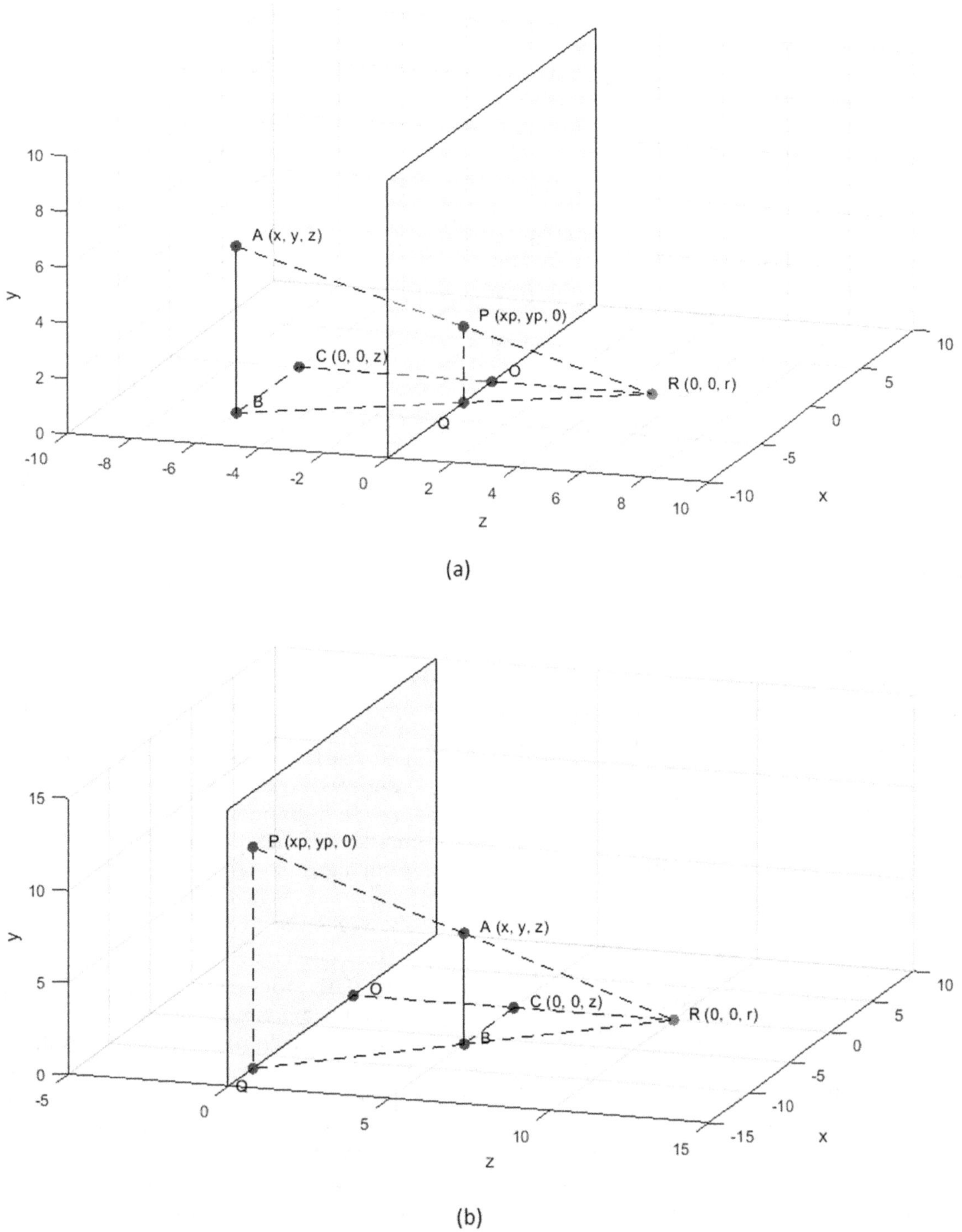

FIGURE 4.56
Perspective projection (a) type 1 and (b) type 2.

This can be represented in terms of homogeneous coordinates $P = M_{xy}.A$ as follows:

$$\begin{pmatrix} x_p \\ y_p \\ z_p \\ 1 \end{pmatrix} = \begin{pmatrix} x \\ y \\ 0 \\ 1-\dfrac{z}{r} \end{pmatrix} = \begin{pmatrix} 1 & 0 & 0 & 0 \\ 0 & 1 & 0 & 0 \\ 0 & 0 & 0 & 0 \\ 0 & 0 & -\dfrac{1}{r} & 1 \end{pmatrix} \begin{pmatrix} x \\ y \\ z \\ 1 \end{pmatrix}$$

Here M_{xy} is the required perspective projection matrix on the $x-y$ plane

4.6 Graphics Applications

Vector graphics play a significant role in various areas of multimedia due to their scalability, versatility and ability to maintain high quality at different sizes. Some common areas within multimedia where vector graphics applications are frequently utilized include but not limited to the following:

Logo Design: Vector graphics are ideal for designing logos because they can be easily resized without losing quality. Logos often need to be displayed in various sizes, such as on business cards, websites and billboards.

Icon Design: Icons used in multimedia, whether for websites, applications or presentations, are often created as vector graphics. This ensures that icons look sharp and clear on different devices and resolutions.

Web Design: Vector graphics are used in Web design for creating illustrations, buttons and other graphical elements. They contribute to a visually appealing and responsive design that can adapt to various screen sizes.

Animations: Vector graphics are commonly employed in multimedia animations. Animated characters, motion graphics and interactive elements can be created using vector-based animation tools, allowing for smooth and scalable animations.

Infographics: Infographics use vector graphics to convey information visually. Charts, graphs and other data visualizations can be created in vector format, enabling easy scaling and modification while maintaining clarity.

Interactive Multimedia Presentations: Vector graphics are often used in interactive presentations, allowing for dynamic and engaging visual content. Interactive elements, such as clickable icons or animated transitions, can be created using vector-based tools.

Print Design: Vector graphics are essential for print materials like brochures, posters and business cards. Print design requires high-resolution images, and vector graphics meet this requirement without loss of quality.

Digital Illustrations: Artists and illustrators use vector graphics applications to create digital illustrations for multimedia projects. The flexibility of vector graphics allows for detailed and expressive artwork.

Cartoon and Comic Design: Vector graphics are commonly used in the creation of cartoons and comics. The ability to easily modify and scale characters and scenes makes vector graphics well-suited for this purpose.

E-learning and Educational Multimedia: Vector graphics find applications in educational multimedia, such as e-learning courses and interactive educational materials. They enable the creation of visually appealing and adaptable content for educational purposes.

E-commerce: In the realm of e-commerce, graphics are the visual linchpin that entices customers. Online retailers leverage high-quality images and videos to showcase products, offer 360-degree views and even allow customers to virtually try on clothing or see how furniture fits in their living space. This visual appeal significantly influences consumer decisions, impacting sales and brand perception.

Advertising: The field of advertising relies heavily on graphics to create eye-catching and memorable campaigns. Graphic designers and illustrators use their skills to craft logos, banners, posters and advertisements that leave a lasting impression. Moreover, digital marketing incorporates graphics into email campaigns, social media posts and website banners to engage the audience and convey messages effectively.

User Interface Design: In the world of user interface (UI) and user experience (UX) design, graphics are fundamental. These designers work meticulously to create intuitive and aesthetically pleasing interfaces for software applications and websites. Through graphical elements like icons, buttons and responsive layouts, they enhance user interaction and navigation, ultimately ensuring a seamless and enjoyable user experience.

Geographical Information Systems (GIS): Graphics are also an essential tool in geographical information systems (GIS), where they are used to map and visualize data related to geographic locations. Whether for urban planning, environmental monitoring or disaster management, GIS professionals rely on maps and spatial data represented through graphics to make informed decisions.

Scientific Research: In the realm of scientific research and medical imaging, graphics enable the visualization of complex data and structures. Researchers use 3D rendering and simulation to model molecular structures, visualize climate patterns or study galaxies. In medicine, medical imaging technologies produce highly detailed graphics for diagnosing diseases, guiding surgical procedures and monitoring patient health.

AR and VR: As technology advances, augmented reality (AR) and virtual reality (VR) are becoming more prevalent. Graphics are the driving force behind these technologies, immersing users in virtual environments, enhancing training and simulations, and enabling interactive experiences in gaming, education and more.

4.7 Legal and Ethical Considerations

When working with vector graphics, there are several legal and ethical considerations that designers and users should be aware of to ensure they are using and distributing content responsibly. Issues related to intellectual property rights, copyright regulations and privacy standards should be kept in mind. Some key points are discussed below (Kane, 2010).

4.7.1 Legal Considerations

Intellectual Property Rights: Ensure that you have the right to use the vector graphics you incorporate into your work. Respect copyrights, trademarks and other intellectual property rights associated with the graphics. Avoid using graphics without proper licensing or permission.

Licensing Agreements: Be aware of the terms and conditions of licensing agreements for vector graphics. Some graphics may be free for personal use but require a license for commercial purposes. Read and adhere to the licensing terms specified by the content creator or provider.

Royalties and Compensation: If you are a graphic designer creating vector graphics for commercial use, ensure that you understand the compensation terms and royalty agreements associated with your work. Respect the rights of other creators and expect fair compensation for your own work.

Attribution: Some vector graphics come with attribution requirements, meaning you must give credit to the original creator. Always check the licensing terms and provide the necessary attribution when required. Failure to do so may result in legal consequences.

Derivative Works: Understand the rules regarding the creation of derivative works based on vector graphics. Some works may have specific guidelines on how they can be modified and used. Respect these guidelines to avoid legal issues.

4.7.2 Ethical Considerations

Privacy Concerns: Be mindful of privacy concerns, especially when using vector graphics that include identifiable individuals or private property. Ensure that you have the necessary permissions to use images that may infringe on someone's privacy rights.

Cultural Sensitivity: Exercise cultural sensitivity when selecting or creating vector graphics. Avoid using images that may be offensive or disrespectful to certain cultures, religions or communities. Consider the potential impact of your work on diverse audiences.

Accuracy and Truthfulness: Ensure that the vector graphics you use accurately represent the intended message. Avoid misleading or deceptive imagery, as this can have legal and ethical implications. Provide clear and truthful information about the content.

Environmental Considerations: Be mindful of the environmental impact associated with the creation and use of vector graphics. Consider using sustainable and eco-friendly design practices, and be aware of any negative environmental consequences related to the production or distribution of your work.

Compliance with Laws and Regulations: Stay informed about relevant laws and regulations related to graphic design, intellectual property and online content. Ensure that your work complies with these legal requirements to avoid legal consequences.

4.8 Challenges and Emerging Trends

Vector graphics have been widely used for their scalability, versatility and ability to maintain quality across different sizes. However, like any technology, vector graphics face challenges and are subject to evolving trends.

4.8.1 Challenges

Complexity of Design: Creating intricate and detailed vector graphics can be time-consuming. As design requirements become more complex, the challenge lies in efficiently producing highly detailed and visually appealing vector illustrations.

Learning Curve: Mastering vector graphics software can be challenging for beginners. The learning curve associated with tools like Adobe Illustrator or CorelDRAW may deter some individuals from exploring the full potential of vector graphics.

Performance in Large Projects: As projects grow in size and complexity, performance issues may arise. Working with numerous layers, intricate paths and extensive details can sometimes lead to slower rendering times and increased system resource usage.

Interoperability: Ensuring seamless interoperability between different vector graphics software and file formats can be a challenge. While widely used formats like SVG (Scalable Vector Graphics) exist, compatibility across various platforms and applications remains an ongoing concern.

Realism in Vector Graphics: Achieving realistic textures and shading in vector graphics can be challenging. While vector graphics excel at clean lines and simplicity, emulating the complexity of realistic textures can be a hurdle.

4.8.2 Emerging Trends

AI Integration: The integration of AI (artificial intelligence) in vector graphics tools is a growing trend. AI can assist designers in automating repetitive tasks, suggesting design elements and even generating preliminary designs based on user inputs.

Enhanced Collaboration: Future vector graphics software is likely to focus on improving collaboration features. Cloud-based collaboration tools, real-time editing and version control are expected to become more advanced, facilitating teamwork among designers.

3D Graphics Evolution: The evolution of vector graphics may involve a greater emphasis on 3D capabilities. Integrating 3D elements seamlessly into vector graphics can open up new possibilities for design in various industries, including gaming, virtual reality and augmented reality.

AR interoperability: The synergy between vector graphics and AR is an emerging trend. Vector graphics' scalability and efficiency make them suitable for AR applications, where lightweight and scalable assets are essential for smooth performance.

Advanced Animation Tools: Improved animation features within vector graphics software are anticipated. As demand grows for animated content in various digital mediums, vector graphics tools may include more sophisticated animation capabilities.

Responsive Design Integration: With the increasing prevalence of responsive design, vector graphics will likely play a crucial role in creating assets that can adapt seamlessly to different screen sizes and resolutions.

Environmental Considerations: Sustainability in design is becoming a focal point. Future trends may involve vector graphics tools incorporating features that promote environmentally friendly practices, such as reducing file sizes and optimizing resource usage.

Cross-Platform Consistency: Efforts to improve cross-platform consistency and compatibility between vector graphics applications are likely to continue. Seamless workflows between different software and operating systems can enhance the efficiency of designers and collaborative projects.

Blockchain for Copyright Protection: Blockchain technology may be used to enhance copyright protection for vector graphics. Implementing blockchain in the metadata of digital assets could provide a more secure and transparent way to track ownership and usage rights.

As technology continues to advance, the landscape of vector graphics will evolve to meet the demands of creative professionals and the changing needs of various industries. Keeping abreast of these challenges and trends is essential for designers and developers working with vector graphics.

4.9 Graphics File Formats

4.9.1 SVG

SVG (Scalable Vector Graphics) [w3.org/Graphics/SVG] is an XML-based vector graphics format, widely used for Web graphics and interactive applications. SVG images are composed of scalable shapes and paths defined using XML markup, making them resolution-independent and suitable for displaying on screens of varying sizes and resolutions. SVG markup consists of elements, attributes and properties that define the structure, appearance and behavior of the graphics. It supports a variety of basic shapes, such as rectangles, circles, ellipses, lines and polygons, as well as complex paths defined by sequences of points and curves. These shapes and paths can be styled and transformed using CSS (Cascading Style Sheets) or inline attributes. SVG images can be styled using CSS, allowing designers to control the appearance of elements such as colors, strokes, fills, gradients and transparency, and support interactivity and animation through the use of event handlers, such as mouse clicks and hover effects, as well as declarative animation elements, such as <animate> and <animateTransform>. Most modern Web browsers support SVG natively, allowing SVG images to be embedded directly into HTML documents using the <svg> element. SVG supports the inclusion of text elements within the graphic, allowing for the display of styled text directly within the image, using CSS properties, such as font-family, font-size, font-weight and text-anchor. Additionally, SVG allows for the embedding of external fonts using the @font-face rule, providing flexibility in typography. SVG supports creation of gradient fills using linear or radial gradients, as well as pattern fills using predefined or custom patterns, allowing for the creation of smooth color transitions and textured effects. It also supports clipping and masking techniques to selectively display or hide parts of an image. Moreover SVG also provides support for filters and effects, such as blur, drop shadow and color matrix (changing color values by multiplying with a matrix of coefficients) that can be applied to elements within the graphic.

4.9.2 PDF

PDF (Portable Document Format) was originally developed by Adobe for documents and subsequently standardized by ISO [www.iso.org/standard/75839.html], supports both vector and raster graphics. It is ideal for documents with mixed content (text, images and vectors) and can include interactive elements. It is often used for document sharing with embedded vector graphics, printing vector-based illustrations and creating electronic presentations. PDF supports the representation of vector graphics using a variety of primitive graphic objects, such as lines, curves, shapes and text. These objects are defined using mathematical formulas rather than a fixed grid of pixels, allowing for scalable and high-quality rendering at any resolution. A graphics state that includes attributes such as color, line width, fill mode and font settings is maintained and can be modified using graphic state operators to control the appearance of vector graphics within the document. PDF also supports transparency and blending modes, allowing for the overlay of vector graphics with varying levels of opacity.

4.9.3 PS, EPS

PS (PostScript) and EPS (Encapsulated PostScript) were developed by Adobe in the 1980s and commonly used for handing vector graphics on monitors and printers [www.adobe.com/jp/print/postscript/pdfs/PLRM.pdf]. The PS file format is essentially a page description language primarily used for describing the appearance of printed pages, including text, vector graphics and images. PS supports the description of vector graphics using mathematical formulas for lines, curves, shapes and text, which enables high-quality output at any resolution. EPS files are essentially containers that encapsulate PostScript content within a framework including additional metadata [www.loc.gov/preservation/digital/formats/fdd/fdd000246.shtml]. This encapsulation allows EPS files to be easily embedded within other documents, such as those created in desktop publishing software, without requiring knowledge of the underlying PostScript language. The encapsulation also allows EPS files to contain both vector graphics and bitmap images, providing greater flexibility in incorporating graphical elements into documents. EPS files can support transparency, allowing for the overlay of graphics with varying levels of opacity. This transparency support enables the creation of layered artwork and complex compositions. EPS files often include a low-resolution preview image, which allows users to quickly view the contents of the file without opening it in a graphics editor. PS files can embed fonts within the file itself, ensuring that text appears correctly even if the recipient does not have the required fonts installed on their system.

4.9.4 FLA, SWF

FLA (Flash Authoring) [www.loc.gov/preservation/digital/formats/fdd/fdd000132.shtml] and SWF (Shockwave Flash) [www.loc.gov/preservation/digital/formats/fdd/fdd000248.shtml] are file formats associated with Adobe Flash, a multimedia platform used for creating animations, interactive websites, games and more. FLA is the native file format used by Adobe Flash Professional (now known as Adobe Animate) for creating and editing multimedia content. These files contain all the assets, timelines, layers, animations, scripts and other elements used to create Flash projects. They primarily consist of vector graphics, which are scalable and can be animated and manipulated using keyframes, tweening and other animation techniques. FLA files organize content into layers and timelines, allowing for the creation of complex animations and interactions. Each layer can contain different elements, such as graphics, text, buttons and movie clips, and timelines control the sequence and timing of these elements. SWF is the file format used to distribute Flash content on the Web. SWF files are exported from FLA files using Adobe Flash Professional (Animate) or other Flash authoring tools. SWF files retain the animations, interactivity and multimedia elements created in the original FLA file. This includes animations, buttons, navigation menus, audio, video and scripted interactions. SWF files are optimized for Web delivery and have relatively small file sizes compared to other multimedia formats, which makes them suitable for embedding in Web pages and delivering rich interactive content over the internet. SWF files can be viewed on various platforms and devices that support Adobe Flash Player or other Flash-compatible software. However, SWF files have been historically associated with security vulnerabilities due to the potential for malicious code execution, as a result, support for Flash Player has been deprecated in modern Web browsers, and Adobe has announced the end-of-life for Flash Player.

4.9.5 AI

AI (Adobe Illustrator) is the native file format for Adobe Illustrator application, and used for saving vector graphics with editing capabilities [www.adobe.com/in/creativecloud/file-types/image/vector/ai-file.html]. AI files primarily contain vector graphics, which are described using mathematical formulas to represent lines, curves, shapes and text. This allows for scalability without loss of quality, making them ideal for artwork that needs to be resized or edited. It supports a layered structure, allowing users to organize artwork into different layers for easier editing and manipulation. Layers can contain individual objects, groups of objects or artwork placed on separate layers for organization and control. Adobe Illustrator documents can contain multiple artboards, each representing a separate canvas for creating and organizing artwork. AI files store information about the size, position and content of each artboard within the document. AI files can be opened and edited in Adobe Illustrator and other compatible software applications, such as Adobe Photoshop and CorelDRAW.

4.9.6 CDR

CDR (CorelDRAW) is a proprietary format used by CorelDRAW application, a popular vector graphics editor developed by Corel Corporation [www.coreldraw.com/en/product/coreldraw]. CDR files primarily contain vector graphics, which are described using mathematical formulas to represent lines, curves, shapes and text, which allows for scalability without loss of quality. CDR files support a layered structure, allowing users to organize artwork into different layers for easier editing and manipulation. Layers can contain individual objects, groups of objects or artwork placed on separate layers for organization and control. CDR files can be opened and edited in CorelDRAW and other compatible software applications like Adobe Illustrator (with some limitations).

4.9.7 WMF

The WMF (Windows Metafile) format is a graphics file format originally developed by Microsoft for storing vector graphics and primarily used in the Windows environment [learn.microsoft.com/en-us/openspecs/windows_protocols/ms-wmf]. WMF files can contain graphical objects defined by the Windows Graphics Device Interface (GDI), such as lines, curves, polygons, rectangles, ellipses and text. These objects are represented using GDI function calls and parameters. In addition to vector graphics, WMF files can also include bitmap images, such as photographs or scanned images.

4.9.8 CGM

CGM (Computer Graphics Metafile) is a free and open file format used for the exchange of vector graphics, standardized as ISO/IEC 8632 [www.iso.org/standard/32378.html]. CGM files are structured documents that consist of a series of graphical elements, such as lines, curves, polygons, text and attributes (e.g., color, line style, fill pattern) which are defined using CGM's syntax and semantics [www.loc.gov/preservation/digital/formats/fdd/fdd000521.shtml]. CGM uses three types of syntactical encoding formats: character-based, used to produce the smallest possible file size for ease of storage and speed of data transmission; binary-encoded, which facilitates exchange and quick access by software applications, clear-text-encoded, designed for human readability and ease of modification using an ASCII text editor. Three versions of CGM files are available: version 1 supports a collection of simple metafile primitives like lines, polylines, arcs, circles, rectangles, ellipses, polygons and text; version 2 can contain composite primitives comprising other primitives; version 3 is for advanced applications, and its metafiles may contain Beziers, NURBS, parabolic and hyperbolic arcs.

4.9.9 OBJ

OBJ (Wavefront Object) [www.loc.gov/preservation/digital/formats/fdd/fdd000507.shtml] is a file format for representing 3D geometry developed by Wavefront Technologies [fileformat.info/format/wavefrontobj/egff.htm]. OBJ files are typically stored in ASCII (plain text) format, making them human-readable and editable with a text editor. Each line in the file represents a different element of the 3D geometry, such as vertices, texture coordinates, normals and faces. The information begins with a list of vertices, which define the 3D coordinates of points in space. Vertices are represented by lines starting with the letter "v" followed by the x, y and z coordinates. The files can optionally include texture coordinates, which specify how textures are mapped onto the surface of the 3D model. Texture coordinates are represented by lines starting with the letter "vt" followed by the u and v coordinates. Faces define the polygons that make up the surface of the 3D model, each face being represented by a line starting with the letter "f" followed by a list of vertex indices that define the vertices of the polygon. OBJ files can reference external material files (MTL files) that define the appearance properties of the 3D model, such as color, reflectivity and transparency.

4.9.10 STL

The STL (Stereolithography) [www.loc.gov/preservation/digital/formats/fdd/fdd000504.shtml] file format was originally developed by 3D Systems [3dsystems.com/quickparts/learning-center/what-is-stl-file] and commonly used for representing 3D models in computer-aided design (CAD) and 3D printing applications. STL files are available in two formats: binary and ASCII; binary STL files store data in a compact binary format, making them more efficient for storage and transmission, while ASCII STL files store data in a human-readable text format, making them easier to read and edit manually. STL files represent 3D models using a collection of triangular facets (also known as polygons). Each facet is defined by three vertices and contains additional information such as normal vectors (used for shading) and attribute data (such as color or material properties). The files provide a mesh representation of 3D geometry, where the surface of the object is approximated by a series of interconnected triangles. The resolution and level of detail of the mesh can vary depending on the complexity of the model and the desired output quality. STL files are also commonly used in the 3D printing industry as they provide a simple and efficient way to represent 3D models for printing. Most 3D printers accept STL files as input and use slicing software to convert the model into printable layers.

4.9.11 FBX

The FBX (FilmBox) [www.loc.gov/preservation/digital/formats/fdd/fdd000558.shtml] file format is a proprietary file format developed by Autodesk [autodesk.com/products/fbx/overview] for storing 3D models, animations and other digital assets used in computer graphics applications. FBX files can store a wide range of 3D data, including geometry, materials, textures, animations, lights, cameras and scene hierarchy, and is supported by a variety of 3D modeling software, animation tools and game engines, including Autodesk Maya, Autodesk 3ds Max, Blender, Unity and Unreal Engine. This interoperability allows FBX files to be exchanged between different software applications without loss of data. The files are available in both binary and ASCII formats; binary FBX files are more compact and efficient for storage and transmission, while ASCII FBX files are human-readable and editable with a text editor. The files store 3D data in a hierarchical structure, representing the relationships between objects, nodes and components in the scene, which allows for the representation of complex scenes with multiple objects, animations and transformations. FBX files support keyframe animation, skeletal animation, blend shapes and other animation techniques commonly used in character animation and rigging. The files can also store material definitions, texture maps and shader properties used to define the appearance of 3D objects.

4.9.12 DAE

The DAE (Digital Asset Exchange) file format, commonly known as Collada, is an open, XML-based file format designed for the exchange of digital assets, including 3D models, animations, textures and metadata, between different 3D modeling and animation software applications. Developed by the Khronos Group [khronos.org/collada], DAE files organize 3D data in a hierarchical structure, representing the relationships between objects, nodes and components in the scene. The files can store geometry data, including vertices, faces, normals and texture coordinates, used to define the shape and structure of 3D objects. Mesh data is represented using <geometry> elements and can include information about materials, textures and shaders. DAE files support keyframe animation, skeletal animation, blend shapes and other animation techniques commonly used in character animation, can store material definitions, texture maps and shader properties used to define the appearance of 3D objects. Moreover DAE files support physics and dynamics simulation data, including rigid body dynamics, collision detection and constraints, which allows for the representation of interactive and physically realistic 3D scenes, such as simulations and games.

4.9.13 MAX

The MAX (3D Sudio MAX) file format is the proprietary file format used by Autodesk's 3ds Max software for storing 3D models, scenes, animations, materials and other project data [adobe.com/in/creativecloud/file-types/image/vector/3ds-file.html]. MAX files can contain a wide range of data, including 3D geometry, cameras, lights, animations, materials, textures, particle systems and scripting information. These files are stored in a binary format, which is optimized for performance and efficiency. It organizes 3D data in a hierarchical structure, representing the relationships between objects, nodes and components in the scene which allows for the representation of complex scenes with multiple objects, animations and transformations. MAX files support the use of layers to organize and manage scene data, which can be used to group related objects, control visibility and apply transformations to multiple objects simultaneously. The Material Editor in 3ds Max allows users to create and edit materials using a node-based interface, and these material definitions are saved within the MAX file. Moreover the files can reference external assets such as textures, images and other 3D files, to enable creation of modular and reusable content across multiple projects.

4.9.14 PLY

The PLY (Polygon) file format developed by Stanford University [graphics.stanford.edu/data/3Dscanrep] is a flexible file format commonly used for storing 3D data, particularly triangular meshes [www.loc.gov/preservation/digital/formats/fdd/fdd000501.shtml]. PLY files can be stored in either ASCII (plain text) or binary format. ASCII files are human-readable and editable with a text editor, making them easier to inspect and modify manually. Binary files are more compact and efficient for storage and transmission, making them suitable for large or complex models. PLY files organize 3D data into elements, where each element represents a type of entity such as vertices, faces, edges or properties. PLY files typically contain vertex data, which defines the 3D coordinates of points in space. Vertex data includes attributes such as position (x, y, z), color (RGB or RGBA), normal vectors, texture coordinates and custom user-defined properties. PLY files also contain face data, which defines the connectivity between vertices to form triangular or polygonal faces. Face data specifies the indices of the vertices that make up each face, as well as additional attributes such as color, material and surface normal.

4.9.15 DWG, DXF

DWG (Drawing) [www.loc.gov/preservation/digital/formats/fdd/fdd000445.shtml] and DXF (Drawing Exchange Format) [www.loc.gov/preservation/digital/formats/fdd/fdd000446.shtml] are file formats developed by Autodesk for storing 2D and 3D design data, primarily used in computer-aided design (CAD) software. DWG is the native proprietary file format used by Autodesk's AutoCAD software. DWG files can contain a wide range of data, including 2D and 3D geometry, annotations, layers, blocks, dimensions, text, materials and metadata. DXF [https://www.adobe.com/in/creativecloud/file-types/image/vector/dxf-file.html] is an open, ASCII-based file format developed by Autodesk for exchanging CAD data between different software applications. It is designed to be a platform-independent and application-independent format, allowing for interoperability between different CAD programs. Like DWG files, DXF files can contain a wide range of data, including 2D and 3D geometry, annotations, layers, blocks, dimensions, text, materials and metadata.

4.9.16 AMF

AMF (Additive Manufacturing File Format) is an open standard XML-based file format specifically designed for additive manufacturing processes, such as 3D printing, standardized as ISO/IEC 52915 standard [www.iso.org/standard/74640.html]. AMF files contain information about the geometry, materials, colors and other characteristics of 3D objects, allowing for precise and accurate representation of digital models intended for additive manufacturing. They can contain a wide range of data, including geometry data, materials, colors, textures, metadata and manufacturing-specific information and represent 3D geometry using a combination of triangles and curved surfaces. The geometry data is defined in terms of vertices, edges and faces, similar to other mesh-based file formats such as STL and OBJ, and can include information about support structures, lattices and other features required for the additive manufacturing process.

4.10 Numerical Problems

4.10.1 2D Transformations

PROBLEM 4.1

A square having vertices (0, 0), (1, 0), (1, 1) and (0, 1) is translated by amounts (−3, 4). Find its new vertices.

Original coordinate matrix: $C = \begin{pmatrix} 0 & 1 & 1 & 0 \\ 0 & 0 & 1 & 1 \\ 1 & 1 & 1 & 1 \end{pmatrix}$

Translation matrix: $T(-3,4) = \begin{pmatrix} 1 & 0 & -3 \\ 0 & 1 & 4 \\ 0 & 0 & 1 \end{pmatrix}$

New coordinate matrix:

$$D = T(-3,4).C = \begin{pmatrix} -3 & -2 & -2 & -3 \\ 4 & 4 & 5 & 5 \\ 1 & 1 & 1 & 1 \end{pmatrix}$$

New vertex coordinates: $(-3,4),(-2,4),(-2,5),(-3,5)$.

PROBLEM 4.2

A quadrilateral having vertices (–1, –1), (1, –2), (1, 2), (–1, 1) is scaled by amounts (–2, 3). Find its new vertices.

Original coordinate matrix: $C = \begin{pmatrix} -1 & 1 & 1 & -1 \\ -1 & -2 & 2 & 1 \\ 1 & 1 & 1 & 1 \end{pmatrix}$

Scaling matrix: $S(-2,3) = \begin{pmatrix} -2 & 0 & 0 \\ 0 & 3 & 0 \\ 0 & 0 & 1 \end{pmatrix}$

New coordinate matrix:

$D = S(-2,3).C = \begin{pmatrix} 2 & -2 & -2 & 2 \\ -3 & -6 & 6 & 3 \\ 1 & 1 & 1 & 1 \end{pmatrix}$

New vertex coordinates: $(2,-3),(-2,-6),(-2,6),(2,3)$.

PROBLEM 4.3

A square having vertices (–1, –1), (1, –1), (1, 1) and (–1, 1) is rotated by angle 30° around the origin along CCW direction. Find its new vertices.

Original coordinate matrix: $C = \begin{pmatrix} -1 & 1 & 1 & -1 \\ -1 & -1 & 1 & 1 \\ 1 & 1 & 1 & 1 \end{pmatrix}$

Rotation matrix:

$R(30^\circ) = \begin{pmatrix} \cos 30 & -\sin 30 & 0 \\ \sin 30 & \cos 30 & 0 \\ 0 & 0 & 1 \end{pmatrix} = \begin{pmatrix} 0.87 & -0.5 & 0 \\ -0.5 & 0.87 & 0 \\ 0 & 0 & 1 \end{pmatrix}$

New coordinate matrix:

$D = R(30^\circ).C = \begin{pmatrix} -0.37 & 1.37 & 0.37 & 1.37 \\ -1.37 & -0.37 & 1.37 & 0.37 \\ 1 & 1 & 1 & 1 \end{pmatrix}$

New vertex coordinates: $(-0.37,-1.37),(1.37,-0.37),(0.37,1.37),(-1.37,0.37)$.

PROBLEM 4.4

A square having vertices (–1, –1), (1, –1), (1, 1) and (–1, 1) is scaled by amounts (–2, 3) about one of its vertices (–1, –1). Find its new vertices.

Original coordinate matrix: $C = \begin{pmatrix} -1 & 1 & 1 & -1 \\ -1 & -1 & 1 & 1 \\ 1 & 1 & 1 & 1 \end{pmatrix}$

Forward Translation matrix: $T(1,1) = \begin{pmatrix} 1 & 0 & 1 \\ 0 & 0 & 1 \\ 0 & 0 & 1 \end{pmatrix}$

Forward Scaling matrix: $S(-2,3) = \begin{pmatrix} -2 & 0 & 0 \\ 0 & 3 & 0 \\ 0 & 0 & 1 \end{pmatrix}$

Reverse Translation matrix: $T(-1,-1) = \begin{pmatrix} 1 & 0 & -1 \\ 0 & 0 & -1 \\ 0 & 0 & 1 \end{pmatrix}$

Composite transformation matrix:

$M = T(-1,-1).S(-2,3).T(1,1) = \begin{pmatrix} -2 & 0 & -3 \\ 0 & 3 & 2 \\ 0 & 0 & 1 \end{pmatrix}$

New coordinate matrix:

$D = M.C = \begin{pmatrix} -1 & -5 & -5 & -1 \\ -1 & -1 & 5 & 5 \\ 1 & 1 & 1 & 1 \end{pmatrix}$

New vertex coordinates: $(-1,-1),(-5,-1),(-5,5),(-1,5)$

PROBLEM 4.5

A square having vertices (–1, –1), (1, –1), (1, 1) and (–1, 1) is rotated by angle 30° along the CCW direction about one of its vertices (–1, –1). Find its new vertices.

Original coordinate matrix: $C = \begin{pmatrix} -1 & 1 & 1 & -1 \\ -1 & -1 & 1 & 1 \\ 1 & 1 & 1 & 1 \end{pmatrix}$

Forward Translation matrix: $T(1,1) = \begin{pmatrix} 1 & 0 & 1 \\ 0 & 0 & 1 \\ 0 & 0 & 1 \end{pmatrix}$

Forward Rotation matrix:

$R(30^\circ) = \begin{pmatrix} \cos 30 & -\sin 30 & 0 \\ \sin 30 & \cos 30 & 0 \\ 0 & 0 & 1 \end{pmatrix} = \begin{pmatrix} 0.87 & -0.5 & 0 \\ -0.5 & 0.87 & 0 \\ 0 & 0 & 1 \end{pmatrix}$

Reverse Translation matrix: $T(-1,-1) = \begin{pmatrix} 1 & 0 & -1 \\ 0 & 0 & -1 \\ 0 & 0 & 1 \end{pmatrix}$

Composite transformation matrix: $M = T(-1,-1).$

$R(30^\circ).T(1,1) = \begin{pmatrix} 0.87 & -0.5 & -0.63 \\ 0.5 & 0.87 & 0.37 \\ 0 & 0 & 1 \end{pmatrix}$

New coordinate matrix:

$D = M.C = \begin{pmatrix} -1 & 0.73 & -0.27 & -2 \\ -1 & 0 & 1.73 & 0.73 \\ 1 & 1 & 1 & 1 \end{pmatrix}$

New vertex coordinates : $(-1,-1),(0.73,0),(-0.27,1.73),(-2,0.73)$

PROBLEM 4.6

A triangle having vertices at (1, 2), (3, 2) and (3, 4) is reflected about the *x*-axis, y-axis and the origin. Find its new coordinates.

Original coordinate matrix: $C = \begin{pmatrix} 1 & 3 & 3 \\ 2 & 2 & 4 \\ 0 & 0 & 1 \end{pmatrix}$

Reflection matrix about x – axis: $F_x = \begin{pmatrix} 1 & 0 & 0 \\ 0 & -1 & 0 \\ 0 & 0 & 1 \end{pmatrix}$

New coordinate matrix: $D_x = F_x.C = \begin{pmatrix} 1 & 3 & 3 \\ -2 & -2 & -4 \\ 0 & 0 & 1 \end{pmatrix}$

For reflection about y – axis: $F_y = \begin{pmatrix} -1 & 0 & 0 \\ 0 & 1 & 0 \\ 0 & 0 & 1 \end{pmatrix}$

New coordinate matrix: $D_y = F_y.C = \begin{pmatrix} -1 & -3 & -3 \\ 2 & 2 & 4 \\ 0 & 0 & 1 \end{pmatrix}$

For reflection about origin: $F_o = \begin{pmatrix} -1 & 0 & 0 \\ 0 & -1 & 0 \\ 0 & 0 & 1 \end{pmatrix}$

New coordinate matrix: $D_o = F_o.C = \begin{pmatrix} -1 & -3 & -3 \\ -2 & -2 & -4 \\ 0 & 0 & 1 \end{pmatrix}$

PROBLEM 4.7

A square having vertices at (−1, −1), (1, −1), (1, 1) and (−1, 1) is subjected to a shear of 1.5 along the *x*-axis and then a shear of 2 along the *y*-axis. Find its new vertices.

Original coordinate matrix: $C = \begin{pmatrix} -1 & 1 & 1 & -1 \\ -1 & -1 & 1 & 1 \\ 1 & 1 & 1 & 1 \end{pmatrix}$

Shear along x – direction: $H_x(1.5) = \begin{pmatrix} 1 & 1.5 & 0 \\ 0 & 1 & 0 \\ 0 & 0 & 1 \end{pmatrix}$

Shear along y – direction: $H_y(2) = \begin{pmatrix} 1 & 0 & 0 \\ 2 & 1 & 0 \\ 0 & 0 & 1 \end{pmatrix}$

New coordinate matrix: $D = H_y.H_x.C$

New coordinates: (-2.5, -6), (-0.5, -2), (2.5, 6), (0.5, 2)

PROBLEM 4.8

Find the new coordinates of a square with vertices (0,0),(1,0),(1,1) and (0,1) under the following transformations: (a) $\begin{pmatrix} 5 & 2 & 5 \\ 2 & 5 & 5 \\ 0 & 0 & 1 \end{pmatrix}$ (b) $\begin{pmatrix} 5 & 2 & 5 \\ 2 & 5 & 5 \\ 5 & 2 & 1 \end{pmatrix}$. Specify the type of transformation in each case.

Original coordinate matrix: $C = \begin{pmatrix} 0 & 1 & 1 & 0 \\ 0 & 0 & 1 & 1 \\ 1 & 1 & 1 & 1 \end{pmatrix}$

(a) Transformation matrix: $M = \begin{pmatrix} 5 & 2 & 5 \\ 2 & 5 & 5 \\ 0 & 0 & 1 \end{pmatrix}$

New coordinate matrix: $D = M.C = \begin{pmatrix} 5 & 10 & 12 & 7 \\ 5 & 7 & 12 & 10 \\ 1 & 1 & 1 & 1 \end{pmatrix}$

New vertices are : $(5.00,5.00),(10.00,7.00),(12.00,12.00),(7.00,10.00)$

Let $x_0 = 5, y_0 = 5, x_1 = 10, y_1 = 7, x_2 = 12, y_2 = 12, x_3 = 7, y_3 = 10$

Now $d_1 = x_1 - x_0 = 5, d_2 = x_2 - x_3 = 5, d_3 = y_1 - y_0 = 2, d_4 = y_2 - y_3 = 2$

Since $d_1 = d_2$ AND $d_3 = d_4$, the transformation is affine in nature.

(b) Transformation matrix: $M = \begin{pmatrix} 5 & 2 & 5 \\ 2 & 5 & 5 \\ 5 & 2 & 1 \end{pmatrix}$

New coordinate matrix: $D_h = M.C = \begin{pmatrix} 5 & 10 & 12 & 7 \\ 5 & 7 & 12 & 10 \\ 1 & 6 & 8 & 3 \end{pmatrix}$

(in homogeneous coordinates)

New coordinate matrix: $D = \begin{pmatrix} 5 & 1.67 & 1.5 & 2.33 \\ 5 & 1.17 & 1.5 & 3.33 \\ 1 & 1 & 1 & 1 \end{pmatrix}$

(in Cartesian coordinates)

New vertices are:
$(5.00,5.00),(1.67,1.17),(1.50,1.50),(2.33,3.33)$

Let $x_0 = 5, y_0 = 5, x_1 = 1.67, y_1 = 1.17, x_2 = 1.5, y_2 = 1.5,$
$x_3 = 2.33, y_3 = 3.33$

Now $d_1 = x_1 - x_0 = -3.33, d_2 = x_2 - x_3 = -0.83,$
$d_3 = y_1 - y_0 = -3.83, d_4 = y_2 - y_3 = -1.83$

Since $d_1 \neq d_2$ AND $d_3 \neq d_4$, the transformation is perspective in nature.

4.10.2 Curves and Splines

PROBLEM 4.9
Find equation of a linear interpolating spline through the points (3, 2) and (8, –4) .

Choose starting equation: $y = a + bx = \begin{pmatrix} 1 & x \end{pmatrix}\begin{pmatrix} a \\ b \end{pmatrix}$

Substitute given points in the equation

$$2 = a + b(3)$$

$$-4 = a + b(8)$$

Write in matrix form $Y = C.A : \begin{pmatrix} 2 \\ -4 \end{pmatrix} = \begin{pmatrix} 1 & 3 \\ 1 & 8 \end{pmatrix}\begin{pmatrix} a \\ b \end{pmatrix}$

Solve the matrix equation
$A = C^{-1}.Y : \begin{pmatrix} a \\ b \end{pmatrix} = \begin{pmatrix} 1.6 & -0.6 \\ -0.2 & 0.2 \end{pmatrix}\begin{pmatrix} 2 \\ -4 \end{pmatrix} = \begin{pmatrix} 5.6 \\ -1.2 \end{pmatrix}$

Substitute the coefficient values in the starting equation:

$$y = 5.6 - 1.2x$$

Verification: In most graphics problems it is usually possible to verify the results obtained by substituting the given data in it. Putting $x = 3$ we get $y = 2$ and putting $x = 8$ we get $y = -4$. Hence, the line does indeed pass through the given points.

PROBLEM 4.10
Find equation of a quadratic interpolating spline through the points (3,2), (6,5) and (8,–4).

Choose starting equation:

$$y = a + bx + cx^2 = \begin{pmatrix} 1 & x & x^2 \end{pmatrix}\begin{pmatrix} a \\ b \\ c \end{pmatrix}$$

Write equations in matrix form

$$Y = C.A : \begin{pmatrix} 2 \\ -4 \\ 5 \end{pmatrix} = \begin{pmatrix} 1 & 3 & 9 \\ 1 & 8 & 64 \\ 1 & 6 & 36 \end{pmatrix}\begin{pmatrix} a \\ b \\ c \end{pmatrix}$$

$$\text{Solve for } A = C^{-1}.Y : \begin{pmatrix} a \\ b \\ c \end{pmatrix} = \begin{pmatrix} -20.8 \\ 10.9 \\ -1.1 \end{pmatrix}$$

Substitute in the starting equation:
$y = -20.8 + 10.9x - 1.1x^2$

Verification: $y(3) = 2, y(6) = 5, y(8) = -4$

PROBLEM 4.11
Find equation of a cubic spline through the points (–1,2), (0,0), (1,–2) and (2,0).

Choose starting equation:

$$y = a + bx + cx^2 + dx^3 = \begin{pmatrix} 1 & x & x^2 & x^3 \end{pmatrix}\begin{pmatrix} a \\ b \\ c \\ d \end{pmatrix}$$

Write equations in matrix form

$$Y = C.A : \begin{pmatrix} 2 \\ 0 \\ -2 \\ 0 \end{pmatrix} = \begin{pmatrix} 1 & -1 & 1 & -1 \\ 1 & 0 & 0 & 0 \\ 1 & 1 & 1 & 1 \\ 1 & 2 & 4 & 8 \end{pmatrix}\begin{pmatrix} a \\ b \\ c \\ d \end{pmatrix}$$

$$\text{Solve for } A = C^{-1}.Y : \begin{pmatrix} a \\ b \\ c \\ d \end{pmatrix} = \begin{pmatrix} 0 \\ -2.67 \\ 0 \\ 0.67 \end{pmatrix}$$

Substitute in the starting equation: $y = -2.67x + 0.67x^3$

Verification: $y(-1) = 2, y(0) = 0, y(1) = -2, y(2) = 0$

PROBLEM 4.12
Find equation of cubic spline through the points (–1,2), (0,0), (1,–2) and (2,0) in parametric form with subdivision ratios $m = 0.1$ and $n = 0.9$.

Choose starting equation written in matrix form:

$$P(t) = a + bt + ct^2 + dt^3 = \begin{pmatrix} 1 & t & t^2 & t^3 \end{pmatrix}\begin{pmatrix} a \\ b \\ c \\ d \end{pmatrix}$$

Write equations in matrix form

$$G = C.A: \begin{pmatrix} -1 & 2 \\ 0 & 0 \\ 1 & -2 \\ 2 & 0 \end{pmatrix} = \begin{pmatrix} 1 & 0 & 0 & 0 \\ 1 & 0.1 & 0.01 & 0.001 \\ 1 & 0.9 & 0.81 & 0.729 \\ 1 & 1 & 1 & 1 \end{pmatrix}\begin{pmatrix} a \\ b \\ c \\ d \end{pmatrix}$$

Solve the equation for

$$A = C^{-1}.G = B.G: \begin{pmatrix} a \\ b \\ c \\ d \end{pmatrix} = \begin{pmatrix} -1 & 2 \\ 12.7222 & -21.4444 \\ -29.1667 & 13.8889 \\ 19.4444 & 5.5556 \end{pmatrix}$$

Substitute the coefficient values in the starting equation

$$x = -1 + 12.7222t - 29.1667t^2 + 19.4444t^3$$

$$y = 2 - 21.4444t + 13.8889t^2 + 5.5556t^3$$

Verification : $x(0) = -1, x(0.1) = 0, x(0.9) = 1, x(1) = 2,$
$y(0) = 2, y(0.1) = 0, y(0.9) = -2, y(1) = 0$

The actual values might differ a bit due to round off errors

PROBLEM 4.13
Find parametric equation of a quadratic Bezier spline through points (1, –1), (4, 3) and (5, –2).

Choose starting equation:

$$P(t) = \begin{pmatrix} 1 & t & t^2 \end{pmatrix}\begin{pmatrix} 1 & 0 & 0 \\ -2 & 2 & 0 \\ 1 & -2 & 1 \end{pmatrix}\begin{pmatrix} P_0 \\ P_1 \\ P_2 \end{pmatrix}$$

Substitute given values in the starting equation:

$$P(t) = \begin{pmatrix} 1 & t & t^2 \end{pmatrix}\begin{pmatrix} 1 & 0 & 0 \\ -2 & 2 & 0 \\ 1 & -2 & 1 \end{pmatrix}\begin{pmatrix} 1 & -1 \\ 4 & 3 \\ 5 & -2 \end{pmatrix}$$

Separating out the components:

$$x(t) = 1 + 6t - 2t^2$$

$$y(t) = -1 + 8t - 9t^2$$

Verification: $x(0) = 1, x(1) = 5, y(0) = -1, y(1) = -2$

PROBLEM 4.14
Find parametric equation of a cubic Bezier spline through points (1, –1), (1, 1), (4, 3) and (5, –2).

Choose starting equation:

$$P(t) = \begin{pmatrix} 1 & t & t^2 & t^3 \end{pmatrix}\begin{pmatrix} 1 & 0 & 0 & 0 \\ -3 & 3 & 0 & 0 \\ 3 & -6 & 3 & 0 \\ -1 & 3 & -3 & 1 \end{pmatrix}\begin{pmatrix} P_0 \\ P_1 \\ P_2 \\ P_3 \end{pmatrix}$$

Substitute given values in the starting equation:

$$P(t) = \begin{pmatrix} 1 & t & t^2 & t^3 \end{pmatrix}\begin{pmatrix} 1 & 0 & 0 & 0 \\ -3 & 3 & 0 & 0 \\ 3 & -6 & 3 & 0 \\ -1 & 3 & -3 & 1 \end{pmatrix}\begin{pmatrix} 1 & -1 \\ 1 & 1 \\ 4 & 3 \\ 5 & -2 \end{pmatrix}$$

Separating out the components:

$$x(t) = 1 + 9t^2 - 5t^3$$

$$y(t) = -1 + 6t - 7t^3$$

Verification: $x(0) = 1, x(1) = 5, y(0) = -1, y(1) = -2$

PROBLEM 4.15

Find the equation of a uniform quadratic B-spline having CPs (1, 4), (4, 6), (5, 2).

Equation of a uniform quadratic B-spline is given by:

$$P(t)=\begin{cases} P_0.\left[\frac{(t-0)^2}{2}\right], 0\le t<1 \\ P_0.\left[\frac{(t-0)(2-t)}{2}+\frac{(t-1)(3-t)}{2}\right]+P_1.\left[\frac{(t-1)^2}{2}\right], 1\le t<2 \\ P_0.\left[\frac{(3-t)^2}{2}\right]+P_1.\left[\frac{(t-1)(3-t)}{2}+\frac{(t-2)(4-t)}{2}\right]+P_2.\left[\frac{(t-2)^2}{2}\right], 2\le t<3 \\ P_1.\left[\frac{(4-t)^2}{2}\right]+P_2.\left[\frac{(t-2)(4-t)}{2}+\frac{(t-3)(5-t)}{2}\right], 3\le t<4 \\ P_2.\left[\frac{(5-t)^2}{2}\right], 4\le t<5 \end{cases}$$

Substituting given values and separating out the x and y components:

$$x(t)=\begin{cases} (1).\left[\frac{(t-0)^2}{2}\right], 0\le t<1 \\ (1).\left[\frac{(t-0)(2-t)}{2}+\frac{(t-1)(3-t)}{2}\right]+(4).\left[\frac{(t-1)^2}{2}\right], 1\le t<2 \\ (1).\left[\frac{(3-t)^2}{2}\right]+(4).\left[\frac{(t-1)(3-t)}{2}+\frac{(t-2)(4-t)}{2}\right]+(5).\left[\frac{(t-2)^2}{2}\right], 2\le t<3 \\ (4).\left[\frac{(4-t)^2}{2}\right]+(5).\left[\frac{(t-2)(4-t)}{2}+\frac{(t-3)(5-t)}{2}\right], 3\le t<4 \\ (5).\left[\frac{(5-t)^2}{2}\right], 4\le t<5 \end{cases}$$

$$y(t)=\begin{cases} (4).\left[\frac{(t-0)^2}{2}\right], 0\le t<1 \\ (4).\left[\frac{(t-0)(2-t)}{2}+\frac{(t-1)(3-t)}{2}\right]+(6).\left[\frac{(t-1)^2}{2}\right], 1\le t<2 \\ (4).\left[\frac{(3-t)^2}{2}\right]+(6).\left[\frac{(t-1)(3-t)}{2}+\frac{(t-2)(4-t)}{2}\right]+(2).\left[\frac{(t-2)^2}{2}\right], 2\le t<3 \\ (4).\left[\frac{(4-t)^2}{2}\right]+(2).\left[\frac{(t-2)(4-t)}{2}+\frac{(t-3)(5-t)}{2}\right], 3\le t<4 \\ (2).\left[\frac{(5-t)^2}{2}\right], 4\le t<5 \end{cases}$$

4.10.3 Properties of Splines

PROBLEM 4.16
Find the length of the curve $y = 3x + 2$ between $x = 1$ and $x = 5$.

$$\text{Length of curve}: L = \int_a^b \sqrt{1+\left(\frac{dy}{dx}\right)^2}\,dx$$

Here $\frac{dy}{dx} = 3$, hence $L = \int_1^5 \sqrt{1+(3)^2}\,dx = \int_1^5 \sqrt{10}\,dx =$ $4\sqrt{10} = 12.65$

PROBLEM 4.17
Calculate area under the curve $y = 10 - x^2$ between the values $x = -1$ and $x = 2$.

$$\text{Area under curve: } A = \int_a^b f(x)\,dx$$

$$\text{Substituting given values, } A = \int_{-1}^{2} \left(10 - x^2\right)dx = 27$$

PROBLEM 4.18
Find the centroid of the area bounded by the curves $y = x^3$, $x = 0$ and $x = 2$.

$$\text{Here area: } A\int_a^b f(x).dx = \int_0^2 x^3.dx = 4$$

Centroid x – coordinate:

$$x_c = \frac{\int_a^b x.f(x).dx}{A} = \frac{\int_0^2 x.x^3.dx}{4} = 1.6$$

Centroid y – coordinate:

$$y_c = \frac{\int_a^b \{f(x)\}^2.dx}{2A} = \frac{\int_0^2 x^6.dx}{2\times 4} = 2.29$$

PROBLEM 4.19
Calculate minimum, maximum and POI of the cubic curve $y = 2 + 13x - 31x^2 + 18x^3$.

From given equation,

$$f(x) = 2 + 13x - 31x^2 + 18x^3$$

$$f'(x) = 13 - 62x + 54x^2$$

$$f''(x) = -62 + 108x$$

Setting $f'(x) = 13 - 62x + 54x^2 = 0$ roots are $r_1 = 0.87, r_2 = 0.28$

Now, $f''(0.87) = -62 + 108(0.87) = -62 + 93.96 = 31.96 > 0$

Thus, there is a minimum point at $x = 0.87$ and $f(0.87) = 1.7$, i.e., (0.87, 1.7)

Again, $f''(0.28) = -62 + 108(0.28) = -62 + 30.24 = -31.76 < 0$

Thus, there is a maximum point at $x = 0.28$ and $f(0.28) = 3.6$, i.e., (0.28, 3.6)

For POI, setting $f''(x) = -62 + 108x = 0$, root $r = 0.574$

Now sign $\{f''(r-\delta)\}$ = sign $\{f''(0.574-0.1)\}$ = sign $\{-62+108(0.474)\}$ = sign$(-10.8) = -1$

And sign $\{f''(r+\delta)\}$ = sign $\{f''(0.574+0.1)\}$ = sign $\{-62+108(0.674)\}$ = sign $(10.8) = +1$

Since signs are opposite, there is a POI at $r = 0.574$

Coordinates of the POI: $[0.574, f(0.574)]$ *i.e.*$(0.574, 2.662)$

4.10.4 3D Transformations

PROBLEM 4.20
A cube with center at origin and vertices at (–1, 1, 1), (1, 1, 1), (1, –1, 1), (–1, –1, 1), (–1, 1, –1), (1, 1, –1), (1, –1, –1) and (–1, –1, –1) is translated by amounts (–2, –1, 3). Find its new vertices.

Original coordinate matrix:

$$C = \begin{pmatrix} -1 & 1 & 1 & -1 & -1 & 1 & 1 & -1 \\ 1 & 1 & -1 & -1 & 1 & 1 & -1 & -1 \\ 1 & 1 & 1 & 1 & -1 & -1 & -1 & -1 \\ 1 & 1 & 1 & 1 & 1 & 1 & 1 & 1 \end{pmatrix}$$

$$\text{Translation matrix: } T(-2,-1,3) = \begin{pmatrix} 1 & 0 & 0 & -2 \\ 0 & 1 & 0 & -1 \\ 0 & 0 & 1 & 3 \\ 0 & 0 & 0 & 1 \end{pmatrix}$$

New coordinate matrix: $D = T(-2,-1,3).C$

$$= \begin{pmatrix} -3 & -1 & -1 & -3 & -3 & -1 & -1 & -3 \\ 0 & 0 & -2 & -2 & 0 & 0 & -2 & -2 \\ 4 & 4 & 4 & 4 & 2 & 2 & 2 & 2 \\ 1 & 1 & 1 & 1 & 1 & 1 & 1 & 1 \end{pmatrix}$$

New coordinates are: $(-3,0,4),(-1,0,4),(-1,-2,4),(-3,-2,4),(-3,0,2),(-1,0,2),(-1,-2,2),(-3,-2,2)$.

PROBLEM 4.21

A cube with center at origin and vertices at (−1, 1, 1), (1, 1, 1), (1, −1, 1), (−1, −1, 1), (−1, 1, −1), (1, 1, −1), (1, −1, −1) and (−1, −1, −1) is scaled by amounts (2, 1, 3). Find its new vertices.

Original coordinate matrix:

$$C=\begin{pmatrix}-1&1&1&-1&-1&1&1&-1\\1&1&-1&-1&1&1&-1&-1\\1&1&1&1&-1&-1&-1&-1\\1&1&1&1&1&1&1&1\end{pmatrix}$$

$$\text{Scaling matrix: } S(2,1,3)=\begin{pmatrix}2&0&0&0\\0&1&0&0\\0&0&3&0\\0&0&0&1\end{pmatrix}$$

New coordinate matrix: $D=S(2,1,3).C$

$$=\begin{pmatrix}-2&2&2&-2&-2&2&2&-2\\1&1&-1&-1&1&1&-1&-1\\3&3&3&3&-3&-3&-3&-3\\1&1&1&1&1&1&1&1\end{pmatrix}$$

New coordinates are: $(-2,1,3),(2,1,3),(2,-1,3),$ $(-2,-1,3),(-2,1,-3),(2,1,-3),(2,-1,-3),(-2,-1,-3)$

PROBLEM 4.22

A cube with center at origin and vertices at (−1, 1, 1), (1, 1, 1), (1, −1, 1), (−1, −1, 1), (−1, 1, −1), (1, 1, −1), (1, −1, −1) and (−1, −1, −1) is rotated by 45° about the x – axis. Find its new vertices.

Original coordinate matrix:

$$C=\begin{pmatrix}-1&1&1&-1&-1&1&1&-1\\1&1&-1&-1&1&1&-1&-1\\1&1&1&1&-1&-1&-1&-1\\1&1&1&1&1&1&1&1\end{pmatrix}$$

Rotation matrix:

$$R_x(45)=\begin{pmatrix}1&0&0&0\\0&\cos 45&-\sin 45&0\\0&\sin 45&\cos 45&0\\0&0&0&1\end{pmatrix}$$

$$=\begin{pmatrix}1&0&0&0\\0&0.71&-0.71&0\\0&0.71&0.71&0\\0&0&0&1\end{pmatrix}$$

New coordinate matrix: $D=R_x(45).C$

$$=\begin{pmatrix}-1&1&1&-1&-1&1&1&-1\\0&0&-1.41&-1.41&1.41&1.41&0&0\\1.41&1.41&0&0&0&0&-1.41&-1.41\\1&1&1&1&1&1&1&1\end{pmatrix}$$

New vertices: $(-1.00,0,1.41),(1.00,0,1.41),$ $(1.00,-1.41,0),(-1.00,-1.41,0),(-1.00,1.41,0),$ $(1.00,1.41,0),(1.00,0,-1.41),(-1.00,0,-1.41)$

PROBLEM 4.23

A cube with center at origin and vertices at (−1, 1, 1), (1, 1, 1), (1, −1, 1), (−1, −1, 1), (−1, 1, −1), (1, 1, −1), (1, −1, −1) and (−1, −1, −1) is rotated by 45° with respect to its vertex (−1, −1, −1) around z –axis. Find its new vertices.

Original coordinate matrix:

$$C=\begin{pmatrix}-1&1&1&-1&-1&1&1&-1\\1&1&-1&-1&1&1&-1&-1\\1&1&1&1&-1&-1&-1&-1\\1&1&1&1&1&1&1&1\end{pmatrix}$$

$$\text{Forward translation: } T(1,1,1)=\begin{pmatrix}1&0&0&1\\0&1&0&1\\0&0&1&1\\0&0&0&1\end{pmatrix}$$

Rotation about z – axis:

$$R_z(\theta)=\begin{pmatrix}\cos 45&-\sin 45&0&0\\\sin 45&\cos 45&0&0\\0&0&1&0\\0&0&0&1\end{pmatrix}$$

$$\text{Reverse translation: } T(-1,-1,-1)=\begin{pmatrix}1&0&0&-1\\0&1&0&-1\\0&0&1&-1\\0&0&0&1\end{pmatrix}$$

Composite transformation:
$M=T(-1,-1,-1).R_z(\theta).T(1,1,1)$

New coordinate matrix: $D=M.C$

New vertices: $(-2.41,0.41,1.00),(-1.00,1.83,1.00),$ $(0.41,0.41,1.00),(-1.00,-1.00,1.00),$ $(-2.41,0.41,-1.00),(-1.00,1.83,-1.00),$ $(0.41,0.41,-1.00),(-1.00,-1.00,-1.00)$

PROBLEM 4.24

A point $C(1, 1, 1)$ is to be rotated by 180° around a line parallel to the y-axis joining points $P(5, 2, 3)$ and $Q(5, 0, 3)$. Find its new coordinates.

$$\text{Original coordinate matrix: } C = \begin{pmatrix} 1 \\ 1 \\ 1 \\ 1 \end{pmatrix}$$

Forward translation to coincide with Y-axis: $T(-5,0,-3)$

Rotation around y-axis: $R_y(180)$

Reverse translation to original location: $T(5,0,3)$

Composite transformation: $M = T(5,0,3).R_y(180).T(-5,0,-3)$

$$\text{New coordinate matrix: } D = M.C = \begin{pmatrix} 9 \\ 1 \\ 5 \\ 1 \end{pmatrix}$$

New coordinates: $(9,1,5)$

PROBLEM 4.25

A cube with center at origin and vertices at (−1, 1, 1), (1, 1, 1), (1, −1, 1), (−1, −1, 1), (−1, 1, −1), (1, 1, −1), (1, −1, −1), (−1, −1, −1) is to be reflected about a plane $z = 3$ parallel to the xy-plane along the z-axis. Find its new vertices.

Translate plane so as to coincide with xy-plane: $T(0,0,-3)$

Reflect about xy-plane, i.e., along z-axis: F_z

Reverse translate plane to original location: $T(0,0,3)$

Composite transformation: $M = T(0,0,3).F_z.T(0,0,-3)$

Original coordinate matrix:

$$C = \begin{pmatrix} -1 & 1 & 1 & -1 & -1 & 1 & 1 & -1 \\ 1 & 1 & -1 & -1 & 1 & 1 & -1 & -1 \\ 1 & 1 & 1 & 1 & -1 & -1 & -1 & -1 \\ 1 & 1 & 1 & 1 & 1 & 1 & 1 & 1 \end{pmatrix}$$

New coordinate matrix: $D = M.C$

New coordinates: $(-1,1,5),(1,1,5),(1,-1,5),(-1,-1,5),(-1,1,7),(1,1,7),(1,-1,7),(-1,-1,7)$

PROBLEM 4.26

A cube with center at origin and vertices at (−1, 1, 1), (1, 1, 1), (1, −1, 1), (−1, −1, 1), (−1, 1, −1), (1, 1, −1), (1, −1, −1) and (−1, −1, −1) is subjected to a shear along the z-axis with parameters (1.2, 2.3). Find its new vertices.

$$\text{Shear matrix along z-axis: } H_z = \begin{pmatrix} 1 & 0 & 0 & 0 \\ 0 & 1 & 0 & 0 \\ 1.2 & 2.3 & 1 & 0 \\ 0 & 0 & 0 & 1 \end{pmatrix}$$

New coordinate matrix: $D = H_z.C$

New vertices:

$(-1.00,1.00,2.10),(1.00,1.00,4.50),(1.00,-1.00,-0.10),(-1.00,-1.00,-2.50),(-1.00,1.00,0.10),(1.00,1.00,2.50),(1.00,-1.00,-2.10),(-1.00,-1.00,-4.50)$

PROBLEM 4.27

Find the transformation for aligning the following vectors with the positive x-axis. Also find the new vector after alignment. (a) $2i + j + 2k$ (b) $2i - j - 2k$.

$(a)\, a = 2, b = 1, c = 2$

$$d = \sqrt{b^2 + c^2} = 2.2361,$$

$$\sin(\alpha) = \frac{b}{d} = 0.4472, \cos(\alpha) = \frac{c}{d} = 0.8944$$

$$\sin(\varphi) = \frac{d}{e} = 0.7454, \cos(\varphi) = \frac{a}{e} = 0.6667$$

$$M = R_y(\varphi).R_x(\alpha) = \begin{pmatrix} 0.6667 & 0.3333 & 0.6667 & 0 \\ 0 & 0.8944 & -0.4472 & 0 \\ -0.7454 & 0.2981 & 0.5963 & 0 \\ 0 & 0 & 0 & 1 \end{pmatrix}$$

$$\text{Original coordinate matrix: } C = \begin{pmatrix} 2 \\ 1 \\ 2 \\ 1 \end{pmatrix}$$

$$\text{New coordinate matrix: } D = M.C = \begin{pmatrix} 3 \\ 0 \\ 0 \\ 1 \end{pmatrix}$$

New vector is: $Q = 3i$

$(b) a = 2, b = -1, c = -2$

$d = \sqrt{b^2 + c^2} = 2.2361, e = \sqrt{a^2 + b^2 + c^2} = 3$

$\sin(\alpha) = \frac{b}{d} = -0.4472, \cos(\alpha) = \frac{c}{d} = -0.8944$

$\sin(\varphi) = \frac{d}{e} = 0.7454, \cos(\varphi) = \frac{a}{e} = 0.6667$

$$M = R_y(\varphi).R_x(\alpha) = \begin{pmatrix} 0.6667 & -0.3333 & -0.6667 & 0 \\ 0 & -0.8944 & 0.4472 & 0 \\ -0.7454 & -0.2981 & -0.5963 & 0 \\ 0 & 0 & 0 & 1 \end{pmatrix}$$

$$\text{Original coordinate matrix}: C = \begin{pmatrix} 2 \\ -1 \\ -2 \\ 1 \end{pmatrix}$$

$$\text{New coordinate matrix } D = M.C = \begin{pmatrix} 3 \\ 0 \\ 0 \\ 1 \end{pmatrix}$$

New vector is: $Q = 3i$

4.10.5 Vectors

PROBLEM 4.28
Find the magnitude and unit vector in the direction of a specified vector $R = 2i - j + 2k$.

Here: $|R| = \sqrt{(a^2 + b^2 + c^2)} = \sqrt{4 + 1 + 4} = 3$

Hence unit vector: $r = (1/3) * (2i - j + 2k) = (2/3)i - (1/3)j + (2/3)k$

PROBLEM 4.29
Calculate angle between two vectors $A = 2i - 3j + k$ and $B = 4i + j - 3k$.

$|A| = \sqrt{4 + 9 + 1} = \sqrt{14}$ *and* $|B| = \sqrt{16 + 1 + 9} = \sqrt{26}$

$\cos(\theta) = (A \bullet B) / (|A|.|B|) = 0.1048, \text{hence } \theta = 83.98^\circ$

PROBLEM 4.30
Calculate the vector perpendicular to both $A = 3i + 5j - 2k$ and $B = 2i - 2j - 2k$.

$$A \times B = (-10 - 4)i + (-4 + 6)j + (-6 - 10)k$$
$$= -14i + 2j - 16k$$

PROBLEM 4.31
Calculate rotation matrix to align vectors with positive x-axis: (a) $-3i + 4j$ (b) $3i - 4j$.

$(a) P = -3i + 4j = (-3, 4)$

$$\theta = 180^\circ - \arctan(4/3) = 126.87^\circ$$

Rotation matrix is: $R(-126.87^\circ)$

Verification: $Q = R(-126.87^\circ).P = (5, 0)$

$(b) P = 3i - 4j = (3, -4)$

$$\theta = -\arctan(4/3) = -53.13^\circ$$

Rotation matrix is: $R(53.13^\circ)$

Verification: $Q = R(53.13^\circ).P = (5, 0)$

PROBLEM 4.32
Calculate rotation matrix to align vectors (a) $3i - 4j$ with positive y-axis (b) $-3i - 4j$ with negative x-axis.

$(a) P = 3i - 4j = (3, -4) \rightarrow \theta = -\arctan\left(\frac{4}{3}\right) = -53.13^\circ$

To align with $+y$ axis, the vector needs to be rotated by $(90 + 53.13)^\circ = 143.13^\circ$ in CCW direction, i.e., rotation matrix is $R(143.13^\circ)$

$(b) P = -3i - 4j = (-3, -4) \rightarrow \theta = \arctan(4/3) = 53.13^\circ$

To align with $-x$ axis, the vector needs to be rotated by 53.13° CW direction, i.e., rotation matrix is $R(-53.13^\circ)$

PROBLEM 4.33

Compute transformation matrix for aligning vector $P = 2i + j + 2k$ with positive z-axis.

Comparing with vector $ai + bj + ck$, we get $a = 2, b = 1$, $c = 2, d = \sqrt{b^2 + c^2} = 2.236, e = \sqrt{a^2 + b^2 + c^2} = 3$

$$\therefore \sin(\alpha) = \frac{b}{d} = 0.447, \cos(\alpha) = \frac{c}{d} = 0.894,$$

$$\sin(\phi) = \frac{a}{e} = 0.667, \cos(\phi) = \frac{d}{e} = 0.745$$

$$R_x(\alpha) = \begin{pmatrix} 1 & 0 & 0 & 0 \\ 0 & \cos\alpha & -\sin\alpha & 0 \\ 0 & \sin\alpha & \cos\alpha & 0 \\ 0 & 0 & 0 & 1 \end{pmatrix} = \begin{pmatrix} 1 & 0 & 0 & 0 \\ 0 & 0.894 & -0.447 & 0 \\ 0 & 0.447 & 0.894 & 0 \\ 0 & 0 & 0 & 1 \end{pmatrix}$$

$$R_y(-\varphi) = \begin{pmatrix} \cos(\varphi) & 0 & -\sin(\varphi) & 0 \\ 0 & 1 & 0 & 0 \\ \sin(\varphi) & 0 & \cos(\varphi) & 0 \\ 0 & 0 & 0 & 1 \end{pmatrix} = \begin{pmatrix} 0.745 & 0 & -0.667 & 0 \\ 0 & 1 & 0 & 0 \\ 0.667 & 0 & 0.745 & 0 \\ 0 & 0 & 0 & 1 \end{pmatrix}$$

Composite transformation:

$$M = R_y(-\varphi).R_x(\alpha) = \begin{pmatrix} 0.745 & -0.298 & -0.596 & 0 \\ 0 & 0.894 & -0.447 & 0 \\ 0.667 & 0.333 & 0.667 & 0 \\ 0 & 0 & 0 & 1 \end{pmatrix}$$

Verification: $Q = M.P = (0, 0, 3)$

4.10.6 Projection

PROBLEM 4.34

Calculate projection matrix and projected coordinates for (a) perspective projection of point $P(-8, 6)$ onto viewline $L: -3x + 12y - 5 = 0$ along viewpoint $V(-3, 11)$ (b) parallel orthographic projection of P on L.

(a) Here, $V = (-3, 11, 1), L = (-3, 12, -5), P = (-8, 6, 1)$

Projection matrix $M = \left[V^T.L - (VL^T).I\right]$

$$= \begin{pmatrix} -3 \\ 11 \\ 1 \end{pmatrix} \begin{pmatrix} -3 & 12 & -5 \end{pmatrix} - \begin{pmatrix} -3 & 11 & 1 \end{pmatrix} \times \begin{pmatrix} -3 \\ 12 \\ -5 \end{pmatrix} \begin{pmatrix} 1 & 0 & 0 \\ 0 & 1 & 0 \\ 0 & 0 & 1 \end{pmatrix}$$

Simplifying, $M = \begin{pmatrix} -127 & -36 & 15 \\ -33 & -4 & -55 \\ -3 & 12 & -141 \end{pmatrix}$ (in homogeneous coordinates)

Original coordinates of point $P = \begin{pmatrix} -8 \\ 6 \\ 1 \end{pmatrix}$

Projected coordinates : $Q = M.P = \begin{pmatrix} 815 \\ 185 \\ -45 \end{pmatrix}$ (in homogeneous coordinates)

Projected coordinates : $Q' = \begin{pmatrix} -18.11 \\ -4.11 \\ 1 \end{pmatrix}$ (in Cartesian coordinates)

Verification: The projected point lies on the view-line: $L(-18.11, -4.11) = 0$

(b) For orthographic projection, the direction of projection should be along the normal of line L. Slope of line $ax + by + c = 0$ is $-\frac{a}{b}$. For line L slope $= 3/12 = 0.25$.

Thus tangent vector $t = (1, 0.25, 1)$. Normal vector $n = R(90) * t = (-0.25, 1, 1)$.

Since parallel projection should be along the normal vector, $V = (-0.25, 1, 0)$.

Projection matrix : $M = \left[V^T.L - (VL^T).I\right]$

$$= \begin{pmatrix} -0.25 \\ 1 \\ 0 \end{pmatrix} \begin{pmatrix} -3 & 12 & -5 \end{pmatrix} - \begin{pmatrix} -0.25 & 1 & 0 \end{pmatrix} \times \begin{pmatrix} -3 \\ 12 \\ -5 \end{pmatrix} \begin{pmatrix} 1 & 0 & 0 \\ 0 & 1 & 0 \\ 0 & 0 & 1 \end{pmatrix}$$

Simplifying, $M = \begin{pmatrix} -12 & -3 & 1.25 \\ -3 & -0.75 & -5 \\ 0 & 0 & -12.75 \end{pmatrix}$ (in homogeneous coordinates)

$$\text{Projected coordinates}: Q = M.P = \begin{pmatrix} 79.25 \\ 14.5 \\ -12.75 \end{pmatrix} \text{(in homogeneous coordinates)}$$

$$\text{Projected coordinates}: Q' = \begin{pmatrix} -6.21 \\ -1.14 \\ 1 \end{pmatrix} \text{(in Cartesian coordinates)}$$

Verification: The projected point lies on the view-line, i.e., $L(-6.21,-1.14)=0$

PROBLEM 4.35

Calculate projection matrix and projected coordinates for (a) perspective projection of point $P(-4,2,2)$ onto viewplane $F: -x+3y+2z-4=0$ and viewpoint $V(2,-1,1)$ (b) parallel orthographic projection of P on F.

(a) Here, $P=(-4,2,2,1), N=(-1,3,2,-4)$,
$V=(2,-1,1,1)$

$$\text{Projection matrix } M = \left[V^T.N-(VN^T).I\right] = \begin{pmatrix} 2 \\ -1 \\ 1 \\ 1 \end{pmatrix}\begin{pmatrix} -1 & 3 & 2 & -4 \end{pmatrix} - \begin{pmatrix} 2 & -1 & 1 & 1 \end{pmatrix}\begin{pmatrix} -1 \\ 3 \\ 2 \\ -4 \end{pmatrix}\begin{pmatrix} 1 & 0 & 0 & 0 \\ 0 & 1 & 0 & 0 \\ 0 & 0 & 1 & 0 \\ 0 & 0 & 0 & 1 \end{pmatrix}$$

$$\text{Simplifying, } M = \begin{pmatrix} 5 & 6 & 4 & -8 \\ 1 & 4 & -2 & 4 \\ -1 & 3 & 9 & -4 \\ -1 & 3 & 2 & 3 \end{pmatrix} \text{(in homogeneous coordinates)}$$

$$\text{Projected coordinates } Q_h = M.P = \begin{pmatrix} -8 \\ 4 \\ 24 \\ 17 \end{pmatrix} \text{(in homogeneous coordinates)}$$

$$\text{Projected coordinates } Q = Q_h / 17 = \begin{pmatrix} -0.47 \\ 0.23 \\ 1.41 \\ 1 \end{pmatrix} \text{(in Cartesian coordinates)}$$

Verification: The projected point lies on the view-plane, i.e., $F(-0.47,0.23,1.41)=0$

(b) For orthographic projection, the direction of projection should be along the normal of plane F, i.e., along N.

Here $P=(-4,2,2,1), N=(-1,3,2,-4)$,
$V=N=(-1,3,2,-4)$

$$\text{Projection matrix } M = \left[V^T.N-(VN^T).I\right] = \begin{pmatrix} -1 \\ 3 \\ 2 \\ -4 \end{pmatrix}\begin{pmatrix} -1 & 3 & 2 & -4 \end{pmatrix} - \begin{pmatrix} -1 & 3 & 2 & -4 \end{pmatrix}\begin{pmatrix} -1 \\ 3 \\ 2 \\ -4 \end{pmatrix}\begin{pmatrix} 1 & 0 & 0 & 0 \\ 0 & 1 & 0 & 0 \\ 0 & 0 & 1 & 0 \\ 0 & 0 & 0 & 1 \end{pmatrix}$$

$$\text{Simplifying, } M = \begin{pmatrix} -13 & -3 & -2 & 4 \\ -3 & -5 & 6 & -12 \\ -2 & 6 & -10 & -8 \\ 0 & 0 & 0 & -14 \end{pmatrix}$$

Projected coordinates $Q_h = M.P = \begin{pmatrix} 46 \\ 2 \\ -8 \\ -14 \end{pmatrix}$ (homogeneous coordinates)

Projected coordinates $Q = Q_h / (-14) = \begin{pmatrix} -3.28 \\ -0.14 \\ 0.57 \\ 1 \end{pmatrix}$ (Cartesian coordinates)

Verification: The projected point lies on the view-plane, i.e., $F(-3.28, -0.14, 0.57) = 0$

4.11 Coding Examples using MATLAB®

4.11.1 2D Transformations

The following example demonstrates 2D translation of a square. The function "legend" designates different color or line types in a graph using textual strings, function "axis" controls appearance of the axes of the plot, "fprintf" prints out strings and values using formatting options, "grid" turns on display of grid lines in a plot, "xlabel" and "ylabel" provide labels along the x – and y –axis (Figure 4.57).

EXAMPLE 4.1 EXAMPLE TO CALCULATE NEW COORDINATES OF A SQUARE WITH VERTICES (0,0), (1,0), (1,1), (0,1) TRANSLATED BY AMOUNTS (-3, 4)

```
clear; clc;
X = [0 1 1 0 0];
Y = [0 0 1 1 0];
C = [X; Y; 1 1 1 1 1];
tx = -3; ty = 4;
T1 = [1 0 tx; 0 1 ty; 0 0 1];
D = T1*C;
fprintf('New vertices : \n');
for i=1:4
    fprintf('(%.2f, %.2f) \n',D(1,i),
       D(2,i));
end

%plotting
plot(C(1,:), C(2,:), 'b--',
   D(1,:),D(2,:), 'r');
xlabel('x');
ylabel('y');
legend('original', 'new');
axis([-6, 6, -6, 6]); grid;
```

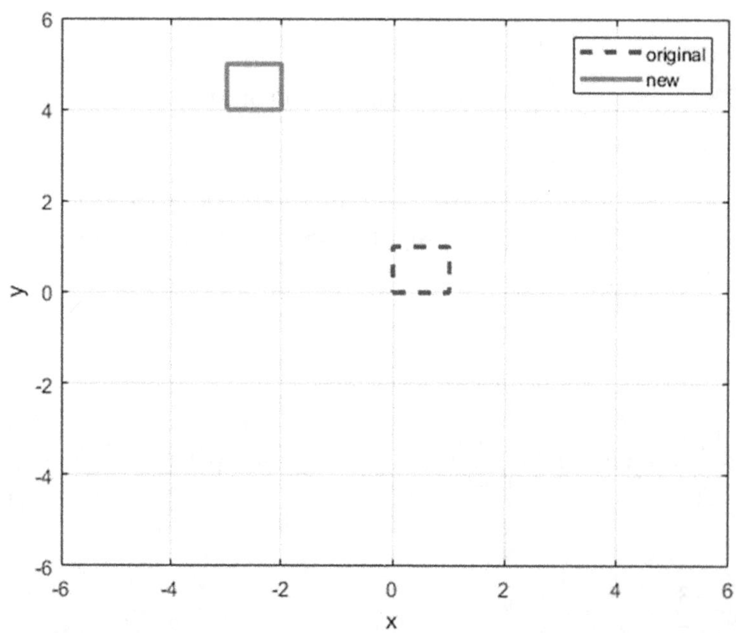

FIGURE 4.57
Plot for Example 4.1

The following example demonstrates 2D scaling of a quadrilateral about the origin (Figure 4.58).

EXAMPLE 4.2 EXAMPLE TO CALCULATE NEW COORDINATES OF A QUADRILATERAL WITH VERTICES (-1,-1), (1,-2), (1,2), (-1,1) SCALED BY AMOUNTS (-2, 3)

```
clear; clc;
X = [-1 1 1 -1 -1];
Y = [-1 -2 2 1 -1];
C = [X;Y; 1 1 1 1 1];
sx = -2;
sy = 3;
S1 = [sx 0 0; 0 sy 0; 0 0 1];
D = S1*C;
fprintf('New vertices : \n');
for i=1:4
    fprintf('(%.2f, %.2f) \n',D(1,i),
       D(2,i));
end

%plotting
plot(C(1,:), C(2,:), 'b--',
   D(1,:),D(2,:), 'r');
xlabel('x');
ylabel('y');
legend('original', 'new');
axis([-6, 6, -6, 6]); grid;
```

The following example demonstrates 2D rotation of a square about the origin. The function "deg2rad" converts degree values to radians (Figure 4.59).

EXAMPLE 4.3 EXAMPLE TO CALCULATE NEW COORDINATES OF A SQUARE WITH VERTICES (-1, -1), (1, -1), (1, 1), AND (-1, 1) AFTER ROTATION BY 30° CCW ABOUT THE ORIGIN

```
clear; clc;
X = [-1 1 1 -1 -1];
Y = [-1 -1 1 1 -1];
C = [X;Y; 1 1 1 1 1];
A = deg2rad(30);
R1 = [cos(A) -sin(A) 0; sin(A) cos(A)
   0; 0 0 1];
D = R1*C;
fprintf('New vertices : \n');
for i=1:4
    fprintf('(%.2f, %.2f) \n',D(1,i),
       D(2,i));
end

%plotting
plot(C(1,:), C(2,:), 'b--', D(1,:),
   D(2,:), 'r');
xlabel('x'); ylabel('y');
legend('original', 'new');
axis([-4, 4, -4, 4]); grid;
axis square;
```

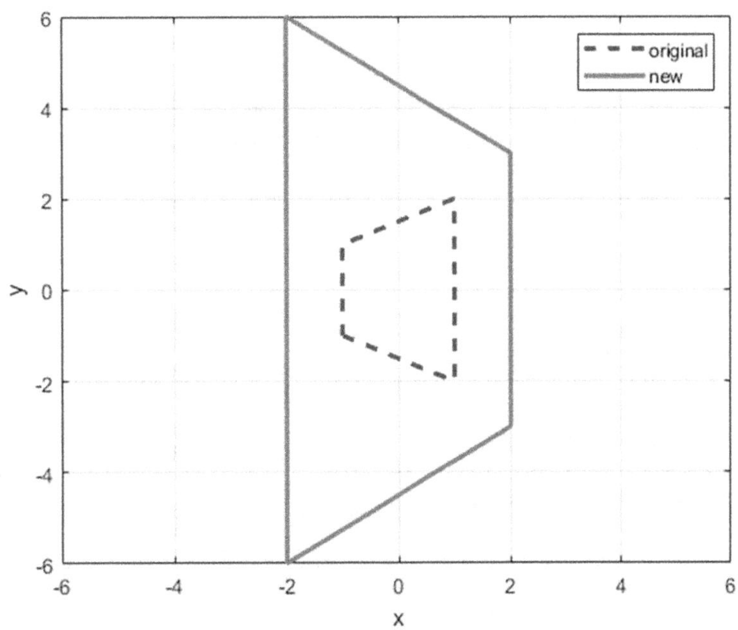

FIGURE 4.58
Plot for Example 4.2

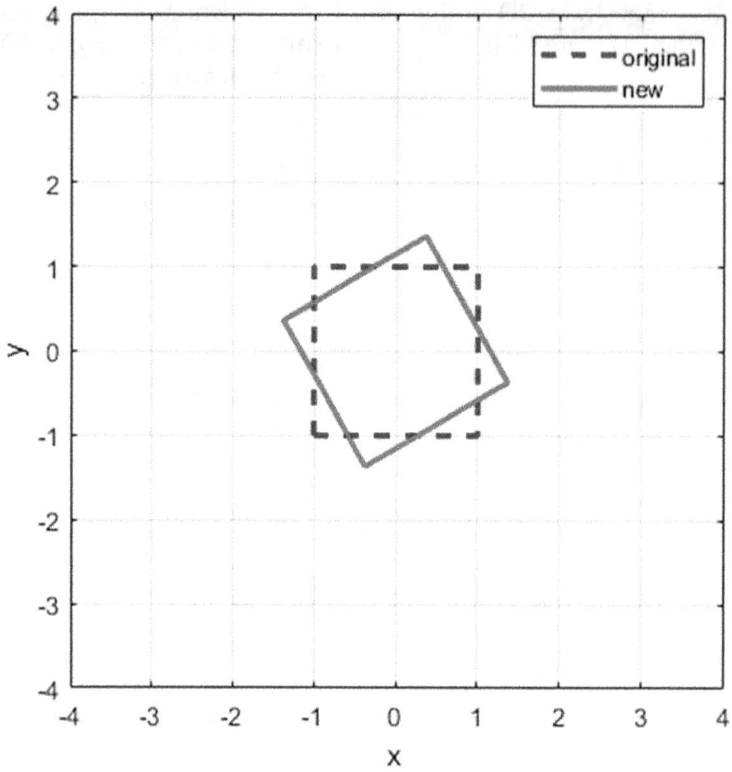

FIGURE 4.59
Plot for Example 4.3.

The following example demonstrates 2D scaling of a square about a fixed point (Figure 4.60).

EXAMPLE 4.4 EXAMPLE TO CALCULATE NEW COORDINATES OF A SQUARE WITH VERTICES (-1, -1), (1, -1), AMOUNTS (-2, 3) ABOUT ONE OF ITS VERTICES (-1, -1)

```
clear; clc;
X = [-1 1 1 -1 -1];
Y = [-1 -1 1 1 -1];
C = [X;Y; 1 1 1 1 1];
sx = -2; sy = 3;
xf = -1; yf = -1;
T1 = [1, 0, -xf ; 0, 1, -yf ; 0, 0, 1];
S1 = [sx, 0, 0 ; 0, sy, 0 ; 0, 0, 1];
T2 = [1, 0, xf ; 0, 1, yf ; 0, 0, 1];
M = T2 * S1 * T1 ;
D = M*C;
fprintf('New vertices : \n');
for i=1:4
    fprintf('(%.2f, %.2f) \n',D(1,i),
       D(2,i));
end

%plotting
plot(C(1,:), C(2,:), 'b--',
   D(1,:),D(2,:), 'r', xf, yf, 'ro');
xlabel('x'); ylabel('y');
legend('original', 'new');
axis([-8, 8, -8, 8]);
axis square; grid;
```

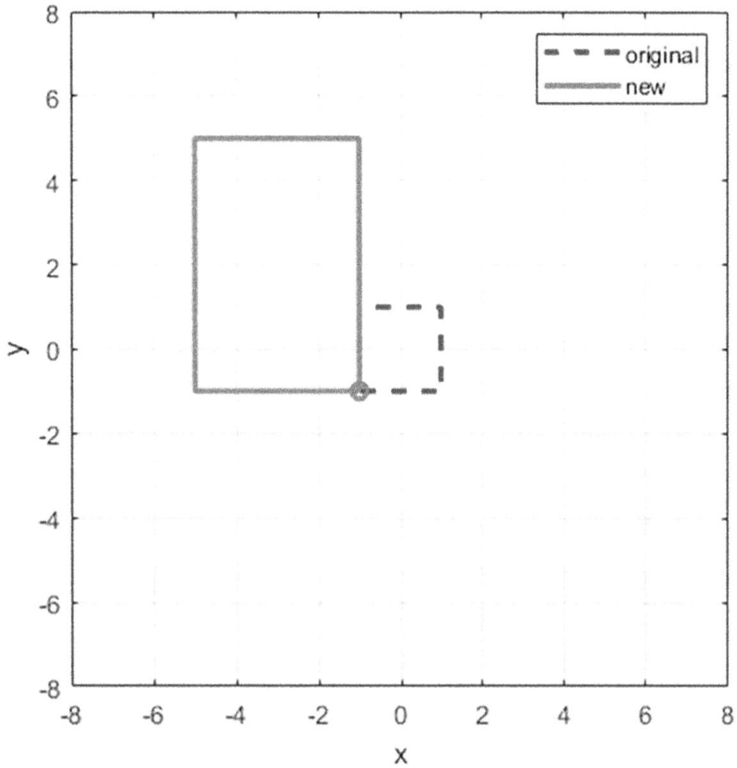

FIGURE 4.60
Plot for Example 4.4.

The following example demonstrates 2D rotation of a square about a fixed point. The functions "cosd" and "sind" calculate the cosine and sine of an angle in degrees instead of radians (Figure 4.61).

EXAMPLE 4.5 EXAMPLE TO CALCULATE NEW COORDINATES OF A SQUARE WITH VERTICES (-1, -1), (1, -1), (1, 1), AND (-1, 1) ROTATED BY ANGLE 30° CCW ABOUT ONE OF ITS VERTICES (-1, -1)

```
clear; clc;
X = [-1 1 1 -1 -1];
Y = [-1 -1 1 1 -1];
C = [X ; Y ; 1 1 1 1 1];
xf = -1;
yf = -1;
A = 30;
T1 = [1, 0, -xf ; 0, 1, -yf ; 0, 0, 1];
R1 = [cosd(A), -sind(A), 0 ; sind(A),
   cosd(A), 0 ; 0, 0, 1];
T2 = [1, 0, xf ; 0, 1, yf ; 0, 0, 1];
M = T2 * R1 * T1 ;
D = M * C;
fprintf('New vertices : \n');
for i=1:4
    fprintf('(%.2f, %.2f) \n',D(1,i),
       D(2,i));
end

%plotting
plot(C(1,:), C(2,:), 'b--',
   D(1,:),D(2,:), 'r', xf, yf, 'ro');
xlabel('x');ylabel('y');
legend('original', 'new');
axis([-4, 4, -4, 4]);
axis square; grid;
```

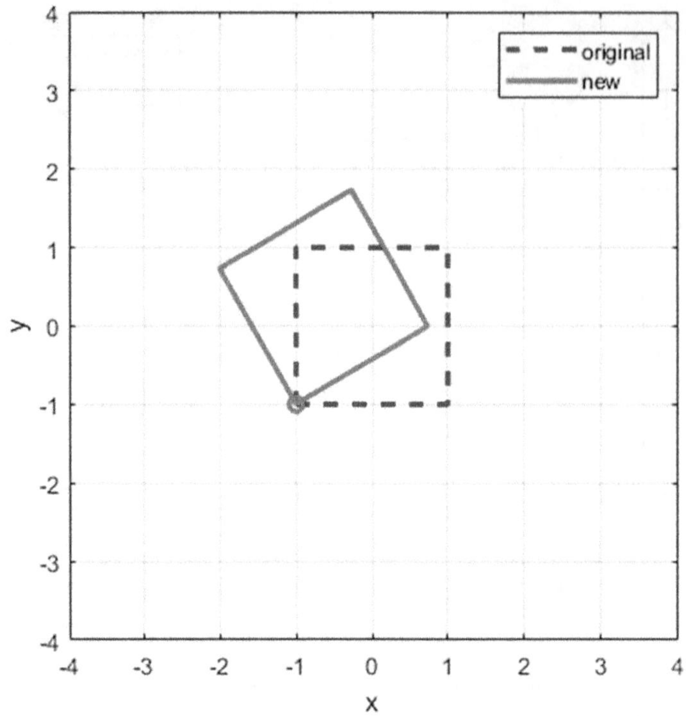

FIGURE 4.61
Plot for Example 4.5.

The following example demonstrates reflection of a triangle about the x-axis, y-axis and the origin (Figure 4.62).

EXAMPLE 4.6 EXAMPLE TO CALCULATE NEW COORDINATES OF A TRIANGLE WITH VERTICES (1, 2), (3, 2), AND (3, 4) AFTER REFLECTION ABOUT X-AXIS, Y-AXIS AND ORIGIN

```
clear; clc;
X = [1, 3, 3, 1];
Y = [2, 2, 4, 2];
C = [X; Y; 1 1 1 1];
Fx = [1 0 0; 0 -1 0; 0 0 1];
Fy = [-1 0 0; 0 1 0; 0 0 1];
Fo = [-1 0 0; 0 -1 0; 0 0 1];
Dx = Fx*C;
Dy = Fy*C;
Do = Fo*C;
fprintf('New vertices X-axis : \n');
for i=1:3
    fprintf('(%.2f, %.2f) \n',Dx(1,i),
  Dx(2,i));
end
fprintf('New vertices Y-axis : \n');
for i=1:3
    fprintf('(%.2f, %.2f) \n',Dy(1,i),
  Dy(2,i));
end
fprintf('New vertices origin: \n');
for i=1:3
    fprintf('(%.2f, %.2f) \n',Do(1,i),
  Do(2,i));
end

%plotting
plot(C(1,:), C(2,:), 'b--',
  Dx(1,:),Dx(2,:), 'r', …
Dy(1,:), Dy(2,:), 'r--', Do(1,:),
  Do(2,:), 'r-.');
xlabel('x'); ylabel('y');
axis([-5, 5, -5, 5]);
legend('original', 'Fx', 'Fy', 'Fo');
axis square; grid;
```

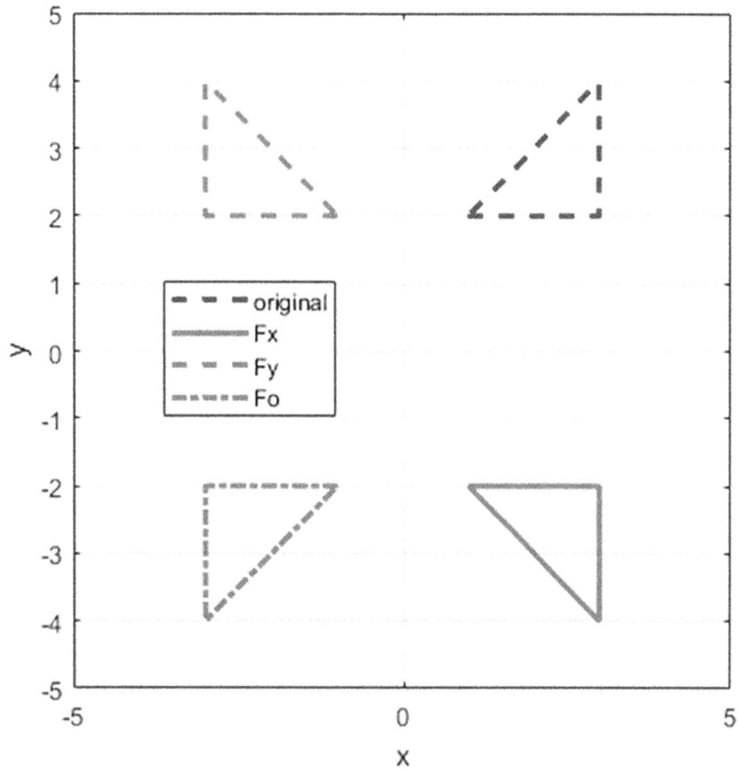

FIGURE 4.62
Plot for Example 4.6.

The following example demonstrates shear of a square along the horizontal and vertical directions (Figure 4.63).

EXAMPLE 4.7 EXAMPLE TO CALCULATE NEW COORDINATES OF A SQUARE WITH VERTICES (-1, -1), (1, -1), (1, 1), AND (-1, 1) AFTER SHEAR AMOUNTS HX = 1.2 AND HY = -1.2

```
clear; clc;
X=[-1 1 1 -1 -1]; Y=[-1 -1 1 1 -1];
C = [X;Y; 1 1 1 1 1];
hx = 1.2; hy = -1.2;
Hx = [1, hx, 0 ; 0, 1, 0 ; 0, 0, 1];
Hy = [1, 0, 0 ; hy, 1, 0 ; 0, 0, 1];
D = Hy*Hx*C;
fprintf('New vertices : \n');
for i=1:4
    fprintf('(%.2f, %.2f) \n',D(1,i),
       D(2,i));
end
plot(C(1,:), C(2,:), 'b--',
   D(1,:),D(2,:), 'r');
xlabel('x');ylabel('y');
legend('original', 'new');
axis equal; grid
```

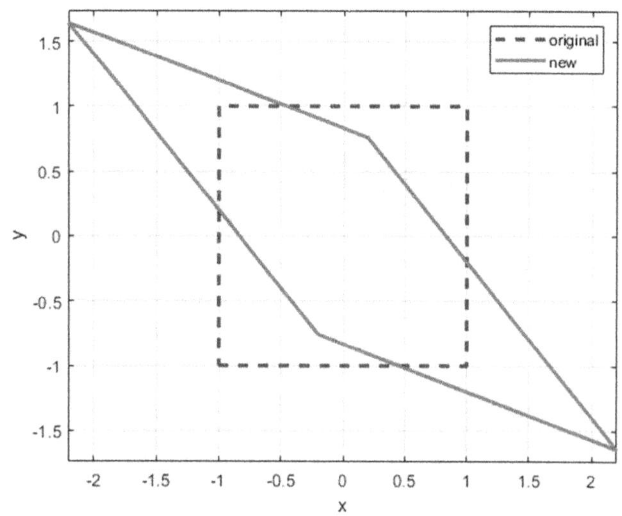

FIGURE 4.63
Plot for Example 4.7.

The following example illustrates the difference between affine and perspective transformations. The function "format" sets the display format in the command window (Figure 4.64).

EXAMPLE 4.8 EXAMPLE TO CALCULATE NEW COORDINATES OF A SQUARE WITH VERTICES (0,0),(1,0),(1,1), AND (0,1) UNDER (A) AFFINE TRANSFORMATION [2 -1 3 ; 2 2 1 ; 0 0 1] (B) PERSPECTIVE TRANSFORMATION [5,4,5 ; 2,5,5 ; 5,2,1]

```
clear; clc; format compact;
% (a)
C = [0 1 1 0 0 ; 0 0 1 1 0 ; 1 1 1 1 1]
M = [2 -1 3 ; 2 2 1 ; 0 0 1]
D = M*C
fprintf('New vertices : \n');
for i=1:4
    fprintf('(%.2f, %.2f) \n', D(1,i),
  D(2,i));
end
subplot(121)
plot (C(1,:), C(2,:), 'b--', D(1,:),
  D(2,:), 'r-'); grid;
legend('original', 'new');
title('affine transformation');
  axis square;
% (b)
M = [5 2 5 ; 2 5 5 ; 5 2 1]
Dh = M*C
for i=1:length(Dh)
    D(:,i) = Dh(:,i)/Dh(3,i);
end
fprintf('New vertices : \n');
for i=1:4
    fprintf('(%.2f, %.2f) \n', D(1,i),
      D(2,i));
end
subplot(122)
plot (C(1,:), C(2,:), 'b--', D(1,:),
  D(2,:), 'r-'); grid;
legend('original', 'new');
title('perspective transformation');
  axis square;
```

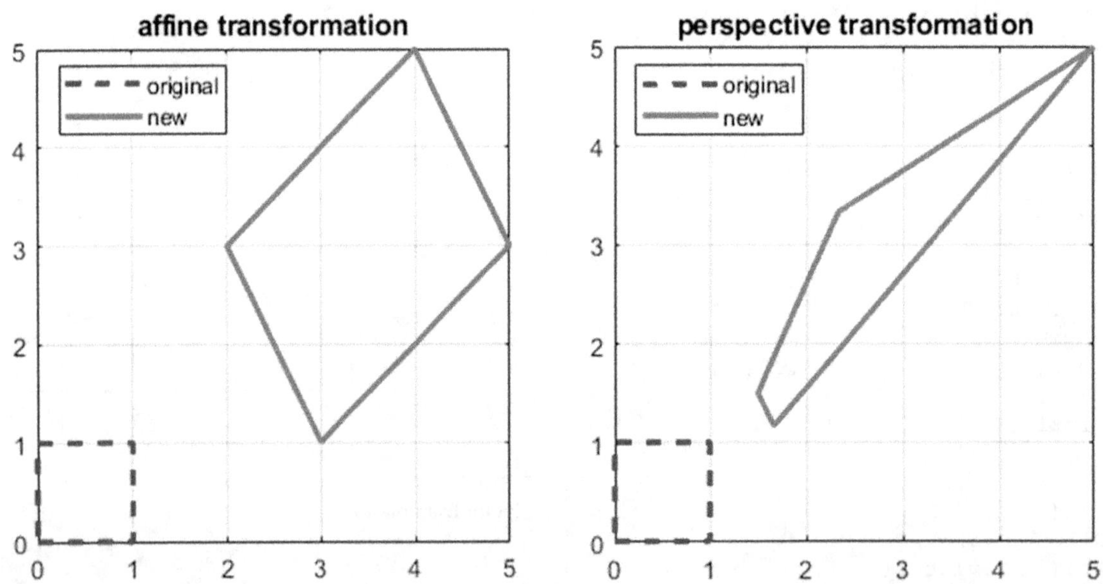

FIGURE 4.64
Plot for Example 4.8.

4.11.2 Curves and Splines

The following example computes the equation of a linear interpolating spline passing through two given points. The function "syms" declares a symbolic variable, "vpa" provides variable precision arithmetic up to 32 bits by default, "linspace" generates a vector of evenly spaced values, "subs" substitutes symbolic variables with a numeric vector, "scatter" produces a 2D scatter plot of points and circles (Figure 4.65).

EXAMPLE 4.9 EXAMPLE TO FIND EQUATION OF LINEAR SPLINE THROUGH THE POINTS (3, 2) AND (8, −4)

```
clear; clc;
syms x;
x1 = 3; y1 = 2;
x2 = 8; y2 = -4;
X = [x1 x2]; Y = [y1 y2];
C = [1 x1; 1 x2];
A = inv(C)*Y';
a = A(1); b = A(2);
fprintf('Required equation : \n');
y = a + b*x;
y = vpa(y)

%plotting
xx = linspace(x1, x2);
yy = subs(y, x, xx);
plot(xx, yy, 'b-'); hold on;
scatter(X, Y, 20, 'r', 'filled');
xlabel('x'); ylabel('y');
grid; axis square;
axis([0 10 -5 3]);
d = 0.5;
text(x1+d, y1, 'P_1');
text(x2+d, y2, 'P_2');
hold off;
```

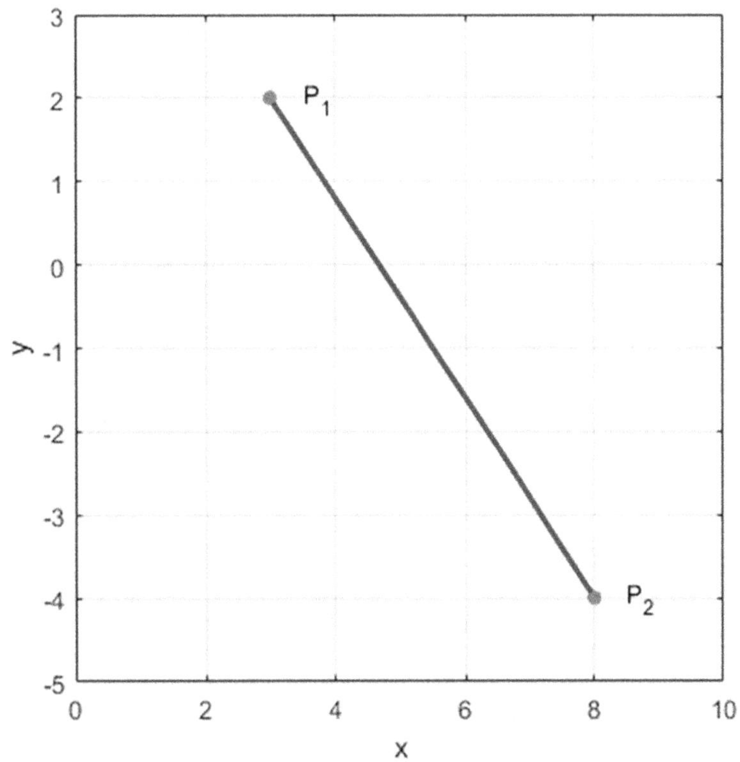

FIGURE 4.65
Plot for Example 4.9.

The following example computes the equation of a quadratic interpolating spline passing through three given points (Figure 4.66).

EXAMPLE 4.10 EXAMPLE TO FIND EQUATION OF A QUADRATIC SPLINE THROUGH POINTS (3, 2), (6, 5) AND (8, –4)

```
clear; clc;
syms x;
x1 = 3; y1 = 2;
x2 = 6; y2 = 5;
x3 = 8; y3 = -4;
X = [x1, x2, x3];
Y = [y1, y2, y3];
C = [1, x1, x1^2; 1, x2, x2^2; 1,
   x3, x3^2];
A = inv(C)*Y';
a = A(1); b = A(2); c = A(3);
fprintf('Required equation : \n');
y = a + b*x + c*x^2; y = vpa(y)

%plotting
d = 0.5;
xx = linspace(x1-2, x3+2);
yy = subs(y, x, xx);
plot(xx,yy, 'b-');
hold on; grid;
scatter(X, Y, 20, 'r', 'filled');
xlabel('x'); ylabel('y');
axis square; axis tight;
text(x1+d, y1, 'P_1');
text(x2+d, y2, 'P_2');
text(x3+d, y3, 'P_3');
hold off;
```

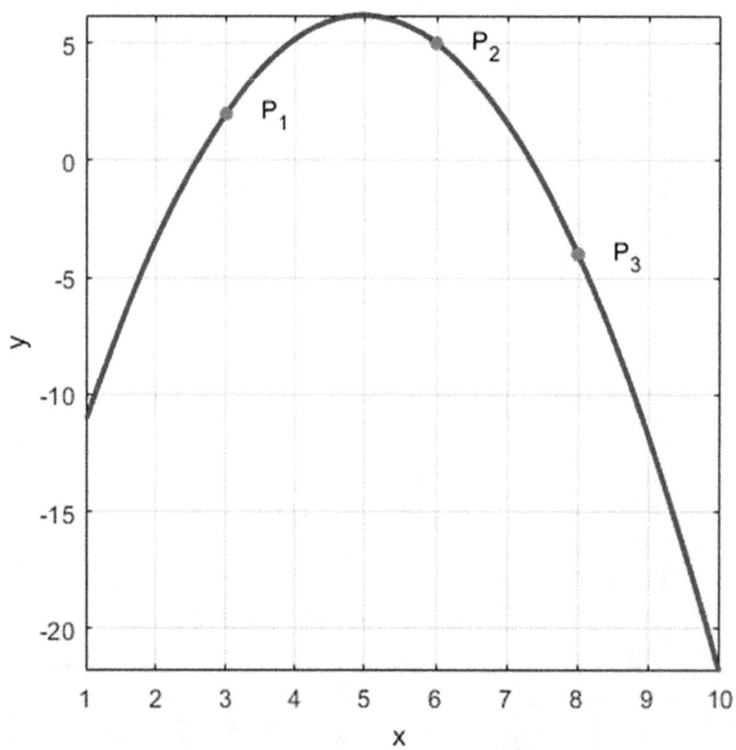

FIGURE 4.66
Plot for Example 4.10.

The following example computes the equation of a cubic interpolating spline passing through four given points (Figure 4.67).

EXAMPLE 4.11 MATLAB EXAMPLE TO FIND EQUATION OF A CUBIC SPLINE THROUGH POINTS (-1, 2), (0, 0) (1, -2) AND (2, 0)

```
clear; clc;
syms x;
x1 = -1; y1 = 2;
x2 = 0; y2 = 0;
x3 = 1; y3 = -2;
x4 = 2; y4 = 0;
X = [x1 ; x2 ; x3 ; x4];
Y = [y1 ; y2 ; y3 ; y4];
C = [1, x1, x1^2, x1^3; 1, x2, x2^2,
   x2^3; 1, x3, x3^2, x3^3; 1, x4,
   x4^2, x4^3];
A = inv(C)*Y;
a = A(1); b = A(2); c = A(3); d = A(4);
fprintf('Required equation : \n');
y = a + b*x + c*x^2 + d*x^3; y =
   vpa(y, 3)

%plotting
X = [x1, x2, x3, x4]; m = min(X); n
   = max(X);
xx = linspace(m - 1, n + 1);
yy = subs(y, x, xx);
plot(xx,yy, 'b');
hold on; grid;
scatter(X, Y, 20, 'r', 'filled');
xlabel('x'); ylabel('y'); axis square;
e = 1;
text(x1, y1+e, 'P_1');
text(x2, y2+e, 'P_2');
text(x3, y3+e, 'P_3');
text(x4, y4+2*e, 'P_4');
hold off;
```

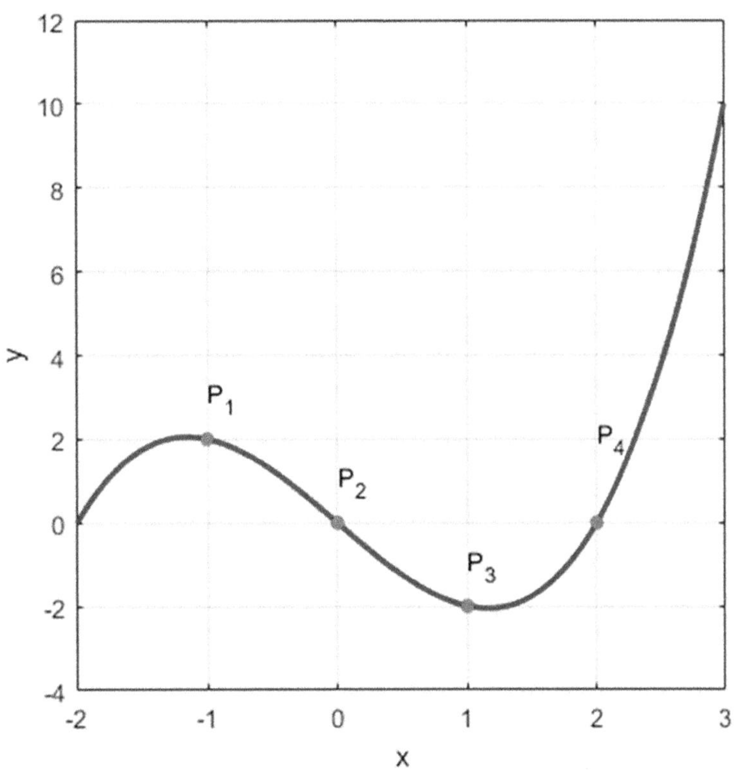

FIGURE 4.67
Plot for Example 4.11.

The following example computes the equation of a cubic interpolating spline passing through four given points in parametric form. The three output plots correspond to two in the parametric domain, i.e., t vs. x and t vs. y and one in spatial domain, i.e., x vs. y. The subdivision ratios specify the fractions in which the curve is divided by the two middle points (Figure 4.68).

EXAMPLE 4.12 EXAMPLE TO FIND PARAMETRIC EQUATION OF A CUBIC SPLINE THROUGH POINTS (-1, 2), (0, 0) (1, -2) AND (2, 0) AND WITH SUB-DIVISION RATIOS M = 0.1 AND N = 0.9

```
clear; clc;
syms t;
x0 = -1; y0 = 2;
x1 = 0; y1 = 0;
x2 = 1; y2 = -2;
x3 = 2; y3 = 0;
m = 0.1; n = 0.9;
P = [x0 y0 ; x1 y1 ; x2 y2 ; x3 y3];
X = [x0 ; x1 ; x2 ; x3]; Y = [y0 ; y1 ;
  y2 ; y3];
C = [1, 0, 0, 0; 1, m, m^2, m^3; 1, n,
  n^2, n^3; 1, 1, 1, 1];
A = inv(C)*P;
ax = A(1,1); ay = A(1,2); bx = A(2,1);
  by = A(2,2);
cx = A(3,1); cy = A(3,2); dx = A(4,1);
  dy = A(4,2);
fprintf('Required equations : \n');
x = ax + bx*t + cx*t^2 + dx*t^3; x =
  vpa(x, 3)
y = ay + by*t + cy*t^2 + dy*t^3; y =
  vpa(y, 3)
%plotting
tt = linspace(0,1);
xx = subs(x, t, tt);
yy = subs(y, t, tt);
subplot(131), plot(tt,xx); grid;
xlabel('t'); ylabel('x'); title('t -
  x'); axis square;
subplot(132), plot(tt,yy); grid;
xlabel('t'); ylabel('y'); title('t -
  y'); axis square;
subplot(133), plot(xx,yy,'b-'); grid;
xlabel('x'); ylabel('y'); title('x -
  y'); axis square;
hold on;
scatter(X, Y, 20, 'r', 'filled');
axis([-2 3 -5 3]);
e = 0.5;
text(x0+e, y0, 'P_0');
text(x1+e, y1, 'P_1');
text(x2+e, y2, 'P_2');
text(x3+e, y3, 'P_3');
hold off;
```

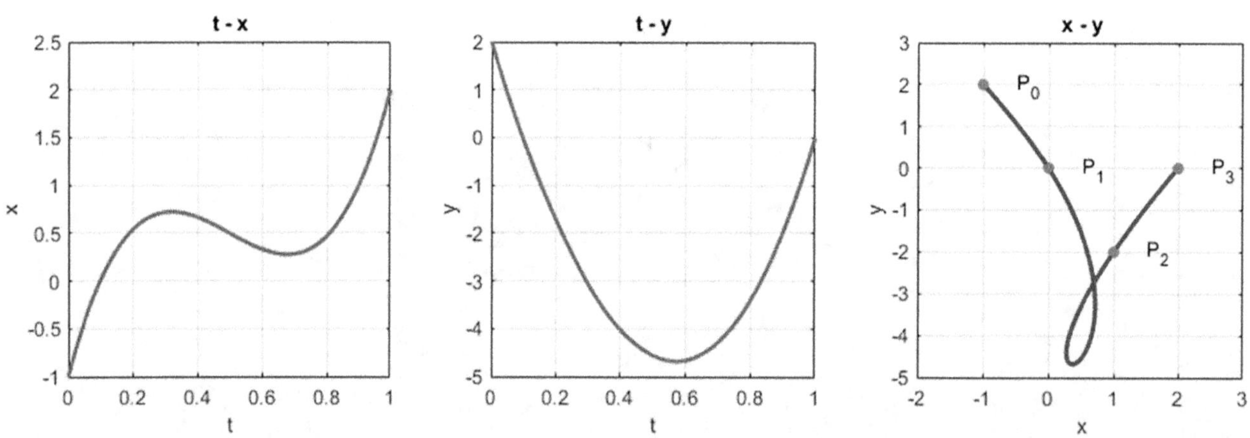

FIGURE 4.68
Plot for Example 4.12.

The following example computes the equation of a quadratic Bezier spline passing through three given points in parametric form, using its known basis matrix (Figure 4.69).

EXAMPLE 4.13 EXAMPLE TO FIND PARAMETRIC EQUATION OF A QUADRATIC BEZIER SPLINE THROUGH POINTS (1, -1), (4, 3) AND (5, -2)

```
clear; clc;
syms t;
P0 = [1, -1]; P1 = [4, 3]; P2 = [5, -2];
X = [P0(1) P1(1) P2(1) ];
Y = [P0(2) P1(2) P2(2) ];
T = [1 t t^2 ];
B = [1 0 0 ; -2 2 0 ; 1 -2 1]; % basis matrix
G = [P0; P1; P2];
P = T*B*G;
fprintf('Required equations :\n');
x = P(1)
y = P(2)

%plotting
tt = linspace(0,1);
xx = subs(x, t, tt);
yy = subs(y, t, tt);
subplot(131), plot(tt, xx); title('t - x');
xlabel('t'); ylabel('x'); axis square;
subplot(132), plot(tt, yy); title('t - y');
xlabel('t'); ylabel('y'); axis square;
subplot(133), plot(xx, yy, 'b-', 'LineWidth', 1.5);
title('x - y');
hold on;
scatter(X, Y, 20, 'r', 'filled');
xlabel('x'); ylabel('y'); axis square;
grid on; d = 0.5;
text(P0(1), P0(2)-d, 'P_0');
text(P1(1)+d, P1(2), 'P_1');
text(P2(1), P2(2)-d, 'P_2');
axis([-1 6 -3 4]);
hold off;
```

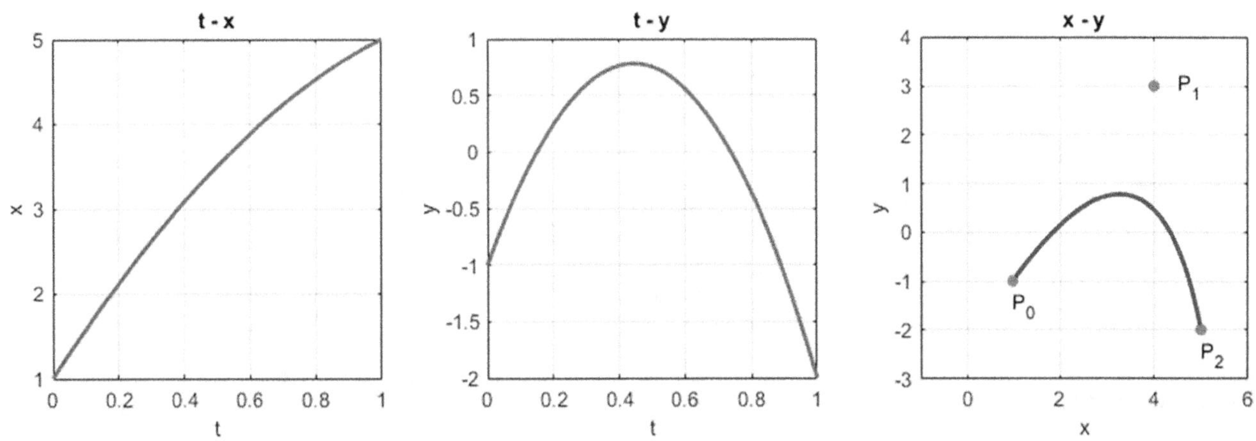

FIGURE 4.69
Plot for Example 4.13.

The following example computes the equation of a cubic Bezier spline passing through four given points in parametric form, using its known basis matrix (Figure 4.70).

EXAMPLE 4.14 EXAMPLE TO FIND PARAMETRIC EQUATION OF A CUBIC BEZIER SPLINE THROUGH POINTS (1, -1), (1, 1), (4, 3), (5, -2)

```
clear; clc;
syms t;
P0 = [1, -1]; P1 = [1, 1]; P2 = [4, 3];
   P3 = [5, -2];
X = [P0(1) P1(1) P2(1) P3(1)];
Y = [P0(2) P1(2) P2(2) P3(2)];
T = [1 t t^2 t^3];
B = [1 0 0 0; -3 3 0 0; 3 -6 3 0; -1 3
   -3 1]; % basis matrix
G = [P0; P1; P2; P3];
P = T*B*G;
fprintf('Required equations :\n');
x = P(1)
y = P(2)

%plotting
tt = linspace(0,1);
xx = subs(x, t, tt);
yy = subs(y, t, tt);
subplot(131), plot(tt, xx);
   title('t - x');
xlabel('t'); ylabel('x'); axis square;
subplot(132), plot(tt, yy);
   title('t - y');
xlabel('t'); ylabel('y'); axis square;
subplot(133), plot(xx, yy, 'b-',
   'LineWidth', 1.5);
xlabel('x'); ylabel('y'); axis square;
   hold on; grid;
scatter(X, Y, 20, 'r', 'filled');
   title('x - y');
axis([0 6 -3 4]);
d = 0.5;
text(P0(1), P0(2)-d, 'P_0');
text(P1(1), P1(2)+d, 'P_1');
text(P2(1), P2(2)-d, 'P_2');
text(P3(1), P3(2)-d, 'P_3');
  hold off;
```

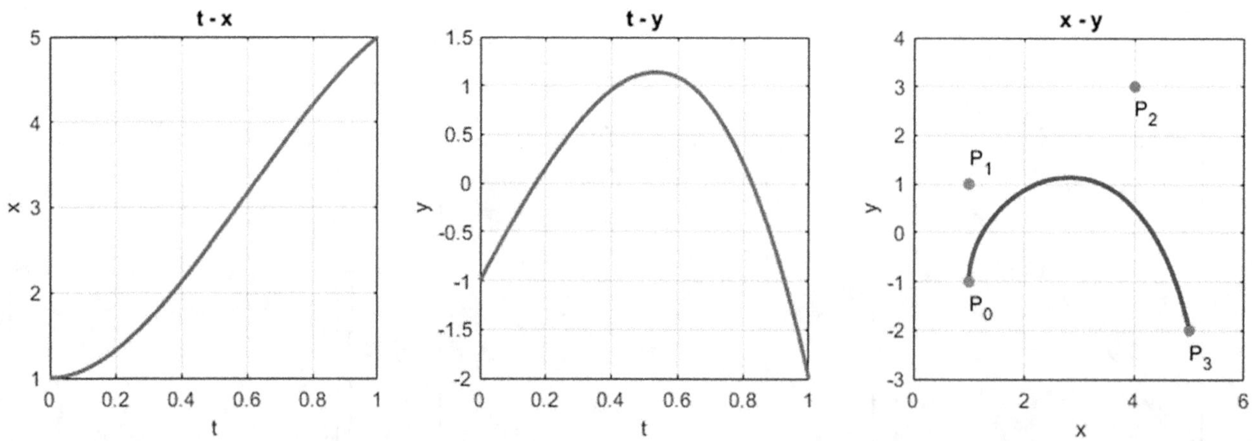

FIGURE 4.70
Plot for Example 4.14.

The following example computes the equation of a uniform quadratic B-spline passing through three given points in parametric form, using its blending functions as defined by the Cox de Boor algorithm. The function "simplify" simplifies a symbolic expression (Figure 4.71).

EXAMPLE 4.15 EXAMPLE TO FIND PARAMETRIC EQUATION OF A UNIFORM QUADRATIC B-SPLINE THROUGH POINTS (1, 4), (4, 6), (5, 2) AND PLOT ITS BLENDING FUNCTIONS

```
clear; format compact; clc;
syms t;

B03A = (t - 0)^2/2;
B03B = (t - 0)*(2 - t)/2 +
   (t - 1)*(3 - t)/2;
B03C = (3 - t)^2/2;

B13B = (t - 1)^2/2;
B13C = (t - 1)*(3 - t)/2 +
   (t - 2)*(4 - t)/2;
B13D = (4 - t)^2/2;

B23C = (t - 2)^2/2;
B23D = (t - 2)*(4 - t)/2 +
   (t - 3)*(5 - t)/2;
B23E = (5 - t)^2/2;

fprintf('Blending functions :\n')

B03 = [B03A, B03B, B03C];
   B03 = simplify(B03)
B13 = [B13B, B13C, B13D];
   B13 = simplify(B13)
B23 = [B23C, B23D, B23E]; B23 =
   simplify(B23)

% Plotting BFs

tta = linspace(0, 1);
ttb = linspace(1, 2);
ttc = linspace(2, 3);
ttd = linspace(3, 4);
tte = linspace(4, 5);
ttf = linspace(5, 6);

B03aa = subs(B03A, t, tta);
B03bb = subs(B03B, t, ttb);
B03cc = subs(B03C, t, ttc);

B13bb = subs(B13B, t, ttb);
B13cc = subs(B13C, t, ttc);
B13dd = subs(B13D, t, ttd);

B23cc = subs(B23C, t, ttc);
B23dd = subs(B23D, t, ttd);
B23ee = subs(B23E, t, tte);

% plotting BFS

figure,
plot(tta, B03aa, 'b-', ttb, B03bb,
   'b--', ttc, B03cc, 'b-.');
hold on;
plot(ttb, B13bb, 'r-', ttc, B13cc,
   'r--', ttd, B13dd, 'r-.');
plot(ttc, B23cc, 'k-', ttd, B23dd,
   'k--', tte, B23ee, 'k-.');
xlabel('t'); ylabel('L'); title
   ('Blending functions');

hold off;

% plotting curve

x0 = 1; x1 = 4; x2 = 5;
y0 = 4; y1 = 6; y2 = 2;

figure,
subplot(131),
plot(tta, x0*B03aa, 'b-', ttb,
   x0*B03bb+x1*B13bb, 'b--', …
    ttc, x0*B03cc+x1*B13cc+x2*B23cc ,
       'b-.', ttd, x1*B13dd+x2*B23dd,
       'b:', tte, x2*B23ee, 'b.-');
       axis square;
xlabel('t'); ylabel('x'); title('t-x');
subplot(132),
plot(tta, y0*B03aa, 'b-', ttb,
   y0*B03bb+y1*B13bb, 'b--', …
    ttc, y0*B03cc+y1*B13cc+y2*B23cc ,
       'b-.', ttd, y1*B13dd+y2*B23dd,
       'b:', tte, y2*B23ee, 'b.-');
       axis square;
xlabel('t'); ylabel('y'); title('t-y');
subplot(133),
plot( x0*B03aa, y0*B03aa, 'b-',
   x0*B03bb+x1*B13bb, y0*B03bb+-
   y1*B13bb, 'b--', …
    x0*B03cc+x1*B13cc+x2*B23cc,
       y0*B03cc+y1*B13cc+y2*B23cc ,
       'b-.', x1*B13dd+x2*B23dd,
       y1*B13dd+y2*B23dd, 'b:',
       x2*B23ee, y2*B23ee,
       'b.-');axis square;
hold; plot(x0, y0, 'r*', x1, y1, 'r*',
   x2, y2, 'r*'); hold off;
  xlabel('x');ylabel('y');title('x-y');
```

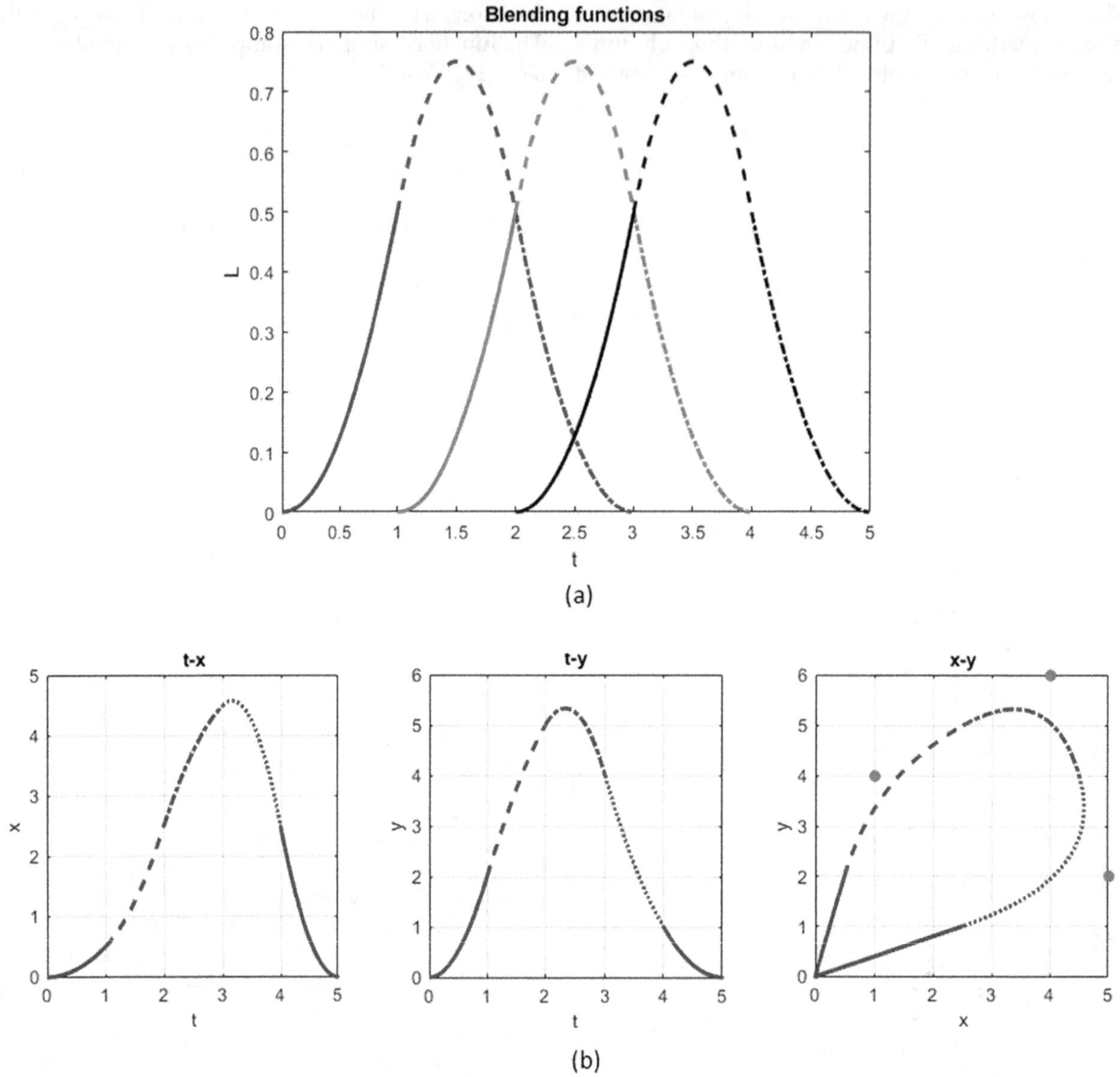

FIGURE 4.71
Plot for Example 4.15.

4.11.3 Properties of Splines

The following example calculates the length of a spline between two given points. The function "diff" performs differentiation and "int" performs integration operation on a symbolic expression, while "sqrt" calculates the square root.

EXAMPLE 4.16 EXAMPLE TO CALCULATE LENGTH OF THE CURVE Y = 3X + 2 BETWEEN X = 1 AND X = 5

```
clear all; clc;
syms x;
y = 3*x+2;
d = diff(y);
e = sqrt(1 + d^2);
f = int(e, 1, 5);
fprintf('Length of curve : %f\n',
eval(f));
```

The following example calculates the area between a spline and the x-axis between two given ordinates. The function "zeros" generates a matrix filled with zeros, "fliplr" flips an array in left–right direction, "fill" fills a polygon with color, "alpha" sets transparency values, "eval" evaluates a symbolic expression (Figure 4.72).

EXAMPLE 4.17 EXAMPLE TO CALCULATE AREA UNDER THE CURVE Y = 10 - X^2 BETWEEN THE VALUES X = -1 AND X = 2

```
clear; clc;
syms x;
y = 10 - x^2;
f = int(y, -1, 2);
eval(f);
fprintf('Area : %f\n', eval(f));

%plotting
xx = linspace(-4, 4);
yy = subs(y, x, xx);
plot(xx, yy);
xlabel('x'); ylabel('y');
grid; hold on;
axis([-5 5, 0 12]);
text(-3, 9, 'y = 10 - x^2');

%filling
x = linspace(-1, 2);
y1 = 10 - x.^2;
y2 = zeros(1,100);
X = [x,fliplr(x)];
Y = [y1,fliplr(y2)];
fill(X,Y,'g');
alpha(0.25);
hold off;
```

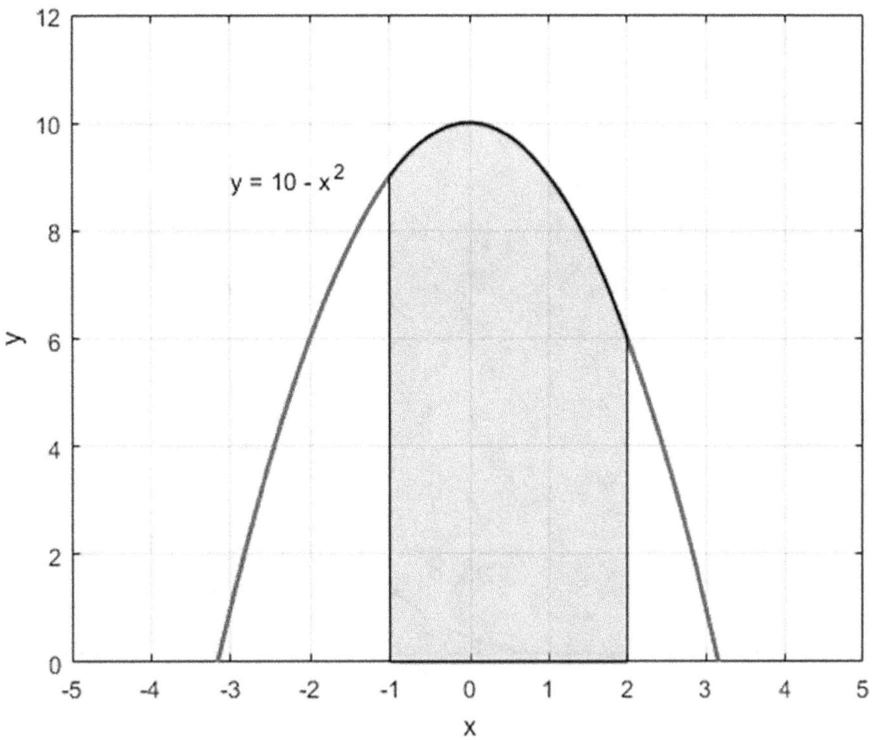

FIGURE 4.72
Plot for Example 4.17.

The following example calculates the centroid of the area between a spline and the x-axis and between two given ordinates (Figure 4.73).

EXAMPLE 4.18 EXAMPLE TO CALCULATE CENTROID OF THE AREA BOUNDED BY THE CURVES Y = X^3, X-AXIS, X = 0 AND X = 2

```
clear; clc;
syms x y;
y = x^3;
a = int(y, 0, 2);
eval(a);
fprintf('Area : %f\n', eval(a));
m1 = int(x*y, 0, 2);
m2 = int(0.5*y^2, 0, 2);
xc = m1/a;
yc = m2/a;
fprintf('Centroid : (%.2f, %.2f) \n',
   eval(xc), eval(yc));

%plotting
xx = linspace(-1, 3);
yy = subs(y, x, xx);
plot(xx, yy);
xlabel('x'); ylabel('y');
grid; hold on;
axis([-1 3, 0 12]);
text(0, 9, 'y = x^3');

%filling
x = linspace(0, 2);
y1 = x.^3;
y2 = zeros(1,100);
X = [x,fliplr(x)];
Y = [y1,fliplr(y2)];
fill(X,Y,'g');
alpha(0.25);
plot(xc, yc, 'r*');
hold off;
```

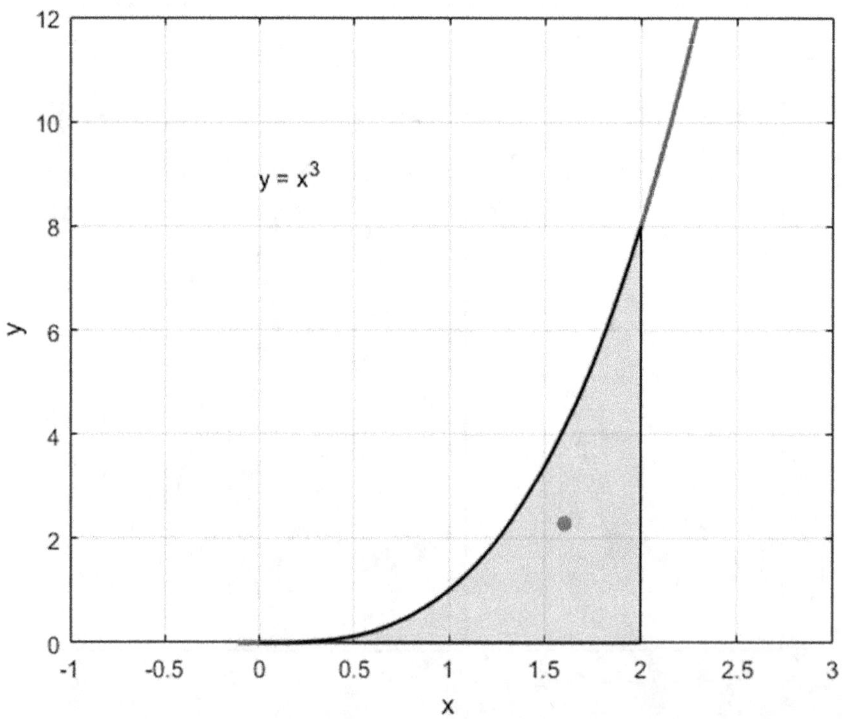

FIGURE 4.73
Plot for Example 4.18.

The following example calculates the coordinates of the critical points of a cubic curve, i.e., the minimum, the maximum and the POI. The function "polyder" differentiates a polynomial, "roots" finds roots of a polynomial equation, "polyval" evaluates value of a polynomial at a point, "sign" returns sign of the argument as +1, 0 or -1 (Figure 4.74).

EXAMPLE 4.19 MATLAB EXAMPLE TO CALCULATE MINIMUM, MAXIMUM AND POI OF THE CUBIC CURVE Y = 2 + 13X - 31X^2 + 18X^3

```
clear; clc;
% ax^3 + bx^2 + cx + d, p = [a,
   b, c, d]
p = [18, -31, 13, 2];
dp = polyder(p);
d2p = polyder(dp);
r = roots(dp);

if polyval(d2p, r(1)) > 0, m1 = 0; else
   m1 = 1; end;
b1 = polyval(p, r(1));
if m1 == 0, fprintf('minimum point :
   (%.2f, %.2f)\n', r(1), b1); end;
if m1 == 1, fprintf('maximum point :
   (%.2f, %.2f)\n', r(1), b1); end;

if polyval(d2p, r(2)) > 0, m2 = 0; else
   m2 = 1; end;
b2 = polyval(p, r(2));
if m2 == 0, fprintf('minimum point :
   (%.2f, %.2f)\n', r(2), b2); end;
if m2 == 1, fprintf('maximum point :
   (%.2f, %.2f)\n', r(2), b2); end;

s = roots(d2p);
s1 = polyval(d2p, s - 0.1);
s2 = polyval(d2p, s + 0.1);
b3 = polyval(p, s);
if (sign(s1) == sign(s2)), fprintf('Not
   a POI');
else fprintf('POI: (%.2f, %.2f)\n', s,
   b3); end;

%plotting
syms x;
y = p(1)*x^3 + p(2)*x^2 +
   p(3)*x + p(4);
X = [r(1), r(2), s];
Y = [b1, b2, b3];
xx = linspace(min([r(1), r(2), s]),
   max([r(1), r(2), s]));
yy = subs(y, x, xx);
plot(xx, yy, 'b-', 'LineWidth', 1.5);
   hold on;
scatter(X, Y, 20, 'r', 'filled');
plot(X, Y, 'ko');
grid; xlabel('x'); ylabel('y');

%labeling
if m1 == 0, text(r(1), b1+0.1,
   'Minimum');
else text(r(1), b1+0.1, 'Maximum');
end;
if m2 == 0, text(r(2), b2+0.1,
   'Minimum');
else text(r(2), b2+0.1, 'Maximum');
end;
text(s, b3+0.1, 'POI');
hold off;
```

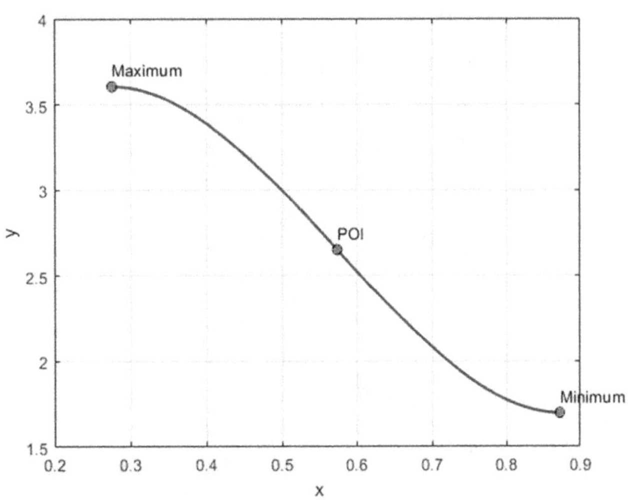

FIGURE 4.74
Plot for Example 4.19.

4.11.4 3D Transformations

The following example calculates the new coordinates of a cube after a translation operation in 3D space. The function "plot3" generates a 3D plot; "zlabel" puts a label on the z–axis with parameter 1.2.

EXAMPLE 4.20 EXAMPLE TO CALCULATE NEW COORDINATES OF THE CUBE WITH VERTICES (-1, 1, 1), (1, 1, 1), (1, -1, 1), (-1, -1, 1), (-1, 1, -1), (1, 1, -1), (1, -1, -1) AND (-1, -1, -1) AFTER TRANSLATION BY AMOUNTS (-2, -1, 3)

```
% with vertices (-1, 1, 1), (1, 1, 1),
  (1, -1, 1), (-1, -1, 1),
% (-1, 1, -1), (1, 1, -1), (1, -1, -1)
  and (-1, -1, -1)
% after translation by amounts
  (-2, -1, 3)
clear; clc;
p1 = [-1,1,1];
p2 = [1,1,1];
p3 = [1,-1,1];
p4 = [-1,-1,1];
p5 = [-1,1,-1];
p6 = [1,1,-1];
p7 = [1,-1,-1];
p8 = [-1,-1,-1];
C = [p1' p2' p3' p4' p5' p6' p7' p8' ;
  1 1 1 1 1 1 1 1 ]
tx = -2; ty = -1; tz = 3;
T1 = [1 0 0 tx ; 0 1 0 ty ; 0 0 1 tz ;
  0 0 0 1];
D = T1*C
fprintf('New vertices : \n');
for i=1:8
    fprintf('(%.2f, %.2f, %.2f) \n',
       D(1,i), D(2,i), D(3,i));
end;
%plotting
C = [p1' p2' p3' p4' p1' p5' p6' p7'
  p8' p5' p8' p4' p3' p7' p6' p2' ;
 1 1 1 1 1 1 1 1 1 1 1 1 1 1 1 1];
D = T1*C;
plot3(C(1,:), C(2,:), C(3,:), 'b',
  'LineWidth', 2); hold on;
plot3(D(1,:), D(2,:), D(3,:), 'r',
  'LineWidth', 2);
xlabel('x'); ylabel('y'); zlabel('z');
legend('original', 'new'); axis equal;
  hold off;
```

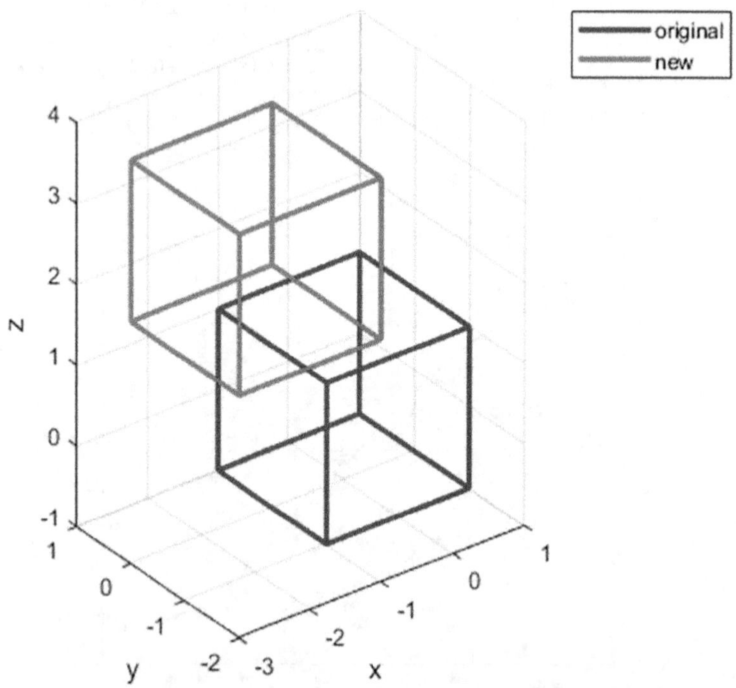

FIGURE 4.75
Plot for Example 4.20.

The following example calculates the new coordinates of a cube after a scaling operation about the origin in 3D space (Figure 4.76).

EXAMPLE 4.21 MATLAB EXAMPLE TO CALCULATE NEW COORDINATES OF A CUBE WITH VERTICES (-1, 1, 1), (1, 1, 1), (1, -1, 1), (-1, -1, 1), (-1, 1, -1), (1, 1, -1), (1, -1, -1) AND (-1, -1, -1) AFTER SCALING BY AMOUNT (2, 1, 3)

```
clear; clc;
p1 = [-1,1,1];
p2 = [1,1,1];
p3 = [1,-1,1];
p4 = [-1,-1,1];
p5 = [-1,1,-1];
p6 = [1,1,-1];
p7 = [1,-1,-1];
p8 = [-1,-1,-1];
C = [p1' p2' p3' p4' p5' p6' p7' p8' ;
   1 1 1 1 1 1 1 1 ]
sx = 2; sy = 1; sz = 3;
S1 =[sx 0 0 0 ; 0 sy 0 0 ; 0 0 sz 0 ;
   0 0 0 1];
D = S1*C

fprintf('New vertices : \n');
for i=1:8
    fprintf('(%.2f, %.2f, %.2f) \n',
       D(1,i), D(2,i), D(3,i));
end;

%plotting
C = [p1' p2' p3' p4' p1' p5' p6' p7'
   p8' p5' p8' p4' p3' p7' p6' p2' ;
 1 1 1 1 1 1 1 1 1 1 1 1 1 1 1 1];
D = S1*C;
plot3(C(1,:), C(2,:), C(3,:), 'b');
   hold on;
plot3(D(1,:), D(2,:), D(3,:), 'r');
xlabel('x'); ylabel('y'); zlabel('z');
legend('original', 'new'); axis equal;
   grid; hold off;
```

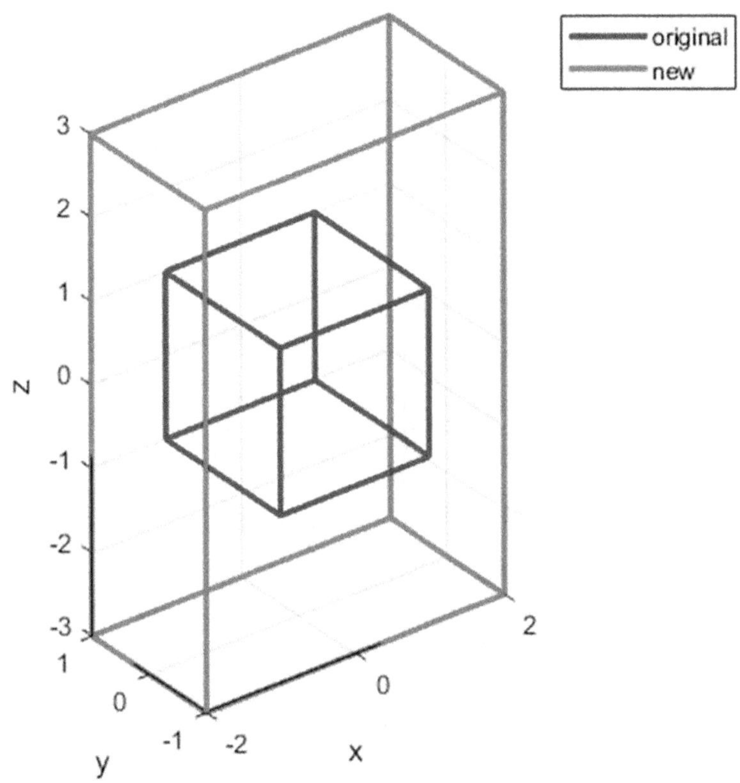

FIGURE 4.76
Plot for Example 4.21.

The following example calculates the new coordinates of a cube after a rotation operation about the origin in 3D space (Figure 4.77).

EXAMPLE 4.22 MATLAB EXAMPLE TO CALCULATE NEW COORDINATES OF A CUBE WITH VERTICES (-1, 1, 1), (1, 1, 1), (1, -1, 1), (-1, -1, 1), (-1, 1, -1), (1, 1, -1), (1, -1, -1) AND (-1, -1, -1) AFTER ROTATION BY 45° ABOUT THE ORIGIN AROUND THE X-AXIS

```
clear; clc;
p1 = [-1,1,1];
p2 = [1,1,1];
p3 = [1,-1,1];
p4 = [-1,-1,1];
p5 = [-1,1,-1];
p6 = [1,1,-1];
p7 = [1,-1,-1];
p8 = [-1,-1,-1];
C = [p1' p2' p3' p4' p5' p6' p7' p8' ;
   1 1 1 1 1 1 1 1 ]

sx = 2; sy = 1; sz = 3;
S1 =[sx 0 0 0 ; 0 sy 0 0 ; 0 0 sz 0 ;
   0 0 0 1];
D = S1*C

fprintf('New vertices : \n');
for i=1:8
    fprintf('(%.2f, %.2f, %.2f) \n',
   D(1,i), D(2,i), D(3,i));
end;

%plotting
C = [p1' p2' p3' p4' p1' p5' p6' p7'
   p8' p5' p8' p4' p3' p7' p6' p2' ;
 1 1 1 1 1 1 1 1 1 1 1 1 1 1 1 1];

A = deg2rad(45);
R1 = [1 0 0 0 ; 0 cos(A) -sin(A) 0 ; 0
   sin(A) cos(A) 0 ; 0 0 0 1];
D = R1*C;
fprintf('New vertices : \n');
for i=1:8
    fprintf('(%.2f, %.2f, %.2f) \n',
   D(1,i), D(2,i), D(3,i));
end;

%plotting
C = [p1' p2' p3' p4' p1' p5' p6' p7'
   p8' p5' p8' p4' p3' p7' p6' p2' ;
 1 1 1 1 1 1 1 1 1 1 1 1 1 1 1 1];
D = R1*C;
plot3(C(1,:), C(2,:), C(3,:), 'b');
   hold on;
plot3(D(1,:), D(2,:), D(3,:), 'r');
xlabel('x'); ylabel('y'); zlabel('z');
legend('original', 'new'); axis equal;
   grid; hold off;
```

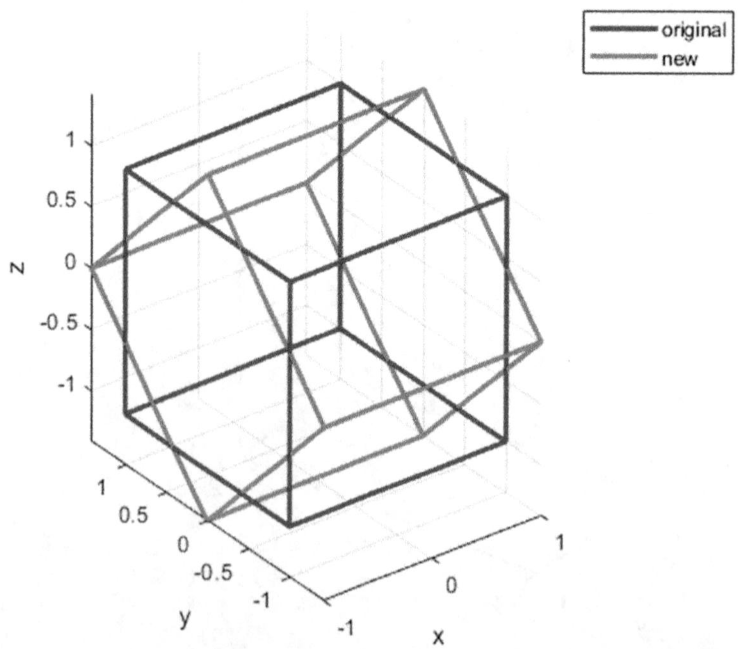

FIGURE 4.77
Plot for Example 4.22.

The following example calculates the new coordinates of a cube after a rotation operation about a fixed point in 3D space (Figure 4.78).

EXAMPLE 4.23 MATLAB EXAMPLE TO CALCULATE NEW COORDINATES OF A CUBE WITH VERTICES (-1, 1, 1), (1, 1, 1), (1, -1, 1), (-1, -1, 1), (-1, 1, -1), (1, 1, -1), (1, -1, -1) AND (-1, -1, -1) AFTER ROTATION BY 45° ABOUT THE POINT (-1,-1,-1) AROUND THE Z-AXIS

```
clear; clc;
p1 = [-1,1,1];
p2 = [1,1,1];
p3 = [1,-1,1];
p4 = [-1,-1,1];
p5 = [-1,1,-1];
p6 = [1,1,-1];
p7 = [1,-1,-1];
p8 = [-1,-1,-1];
C = [p1' p2' p3' p4' p5' p6' p7' p8' ;
   1 1 1 1 1 1 1 1 ]

tx = -1; ty = -1; tz = -1;
T1 = [1 0 0 -tx ; 0 1 0 -ty ; 0 0 1
   -tz ; 0 0 0 1];
A = 45;
R1 = [cosd(A) -sind(A) 0 0 ; sind(A)
   cosd(A) 0 0 ; 0 0 1 0 ; 0 0 0 1];
T2 = [1 0 0 tx ; 0 1 0 ty ; 0 0 1 tz ;
   0 0 0 1];
M = T2*R1*T1;
D = M*C;
fprintf('New vertices : \n');
for i=1:8
    fprintf('(%.2f, %.2f, %.2f) \n',
   D(1,i), D(2,i), D(3,i));
end;

%plotting
C = [p1' p2' p3' p4' p1' p5' p6' p7'
   p8' p5' p8' p4' p3' p7' p6' p2' ;
 1 1 1 1 1 1 1 1 1 1 1 1 1 1 1 1];
D = M*C;
plot3(C(1,:), C(2,:), C(3,:), 'b');
   hold on;
plot3(D(1,:), D(2,:), D(3,:), 'r');
xlabel('x'); ylabel('y'); zlabel('z');
legend('original', 'new'); axis equal;
   grid; hold off;
```

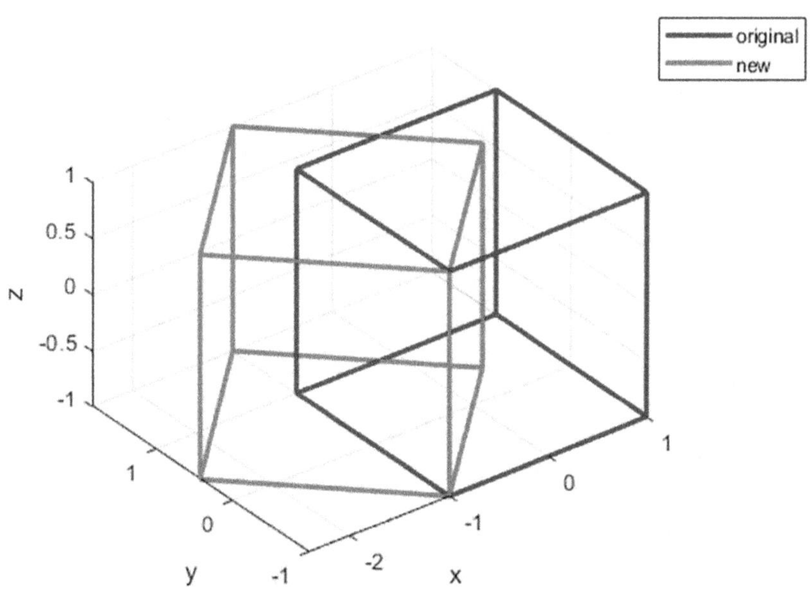

FIGURE 4.78
Plot for Example 4.23.

The following example calculates the new coordinates of a point after rotation around a line parallel to the y-axis. The function "line" draws a line from one point to another (Figure 4.79).

EXAMPLE 4.24 EXAMPLE TO CALCULATE NEW COORDINATES OF A POINT C(1,1,1) AFTER ROTATION BY 180° AROUND A LINE PARALLEL TO THE Y-AXIS JOINING POINTS P(5, 2, 3) AND Q(5, 0, 3)

```
clear; clc;
p = [1,1,1];
C = [p' ; 1];
P = [5, 2, 3];
Q = [5, 0, 3];
tx = -Q(1); ty = -Q(2); tz = -Q(3);
T1 = [1 0 0 tx ; 0 1 0 ty ; 0 0 1 tz ; 0 0 0 1];
A = deg2rad(180);
R1 = [cos(A), 0, sin(A), 0 ; 0, 1, 0, 0 ; -sin(A), 0, cos(A), 0 ; 0, 0, 0, 1];
T2 = inv(T1);
M = T2*R1*T1;
D = M*C;
fprintf('New vertices : \n')
fprintf('(%.2f, %.2f, %.2f) \n', D(1,1), D(2,1), D(3,1));

%plotting
plot3(C(1,:), C(2,:), C(3,:), 'bo', 'MarkerFaceColor', 'b'); hold on;
plot3(D(1,:), D(2,:), D(3,:), 'ro', 'MarkerFaceColor', 'r'); grid;
line([5, 5], [2, 0], [3, 3], 'LineWidth', 2);
plot3(P(1), P(2), P(3), 'ko');
plot3(Q(1), Q(2), Q(3), 'ko');
xlabel('x'); ylabel('y'); zlabel('z');
legend('original', 'new'); axis equal; hold off;
```

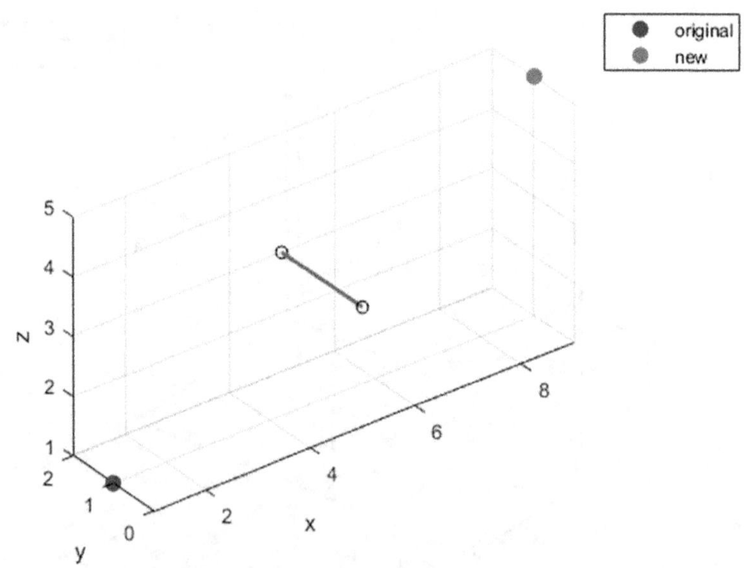

FIGURE 4.79
Plot for Example 4.24.

The following example calculates the new coordinates of a cube after reflection about a plane parallel to the xy-plane along the z-axis (Figure 4.80).

EXAMPLE 4.25 EXAMPLE TO CALCULATE NEW COORDINATES OF THE CUBE WITH VERTICES (-1, 1, 1), (1, 1, 1), (1, -1, 1), (-1, -1, 1), (-1, 1, -1), (1, 1, -1), (1, -1, -1) AND (-1, -1, -1) AFTER REFLECTION ABOUT A PLANE Z = 3 PARALLEL TO THE XY-PLANE ALONG THE Z-AXIS

```
clear; clc;
p1 = [-1,1,1];
p2 = [1,1,1];
p3 = [1,-1,1];
p4 = [-1,-1,1];
p5 = [-1,1,-1];
p6 = [1,1,-1];
p7 = [1,-1,-1];
p8 = [-1,-1,-1];
C = [p1' p2' p3' p4' p5' p6' p7' p8' ;
   1 1 1 1 1 1 1 1 ];

tx = 0; ty = 0; tz = -3;
T1 = [1, 0, 0, tx ; 0, 1, 0, ty ; 0, 0,
   1, tz ; 0, 0, 0, 1];
Fz = [1, 0, 0, 0 ; 0, 1, 0, 0 ; 0, 0,
   -1, 0 ; 0, 0, 0, 1];
T2 = [1, 0, 0, -tx ; 0, 1, 0, -ty ; 0,
   0, 1, -tz ; 0, 0, 0, 1];
M = T2 * Fz * T1;
D = M*C;

fprintf('New vertices : \n');
for i=1:8
 fprintf('(%.2f, %.2f, %.2f)
   \n',D(1,i), D(2,i), D(3,i));
end

%plotting
C = [p1' p2' p3' p4' p1' p5' p6' p7'
   p8' p5' p8' p4' p3' p7' p6' p2' ;
 1 1 1 1 1 1 1 1 1 1 1 1 1 1 1 1];
D = M*C;
plot3(C(1,:), C(2,:), C(3,:), 'b');
   hold on;
plot3(D(1,:), D(2,:), D(3,:), 'r'); grid;
xlabel('x'); ylabel('y'); zlabel('z')
legend('original', 'new'); axis equal;
   hold off;
```

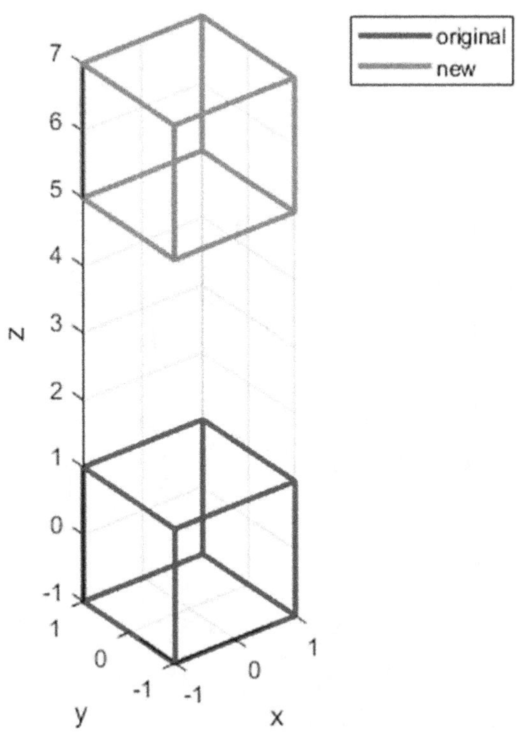

FIGURE 4.80
Plot for Example 4.25.

The following example calculates new coordinates of a cube after shear along the z-axis (Figure 4.81).

EXAMPLE 4.26 EXAMPLE TO CALCULATE NEW COORDINATES OF THE CUBE WITH VERTICES (-1, 1, 1), (1, 1, 1), (1, -1, 1), (-1, -1, 1), (-1, 1, -1), (1, 1, -1), (1, -1, -1) AND (-1, -1, -1) AFTER SHEAR ALONG Z-AXIS WITH PARAMETER 1.2

```
clear; clc;
p1 = [-1,1,1];
p2 = [1,1,1];
p3 = [1,-1,1];
p4 = [-1,-1,1];
p5 = [-1,1,-1];
p6 = [1,1,-1];
p7 = [1,-1,-1];
p8 = [-1,-1,-1];
C = [p1' p2' p3' p4' p5' p6' p7' p8' ;
   1 1 1 1 1 1 1 1 ];

h = 1.2;
H = [1, 0, 0, 0 ; 0, 1, 0, 0 ; 0, h, 1,
   0 ; 0, 0, 0, 1];
D = H*C;

fprintf('New vertices : \n');
for i=1:8
 fprintf('(%.2f, %.2f, %.2f)
   \n',D(1,i), D(2,i), D(3,i));
end

%plotting
C = [p1' p2' p3' p4' p1' p5' p6' p7'
   p8' p5' p8' p4' p3' p7' p6' p2' ;
 1 1 1 1 1 1 1 1 1 1 1 1 1 1 1 1];
D = H*C;
plot3(C(1,:), C(2,:), C(3,:), 'b',
   'LineWidth', 2); hold on;
plot3(D(1,:), D(2,:), D(3,:), 'r',
   'LineWidth', 2);

xlabel('x'); ylabel('y'); zlabel('z');
legend('original', 'new');
axis equal; hold off;
```

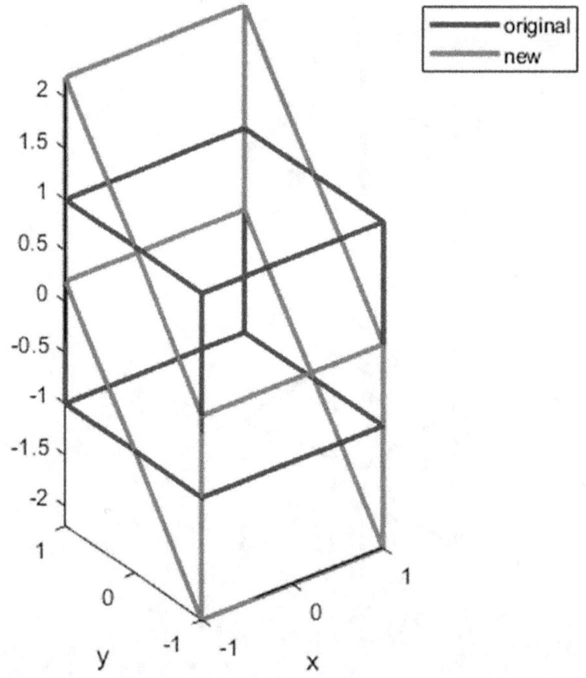

FIGURE 4.81
Plot for Example 4.26.

4.11.5 Vectors

The following example calculates the unit vector along the direction of a given vector.

The function "norm" calculates the magnitude of a vector, "quiver3" plots vectors as arrows in 3D space (Figure 4.82).

The following example calculates the angle between two vectors. The function "dot" returns the dot product of two vectors.

EXAMPLE 4.27 EXAMPLE TO CALCULATE UNIT VECTOR ALONG DIRECTION OF A GIVEN VECTOR R = 2I - J + 2K

```
clear; clc;
R = [2, -1, 2];
nR = norm(R);
fprintf('Magnitude : %f \n', nR);
r = R/nR;
fprintf('Unit vector : (%f, %f, %f)\n',
   r(1), r(2), r(3));
quiver3(0, 0, 0, R(1), R(2), R(3), 1,
   'b', 'LineWidth', 1.5);
hold on;
quiver3(0, 0, 0, r(1), r(2), r(3), 1,
   'r', 'LineWidth', 1.5);
hold off;
xlabel('x'); ylabel('y'); zlabel('z');
```

EXAMPLE 4.28 EXAMPLE TO CALCULATE ANGLE BETWEEN TWO VECTORS A = 2I - 3J + K AND B = 4I + J - 3K

```
clear; clc;
A = [2, -3, 1];
B = [4, 1, -3];
C = dot(A, B);
nA = norm(A);
nB = norm(B);
D = C/(nA*nB);
angle = acosd(D);
fprintf('Angle : %f deg\n', angle);
```

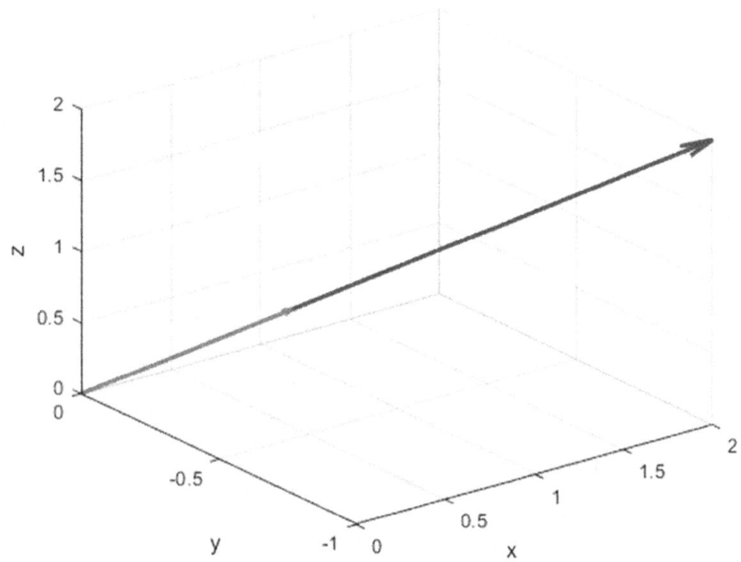

FIGURE 4.82
Plot for Example 4.27.

The following example computes a vector perpendicular to two given vectors. The function "cross" returns the cross product of two vectors.

EXAMPLE 4.29 EXAMPLE TO CALCULATE THE VECTOR PERPENDICULAR TO BOTH VECTORS A = 3I + 5J - 2K AND B = 2I - 2J - 2K

```
clear; clc;
A = [3, 5, -2];
B = [2, -2, -2];
C = cross(A, B)
%verification
dot(C,A) % should be 0
dot(C,B) % should be 0
```

The following examples compute the rotation matrix to align a 2D vector with a primary axis.

EXAMPLE 4.30 EXAMPLE TO CALCULATE ROTATION MATRIX TO ALIGN VECTORS WITH POSITIVE X-AXIS : (A) -3I + 4J (B) 3I - 4J

```
P = [-3, 4]
B = pi - atan(abs(P(2))/abs(P(1)));
ang = rad2deg(B)
A = -B;
R = [cos(A) -sin(A) 0 ; sin(A)
   cos(A) 0 ; 0 0 1];
P = [3, -4]
B = -atan(abs(P(2))/abs(P(1)));
ang = rad2deg(B)
A = -B;
R = [cos(A) -sin(A) 0 ; sin(A)
   cos(A) 0 ; 0 0 1];
```

EXAMPLE 4.31 EXAMPLE TO CALCULATE ROTATION MATRIX TO ALIGN VECTORS (A) 3I - 4J WITH POSITIVE Y-AXIS (B) -3I - 4J WITH NEGATIVE X-AXIS

```
clear; clc;
P = [3, -4]
B = atan(abs(P(2))/abs(P(1)));
A = B + pi/2;
R = [cos(A) -sin(A) 0 ; sin(A)
   cos(A) 0 ; 0 0 1];

P = [-3, -4]
B = atan(abs(P(2))/abs(P(1)));
A = -B;
R = [cos(A) -sin(A) 0 ; sin(A)
   cos(A) 0 ; 0 0 1];
```

The following example computes the rotation matrix to align a 3D vector with a primary axis. The function "asin" calculates inverse sine in radians.

EXAMPLE 4.32 EXAMPLE TO COMPUTE TRANSFORMATION FOR ALIGNING VECTOR 2I + J + 2K WITH POSITIVE Z-AXIS

```
clear; clc;
P = [2; 1; 2; 1];
a = P(1);
b = P(2);
c = P(3);
d = sqrt(b^2 + c^2);
A = asin(b/d);
A = acos(c/d);
R1 = [1 0 0 0; 0 cos(A) -sin(A) 0; 0
   sin(A) cos(A) 0; 0 0 0 1];
e = sqrt(a^2 + d^2);
B = asin(a/e);
R2 = [cos(B) 0 -sin(B) 0; 0 1 0 0;
   sin(B) 0 cos(B) 0; 0 0 0 1];
fprintf('Transformation matrix : \n');
M = R2*R1
fprintf('New vector : \n');
Q = M*P
```

4.11.6 Projection

The following example computes the 2D projection matrix and projected coordinates for an orthographic and a perspective projection of a point onto a given view-line. The function "eye" generates an identity matrix of specified size with ones along the main diagonal and zeros elsewhere (Figure 4.83).

EXAMPLE 4.33 EXAMPLE TO CALCULATE 2D PROJECTION MATRIX AND PROJECTED COORDINATES FOR (A) PERSPECTIVE PROJECTION OF POINT P(-8,-6) ONTO VIEWLINE L : -3X + 12Y - 5 = 0 AND VIEWPOINT V(-3, 11) (B) PARALLEL ORTHOGRAPHIC PROJECTION OF P ON L

```
clear all; clc; format compact;
P = [-8, 6, 1];
L = [-3, 12, -5];
syms x y;
f = -3*x + 12*y - 5;

% (a) perspective projection
V = [-3, 11, 1];
M = V'*L - V*L'*eye(3);
Q = M*P';
```

```
Qc = Q/Q(3)
y1 = (-L(1)*x - L(3))/L(2);
xx = -20:10;
yy = subs(y1, x, xx);

%plotting
y1 = (-L(1)*x - L(3))/L(2);
xx = -20:10;
yy = subs(y1, x, xx);
plot(xx, yy, 'b-', 'LineWidth', 1.5);
hold on; grid;
scatter(P(1), P(2), 20, 'r', 'filled');
scatter(V(1), V(2), 20, 'r', 'filled');
scatter(Qc(1), Qc(2), 20, 'r',
   'filled');
plot([V(1), P(1)], [V(2),
   P(2)], 'k--');
plot([P(1), Qc(1)], [P(2),
   Qc(2)], 'k--');
xlabel('x'); ylabel('y'); axis equal;
text(-2, 1, 'L', 'FontSize', 15);
text(P(1)+0.5, P(2), 'P');
text(Qc(1)+0.5, Qc(2), 'Q');
text(V(1)+0.5, V(2), 'V');

%verification
f = -3*x + 12*y - 5;
vrf1 = subs(f, [x, y], [Qc(1), Qc(2)])

% (b) orthographic projection
m = -L(1)/L(2); % slope
t = [1, m, 1]; % tangent
```

```
R90 = [cosd(90) -sind(90) 0 ; sind(90)
   cosd(90) 0 ; 0 0 1];
n = R90*t'; % normal
V = [n(1), n(2), 0];
M = V'*L - V*L'*eye(3);
Q = M*P';
Qc = Q/Q(3)

%plotting
figure
syms x y;
y1 = (-L(1)*x - L(3))/L(2);
xx = -10:10;
yy = subs(y1, x, xx);
plot(xx, yy, 'b-', 'LineWidth', 1.5);
hold on; grid;
quiver(P(1), P(2), V(1), V(2));
quiver(V(1), V(2), V(1), V(2));
scatter(P(1), P(2), 20, 'r', 'filled');
scatter(V(1), V(2), 20, 'r', 'filled');
scatter(Qc(1), Qc(2), 20, 'r',
   'filled');
plot([P(1), Qc(1)], [P(2),
   Qc(2)], 'k--');
text(Qc(1)+0.5, Qc(2), 'Q');
text(V(1)+0.5, V(2), 'V');
text(P(1)+0.5, P(2), 'P');
text(-2, 1, 'L', 'FontSize', 15);
xlabel('x'); ylabel('y'); axis equal;

%verification
f = -3*x + 12*y - 5;
vrf2 = subs(f, [x, y], [Qc(1), Qc(2)])
```

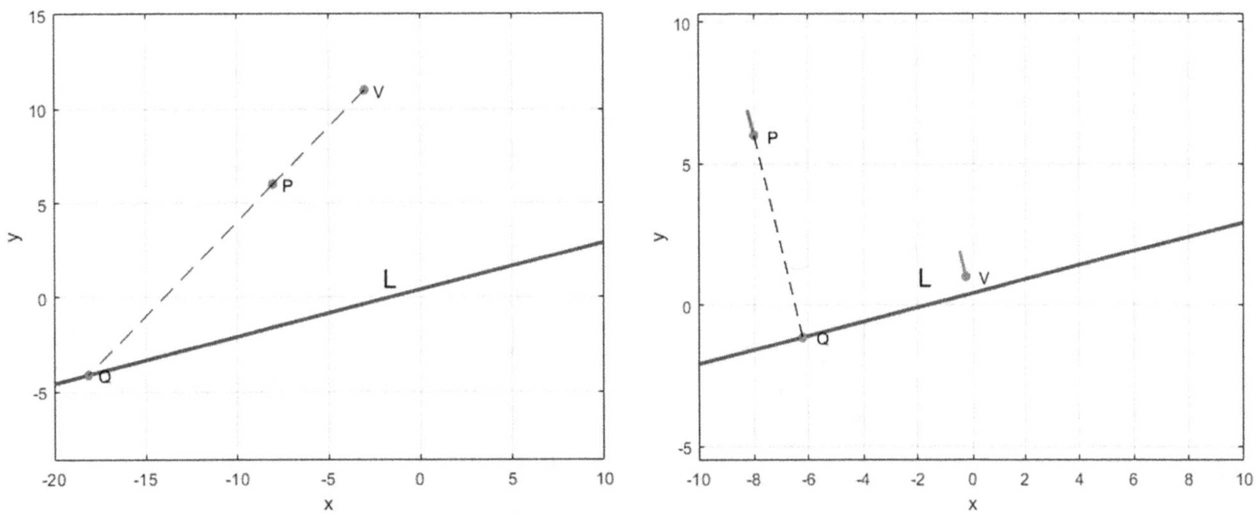

FIGURE 4.83
Plot for Example 4.33.

The following example computes the 3D projection matrix and projected coordinates for an orthographic and a perspective projection of a point onto a given view-plane. The functions "plot3" generates a 3D line plot, "quiver3" generates a 3D arrow plot, "fimplicit3" generates a 3D plot of an implicit function (Figure 4.84).

EXAMPLE 4.34 EXAMPLE TO CALCULATE 3D PROJECTION MATRIX AND PROJECTED COORDINATES FOR (A) PERSPECTIVE PROJECTION OF POINT P(-4,2,2) ONTO VIEWPLANE F : -X + 3Y + 2Z - 4 = 0 AND VIEWPOINT V(2, -1, 1) (B) PARALLEL ORTHOGRAPHIC PROJECTION OF P ON F (A) PERSPECTIVE PROJECTION

```
clear all; clc; format compact;
N = [-1, 3, 2, -4];
P = [-4, 2, 2, 1];
syms x y z;
f = -x + 3*y +2*z - 4;
% (a) perspective projection
V = [2, -1, 1, 1];
M = V'*N - V*N'*eye(4);
Qh = M*P';
Q = Qh/Qh(4)
figure
plot3(P(1), P(2), P(3), 'ro');
hold on; grid; view(-66, 30);
xlabel('x'); ylabel('y'); zlabel('z');
plot3(Q(1), Q(2), Q(3), 'ro');
plot3(V(1), V(2), V(3), 'ro');
plot3([V(1) P(1)], [V(2) P(2)], [V(3)
   P(3)], 'k--');
quiver3(0, 0, 2, N(1), N(2), N(3));
text(P(1), P(2), P(3)+0.5, 'P');
text(Q(1), Q(2), Q(3)+0.5, 'Q');
text(V(1), V(2), V(3)+0.5, 'V');
text(N(1), N(2), N(3)+2, 'N');

%verification
vrf1 = subs(f, [x, y, z], [Q(1),
   Q(2), Q(3)])
fimplicit3(f, 'MeshDensity', 2,
   'FaceColor', 'y', 'FaceAlpha',0.3);

% (b) orthographic projection
V = [N(1), N(2), N(3), 0];
M = V'*N - V*N'*eye(4);
Qh = M*P';
Q = Qh/Qh(4)
figure
plot3(P(1), P(2), P(3), 'ro');
hold on; grid; view(-80, 25);
quiver3(0, 0, 2, N(1), N(2), N(3));
quiver3(V(1), V(2), V(3), V(1),
   V(2), V(3));
plot3(Q(1), Q(2), Q(3), 'ro');
plot3(V(1), V(2), V(3), 'ro');
plot3([Q(1) P(1)], [Q(2) P(2)], [Q(3)
   P(3)], 'k--');
xlabel('x'); ylabel('y'); zlabel('z');
text(P(1), P(2), P(3)+0.5, 'P');
text(Q(1), Q(2), Q(3)+0.5, 'Q');
text(V(1), V(2), V(3)+0.5, 'V');
text(N(1), N(2), N(3)+2, 'N')

%verification
vrf2 = subs(f, [x, y, z], [Q(1),
   Q(2), Q(3)])
fimplicit3(f, 'MeshDensity', 2,
   'FaceColor', 'y', 'FaceAlpha',0.3);
hold off;
```

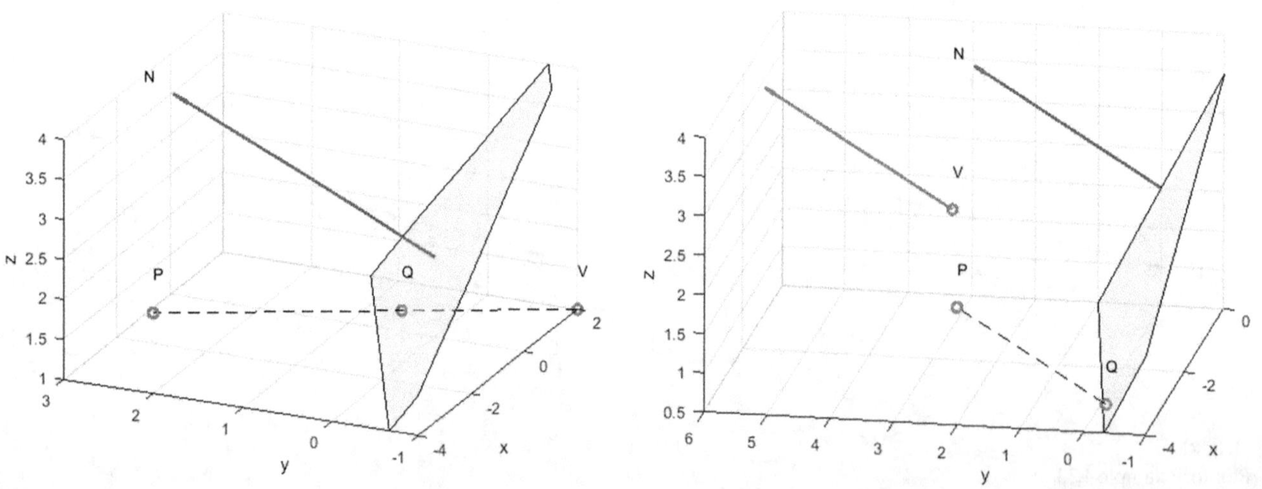

FIGURE 4.84
Plot for Example 4.34.

Review Questions

- Trace the historical evolution of graphics highlighting the salient events.
- What are the utilities of graphics in a multimedia presentation?
- Differentiate between raster and vector graphics.
- Discuss the functionalities of the components of a graphics system.
- Differentiate characteristics of 2D and 3D graphics.
- How is a 2D coordinate system different from a 3D coordinate system?
- Explain how line drawing algorithms generate straight lines between given points.
- How can circle drawing algorithms efficiently draw circles on screens?
- What the utilities of filling and clipping algorithms?
- Discuss how new coordinates of a point is calculated under various 2D transformations.
- Differentiate between scaling and shearing.
- What are homogeneous coordinates, and what are its advantages?
- What is meant by fixed point rotation and fixed point scaling?
- Differentiate between affine and perspective transformations.
- What are splines and how many categories of splines exist?
- How can splines be represented mathematically?
- Differentiate between implicit, explicit and parametric polynomial equations.
- Given two points, how is equation of a linear interpolating spline calculated?
- How can equation of a quadratic interpolating spline be calculated from three points?
- How can equation of a cubic interpolating spline be calculated in parametric form?
- What is meant by blending functions, and what are their utilities?
- How can equations of quadratic Bezier spline be derived from Bernstein polynomials?
- Explain the steps how the basis matrix of a cubic Bezier spline be derived.
- What are the major drawbacks of Bezier splines and how are these addressed?
- Discuss how the Cox de Boor algorithm used to derive B-spline equations?
- How can equations of a uniform quadratic B-spline be computed?
- What is a knot vector and how are its values determined?
- Discuss how the degree of a B-spline is independent of its number of control points.
- Differentiate between uniform, non-uniform and open-uniform B-splines.
- How can spline equations be converted from one spline type to another?
- How can the length of a spline between two given points be calculated?
- How can the area between a spline and the primary axis be calculated?
- How can the centroid coordinates of a bounded area be derived?
- What are the conditions to be satisfied to determine critical points of a spline?
- What are fractals and how are their dimensions determined?
- Explain giving examples how a 3D surface can be generated from 2D shapes.
- What are geometric primitives and modifiers in connection with 3D modeling?
- Discuss the processes of lathing, lofting and extrusion for creating 3D surfaces.
- Discuss how the transformation matrices of 3D transformations can be derived.
- How can 3D transformation matrices for rotation parallel to primary axes be derived?
- Derive 3D transformation matrices for reflection about the primary planes.
- What are vectors? How can resultant of multiple vectors be computed?
- What is vector dot product? How can it be used to find angle between two vectors?
- What is vector cross product? How can direction of the resultant be determined?
- Explain whether following operations are valid: (a) $(a \bullet b) \times c$ (b) $(a \times b) \bullet c$
- How the angle of the vectors $\pm ai \pm bj$ with respect to the primary axes be calculated?
- Derive the transformation matrix to align the vector $ai + bj + ck$ with positive z-axis.

- Mention the steps to calculate transformation matrix of rotation around a 3D vector.
- Differentiate between parallel and perspective projection.
- Differentiate between orthographic, axonometric and oblique projections.
- How can homogeneous vector equations be used to determine projected coordinates?
- How are parallel multi-view projections different from parallel axonometric projections?
- Explain foreshortening factors? Differentiate isometric, diametric, trimetric projections.
- What are the characteristics of cavalier and cabinet projections?
- What is a PRP in connection with perspective projection?
- Discuss some of the major applications of graphics.
- Mention some of the legal and ethical considerations in the field of graphics.
- What some of the challenges and emerging trends in the field of graphic design?
- Mention the characteristics of some of the major graphic file formats.

References

Chakraborty, S., *Fundamentals of computer graphics*, Everest Publishing House, 2010.

Boor, C., Subroutine package for calculating with B-splines, Tech Rep. LA-4728-MS, Los Alamos Sci. Lab, Los Alamos, NM, pp. 109–121, 1971.

Foley, J. D., A. van Dam, S. K. Feiner, et al. 1995. *Computer graphics: Principles and practice*. Addison-Wesley Professional, 1990.

Godse, A. P., D. A. Godse, *Computer graphics and multimedia*, Technical Publications, 2021.

Hearn, D. & M. P. Baker, *Computer graphics, C version* 2nd edition. Prentice Hall, 1996.

Kane, E. M., *Ethics: A graphic designer's field guide*, Simon & Schuster, 2010

Mandelbrot, B. B., *The fractal geometry of Nature*, W H Freeman and Co., 1982.

Marsh, D., *Applied geometry for computer graphics and CAD*, Springer, 2005.

Mathews, J. H. & C. D. Fink, *Numerical methods using MATLAB*, Prentice Hall, 2004.

O'Rourke, M., *Principles of three dimensional computer animation*, W. W. Norton & Company, 2003.

Olive, J., *Maths: A student's survival guide*, Cambridge University Press, 2003.

Rovenski, V., *Modeling of curves and surfaces with MATLAB*. Springer, 2010.

Shirley, P., *Fundamentals of computer graphics*. AK Peters/CRC Press, 2002.

5

Audio

5.1 Audio Fundamentals

5.1.1 Key Terms

We begin with a snapshot of the important terms relevant to the digital audio, to present the entire chapter in a nutshell. These terms will be expanded in the following sections of the chapter in their proper contexts.

Adaptive DPCM: Adaptive Differential Pulse Code Modulation (ADPCM) is a coding scheme that adjusts the quantization levels of the signal based on the changing characteristics of the input. By adapting to the input signal's dynamics, ADPCM optimizes the encoding process, providing a more efficient representation of audio signals with a reduced data rate compared to traditional PCM.

Amplifier: An audio amplifier is an electronic device designed to increase the strength of audio signals, making them powerful enough to drive speakers or other output devices. It takes a weak input signal, such as from a microphone or audio source, and amplifies it to produce a higher-powered output signal for better sound reproduction.

Amplitude: The amplitude of a sound wave refers to the maximum displacement or distance a particle in a medium moves from its rest position as the sound wave passes through. In the context of a waveform, it represents the peak height of the wave and correlates with the perceived loudness of the sound, with higher amplitudes corresponding to louder sounds.

Audio file formats: Audio file formats are standardized structures for encoding and storing digital audio data, determining how audio information is compressed, organized and stored. Common examples include MP3, WAV and FLAC, each with different characteristics and compression methods suitable for various applications in digital audio.

Connectors: Audio connectors are physical interfaces used to establish electrical connections between audio devices, facilitating the transfer of audio signals. Common examples include connectors like 3.5mm jacks, RCA plugs and XLR connectors, each serving different purposes and applications in audio equipment.

Decibel: The decibel (dB) is a logarithmic unit used to measure the intensity or amplitude of sound or the magnitude of a physical quantity. In the context of sound, it quantifies the relative loudness or volume, with an increase of 10 dB representing a tenfold increase in sound intensity.

Differential PCM: Differential Pulse Code Modulation (DPCM) is a signal encoding technique that represents the difference between consecutive samples rather than encoding each sample independently. By encoding the changes or differentials between successive samples, DPCM reduces the amount of data required for transmission or storage, making it an efficient method for compressing and transmitting audio signals.

FIR filter: A Finite Impulse Response (FIR) audio filter is a type of digital filter used in signal processing to modify the frequency response of an audio signal. It operates by convolving the input signal with a finite-length sequence of coefficients, producing an output signal that is a weighted sum of past input samples, allowing precise control over the filter characteristics.

Frequency: The frequency of a sound wave is the number of cycles or vibrations per unit of time, typically measured in Hertz (Hz). Higher frequencies correspond to higher-pitched sounds, while lower frequencies correspond to lower-pitched sounds in the audible range.

Hertz: Hertz (Hz) is the unit of frequency, representing the number of cycles or oscillations per second in a wave. In the context of sound, one Hertz equals one cycle per second, determining the pitch of the sound where higher Hertz values correspond to higher frequencies and vice versa.

DOI: 10.1201/9781003588030-5

IIR filter: An Infinite Impulse Response (IIR) audio filter is a type of digital filter used in signal processing that relies on recursive feedback to modify the frequency response of an audio signal. Unlike FIR filters, IIR filters use feedback, allowing them to achieve similar frequency shaping with fewer coefficients, making them computationally efficient.

Loudness: Loudness in audio refers to the perceived intensity or volume of a sound. It is influenced by the amplitude of the sound wave, with greater amplitudes generally perceived as louder, while lower amplitudes are perceived as softer.

Loudspeaker: A loudspeaker, commonly known as a speaker, is an electroacoustic transducer that converts electrical audio signals into sound waves, producing sound for listeners. It typically consists of a diaphragm or cone that vibrates in response to the electrical signal, creating pressure waves in the air that we perceive as sound.

Masking: Audio masking occurs when the presence of one sound, known as the masker, makes another sound, the target, less audible or even inaudible to a listener. This phenomenon is often utilized in audio engineering and psychoacoustics to manipulate perception, such as in noise reduction or when designing audio compression algorithms.

Microphone: A microphone is a transducer that converts sound waves into electrical signals, capturing audio input for recording or amplification. It typically employs a diaphragm or other acoustic sensing element to convert variations in air pressure caused by sound into corresponding electrical voltages.

MIDI: MIDI (Musical Instrument Digital Interface) is a protocol that enables electronic musical instruments, computers and other devices to communicate and synchronize with each other. It uses a standardized set of commands and messages to transmit musical information, allowing for the creation, recording and playback of music in a digital environment.

Noise gate: A noise gate is an audio processing device or software tool that automatically reduces or mutes the volume of a signal when it falls below a certain threshold, helping eliminate unwanted background noise during quiet passages. It is commonly used in audio production to enhance the clarity of recordings by suppressing noise during pauses or softer sections.

Phase: Phase in a sound wave refers to the relative position of a point in the wave cycle at a specific moment in time. When two sound waves are in phase, their corresponding points align, reinforcing each other and resulting in constructive interference; when out of phase, they may cancel each other out through destructive interference.

Pitch: Audio pitch refers to the perceived frequency of a sound, determining whether it is high or low. Higher pitch corresponds to higher frequencies, while lower pitch corresponds to lower frequencies in the audio spectrum.

Polar plot: Polar plots of microphones visually represent the directional sensitivity or pickup pattern of a microphone across various angles. These plots illustrate how a microphone captures sound from different directions, helping users understand the microphone's response to incoming audio signals in terms of directionality and sensitivity.

Progressive wave: A type of wave which progresses forward in space from one place to another. A progressive wave is therefore associated with two types of motions: the oscillation of the particles of the wave about their mean position, and the motion of the wave itself in space.

Pulse code modulation (PCM): Pulse Code Modulation (PCM) is a method used to digitally represent analog signals, such as audio or voice, by encoding the amplitude of the signal at regular intervals. In PCM, the analog signal is sampled, and each sample is quantized and assigned a binary code, allowing for accurate digital representation and reconstruction of the original analog waveform.

Sound card: A sound card, or audio interface, is a hardware component in a computer or external device that enables the input and output of audio signals. It processes and converts digital and analog audio information, facilitating tasks such as playback, recording and the connection of speakers, microphones and other audio peripherals.

Sound wave: A sound wave is a longitudinal wave that carries mechanical energy through a medium, typically air, and is created by the vibrations of a source. It is characterized by properties such as frequency, amplitude and wavelength, determining the pitch, loudness and tone of the audible sound.

Spectral analysis: Spectral audio analysis involves examining the frequency components of an audio signal, breaking it down into its individual frequency components to analyze its spectral content. This analysis provides insights into the distribution of frequencies, helping in tasks such as identifying specific sounds, measuring tonal characteristics and understanding the overall frequency composition of the audio.

Sub-woofer: A subwoofer is a specialized loudspeaker designed to reproduce low-frequency sounds, particularly deep bass, in an audio system. Its large driver and enclosure are dedicated to handling low-frequency ranges, providing a richer and more immersive audio experience, especially in home theatre or music systems.

Surround sound: Surround sound refers to a multi-channel audio system that immerses listeners in a three-dimensional audio experience by utilizing multiple speakers strategically placed around the listening area. This technology aims to create a sense of spatial depth and directionality, enhancing the realism and immersion in audio-visual content.

Synthesizer: A digital synthesizer is an electronic musical instrument that generates sound using digital signal processing techniques. It can emulate a wide range of sounds by manipulating digitally generated waveforms, offering versatility and flexibility in sound design for music production.

Temporal filter: A temporal audio filter is a processing technique that manipulates the time domain characteristics of an audio signal, affecting its timing and temporal aspects. This type of filter can be used to modify the time-based features of sound, such as attack and decay, providing control over the dynamics and transients in the audio signal.

Tweeter: A tweeter is a type of loudspeaker designed to reproduce high-frequency sounds or treble in an audio system. It is typically smaller than woofers and is responsible for producing the higher-pitched audio frequencies to achieve a balanced and full-range sound output in a speaker system.

Waveform: An audio waveform is a graphical representation of a sound wave, illustrating how the air pressure variations corresponding to the sound change over time. It depicts the amplitude and frequency characteristics of the sound, providing a visual representation of the audio signal.

Windowing: In signal processing, windowing is a technique that involves multiplying a signal, or a portion of a signal, by a mathematical function called a window. This process helps reduce distortions and artifacts introduced during the analysis of finite segments of a signal, especially when using techniques like the Fourier Transform.

Woofer: A woofer is a type of loudspeaker designed to reproduce low-frequency sounds or bass in an audio system. It is characterized by its larger size and is dedicated to handling lower-frequency ranges to enhance the overall audio experience, particularly in music or home theatre systems.

5.1.2 Historical Evolution

1950s–1970s: The foundations of digital audio processing were laid in the mid-20th century with the advent of digital computers. Researchers explored methods to convert analog audio signals into digital form for efficient storage and processing. Max Mathews, often regarded as the father of computer music, created the first computer-generated musical sounds using an IBM 704 computer in the late 1950s.

1970s–1980s: Pulse Code Modulation (PCM) emerged as a key technology for digitizing audio signals. The 16-bit PCM audio standard was introduced, allowing for high-fidelity audio representation. This era also witnessed the commercial introduction of the Compact Disc (CD) in the early 1980s, marking a pivotal moment in the digital audio revolution by providing a standardized digital format for audio distribution.

1980s–1990s: The advent of dedicated Digital Signal Processors (DSPs) in the 1980s brought about a significant shift in digital audio processing. DSP chips enabled real-time processing of audio signals, leading to the development of digital audio effects, equalization and other sophisticated manipulations. This era also saw the rise of digital audio workstations (DAWs), empowering musicians and producers with powerful tools for recording and editing digital audio.

1990s–2000s: The development of the MP3 (MPEG-1 Audio Layer III) compression standard in the 1990s revolutionized the distribution of audio over the internet. MP3 allowed for efficient compression of audio files without significant loss of quality, facilitating the rise of online music distribution and the transition from physical media to digital downloads.

2000s–Present: The 21st century witnessed the proliferation of surround sound technologies, offering immersive audio experiences in home theatres and cinemas. Advanced audio codecs, such as Dolby TrueHD and DTS-HD, further elevated audio quality in the context of high-definition multimedia. The integration of digital audio processing into consumer devices, including smartphones and smart speakers, became widespread.

2010s–Present: The advent of high-speed internet and cloud computing has transformed how audio is processed and distributed. Streaming services, employing sophisticated algorithms and adaptive bitrate streaming, have become dominant, offering users instant access to vast libraries of high-quality audio content. Cloud-based audio processing has also enabled real-time collaboration in music production and advanced audio analysis techniques.

2020s–Present: The current landscape explores spatial audio technologies and their integration with virtual reality (VR) and augmented reality (AR) platforms. Object-based audio, 3D audio rendering and personalized sound experiences are at the forefront, promising a new dimension in immersive digital audio processing.

5.1.3 Basic Concepts

5.1.3.1 Sound Waves

Sound is a form of energy that travels through a material medium, such as air, water or solids, in the form of waves. As sound energy propagates through the medium, it sets up alternate regions of compression and rarefaction by shifting the particles of the medium, e.g., molecules of air. This is pictorially represented as a wave, the upper part (i.e., the crest or positive peak) denoting a compression and the lower part (i.e., the trough or negative peak) denoting a rarefaction.

"Sound is an alteration in pressure, particle displacement or particle velocity propagated in an elastic material" (Rossing et al., 2011). Since a sound wave actually represents a disturbance of the medium particles from their original positions (i.e., before the wave started), it cannot exist in vacuum. Sound waves have two characteristic properties. Firstly, they are said to be longitudinal waves, which means that the direction of propagation of sound is the same as the direction along which the medium particles oscillate. This is in contrast to transverse waves, like light, where the wave moves in a direction perpendicular to the oscillation of the particles. Secondly, sound waves are also referred to as mechanical waves. This means that they need a material medium to propagate from one place to another and are capable of being compressed and expanded like springs. When they are compressed, the peaks come closer together, while on expansion the peaks move further apart. Sound waves are characterized by their fundamental properties like amplitude, frequency, waveform as well as their relative phases (Figure 5.1).

5.1.3.2 Types of Sounds

In general, sounds that we hear can be broadly classified into three categories: speech, music and environmental sounds. Speech is uttered by a human and

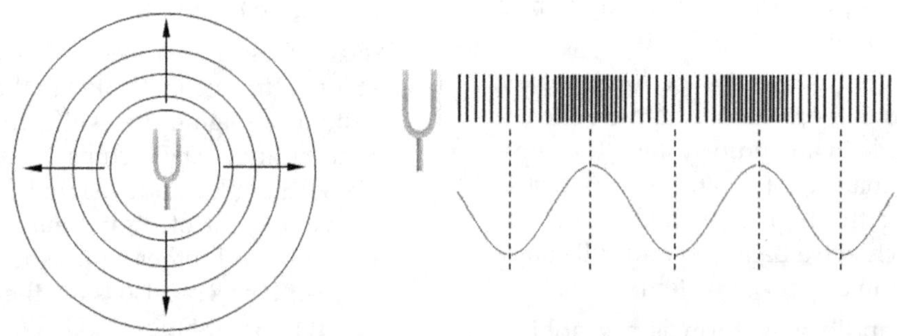

FIGURE 5.1
Propagation of sound waves.

generated from the human voice box; music originates from musical instruments like guitar, flute, violin, usually being generated from vibrating strings, plates or air columns; environmental sounds are anything other than speech and music and include noises we normally hear in our daily lives. Environmental sounds can again be divided into two broad subtypes: those originating from inorganic sources, like sounds of horns, bells, vehicles, explosions and those originating from organic sources, like sounds of birds, animals, laughter, clapping and so on. In recent times, we can also probably think of a fourth category of synthetic sounds generated from computers and digital audio instruments like various types of clicking, alert and beeping sounds, as well as electronic music from synthesizers (Figure 5.2).

5.1.3.3 Amplitude

Amplitude of a wave is the maximum displacement of a particle in the path of a wave and indicates the peak height of the wave. Subsequently, we will use the term "amplitude" to mean particle displacement. The physical manifestation of amplitude is the intensity of energy of the wave; for sound waves, this corresponds to the loudness of sound, larger the energy of the sound wave, more will be its amplitude and louder will it sound in our ears. Loudness is measured in a unit called, decibel, denoted by dB and involves comparing the intensity of a sound with the faintest sound audible by the human ear, expressing the ratio as a logarithmic value. A 60 dB sound has energy content about a million times that of the softest audible sound, while the total range of human hearing is 120 dB. In the following figure, the waveform in the second row has amplitude of one-third of the waveform in the first row.

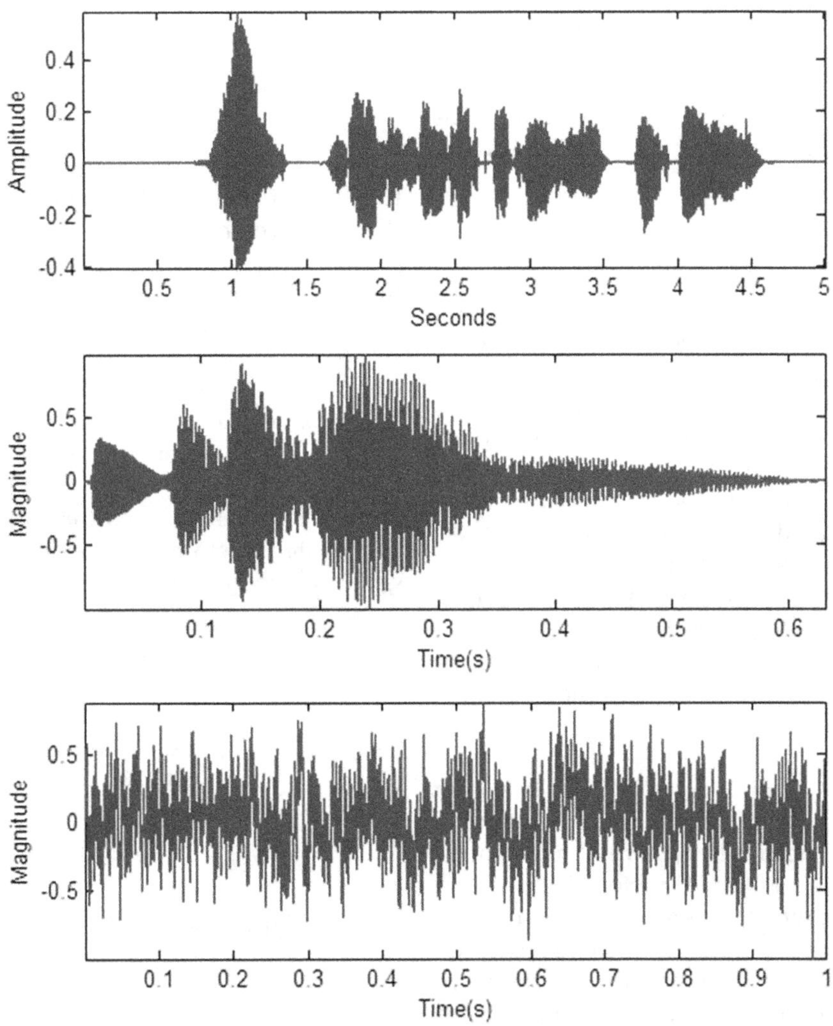

FIGURE 5.2
Sound waves of speech, music and noise.

5.1.3.4 Frequency

This measures the number of vibrations of a particle in the path of a wave in one second. The physical manifestation of frequency of a sound wave is the pitch of sound. A high-pitched sound, like that of a whistle, has higher frequency than a dull flat sound, like the sound of a drum. Frequency is measured in a unit called Hertz and denoted by Hz, a sound of 1 Hz being produced by an object vibrating at the rate of 1 oscillation per second. The total range of human hearing lies between 20 Hz at the lower end to 20,000 Hz (or 20 kHz) at the higher end, which means that we can hear sounds produced from objects vibrating at the rate of 20 to 20000 oscillations per second. Frequencies below the audible range are called infrasonic/subsonic, frequencies above the audible range are called ultrasonic/supersonic. On compression, the frequency of sound increases and appears more high pitched to our ears, while on expansion, the frequency decreases making it appear more dull and flat. This is known as the Doppler effect and enables us to ascertain whether a sound source is moving toward or away from us, e.g., whistle of a moving train. In the following figure, the waveform in the second row has a frequency three times that of the waveform in the first row.

5.1.3.5 Phase

Phase denotes the relative position of a point on a sound wave at a specific moment. Two points on a wave having the same state of oscillation are said to be in the same phase, for example two consecutive peaks. The spatial distance between two consecutive points in a sound wave that are in phase is called the wavelength (λ). It is inversely proportional to frequency and can be computed using the relation $\lambda = v / f$, where v represents the speed of sound in the given medium. Two different sound waves can be in-phase, when they rise or fall together and can generate constructive interference; otherwise, if they are out of phase they result in destructive interference.

5.1.3.6 Tone and Note

A tone is a sound having a single frequency. A tone can be represented pictorially by a wavy curve called a sinusoidal wave. An example of a tone is the sound produced when a tuning fork is struck with a padded hammer. The sinusoidal nature of the curve is derived from the fact that a tone is produced from a kind of vibratory motion called Simple Harmonic Motion (SHM), which can be described by a sine function. A single frequency sound can be described by the equation $y = a.\sin(\omega t - \theta)$, where a is the amplitude, ω is the angular frequency given by $\omega = 2\pi f$, f being the linear frequency and θ is the phase lag. In the following figure the sinusoidal waves in first and second rows are examples of tones.

A composite mixture of various tones of varying amplitudes and frequencies is called a note. The waveform of a note can be derived from the resultant or sum of all its tonal components. The lowest frequency of a note is called the fundamental frequency. In the following figure the third and fourth rows depict composite notes derived from tonal components in the first and second rows.

5.1.3.7 Waveform

Waveform indicates the actual shape of the wave when represented pictorially. Shapes of the waves can be sinusoidal, square, triangular, sawtooth and so on, while complex sounds can be of any arbitrary and irregular shape. The physical manifestation of waveform is the quality or timbre of sound. This helps us distinguish between sounds coming from different instruments like a guitar and a violin. The pictorial representation of the waveform depends on the amplitude and frequency of the tonal components as well as their relative phase differences. The Fourier Theorem named after French mathematician Jean-Baptiste Joseph (Fourier, 1822) proposes that any periodic signal can be represented as weighted sums of sinusoidal components. The summation of known weighted components to derive an arbitrary function is called Fourier synthesis, whereas the process of deriving the weights for describing a given function is called Fourier analysis. The collection of weighted sinusoidal terms is called the Fourier series. Some common composite waveforms and their tonal components are given below (Figure 5.3):

$$\text{Square wave}: \cos t - \frac{1}{3}\cos 3t + \frac{1}{5}\cos 5t - \frac{1}{7}\cos 7t + \ldots$$

$$\text{Triangular wave}: \cos t + \frac{1}{9}\cos 3t + \frac{1}{25}\cos 5t + \ldots$$

$$\text{Sawtooth wave}: \sin t - \frac{1}{2}\sin 2t + \frac{1}{3}\sin 3t - \frac{1}{4}\sin 4t + \ldots$$

$$\text{Half}-\text{rectified wave}: 1 + \frac{\pi}{2}\cos t + \frac{2}{3}\cos 2t - \frac{2}{15}\cos 4t + \frac{2}{35}\cos 6t - \ldots$$

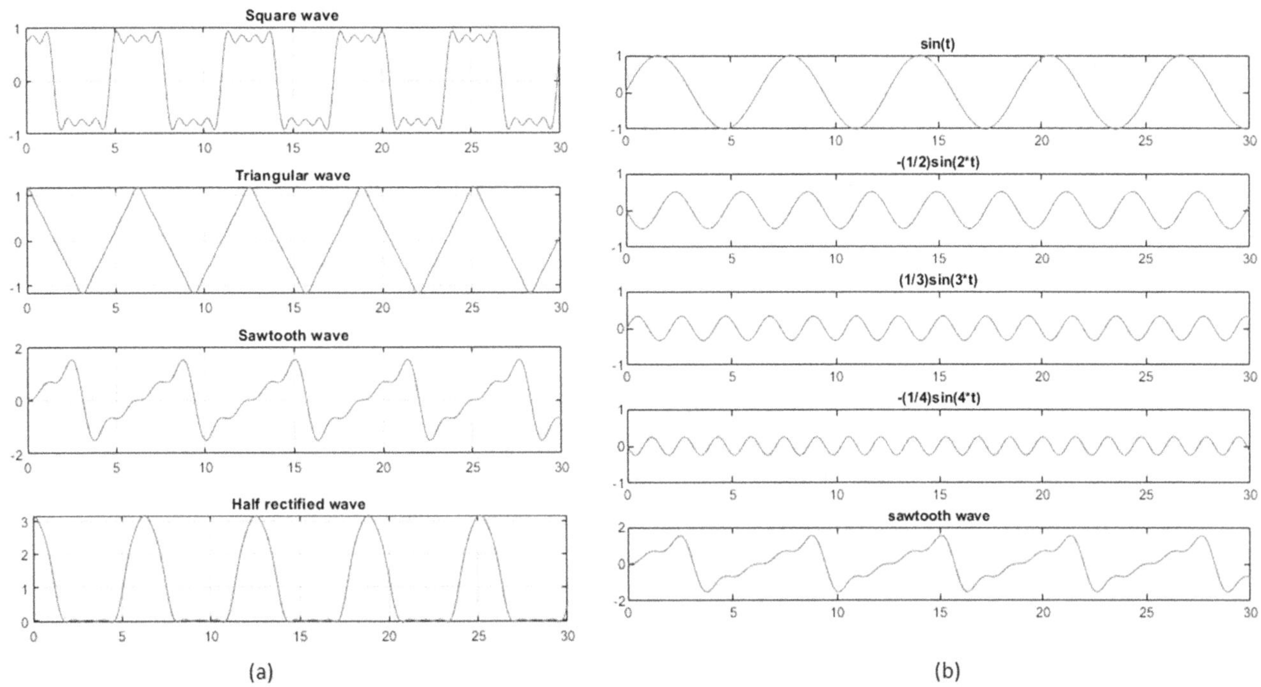

FIGURE 5.3
(a) Composite waveforms (b) tonal components of the sawtooth wave.

5.1.3.8 Acoustic Principles

Acoustics is the branch of physics that deals with the study of sound and its transmission, production and effects. The field encompasses a wide range of phenomena related to mechanical waves in gases, liquids and solids (Olson, 1957).

Sound waves can undergo reflection and refraction when encountering obstacles or changes in the medium. Reflection occurs when sound waves bounce off surfaces, refraction is the bending of sound waves due to changes in the medium, and diffraction is the bending of sound waves around obstacles.

When two or more sound waves overlap, they exhibit superposition and interference. Constructive interference occurs when waves are in phase and reinforce each other, leading to increased amplitude and louder sounds, while destructive interference when waves are out of phase, results in reduced amplitude and quieter sounds.

Resonance occurs when an object vibrates at its natural frequency, absorbing energy efficiently. Resonance is responsible for the production of sound in musical instruments and is exploited in acoustic designs to enhance the quality of sound in spaces. Materials exhibit varying degrees of absorption of sound waves. Soft, porous materials absorb sound, reducing its reflection and preventing echoes, hard, reflective surfaces, on the other hand, contribute to more sound reflection.

Sound propagates differently in solids, liquids and gases due to variations in the medium's density and elasticity. In general, sound travels fastest in solids, followed by liquids, and slowest in gases. Sound waves can pass through materials referred to as transmission. The ability of a material to transmit sound depends on its density and thickness. The speed of sound varies with the medium it travels through. For instance, in dry air at room temperature, sound travels at approximately 343 meters per second (m/s).

The Doppler effect describes the change in frequency (pitch) of a sound wave in relation to the motion of the source or observer. An approaching sound source or observer experiences a higher frequency (shorter wavelength) as the waves get compressed, while a receding source or observer experiences a lower frequency (longer wavelength) as the waves get elongated.

5.1.3.9 Music and Noise

In general periodic or symmetrical vibration produce sounds which seems musical to the human ear, which irregular or non-periodic vibrations generate noise. It has also been observed that presence of more harmonic content adds to the richness of musical sound, which is referred to as harmony. The lowest frequency of a note is called the fundamental frequency; all the other frequencies are called overtones. Frequencies of some overtones may be integral multiples of the fundamental frequency, which are called harmonics. White noise is a signal that has the same energy or power for any frequency value, i.e., constant power density. A noise with decreasing power density with frequency is called red noise while a noise with increasing power density with frequency is called blue noise.

5.1.3.10 Loudness and Decibel

Loudness is a perceptual property of sound dependent on its energy, measured in a unit called decibels. It involves comparing the intensity of a sound with the faintest sound audible by the human ear and expressing the ratio as a logarithmic value. If P_1 be the power or energy content of a signal in absolute units and P_2 be the corresponding value for a reference signal, then the power in decibel is given by: $P_{dB} = 10\log(P_1/P_2)$. If the intensity of energy of the signal is expressed in terms of amplitude values then $P_{dB} = 20\log(A_1/A_2)$, as power is proportional to square of the amplitude. In real-life calculation, the denominator P_2 or A_2 corresponds to the power or amplitude of the softest audible sound that the average human ear can hear, and has a power of about 10^{-12} watt/sq. meter. Thus, a 60 dB sound has 10^6 times the energy content of the softest audible sound.

5.1.3.11 Dynamic range

It is the ratio between the smallest and largest possible values of a variable quantity. In acoustics, the term dynamic range is used to mean the ratio of maximum amplitude of undistorted sound in audio equipment like microphone or loudspeaker to the amplitude of the quietest sound possible which is often determined by inherent noise characteristics of the device. Often expressed in decibels (dB), the dynamic range of human hearing is considered around 120 dB. In practice, it is difficult to achieve this full dynamic range using electronic equipment. For example the dynamic range of a magnetic tape is of the order of 55 dB. Dynamic range compression (DRC) used in electronic equipment work like an automatic volume control, i.e., loud sounds over a certain threshold are reduced (while quiet sounds remain unchanged) and quiet sounds below a certain threshold are increased (while loud sounds remain unchanged). The amount of reduction using DRC is called the gain reduction and expressed as a ratio; e.g., a ratio of 2:1 means that if the input sound level is 2 dB above the threshold then the output sound level is 1 dB.

5.1.3.12 Minimum threshold

The minimum threshold is the least audible sound that the normal human ear can detect and hear, associated with an energy level of 10^{-12} watt/m^2. The sensitivity of the human ear is, however, frequency-dependent. Maximum sensitivity occurs at 1 to 5 kHz with relative insensitivity at low and high frequencies. This means that a 20 Hz tone would have to be much louder than a 1 kHz tone to be barely audible. The minimum threshold values, i.e., the amplitudes of the least audible sounds when plotted against frequency values gives rise to the minimum threshold curve. The upper portion denotes the audible region, while the lower portion denotes the inaudible region. The minimum value on the curve occurs around the frequency of 1 kHz where the sensitivity of the human ear is the greatest.

5.1.3.13 Masking

Masking originates due to the limitation of the human ear which prevents us from hearing two sounds of differing loudness but close in frequency or time. Frequency masking occurs because an audible sound has a tendency to distort the threshold curve and shift it upward so that a lower amplitude sound having similar frequency values would fall below the threshold level of the curve and hence would be rendered inaudible. The human ear contains about 30,000 hair cells that detect local vibrations and convey audio information to the brain via electrical impulses. These hair cells respond to the strongest stimulation in their local region. The amount of distortion of the curve is restricted to a small region surrounding the strongest sounds. The entire range of audible frequencies is divided into a number of such regions, known as critical bands. Critical bands are much narrower at low frequencies than at high frequencies, and width of a critical band, determine the extent of the distortion of the threshold curve. They are approximately 100 Hz wide for frequencies from 20 to 400 Hz and about 1 kHz wide for frequencies from 4 kHz to 5 kHz. Within a critical band of frequencies, only the strongest sound will be heard while the others are subdued. The louder sound is called masker while the quieter sound is called masked (Figure 5.4).

5.1.3.14 Sound as Progressive Wave

Sound is a progressive equation as the wave-front progresses forward in space from one place to another. Therefore there are two types of motions associated with a sound wave: the oscillations of the particles of the medium about their mean positions and the

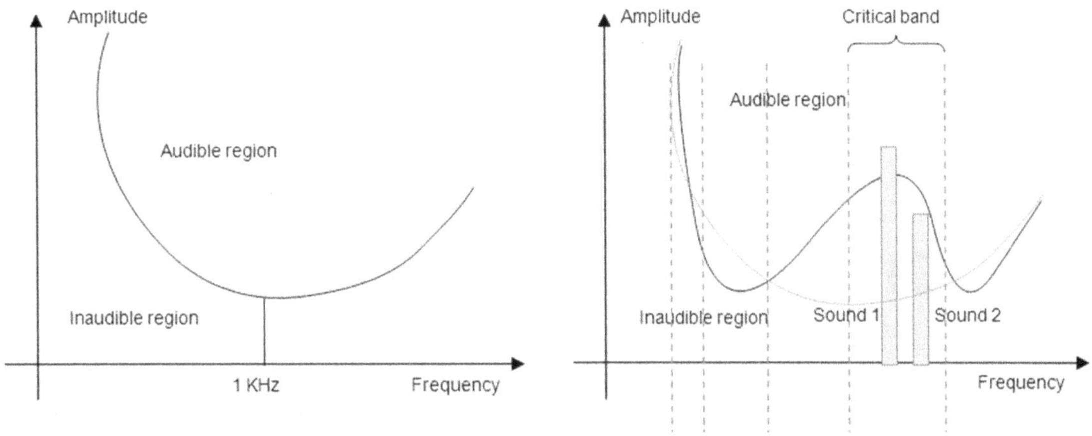

FIGURE 5.4
Minimum threshold curve and masking.

motion of the entire wave forward. A single sound wave (tone) is represented by a sinusoidal curve and is describe by equation: $y = a.\sin(\omega t)$, where 'a' is the amplitude, 'ω' is the angular frequency and 't' is the time. The concept of angular frequency is derived from the fact that a sinusoidal wave is produced by a simple harmonic motion (SHM) of an oscillating spring loaded weight attached to a particle P rotating along a circle at uniform speed, by a flexible string. As the particle rotates once around the circle, the weight makes one oscillation and the mark it leaves on a moving paper in the background is one cycle of a sinusoidal wave. Thus one cycle of the wave is produced by one complete revolution of P, i.e., 2π radians. To generate a wave of frequency f (f cycles/s) P must move at the speed of $2\pi f$ radians/s which is defined as the angular frequency, i.e., $\omega = 2\pi f$ radians/s. Since the distance spanning across one cycle of the wave is the wavelength λ, the distance travelled by the wave in one second is $v = \lambda.f$ which is defined as its linear velocity. This motion of the wave is assumed to be along the positive x-axis from left to right, so each particle lags in phase with respect to the particle on the left. If θ be the phase lag between two particles separated by distance x, then equation of the wave taking into account all the particle becomes:

$$y = a.\sin(\omega t - \theta)$$

Now phase difference between two particles separated by wavelength λ is 2π, hence phase difference between particles separated by distance x is: $(2\pi / \lambda)x$. Equating this to θ the equation of the progressive wave can be written as:

$$y = a.\sin(\omega t - 2\pi x / \lambda)$$

Since the angular frequency $\omega = 2\pi f = 2\pi / T$ where $T = 1/f$ is the time period of the wave, an alternate form of the above equation can also be:

$$y = a.\sin\{2\pi(ft - x/\lambda)\} = a.\sin\{2\pi(t/T - x/\lambda)$$

For a particular value of time t, the equation describes a snapshot of the wave at one instant where each value of x describes the state of a particle in the path of the wave at that instant. For a particular value of x, the equation describes the motion of a single particle over time t.

5.2 Audio I/O

Audio capture and recording serve as the foundation of audio production in multimedia technology. To process sound, environmental sound waves need to be converted to electrical signals. This is done using a device called microphone. The electrical outputs from the microphone are proportional to the intensity of the sound energy. These voltage levels are usually quite small and are boosted up using an amplifier arrangement. During audio playback the electrical signals are converted back to environmental sound using a loudspeaker arrangement (Huber & Runstein, 2017).

5.2.1 Microphones

A microphone is a transducer that converts variations in air pressure, or sound waves, into an electrical signal. The basic principle of how a microphone works involves the conversion of acoustic energy into electrical energy through the movement of specific components within the microphone. When a sound is

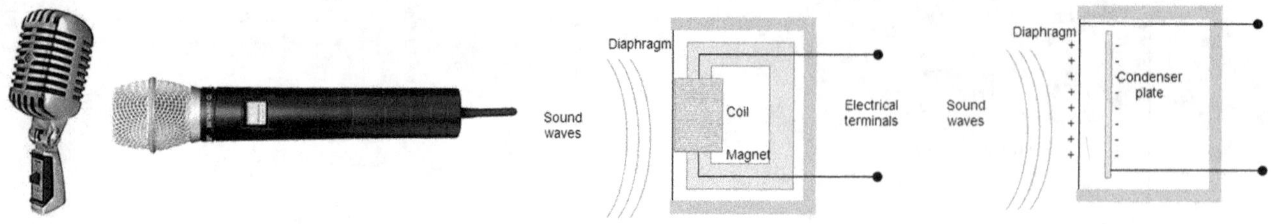

FIGURE 5.5
Microphone structural types (a) dynamic type (b) condenser type.

produced, it generates variations in air pressure known as sound waves. These waves consist of compressions and rarefactions, which are regions of high and low pressure, respectively. The diaphragm is a thin, flexible membrane that is a crucial component of most microphones. It is positioned at the front of the microphone and acts as a barrier between the external environment and the internal components. The diaphragm is typically made of materials like plastic, metal or mylar. When sound waves hit the diaphragm, they cause it to vibrate or move back and forth. The movement of the diaphragm corresponds to the changes in air pressure caused by the incoming sound waves. The diaphragm is connected to a transducer mechanism, which generates an electrical current proportional to the diaphragm's movement. This electrical signal is an analog representation of the original sound and contains information about the frequency, amplitude and other characteristics of the sound. The electrical signal is then transmitted through the microphone's output connections.

5.2.1.1 Structural Types

Based on structural aspects, microphones are broadly divided into moving coil and condenser types. Moving coil or dynamic microphones are rugged and versatile transducers known for their durability. They operate based on electromagnetic induction, utilizing a diaphragm attached to a coil within a magnetic field. When sound waves hit the diaphragm, it moves, causing the coil to move within the magnetic field, this movement induces an electrical current, generating the microphone signal. This design makes dynamic microphones ideal for capturing loud sound sources, such as musical instruments and live performances, and can handle high sound pressure levels (SPL) without distortion, making them a staple in live sound reinforcement. Condenser microphones are prized for their sensitivity and accuracy; they have a diaphragm, which is typically very thin and lightweight, placed close to a back-plate, forming a capacitor. The electrical charge on the capacitor varies with the movement of the diaphragm in response to sound waves, and an external power source is required to maintain the charge (Figure 5.5). These microphones excel in capturing light and subtle sound, making them the preferred choice for studio recording (Huber & Runstein, 2017).

5.2.1.2 Functional Types

Based on functional aspects, microphones can be divided into omnidirectional, bidirectional and unidirectional. An omnidirectional microphone is equally sensitive toward sounds coming from all directions and suitable for wildlife recording and conference proceedings. It consists of a container open at one end, containing a diaphragm inside. Sounds coming from all directions enter through the opening and impinge on the diaphragm causing it to vibrate. For a fixed distance, sounds from all directions produce the same vibration in the diaphragm and hence the same electrical output. A bidirectional microphone is sensitive toward sounds coming from the front and rear while rejecting sound from the sides, and suitable for interview setups. It consists of a container with a diaphragm inside and two openings on opposite sides. Sounds from both the openings create a differential force to vibrate the diaphragm; however, sounds from the sides create equal and opposite pressures to inhibit vibration. Unidirectional microphones are sensitive toward sounds coming from only the front making them suitable for situations where background noise rejection is essential like studio vocals. It consists of a resistive material on one side of the diaphragm to dampen sounds from the rear resulting in the microphone being sensitive to sounds only from the front (Figure 5.6).

5.2.1.3 Polar Plots

The polar pattern, or polar plot, of a microphone defines how its sensitivity varies with the direction of incoming sound. Omnidirectional microphones have a circular polar pattern, capturing sound equally from all directions. Bidirectional microphones capture sound equally from the front and back while rejecting

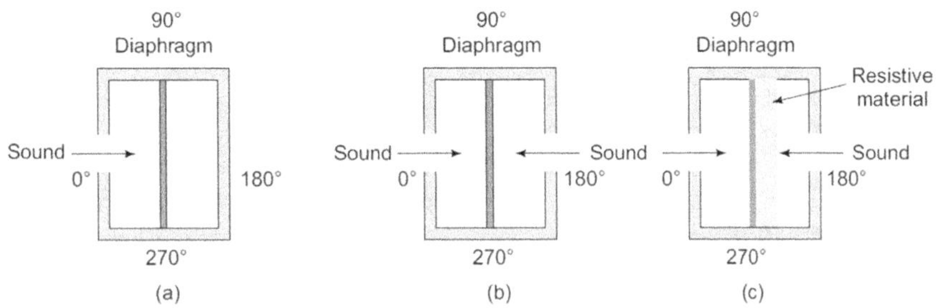

FIGURE 5.6
Microphone functional types (a) omnidirectional (b) bidirectional (c) unidirectional.

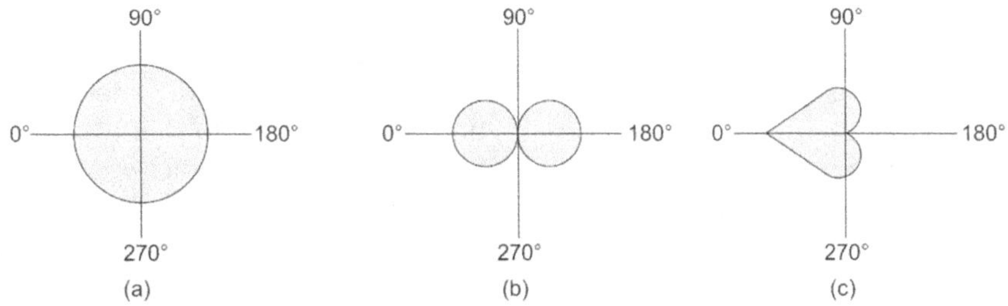

FIGURE 5.7
Polar plots (a) omnidirectional, (b) bidirectional, (c) unidirectional.

sound from the sides which makes their polar plot resemble a figure "8" along the horizontal. Unidirectional microphones have sensitivity maximum at the front and minimum at the rear, and decrease gradually from the front to the rear, resulting in a decreased, but non-zero, value at the sides. The polar plot is heart-shaped, due to which such microphones are also known as cardioid microphones (Figure 5.7).

5.2.2 Amplifiers

Audio amplifiers are electronic devices that increase the amplitude of audio signals, making them suitable for driving speakers or other output devices. The amplifier ensures that weak audio signals from sources like microphones, musical instruments or audio sources are powerful enough to drive speakers and produce audible sound. The input stage is responsible for receiving the weak audio signal from the source. This stage often includes components like coupling capacitors to block DC components and ensure that only the AC audio signal passes through. The heart of the amplifier, the amplification stage, increases the amplitude of the audio signal. This stage typically involves electronic components like transistors or operational amplifiers (op-amps). In analog amplifiers, the amplification is achieved through the use of active devices, such as transistors configured in various amplifier configurations (common emitter, common collector, etc.). Many amplifiers incorporate feedback networks to stabilize the amplification process and control the frequency response. Feedback helps in achieving a more linear and predictable performance. Some amplifiers include tone control circuits, such as bass and treble adjustments, to allow users to customize the audio frequency response according to their preferences. The volume control circuit allows users to adjust the output level of the amplifier. This can be achieved using a potentiometer (variable resistor) in the signal path. The output stage is responsible for delivering the amplified signal to the load, usually speakers. This stage often employs power transistors or other power devices capable of handling higher current and power levels. The power supply provides the necessary voltage and current to the various stages of the amplifier.

The audio amplifier begins by receiving a weak audio signal from a source, such as a microphone or audio source. The input signal is then amplified in the amplification stage. The amplification factor is determined by the characteristics of the active devices (transistors, op-amps) and the feedback network. If present, tone control circuits and volume control circuits adjust the tonal balance and overall output level of the amplifier. The amplified signal is sent to the output stage, which is capable of driving the connected load, typically speakers. The power supply ensures a stable and regulated voltage for the amplifier's operation, contributing to overall performance and efficiency.

Audio amplifiers are classified into different classes based on their operational characteristics. The primary amplifier classes are Class-A, Class-B, Class-AB and Class-D. Each class has its own set of working principles, advantages and limitations. In a Class-A amplifier, the active device (usually a transistor) conducts throughout the entire 360 degrees of the input signal cycle. The transistor remains on for the entire signal cycle, conducting even when there is no input signal. This ensures that there is always current flowing through the output device, eliminating crossover distortion. Class-A amplifiers are known for their excellent linearity, producing minimal distortion. They are, however, less efficient as the transistor is always conducting, leading to higher power dissipation.

In a Class-B amplifier, the active devices (usually a pair of transistors or tubes) conduct only for half of the input signal cycle. One device conducts during the positive half-cycle, and the other conducts during the negative half-cycle. This eliminates the DC bias present in Class-A, but it introduces crossover distortion at the point where one device hands over to the other. Class-B amplifiers are more efficient than Class-A, as the devices only conduct during half of the cycle. However, the issue of crossover distortion needs to be addressed for optimal performance.

Class-AB amplifiers aim to combine the linearity of Class-A with the efficiency of Class-B. They use a small bias current to keep the active device conducting slightly even when there is no input signal, reducing crossover distortion. Class-AB amplifiers provide better efficiency compared to Class-A. The biasing helps reduce crossover distortion, making them suitable for applications requiring a balance between efficiency and linearity.

Class-D amplifiers, also known as switching amplifiers, use pulse-width modulation (PWM) or pulse-density modulation to amplify the input signal. The audio signal is converted into a series of pulses with varying widths, and these pulses control the output devices (transistors) to reproduce the amplified signal. Class-D amplifiers are highly efficient, as the output devices are either fully on or fully off, minimizing power dissipation. They are often more compact and lighter than analog amplifiers.

Each amplifier class has its own set of advantages and trade-offs, and the choice of which class to use depends on the specific requirements of the application, such as power efficiency, linearity and size constraints. Class-A and Class-AB amplifiers are often preferred in high-fidelity audio applications, while Class-D amplifiers are popular in applications where power efficiency is critical (Figure 5.8).

5.2.3 Loudspeakers

A loudspeaker is a device that converts electrical energy back to acoustic energy and, therefore, functions just opposite to that of a microphone. Electrical signals from an amplifier or a playback system are fed to the loudspeaker based on which it generates environmental sound whose loudness is proportional to the amplitude of the source electrical signal. The dynamic loudspeakers are based on the traditional design of a wire coil and a paper cone. A cone made of paper or fiber, known as the diaphragm, is attached to a coil of wire, kept near a permanent magnet. When current from a source system is passed through the coil, a magnetic field is generated around the coil, this field interacts with the magnetic field of the permanent magnet generating vibrating forces that oscillate the diaphragm. The diaphragm oscillates in the same frequency as the original electrical signal and, therefore, reproduces the same sounds that had been used to encode the signal in the first place. All these components are enclosed in a container that additionally includes a suspension system that provides lateral stability to the vibrating components (Figure 5.9).

Due to resonance characteristics, the physical properties of a vibrating element makes it suitable to reproduce sounds of a specific frequency range, instead of the entire 20 kHz human audible range. Thicker and heavier diaphragms are suitable for low-frequency sounds while thinner and lighter elements are suitable for high frequencies. Thus, to get a good response over the entire audible range, a loudspeaker is divided into smaller units, each of which is tuned for a small

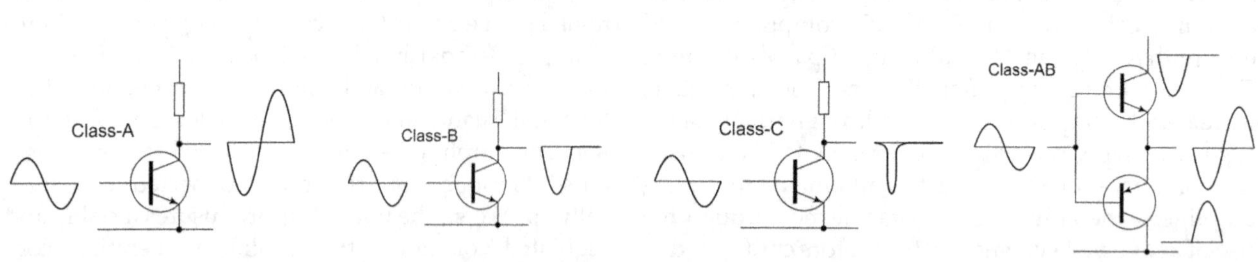

FIGURE 5.8
Types of amplifiers.

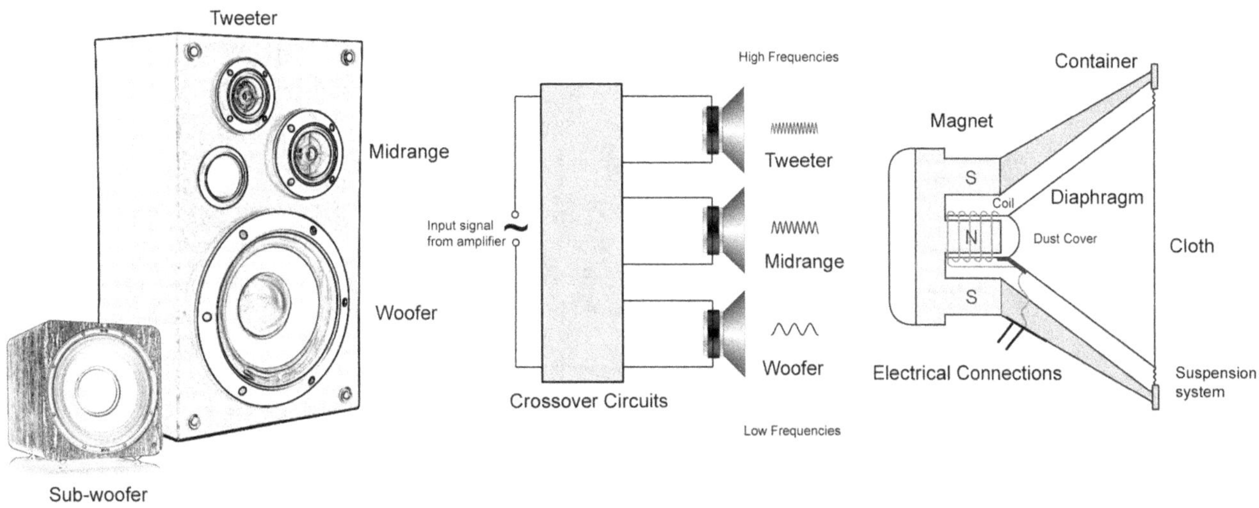

FIGURE 5.9
Loudspeakers.

frequency range. Through the use of filters known as crossover circuits, appropriate frequencies are filtered from the input signal and fed to corresponding units. These units are the following: (1) Woofers handle low frequencies, ranging from 20 Hz to 400 Hz. Such low frequency sounds are known as bass. (2) Mid-range speakers are designed to handle middle frequency ranges between 400 Hz and 4kHz. (3) Tweeters are designed to handle high frequency ranges between 4 kHz and 20 kHz. Such high-frequency sounds are known as treble. Since the high-frequency sounds have short wavelengths, they have high directional properties and hence placement of tweeter units becomes critical for good perceived sound quality. (4) Modern speaker systems often include a subwoofer for handling the very low frequencies below 100 Hz. The long wavelengths of the subwoofer sounds make it impossible for the user to perceive the direction of the sound source. Hence, a single subwoofer unit is sufficient irrespective of the number of channels in a music system, leading to designations such as 5.1 system, where the.1 refers to the single subwoofer corresponding to the 5 other channels (Toole, 2017).

Home audio systems utilize various types of speaker drivers to reproduce sound accurately and efficiently. Three common types of drivers used in home audio systems are dynamic cone drivers, ribbon drivers and horn speakers. Dynamic cone drivers are the most widely used type where a diaphragm is connected to a voice coil, the coil moves within a magnetic field, producing sound vibrations. Dynamic cone drivers are known for their versatility and ability to reproduce a wide range of frequencies. Ribbon drivers use a thin metal ribbon suspended in a magnetic field, as electrical current passes through the ribbon, it moves, generating sound. Ribbon drivers are known for their fast response and accurate reproduction of high frequencies. Horn speakers use a flared structure (horn) to amplify sound waves, allowing for greater efficiency. They are often used in public address systems and high-fidelity audio setups.

Most headphones and earphones use dynamic drivers to convert electrical signals into sound. These drivers consist of a diaphragm and a coil in a magnetic field, producing sound vibrations. In high-end headphones, planar magnetic drivers provide improved accuracy and response. These drivers use a thin, lightweight diaphragm with a planar magnetic array, resulting in lower distortion and enhanced clarity. Found in premium electrostatic headphones, electrostatic drivers use an ultra-thin diaphragm between two electrically charged plates. They deliver exceptional detail and speed but often require dedicated amplifiers.

Widely used for wireless audio, Bluetooth technology [www.bluetooth.com] enables seamless connections between devices. Bluetooth codecs, such as aptX [www.aptx.com] enhance the quality of wireless audio transmission. High-quality audio streaming is achieved through Wi-Fi [www.wi-fi.org] technologies. Devices like smart speakers often use Wi-Fi for multi-room audio and high-resolution playback. Advanced wireless protocols like AirPlay [www.apple.com/airplay] and Chromecast [support.google.com/chromecast] provide high-fidelity audio streaming and multi-device synchronization, enhancing the overall user experience.

Digital signal processing is used to manipulate and enhance audio signals, and enables features like room correction, bass management and virtual surround

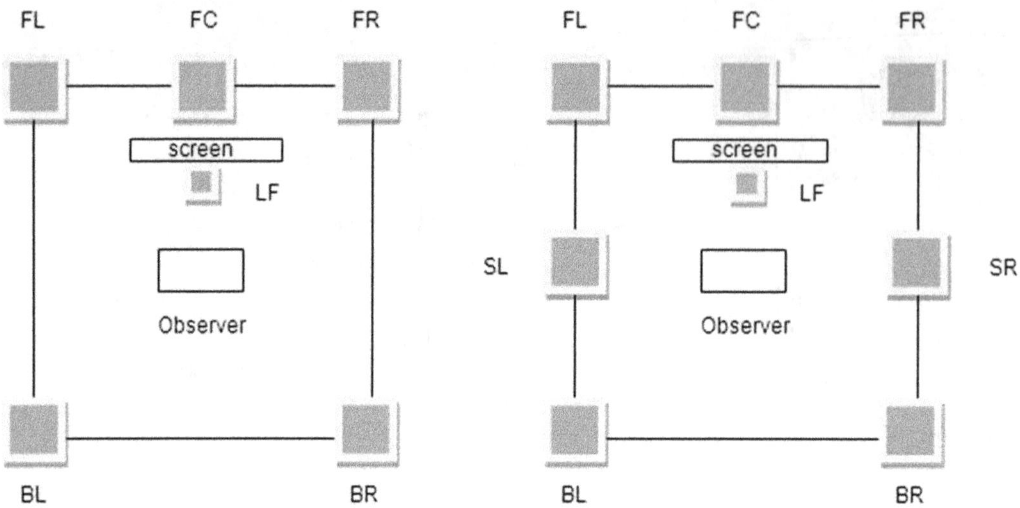

FIGURE 5.10
Surround sound schemes.

sound. Technologies like Audyssey [audyssey.com] and Dirac [dirac.com/live] aim to correct for acoustic anomalies in a room, optimizing audio playback for the specific characteristics of the listening environment. Audio equalization allows users to adjust frequency response using parametric equalizers for precise control over specific frequency bands, allowing for fine-tuning of audio output. In gaming, technologies like binaural audio and HRTF (Head-Related Transfer Function) aim to create a more immersive 3D audio experience, enhancing spatial awareness for gamers.

5.2.4 Surround Sound Technologies

Surround sound systems are designed to simulate a 3D audio environment by placing multiple speakers at strategic locations around the room, thereby immersing the listener to a more engaging experience. Human auditory systems relies on cues like inter-aural time difference (ITD) and inter-aural level difference (ILD) to determine the location of the sound source in 3D space. Surround sound systems use such parameters to replicate spatial audio and a sense of directionality. Multiple audio channels are assigned specific roles like front, back, left, right to generate sound localization. These arrangements are referred to as 5.1 or 7.1 systems. The former consists of five speakers placed with respect to the observer at front-center (FC), front-left (FL), front-right (FR), back-left (BL) and back-right (BR) along with a low-frequency sub-woofer in the middle, while the latter consists of two additional speakers at side-left (SL) and side-right (SR). The sub-woofer, responsible for reproducing low-frequency effects (LFE) like deep bass, which have omnidirectional properties, allows for flexibility in their placements (Cardone, 2021) (Figure 5.10).

Early surround sound systems like Dolby Pro Logic and Dolby Digital relied on channel-based format which was effective for creating directional audio but had limitations in reproducing height information. Object-based audio technologies like Dolby Atmos [www.dolby.com/technologies/dolby-atmos] and DTS:X [www.dts.com/dtsx] represent audio as objects in 3D space, which allow designers to specify location and movement of individual audio objects independently creating a more dynamic experience. Ambisonics is a full-sphere surround sound technique that captures audio information from all directions and utilizes a spherical coordinate system to represent sound sources in three dimensions. Ambisonic recordings can be decoded for playback on various speaker configurations or for use in virtual reality environments, ensuring a high degree of flexibility in audio reproduction.

Introduced in the early 1990s, Dolby Digital (AC-3) is a widely adopted audio compression technology, and supports up to 5.1 channels (front left, front center, front right, rear left, rear right and a subwoofer). It is commonly used in DVDs, Blu-ray discs and digital broadcasting. A high-definition audio codec, Dolby TrueHD supports up to 7.1 channels of lossless audio, and often found in Blu-ray discs, providing superior audio quality for home theatre systems. Similar to Dolby Digital, DTS Digital Surround is a widely used audio codec in DVDs, Blu-ray discs and digital broadcasting, supports up to 5.1 channels and is known for its high-quality audio, while DTS-HD Master Audio is a high definition audio codec and supports 7.1 channels of lossless audio. Developed by Lucasfilm, THX

Surround [www.thx.com] is a set of audio and video standards aimed at ensuring high-quality reproduction of content in cinemas and home theatres. THX Surround typically includes configurations like THX Spatial Audio [www.thx.com/spatial-audio] for home theatres, providing a cinematic audio experience. Virtual surround sound technologies like Dolby Headphone [www.dolby.com/experience/headphones] and DTS Headphone:X [www.dts.com/dts-headphonex] simulate a surround sound experience through stereo headphones.

5.2.5 Sound Card

A sound card, also known as an audio interface or audio card, is a hardware component that facilitates audio input and output for a computer. It features various input and output ports that enable connectivity with different audio devices, as well as the necessary components for digitization of sound.

5.2.5.1 I/O Ports

Microphone In port: A 3.5mm (1/8-inch) or 6.35mm (1/4-inch) jack designated for connecting external microphones. Some sound cards may also have XLR inputs for professional microphones. Used for capturing audio from microphones, whether for voice recording, podcasting, or musical instrument recording.

Line-In: A 3.5mm (1/8-inch) or 6.35mm (1/4-inch) stereo jack for connecting line-level audio sources, such as CD players, musical instruments, or other audio playback devices. It is useful for capturing audio from external sources other than microphones.

Speaker/Line-Out: A 3.5mm (1/8-inch) or 6.35mm (1/4-inch) stereo jack for connecting external speakers, headphones, or audio playback devices, used to send audio signals to speakers or headphones for monitoring or playback.

Line-Out (Rear or Surround): Additional line-out ports, often labeled for rear, surround, or other channels, found in 5.1, 7.1 or surround sound setups, used in multi-channel audio setups, such as home theatre systems or surround sound configurations.

Digital Output (SPDIF or Optical Out): A digital audio output port, often in SPDIF (Sony/Philips Digital Interface) or optical format, for connecting to external digital audio equipment or home theatre systems. It transmits digital audio signals without the need for analog conversion, maintaining signal quality.

MIDI Input/Output: MIDI (Musical Instrument Digital Interface) ports, often in the form of 5-pin DIN connectors, for connecting MIDI devices like keyboards, synthesizers or controllers. It facilitates communication between the computer and MIDI-capable musical instruments or controllers.

Firewire/USB Inputs and Outputs: Some audio interfaces have additional input and output options via Firewire (IEEE 1394) or USB connections. Enables connectivity with external audio devices or expands the number of available input and output channel.

5.2.5.2 Components

Analog-to-Digital Conversion (ADC): At the heart of a sound card's architecture lies the Analog-to-Digital Converter (ADC), responsible for transforming analog audio signals from sources such as microphones or musical instruments into digital data that can be processed by the computer. The quality of the ADC greatly influences the overall sound quality captured by the sound card.

Memory Bank: This denotes the local memory of the sound card for storing audio data during digitization and playback of sound files. When digital audio files needs to be played back, the audio data is first stored in the memory buffer before being processed by the Digital-to-Analog Converter (DAC) for conversion to analog format. Again, when an analog input is digitized, the digital audio data is temporarily stored in the memory buffer before being written to the hard disk as a file.

Digital Signal Processor (DSP): Sound cards often incorporate a Digital Signal Processor (DSP), which is a specialized microprocessor designed to handle the mathematical computations involved in audio processing. The DSP executes various algorithms for tasks such as equalization, spatialization and effects processing. The inclusion of a DSP enhances the sound card's capability to manipulate audio signals in real time.

Digital-to-Analog Conversion (DAC): On the output side, the Digital-to-Analog Converter (DAC) plays a crucial role. It converts digital audio data back into analog signals that can be sent to speakers or headphones. Similar to

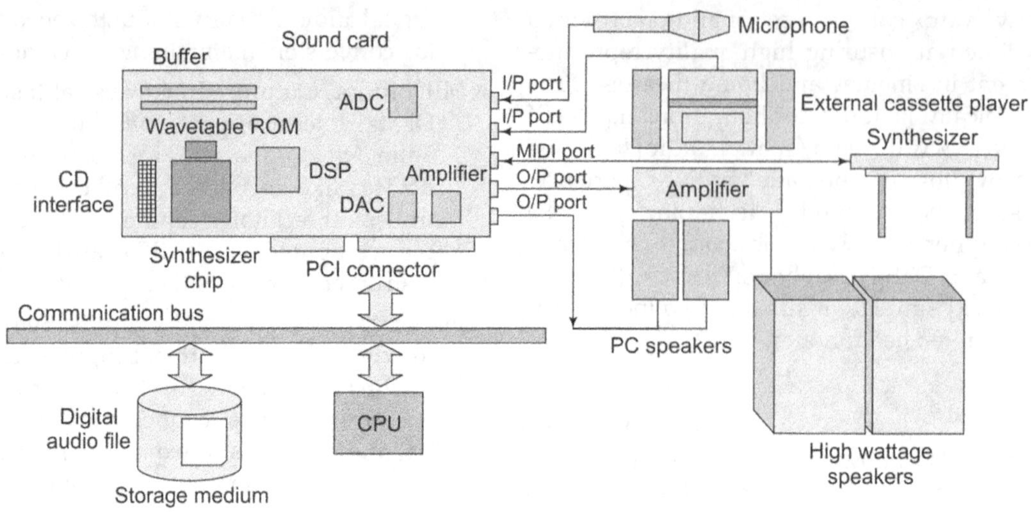

FIGURE 5.11
Sound card interfaces.

the ADC, the quality of the DAC significantly impacts the fidelity of the audio playback.

MIDI Synthesizer chip: A MIDI synthesizer chip is necessary to recognize MIDI sequences recorded onto the disk or input from an external synthesizer. MIDI files don't contain actual audio data but rather musical instructions. This chip interprets the instructions and generates the required sounds (Figure 5.11).

5.2.6 Digital Audio Representation

5.2.6.1 Audio Digitization

The digitization of sound by a sound card involves converting analog audio signals into digital data that can be processed, stored and manipulated by a computer. The process typically follows these key steps:

Analog Sound Source: The sound digitization process starts with an analog sound source, such as a microphone, musical instrument or another analog audio device. The sound waves generated by the source represent variations in air pressure.

Analog-to-Digital Conversion (ADC): The analog audio signal is then directed to the Analog-to-Digital Converter (ADC) on the sound card. The ADC is a crucial component responsible for transforming the continuous analog signal into discrete digital data. This involves two main steps: sampling and quantization.

Sampling: The ADC samples the amplitude of the analog signal at regular intervals, capturing a snapshot of the waveform at each instance. The rate at which these samples are taken is known as the sample rate, measured in Hertz (Hz).

Quantization: The amplitude values obtained from sampling are then quantized, meaning they are assigned specific numerical values. The number of bits used for quantization determines the precision of each sample and is known as the bit depth. A higher bit depth allows for a more accurate representation of the analog signal.

Digital Data Representation: The result of the ADC process is a stream of digital data representing the sampled and quantized audio signal. Each sample is typically represented as a binary number, with the bit depth determining the range and precision of these values.

Digital Signal Processor (DSP): The Digital Signal Processor (DSP), a specialized microprocessor, coordinates the activities of the sound card. It can also perform mathematical operations on the digital audio data, such as equalization, filtering and compression in real time.

Transmission: The processed digital audio data is typically stored temporarily in a buffer before being transmitted to the computer's central processing unit (CPU) This transfer can occur through various interfaces, such as PCI, USB or PCIe, depending on the design of the sound card.

Software Processing: Once within the computer, the digitized audio data can be processed further by audio software. This might include editing, mixing, applying effects or other manipulations depending on the user's preferences or the requirements of a specific application.

Storage or Real-Time Playback: The digitized audio data can be stored as a file on the computer's storage system in formats like WAV, MP3 or others. Alternatively, the data can be played back in real time through speakers or headphones for immediate auditory perception.

5.2.6.2 Digital Audio Parameters

We have already discussed in Chapter 1 how an analog quantity is converted to digital form through the processes of sampling, quantization and code-word generation. It was seen that the digital form is a degraded version of the analog form because of quantization error; however, quality can be improved by increasing sampling rate. The upper value of sampling rate is limited by the hardware/software capabilities and economic considerations. However, the question that whether there is a lower limit of sampling rate below which the quality of the digital quantity becomes unacceptable arises is answered by Nyquist's sampling theory, i.e., sampling frequency needs to be twice the input frequency. We know that the full range of human hearing ranges from 20 Hz to 20 kHz. Thus, to be able to represent the entire range digitally, minimum sampling frequencies should be around 40 kHz. In practical systems a slightly higher frequency in the range of 44–48 kHz is employed during sampling. However, it is not necessary that we always sample at 44 kHz. This is true only when we want to represent all the frequencies the human ear responds to and is used mainly for recording musical instruments. For other purposes, e.g., for recording human speech, we can use a much lower sampling rate of the order of 11 kHz as we know human voice does not contain frequency components beyond 5.5 kHz. Although we have seen that increasing the sampling resolution increases the accuracy of the digital signal with respect to the analog input signal, it also increases the file size which in turn increases the cost of storage and manipulation. For practical purposes, unless we require extremely fine reproductions, bit depths of 8 bits and 16 bits are sufficient for our purposes. Digital audio offers several advantages over analog audio, including: (Cardone, 2021) Noise Reduction: Digital systems are less susceptible to noise and interference. (Cobussen & Nielsen, 2016) Editing and Processing: Digital audio can be easily edited and processed using software. (Davies, 2009) Storage and Reproduction: Digital audio is easily stored and transmitted in various formats. (Fourier, 1822) Durability: Digital media is less prone to wear and degradation over time (Pohlmann, 2010).

Let f be the frequency of the analog audio signal. During digitization, the minimum sampling rate F should be twice the signal frequency as per Nyquist's postulate. Hence:

$$F = 2f$$

Let b be the bit depth of the audio, and c be the number of channels. For mono sound, $c = 1$; for stereo, $c = 2$; and for multi-channel audio like surround sound, c can have higher values. Then data rate D of the digitized audio signal is the amount of data flowing per second in bits/second:

$$D = F.b.c$$

Let T be the duration of audio in seconds. Then number of samples N in the audio is given by

$$N = F.T$$

Let S be the file size of the audio on bits. The file size is derived by multiplying the data rate with the total duration:

$$S = D.T = F.b.c.T = 2f.b.c.t$$

5.2.6.3 CD Quality Audio

It is clear from the above equations that increasing the sampling rate and resolution, increases file size. This requires higher storage space and greater processing power. As a sample calculation we can consider the following: For an audio-CD, sampling is done at 44.1 kHz, 16-bit resolution and stereo mode. Thus, for a 1-minute sound clip we require a storage space of (44100 samples/second) × (60 second) × (16 bits/sample) × (2 channels) which is equal to 84672000 bits, or (84672000/8) = 10584000 bytes which is roughly equal to (10584000/(1024 × 1024)) = 10 MB. This gives us a thumb rule that each minute of CD quality audio requires 10 MB of storage space. Also the data rate for smooth playback is: (44100 samples/second) × (16 bits/sample) × (2 stereo channels) or 1.4 M bits/second. It may be noted here that the NTSC and PAL standards developed for TV transmission were in a way responsible for creating the standard sampling rate of 44,100 Hz for CD quality digital audio in the later part of 1970. This value of 44.1 kHz was thought to be compatible with both the standards due to the following reasoning. Although the NTSC proposes 525 horizontal lines per frame, i.e., 262 lines per field, taking into account the landing zones for the electron beam during raster scanning, there are actually 245 active lines per field which together with 30 frames per second, i.e., 60 fields per second, and three audio samples being encoded per video line, leads to a total of $245 \times 60 \times 3 = 44{,}100$ audio samples per second. Again for PAL which proposes 625 lines per frame, i.e., 312 lines per field, out of which 294 are active lines, and 25 frames per second, i.e., 50 fields per second, and three audio samples being encoded per video line, lead to a total of $294 \times 50 \times 3 = 44{,}100$ audio samples per second. Because of these computations, 44.1 kHz was considered to the best usable value compatible with the existing standards during the 1970s.

5.2.7 Audio Transmission

To convey digital audio data in real time between different hardware devices, there must be both a data communications channel and common clock synchronization. In addition, the interconnection requires an audio format recognized by both transmitting and receiving devices. Some important aspects are discussed below:

5.2.7.1 AES/EBU

The AES/EBU (Audio Engineering Society/European Broadcasting Union) standard is a digital audio interconnection standard used primarily in professional audio applications, such as studio recording, broadcasting and live sound reinforcement. It defines a digital audio interface for transmitting two channel uncompressed, linear pulse-code modulation (PCM) audio data between professional audio equipment. It allows for the high-quality transmission of audio signals with minimal degradation and interference, and specifies the electrical characteristics of the interface, including voltage levels, impedance and signal timing. The standard typically uses balanced, differential signaling over 110 ohm twisted-pair cables with XLR connectors, or 75 ohm BNC connector, and supports various sampling rates and bit depths for digital audio signals, including common rates such as 44.1 kHz (CD-quality), 48 kHz (standard for digital audio), and higher rates for high-resolution audio applications; bit depths typically range from 16 to 24 bits per sample. AES/EBU defines the format for transmitting digital audio data, including the arrangement of audio samples, synchronization signals and error detection/correction mechanisms and is widely adopted in professional audio equipment and is compatible with a variety of digital audio devices, including digital audio workstations (DAWs), audio interfaces, mixing consoles, digital signal processors (DSPs) and digital tape machines. The current version of the standard AES3 [www.aes.org/publications/standards/search.cfm?docID=13] has been incorporated as the standard IEC 60958 [webstore.iec.ch/publication/24413]. A consumer-grade variant of the standard is known as S/PDIF.

5.2.7.2 S/PDIF

The S/PDIF (Sony/Philips Digital Interface) audio standard is a digital audio interface is a consumer-grade variant of the AES3 used for consumer electronics applications. S/PDIF allows for the transmission of digital audio signals over coaxial cables or optical fibers. It provides a means of connecting audio sources, such as CD players, DVD players, Blu-ray players, digital audio players and computers, to audio receivers, soundbars, amplifiers and other audio equipment. The signal is transmitted either a coaxial cable using RCA or BNC connectors or a fiber optic cable using TOSLINK connectors. S/PDIF can carry two channels of uncompressed PCM audio or compressed 5.1 channel surround sound, as used in Dolby or DTS systems.

5.2.7.3 Audio Cables and Connectors

TRS (Tip-Ring-Sleeve) connectors, also known as 1/4-inch or 3.5 mm audio jacks, are commonly used for analog audio connections in various audio equipment, including headphones, microphones, musical instruments, amplifiers and audio interfaces. TRS connectors consist of three main sections: the tip, the ring and the sleeve. For stereo audio, the tip carries the left channel (L) or signal, the ring carries the right channel (R) or signal, and the sleeve serves as the common ground or return path for the signals. TRS connectors come in two main sizes: 1/4-inch (6.35 mm) and 3.5 mm (1/8-inch). The 1/4-inch TRS connectors are commonly used in professional audio equipment, musical instruments and amplifiers, while the 3.5 mm TRS connectors are more commonly found in consumer audio devices, headphones, smartphones and portable audio players. In some cases a smaller variant of 2.5 mm (1/10-inch) TRS connector is also used to connect smaller portable devices and compact headphones, while other variants like TS (tip sleeve) may be used for mono audio and TRRS (tip ring ring sleeve) may be used for a headset with microphone or a single cable carrying both video and stereo audio (Figure 5.12).

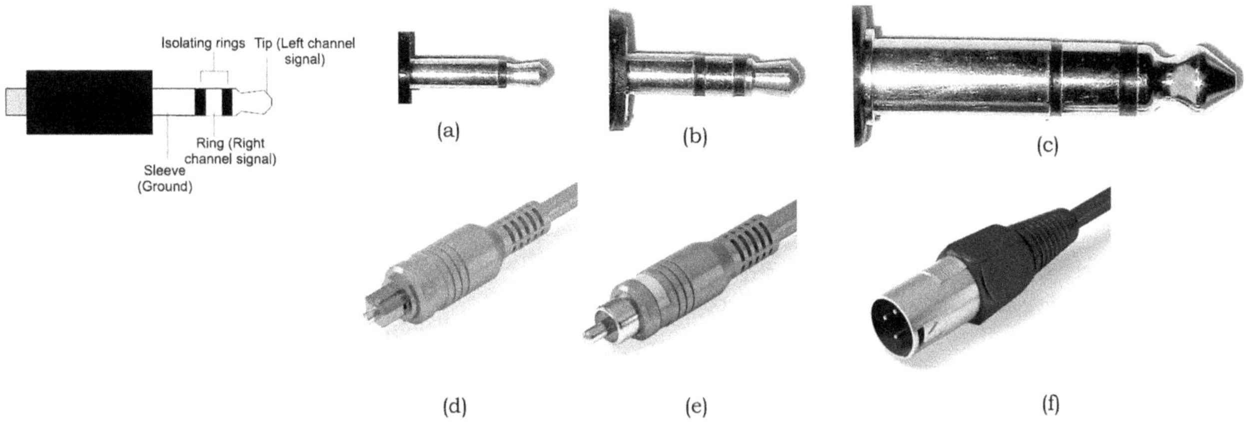

FIGURE 5.12
Audio connectors with TRS schematic (a) TS 2.5 mm, (b) TRS 3.5 mm, (c) TRS 6.35 mm, (d) TOSLINK (e) RCA (f) XLR.

5.2.8 Musical Instrument Digital Interface (MIDI)

Musical Instrument Digital Interface (MIDI) is a protocol for interfacing digital musical instruments like synthesizers to digital computers. It was first introduced in the early 1980s and has since become a crucial component in the world of electronic music production. Over the years, MIDI has undergone several revisions and extensions to accommodate the evolving needs of the music industry. The original MIDI 1.0 specification, introduced in 1983, laid the foundation for basic musical communication. Subsequent revisions included the introduction of General MIDI (GM) in 1991, which standardized instrument sounds across devices, ensuring consistent playback. The most recent significant update is the introduction of MIDI 2.0. Adopted in 2020, MIDI 2.0 represents a major leap forward in terms of capabilities and flexibility. Unlike its predecessor, MIDI 2.0 uses a bidirectional protocol, allowing devices to communicate more nuanced musical information, system updates and parameter changes in both directions. Additionally, MIDI 2.0 supports higher resolution, enabling more precise control over musical elements. The MIDI protocol has three major portions: hardware, messages and file format. Technical issues and updates are handled by the MIDI Manufacturers Association (MMA) [www.midi.org] (Rumsey, 2003).

5.2.8.1 MIDI Hardware

The first part called hardware specifications outlines the cables, connectors, signal formats and pin layouts required for connecting one MIDI device to another. A MIDI controller is a keyboard-like device which when played by pressing keys generates a set of digital instructions defining how sound is to be played. The sound module interprets the instruction and generates the required sound. MIDI hardware communication primarily occurs through 5-pin DIN connectors. These connectors carry three separate communication channels: MIDI IN, MIDI OUT and MIDI THRU. The MIDI IN port receives incoming MIDI data, the MIDI OUT port transmits outgoing data and the MIDI THRU port replicates the incoming data for daisy-chaining multiple devices. MIDI cables, featuring a standard 5-pin DIN connector on each end, carry the electrical signals between MIDI-compatible devices. The use of separate connectors for input and output ensures unidirectional communication, maintaining the integrity of MIDI data flow. MIDI communication relies on a current loop electrical interface. The electrical specifications of the MIDI hardware protocol include a voltage range of approximately 0 to 5 volts. A logical '0' is represented by a current flow of at least 5 mA, while a logical "1" is indicated by the absence of current flow. This current loop design helps mitigate interference and noise issues common in musical environments. The MIDI interface utilizes opto-isolation to further enhance signal integrity. This involves the use of optocouplers to isolate the electronic circuits of different devices, protecting them from potential electrical issues such as ground loops and voltage fluctuations. Common MIDI hardware devices include controllers, synthesizers, sound modules, interface adapters, merger and splitters.

MIDI Controllers: These devices include keyboards, drum pads and other input devices that generate MIDI data based on user interaction. MIDI controllers typically have MIDI OUT ports to send data to synthesizers or computers. A MIDI controller is a device that is played as an instrument, like a keyboard. However, unlike a piano keyboard, the keys when pressed do not directly generate sound based on physical processes like vibration, but generate a set of digital instructions which define how sound is to be created.

Sequencers and sound Modules: These devices receive MIDI data through their MIDI IN ports, translating the information into audio signals. Sequencers allow MIDI data sequences to be captured, stored, edited, combined and replayed. Sound modules interpret MIDI instructions and produce sound typically from a wavetable chip inside it.

MIDI Interface adapters: External MIDI interface adapters, bridge the gap between MIDI hardware and computers. They often provide USB or serial connectivity and allow MIDI data to be transferred bidirectionally, enabling integration with digital audio workstations (DAWs) and software instruments.

MIDI Merger and Splitter Boxes: Merger boxes combine multiple MIDI inputs into a single output, facilitating the integration of multiple controllers. Splitter boxes, on the other hand, divide a single MIDI input into multiple outputs, useful for controlling multiple devices simultaneously (Figure 5.13).

5.2.8.2 MIDI Channels

MIDI uses concept of logical channels to facilitate communication between devices. MIDI channels are essentially communication pathways such that each channel can carry distinct musical information. Devices set to the same channel respond to the messages while others remain unaffected. MIDI channels contribute to polyphony by allowing simultaneous transmission of multiple notes, but each channel is associated with a specific instrument sound, for example one channel may be set for piano sounds and another channel for drum sounds. A MIDI sequencer can record data from multiple channels onto separate tracks for later editing. The concept of channels can be thought to be analogous to layers in an image editor with the idea that separate entities can be manipulated independently within a larger composition. As per MIDI 1.0 specifications, number could be maximum 16, but MIDI 2.0 has the potential to support a larger number of channels.

5.2.8.3 MIDI Message Format

The second part, called the message format, defines how the musical information traveling from one device to another needs to be coded. The message format uses a three-byte structure where the first byte defines the actual note to be played, while the remaining two bytes define additional related information like the note number and velocity (pressure). The MIDI protocol relies on this standardized message format to facilitate communication between electronic musical instruments and devices. Each MIDI message is a concise packet of information that instructs devices on various musical events and control parameters. A standard MIDI message consists of three bytes transmitted serially at a rate of 31.25 kbps. These bytes are categorized as follows:

Status Byte (8 bits): The first byte in a MIDI message is the status byte, which indicates the type of message being sent. It begins with the status bit (always set to 1) followed by a 3-bit command, specifying the nature of the message (e.g., note-on, note-off, control change). The remaining 4 bits represent the MIDI channel (1 to 16).

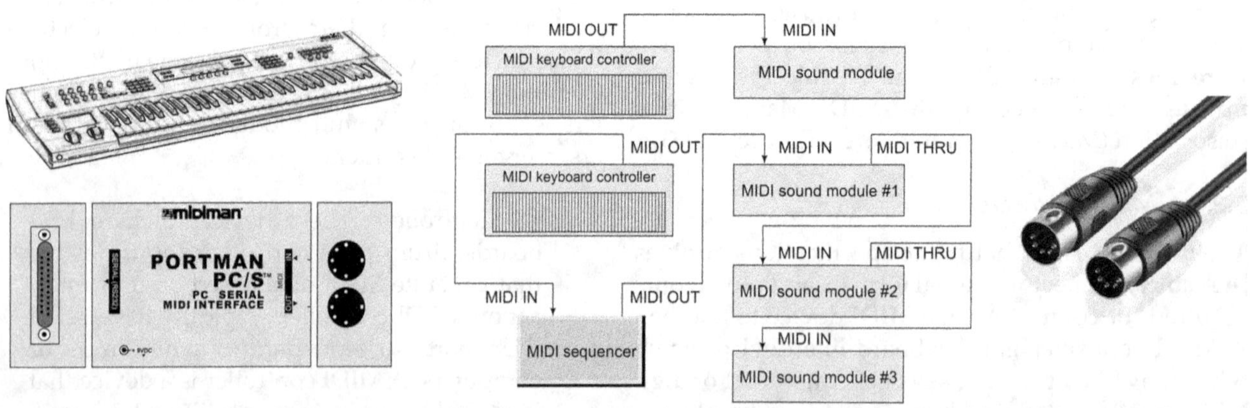

FIGURE 5.13
MIDI hardware.

Data Byte 1 (8 bits): The second byte, also known as the data byte 1, follows the status byte and carries additional information depending on the type of message. For example, in a note-on message, this byte represents the note number, while in a control change message, it corresponds to the controller number.

Data Byte 2 (8 bits): The third byte, or data byte 2, follows data byte 1 and provides further information based on the message type. For note-on and note-off messages, it represents the velocity or pressure, while for control change messages, it specifies the new value of the controller.

MIDI messages are categorized as channel message or system message. Channel messages are those that apply to a specific channel, and the channel number is included in the status byte for these messages. System messages are not channel specific, but apply to the system as a whole, and no channel number is indicated in their status bytes. Channel messages may be further classified as being either channel voice messages, or channel mode messages. Channel Voice Messages carry musical performance data, and these messages comprise most of the traffic in a typical MIDI data stream. The messages in this category include the Note On, Note Off, Polyphonic Aftertouch, Pitch Bend, Program Change, Channel Pressure Aftertouch and the Control Change messages. A Note On message, having status byte range 0x90 to 0x9F, is used to signal start of a musical note and specifies which note to play, on which channel and with what velocity (intensity or pressure). Similarly a Note Off message, having status byte range 0x80 to 0x8F, is used to signal stop playing a musical note. A Polyphonic Aftertouch message, with range 0xA0 to 0xAF, indicates amount of pressure to be applied on a key; a Control Change message, 0xB0 to 0xBF, is used to control a wide variety of functions, e.g., to expand the number of different instrument sounds and to edit sound in specific ways; a Program Change message, 0xC0 to 0xCF, indicate changing the preset program; a Channel Pressure Aftertouch message, 0xD0 to 0xDF, indicates pressure for all keys on a channel; a Pitch Bend message, 0xE0 to 0xEF, indicates change of pitch.

Channel Mode messages are a subset of Control Change message and has a status byte value of 0xB0. They use a controller number to indicate the function required. Controller number 121 is used to reset all controllers. Controller number 122 is used to enable or disable local control (In a MIDI synthesizer which has its own keyboard, the functions of the keyboard controller and the synthesizer can be isolated by turning Local Control off). Controller numbers 124 through 127 are used to select between omni mode On or Off, and to select between the mono mode or poly mode of operation. When omni mode is On, the synthesizer will respond to incoming MIDI data on all channels. When omni mode is Off, the synthesizer will only respond to MIDI messages on one channel. When poly mode is selected, incoming Note On messages are played polyphonically. This means that when multiple Note On messages are received, each note is assigned its own voice (subject to the number of voices available in the synthesizer). The result is that multiple notes are played at the same time. When mono mode is selected, a single voice is assigned per MIDI channel. This means that only one note can be played on a given channel at a given time.

System messages are classified as being System Common messages and System Real-time messages. System Common messages provide a way to communicate general information relevant to the entire MIDI systems. Examples include: Song Position Pointer (0xF2), Song Select (0xF3), Tune Request (0xF6). System Real-time messages provide a way to communicate information related to timing and synchronization. Examples include: Timing Clock (0xF8), Start (0xFA), Continue (0xFB), Stop (0xFC), Active Sensing (0xFE), System Reset (0xFF) (Figure 5.14).

5.2.8.4 MIDI File Format

The third part called file format defines how MIDI instructions are stored in a MIDI file. A MIDI file has the.MID or.MIDI extension. It serves as a standardized means to store musical information, enabling the exchange and playback of complex musical compositions across different platforms and software applications. A MIDI file is a binary file that organizes musical information into a structured format. It consists of a series of "chunks", each serving a specific purpose. The two primary types of chunks are the Header Chunk and the Track Chunks. A header chunk, identified by a chunk type of "MThd", indicates the type of MIDI file (0, 1 or 2) and specifies the total number of tracks in the MIDI file, as well as the timing resolution which indicates the number of divisions per quarter note (analogous to number of frames per second in video). The track chunk, identified by a chunk type of "MTrk", consists of MIDI events and messages encoded in a serialized fashion. Standard MIDI File Types can be of three types:

- Format 0: Single track representing a complete musical composition.

STATUS BYTE				DATA BYTES	
1st Byte Value			Function	2nd Byte	3rd Byte
Binary	Hex	Dec			
10000000	80	128	Chan 1 Note off	Note Number (0-127)	Note Velocity (0-127)
10000001	81	129	Chan 2 "		
10000010	82	130	Chan 3 "	"	"
10000011	83	131	Chan 4 "	"	"
10000100	84	132	Chan 5 "	"	"
...					
10010000	90	144	Chan 1 Note on	"	"
10010001	91	145	Chan 2 "	"	"
10010010	92	146	Chan 3 "	"	"
10010011	93	147	Chan 4 "	"	"
10010100	94	148	Chan 5 "	"	"
...					
11110110	F6	246	Tune request	NONE	NONE
11110111	F7	247	End of SysEx (EOX)	"	"
11111000	F8	248	Timing clock	"	"
11111001	F9	249	Undefined (Reserved)	"	"
11111010	FA	250	Start	"	"
11111011	FB	251	Continue	"	"
11111100	FC	252	Stop	"	"
11111101	FD	253	Undefined (Reserved)	"	"
11111110	FE	254	Active Sensing	"	"
11111111	FF	255	System Reset	"	"

FIGURE 5.14
MIDI message format.

- Format 1: Multiple tracks, each containing a different musical voice or element.
- Format 2: Multiple tracks but used for patterns or sequences rather than complete compositions.

5.2.8.5 Key Features of MIDI 2.0

MIDI 1.0, while ground-breaking in its time, faced limitations in terms of data resolution, expressive capabilities and flexibility. Recognizing the need for an upgrade the MMA collaborated with the Association of Music Electronics Industry (AMIE) to develop the MIDI 2.0 standard, which allows for bidirectional communication, higher resolution and precision in data transmission, access to a broader range of parameters and concept of profiles, among other features [www.midi.org/details-about-midi-2-0-midi-ci-profiles-and-property-exchange-updated-june-2023].

Bidirectional Communication: MIDI 2.0 allows devices to send and receive messages, fostering more interactive and dynamic communication between instruments and controllers.

Increased Resolution: MIDI 2.0 supports 32-bit resolution for parameter values, providing finer control over musical expression and nuances.

Expanded Expressiveness: Allows for a broader range of parameters including enhanced control over articulation, dynamics and a more extensive set of controllers.

Profiles: MIDI 2.0 introduces the concept of profiles, allowing devices to define and share specific sets of capabilities, making it easier for instruments to work seamlessly together.

Backward Compatibility: Despite its significant enhancements, MIDI 2.0 remains backward compatible with MIDI 1.0, ensuring that existing MIDI equipment can still function in a MIDI 2.0 environment.

5.3 Audio Editing and Processing

Digital audio editing is the process of manipulating and modifying sound using computer-based software.

It involves tasks such as cutting, copying, pasting and rearranging audio segments to enhance or alter the original recording. Additionally, digital audio editing allows for the application of various effects, equalization and mastering techniques to achieve desired audio quality and creative outcomes (Jackson, 2015).

5.3.1 Segmentation

Since the characteristics of an audio signal change over time, the first step of audio processing involves segmenting the entire audio signal into segments called audio frames and then processing each frame individually. Suppose a digital audio signal x contains n samples represented as:

$$x = [x(1), x(2)\ldots, x(n)]$$

The audio file needs to be partitioned into m number of audio frames, duration of each frame being tf seconds. If fs be the sampling rate of the audio, then number of samples per frame $nf = tf * fs$ and number of frames in the file is $m = n / nf$. The first frame starts with sample index number 1 and ends with sample index nf, the second frame from $nf + 1$ to $2nf$, the third frame from $2nf + 1$ to $3nf$ and so on. Then the k-th frame starts with sample index $(k-1)*nf$ and ends at $(k*nf)$.

$$f1 = \{1, nf\},$$

$$f2 = \{nf + 1, 2nf\}$$

$$f3 = \{2nf + 1, 3nf\}$$

$$\ldots$$

$$fk = \{(k-1)*nf, k*nf\}$$

If each of these frames is processed individually, say, undergo normalization, and then re-joined again, then there is a discontinuity between neighboring frames. This is audible to the human ear as a clicking sound. One solution to this is for the frames to partially overlap with each other. Overlap means that instead of straightforward segmentation of the audio vector into sequential frames, each new frame is made to contain a part of the previous frame and part of the next frame. Overlapping ensures that the fringe effects are reduced. The degree of overlap (usually expressed as a percentage) describes the amount of the previous frame that is repeated in the following frame. Overlaps of 25% and 50% are common. However, this leads to another problem, i.e., we end up with more audio: a 50% overlap doubles the number of frames that need to be processed. The work-around for many of the segmentation and overlap problems is windowing prior to reassembly. A judicious choice of window alleviates the joining together of overlapped, processed frames (Figure 5.15).

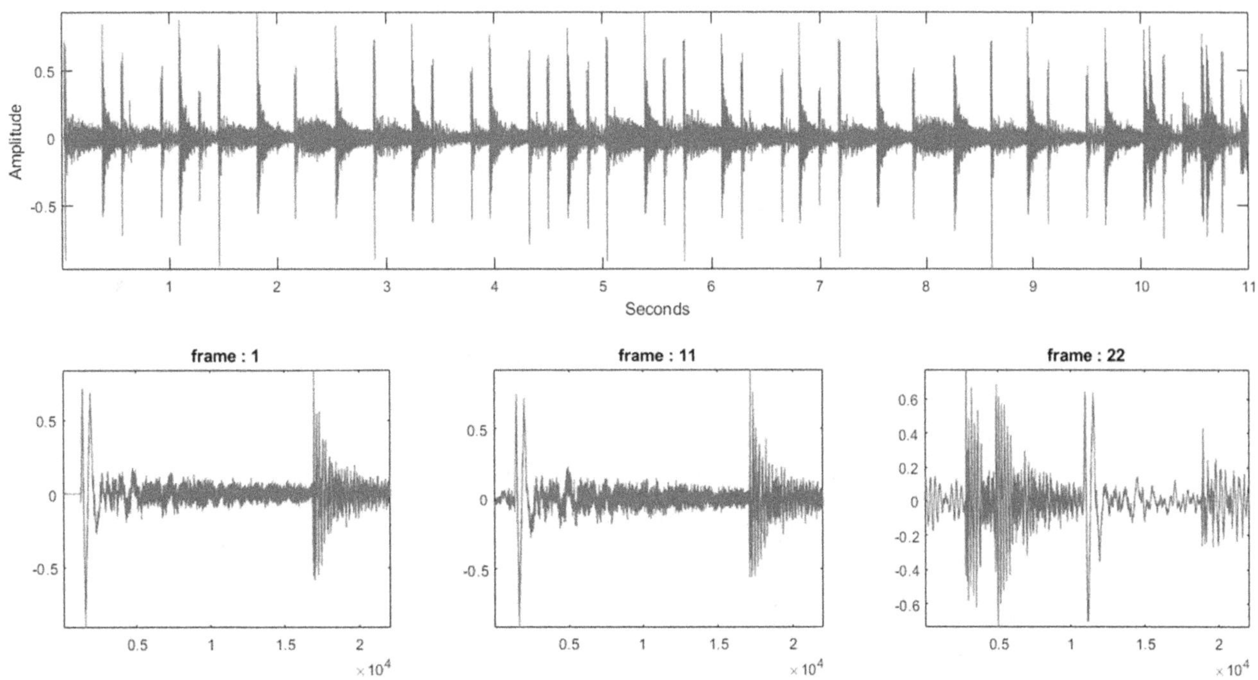

FIGURE 5.15
Audio segmentation.

5.3.2 Windowing

A window function is a function to isolate and analyze a small part of a signal or its spectrum. Usually, the values of the signal outside the window are zero or rapidly tend toward zero. The analysis is usually done by multiplying the signal with the window coefficients (Figure 5.16).

Rectangular window: The simplest window is the rectangular window, which has the value 1 over the width and 0 elsewhere:

$$w(x) = 1, 0 \le x \le N$$

$$w(x) = 0, \text{elsewhere}$$

Bartlett window: The Bartlett window is a triangular window defined as follows:

$$w(x) = 2x / N, 0 \le x \le N / 2$$

$$w(x) = 2 - 2x / N, N / 2 \le x \le N$$

Gaussian window: The Gaussian window is defined as follows, where σ is the standard deviation of the Gaussian curve:

$$w(x) = \exp\left(-x^2 / 2\sigma^2\right), -(N-1)/2 \le x \le (N-1)/2$$

Hamming window: The Hamming window is defined as follows:

$$w(x) = 0.54 - 0.46.\cos\left(2\pi x / N\right), 0 \le x \le N$$

Flat-top window: The Flat-top window is defined as follows where representative values of the coefficients are $a_0 = 0.215, a_1 = 0.416, a_2 = 0.277, a_3 = 0.083, a_4 = 0.007$:

$$w(x) = a_0 - a_1.\cos\left(\frac{2\pi x}{N-1}\right) + a_2.\cos\left(\frac{4\pi x}{N-1}\right) - a_3.\cos\left(\frac{6\pi x}{N-1}\right) + a_4.\cos\left(\frac{8\pi x}{N-1}\right), \quad 0 \le x \le N-1$$

Blackman window: The Blackman window of length N is defined as follows:

$$w(x) = 0.42 - 0.5.\cos\left(\frac{2\pi x}{N-1}\right) + 0.08.\cos\left(\frac{4\pi x}{N-1}\right), \quad 0 \le x \le N-1$$

5.3.3 Noise Gate

A noise gate is an audio processing tool used to control the level of background noise in an audio signal.

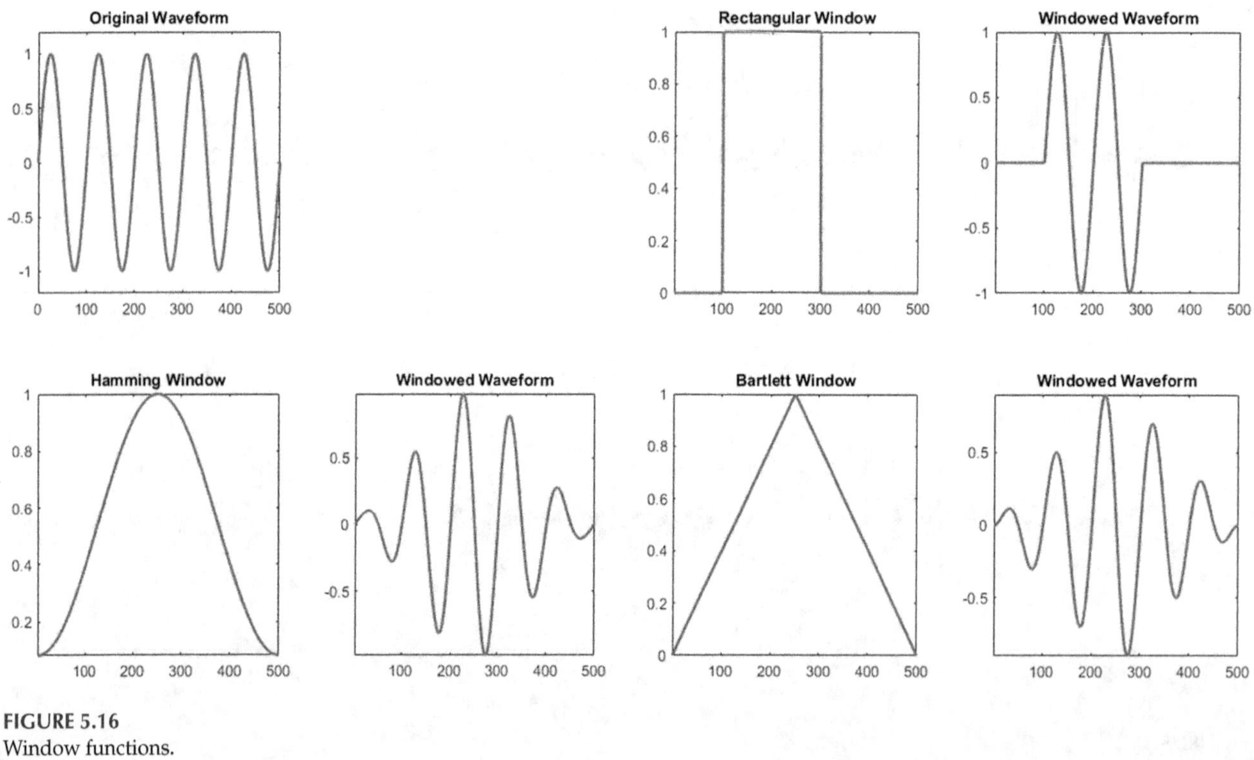

FIGURE 5.16
Window functions.

It operates by selectively allowing or blocking the passage of audio signals based on their amplitude. The user or the operator sets a threshold level on the noise gate. This threshold represents the amplitude below which the audio signal is considered to be background noise. The noise gate continuously monitors the amplitude of the incoming audio signal. When the signal level falls below the set threshold, the gate is triggered to close. When the gate is closed, it attenuates or blocks the passage of the audio signal. This means that any signal below the threshold is reduced in volume or muted. Again when the signal rises above the threshold amplitude, the gate opens to allow the signal to pass through. A noise gate therefore does not remove noise from the signal itself, when the gate is open both the signal and noise pass through. However, the noise is not noticeable because of the higher amplitude of the signal. A noise becomes noticeable when signal amplitude decreases and that is when the gate closes to block both signal and noise.

Parameters used to control the opening and closing of the gate, include the attack time and release time. The attack time defines the length of time it takes for the gate to change from closed to fully open, i.e., the fade-in duration. Likewise the release time determine how quickly the gate closes from fully open condition, i.e., the fade-out duration. An optional hold time is used to specify how long the gate will continue to remain open even after the signal falls below the threshold. This is to ensure that the gate does not close during short pauses between words or sentences in a speech signal. After the hold time has elapsed, if the signal still remains below the threshold, then only the release period commences. A shorter attack time means that the noise gate responds more quickly to incoming signals that cross the threshold providing a faster transition from closed to open gate. This can be beneficial in situations where it is desired to quickly let through transient sounds like the initial attack of a musical instrument. A longer attack time results in a slower response gradually allowing the signal to pass through. This can be useful where a gradual transition is desirable. A shorter release time means that the noise gate responds quickly to the signal dropping below the threshold. This can be useful in situations where it is desirable to rapidly suppress noise between transient sounds. A longer release time leads to a slower response gradually attenuating the signal. This can be useful in scenarios where a more gradual decay of the signal is desired to avoid abrupt changes or unnatural artifacts. The choice of the attack and release times depends on the characteristics of the audio signal and the desired outcome. It is often adjusted to find a balance between effectively reducing unwanted noise and allowing for a natural and smooth opening and closing of the gate without creating noticeable artifacts in the audio (Figure 5.17).

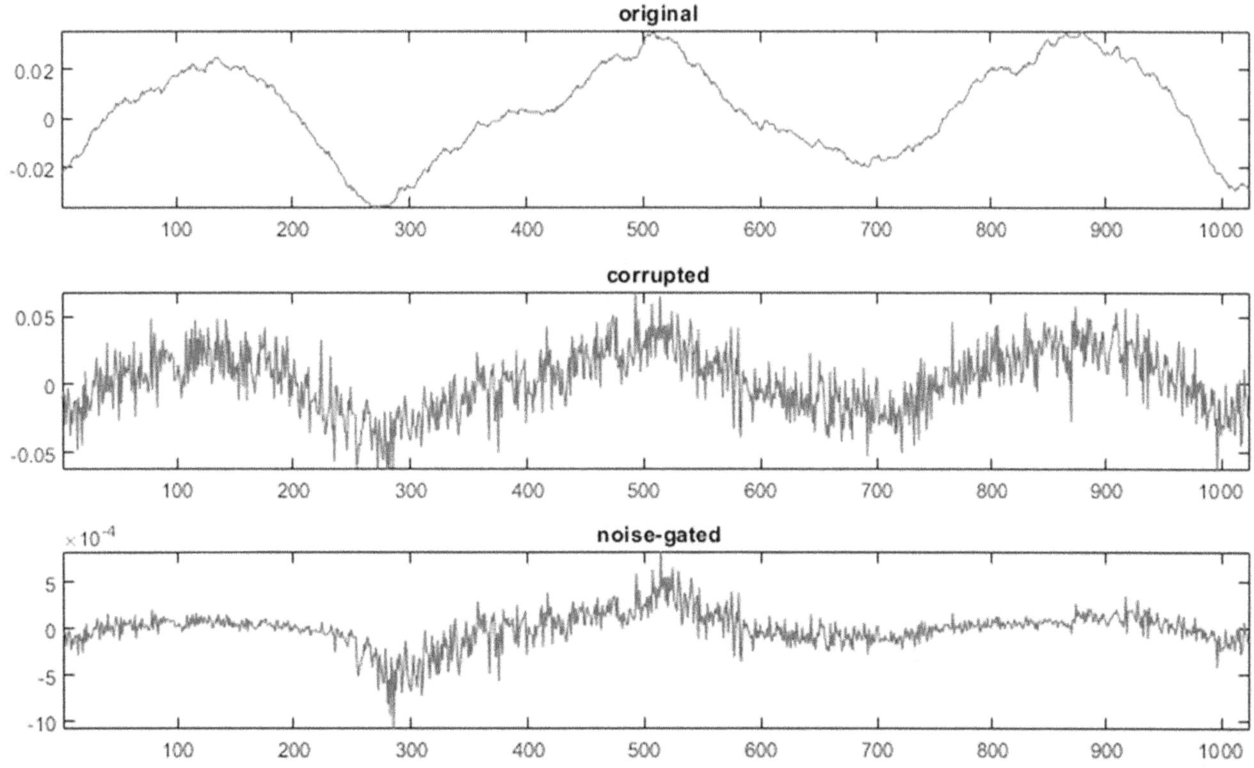

FIGURE 5.17
Application of a noise gate on a noisy signal.

5.3.4 Dynamic Range Compressor (DRC)

The dynamic range of an audio signal is the ratio between the loudest and softest parts. Signals with large dynamic range can be fitted in a narrower range of recording media using a process called dynamic range compression. A dynamic range compressor (DRC) reduces the dynamic range by attenuating the louder parts. The compressor continuously monitors the amplitude of the incoming audio signal. The user or the compressor itself sets a threshold level. When the input signal exceeds this threshold, compression is applied. The ratio control determines the degree of compression once the signal surpasses the threshold. For example, a 4:1 ratio means that for every 4 dB above the threshold, the output will only increase by 1 dB. The attack time determines how quickly the compressor responds to an input signal exceeding the threshold. A shorter attack time responds more quickly, while a longer attack time lets some transients pass through uncompressed. The release time controls how quickly the compressor stops attenuating the signal once it falls below the threshold. A shorter release time may result in a more noticeable pumping effect, while a longer release time may sound more natural. To compensate for the attenuation caused by compression, an output gain control allows the user to boost the overall signal level.

Similar to the compressor, the dynamic range expander (DRE) monitors the amplitude of the incoming audio signal. The user or the expander itself sets a threshold level. When the input signal falls below this threshold, expansion is applied. The ratio control determines the degree of expansion once the signal falls below the threshold. For example, a 4:1 ratio means that for every 4 dB below the threshold, the output will only decrease by 1 dB. The attack time sets how quickly the expander responds to an input signal falling below the threshold. A shorter attack time reacts more quickly, while a longer attack time may let softer transients pass through unaffected. Similar to the compressor, the release time controls how quickly the expander stops boosting the signal once it rises above the threshold. To compensate for the expansion, an output gain control allows the user to adjust the overall signal level. Some expanders include a hold control, which delays the return to normal operation after the signal falls below the threshold. This can help maintain a consistent background noise level (Figure 5.18).

Compressors are commonly used in audio production to control the dynamic range of vocals, instruments and overall mix. They are used to enhance sustain, control transients, and ensure a more consistent overall level. Expanders are employed to reduce background noise in recordings or to add dynamics to a signal. They can be used in broadcasting to reduce the noise between spoken words or to emphasize softer elements in a mix.

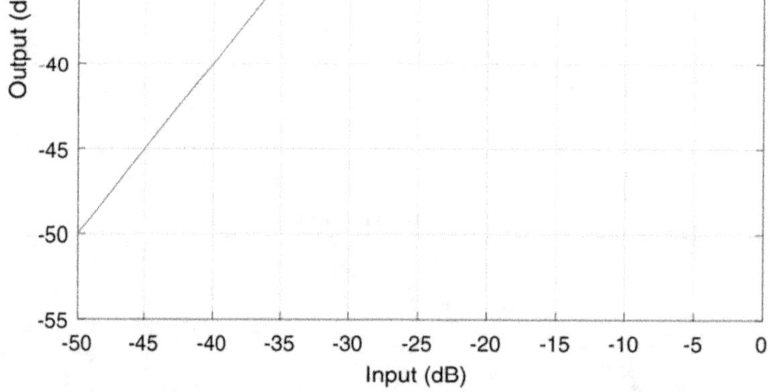

FIGURE 5.18
I/O characteristics of a dynamic range compressor.

5.3.5 Spectral Analysis

Audio spectral analysis is a process that involves examining the frequency content of an audio signal over time. It provides a visual representation of the distribution of frequencies in an audio signal, commonly displayed as a spectrogram or frequency spectrum. Spectral analysis is crucial in audio processing for tasks such as equalization, filtering, compression and understanding the overall frequency characteristics of a sound.

Time-Frequency Representation: Audio signals are dynamic and change over time. Spectral analysis captures this dynamic nature by representing the frequency content of the signal at different time intervals. Time-Frequency representations, such as spectrograms, display the evolution of frequencies over time.

Short-Time Fourier Transform (STFT): The Short-Time Fourier Transform is a widely used technique for audio spectral analysis. It involves dividing the audio signal into short overlapping segments, and for each segment, applying the Fourier Transform to convert the signal from the time domain to the frequency domain. The resulting spectrum for each time segment provides information about the frequency components present during that interval.

Spectrogram Display: A spectrogram is a visual representation of the STFT output, where time is represented on the horizontal axis, frequency on the vertical axis and the intensity of the colors or shading represents the amplitude of the corresponding frequencies. Bright areas in the spectrogram indicate higher energy or amplitude at specific frequencies during particular time intervals (Figure 5.19).

Peak Detection and Analysis: Spectral analysis allows the identification of prominent peaks or spikes in the frequency content. These peaks represent dominant frequencies or harmonics in the signal. Peak detection algorithms can be employed to identify and analyze specific frequencies or frequency ranges.

Equalization: Spectral analysis is crucial for equalization, a process where the balance of frequencies in an audio signal is adjusted.

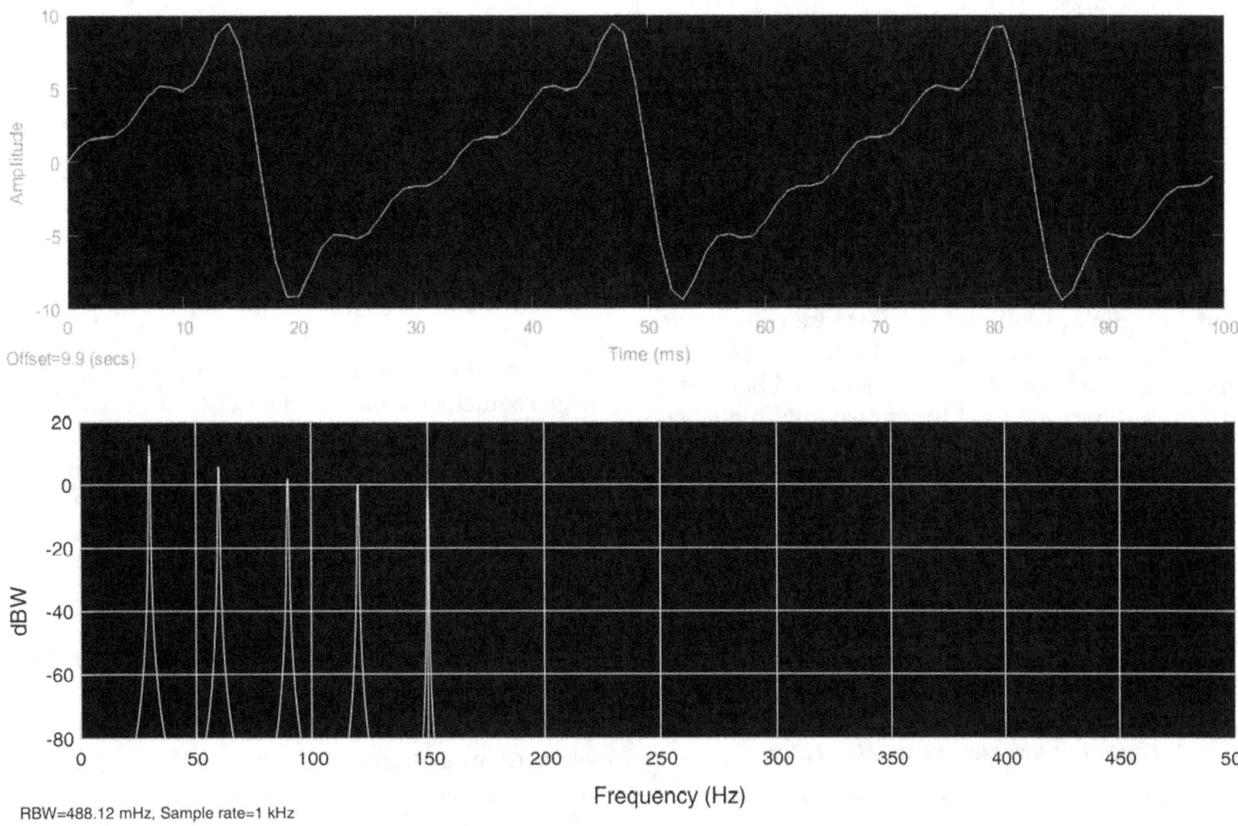

FIGURE 5.19
Spectrum analyzer.

Graphic equalizers, parametric equalizers and other equalization tools use spectral analysis to display and manipulate frequency components.

Filtering: Spectral analysis helps design and implement, various types of filters, such as high-pass, low-pass and band-pass filters. Filters modify the frequency content of a signal based on its spectral characteristics.

Pitch Detection: Spectral analysis aids in pitch detection by identifying the fundamental frequency and harmonics in a signal. This is essential in tasks such as tuning musical instruments or analyzing vocal pitch.

Audio Effects: Various audio effects, such as chorus and reverb, rely on spectral analysis to modify the frequency content of a signal over time. Spectral processing is employed to create unique soundscapes and textures.

Speech and Audio Recognition: Spectral analysis is used in speech and audio recognition systems to extract relevant features from the frequency domain for pattern recognition and classification.

Quality Control: In audio production, spectral analysis is employed for quality control purposes. It helps identify issues such as unwanted noise, distortion or frequency imbalances.

5.3.6 Temporal Filters

A temporal filter takes in a time-domain signal, modifies the frequency content and returns a new time-domain signal, usually for the purpose of removing high-frequency noise. Functionally filters are of four types: high-pass, low-pass, band-pass and band-stop. High-pass filters are used to remove low frequencies below a specified threshold, low-pass filters are used to remove high frequencies above a specified threshold, band-pass filters are used to allow a range of frequencies within a lower and an upper threshold, and band-stop filters block a range of frequencies within a lower and an upper threshold. Structurally the filters can be of two types: finite impulse response and infinite impulse response (Smith, 2006).

5.3.6.1 Finite Impulse Response (FIR) Filter

Finite Impulse Response (FIR) filters are characterized by a finite impulse response, meaning that the filter's output is determined by a finite number of past and present input samples. The output of an FIR filter is the result of convolving the input signal with a set of coefficients, representing the filter's impulse response. FIR filters can be designed to have a linear phase response, which means that all frequencies experience the same amount of delay. This property is desirable in applications where preserving the phase relationships of different frequency components is crucial, such as in audio equalization. FIR filters are commonly used in applications where linear phase and precise control over the frequency response are essential. This includes audio equalization, filtering and certain types of audio effects. Designing FIR filters can be computationally more demanding, especially for filters with a large number of coefficients (Figure 5.20).

A FIR filter is represented by the relation $y = H(b,x)$ and takes an n-element input signal x, i.e., $x = [x(1),\ldots,x(n)]$ and uses an m-element filter coefficient b, i.e., $b = [b(1),\ldots,b(m)]$. The n-element output produced $y = [y(1),\ldots,y(n)]$ is a linear combination of the input and filter coefficients such that the i-th output element is given by:

$$y(i) = b(1).x(i) + b(2).x(i-1) + \ldots + b(m).x(i-m+1)$$
$$= \sum_{k=1}^{m} b(k).x(i-k+1)$$

5.3.6.2 Infinite Impulse Response (IIR) filter

Infinite Impulse Response (IIR) filters have an infinite impulse response, meaning that the filter's output depends on an infinite number of past input samples. The output of an IIR filter is determined by recursively feeding back its output into the filter, creating a feedback loop. The presence of a feedback loop in IIR filters can lead to a more efficient implementation with fewer coefficients compared to FIR filters. IIR filters generally introduce nonlinear phase distortion, where different frequency components experience different amounts of delay. IIR filters are widely used in audio processing applications where computational efficiency is critical. This includes tasks such as real-time filtering, audio compression and various audio effects. Designing IIR filters is often computationally less intensive compared to FIR filters, especially for filters with a small number of poles and zeros.

An IIR filter is represented as $y = H(b,a,x)$, takes an n-element input signal x, i.e., $x = [x(1),\ldots,x(n)]$, and uses m-element filter coefficients a and b, i.e., $a = [a(1),\ldots,a(m)]$ and $b = [b(1),\ldots,b(m)]$. The n-element output produced $y = [y(1),\ldots,y(n)]$ is a

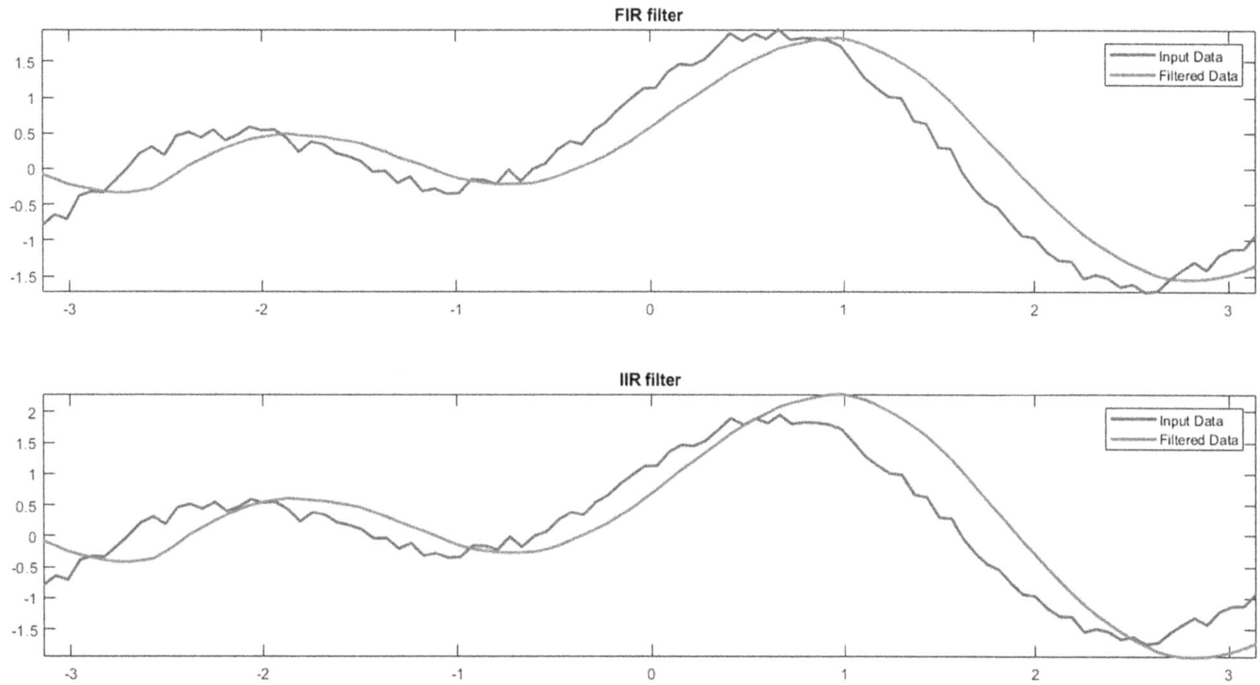

FIGURE 5.20
Filtering using FIR and IIR filters.

non-linear combination of the input and filter coefficients given by:

$$a(1).y(i)+a(2).y(i-1)...+a(m).y(i-(m-1)) \\ =b(1).x(i)+b(2).x(i-1)+...+b(m).x(i-(m-1))$$

Written in the compact form, where by convention a(1) = 1 :

$$y(i)=\sum_{k=1}^{m}b(k).x(i-k+1)-\sum_{k=2}^{m}a(k).y(i-k+1)$$

5.3.7 Common Editing Tasks

Cutting and Trimming: Removing unwanted sections, pauses or mistakes from audio clips. This is done using a cut tool, trim tool or razor tool in an audio editing software.

Adjusting Volume Levels: Balancing the volume of different audio tracks or sections. Volume controls, faders or gain adjustments are used for this.

Applying Fade-In and Fade-Out: Gradually increasing or decreasing the volume at the beginning or end of audio clips. Fade controls or automation features are used for this.

Equalization (EQ): Adjusting the balance of frequencies in audio clips. Graphic or parametric equalizers are used.

Adding Effects: Applying audio effects to enhance or modify the sound. Reverb, delay, chorus or specialized audio effects are used.

Noise Reduction: Removing or reducing unwanted background noise or hum. Noise reduction plugins or noise gates are used.

Pitch Correction: Adjusting the pitch of vocals or instruments using pitch correction plugins.

Time Stretching and Compression: Adjusting the speed or duration of audio clips, using Time-stretching algorithms or time compression/expansion features.

Editing Multi-Track Projects: Arranging and synchronizing multiple audio tracks for combining vocals, music and sound effects for a cohesive audio mix.

Adjust Panning: Determines which part of the audio plays in which speaker or both speakers.

Exporting and Rendering: Converting the edited audio project into a final audio file, using Export settings and rendering options, for preparing the audio for distribution on various platforms or devices.

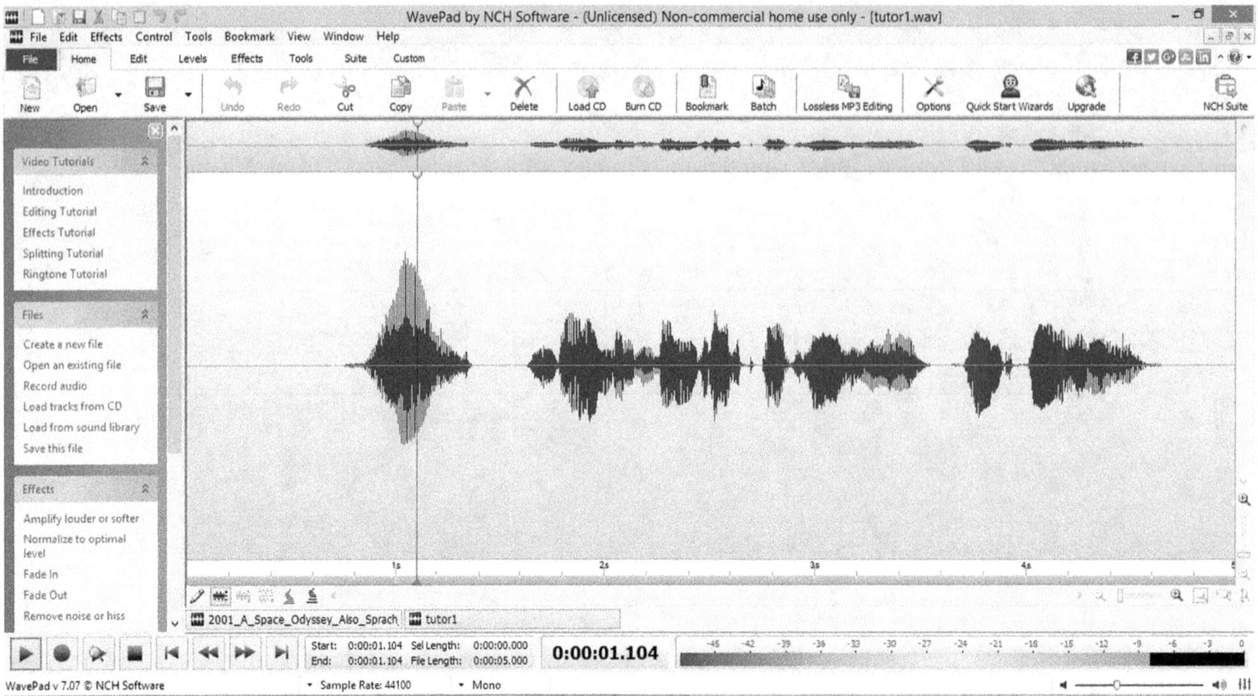

FIGURE 5.21
Typical GUI-based audio editor interface.

Adding Sound Effects: Integrating sound effects like echo, chorus and filters to enhance the auditory experience, using sound effect libraries, for creating a more immersive audio environment, emphasizing specific actions or enhancing storytelling (Figure 5.21).

5.4 Audio Applications

5.4.1 Audio in AR and VR

In augmented reality (AR) and virtual reality (VR), audio applications play a crucial role in creating immersive and realistic experiences. Spatial audio technologies enable the placement and movement of sounds in a three-dimensional space, enhancing the user's perception of depth and directionality within the virtual environment. These applications are essential for creating a convincing and engaging sensory experience, providing users with a more immersive and realistic audio environment in AR and VR scenarios (Kim et al., 2019).

Enhancing Immersion: Audio is essential for creating a sense of presence and immersion in VR and AR. Realistic audio cues that match visual information help users perceive the virtual or augmented world as more convincing and interactive.

Providing Contextual Information: Audio provides contextual information about the virtual environment. Sounds can indicate the proximity of objects, the direction of movement or the spatial layout of the surroundings, enhancing the user's understanding of the space.

Spatial Audio: Spatial audio refers to audio techniques that simulate sound sources in a 3D space, allowing users to perceive the direction, distance and movement of sounds. It relies on binaural audio, Head-Related Transfer Functions (HRTFs) and accurate sound source positioning.

Head-Related Transfer Functions (HRTFs): HRTFs are mathematical representations of how sound interacts with the listener's head and ears. In VR and AR, real-time HRTFs are used to adapt audio based on the user's head movements, ensuring that sounds match their changing perspective.

Ambisonics: Ambisonics is a popular spatial audio technology for VR and AR. It captures sound from all directions and allows for post-production manipulation of sound fields. Ambisonics enhances the sense of presence in virtual environments.

Object-Based Audio: Object-based audio systems enable sound designers to place audio objects in a 3D space. These objects can be tied to virtual entities in the VR or AR world, allowing for dynamic and interactive audio experiences.

5.4.2 Audio in Gaming

In gaming, audio applications are fundamental for creating immersive and interactive experiences. Advanced audio technologies, such as 3D spatial sound, contribute to the sense of realism by allowing players to perceive the direction and distance of in-game sounds. Additionally, dynamic soundscapes and adaptive audio responses enhance gameplay by providing auditory cues, feedback and atmosphere, contributing significantly to the overall gaming experience (Somberg, 2010).

Role of Sound Design: Sound design is the art of creating audio elements for games, including music, sound effects and voiceovers. It enhances storytelling, character development and environmental immersion.

Emotional Impact: Well-designed audio can evoke emotions in players, enhancing their connection to the game world. It can build tension, excitement and empathy through carefully crafted soundscapes.

Dynamic Soundtracks: Dynamic soundtracks adjust in response to gameplay events, creating a personalized and immersive experience. This technique is used to maintain player engagement and adapt to changing scenarios.

Reactive Sound Effects: Reactive sound effects change based on player actions, providing feedback and reinforcing in-game events. Interactive audio elements contribute to player agency and engagement.

Realism and Immersion: Spatial audio techniques, such as binaural audio and Head-Related Transfer Functions (HRTFs), create 3D soundscapes that enhance realism and immersion. They allow players to locate audio sources and react accordingly.

5.4.3 Audio Accessibility

Audio accessibility involves designing and implementing features to ensure that digital content, applications and services are usable and inclusive for individuals with hearing impairments or disabilities. This includes providing alternative formats, such as captions or transcripts, for audio content, making interfaces compatible with screen readers, and incorporating features like adjustable volume levels or visual indicators for important auditory information. By prioritizing audio accessibility, developers and content creators aim to make their products more inclusive and accessible to a diverse range of users, fostering a more equitable digital experience.

Inclusive Communication: Audio accessibility ensures that information and communication are inclusive and accessible to all, regardless of their hearing abilities. It promotes equal access to content and services.

Legal and Ethical Obligations: In many countries, there are legal obligations to provide accessible content. Beyond legal requirements, it is an ethical responsibility to make content inclusive for everyone (Web Content Accessibility Guidelines).

Web Content Accessibility Guidelines (WCAG): The WCAG provide a set of internationally recognized guidelines for making Web content, including audio, accessible to individuals with disabilities. These guidelines cover aspects like audio descriptions, captions and text alternatives (W3C).

Section 508: Section 508 of the Rehabilitation Act in the United States mandates that federal agencies provide accessible content, including audio, to employees and the public (U.S. Access Board).

Screen Readers: Screen readers are assistive technologies that convert digital text, including audio content, into synthesized speech or Braille output. They allow individuals with visual impairments to access audio content.

Hearing Aids and Cochlear Implants: Hearing aids and cochlear implants are assistive technologies that help individuals with hearing impairments to hear and understand audio content more clearly.

Best Practices for Audio Accessibility: Including text transcripts alongside audio content allows individuals with hearing impairments to read the spoken words and access the information. Adding captions and subtitles to audio and video content provides a textual representation of the spoken words, making it accessible to individuals with hearing disabilities (W3C). Audio descriptions are narrated descriptions of visual elements in audio or video content. They enable individuals with visual impairments to understand the visual context of the content. Audio descriptions are essential in media, including movies and television, to ensure that individuals with visual impairments can follow the storyline and understand the visual elements (American Council of the Blind).

5.5 Legal and Ethical Considerations

Digital audio applications have become integral to various industries, ranging from entertainment and education to communication and accessibility. As these applications evolve, it is crucial to navigate the legal and ethical landscape surrounding digital audio content. Legal and ethical considerations encompass issues related to copyright, licensing and privacy. Adhering to copyright laws is crucial to ensure that audio content is used in compliance with intellectual property regulations. Ethical considerations involve obtaining informed consent for recording, respecting privacy rights and avoiding the unauthorized use or manipulation of audio content in ways that may cause harm or infringe on individuals' rights. It is essential for creators, businesses and users to navigate these considerations responsibly to maintain a fair and ethical soundscape in various contexts (Davies, 2009; Cobussen & Nielsen, 2016).

5.5.1 Legal Considerations

Intellectual Property Rights: Digital audio content, including music, podcasts and sound recordings, is subject to copyright laws. Ensure proper licensing and permissions for the use, reproduction and distribution of copyrighted material.

Licensing Agreements: Adhere to the terms and conditions outlined in licensing agreements, whether for the use of music in applications, audio software or any other audio-related content.

Royalties and Compensation: Ensure fair compensation and adherence to royalty agreements for musicians, composers and other contributors involved in the creation of audio content.

Fair Use Doctrine: Understand the concept of fair use, especially when it comes to sampling or using excerpts of copyrighted material. Fair use allows limited use of copyrighted material without permission for purposes such as commentary, criticism, news reporting, or education.

Disability Laws: Comply with accessibility requirements outlined in laws like the Americans with Disabilities Act (ADA), ensuring that digital audio applications are accessible to users with disabilities.

Data Protection and Privacy Laws: Adhere to data protection and privacy laws, ensuring that any collection, storage, or processing of user data within digital audio applications complies with relevant regulations, such as GDPR or CCPA.

5.5.2 Ethical Considerations

Inclusive Design: Prioritize inclusive design to ensure that digital audio applications are accessible to users with diverse needs, including those with visual or hearing impairments.

Representation and Diversity: Avoid perpetuating stereotypes and ensure representation and diversity in the creation and use of audio content. Consider the cultural implications of audio choices to avoid unintentional bias.

Transparency: Be transparent about the data collected, the purpose of data usage and any potential impacts on privacy. Users should have a clear understanding of how their audio data is being handled.

User Consent: Obtain explicit and informed consent from users before collecting any audio data. Clearly communicate how the collected data will be used and provide users with the option to opt out.

AI and Bias: Be aware of and actively work to mitigate biases in AI algorithms used in audio applications. Biased algorithms can perpetuate social inequalities, particularly in voice recognition systems.

Security Measures: Implement robust security measures to protect user data and prevent unauthorized access. Security breaches in audio applications can lead to privacy concerns and legal ramifications.

Education and Awareness: Educate users about the potential risks and ethical considerations associated with digital audio applications. This can foster a more informed and responsible user base.

Impact on Mental Health: Be mindful of the potential impact of audio content on mental health. Consider incorporating features that promote positive user experiences and well-being.

Community Engagement: Engage with the user community to gather feedback on ethical considerations. Involving users in decision-making processes can lead to more responsible and community-driven practices.

Public Perception: Consider the public perception of digital audio applications. Ethical practices contribute to a positive public image, fostering trust and long-term success.

Navigating the legal and ethical landscape of digital audio applications is imperative to build sustainable and responsible solutions. By prioritizing compliance with intellectual property laws, ensuring inclusivity and upholding ethical principles, developers and content creators contribute to a digital audio landscape that respects user rights, fosters diversity and enhances the overall user experience.

5.6 Challenges and Emerging Trends

As digital audio technology continues to evolve, it faces both exciting opportunities and complex challenges. From improving audio quality to addressing emerging trends, the digital audio landscape is dynamic and multifaceted (Schutze & Schutze, 2018).

5.6.1 Challenges

Compression vs. Quality: Balancing the need for audio compression to save bandwidth and storage space with the demand for high-quality audio remains a significant challenge. Striking the right balance is crucial for various applications, from streaming services to mobile apps.

Immersive Audio Adoption: While technologies like Dolby Atmos and DTS:X offer immersive audio experiences, widespread adoption faces hurdles. Content creation, device compatibility and consumer awareness are challenges to achieving mainstream adoption of immersive audio.

Interoperability and Standards: Ensuring interoperability among various audio devices and platforms is challenging, especially with the proliferation of diverse audio formats and standards. Achieving a seamless experience across different devices remains an ongoing challenge.

Personalization and Privacy: As personalization in audio content delivery becomes more sophisticated, ensuring user privacy and consent is a challenge. Balancing the customization of user experiences with privacy concerns requires careful consideration.

Audio Quality in Streaming: While streaming services have become dominant, ensuring consistent high audio quality, especially for audiophiles, poses a challenge. Bandwidth limitations and the need for efficient compression algorithms are areas of focus.

AI-Generated Audio Challenges: The use of AI in generating audio content introduces challenges related to ethical considerations, potential biases and the need for human-like expressiveness. Striking a balance between automated audio generation and maintaining artistic integrity is an ongoing challenge.

5.6.2 Emerging Trends

Spatial Audio and 3D Sound: The future of audio technology lies in spatial audio and 3D sound experiences. Technologies like binaural audio and object-based audio aim to create immersive, three-dimensional soundscapes for a more realistic and engaging user experience.

Voice-Controlled Interfaces: With the rise of smart speakers and voice assistants, voice-controlled interfaces are becoming increasingly prevalent. The integration of natural language processing and AI enhances the user experience and accessibility of digital audio applications.

Personalized Audio Experiences: The future holds more advanced personalization in audio content delivery. AI-driven algorithms will analyze user preferences and habits to curate personalized playlists, recommend content and adapt audio experiences to individual preferences.

Haptic Feedback: Some headphones and devices incorporate haptic feedback to provide tactile sensations in response to audio signals. This enhances the overall sensory experience, particularly in gaming and virtual reality applications.

Augmented Reality (AR) Audio: AR technology extends beyond visuals to include audio augmentation. AR audio applications, such as spatialized audio in AR glasses, promise to provide more interactive and context-aware audio experiences in the real world.

Blockchain for Music Rights: Blockchain technology is increasingly being explored to address issues of copyright and royalties in the music industry. Smart contracts and decentralized platforms could offer transparent and fair compensation to artists and content creators.

AI-Enhanced Audio Production: AI is playing a growing role in audio production, assisting in tasks such as sound design, mixing and mastering. AI-powered tools can enhance efficiency and creativity in the creation of audio content, including noise cancellation, upscaling audio quality and creating personalized sound profiles based on user preferences.

Biometric Sound Analysis: The use of biometric sound analysis for health monitoring and emotional well-being is an emerging trend. Audio signals can be analyzed to detect physiological and emotional states, opening new possibilities for healthcare and personal wellness applications.

Edge Computing for Low-Latency Audio: Edge computing is gaining prominence to address latency concerns in real-time audio applications. By processing audio data closer to the source, edge computing reduces latency, making it suitable for applications like live streaming and virtual communication.

Environmental Sound Recognition: With a growing focus on ambient computing, environmental sound recognition is gaining traction. Devices equipped with the ability to recognize and respond to environmental sounds could enhance user experiences in smart homes and IoT applications.

Inclusive Audio Design: Emphasizing inclusivity, future trends in audio technology will focus on creating content that is accessible to individuals with diverse abilities. This includes advancements in audio description technologies and features that cater to users with hearing impairments.

Digital audio technology is at the forefront of innovation, offering new and immersive experiences. Overcoming current challenges and embracing newer trends will shape the industry, ensuring that digital audio continues to captivate and enhance the way we consume and interact with sound in the digital age. As consumer demands for high-fidelity, convenient and immersive audio experiences grow, these technologies will play a crucial role in shaping the future of how we listen and interact with sound.

5.7 Audio File Formats

5.7.1 AAC

AAC (Advanced Audio Coding) is a part of the MPEG-2 audio standard and uses the file extension. AAC [mpeg.chiariglione.org/standards/mpeg-2/advanced-audio-coding]. It is not compatible to MPEG-1 standards like MP3 and is believed to be an improved version of MP3 providing better sound quality at same bit rates, as evidenced from results of listening tests. Its improvements over MP3 include more sampling frequencies of 8–96 kHz compared to 16–48 kHz used in MP3, support for multi-channel sound compared to 2 channels by MP3, higher efficiency coding using MDCT compared to DCT in MP3, better handling of audio frequencies above 16 kHz. The AAC format was subsequently updated in MPEG-4 (Audio) Part-3, with the addition of perceptual noise substitution (PNS) and a long term predictor (LTP).

5.7.2 AIFF

AIFF (Audio Interchange File Format) is a file format standard used for storing audio data on personal computers. The format was co-developed by Apple based on the IFF (Interchange File Format), a generic file structure developed by Electronic Arts in 1985 for the 68k processor series used in Macintosh systems [www.mmsp.ece.mcgill.ca/Documents/AudioFormats/AIFF/Docs/AIFF-1.3.pdf]. The audio data in an AIFF file is uncompressed so the files tend to be much larger than files that use lossless or lossy compression formats. Types of chunks found in AIFF files include common chunk, sound data chunk, marker chunk, instrument chunk, comment chunk, name chunk, author chunk and copyright chunk.

5.7.3 AMR

AMR (Adaptive Multi Rate) [datatracker.ietf.org/doc/html/rfc4867] is a patented file format for speech coding and adopted by 3GPP as the standard speech CODEC for mobile phones, in 1999. It supports a sampling frequency of 8 kHz at 13-bit depth and is partitioned into 20 ms audio frames each containing 160 samples. It uses 8 different CODECs having different bit-rates ranging from 4.75 kbps to 12.2 kbps, such as ACELP (algebraic code excited linear prediction), DTX (discontinuous transmission) and VAD (voice activity detection). The patents are held by several companies, including Nokia Corp., Voice Age and Ericsson. AMR-WB (AMR-Wideband) [www.itu.int/rec/T-REC-G.722.2] is an extension of the AMR which provides improved speech quality due to a wider speech bandwidth of 50–7000 Hz.

5.7.4 APE

APE (Monkey's Audio) is a lossless audio format and uses the.APE extension [www.monkeysaudio.com]. APE files generally achieve compression rates slightly better than FLAC and significantly better than SHN; however, both encoding and decoding are somewhat slower. Although APE is a freeware, it has a non-free software license and hence is not included in most operating systems that rely on free software, compared to FLAC that comes pre-installed in most Linux distributions. The APEv2 tag was originally developed for the Musepack (MPC) file format as a metadata container for storing information like title, artist and track number, and was later adopted for the Monkey's audio file format. Recently it has emerged as an alternative to the ID3 tags for the MP3 files. The main advantage of the APEv2 tag over the ID3 tag is that the latter has a very rigid structure and the changes in each version is often contradictory to those of an earlier version, in comparison the APEv2 provides for a much more flexible structure.

5.7.5 DLS

DLS (DownLoadable Sounds) format provides a means for game developers and composers to add their own custom sounds to the General MIDI sound set stored in a sound card's ROM [www.midi.org/dls]. DLS-compatible devices will automatically download these custom sounds from card, disk or CD-ROM into system RAM, allowing MIDI music to be freely augmented with new instrument sounds, dialog or special effects – thus providing a universal interactive playback experience, along with an unlimited palette of sounds. At the same time, it enables the wavetable synthesizers in computer sound cards to deliver improved audio at no additional cost. The DLS specifications define a sound data format and the required synthesizer features for accurate playback on any DLS compatible device.

5.7.6 FLAC

FLAC (Free Lossless Audio Codec) is a popular lossless audio file format, well supported by many software and hardware audio products [www.xiph.org/flac]. FLAC is distinguished from general lossless algorithms such as ZIP and gzip in that it is specifically designed for the efficient packing of audio data. FLAC achieves compression rates of 30–70%. FLAC's technical strengths versus other lossless CODECs lie in its ability to be streamed, as well as a fast decode time that is independent of compression level.

5.7.7 MID

MID (MIDI) files are textual files that contain instructions on how to play a piece of music on digital musical instruments, published by MMA (MIDI Manufacturers Association) [www.midi.org/midi-2-0]. The actual music is generated from a digital synthesizer chip that can recognize the instructions and retrieve (or create) corresponding audio samples using a repository of sounds. Hence, the files are very compact in size and ideal for Web applications. The sound repository must conform to the instrument palette specified by the GM standard for portability between different MIDI sound generators. MIDI Karaoke that use the.KAR extension, is an unofficial extension to the MID format used to add synchronized lyrics to standard MIDI files.

5.7.8 MP3

MP3 (MPEG-1 Audio Layer III) file format is based on the MPEG (Motion Pictures Expert Group) audio standard [mpeg.chiariglione.org/standards/mpeg-1/audio]. It is a lossy compression format using a perceptual CODEC that removes portions of an audio file not perceivable by human beings to reduce the file size. Most encoders allow encoding profiles with different levels of compression. For example, bit rates of 28.9, 64, 112, 128, 192 and 320 kbps may be allowed. MP3 can compress a typical song to about 5 MB with a compression ratio of 10:1 that can be easily downloaded from the Internet and provides a popular way of distributing music files. Moreover, it provides good audio quality and at 64 kbps is comparable to CD quality. The MP3 algorithm does not specify means for encryption or copy protection, and thus content may be copied indefinitely. Although the decoding algorithm and file format are well defined, the standard does not include a precise specification for the encoder, due to which there are many MP3 encoders available, each producing files of differing quality.

5.7.9 M4A, M4P

M4A (MPEG-4 Audio, Part-14) is a container file format, part of the MPEG-4 audio standard [mpeg.chiariglione.org/standards/mpeg-4/audio] and uses the Apple Lossless Audio Codec (ALAC) or Apple Lossless Encoder (ALE), developed by Apple Computer for lossless encoding of digital music. Apple Lossless data is stored within an MP4 container with the filename extension M4A. It does not utilize any digital rights management scheme, but by the nature of the container, it is thought that DRM (digital rights management) can be applied to ALAC much the same way it can with other files in QuickTime containers. The format uses LPC to compress files and uses 40–60% of the space of the original uncompressed files. The normal extension for any MPEG-4 file is.MP4, which is also mentioned in the MPEG-4 standard. The.M4A [mp4ra.org] file extension has been popularized by Apple, which started using it in their iTunes software and iPod music players to distinguish between MPEG-4 Video and Audio files. When these files have Digital Rights Management (DRM) restrictions applied to them, their extension is changed to.M4P, the P standing for protected.

5.7.10 MPC

MPC (Musepack) is an open-source version of MP2 (MPEG-1 layer II) format [www.musepack.net]. Unlike MP2, it, however, uses Huffman coding (like MP3), noise substitution techniques (like MPEG-4 AAC) and variable bit rate between 3 Kbps and 1.3 Mbps. The psycho-acoustic model of MPC is based on that of MP2 but is enhanced due to a number of additional components like CVD (Clear Voice Detection) and ANS (Adaptive Noise Shaping). MPC uses the APEv2 metadata container, and is also a streamable format.

5.7.11 OGG

OGG (Ogg Vorbis) is a free and open audio compression project [www.xiph.org/vorbis] and is part of their Ogg effort to create free and open multimedia and signal processing standards. Ogg Vorbis is completely free from licensing or patent issues associated with formats like MP3. The Ogg Vorbis format is popular among open-source communities, and due to its higher fidelity and completely free nature, it is considered to be a natural replacement for the MP3 format. In the commercial sector, Ogg Vorbis is set to replace MP3 as the de facto standard audio CODEC, with many newer video game titles employing Ogg Vorbis as opposed to MP3. Vorbis uses the Modified Discrete Cosine transform (MDCT) for converting sound data from time- to frequency-domain.

5.7.12 OMG, OMA, AA3

.OMG, .OMA and.AA3 are file formats used to store information on Minidiscs and other Sony-branded audio players using the ATRAC (Adaptive TRansform Acoustic Coding) audio compression algorithm [www.sony.net/Products/ATRAC3]. ATRAC uses modified discrete cosine transform to represent encoded audio. ATRAC files can be played back on IBM compatible PC using the RealAudio software or the Liquid Audio plug-in module for Winamp. ATRAC1 supports full stereo encoding with a data rate of 292 kbps. The quality is generally transparent for most people, meaning that it is not possible to tell an ATRAC encoding from the source. ATRAC3 LP2 mode uses a 132 kbps data rate with a quality similar to that of 128 kbps MP3. ATRAC3 LP4 mode reduces the data rate to 66 kbps (half that of LP2), partly by using joint stereo coding and a lowpass filter of around 13.5 kHz. ATRAC3plus is used in Sony Hi-MD Walkman devices and CD players and is thought to use a hybrid sub-band/MDCT compression scheme.

5.7.13 OFR

OFR (OptimFROG) is a proprietary lossless audio CODEC optimized for high compression ratios [www.losslessaudio.org]. As reported on its official site, OptimFROG obtains asymptotically the best lossless audio compression ratios. The compression ratios that can be obtained from OptimFROG generally range from 25% (silent classical music) to 70% (loud rock music) of the original audio file size. As reported on its website, OptimFROG uses a new audio compression technology, the generalized stereo decorrelation concept (together with the optimal predictor). OptimFROG DualStream is a lossy CODEC, aimed to fill the gap between perceptual coding and lossless coding. OptimFROG DualStream has an option to produce a correction file. This file can be used, in combination with the main lossy-encoded file, for lossless decoding.

5.7.14 OPUS

Opus is a versatile audio compression format [www.opus-codec.org] that supports both lossless and lossy compression, developed by the Xiph.Org foundation and standardized by the IETF as RFC 6716 [datatracker.ietf.org/doc/html/rfc6716]. Opus supports bitrates from 6 kbps to 510 kbps, sampling rates from 8 kHz to 48 kHz, audio frame sizes from 2.5 ms to 60 ms, constant bitrates (CBR) and variable bitrates (VBR). It combines LPC-based SILK algorithm developed by Skype/Microsoft and the MDCT-based CELT algorithm developed by Xiph.Org foundation. It is particularly well-suited for real-time applications like VoIP and online gaming, due to its low latency and excellent audio quality. Opus can achieve a wide range of compression ratios, depending on the desired trade-off between audio quality and file size.

5.7.15 RA

RA (RealAudio) is a proprietary audio format [www.loc.gov/preservation/digital/formats/fdd/fdd000055.shtml] developed by RealNetworks [www.real.com]. It is especially designed to conform to low bandwidths, and it can be used as a streaming audio format, i.e., played at the same time as it is downloaded. Many radio stations use RealAudio to stream their programming over the Internet in real time. The main player for RealAudio content is RealNetworks' RealPlayer. RealAudio files are compressed using several different audio CODECs: the earlier versions used linear predictive coding (LPC), while later versions incorporated the ATRAC3 and MPEG-4 AAC CODEC. RealAudio supports streaming by using the standard Real Time Streaming Protocol (RTSP) to manage the connection and a proprietary protocol Real Data Transport (RDT) from RealNetworks to send the actual audio data.

5.7.16 SPX

SPX (Speex) is a patent free audio compression format designed for speech coding [www.speex.org]. It was designed for VoIP applications that mean that it needed to handle lost packets. CELP was chosen as the encoding technique for supporting both low bit rates (e.g., 5 Kbps) and high bitrates (e.g. 16 Kbps). Speex supports three sampling rates: 8 kHz (narrowband), 16 kHz (wideband) and 32 kHz (ultra-wideband). The quality is controlled by a quality parameter ranging from 0 to 10. The encoder can operate at several complexity levels. The quality is better at high complexity levels that, however, require higher CPU resources. It supports Variable Bit Rates (VBR) that mean that it can use higher bit rates for specific sounds for improving quality. Speex has a component called VAD (Voice Activity Detection) that allows the encoder to detect the presence of speech or silence and accordingly adjust bit rates. Another feature called DTX (discontinuous transmission) allows the encoder to stop and start transmission asynchronously.

5.7.17 TTA

TTA (The True Audio) is a free, simple real-time lossless audio format supporting multichannel 8, 16 and 24-bit data of uncompressed input files [www.tausoft.org]. It uses a real-time encoding/decoding algorithm allowing fast operation speed and minimal system requirements. It can be compiled and executed on several different platforms with free and open-source code and documentation. The compression ratio is generally in the range between 30% and 70% of the original. TTA format supports both ID3v1 and ID3v2 information tags. The TTA file header contains a unique format identifier, which is followed by two metadata blocks.

5.7.18 VOC

VOC (Voice Creative) is a lossless file format used with Creative [www.creative.com] Sound Blaster sound cards to encode speech recordings. Sound up to 16-bit stereo is supported along with compressed formats. These files can contain markers for looping and synchronization markers for multimedia applications. Initially, VOC files used LPC (linear predication) to losslessly compress the files; however, later versions used CELP (code excited linear prediction).

5.7.19 WV

WV (WavPack) is a free, open-source lossless audio compression format, which allows users to compress (and restore) both 16-bit and 24-bit audio files in the. WAV format [www.wavpack.com]. It also supports multichannel streams and high-frequency sampling rates. Like other lossless compression schemes, the data reduction varies with the source, but is generally between 25% and 50%. WavPack also incorporates a unique "hybrid" mode that provides all the advantages of lossless compression with an additional bonus. Instead of creating a single file, this mode creates both a relatively small, high-quality lossy file that can be used all by itself, and a "correction" file that (when combined with the lossy file) provides full lossless restoration. For some users, this means never having to choose between lossless and lossy compression.

5.7.20 WMA

WMA (Windows Media Audio) is a proprietary compressed audio file format used by Microsoft [learn.microsoft.com/en-us/windows/win32/medfound/about-the-windows-media-codecs]. It was initially a competitor to the MP3 format, but with the introduction of Apple's iTunes Music Store, it has positioned itself as a competitor to the Advanced Audio Coding (AAC) format used by Apple. It is a proprietary technology part of the Windows Media framework. An initial reason for the development of WMA might have been that MP3 technology is patented and has to be licensed from Thomson for inclusion in the Microsoft Windows operating system. A WMA file is almost always encapsulated in an Advanced Systems Format (ASF) file. The resulting file may have the filename suffix WMA or ASF with the WMA suffix being used only if the file is strictly audio. WMA features digital rights management using a combination of elliptic curve cryptography key exchange, DES block cipher, and the SHA-1 hashing function.

5.7.21 WAV

WAV (Waveform) audio format is a Microsoft and IBM audio file format standard for storing audio on PCs [learn.microsoft.com/en-us/windows-hardware/drivers/audio/extensible-wave-format-descriptors]. It is a variant of the RIFF bitstream format method for storing data in "chunks", and thus also close to the IFF and the AIFF format used on Macintosh computers. The RIFF format acts as a "wrapper" for various audio compression CODECs. It is the main format used on Windows systems for raw audio. It is an expandable format that supports multiple data formats and compression schemes. It is used for uncompressed 8-, 12- and 16-bit audio files both mono and multi-channel, at a variety of sampling rates including 44.1 kHz. Though a WAV file can hold audio compressed using some lossless CODECs like DPCM and ADPCM, by far the most common format is PCM audio data. Since PCM uses an uncompressed, lossless storage method that keeps all the samples of an audio track, professional users or audio experts may use the WAV format for maximum audio quality.

5.7.22 XMF

XMF (Extensible Music Format) is a container format [www.midi.org/extensible-music-format-xmf] developed by MMA containing one or more MIDI files, DLS files, WAV and other digital audio files to create a collection of all resources needed to present a musical piece, an interactive Web page soundtrack or any other piece of media using pre-produced sound elements. The Mobile XMF is an XMF format developed specifically for mobile phones. Interactive XMF is the world's first open format for interactive audio content.

5.8 Numerical Problems

5.8.1 Sound Waves

PROBLEM 5.1

The equation of a progressive wave is: $y = 8\sin(140\pi t - 0.08\pi x)$ where x and y are in cm and t in seconds. Find the amplitude, frequency, wavelength and speed of the wave.

Equation of a progressive wave :
$y = a\sin\{2\pi(t/T - x/\lambda)\}$

Comparing : amplitude $a = 8\,\text{cm}$

Also, $2/T = 140$, which implies, $T = 1/70$ second

Hence frequency $f = 1/T = 70\,\text{Hz}$

Again, $2/\lambda =$ 0.08, which implies, wavelength $\lambda = 25\,\text{cm}$

Hence, speed $v = \lambda f = 70 \times 25 = 1750\,\text{cm/s}$

PROBLEM 5.2

A body vibrating with a particular frequency generates waves having wavelength 20 cm in a medium A travelling at 160 m/s. Calculate the wavelength of the wave it will generate in another medium B propagating with a velocity 240 m/s.

Let f be the constant frequency of the wave, generated by the vibrating source.

But when the wave travels in different media, it can have different velocities and hence different wavelengths

Velocity of the wave in the two media are: $vA = (\lambda A)f$ and $vB = (\lambda B)f$

Hence $vB/vA = \lambda B/\lambda A$

Thus $\lambda B = \lambda A(vB/vA) = 20(240/160) = 30$ cm

PROBLEM 5.3

Equation of the simple harmonic oscillation of a source is $y = 15\sin 100\pi t$ cm. (a) Write equation of oscillation of a point 150 m from the source (b) Write equation of the wave at a time $t = 0.04$ sec from start. The oscillations propagate with a velocity of 300 m/s.

Here $a = 15\,\text{cm}$, $\omega = 100\pi$. Hence $f = \omega/2\pi = 50$ which gives $T = 1/50$.

Also $\lambda = v/f = 300/50 = 6$ m $= 600$ cm

Equation of the progressive wave :

$$y = a\sin\{2\pi(t/T - x/\lambda)\}$$
$$= 15\sin\{2\pi(50t - x/600)\}$$

(a) For $x = 15000\,\text{cm}, y = 15\sin\{2\pi(50t - 15000/600)\}$
$= 15\sin\{2\pi(50t - 25)\} = 15\sin(100\pi t - 50\pi)$
(b) For $t = 0.04$ sec, $y = 15\sin\{2\pi(50*0.04 - x/600)\}$
$= 15\sin(4\pi - x\pi/300)$

5.8.2 Digital Audio

PROBLEM 5.4

An audio signal is digitized at a sampling rate of 44.1 kHz, a bit depth of 16 and in stereo mode. Calculate the space occupied by 1 minute of the audio and its data rate for playback.

Here, $F = 44100$ Hz, $b = 16, c = 2, T = 60$ seconds

Data rate $D = F.b.c$ = (44100 samples/second)(16 bits/sample)(2 channels) = 1411200 bps = 1.4 Mbps

File size $S = D.T$ = (1411200 Mbits/second)(60 second) = 84672000 bits = 10.09 MB

(This forms the general rule of thumb that each minute of uncompressed audio takes up approximately 10 MB for audio-CD quality.)

PROBLEM 5.5

An audio signal is recorded on a computer in stereo mode using a bit depth of *b* such that its data rate is *R* KB/s. Find an expression for the average frequency of the signal.

Let the average frequency be f and sampling rate be F.

Then by Nyquist's theorem, $F = 2f$

Since the audio is in stereo mode, number of channels $c = 2$

Data rate $D = F.b.c = (2f)(b)(2)$ bits/second = $(2f)(b)(2)/(8 \times 1024) = f.b/2048$ KB/s

Equating to R, we get $f = 2048R/b$

PROBLEM 5.6

An audio clip has a duration of 8 minutes. The highest frequency in the sound wave is 15 kHz. This is to be sampled using 8 bits per sample and in stereo mode. Estimate the minimum data rate in KB/s required to playback the digital file, and the file size in MB.

Here, $f = 15\,\text{kHz}, b = 8, c = 2, T = 8\,\text{minutes}$.

Sampling rate $F = 2f = 30\,\text{kHz}$

Data rate $D = F.b.c = (30000 \times 8 \times 2)/(8 \times 1024)$ = 58.6 KB/s

File size $S = F.b.c.t = (30000)(8)(2)(8 \times 60)/(8 \times 1024 \times 1024) = 27.46\,\text{MB}$

PROBLEM 5.7

An uncompressed audio file in WAV format with a duration of 4 minutes has file size of 48 megabytes (MB). Calculate the average bit rate.

File size in bits = 48 * 1024 * 1024 * 8 = 402,653,184 bits

Bit rate = 402,653,184 bits/(4*60) sec = 1677721 bps = 1.67 Mbps

PROBLEM 5.8:

The levels of the individual instrument tracks during a recording are as follows: Guitar (track 1) = -3 dB, Vocals (track 2) = -6 dB, Drums (track 3) = -4 dB, Bass (track 4) = -5 dB. Calculate the overall level (in dB) of the mixed audio.

Loudness in dB = $10.log_{10}$ (Amplitude levels). Here amplitude levels are:

$$\text{Track1}: 10^{\left(-\frac{3}{10}\right)} = 0.501$$

$$\text{Track2}: 10^{\left(-\frac{6}{10}\right)} = 0.251$$

$$\text{Track3}: 10^{\left(-\frac{4}{10}\right)} = 0.398$$

$$\text{Track4}: 10^{\left(-\frac{5}{10}\right)} = 0.316$$

Total amplitude: 0.501 + 0.251 + 0.398 + 0.316 = 1.466

$\text{Overall Level}(\text{in dB}) = 10 * \log_{10}(1.466) = 1.66\,\text{dB}$

5.8.3 Audio Editing

PROBLEM 5.9

Consider an audio signal with 5 sample values $[1,2,3,4,5]$. It is to be filtered with a filter $b = [1,-0.5]$. Find the output.

Here $y(i) = b(1).x(i) + b(2).x(i-1) + \ldots$
$+ b(m).x(i-m+1)$

$$y(1) = b(1).x(1) + b(2).x(0) = (1)(1) + (-0.5)(0) = 1$$

$$y(2) = b(1).x(2) + b(2).x(1) = (1)(2) + (-0.5)(1) = 1.5$$

$$y(3) = b(1).x(3) + b(2).x(2) = (1)(3) + (-0.5)(2) = 2$$

$$y(4) = b(1).x(4) + b(2).x(3) = (1)(4) + (-0.5)(3) = 2.5$$

$$y(5) = b(1).x(5) + b(2).x(4) = (1)(5) + (-0.5)(4) = 3$$

Output $y = [1, 1.5, 2, 2.5, 3]$

PROBLEM 5.10

Consider an audio signal with 5 sample values $[1,2,3,4,5]$. It is to be filtered with a filter having $a = [1,-1], b = [1,-0.5]$. Find the output.

$$a(1).y(1) = b(1).x(1) i.e. y(1) = 1$$

$$a(1).y(2) + a(2).y(1) \\ = b(1).x(2) + b(2).x(1) i.e. y(2) = 2.5$$

$$a(1).y(3) + a(2).y(2) + a(3).y(1) \\ = b(1).x(3) + b(2).x(2) + b(3).x(1) i.e. y(3) = 4.5$$

$$a(1).y(4) + a(2).y(3) + a(3).y(2) + a(4).y(1) \\ = b(1).x(4) + b(2).x(3) + b(3).x(2) + b(4).x(1) i.e. y(4) \\ = 7$$

$$a(1).y(5) + a(2).y(4) + a(3).y(3) + a(4).y(2) \\ + a(5).y(1) = b(1).x(5) + b(2).x(4) \\ + b(3).x(3) + b(4).x(2) + b(5).x(1) i.e. y(5) = 10$$

Output $y = [1, 2.5, 4.5, 7, 10]$

PROBLEM 5.11

The Bartlett window is given by the following function: $\omega(n) = (1/k)\{k - |n-k|\}$, $0 \le n \le N$, where $k = (N-1)/2$. Find the points of the Bartlett window for $N = 7$.

$\omega(0) = (2/6)\{(6/2) - |0 - 6/2|\} = (1/3)\{3 - 3\} = 0$
$\omega(1) = (2/6)\{(6/2) - |1 - 6/2|\} = (1/3)\{3 - 2\} = 1/3$
$\omega(2) = (2/6)\{(6/2) - |2 - 6/2|\} = (1/3)\{3 - 1\} = 2/3$
$\omega(3) = (2/6)\{(6/2) - |3 - 6/2|\} = (1/3)\{3 - 0\} = 1$
$\omega(4) = (2/6)\{(6/2) - |4 - 6/2|\} = (1/3)\{3 - 1\} = 2/3$
$\omega(5) = (2/6)\{(6/2) - |5 - 6/2|\} = (1/3)\{3 - 2\} = 1/3$
$\omega(6) = (2/6)\{(6/2) - |6 - 6/2|\} = (1/3)\{3 - 3\} = 0$

5.9 Coding Examples using MATLAB

Audio processing functions in MATLAB® can be divided into two broad categories: basic MATLAB (BM) functions and Audio System Toolbox (AST) functions. The BM functions are a set of basic tools used for performing preliminary mathematical matrix operations and graphical plotting operations. The AST provides algorithms and tools for the design, simulation and desktop prototyping of audio processing systems and includes a set of more advanced tools for specialized processing tasks like compressor, expander, noise gate, spectrum analyzer and synthesizer. The audio file formats supported by MATLAB includes WAVE (.wav), OGG (.ogg), FLAC (.fac), AIFF (.aif), MP3 (.mp3) and MPEG-4 AAC (.m4a, mp4). Most of the audio files used in the examples are included in the MATLAB package and do not need to be supplied by the user. The audio samples used in this book are available in the following folder: (matlab-root)/toolbox/audio/samples/

5.9.1 Sound Waves

The following example displays a couple of sinusoidal tones and combines them to form composite notes. The first combination occurs when both the tones are in phase, while in the second combination they are 180 degrees out of phase (Figure 5.22).

EXAMPLE 5.1 MATLAB EXAMPLE TO DISPLAY SINUSOIDAL TONES AND COMPOSITE NOTES

```
clear; clc;
t = 1 : 0.1 : 50;
subplot(411), plot(t, sin(t));
   ylabel('sin(t)');
subplot(412), plot(t, 0.3*sin(3*t));
ylabel('0.3sin(3t)'); axis([0, 50,
   -1, 1]);
subplot(413), plot(t, sin(t) +
   0.3*sin(3*t));
ylabel('sin(t) + 0.3sin(3t)');
subplot(414), plot(t, sin(t) +
   0.3*sin(3*t - pi));
ylabel('sin(t) + 0.3sin(3t-\pi)');
```

The following example displays a number of composite waveforms using a combination of sinusoidal terms in a Fourier series (Figure 5.23).

EXAMPLE 5.2 MATLAB EXAMPLE TO GENERATE COMMON WAVEFORMS USING FOURIER SERIES

```
clear; clc;
t = 0:0.1:30;
figure,
a = cos(t) - (1/3)*cos(3*t) +
   (1/5)*cos(5*t) - (1/7)*cos(7*t) ;
b = cos(t) + (1/9)*cos(3*t) +
   (1/25)*cos(5*t) + (1/49)*cos(7*t);
c = sin(t) - (1/2)*sin(2*t) +
   (1/3)*sin(3*t) - (1/4)*sin(4*t);
subplot(311), plot(t, a); title('Square
   wave'); grid;
subplot(312), plot(t, b);
   title('Triangular wave'); grid;
subplot(313), plot(t, c);
   title('Sawtooth wave'); grid;
```

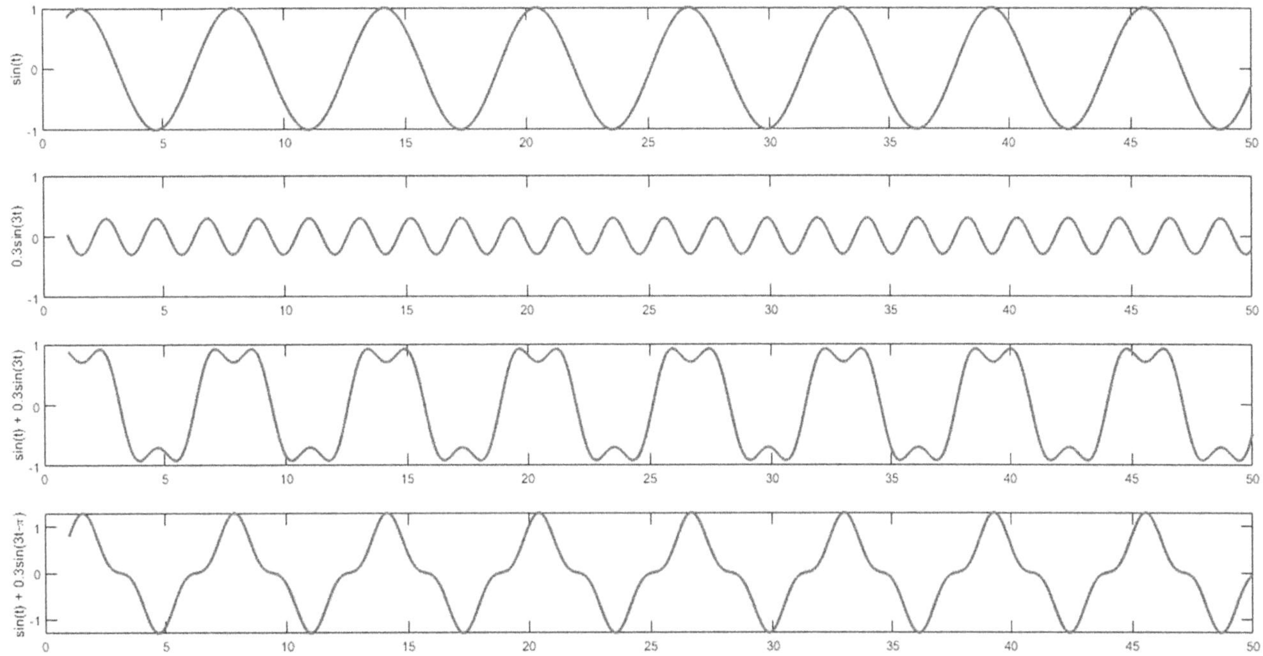

FIGURE 5.22
Output of Example 5.1.

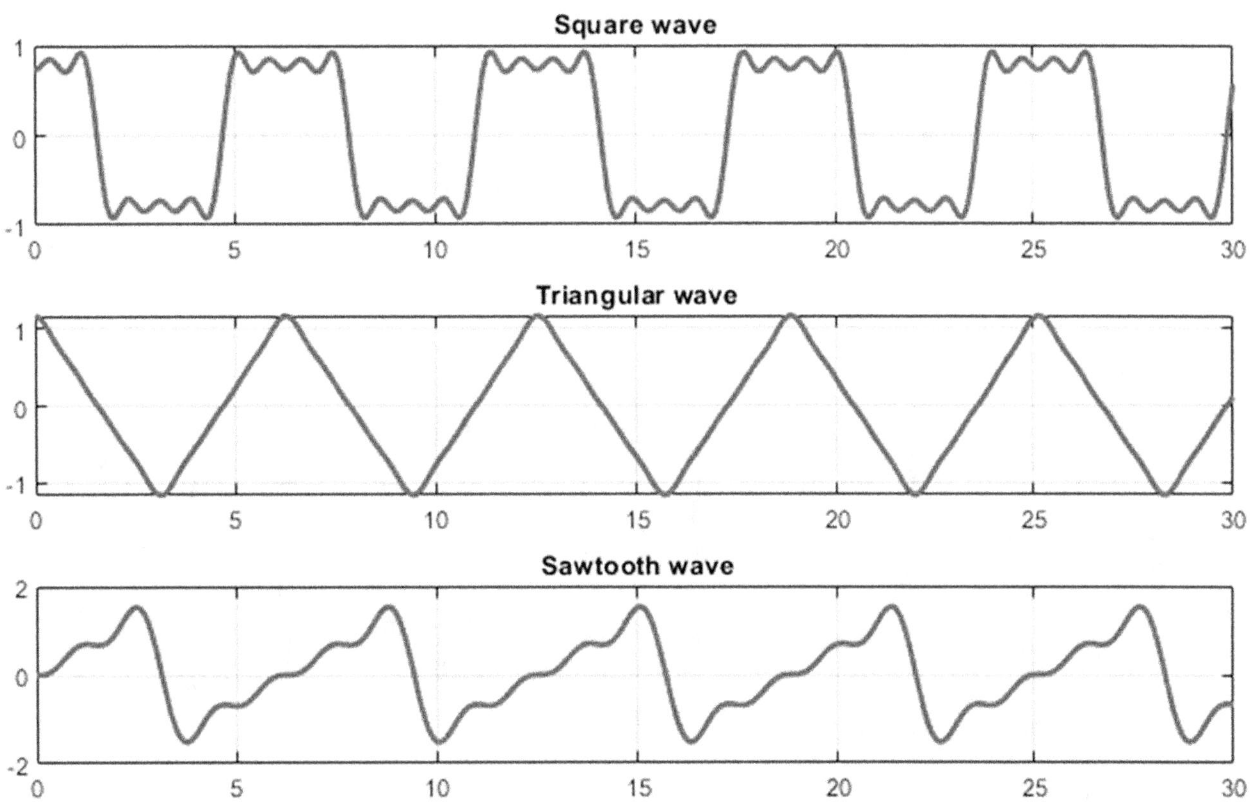

FIGURE 5.23
Output of Example 5.2.

5.9.2 Audio I/O

The following example illustrates playing a sound file and displaying its waveform. The function "audioread" is used to read audio from a specified file and returns the data matrix and the sample rate of the audio, "sound" is used to play the audio by specifying the data matrix and the sample rate, "audioinfo" displays information about the audio file like sample rate, total number of samples, duration in seconds, bits per sample, number of channels and compression method (Figure 5.25).

EXAMPLE 5.3 MATLAB EXAMPLE TO PLAY A SOUND FILE AND PLOT ITS WAVEFORM

```
clear; clc;
f = 'Counting-16-44p1-mono-15secs.wav';
[x, fs] = audioread(f);
sound(x, fs);
audioinfo (f)
figure, plot(x);
xlabel('Samples'); ylabel('Amplitude');
   axis tight;
```

The following example demonstrates speech recording and storing it as a file. The function "audiorecorder" creates an audio object for recording sound using the specified sample rate, bit depth and number of channels, "recordblocking" holds control for the audiorecorder object to record audio for the specified duration in seconds, "getaudiodata" stores the recorded audio signal in a numeric array, "play" plays an audio recording. By default, the data type of the numeric array is "double" and the values of the audio samples range from −1 to +1. The function "audiowrite" is used to write the audio data to a specified filename.

EXAMPLE 5.4 MATLAB EXAMPLE TO DEMONSTRATE SPEECH RECORDING

```
clear; clc;
fs = 44100; bs = 16; ch = 1;
ar = audiorecorder(fs, bs, ch);
get(ar);
% Record your voice for 5 seconds.
disp('Start speaking.')
recordblocking(ar, 5);
disp('End of Recording.');
pause(10);
% Play back the recording.
play(ar);
% Plot the waveform.
r = getaudiodata(ar);
plot(r);
% Write audio to file
audiowrite('myrec.mp4', r, fs);
```

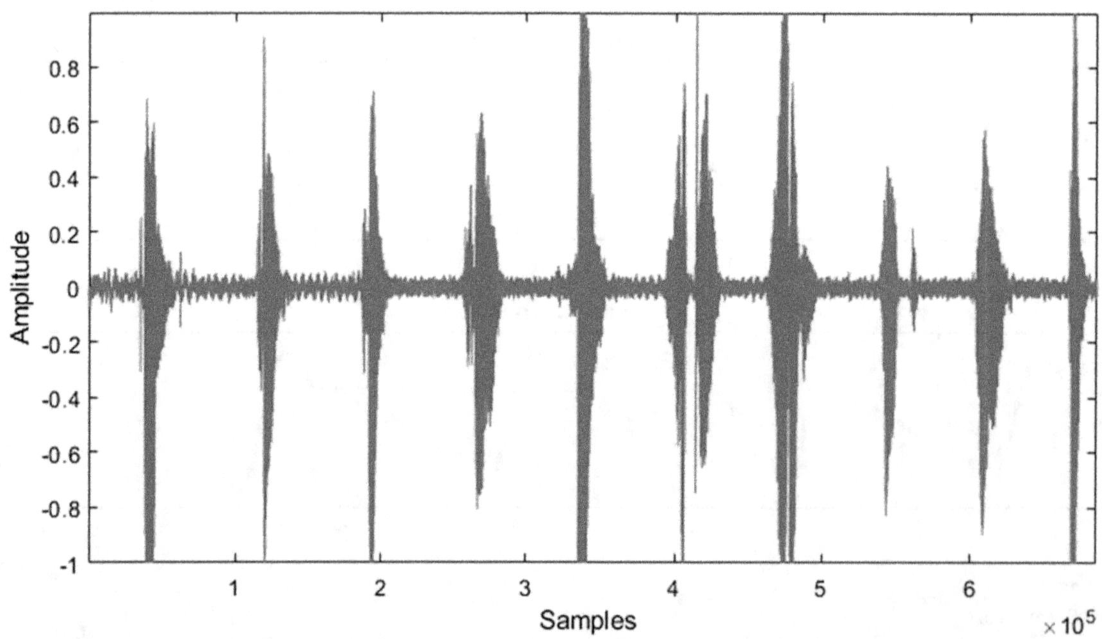

FIGURE 5.24
Output of Example 5.3.

5.9.3 Audio Segmentation

The following example 5.5 splits an audio file into non-overlapping frames of 0.5 second duration each and displays the first frame, last frame and middle frame. The number of samples is divided by the sampling rate (fs) to return the duration in seconds (t1) which is then rounded to an integer number (t2). The newly computed number of samples (lenx) is used to isolate the relevant samples (newx) from the original file. The number of samples in each audio frame (e) is used to calculate the number of audio frames (f) (Figure 5.26).

5.9.4 Window Functions

The following example shows pictorial representations of a number of window functions. The function "window" is used to generate a window of the specified type and width (Figure 5.27).

EXAMPLE 5.5 MATLAB EXAMPLE TO PARTITION AUDIO INTO NON-OVERLAPPING FRAMES

```
clear; clc;
fn = 'Counting-16-44p1-
   mono-15secs.wav';
[x, fs] = audioread(fn);
t1 = length(x)/fs;
t2 = floor(t1);
len_x = t2*fs;
new_x = x(1:len_x);
e = 0.5*fs; % samples per audio frame
f = floor(len_x/e); % Total no. of
   audio frames/file
t = [1:len_x]/fs;
for c = 0 : f-1 % do for all frames
seg{c+1} = new_x(c*e+1:(c+1)*e);
end

% plotting
subplot(2,3,[1:3]), plot(t,new_x);
xlabel('Seconds'); ylabel('Amplitude');
   axis tight;
subplot(234), plot(seg{1}), axis tight;
   title('frame : 1');
subplot(235), plot(seg{round(f/2)}),
   axis tight;
title(['frame : ',
   num2str(round(f/2))]);
subplot(236), plot(seg{f}), axis tight;
title(['frame : ', num2str(f)]);
```

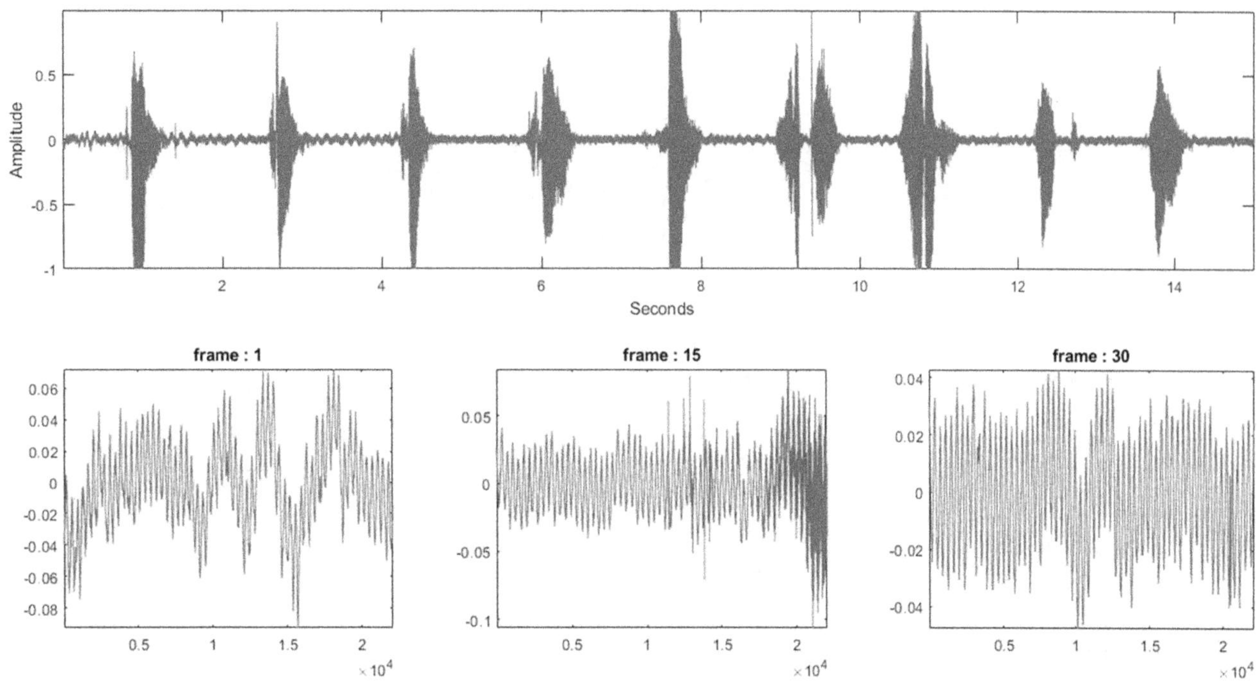

FIGURE 5.25
Output of Example 5.5.

EXAMPLE 5.6 MATLAB EXAMPLE TO PLOT DIFFERENT WINDOW FUNCTIONS

```
clear; clc;
t = 0:500;
y = sin(2*pi*t/100);
h1 = window(@rectwin,300);
h1(1:100) = 0; h1(451:501)= 0; y1 = y.*h1';
h2 = window(@hamming,501); y2 = y.*h2';
h3 = window(@bartlett,501); y3 = y.*h3';
h4 = window(@flattopwin,501); y4 = y.*h4';
h5 = window(@blackman,501); y5 = y.*h5';
figure,
subplot(341), plot(t,y);
axis([0 500 -1.2 1.2]);
title('Original Waveform');
subplot(343), plot(h1); title('Rectangular Window'); axis tight;
subplot(344), plot(y1); title('Windowed Waveform'); axis tight;
subplot(345), plot(h2); title('Hamming Window'); axis tight;
subplot(346), plot(y2); title('Windowed Waveform'); axis tight;
subplot(347), plot(h3); title('Bartlett Window'); axis tight;
subplot(348), plot(y3); title('Windowed Waveform'); axis tight;
subplot(349), plot(h4); title('Flat-top Window'); axis tight;
subplot(3,4,10), plot(y4); title('Windowed Waveform'); axis tight;
subplot(3,4,11), plot(h5); title('Blackman Window'); axis tight;
subplot(3,4,12), plot(y5); title('Windowed Waveform'); axis tight;
```

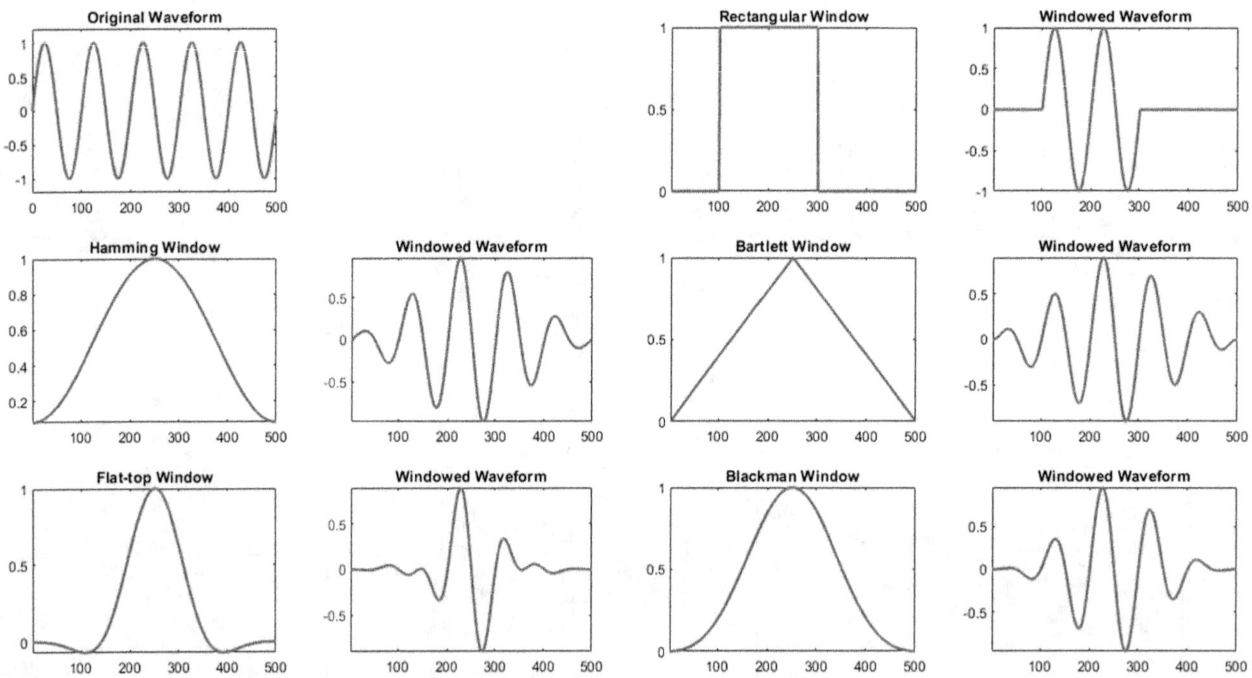

FIGURE 5.26
Output of Example 5.6.

5.9.5 Measuring Loudness

The following example calculates the momentary, short-term and integrated loudness of an audio signal and plots the results for visualization. The function "loudnessMeter" calculates the momentary loudness, short-term loudness, integrated loudness and true-peak value of an audio signal, "release" releases a resource. The values are expressed in loudness units relative to full scale (LUFS). Peak value is measured in dB (Figure 5.28).

EXAMPLE 5.7 MATLAB EXAMPLE TO CALCULATE LOUDNESS

```
clear; clc;
fn = 'RockDrums-44p1-
   stereo-11secs.mp3';
[a, sr] = audioread(fn);
r = dsp.AudioFileReader(fn);
lm = loudnessMeter('SampleRate',r.
   SampleRate);
momentary = [];
shortTerm = [];
integrated = [];
nf = 0; % number of frames
sf = r.SamplesPerFrame;
fs = r.SampleRate;
while ~isDone(r) % do for each frame
 nf = nf + 1;
 x = r();
 [m,s,i,n,p] = lm(x);
 momentary = [momentary; m];
 shortTerm = [shortTerm; s];
 integrated = [integrated; i];
end
release(r)
ns = nf * sf; % number of samples
td = ns/fs; % time duration
t = linspace(0,td,length(momentary));
subplot(211), plot(a); axis tight;
subplot(212),
plot(t,[momentary,shortTerm,in
   tegrated])
title('Loudness Measurements')
legend('Momentary','Short-
   term','Integrated')
xlabel('Time (seconds)')
ylabel('LUFS')
axis tight;
```

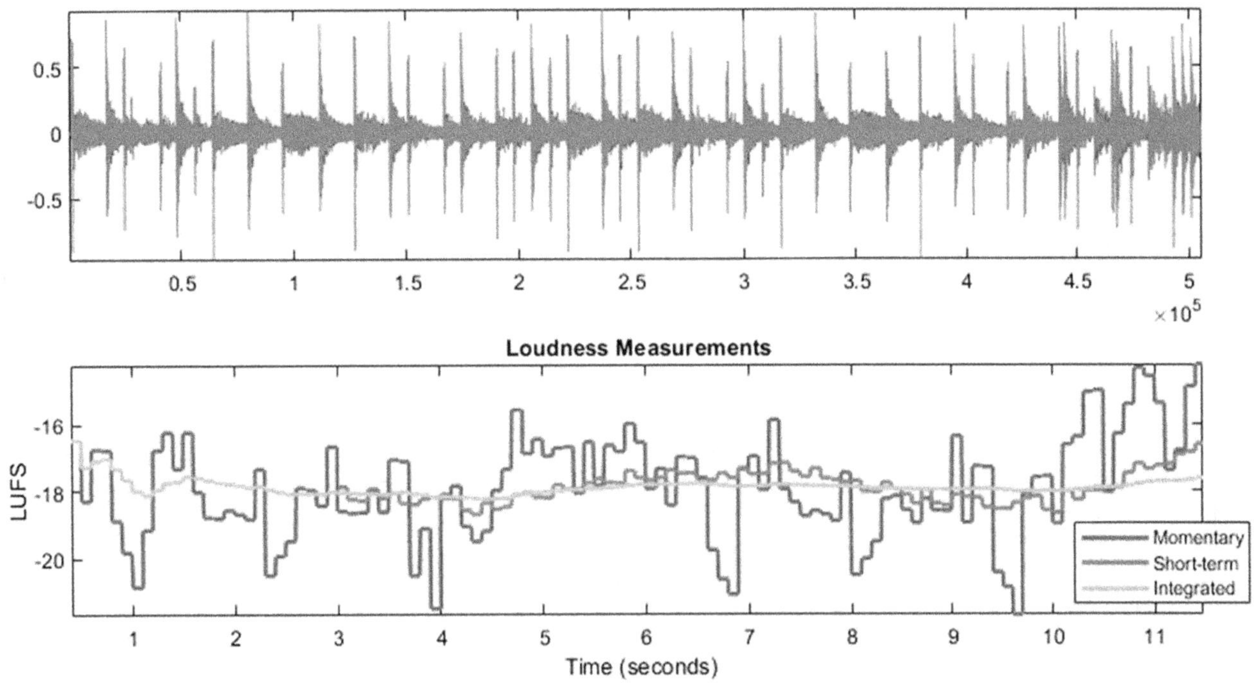

FIGURE 5.27
Output of Example 5.7.

5.9.6 Temporal Filters

The following example computes averages along a vector of data by sliding a window of width ω and computing averages of the data contained within each window using the FIR and IIR schemes. The function "filter" is used to implement a 1D filter on a 1D signal, "ones" creates an array of all ones, "rng" initializes a random number generator. A moving-average filter is a common method used for smoothing noisy data (Figure 5.29).

EXAMPLE 5.8 MATLAB EXAMPLE TO REMOVE NOISE USING FILTERS

```
clear; clc;
t = linspace(-pi,pi,100);
rng default %initialize random number generator
x = sin(t) + 0.25*rand(size(t)); % add noise to signal

% FIR filter
a1 = 1;
w = 10; b = (1/w)*ones(1,w);
y1 = filter(b,a1,x);
figure,
subplot(211),
plot(t,x); hold on; plot(t,y1);
legend('Input Data','Filtered Data')
title('FIR filter'); hold off;

% IIR filter
a2 = [1, -0.2];
y2 = filter(b,a2,x);
subplot(212),
plot(t,x); hold on; plot(t,y2);
legend('Input Data', 'Filtered Data')
title('IIR filter'); hold off;
```

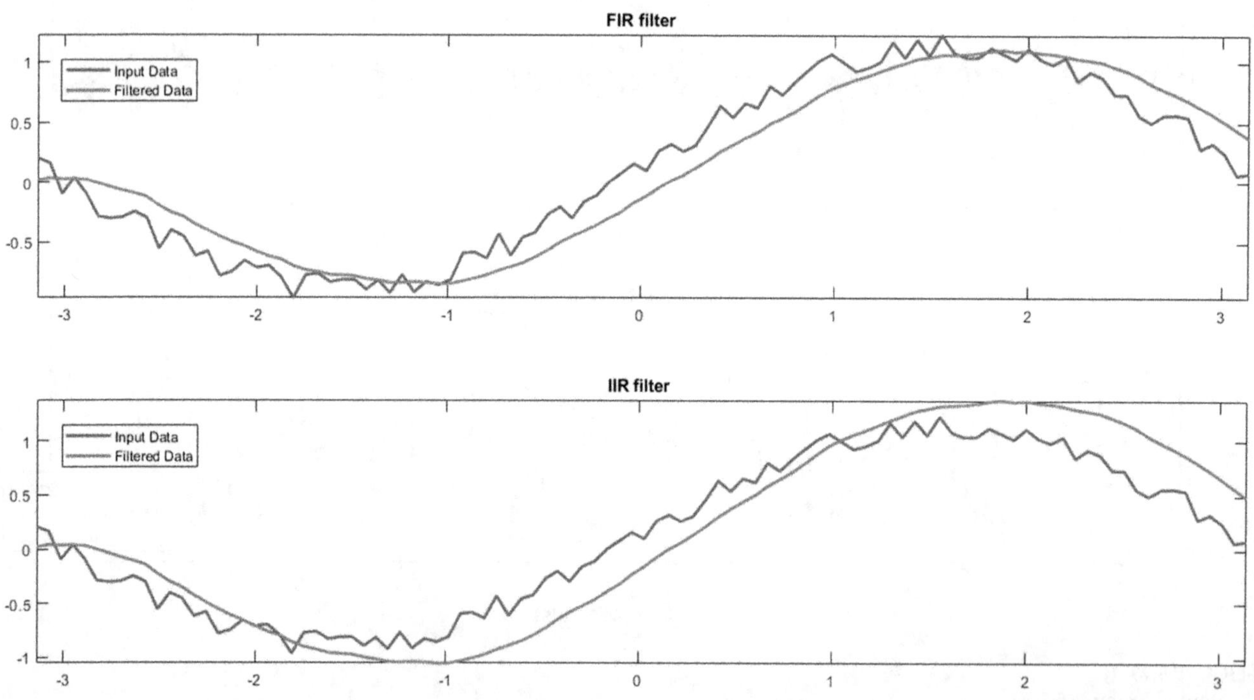

FIGURE 5.28
Output of Example 5.8.

5.9.7 Spectral Analysis

The following example shows a composite note being generated by adding three sinusoidal tones with frequencies of 50 Hz, 120 Hz and 150Hz and amplitudes of 0.6, 0.4 and 0.2, respectively. The composite note is transformed to the frequency domain using forward DFT and its frequency components are extracted, after which it is converted back to time domain using inverse DFT. The functions "fft" and "ifft" are used to implement the forward DFT and inverse 1D DFT (Figure 5.30).

EXAMPLE 5.9 MATLAB EXAMPLE TO DISPLAY FREQUENCY COMPONENTS

```
clear; clc;
k = 1000;
Fs = k; % Sampling frequency
T = 1/Fs; % Sampling period
L = 1500; % Length of signal
t = (0:L-1)*T; % Time vector
x1 = 0.6*sin(2*pi*50*t); % First
   component
x2 = 0.4*sin(2*pi*120*t); % Second
   component
x3 = 0.2*sin(2*pi*150*t); % Third
   component
figure,
subplot(321),
plot(x1(1:k/10)); axis([1, k/10, -1,
   1]); grid; title('x1');
subplot(323),
plot(x2(1:k/10)); axis([1, k/10, -1,
   1]); grid; title('x2');
subplot(325),
plot(x3(1:k/10)); axis([1, k/10, -1,
   1]); grid; title('x3');
subplot(322),
X = [x1+x2+x3];
plot(t(1:k/10),X(1:k/10)); grid;
   title('X');
subplot(324),
Y = fft(X);
P2 = abs(Y/L);
P1 = P2(1:L/2+1);
P1(2:end-1) = 2*P1(2:end-1);
f = Fs*(0:(L/2))/L;
plot(f,P1); grid; title('Y');
xlabel('f (Hz)')
ylabel('|P1(f)|')
subplot(326),
y = ifft(Y);
plot(t(1:k/10),y(1:k/10)); grid;
   title('y');
```

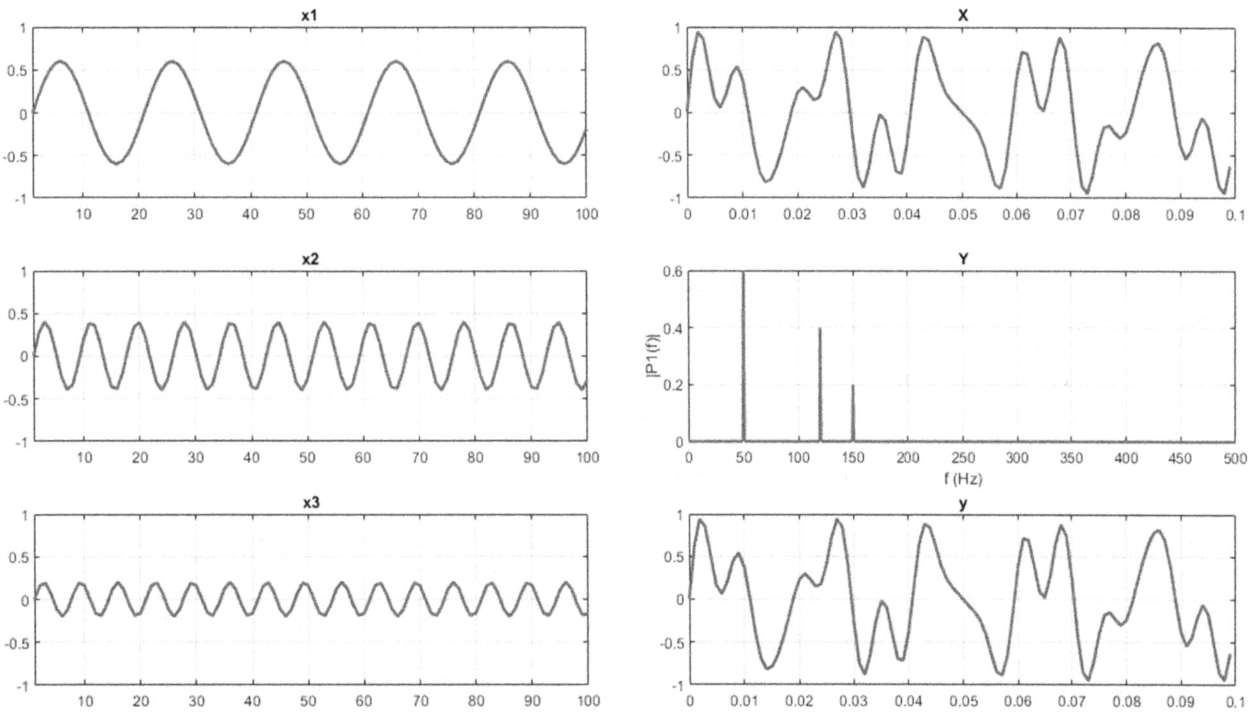

FIGURE 5.29
Output of Example 5.9.

In the following example, a square wave is digitized using 200 samples and it is transformed to the frequency domain using DFT. The real and imaginary parts of the coefficients A and B are extracted and plotted along with the signal waveform. The cosine and sine basis functions are then computed, each of which has 200 components, out of which 8 components are displayed: 1, 2, 3, 4, 5, 10, 50, 100. The function "fft" calculates the fast Fourier transform, "imag" depicts the imaginary part of a complex number, "real" depicts the real part, "cell" creates a cell array and "numel" returns the number of array elements (Figure 5.24).

EXAMPLE 5.10 MATLAB EXAMPLE TO DISPLAY DFT BASIS FUNCTIONS

```
clear; clc;
% square wave
t = 0 : 0.1 : 20;
x = sin(t) + (1/3)*sin(3*t) +
   (1/5)*sin(5*t) + (1/7)*sin(7*t);
N = numel(x);
X = fft(x);
A = real(X);
B = -imag(X);
C = cell(1,N);
for k=0:N-1
for i=0:N-1
    C{k+1} = [C{k+1}, cos(2*pi*i*k/N)];
end
end
S = cell(1,N);
for k=0:N-1
for i=0:N-1
    S{k+1} = [S{k+1}, sin(2*pi*i*k/N)];
end
end
figure,
subplot(441), plot(C{1}); axis tight;
   title('C (1)');
subplot(442), plot(C{2}); axis tight;
   title('C (2)');
subplot(443), plot(C{3}); axis tight;
   title('C (3)');
subplot(444), plot(C{4}); axis tight;
   title('C (4)');
subplot(445), plot(C{5}); axis tight;
   title('C (5)');
subplot(446), plot(C{10}); axis tight;
   title('C (10)');
subplot(447), plot(C{50}); axis tight;
   title('C (50)');
subplot(448), plot(C{100}); axis tight;
   title('C (100)');
subplot(449), plot(S{1}); axis tight;
   title('S (1)');
subplot(4,4,10), plot(S{2}); axis
   tight; title('S (2)');
subplot(4,4,11), plot(S{3}); axis
   tight; title('S (3)');
subplot(4,4,12), plot(S{4}); axis
   tight; title('S (4)');
subplot(4,4,13), plot(S{5}); axis
   tight; title('S (5)');
subplot(4,4,14), plot(S{10}); axis
   tight; title('S (10)');
subplot(4,4,15), plot(S{50}); axis
   tight; title('S (50)');
subplot(4,4,16), plot(S{100}); axis
   tight; title('S (100)');
```

The following example illustrates generation of audio spectrograms. The function "chirp" generates a waveform with variable frequency, "spectrogram" generates a spectrogram using short-time Fourier transform. The general syntax is the following: chirp(t, f0, t1, f1, 'method'), where f0 is the instantaneous frequency at time t0, f1 the instantaneous frequency at time t1 and "method" specifies the interpolation type (Figure 5.31).

EXAMPLE 5.11 MATLAB EXAMPLE TO GENERATE SPECTROGRAMS

```
clear; clc;
figure,
t = 0:1/1e3:2;
y1 = chirp(t,0,1,250);
subplot(311),spectrogram(y1,256,250,25
   6,1e3,'yaxis')
y2 = chirp(t,100,1,200,'quadratic');
subplot(312),spectrogram(y2,256,250,25
   6,1e3,'yaxis')
y3 = chirp(t,400,1,300,'quadratic');
subplot(313),spectrogram(y3,256,250,25
   6,1e3,'yaxis')
```

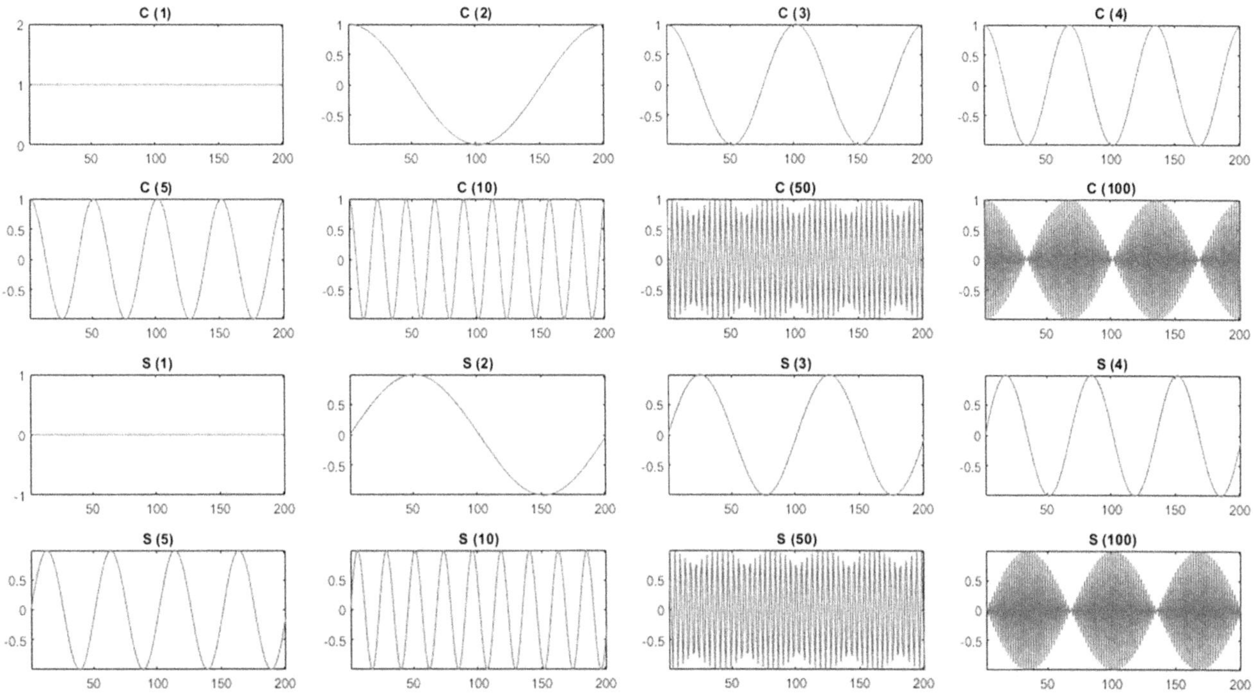

FIGURE 5.30
Output of Example 5.10.

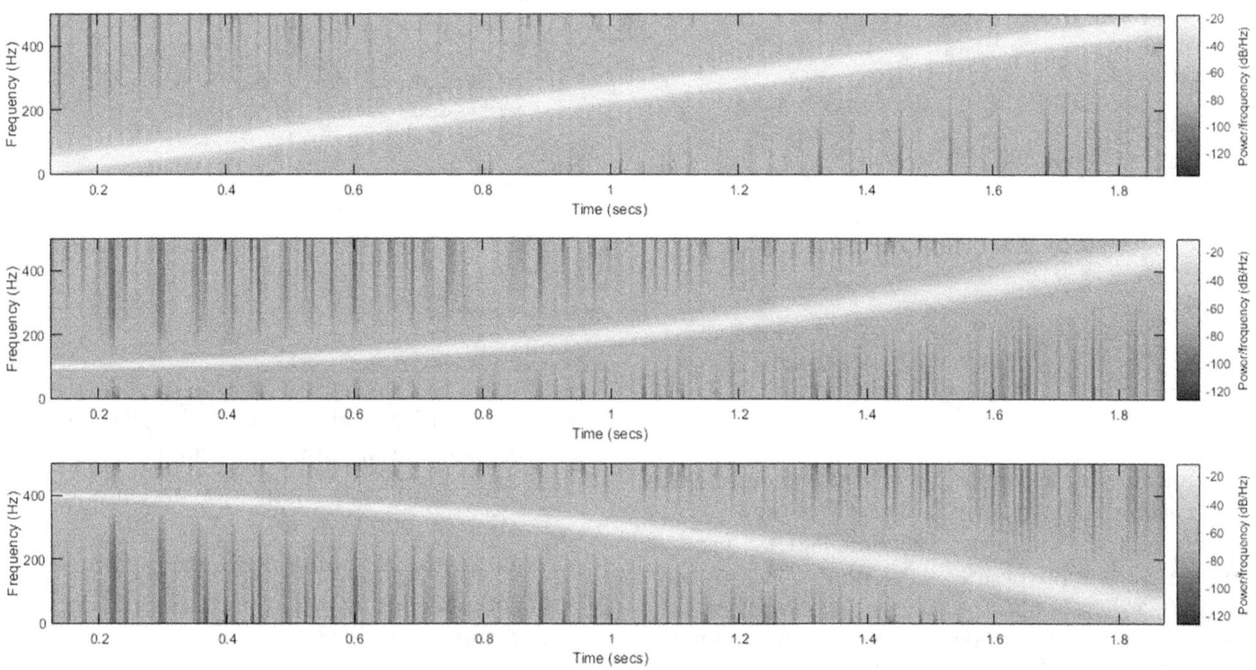

FIGURE 5.31
Output of Example 5.11.

5.9.8 MIDI

The following example illustrates playing notes on a MIDI device by using MIDI messages. The function "mididevinfo" displays a table containing information about a list of MIDI devices attached to the system. The function "mididevice" is used to create an interface to one or more of the MIDI devices listed. The function "midimsg" is used to send and receive MIDI messages to one or more of the MIDI devices listed. The function "midisend" is used to send a MIDI message to one or more of the listed devices.

EXAMPLE 5.12 MATLAB EXAMPLE FOR PLAYING NOTES ON A MIDI DEVICE

```
clear; clc;
mididevinfo
device = mididevice('Microsoft MIDI
   Mapper');
channel = 1; velocity = 64;
   duration = 1; timestamp = 1;
note = 60;
msg = midimsg('Note', channel, note,
   velocity, duration, timestamp)
midisend(device, msg);
note = 61;
msg = midimsg('Note', channel, note,
   velocity, duration, timestamp)
midisend(device, msg);
note = 62;
msg = midimsg('Note', channel, note,
   velocity, duration, timestamp)
midisend(device, msg);
note = 63;
msg = midimsg('Note', channel, note,
   velocity, duration, timestamp)
midisend(device, msg);
note = 64;
msg = midimsg('Note', channel, note,
   velocity, duration, timestamp)
midisend(device, msg);
```

The following example plays a set of eight notes using different instruments. The "ProgramChange" option of the "midimsg" function can be used to change the sound of the instruments. The General MIDI (GM-1) standard defines a set of 128 sounds each with a unique number to identify it Although the GM1 does not define the actual characteristics of each sound, the names in parenthesis are intended only as guides: 6 (harp), 8 (celesta), 14 (bells), 18 (organ), 48 (string), 55 (orchestra), 61 (brass), 73 (flute) and so on. The sound effects include 122 (sea shore), 123 (bird tweet), 124 (telephone ring), 126 (applause), 127 (gunshot) and so on.

EXAMPLE 5.13 MATLAB EXAMPLE FOR PLAYING DIFFERENT INSTRUMENTS ON A MIDI DEVICE

```
clear; clc;
device = mididevice('Microsoft GS
   Wavetable Synth');
melody = [61,62,63,64,65,66,67,68];
channel = 5;
velocity = 120;
duration = 1;
timestamp = 1;
n = numel(melody);
pc = [6,8,14,18,48,55,61,73,76,80,91,9
   8,100,102,112,117,118,115,122,123,12
   4,126,127];
counter=1;
for count=1:numel(pc)
    programChangeMessage =
   midimsg('ProgramChange',1,
   pc(counter));
    midisend(device,programChang
   eMessage);
for i = 1:n
    idx = (2*i-1):(2*i);
    msgArray1(idx) = midimsg('Note',1,
   melody(i),velocity,duration,i);
    msgArray2(idx) =
   midimsg('Note',1,melody
   (9-i),velocity,duration,i);
end
    midisend(device,msgArray1)
    midisend(device,msgArray2)
    counter=counter+1;
end
```

Review Questions

- Trace the historical evolution of digital audio processing highlighting important events.
- Discuss amplitude, frequency and phase in relation to sound waves.
- What are the key points of acoustic principles?
- What is meant by minimum threshold curve and audio masking?
- How can sound be represented as a progressive wave?
- What is meant by CD quality audio, and what are its sampling parameters?
- What is the working principle of a microphone? What does its polar plot indicate?

- Discuss the various structural types and functional types of microphones.
- How does an audio amplifier work? Discuss the various classes of the same.
- Why is a loudspeaker divided into multiple structural units?
- What is meant by surround sound? Discuss technologies in this field.
- What are the I/O ports in a sound card and what are their functions?
- Discuss functions and workflow of major components of a sound card.
- Discuss the various aspects of the MIDI standard and key features of MIDI 2.0.
- Differentiate between the various types of MIDI messages.
- Mention some of the common audio editing tasks offered by a GUI-based software.
- What is meant by audio segmentation and why is it necessary?
- Mention the characteristics of various windowing functions.
- What is a noise gate, and what are its activation parameters?
- How does a dynamic range compressor help to improve sound quality?
- What are the applications of spectral analysis of audio?
- Differentiate between the FIR and IIR temporal filters.
- Discuss in brief some of the major applications of audio in recent times.
- What are the legal and ethical considerations for digital audio processing?
- Mention some of the challenges and emerging trends in audio processing.
- Discuss some of the characteristics of major audio file formats.

References

Cardone, E.P., *The art and science of surround and stereo recording*, Springer Vienna, 2021.

Cobussen, M., N. Nielsen, *Music and ethics*, Routledge, 2016.

Davies, M.J., *Legal issues in the music industry*, BuzzGig LLC, 2009.

Fourier, J.B.J., *Theorie analytique de la chaleur*, Chez Firmin Didot, 1822.

Huber, D.M., R. Runstein, *Modern recording techniques*, Routledge, 2017.

Jackson, W., *Digital audio editing fundamentals*, APress, 2015.

Kim, H., L. Remaggi, P. Jackson & A. Hilton, "Immersive spatial audio reproduction for VR/AR using room acoustic modelling from 360° images", *IEEE Conference on Virtual Reality and 3D User Interfaces (VR)*, pp. 120–126, 2019.

Olson H. F., "*Acoustical Engineering*", Van Nostrand, Princeton, N.J., 1957.

Pohlmann, K., *Principles of digital audio*, McGraw-Hill, 2010.

Rossing, T., R. Moore & P. Wheeler, *Science of sound*, Pearson, 2011.

Rumsey, F., *Desktop audio technology: Digital audio and MIDI principles*, Routledge, 2003.

Schutze, S., A.I. Schutze, *New realities in audio: A practical guide for VR, AR, MR and 360 video*, CRC Press, 2018.

Smith, J.O., *Introduction to digital filters: With audio applications*, Createspace Independent Publishers, 2006.

Somberg, G. (editor), *Game audio programming: Principles and practices*, CRC Press, 2010.

Toole, F.E., *Sound reproduction: The acoustics and psychoacoustics of loudspeakers and rooms*, Routledge, 2017.

6

Video

6.1 Video Fundamentals

6.1.1 Key Terms

We begin with a snapshot of the important terms relevant to the digital video, to present the entire chapter in a nutshell. These terms will be expanded in the following sections of the chapter in their proper contexts.

Chroma sub-sampling: Chroma sub-sampling in video refers to the practice of representing color information at a lower resolution than brightness information. It involves reducing the amount of sampled color information while retaining the full resolution of brightness (luminance), which helps in compressing video data while maintaining acceptable image quality.

Chrominance: Chrominance, often referred to as chroma, represents the color information in a video signal, separate from the luminance (brightness) information. It includes the hue and saturation components, providing the color details that, when combined with luminance, form a complete representation of a video image.

HDMI: HDMI (High Definition Multimedia Interface) is an audio/video interface for transmitting digital data between devices, presenting digital alternative to composite video, component video, S-video and VGA connectors. HDMI connects set-top boxes, Blu-Ray disc players, HD DVD players, personal computers, games consoles, etc.

Luminance: Luminance, often referred to as Y or Y′, represents the brightness or grayscale component in a video signal, separate from the color information (chrominance). It conveys the intensity or lightness of an image and is a key element in the overall representation of visual content in video.

NTSC: NTSC, or National Television System Committee, is a video standard used primarily in North America and some other regions, defining the technical specifications for analog television broadcasting. It specifies a video format with a frame rate of approximately 30 frames per second and a resolution of 525 lines, utilizing interlaced scanning for the transmission of color television signals.

PAL: PAL, or Phase Alternating Line, is a video standard used in many parts of the world, including Europe and Asia, defining the technical specifications for analog television broadcasting. PAL employs a frame rate of approximately 25 frames per second and a resolution of 625 lines, utilizing interlaced scanning for the transmission of color television signals.

S-Video: Super-video (S-video) is an analog video signal format where the luminance and chrominance portions are transmitted separately using multiple wires instead of the same wire as for composite video. This provides a better video quality than composite video because of reduced interference but the cable is more expensive, and is usually found in high-end equipment.

SMPTE timecode: SMPTE (Society of Motion Picture and Television Engineers) timecode is a standardized system for labeling individual frames of a video or film production with a unique identifier, facilitating precise synchronization and editing in post-production. It uses a specific timecode format, typically displayed as hours, minutes, seconds and frames, allowing for accurate referencing and coordination of audio and video elements in the production process.

Streaming: Video streaming is the continuous transmission of video content over the internet in real time, allowing users to watch videos without downloading them first. It involves the compression, transmission and playback of video data, providing a seamless and on-demand viewing experience for users across various devices.

Video capture card: A video capture card is a hardware device that allows the input of external video signals, such as those from cameras, VCRs or game consoles, into a

DOI: 10.1201/9781003588030-6

computer for processing, recording or broadcasting. It converts analog video signals into digital format, enabling video content to be utilized or manipulated on a computer.

Video color spaces: Video color spaces define how colors are represented in a video signal by assigning numerical values to the components of each color. Common video color spaces include RGB (Red, Green, Blue) and YUV, with YUV being particularly used in video compression and broadcasting due to its separation of luminance and chrominance information.

Video file formats: Video file formats are standardized structures for encoding and storing digital video data, defining how video information is compressed, organized and stored. Common examples include formats like MP4, AVI and MKV, each employing different compression methods and settings suitable for various applications in digital video.

YCbCr: YCbCr is a video signal representation that separates luminance (Y) from chrominance (Cb and Cr), allowing for efficient compression and transmission of video content. It is commonly used in video encoding standards like MPEG and is advantageous for separating brightness and color information in digital video processing.

YIQ: YIQ is a color space used in NTSC television broadcasting to represent color information by separating it into luminance (Y) and two chrominance components (I and Q). The Y component represents brightness, while I and Q represent the color information, allowing for efficient transmission and processing of color television signals.

YUV: YUV is a color space that separates image brightness (luminance, Y) and color information (chrominance, U and V) to represent colors in a video signal in PAL television broadcasting. It is commonly used in video compression and broadcasting, providing an efficient way to transmit and process color information separately from brightness.

6.1.2 Historical Evolution

The historical evolution of digital video processing spans several decades, witnessing remarkable advancements that have transformed the landscape of video capture, editing and distribution.

1960s–1970s: The groundwork for digital video processing was laid in the 1960s and 1970s with early experiments in video digitization. Researchers explored techniques to convert analog video signals into digital form, marking the inception of digital video processing.

1980s: The 1980s saw the establishment of digital video standards, including formats like MPEG-1, which laid the foundation for efficient video compression and transmission. This era also witnessed the introduction of the first digital video cameras and the transition from analog to digital video editing systems.

1990s: The 1990s marked a significant shift with the widespread adoption of digital video editing technologies. Non-linear editing (NLE) systems replaced traditional linear editing methods, allowing for greater flexibility, precision and the ability to manipulate digital video files directly on computers.

1990s–2000s: Digital television (DTV) standards were introduced in the 1990s, paving the way for enhanced image quality and interactive features. Additionally, the DVD format, with its digital video encoding, became a popular medium for distributing high-quality video content.

2000s: The 2000s witnessed the widespread adoption of high-definition (HD) video, offering significantly improved resolution and image quality. Blu-ray Discs, with their large storage capacity and advanced video compression (H.264), became the standard for high-quality video distribution.

2010s: The advent of high-speed internet and improved video compression algorithms led to the rise of streaming services. Platforms like YouTube, Netflix and others revolutionized how people consume video content, with adaptive streaming and on-demand access becoming integral to the digital video landscape.

2020s–Present: The present era is characterized by the widespread adoption of 4K and 8K resolution videos. These formats offer even higher resolution and clarity, contributing to an immersive viewing experience. The development of HEVC (High-Efficiency Video Coding) further optimized video compression for higher resolutions. As we move into the future, digital video processing is converging with immersive technologies like virtual reality (VR) and augmented reality (AR).

These technologies demand advanced video processing capabilities to deliver realistic and interactive visual experiences.

6.1.3 Basic Concepts

6.1.3.1 Frame and Frame Rate

Video consists of a set of still images called frames which are displayed to the user one after another at a specific speed called the frame rate measured in frames per second, shortened to fps. If displayed at a fast enough rate, the human eye cannot distinguish the individual images as separate entities but merges them together creating an illusion of moving images, because of the phenomenon of persistence of vision (PoV). It has been observed that the frame rate should be around 25 to 30 fps for perceiving a smooth motion without gaps or jerks. Audio is added and synchronized with the apparent movement of images to create a complete video sequence (Figure 6.1). A video file therefore consists of multiple images and one or more audio tracks. One disadvantage of handling so much information together is an increase in file size and consequently large amount of processing resources to handle them. For example, a 1-minute video file consisting of 30 frames each 640 by 480 pixels in size and using 24-bit color information takes up more than 1582 MB of space. Audio sampled at 44,100 Hz adds another 10 MB to the file every minute. Moreover, playback of the video file requires a bandwidth of around 30 MB/s. Schemes of compression therefore are very important for video to handle such large overheads.

6.1.3.2 Motion Video and Motion Picture

When visual and audio information is recorded in the form of electrical signals onto magnetic storage, and/or transmitted along wires or broadcast over TV channels, then such representation of video is specified using the term "motion video" to distinguish it from another kind of representation called motion picture used in cinema theatres where video frames are recorded onto celluloid film using a photo-chemical process. Motion video in the form of electrical signals is generated from an analog video camera and stored in magnetic tapes like video cassettes and later played back using video cassette player (VCP). TV transmission is also a popular example of motion video display. Earlier generation analog video cameras used vacuum tubes called cathode ray tubes (CRT) to generate these signals, which can then be fed to a monitor to display the video, while audio was recorded separately using a microphone and fed to loud-speakers for generation of sound. New generation video cameras replace CRTs with electronic photo-sensors called charge coupled devices (CCD) which generate electrical signals roughly proportional to the intensity of light falling on them. Signals from a CCD array are collected sequentially and sent to a monitor for display.

6.1.3.3 Component Video and Composite Video

Component video refers to three separate RGB signals corresponding to the primary colors red, green and blue, generated from an analog video device like a camera which can be fed to a color monitor using three separate cables, to display an image on screen. Inside the monitor, these signals are used to activate a color generation system like CRT electron guns or LCD elements for color reproduction. Composite video on the other hand is a scheme where the three RGB signals are combined into a single signal called YC signal, carrying luminance and chrominance information, pertaining to brightness and color, which can be transmitted using a single cable or broadcast channel. Composite signals are more convenient and efficient to transmit from one place to another, at the

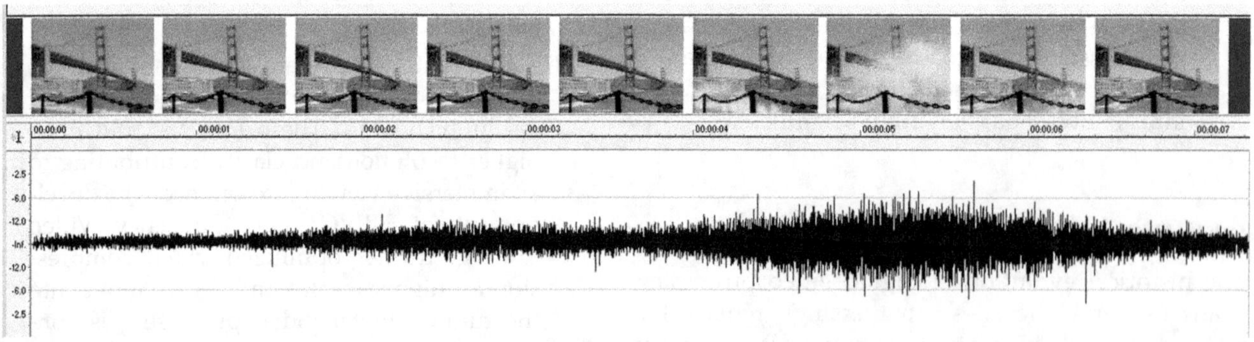

FIGURE 6.1
Video as a combination of image frames and synchronized audio.

receiving end they again need to be reverted back to RGB signals for being displayed on a monitor screen (Figure 6.2).

6.1.3.4 YC Signal Format

The YC signal format represents video information in terms of luminance Y and chrominance C. The advantages of this format over the RGB format included the fact that both Y and C could be transmitted over a single cable or channel, and therefore arrived exactly at the same instant at the receiving end. This was done by splitting the typical 6 MHz bandwidth of a TV channel into two parts, 0 to 4 MHz was allotted to Y and 1.5 MHz for C, the remaining 0.5 MHz being used for audio. The reason behind this unequal distribution was because of the fact that the human eye was more sensitive toward the Y information and less toward the C information. Another advantage of the YC signal format was that only the Y part of the signal could be used to cater to the B/W TV sets while both Y and C could be used to cater to the color TV sets. This meant that only a single transmission system was required and only a filter at the receiving end could be used to remove the color signal for monochrome viewing. Due to the usage of a single transmission cable, cost of the system could also be reduced.

The Y signal representing the grayscale intensity can be computed using a linear combination of the RGB signals. After experimenting with a number of combinations and keeping in mind that the human eye was more sensitive toward the green part of the color spectrum, it was finally standardized as per the ITU-T Rec. 601 (1982) [www.itu.int/rec/R-REC-BT.601-7-201103-I/en], that Y would be composed of 60% of G, 30% of R and 10% of B resulting in the relation: $Y = 0.299R + 0.587G + 0.114B$. The color information was represented using two sub-components called Cb and Cr and defined as follows: $Cb = B - Y$ and $Cr = R - Y$. Accordingly, the composite video format, requiring a single cable or channel for transmission, is specifically referred to as using the YCbCr signal format. Most of the analog video equipment used today for transmitting video signals use the composite video cable and connector for interfacing, e.g., between VCP and TV (Figure 6.3).

6.1.3.5 Chroma Sub-sampling

Conversion of RGB to the YC signal format has another important advantage: the possibility of using

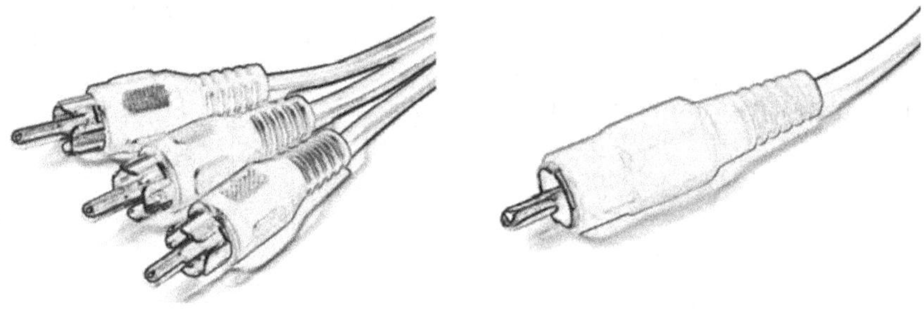

FIGURE 6.2
Component video and composite video cables.

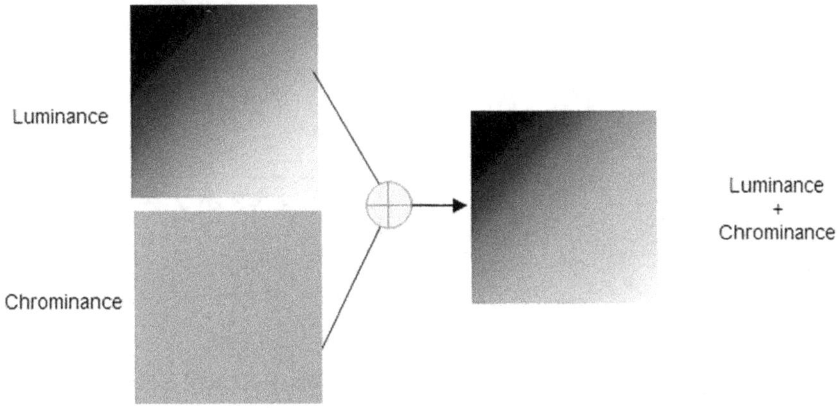

FIGURE 6.3
Luminance and chrominance in YC signals.

less bandwidth by reducing color information. Studies have shown that the human eye is more sensitive to luminance (brightness) information than to chrominance (color) information. This finding is exploited to reduce color information during video transmission, a process referred to as chroma sub-sampling. The reduction in color information is denoted by a set of three numbers expressed as a ratio A:B:C. The numbers denote the amount of luminance and chrominance information within a window on the screen usually 4 pixels wide and 2 pixels high. Common values include 4:2:2 which imply that within a sliding 4 × 2 window, there are 4 pixels containing Y information along the first row, 2 pixels of C information along the first row and 2 pixels of C information along the second row. Essentially, this means while all the pixels contain brightness information, color information is reduced to half along the horizontal direction. Other values frequently used are 4:1:1 and 4:2:0. The first set indicates one-fourth color information horizontally, while the second set indicates half-color information both along the horizontal and vertical directions. Obviously, a value of 4:4:4 indicates no reduction in color information (Figure 6.4).

6.1.3.6 NTSC TV Standard

NTSC (National Television Systems Committee) is a television broadcasting system [www.ntsc-tv.com] used in a number of countries including Korea, Japan, Canada, North America, parts of South America, Mexico and the Caribbean islands, created by an industry-wide standardization body. It was set up in 1940 by the Federal Communication Commission (FCC) in the United States to establish a nationwide standard for black-and-white TV transmission. It specified a standard using 525 horizontal lines, 30 frames per second, 2 interlaced fields per frame (also called 2:1 interlacing), 262.5 lines per field, 60 fields per second, an aspect ratio of 4:3 and frequency modulation for the audio signal (frequency modulation is a form of modulation which represents information as variations in the instantaneous frequency of a carrier wave). Although, each frame in an NTSC video consists of 525 horizontal lines, however, only 480 of them are actively used for generating the picture on the screen, the rest being used for synchronization and vertical retrace. In color transmission, the luminance signal Y is derived based on the ITU-T Rec. 601 (1982) mentioned above. Since the human eye is most sensitive to variations in luminance, the Y signal is allowed a bandwidth of 0–4.2 MHz. The chrominance part of the signal is represented by two 3.58 MHz sub-components known as I (in-phase) and Q (quadrature). I and Q signals are amplitude modulated in quadrature (QAM) onto the sub-carrier wave. The I signal is in phase with the carrier wave and the Q is in quadrature, i.e., 90 degrees out of phase with the sub-carrier signal. I physically represents the orange-cyan axis (positive I is orange, negative I is cyan) and is band-limited to 1.3 MHz while Q physically represents the magenta-green axis (positive Q is magenta, negative Q is green) and its bandwidth is limited to 0.6 MHz. I and Q can be defined in terms of R, G and B. I and Q can be defined in terms of R, G and B.

$$Y = 0.299R + 0.587G + 0.114B$$

$$I = 0.597R - 0.274G - 0.321B$$

$$Q = 0.211R - 0.523G + 0.311B$$

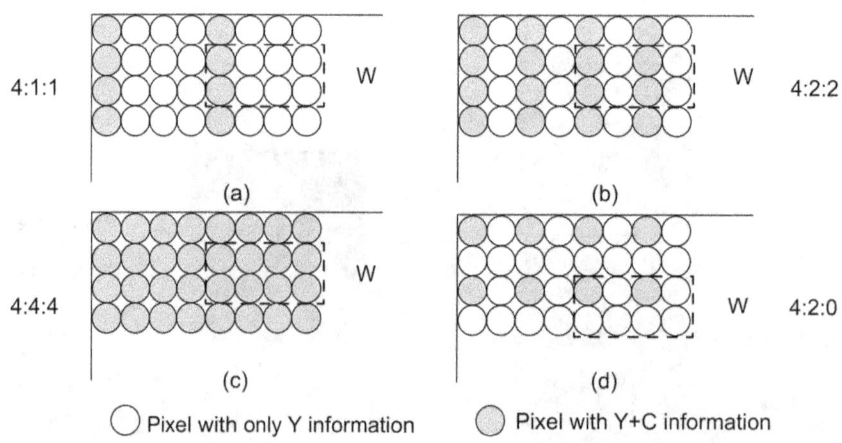

FIGURE 6.4
Chroma sub-sampling.

6.1.3.7 PAL TV Standard

PAL (Phase Alternation Lines – sometimes the terms Alternate or Alternating are also used) is a TV broadcasting standard used in Europe, Asia, Africa and Australia. PAL was developed by Walter Bruch at Telefunken in Germany, and first introduced in 1967. French electronics manufacturer Thomson later bought Telefunken. The PAL system uses 625 horizontal lines at 25 frames per second, 2:1 interlacing with 2 fields per frame, 4:3 aspect ratio and a chroma subsampling scheme of 4:2:2. Similar to NTSC, PAL also uses a luminance component Y derived from NTSC standard. The chrominance part of the signal is represented by two 4.43 MHz sub-components known as U (in-phase) and V (quadrature). The U and V signals are amplitude modulated in quadrature onto the subcarrier wave. Both U and V are band-limited to 1.3 MHz each, while the composite video signal may have bandwidths of 4.2, 5, 5,5 or 6 MHz depending on the specific standard used. U and V can be defined in terms of R, G and B (Slater, 1991).

$$Y = 0.29900R + 0.58700G + 0.11400B$$

$$U = -0.14713R - 0.28886G + 0.43600B$$

$$V = 0.61500R - 0.51499G - 0.10001B$$

6.2 Video I/O

Video input and capture techniques involve the process of acquiring video footage or streams from various sources. These techniques are commonly used in areas such as filmmaking, live broadcasting, video production, surveillance and computer vision applications. Digitizing video, in general, requires a video capture card and associated recording software. The capture card is usually installed at the PC end, which accepts analog video from a source device and converts it into a digital file using recording software. Alternatively, the capture card can be inside a digital video camera, which is capable of producing a digital video output and recording it onto a tape. The digital output from a digital video camera can also be fed to a PC after necessary format conversion.

6.2.1 Video Camera

Analog video cameras are used to record a succession of still images and then convert the brightness and color information of the images into electrical signals. There were two types: the earlier ones using cathode ray tubes (CRT) for video capture and the later ones using charge coupled devices (CCD) as the capture sensor (Musburger, 2012).

6.2.1.1 CRT-based

In the earlier generation of cameras, the CRT itself functioned as the primary image sensor, capturing light and converting it into electrical signals for further processing. The face of the CRT acted as a photoconductive surface sensitive to light. When exposed to light, it generated electrical charges proportionate to the intensity of the incoming light. The electrical charges on the CRT's surface caused the emission of electrons, forming an electron image representing the captured scene. The emitted electron signals underwent amplification and modulation to enhance the signal quality and prepare it for transmission or recording. Analog signals were converted into discrete scan lines for compatibility with display devices. The CRT generated an output voltage which could be fed to a display device or recorded on magnetic storage. For color camera, three separate R, G, B signals were generated at the output.

6.2.1.2 CCD-based

As technology progressed, dedicated image sensors like CCDs became more prevalent due to their higher resolution and efficiency. CCDs capture light and convert it into electrical signals, providing the basis for analog video. A lens system focuses light onto the CCD, determining aspects like focus, zoom and depth of field. Analog circuits process the electrical signals from the CCD, including amplification, color correction and synchronization. A scan conversion process converts the continuous analog signals into discrete scan lines, suitable for display and transmission. These devices were called "camcorders" as they contained the recording media within the same container (Kallen, 2014). Analog video camcorders were prevalent before the widespread adoption of digital technologies, providing a means to capture and record video content on analog formats. Analog video camcorders recorded video in analog format, storing information as continuous electrical signals on magnetic storage media. Analog camcorders typically had built-in microphones for recording audio, some models with an input for external microphones to enhance audio quality. Camcorders commonly used VHS or VHS-C tapes for recording. VHS-C tapes were smaller versions of VHS tapes. Compact 8mm tapes and the improved Hi8 tapes were also used, offering better video quality compared to VHS formats. Professional-grade camcorders often used Betacam, while Betamax was a consumer format. Sony's Video8 and Digital8 formats also gained popularity, especially for personal use. The recording time depended on the length of the tape, with common options like 30 minutes, 60 minutes and 120 minutes. The camcorder's CCD sensor captured the analog video signal, including luminance and chrominance information. Analog video signals were processed within the camcorder, adjusting color balance, contrast and other parameters. The processed analog signal was modulated onto the recording medium, typically a magnetic tape, using helical scan recording technology. During playback, the recorded signal was read from the tape, converted back into analog form and displayed on a monitor or TV. Analog camcorders had lower resolution compared to digital counterparts, typically offering Standard Definition (SD) video quality. Analog signals were susceptible to interference, leading to issues like snow or color distortion in low-quality recordings.

6.2.1.3 Image Capture Sensors

The image sensor is either he CMOS or CCD type. Common in modern cameras, CMOS (Complementary Metal-Oxide-Semiconductor) sensors are versatile and energy-efficient, providing high-quality image capture. Light incident on the CMOS sensors generates electrical charges in proportion to the intensity of the light. Each pixel's charge is read out individually, creating a digital representation of the captured scene. Still used in some professional applications, CCD sensors offer excellent image quality but may consume more power. CMOS sensors have a more complex structure, with each pixel containing its own photodiode and amplification circuitry, and can be manufactured using standard semiconductor processes, making them more cost-effective to produce in large volumes. CCD sensors have a simpler structure, with a single amplifier shared among all pixels in the sensor, and traditionally require more complex manufacturing processes, making them potentially more expensive to produce compared to CMOS sensors. Because of the dedicated amplifier, parallel readout of pixel values is possible which leads to faster readout speeds. CCD sensors on the other hand, use a serial process for readout, transferring charge from pixel to pixel before reaching the amplifier. This can result in slower readout speeds. Moreover, CMOS sensors generally have lower power consumption because they only draw power when pixels are actively being read, whereas, CCD sensors typically have higher power consumption because they require continuous power for the entire row during readout. CCD sensors were traditionally known for better low-light performance, but this advantage has diminished with advancements in CMOS technology. Overall, CCD have traditionally produced better image quality in certain scenarios, specially good low-light performance, and suitability for specialized applications, however, have higher power consumption, slower readout speeds and potential higher manufacturing costs. CMOS sensors on the other hand, have lower power consumption, faster readout speeds, cost-effective manufacturing and versatility for various applications, however had challenges in low-light performance, but recent advancements have mitigated this to a large extent.

6.2.1.4 Digital Camera

Modern digital video cameras have evolved significantly from their analog predecessors, leveraging advanced technologies to capture, process and store high-quality video content. Main components and features include the following:

Imaging Sensor: At the heart of a digital video camera lies the imaging sensor, typically a Charge-Coupled Device (CCD) or a Complementary Metal-Oxide-Semiconductor (CMOS) sensor. These sensors convert light into electrical signals, capturing the image. CMOS sensors, in particular, have gained prominence due to their lower power consumption and ease of integration.

Resolution and Pixel Count: Resolution is a critical factor in determining the clarity of video footage. Digital video cameras offer varying resolutions, commonly expressed in terms of pixels (e.g., 1080p, 4K). Higher pixel counts result in sharper images and increased detail. Video resolutions are commonly standardized, such as Full HD (1920 × 1080) or Ultra HD/4K (3840 × 2160).

Optics and Lenses: High-quality lenses are crucial for capturing sharp and well-defined images. Digital video cameras often feature interchangeable lenses to cater to diverse shooting scenarios. The aperture, focal length and lens quality impact depth of field, low-light performance and overall image clarity.

Image Processor: The image processor handles the data from the imaging sensor, applying various enhancements and adjustments. It plays a key role in image quality, color reproduction and the camera's overall performance. Advanced image processing algorithms can reduce noise, enhance dynamic range and improve low-light capabilities.

Video Compression: Digital video cameras employ compression algorithms to reduce the size of video files without significant loss of quality. Common video compression standards include H.264 and H.265 (HEVC). These codecs balance file size and video quality, ensuring efficient storage and transmission.

Frame Rate and Shutter Speed: Frame rate determines the number of frames captured per second. Common frame rates include 24fps (frames per second) for cinematic content and 30fps or 60fps for standard video. Shutter speed, a related parameter, influences motion blur and exposure. Both factors contribute to the overall visual aesthetics of the captured video.

Autofocus and Manual Focus Systems: Digital video cameras feature autofocus systems that automatically adjust focus based on the subject's distance. Manual focus capabilities are also essential for professional videographers who require precise control over focus points, especially in dynamic shooting situations.

White Balance and Color Grading: White balance ensures accurate color representation by compensating for varying lighting conditions. Digital video cameras often include manual and automatic white balance settings. Additionally, color grading features enable videographers to manipulate colors in post-production, enhancing creative expression.

Audio Capture and Microphones: Digital video cameras are equipped with built-in microphones or external audio input ports. Professional videographers may use external microphones for improved audio quality. Audio capture capabilities, including manual audio level controls and audio monitoring, contribute to a well-rounded video production.

Connectivity and Storage: Digital video cameras offer various connectivity options, such as USB, HDMI or SDI, facilitating data transfer and external device integration. Storage options include internal memory, SD cards or external hard drives, allowing videographers to store large video files conveniently.

User Interface and Controls: The user interface comprises controls, menus and displays that enable users to configure camera settings. Touchscreens, physical buttons and dials provide intuitive control over exposure, focus and other parameters, enhancing the user experience.

EVF: An Electronic Viewfinder (EVF) or LCD screen provides real-time previews of the captured scene, aiding in composition and framing. Touchscreen interfaces allow users to access menus, adjust settings and control various functions directly on the display.

Storage: Video files are typically saved in formats like MP4, MOV or AVCHD, ensuring compatibility with various playback devices and editing software. Many modern cameras support 4K (3840 × 2160 pixels) or even higher resolutions, providing detailed and crisp video quality. Some cameras can capture high-speed video at frame rates well above the standard 24 or 30 frames per second (fps).

Apart from the image sensor, a digital camera has a lens system, often with adjustable focal lengths and apertures, focuses incoming light onto the image sensor. Some cameras incorporate optical image stabilization (OIS) mechanisms to compensate for handshakes or vibrations. A Digital Signal Processor (DSP) processes the electronic signals from the image sensor, performing tasks such as noise reduction, color correction and image enhancement. Automatic adjustments to white balance and exposure settings optimize the image for different lighting conditions. Modern digital video cameras use digital storage media, such as SD cards or internal solid-state drives (SSDs), to store captured video files. Video files are often compressed using codecs to optimize storage space without significant loss of quality. Intelligent algorithms can detect and track faces or objects within the frame, ensuring they remain in focus. Built-in wireless connectivity allows for seamless file transfer, remote control and live streaming directly from the camera to other devices or online platforms.

6.2.2 Video Capture Card

A video capture card, also known as a capture card or capture board, is a hardware device that allows to capture and record video signals from external sources such as cameras, gaming consoles or other video playback devices (Leggett, 2020). A video capture card serves as an interface between analog video sources (such as cameras, VCRs or gaming consoles) and a computer, allowing users to digitize, process and store video content. The architecture of a video capture card can vary, but here are the main components typically found in such devices:

Video Input Ports: Composite Video (RCA) is a standard analog video input often used for connecting devices like VCRs or older video cameras. In some cases S-Video (Mini-DIN) accepts S-Video signals, providing better quality than composite video. Component Video (RCA or BNC) connectors support separate Y, Pb, Pr component video signals, offering high-quality input. Some modern capture cards include HDMI input ports, allowing direct connection to digital sources like cameras or gaming consoles.

Audio Input Ports: RCA or 3.5mm jacks are provided for capturing accompanying audio signals. In cases where HDMI is used, audio signals can be embedded within the HDMI stream and captured simultaneously.

Video Processor: The video processor is responsible for processing and digitizing the incoming analog video signals. It converts analog signals into digital format for further processing and storage.

Analog-to-Digital Converter (ADC): The ADC is a crucial component that converts analog video signals into digital data. This is necessary because modern computers and storage devices work with digital data.

Memory (RAM): Video capture cards typically include on-board memory to temporarily store the digitized video data before it is transferred to the computer's main memory or storage.

Video Encoder: The video encoder compresses the digitized video data using various compression algorithms (such as H.264 or MPEG) to reduce file sizes and make them suitable for storage and streaming.

Output Ports: PCIe/PCI/USB/Thunderbolt enables video capture cards to connect to a computer through various interfaces. PCIe (PCI Express) and PCI cards are internal and installed directly on the motherboard, while USB and Thunderbolt variants offer external connectivity.

Driver and Software: Video capture cards come with drivers that allow the operating system to communicate with the hardware. Additionally, manufacturers often provide software for capturing, editing and streaming video content (Figure 6.5).

6.2.3 Video Digitization

Video digitization is the process of converting analog video signals into digital format. This process is crucial for preserving and modernizing video content, making it compatible with digital systems and storage. Here are the general steps involved in video digitization:

Source Connection: Connect the analog video source (e.g., VHS player, camcorder, analog camera) to the input port of the capture card via composite, S-Video, component video cables.

Audio Connection: If capturing audio, connect the analog audio source to the corresponding input port on the capture card using RCA or 3.5mm jacks.

Digital Source Connection: For HDMI sources, connect the device directly to the HDMI input port on the capture card.

Computer Connection: Install the video capture card into the appropriate slot on the motherboard (PCI or PCIe) or connect it externally via USB or Thunderbolt.

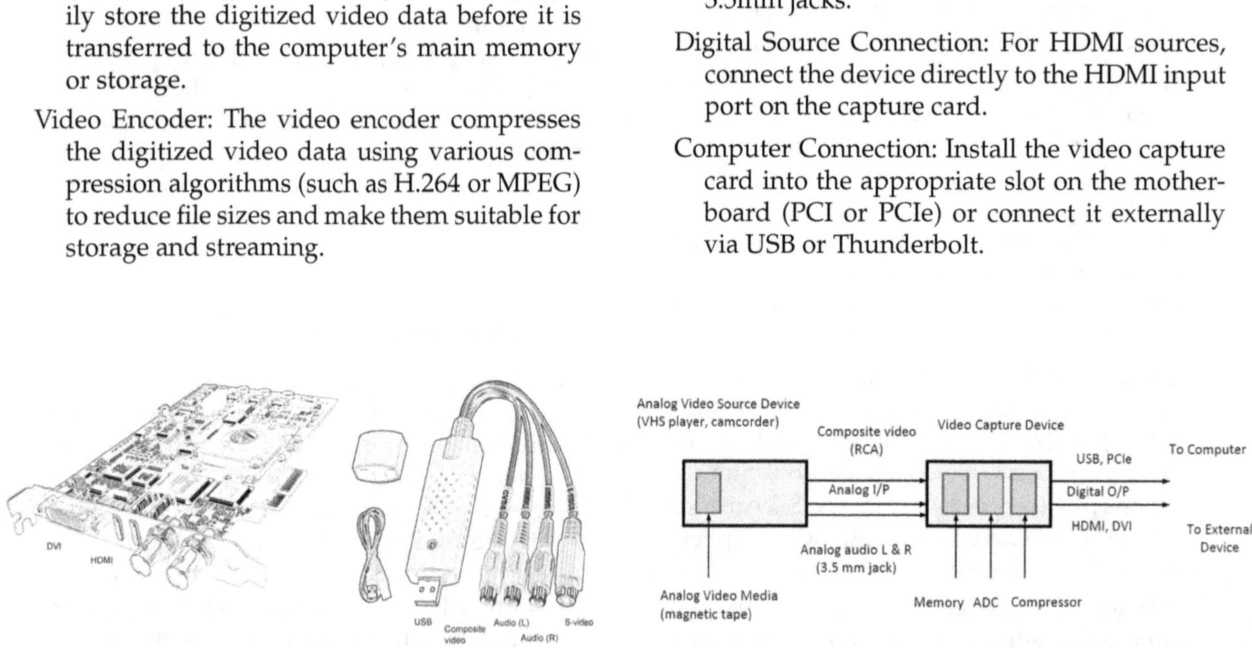

FIGURE 6.5
Video capture card interfaces.

Driver Installation: Ensure the capture card is compatible with the operating system. Install the necessary drivers provided by the card manufacturer. Configuration: Adjust settings such as resolution, frame rate and audio preferences through the installed driver software.

Video Digitization Process: The capture card digitizes the incoming analog video signals using an Analog-to-Digital Converter (ADC). The incoming analog video signal may need processing to ensure it is compatible with the digitization device. This processing may include adjustments for color balance, brightness, contrast and other parameters.

Data Transfer: The digitized video data is transferred to the computer through the chosen interface (PCIe, USB, etc.).

Processing: Video processing tasks, such as compression and color correction, may be handled by the video processor or encoder of the capture card or the computer's CPU.

Software Applications: Use dedicated capture software or video editing applications to initiate the capturing process, adjust settings and monitor the input.

Quality Considerations: Set the capture card to the desired resolution and frame rate, ensuring optimal video quality. Bitrate and Compression: Adjust bitrate and compression settings to balance file size and video quality.

Storage or Transmission: The digitized and, if applicable, compressed video data is stored in a digital format. It can be saved on a computer's hard drive, external storage device or transmitted over a network for live streaming or remote viewing.

Metadata Addition (Optional): Metadata, such as timecodes, captions and other descriptive information, may be added to the digitized video for organization and retrieval purposes.

6.2.4 Video Capture Software

In conjunction with video capture cards, manufacturers often provide bundled capture software that complements the hardware, offering users a comprehensive solution for capturing, editing and managing digital video content. Below is an overview of the typical features found in video capture software bundled with video capture cards:

Device Detection and Configuration: The software automatically identifies and configures settings for the connected video capture card. Allows users to manually adjust settings such as input type, resolution and frame rate.

Capture Control: Initiates and terminates the video capture process, and allows pausing and resuming the recording without creating separate files.

Video Source Selection: Enables users to choose the video source, whether it's composite, S-Video, component or HDMI, as well as the audio source for capturing accompanying audio.

Preview and Monitoring: Displays a live preview of the incoming video feed on the computer screen, and overlays information such as resolution, frame rate and recording status on the preview window.

Capture Settings: Allows users to set the desired video resolution and frame rate for recording, and adjusts the bitrate and compression settings to control file size and video quality.

Audio Controls: Manages audio volume level adjustments during capture, and configures audio settings such as sample rate and bitrate.

File Management: Offers options for naming captured files, and allows users to choose the directory where captured videos are stored.

Editing and Post-Processing: Provides simple editing tools for trimming, cutting and merging video clips, and offers basic filters and effects to enhance the captured video.

Export and Sharing: Supports various video file formats for compatibility with editing software and playback devices, may facilitate sharing directly to online platforms or social media.

User Interface: A user-friendly interface with clear navigation and easy access to essential features, allows users to customize the interface based on personal preferences.

Live Streaming (Optional): Some capture software includes live streaming capabilities, enabling users to broadcast content in real time.

Documentation and Help: Provides access to a comprehensive user manual for reference, and links to online support resources, forums or direct customer support.

Firmware and Software Updates: Enables automatic checking and updating of both capture card firmware and software for bug fixes and feature enhancements.

6.2.5 Video Playback

Video output and playback are crucial components in the consumption of digital video content. Whether for entertainment, education or professional purposes, the quality and seamless delivery of video play a significant role in the viewer's experience.

Display Devices: The output of digital video is often viewed on various display devices, ranging from traditional monitors and television screens to more modern devices like smartphones, tablets and projectors. Each device has specific characteristics, including resolution, aspect ratio and color reproduction, which impact how the video appears to the viewer.

Connectivity: Different video output interfaces are used to connect devices to displays. Common interfaces include HDMI (High-Definition Multimedia Interface), DisplayPort, VGA (Video Graphics Array) and more. The choice of interface depends on the compatibility of the devices being connected.

Resolution Matching: To ensure optimal viewing quality, it's important to match the resolution of the video content with the native resolution of the display device. This helps prevent issues such as pixelation or stretching.

Media Players: Media players are software applications or hardware devices designed for the playback of digital video files. Popular media players include VLC Media Player, Windows Media Player, QuickTime and various streaming platforms like YouTube and Netflix.

CODEC Compatibility: Video files are often encoded using specific codecs, and the media player must support these codecs to decode and play the content properly. Common video codecs include H.264, H.265, VP9 and more.

Streaming Services: With the rise of high-speed internet, video streaming services have become increasingly popular. These services deliver video content in real time over the internet, allowing users to watch videos without downloading the entire file. Popular streaming platforms include Netflix, Hulu, Amazon Prime Video and YouTube.

Bitrate and Compression: The bitrate of a video file affects its quality and file size. Higher bitrates generally result in better quality but may require more bandwidth for streaming. Compression techniques, such as those used in streaming services, balance quality and file size for efficient delivery.

Interactive Elements: Some video content includes interactive elements, allowing viewers to engage with the video. This may include clickable links, annotations or interactive overlays that provide additional information or lead to related content.

Subtitle and Closed Captioning: Subtitles and closed captioning enhance accessibility by providing text representation of spoken dialogue and sound effects. Video players often support multiple languages and styles for subtitles.

6.2.6 Video Transmission

Video transmission is the process of sending information from one point to another enabling real time communication and content delivery over large distances. Analog transmission involves continuously varying signals, often susceptible to degradation and interference. Digital transmission converts video signals to binary data enabling more reliable transmission and the ability to incorporate compression and error correction techniques (Weynand & Weise, 2012).

6.2.6.1 Analog Video Transmission

RGB signals for color reproduction worked well when transmitted over short distances, typically over a few meters. However, when these signals were needed to be transmitted over large distances spanning several kilo meters like in TV transmission, a number of challenges were encountered. First, three separate copper cables running over several kilo meters made the system costly. Second, three separate signals transmitted along the three cables did not arrive exactly at the same instant of time at the receiving end due to differences in attenuation factors, with the result that the images were frequently out of sync and distorted. Third, when color TV transmission started in several countries, the earlier monochrome system of black & white (B/W) TV also continued side by side, so that a need was felt to design a signal format which can cater to both systems at once. To deal with all these problems, a new signal format was developed which was called composite video and the signals were called YC signals. Y indicated the luminance or intensity signal and C indicated the chrominance or color signal. YC signals could be transmitted over a single cable or channel. Only Y with C filtered out could be used to drive a B/W color TV while both Y and C are used for color TV reproduction.

As per the ITU-T Rec. 601 (1982) [itu.int/rec/R-REC-BT.601-7-201103-I/en], Y can be represented as a linear combination of R, G, B components according to the relation: Y = 0.299R + 0.587G + 0.114B. The color information was represented using two components called the color difference signals. It consisted of two color sub-components called Cb and Cr and defined as follows: Cb = B - Y and Cr = R - Y. Physically, the Y signal is obtained by passing the R, G, B current signals from the respective camera output through a resistor bridge. An impedance of 30k ohm is connected in parallel to each of the signals R, G and B output from the tube camera. Hence, the output is a combination of {30/(70 + 30)}R, {30/(20 + 30)}G, {30/(270 + 30)}B, i.e., 0.3R + 0.6G + 0.1B approximately. The color-difference signals are generated by inverting Y using an inverter and adding the inverted signal separately to R and B to obtain (R – Y) and (B – Y) (Figure 6.6).

The RGB output signals from a video camera are transformed to YC format which could be efficiently transmitted over large distances over a single channel. The bandwidth of the channel is divided into two parts: the lower 70% was allocated to Y since the human eye is most sensitive to variations in luminance, while the upper 40% was allocated to C with a small overlap between the two. At the receiving end for a B/W TV, the C component is discarded and only the Y component is used to display a grayscale image. For a color TV, the YC components are again converted back to RGB signals which are used to drive the electron guns of a CRT. Physically, the Y signal is obtained by passing the R, G, B current signals from the respective camera tubes through a resistor bridge. At the receiving end for a B/W TV, the C component is discarded and only the Y component is used to display a grayscale image. For a color TV, the YC components are again converted back to RGB signals which are used to drive the electron guns of a CRT.

6.2.6.2 Digital Video Transmission

Digital video transmission involves the efficient and reliable transfer of video data from a source to a destination, typically over various communication networks. Key components involved include:

Data Compression: Compression is crucial for minimizing the amount of data required to represent video content, reducing bandwidth requirements and transmission times. Video codecs like H.264 (AVC) or H.265 (HEVC) are widely used for efficient compression, balancing quality and file size.

Packetization: Involves breaking down video data into smaller packets for transmission over networks. Packets typically include headers with information like source and destination addresses, sequence numbers and payload data.

Transmission Protocols: TCP (Transmission Control Protocol) is a reliable, connection-oriented protocol suitable for applications where data integrity is crucial. It ensures that data arrives intact and in the correct order, but may introduce latency. UDP (User Datagram Protocol) is a connectionless, lightweight protocol ideal for real-time applications where low latency is critical, and provides faster transmission with less overhead but does not guarantee delivery or order.

Streaming Protocols: RTSP (Real-Time Streaming Protocol) is a protocol designed for controlling the delivery of streaming media, often used in conjunction with RTP. It supports live streaming and on-demand media, offering flexibility in content delivery. RTP (Real-time Transport Protocol) focuses on the real-time transmission of audio and video data. It supports synchronization of multiple streams and is widely used in VoIP and video conferencing.

Error Correction: Forward Error Correction (FEC) involves techniques that add redundant information to transmitted data to enable the receiver to correct errors without retransmission. It improves reliability by correcting

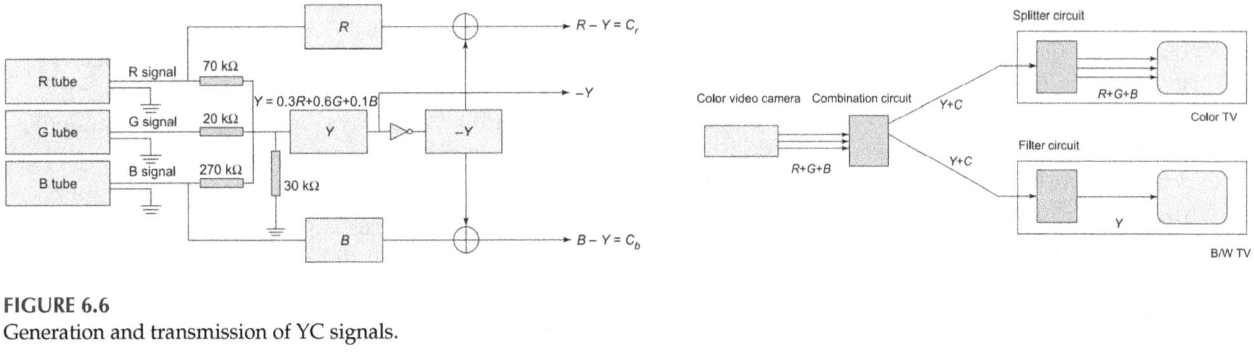

FIGURE 6.6
Generation and transmission of YC signals.

errors at the receiving end without requesting retransmission. Automatic Repeat reQuest (ARQ) is a method where the receiver detects errors and requests the sender to retransmit the affected data. It ensures data integrity by retransmitting lost or corrupted packets.

Quality of Service (QoS): QoS mechanisms prioritize certain types of traffic, ensuring a consistent level of service for time-sensitive applications like video streaming. Network routers and switches may implement QoS policies to prioritize video traffic over non-real-time data.

Adaptive Bitrate Streaming (ABR): A technique that dynamically adjusts the quality of a video stream based on the viewer's network conditions. Content Delivery Networks (CDNs) and streaming servers deliver multiple versions of a video at different bitrates, allowing devices to switch based on available bandwidth.

Encryption: Involves protocols like HTTPS for secure Web-based transmissions, and encryption standards such as TLS or AES for securing video data during transmission to prevent unauthorized access or tampering.

Latency Management: Minimizing delays between video capture and playback, critical for applications like video conferencing and live broadcasting. Involves low-latency codecs, optimized network protocols and edge computing technologies contribute to reduced transmission delays.

Content Delivery Networks (CDNs): Networks of geographically distributed servers that work together to deliver digital content, including video, to users. CDNs cache and serve video content from servers closer to end-users, reducing latency and improving content delivery speed.

6.2.6.3 Video Cables and Connectors

VGA (Video Graphics Array): VGA is an analog video interface that was widely used for connecting computers to monitors. VGA connectors have 15 pins arranged in three rows. VGA supports lower resolutions compared to digital interfaces, typically up to 1600 × 1200.

RCA (Radio Corporation of America): RCA connectors are widely used for analog audio and video signals. RCA connectors are typically color-coded, with red and white for audio and yellow for composite video. RCA connectors are commonly used for lower-resolution analog video signals.

S-Video: S-Video is an analog video signal format that encodes luminance and chrominance signals on two separate channels. These have four pins, two of which carries intensity and color information and the other two being the corresponding ground wires. The pins are housed in a cylindrical DIN connector containing a metal shielding.

HDMI (High-Definition Multimedia Interface): HDMI is a widely used digital interface for transmitting high-definition audio and video signals between devices. HDMI connectors come in various sizes, with Type A (standard), Type C (mini) and Type D (micro) being the most common. HDMI supports a range of video resolutions, including 4K and beyond. It can also carry audio signals and support features like Ethernet and CEC (Consumer Electronics Control).

DisplayPort: DisplayPort is a digital audio/video interface designed to replace older interfaces like VGA and DVI. DisplayPort connectors are rectangular with one corner cut off for orientation. Mini DisplayPort is a smaller variant. DisplayPort supports high resolutions, including 8K. It can carry audio, and newer versions support features like Adaptive Sync for variable refresh rates.

DVI (Digital Visual Interface): DVI is a digital interface commonly used for connecting computer monitors to video sources. DVI connectors come in three main types: DVI-D (digital), DVI-I (integrated digital and analog) and DVI-A (analog). DVI supports various resolutions, including 1080p. DVI-D and DVI-I can support both digital and analog signals.

Thunderbolt: Thunderbolt is an interface that supports high-speed data transfer, video output and power delivery over a single cable. Thunderbolt uses a USB Type-C connector, making it versatile and compatible with various devices. Thunderbolt supports high-resolution displays, and the latest versions offer impressive data transfer rates.

USB Type-C: USB Type-C is a versatile connector used for various purposes, including data transfer, power delivery and video output. The small, reversible USB Type-C connector is becoming more common in devices. USB

Type-C can support video output using protocols like DisplayPort or Thunderbolt, making it a multifunctional connector.

RJ45 (HDBaseT): Ethernet cables, commonly used for network connections, are also utilized in the HDBaseT standard for transmitting high-quality audio and video signals. RJ45 connectors are used for Ethernet cables. HDBaseT can transmit high-definition video, audio, power and control signals over long distances using standard Ethernet cables.

SDI (Serial Digital Interface): SDI is a professional-grade digital video interface used in broadcast and production environments. Typically it employs BNC connectors for coaxial cables, and supports various video resolutions, including standard and high definition. It is also known for its robustness and reliability in professional video production, often used for live broadcasting.

FireWire (IEEE 1394): FireWire, also known as IEEE 1394 or i.LINK, is a high-speed serial interface that supports both data and video transmission. Typically uses a 4-pin or 6-pin connector for smaller devices and a 9-pin connector for larger applications, and capable of transmitting standard and high-definition video signals. Initially popular for video cameras and external storage devices, offering high bandwidth and isochronous data transfer, making it suitable for real-time applications, however, later on largely been superseded by other interfaces like USB and Thunderbolt in recent years (Figure 6.7).

6.3 Video Editing and Processing

6.3.1 Image Processing Tasks

Video editing involves the manipulation and enhancement of visual and auditory elements to create a cohesive and engaging final product. Image processing tasks play a crucial role in refining the visual aspects of video content. Below is an overview of image processing tasks commonly employed in video editing:

Color Grading: Adjusting the color balance, contrast, brightness and saturation to achieve a desired look or mood in the video. Color grading involves the use of color correction tools, curves and color wheels to manipulate the color information in each frame.

Exposure Adjustment: Correcting the overall brightness and darkness levels of a video, ensuring optimal visibility and clarity. Exposure adjustments can be achieved through controls like gamma correction, levels adjustment and histogram manipulation.

White Balance Correction: Balancing the color temperature of a video to ensure accurate representation of white colors. White balance correction compensates for variations in lighting conditions, such as indoor and outdoor scenes, by adjusting the color temperature of the footage.

Image Stabilization: Reducing the impact of camera shake or jitter in video footage to create smoother and more visually pleasing sequences. Image stabilization algorithms analyze motion patterns and adjust frames to align and stabilize the overall video.

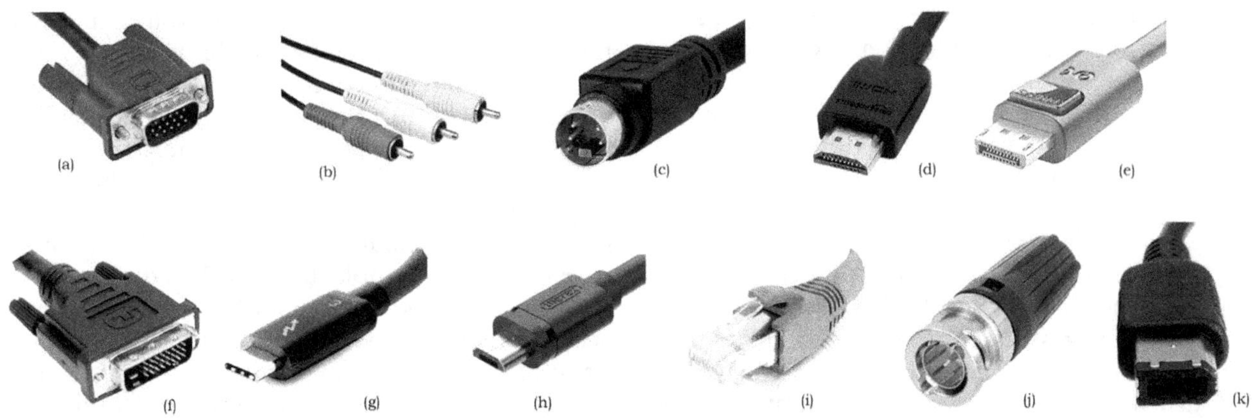

FIGURE 6.7
Video connectors: (a) VGA, (b) RCA, (c) S-Video, (d) HDMI, (e) DisplayPort, (f) DVI, (g) Thunderbolt, (h) USB type-C, (i) RJ-45, (j) DVI (k) Firewire.

Sharpening: Enhancing the clarity and detail of video frames by emphasizing edges and fine features. Sharpening algorithms apply localized adjustments to image contrast, enhancing the perception of sharpness.

Blurring: Intentionally reducing the clarity or focus of specific areas in a video for creative or privacy reasons. Gaussian blur or other blurring techniques can be applied to soften details in selected regions.

Image Overlay and Watermarking: Adding graphics, logos or watermarks to video frames for branding or copyright purposes. Image overlay involves positioning and blending external images onto video frames, while watermarking techniques ensure visibility without significant interference with the main content.

Chroma Keying (Green Screen): Replacing a specific color (often green or blue) in the video with another image or background. Chroma keying algorithms identify and remove the specified color, allowing the insertion of alternative backgrounds or visuals.

Image Cropping and Resizing: Adjusting the dimensions of video frames by cropping unwanted areas or resizing to fit specific aspect ratios. Cropping involves removing portions of the frame, while resizing adjusts the overall dimensions of the video.

Special Effects: Adding creative elements such as filters, overlays or animations to enhance the visual appeal of the video. Special effects are achieved through a combination of image processing techniques, including blending modes, filters and layering.

Face Recognition and Tracking: Identifying and tracking human faces within the video, enabling various applications like automatic focus adjustments or facial effects. Face recognition algorithms analyze video frames, detecting and tracking faces based on predefined characteristics.

Since video frames are individual images, image processing techniques can be applied to each frame and compiled back to the video. We have seen earlier that color RGB images can be stored as 3D arrays, each dimension for one of the color channels. Extending the idea, a video can be stored as 4D arrays, the first three dimensions pertaining to color, and the fourth dimension for the frame number of the video clip. Each frame of the video can be read into memory and then common image processing tasks like color conversion, edge detection, intensity corrections and noise reduction can be applied to it, after which it can be written back to the video sequence. Since the fourth parameter of the 4D array indicates the frame number, this can be displayed over the frame specifying a size and location, as well as other text.

6.3.2 Timebase

In the natural world, we experience time as a continuous flow of events. However, working with video requires precise synchronization; so it is necessary to measure time using precise numbers. Familiar time increments like hours, minutes and seconds are not precise enough as each second might contain several events. When editing video, several source clips may need to be imported to create the output clip. The source-frame rates of these source clips determine how many frame rates are displayed per second within these clips. Source frame rates can be different for different types of clips, for example, motion film (24 fps), PAL (25 fps), NTSC (29.97 fps), CD applications (30 fps) and Web applications (15 fps). In a video editing project file, there is a single and common timeline where all the imported clips are placed. A parameter, called the timebase, determines how time is measured and displayed within the editing software. For example, a timebase of 30 means each second is divided into 30 units. The exact time at which an edit occurs depends on the timebase specified for the particular project. Since there needs to be a common timebase for the video editor timeline, source clips whose frame rates do not match with the specified timebase need adjustments.

If the timebase fps is same as that of the source fps, every frame is the source is represented as it is in the timebase without any need for adjustments. If the timebase fps is half of the source fps then every alternate frame in the source would need to be discarded. If the timebase fps is greater than the source fps, some frames in the source need to be duplicated to match the increase in the frame count displayed per second. On the other hand, if the timebase fps is smaller than the source fps, some frames in the source need to be discarded to match the decrease in the frame count displayed per second. These changes are as far as possible equally distributed over the entire length of the source clip. For example if the timebase fps is 30, and source fps is 24 then every fourth frame in the source needs to be duplicated to increase the count by 6, i.e., frames 1, 5, 9, 13, 17, 21. If the timebase fps is 15, and source fps is 24 then approximately every third frame in the source needs to be discarded to decrease the count by 9, i.e., frames 3, 6, 8, 11, 13, 16, 18, 21, 23 (Figure 6.8).

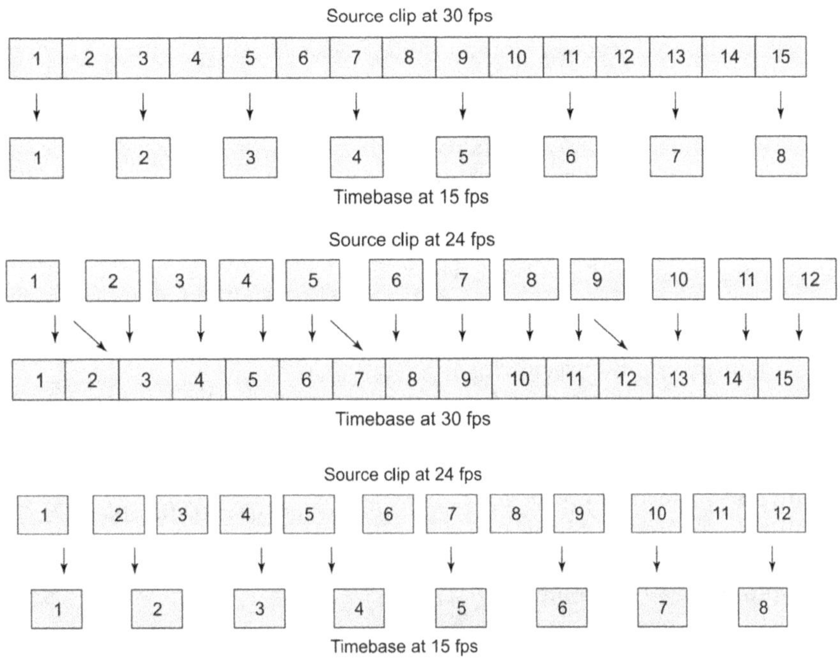

FIGURE 6.8
Timebase adjustments of video frames.

6.3.3 SMPTE Timecode

Time code defines how frames in a movie are counted and affects the way you view and edit a clip. A standard way to represent time code have been developed by a global body called Society of Motion Pictures and Television Engineers (SMPTE) [www.smpte.org] and represent time code by a set of numbers in the format hh:mm:ss:ff. The numbers represent hours, minutes, seconds and frames, and are added to video to enable precise editing, e.g., 00:03:51:03. When NTSC color systems were developed, the frame rate was changed by a tiny amount from 30 fps to 29.97 fps to eliminate the possibility of crosstalk between the audio and color information. This poses a problem since this small difference will cause SMPTE time and real time (what the clock reads) to be different over long periods. Because of this, two methods are used to generate SMPTE time code in the video world: Drop Mode and Non-Drop Mode.

6.3.3.1 Non-Drop Mode

In Non-Drop Mode, the time-code frames are always incremented by one in exact synchronization to the frames of your video. However, since the video actually plays at only 29.97 frames per second (rather than 30 frames per second), SMPTE time (i.e., time stamped on the video frames) will increment at a slower rate than real-world time (i.e., time displayed by the clock). This is because time on the video frames is stamped as 30 frames per second (the "second" value increments after thirty "frame" values, i.e., 00:00:00:00 … 00:00:00:29, 00:00:01:00 … 00:00:01:29, 00:00:02:00 …) but since the video plays at 29.97 fps, the increment in the "second" value actually occurs after (30/29.97) or 1.001 seconds. This will lead to an SMPTE time versus real time discrepancy. After a while, we could look at the clock on the wall and notice it is farther ahead than the time displayed by the SMPTE timecodes. In one hour, there is a discrepancy of (0.03 × 60 × 60) or 108 frames or 3.6 seconds between real time and SMPTE time.

6.3.3.2 Drop Mode

The Drop Mode time code attempts to compensate for the discrepancy between real-world time and SMPTE time by "dropping" frames from the sequence of SMPTE frames in order to catch up with real-world time. What this means is that occasionally in the SMPTE sequence of time, the SMPTE time will jump forward by more than one frame number. The time is adjusted forward by two frames on every minute boundary except 00, 10, 20, 30, 40 and 50. Thus, when SMPTE Drop time increments from 00:01:59:29, the next value will be 00:02:00:02 in SMPTE Drop rather than 00:02:00:00 in SMPTE Non-Drop. No frames are lost, because drop-frame time code does not actually drop frames, only frame numbers. To distinguish from the non-drop type, the numbers are separated by semicolons instead of colons, i.e., 00;02;00;02.

To illustrate the scenario, let us take a simple example. Assume a video clip having 15 frames stamped with a timecode with a frame rate of 5 frames/second. The frame sequence using a format (second : frame) is 1:1, 1:2, …, 1:5, 2:1, 2:2, …, 2:5, 3:1, 3:2, …, 3:5. Now suppose the video actually plays at 4 frames/second instead of the stamped rate of 5 frames/second. This would lead to a discrepancy between the stamped time and actual time such that in second number 2 we would see the frame stamped 1:5, in second number 3 we would see the frames 2:4 and 2:5 and so on. This situation is similar to a non-drop mode scenario. To rectify the discrepancy, the frames are stamped in a different manner to maintain synchronization with the real time, in the process dropping some of the frame numbers, e.g., after 1:4 instead of 1:5 we get 2:1. This situation is similar to a drop-mode scenario. Notice that none of the frames are actually dropped, only some of the frame numbers are eliminated, e.g., 1:5, 2:5, etc., do not exist. This scheme is designated with a semi-colon between the numbers instead of a colon (Figure 6.9).

6.3.4 Video Color Spaces

As discussed earlier RGB information can be converted to YCbCr color space using specified color conversion matrices (Poynton, 1996). YCbCr is related to RGB, according to the following relations:

$$Y = 0.299R + 0.587G + 0.114B$$

$$Cb = B - Y$$

$$Cr = R - Y$$

Substituting the value of Y in the second and third equations, we derive the following:

$$Y = 0.299R + 0.587G + 0.114B$$

$$Cb = -0.299R - 0.587G + 0.886B$$

$$Cr = 0.701R - 0.587G - 0.114B$$

The inverse relations are derived as follows:

$$R = Y + Cr$$

$$B = Y + Cb$$

$$G = Y - 0.1942Cb - 0.5094Cr$$

The National Television Systems Committee (NTSC) established in 1940, is a world standard body for

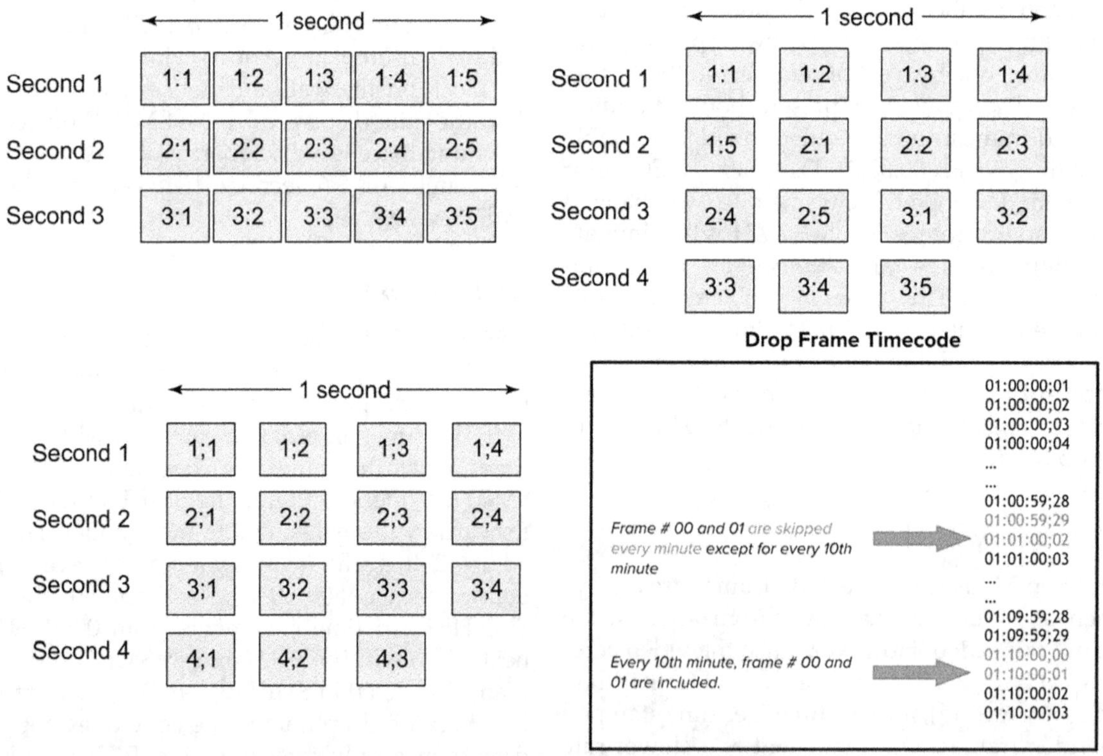

FIGURE 6.9
Adjustment of video timecodes.

analog television broadcasting in a number of countries, including the United States, Canada, Korea and Japan. To establish a color transmission standard, the luminance information is calculated from the RGB signals using the Y equation given above, while the chrominance part is represented using two subcomponents named I (in-phase) and Q (quadrature-phase). YIQ is related to RGB, according to the following relations. Currently these conversion relations are part of the ITU-R BT.1700 standard (www.itu.int/rec/R-REC-BT.1700-0-200502-I/en).

$$Y = 0.299R + 0.587G + 0.114B$$

$$I = 0.597R - 0.274G - 0.321B$$

$$Q = 0.211R - 0.523G + 0.311B$$

The inverse relations are:

$$R = Y + 0.956I + 0.621Q$$

$$G = Y - 0.272I - 0.647Q$$

$$B = Y - 1.106I + 1.706Q$$

Phase Alternation Lines (PAL) is the other major TV transmission standard used in Europe, Asia, Africa and Australia. PAL uses the same luminance definition as NTSC but its chrominance sub-components named U and V are different. YUV is related to RGB, according to the following relations. Currently these conversion relations are part ITU-R BT.601 standard (www.itu.int/rec/R-REC-BT.601-7-201103-I/en) (Figure 6.10).

$$Y = 0.29900R + 0.58700G + 0.11400B$$

$$U = -0.14713R - 0.28886G + 0.43600B$$

$$V = 0.61500R - 0.51499G - 0.10001B$$

The inverse relations are:

$$R = Y + 1.140V$$

$$G = Y - 0.395U - 0.581V$$

$$B = Y + 2.032U$$

Note:
It needs to be noted here that the NTSC and PAL standards developed for TV transmission were in a way responsible for creating the standard sampling rate of 44,100 Hz for CD quality digital audio in the later part of 1970. This value of 44.1 kHz was thought to be compatible with both the standards due to the following reasoning. Although the NTSC proposes 525 horizontal lines per frame, i.e., 262 lines per field, taking into account the landing zones for the electron beam during raster scanning, there are actually 245 active lines per field which together with 30 frames per second, i.e., 60 fields per second, and three audio samples being encoded per video line, leads to a total of 245 × 60 × 3 = 44,100 audio samples per second. Again for PAL which proposes 625 lines per frame, i.e., 312 lines

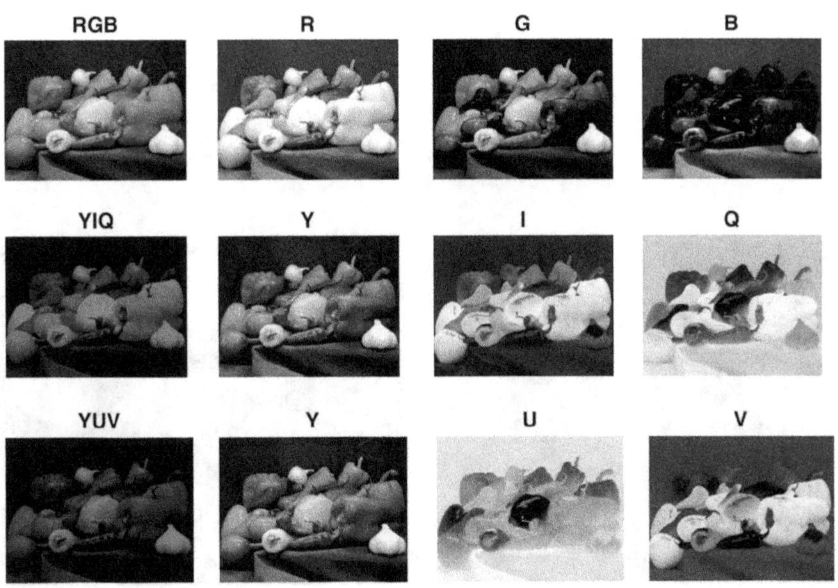

FIGURE 6.10
Video color spaces.

per field, out of which 294 are active lines, and 25 frames per second, i.e., 50 fields per second, and three audio samples being encoded per video line, leads to a total of 294 × 50 × 3 = 44,100 audio samples per second. Because of these computations, 44.1 kHz was considered to the best usable value compatible with the existing standards during the 1970s.

6.3.5 Blob Detection

In computer vision, the term "object detection" relates to detecting the presence of well-known semantic entities like cars, chairs, tables and people in images and videos (Dasiopoulou et al., 2005), usually for the purpose of annotation, classification and retrieval. Each class of object is characterized by a set of unique features and machine learning algorithms like neural networks are trained to look for those features in images and video frames (Zhang, 2018). The first step toward object detection is called blob detection, where a blob is a region in a digital image that differs in intensity or color from its surrounding regions. Once a blob is detected, it can be segmented from the rest of the image and then further processed to identify the semantic nature of the object represented by the region. One of the most common blob detectors is the Laplacian of Gaussian (LoG) operator. The input image $f(x,y)$ is first convolved with a Gaussian kernel $h(x,y)$:

$$g(x,y) = f(x,y) \otimes h(x,y)$$

where $h(x,y)$ is defined as follows:

$$h(x,y) = \exp\left(-\frac{x^2+y^2}{2\sigma^2}\right)$$

The Laplacian operator ∇^2 is the double derivative of the argument; in this case the operator is applied to the Gaussian convolved image:

$$\nabla^2 f(x,y) = \frac{\partial^2 f(x,y)}{\partial x^2} + \frac{\partial^2 f(x,y)}{\partial y^2}$$

This usually results in strong positive responses for dark regions and strong negative responses for bright regions. However, the main problem in applying the blob detector is that the operator response is strongly dependent on the relative sizes of the blob regions and the size of the Gaussian kernel. Since the size of a prospective blob region is unknown for an arbitrary image, a multi-scale approach is adopted; i.e., a number of different sizes of the LoG kernel are used to observe which scale produces the strongest response. A collection of such different sizes or scales is called the scale space (Figure 6.11).

6.3.6 Human Detection

To identify un-occluded people in upright positions, the human detector uses the HOG (histogram of oriented gradients) features and a trained Support Vector Machine (SVM) classifier (Dalal & Triggs, 2005). The method is based on evaluating normalized local histograms of image gradient orientations. For a pixel at location (x,y) with intensity $f(x,y)$, the gradient magnitude g and orientation θ is given as follows:

$$gx = \frac{\partial f(x,y)}{\partial x} = \{f(x+1,y) - f(x-1,y)\}$$

$$gy = \frac{\partial f(x,y)}{\partial y} = \{f(x,y+1) - f(x,y-1)\}$$

$$g = \sqrt{gx^2 + gy^2}, \theta = \arctan(gy / gx)$$

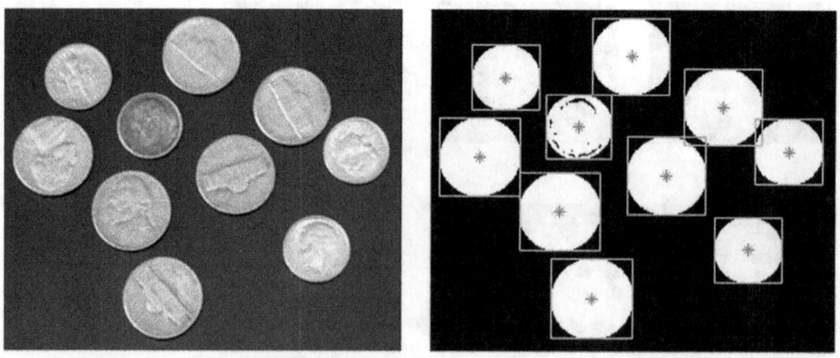

FIGURE 6.11
Blob detection.

An image of an upright person, standing or walking, is typically assumed to be 64 × 128 pixels in dimensions, which is divided into rectangular cells, each 8 × 8 pixels in size. Hence, there would be eight cells along the width and 16 cells along the height. A collection of 2 × 2 cells constitute one block, i.e., each block is 16 × 16 pixels in size. Blocks are considered with 50% overlap and within each block, the pixel orientations are quantized into nine bins ranging over angles 0°–180°, i.e., with 20° angular separation. The vote for the histogram bins is the gradient magnitude. The final feature vector is a concatenation of all the histograms in each block (Figure 6.12).

6.3.7 Face Detection

The Viola–Jones algorithm (Viola & Jones, 2001) was proposed to detect people's faces, noses, eyes, mouth or upper body. It is most suitable to detect object categories whose aspect ratio does not vary too much. It uses a sliding window to decide whether the window contains the object of interest. The size of the window may vary to accommodate objects at different scales but its aspect ratio remains fixed. The cascade classifier consists of a collection of learners, and each stage is trained using a technique called boosting. Each learner labels the region within the current window as either positive or negative. If the label is positive, the classifier passes the region to the next stage, and if the label is negative, the classification of the region completes and the window is shifted to the next position. The classifier reports an object found at the current window location when all the stages of the classifier reports the region as positive. A cascade classifier needs to be trained using a set of positive samples and a set of negative samples. The Viola–Jones algorithm can detect a variety of objects; however, it was primarily motivated by the problem of human face detection. A constraint for this is that the faces should be frontal, upright and un-occluded. The algorithm uses the Haar-like features developed from the concept of Haar wavelets (Haar, 1910) and takes the form of rectangular regions at specific locations in a detection window. Features consist of sums of pixel intensities in different regions and differences between these sums, which are then used to categorize subsections of the image. For example, for a human face, regions like the eyes are darker than neighboring regions like the cheeks, so sum of pixel intensities within a rectangle placed above the eyes would be different than those placed above the cheeks by a specified threshold, which if true, signals to the system what part of the face this might be. Because Haar-like features are weak learners with low classification rates, a large number of such features are organized to form a "cascade" for good classification. However, because of their simplicity, the calculation speed is quite high. Moreover, due to the use of summed up tables or integral images (Crow, 1984), a Haar-like feature of any size can be calculated in constant time, depending on the number of rectangles present. An integral image is a 2D lookup table in the form of a matrix with the same size as the original image, such that the value at any point is the sum of all pixels located on the upper-left region of the original image. This allows computation of rectangular areas at any position or scale using only four lookups. For example, to calculate the area enclosed within the rectangle bounded by the upper-left vertex A, upper-right vertex B, lower-right vertex C and lower-left vertex D of an integral image I we can perform sum = I(C) + I(A) − I(B) − I(D). Viola–Jones uses three types of features in their computations: 2-rectangle, 3-rectangle and 4-rectangle which respectively need 6, 8 and 9 lookups to calculate their sums (Figure 6.13).

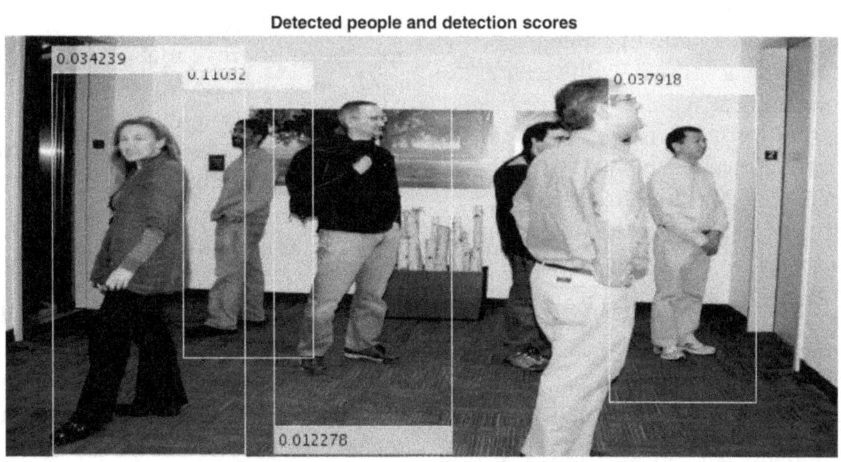

FIGURE 6.12
Human detection.

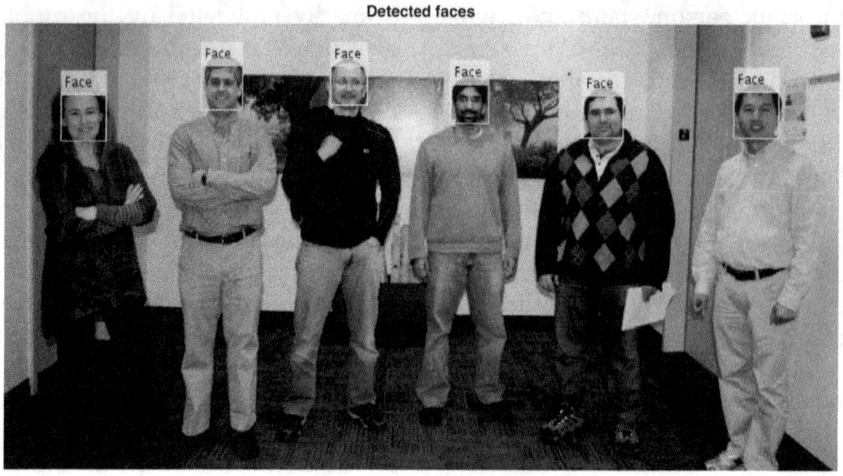

FIGURE 6.13
Face detection.

6.3.8 Histogram-Based Motion Tracker

The histogram-based tracker uses the histogram of pixel values of an object in an initial video frame to track it over the subsequent frames using the mean-shift algorithm. The mean-shift algorithm (Comaniciu & Meer, 2002) is a non-parametric technique (i.e., cannot be calculated from parameters of an equation) proposed for finding an area of a feature space where the density of the feature points is the highest. The process starts with an initial window in the feature space with a known center and a centroid which is calculated based on the distribution of the data points within the window area. Typically these two will not match, and the window is shifted so that its center coincides with the calculated centroid. Based on the new data distribution within the window, the centroid is re-calculated and the window re-shifted. This process continues in an iterative manner until the window center coincides with the centroid when the window is deemed to be over the region of maximum density. However, it requires knowing the size of the object to be tracked, which is defined by the user at the initialization by specifying a window size and location. The data distribution map is obtained after a back-projection of a color model which is typically the histogram of the color that needs to be identified. The color is usually represented in the HSV color space, and the histogram based on the hue-saturation (h,s) values becomes the model histogram in the initial frame. The model histogram depicts that for each value of (h,s) pair in the initial window, what is the probability of the pixel occurring, i.e., how many pixels have that value of (h,s) in the initial window. This histogram is then applied over other frames to find the areas containing the same color. This process is called histogram back projection. After the process completes, the brightest regions in the test frame correspond to the highest probability of finding the object of the initial frame in the test frame. This process is continued for all frames. One problem with the mean-shift algorithm is that the window size and orientation remain the same over all the frames, whereas the actual object being tracked may change in both size (e.g. moving closer or farther from the camera) and orientation (e.g. upright or rotated). To handle this, a modified version of the mean-shift known as the continuously adaptive mean-shift (CAMshift) has been proposed (Bradski, 1998) which updates the size and orientation of the window in each frame by computing the major axis and its angle of inclination of the best fitting ellipse to the window (Figure 6.14).

6.3.9 Optical Flow–Based Motion Tracker

Optical flow is a technique used for determining motion of objects in a video by measuring the change in pixel intensities over a set of frames. The underlying assumption is that a pixel at location (x,y) and time t in one video frame will have moved by amount Δx and Δy in some other frame at Δt if there is a relative motion between an object and the observer, but its intensity or brightness will remain the same. If $I(x,y,t)$ be the intensity of a pixel in one frame, then the brightness constraint can be written as:

$$I(x,y,t) = I(x+\Delta x, y+\Delta y, t+\Delta t)$$

Assuming the movement to be small, using the Taylor series expansion and ignoring the higher-order terms we have:

$$I(x+\Delta x, y+\Delta y, t+\Delta t) =$$

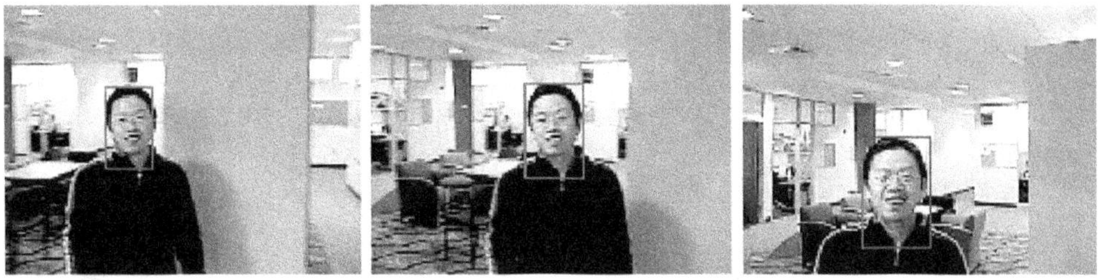

FIGURE 6.14
Histogram-based Motion tracker.

$$I(x,y,t)+(\partial I/\partial x)\Delta x+(\partial I/\partial y)\Delta y+(\partial I/\partial t)\Delta t$$

$$\frac{\partial I}{\partial x}\Delta x+\frac{\partial I}{\partial y}\Delta y+\frac{\partial I}{\partial t}\Delta t=0$$

$$\left(\frac{\partial I}{\partial x}\right)\left(\frac{\Delta x}{\Delta t}\right)+\left(\frac{\partial I}{\partial y}\right)\left(\frac{\Delta y}{\Delta t}\right)+\left(\frac{\partial I}{\partial t}\right)\left(\frac{\Delta t}{\Delta t}\right)=0$$

$$I_x.V_x+I_y.V_y+I_t=0$$

Here, I_x, I_y, I_t are the partial derivatives of the image and V_x, V_y are the components of the optical flow velocity. The two unknowns V_x and V_y cannot be solved from one equation and hence there are a number of methods which introduce additional constraints for estimating the optical flow. The Horn–Schunck method (Horn & Schunck, 1981) assumes that the optical flow is smooth over the entire image and estimates the velocities V_x and V_y by minimizing a global energy functional using an iterative process. The Farneback method (Farneback, 2003) approximates each neighborhood of both frames by quadratic polynomials, and then a method to estimate displacement fields from the polynomial expansion coefficients is derived. The Lucas-Kanade (Lucas & Kanade, 1981) method divides the original image into smaller sections and assumes a constant velocity in each section, after which it performs a weighted least-square fit of the optical flow constraint equation to a constant model for V_x, V_y in each section (Figure 6.15).

6.3.10 Common Editing Tasks

Video editing involves manipulating and arranging video footage to create a coherent and engaging final product. Different projects may require various editing tasks, ranging from simple adjustments to complex visual effects (Jackson, 2016). Here are some common video editing tasks that can be done using GUI-based video editing application software (Figure 6.16):

Cutting and Trimming: Removing unwanted segments or portions from video clips, using Cut tool, trim tool or the razor tool in editing software, for Eliminating unnecessary content, refining pacing or shortening video duration.

Joining and Concatenating: Combining multiple video clips into a seamless sequence using Join or concatenate functions in editing software for Creating a continuous narrative or combining various scenes.

Adding Transitions: Smoothly transitioning between different video clips or scenes using Fade-ins, fade-outs, wipes, dissolves or specialized transition effects for Enhancing visual flow and maintaining viewer engagement.

Applying Video Effects: Involves adding visual enhancements or altering the appearance of video clips, using color correction filters and special effects for adjusting color balance,

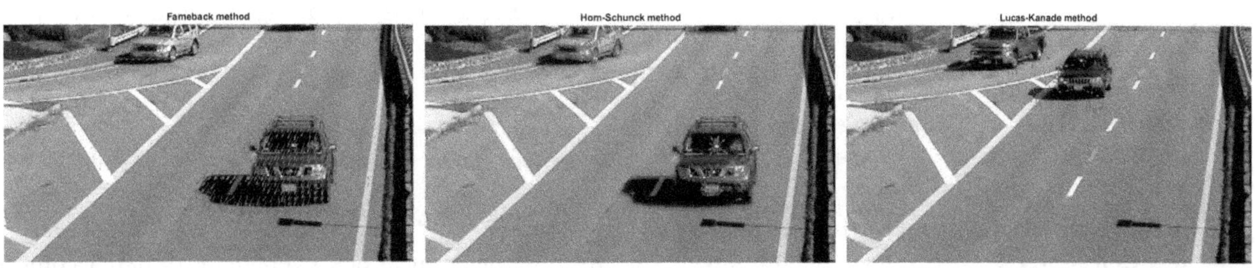

FIGURE 6.15
Optical flow–based Motion tracker.

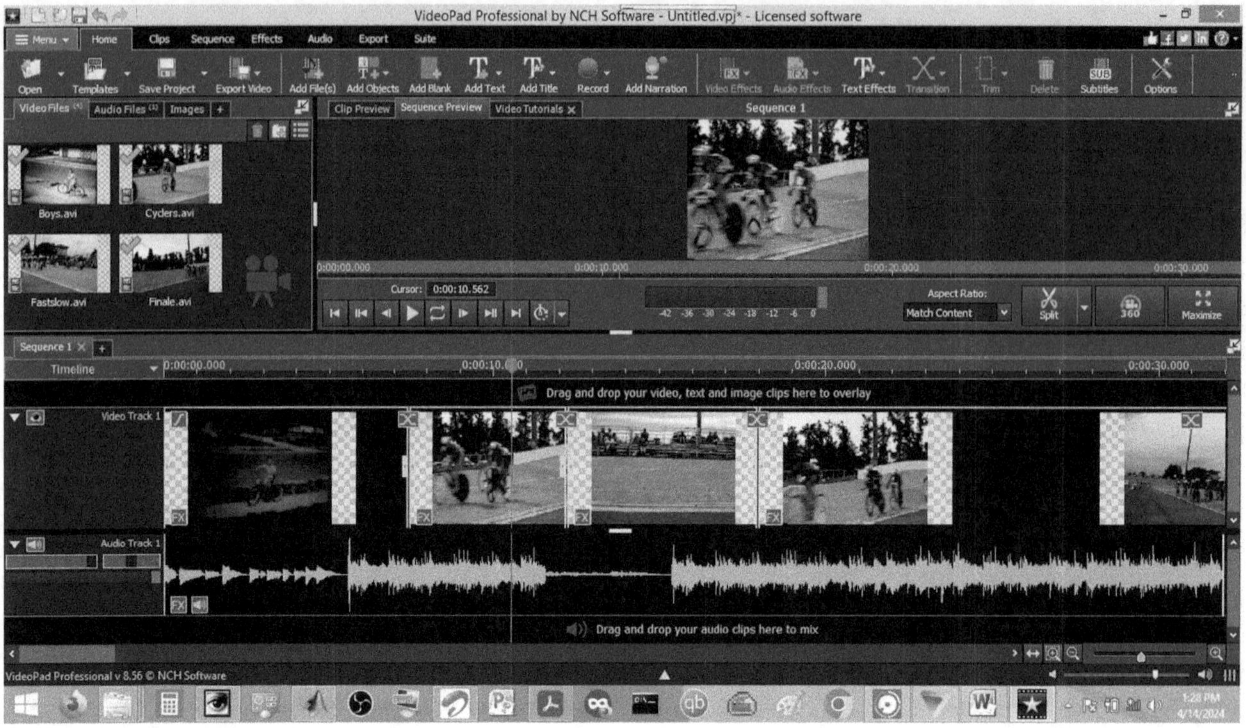

FIGURE 6.16
Typical GUI-based video editor interface.

enhancing visual aesthetics or creating specific looks.

Overlaying Text and Graphics: Adding text, titles, logos or graphics to the video using Text tools, graphics import and overlay features for providing context, adding branding elements or conveying information.

Adjusting Speed and Time Remapping: Altering the playback speed of video clips using speed controls, time remapping features for creating slow-motion or fast-motion effects, adjusting pacing.

Audio Editing: Adjusting volume, adding or removing audio tracks, applying effects using Audio meters, fade controls, equalization and audio effects for ensuring balanced audio levels, adding music or incorporating sound effects.

Split Screen and Picture-in-Picture: Displaying multiple video clips simultaneously on the screen using Split-screen layouts, picture-in-picture features for comparing scenes, showing multiple perspectives or creating dynamic visual compositions.

Blue/Green Screen (Chroma Keying): Removing a background from video footage and replacing it with another using Chroma key effect or green screen features for creating visual effects, placing actors in different environments or adding virtual backgrounds.

Exporting and Rendering: Converting the edited project into a final video file using Export settings and render options for preparing the video for distribution on various platforms or devices.

Adding Subtitles and Captions: Incorporating text on the screen to provide context or aid accessibility using Subtitle editors, captioning tools for making videos more accessible, providing translations or adding additional information.

Masking and Rotoscoping: Creating masks to isolate and manipulate specific areas of the frame using masking tools, rotoscoping techniques for applying effects selectively, isolating subjects or adding visual elements to specific areas.

6.4 Video Applications

Multimedia applications leverage the dynamic combination of various media elements to create engaging and interactive user experiences. Among these elements, video stands out as a powerful tool for conveying information, telling stories and enhancing the overall impact of multimedia applications.

Educational Multimedia: In educational settings, multimedia applications often integrate video content to facilitate effective learning experiences. Educational videos can explain complex concepts, showcase experiments and provide virtual tours, making learning more engaging and accessible. Platforms like Khan Academy utilize video extensively to supplement traditional educational methods.

Entertainment and Gaming: Video plays a central role in entertainment multimedia applications, including video games and interactive experiences. Cinematic cut scenes, trailers and in-game animations contribute to the storytelling aspect of gaming, immersing players in rich narratives. Streaming services like Twitch have further transformed gaming into a multimedia experience by combining live video, chat interactions and social engagement.

Communication and Collaboration: Multimedia applications in communication and collaboration leverage video to enhance virtual interactions. Video conferencing tools such as Zoom, Microsoft Teams and Skype use real-time video to facilitate remote communication, making virtual meetings more personal and effective. Collaborative platforms may also integrate video for interactive discussions and presentations.

Marketing and Advertising: Digital video has become a cornerstone of marketing and advertising strategies. Multimedia applications enable the creation of promotional videos, advertisements and branded content. Social media platforms leverage video content for targeted advertising, and platforms like Instagram and TikTok thrive on short-form video content for marketing purposes.

Healthcare and Training: In healthcare, multimedia applications incorporate video for training purposes, patient education and virtual simulations. Medical professionals use video content to demonstrate surgical procedures, train staff and communicate with patients. Virtual reality applications provide immersive medical training experiences through interactive video simulations.

Augmented and Virtual Reality (AR/VR): Video is fundamental to the immersive experiences created by augmented and virtual reality applications. AR applications overlay digital information onto the real world through video captured by device cameras. VR applications use 360-degree videos to transport users to virtual environments. Examples include VR tours, training simulations and AR-enhanced navigation applications.

Social Media Platforms: Social media platforms heavily rely on video content for user engagement. Platforms such as YouTube, Instagram and TikTok are driven by user-generated video content. Live video streaming on platforms like Facebook Live and Twitter's Periscope allows real-time interaction, contributing to the multimedia nature of social media.

Museums and Exhibitions: Multimedia applications are transforming the museum and exhibition experience. Video installations, interactive displays and virtual walkthroughs enhance visitor engagement. Digital video content is used to provide historical context, share stories and create immersive exhibits in cultural institutions.

Real Estate and Virtual Tours: In the real estate industry, multimedia applications leverage video for virtual property tours. Video walkthroughs give potential buyers a realistic sense of a property's layout and features, enhancing the property viewing experience. This approach is increasingly popular in online real estate listings.

Video's integration into multimedia applications has revolutionized how information is presented, experiences are delivered and interactions take place across various domains. As technology continues to advance, the seamless integration of video into multimedia applications will likely open new avenues for creativity, education, communication and entertainment. The dynamic synergy of multimedia elements, with video at its core, continues to shape the way we engage with and experience digital content.

6.5 Legal and Ethical Considerations

Legal and ethical considerations in video production involve adherence to copyright laws, securing proper licensing for content, and respecting privacy rights. Creators must ensure they have the right to use any video material, including footage, music or images, and comply with intellectual property regulations. Ethical concerns include obtaining informed consent for filming, avoiding misrepresentation and respecting the privacy of individuals featured in the video to uphold responsible and respectful content creation practices (Taskiran & Pinarbasi, 2021).

6.5.1 Legal Considerations

Copyright and Intellectual Property: Respect for copyright laws is paramount when creating and sharing digital video content. Unauthorized use of copyrighted material, including music, images and footage, can lead to legal consequences. Proper licensing and permissions should be obtained for any copyrighted material used in video production.

Privacy Laws: Recording and sharing videos may involve capturing people, private property or sensitive information. Understanding and adhering to privacy laws and obtaining consent when necessary are critical to avoid legal issues.

Defamation: Content creators must be cautious not to produce videos that harm the reputation of individuals or organizations. Defamatory statements, false accusations or misleading information can lead to legal action.

Terms of Service and Platform Policies: When uploading videos to online platforms, users are bound by the terms of service and community guidelines of those platforms. Violating these terms may result in content removal, account suspension or other penalties.

Fair Use: Understanding the principles of fair use is crucial. While it allows for the limited use of copyrighted material for purposes such as commentary, criticism or education, it is a nuanced legal concept that requires careful consideration.

Accessibility Compliance: Ensuring that digital videos comply with accessibility standards is not only ethically responsible but also legally required in many jurisdictions. This includes providing closed captions for the hearing impaired and making content accessible to individuals with disabilities.

6.5.2 Ethical Considerations

Accuracy and Truthfulness: Maintaining the accuracy and truthfulness of video content is an ethical obligation. Misleading information, deepfakes or manipulative editing techniques can erode trust and have societal consequences.

Informed Consent: Obtaining informed consent from individuals appearing in videos is an ethical practice. This is especially important in situations where the content may be sensitive or portray individuals in a potentially negative light.

Sensitivity to Cultural Differences: Digital videos may be viewed globally, and content creators should be sensitive to cultural differences. Avoiding stereotypes, respecting cultural norms and considering diverse perspectives contribute to ethical video production.

Minimizing Harm: Content creators should consider the potential impact of their videos on viewers and society at large. Minimizing harm involves avoiding content that may incite violence, discrimination or harm to individuals or communities.

Child Protection: Special care must be taken when featuring children in videos. Ethical considerations include protecting their privacy, obtaining parental consent and avoiding content that could exploit or harm minors.

Social Responsibility: Video creators and platforms have a social responsibility to contribute positively to society. This involves avoiding content that promotes hate speech, discrimination or harmful behaviors.

Navigating the legal and ethical landscape of digital video requires a combination of legal awareness, ethical responsibility and a commitment to integrity. Content creators, distributors and consumers alike play a role in upholding these considerations to ensure that the digital video landscape remains a space of creativity, expression and responsible communication. Staying informed about evolving laws and ethical standards is essential as the digital video landscape continues to evolve.

6.6 Challenges and Emerging Trends

6.6.1 Challenges

Bandwidth Limitations: Streaming high-quality video content demands substantial bandwidth. In regions with limited internet infrastructure, users may face challenges in accessing or streaming high-resolution videos seamlessly.

Storage and Processing Power: High-resolution videos and emerging technologies like 8K demand significant storage space and processing power. This poses challenges for both content creators and consumers, especially those using devices with limited storage capacity.

Copyright Infringement and Piracy: Digital video content is susceptible to copyright infringement and piracy. Illegitimate distribution of copyrighted material poses challenges for content creators and distributors, impacting revenue streams and intellectual property rights.

Quality of Experience (QoE): Ensuring a consistent and high-quality viewing experience across various devices and network conditions is a continuous challenge. Factors like buffering, latency and resolution can affect the overall quality of the user experience.

Security and Privacy Concerns: As digital video platforms and streaming services collect user data, concerns about privacy and security arise. Protecting sensitive information and preventing unauthorized access to content are ongoing challenges in the digital video landscape.

6.6.2 Emerging Trends

5G and Edge Computing: The rollout of 5G networks will significantly enhance data transfer speeds and reduce latency, leading to improved streaming quality. Coupled with edge computing, this advancement will enable faster content delivery and more immersive experiences.

Virtual and Augmented Reality Integration: The integration of virtual reality (VR) and augmented reality (AR) technologies into digital video is a growing trend. This includes immersive 360-degree videos, interactive VR experiences and AR overlays on live video content.

Enhanced Compression Technologies: Continued advancements in video compression technologies, such as the development of more efficient codecs, will enable higher quality video streaming at lower bitrates. This is crucial for delivering high-resolution content while optimizing bandwidth usage. Personalized and Interactive Content: The future of digital video involves more personalized and interactive content. Content recommendation algorithms, interactive storytelling and user-driven narratives will provide viewers with customized and engaging experiences.

Artificial Intelligence (AI) and Machine Learning (ML): AI and ML technologies will play a significant role in video production and editing. Automated video editing, content analysis for better recommendations and deep learning algorithms for enhanced video quality are areas where these technologies will have a substantial impact.

Blockchain for Content Distribution: Blockchain technology holds the potential to revolutionize content distribution by providing a secure and transparent platform. Decentralized video platforms, content authentication and transparent royalty systems are potential applications.

Immersive Audio Experiences: The evolution of audio technologies, including spatial audio and 3D sound, will contribute to more immersive video experiences. These advancements enhance the audio-visual synchronization and overall realism of digital video content.

Sustainable Video Production: With increasing environmental concerns, there is a growing trend toward sustainable video production. This involves minimizing the environmental impact of video creation, distribution and storage through energy-efficient processes and eco-friendly technologies.

The challenges and future trends in digital video reflect the dynamic nature of this rapidly evolving field. As technology continues to advance, addressing challenges related to bandwidth, storage, security and privacy will be crucial. Simultaneously, embracing emerging trends such as 5G, VR, AI and sustainable practices will shape the future landscape of digital video, offering new possibilities for creativity, engagement and user experience. Content creators, industry stakeholders and technology developers will play pivotal roles in navigating and shaping the future of digital video.

6.7 Video File Formats

Video file formats are integral to the multimedia landscape, providing a standardized way to store, transmit and play digital video content. The diverse range of video formats caters to various needs, whether it be optimized streaming, high-quality playback or compatibility across different platforms and devices.

6.7.1 MP4

MP4 (MPEG-4 Part 14) [mpeg.chiariglione.org/standards/mpeg-4/mp4-file-format] is a digital container format, formally ISO/IEC 14496-14 [www.iso.org/standard/79110.html] commonly used for online streaming services, video sharing platforms and mobile devices. Its compatibility extends across a wide array of devices, making it a universal choice for video distribution. First released in 2003, MPEG-4 Part 14 is an extension of the ISO Base File Format [mpeg.chiariglione.org/standards/mpeg-4/iso-base-media-file-format] MPEG-4 Part 12 formally ISO/IEC 14496-12 [www.iso.org/standard/83102.html] which defines a general structure for time-based media files. While the only file format defined by the standard is .MP4 other filename extensions like .M4A, .M4P and .M4V are also used. MP4 commonly employs the H.265 / H.264 video codecs and MPEG-4 Part 3 audio codecs, striking a balance between compression efficiency and video quality. This makes it suitable for delivering high-quality content over the internet.

6.7.2 AVI

AVI (Audio Video Interleave), is a proprietary Microsoft container format [learn.microsoft.com/en-us/windows/win32/directshow/avi-file-format] introduced in 1992 as part of its Video for Windows software. Although an older format, is still relevant in scenarios where compatibility with legacy systems or specific software is crucial. It supports multiple audio and video streams, making it versatile but less efficient in compression compared to newer formats. The AVI format is based on the RIFF (resource interchange file format) which divides the file data into chunks, each chunk identified by a tag. AVI files can use various video codecs, providing flexibility in codec selection based on specific requirements, although it lacks support for certain features like timecode and B-frames.

6.7.3 MKV

MKV (Matroska Video) is a royalty-free and open container format [www.matroska.org] first released in 2001 that can hold multiple audio, video, image and text subtitles in one file. The name is derived from a Russian word meaning hollow wooden dolls. Its open-source nature allows for flexibility in supporting various audio and video codecs, making it ideal for storing high-definition and Blu-ray quality content. MKV supports advanced features such as subtitles, multiple audio tracks and chapter markers, making it a comprehensive container for high-quality multimedia.

6.7.4 MOV

MOV is a multimedia container format developed by Apple Inc. for storing audio, video and text data [www.apple.com/quicktime]. It is closely associated with the QuickTime multimedia framework and is commonly used for storing movies, video clips and other multimedia content on Apple devices and platforms. MOV is a container format, supporting multiple types of data streams, including audio, video, text and metadata, including popular codecs such as H.264 for video and AAC for audio. MOV files consist of a hierarchical structure of atoms, which are data structures that contain metadata, media samples and other information about the content stored in the file. Atoms can be nested within each other to represent the relationships between different components of the multimedia content. MOV files are widely supported by Apple devices and software, including macOS, iOS, QuickTime Player and Final Cut Pro. The MPEG-4 file format specification was created on the basis of the QuickTime format specification published in 2001.

6.7.5 WebM

WebM is an open, royalty-free media file format designed for use with HTML5, developed by the WebM Project [www.webmproject.org], sponsored by Google. WebM files are widely used for streaming video content on the Web due to their high-quality compression and broad support across various platforms and browsers, including Google Chrome, Mozilla Firefox and Microsoft Edge. WebM files typically use the VP8 or VP9 video codec for video compression and the Vorbis or Opus audio codec for audio compression. These codecs are optimized for efficient compression while maintaining high visual and audio quality. WebM files are based on the Matroska multimedia container format which allows for the inclusion of multiple audio, video and subtitle streams within a single file. They are well suited for streaming over the internet, supported by adaptive streaming technologies such as Dynamic Adaptive Streaming over HTTP (DASH) and HTTP Live Streaming (HLS).

6.7.6 WMV

WMV (Windows Media Video) is a video compression format developed by Microsoft for storing and streaming audiovisual content. It is part of the Windows Media framework and is widely used for delivering video content over the internet, as well as for storing video files on Windows-based systems. WMV files use codecs such as Windows Media Video 9, and Windows Media Video Advanced Profile for video compression. WMV files are stored in the Advanced Systems Format (ASF), which is a container format developed by Microsoft for storing audio and video content. The ASF format allows for the inclusion of multiple audio and video streams, as well as metadata and other auxiliary data [https://learn.microsoft.com/en-us/windows/win32/wmformat/overview-of-the-asf-format]. WMV files are essentially ASF files that contain video streams encoded using Microsoft's Windows Media Video codecs. This integration allows WMV files to leverage the features and capabilities of the ASF container format, including its support for streaming, DRM and synchronization. WMV files consist of a hierarchical structure of objects, including header objects, data objects and index objects, and support variable bitrate (VBR) and constant bitrate (CBR) encoding modes, allowing content creators to control the quality and file size of the resulting video. WMV files are widely supported by Microsoft Windows-based systems and software, including Windows Media Player, Windows Movie Maker and Microsoft Edge browser.

6.7.7 FLV

FLV (Flash Video) [www.adobe.com/products/flashplayer/end-of-life.html] is a container file format developed by Adobe Systems for delivering video content over the internet using Adobe Flash Player or Adobe AIR platforms. The FLV format was commonly used for streaming video content on websites and other online platforms due to its relatively small file size and widespread support and typically used codecs such as Sorenson Spark, On2 VP6 or H.264 for video compression, and MP3, AAC or PCM for audio compression. FLV files are based on the Adobe Flash Video File Format, which is a binary format designed to store audio, video and metadata within a single file. The structure of an FLV file consists of a header followed by a series of tags, each containing audio, video or metadata information. Flash technology, including FLV files, became outdated as newer and more efficient Web standards and technologies emerged. HTML5, CSS and JavaScript have largely replaced Flash for multimedia content delivery due to their better performance, security and cross-platform compatibility. With the rise of alternative technologies and the increasing adoption of mobile devices, the usage of Flash Player and FLV files declined significantly. The shift away from Flash Player and FLV files was also influenced by industry trends and standards organizations advocating for open, interoperable and secure Web technologies.

6.7.8 3GP, 3G2

3GP [www.3gpp.org/dynareport?code=26-series.htm] and 3G2 [www.3gpp2.org/Public_html/Specs/index.cfm] are multimedia container formats designed for storing audiovisual content, primarily optimized for delivery over mobile networks. These formats are commonly used for streaming video content on mobile devices, such as smartphones and tablets, and are supported by a wide range of mobile platforms and devices. Developed by the 3rd Generation Partnership Project for mobile devices, it is based on the MPEG-4 Part 12 container format and is designed to contain audio and video streams, as well as text and other multimedia content. 3G2 (Third Generation Partnership Project 2) is based on the MPEG-4 Part 14 container format and is similar to 3GP but includes additional features and capabilities.

6.8 Numerical Problems

PROBLEM 6.1

Consider a TV camera where the maximum intensity of a color signal is represented by 1 volt. An unsaturated magenta signal is formed by mixing 70% R, 20% G and 60% B. What is the luminance output voltage for the signal? What would this value if the magenta color is saturated?

Maximum output value of a color signal is assumed to be 1 volt.

For unsaturated magenta, R = 0.7 volt, G = 0.2 volt, B = 0.6 volt.

$Y = 0.3(0.7) + 0.59(0.2) + 0.11(0.6) = 0.394$ volt.

Since 0.5 volt represents a middle gray shade, the unsaturated magenta color would be represented by a dark gray shade (39.4% gray)

Saturated magenta consists of 100% red and 100% blue, i.e., R = 1 volt, B = 1 volt. From equation (6.2), $Y = 0.3(1) + 0.1(1) = 0.4$ volt (40% gray)

PROBLEM 6.2

Calculate bit rate and storage space required for a 1-hour movie in NTSC format, assuming 4:2:2 chroma sub-sampling, according to CCIR-601 recommendations.

NTSC format has 720 x 480 pixels at 30 frames/second.

Since sub-sampling scheme is 4:2:2, in one frame there are 720 x 480 pixels of Y and 360 x 480 pixels each of Cb and Cr

As per CCIR-601, sampling rate is 13.5 MHz for Y and 6.75 MHz for each of C components, with 8 bits per sample.

Hence, bit rate is [13.5 × 10^6 + 2(6.75 × 10^6)] × 8 = 216 Mbps

Memory required per line: (24 × 360) + (8 × 360) = 11520 bits or 1440 bytes

Memory required per frame each made of 480 lines: 1440 × 480 = 691.2 KB

Memory required to store 1 hour of movie: 691.2 × 30 frames/s × 3600 s = 112 GB

PROBLEM 6.3

An NTSC encoded video clip has a frame size of 720 × 480 pixels and is digitized using a bit depth of 8 bits for each of Y, Cb and Cr, and a chroma sub-sampling scheme of 4:2:2. Calculate the file size of 1 minute of the video clip and the total time taken for it to be transmitted over a 2 Mbps transmission line.

The frame size of the NTSC encoded video is 720 × 480 pixels, and frame rate is 30 fps. Chroma sub-sampling scheme is 4:2:2, and bit depth is 8 bits for each of Y, Cb and Cr.

In a single line of the video frame, 360 pixels have 24 bits (Y + Cb + Cr) and 360 pixels have 8 bits (Y).

Memory required per line = (24 × 360) + (8 × 360) = 11520 bits = 1440 bytes

Memory required per frame = 1440 × 480 = 691200 bytes = 11520 × 480 = 5529600 bits

Memory required to store one second of the video = 5529600 × 30 frames/second = 165888000 bits = 19.77 MB

Memory required to store 1 minute of the video = 165888000 × 60 = 9953280000 bits = 1186.2 MB

Time taken to transmit this over a 2 Mbps line = (9953280000/2000000) second = 4976.64 second = 1.38 hours

PROBLEM 6.4

Repeat the previous problem for chroma sub-sampling scheme of 4:2:0

The frame size of the NTSC encoded video is 720 × 480 pixels, and frame rate is 30 fps. Chroma sub-sampling scheme is 4:2:0, and bit depth is 8 bits for each of Y, Cb and Cr

There are two types of video lines: those with C information and those without C information

For the first type, 360 pixels have 24 bits (Y + Cb + Cr) and 360 pixels have 8 bits (Y)

Memory required per line = (24 * 360) + (8 * 360) = 11520 bits = 1440 bytes

For the second type, 720 pixels have 8 bits (Y)

Memory required per line = (8 × 720) = 5760 bits = 720 bytes

Memory required per frame = (1440 × 240) + (720 × 240) = 518400 bytes (since there are 240 lines of each type) = 4147200 bits

Memory required to store one second of the video = 518400 × 30 frames/second = 15552000 bytes = 14.83 MB = 124416000 bits

Memory required to store 1 minute of the video = 14.83 × 60 = 889.8 MB = 7464960000 bits

Time taken to transmit this over a 2 Mbps line = (7464960000/2000000) seconds = 3732.48 seconds = 1.04 hours

6.9 Coding Examples using MATLAB

Video processing functions in MATLAB® can be divided into two broad categories: basic MATLAB functions and Computer Vision System Toolbox (CVST) functions. The BM functions are a set of basic tools used for performing preliminary mathematical matrix operations and graphical plotting operations. The CVST, which provides algorithms, functions and apps for designing and simulating computer vision and video processing systems, includes a set of more advanced tools for specialized processing tasks like blob analysis, object detection and motion tracking. The video file formats supported by MATLAB includes MPEG-1 (.mpg), Windows Media® Video (.wmv), MPEG-4 including H.264 encoded video (.mp4, .m4v), Apple QuickTime Movie (.mov), 3GPP and Ogg Theora (.ogg). Most of the video files used in the examples are included in the MATLAB package and do not need to be supplied by the user. The inbuilt media files are included in the folders: (matlab-root)\toolbox\vision\visiondata.

6.9.1 Video I/O

The most basic way to play a video file is to use the function "implay" with a specified filename. The function "mmfileinfo" can be used to extract information about the file, e.g., the audio and video structures. In the following example, this is indicated as method-1. The function "VideoReader" can be used to read a video file, which creates a VideoReader object. Properties of the object can be used to retrieve video information like duration, frame height and width, file path, frame rate, number of frames, file format and so on. The "read" method can be used to read the video data which is stored in a 4D array containing the frame height, frame width, color channel index and frame index. The function "implay" can then be used to play the video data. For playing a subset of the frames, the start-frame and end-frame can be specified. A value of "Inf" for the end-frame plays the video until the end. In the following example, this is indicated as method-2 (Figure 6.17).

Alternatively, the "readFrame" function can be used to read each frame individually and play them back using a loop. Each frame returned is represented as a 3D array for a color image, and the operation is to be repeated depending on the total number of frames to be displayed. The total number of frames can be extracted from the property "NumberOfFrames". A counter can be used to display the corresponding frame number in the title field of the figure window (Figure 6.18).

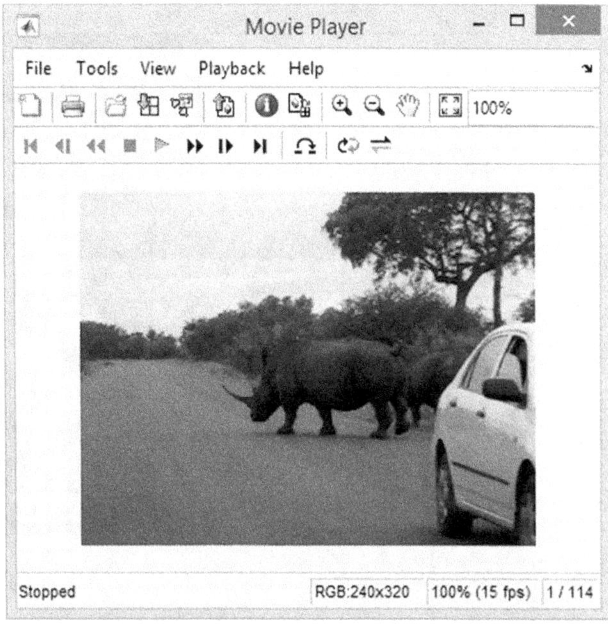

FIGURE 6.17
Output of Example 6.1.

EXAMPLE 6.1 EXAMPLE TO PLAY A VIDEO AND GET SOME VIDEO INFORMATION

```
clear; clc;
fv = 'rhinos.avi';
fa = 'RockDrums-44p1-stereo-
   11secs.mp3';

% method-1
implay(fv);
ia = mmfileinfo(fa); ia.Audio
iv = mmfileinfo(fv); iv.Video

% method-2
vr = VideoReader(fv); % video
   reader object
d = vr.Duration
h = vr.Height
w = vr.Width
p = vr.Path
bp = vr.BitsPerPixel
fr = vr.FrameRate
nf = vr.NumberOfFrames
fo = vr.VideoFormat
ff = vr.getFileFormats
v = read(vr); % 4-D array containing
   video frames
implay(v)
sf = 11; % start frame
ef = 50; % end frame
cv1 = read(vr,[sf, ef]);
cv2 = read(vr,[50, Inf]);
implay(cv1) % Total frame numbers
   indicated in status bar
implay(cv2) % Total frame numbers
   indicated in status bar
```

EXAMPLE 6.2 EXAMPLE FOR A VIDEO FRAME COUNTER

```
clear; clc;
fn = 'rhinos.avi';
vr = VideoReader(fn); % video
   reader object
nf = vr.NumberOfFrames; % number
   of frames
fr = vr.FrameRate; % frame rate
du = vr.Duration; % video duration
of = 2.5; % time offset in seconds from
   beginning

vr = VideoReader(fn);
fi = 0;
for i = 1:nf
    vf = readFrame(vr); % video frame
    fi = fi + 1; % frame index number
    image(vf); title(fi); axis square;
    pause(1/fr);
end
```

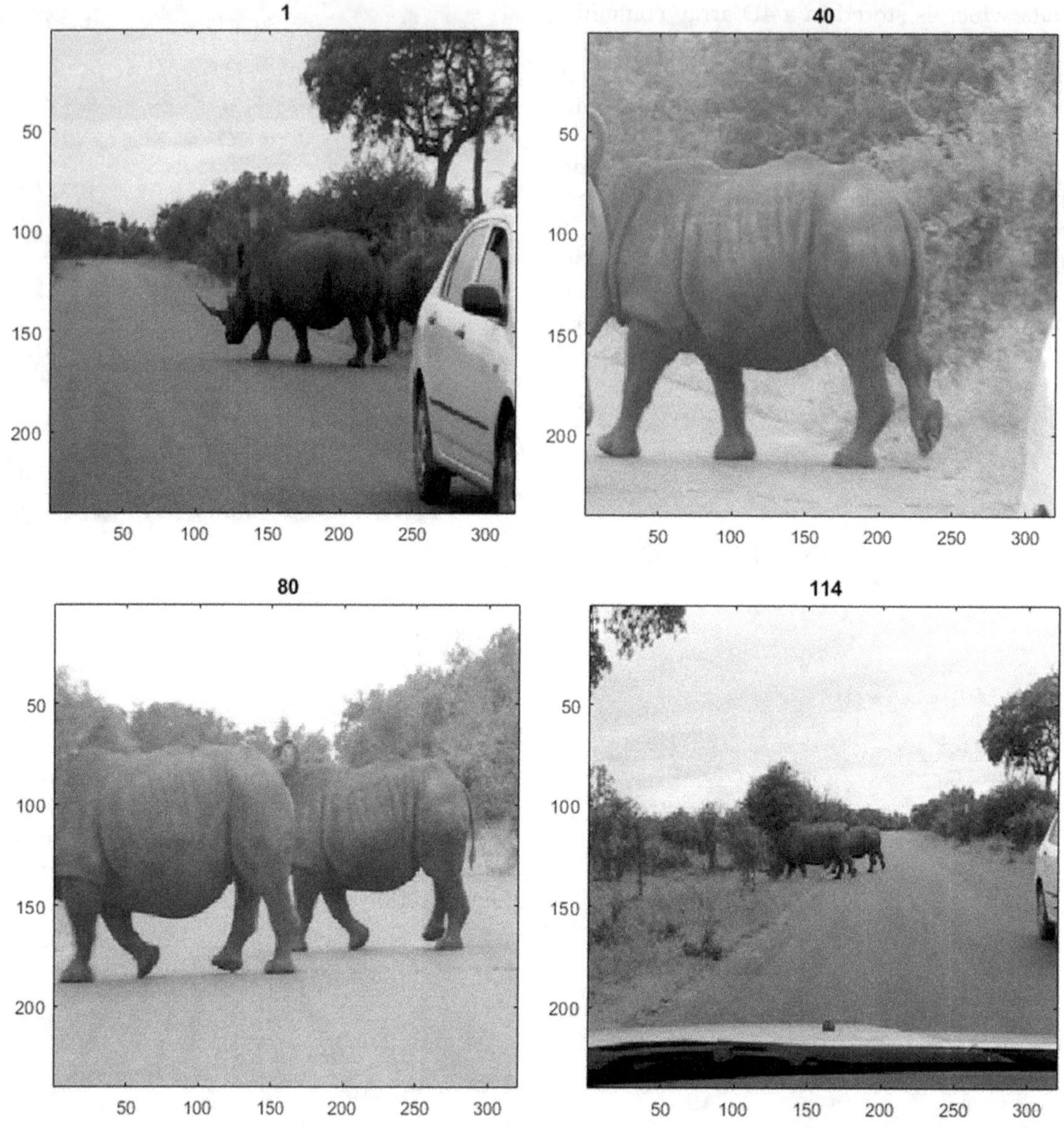

FIGURE 6.18
Output of Example 6.2.

The function "VideoWriter" can be used to write video files and creates a VideoWriter object. Properties of the object can be used to specify filename, file format, compression ratio, duration and so on. The methods "open" and "close" can be used to open a file for writing video data and close the file after writing video data. The function "writeVideo" is used to write the actual video data to the file (Figure 6.19).

EXAMPLE 6.3 EXAMPLE TO CREATE VIDEO FRAMES FROM GRAPHICAL PLOTS

```
clear; clc;
v = VideoWriter('newv.avi');
open(v);
for i = 1:15
    plot(rand(10,5), 'o'); title(i);
    f(i) = getframe;
    writeVideo(v, f);
end
close(v);
fps = 12;
implay('newv.avi', fps);
```

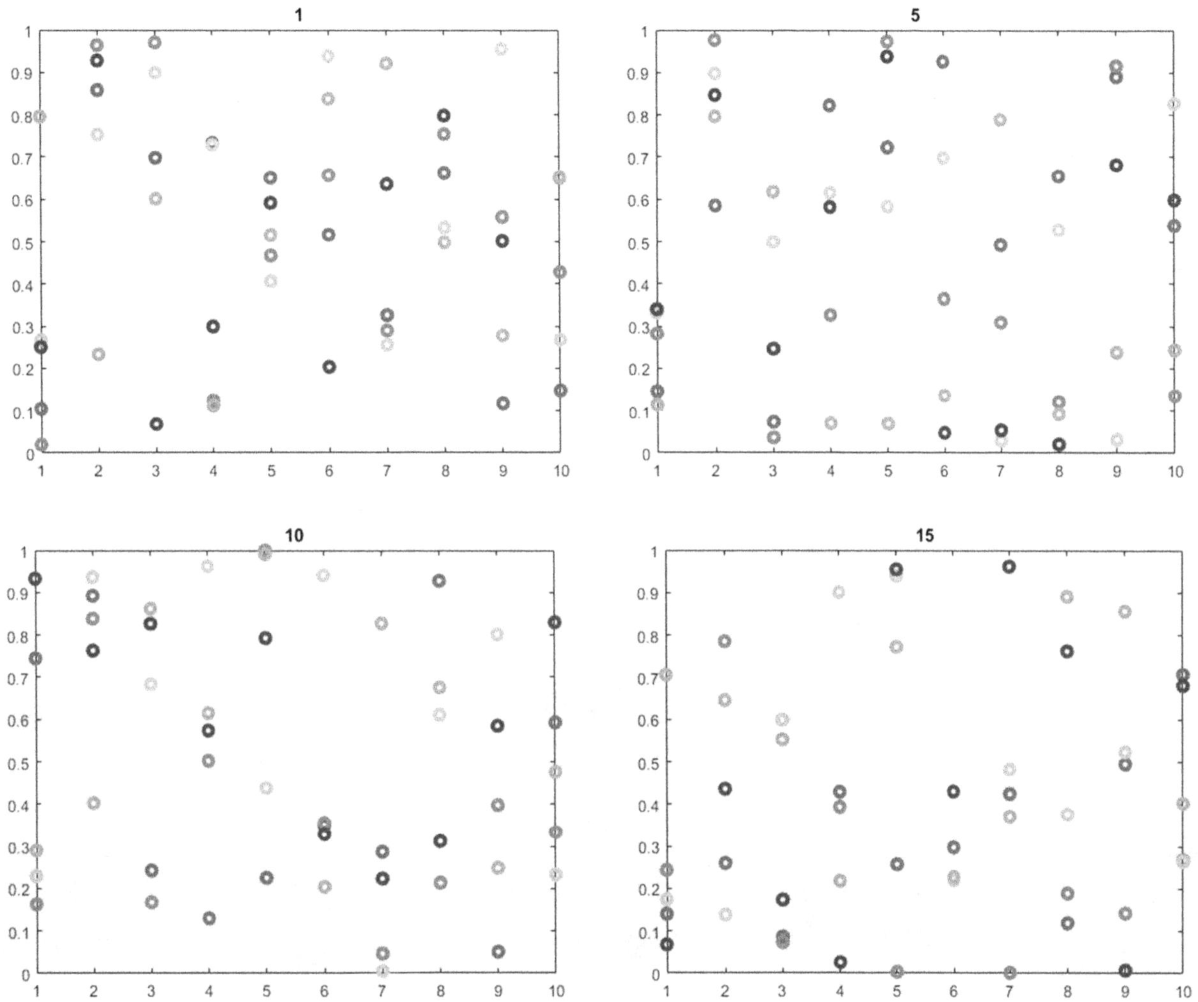

FIGURE 6.19
Output of Example 6.3.

6.9.2 Processing Video Frames

Since video frames are individual images, image processing techniques can be applied to each frame and compiled back to the video. The following example shows specific frames of a video being modified (inverted) and then written back to another video sequence. The function "imadjust" adjusts image intensity or color, "imshow" displays the frames in a figure window, "implay" plays the video sequence (Figure 6.20).

EXAMPLE 6.4 EXAMPLE TO INVERT EVERY 5-TH FRAME OF A VIDEO

```
clear; clc;
vr = VideoReader('rhinos.avi');
nf = vr.NumberOfFrames;
v = read(vr);
g = v;
for k = 1:5:nf
    g(:,:,:,k) = imadjust(v(:,:,:,k),
    [0, 1], [1, 0]);
end
k = 0;
for r = 1:5
    for c = 1:5
        k = k + 1;
        subplot(5, 5, c+(r-1)*5),
        imshow(g(:,:,:,k)); title(k)
    end
end
implay(g);
```

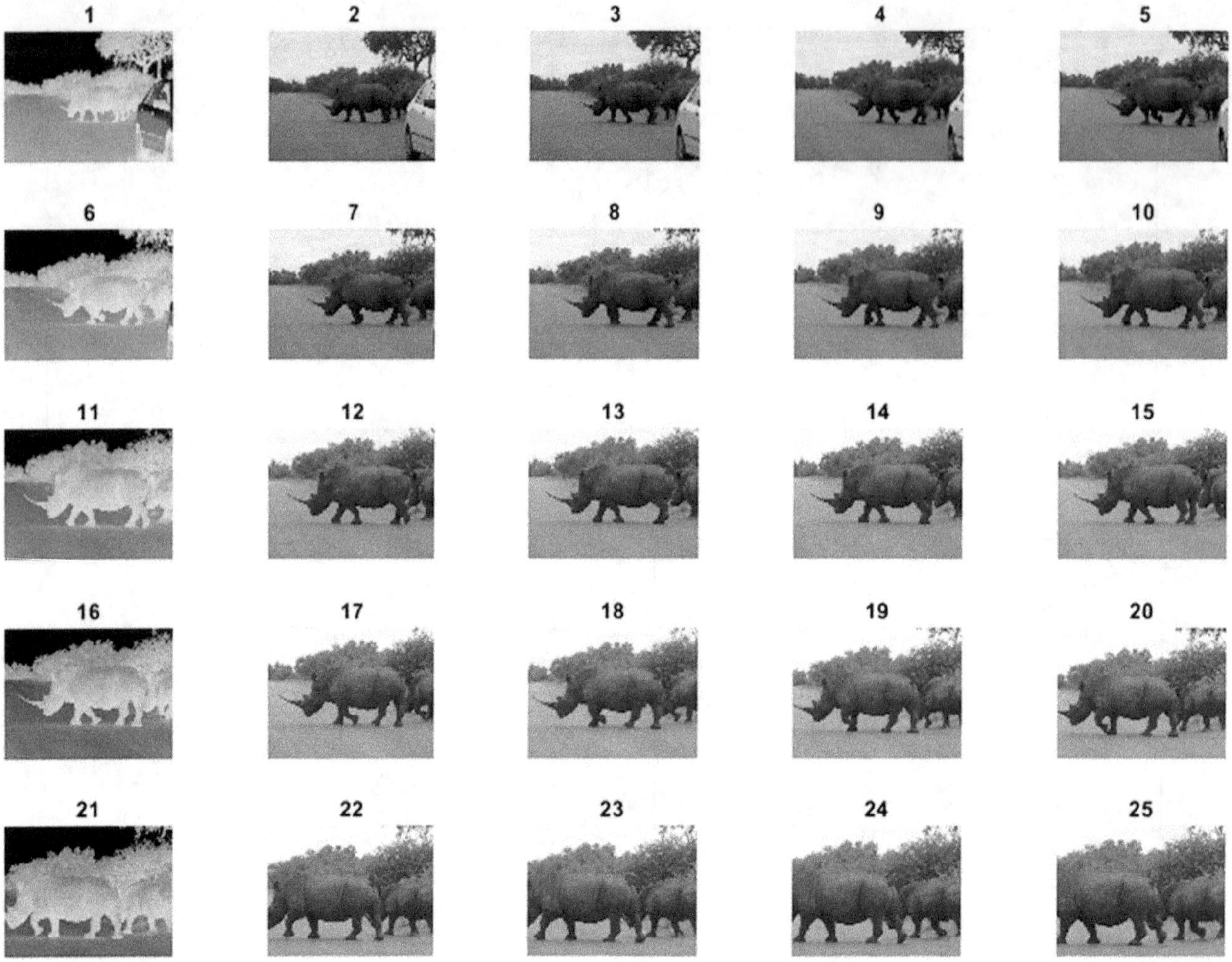

FIGURE 6.20
Output of Example 6.4.

The following example displays frame numbers at the bottom right of each frame of a video. The position, color, opacity and font size are specified as arguments for each frame, and the process is repeated for all frames in a loop structure. The function "insertText" is used to insert text in images and video frames (Figure 6.21).

EXAMPLE 6.5 EXAMPLE TO INSERT TEXT AT SPECIFIC LOCATIONS IN FRAMES

```
clear; clc;
vr = VideoReader('xylophone.mp4');
nf = vr.NumberOfFrames;
fw = vr.Width;
fh = vr.Height;
v = read(vr);
position = [0.75*fw, 0.75*fh];
for k = 1:nf
    g(:,:,:,k) = insertText(v(:,:,:,k),
    position, num2str(k), ...
    'FontSize',20,'BoxColor','red',...
    'BoxOpacity',0.5,'TextColor','
white');
end
implay(g);
```

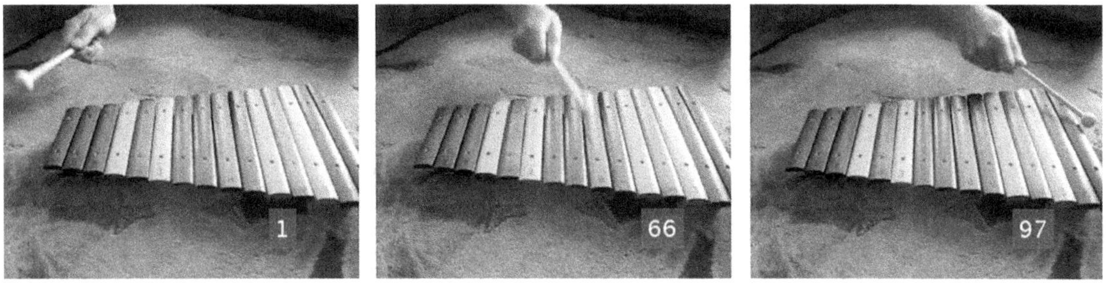

FIGURE 6.21
Output of Example 6.5.

The frames of a video can be selectively played at a specified frame rate. The following example shows only the odd frames, and even frames of a video are selected and played back at a frame rate 10% of the original fps. The frame numbers reflect the odd and even sets (Figure 6.22).

EXAMPLE 6.6 EXAMPLE TO PLAY ONLY ODD VIDEO FRAMES

```
clear; clc;
vr = VideoReader('xylophone.mp4');
nf = vr.NumberOfFrames;
fw = vr.Width;
fh = vr.Height;
fr = vr.FrameRate;
v = read(vr);
position = [0.75*fw, 0.75*fh];
for k = 1:nf
    g(:,:,:,k) = insertText(v(:,:,:,k),
position, num2str(k), ...
     'FontSize',20,'BoxColor','red',...
     'BoxOpacity',0.5,'TextColor',
     'white');
end
j=1;
for k = 1:2:nf % select odd frames
    m(:,:,:,j) = g(:,:,:,k);
    j = j+1;
end
implay(m, fr/10);
```

The following example shows a color video being converted to grayscale, then to binary and finally an edge detection filter being applied to the binary frames. The processed frames are then compiled back to a video structure. The function "rgb2gray" converts RGB color images to grayscale, "im2bw" converts a grayscale image to binary, "edge" finds edges in a binary image (Figure 6.23).

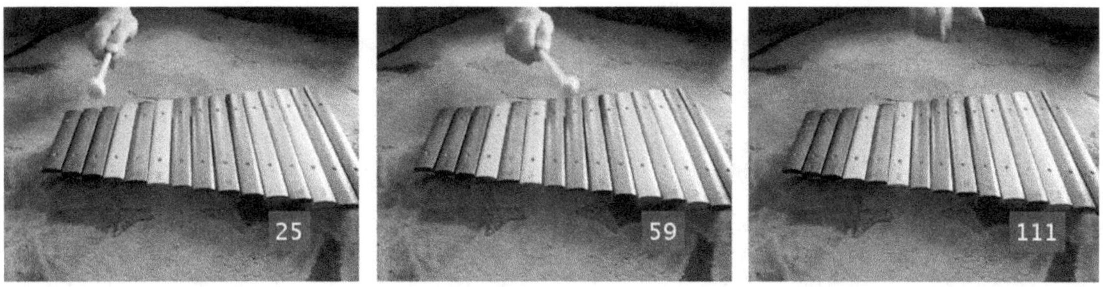

FIGURE 6.22
Output of Example 6.6.

EXAMPLE 6.7 EXAMPLE TO CONVERT VIDEO COLOR TO GRAYSCALE AND BINARY

```
clear; clc;
fn = 'viplanedeparture.mp4';
vr = VideoReader(fn);
nf = vr.NumberOfFrames;
v = read(vr);
for k = 1:nf
    w(:,:,:,k) = rgb2gray(v(:,:,:,k));
end
implay(w);
for k = 1:nf
    u(:,:,:,k) = im2bw(w(:,:,:,k));
end
implay(u);
for k = 1:nf
    x(:,:,:,k) = edge(u(:,:,:,k),
'sobel');
end
implay(x);
```

6.9.3 Video Color Spaces

The following example converts an RGB color image to YCbCr color space and displays it along with the individual color channels. The functions "rgb2ycbcr" and "ycbcr2rgb" convert RGB image to YCbCr color space and vice versa (Figure 6.24).

EXAMPLE 6.8 EXAMPLE FOR RGB TO YCBCR COLOR CONVERSION

```
clear; clc;
vr = VideoReader('xylophone.mp4');
nf = vr.NumberOfFrames;
v = read(vr);
for k = 1:nf
    YCbCr(:,:,:,k) =
rgb2ycbcr(v(:,:,:,k));
end
implay(YCbCr);
```

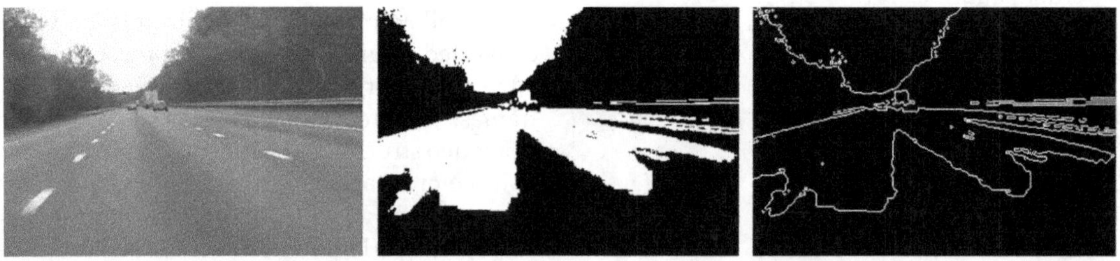

FIGURE 6.23
Output of Example 6.7.

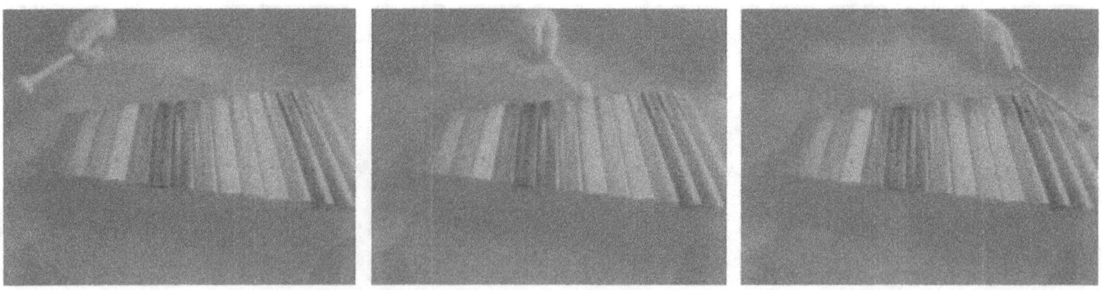

FIGURE 6.24
Output of Example 6.8.

The following example illustrates the conversion using still images. Each channel is separated out and displayed individually. The functions "rgb2ntsc" and "ntsc2rgb" convert RGB image to NTSC color space and vice versa (Figure 6.25).

EXAMPLE 6.9 EXAMPLE FOR RGB TO YIQ COLOR CONVERSION

```
clear; clc;
vr = VideoReader('xylophone.mp4');
nf = vr.NumberOfFrames;
v = read(vr);
for k = 1:nf
    NTSC(:,:,:,k) =
    rgb2ntsc(v(:,:,:,k));
end
implay(NTSC);
```

6.9.4 Blob Analysis

The following example detects bright regions over a dark background and computes some shape properties of these regions. The computed values are displayed beside each region after enclosing them within bounding boxes. The function "num2string" converts numbers to strings, "strcat" concatenates strings horizontally, "vision.BlobAnalysis" detects objects in a binary image and analyzes a number of properties for each object, like area, centroid, bounding box, major axis length, minor axis length (of the ellipses that have the same normalized second central moments as the object itself), orientation (angle between major axis and X-axis), eccentricity and perimeter (Figure 6.26).

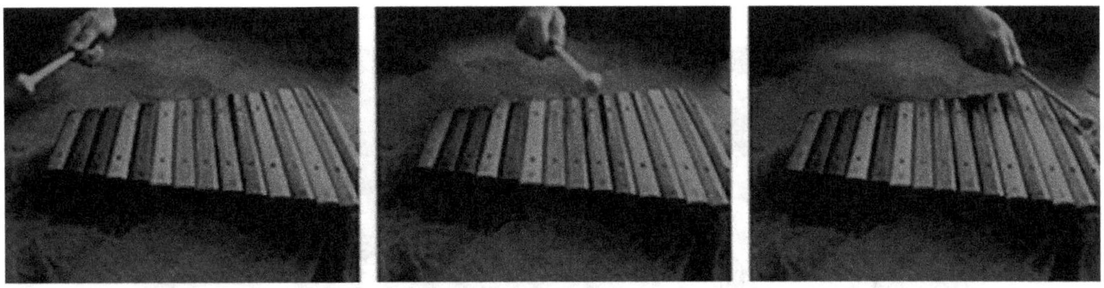

FIGURE 6.25
Output of Example 6.9.

EXAMPLE 6.10 EXAMPLE TO DEMONSTRATE BLOB ANALYSIS

```
clear; clc;
h = vision.BlobAnalysis;
I = imread('circlesBrightDark.png');
b = im2bw(I, 0.7);
h.MajorAxisLengthOutputPort = true;
h.MinorAxisLengthOutputPort = true;
h.OrientationOutputPort = true;
h.EccentricityOutputPort = true;
h.EquivalentDiameterSquaredOutputPort = false;
h.ExtentOutputPort = false;
h.PerimeterOutputPort = true;
[area, ctrd, bbox, maja, mina, orie, ecce, peri] = step(h, b)
c = insertShape(double(b), 'Rectangle', bbox, 'Color', 'green');
figure, imshow(c); hold on;
for i = 1:3
    plot(ctrd(i,1), ctrd(i,2), 'r*');
end
x1 = ctrd(1,1)+100;
```

```
x2 = ctrd(2,1)+100;
x3 = ctrd(3,1)-60;
y1 = ctrd(1,2);
y2 = ctrd(2,2);
y3 = ctrd(3,2)-100;

A1 = num2str(area(1)); A2 = num2str(area(2)); A3 = num2str(area(3));
M1 = num2str(maja(1)); M2 = num2str(maja(2)); M3 = num2str(maja(3));
P1 = num2str(peri(1)); P2 = num2str(peri(2)); P3 = num2str(peri(3));
e1 = num2str(ecce(1)); e2 = num2str(ecce(2)); e3 = num2str(ecce(3));

s1 = strcat('A= ', A1,', M=', M1,', P=', P1, ', e=', e1);
s2 = strcat('A= ', A2,', M=', M2,', P=', P2, ', e=', e2);
s3 = strcat('A= ', A3,', M=', M3,', P=', P3, ', e=', e3);

text(x1, y1, s1, 'Color', 'yellow');
text(x2, y2, s2, 'Color', 'yellow');
text(x3, y3, s3, 'Color', 'yellow');

ellow');
```

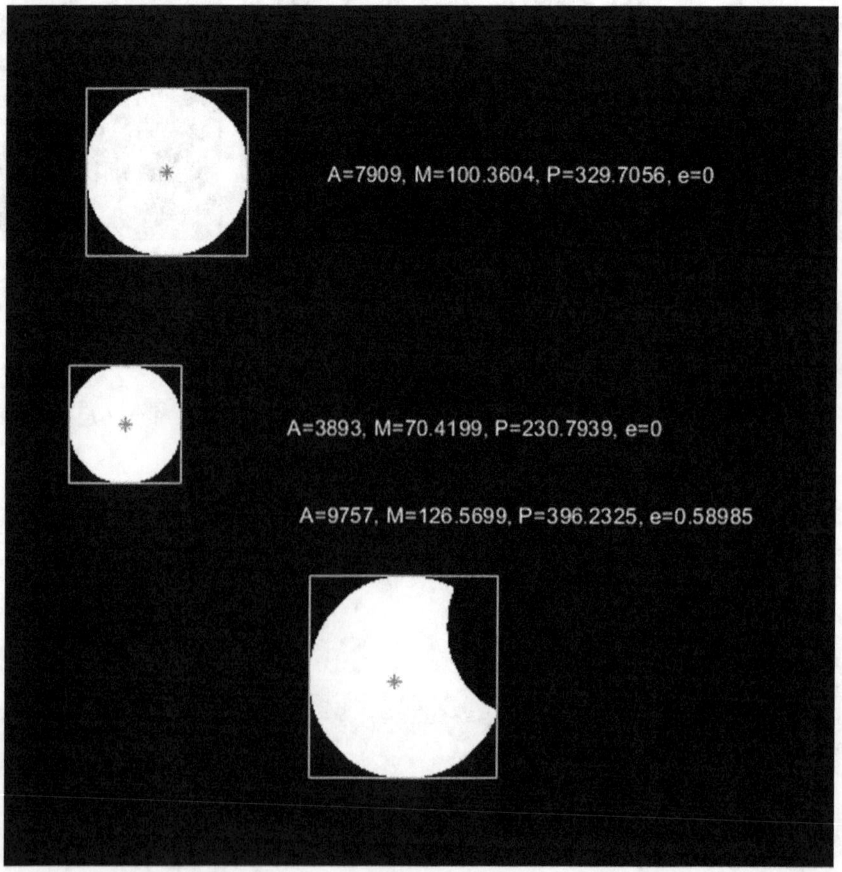

FIGURE 6.26
Output of Example 6.10.

6.9.5 Foreground Detector

The following example detects a foreground object from each frame of a video and inserts a bounding box to demarcate it. The function "vision.ForegroundDetector" computes a foreground mask by determining whether individual pixels are part of the background or foreground, "vision.VideoFileReader" reads video from a file, "vision.VideoPlayer" plays a video. It uses a specified number of initial video frames for training the background model and GMM to create a foreground mask. The mask is used to create bounding box parameters based on which the function "insertShape" draws designated shapes with specified colors on to the video frames (Figure 6.27).

EXAMPLE 6.11 EXAMPLE FOR FOREGROUND DETECTOR

```
clear; clc;
fn = 'visiontraffic.avi';
vr = vision.VideoFileReader(fn, 'VideoO
     utputDataType','uint8');
fd = vision.ForegroundDetector;
ba = vision.BlobAnalysis('CentroidOutpu
     tPort', false, ...
    'AreaOutputPort', false, ...
    'BoundingBoxOutputPort', true, ...
    'MinimumBlobArea', 100);
vp = vision.VideoPlayer();
while ~isDone(vr)
    frame = vr();
    mask = fd(frame);
    bbox = ba(mask);
    out = insertShape(frame,'FilledRec
    tangle', ...
        bbox, 'Color', 'white',
'Opacity',0.3);
    vp(out);
end
release(vp);
release(vr);
```

6.9.6 Histogram-Based Motion Tracking

The following example shows a human face being tracked in each frame of an input video. The function "vision.HistogramBasedTracker" incorporates the CAMShift algorithm for object tracking. Based on the HSV equivalent of an initial frame and an initial search region, the "initializeObject" method generates a 16-bin histogram, which is used by the tracker to return the bounding box (bbox) coordinates of the target object in each frame of the video. These coordinates are used to generate a rectangular shape with specified border color and inserted into the frame which is then displayed by the player object (vp) within a Video Player window. Each frame is displayed likewise with a pause in between (Figure 6.28).

EXAMPLE 6.12 EXAMPLE FOR HISTOGRAM BASED MOTION TRACKING

```
clear; clc;
vr = vision.VideoFileReader('vipcolorse
   gmentation.avi');
vp = vision.VideoPlayer();
si = vision.ShapeInserter('BorderColor'
   ,'Custom', ...
    'CustomBorderColor',[1 0 0]);
objectFrame = vr();
objectHSV = rgb2hsv(objectFrame);
objectRegion = [40, 45, 25, 25];
tr = vision.HistogramBasedTracker;
initializeObject(tr, objectHSV(:,:,1) ,
objectRegion);
while ~isDone(vr)
    frame = vr();
    hsv = rgb2hsv(frame);
    bbox = tr(hsv(:,:,1));
    out = si(frame,bbox);
    vp(out);
    pause(0.1)
end
```

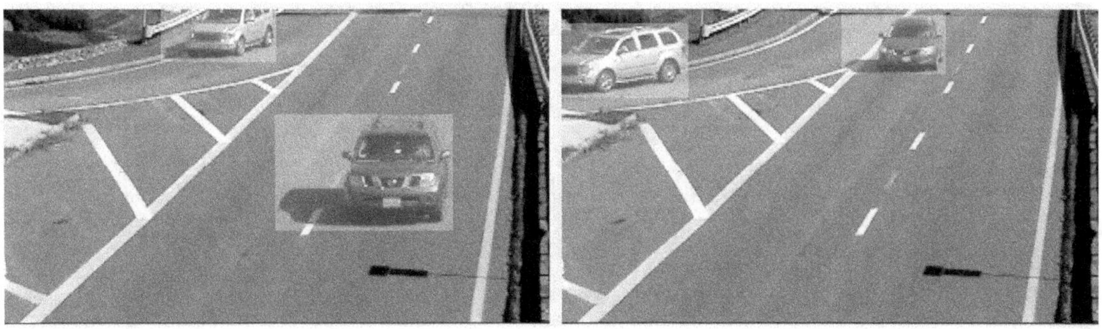

FIGURE 6.27
Output of Example 6.11.

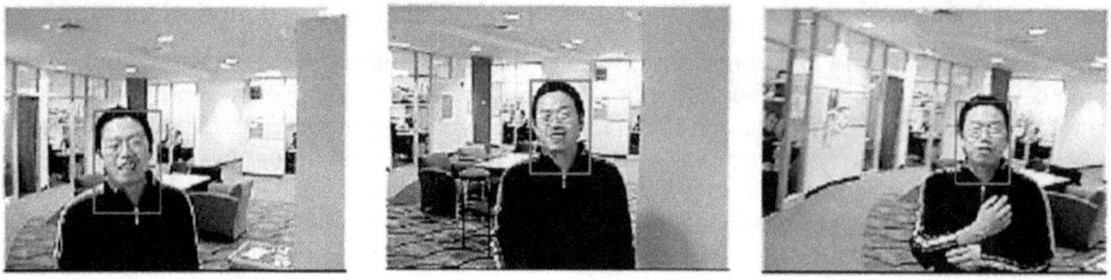

FIGURE 6.28
Output of Example 6.12.

6.9.7 Optical Flow–Based Motion Tracking

The following example illustrates creating optical flow objects and using five frames for estimation. The functions "opticalFlowFarneback" and "opticalFlowHS" are used to estimate the direction and speed of a moving object from one video frame to another using the Farneback algorithm and the Horn–Schunck algorithm. The "estimateFlow" method estimates the optical flow of the video frame with respect to the previous frame. The function "plot" . The parameter "DecimationFactor" controls the number of arrows, and the parameter "ScaleFactor" controls the length of arrows (Figure 6.29).

EXAMPLE 6.13 EXAMPLE FOR OPTICAL FLOW BASED MOTION TRACKING

```
clear; clc; fn = 'visiontraffic.avi';
vr = VideoReader(fn); v = read(vr);
for k = 155:160
    w(:,:,:,k-154) =
rgb2gray(v(:,:,:,k));
end
% Farneback method
figure,
off = opticalFlowFarneback;
for i = 1:5
    vf = w(:,:,:,i);
    of1 = estimateFlow(off,vf);
    subplot(121),
    imshow(vf); hold on;
    title('Farneback method');
    plot(of1,'DecimationFactor',[10
    10],'ScaleFactor',2);
    hold off;
end
% Horn-Schunck method
ofh = opticalFlowHS;
for i = 1:5
    vf = w(:,:,:,i);
    of2 = estimateFlow(ofh,vf);
    subplot(122),
    imshow(vf); hold on; title('Horn-
    Schunck method');
    plot(of2,'DecimationFactor',[2
    2],'ScaleFactor',30);
    hold off;
end
```

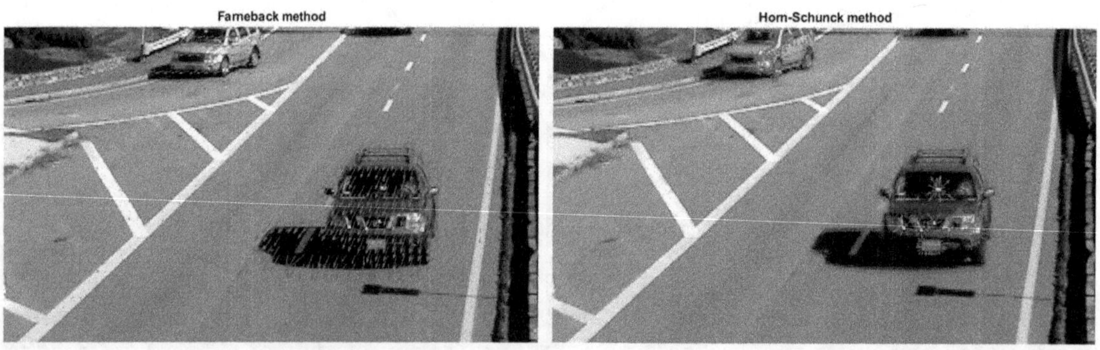

FIGURE 6.29
Output of Example 6.13.

Review Questions

- Trace the historical evolution of digital video processing highlighting salient events.
- What are meant by frame and frame rate in connection with video playback?
- Distinguish between component video and composite video.
- What is the Y-C signal format and how is it derived from RGB signals?
- Explain various schemes of chroma sub-sampling and their benefits.
- Discuss major TV transmission standards and their specifications.
- Explain the working principles of video camera.
- Mention key components and features of a digital video camera.
- What are the functions of a video capture card?
- Mention in brief the video digitization process.
- What are some of the features of a typical video capture software?
- Explain how video transmission takes place.
- Discuss key components involved in digital video transmission.
- Mention some of the popular video interface connectors used today.
- What are some of the common video editing tasks done using a GUI-based software?
- What is meant by timebase adjustments in connection with video editing?
- Distinguish between drop mode and non-drop mode SMPTE timecode.
- What are some of the major video color spaces in use today?
- Explain how blob detection can be done using LoG kernels.
- Explain how HOG features can be used for human detection.
- Explain how the Viola–Jones algorithm can be used for face detection.
- Explain the principle of operation of the histogram-based motion tracker.
- Discuss how optical flow–based motion trackers can be used to track moving objects.
- Mention some of the major video-based applications used in recent times.
- Discuss legal and ethical considerations for creation and distribution of digital video.
- Mention some of the challenges and emerging trends in using video content.
- Mention major video file formats in use today.

References

Bradski, G. R., Computer vision face tracking for use in a perceptual user interface, *IEEE Workshop on Applications of Computer Vision*, pp. 214–219, 1998.

Comaniciu, D., P. Meer, Mean Shift: A robust approach toward feature space analysis, *IEEE Transactions on Pattern Analysis and Machine Intelligence (PAMI)*, vol. 24, no. 5, pp. 603–619, 2002.

Crow, F., Summed up tables for texture mapping, *Proceedings of the SIGGRAPH*, vol. 18, no. 3, pp. 207–212, 1984.

Dalal, N. & B. Triggs. Histograms of oriented gradients for human detection, *IEEE Computer Society Conference on Computer Vision and Pattern Recognition*, vol. 1, pp. 886–893, 2005.

Dasiopoulou, S., et al., Knowledge-assisted semantic video object detection, *IEEE Transactions on Circuits and Systems for Video Technology*, vol. 15, no. 10, pp. 1210–1224, 2005.

Farneback, G., "Two-frame motion estimation based on polynomial expansion", *Proceedings of the 13th Scandinavian Conference on Image Analysis*, 2003.

Haar, A., Zur Theorie der orthogonalen Funktionensysteme, *Mathematische Annalen*, vol. 69, pp. 331–371, 1910

Horn, B. K. P. & B. G. Schunck, Determining optical flow, *Artificial Intelligence*, vol. 17, pp. 185–203, 1981

Jackson, W., *Digital video editing fundamentals*, Apress, 2016.

Kallen, S. A., *Digital cameras and camcorders*, Lucent Books, 2014.

Leggett, E. R., *Digitization and digital archiving*, Rowman & Littlefield, 2020.

Lucas, B. D. and Kanade, T., An iterative image registration technique with an application to stereo vision, *Proceedings of Imaging Understanding Workshop*, pp. 121–130, 1981.

Musburger, R. B., *Single-camera video production*, CRC Press, 2012.

Poynton, C., *"A Technical Introduction to Digital Video"*, John Wiley & Sons Inc., p. 175, 1996.

Slater, J., *Modern television systems*, CRC Press, 1991.

Taskiran, M. N., F. Pinarbasi, *Multidisciplinary approaches to ethics in the digital era*, IGI Global, 2021.

Viola, P., M. J. Jones, Rapid object detection using a boosted cascade of simple features, *Proceedings of the 2001 IEEE Computer Society Conference on Computer Vision and Pattern Recognition (CVPR)*, vol. 1, pp. 511–518, 2001.

Weynand, D., M. Weise, *How video works*, CRC Press, 2012.

Zhang, S., Single shot refinement neural network for object detection, *Proceedings of the IEEE Conference on Computer Vision and Pattern Recognition (CVPR)*, pp. 4203–4212, 2018.

7

Animation

7.1 Animation Fundamentals

7.1.1 Key Terms

We begin with a snapshot of the important terms relevant to the 2D and 3D animation, to present the entire chapter in a nutshell. These terms will be expanded in the following sections of the chapter in their proper contexts.

Animation file formats: Vector animation file formats store animations using mathematical descriptions of shapes and movements, allowing for scalability without loss of quality. Examples include SVG (Scalable Vector Graphics) and Flash (SWF), offering a versatile and efficient way to represent animated graphics in digital media.

Atmospheric effects: Atmospheric effects in 3D modeling involve simulating the interaction of light with atmospheric elements to enhance realism in rendered scenes. Techniques such as fog, haze and volumetric lighting are employed to replicate the visual impact of atmospheric conditions, contributing to a more immersive and visually compelling environment.

Camera movements: Camera movements in 3D animation involve changing the position, orientation or focal length of the virtual camera to create dynamic and visually engaging shots. These movements, such as pans, tilts, zooms and tracking, contribute to the storytelling and visual appeal of the animation by controlling the viewer's perspective within the virtual space.

Hierarchical animation: Hierarchical animation in computer graphics involves organizing a model's components into a hierarchical structure, allowing for efficient and controlled animation by moving or rotating parts relative to their parent components. This approach simplifies the animation process, providing a structured way to manage complex movements and transformations in a 3D model.

Inverse kinematics (IK): Inverse Kinematics (IK) is a technique in computer graphics and robotics used to calculate the joint angles of an articulated structure to achieve a desired end-effector position. It is particularly useful in character animation and robotic systems, providing a way to control and animate complex movements by specifying the goal positions or orientations of specific parts of the structure.

Keyframing: Keyframing is the technique of setting keyframes at specific points in time to define an object's properties. Animators create motion by specifying keyframes, and the animation software generates the frames in between (tweening).

Motion path: Motion paths in animation define the trajectory or route that an animated object follows over time. By specifying the path, animators can control the movement of objects in a smooth and predictable manner, enhancing the visual storytelling and dynamics of the animation.

Onion skinning: A technique in animation that displays multiple frames of an animation simultaneously, allowing animators to see the current frame overlaid with the preceding and succeeding frames. This visual aid helps animators maintain consistency in movement, easing the process of creating smooth and fluid animations by providing a reference to the previous and upcoming frames.

Painter's algorithm: The Painter's algorithm is a rendering technique used in computer graphics to determine the visibility of surfaces and their order of rendering. It works by sorting and rendering surfaces from the farthest to the nearest in the scene, simulating the approach of a painter who first paints the background and then adds elements in the foreground.

Parameter Curve Editing: Parameter curve editing in computer graphics involves manipulating the parameters of a curve, such as control points or coefficients, to modify its shape and characteristics. This interactive process

DOI: 10.1201/9781003588030-7

allows users to finely control the appearance of curves, making it a valuable tool in design and animation applications.

Particle systems: Particle systems in computer graphics are simulations of individual entities, often representing objects like raindrops, sparks, or fire, that collectively create dynamic visual effects. These systems use algorithms to govern the behavior, motion and appearance of the particles, contributing to the realistic rendering of complex phenomena in animations and simulations.

Ray casting algorithm: The Ray Casting algorithm is a rendering technique in computer graphics that simulates the tracing of rays from the viewer's eye into a scene to determine the intersections with surfaces. By calculating these intersections, it generates the pixel values for rendering a 3D scene, providing a method for realistic rendering and shading effects.

Ray tracing algorithm: Ray tracing is a rendering algorithm in computer graphics that simulates the way light interacts with objects to generate realistic images. It traces the path of rays of light as they travel through a scene, calculating their interactions with surfaces, Reflections, and refractions, resulting in visually accurate renderings with realistic lighting and shadows.

Rendering: Rendering in computer graphics is the process of generating an image from a three-dimensional model or scene using specialized algorithms and calculations. It involves the simulation of lighting, shading, and other visual effects to produce the final 2D representation that can be displayed on a screen or in printed media.

Shading algorithm: A shading algorithm in computer graphics determines the colors and intensities of pixels in a rendered image, considering factors like lighting, material properties, and the orientation of surfaces. It plays a crucial role in creating realistic visual effects by simulating how light interacts with objects in a virtual environment.

Space warp: In 3D animation, a space warp refers to a type of deformer or modifier that can be applied to objects or geometry to distort or manipulate their shape in various ways. Space warps are often used to create special effects, simulate dynamic movements or control the overall behavior of objects within a scene.

Shape changes: Shape changes in 3D animation involve altering the form or appearance of an object or character over time. This dynamic transformation is achieved through techniques such as morphing, skeletal deformation, or blend shapes, allowing animators to create fluid and expressive movements in characters or objects within a 3D scene.

Tweening: Tweening, short for "in-between" is a technique in animation where intermediate frames are generated to create smooth transitions between keyframes. It is commonly used to achieve fluid motion in animation by automatically interpolating the frames between two key poses.

Z-buffer algorithm: The Z-buffer algorithm is a depth-buffering technique used in computer graphics for hidden surface removal during rendering. It involves assigning a depth value (Z-coordinate) to each pixel in the scene, allowing the renderer to determine which surfaces are visible and which are hidden based on their depth values.

Zones of vision: Zones of vision in computer graphics, often referred to as a frustum, represent the viewing volume that is visible to a camera or viewer. It is a pyramidal shape defined by the camera's position, orientation and field of view, encompassing the space where objects are rendered within a scene.

7.1.2 Historical Evolution

1800s–1910s: The foundations of 2D animation were laid in the late 19th and early 20th centuries through pioneering experiments with moving images. Inventors like Eadweard Muybridge and J. Stuart Blackton used sequential photographs and drawings to create short animated sequences, setting the stage for the art form.

1920s–1930s: The 1920s saw the emergence of hand-drawn animation with the creation of characters like Felix the Cat. However, it was Walt Disney's introduction of synchronized sound in *Steamboat Willie* (1928), featuring Mickey Mouse, that marked a significant milestone in animation history.

1930s–1950s: The 1930s to the 1950s are often referred to as the Golden Age of Animation. Major animation studios, including Disney, Warner Bros., and MGM, produced iconic characters such as Bugs Bunny, Daffy Duck, and Tom and Jerry. Technological advancements allowed for smoother animation and the introduction of color.

1950s–1960s: As television became a dominant medium in the 1950s, animation studios embraced limited animation techniques to produce content more cost-effectively. Hanna-Barbera, for instance, created popular TV cartoons like *The Flintstones* and *Yogi Bear* using limited animation.

1960s–1970s: The 1960s and 1970s witnessed a surge in experimental animation. Artists explored abstract and avant-garde animation styles. Notable works include Norman McLaren's *Pas de Deux* (1968) and the rise of independent animators like Ralph Bakshi with films like *Fritz the Cat* (1972).

1980s: The 1980s marked the introduction of computer-assisted animation techniques. Disney's *The Great Mouse Detective* (1986) featured the first major use of computer-generated imagery (CGI) in a feature film. Computer technology began to complement traditional hand-drawn animation processes.

1980s–1990s: The late 1980s to the mid-1990s are known as the Disney Renaissance, characterized by a resurgence of critically and commercially successful animated films. Hits like *The Little Mermaid* (1989), *Beauty and the Beast* (1991) and *The Lion King* (1994) showcased a blend of traditional animation and new technologies.

1990s–Present: The late 1990s and early 2000s witnessed a shift toward digital animation. Pixar's *Toy Story* (1995) became the first feature-length film created entirely using computer-generated imagery. Digital tools allowed for greater flexibility and creativity in the animation process.

1990s–2000s: With the rise of the internet, Web animation gained popularity. Macromedia Flash, introduced in the late 1990s, became a widely used platform for creating interactive and animated Web content. Flash animations were prevalent on websites and played a significant role in online entertainment.

2000s–Present: In the contemporary era, 2D animation continues to thrive in various forms. While feature films like *The Princess and the Frog* (2009) maintain the traditional hand-drawn style, animated TV series, Web series and short films explore diverse storytelling and artistic approaches.

The evolution of 3D animation is another captivating journey that spans from early experiments with computer graphics to the dazzling visual effects of contemporary cinema and animation.

1960s–1970s: The roots of 3D animation can be traced back to the 1960s and 1970s when computer scientists and researchers began experimenting with wireframe models. Ivan Sutherland's *Sketchpad* (1963) and the development of computer graphics algorithms set the stage for three-dimensional computer-generated imagery.

1970s–1980s: In the 1970s, advancements in 3D wireframe modeling techniques allowed for the creation of more complex geometric shapes. The Utah Teapot, a famous computer graphics model, became an iconic symbol of early 3D computer graphics.

1980s: The 1980s witnessed significant progress in solid modeling and rendering techniques. Ray-tracing algorithms, such as those developed by James Kajiya in 1986, simulated the behavior of light, leading to more realistic 3D rendered scenes.

1980s–1990s: Computer-Aided Design (CAD) systems in the 1980s contributed to the growth of 3D modeling. These systems were initially used in fields like architecture and engineering for precise visualization and simulation of three-dimensional structures.

1980s–1990s: The 1980s saw the establishment of Pixar Animation Studios, a pivotal player in the evolution of 3D animation. Pixar's short film named *Luxo Jr.* (1986) showcased the potential of 3D character animation. Pixar later collaborated with Disney to create the ground-breaking feature film *Toy Story* (1995), the first entirely computer-animated feature film.

1990s: The 1990s witnessed the integration of real-time 3D graphics in video games. The introduction of advanced graphics processing units (GPUs) and game engines allowed for the creation of immersive 3D environments, transforming the gaming industry.

2000s: The 2000s brought about advancements in 3D animation software, making the creation of 3D content more accessible to artists and animators. Software like Autodesk Maya, 3d Studio Max and Cinema 4D became industry standards, offering robust tools for modeling, animation, and rendering. Motion capture technology became increasingly prevalent in the 2000s, enabling the capture of real-world movements for use in 3D animation. This technology enhanced the realism of character animation in films, video games, and other media.

2010s–Present: The 2010s and beyond have seen advancements in global illumination techniques and realistic rendering. Technologies like physically based rendering (PBR) contribute to achieving lifelike lighting and materials in 3D scenes, enhancing the visual quality of animated content.

2020s-Present: In the present era, virtual reality (VR) has become an exciting frontier for 3D animation. VR experiences leverage immersive 3D environments, and technologies like augmented reality (AR) further integrate 3D animated elements into the real world.

7.1.3 Basic Concepts

7.1.3.1 Key-frames and Tweening

In traditional animation, lead animators or experts draw the most important frames or key-frames, which define the frames where the course of action changes. The intermediate frames between the keyframes are drawn by the assistant animators. This process is called tweening, which has been derived from the word "in-between" (Figure 7.1). For example, for depicting the motion of the rectangle moving from the upper left corner to the lower right corner of the frame and at the same time changing its size and angular orientation, the key-frames specify its initial and final states, while the middle frames are the tweened frames, which display intermediate states of the rectangle. The total number of intermediate frames determines the smoothness or quality of the motion, and this together with the frame rate consideration, determine the duration of playback. It has been observed that 18 increments of movement projected at 24 frames per second give a lifelike result. To save time and money, some animators use double-framing. They draw nine motion increments and then photograph each frame twice. The result is less smooth but still acceptable. Triple-framing using only 6 increments that are each made into three frames is used almost exclusively for student work. In earlier days, all drawings were done by hand and then photographed on

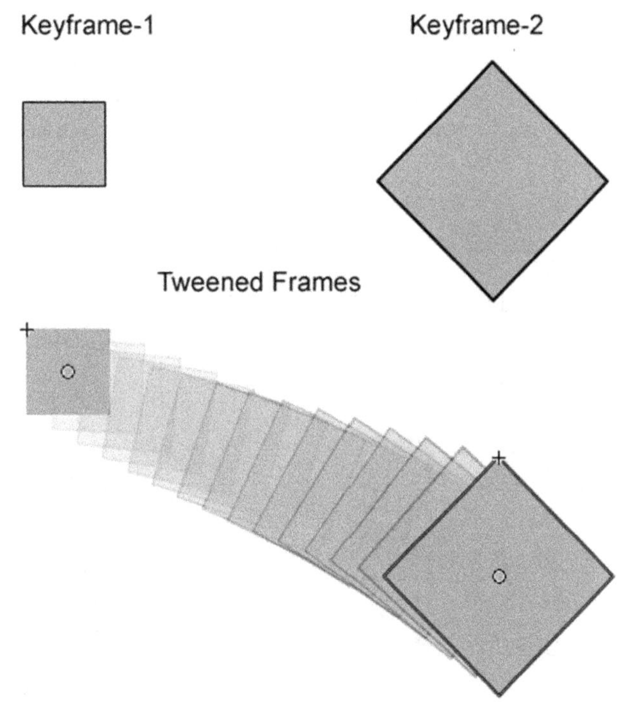

FIGURE 7.1
Keyframes and tweening.

film or tape. Nowadays, with the advent of digital computers, key-frames and tweening may be made using graphic software, saved as files inside the computer and played back on the screen at varying frame rates. On one hand, this can save a lot of time and energy, make the drawings more accurate and provide all the facilities of digital editing.

7.1.3.2 Cel Animation

Cel animation is a term derived from traditional animation. Cel comes from the word "celluloid", the material that made up early motion picture film, and refers to the transparent piece of film that is used in hand-drawn animation. Animation cels are generally layered, one on top of the other, to produce a single animation frame. Layering enables the animator to isolate and redraw only the parts of the image that change between successive frames. A frame consists of the background cel and the overlying cels and is like a snapshot of the action at one instant of time. To depict movement, only a portion, typically the foreground cel, can be changed between frames without changing the background cel (Figure 7.2).

7.1.3.3 Rotoscoping and Bluescreening

Rotoscoping was an early animation technique, which enabled animators and video editors to trace the contour of objects on each frame of an animation and video sequence to create a silhouette called a matte. The traced contour would then be replaced by something else to produce a special visual effect. The technique was first used around 1914 to place live characters over synthetic backgrounds. Rotoscoping has been used as a tool for special effects in action movies. One example was in the original Star Wars movie in 1977 where it was used to create the glowing light-sabre effect by creating a matte based on sticks held by actors. Nowadays, this technique has largely been superseded by the bluescreen technique. However, it can still be used in special cases where bluescreening will not be accurate enough. Bluescreening is a technique for shooting live action against an even-colored blue background and then replacing the background by another image. This is extensively used nowadays as chroma-keying using digital editing tools whereby the background color is selected by a selection tool and replaced by pasting over with some other background. Blue is normally used for people because human skin has very little blue color in it. Sometimes when the scene itself contains objects with blue color, other colors like green and orange can be used instead.

7.1.3.4 Stop-Motion Animation

Stop-motion animation is a technique by which a physical object is manipulated in each frame by small increments which creates an illusion that the object is moving on its own when the frames are played back as a continuous sequence. A popular variety of this kind of animation is clay-mation where clay figures are animated by changing their position and shape slightly in each frame. Nowadays, stop motion is being replaced by the use of computers to move parts of a computer-generated model between each frame, instead of moving a physical model by hand. Famous examples include "Wallace and Gromit" and "The Nightmare Before Christmas".

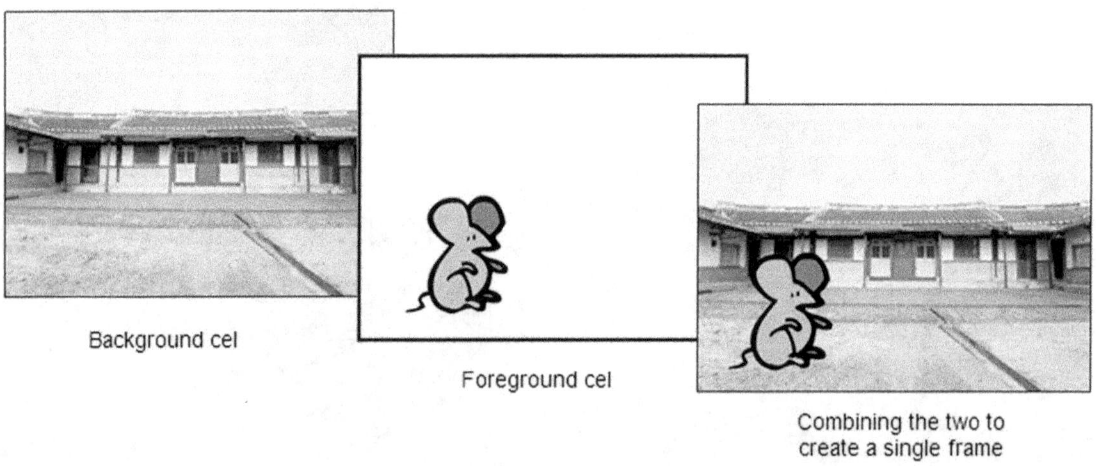

FIGURE 7.2
Cel animation.

7.1.3.5 Flipbook Animation

A flipbook is a book with a series of pictures varying gradually from one page to the next, so that when the pages are turned rapidly, the pictures appear to animate, simulating motion or some other change. This is called flipbook animation. Flipbooks are often illustrated books for children, but may also be geared toward adults and employ a series of photographs rather than drawings. Flipbooks are essentially a primitive form of animation. Like motion pictures, they rely on persistence of vision to create the illusion that continuous motion is being seen rather than a series of discontinuous images being exchanged in succession. Because of this, flipbook images will only appear on one side of the book's pages, so that rather than "reading" left to right, a viewer simply stares at the same location of the pictures in the flipbook as the pages turn. The book must also be flipped with enough speed for the illusion to work, so the standard way to "read" a flipbook is to hold the book with one hand and flip through its pages with the thumb of the other hand.

7.1.3.6 Motion Cycling

Human and animal motion, such as walking, running and flying, is mainly a repetitive action that is best represented by a cycle. A walk cycle requires 8 to 12 frames. The sequence usually falls into two halves. The first half begins at an extreme (frames 1–2): the feet are at their farthest apart, with the back toe and front heel touching the ground. In the remainder of the first half (frames 3–4), the legs trade position. So do the arms, but when the left leg is forward, the right arm is forward, and vice versa. The second half of the cycle (frames 5–8) is simply a variation of the first half, but with arms and legs reversed. The finished walking character can be used as a moving cell, i.e., a sprite. For the flying sequence the first four frames depict the wings going up and the next four frames show the wings flapping down (Figure 7.3).

7.1.3.7 Principles of Animation

The art of animation is not just about moving pictures; it's about creating the illusion of life and motion. The principles of animation serve as the foundation for achieving this illusion, making animations believable and engaging. Developed by Disney animators Frank Thomas and Ollie Johnston in their book *The Illusion of Life: Disney Animation* (Thomas & Johnston, 1981), these principles have become a guiding light for animators across the globe.

Squash and Stretch: Squash and stretch is one of the most fundamental principles. It involves giving objects weight and flexibility. When an object moves or deforms, it should follow the laws of physics. For example, when a ball bounces, it stretches on impact and squashes when it hits the ground.

Anticipation: Anticipation is the act of preparing the audience for an action. It allows viewers to anticipate what will happen next. For example, before a character jumps, they often crouch down slightly to indicate their intention.

Staging: Staging involves presenting an idea or action clearly to the audience. It ensures that the audience's attention is directed to the most important elements in the scene. Effective staging eliminates confusion and keeps the viewer engaged. For example, in a fight scene, the primary action, such as a punch, should be prominently staged, ensuring the audience's focus is on the impact. Background elements should support, not distract from, the central action.

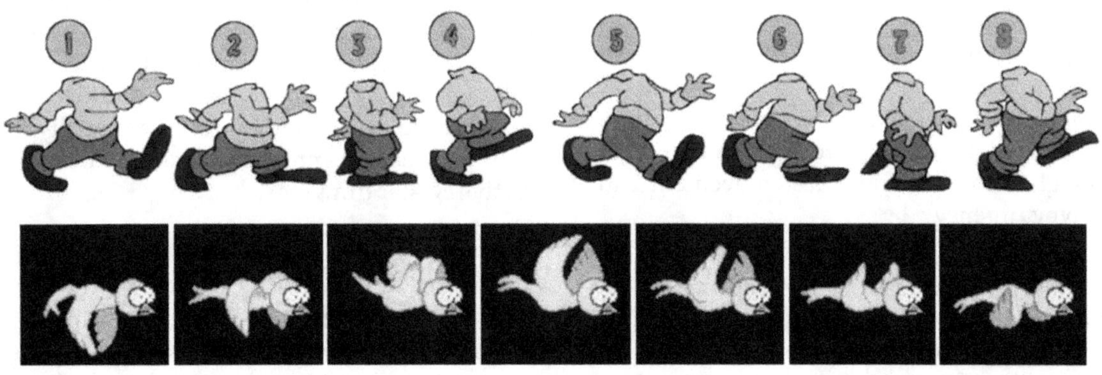

FIGURE 7.3
Examples of motion cycling.

Straight-Ahead and Pose-to-Pose Animation: Straight-ahead animation involves creating each frame in sequence, while pose-to-pose animation starts with keyframes and then fills in the intermediate frames. The choice between these techniques depends on the desired effect and efficiency.

Follow Through and Overlapping Action: Follow through occurs when an object continues to move after the main action has stopped, and overlapping action involves multiple parts of an object moving at different rates. These principles make animations appear more natural and less rigid. For example, when a dog suddenly stops running, its ears, tail and fur continue moving momentarily before they come to rest, adding a realistic touch to the motion.

Slow In and Slow Out (Ease In and Ease Out): Slow in and slow out refer to the gradual acceleration and deceleration of an object's motion. This principle mimics real-world physics and makes movements look smoother and more realistic. For example, a car accelerating from a complete stop doesn't immediately reach its maximum speed. It starts slowly, accelerates and then gradually slows down when coming to a stop.

Arcs: Arcs represent the curved path that objects often follow during motion. Emphasizing arcs in animation adds fluidity and naturalness to movement. For example, when a figure skater spins, their arms describe a graceful arc in the air. In animation, movements such as a character swinging a sword should follow curved paths for a more natural look.

Secondary Action: Secondary actions are additional motions that complement the main action. For example, when a character walks, their clothing and hair may sway in response to the movement.

Timing: Timing determines the speed and rhythm of actions. It helps convey emotions, weight and the character's state of mind. A slow, deliberate movement can express thoughtfulness, while a fast movement can convey urgency.

Exaggeration: Exaggeration involves pushing actions and expressions beyond reality to make them more interesting and expressive. It's a key tool for emphasizing emotions and storytelling. For example, in a cartoon, a character might be so surprised that their eyes pop out of their head. This exaggeration of the character's reaction enhances the comedic effect.

Solid Drawing: Solid drawing focuses on giving characters and objects a three-dimensional appearance. Animators must understand form, anatomy and perspective to achieve convincing solidity. For example, when a character turns, their form should show volume and depth to give the illusion of a solid figure.

Appeal: Appeal is the quality that makes characters and objects attractive and relatable to the audience. Creating characters with unique and memorable traits adds to their appeal. For example, Mickey Mouse's iconic design, with large round ears and friendly eyes, makes him instantly recognizable and endearing to audiences.

7.1.3.8 Computer Animation

Computer-assisted animation can be based on the key-frame concept. The great advantage of computer assisted animation is that in-between frames are created by the animation program itself, not by junior animators doing a lot of tedious work. Computer animation software typically simulates the process of traditional cell-based animation, by placing the animated object on a timeline to depict the flow of time. A playback head moves across the timeline to display each of the frames one after another. You create keyframes by picking a set of points on the timeline and then choosing values for time-varying parameters such as position, size, orientation and color at these points. The computer generates or tweens intermediate frames between the key-frames by interpolating the parameter values from one key-frame to the next. Because key-frames mark transitions between properties, it is important to make these transitions appear smooth. To ensure smooth transitions between frames, each frame must be carefully aligned or registered with other frames. A registration point is a point on each cell that lines up with the same point on every other cell. Computer animation programs usually have grid and alignment commands to help animators to correctly register drawings.

7.1.3.9 Path-Based Animation

With the advent of computers for creating animation, we have another class of animation that differs from the traditional cell-based animation. Such animation is called path animation as it generally involves a path, straight or curved, over which a graphical object moves. The path is typically represented as splines and hence such animations are typically vector-based; i.e., the animation is not stored as a collection of key-frames and tweened frames, but as a set of spline equations over which the object is made to move during playback. In the simplest cases, the appearance of the object does not change, and hence it can simply be a single static graphical drawing, which is made to move along the specified path. In more complex cases, the object can be dynamically made to change its appearance based on its location on the path, for example, a bouncing ball can appear round when in the air but become flattened as it strikes the ground (Figure 7.4b). If the object itself needs to change in appearance then the fixed graphics is replaced by a movie clip containing multiple frames, e.g., frames and the entire movie clip is made to move along the spline path (Figure 7.4).

7.1.3.10 3D Animation

3D modeling is a fundamental step in 3D animation, involving the creation of digital objects, characters, and environments (Zeman, 2015). Modelers use specialized software tools to define the shape, structure and appearance of these elements. Techniques include creating 3D structures from pre-defined 3D objects called geometrical primitives as well as creating 3D structures from 2D shapes. The former method involve using modifiers like taper, bend, twist as well as transformations, Boolean operations, arrays to create complex objects from simpler ones. The latter method involves processes like lathing, lofting and extrusion to convert shapes to surfaces.

Once the 3D surface is modeled surface color and texture are applied to impart realistic appearances. Techniques involve determining surface color, background color, determining surface type like opaque, translucent or transparent, reflectivity and refractivity, and texture mapping.

Lighting involves determining the types of lights in the 3D scene, their distances and angles of lighting, shading and illumination, casting of shadows. The next step involves placing the cameras, defining their types, focal lengths, zooming ratios, center of interests. Animation can be frame-based or path-based, and needs to define how each object needs to behave over time, how their appearances change over time, whether the lights and camera moves, if so defining their trajectories and speeds.

Rendering is the process of creating 2D images from 3D models. Various techniques are used to achieve realistic results. Rendering algorithms like ray-casting and ray-tracing determine how each object looks based on their surface characteristics as well as considering proximity to lights, reflective surfaces, shading and shadows of neighboring objects, occlusion of overlapping objects.

7.2 2D Animation

7.2.1 Interpolations

A key-frame-based software system creates the in-between frames of an animation by interpolating the transformation values from one key-frame to the next (O'Rourke, 2003). An object is 10 m away from the observer at key-frame 1 (Kf 1) and 0 m from the observer at key-frame 60 (Kf 60). The animator specifies all the nine transformation parameters to the software both at Kf 1 and Kf 60. The software then computes the values of the parameters from frame 2 to frame 59 by interpolation. The simplest kind of interpolation, called linear interpolation, gets its name from the fact that if you draw a graph of the relationship between the two parameters (i.e., frame numbers and transformation values), you get a straight line. In interpolating, say, from frame 1 to frame 60, frame 30 (f 30) which is halfway between frames 1 and 60,

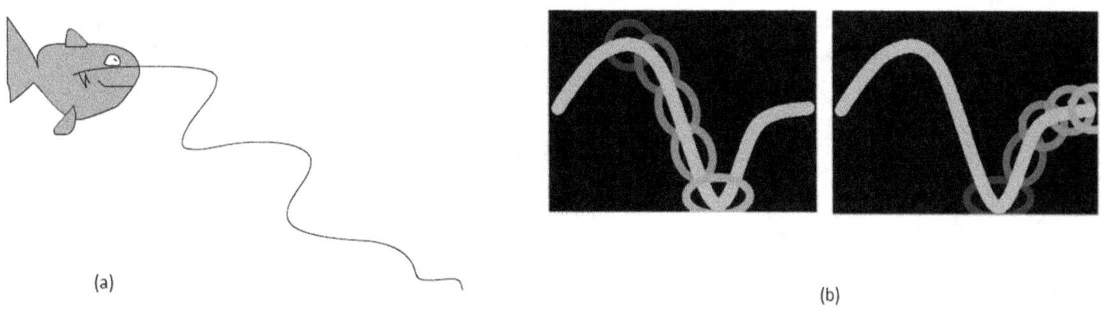

FIGURE 7.4
(a) Path-based animation (b) dynamically changing object.

receives transformation values that are half of the difference between the values at frame 1 and the values at frame 60. The rate at which the distance is changing, i.e., speed, stays the same over the length of the entire interpolation. Thus, if the translation along X-axis TX changes by 2 m in the first ten frames, then TX also changes by 2 m between frames 50 and 60. Once key-frames have been defined and in-betweens generated, the animator would normally want to view the animation to evaluate it. Upon seeing the motion preview, the animator may decide to change one of the key-frames and save it as a new key-frame overwriting the old key-frame. If the speed needs to vary over the range of frames, a third key-frame is required in between, say, at frame 30. The object moves from frame 1 to frame 30 at a specific speed and then accelerates to a faster speed so that it reaches the destination before frame 60, e.g., at frame 45. There is an abrupt change of speed at frame 30, and so frame 30 becomes another key-frame, denoted as Kf 30, as it changes some of transformation parameters as defined in Kf 1 (Figure 7.5).

If your requirement is that the cube should move smoothly through various positions without any abrupt changes, then the solution is a spline interpolation. If you ask the computer to calculate a curve through these control points as a spline interpolation rather than a linear interpolation you get the smooth curvature — the smooth change in TX. Since there is no abrupt change in the curve, the cube translates smoothly from one point to another over the entire length of the sixty-frame animation. At first, it moves slowly (horizontal portion of the graph near frame 1) and then slowly picks up speed, the maximum being toward the end of the trajectory (vertical portion of the graph near frame 60). In addition to linear and spline interpolations, other interpolations along with distinct terminology attached to them are commonly used. In animation, you often want some change to accelerate slowly. Such changes are known as ease-in. This is indicated by a flat curve which slowly increases in slope. The opposite of an ease-in is an ease-out, in which the change decelerates. This is indicated by the steep-sloped line which slowly flattens out. Combining an ease-in and an ease-out produces an interpolation called an ease-in-out (which looks like an S-shaped curve) in which the value changes slowly at first then more quickly and then slowly again.

7.2.2 Parameter Curve Editing

In a key-frame-based animation system, the most common way to define the movement and timing of an object is to transform the object manually (e.g., drag to scale by mouse or enter scale parameters) until it looks right visually and then save each set of transformations as a key-frame. There is another very common and powerful approach to defining the movement and timing of an animation. We saw in a previous section that it is possible to represent the changes in a given transformation parameters as a graph, with the changes in the value of a parameter plotted against time. The alternate approach to defining animation takes advantages of this sort of graphical representation. The underlying concept of this graphical approach is that any change made to the parameter graph causes a corresponding change in the animation. Imagine that the height SY (i.e., scale along y-axis) of a cylinder increases and then decreases. Using a system that allows parameter-graph editing, you can select control points that represents specific key-frames and pull them up or down to change the value of the SY parameter. Doing so immediately changes the height of the cylinder at that frame (O'Rourke, 2003) (Figure 7.6).

It is also possible to push or pull a control point horizontally in the direction of time. If you select and drag the control point at frame 30 to the left leaving the point at frame 10, the height that the cone attains does not change. However, the timing of the animation changes so that the cylinder achieves maximum height n only 10 frames, instead of the 30 frames it originally took, i.e., thrice as fast as the original animation. Moreover, the cylinder reverts back to the lower height more slowly in 50 frames instead of 30 frames. In parameter curve-editing systems, it is normally possible to edit a curve in all the same ways that you might edit a curve for modeling purposes. For example, you might insert new control points into the curve, thereby changing the shape of the curve,

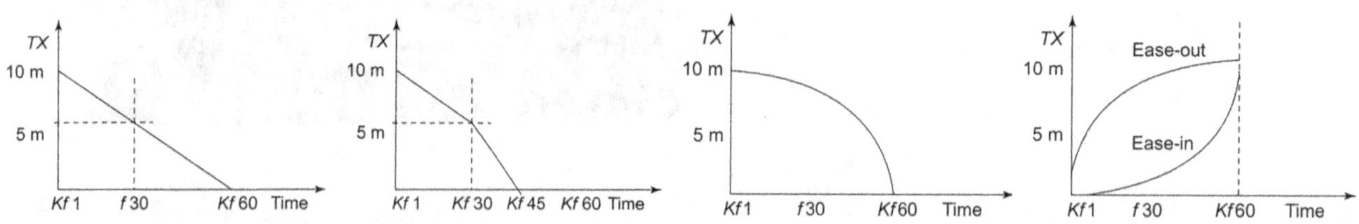

FIGURE 7.5
Linear and spline-based interpolations.

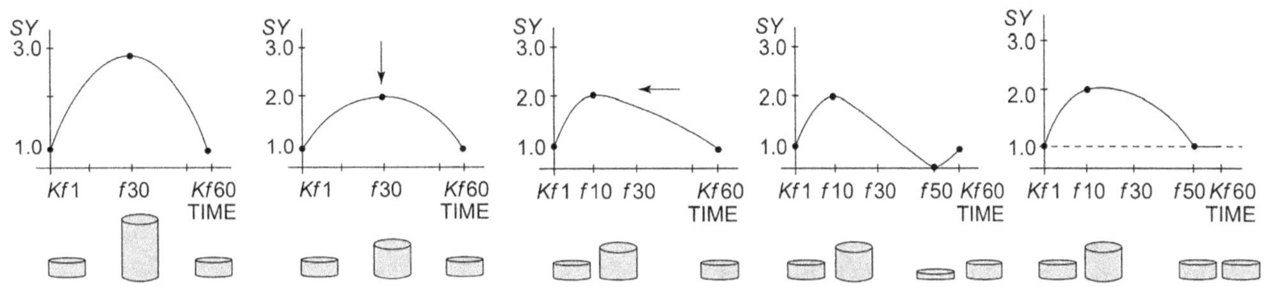

FIGURE 7.6
Parameter curve editing.

as well as the animation controlled by the graph. Most systems also allow you to select the type of interpolation used between any two control points. Any combination of interpolation types may be used between frames. For example, between one pair of control points, the interpolation might be a spline. Between another pair of control points, the interpolation may be linear. This technique is particularly useful when you want an element of your animation to change for a certain amount of time, but then to remain unchanging for another period of time. It is often found that during playback, an animation or section of animation is too fast or too slow. Most systems provide you with some ready way to lengthen or shorten a sequence of animation, effectively changing the timing to make an action slower or faster. This editing capability is usually called scaling the animation. If the scale factor is two, for example, the sequence becomes twice as long, that is, twice as slow.

7.2.3 Hierarchical Animation

Many models are more complex than a simple one-piece object. These models consist of several parts which you need to organize into a hierarchical structure in order to gain more control over the transformations you apply to different elements of the model. Animating a hierarchical model is conceptually just an extension of the technique of animating a simple one-piece model. Consider a graphical object representing a table with five members as shown below. When rotating the table by a specific angle, each of the members rotates about its own local origin, called pivot point. The result is not what is desired. The same things happen if each element is scaled about its individual pivot points. To produce the desired result, all the parts of the table must transform about a single origin. The solution is to organize the model into a hierarchical structure. The whole table is at the top level of the structure and the separate elements are at the lower levels. The whole system can have a collective pivot point (larger cross) about which it rotates as a whole. The transformation of the Table object propagates downward to the lower level objects, which are, however, always relative to the local origin of the Table. Within such a hierarchy, each element is called a child node of the Table object. All the five lower-level nodes consist of both a transformation matrix (rectangle) and some geometry (oval). The Table object, however, consists only of a transformation matrix but no geometry, because it is purely a logical grouping of several sub-elements (O'Rourke, 2003) (Figure 7.7).

7.2.4 Inverse Kinematics (IK)

In some situations, the guideline of the previous section, i.e., selecting each node of the hierarchy, transforming that node, and saving the transformation, is cumbersome. Consider the simple arm model in one position and think about moving that model to another position. In real life, you intuitively think of

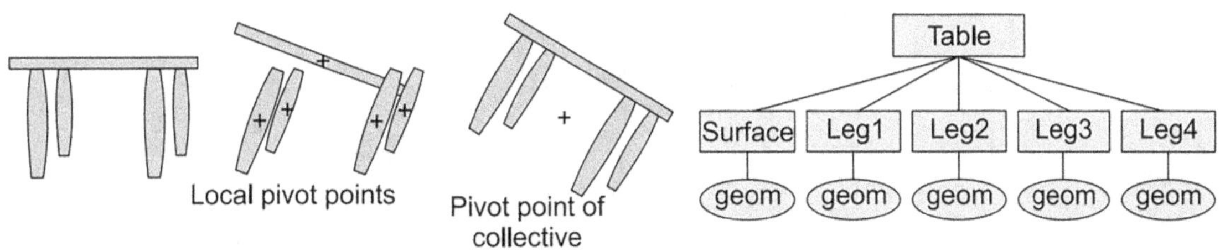

FIGURE 7.7
Hierarchical animation.

this kind of movement as "I moved my hand from here to there" and not as "I rotated my upper arm, then I rotated my lower arm, then I rotated my hand". Thus, the position of the hand determines the position of the arm joints, because all the parts of the arm are connected and remain so as the arm moves. If the hand moves, the lower arm must follow; if the lower arm moves, the upper arm must follow. You know this intuitively and that is why you want to place the hand and let the joints follow, rather than individually rotating each joint in order to get the hand to a specific location. The technique that implements this approach is called inverse kinematics. "Kinematics" refers to the mechanical study of motion while "inverse" refers to the fact that the flow of transformations within the hierarchical model is calculated in the opposite direction to the normal calculations. While in the previous section, the rotation of the table object (parent node) determined the final positions of the legs (child node), in this case the rotation of the hand (child node) determines the final position of the upper arm (parent node). Normally, you think of the transformations of a hierarchy as propagating downward through the hierarchy. The transformations of LowerArm should affect Hand but those of Hand should have no effect on LowerArm. In an inverse kinematics model, however, the transformations applied to the lowest level, Hand, determines, the transformations of LowerArm. The calculations of the transformations travel upward through the hierarchy. The standard downward propagation of transformations is sometimes referred to as forward kinematics to emphasize this difference. Since the hierarchy of an IK model behaves in a chainlike fashion, with each joint following the movement of its neighboring joint, the hierarchy is often called a chain. Each joint or node is referred to as a link in the chain. The end point of the final link in an IK chain — the point that you move — is called the effector, because this point effects the transformations of the various joints. The starting point of the first link in the chain — the one point of the whole chain that is fixed — is called the root of the chain. The root is also the pivot point of the entire chain. IK is frequently applied to human and other animal bodies. Since joints of the body cannot move in unrestricted directions — the human elbow, for example, does not bend beyond approximately 180 degrees — it is common for a 3D animation system to impose a 180-degree rotation constraint on the joints of all inverse kinematic models (O'Rourke, 2003) (Figure 7.8).

7.2.5 Motion Paths

The concept of motion paths allows you to define a path that an object moves along. The path is drawn in space using the standard curve-drawing techniques. This path, usually called the motion path of the object, represents the path along which the object will move. The animator indicates the object that should move along the path and specifies the number of frames over which the motion should take place. The computer then interpolates the in-between location of the object along that path for each in-between frame of the sequence. For example, suppose you draw a motion path and assign it to a cube, beginning at frame 1 and ending at frame 100. If you use a standard linear interpolation, then at frame 50 that represents half of the total time, the cube will be located halfway along the path. This moves the cube along the path at a constant rate of speed throughout the length of the animation. Most systems also provide a technique for controlling the rate of movement by adjusting the interpolation of a second curve, called a timing curve, which represents the rate of movement along the path (Figure 7.9a). The timing curve plots time on one axis and the percentage of distance on the path along the other axis. By editing and changing the timing curve, you change the rate of movement of the object along the path. For example, by changing the linear curve to an ease-in interpolation curve, the animator specifies that the cube still follows the same motion path but doing so at a different rate of speed, moving in slowly at first and then picking up speed covering a great distance in the final frames of the animation. If the timing curve is flattened and made horizontal over a certain range of frames, the object remains at the same location on the path for that range. If the timing curve slopes downward, the object moves backward. Another issue of

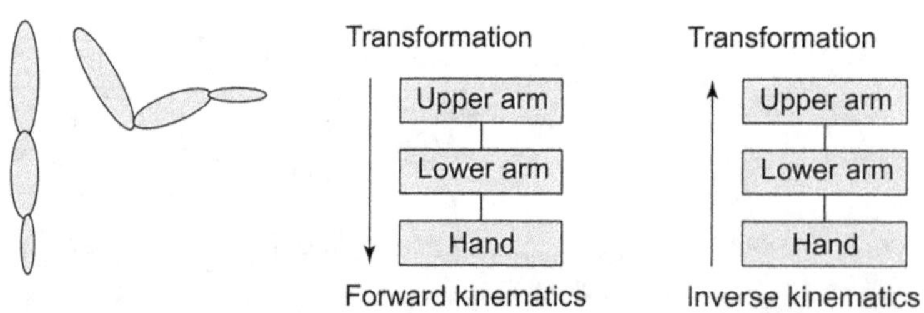

FIGURE 7.8
Inverse kinematics.

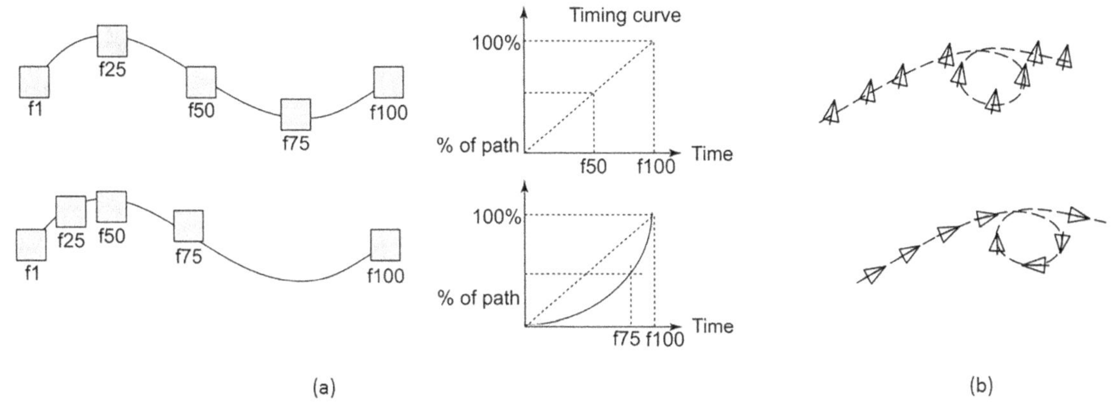

FIGURE 7.9
(a) Motion paths with timing curves (b) changing orientation of object

importance that must be considered when animating an object along a motion path is the orientation of the object relative to the path. Suppose you are animating a paper airplane along a motion path. Undoubtedly you want the nose of the airplane to stay on the path, i.e., to remain tangent to the curve. Some systems do this by default. Other systems by default always keep the object in the original orientation of the object as it moves along the path, and must be manually adjusted using parameters (O'Rourke, 2003) (Figure 7.9b).

7.2.6 Common Editing Tasks

Some common animation related tasks that can be performed using GUI-based animation software without the need for extensive coding are discussed below (Figure 7.10).

Using Timeline: The timeline contains a sequence of frames for simulating the flow of time using a playback head which moves from left to right. As the head moves over specific key frames, characteristics attached to these frames are applied to relevant graphical objects thereby changing their motion and/or shape as well as using them as triggers for event-based actions.

Motion Tweening: Involves linear movement of graphical objects over time along with changes in their characteristics like size and orientation.

Shape Tweening: Involves change of shape over time. In some cases both position and shape can be changed simultaneously.

Layering: Involves assigning objects to different layers for vertical ordering, i.e., determining which objects should come in front and which should go behind others.

Motion Guide: Involves specifying movement of objects along specific straight or curved paths.

Color Cycling: Involves tweening of multiple colors defined over keyframes.

Text Tweening: Involves tweening of alphanumeric characters over time.

Easing effects: Involves specifying ease-in (accelerated) and ease-out (decelerated) motion over time.

Buttons and Sounds: Involves creation of clickable buttons for triggering events and playback of sounds.

Masking: Involves editing changes visible within specific areas of the stage.

Transparency: Displaying partially transparent objects through use of alpha channels.

Interactivity: Using an associated programming language to define interactivity over space and time.

7.3 3D Animation

7.3.1 Modeling Surfaces

Surfaces define the shape and contour of the 3D graphical objects and models, and have two broad aspects to them: topology/structure and characteristics/appearance. The most basic type of surface is a flat surfaces commonly represented by a plane. Alternatively, we can have curved surfaces modeled using two splines u and v along orthogonal directions. Depending on the types of splines used, surfaces may be named accordingly, e.g., Bezier surfaces or B-spline surfaces. Spline-based surfaces often have a grid of

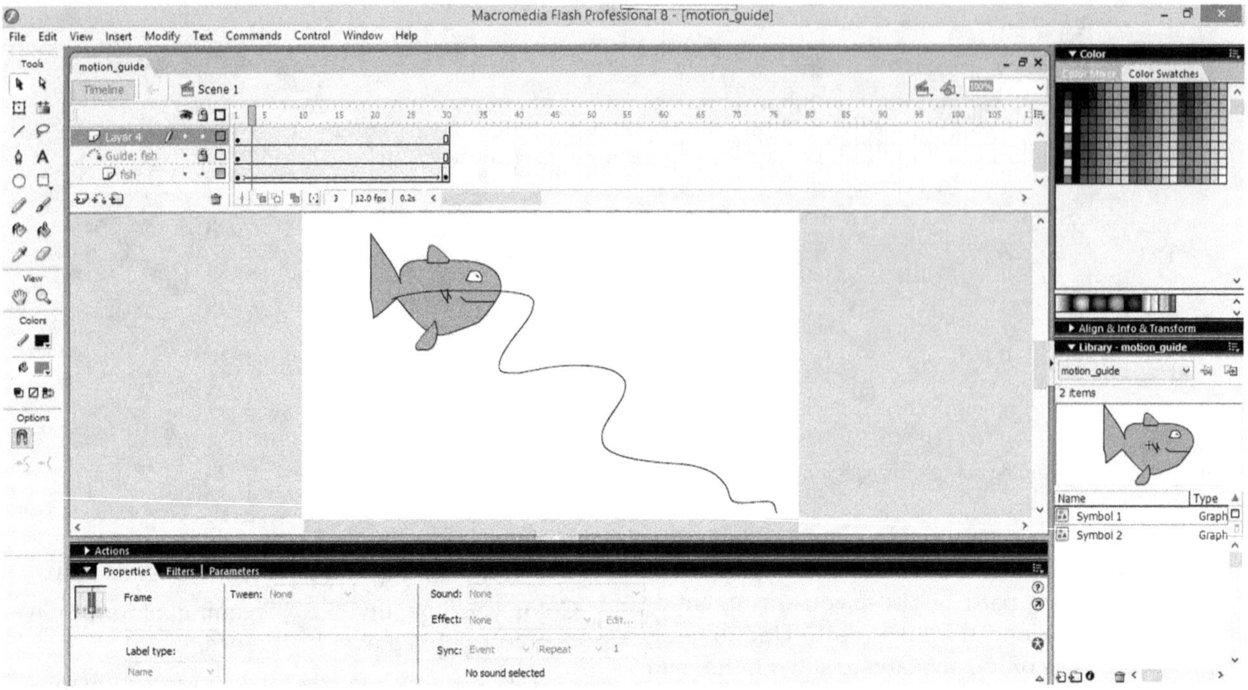

FIGURE 7.10
Typical GUI-based 2D animation editor interface.

control points associated with them using which the shape of the surface may be modified (Foley, 1995). Curved surfaces can be categorized into two broad types based on their mathematical representation: implicit and parametric. Implicit surfaces have equations of the form $f(x,y,z)=0$, while parametric surfaces are represented using parametric variables, namely, $x(u,v), y(u,v), z(u,v)$. Surfaces can also be categorized based on methods of generation, e.g., extrusion and revolution. Apart from the surface topology, this section also takes a look at surface appearances. Surface appearances are determined by color, texture and lighting. Texture mapping provides a realistic look to a surface and is extensively used in 3D graphical models, e.g., wooden table or metal plate. Lighting determines the brightness and shading aspects of a surface.

7.3.1.1 Flat Surfaces

To derive the Cartesian equation of a plane consider ON is the perpendicular from origin O onto the plane at N and let n be the unit vector along ON. Let length of ON be D. Let P be any arbitrary point on the plane and let r be its position vector. Also let the angle between ON and OP be θ.

Computing dot product between r and n we get:

$$r \bullet n = |r||n| \cos(\theta) = r.1.\cos(\theta) = D$$

The above equation shows that the dot product of the position vector of any point P on the plane and the unit normal vector equals the perpendicular distance D of the plane from the origin. If $n = n_1 i + n_2 j + n_3 k$ and $r = xi + yj + zk$ then:

$$r \bullet n = x.n_1 + y.n_2 + z.n_3 = D$$

The general form of the Cartesian equation of a plane is given by (Hearn and Baker, 1996): $Ax + By + Cz = D$

Comparing we get:

$$A = n_1$$

$$B = n_2$$

$$C = n_3$$

This implies that the coefficients of the Cartesian equation of a plane are equal to the components of the unit normal vector from the origin onto the plane (Figure 7.11).

7.3.1.2 Curved Parametric Surfaces

A 2D curve is represented in parametric form as $C(t) = \{x(t), y(t)\}$, where t is the parametric variable. A parametric surface is an extension of this concept to 3D. Instead of a single variable t now we have two parametric variables u, v, and instead of two functions

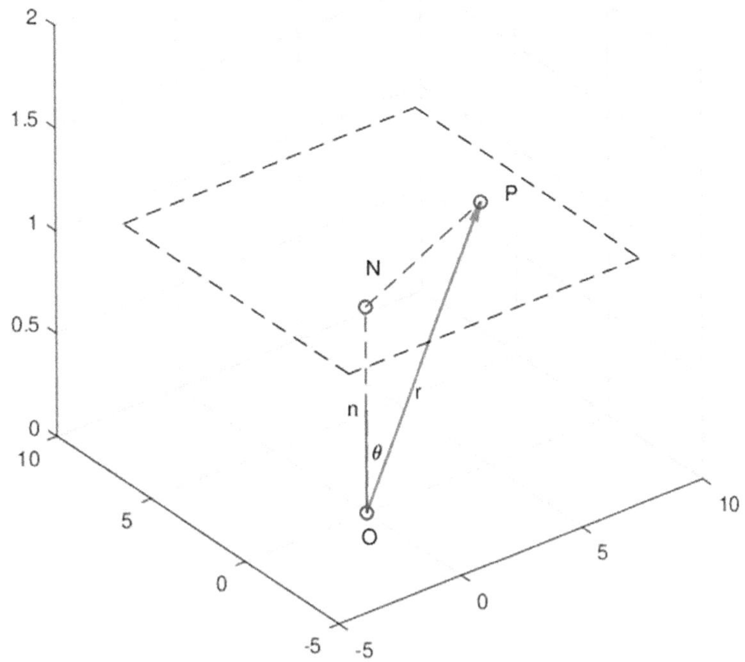

FIGURE 7.11
Determining equation of a flat plane surface.

$x(t)$ and $y(t)$, we have three functions $x(u,v), y(u,v)$ and $z(u,v)$ which together generate a surface $S(u,v)$ in 3D space.

$$S(u,v) = \{x(u,v), y(u,v), z(u,v)\}$$

A popular type of parametric surface is a Bezier surface generated from two Bezier splines along orthogonal directions. A quadratic Bezier spline with three control points is given by:

$$C(t) = \left\{(1-t)^2,\ 2t(1-t),\ t^2\right\} \begin{pmatrix} P_0 \\ P_1 \\ P_2 \end{pmatrix}$$

A bi-quadratic Bezier surface associated with two orthogonal Bezier splines and a grid of 3 by 3 or 9 control points is given by the following (Figure 7.12):

$$S(u,v) = \left\{(1-u)^2,\quad 2u(1-u),\quad u^2\right\}. \begin{pmatrix} P_{00} & P_{01} & P_{02} \\ P_{10} & P_{11} & P_{12} \\ P_{20} & P_{21} & P_{22} \end{pmatrix} . \begin{Bmatrix} (1-v)^2 \\ 2v(1-v) \\ v^2 \end{Bmatrix}$$

Likewise a cubic Bezier surface would be associated with a grid of 4 by 4 or 16 CPs.

7.3.1.3 Curved Implicit Surfaces

Apart from parametric surfaces, the other type of surfaces most frequently encountered in graphics is called implicit surfaces and their equations are of the form $f(x,y,z) = 0$. The second-degree implicit equations are also called quadric surfaces (Hearn & Baker, 1996) (Rovenski, 2010) and have a general form shown below, where A to J are constants.

$$Ax^2 + By^2 + Cz^2 + Dxy + Eyz + Fzx + Gx + Hy + Iz + J = 0$$

Some commonly used quadric surfaces are listed below, where k is a constant (Figure 7.13).

Ellipsoid: $ax^2 + by^2 + cz^2 = k$
Elliptic cone: $ax^2 + by^2 - cz^2 = 0$
Hyperboloid: $ax^2 + by^2 - cz^2 = -k$
Elliptic paraboloid: $ax^2 + by^2 - z = 0$
Elliptic cylinder: $ax^2 + by^2 = k$
Parabolic cylinder: $ax + by^2 = k$

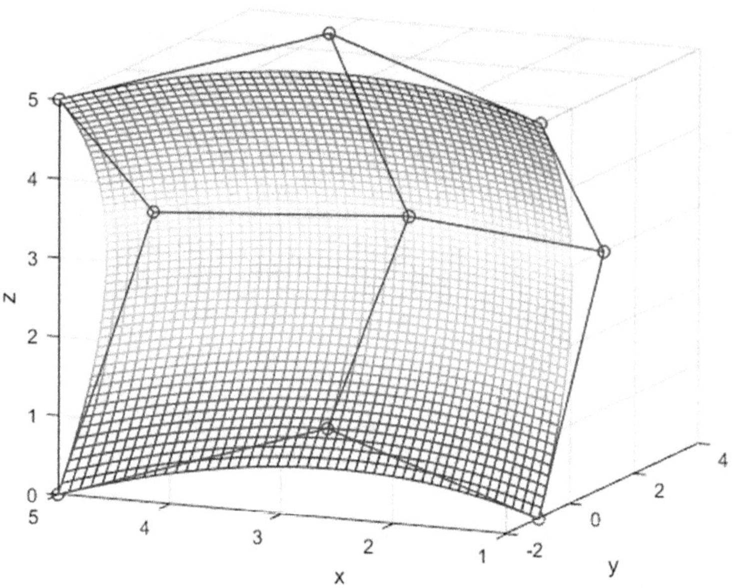

FIGURE 7.12
Bi-quadratic Bezier surface.

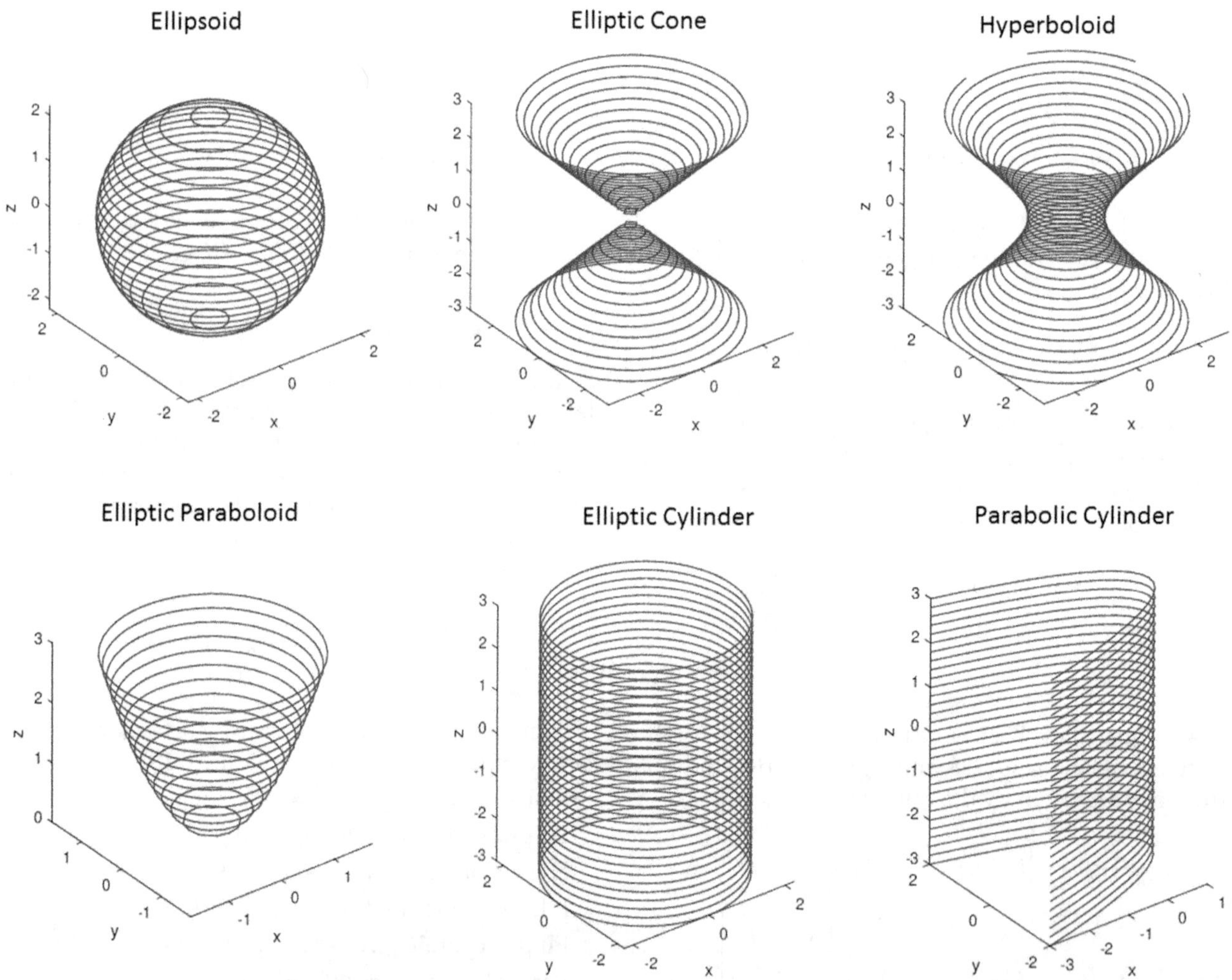

FIGURE 7.13
Implicit surfaces.

7.3.1.4 Extruded Surfaces

Extruded surfaces are created when a 2D plane curve is moved along a straight line in a direction perpendicular to the plane (O'Rourke, 2003). Depending on the moving curve, extruded surfaces can either be flat or curved. If the generating curve is represented as $C(u)=[x(u),y(u)]$, then the resulting surface is expressed in parametric form as:

$$S(u,v)=\{x(u),y(u),v\}$$

Here, $0 \le u \le 1, 0 \le v \le h$, where u is along the plane containing the curve and v is perpendicular to the plane, and h is the maximum distance by which the curve is moved. For example if a circle moves perpendicular to its plane, then it generates a cylinder (Figure 7.14a).

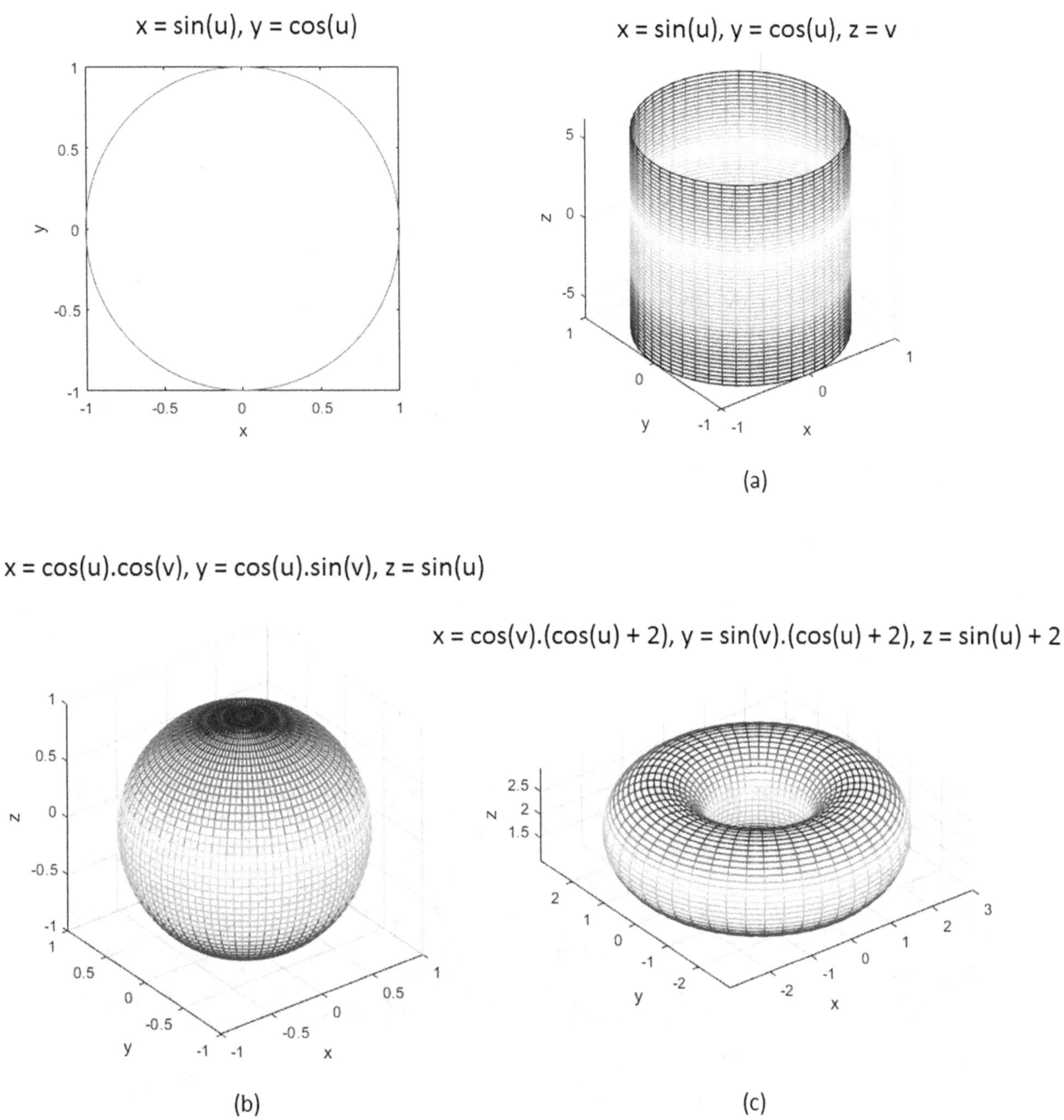

FIGURE 7.14
2D curve with (a) extruded surface (b) surface of revolution (c) revolved with offset.

7.3.1.5 Surfaces of Revolution

Surfaces of revolution are created when a 2D plane curve is rotated about an axis (O'Rourke, 2003) (Rovenski, 2010). If the generating curve is represented as $C(u)=[x(u),y(u)]$, then the resulting surface is expressed in parametric form as:

$$S(u,v)=\{x(u).\cos v, x(u).\sin v, y(u)\}$$

Here, $0 \le u \le 1, 0 \le v \le 2\pi$. If $v \ge 2\pi$, the surface is closed, if $v < 2\pi$ the surface is open. For example if a circle revolves about an axis through its center, then it generates a sphere (Figure 7.14b). In some cases the revolution can occur about an axis outside the curve. If a circle revolves about an axis with an offset from its center, then it generates a torus (Figure 7.14c).

7.3.2 Surface Color

The first characteristic of a surface is the color. This is specified in terms of RGB triplets which can either be entered as numerical values or by dragging a set of sliders. Some programs also offer the possibility of defining color in terms of hue, saturation and lightness. Diffuseness is a measure of how much light reflects from a surface. A surface with a small diffuse component will be darker, because it reflects less light, than a surface with a large diffuse component. You usually specify diffuseness often with a slider bar, as a number between zero and one. A higher value means that more light reflects off the surface. Another parameter called specularity controls how shiny the surface is. While diffuseness controls the overall brightness of the surface, a specular value is used to control the brightness of the highlights. Specularity is also specified as a number between 0 and 1. A plastic surface will in general have lower specularity than a metallic surface. Different materials actually have different highlight colors, e.g., plastic tends to reflect a white highlight, while aluminum tends to reflect a highlight of the same color as the color of the aluminum. Some systems thus allow you to specify highlight colors. These are usually specified using the standard RGB sliders (Figure 7.15). Shiny surfaces in addition to having highlights also tend have reflectivity; i.e., it will have reflections of objects around it. Not all shiny surfaces are equally reflective. Shiny plastic is less reflective than an equally shiny stainless steel. This is usually controlled by a slider ranging from 0 to 1. 0 is a surface that does not reflect the surface at all while 1 is a perfectly reflective mirror. A surface can also be opaque or transparent, and a transparency parameter allows you to control this characteristic. Here also, a number from 0 to 1 is used, 0 being a completely opaque object while 1 being a perfectly transparent object. Another surface characteristic of transparent objects allow you to specify how light bends as it passes from one material to another. This parameter is called refractivity which makes use of the refractive index values of the real world. Air has a RI of 1, a material with RI greater than 1 bends light in a concave manner, a material with RI less than 1 bends light in a convex manner. To render light-emitting surfaces like a light bulb, most systems provide a parameter called incandescence. This parameter is also specified with a number from 0 to 1, and adds certain amount of brightness to the original color of the surface (O'Rourke, 2003).

7.3.3 Surface Texture

Texture mapping is a process of applying an image, referred to as the texture, onto a surface, usually for the purpose of making the surface more realistic in appearance (Shirley & Morley, 2003). The texture being an image is a rectangular 2D matrix of pixel

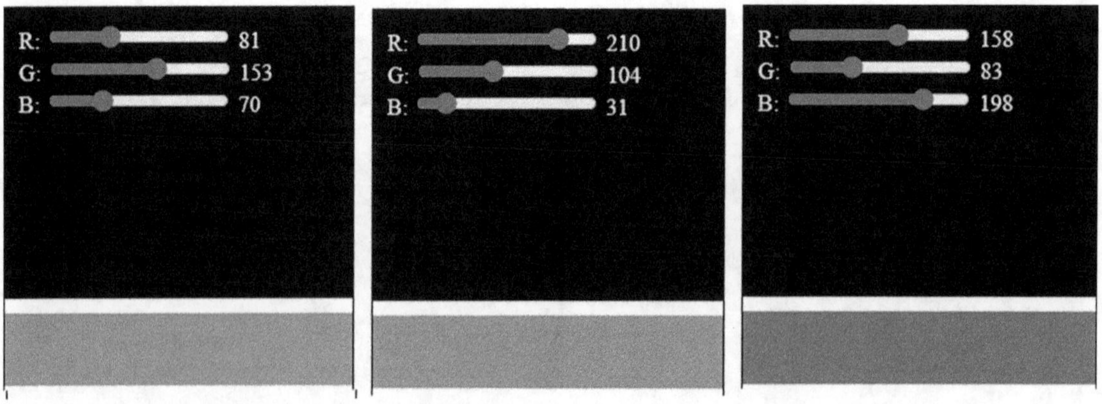

FIGURE 7.15
Specifying surface color.

values, usually represented using (u,v) coordinate values while the surface, can be of any arbitrary shape in 2D or 3D and is represented using (x,y) or (x,y,z) coordinate values respectively (Figure 7.16). To determine which part of the image is applied to which part of the surface a mapping between (u,v) and (x,y,z) values is necessary to maintain homogeneous integrity (O'Rourke, 2003). There are two broad ways: projection mapping and parameterized mapping.

7.3.3.1 Projection Texture Mapping

In projection texture mapping, the texture image is projected through space onto a surface. Wherever the texture image hits the surface of the model the surface takes on the colors of that section of the texture image. In planar projection mapping, the texture image is projected along each of the three axes – x, y and z onto a flat planar surface. One limitation of this is only a flat surface perpendicular to the direction of projection receives a completely accurate mapping of the texture image. For surfaces along other directions the texture pattern streaks along the sides. For multidirectional mapping a cylindrical or spherical projection mapping can be used where the texture image is bent along a cylindrical or spherical surface and then projected inward onto the actual 3D surface (Figure 7.17).

7.3.3.2 Parametric Texture Mapping

An alternative technique called parameterized texture mapping is analogous to stretching a flat sheet of rubber containing the texture pattern over the three dimensional surface. The basic idea involves dividing both the texture and the surface into a number of rectangular cells and then applying each cell of the texture to the corresponding cell on the surface. This provides a number of parameters using which the mapping process can be controlled. The scale parameter determines the size of the texture with respect to the surface. The default value is 1, which means the texture occupies 100% of the surface. A scale of 0.5 means that the texture occupies

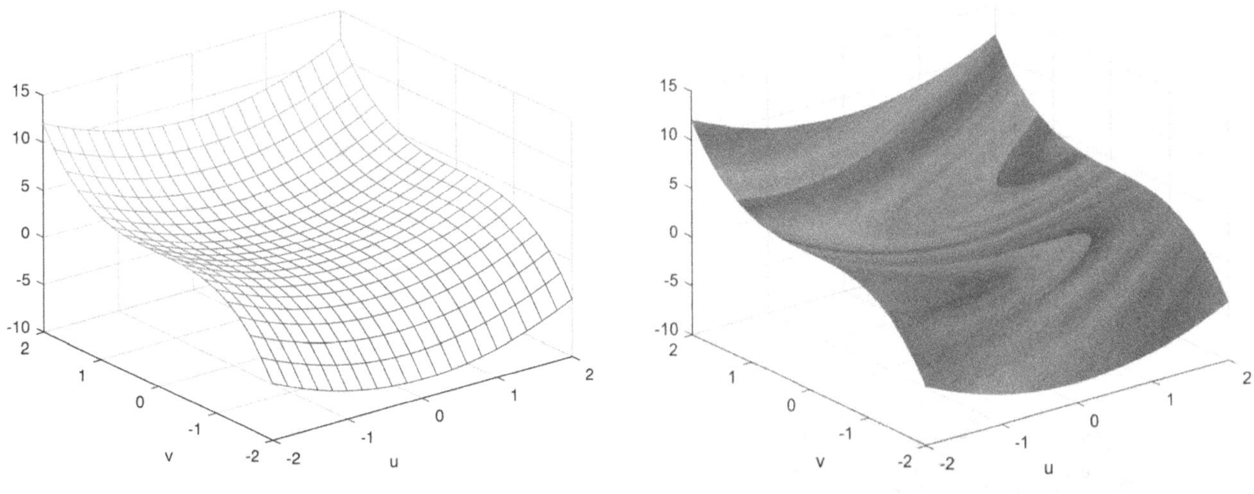

FIGURE 7.16
Surface texture.

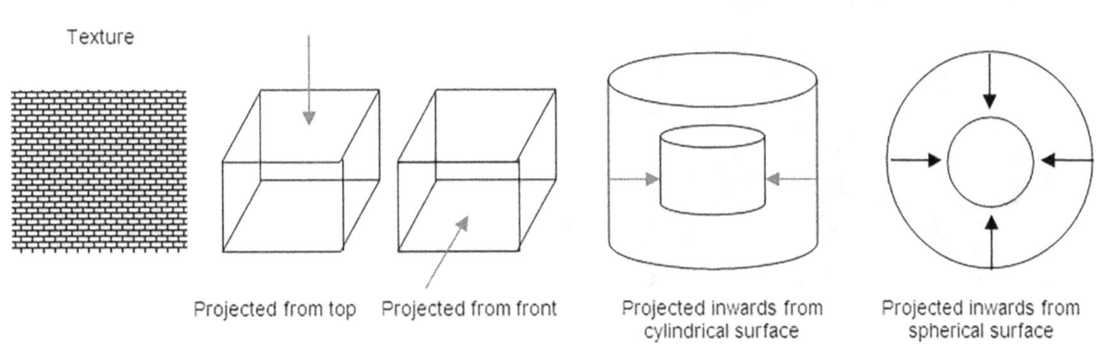

FIGURE 7.17
Projection texture mapping.

50% of the surface along both horizontal and vertical directions. A scale of 0.25 means 25% coverage in either direction. The placement parameter specifies where on the surface the mapping process should begin. The default value of (0,0) indicates the mapping starts at the origin of the surface, say, at bottom-left corner. For a scaling of 0.25, the start point may be shifted to (0.5, 0) meaning horizontal middle and vertical bottom. Such shifting is usually referred to as offset. To begin from top-right corner offset needs to be (0.75, 0.75). A third parameter called wrapping specifies whether the texture repeats or wraps around the surface. With a scale of 1 and offset of (0,0), no wrapping is required. With a scale of 1 and offset (0.5,0), the image starts halfway across the surface in horizontal direction and wraps around so that the right half of the image appears on the left half of the surface. With offset of (0.5,0.5), the image wraps around in both horizontal and vertical directions. If wrapping is switched off, only a portion of the image is visible on the surface (Figure 7.18).

7.3.3.3 Mapping Transformation

Consider a texture described by normalized (u,v) coordinates in the range [0, 1] applied to a 2D surface described by (x,y) coordinates using an affine transformation which keeps parallel lines intact. The corners of the rectangular texture image have (u,v) coordinates of (0, 0), (1, 0), (1, 1), (0, 1), and these points are to be mapped to a 2D surface in the form of a parallelogram having (x,y) coordinates $(x_0,y_0),(x_1,y_1),(x_2,y_2),(x_3,y_3)$ such that $|x_1 - x_0| = |x_2 - x_3|$ and $|y_1 - y_0| = |y_2 - y_3|$ to make the mapping transformation affine in nature. An affine transformation is given by the following (Figure 7.19):

$$\begin{pmatrix} x \\ y \\ 1 \end{pmatrix} = \begin{pmatrix} a & b & c \\ d & e & f \\ 0 & 0 & 1 \end{pmatrix} \begin{pmatrix} u \\ v \\ 1 \end{pmatrix}$$

From the above we have:

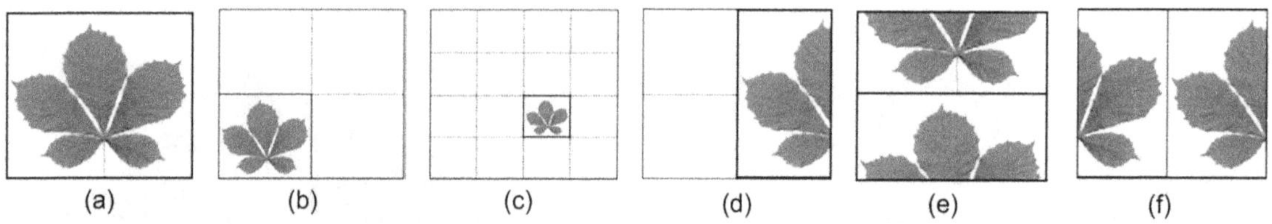

FIGURE 7.18
Parameterized texture mapping.

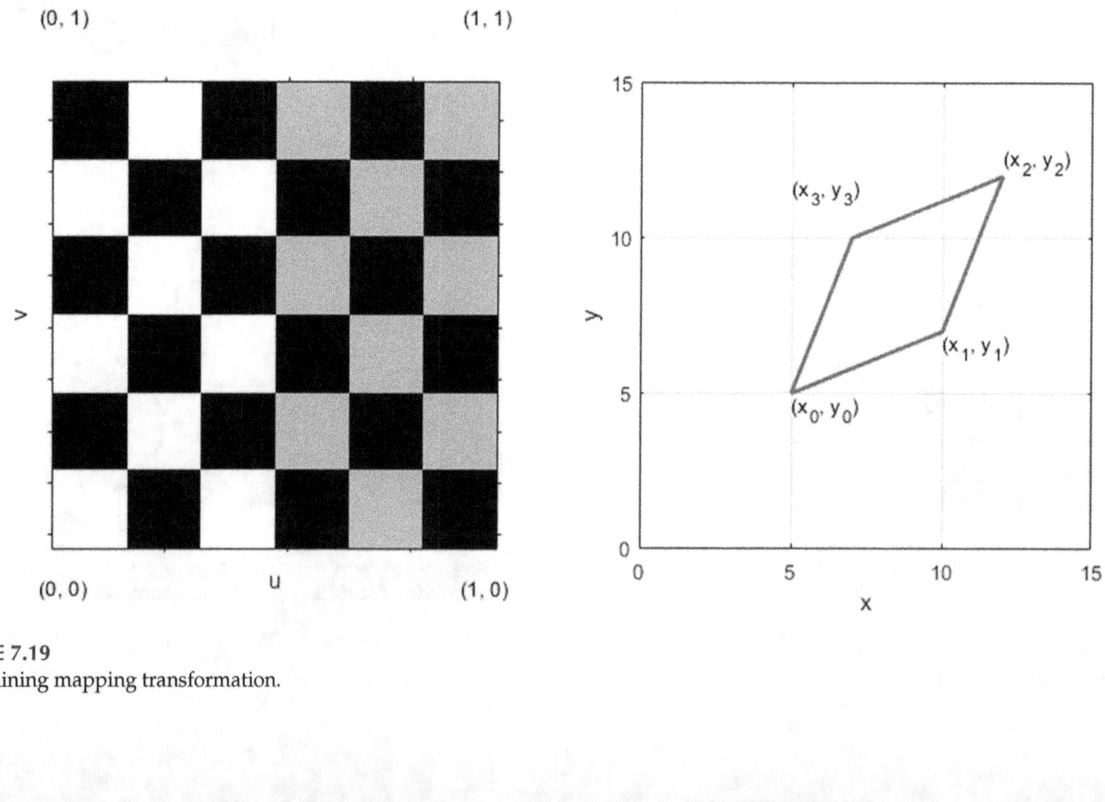

FIGURE 7.19
Determining mapping transformation.

$$x = au + bv + c$$

$$y = du + ev + f$$

Plugging in the given boundary conditions (BC), we can solve for the unknown coefficients a,b,c,d,e,f as follows:

BC-1: $u = 0, v = 0$ is mapped to $x = x_0, y = y_0$ which implies $c = x_0$ and $f = y_0$

BC-2: $u = 1, v = 0$ is mapped to $x = x_1, y = y_1$ which implies $a = x_1 - x_0$ and $d = y_1 - y_0$

BC-3: $u = 0, v = 1$ is mapped to $x = x_3, y = y_3$ which implies $b = x_3 - x_0$ and $e = y_3 - y_0$

Substituting in the starting equation:

$$\begin{pmatrix} x \\ y \\ 1 \end{pmatrix} = \begin{pmatrix} x_1 - x_0 & x_3 - x_0 & x_0 \\ y_1 - y_0 & y_3 - y_0 & y_0 \\ 0 & 0 & 1 \end{pmatrix} \begin{pmatrix} u \\ v \\ 1 \end{pmatrix}$$

7.3.4 Lights and Illumination

7.3.4.1 Light Parameters

In order to see a scene or any objects within that scene, one must define lights. The parameters and types of light that can be specified in 3D graphics software are discussed below. The first characteristic to specify is position in terms of XYZ coordinates of the light. Positioning can also be done with the mouse pointer. The next parameter is intensity, which is specified as a range of numbers. For example, if the range is 0.0 to 1.0 then an intensity of 1.0 produces an extremely bright light while 0.0 turns the light off. A third parameter is the color, specified as an RGB set of numbers. Thus, RGB = (255,255,0) describes pure yellow, and RGB = (255,255,255) is pure white. A parameter called decay or fall-off provides a measure of how light fades with distance. A decay value of zero means that there is no decay and light continues forever with same intensity. The larger the decay value, the more quickly it fades with distance. A spread parameter controls the width of a light cone. The spread of a spotlight is a measure of the angle between the opposite sides of the cone. A direction parameter specifies how light rays travel from the source to the destination. Direction controls the appearance of the shadows. Some light like ambient light does not have any specific directions. Another parameter called drop-off indicates how the intensity of the light decreases from the center of a light cone to the edges. A drop-off value of zero produces a hard-edged demarcation between the dark and light portions. A drop-off value greater than zero, produces a gradual change from dark to light using certain fuzziness. A glow parameter can be adjusted to create luminous effects. Adjustable sub-parameters include intensity of glow, how far the glow spreads and shape of the glow. The glow parameters are separate from the intensity or decay of the point light itself. Another effect available in some systems enables to simulate lens flare that occurs on the lens of a camera facing directly into a light. If the lens flare parameter has been turned on, a hot spot of light will be rendered.

7.3.4.2 Light Types

Most 3D computer systems offer a range of light types that attempt to simulate the different types of real light. The most common type of light in a graphics system is the point light. It simulates effect of a light bulb at a specific point in space by radiating light equally in all directions. Intended to simulate the fact that light from a bulb fades with distance, point light includes the decay or fall-off parameter. A point light does not have any size or shape. 3D systems allow you to treat the point light as a logical object; i.e., you can select it, delete it, move it, etc., by providing some iconic representation of the light.

A second type of light, called a spotlight, has all the parameters of a point light plus some additional parameters to simulate the effects of a spotlight in the real world. A spotlight throws light in a cone-shaped beam and has a spread associated with it. A spotlight also throws light in a certain direction. You change the direction by rotating the spotlight. Objects that lie outside the cone do not receive any of the light from the spotlight. Just as point lights, spotlights also fade with distance and have decay parameters. But spotlights have another fade parameter called drop-off.

Another type of light provided by some systems is called an area light, which simulates light emanating from an entire area, like banks of fluorescent light or screens of television screens. It emits a rectangular beam instead of a conical beam of a spotlight.

An ambient light simulates the overall amount of daylight. An ambient light does not emanate from a specific location in space, nor does it flow in a specific direction. Consequently, when defining the ambient light you specify only the intensity and color parameters. Because of the directionless properties of an ambient light, all sides of an object are lit equally. By itself, therefore, ambient light cannot provide a realistic rendering of a scene; rather, it is to be used in conjunction with other lights.

A directional light is considered to be located infinitely away, simulating the great distance of the sun. In this it resembles ambient light, which has no location. But unlike an ambient light, directional light has direction, which is indicated by an arrow. Thus, it

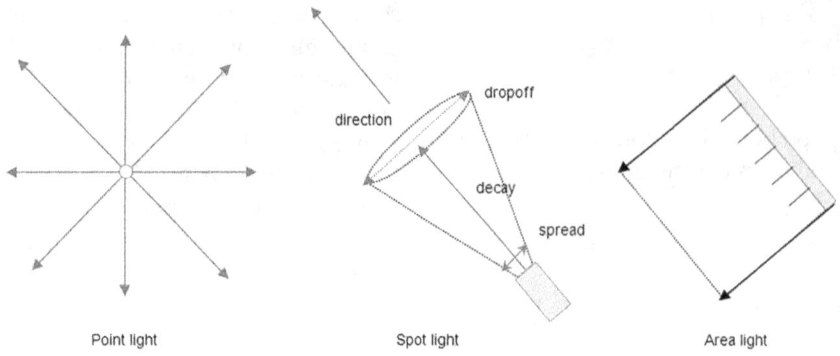

FIGURE 7.20
Light types.

more accurately simulates sunlight. Unlike other lights like spotlights and area lights, which also have direction but throw light only in certain circumscribed regions, directional lights throw equal amounts of light everywhere (Figure 7.20).

In scenes where multiple objects are to be rendered, considerations of shading and shadows come into play. Shading is the effect on the surface of an object as the surface goes from lighter to darker. If there are several objects in a scene, each object not only is shaded but might also cast shadows on other objects. The most common way to turn shadow casting on or off is through a parameter associated with each light. When you define any type of light, you specify whether or not this particular light cast shadows. Shadows play a crucial role in conveying information about the three-dimensional placement of objects.

7.3.4.3 Reflection

let PA indicate the direction of an incident light ray striking the surface at P making an angle θ with the normal along PC and let PD indicate the direction of the reflected ray such that PA = PD. Let AC be parallel to PD and CD be parallel to PA intersecting at C. Project PA onto N at B and extend PB to C. Writing in terms of vectors, let L and R represent the unit vectors for incidence and reflected rays and N is the unit vector along the normal. The laws of Reflection dictate that angles of incidence and Reflection have to be equal and also the incident ray, reflected ray and surface normal should lie on the same plane. According to the triangle rule for vectors, R = PC + CD. The projection of L onto N is given by $(L\cos\theta).N$ = PB. Hence,

$$PC = 2PB = 2\left(|L|.\cos\theta\right)N.$$

Also, $CD = -L$. Combining these expressions, we get the following, remembering that vectors L, N, and R are the unit vectors and have magnitude 1:

$$R = PC + CD = 2PB + CD = 2\left(|L|.\cos\theta\right)N - L$$
$$= 2\left(|L||N|.\cos\theta\right)N - L = 2(L \bullet N)N - L$$

This allows us to calculate the reflected ray given the incident ray and normal to the surface (Figure 7.21).

7.3.4.4 Illumination Model

Lights are responsible for surface illumination. This determines the brightness of a surface given the parameters regarding the light sources such as the light intensity, angle of incidence light, angle of the observer looking at the surface, and also the reflectance properties of the surface. An illumination model takes these parameters as input and produces an output regarding the brightness of the surface. Since the brightness depends on the angle of reflected light and the viewpoint of the observer in some cases, we need to derive a mathematical model for this purpose (Shirley & Morley, 2003).

Intensity at any point on the surface depends on three types of reflections: ambient reflection, diffuse reflection and specular reflection (Hearn & Baker, 1996). Ambient reflection assumes that all objects receive the same amount of light from all directions and simulates a constant background illumination. Intensity I_a at any point P on the surface due to ambient Reflection is given by the following, where L_a denotes the intensity of ambient light, and $0 \le k_a \le 1$ is the ambient reflection coefficient of a surface which measures what percentage of the incident ambient light the surface reflects (Foley et al., 1990):

$$I_a = L_a.k_a$$

Diffuse reflection occurs when directional light falling on the surface is scattered in all directions equally. In this case the amount of reflection depends on the angle θ of the incident light. For a small value of ,

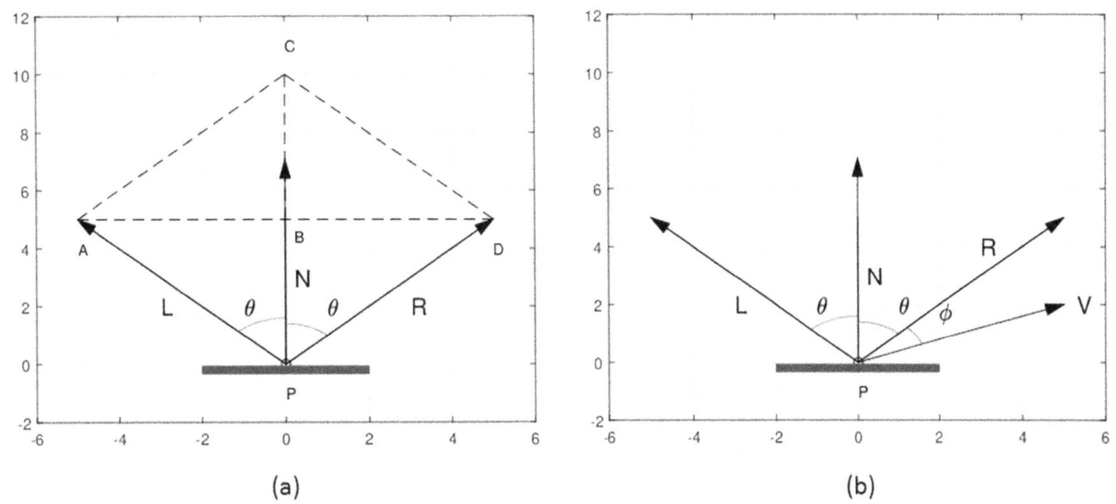

FIGURE 7.21
Relation between incident ray, reflected ray, viewing direction and normal.

most of the light would bounce back along the same path and observed intensity would be high. For large values of θ most of the light would be scattered along other direction and observed intensity would be small, hence the intensity is proportional to $\cos\theta$. Intensity I_d at any point P on the surface due to diffused Reflection is given by the following, where L_p is the intensity of source light and $0 \le k_d \le 1$ is the diffused Reflection coefficient of a surface which measures what percentage of the incident diffused light the surface reflects:

$$I_d = L_p.k_d.\cos\theta = L_p.k_d.(L \bullet N)$$

Specular reflection occurs when light is reflected at a certain angle from a shiny surface. A shiny surface behaves like an imperfect mirror and produces specular highlights, which is actually the image of the light source itself reflected from the surface. Unlike diffuse Reflection, specular Reflection is dependent on position of viewer. Let V be the unit vector along the viewing direction and φ be the angle between V and R (Figure 7.21b). Observed intensity would be highest when the observer views the surface exactly along the reflected ray, i.e., $\varphi = 0$ but intensity would reduce as φ increases and the observer moves further away from the reflected light, hence intensity is proportional to $\cos\varphi$. Intensity I_s at any point P on the surface due to specular reflection is given by the following, where L_p is the intensity of source light and $0 \le k_s \le 1$ is the specular reflection coefficient of a surface, φ is the angle between V and R and m is a positive number dependent on the material of the surface:

$$I_s = L_p.k_s.(\cos\varphi)^m = L_p.k_s.(R \bullet V)^m$$

Hence, total intensity I of the surface is the combined effect of all the above factors:

$$I = I_a + I_d + I_s$$

7.3.5 Camera and Vision

7.3.5.1 Camera Location and Movements

When you create a computer rendering of a three-dimensional scene, you first define the point of view from which the scene is to be observed. A point of view consists of two factors: "where you are standing (location)" and "what you are looking at (subject)". The first factor is called Camera Location (CL) and the second factor is called Center Of Interest (COI). Both of these are points in space and defined as triplets of XYZ coordinates. To illustrate, consider yourself standing in front of a house and looking at a chimney. If you now go behind the house and look at the same chimney, you see a different view of the same object. This is a case of changing the CL while keeping the COI same. Now, reverse the situation and keep the CL constant, but change the COI factor, i.e., you stand in front of the house but once look at the chimney and later look at a window instead. Most 3D software allows you to specify both CL and COI either by typing in those numbers explicitly or by positioning the camera by a pointing device. The rectangular icon represents the camera location and the circle with cross-hairs represents the camera's center of interest. There are a number of standard camera movements in 3D animation scenarios. Movements can be broadly classified as linear movements and circular movements. . In the following we assume that x-axis is along the horizontal (left-right),

y –axis is along the vertical (up-down), z –axis (line of sight) is perpendicular to the plane of the screen (forward-backward) (O'Rourke, 2003) (Figure 7.22).

Linear movements can be of the following types:

- Track : Move horizontally along x-axis to the left or right
- Crane : Move vertically along y-axis up or down
- Dolly : Move along z-axis towards or away from the subject

Circular movements can be of the following types:

- Tilt : Rotate about x-axis and looks up or down
- Pan : Rotate about y-axis and looks left or right
- Roll: Rotate about z-axis clockwise or anti-clockwise
- Orbit: Rotate about the subject (COI) in a circular path

One additional camera parameter, called zoom, simulates the effect of a zoom lens. Zooming-in magnifies the image and makes objects appear closer while zooming-out makes the objects appear farther.

Apart from animating objects over time, it is also possible to animate camera parameters, such as point of view from which the scene is observed, over time. The simplest approach followed by 3D systems is to use a basic key-framing technique for the camera just as for individual objects. Most systems treat the camera as an object and allow you to manipulate it like translating or rotating. The settings of the camera are then saved as key-frames. The computer then interpolates the in-between camera positions for each frame that lies between the key-frames. Any of the parameters that define a camera – location, direction, FOV, focal length – normally can be animated with this basic key-frame approach. The series of figures represents a camera animation. Between the first and second panels, the camera rotates around the COI, while between the second and third panels, the camera zooms in, i.e., the FOV changes.

7.3.5.2 Zones of Vision

The human field of view can be thought as a cone-shaped area called the cone of vision. Objects that lie within the cone of vision are visible; objects that lie outside the cone are not visible. In computer graphics, the cone of vision becomes a pyramid of vision in order to conform to the rectangular shape of the computer monitor. The shape of the pyramid is the angle from top to bottom of the pyramid, referred to as the field-of-view (FOV) angle or FOV measured in angles. When you view a scene, some objects appear in focus and some appear out of focus. Some rendering programs reproduce this effect through a parameter called depth of field. Depth of field is specified by two numbers: the first represents the nearest distance at which objects will be in focus, and the second represents the farthest distance at which they will be in focus. An important characteristic of the camera is that when a program renders a scene, it must restrict the scene to a finite three-dimensional space. This is necessary because a program dealing with infinite space would continue rendering forever. The most basic restriction imposed by a rendering program is determined by the four edges of the computer screen. The program looks through this screen as if through a window and then deals with only that space viewable through the window. An invisible vertical plane called the far clipping plane defines the distance beyond which nothing is rendered. Objects farther away than

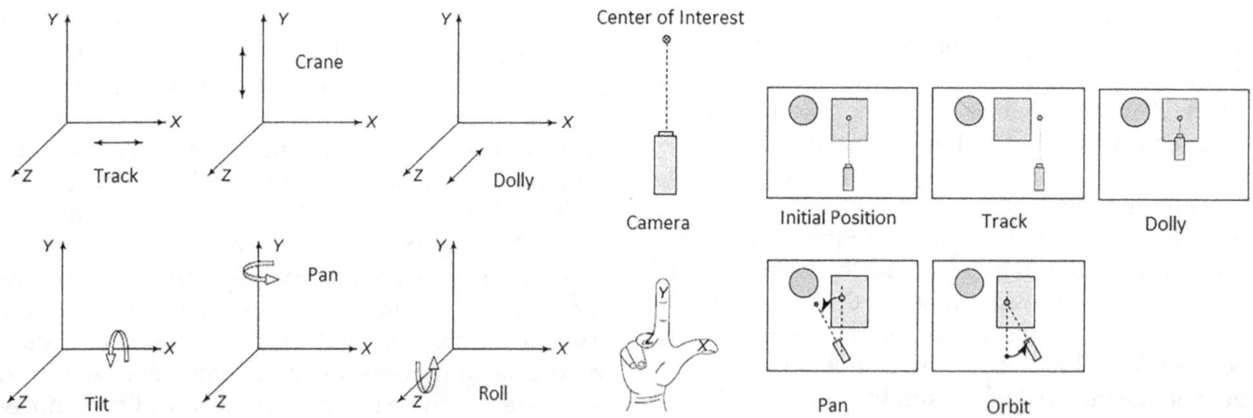

FIGURE 7.22
Linear and circular camera movements.

the far clipping plane are said to be clipped. Sometimes a near clipping plane prevents objects closer to it from being rendered. Combining the clipping by the edges of the screen and those by the far and near clipping planes, you end up with a viewable world in the shape of a truncated pyramid (Figure 7.23).

Cameras of graphics systems also permit you to animate the locations of the far and near clipping planes. This may be done to improve the Z-buffer rendering resolution of a scene. The larger the amount of space to be dealt by the Z-buffer, the less accurate this information will be, because the algorithm divides the space into a fixed number of subdivisions. The specific number of subdivisions used is determined by the amount of memory utilized for each pixel. For example, for displaying a bird flying from a large distance, the clipping planes may be initially set very far apart, but as the bird comes closer, animating the back clipping plane to stay close to the bird improves the Z-buffer rendering resolution and results in a more accurate rendering. Motion-path animation can also be applied to a camera. For example, to show a car-chase sequence, the camera can itself move like a car. Some complexities, however, arise when you think of camera path animation. A camera has both location and COI. If the camera always looks to the front as it moves along a path, it may produce an effect that is too mechanical. Like a rider, the gaze of the camera may slide from one side of the path to the other. Some systems allow you to get this effect by specifying a separate path for the COI. Another aspect to consider with the motion paths is the issue of tilt or roll of the camera. Some systems allow you to specify the tilting as a set of rotational values that can be created either automatically through a menu selection or by setting key-frames (Figure 7.24).

7.3.6 Creating Animation

Like 2D animation, 3D animation can also be generally of two types: keyframe-based and path-based. In the first type a set of keyframes are specified over the duration of animation along with the set of characteristics that needs to change at each keyframe and the system then tweens over these changes. In the second type a path is specified along which the object needs to move and characteristics are specific only at the start and end of the path without individual key-frames along the path, the system then tweens these properties over the length of the path. Rendering is the final step when the vector objects are converted to pixels to be displayed on screen.

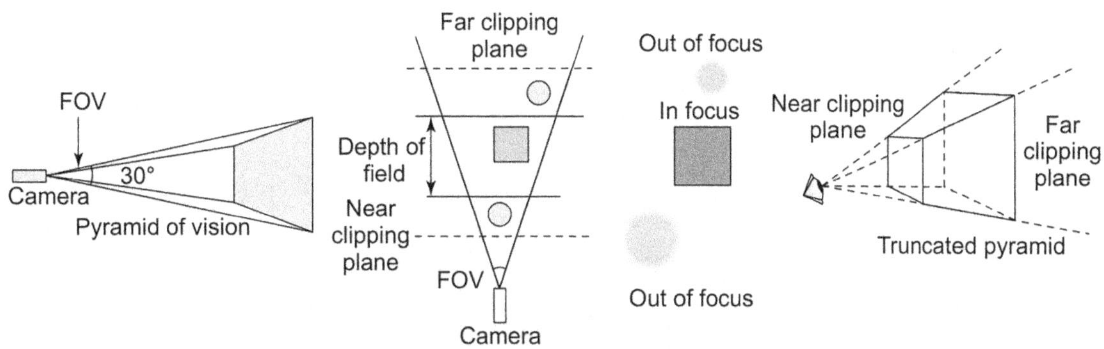

FIGURE 7.23
Zones of vision.

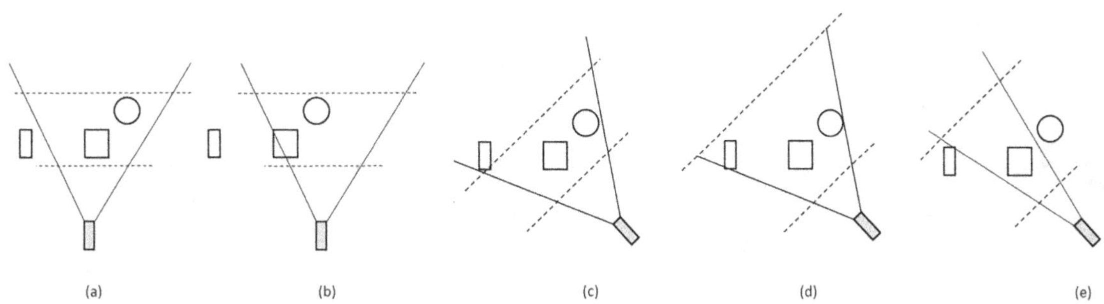

FIGURE 7.24
Animating camera parameters. (a) initial position (b) translation (c) rotation (d) changing clipping planes (e) changing FOV angle.

7.3.6.1 Keyframe and Path-Based Animation

Animators define keyframes which represent specific poses or states of objects, and serve as the reference points for the animation sequence. The software interpolates between these keyframes to generate the motion between them. The interpolation can be linear or follow custom curves, with uniform motion or accelerated/decelerated motion. Easing in/out controls the acceleration and deceleration in the motion thereby adding realism to the scenario. In path-based animation, animators create paths using tools provided by the software and attach the objects to the path specifying how object characteristics and orientations should change over the path but do not create individual keyframes for the purpose.

7.3.6.2 Particle Systems

Many phenomena like cloud, rain, spray, smoke, gas, steam and fire cannot be modeled easily as surfaces. The particle system technique found on many 3D system packages handle these types of phenomena that consist of masses of molecule-sized particles rather than surfaces. Defined to exist and move in a three-dimensional space, these particles, which are too small to be seen individually, will become visible only if present in sufficient numbers. When the rendering program processes the model information for a given frame, it looks at each pixel of screen space and calculates whether enough particles are present at that location to be visible. If so, pixels are colored appropriately and rendered. In defining a particle system, several parameters need to be specified, for example, number of particles, color of the particles, speed and direction of movement, as well as a randomness factor. Some systems allow the movement of the particles to be affected by other related factors like wind and gravity (Figure 7.25).

7.3.6.3 Space Warps

High-end 3D packages offer particle-like modeling functions, which operate on actual surfaces but manipulate surfaces like particles. These are called space warps, e.g., waves, ripple, bomb. The most common of these functions is a bomb (or explosion) in which each surface is broken into many small surfaces which expand outward in an exploding pattern. Important parameters controlling the explosion are the strength of explosion, intensity, minimum and maximum fragment sizes, speed, distance which the pieces travel, spin velocity, effect of gravity and others. Usually, a randomness factor can be specified, which ensures that not all pieces are of uniform

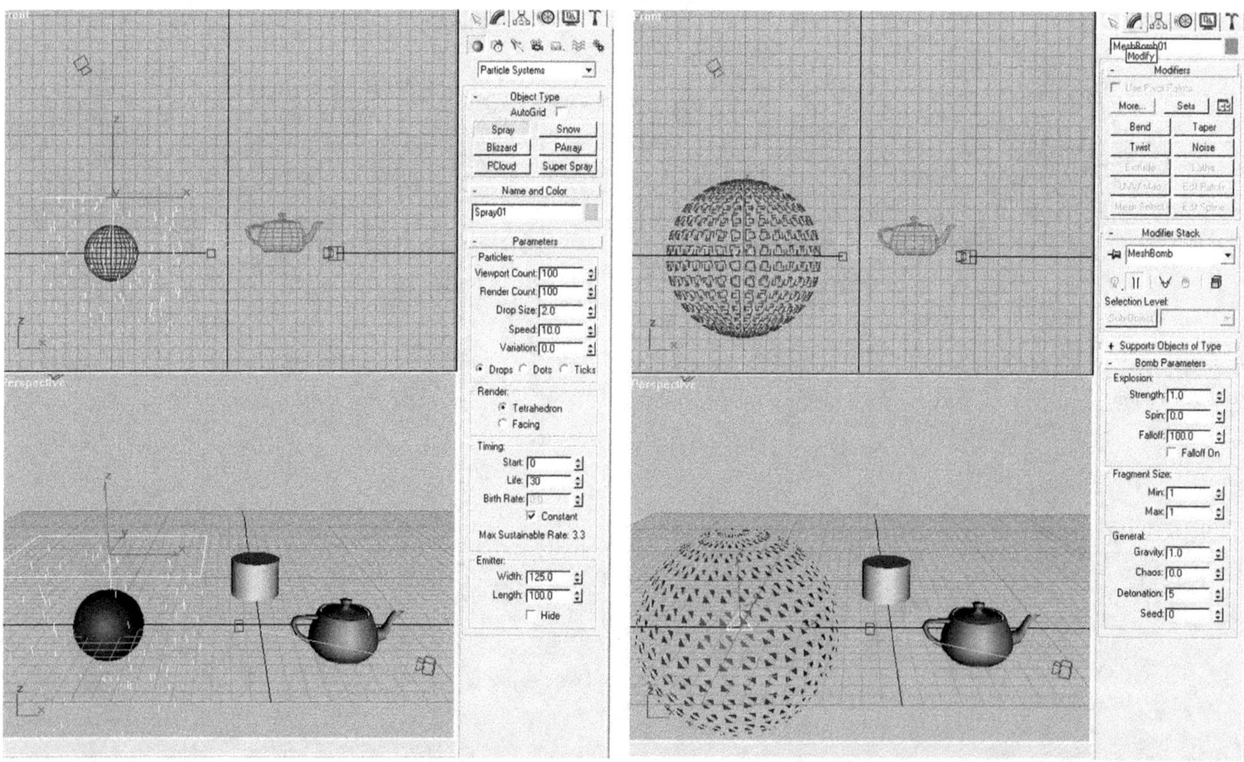

FIGURE 7.25
Particle systems and space warp.

structure, and they are moving at different speeds and in different directions.

7.3.6.4 Atmospheric Effects

Many 3D computer graphics images have a distinctive crystal-clear quality. Sometimes, this clarity is intended by the artist but sometimes it is not desirable and creates an appearance of unreality and falseness. In the real world, the perceived colors of objects change depending on the distance of the objects from the viewer. This is produced by the scattering of the light rays by the tiny air molecules of the atmosphere. Because they typically render only surfaces, 3D computer rendering programs often have difficulty handling this sort of atmospheric effects. To address this problem, some high-end software packages incorporate density maps which simulate fog or haze and change visibility of objects along with distance from the viewer. Parameters for specifying atmospheric haze might include the distance at which an object will be completely obscured, and whether the density of the fog changes linearly or non-linearly with distance and along which direction.

7.3.7 Rendering

Rendering is a process of converting the graphical objects stored as mathematical entities into pixel data which can be displayed on screen. It has already been mentioned that graphics is stored internally in a computer in the form of mathematical expressions and vectors. However, when the graphics need to be displayed on a monitor screen, the mathematical data needs to be converted to pixel-based data, which are then mapped to the monitor pixels for a visual representation of the data. Rendering algorithms refer to computational techniques used to generate images or sequence of frames from 3D models and scenes created using vector-based approaches; i.e., it converts vector data to pixel data. These algorithms determine how light interacts with objects in virtual environments simulating realistic shading, reflection and refraction. By employing rendering algorithms animators can create visually compelling and lifelike animations. Depending on the amount and complexities of the stored data, rendering can occupy varying amounts of time, e.g., from few seconds to several hours or even more (Akenine-Moller et al., 2008).

7.3.7.1 Rendering Types

The simplest form of rendering is the wire-frame rendering where the graphical object is assumed to be made up of only edges and no surfaces. Wire-frame rendering represents an object using connected line segments, straight or curved, giving the appearance of wires connected together, hence the name. The advantage of wire-frame rendering is that a small amount of information needs to be displayed and hence the rendering process is usually very fast, fast enough to allow real-time interaction with the object or model. The rendered output is often referred to as the wire-frame model. The disadvantage of wireframe rendering is that the output does not have surfaces and, hence, is not a realistic representation of the actual graphical object but simply a skeleton structure of it. Moreover, wire-frame models can sometimes be ambiguous as to the actual structure of the object, since it might be difficult to tell which of the wires are in front and which are to the rear.

Hidden-line rendering is a slightly more advanced form of wire-frame rendering, where the model is still represented using wire-like lines for edges, but it is assumed that the object has surfaces and surfaces can hide edges behind them. Although the surfaces themselves are not shown, the edges at the rear of the surfaces are assumed to be hidden and the corresponding lines are removed. Hidden-line models are an improvement over wire-frame models in that it gives the viewer some idea as to which surfaces and edges are in front and which are at the back. However, it requires additional computations to determine these and hence hidden-line models might require more time and resources to be displayed than wire-frame models.

Shaded rendering is more advanced then hidden-line rendering where the model is shown to have surfaces in addition to edges. The surfaces are displayed as shaded polygons, and the shading is performed depending on the number and distance of the light sources around the object, as well as the orientation of light rays with respect to the surface. Determining the shaded look of the surface is obviously more computation intensive than hidden-line rendering and, hence, would be slower to render. Moreover, when an object is moved in 3D space, the shading computations have to be redone at each different location of the object. Some graphics software provides a way around this to reduce computations by displaying the shaded look only at the first and last points of the motion path, while displaying the wire-frame model at the intermediate or transient positions (Glassner, 1995) (Figure 7.26).

7.3.7.2 Ray-Casting Algorithm

Ray casting is one of the most popular and widely used algorithms for rendering an entire 3D scene. It works by looking at each pixel one after another and calculating the color that the pixel should have,

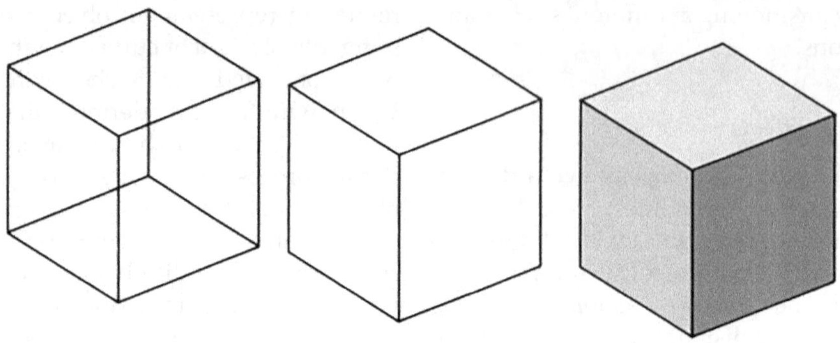

FIGURE 7.26
Wireframe, hidden-line and shaded rendering.

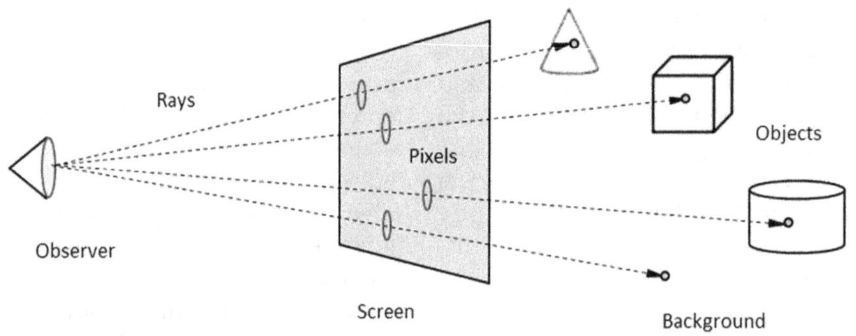

FIGURE 7.27
Ray casting.

depending on the parameters specified when the 3D scene was created. This approach is called scan-line rendering, and it enables the viewer to see the pixels filling in one by one and line by line. A ray is cast through the first pixel of the first scan line, as if the eye was looking through a tiny, pixel-sized window into the three-dimensional world. The eye then follows the ray until the ray either hits an object or exits from the viewable world. If the ray hits an object, the program calculates the color of the object at the point where it has been hit using a shading algorithm. This color becomes the color of the pixel through which the ray has been cast. The algorithm steps through all the pixels of the image in the same fashion, casting a ray through each one and calculating its color (Roth, 1982) (Figure 7.27).

7.3.7.3 Ray-Tracing Algorithm

Ray-casting algorithm scans produce very sophisticated renderings, but they have one fundamental limitation: they deal with the shading of each object as if it existed in isolation and that other objects do not have any effect to the object being rendered. As a result, creating effects that involves interaction of multiple objects becomes a problem like Reflections, shadows and transparency. A different category of rendering algorithm called ray tracing addresses this problem by dealing with all the objects in a scene simultaneously. When you look at a specific point on a surface, the color at that point is affected not only by the light falling from the light source, but also by the light bouncing onto it from nearby surfaces. As with the ray-casting technique, a ray is projected from the eye through the pixel and into the scene and hits the first surface. If the surface has been defined as somewhat reflective, the ray bounces off it and hits the second object, which might have been defined as partially reflective and partially transparent. This contact generates two ray paths: one bounces off it and the other passes through it and hits the third object. In order to calculate the color of the pixel at the point where the ray first hit it, you begin by calculating the color of the first object at the point indicated, which in turn is affected by the color of the second object, which in turn is influenced by the color of the third object. You also need to know the color of the space around the objects since rays from the surrounding space also hit the cube. Because the calculation of each surface point takes into consideration all the different surfaces in the scene, the effects of all those surfaces show up in the final rendering. Shadows, reflections and transparency are all automatically calculated by the ray-tracing technique. In a complex scene with a great many objects, ray tracing can become immensely complex. If you continue tracing the path of a ray in such a scene, the ray can go on bouncing off and through hundreds of objects, creating paths so complex that can be impractical to render. Consequently, most ray-tracing programs ask you to define the maximum number of bounces that each ray should follow. This is called the depth of the ray tracing. The larger the depth, the more accurate but also more time-consuming the rendering. If the depth is zero—that is, if no bounces are followed—the ray traces becomes effectively the same as a ray caster (Shirley & Morley, 2003) (Figure 7.28).

7.3.7.4 Shading Algorithms

A shading algorithm determines the shaded look of surfaces. A shading algorithm determines the color of each point of the surface by looking at the amount and angle of light falling on the surface, as well as the colors of the light and surface. The simplest form of shading is called faceted shading in which it is assumed that any flat surface will have the same color at all points. To calculate shading, the algorithm needs to determine the surface direction, i.e., whether the surface faces toward or away from light, and accordingly, it will appear lighter or darker. It determines the direction by calculating the angle between the surface normal (line perpendicular to the surface) and the direction of light. A flat surface has a single surface normal and it is comparatively easier to determine its shading, but a curved surface is more complicated as the direction of the surface changes continuously. For a curved surface, a shading algorithm uses polygonal approximation to decompose the curved surface into a number of polygons, and then shade each polygon based on the direction of its surface normal. Polygonal approximations, however, can present a problem. If the polygons are rendered with faceted shading, the actual shape of the polygons becomes apparent, which results in a smoothly curved surface taking on a faceted look. To improve the shading, a smooth-shading algorithm is used which uses the average of the two normals of two surfaces to calculate an intermediate shading at the connecting edge. This produces a smoother progression of shading along the surface from one polygon to the next, even though the surface is still made up of flat polygons (Chakraborty, 2010) (Figure 7.29).

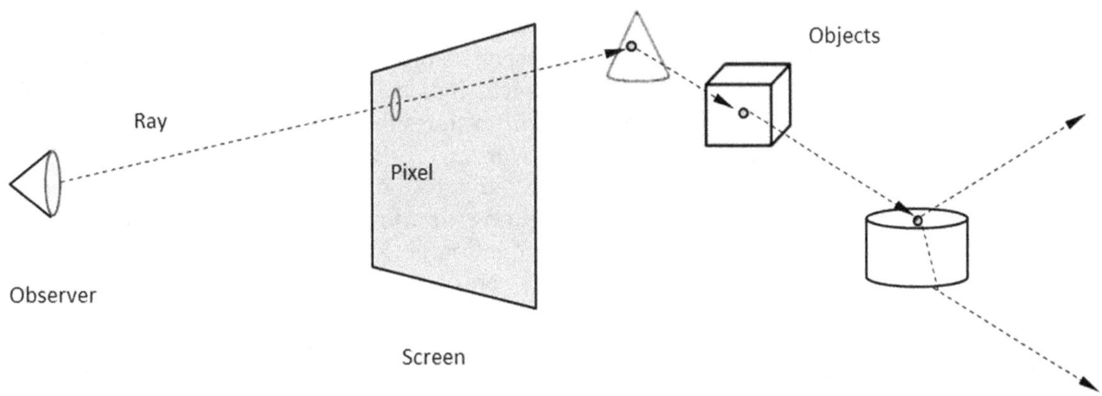

FIGURE 7.28
Ray tracing.

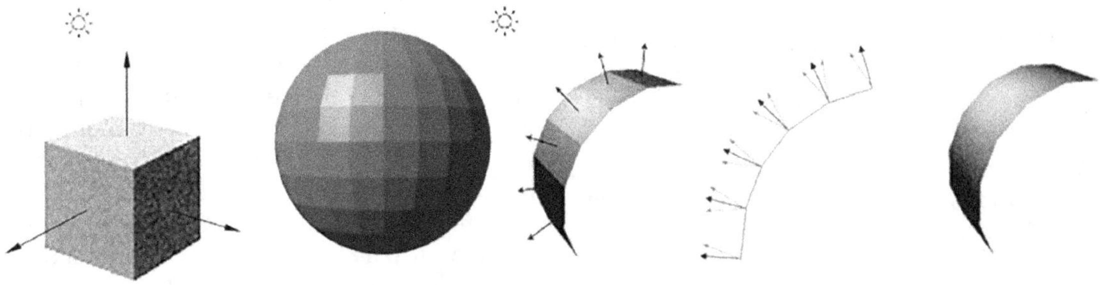

FIGURE 7.29
Shading.

7.3.7.5 Gouraud Shading Algorithm

One of the most popular smooth shading algorithms is the Gouraud shading algorithm, proposed by Henri Gouraud (Gouraud, 1971) in which pixel intensity at a point on the scan line is calculated by interpolating intensity values from neighboring points. Intensity at the point P is linearly interpolated from intensities at points A and B. Similarly, intensity at the point Q is linearly interpolated from intensities at points B and C. An interior point R is then assigned an intensity value that is linearly interpolated from intensities at points P and Q. If point P divides AB in ratio $u:1-u$, where $0 \le u \le 1$, then intensity at P can be calculated as follows.

$$I_P = u.I_B + (1-u).I_A$$

Similarly intensity at Q which divides BC in ratio $v:1-v$, where $0 \le v \le 1$, then intensity at Q can be calculated as follows

$$I_Q = v.I_C + (1-v).I_B$$

Finally if R divides PQ in ratio $w:1-w$, where $0 \le w \le 1$, then intensity at R can be calculated as follows

$$I_R = w.I_Q + (1-w).I_P$$

For a neighboring point R′ with ratio w' the intensity can be calculated incrementally from intensity at R, where $\Delta w = w' - w$:

$$I_{R'} = I_R + \Delta w.(I_Q - I_P)$$

7.3.7.6 Phong Shading Algorithm

A drawback of Gouraud shading is that if two points happen to have the same intensity then all intermediate points will be imposed the same value by linear interpolation and the surface appears flat. An alternative algorithm called Phong shading algorithm, proposed by Bui Tuong Phong, considered more accurate than Gouraud shading, works by interpolating the normal along a scan line rather than intensity values. If N_P, N_Q, N_R are the normals to the surface at points P, Q, R, respectively, then as per the logic of the previous equations we have the following relations (Phong, 1975).

$$N_P = u.N_B + (1-u).N_A$$

$$N_Q = v.N_C + (1-v).N_B$$

$$N_R = w.N_Q + (1-w).N_P$$

An illumination model is applied to the interpolated normal directions to calculate intensity at the corresponding points. An illumination model provides a procedure to calculate intensity of a point on a surface given information about the light source and the surface properties. In a graphics/animation package, an illumination model is used to calculate pixel values of all points in a 3D scene. To calculate light intensity at a point, three factors are usually taken into consideration: ambient light, diffuse reflection, and specular reflection.

7.3.7.7 Painter's Algorithm

In general, most scenes consist of several objects in which case the rendering algorithm also needs to decide which objects should be rendered in front of other objects. For rendering of scenes with multiple objects, one approach is to sort all the objects by depth so that the rendering program can start rendering those objects that are farthest away. Once rendered, each new object covers up distant objects that have already been rendered. This procedure resembles the way a painter might complete the background of a scene before painting objects in the foreground and, as such, it is called the painter's algorithm. The algorithm states that if two polygons P and Q are found to overlap, it is tested whether P is completely behind Q relative to the viewing plane. This is done by substituting coordinates of all vertices of P into the plane equation of Q and checking the sign of the result. If P is completely behind Q then P is painted first, otherwise P and Q are swapped and Q is painted first. If some parts of P are behind Q, while other parts are in front then P is split into two polygons P1 and P2 and these replace P. The tests are repeated using components P1 and P2. The painter's algorithm is often used in conjunction with a Binary Space Partition (BSP) tree which provides an efficient method to determine which surfaces are in front or back of other surfaces. A BSP tree uses a plane attached to a surface to partition the space into two sets of objects, one in front and one at the back relative to the viewing plane. Each of these spaces is again partitioned by another plane and a binary tree is constructed with front objects on left branches and rear objects on right branches. When the BSP tree is complete, it is processed by selecting surfaces for display in the order back to front (Foley et al., 1990) (Figure 7.30).

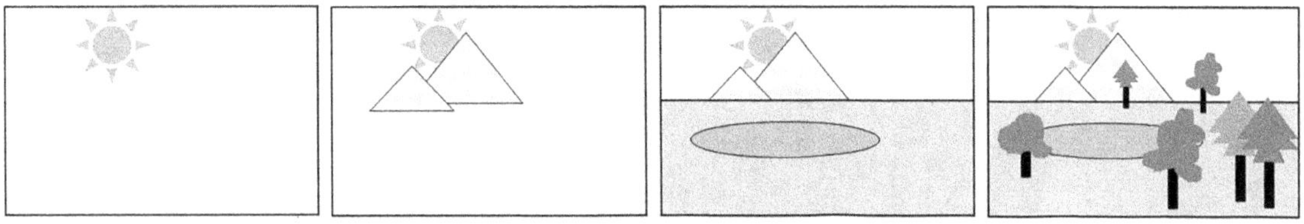

FIGURE 7.30
Painter's algorithm-based rendering.

7.3.7.8 Z-Buffer Algorithm

To presort objects by depth can be very time-consuming, particularly with a scene involving a large number of objects because each polygon of each object has to be sorted by depth. An alternative solution to this problem is known as the Z-buffer algorithm. The Z-buffer stores depth of each pixel from the observer, in memory during creation. For each pixel position (x,y) on the view-plane, object depths are determined by comparing their z-values. Assuming viewing direction along the negative Z-axis, intensity value at (x,y) should correspond to the closest polygon P1 represented by the largest z-value. Two buffers are used: a depth buffer used to store depth values for each (x,y) position, and an intensity buffer to store corresponding intensity values. The algorithm can be stated as follows:

- Initialize screen to background color, i.e., fill intensity buffer with some constant value: $I_{buf}(x,y) = I_{bkg}, forall(x,y)$
- Initialize depth buffer to back clipping plane, i.e., fill depth buffer with some constant small value: $Z_{buf}(x,y) = Z_{bkg}, forall(x,y)$. Frequently $Z_{bkg} = 0$.
- For each pixel of each polygon initialize scan conversion process; i.e., for each pixel (x,y) calculate its depth $z(x,y)$. Depth values for a surface is calculated from its plane equation: $z = (-Ax - By - D)/C$.
- If $z(x,y) \geq Z_{buf}(x,y)$ set $Z_{buf}(x,y) = z(x,y)$ and set value of intensity buffer at (x,y) to pixel value of the point: $I_{buf}(x,y) = I(x,y)$.

The process is repeated until all pixels have been processed. The actual rendering involves displaying intensity at (x,y) corresponding to the largest depth value of $z(x,y)$. If two points have the same z-value then the second point is displayed as the color is changed if $z(x,y) \geq Z_{buf}(x,y)$ is true; however, for some implementations a condition of $z(x,y) > Z_{buf}(x,y)$ might be used for change. The figure below shows a grid of 4 by 4 pixels where the values indicate depth values. A indicates pixels with depth values 0 (background) and 5 (foreground). A polygon B with depth values shown is superimposed on A. The final values rendered is shown in C where at each pixel location the depth values of B are compared and the pixel values of A and the pixel with the higher or same value as A is retained in the final rendering (Foley et al., 1990) (Figure 7.31).

7.3.8 Common Editing Tasks

Some of the common 3D animation tasks that can be performed using a typical GUI-based 3D animation software are discussed below (Figure 7.32).

Primitives: Working with geometric primitives and using various transformations to create complex models.

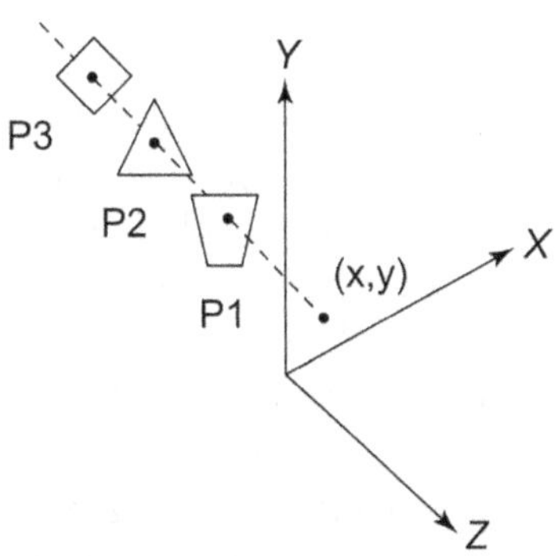

A		B		C
5 5 5 0		3 4 3 0		5 5 5 0
5 5 5 0		6 5 4 0		6 5 5 0
5 5 0 0	+	7 6 5 0	=	7 6 5 0
0 0 0 0		0 0 0 0		0 0 0 0

FIGURE 7.31
Z-buffer-based rendering.

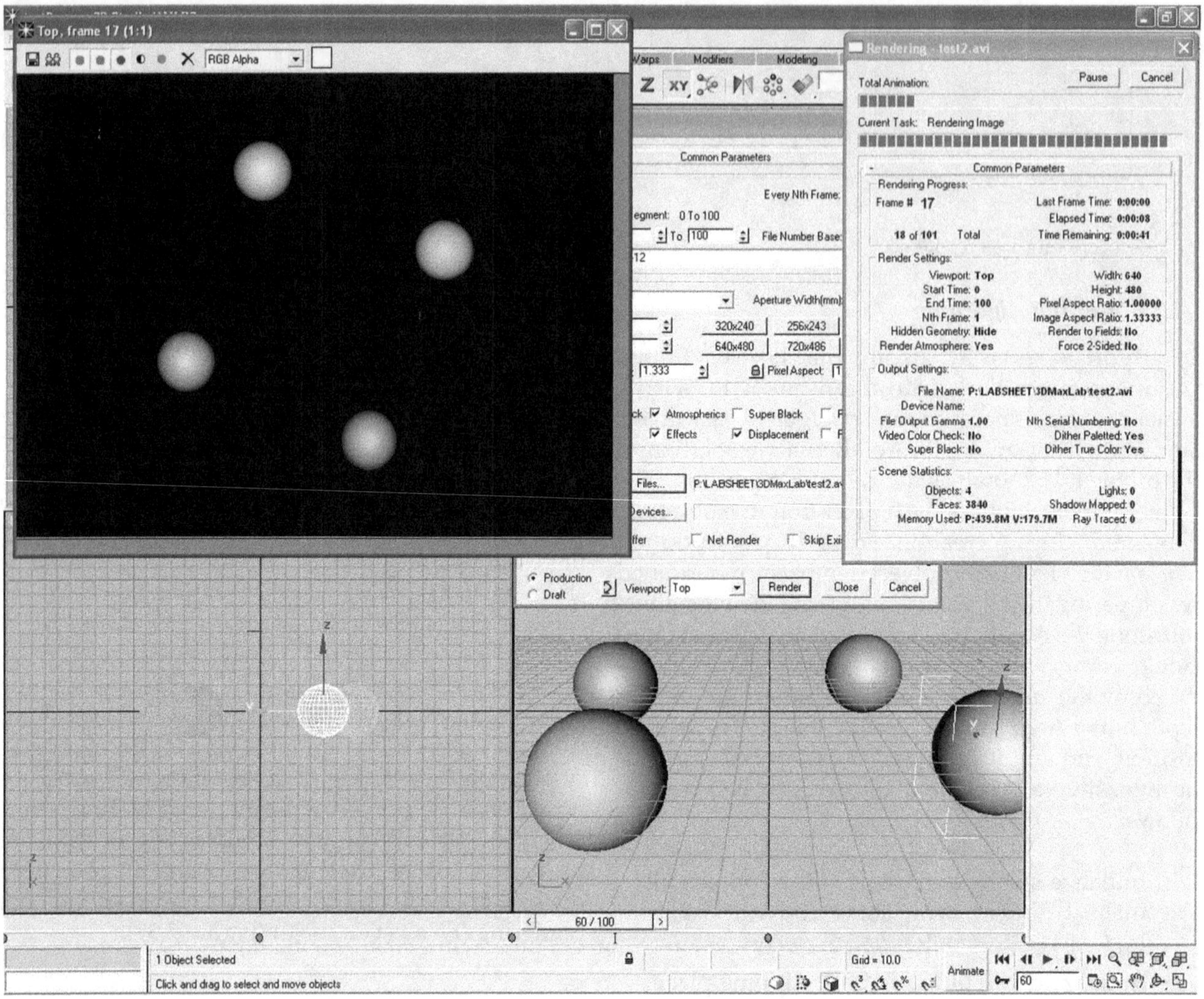

FIGURE 7.32
Typical GUI-based 3D animation editor interface.

Arrays: Creating 1D, 2D and 3D linear, circular and spiral arrays of repeating objects.

Extrusion: Creating 3D models and surfaces from 2D shapes through extrusion.

Lathing: Creating 3D models and surfaces from 2D shapes through lathing about different axes.

Lofting: Creating 3D models and surfaces by moving 2D shapes along various trajectories and paths.

Boolean operations: Combining multiple 3D models to create compound objects using unions, intersections, addition and subtraction.

Surface texture: Applying surface texture over 3D surfaces by selecting textures from a materials library. Also includes creation of transparent and metallic objects.

Lighting: Specifying illumination and shading of a 3D scene by defining light parameters like location, type, color, intensity, direction.

Camera: Defining the viewpoints of the 3D scene by specifying camera locations and center of interests as well as parameters like focal length, FOV angles, zoom ratios.

Animation: Creating animation by specifying keyframes and motion guides, locations in 3D space and time intervals for changes to take place

Particle systems: Defining particle systems to simulate effects of rain, fog, spray, wind.

Space warps: Defining explosion effects by using space warps and specifying parameters like intensity, number and size of fragments, spin, falloff, effect of gravity.

7.4 Animation Applications

Both 2D and 3D animations contribute significantly to the versatility and impact of multimedia applications, catering to diverse industries and enhancing various forms of digital content. The choice between 2D and 3D often depends on the specific requirements and objectives of the multimedia project.

7.4.1 2D Animation

Web Design and User Interface (UI): 2D animations are employed in Web design to create interactive and visually appealing user interfaces. Animated buttons, transitions and illustrations enhance the overall user experience.

E-Learning and Educational Content: In educational multimedia applications, 2D animations are used to simplify complex concepts, create engaging tutorials and make learning materials more interactive and memorable.

Advertising and Marketing: 2D animations are frequently used in digital marketing campaigns, explainer videos and advertisements. They convey messages in a concise and entertaining manner, increasing audience engagement.

Mobile Apps: Many mobile applications leverage 2D animations for onboarding processes, in-app transitions and interactive elements. Animated icons and visual feedback enhance the overall user experience.

Social Media Content: 2D animations are popular on social media platforms for creating shareable and engaging content. Animated infographics, short stories and visualizations are effective for grabbing attention.

Presentations and Slideshows: 2D animations are used to make presentations more dynamic and engaging. Animated charts, diagrams and transitions can enhance the clarity and impact of the content.

Interactive Multimedia Storytelling: 2D animations are integrated into interactive multimedia storytelling applications, such as digital books and interactive websites, to enhance the narrative and captivate the audience.

7.4.2 3D Animation

Virtual Reality (VR) and Augmented Reality (AR): 3D animations are crucial in VR and AR applications, providing immersive experiences. They are used in gaming, simulations and interactive educational content.

Architectural Visualization: 3D animations are utilized in architectural multimedia applications to visualize and showcase building designs. Clients can experience a virtual walkthrough of structures before they are built.

Gaming and Entertainment: 3D animations are a cornerstone of video games and multimedia entertainment. They bring characters, environments, and cinematic sequences to life, creating a rich and engaging gaming experience.

Product Visualization and Prototyping: 3D animations help showcase products from various angles, demonstrate functionality and simulate prototypes. This is particularly common in industries like manufacturing and product design.

Medical and Scientific Visualization: In multimedia applications within the medical field, 3D animations are used to visualize complex biological processes, surgical procedures and medical concepts for educational and training purposes.

Animated Simulations: Animated simulations, such as those in physics or engineering applications, often use 3D animations to visually represent dynamic processes and scenarios.

Digital Art and Installations: Artists and designers use 3D animations in multimedia installations and digital art projects to create visually stunning and immersive experiences.

Film and TV Production: 3D animations are extensively used in multimedia productions for special effects, CGI (computer-generated imagery) and creating fantastical worlds in films and television shows.

7.5 Legal and Ethical Considerations

Legal considerations in both 2D and 3D animation are crucial to ensure compliance with intellectual property laws, contractual agreements, and other legal standards. Here are key legal considerations for both types of animation:

7.5.1 Legal Considerations

Legal considerations in animation encompass issues related to adherence to copyright laws, licensing agreements and intellectual property rights. Animators are required to navigate legal frameworks to ensure they have the right to use specific characters, music or other elements in their work. Additionally contracts, fair use principles and compliance with industry regulations play a crucial role is addressing legal aspects within the animation field (Burr, 2004).

Intellectual Property (IP) Rights: Respect the intellectual property rights of others and ensure that you have the right to use any characters, designs or elements in your animation. Obtain necessary permissions, licenses, or create original content to avoid copyright infringement.

Copyright Issues: Be aware of copyright laws and ensure that your animation does not infringe on the copyright of existing works. Obtain permission to use copyrighted material or create original content. Understand fair use principles where applicable.

Licensing Agreements: Adhere to the terms and conditions specified in licensing agreements associated with any assets used in the animation. Review and comply with licensing agreements to avoid legal issues related to the use of licensed content.

Contracts and Agreements: Clearly define the terms of engagement and ownership in contracts when collaborating with others on an animation project. Draft comprehensive contracts that address intellectual property rights, compensation and other relevant terms.

Model Releases: If your animation involves recognizable individuals, be aware of the need for model releases. Obtain written consent from individuals appearing in the animation, especially for commercial or public use.

Defamation and Privacy Laws: Be cautious about creating content that could be defamatory or infringe on an individual's privacy rights. Ensure that your animation does not depict individuals in a false or harmful light and respect privacy laws.

Trademark Issues: Avoid the unauthorized use of trademarks or brand logos that could lead to trademark infringement. Obtain permission if necessary, or create original content that does not involve the unauthorized use of trademarks.

Distribution and Licensing: Understand the legal aspects of distributing and licensing your animation, especially for commercial purposes. Comply with distribution platforms' terms of service, and clearly define licensing terms if you are licensing your animation.

Age-Appropriate Content: Ensure that your animation's content is age-appropriate, especially if it is targeted at children. Adhere to relevant regulations and guidelines to avoid legal issues related to inappropriate content.

Contractual Disputes: Anticipate and address potential contractual disputes with collaborators, clients or distributors. Clearly outline dispute resolution mechanisms in contracts and seek legal advice if conflicts arise.

Technology and Digital Rights Management: Protect your animation from unauthorized distribution or use through digital rights management (DRM) and other technological measures. Implement DRM solutions to control access and usage of your animation, if applicable.

Understanding and addressing these legal considerations will help creators, animators, and studios navigate the complex legal landscape associated with 2D and 3D animation, reducing the risk of legal disputes and ensuring ethical and responsible content creation. Consulting with legal professionals specializing in intellectual property and entertainment law is advisable to ensure comprehensive legal protection.

7.5.2 Ethical Considerations

Ethical considerations in animation involve decisions about content, representation and the impact of the animated work on the audience. Animators must weigh the potential effects of their creations on the cultural sensitivities, avoiding stereotypes or offensive depictions. Additionally ethical choices may extend to workplace practices, ensuring fair treatment of animators and promoting diversity in character design and storytelling (Wilkins et al., 2021).

Representation and Diversity: Ensure diverse and authentic representation of individuals and cultures in animation. Avoid perpetuating stereotypes and actively work to include diverse perspectives in character design and storytelling.

Cultural Sensitivity: Approach the representation of cultures with sensitivity and avoid cultural appropriation. Conduct thorough research, collaborate with cultural experts and seek feedback to ensure accurate and respectful portrayals.

Social Impact: Be aware of the potential impact of your animation on society, particularly concerning sensitive topics or controversial themes. Consider the potential consequences of your work and strive to contribute positively to social discourse. Child Protection: Exercise caution when creating content that involves minors, ensuring that it is age-appropriate and complies with child protection laws. Adhere to legal standards, obtain necessary permissions, and prioritize the well-being of young audiences.

Informed Consent: Obtain informed consent from individuals involved in the creation or representation of characters, especially if their likeness is used. Clearly communicate how characters will be portrayed and seek permission when necessary. Authenticity in Animation Styles: Be transparent about the animation style used and avoid misleading audiences about the nature of the animation. Clearly communicate the artistic choices made in the animation process.

Environmental Impact: Consider the environmental impact of 2D animation production, including paper usage and waste. Adopt sustainable practices, such as digital animation techniques and environmentally friendly materials.

Realism and Misrepresentation: Be mindful of the ethical implications of creating hyper-realistic or manipulated content that may mislead viewers. Clearly disclose any manipulations or alterations made to content and consider the potential impact on perception.

Privacy in Motion Capture: Respect the privacy of individuals involved in motion capture for realistic animations. Obtain informed consent, clearly communicate the purpose of motion capture and protect the privacy of participants.

Deepfakes and Misuse of Technology: Avoid the misuse of technology, such as creating deepfakes that could be used for deceptive or harmful purposes. Use technology responsibly and consider the potential consequences of creating misleading or falsified content.

Accessibility: Ensure that 3D animations are accessible to diverse audiences, including those with disabilities. Incorporate accessibility features, such as subtitles and audio descriptions, to make animations inclusive.

7.6 Challenges and Emerging Trends

7.6.1 2D Animation

7.6.1.1 Challenges

Competing with 3D Animation: 2D animation often faces competition with the widespread popularity of 3D animation. Some audiences may perceive 2D animation as outdated, posing a challenge for its marketability.

Complex Scene Creation: Creating complex and detailed scenes in 2D animation can be time-consuming. Achieving the same level of visual richness as in 3D animation may require more intricate hand-drawn work.

Limited Depth Perception: 2D animation can sometimes lack the depth perception that 3D animation effortlessly achieves. This limitation may impact the immersive quality of certain scenes.

Sustainability in Production: Maintaining a sustainable production pipeline for 2D animation, especially for large-scale projects, can be challenging. Balancing efficiency and quality is crucial.

Adapting to New Technologies: Staying up-to-date with new technologies, such as augmented reality (AR) and virtual reality (VR), can be more challenging for 2D animation compared to 3D animation.

7.6.1.2 Emerging Trends

Mixed Media and Techniques: The future of 2D animation might involve blending traditional hand-drawn techniques with digital tools, creating unique and visually compelling styles.

Interactive 2D Animation: With the rise of interactive content, 2D animation could evolve to include more interactive elements, allowing audiences to engage with the storytelling process.

Augmented Reality (AR): Integrating 2D animation with AR experiences can offer new possibilities, providing interactive and immersive content for users in real-world environments.

7.6.2 3D Animation

7.6.2.1 *Challenges*

High Production Costs: 3D animation often requires significant financial investment due to the cost of specialized software, hardware and skilled personnel.

Learning Curve: Mastering 3D animation software can be complex and time-consuming, potentially posing a barrier for new artists entering the field.

Rendering Times: Rendering intricate 3D scenes can be time-consuming, especially for high-quality animations. Efficient rendering solutions are continually sought to minimize production time.

Realism Expectations: The constant push for more realistic animations can be challenging, requiring advancements in technology and techniques to meet audience expectations.

7.6.2.2 *Emerging Trends*

Real-Time Rendering: Advancements in real time rendering technologies will continue to make it possible to create high-quality 3D animations more efficiently.

Virtual Production Techniques: The integration of virtual production techniques, as seen in films like *The Mandalorian*, is likely to become more common, blending physical and digital elements seamlessly.

Immersive Experiences: 3D animation will likely play a significant role in the development of immersive experiences, including virtual reality (VR) and augmented reality (AR) applications.

AI and Automation: The use of artificial intelligence (AI) and automation in 3D animation processes may increase, streamlining certain aspects of production and making animation more accessible.

Hybrid Animation Styles: Experimentation with hybrid styles that blend 2D and 3D animation elements could become more common, offering unique visual aesthetics.

Blockchain for Animation Production: The use of blockchain technology for animation production, providing transparent and secure asset management, could become more prevalent.

Both 2D and 3D animation will likely continue to evolve and coexist, with each addressing unique challenges and contributing to a diverse and innovative animation landscape. The future holds exciting possibilities as technology advances and creative boundaries are pushed.

7.7 Animation File Formats

7.7.1 SVG

Scalable Vector Graphics (SVG) [www.w3.org/Graphics/SVG/] is a set of XML-based specifications for describing 2D vector graphics, and supports the ability to change vector graphics over time, to create animated effects [www.w3.org/TR/SVG/animate.html]. Using SVG's animation elements (svg-animation) [svgwg.org/specs/animations/], SVG document fragments can describe time-based modifications to the document's elements. Using the various animation elements, authors can define motion paths, or interpolate the element's attributes and style properties. These effects can be chained together or triggered in response to other events in the document.

7.7.2 FLA, SWF

The Flash (FLA) [adobe.com/products/flashruntimes.html] and Shockwave Format (SWF) [open-flash.github.io/mirrors/swf-spec-19.pdf] are file formats to store editable and non-editable vector-based animation created by Adobe Flash application software. Adobe Flash, later renamed as Adobe Animate, contains a timeline where keyframes can be specified and using which animation content can be created based on motion tweening and shape tweening options. Path-based animation can also be created by using motion guides. Interactive elements can be created using Flash's integrated object-based programming language ActionScript. The SWF format is a distributable format which can be played back either using a standalone shockwave player or via a Web browser using a SWF plug-in. The use of vector format makes the file smaller consuming less bandwidth, and its capability for being streamed makes it an ideal choice for Web graphics and animation. Nowadays, however, Flash content is no longer actively supported by modern browsers having being superseded by SVG and HTML5.

7.7.3 Animated GIF

Animated GIF is a variant of the GIF file format, an 8-bit image file format introduced by CompuServe in 1987, and later enhanced in 1989 [www.w3.org/Graphics/GIF/spec-gif89a.txt]. GIF files are capable of storing multiple 8-bit images in a single file and then later playing them back at a specific speed, which leads to the generation of animation. Animated GIF files are extensively used on the Web to display simple animations. One drawback of animated GIF files is that they do not support audio and interactivity. To facilitate displaying animations, the GIF89a spec added the Graphic Control Extension (GCE), which allows the images (frames) in the file to be painted with time delays, forming a video clip. Each frame in an animation GIF is introduced by its own GCE specifying the time delay to wait after the frame is drawn. To enable an animation to loop, Netscape added the Netscape Application Block (NAB) to specify the number of times the sequence of frames should be played (1 to 65535 times) or continuously. Since GIF is an image format, the animations so produced are raster-based instead of vector-based.

7.7.4 Animated PNG

Animated PNG [wiki.mozilla.org/APNG_Specification] is an extension of PNG that supports basic animations. The first frame of an APNG file is stored as a normal PNG stream, so most standard PNG decoders are able to display the first frame of an APNG file. APNG supports 24-bit images and 8-bit transparency. An APNG stream is a normal PNG stream with three additional chunk types describing the animation and providing additional frame data. One of the key components of APNG is the Animation Control Chunk, which is used to specify the timing and ordering of frames within the animation. This chunk contains information such as the frame delay, frame disposal method (how the previous frame is handled), and whether the frame includes transparency information. When rendering an APNG animation, each frame is displayed for the specified duration before transitioning to the next frame. The rendering process takes into account any transparency information to correctly composite each frame over the previous ones, allowing for smooth animations with varying levels of transparency, hence like an animated GIF file the animation is raster-based instead of vector-based.

7.7.5 MNG

Multiple-image Network Graphics (MNG) [www.libpng.org/pub/mng/spec] is a multiple-image member of the PNG (Portable Network Graphics) format family. It can contain animations, slide shows or complex still frames, comprising multiple PNG single-image data streams. It uses the same chunk structure that is defined in the PNG specification, and share other features of the PNG format, due to which Any PNG decoder must be able to decode MNG. It provides a mechanism for reusing image data without having to retransmit it. Multiple images can be composed into a "frame" and a group of images can be used as an animated "sprite" that moves from one location to another in subsequent frames. MNG can store images in a highly compressible "Delta-PNG" format which defines an image in terms of a parent PNG and the differences from that image. This provides a much more compact way of representing subsequent images than using a complete PNG data stream for each.

7.7.6 FBX

Filmbox (FBX) [www.autodesk.com/products/fbx/overview] is a proprietary format used for 3D animation and modeling owned by Autodesk. It's supported by many 3D software applications and allows for the exchange of 3D models, animations and scenes. It was designed to facilitate higher-fidelity data exchange between 3ds Max, Maya, MotionBuilder, Mudbox and other propriety and third-party software.

7.7.7 MAX

3D Studio MAX (MAX) is a proprietary format native to Autodesk 3d Studio Max [www.autodesk.in/products/3ds-max/overview] and store complete 3D scenes, including models, textures, lights, cameras and animations. The MAX file format was developed by Autodesk for the 3dS MAX application, which is a 3D modeling, animation, and rendering solution used to create 3D animation for game development, design visualization, feature film and television effects, and education.

7.7.8 DAE

Collada (Collaborative Design Activity) [www.khronos.org/collada] is an open standard that supports the exchange of 3D assets, including animations, between different 3D applications using DAE (Digital Asset Exchange) files. The key features include mesh geometry, physics, textures, animation capabilities and effects, as well as options to apply different shaders, skinning and instantiation. A DAE file can store a diverse range of content, including images, textures and 3D models, but the format's biggest selling point is its compatibility across multiple platforms, i.e., a standard way to store 3D assets.

7.8 Numerical Problems

7.8.1 Surfaces

PROBLEM 7.1

A parametric surface $S(u,v)=(u-v,u+v,u^2-v^2)$ is translated using $T(3,5,4)$ and then rotated about the z-axis by 90°. Find the parametric representation of the resulting surface.

Translation matrix : $T(3,5,4)$

Rotation matrix: $R_z(90)$

Composite transformation matrix:

$$M = R_z(90).T(3,5,4) = \begin{pmatrix} 0 & -1 & 0 & -5 \\ 1 & 0 & 0 & 3 \\ 0 & 0 & 1 & 4 \\ 0 & 0 & 0 & 1 \end{pmatrix}$$

Original curve: $P = \begin{pmatrix} u-v \\ u+v \\ u^2-v^2 \\ 1 \end{pmatrix}$

Modified curve: $Q = M.P = \begin{pmatrix} u-v-5 \\ u-v+3 \\ u^2-v^2+4 \\ 1 \end{pmatrix}$

Required curve equation: $S(u,v) = (u-v-5,\ u-v+3,\ u^2-v^2+4)$

PROBLEM 7.2

Find the equation of a bi-linear Bezier surface using the following control points: P_{00} = (0,0,1), P_{01} = (1,1,1), P_{10} = (1,0,0), P_{11} = (0,1,0)

For bi-linear Bezier surface:

$$S(u,v)=\begin{bmatrix}1-u, & u\end{bmatrix}\begin{bmatrix}P_{00} & P_{01} \\ P_{10} & P_{11}\end{bmatrix}\begin{bmatrix}1-v \\ v\end{bmatrix}$$

Substituting values and separating into components:

$$x(u,v)=\begin{bmatrix}1-u, & u\end{bmatrix}\begin{bmatrix}0 & 1 \\ 1 & 0\end{bmatrix}\begin{bmatrix}1-v \\ v\end{bmatrix} = u+v-2uv$$

$$y(u,v)=\begin{bmatrix}1-u, & u\end{bmatrix}\begin{bmatrix}0 & 1 \\ 0 & 1\end{bmatrix}\begin{bmatrix}1-v \\ v\end{bmatrix} = v$$

$$z(u,v)=\begin{bmatrix}1-u, & u\end{bmatrix}\begin{bmatrix}1 & 1 \\ 0 & 0\end{bmatrix}\begin{bmatrix}1-v \\ v\end{bmatrix} = 1-u$$

Required surface equation:
$S(u,v)=(u+v-2uv, v, 1-u)$

PROBLEM 7.3

Find point(s) of intersection between the hyperboloid $2x^2+3y^2-z^2=16$ and the parametric line $(t-4,t-5,t+10)$.

For any point on the line: $x=t-4, y=t-5, z=t+10$

At point of intersection this also should satisfy the equation of the surface

Substituting: $2(t-4)^2+3(t-5)^2-(t+10)^2=16$

Simplifying: $4t^2-66t-9=0$ whose solutions are: $t=-0.1353, 16.6353$

Substituting, points of intersection are: (-4.135255, -5.135255, 9.864745) and (12.635255, 11.635255, 26.635255)

Verification:

$$2(-4.135255)^2+3(-5.135255)^2-(9.864745)^2=16$$

$$2(12.635255)^2+3(11.635255)^2-(26.635255)^2=16$$

PROBLEM 7.4

Find equation of the surface generated when circle $x=sin(u), y=cos(u)$ (a) is extruded perpendicular to its plane to form a cylinder (b) rotated upon its axis to form a sphere.

$(a) x=\sin(u); y=\cos(u); z=v;$

$S(u,v)=(x,y,z)=\{\sin(u),\cos(u),v\}$

Here, $0 \le u \le 1, 0 \le v \le h$, where u is along the plane containing the curve and v is perpendicular to the plane, and h is the maximum distance by which the curve is moved.

$(b) x=\cos(u).\cos(v); y=\cos(u).\sin(v); z=\sin(u)$

$S(u,v)=(x,y,z)$

$=\{\cos(u).\cos(v),\cos(u).\sin(v),\sin(u)\}$

Here, $0 \le u \le 1, 0 \le v \le 2\pi$. If v equal to or greater than 2π the surface is closed, otherwise it is open.

PROBLEM 7.5

Derive a transformation for mapping a texture with (u,v) coordinates (0, 0), (1, 0), (1, 1), (0, 1) to a surface with (x,y) coordinates of (5, 5), (10, 7), (12, 12), (7, 10). Also for the texture point $(u=0.6, v=0.7)$, find the corresponding point on the surface.

Surface coordinates: $(x_0,y_0)=(5,5), (x_1,y_1)=(10,7), (x_2,y_2)=(12,12), (x_3,y_3)=(7,10)$

Now $(x_1-x_0)=5, (x_2-x_3)=5, (y_1-y_0)=2, (y_2-y_3)=2$

Since $(x_1-x_0)=(x_2-x_3)$ and $(y_1-y_0)=(y_2-y_3)$ the mapping transformation is affine in nature.

For affine transformation matrix

$$M = \begin{bmatrix} x_1 - x_0 & x_3 - x_0 & x_0 \\ y_1 - y_0 & y_3 - y_0 & y_0 \\ 0 & 0 & 1 \end{bmatrix} = \begin{bmatrix} 5 & 2 & 5 \\ 2 & 5 & 5 \\ 0 & 0 & 1 \end{bmatrix}$$

$$x = 5u + 2v + 5$$

$$y = 2u + 5v + 5$$

$$\text{For}(u = 0.6, v = 0.7),$$

$$y = 2(0.6) + 5(0.7) + 5 = 9.7$$

Verification: $x(0,0) = 5$, $y(0,0) = 5$, $x(0,1) = 7$, $y(0,1) = 10$, $x(1,0) = 10$, $y(1,0) = 7$, $x(1,1) = 12$, $y(1,1) = 12$

7.8.2 Lights

PROBLEM 7.6

Calculate the reflected ray and angle of reflection for an incident ray of $L = -i + 2j - k$ and a normal of $N = j$. Verify that angles of incidence and reflection are equal.

Here $L = -i + 2j - k$ and $N = j$

Now$L \bullet N = 2$

Reflected ray: $R = 2(L \bullet N)N - L = 4j - (-i + 2j - k) = i + 2j + k$

Angle of incidence:

$\cos\theta = (L \bullet N)/(|L||N|) = 2/(\sqrt{6}) = 0.82$, i.e., $\theta = 35.26°$

Angle of reflection:

$\cos\theta = (R \bullet N)/(|R||N|) = 2/(\sqrt{6}) = 0.82$

PROBLEM 7.7

Light is incident along $L = -i + 2j - k$ at a point on a surface with normal $N = j$. Calculate the intensity at the point if the source light is 10 times more intense than the ambient light. Assume viewing direction as $V = i + 1.5j + 0.5k$ and $k_a = 0.15, k_d = 0.4, k_s = 0.8, m = 5$.

Incident ray is $L = -i + 2j - k$, hence unit vector $L_u = L/|L| = (-0.41, 0.81, -0.41)$

Normal is $N = j$, hence unit vector $N_u = N/|N| =$ (0, 1, 0)

Reflected ray unit vector $R_u = 2(L_u \bullet N_u)N_u - L_u =$ (0.41, 0.81, 0.41)

Viewing direction is $V = i + 1.5j + 0.5k$. Hence, unit vector $V_u = V/|V| = (0.53, 0.80, 0.27)$

Now, $L_u \bullet N_u = (-0.41, 0.81, -0.41) \bullet (0,1,0) = 0.81$ and $R_u \bullet V_u = (0.41, 0.81, 0.41) \bullet (0.53, 0.80, 0.27) = 0.98$.

Intensity due to ambient reflection: $I_a = L_a.k_a =$ (1)(0.15) = 0.15

Intensity due to diffused reflection:

$I_d = L_p.k_d.(Ln \bullet Nn) = 10 \times 0.25 \times 0.8165 = 2.0412$

Intensity due to specular reflection:

$I_s = L_p.k_s.(Rn \bullet Vn)^5 = 10 \times 0.5 \times 0.9820^5 = 4.5655$

Total intensity : $I = I_a + I_d + I_s = 6.7567$

Thus, the total intensity on the surface is approximately 67.5% of the source intensity.

7.9 Coding Examples using MATLAB®

7.9.1 Surfaces

The following example illustrates transformation of 3D surfaces. The function "ezmesh" creates a mesh of points, "deg2rad" converts degree values to radians, "eval" evaluates and expression (Figure 7.33).

EXAMPLE 7.1 EXAMPLE TO CALCULATE THE NEW EQUATION OF PARAMETRIC SURFACE S = (U - V, U + V, U^2 - V^2) AFTER TRANSLATION USING T(3,5,4) AND ROTATION ABOUT Z-AXIS BY 90°

```
clear; clc; syms u v;
tx = 3; ty = 5; tz = 4;
A = deg2rad(90);
P = [u - v ; u + v ; u^2 - v^2 ; 1]
T1 = [1, 0, 0, tx ; 0, 1, 0, ty ; 0, 0, 1, tz ; 0, 0, 0, 1];
R1 = [cos(A), -sin(A), 0, 0 ; sin(A), cos(A), 0, 0 ;
     0, 0, 1, 0 ; 0, 0, 0, 1];
M = R1*T1;
Q = R1*T1*P;
Q = eval(Q)
subplot(121)
ezmesh(P(1), P(2), P(3)); title('Original'); view(-13, 48); axis square;
subplot(122)
ezmesh(Q(1), Q(2), Q(3)); title('New'); view(-13, 48); axis square;
```

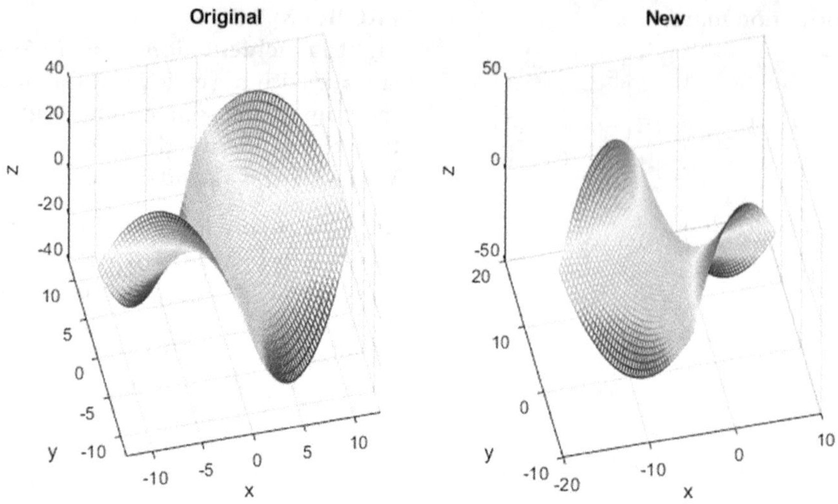

FIGURE 7.33
Output of Example 7.1.

The following example illustrates generation of a bi-linear Bezier surface. The function "syms" declares symbolic variables, "plot3" generates a 3D plot and "text" inserts textual descriptions in the plots (Figure 7.34).

The following example illustrates computation of intersection points on implicit surfaces. The function "solve" generates a solution for an equation and computes its roots, "ezplot3" plots symbolic variables in 3D environments, "subs" substitutes symbolic

EXAMPLE 7.2 EXAMPLE TO CALCULATE EQUATION OF BI-LINEAR BEZIER SURFACE PASSING THROUGH CONTROL POINTS P00 = (0, 0, 1), P01 = (1, 1, 1), P10 = (1, 0, 0), P11 = (0, 1, 0)

```
clear; clc;
P00 = [0,0,1];
P01 = [1,1,1];
P10 = [1,0,0];
P11 = [0,1,0];
syms u v;
x00 = P00(1); x01 = P01(1); x10 = P10(1); x11 = P11(1);
y00 = P00(2); y01 = P01(2); y10 = P10(2); y11 = P11(2);
z00 = P00(3); z01 = P01(3); z10 = P10(3); z11 = P11(3);
x = [1-u, u]*[x00, x01 ; x10, x11]*[1-v ; v]; x = simplify(x)
y = [1-u, u]*[y00, y01 ; y10, y11]*[1-v ; v]; y = simplify(y)
z = [1-u, u]*[z00, z01 ; z10, z11]*[1-v ; v]; z = simplify(z)
ezmesh(x, y, z, [0,1,0,1]); title(""); hold on;

plot3([P00(1) P01(1)], [P00(2) P01(2)], [P00(3) P01(3)], ...
    'b-', 'LineWidth', 2);
plot3([P00(1) P01(1)], [P00(2) P01(2)], [P00(3) P01(3)], 'bo');
plot3([P10(1) P11(1)], [P10(2) P11(2)], [P10(3) P11(3)], ...
    'b-', 'LineWidth', 2);
plot3([P10(1) P11(1)], [P10(2) P11(2)], [P10(3) P11(3)], 'bo');
text(x00+0.2, y00, z00, 'P00');
text(x01+0.2, y01, z01, 'P01');
text(x10-0.1, y10, z10+0.2, 'P10');
text(x11, y11, z11-0.1, 'P11');
hold off;
```

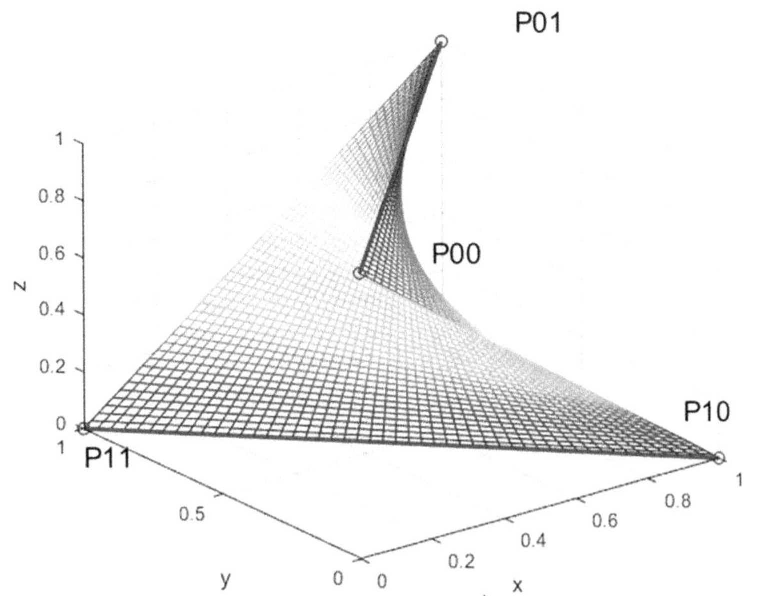

FIGURE 7.34
Output of Example 7.2.

variables with numerical values, "ezmesh" creates a mesh of points, "view" specifies the horizontal and vertical angles for viewing a 3D scene, "ezplot" generates plots of symbolic variables, "colormap" specifies the color palette to use, "hold" temporarily holds the plot for further inputs before displaying the results, "eval" evaluates an expression (Figure 7.35).

EXAMPLE 7.3 EXAMPLE TO CALCULATE POINT(S) OF INTERSECTION BETWEEN THE HYPER-BOLOID 2X^2 + 3Y^2 - Z^2 = 16 AND THE PARAMETRIC LINE (T-4, T-5, T+10)

```
clear; clc;
syms t;
x = t - 4; y = t - 5; z = t + 10;
P = 2*x^2 + 3*y^2 - z^2 - 16;
R = solve(P);
R1 = R(1); eval(R1);
R2 = R(2); eval(R2);
X1 = subs(x, 't', R1); X1 = eval(X1);
Y1 = subs(y, 't', R1); Y1 = eval(Y1);
Z1 = subs(z, 't', R1); Z1 = eval(Z1);
X2 = subs(x, 't', R2); X2 = eval(X2);
Y2 = subs(y, 't', R2); Y2 = eval(Y2);
Z2 = subs(z, 't', R2); Z2 = eval(Z2);
fprintf('Point of intersection 1 : \n a
   = (%f, %f, %f)\n', ...
    X1, Y1, Z1);
fprintf('Point of intersection 2 : \n b
   = (%f, %f, %f)\n', ...
    X2, Y2, Z2);

%verification
vrf1 = subs(P, [x, y, z], [X1, Y1,
   Z1]); eval(vrf1)
vrf2 = subs(P, [x, y, z], [X2, Y2,
   Z2]); eval(vrf2)

%plotting
syms u v;
x = u;
y = v;
z = sqrt(2*u^2 + 3*v^2 - 16);
k = 30; ezmesh(x,y,z,
   [-k,k,-k,k,-k,k]);
hold on;
ezplot3('t-4', 't-5', 't + 10',
   [-40, 40]);
view(20, 64); hold off;
   colormap('jet');

y = v;
z = sqrt(2*u^2 + 3*v^2 - 16);
k = 30; ezmesh(x,y,z,
   [-k,k,-k,k,-k,k]);
hold on;
ezplot3('t-4', 't-5', 't + 10',
   [-40, 40]);
view(20, 64); hold off;
   colormap('jet');
```

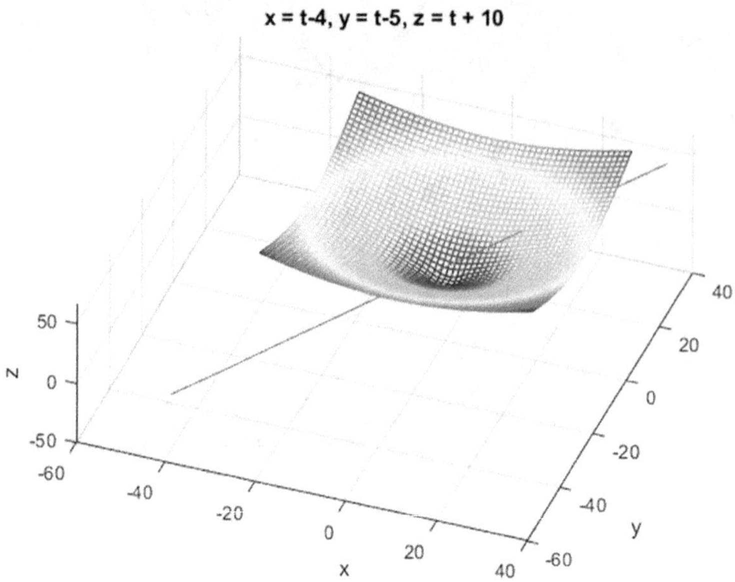

FIGURE 7.35
Output of Example 7.3.

The following example illustrates generation of extruded surfaces. The function "ezplot" generates plots of symbolic variables, "colormap" specifies the color palette to use, "ezmesh" creates a mesh of points, "axis" specifies aspect ratio of the axis (Figure 7.36).

EXAMPLE 7.4 EXAMPLE TO CALCULATE EQUATION OF THE CYLINDRICAL SURFACE FORMED BY THE GENERATING CIRCLE X = SIN(U), Y = COS(U) IS EXTRUDED PERPENDICULAR TO ITS PLANE

The following example illustrates generation of surfaces of revolution. The function "ezplot" generates plots of symbolic variables, "colormap" specifies the color palette to use, "ezmesh" creates a mesh of points, "axis" specifies aspect ratio of the axis (Figure 7.37).

```
clear; clc;
syms u v;
x1 = sin(u); y1 = cos(u); z1 = v;
C1 = [x1, y1]
S1 = [x1, y1, z1]

subplot(121), ezplot(C1(1), C1(2));
   axis square; colormap('jet');
subplot(122), ezmesh(S1(1), S1(2),
   S1(3)); axis square;
```

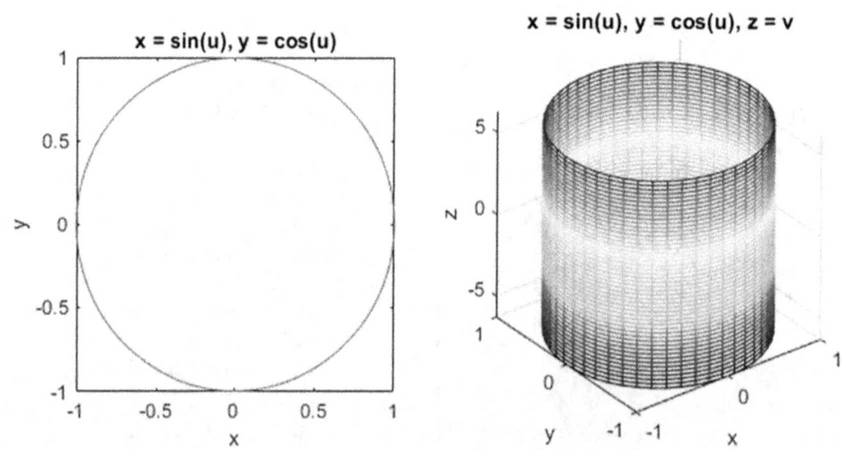

FIGURE 7.36
Output of Example 7.4.

The following examples illustrate texture mapping on plane surfaces. The function "patch" generates filled polygons, "scatter" generates a scatter plot, "grid" generates grid lines (Figure 7.38).

EXAMPLE 7.5 EXAMPLE TO CALCULATE EQUATION OF THE SPHERICAL SURFACE FORMED BY REVOLVING THE GENERATING CIRCLE X = SIN(U), Y = COS(U) AROUND ITS AXIS

```
clear; clc;
syms u v;
x = cos(u); y = sin(u);
C = [x, y];
S = [x*cos(v), x*sin(v), y];
figure,
subplot(121), ezplot(C(1), C(2));
   axis square;
subplot(122), ezmesh(S(1), S(2), S(3));
   axis square;
colormap(jet);
```

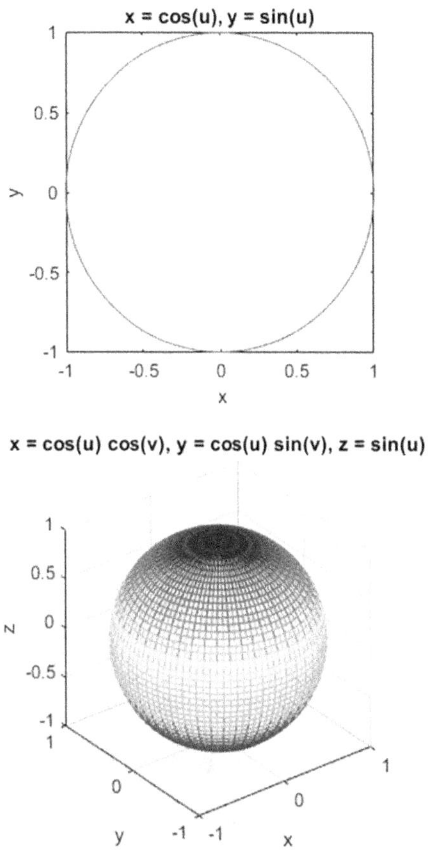

FIGURE 7.37
Output of Example 7.5.

EXAMPLE 7.6 EXAMPLE TO CALCULATE MAPPING RELATION BETWEEN TEXTURE WITH COORDINATES (0, 0), (1, 0), (1, 1), (0, 1) AND SURFACE WITH COORDINATES (5, 5), (10, 7), (12, 12), (7 , 10). ALSO FOR THE TEXTURE POINT (0.6, 0.7) TO CALCULATE THE CORRESPONDING POINT ON THE SURFACE

```
clear; clc;
x0 = 5; y0 = 5;
x1 = 10; y1 = 7;
x2 = 12; y2 = 12;
x3 = 7; y3 = 10;

M = [x1-x0, x3-x0, x0 ; y1-y0, y3-y0, y0 ; 0, 0, 1]

d1 = x1 - x0; d2 = x2 - x3;
if d1 == d2
fprintf('Transformation is affine\n');
else
fprintf('Transformation is perspective\n');
end
```

```
X1 = M*[0.6 ; 0.7 ; 1];
fprintf('For u=0.6, v=0.7, (x,y) = (%.2f, %.2f) \n', X1(1),X1(2) );

subplot(121)
x = [0 1 1 0];
y = [0 0 1 1];
c = [0 4 6 8];
colormap(jet);
patch(x,y,c); hold on;
scatter(0.6, 0.7, 20, 'r', 'filled');
axis square; hold off;
subplot(122)
x = [5 10 12 7];
y = [5 7 12 10];
c = [0 4 6 8];
colormap(jet);
patch(x,y,c); hold on;
scatter(X1(1), X1(2), 20, 'r', 'filled');
axis square; grid; hold off;
```

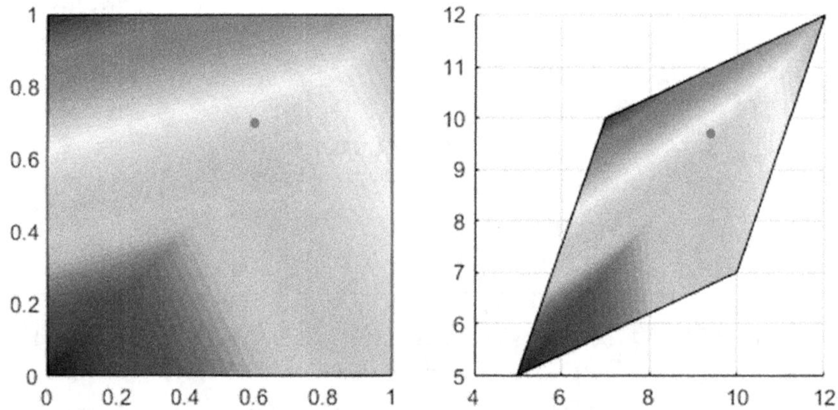

FIGURE 7.38
Output of Example 7.6.

The following examples illustrate texture mapping on non-planar surfaces. The function "warp" displays an image as a texture mapped surface, "load" loads data from file, "meshgrid" generates 2D grid coordinates, "imshow" displays an image (Figure 7.39).

EXAMPLE 7.7 EXAMPLE TO CALCULATE TEXTURE MAPPING FOR A NON-PLANAR SURFACE

```
clear; clc; load trees;
[x, y] = meshgrid(-100:100, -100:100);
S = -(x.^3 + y.^3);
figure, subplot(121),

imshow(X, map);
subplot(122), warp(x, y, S, X, map);
axis square; view(-20, 30); grid;
xlabel('x'); ylabel('y'); zlabel('z');
```

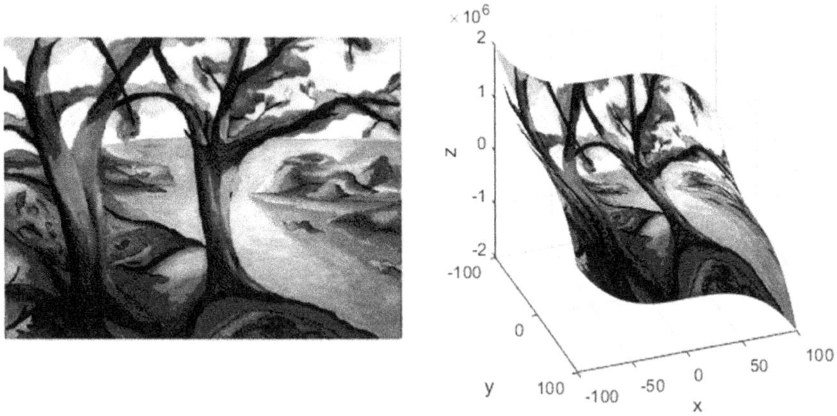

FIGURE 7.39
Output of Example 7.7.

7.9.2 Lights

The following example illustrates calculation of reflected light rays. The function "norm" returns the magnitude of a vector, "dot" calculates dot product of two vectors, "quiver3" draws an arrow in 3D space and "plot3" generates a 3D plot (Figure 7.40)

EXAMPLE 7.8 EXAMPLE TO CALCULATE THE REFLECTED RAY AND ANGLE OF REFLECTION FOR INCIDENT RAY OF L = -I + 2J - K AND NORMAL OF N = J

```
clear; clc;
L = [-1, 2, -1]; Lu = L/norm(L); L = Lu;
N = [0, 1, 0]; Nu = N/norm(N); N = Nu;
Ru = 2*dot(Lu,Nu)*Nu - Lu; R = Ru;
fprintf('Reflected ray : (%.2f)i + (%.2f)j +(%.2f)k \n', ...
    R(1), R(2), R(3));
ci = dot(L, N); ai = acosd(ci);
cr = dot(R, N); ar = acosd(cr);
fprintf('Angle of incidence : %.2f deg\n', ai);
fprintf('Angle of Reflection : %.2f deg\n', ar);

%plotting
quiver3(0, 0, 0, L(1), L(2), L(3)); hold on;
quiver3(0, 0, 0, R(1), R(2), R(3));
quiver3(0, 0, 0, N(1), N(2), N(3));
plot3(0, 0, 0, 'bo'); grid on;
xlabel('i'); ylabel('j'); zlabel('k');
text(L(1), L(2), L(3), 'L');
text(N(1), N(2), N(3), 'N');
text(R(1), R(2), R(3), 'R');
hold off;
```

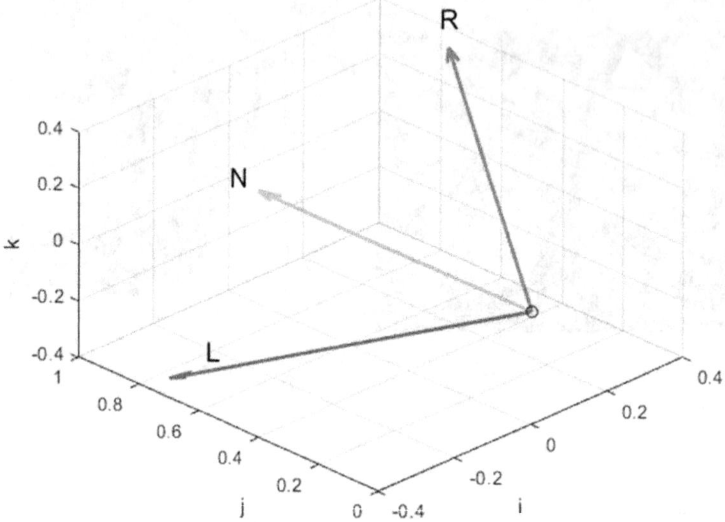

FIGURE 7.40
Output of Example 7.8.

The following example illustrates calculation of surface illumination. The function "norm" returns the magnitude of a vector; "dot" calculates dot product of two vectors.

EXAMPLE 7.9 EXAMPLE TO CALCULATE ILLUMINATION AT A POINT ON A SURFACE

```
% given incident ray L = -i + 2j - k, normal N = j, viewing direction
% V = i + 1.5j + 0.5k, L_p = 10*L_a, k_a = 0.15, k_d = 0.4, k_s = 0.8,
% m = 5

clear; clc;
L = [-1, 2, -1]; Lu = L/norm(L);
N = [0, 1, 0]; Nu = N/norm(N);
V = [1, 1.5, 0.5]; Vu = V/norm(V);
Ru = 2*dot(Lu,Nu)*Nu - Lu;
La = 1;
Lp = 10
ka = 0.15;
kd = 0.25;
ks = 0.5;
m = 5;
fprintf('Ambient intensity : \n');
Ia = La*ka
fprintf('Diffused intensity : \n');
Id = Lp*kd*dot(Lu,Nu)
fprintf('Specular intensity : \n');
Is = Lp*ks*(dot(Ru,Vu))^m
fprintf('Total intensity : \n');
I = Ia + Id + Is
```

Review Questions

- Trace the historical evolution of animation highlighting major events.
- Explain the concepts of keyframes and tweening.
- Discuss major 2D animation techniques like cel animation and motion cycling.
- Discuss how the principles of animation serve as a foundation for creating the illusion of life.
- Explain how the advent of computers led to the development of path animation.
- What are the basic steps for creating 3D animation?
- What role do interpolations play in the creation of animation?
- How can parameter curve editing be used as an alternative to frame-based animation?
- Explain the terms: hierarchical animation and inverse kinematics
- What parameters are necessary for specifying motion paths?
- Mention some common animation tasks that can be performed using a typical GUI-based 2D animation software.
- What are zones of vision in the context of 3D animation?
- Discuss the various linear and circular camera movements possible in 3D animation.
- Discuss how techniques like atmospheric effects, particle systems and space warps help to incorporate realistic effects in 3D animation.
- What is meant by rendering, and how many types of rendering are used?
- Distinguish between ray-casting and ray-tracing algorithms.
- What is a shading algorithm? Distinguish between two major types of shading algorithms.
- Distinguish between two major types of rendering algorithms.
- Mention some common animation tasks that can be performed using a typical GUI-based 3D animation software.
- Discuss some of the common applications of 2D and 3D animation.
- What are the key legal and ethical considerations in the field of animation?
- Discuss the major challenges and emerging trends for 2D and 3D animation.
- Mention some popular file formats for storage and playback of vector animation.

References

Akenine-Moller, T., E. Haines & N. Hoffman, *Real time rendering*, CRC Press, 2008

Burr, S.L., *Entertainment Law in a nutshell*, West Group, 2004

Chakraborty, S. *Fundamentals of computer graphics*, Everest Publishing House, 2010.

Foley, J.D., A. van Dam, S.K. Feiner, et al. *Computer graphics: Principles and practice*. Addison-Wesley Professional, 1990.

Glassner, A.S., *Principles of digital image synthesis*, Morgan Kauffman Publishers, 1995

Gouraud, H., Continuous shading of curved surfaces, *IEEE Transactions on Computers*, vol. C-20, no. 6, pp. 623–629, 1971.

Hearn, D., M.P. Baker. *Computer Graphics, C Version* Second edition, Prentice Hall, 1996.

O'Rourke, M., *Principles of three dimensional computer animation*, W. W. Norton & Company, 2003.

Phong B T, Illumination for computer generated pictures, *Communication of the ACM*, vol. 18, no. 6, pp. 311–317, 1975.

Roth S D, Ray casting for modelling solids, *Computer Graphics and Image Processing*, Elsevier, vol. 18, no. 2, pp. 109–144, 1982.

Rovenski, V., *Modeling of curves and surfaces with MATLAB*, Springer Germany, 2010.

Shirley, P., R.K. Morley, *Realistic ray tracing*, A K Peters/CRC Press, 2/e, 2003.

Thomas, F., O. Johnston, The illusion of life: Disney animation, *Hyperion*, 1981, reprint 1997.

Wilkins L, C. Painter, P. Patterson, *Media ethics: Issues and cases*, Rowman & Littlefield, 2021.

Zeman, N.B., *Essential skills for 3D modeling, rendering and animation*, CRC Press, 2015.

8

Compression

8.1 Compression Fundamentals

8.1.1 Key Terms

We begin with a snapshot of the important terms relevant to compression, to present the entire chapter in a nutshell. All these terms will be expanded in the following sections of the chapter in their proper contexts.

AAC: Advanced Audio Coding (AAC) is a standardized lossy compression format designed to achieve better audio quality than its predecessor MP3, at similar bit rates. Widely used in various applications AAC is known for its efficiency in delivering high-quality audio with reduced file sizes.

AVC: Advanced Video Coding (AVC), also known as H.264, is a widely used video compression standard that efficiently compresses and decompresses digital video. It provides high video quality at lower bit rates, making it suitable for various applications, including video streaming, broadcasting and video conferencing.

CODEC: Short for coder-decoder, it is a software or hardware tool that compresses or decompresses digital media files, it is essential for efficient transmission, storage and playback of audio and video content by encoding the data at source and decoding it at the destination.

DCT: Discrete Cosine Transform (DCT) is a mathematical transformation used in image and signal processing to convert spatial-domain data like pixel values in an image, into frequency domain coefficients. It is a key component in image compression algorithms such as JPEG, where the DCT helps represent the image in a more compact form for efficient storage and transmission.

DPCM: Differential Pulse Code Modulation (DPCM) is a digital signal encoding method that quantizes the difference between consecutive samples rather than each sample individually. This technique efficiently compresses audio signals by encoding the changes in amplitude reducing the data for storage or transmission.

DWT: Discrete Wavelet Transform (DWT) is a mathematical technique used in signal processing to transform and analyze signals in terms of wavelets, which are small localized waves with finite duration. DWT allows for multi-resolution analysis of a signal providing both frequency and time domain information, making it useful in various applications including image and audio compression.

Fractal compression: Fractal compression is a technique that uses fractal geometry to efficiently compress and decompress images. It represents images as iterated transformations, capturing self-replicating patterns to achieve compression, and has been applied in various fields, including image compression and texture synthesis.

HEVC: High Efficiency Video Coding (HEVC), also known as H.265, is a video compression standard designed to improve upon the efficiency of its predecessor, H.264. HEVC achieves higher compression ratios while maintaining high video quality, making it suitable for applications like 4K and 8K video streaming and storage.

Huffman Coding (HC): Huffman coding is a variable-length encoding algorithm used for lossless data compression, assigning shorter codes to more frequent symbols and longer codes to less frequent symbols. By efficiently representing the information in this manner, Huffman coding reduces the overall size of the encoded data, making it a widely used technique in compression algorithms.

JPEG: Joint Photographic Experts Group (JPEG) is a widely used image compression standard that employs lossy compression to reduce file sizes while maintaining a visually acceptable level of quality. It achieves this by selectively discarding image data, particularly in areas less sensitive to human perception, resulting in efficient compression for photographic images.

DOI: 10.1201/9781003588030-8

Lempel-Ziv Coding (LZ): Lempel-Ziv coding is a family of lossless data compression algorithms that includes popular methods like LZ77 and LZ78. These algorithms work by replacing repeated occurrences of data with references, resulting in efficient compression and widely used in various compression formats, such as gzip and DEFLATE.

Lossless compression: A data compression method that reduces the size of files without sacrificing any original data, ensuring that the compressed file can be perfectly reconstructed to its original form. This type of compression is commonly used in applications where preserving every bit of the original information is crucial, such as archival storage or medical imaging.

Lossy compression: A data compression method that achieves smaller file sizes by discarding some of the original data, often sacrificing certain details that may be less perceptible to human senses. This technique is commonly used in image, audio and video compression where a balance is struck between file size reduction and acceptable loss of quality for practical storage and transmission.

Macroblock: In video compression, a macroblock is a fixed-size block of pixels used as a unit for motion compensation. It represents a spatial area in a frame and is employed to reduce redundancy in video data, allowing for efficient compression in video coding standards like MPEG and H.264/AVC.

Motion compensation: Motion compensation is a technique used in video compression to reduce temporal redundancy by estimating and compensating for the motion of objects between consecutive video frames. By predicting the movement of pixels, motion compensation helps achieve efficient compression, allowing for the representation of video sequences with reduced data.

M-JPEG: Motion JPEG (M-JPEG) is a video compression format that compresses each frame of a video as a separate JPEG image. While less efficient in terms of compression compared to other video codecs, M-JPEG is simple and straightforward, making it suitable for certain applications where individual frame access is crucial, such as in medical systems or surveillance footage analysis.

MP3: Short for MPEG-1 Audio Layer III, MP3 is a popular audio compression format that used perceptual coding to significantly reduce file sizes while maintaining reasonable sound quality. It achieves compression by removing redundant information and is widely used for music storage and playback in various devices.

MPEG-1 Audio: MPEG-1 Audio is a compression standard for digital audio defined by the Moving Picture Experts Group (MPEG). It introduced the MP3 format, a widely used and efficient method for compressing audio files without significant loss of quality, revolutionizing the distribution and consumption of digital music.

MPEG-1 Video: MPEG-1 Video is a compression standard developed by the Moving Picture Experts Group for the encoding of digital video. It was one of the first widely adopted video compression formats, commonly used in early digital video applications and the creation of Video CDs.

MPEG-2 Audio: MPEG-2 Audio is a standard for compressing digital audio data, developed by the Moving Picture Experts Group. It is commonly used in various applications such as DVDs, digital television broadcasts and video streaming to efficiently encode audio while maintaining a good balance between compression and sound quality.

MPEG-2 Video: MPEG-2 Video is a widely used compression standard developed by the Moving Picture Experts Group for encoding digital video. Commonly utilized in broadcast television, DVDs and digital video broadcasting, MPEG-2 provides efficient compression with good video quality, making it a foundational standard in various multimedia applications.

MPEG-4 Video part 2: MPEG-4 Video Part 2, also known as Advanced Simple Profile (ASP), is a compression standard within the MPEG-4 suite, focusing on efficient video compression with enhanced features. It includes various tools for video coding and supports functionalities like object-based coding and interactivity, making it suitable for applications such as video streaming, digital television and multimedia content creation.

MPEG-4 Video part 10: MPEG-4 Video Part 10, commonly known as H.264 or AVC (Advanced Video Coding), is a widely adopted video compression standard developed by the Moving Picture Experts Group.

Renowned for its high compression efficiency and quality, H.264 is extensively used in various applications, including video streaming, video conferencing and broadcasting.

Psycho acoustic model: An algorithmic model, used in MP3, that exploits characteristics of human hearing to discard audio data that is less perceptually significant. By analyzing the frequency and amplitude perception of the human ear, the model allows compression algorithms to remove certain details from files resulting in smaller file sizes without significant loss in perceived quality.

Quadtree Segmentation: A spatial partitioning technique used in image and graphics processing to recursively divide visual data into four quadrants until a desired level of detail is reached or certain criteria are fulfilled. This hierarchical data structure is employed for efficient representation and analysis of image and graphics.

Run Length Encoding (RLE): Run-Length Encoding (RLE) is a simple compression algorithm that represents consecutive identical elements in a data stream as a single value and its count. It is often used for compressing images, where sequences of repeated pixels can be efficiently encoded by indicating the pixel value and the number of times it repeats in a run.

Vector Quantization (VQ): Vector Quantization (VQ) is a data compression technique that represents a set of data points by a smaller set of prototype vectors. By associating each data point with the nearest prototype vector, vector quantization efficiently reduces the amount of data needed to represent the original set, commonly employed in image and video compression.

8.1.2 Historical Evolution

Digital compression technology has undergone a remarkable evolution, driven by the need to efficiently store, transmit and manage digital data. Here is an overview of the key milestones in the historical development of digital compression technology:

1940s–1950s: The foundational concepts of data compression began to emerge in the late 1940s and early 1950s with the advent of digital computers. Researchers explored basic techniques to reduce the size of data for efficient storage and transmission. In 1952, David A. Huffman introduced Huffman coding, a popular algorithm for lossless data compression. It efficiently assigned variable-length codes to different symbols based on their frequency of occurrence, significantly reducing the overall bit length of data.

1960s: Run-Length Encoding, a simple, yet effective, compression technique, gained popularity in the 1960s. It involved encoding consecutive repeated elements with a single data value and count, reducing redundancy in data representation.

1970s: The 1970s saw the introduction of Differential Pulse Code Modulation (DPCM) techniques, where only the difference between consecutive data points was encoded. This approach reduced the amount of information needed to represent audio and image signals.

1980s: The 1980s marked a shift toward lossy compression methods, where some data is discarded to achieve higher compression ratios. Transform coding techniques, such as the Discrete Cosine Transform (DCT) used in JPEG compression, became prevalent for image and video compression.

1990s: The 1990s witnessed the establishment of the Moving Picture Experts Group (MPEG), which introduced widely adopted standards for video compression. MPEG-1, MPEG-2 and, later, MPEG-4 played a significant role in the compression of digital video content.

1990s–2000s: Wavelet-based compression algorithms, such as those used in JPEG2000, gained prominence in the late 1990s and 2000s. These methods offered advantages in preserving image quality at various resolutions.

2000s–Present: The 2000s saw the development of Advanced Video Coding (AVC), also known as H.264, which became a widely used standard for video compression. High-Efficiency Video Coding (HEVC or H.265), introduced in 2013, further improved compression efficiency, enabling higher-quality video at lower bit rates.

2010s–Present: The rise of online content delivery and streaming services in the 2010s emphasized the importance of efficient compression for delivering high-quality media over the internet. Adaptive bitrate streaming and advanced compression algorithms have become essential for optimizing user experience.

2020s–Present: In recent years, artificial intelligence and machine learning techniques have been applied to compression algorithms. These methods, such as neural network-based compression, aim to achieve even greater compression efficiency while maintaining perceptual quality.

8.1.3 Basic Concepts

Compared to text files, other media files like image, audio, and video take up a large amount of disk space. A typical 5-page document file occupies 75 KB of space, whereas a single image can take up about 1.4 MB, a 1-minute audio clip can take up over 10 MB and a 1-minute video clip can take up 2 GB of disk space. It is quite difficult working with such huge files because of two reasons: first, due to their huge sizes, storage requirements increase rapidly thereby increasing the cost, and second, even if there is adequate storage space, such files require large data transfer rates that may be beyond the capabilities of both the processor and the hard disk. Due to these facts it is customary to subject the media files to a process called compression. Compression reduces their file sizes using mathematical algorithms, after which it becomes much more efficient to manipulate these files. On one hand compression reduces the data storage requirements, and on the other hand the data rate for transmission and playback. The amount of compression which can be achieved depends both on the original media data and on the compression technique applied. There are various compression methods available and the compression factors can vary from two times to over ten times. Compression techniques typically exploit the redundancies associated with a file which can be statistical or perceptual, and can broadly divided into two categories based on how they manipulate the file data, namely, lossless and lossy. Compression algorithms can also be spatial or temporal depending on which type of data they have been designed to operate on.

8.1.3.1 CODEC

To compress the file and reduce its size, it needs to be filtered through specialized software called a CODEC, which is short for Compression/Decompression or Coder/Decoder. The software reads the media data and applies mathematical algorithms to reduce its size. The compressed media is stored on the disk or other storage media, usually as a different file type and extension. When the media needs to be displayed or played back either as stand-alone media or as part of a presentation, the same software is again used to decompress the data which was previously compressed. The decompression process is necessary because the playback devices like the monitor or speakers cannot directly handle compressed data. The decompression process typically takes place in the memory or buffer so that the original compressed file stays intact (Figure 8.1).

8.1.3.2 Lossless Compression

Lossless compression is a data compression technique that retains all the original data after compression and ensures perfect reconstruction upon decompression. It achieves compression by identifying and removing redundancies in the data without sacrificing any information. The data is manipulated in a way that they occupy less space and can again be reverted back to their original state. The advantage of lossless compression is that the original data stays intact without degradation of quality and can be reused multiple times. The disadvantage is that the compression achieved is not very high and may be typically of the order of 2 to 5 times. Lossless compression is used where media quality is of utmost importance and the larger space requirements may be justified. For example, in health informatics, quality of digitally stored medical images like X-ray plates and ultra-sonographs is crucial for proper diagnosis. Examples of lossless compression

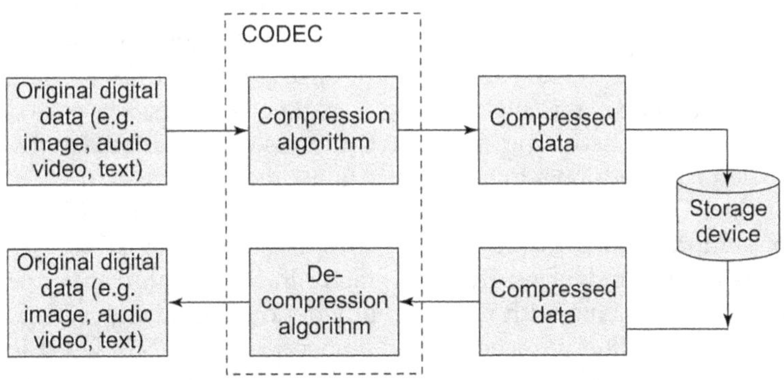

FIGURE 8.1
CODEC.

techniques include: Run-Length Encoding (RLE), Lempel-Ziv (LZ) compression algorithms (e.g., LZ77, LZ78, LZW) and Huffman coding for text, PNG (Portable Network Graphics) and TIFF (Tagged Image File Format) for images, FLAC (Free Lossless Audio Codec) for audio and HuffYUV for video.

8.1.3.3 Lossy Compression

Lossy compression, on the other hand, sacrifices some amount of data in order to achieve higher compression ratios. It involves discarding certain details that are deemed less perceptible to the human senses or less critical to the overall understanding of the content. After decompression, the original data cannot be recovered which leads to a degradation of media quality. However, if done correctly the quality loss may not be immediately apparent because of the limitations of the human eye and ears, and also because of the tendency of the human senses to bridge the gaps in information. An important consideration is how much information can be lost before it is perceptible to the human senses, and this is usually specified using a quality parameter. Compression ratios of the order of 10 to 50 times may be achieved by this method. Lossy compression is usually used where media quality may be sacrificed to a certain extent for reducing space requirements, like in multimedia educational or corporate presentations and Web-page content. Examples of lossy compression techniques include: JPEG (Joint Photographic Experts Group) for images, MP3 (MPEG Audio Layer III) for audio, MP4 (MPEG-4) for video.

8.1.3.4 Redundancies

The fundamental logic behind compression schemes lies in the strategic exploitation of redundancies present in data, a process crucial for achieving efficient compression and minimizing storage space or transmission bandwidth requirements. These redundancies can be broadly categorized into two types: statistical and perceptual. Statistical redundancies stem from the likelihood of certain symbols or patterns occurring more frequently than others in a given dataset. Compression algorithms capitalize on this non-uniform distribution of symbols by assigning shorter codes to more common elements and longer codes to less common ones. Huffman Coding and Arithmetic Coding are examples of compression techniques that focus on minimizing statistical redundancies. By representing frequently occurring elements with shorter codes, the overall average code length is reduced, contributing to a more compact representation of the data. Perceptual redundancies refer to redundancies that arise from limitations in human perception. In multimedia applications, especially in image and audio compression, certain details may be redundant or imperceptible to the human senses. Compression algorithms exploit these perceptual redundancies to discard or approximate less critical information. For instance, in image compression, the removal of high-frequency components through techniques like DCT results in perceptual compression where the loss of certain details is often imperceptible to the human eye. Similarly, in audio compression, the removal of frequencies beyond the perceptual threshold contributes to the compact representation of the audio signal without significant perceived loss in quality.

Redundancies can also be classified as spatial or temporal. Spatial redundancy occurs when neighboring data elements within a spatial domain exhibit similarity or redundancy. It is particularly relevant in spatial data, such as images or two-dimensional arrays, where neighboring elements often exhibit similarity or redundancy. In images, adjacent pixels often share similar color values. Spatial redundancy can manifest as patterns, structures or textures within the data. These repetitive elements can be exploited to reduce the amount of information that needs to be stored or transmitted. Temporal redundancy refers to the repetitive nature of information over time in a data sequence. This concept is particularly relevant in scenarios where data evolves or changes gradually, allowing for the identification and removal of redundant information. Audio sequences may contain similar sample values or video sequences can contain similar frames over a period of time.

8.1.3.5 Measurements

Evaluation of compression algorithms is essential to understand their effectiveness and performance. Various metrics are employed to quantify the compression quality and efficiency of a given algorithm. These metrics provide insights into how well the algorithm preserves the original information and how much compression it achieves. Below are some commonly used compression measurement metrics:

Compression ratio (CR): A fundamental metric that represents the ratio of the original uncompressed data (U) size to the compressed data size (C), i.e., $CR = U / C$. A higher compression ratio indicates more effective compression. It can be denoted as a fraction or a ratio, e.g., 10/4 or 2.5:1.

Compression Factor (CF): Denotes the reciprocal of compression ratio: $CF = C / U$. A lower compression factor indicates more effective compression. It is usually denoted as a fraction, e.g., 0.4.

Space Savings (SS): Used to indicate the reduction in size relative to the uncompressed size: $SS = (U - C) / U = 1 - CF$. A higher space savings indicates more effective compression. It is usually denoted as a percentage value, e.g., 60%.

Bit Rate: In case of data transmissions or streaming data where file sizes may not be known, compression can be measured by the ratio of the data rate of the compressed to the uncompressed data. Lower bit rates suggest better compression efficiency, as it implies that fewer bits are required to represent the same information. For example, data rate of uncompressed CD-quality audio is 1.4112 Mbps, while an MP3 compressed stream can have a data rate of 128 kbps, leading to a compression ratio of $(1.4112 \times 1000)/(28) = 11.025$.

8.1.3.6 Entropy

The term "entropy" originated in context to thermodynamics, where it is used to mean a measure of energy in a physical system that cannot be used to do useful work. It is also used to depict the disorder in the system. The SI unit of entropy is joules per Kelvin (J/K) which is the same unit as heat capacity. In context to information technology, the term is used to depict randomness in a signal, which in turn provides a measure of how much useful information can be carried by a signal. Suppose a signal is used to transmit a text string from a source to a destination. As a single character, say, "c", passes along an observer, it cannot be predicted with accuracy what the next character would be. Entropy is a measure of this randomness in the signal. Statistical probability models can, however, be used to provide a guess as to what the next character might be by looking at the probabilities of all the characters present. This was suggested by C E Shannon in his 1948 paper entitled "A Mathematical Theory of Communication" (Shannon, 1948), in which he derives a definition of entropy in terms of a discrete random event x having possible states $1,\ldots,n$: the entropy is the weighted sum across all symbols $c(i)$ with non-zero probability $p(i)$:

$$H = -\Sigma p(i) . \log_2 p(i)$$

As a consequence of Shannon's source coding theorem, the entropy is a measure of the smallest code-word length that is theoretically possible for the given alphabet with associated weights.

8.2 Text Compression

Text compression methods attempt to reduce size of a text file exploiting redundancies in the textual pattern or assigning smaller storage space to more frequently occurring data patterns. Techniques include RLE, Huffman coding and LZW algorithm. Text compression schemes are always lossless due to the obvious reason that lossy methods can distort or modify the textual content which is not desirable.

8.2.1 Run Length Encoding (RLE)

Run-Length Encoding is a simple and effective technique used for compressing text data by encoding consecutive, identical characters as a single value followed by the count of occurrences. This method takes advantage of redundancy present in text data, where sequences of the same character are common. In the encoding process, consecutive identical characters, known as "runs", are identified. The algorithm scans the text and locates these runs to be encoded. The runs are then represented by a pair of values – the character itself and the count of its consecutive occurrences. For example, if the original text contains the sequence "AAAABBBCCDAA", it can be encoded as "4A3B2C1D2A." RLE excels in compressing text data with long sequences of repeated characters, i.e., in scenarios where consecutive characters are the same, RLE achieves high compression ratios by replacing those sequences with a compact representation. However, RLE is less effective when the text contains minimal repeated characters, in which case, the overhead of encoding each character individually can outweigh the benefits of compression, leading to larger compressed files. Choosing an appropriate threshold for the length of runs is crucial. If the threshold is too short, the encoding may result in increased file size due to the overhead of encoding short runs. Decompression involves scanning the encoded data and reconstructing the original text by expanding the encoded runs. The algorithm reads the count associated with each character and replicates it accordingly. RLE is a lossless compression technique, ensuring that the original data can be perfectly reconstructed after decompression.

8.2.2 Huffman Coding

The Huffman coding (HC) method assigns variable-length codes to characters based on their probabilities of occurrence in the text, proposed by David A Huffman in a paper published in 1952 (Huffman, 1952). Huffman coding uses a specific method for choosing the representation for each symbol, resulting in a "prefix free" manner; i.e., the bit string representing some particular symbol is never a prefix of the bit string representing any other symbol. Given a set of symbols (characters) and their weights (probabilities) the objective is to find a prefix-free code with minimum expected codeword length. Mathematically, given a set of characters of size n, $A = \{a_1, a_2, \ldots, a_n\}$ and weights (probabilities) $W = \{w_1, w_2, \ldots, w_n\}$, the output needs to a set of binary codewords $C = \{c_1, c_2, \ldots, c_n\}$, where c_i is the codeword for a_i having probability of occurrence w_i, $i = \{1,2,\ldots,n\}$, the procedure consists of the following steps:

- Step 1: Arrange the characters in the descending order of frequencies
- Step 2: Assign code values 1 and 0 to the last two items in the list
- Step 3: Replace the items by adding their weights up and inserting a new item in the proper sorted position in the list
- Step 4: Repeat the previous steps until there are only two items in the list
- Step 5: Codeword of each character is a concatenation of the code values traversing the lists from bottom to top

To illustrate with an example, consider the following characters along with their probabilities (p) of occurrence in parenthesis: A (0.1), B (0.15), C (0.3), D (0.16), E (0.29).

Prepare sorted list: C (0.3), E (0.29), D (0.16), B (0.15), A (0.1)

Assign code values: C (0.3), E (0.29), D (0.16), B (0.15) [1], A (0.1) [0]

Add and replace: C (0.3), E (0.29), AB (0.25), D (0.16)

Assign code values: C (0.3), E (0.29), AB (0.25) [1], D (0.16) [0]

Add and replace: ABD (0.41), C (0.3), E (0.29)

Assign code values: ABD (0.41), C (0.3) [1], E (0.29) [0]

Add and replace: CE (0.59), ABD (0.41)

Assign code values: CE (0.59) [1], ABD (0.41) [0]

The process is stopped since there are only two items in the list. Codewords are generated by concatenating code values for each character traversing from right to left (Figure 8.2). The variable length codewords are as follows whose width (w) vary from 2 for characters with higher frequencies, i.e., C, D, E, to 3 for characters with lower frequencies, i.e., A, B:

Codeword A: 010, codeword B: 011, codeword C: 11, codeword D: 00, codeword E: 10

A pictorial representation of the encoding process is shown below.

Since there are 5 characters, fixed length is 3 bits/character

Code words are: 000, 001, 010, 011, 100

After compression, average bits/character = w(A)*p(A) + w(B)*p(B) + w(C)*p(C) + w(D)*p(D) + w(E)*p(E) = 3(0.1) + 3(0.15) + 2(0.3) + 2(0.16) + 2(0.29) = 0.3 + 0.45 + 0.6 + 0.32 + 0.58 = 2.25.

Hence, compression ratio CR = 3/2.25 = 1.33.

For comparison, Shannon's entropy value gives the smallest bits/character for this scenario:

$$H = \sum_i \left[-p_i.\log_2(p_i)\right] = -(0.1)\log_2(0.1) - (0.15)\log_2(0.15) - (0.3)\log_2(0.3) - (0.16)\log_2(0.16) - (0.29)\log_2(0.29) = 2.205$$

As a consequence of Shannon's source coding theorem, the entropy is a measure of the smallest codeword length that is theoretically possible for the given alphabet with associated weights. In this example, the weighted average codeword length calculated by Huffman coding is 2.25 bits per symbol, only slightly larger than the calculated entropy of 2.205 bits per symbol.

The process of decompression is simply a matter of translating the stream of codewords to individual

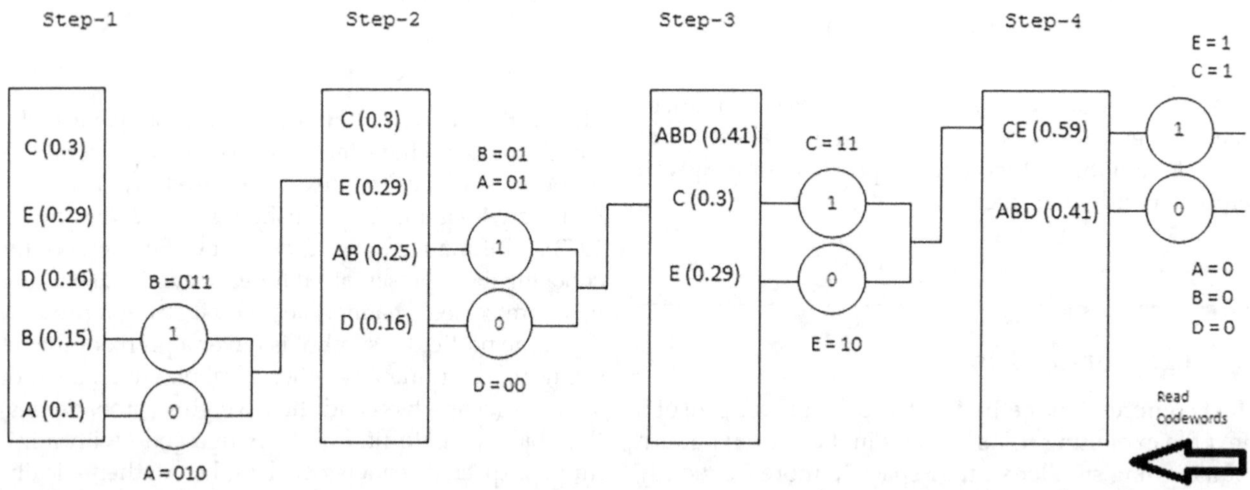

FIGURE 8.2
Huffman coding.

characters. For this, either the Huffman table with the mapping between the characters and codewords is sent to the decoder, or alternatively, at the decoder end the Huffman tree is reconstructed using the probability values of the characters.

8.2.3 Dictionary-Based Coding

While probabilistic coding techniques like HC try to represent frequently occurring symbols with shorter codes, dictionary-based coding techniques try to identify repeated sequence of symbols in the input signal and then represent them with references to previously occurring symbols stored in a dictionary. The dictionary holds strings of symbols, which might be alphanumeric characters in text files or pixel values in image files or audio samples in sound files, and then encode strings in the input signal using index/pointers/tokens of identical strings in the dictionary. There are several variants of this class of methods classified based on static dictionary and dynamic dictionary. A static dictionary is permanent sometimes allowing addition of strings but no deletion, whereas a dynamic dictionary allows for additions and deletions of entries to adapt to the input signal; hence, they are also referred to as adaptive. Lempel-Ziv compression is a family of algorithms widely used for compression using dynamic dictionaries. These algorithms, including LZ77 and LZ78, named after Abraham Lempel and Jacob Ziv in 1977 and 1978, are known for their ability to detect and eliminate redundancy in a given text by replacing repeated strings of symbols, and it can be shown that compression of strings instead of individual characters yield better compression results (Salomon, 2004).

8.2.3.1 LZ77

LZ77, also referred to as sliding window or LZ1, works by searching for repeated sequences of characters (Ziv and Lempel, 1977). At any point within the document to be compressed, the encoder keeps track of a set of previous characters kept in a reserved memory space, referred to as the sliding window. The window below is divided into two parts: the part on the left is called the search buffer (SB) which is the current dictionary, and it always includes symbols that have recently been input and encoded. The part on the right is the look-ahead buffer (LAB), containing text yet to be encoded. The algorithm searches the SB for the longest match with the beginning of the LAB, when a match is found, a 3-field token is generated which is the triplet <offset, length, symbol> where "offset" represents the distance between the matched symbols, "length" represents the length of characters matched and "symbol" represents the next symbol to be encoded in the LAB. The token is written to the output stream and the window is shifted to the right. The process continues until all the symbols in the LAB have been processed. An example for the string "abracadabra#" is shown below to illustrate the process, where # is the end of string marker.

In step 5 the nearest matching "a" is tokenized with an offset of 2 and length 1, while in step 6 the largest matching length is tokenized with offset 7 and length 4. The decoder is much simpler: it looks at a token, finds the match in its buffer, writes the match and the third token field on the output stream, then shifts the matched string and the third field into the buffer. For example, after the first two steps token <0,0,r> in step 3 generates the decoded string as "abr", token <3,1,c> in step 4 generates a matched "a" with an offset 3, length 1 followed by "c" producing a decoded string "abrac", token <2,1,d> in step 5 generates a matched "a" with offset 2 length 1 followed by "d" producing a decoded string "abracad". Finally in step 6 token <7,4,#> generates 4 matching characters at an offset of 7, i.e., "abra", followed by "#" producing a decoded string "abracadabra#".

8.2.3.2 LZ78

One of the drawbacks of LZ77 is that it makes an implicit assumption that patterns in the input sequence occurs close together. For data that do not satisfy this assumption, the previous occurrence of a matching sequence may have already shifted out of the search buffer and hence cannot be processed. Another disadvantage is that LAB must be kept small otherwise the

TABLE 8.1
LZ77 Encoding

Search Buffer (SB)							Look Ahead Buffer (LAB)						Steps	Token
							a	b	r	a	c	a	1	<0,0,a>
						a	b	r	a	c	a	d	2	<0,0,b>
					a	b	r	a	c	a	d	a	3	<0,0,r>
				a	b	r	a	c	a	d	a	b	4	<3,1,c>
		a	b	r	a	c	a	d	a	b	r	a	5	<2,1,d>
a	b	r	a	c	a	d	a	b	r	a	#		6	<7,4,#>

TABLE 8.2
LZ78 Encoding

Dictionary		Token	Dictionary		Token
index	**string**		**index**	**string**	
1	a	(0, a)	5	ad	(1, d)
2	b	(0, b)	6	ab	(1, b)
3	r	(0, r)	7	ra	(3, a)
4	ac	(1, c)	8	#	(0, #)

encoder would be become slower since searching takes longer. The LZ78, also referred to as LZ2 (Ziv and Lempel, 1978) was designed to overcome these limitations and does not use any buffers or sliding windows. The dictionary starts empty; the encoder generates a 2-field token <index, symbol>: the first field is an index to the matched item and the second is the code of the next symbol. In general, the current symbol is read and becomes a one-symbol string. The encoder then tries to find it in the dictionary, if found, the next symbol is read and concatenated with the first to form a two-symbol string that the encoder then tries to locate in the dictionary. As long as those strings are found in the dictionary, more symbols are read and concatenated to the string. At a certain point the string is not found in the dictionary, so the encoder adds it to the dictionary and outputs a token with the last dictionary match index as its first field, and the last symbol of the string as its second field. The last character of the string written to the dictionary will be the one that broke the match. In general, the dictionary starts with short strings, but as more text is being input and processed, longer and longer strings are added to it. The size of the dictionary can either be fixed or may be determined by the size of the available memory. A large dictionary may contain more strings and allow longer matches but makes the process slower. The following illustrates the process for the string "abracadabra#".

The decoder looks at the first token (0, a) and generates decoded string "a", from second token (0, b) generates "ab", from third token (0, r) generates "abr", from fourth token (1, c) looks up index 1 and inserts "a" then appends "c" making the decoded string as "abrac", from fifth token (1, d) looks up index 1 and inserts "a" then appends "d" making the decoded string as "abracad", from sixth token (1, b) looks up index 1 and inserts "a" then appends "b" making the decoded string as "abracadab", from seventh token (3, a) looks up index 3 and inserts "r" then appends "a" making the decoded string as "abracadabra", finally inserts the end-of-string marker # from the eighth token.

While LZ77 only uses the characters previous to the current position to populate the dictionary, the LZ78 algorithm also looks at the next or subsequent characters and inserts them into the dictionary using additional codes if necessary.

8.2.3.3 LZW

The most popular form of LZ78 algorithm is the LZW algorithm, a result of modifications made by Terry Welch (1984). The LZW coding (Lempel–Ziv–Welsh) coding algorithm starts by initializing the dictionary to all the symbols in the alphabet and generates a 1-field token which is an index to the dictionary. In case of 8-bit symbols the first 256 entries are occupied before any input can be processed. The encoder inputs symbols one by one and accumulates them in a string I. After each symbol is input and is concatenated to I, the dictionary is searched for string I. As long as I is found in the dictionary, the process continues, at a certain point, adding the next symbol x causes the search to fail; at this point the encoder (1) outputs the dictionary pointer that points to string I, (2) saves string Ix in the next available dictionary entry and (3) initializes string I to symbol x. The following illustrates the process for the string "abracadabra#" assuming entries

TABLE 8.3
LZW Encoding

Step	Input I	In Dict ?	New Entry	Token O/P	Step	Input I	In Dict ?	New Entry	Token O/P
1	a	Y			11	a	Y		
2	ab	N	256-ab	97 (a)	12	ad	N	261-ad	97 (a)
3	b	Y			13	d	Y		
4	br	N	257-br	98 (b)	14	da	N	262-da	100 (d)
5	r	Y			15	a	Y		
6	ra	N	258-ra	114 (r)	16	ab	Y		
7	a	Y			17	abr	N	263-abr	256 (ab)
8	ac	N	259-ac	97 (a)	18	r	Y		
9	c	Y			19	ra	Y		
10	ca	N	260-ca	99 (c)	20	ra#	N	264-ra#	258 (ra)
					21				

0 to 255 are already filled up using the ASCII character set and # is the end of string indicator:

For decoding the first token 97 produces decoded string "a", the second token 98 produces "b", third token 114 produces "r", fourth token 97 produces "a", fifth token 99 produces "c", sixth token 97 produces "a", seventh token 100 produces "d", eight token 256 produces "ab", ninth token 258 produces "ra", tenth token 265 produces "#", so concatenating all the symbols the original string can be retrieved, namely, "abracadabra".

8.3 Image Compression

Image compression is a vital area within multimedia technology that addresses the challenge of reducing the size of digital images while maintaining acceptable visual quality. Effective image compression is crucial for various applications, including image storage, transmission over networks, and multimedia content delivery. Image compression techniques encompass both lossless and lossy methods, each tailored to different requirements and constraints. Lossless compression algorithms aim to reduce file size without sacrificing any image quality, making them suitable for applications where accuracy is important, such as medical imaging or archival storage. Common lossless methods include RLE which replaces sequences of identical pixels with a single value and count, HC which represents frequently occurring pixel values with shorter codes, and LZW which identifies and replaces repetitive patterns within the image data. Lossy compression, on the other hand, selectively discards less critical image information to achieve higher compression ratios, making it ideal for applications where slight degradation in image quality is acceptable, such as Web graphics or digital photography. Popular lossy compression techniques include the DCT used in JPEG compression, which converts image data into frequency components and quantizes high-frequency components, and wavelet-based methods used in JPEG 2000, which offers improved compression efficiency and scalability. The choice between lossless and lossy compression depends on factors such as the intended use of the image, desired compression ratio and acceptable level of image degradation.

8.3.1 Lossless Image Compression

Lossless image compression is a class of methods used to reduce the size of digital images without sacrificing any image quality, by employing various mathematical and statistical methods to encode the image data in a more efficient manner while preserving all original pixel information. These methods typically exploit redundancies within the image data, such as spatial redundancies between neighboring pixels or temporal redundancies in sequences of images. Common lossless compression algorithms include LZW, RLE and Huffman coding. Lossless compression is often preferred for applications where image fidelity is critical, such as medical imaging, archival storage and professional photography. However, lossless compression typically achieves lower compression ratios compared to lossy compression techniques.

8.3.1.1 Run-Length Encoding

RLE is suitable to compress binary images like fax documents as they contain small black areas (characters) over a large white background. Images containing large areas of single colors, like maps, charts, logos, can also be efficiently compressed using RLE. The areas containing single colors consist of a number of pixels having the same RGB value, so instead of storing all the individual pixel values, only a single pixel value along with a count value as to how many times to repeat the pixel value, can be used to effectively compress those image portions. For example, 100R-50G-60Y could represent the image containing 100 pixels of red followed by 50 pixels of green followed by 60 pixels of yellow. RLE is usually not suitable for continuous tone photographic images containing a large number of varying colors. Also, large images containing RLE might take longer time to be rendered on the screen as the graphics system needs to decode the occurrence numbers and generate the additional pixel values. Another drawback of RLE is that the decoding needs to be sequential, as to generate pixel values from a specific point within the image the decoder needs to calculate how many pixels are present before that point.

8.3.1.2 Huffman Coding

For images, which are not binary but contain limited number of pixel values distributed throughout the image, Huffman coding can be used to generate variable length codes for each pixel based on their frequencies of occurrences. The compression ratio in this case depends on the frequency distribution of pixel values and the size of the Huffman codes and can vary significantly based on the image content. The process starts with the analysis of the input pixels to determine their frequencies of occurrences: for grayscale images frequency analysis of each pixel intensity in the image is carried out, for color images frequency analysis for each color channel is done separately. It might be noted here that in some cases the RGB color space may be converted to another color space like

YCbCr more suitable for human vision. The Huffman tree is constructed and a code word is assigned to each pixel intensity value, based on its position in the tree, more frequent pixel values being assigned shorter codes and less frequent pixel values longer codes. During the encoding phase each pixel value in the image is replaced by its Huffman code resulting in a sequence of variable length code words representing the original image data. The Huffman code words are either stored in a dictionary which is used during the decoding phase, or alternatively the Huffman tree is reconstructed at the decoder to map the codes back to the pixel values.

8.3.1.3 Dictionary-Based Coding

LZ coding used in image formats like GIF, PNG and TIFF, typically involves identifying repetitive patterns or sequences of data within the image and replaces them with references to previously coded data kept in a dictionary. For a static dictionary, the encoding process is a 2 pass method. In the first pass, the source image is read and a list of distinct pixel values and their frequencies are prepared, the list is sorted in descending order of frequencies and can have a maximum of 256 entries to cater to 8-bit images like GIF, after which it is written to the compressed file preceded by a 1-byte integer to represent its length. In the second pass the index of the entries in the dictionary, a number in the range [0, 255], which match with input sequences in the source file, are written to the compressed file. The decompression process is more straightforward, the decompressor decodes each index from the compressed file by locating the actual symbols from the dictionary. PNG images utilize a predictive filtering scheme predicts each pixel's value based on neighboring pixels, before applying LZ compression. This predictive filtering reduces spatial redundancy within the image after which LZ coding is applied to further compress the image data.

8.3.1.4 Differential Coding

The Differential Pulse Code Modulation (DPCM), invented by C Chapin Cutler at Bell Labs in 1950, does not code a sample value directly but instead codes the difference between the actual value of the sample and a prediction of that value; hence, it is also called predictive coding technique. The predicted value is derived from the previous sample value. The difference between the predicted and the actual value is called the prediction error. The differential coding method is particularly well suited for signals in which successive values do not differ too much from each other, e.g., image containing smoothly varying colors like gradients. Usually, for natural images or sounds, neighboring image pixels or sound samples are highly correlated; i.e., they do not differ very much. Hence, we expect the variance of the difference signal to be smaller than the original signal. At the decoder, the difference is added back to get the original values.

8.3.2 Lossy Image Compression

JPEG (Joint Photographers Expert Group) [www.jpeg.org] is the ISO/IEC international standard 10918-1 [www.iso.org/standard/18902.html] developed in 1992 in collaboration with the International Telecommunication Union (ITU) [www.itu.int/rec/T-REC-T.81]. JPEG is a compression standard for continuous-tone grayscale or color images. It uses a combination of discrete cosine transform, quantization, run length encoding and Huffman encoding techniques, and supports several modes of operation including lossless and various types of lossy modes. Its performance depends on the complexity of the image. Normally image compression ratio is around 20:1. JPEG has been designed for photographic color images with a large number of varying color or grayscale shades and will not perform well on bitonal images or line drawings. The JPEG encoding process involves several steps to compress digital images while balancing between file size and image quality. Initially, the image undergoes color space conversion, typically from RGB to YCbCr, which separates luminance (Y) and chrominance (Cb and Cr) components for reducing redundancy, as the human eye is more sensitive to changes in luminance than chrominance. Next, the image is divided into blocks, typically 8 × 8 pixels in size, and each block undergoes a DCT, which converts spatial pixel data into frequency components. The DCT results in most image information being concentrated in the lower-frequency coefficients, enabling more efficient compression. Quantization follows, where the DCT coefficients are divided by a quantization matrix, allowing for the reduction of high-frequency components that contribute less to perceived image quality. This step introduces lossy compression by discarding information, but it's the primary contributor to compression efficiency. Then, the quantized coefficients are further compressed using entropy encoding techniques like DPCM, RLE and Huffman coding, which exploit statistical redundancies within the data. Finally, additional steps such as header information encoding and inclusion of error checking codes are applied to complete the JPEG encoding process, resulting in a compressed file ready for storage or transmission.

8.3.2.1 JPEG Overview

8.3.2.1.1 Block Preparation

An image is represented by one or more 2D arrays of pixel values. For continuous tone grayscale images or color images using a CLUT there will be a single array consisting of 8-bit values for each pixel of the image. For color images, without a CLUT, there will be three 2D arrays of pixel values corresponding to R, G and B sub-components. An alternative form of representation for color images used for video signals is the YCbCr format, which also consists of three 2D arrays, but here the arrays corresponding to Cb and Cr is usually smaller than that for Y, so as to reduce the bandwidth of the chrominance signals compared to luminance signals. The block preparation step breaks each 2D array of the image into individual blocks of 8 x 8 pixels per block. These blocks are in preparation of the next step where DCT is applied to each block individually instead of to the entire image as a whole (Figure 8.3).

8.3.2.1.2 Discrete Cosine Transform

In this step, a 2D DCT is used to convert each block from the spatial to the frequency domain. Before computing the DCT however, values of each 8 × 8 block are shifted from the positive range of [0, 255] to one centered on zero, i.e., [-128, 127]. This is done by subtracting 128 from each value and reduces the dynamic range requirements in the DCT processing stage.

The forward 2D DCT is computed according to the following relation:

$$F(u,v) = \alpha_u.\alpha_v.\sum_{x=0}^{M-1}\sum_{y=0}^{N-1} f(x,y) .\cos\left\{\frac{(2x+1)\pi u}{2M}\right\}.\cos\left\{\frac{(2y+1)\pi v}{2N}\right\}$$

Here $F(u,v)$ is the DCT coefficient at frequency indices (u,v), $f(x,y)$ is the pixel value of the input image at coordinates (x,y), M and N are the dimensions of the image, u and v are the frequency indices, ranging from 0 to M-1 and 0 to N-1 respectively, angular arguments are in radians, and $\alpha_u = \sqrt{\frac{1}{M}}\text{for } u = 0, \alpha_u = \sqrt{\frac{2}{N}}\,for\, u \neq 0,$ $\alpha_v = \sqrt{\frac{1}{N}}\text{ for } v = 0, \alpha_v = \sqrt{\frac{2}{N}}\text{ for } v \neq 0$ are normalizing scale factors to make the transformation orthonormal. For the 8 × 8 block we have putting $M = N = 8$:

$$F(u,v) = \alpha_u.\alpha_v.\sum_{x=0}^{7}\sum_{y=0}^{7} f(x,y) .\cos\left\{\frac{(2x+1)\pi u}{16}\right\}.\cos\left\{\frac{(2y+1)\pi v}{16}\right\}$$

$$\alpha_u = \frac{1}{2}\sqrt{\frac{1}{2}}\text{for } u = 0, \alpha_u = \frac{1}{2}\text{for } u \neq 0,$$

$$\alpha_v = \frac{1}{2}\sqrt{\frac{1}{2}}\text{for } v = 0, \alpha_v = \frac{1}{2}\text{for } v \neq 0$$

The first frequency component term is called the DC coefficient and is proportional to the average of all pixel values, while the other frequency component terms are called AC coefficients. The coefficients are arranged according to increasing horizontal frequencies from left to right and increasing vertical frequencies from top to bottom. Since an 8 by 8 block of pixels occupies a very small area, approximately 5 mm by 5 mm, variation of color or brightness within the block will be generally small; hence, most AC coefficients will be quite small or zero and the DC

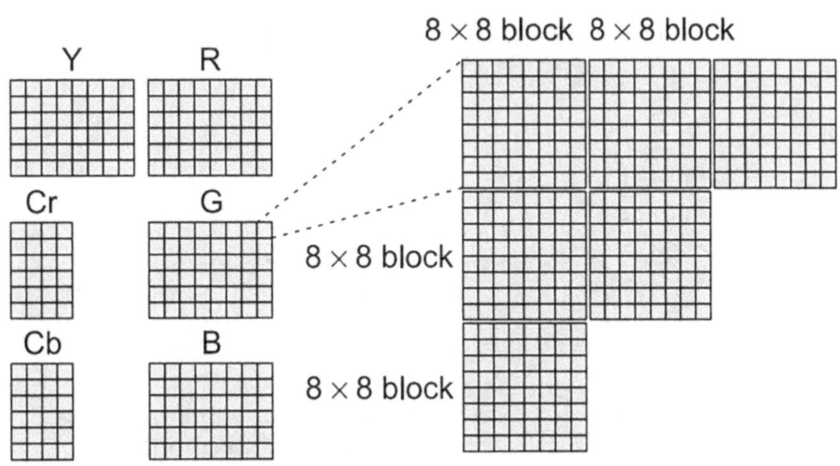

FIGURE 8.3
JPEG: Block preparation step.

coefficient values of neighboring blocks will be same or similar (Figure 8.4).

8.3.2.1.3 Quantization

So far no information has been lost. If the image is stored as such and then the inverse transform is applied, the initial image will be recovered in its exact form (in practice, small losses do occur owing to the use of fixed point arithmetic). The human eye responds primarily to the DC coefficients and lower spatial frequency coefficients. Thus, if the magnitude of a higher frequency coefficient is below a certain threshold, the eye will not detect it. This property is exploited in the quantization phase by dropping (i.e., setting to zero) the higher spatial frequency coefficients in the transformed array whose amplitudes are less than a predefined threshold value.

8.3.2.1.4 Zigzag Scan

After the DCT stage, the remaining stages involve entropy encoding. The entropy-coding algorithms operate on a one-dimensional string of values, i.e., a vector. The output of the quantization stage is, however, a 2D array. Hence, to apply an entropy scheme, the array is to be converted to a 1D vector. This operation is known as vectoring. Values in the upper-left corner of the array are non-zero while values in the lower-right corner of the array are mostly zero. Thus, a simple scan row by row from left to right would lead to a mixture of zero and non-zero values in the 1D vector, which would not be optimum for compression at a later stage. To cluster together zero and non-zero values a zigzag scan of the array is performed. The scanning is started from the top-left value and proceeds in the manner shown. The grouping together of similar values is exploited at a later stage (Figure 8.5).

8.3.2.1.5 Differential Pulse Code Modulation

There is one DC coefficient per block. The DC coefficient is a measure of the mean value of the 64 values of that block. Hence, it is the largest coefficient and because of its importance it is kept as high as possible during the quantization phase. Because of the small physical area covered by each block, the DC coefficient varies slowly from one block to the next. To exploit this similarity, the sequence of DC coefficients is encoded in DPCM mode. This means that the difference between the DC coefficient of each block and the adjacent block is computed and stored. This scheme helps to reduce the number of bits required to encode the relatively large magnitudes of the DC coefficients.

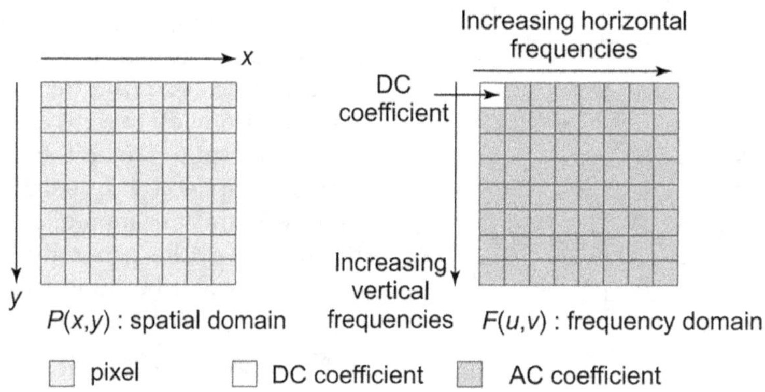

FIGURE 8.4
JPEG: DCT step.

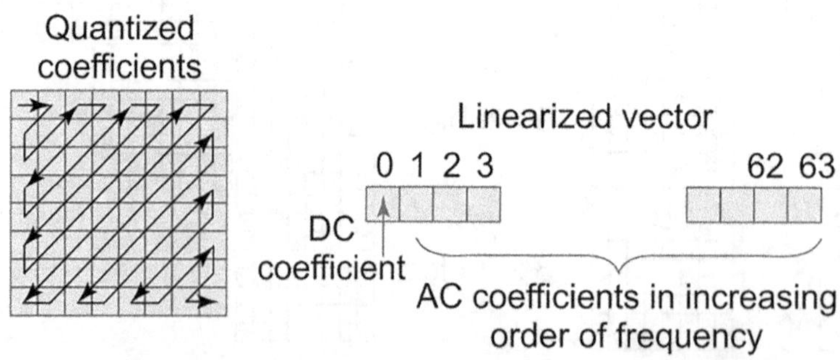

FIGURE 8.5
JPEG: Zigzag scan.

8.3.2.1.6 Run-Length Encoding

After the quantization step, only some of the AC coefficients have survived while others have been reduced to zero. The surviving values of each block are to be stored. However, many of the values might be same and to take advantage of this they are run length encoded. Due to the zigzag scan the AC coefficients of each block have been grouped in such a way that the zero values have been clustered together. To exploit this arrangement, they are encoded using the RLE scheme.

8.3.2.1.7 Huffman Coding

The final step consists of applying a Huffman encoding scheme which allocates variable length codes and requires a code table. This is applied to both the differential encoded DC coefficients of different blocks as well as the AC coefficients within each block.

8.3.2.2 JPEG Encoder

The JPEG encoder summarizes the encoding steps. The input image is split into 8 by 8 blocks of pixels. Forward DCT converts each block into frequency components and generates DC and AC coefficients. The quantization step utilizing a table of threshold values is used to reduce the data of each block by discarding the high frequency coefficients. The remaining coefficients are converted to a one-dimensional vector using a zigzag scan to cluster together similar values. The DC coefficients, being similar in value, are compressed using DPCM coding, while the AC coefficients having a lot of repeated values are exploited using RLE encoding. The final code word is allotted variable-length codes using Huffman encoding, and then associated with a frame packing step which allocates error checking codes before being stored as the compressed JPEG image (Figure 8.6).

8.3.2.3 JPEG Decoder

The JPEG decoder is made up of stages that are simply the corresponding decoder sections of those used in the encoder. On receipt of the encoded bit-stream, the frame decoder first identifies the control information and tables within the various headers. The Huffman decoder uses the Huffman table to decode the code words, after which the DPCM decoder generates the dc coefficients and the RLE decoder generates the AC coefficients. The inverse zigzag scan puts back the 64 DCT coefficients in the form of a matrix with 8 × 8 dimensions. The de-quantizer uses the quantization table to recreate the coefficient values that have not been removed. The IDCT block converts the frequency-domain components to the spatial domain to display the image as pixel values.

8.4 Graphics Compression

Graphic compression methods like quadtree segmentation and fractal compression offer innovative approaches to reducing the size of digital vector graphics files while preserving their visual fidelity. Quadtree segmentation divides the graphics content into smaller blocks recursively until a termination condition is met, such as reaching a predefined threshold for block size or achieving a desired level of detail. This hierarchical structure allows for efficient representation of both smooth areas and detailed regions in the image. Fractal compression, on the other hand, exploits self-similarity within the graphics by encoding it as a set of mathematical transformations, applied iteratively to a base image. These transformations generate a fractal code, which can be decoded to reconstruct the original content.

FIGURE 8.6
JPEG encoder and decoder.

8.4.1 Quadtree Segmentation (QT)

The quadtree is a popular data structure often used to store 2D graphics in an efficient way. On one hand, it is a means of compression by storing the graphics data using a lower number of bits, especially providing considerable savings in storage space when the graphics contains large areas of single color. On the other hand, it creates a hierarchical tree-like structure, which makes accessing, modifying, zooming and deleting specific areas of the graphics quicker and easier. As the name suggests, a quadtree divides a graphical region into four equal quadrants and successively repeats the process until a region contains homogeneous data after which it is not divided any further. Each of the regions is represented as a node in the quadtree. If a region is subdivided, the corresponding node in the sub-tree contains four child nodes representing the four sub-quadrants into which it is divided.

8.4.1.1 QT Encoder

As an example, let us consider the graphical region shown. It is an 8 by 8 region where the small squares represent pixels. Since, it is a binary graphics, the pixels can be either black or white. If we represent white by "0" and black by "1", then it requires 64 bits to store the graphical section without any compression. As mentioned before, a node in the quadtree represents a region of a graphical image. A node can either be white if the region the node represents contains only white pixels, or black if the region contains only black or gray pixels, or if the region contains a mixture of white and black pixels. The following section discusses how the encoder works and how much compression is achieved.

The top-most node represents the entire image 8 by 8 in size and is colored gray since it is a mixture of white and black pixels. The image is then divided into four quadrants of 4 by 4 pixels in each quadrant. We arbitrarily select an order to count the quadrants: in this case NW is 1, NE is 2, SE is 3, SW is 4 in a clockwise manner. Any order can be used provided that the decoding is also done in the same order. Quadrant 1 (Q1) is fully white and so it is represented using a white node, quadrant 2 (Q2) contains both types of pixels and so it is represented using a gray node, Q3 is also represented using a gray node while Q4 is fully black and so it is represented using a black node. This comprises the row 2 of the tree under the root node. Q1 and Q4 being homogeneous (all pixels of same color) are not divided further. Q2 and Q3 are further divided into four quadrants, each 2 by 2 in size and depending on whether they are homogeneous or heterogeneous, are assigned colors white/black or gray. This comprises row 3 of the quadtree. In this case, Q23 and Q33 are gray while the remaining are homogeneous. In row 4 of the table, the gray nodes of row 3, i.e., Q23 and Q33 are further subdivided into sections 1 by 1 in size and assigned appropriate colors. Since, each section in row 4 is an individual pixel they cannot be subdivided any further, and the tree structure is complete. To represent the quadtree using code values, we arbitrarily assign value "1" for a gray (heterogeneous) node, and "0" for a homogeneous node. A homogeneous node can either be white in which case it is assigned value "00" or black in which case it is assigned value "01". Starting now from the top node and traversing the tree from top to down and left to right, we write the following code strings to represent it: Starting from left "1" is the gray node of row 1, after which there are four values representing the four nodes in row 2 (within square brackets). These values are 00 (Q1), 1 (Q2), 1 (Q3), 01 (Q4). Q2 is followed by a set of four values (within braces) which are: 00 (Q21), 00 (Q21), 1(Q23), 01 (Q24). Similarly, Q3 is followed by a set of four values (within braces) which are 01 (Q31), 00 (Q32), 1 (Q33), 00 (Q34). Next Q23 is followed by a set of four values (within parenthesis) which are 01 (Q231), 00 (Q232), 00 (Q233), 00 (Q234), Similarly, Q33 is followed by a set of four values (within parenthesis) which are 00 (Q331), 00 (Q332), 01 (Q333), 00 (Q334). On careful observation, we see that the entire quadtree structure can be represented by the above string without using the brackets, namely, 1001000010100000001101001000001000001. The brackets are redundant as the first 1 represents gray (root), 00 represent white (Q1), 1 represents gray (Q2) since 10 does not have any meaning, so 1 is to be taken individually, 00 after 1 represents white (Q21), and so on. The entire data is, therefore, represented using 37 bits which implies a compression ratio of 64/37 or 1.73 (Figure 8.7).

8.4.1.2 QT Decoder

To decode a quadtree and get back the original data, we start with a blank 8 by 8 gray section. We take values in pairs 00 and 01 and put underlines below them but leave an individual "1" as it is, remembering that "10" is not a valid value. Then we put brackets after each individual "1" remembering there can be four such values following a "1". If we encounter another individual "1" within the bracket, we again use a different bracket to demarcate those four values following the 1.

Step 1: For re-building the graphics, we see that the first value after the root 1 is 00; hence, we color Q1 fully white. A value of 1 for Q2

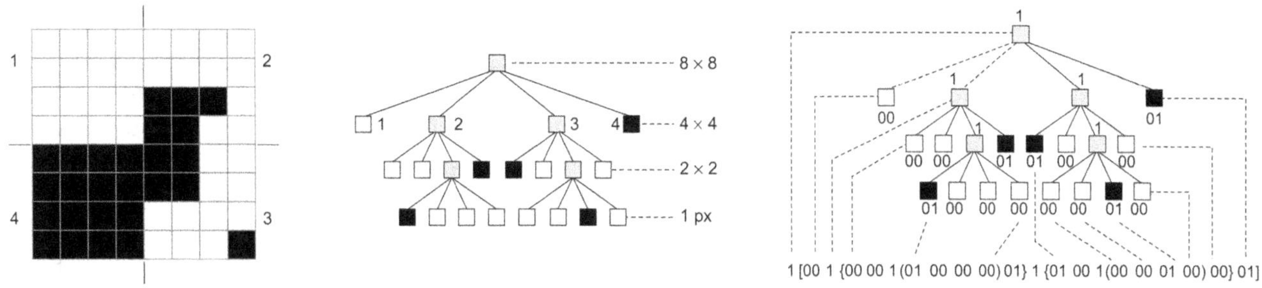

FIGURE 8.7
Quadtree encoding.

and Q3 means a mixture of black and white, so we keep them gray. A value of 01 for Q4 means that we can color it black. This gives us the step 1 partial figure.

Step 2: We look at the data following the "1" for Q2 and see that 00 means Q21 is white, 00 means Q22 is white, 1 means Q23 is gray and we do not color that for the time being, 01 means Q24 is black. Similarly, looking at the data following the 1 for Q3, we see that 01 means Q31 is black, 00 means Q32 is white, 1 means Q33 is gray and 00 means Q34 is white. This gives us the step 2 partial figure.

Step 3: We look at the 1 representing Q23 and see that it is followed by 01 (Q231), 00 (Q232), 00 (Q233), 00 (Q234) and color the pixels accordingly. We then look at the 1 representing Q33 and see that it is followed by 00 (Q331), 00 (Q332), 01 (Q333), 00 (Q334) and color the pixels accordingly. This gives us the step 3 figure which is the complete representation of the decoded figure (Figure 8.8).

8.4.2 Fractal Compression

Fractal compression is a unique and innovative approach to image and data compression that leverages the self-replicating properties of fractals to achieve high compression ratios while preserving image quality. Unlike traditional compression methods that rely on mathematical techniques and transformations, fractal compression uses fractal transformations to encode and decode images. Fractals exhibit self-similarity, meaning that they contain smaller copies of themselves, at different scales. This property allows for the efficient encoding of images through the replication of fractal patterns. Iterated Function Systems (IFS) are at the core of fractal compression, which consists of a set of mathematical transformations applied iteratively to generate a fractal pattern that approximates the original image. Fractal compression has found applications in various domains, including: image compression, medical imaging, geographical information systems, remote sensing, art and design. Fractal compression techniques vary in complexity and efficiency. Three common approaches are: standard fractal compression, vector quantization fractal compression and progressive fractal compression (Falconer, 2003).

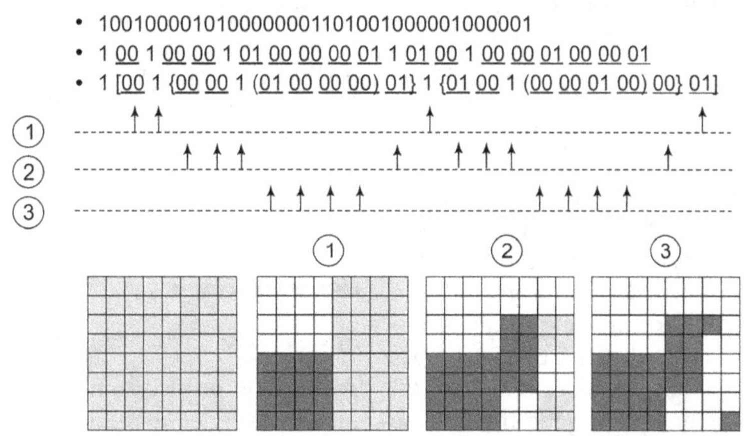

FIGURE 8.8
Quadtree decoding.

8.4.2.1 Standard Method

Standard fractal compression is the most basic form of fractal compression. It involves partitioning an image into smaller blocks, called range blocks, and searching for similar patterns, called domain blocks, within the image. Each range block is replaced by a scaled and transformed domain block, and the process is repeated until the entire image is encoded. The steps are as follows: (1) Image Partitioning: Divide the image into non-overlapping range blocks and domain blocks. The range blocks are the regions of the image that will be encoded, while domain blocks are the patterns we search for within the image. (2) Block Matching: For each range block, search for the best-matching domain block within the image. This is typically done by measuring the mean squared error (MSE) or other similarity metrics between the range block and potential domain blocks. (3) Transformation: Scale and transform the selected domain block to fit the range block. The transformation includes translation, rotation and scaling. The transformation parameters are recorded. (4) Iteration: Repeat the block matching and transformation steps for all range blocks. Iterate this process to refine the image representation, improving the match between range and domain blocks. (5) Decoding: To decode the image, apply the inverse transformation to the range blocks. Combine the transformed blocks to reconstruct the original image.

8.4.2.2 Vector Quantization (VQ) Method

Vector quantization fractal compression improves compression efficiency by using vector quantization to represent domain blocks. Instead of searching for an exact match, it quantizes domain blocks into code vectors, resulting in higher compression ratios. The steps are as follows: (1) Codebook Creation: Create a codebook of representative domain blocks. This codebook is generated by clustering similar domain blocks from the image. (2) Vector quantization: Quantize each domain block to the nearest code vector in the codebook. This replaces the domain blocks with code vectors. (3) Block Matching: For each range block, search for the best-matching code vector within the codebook. This is done by measuring the similarity between the range block and the code vectors. (4) Transformation: Scale and transform the selected code vector to fit the range block, just like in standard fractal compression. (5) Iteration: Repeat the block matching, transformation and quantization steps for all range blocks. Iterate this process to refine the image representation. (6) Decoding: Decode the image by applying the inverse transformation to the transformed code vectors and combining them to reconstruct the original image.

8.4.2.3 Progressive Method

Progressive fractal compression focuses on optimizing the encoding and decoding process for faster compression. It uses hierarchical structures to progressively refine the image representation, allowing users to view an approximation of the image before the compression process is complete. The steps are as follows: (1) Multi-resolution Pyramid: Create a multi-resolution pyramid of the image. This pyramid includes multiple versions of the image, each with varying levels of detail. (2) Progressive Encoding: Start by encoding the coarsest (lowest-resolution) version of the image. This provides a rough approximation of the image. As compression continues, refine the image representation by encoding higher-resolution versions. (3) Progressive Decoding: On the decoding side, users can view the coarsest version of the image while the compression process is on-going. The image progressively improves in quality as more data is transmitted. (4) Balancing Quality and Compression: Progressive fractal compression allows users to balance image quality and compression time. Users can stop the compression process at any point to get the desired quality level.

8.4.2.4 Challenges and Directions

Despite its potential, fractal compression has faced challenges related to encoding and decoding speed, making it less suitable for real-time applications. Future directions in fractal compression research aim to address these challenges and explore applications in emerging fields like virtual reality and augmented reality. Challenges include: (1) Encoding and Decoding Speed: Fractal compression can be computationally intensive, especially for large images and research is focused on optimizing algorithms and leveraging hardware acceleration to improve speed. (2) Quality Control: Ensuring consistent image quality across different compression levels and applications is a challenge and future research aims to develop better quality control mechanisms. Exploring how fractal compression can be applied to emerging data types, such as 3D point clouds, genomics data and immersive media, is a growing area of research.

8.5 Audio Compression

Audio compression encompasses a variety of techniques designed to reduce the size of digital audio files while maintaining acceptable audio quality. Lossless compression methods aim to achieve compression without any loss of audio data, making them suitable for applications where fidelity is critical, such as professional audio production or archival storage. Common lossless compression algorithms include FLAC (Free Lossless Audio Codec) and ALAC (Apple Lossless Audio Codec), which employ techniques like predictive modeling and entropy coding to encode audio data efficiently. Lossy compression methods, on the other hand, sacrifice some audio information to achieve higher compression ratios, making them suitable for applications where file size is a primary concern, such as streaming audio over the internet or storing large music libraries on portable devices. Popular lossy compression algorithms include MP3 (MPEG Audio Layer III), which utilizes perceptual coding techniques to discard audio data that is less audible to the human ear, and AAC (Advanced Audio Coding), which offers improved compression efficiency and audio quality compared to MP3. The choice between lossless and lossy compression depends on factors such as the intended use of the audio, desired compression ratio and acceptable level of audio degradation.

8.5.1 Lossless Audio Compression

Lossless audio compression is a method employed to reduce the size of digital audio files without compromising any audio fidelity and aim to preserve all original audio information. The main application of lossless audio compression is to create high-quality master recordings of speech and music for archival purposes so that subsequent copies can be made without introducing compression artifacts. Differential or predictive modeling is a fundamental technique used in lossless audio compression, where the audio encoder predicts each audio sample based on previous samples or a model of the signal. The difference between the predicted sample and the actual sample, known as the prediction error or residual, is then encoded and stored. Entropy coding techniques such as Huffman coding or arithmetic coding assign variable-length codes to the prediction errors based on their probabilities of occurrence. By assigning shorter codes to more frequent symbols or errors, entropy coding reduces the overall number of bits required to represent the audio data. Common lossless audio compression formats include FLAC (Free Lossless Audio Codec), ALAC (Apple Lossless Audio Codec) and MPEG-4 lossless schemes, among others.

8.5.1.1 Pulse Code Modulation (PCM)

Pulse Code Modulation (PCM) is a method used to digitally represent analog signals, such as audio or voice, by encoding the amplitude of the signal at regular intervals. In PCM, the analog signal is sampled, and each sample is quantized and assigned a binary code, allowing for accurate digital representation and reconstruction of the original analog waveform. According to the Nyquist-Shannon sampling theorem, the sampling frequency must be at least twice the highest frequency component of the analog signal to accurately reconstruct the original signal. Once the analog signal is sampled, each sample's amplitude is quantized into a finite set of discrete levels. This process involves rounding the sampled amplitude to the nearest quantization level. The number of quantization levels determines the resolution and dynamic range of the digital signal. Higher resolution results in more accurate representation of the analog signal but requires more bits per sample. The quantized samples are then encoded into digital binary code. Each sample is represented by a binary number, with the number of bits per sample determined by the quantization process. On a computer the sound is stored as a vector of samples each sample represented as a 16-bit value, and the timing between the samples being determined by the sample rate.

8.5.1.2 Differential PCM (DPCM)

DPCM (Differential Pulse Code Modulation), invented by C Chapin Cutler at Bell Labs in 1950, does not code a sample value directly but instead codes the difference between the actual value of the sample and a prediction of that value. Hence, it is also called the predictive coding technique. The predicted value is derived from the previous sample value. The difference between the predicted and the actual value, called the prediction error, is quantized using PCM techniques. The differential coding method is particularly well suited for signals in which successive values do not differ too much from each other, like natural images or sounds, where the neighboring image pixels or sound samples are highly correlated; i.e., they do not differ very much in value. Hence, the variance of the difference signal is expected to be smaller than the original signal, which implies fewer bits are required for quantization, leading to data compression. In the encoder the register holds the previous sample value, say, 6. The current sample value, say, 8, is fed as input and its difference with the register content is computed in the subtractor, i.e., +2 which is the DPCM output. The DPCM value (+2) is also fed to an Adder along with the register content (6) to provide the sample value (8) for the next computation. This value (8) is fed to the register and is used as the previous value for the next computation. For decoding, the register holds the previous value of the decoded PCM

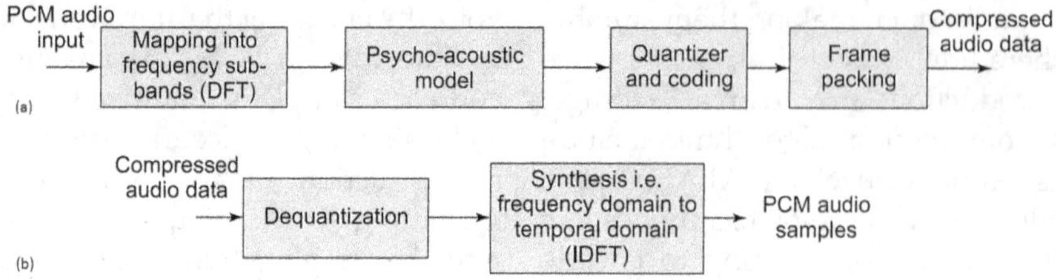

FIGURE 8.9
DPCM (a) working principle (b) encoder (c) decoder.

sample, say, 6, which is added to the current DPCM difference value (say +2) to obtain the current sample value (8). The current sample value is next fed to the register to act as the previous sample value for the next computation, i.e., 8 stored in the Register is added to the DPCM value of +4 to generate the next PCM value of 12, and so on (Figure 8.9).

8.5.1.3 Adaptive DPCM (ADPCM)

Adaptive Differential Pulse Code Modulation (ADPCM) is an extension of DPCM that dynamically adjusts its encoding parameters based on the input signal characteristics. ADPCM improves compression efficiency by adaptively selecting prediction coefficients and quantization step sizes. This adaptation may involve updating prediction coefficients or selecting different prediction algorithms based on the signal's local characteristics. ADPCM adjusts the quantization step size based on the magnitude of the prediction error or other signal properties. This adaptive quantization ensures that more bits are allocated to significant prediction errors while fewer bits are used for smaller errors, improving the signal-to-noise ratio. The adaptively quantized prediction errors are encoded using PCM encoding schemes. ADPCM is particularly useful for compressing speech and audio signals with varying dynamics and characteristics. It achieves higher compression ratios than traditional PCM and DPCM while maintaining acceptable audio quality. ADPCM is widely used in telecommunications, voice over IP (VoIP), digital audio recording and video conferencing systems.

8.5.1.4 Free Lossless Audio Codec (FLAC)

FLAC (Free Lossless Audio Codec) [www.flac.sourceforge.net] is distinguished from general lossless algorithms such as ZIP and GZIP in that it is specifically designed for the efficient packing of audio data. While ZIP may compress a CD-quality audio file 20–40%, FLAC achieves compression rates of 30–70%. FLAC uses linear prediction to convert the audio samples to a series of small, uncorrelated numbers (known as the residual) which are stored efficiently using Golomb–Rice coding. It also uses RLE for blocks of identical samples such as silent passages. FLAC's technical strengths versus other lossless CODECs lie in its ability to be streamed, as well as a fast decode time that is independent of compression level. Linear prediction is a mathematical operation where future values are estimated as a linear function of previous samples. Golomb coding is a form of entropy coding invented by Solomon W Golomb that is optimal for alphabets following geometric distribution. It uses a tunable parameter to divide an input value into two parts: the quotient and remainder. The quotient is encoded using unary coding while the remainder in truncated binary coding.

8.5.1.5 Apple Lossless Audio Codec (ALAC)

Apple Lossless Audio Codec (ALAC) [macosforge.github.io/alac] or Apple Lossless Encoder (ALE), is an audio CODEC developed by Apple Computer for lossless encoding of digital music and is stored within an MP4 (MPEG-4 Layer 14) container with the filename extension.M4A. However, it is not a variant of AAC; it uses linear prediction and can achieve compression of 2 to 3 times. It is commonly used for preserving high-fidelity audio in Apple devices and ecosystems. The ALAC algorithm predicts the value of each audio sample based on the previous samples, the difference between the predicted value and the actual value, called the prediction residual, are then quantized. The quantized residuals are further compressed using entropy techniques. ALAC also encodes embedded metadata like album artwork and track information which are stored alongside the compressed audio data.

8.5.1.6 MPEG-4 SLS

MPEG-4 SLS (Scalable Lossless) [www.chiariglione.org/mpeg/technologies/mpeg-4/mp04-sls/index.htm] coding is an extension of MPEG-4 Audio standard to allow lossless audio compression. It allows both a lossy and lossless layer for backward compatibility to MPEG-4 AAC. On top of the core MPEG-4 AAC CODEC, a scalable extension layer increases the signal-to-noise ratio reaching lossless qualities with an average compression ratio of about 58%. The scalability enables transmission of the audio stream to several recipients at different bandwidths. The SLS algorithm is a scalable transform-based coder, providing a gradual refinement of the description of the transform coefficients, starting with perceptually weighted reconstruction levels provided by the AAC core bit-stream, up to the resolution of the original input signal. In order to achieve lossless reconstruction, the SLS decoder uses an inverse Integer MDCT (IntMDCT) transform, and deterministic versions of several tools used for AAC-core bit-stream decoding.

8.5.1.7 MPEG-4 ALS

MPEG-4 ALS (Audio Lossless) is an extension of MPEG-4 Part-3 Audio [www.iso.org/standard/76383.html] to allow lossless audio compression. It is similar to FLAC and uses linear predictive coding and Golomb Rice coding. Its main features include support for 32 bits, multi-channels, tagging, streaming, arbitrary sampling rates up to 192 kHz, error correction schemes, optional storage in MP4 container, possibility of being multiplexed with video data (Liebchen et al., 2005).

8.5.1.8 OptimFROG

OptimFROG (OFR) [www.losslessaudio.org] is a proprietary lossless audio CODEC optimized for high compression ratios. As reported on its official site, OptimFROG obtains asymptotically the best lossless audio compression ratios. The compression ratios which can obtained with OptimFROG are generally ranging from 25% (silent classical music) to 70% (loud rock music) of the original audio file size. This is less compared with high-quality MP3 files (~176 Kb); however, being lossless it produces perfect copies of the original music. As reported on its website, OptimFROG uses a new audio compression technology, the generalized stereo de-correlation concept (together with the optimal predictor), which was first introduced with OptimFROG in 2001. At the time of its introduction, the new technology yielded significant better (~1.5%) compression than existing state-of-the-art lossless audio compressors. OptimFROG DualStream is a lossy CODEC, aimed to fill the gap between perceptual coding and lossless coding, having an option to produce a correction file. This file can be used, in combination with the main lossy encoded file, for lossless decoding.

8.5.1.9 Monkey's Audio (APE)

Monkey's Audio [www.monkeysaudio.com] is a lossless audio compression CODEC which use the ".APE" extension. It generally achieves compression rates that are slightly better than FLAC and significantly better than SHN. Both encoding and decoding are generally somewhat slower than with FLAC or SHN, and the decoder is problematic to implement on portable digital audio players. It suffers from relatively slow seeking, depending on the compression level chosen. The APE tag was originally developed for the Musepack (MPC) file format as a metadata container for storing information like title, artist and track number, and was later adopted for the Monkey's Audio file format as APEv2. Recently it has emerged as an alternative to the ID3 tags for the MP3 files. The main advantage of the APEv2 tag over the ID3 tag is that the latter has a very rigid structure and the changes in each version is often contradictory to those of an earlier version, e.g., a player supporting ID3v2.2 may not correctly read the ID3v2.3 format. In comparison, the APEv2 provides for a much more flexible structure.

8.5.1.10 True Audio (TTA)

TTA (The True Audio) [www.true-audio.com] is a free, simple real-time lossless audio CODEC supporting multichannel 8, 16 and 24-bit data of uncompressed WAV input files. It uses a real-time encoding/decoding algorithm allowing fast operation speed and minimal system requirements. The compression ratio is generally in the range between 30% and 70% of the original. After block decomposition, the data are subjected to intra-channel de-correlation and then transferred to prognosis stage. On this stage, the modeling of input signal is realized by a two-step adaptive filter. The difference between original and prognosis signal is transferred to entropy encoder. The residue signal is compressed by Rice coding.

8.5.1.11 WavPack (WV)

WavPack [www.wavpack.com] is a free, open-source lossless audio compression format which allows users to compress (and restore) both 16-bit and 24-bit audio files in the.WAV format. It also supports multichannel streams and high frequency sampling rates. Like other lossless compression schemes the data reduction varies with the source, but is generally between 25% and 50% for typical popular music and somewhat better than that for classical music and other sources with greater dynamic range. WavPack also incorporates a unique "hybrid" mode that provides all the advantages of lossless compression with an additional bonus. Instead of creating a single file, this mode creates both a relatively small, high-quality lossy file that can be used all by itself, and a "correction" file that (when combined with the lossy file) provides full lossless restoration. For some users, this means never having to choose between lossless and lossy compression. WavPack support was added to WinZip ver. 11. To ensure lossless mode and high operational speeds, WavPack avoids floating-point operations and is based entirely on integer math. In the default mode, it uses a weighted prediction scheme based on previous samples. For stereo sound, correlation between the left and right channels is further exploited. WavPack's encoder does not require data to be buffered ahead of encoding; it converts each sample directly to bit codes. This is computationally more efficient than Rice coding and is better for applications where coding delay is critical.

8.5.1.12 Shorten (SHN)

Shorten is an audio CODEC used to losslessly compress CD-quality audio files (44.1 kHz 16-bit stereo PCM). It is a compressed data file format similar to ZIP and RAR, but is optimized for compressing audio data [mi.eng.cam.ac.uk/reports/svr-ftp/auto-pdf/robinson_tr156.pdf]. More mature lossless audio CODECs such as FLAC, Monkey's Audio and TTA have become popular recently, although Shorten remains a popular format due to the large number of live shows in circulation encoded as Shorten files. Some applications require the lossless digital output that such CODECs provide. Shorten files use the.SHN file extension. The Shorten algorithm and the reference code that implement it were developed by Tony Robinson of SoftSound Ltd. and were made available under a generous non-commercial license. It has since been extended by Wayne Stielau to include seek tables so that one may seek within individual tracks when playing the files on one's computer.

8.5.2 Lossy Audio Compression

Lossy audio compression is a class of techniques used to reduce the size of digital audio files by selectively discarding some audio data that is considered less perceptually significant. Unlike lossless compression methods, which aim to preserve all original audio information, lossy compression sacrifices some audio fidelity in favor of achieving higher compression ratios. One of the key methods employed is perceptual coding, which takes advantage of the limitations of human auditory perception to remove audio data that is deemed less audible or less relevant to the listener. Perceptual coding techniques often involve frequency analysis of the audio signal for dividing the audio signal into frequency bands and discard high-frequency components that are less perceptible to the human ear. Additionally, psychoacoustic models are used to analyze characteristics of the audio signal and determine which components can be safely removed without significantly impacting perceived audio quality. Popular lossy audio compression formats include MP3 (MPEG Audio Layer III), AAC (Advanced Audio Coding) and OGG Vorbis, which offer varying levels of compression efficiency and audio quality. Lossy compression is commonly used in applications where reducing file size is a priority, such as streaming audio over the internet or storing large music libraries on portable devices, and where a certain level of audio degradation is acceptable.

8.5.2.1 MPEG Audio Overview

8.5.2.1.1 Time-Frequency Analysis

The Time-Frequency Analysis stage in MPEG audio compression employs techniques to transform the audio signal from the time domain to the frequency domain. Initially, the audio signal is segmented into overlapping audio frames of fixed duration, such as 20 milliseconds. Common window functions like the Hann window are applied to each frame to minimize spectral leakage and artifacts caused by abrupt signal transitions at frame boundaries. The windowed frames undergo MDCT (Modified DCT) a variant of the DCT optimized for signal processing applications. MDCT operates on overlapping audio segments and is favored due to its ability to achieve high frequency resolution with minimal temporal artifacts. The MDCT generates frequency coefficients representing the audio signal's spectral content. The number of coefficients produced by the MDCT corresponds to the frequency resolution of the analysis. Higher frequency resolution allows for more precise representation at the cost of increased computational complexity and data volume. Overlapping frames are essential to minimize artifacts at audio frame boundaries. Typically, frames overlap by 50%, ensuring that each sample contributes to multiple MDCT outputs. After processing, the MDCT outputs are overlapped and added to reconstruct the audio signal in the time domain.

8.5.2.1.2 Psycho-acoustic Analysis

A psychoacoustic model analyzes the frequency and amplitude characteristics of the audio signal and takes into account various auditory phenomena, using perceptual coding to mimic human auditory perception. At its core perceptual coding relies on psycho-acoustic phenomena like masking. Masking originates due to the limitation of the human ear which prevents us from hearing two sounds of differing loudness but close in frequency or time. Frequency masking occurs because an audible sound has a tendency to distort the threshold curve and shift it upward so that a lower amplitude sound having similar frequency values would fall below the threshold level of the curve and hence would be rendered inaudible. The human ear contains about 30,000 hair cells that detect local vibrations and convey audio information to the brain via electrical impulses. These hair cells respond to the strongest stimulation in their local region. The amount of distortion of the curve is restricted to a small region surrounding the strongest sounds. The entire range of audible frequencies is divided into a number of such regions, known as critical bands. Critical bands are much narrower at low frequencies than at high frequencies, and width of a critical band, determine the extent of the distortion of the threshold curve. They are approximately 100 Hz wide for frequencies from 20 Hz to 400 Hz and about 1 kHz wide for frequencies from 4 kHz to 5 kHz. Within a critical band of frequencies, only the strongest sound will be heard while the others are subdued. The louder sound is called masker while the quieter sound is called masked.

The model identifies these masking thresholds for each frequency band, determining the amount of masking that occurs and the frequency ranges affected. By quantifying these masking effects, the psychoacoustic model determines the perceptual importance of each frequency component. Another consideration is temporal masking where a loud sound can mask quieter sounds occurring shortly before or after it in time. The psychoacoustic model assesses temporal masking thresholds to account for these effects, ensuring that perceptually significant audio information isn't discarded due to transient sounds. Furthermore, the model takes into account the characteristics of different audio signals, such as tonal components (e.g., musical tones) and non-tonal components (e.g., noise), different masking thresholds are applied based on the presence and characteristics of tonal and non-tonal components within the audio signal. Additionally, the model also takes into account the properties of the human ear, such as frequency selectivity and loudness perception, and incorporates frequency weighting functions and loudness models to accurately represent how humans perceive sound at different frequencies and volume levels.

8.5.2.1.3 Quantization

Based on the psychoacoustic analysis, quantization is applied to the frequency components. Quantization reduces the precision of the frequency coefficients, effectively discarding information that is deemed less perceptually significant. This step introduces quantization noise, which may affect audio quality, but it's carefully controlled to minimize perceptual impact. Scale-factors are calculated for each group of frequency components to adjust the quantization step size. Scale-factors ensure that the quantization noise is distributed appropriately across different frequency bands, maintaining a consistent level of perceived audio quality.

8.5.2.1.4 Huffman Coding

The quantized frequency coefficients, along with the scale-factors and other necessary information, are encoded using Huffman coding. Huffman coding assigns variable-length codes to different symbols based on their probabilities of occurrence, resulting in more efficient representation of the audio data. Huffman tables used for encoding are typically optimized to achieve high compression ratios while minimizing the impact on audio quality.

8.5.2.2 MPEG-1 Audio

The Motion Pictures Expert Group (MPEG-1) Audio standard [mpeg.chiariglione.org/standards/mpeg-1/audio], defined in ISO Recommendation 11172-3 [www.iso.org/obp/ui/en/#iso:std:iso-iec:11172:-3:ed-1:v1:en] provides lossy compression algorithms for digital audio. Using a transform-coding algorithm (DFT or DCT), the PCM samples are converted to a set of frequency components for each sub-band. Then using known hearing thresholds and masking properties of each sub-band, a psycho-acoustic model determines various masking effects of the input signal. After discarding those frequency components whose amplitudes are below the audible threshold, the remaining components are sent to a quantizer block to determine the bit allocations for the components. Variable bit allocations are used in such a way that frequency components in the regions of highest sensitivity can be quantized with more bits. After the components are encoded, they are included in frames, whose headers carry information like error-correction codes.

In the decoder the magnitude of the frequency components are determined by the de-quantizers. These are then passed through a synthesis bank, which employs an Inverse Transform algorithm (IDFT or IDCT) to produce the PCM samples. The PCM samples are then converted to an analog signal. We notice that the psycho-acoustic model is not required at the decoder. This not only reduces the cost of the decoder but also makes it independent to the specific type of model used at the encoder. Because analysis is done within frequency bands, the method is also known as

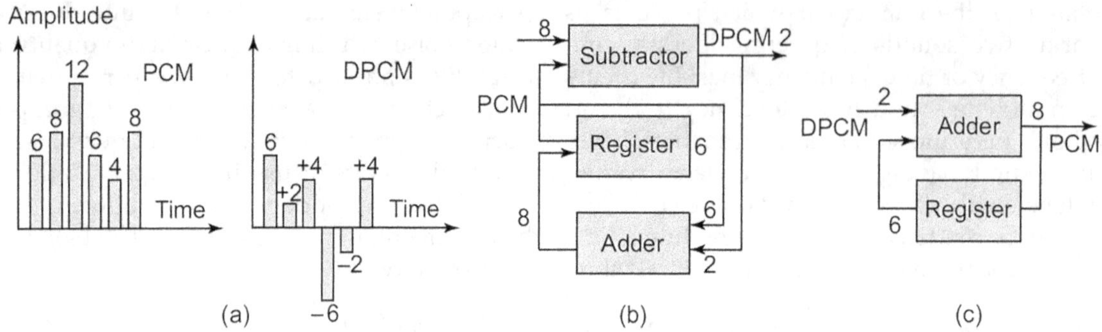

FIGURE 8.10
MPEG audio (a) encoder and (b) decoder.

sub-band coding. There are three different layers pertaining to three levels of complexities for the algorithms. All of them are based on the principle of the perceptual coder as described above. Layer I is the basic mode and Layer II and Layer III have increasing levels of complexities associated with them, which in turn produces a corresponding increase in levels of compression for the same perceived audio quality (Figure 8.10).

- MPEG-1 Audio Layer I (MP1): Layer I describes the least sophisticated method that requires relatively high data rates of about 192 kbps/channel. The compression ratio is about 4:1 and the quality is same as that of digital audio cassette.
- MPEG-1 Audio Layer II (MP2): The MPEG-1 Layer II encoding project was initiated by Fraunhofer IIS. The project was financed by the European Union as part of the EUREKA research program, commonly known as EU-147. In 1991, there were two proposals: MUSICAM (which later came to known as Layer II) and ASPEC (adaptive spectral perceptual entropy coding). MUSICAM was chosen because of its simplicity and error resistance. In 1993, MP2 (MPEG-1 Layer II) files first appeared on the Internet and were often played back using the Xing MPEG Player, and later in a program in UNIX called MAPlay released in 1994. Initially, the only encoder available for MP2 production was Xing encoder. The bit rate for Layer-2 is about 128 kbps/channel, the compression ratio ranges from 6:1 to 8:1 and the quality same as that of digital audio broadcasting.
- MPEG-1 Audio Layer III (MP3): The MPEG-1 Layer III algorithm, also widely known as MP3, allow different levels of compression using a number of different bit rates, namely, 28.9, 64, 112, 128, 192 and 320 kbps. Higher bit rates may provide stereo playback at 44.1 sampling frequency whereas lower rates will not. MP3 can compress a typical song to about 5 MB so it can be MODEM downloaded in about 5 minutes. Moreover it provides good audio quality comparable to Audio-CD. The MP3 algorithm does not specify means for encryption or copy protection, thus content may be copied indefinitely. Many shareware applications are available to encode and decode MP3 files. Beginning in the first half of 1995, MP3 files began flourishing on the Internet. Most listeners accept the MP3 bit rate of 64 kbps/channel as near CD quality, which provides a compression ratio of approximately 10:1, although listening tests show that with a bit of practice most people can distinguish the MP3 files from the CD original. We have seen above that the decoder for perceptual coding is independent of the encoder. The MPEG-1 Audio standard does not include a precise specification for an MP3 encoder. The decoding algorithm and file format are, however, well defined. Implementers of the standard are supposed to devise the algorithms themselves. As a result, there are many MP3 encoders available each producing files of differing quality.

8.5.2.3 MPEG-2 Audio

The MPEG-2 audio standard [mpeg.chiariglione.org/standards/mpeg-2/audio] was designed for applications ranging from digital HDTV television transmission to Internet downloading. It uses lower sampling frequencies (16 kHz, 22.05 kHz, 24 kHz) providing better sound quality at low bit rates (below 64 Kbps/channel). The MPEG-2 standard encompasses the MPEG-1 standard using the same coding and decoding principles as MPEG-1. It has two variants: MPEG-2

Part 3 approved in 1994 and MPEG-2 Part 7 approved in 1997. It contains two variants: MPEG-2 BC and MPEG-2 AAC.

MPEG-2 Part 3 (MPEG-2 BC): Defined as standard ISO/IEC 13818-3 [www.iso.org/standard/26797.html], this is a backward compatible extension of MPEG-1 to multichannel sound with support for five full bandwidth channels and one low frequency channel, referred to an 5.1 channel. This part of the standard is known as MPEG-2 BC (backward compatible) and can be read and decoded by an MPEG-1 decoder. MPEG-2 BC has the standard three layer structure of MPEG-1. When decoding an MPEG-2 BC stream, an MPEG-1 decoder will combine all the multi-channels into two stereo channels. Due to the compatibility MPEG-1 audio can be used together with MPEG-2 video and conversely MPEG-2 BC audio can be used with MPEG-1 video. When the MPEG-2 audio standard was published in 1995, it was discovered there were scopes of improvements on certain functionalities. Accordingly, a Second Edition of the MPEG-2 BC was developed with some minor corrections, involving improvements in cross-talk and the low-frequency channel.

MPEG-2 Part 7 (MPEG-2 AAC): Defined as standard ISO/IEC 13818-7 [www.iso.org/standard/43345.html], this is a new coding scheme which is not backward compatible with MPEG-1, and known as Advanced Audio Scheme (AAC). Due to removal of compatibility constraints, MPEG-2 AAC is considered to be an improved standard compared to MPEG-2 BC providing very high audio quality at 64 Kbps/channel for multichannel operation. It provides support for 48 main audio channels, 16 low-frequency effects (LFE) channels and 16 multi-lingual channels. MPEG-2 AAC implements three different coder complexity and performance schemes called profiles.

8.5.2.4 MPEG-4 Audio

MPEG-4 Audio or MPEG-4 Part 3 or MPEG-4 AAC (Advanced Audio Coding) standard [mpeg.chiariglione.org/standards/mpeg-4/audio] formally ISO/IEC 14496-3 [www.iso.org/standard/76383.html] first released in 1999, includes a variety of audio coding standards and targets different requirements and applications like natural sound, synthetic sound, low-bitrate, high-quality, speech, music, interactive content and so on. It consists of a number of object types and profiles. The object types allows for representation and coding of signals with different characteristics and requirements ranging from speech and music to synthetic sounds and interactive content, and each profile supports different sets of object types.

The main object types include the following: Speech and General Audio Coding (SA), Low-Complexity Spectral Band Replication (SBR), Parametric Audio Coding (PAR) Structured Audio (SAOL), Transform weighted interleave Vector Quantization (TwinVQ), Code Excited Linear Prediction (CELP), Harmonic Vector eXcitation Coding (HVXC), MPEG Surround, Audio Lossless Coding (ALS) and Scalable Lossless (SLS).

SA is optimized for speech signals and simple audio content. It employs low-complexity coding techniques such as linear predictive coding (LPC) and code-excited linear prediction (CELP) to efficiently encode speech signals and suitable for applications like teleconferencing, voice-over-IP (VoIP) and low-bitrate speech transmission.

SBR enhances the coding efficiency of MPEG-4 Audio by generating a parametric side information stream that describes the high-frequency components not explicitly coded in the main audio bitstream; by combining this side information with a lower-frequency core audio signal, SBR achieves significant compression gains while maintaining audio quality, particularly at lower bit rates.

PAR represents audio signals using a set of perceptually relevant parameters instead of directly coding the audio waveform; it extracts and encodes parameters related to spectral envelope, pitch and excitation, allowing for efficient representation of audio signals with tonal components and transient sounds, which makes it suitable for applications requiring low bit rates and scalability, such as digital broadcasting and mobile streaming.

SAOL enables the representation and synthesis of complex audio signals using procedural audio synthesis techniques and defines a high-level programming language for describing audio synthesis algorithms and interactive audio behaviors.

TwinVQ employs a combination of vector quantization and spectral shaping techniques to encode audio signals efficiently; the input audio signal is transformed into a time-frequency representation using filter banks, after which it utilizes a unique vector quantization approach to code the spectral coefficients, which groups them into vectors and quantizes them jointly to achieve better compression efficiency.

CELP operates on the principle of modeling and synthesizing speech signals using a compact codebook of excitation vectors; in the encoding process,

CELP analyzes the input speech signal and extracts parameters such as pitch, spectral envelope and residual signal, which are then used to synthesize the speech signal at the decoder using a compact codebook of excitation vectors, which are selected based on their similarity to the residual signal.

HVXC is a speech coding algorithm operating at very low bitrates of 2–4 kbps; in the encoding process, the input speech signal is analyzed to extract parameters such as pitch, spectral envelope and voicing information which are then used to synthesize the speech signal at the decoder using a sinusoidal model for voiced segments and a noise-like model for unvoiced segments.

MPEG Surround, formally ISO/IEC 23003-1 [www.iso.org/standard/44159.html] or MPEG-D part 1 [mpeg.chiariglione.org/standards/mpeg-d] also known as Spatial Audio Coding, provides a scheme to extend mono and stereo sounds to multi-channel audio by adding multi-channel information to the core bit-stream. In the encoding process, MPEG Surround extracts spatial cues and directional information from the input audio signal, such as inter-channel time and level differences, which are then encoded using parametric techniques and transmitted alongside the mono or stereo downmix signal. At the decoder, the spatial cues are decoded and combined with the downmix signal to recreate the original multi-channel audio.

ALS utilizes predictive modeling techniques to forecast future audio samples based on past samples to allow for lossless audio coding. The difference between the predicted and actual samples, known as the prediction residual, is then encoded using lossless compression algorithms such as Rice Golomb coding. Two predictors are used: a short-term predictor based on LPC and a long-term predictor with weighted residuals each with its own delay.

SLS allows both a lossy and lossless correction layers for backward compatibility to MPEG-4 AAC. On top of the core MPEG-4 AAC CODEC, a scalable extension layer increases the signal-to-noise ratio reaching lossless qualities with an average compression ratio of about 58%. The scalability enables transmission of the audio stream to several recipients at different bandwidths.

The major profiles include: main, scalable sample rate (SSR), high efficiency AAC (HE-AAC) and HE-AAC v2. The Main Profile is the baseline profile for MPEG-4 Audio, offering a wide range of audio coding tools suitable for general-purpose audio compression. It includes support for various object types such as Speech and General Audio Coding (SA), Low-Complexity Spectral Band Replication (SBR) and Parametric Audio Coding (PAR). The Main Profile provides a comprehensive solution for encoding diverse audio content, from speech and music to synthetic sounds and interactive audio. The Scalable Sample Rate (SSR) Profile is tailored for applications requiring scalability in audio quality and bitrate. It enables the encoding of audio content at multiple sample rates, allowing for efficient transmission and playback on devices with different capabilities and network conditions. The SSR Profile is beneficial for streaming media, digital broadcasting and adaptive bitrate streaming services where adaptive quality is desired. The High Efficiency AAC (HE-AAC) Profile is optimized for high-quality audio compression at low bit rates. It combines the Low-Complexity Spectral Band Replication (SBR) object type with Advanced Audio Coding (AAC) to achieve superior compression efficiency while maintaining audio quality, particularly in bandwidth-constrained environments. HE-AAC is widely used in digital broadcasting, mobile streaming and internet radio where bandwidth efficiency is critical. Building upon the HE-AAC Profile, the High Efficiency AAC v2 (HE-AAC v2) Profile introduces additional enhancements to further improve compression efficiency and audio quality. HE-AAC v2 incorporates Parametric Stereo (PS) coding, which efficiently encodes stereo audio signals with spatial image enhancement. It also supports seamless bitrate switching, allowing for smooth transitions between different quality levels during streaming.

8.6 Video Compression

Compression of digital video involves compression of the visual as well as the associated audio information. The visual information is contained within a series of frames, each of which is a still image. Hence, compression of the frames, require image-compression algorithms, i.e., spatial redundancies within each image frame are detected and removed to compress the frames individually. This is called intra-frame compression, as compression occurs within each frame. Additionally, redundancies occurring due to the correlation that exists between successive frames are also exploited, e.g., similarities that might exist between portions of different frames. Compression that employs such temporal redundancies (occurring at different points in time) is called inter-frame compression. Video compression is mostly lossy although some lossless schemes also exist. Along with the visual information, the associated audio signals in a video is also compressed using audio compression algorithms.

8.6.1 Lossless Video Compression

Lossless video compression is a method employed to reduce the size of video files without sacrificing any visual quality. Unlike lossy compression techniques, which discard some data during the encoding process, lossless compression algorithms aim to retain all original video information. This is achieved through various coding techniques that exploit redundancies and patterns within the video frames. One common approach is predictive coding, where each frame is encoded based on the difference between its pixel values and predictions made from neighboring pixels or previous frames. This prediction error, along with additional encoding parameters, is then compressed using entropy coding methods such as Huffman coding or arithmetic coding. Other techniques like spatial and temporal redundancy reduction, differential pulse-code modulation (DPCM) and RLE may also be employed to further compress the data. While lossless compression typically results in larger file sizes compared to lossy compression, it ensures that the original video content can be perfectly reconstructed during decoding, making it suitable for applications where preserving visual fidelity is paramount, such as medical imaging, archival storage and professional video editing. Common lossless audio compression formats include HuffYUV and Lagarith.

8.6.1.1 HuffYUV

HuffYUV [www.videohelp.com/software/HuffYUV] is a lossless video CODEC, first released in 2000, used to compress video in AVI format using YUV color space. Similar to lossless JPEG, the algorithm predicts each sample and the error is encoded using Huffman coding scheme. Every frame is intra-coded so there are no inter-frame dependencies. In this respect, it is similar to Motion JPEG, however, unlike MJPEG which is lossy, HuffYUV is lossless. The error signal in each channel is encoded with its own Huffman table. These tables are then stored in the output files and used when decompressing. In addition to YUV color space, it can also work with RGB data.

8.6.1.2 Lagarith

Lagarith [lags.leetcode.net/codec.html] is an open-source lossless video CODEC, first released in 2004, considered to be more efficient than HuffYUV. Like HuffYUV it avoids inter-frame prediction, and encodes–decodes each frame separately. To avoid color space conversions, thereby introducing possible round-off errors, it supports both YUV and RGB color spaces.

8.6.2 Lossy Video Compression

Lossy video compression is a method used to reduce the size of video files by selectively discarding some information that is deemed less perceptually significant, thereby achieving higher compression ratios compared to lossless compression techniques. Unlike lossless compression, where the goal is to retain every detail of the original video, lossy compression introduces some degree of data loss during the encoding process. This is typically accomplished by exploiting perceptual redundancies and limitations of human visual perception. Lossy compression algorithms often employ techniques such as spatial and temporal sub-sampling, quantization and transform coding to achieve compression. For example, spatial sub-sampling reduces the resolution of color information, temporal sub-sampling reduces the frame rate, quantization reduce the precision of pixel values, and transform coding, such as DCT or wavelet transform, helps to remove high frequency components. While lossy compression results in some loss of visual quality, the degree of loss can be controlled by adjusting compression parameters such as bit rate, quantization levels and encoding settings. Lossy compression is widely used in applications where high compression ratios are required, such as video streaming, video conferencing, digital television broadcasting and online video sharing platforms. The trade-off between compression efficiency and visual quality is carefully balanced to ensure that the compressed video remains perceptually acceptable for its intended use. Popular lossy audio compression formats include MP4 (MPEG-4 Part 2), H.265 (HEVC), VP9 and AV1.

8.6.2.1 MPEG Video Overview

8.6.2.1.1 Macroblocks and Motion Estimation

Each video frame is partitioned into rectangular blocks called macroblocks. A typical size that is mostly used is 16 × 16 pixels. Each macroblock is associated with a vector describing its location in the next frame. During encoding, motion estimation algorithms analyze each macroblock in the current frame and search for the best match in one or more reference frames, usually the preceding frame or frames. The motion estimation process determines the displacement of each macroblock by calculating a motion vector, which represents the horizontal and vertical offset required to align the macroblock with its best match in the reference frame(s). The compression algorithm starts from the original location of the block in the current frame and searches the next frame to identify where the block has moved. If the exact block is found then only a motion vector is stored with information about the displacement of the block. If the exact block cannot be found (as some of the pixel values within the block might have changed), the best match is selected and the difference of the pixel values between the original and the changed block is computed. Next, both the motion vector and the differential block information, called block residual, is encoded. The motion vectors are encoded and transmitted along with the prediction residuals to the decoder. At the decoder, motion compensation uses the motion vectors and the residuals to reconstruct the frames. This process efficiently reduces temporal redundancy by transmitting only the prediction residuals and motion vectors, resulting in significant compression gains.

8.6.2.1.2 I-frame Coding

I-frames (intracoded frames) are coded without any reference to other images, so they act as key-frames. MPEG makes use of JPEG coding for I-frames with compression ratios from 10:1 to 20:1. They can be used as a reference for other frames. In a video stream, I-frames are present at regular intervals in order to allow for the possibility of the contents being corrupted during transmission. The collection of frames between successive I-frames is known as Group of Pictures (GOP), and typical values range from 3 to 12.

8.6.2.1.3 P-frame Coding

P-frames (predictive frames) require information from the previous I- and/or P-frame for encoding and decoding. By exploiting temporal redundancies, the achievable compression ratio is higher than that of the I-frames. P-frames can be accessed only after the referenced I- or P-frame has been decoded. Encoding of P-frames is done using a combination of frame differencing and motion compensation. The number of P-frames in a GOP is, however, limited since any error present in a P-frame will be propagated to the next. The number of frames between a P-frame and the preceding I- or P-frame is called prediction span and typical values range from 1 to 3. Typical compression ratios range from 20:1 to 30:1.

8.6.2.1.4 B-frame Coding

B-frames (bidirectional predictive frames) require information from the previous and following I and/or P-frame for encoding and decoding. The highest compression ratio is attainable by using these frames. B-frames are never used as reference for other frames. Reference frames must be transmitted first. Thus transmission order and display order may differ. The first I-frame must be transmitted first followed by the next P-frame and then by the B-frames. Thereafter the second I-frame must be transmitted. Typical compression ratios range from 30:1 to 50:1 (Figure 8.11).

8.6.2.1.5 D-frame coding

A fourth type of frame known as D-frames (dc coefficient frame) is used in VoD applications. These are used to display the content when the user rewinds or fast-forwards through the movie and are ignored during the normal decoding of frames. The D-frames are highly compressed and inserted at regular intervals throughout the stream. They consist of only the encoded dc coefficients during the DCT phase and, hence, are necessarily of low resolution that can be decoded at higher speeds.

8.6.2.2 Motion-JPEG

M-JPEG or Motion JPEG [datatracker.ietf.org/doc/html/rfc2435] is a simple video compression scheme

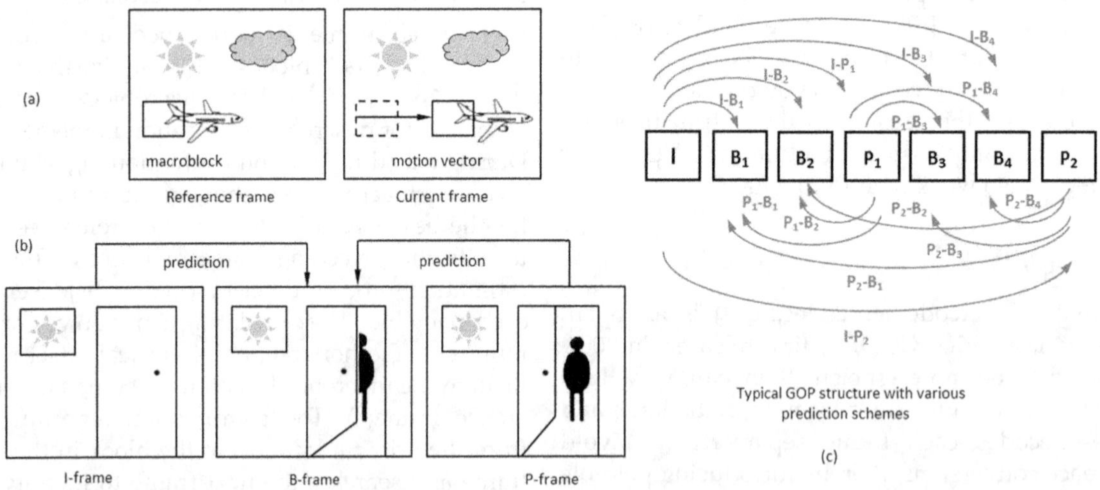

FIGURE 8.11
MPEG video compression scheme.

where each frame is coded separately as a JPEG image and then combined together into a video file. It uses only intra-frame compression where each frame is compressed using the lossy JPEG algorithm based on the DCT, before a perceptual model based on the human visual system discards high-frequency information, i.e., sharp changes in intensity and color. M-JPEG, however, avoids inter-frame compression where redundancy over successive frames is exploited. This limits its efficiency to compression ratios of around 1:20, whereas modern CODECs based on inter-frame compression can achieve compression values of around 1:50. One advantage of this is that its video quality is not degraded by fast or random motion in the video content, as is the case with CODECs like MPEG based on inter-frame compression. Originally developed for multimedia PC applications, M-JPEG has since been superseded by more advanced CODECs and nowadays mainly used in digital cameras and portable devices. It could not be standardized similar to standards like MPEG because of lack of documentation; however, RFC2435 above from IETF describes the RTP payload format for JPEG compressed video and can be consulted as reference material.

8.6.2.3 H.261

The H.261 [www.itu.int/rec/T-REC-H.261/en] was developed by ITU-T in 1988 for video-telephony and videoconferencing applications in an ISDN environment. The target bit rates are multiples of 64 kbps, and supported two frame sizes, the CIF (Common Intermediate Format) 352 × 288, and Quarter CIF (QCIF) 176 × 144. It used the DCT-based algorithms to remove intra-frame redundancy and motion compensation to remove inter-frame redundancy, did not use B-frames, as the encoder-to-decoder delay is a critical issue for lip synchronization. H.261 was the first standard in which the concept of macroblocks of 16 × 16 pixels appeared, along with 4:2:0 sub-sampling with YCbCr color space, and formed the basis of all subsequent video coding standards developed over time like MPEG-1 Part 2, H.262/MPEG-2 Part 2, H.263, MPEG-4 Part 2, H.264/MPEG-4 Part 10, H.265/HEVC.

8.6.2.4 MPEG-1 Video/MPEG-1 Part 2

The MPEG-1 video standard [mpeg.chiariglione.org/standards/mpeg-1/video] was completed in 1991 with the development of the ISO/IEC specification 11172-2 [www.iso.org/standard/22411.html] which was the standard for coding of moving pictures and associated audio for digital storage at about 1.5 Mbps. This provides for a VHS-quality video and audio suitable for CD-ROM applications and SD TV. To suit a range of applications, the user can specify a set of input parameters including frame size and frame rate. Important features provided by MPEG-1 include frame-based random access of video, fast-forward/fast-reverse searches, reverse playback of video, and editability of the compressed bit-stream. To achieve a high-compression ratio, both intra-frame and inter-frame redundancy are exploited. During the encoding phase, the color space of the frames is first converted from RGB to YCbCr. The digitized content of the Y array associated with each frame are first divided into a 2-dimensional array of 16 × 16 pixels known as the macroblock. For a 4:1:1 chroma sub-sampling scheme, the related Cb and Cr arrays each become 8 × 8 pixels in size. A macroblock, therefore, consists of four DCT blocks for luminance (i.e., 16 × 16 block of Y) and one DCT block each of the two chrominance signals (8 × 8 block of Cb and 8 x 8 block of Cr), i.e., a total of 6 DCT blocks. Each macroblock has an address associated with it. Though it offers a large variety of sizes, the coder is optimized to the SIF (Source Input Format) with resolutions of up to 352 × 288 pixels. Although the SIF calls for a horizontal resolution of 360 pixels, however, since each frame is divided into macroblocks of 16 × 16 pixels, the horizontal resolution is reduced from 360 to 352 pixels to produce an integral number of 22 macroblocks. A complete video stream is known as a sequence, which consists of a string of GOPs. Each GOP comprises a string of I, P and B frames. Each frame is made of a number of macroblocks, and each macroblock is made of a number of 8 × 8 pixel blocks.

8.6.2.5 MPEG-2 Video/MPEG-2 Part 2/H.262

MPEG-2 standard [mpeg.chiariglione.org/standards/mpeg-2/video] is formally referred to as ISO/IEC 13818-2 [https://www.iso.org/standard/61152.html] was first released in 1996. Specifically the MPEG-2 was developed to provide video quality not lower than and up to HDTV quality. Its target bit rates are 2 to 15 Mbps and it is optimized at 4 Mbps. The ITU-T Recommendations H.262 [www.itu.int/rec/T--REC-H.262] is identical to the ISO 13818-2. The basic coding structure of MPEG-2 video is the same as that of MPEG-1, that is, inter-frame and intra-frame compression with I, P and B frames. However, the design was aimed to remove some of the limitations of MPEG-1 Video as below: (1) Audio compression scheme limited to two stereo channels. (2) No standardized support for interlaced video. (3) Only one standard profile related to frame resolution and bit rate. (4) Support for only one color space YCbCr 4:2:0.

The most important differences with respect to MPEG-1 include the following: (1) Field/frame prediction modes for supporting interlaced video: Here each frame consists of two fields, a top field and a bottom field. Each field can be predicted from either field of the previous anchor frame. (2) Field/frame DCT coding syntax: Allows adaptive selection whether DCT is to be applied at the field level or the frame level. (3) Pan: Provides for parameters used to display a specified rectangle within a frame thereby including the option for panning. For example, a "4:3" region may be used to pan a "16:9" frame. (4) Scalability: MPEG-2 has several scalability features that includes spatial scalability (allows multi-resolution coding), temporal scalability (allows multiple field interlacing), SNR scalability (encoding at multiple quality levels). (5) Error concealment: Features for concealing errors in a noisy channel environment.

MPEG-2 has potentials to support a wide range of applications from mobile devices to HDTV; however, for each application it is unrealistic and too expensive to support all its features. To allow applications to support only subsets of the standard, a number of levels and profiles have been defined. The profiles specify information like coding scheme, chroma scheme, aspect ratio, while levels specify quantitative parameters like resolution, bit depth and frame rate. Some of the important profiles and levels are shown below:

Simple profile (SP): frames (I, P), chroma (4:2:0), aspect ratio (4:3/16:9)

Main profile (MP): frames (I, P, B), chroma (4:2:0), aspect ratio (4:3/16:9)

High profile (HP): frames (I, P, B), chroma (4:2:0/4:2:2), aspect ratio (4:3/16:9)

Low Level (LL): frame rates (23-30 Hz), frame size (352 × 288), bit-rate (4 Mbps)

Main Level (ML): frame rates (23-30 Hz), frame size (720 × 576), bit-rate (15 Mbps)

High Level (HL): frame rates (23-60 Hz), frame size (1920 × 1152), bit-rate (80 Mbps)

An application specifies its capabilities in terms of profiles and levels usually specified as profile@level, as for example:

Mobile handsets: SP@LL

Personal digital assistants (PDA): SP@ML

Set-top boxes (STB): MP@LL

Digital video broadcasting (DVB): MP@ML

HDTV: MP@HL

8.6.2.6 H.263

The H.263 [www.itu.int/rec/T-REC-H.263/en] was first released in 1996 and was specifically designed for very low bit rate applications like video-telephony, video-conferencing, interactive games, surveillance video, below 64 Kbps for use over wireless and public switched telephone networks. The frame formats used are QCIF and sub-QCIF (S-QCIF). As with H.261, since each frame is divided into macroblocks of 16 by 16 pixels, the horizontal resolution is reduced from 180 to 176 to produce an integer number of 11 macroblocks. Using 4:2:2 chroma sub-sampling scheme, the spatial resolutions become: Y = 176 × 144, Cb = Cr = 88 × 72 for QCIF and Y = 128 × 96, Cb = Cr = 64 × 48 for S-QCIF. Progressive scanning is used with a frame refresh rate of either 15 or 7.5 fps. The encoder is similar to H.261 encoder with the inclusion of some additional features given below: (1) Combined PB frames: To obtain higher levels of compression than H.261, H.263 which use B-frames. To use a high frame rate, neighboring P and B frames can be encoded as a single entity. (2) Unrestricted motion vectors: Motion vectors are allowed to point outside the frame area. (3) Error handling: An improved capability for handling errors. (4) Limiting errors: The concept of Group of Macroblocks (GOB) to restrict errors in one GOB from affecting other areas of the frame.

8.6.2.7 MPEG-4 Video/MPEG-4 Part 2

MPEG-4 Video (Part 2) standard [mpeg.chiariglione.org/standards/mpeg-4/video] formally ISO/IEC 14496-2 [www.iso.org/standard/39259.html] is a video-compression technology developed by MPEG first released in 1999. Similar to MPEG-1 and MPEG-2, it is also discrete cosine transform compression standard. Several popular codecs, including DivX [www.divx.com], Xvid [www.xvid.com], and 3ivx [www.3ivx.com], implement this standard. To address various applications ranging from low-quality, low-resolution surveillance cameras to high-definition TV broadcasting and DVDs, many video standards group features into profiles and levels. MPEG-4 Part 2 has approximately 21 profiles, including profiles called Simple, Advanced Simple, Main, Core, Advanced Coding Efficiency, Advanced Real Time Simple and several levels in each profile. For example, for Simple Profile (SP), maximum bitrate and maximum frame size ranges from 64 kbps/QCIF (176 × 144) at level 0 to 12 Mbps/720p (1280 × 720) at level 6, for Advanced Simple Profile (ASP) the corresponding range of values are 128 kbps/QCIF (176 × 144) to 8 Mbps/(720 × 576).

8.6.2.8 MPEG-4 Video/MPEG-4 Part 10/ AVC/H.264

MPEG-4 Part 10 [mpeg.chiariglione.org/standards/mpeg-4/advanced-video-coding] is a high-compression digital video codec standard written by the ITU-T Video Coding Experts Group (VCEG) together with the ISO/IEC Moving Picture Experts Group (MPEG) as the product of a collective partnership effort known as the Joint Video Team (JVT), first released in 2004. The ITU-T H.264 standard [www.itu.int/rec/T-REC-H.264] and the ISO/IEC MPEG-4 Part 10 standard, formally, ISO/IEC 14496-10 [www.iso.org/standard/83529.html], are technically identical, and the technology is also known as AVC, for Advanced Video Coding (Marpe et al., 2005): The intent of H.264/AVC project has been to create a standard that would be capable of providing good video quality at bit rates that are substantially lower (e.g., half or less) than what previous standards would need (e.g., relative to MPEG-2, H.263 or MPEG-4 Part 2). An additional goal was to do this in a flexible way that would allow the standard to be applied to a very wide variety of applications (e.g., for both low and high bit rates, and low- and high-resolution video) and networks/systems (e.g., for broadcast, DVD storage, RTP/IP packet networks and ITU-T multimedia telephony systems).

Some of the key features of the standard are as follows:

High compression efficiency: It offers significantly improved compression efficiency compared to its predecessors, allowing for higher-quality video at lower bitrates, which makes it ideal for streaming applications where bandwidth is limited.

Flexible Macrobook Ordering (FMO): It introduces FMO, allowing for different methods of partitioning macroblocks within a frame, which can improve error resilience and enable better handling of packet loss in network transmission.

Fidelity Range Extensions (FRExt): It supports FRExt which enabled higher color depths and sub-sampling schemes of 4:2:2 and 4:4:4.

Multiple Reference Frames: It supports multiple reference frames, allowing a frame to be predicted from multiple past frames, which enhance the quality of motion compensation, leading to better video quality, especially in scenes with high motion.

Variable block size Motion Compensation: It supports motion compensation with variable block sizes ranging from 16 × 16 to 4 × 4 enabling smoother segmentation of moving regions.

Advanced entropy coding: It uses advanced entropy coding techniques, including Context Adaptive Variable Length Coding (CAVLC) and Context Adaptive Binary Arithmetic Coding (CABAC), to further improve compression efficiency.

Scalability and Multiview: It supports scalability, allowing for the encoding of video streams at different resolutions and quality levels from a single source. It also supports multiview video coding, enabling the encoding of multiple views of a scene for applications like 3D video.

Deblocking filter: It includes a deblocking filter that helps reduce artifacts at block boundaries, resulting in smoother and more visually appealing images.

8.6.2.9 H.265/HEVC/MPEG-H Part 2

High Efficiency Video Coding (HEVC) [mpeg.chiariglione.org/standards/mpeg-h/high-efficiency-video-coding] also known as H.265 [www.itu.int/rec/T-REC-H.265] is a video compression standard designed as a successor of Advanced Video Coding (AVC) /H.264/MPEG-4 Part 10 and first released in 2013. HEVC achieves significant improvements in compression efficiency as compared to H.264 with support for variable block sizes, improved prediction modes, quadtree based block partitioning, improved motion compensation, advanced filtering to reduce artifacts, advanced scalability extensions to enable transmission of video streams with different resolutions and frame rates. HEVC videos can be included in various container formats like MP4, Quicktime and Matroska and can reduce bitrate requirements by half with comparable quality as compared to its predecessor H.264/AVC. Tiles allow for parallel processing of rectangular grids of the frame and a single entropy encoder CABAC (context-adaptive binary arithmetic coding) helps maintain higher throughput while maintaining higher compression efficiency. Compared to 8 directional modes for intra-frame prediction used in H.264, HEVC uses 33 directional modes and has more improved motion vector prediction (16-bit) compared to 8-bit in H.264. It defines 13 levels of bitstream constraints with the lowest level supporting 128 kbps bit-rate and 176 × 144 (QCIF) resolution to the maximum of around 800 Mbps and 8192 × 4320 resolution at the highest level. HEVC defines a signed 16-bit range for both horizontal and vertical motion vectors and allows for two motion vector modes: AMVP (Advanced Motion Vector Prediction) mode allows data from both reference frame and adjacent prediction blocks, and merge mode allows data from neighboring prediction blocks. The deblocking filter (DBF) applies to 8 × 8 sample block in contrast to the DBF in H.264 which applies to a 4 × 4 block, and a SAO (Sample Adaptive Offset) filter applied after the DBF allows for better reconstruction of the original signal amplitudes (Puri and Majumder, 2012).

8.6.2.10 H.266/VVC/MPEG-I Part 3

Versatile Video Coding (VVC) [mpeg.chiariglione.org/standards/mpeg-i/versatile-video-coding] also known as H.266 [www.itu.int/rec/T-REC-H.266] is a video compression standard designed as a successor of HEVC/H.265 and first released in 2020. It provides support for resolutions up to 16K (15360 × 8640) and 360° videos. It supports several color spaces including YCbCr, wide color gamut and HDR (high dynamic range).

8.6.2.11 Ogg Theora

Ogg Theora [www.theora.org] is a video compression format developed by Xiph foundation and first released in 2004. Based on On2 Technologies' VP3 codec, Ogg Theora competes with MPEG-4 (XviD and DivX), RealVideo and Windows Media Video (WMV). It uses a variable bitrate DCT based scheme with chroma sub-sampling but does not support interlacing and avoids B-frames. It is a royalty-free open standard and is most commonly packaged in the Ogg container along with the Ogg Vorbis audio streams. It employs fixed block sizes and simple motion compensation with constant bit rate resulting in potentially lower compression efficiency than more modern codecs, especially for high-motion content.

8.6.2.12 VC-1

VC-1 [datatracker.ietf.org/doc/html/rfc4425] is the informal name of the SMPTE 421M video codec standard, initially developed as a proprietary video format by Microsoft and later released as a formal SMPTE standard video format in 2006 [learn.microsoft.com/en-us/windows-hardware/drivers/display/vc-1]. VC-1 is an evolution of the conventional DCT-based video codec design also found in H.261, H.263, MPEG-1, MPEG-2 and MPEG-4 Part 2. The main goal of VC-1 development and standardization is to support the compression of interlaced content without first converting it to progressive, making it more attractive to broadcast and video industry professionals. Both HD DVD and Blu-Ray Disc had adopted VC-1 as a video standard. VC-1 is also supported by Microsoft XBox 360 and Sony Playstation 3 game consoles. It has a number of profiles and levels each with its specific resolution and bit-rate to suit a number of varied applications. Simple profile ranges from 96 kbps bit rate and frame resolution of 176 × 144 to 384 kbps and 352 × 288. Main profile ranges from 2 Mbps and 320 × 240 to 20 Mbps and 1920 × 1080 (1080p). Advanced profile ranges from 2 Mbps and 352 × 288 to 135 Mbps and 2048 × 2048.

8.6.2.13 VP-9

VP9 is an open and royalty-free compression format developed by Google [www.webmproject.org/vp9] as an open-source alternative to H.265/HEVC standard and first released in 2013. It introduces new features like larger block sizes for better motion compensation, variable block size transform coding, adaptive loop filtering techniques to reduce artifacts, divides the video into smaller tiles allowing for parallel processing of each tile, high bit-depth per channel for better color reproduction, and, scalable coding allowing for transmission of video streams with different resolutions. It supports a number of color spaces like sRGB, YCbCr, Rec. 601, Rec. 709, Rec. 2020 and Rec. 2021.

8.6.2.14 AV-1

AV-1 is a royalty-free video compression codec [www.aomedia.org/av1] developed by Alliance for Open Media (AOMedia). First released in 2018, it is designed to provide high compression efficiency without compromising on quality making it suitable for streaming over the Internet. It is based on the traditional block based frequency transform with some new features like CDEF (constrained directional enhancement filter) which reduces blocking artifacts, compound prediction which blends together predictions from two different reference frames, asymmetric partitioning to better adapt to characteristics of different video sequences, warped motion compensation for more accurate motion prediction of complex patterns, and adaptive quantization to allocate bits more efficiently to critical areas of the frame.

8.7 Numerical Problems

PROBLEM 8.1

The LZ compression scheme is used to compress a text document. The dictionary table contains 1024 entries. The average characters per word in the document, is 5. Calculate the compression achieved.

The dictionary table contains 1024 entries. Hence, it is represented by a 10-bit code word (2^10 = 1024). Thus, the index of each word in the document is a 10-bit number.

If the compression scheme was not applied, each character would have been represented by a 7-bit ASCII code.

Since there is an average of 5 characters per word, each word would need to be represented by a 35-bit number.

However, after compression each word is represented by a 10-bit number.

Hence, the compression ratio is 35:10 or 3.5:1.

PROBLEM 8.2

A document contains letters A through F with frequencies as indicated: A: 0.25, B: 0.1, C: 0.2, D: 0.15, E: 0.26, F: 0.04. (a) Use Huffman coding to derive a code word set (b) Find average number of bits per code word. (c) Find the minimum number of bits required assuming fixed-length code words.

(a) Here A(0.25), B(0.1), C(0.2), D(0.15), E(0.26), F(0.04)

Arrange in descending order: E(0.26), A(0.25), C(0.2), D(0.15), B(0.1), F(0.04)

Assign codewords to the last two items: E(0.26), A(0.25), C(0.2), D(0.15), B(0.1)[1], F(0.04)[0]

Combine and insert back into sorted list: E(0.26), A(0.25), C(0.2), D(0.15), BF(0.14)

Assign codewords: E(0.26), A(0.25), C(0.2), D(0.15)[1], BF(0.14)[0]

Combine and insert back: BDF(0.29), E(0.26), A(0.25), C(0.2)

Assign codewords: BDF(0.29), E(0.26), A(0.25)[1], C(0.2)[0]

Combine and insert back: AC(0.45), BDF(0.29), E(0.26)

Assign codewords: AC(0.45), BDF(0.29)[1], E(0.26)[0]

Combine and insert back: BDEF(0.45), AC(0.45)

Assign codewords: BDEF(0.45)[1], AC(0.45)[0]

The code word for each character are listed in order traversing from the leaf node to the root node:

w(A):01, w(B):1101, w(C):00, w(D):111, w(E):10, w(F):1100

(b) Average number of bits per code word:

2(0.25) + 4(0.1) + 2(0.2) + 3(0.15) + 2(0.26) + 4(0.04) = 0.50 + 0.40 + 0.40 + 0.45 + 0.52 + 0.16 = 2.43

(c) Since there are 6 different characters, using fixed-length code words, minimum number of bits per word is 3 (since 2^3 = 8)

PROBLEM 8.3

Use LZ77 codes to encode and decode the following text string: sir_sid_eastman

Steps	SB	LAB	Token
1		sir_sid_eastman	<0,0,s>
2	s	ir_sid_eastman	<0,0,i>
3	si	r_sid_eastman	<0,0,r>
4	sir	_sid_eastman	<0,0,_>
5	sir_	sid_eastman	<4,2,d>
6	sir_sid	_eastman	<4,1,e>
7	sir_sid_e	astman	<0,0,a>
8	sir_sid_ea	stman	<6,1,t>
9	sir_sid_east	man	<0,1,m>
10	sir_sid_eastm	an	
11	sir_sid_eastman		

Steps	Token	Decoded output (count from right to left)
1	<0,0,s>	s
2	<0,0,i>	si
3	<0,0,r>	sir
4	<0,0,_>	sir_
5	<4,2,d>	sir_sid
6	<4,1,e>	sir_sid_e
7	<0,0,a>	sir_sid_ea
8	<6,1,t>	sir_sid_east
9	<0,1,m>	sir_sid_eastm
10	<4,1,n>	sir_sid_eastman

PROBLEM 8.4

Use LZ78 codes to encode and decode the following text string: sir_sid_eastman

Index	String	Token	Index	String	Token
1	s	(0,s)	7	_e	(4,e)
2	i	(0,i)	8	a	(0,a)
3	r	(0,r)	9	st	(1,t)
4	_	(0,_)	10	m	(0,m)
5	si	(1,i)	11	an	(8,n)
6	d	(0,d)			

Index	Token	Decoded output	Index	Token	Decoded output
1	(0,s)	s	7	(4,e)	_e
2	(0,i)	i	8	(0,a)	a
3	(0,r)	r	9	(1,t)	st
4	(0,_)	_	10	(0,m)	m
5	(1,i)	si	11	(8,n)	an
6	(0,d)	d			

PROBLEM 8.5
Use LZW codes to encode and decode the following text string: sir_sid_eastman

Step	Input I	In Dict ?	New Entry	Token O/P	Step	Input I	In Dict ?	New Entry	Token O/P
1	s	Y			16	e	Y		
2	si	N	256-si	115 (s)	17	ea	N	263-ea	101 (e)
3	i	Y			18	a	Y		
4	ir	N	257-ir	105 (i)	19	as	N	264-as	97 (a)
5	r	Y			20	s	Y		
6	r_	N	258-r_	114 (r)	21	st	N	265-st	115 (s)
7	_	Y			22	t	Y		
8	_s	N	259-_s	95 (_)	23	tm	N	266-tm	116 (t)
9	s	Y			24	m	Y		
10	si	Y			25	ma	N	267-ma	109 (m)
11	sid	N	260-sid	256 (si)	26	a	Y		
12	d	Y			27	an	N	268-an	97 (a)
13	d_	N	261-d_	100 (d)	28	n	Y		
14	_	Y			29	n#	N		110 (n)
15	_e	N	262-_e	95 (_)					

Steps	Token	Decoded output	Steps	Token	Decoded output
1	115	s	8	101	e
2	105	i	9	97	a
3	114	r	10	115	s
4	95	_	11	116	t
5	256	si	12	109	m
6	100	d	13	97	a
7	95	_	14	110	n

PROBLEM 8.6
Consider a section of a grayscale image containing 100 pixels with 8 different gray levels indicated by symbols A to H using 3 bits per pixel. Calculate the minimum bits per pixel using Shannon's entropy equation if the number of occurrences of gray values is as follows: A (2), B (8), C (15), D (20), E (40), F (5), G (7), H (3).

The probability values for the gray values are: p(A) = 0.02, p(B) = 0.08, p(C) = 0.15, p(D) = 0.2, p(E) = 0.4, p(F) = 0.05, p(G) = 0.07, p(H) = 0.03

As per Shannon's entropy equation

$$H = -\Sigma p(i).\log_2 p(i) = -0.02\log_2(0.02) - 0.08\log_2(0.08) - 0.15\log_2(0.15) - 0.2\log_2(0.2) - 0.4\log_2(0.4) - 0.05\log_2(0.05) - 0.07\log_2(0.07) - 0.03\log_2(0.03)$$

$$H = -0.02(-5.64) - 0.08(-3.64) - 0.15(-2.74) - 0.2(-2.32) - 0.4(-1.32) - 0.05(-4.32) - 0.07(-3.84) - 0.03(-5.06)$$

$$H = 0.11 + 0.29 + 0.41 + 0.46 + 0.53 + 0.22 + 0.27 + 0.15 = 2.44$$

Thus the minimum bits per pixel for the given probabilities is 2.44

PROBLEM 8.7
Consider two pixels with grayscale intensities p_1 and p_2 having probabilities 0.8 and 0.2 respectively within an image. Calculate the Huffman codes of all combinations of the pixels taken two at a time.

If the pixels are encoded individually, a variable-size encoder would assign 1-bit codes to each of the pixels. We now generate all combinations of the two pixels taken two at a time along with their probability values:

Combination c1: p_1p_1, probability: $0.8 \times 0.8 = 0.64$

Combination c2: p_1p_2, probability: $0.8 \times 0.2 = 0.16$

Combination c3: p_2p_1, probability: $0.2 \times 0.8 = 0.16$

Combination c4: p_2p_2, probability: $0.2 \times 0.2 = 0.04$

Assigning Huffman codes:

c1(0.64), c2 (0.16), c3(0.16), c4(0.04)

c1(0.64), c2 (0.16), c3(0.16) [1], c4(0.04) [0]

c1(0.64), c3c4(0.2) [1], c2 (0.16) [0]

c1(0.64) [1], c2c3c4(0.36) [0]

This gives the codewords as follows: c1 (1), c2 (00), c3 (011), c4 (010)

The average size of the Huffman code per combination is: 1(0.64) + 2(0.16) + 3(0.16) + 3(0.04) = 1.56 bits which implies 0.78 bits/pixel.

This shows that better compression results are obtained by encoding combinations of the pixels instead of the individual pixels themselves.

PROBLEM 8.8

Repeat the previous problem considering all combinations of the pixels taken three at a time.

Combinations of the two pixels taken three at a time along with their probability values:

Combination c1: $p_1p_1p_1$, probability: $0.8 \times 0.8 \times 0.8 = 0.512$

Combination c2: $p_1p_1p_2$, probability: $0.8 \times 0.8 \times 0.2 = 0.128$

Combination c3: $p_1p_2p_1$, probability: $0.8 \times 0.2 \times 0.8 = 0.128$

Combination c4: $p_1p_2p_2$, probability: $0.8 \times 0.2 \times 0.2 = 0.032$

Combination c5: $p_2p_1p_1$, probability: $0.2 \times 0.8 \times 0.8 = 0.128$

Combination c6: $p_2p_1p_2$, probability: $0.2 \times 0.8 \times 0.2 = 0.032$

Combination c7: $p_2p_2p_1$, probability: $0.2 \times 0.2 \times 0.8 = 0.032$

Combination c8: $p_2p_2p_2$, probability: $0.2 \times 0.2 \times 0.2 = 0.008$

Assigning Huffman codes:

c1 (0.512), c2 (0.128), c3 (0.128), c5 (0.128), c4 (0.032), c6 (0.032), c7 (0.032), c8 (0.008)

c1 (0.512), c2 (0.128), c3 (0.128), c5 (0.128), c4 (0.032), c6 (0.032), c7 (0.032) [1], c8 (0.008) [0]

c1 (0.512), c2 (0.128), c3 (0.128), c5 (0.128), c7c8 (0.04), c4 (0.032) [1], c6 (0.032) [0]

c1 (0.512), c2 (0.128), c3 (0.128), c5 (0.128), c4c6 (0.064) [1], c7c8 (0.04) [0]

c1 (0.512), c2 (0.128), c3 (0.128), c5 (0.128) [1], c4c6c7c8 (0.068) [0]

c1 (0.512), c4c5c6c7c8 (0.196), c2 (0.128) [1], c3 (0.128) [0]

c1 (0.512), c2c3 (0.256) [1], c4c5c6c7c8 (0.196) [0]

c1 (0.512) [1], c2c3c4c5c6c7c8 (0.452) [0]

Codewords:

c1 (1), c2 (011), c3 (010), c4 (00011), c5 (001), c6 (00010), c7 (00001), c8 (00000)

The average size of the Huffman code per combination is: $1 \times 0.512 + 3 \times 3 \times 0.128 + 3 \times 5 \times 0.032 + 5 \times 0.008 = 2.184$ bits per string, which equals 0.728 bits per symbol.

PROBLEM 8.9

Consider a 3-bit 100 pixel image containing 8 different gray levels A to H whose histogram is given by [2, 9, 12, 20, 25, 16, 12, 4]. Calculate how much compression can be achieved using Huffman codes.

E (25), D (20), F (16), C (12), G (12), B (9), H (4), A (2)

E (25), D (20), F (16), C (12), G (12), B (9), H (4) [1], A (2) [0]

E (25), D (20), F (16), C (12), G (12), B (9) [1], AH (6) [0]

E (25), D (20), F (16), ABH (15), C (12) [1], G (12) [0]

E (25), CG (24), D (20), F (16) [1], ABH (15) [0]

ABFH (31), E (25), CG (24) [1], D (20) [0]

CDG (44), ABFH (31) [1], E (25) [0]

ABEFH (56) [1], CDG (44) [0]

Codewords (Figure 8.12):

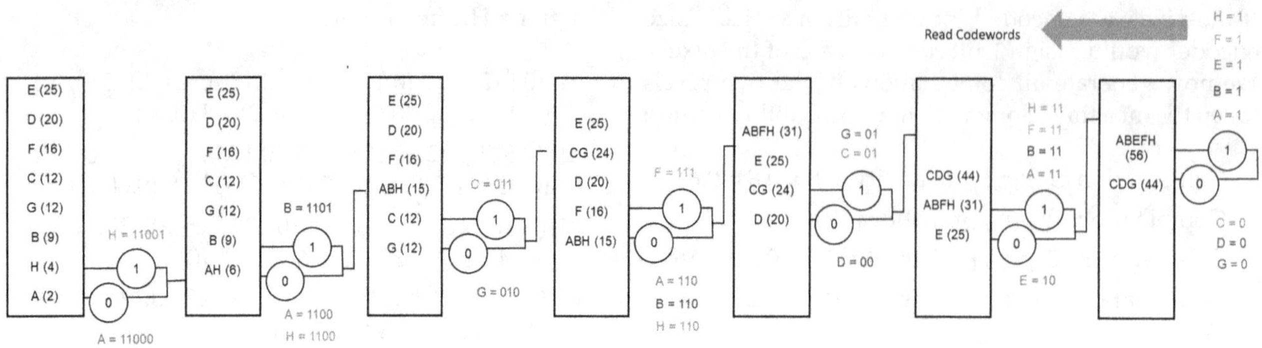

FIGURE 8.12
Huffman Coding (Problem 8.9).

A (11000), B (1101), C (011), D (00), E (10), F (111), G (010), H (11001)

The average size of the Huffman code: $(2 \times 5 + 9 \times 4 + 12 \times 3 + 20 \times 2 + 25 \times 2 + 16 \times 3 + 12 \times 3 + 4 \times 5)/100 = (10 + 36 + 36 + 40 + 50 + 48 + 36 + 20)/100 = 276/100 = 2.76$ bits/pixel

$\therefore$ Compression ratio $= 3/2.76 = 1.087$

PROBLEM 8.10

Using an 8 × 8 image block show sample calculations to illustrate the process of DCT, quantization and inverse DCT operations.

Consider sample 8 × 8 image section as shown below:

$$\begin{pmatrix} 62 & 55 & 55 & 54 & 49 & 48 & 47 & 55 \\ 62 & 57 & 54 & 52 & 48 & 47 & 48 & 53 \\ 61 & 60 & 52 & 49 & 48 & 47 & 49 & 54 \\ 63 & 61 & 60 & 60 & 63 & 65 & 68 & 65 \\ 67 & 67 & 70 & 74 & 79 & 85 & 91 & 92 \\ 82 & 95 & 101 & 106 & 114 & 115 & 112 & 117 \\ 96 & 111 & 115 & 119 & 128 & 128 & 130 & 127 \\ 109 & 121 & 127 & 133 & 139 & 141 & 140 & 133 \end{pmatrix}$$

The values in the image are in the range [0, 255]. To make the values centered around zero, 128 is subtracted from each value to bring them within the range [-128, 127]. After this step the new values are as follows:

$$\begin{pmatrix} -66 & -73 & -73 & -74 & -79 & -80 & -81 & -73 \\ -66 & -71 & -74 & -76 & -80 & -81 & -80 & -75 \\ -67 & -68 & -76 & -79 & -80 & -81 & -79 & -74 \\ -65 & -67 & -68 & -68 & -65 & -63 & -60 & -63 \\ -61 & -61 & -58 & -54 & -49 & -43 & -37 & -36 \\ -46 & -33 & -27 & -22 & -14 & -13 & -16 & -11 \\ -32 & -17 & -13 & -9 & 0 & 0 & 2 & -1 \\ -19 & -7 & -1 & 5 & 11 & 13 & 12 & 5 \end{pmatrix}$$

2D DCT now applied to the image block as per the relation below and the resulting values are rounded to one place of decimal.

$$F(u,v) = \alpha_u.\alpha_v.\sum_{x=0}^{7}\sum_{y=0}^{7} f(x,y) .\cos\left\{\frac{(2x+1)\pi u}{16}\right\}.\cos\left\{\frac{(2y+1)\pi v}{16}\right\}$$

Here $\alpha_u = \frac{1}{2}\sqrt{\frac{1}{2}}$ $for\, u = 0, \alpha_u = \frac{1}{2}$ $for\, u \neq 0$, $\alpha_v = \frac{1}{2}\sqrt{\frac{1}{2}}$ $for\, v = 0, \alpha_v = \frac{1}{2}$ $for\, v \neq 0$ are normalizing scale factors to make the transformation orthonormal.

The resulting DCT coefficient matrix is shown below. The top left value is the DC coefficient.

$$\begin{pmatrix} -369.6 & -29.7 & -2.6 & -2.5 & -1.1 & -3.7 & -1.5 & -0.1 \\ -231.1 & 44.9 & 24.5 & -0.3 & 9.3 & 3.9 & 4.3 & -1.4 \\ 62.8 & 8.5 & -7.6 & -2.7 & 0.3 & -0.4 & 0.5 & -0.8 \\ 12.5 & -14.6 & -3.5 & -3.4 & 2.4 & -1.3 & 2.7 & -0.4 \\ -4.9 & -3.9 & 0.9 & 3.6 & 0.1 & 5.1 & 1.1 & 0.5 \\ -0.5 & 3.2 & -1.4 & 0.2 & -1.1 & -1.5 & -1.1 & 0.9 \\ 4.4 & 2.3 & -1.7 & -1.6 & 1.1 & -2.7 & 1.1 & -1.4 \\ -10.2 & -1.8 & 5.9 & -0.4 & 0.3 & 0.4 & -1.0 & 0 \end{pmatrix}$$

A typical quantization matrix to bring about around 50% compression of the JPEG image is:

$$\begin{pmatrix} 16 & 12 & 14 & 14 & 18 & 24 & 49 & 72 \\ 11 & 12 & 13 & 17 & 22 & 35 & 64 & 92 \\ 10 & 14 & 16 & 22 & 37 & 55 & 78 & 95 \\ 16 & 19 & 24 & 29 & 56 & 64 & 87 & 98 \\ 24 & 26 & 40 & 51 & 68 & 81 & 103 & 112 \\ 40 & 58 & 57 & 87 & 109 & 104 & 121 & 100 \\ 51 & 60 & 69 & 80 & 103 & 113 & 120 & 103 \\ 61 & 65 & 56 & 62 & 77 & 92 & 101 & 99 \end{pmatrix}$$

Dividing the DCT matrix by the quantization matrix, element by element, and rounding the values to the nearest integer, we obtain the quantized matrix as below:

$$\begin{pmatrix} -23 & -2 & 0 & 0 & 0 & 0 & 0 & 0 \\ -21 & 4 & 2 & 0 & 0 & 0 & 0 & 0 \\ 6 & 1 & 0 & 0 & 0 & 0 & 0 & 0 \\ 1 & -1 & 0 & 0 & 0 & 0 & 0 & 0 \\ 0 & 0 & 0 & 0 & 0 & 0 & 0 & 0 \\ 0 & 0 & 0 & 0 & 0 & 0 & 0 & 0 \\ 0 & 0 & 0 & 0 & 0 & 0 & 0 & 0 \\ 0 & 0 & 0 & 0 & 0 & 0 & 0 & 0 \end{pmatrix}$$

These values are read off in a zigzag manner during conversion to a one dimensional matrix for subsequent entropy coding steps.

[-23, -2, -21, 6, 4, 0, 0, 2, 1, 1, 0, -1, 0, 0, 0, …]

To generate the compressed image from the quantized matrix, the quantized matrix is multiplied element by element with the quantization matrix to obtain the de-quantized matrix as below:

$$\begin{pmatrix} -368 & -24 & 0 & 0 & 0 & 0 & 0 & 0 \\ -231 & 48 & 26 & 0 & 0 & 0 & 0 & 0 \\ 60 & 14 & 0 & 0 & 0 & 0 & 0 & 0 \\ 16 & -19 & 0 & 0 & 0 & 0 & 0 & 0 \\ 0 & 0 & 0 & 0 & 0 & 0 & 0 & 0 \\ 0 & 0 & 0 & 0 & 0 & 0 & 0 & 0 \\ 0 & 0 & 0 & 0 & 0 & 0 & 0 & 0 \\ 0 & 0 & 0 & 0 & 0 & 0 & 0 & 0 \end{pmatrix}$$

This is now subjected to the inverse DCT operation as per the relation below, to return back to spatial domain values from frequency domain coefficient values:

$$f(x,y) = \sum_{u=0}^{7}\sum_{v=0}^{7}\alpha_u.\alpha_v.F(u,v)$$

$$.\cos\left\{\frac{(2x+1)\pi u}{16}\right\}.\cos\left\{\frac{(2y+1)\pi v}{16}\right\}$$

Here $\alpha_u = \frac{1}{2}\sqrt{\frac{1}{2}} for\, u = 0, \alpha_u = \frac{1}{2} for\, u \neq 0,$

$\alpha_v = \frac{1}{2}\sqrt{\frac{1}{2}} for\, v = 0, \alpha_v = \frac{1}{2} for\, v \neq 0$

The matrix obtained after IDCT is shown below:

$$\begin{pmatrix} -61 & -66 & -73 & -78 & -81 & -80 & -77 & -75 \\ -64 & -68 & -74 & -80 & -83 & -83 & -81 & -79 \\ -67 & -69 & -74 & -78 & -80 & -80 & -79 & -78 \\ -67 & -67 & -67 & -67 & -66 & -64 & -63 & -62 \\ -60 & -57 & -53 & -48 & -43 & -39 & -36 & -35 \\ -45 & -40 & -33 & -25 & -18 & -14 & -12 & -11 \\ -26 & -21 & -13 & -5 & 0 & 2 & 2 & 1 \\ -13 & -8 & -1 & 6 & 9 & 9 & 6 & 4 \end{pmatrix}$$

The final compressed image to be display is obtained is obtained 128 to each value:

$$\begin{pmatrix} 67 & 62 & 55 & 50 & 47 & 48 & 51 & 53 \\ 64 & 60 & 54 & 48 & 45 & 45 & 47 & 49 \\ 61 & 59 & 54 & 50 & 48 & 48 & 49 & 50 \\ 61 & 61 & 61 & 61 & 62 & 64 & 65 & 66 \\ 68 & 71 & 75 & 80 & 85 & 89 & 92 & 93 \\ 83 & 88 & 95 & 103 & 110 & 114 & 116 & 117 \\ 102 & 107 & 115 & 123 & 128 & 130 & 130 & 129 \\ 115 & 120 & 127 & 134 & 137 & 137 & 134 & 132 \end{pmatrix}$$

This indicates to an absolute error between the input image and compressed image of:

$$\begin{pmatrix} 5 & 7 & 0 & 4 & 2 & 0 & 4 & 2 \\ 2 & 3 & 0 & 4 & 3 & 2 & 1 & 4 \\ 0 & 1 & 2 & 1 & 0 & 1 & 0 & 4 \\ 2 & 0 & 1 & 1 & 1 & 1 & 3 & 1 \\ 1 & 4 & 5 & 6 & 6 & 4 & 1 & 1 \\ 1 & 7 & 6 & 3 & 4 & 1 & 4 & 0 \\ 6 & 4 & 0 & 4 & 0 & 2 & 0 & 2 \\ 6 & 1 & 0 & 0 & 2 & 4 & 6 & 1 \end{pmatrix}$$

This illustrates that retaining only about 8 out of the 64 DCT coefficients corresponds to a mean error of only about 3.26% with respect to the original image.

PROBLEM 8.11

For the E-section superimposed on a 8 × 8 grid, derive a quadtree representation and calculate the compression achieved.

				G					
B	G				G				B
	B	B	G WWBB	G WWBB	G BBWW	G BBWW	B	B	

For the E-section in Figure 8.13, the quadtree representation is as shown below where the letters B, G, W designate Black, Gray and White, B and W being homogeneous and do not need splitting while G being heterogeneous and needs further splitting into sub-quadrants:

The first row represents the entire section and is designated as G, the second row represents the quadrants 1, 2, 3, 4 and labeled as B, G, G, B. The third row represents the second quadrant which is split into sub-quadrants B, B, G, G; and the third quadrant which is split into sub-quadrants G, G, B, B. Finally the last row represents sub-quadrants 2.3 (W, W, B, B), 2.4 (W, W, B, B), 3.1 (B, B, W, W) and 3.2 (B, B, W, W).

For encoding the quadtree we use 1 for G, 00 for W, 01 for B. The steps are shown below each step corresponding to each row in the quadtree:

				1					
01	1				1				01
	01	01	1 00,00,01,01	1 00,00,01,01	1 01,01,00,00	1 01,01,00,00	01	01	

Step 1: 1

Step 2: 01, 1, 1, 01

Step 3: 01, 1(01,01,1,1), 1(1,1,01,01), 01

Step 4: 01, 1(01,01, 1(00,00,01,01), 1(00,00,01,01)), 1(1(01,01,00,00), 1(01,01,00,00), 01, 01)), 01

$$01,1\big(01,01,1(00,00,01,01),1(00,00,01,01)\big)$$
$$,1\big(1(01,01,00,00),1(01,01,00,00),01,01\big)),01$$

Note that the parenthesis, comma and spaces are not required for the actual encoding; these have been inserted for our convenience. The actual code can be written as: 01101011000001011000001011 1010100001010100000010101, which requires 50 bits as opposed to the original graphics section of 8 × 8 or 64 pixels. Hence, compression ratio is 64/50 = 1.28. The decoding can be done as follows:

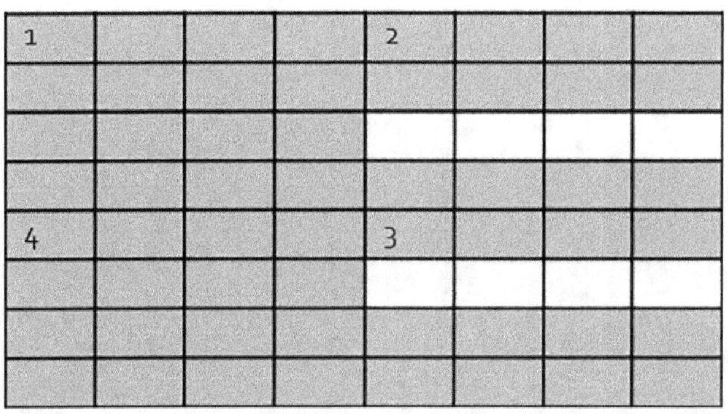

FIGURE 8.13
E-section (Problem 8.11).

PROBLEM 8.12

Using a sinusoidal audio waveform show sample calculations to illustrate the process of DCT, quantization and inverse DCT operations.

Consider 10 samples from a cosine shaped audio waveform ranging from 0 to 2π with maximum amplitude of 10 units as shown below rounded to the nearest integer:

$$x = (10,8,2,-5,-9,-9,-5,2,8,10)$$

Taking DCT of the signal we get following DCT coefficients:

$$(3.79,0,22.99,0,-1.89,0,-1.07,0,-0.10,0)$$

Using a threshold of 2, all coefficients whose absolute value is less than 2 is set to zero. The quantized DCT signal becomes:

$$(3.79,0,22.99,0,0,0,0,0,0,0)$$

Taking IDCT of the above we get the reconstructed signal as follows:

$$r = (10.98, 7.25, 1.2, -4.85, -8.58, -8.58, -4.85, 1.2, 7.25, 10.98)$$

The sum square error between the original and reconstructed signal is given by:

$$e = \sum_i (x_i - r_i)^2 = 4.744$$

PROBLEM 8.13

An MPEG-1 video has a frame sequence: IBBPBBPBBPBBI... For average compression ratios of 10:1 (I), 20:1 (P) and 50:1 (B), derive average bit rate generated by the encoder for PAL format (assume frame size 352 by 288 and chroma scheme 4:2:2).

The GOP size is 12 out of which there are 1 I-frame, 3 P-frames, 8 B-frames

Net compression factor: 1(1/10) + 3(1/20) + 8(1/50) = 0.1 + 0.15 + 0.16 = 0.41

Average compression factor/frame: 0.41/12 = 0.034

Data per row without compression: (24)(352/2) + (8)(352/2) = 5632 bits

Data per frame without compression: (5632)(288) = 1622016 bits

Data per frame with compression: (1622016)(0.034) = 55148.5 bits/frame

Bit rate at 25 fps: (55148.5 bits/frame)(25) = 1.378 Mbps

8.8 Coding Examples using MATLAB®

8.8.1 Run Length Encoding (RLE)

The following example illustrates RLE compression. A string containing repeated characters is fed as an input to the encoder and the output displays the actual characters preceded by the number of repetitions. The decoder reverts the original string from the encoded output. The function "disp" displays the value of a variable, "input" accepts an input from the user (Example 8.1),

EXAMPLE 8.1 EXAMPLE TO DEMONSTRATE RLE ENCODING AND DECODING

```
% RLE encoder
clc; clear;
a = input('Enter the array:');
% [8 8 8 2 2 2 2 5 5 1 1 1 1 1]
b = [];
c = 1;
for i = 1:length(a)-1
    if(a(i) == a(i+1))
       c = c+1;
    else
       b = [b, c, a(i),];
    c = 1;
    end
end

b = [b, c, a(length(a))];
disp(b);
% RLE decoder
clc; clear;
a = input('Enter the array:');
b = []; % [3 8 4 2 2 5 5 1]
for i = 1:2:length(a)
    b = [b a(i)];
end
c = [];
for i = 2:2:length(a)
    c = [c a(i)];
end
u = [];
for i = 1:length(b)
    n = b(i);
    r = c(i);
    for q = 1:n
        u = [u r];
    end
end
u
```

8.8.2 DCT-Based Compression

The following example illustrates DCT based image compression. The image is first converted to 8 by 8 blocks of DCT coefficients, then quantized using a quantization matrix for a typical compression of 50%. Inverse DCT is then used on the quantized image to generate the compressed image, which is then displayed alongside the original image. The function "imread" reads an image from a file, "rgb2gray" converts RGB color image to grayscale, "blockproc" processes individual blocks in images, "dct2" and "idct2" computes the forward and inverse 2D DCT The "./"

symbol indicates element wise operation; i.e., each element of the preceding matrix is divided by the corresponding element of the following matrix; hence, their dimensions need to be equal (Figure 8.14).

The following example illustrates 2D DCT on a sample 8 × 8 image block after its values are shifted from the range [0, 255] to being centered across zero using the range [-128, 127] (Example 8.3).

EXAMPLE 8.2 DCT BASED COMPRESSION

```
clear; clc;
% Read the input image
inputImage = imread('peppers.png');

% Convert the input image to grayscale if it's a color image
if size(inputImage, 3) == 3
    inputImage = rgb2gray(inputImage);
end

% Perform DCT on image blocks (8x8 blocks)
dctImage = blockproc(inputImage, [8 8], @(block) dct2(block.data));

% Quantize DCT coefficients (adjust quantization matrix for different
compression levels)
compressionLevel = 1; % Increase for higher compression

% Typical quantization matrix  for around 50% compression
quantizationMatrix = [
    16  12  14  14  18  24  49  72;
    11  12  13  17  22  35  64  92;
    10  14  16  22  37  55  78  95;
    16  19  24  29  56  64  87  98;
    24  26  40  51  68  81 103 112;
    40  58  57  87 109 104 121 100;
    51  60  69  80 103 113 120 103;
    61  65  56  62  77  92 101  99
];
quantizedImage = blockproc(dctImage, [8 8], @(block) round(block.data ./
(quantizationMatrix * compressionLevel)));

% Perform inverse DCT to reconstruct the compressed image
reconstructedImage = blockproc(quantizedImage, [8 8], @(block) idct2(block.data));

% Display original and compressed images
figure;
subplot(1, 2, 1);
imshow(inputImage);
title('Original Image');
subplot(1, 2, 2);
imshow(reconstructedImage,[]);
title('Compressed Image');
```

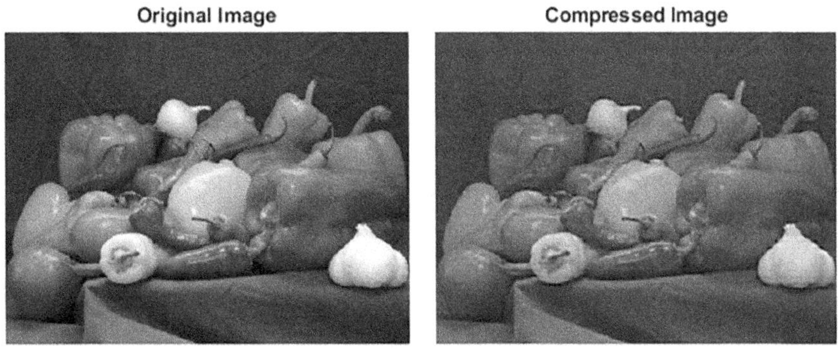

FIGURE 8.14
Output of Example 8.2.

EXAMPLE 8.3 DCT COMPRESSION ON SAMPLE IMAGE BLOCK

```
clear; clc;
% Read the input image
inputImage = [  62  55  55  54  49  48  47  55;
                62  57  54  52  48  47  48  53;
                61  60  52  49  48  47  49  54;
                63  61  60  60  63  65  68  65;
                67  67  70  74  79  85  91  92;
                82  95  101 106 114 115 112 117;
                96  111 115 119 128 128 130 127;
                109 121 127 133 139 141 140 133;
                ]
shiftedImage = inputImage - 128;

% Perform DCT on image blocks (8x8 blocks)
dctImage = dct2(shiftedImage)
roundedImage = round(dctImage,1)

% Typical quantization matrix  for around 50% compression
quantizationMatrix = [
    16  12  14  14  18  24  49  72;
    11  12  13  17  22  35  64  92;
    10  14  16  22  37  55  78  95;
    16  19  24  29  56  64  87  98;
    24  26  40  51  68  81  103 112;
    40  58  57  87  109 104 121 100;
    51  60  69  80  103 113 120 103;
    61  65  56  62  77  92  101 99
]
quantizedImage = round(roundedImage ./ quantizationMatrix)

% dequantize
dequantizedImage = quantizedImage .* quantizationMatrix

% Perform inverse DCT to reconstruct the compressed image
reconstructedShiftedImage = round(idct2(dequantizedImage))

reconstructedImage = reconstructedShiftedImage + 128
% Display original and compressed images
figure;
```

```
subplot(1, 2, 1);
imshow(uint8(inputImage));
title('Original Image');
subplot(1, 2, 2);
imshow(uint8(reconstructedImage));
title('Reconstructed Image');
```

The following example illustrates DCT, quantization and IDCT on a 1D sinusoidal audio waveform (Example 8.4)

8.8.3 2D DCT Basis Functions

The following example demonstrates how to display the 8 by 8 2D DCT basis matrices as images. The first matrix on the top-left is the DC function, while the others have sinusoidal components, the horizontal frequency increasing from left to right and vertical frequency increasing from top to bottom (Figure 8.15).

EXAMPLE 8.4 DCT COMPRESSION ON AUDIO SIGNAL

```
clear; clc;
% Generate a sine wave signal
t = linspace(0, 2*pi, 10); % 10 values
signal = 10*cos(t);
signal = round(signal);

% Perform Discrete Cosine Transform (DCT)
dct_signal = dct(signal);
dct_original_signal = dct_signal;

% Set a threshold for compression
threshold = 2;

% Find the indices where the DCT coefficients are below the threshold
indices = find(abs(dct_signal) < threshold);

% Set those coefficients to zero
dct_signal(indices) = 0;

% Reconstruct the signal using inverse DCT
reconstructed_signal = idct(dct_signal);

% Plot original and reconstructed signals
subplot(2,1,1);
plot(signal);
title('Original Signal');

subplot(2,1,2);
plot(reconstructed_signal);
title('Reconstructed Signal');

se = sumsqr(signal - reconstructed_signal) % error
```

EXAMPLE 8.5 2D DCT BASIS FUNCTIONS

```
clear; clc;
% Define the size of the block
block_size = 8;

% Generate basis functions
basis_functions = zeros(block_size, block_size, block_size, block_size);

for u = 0:block_size-1
    for v = 0:block_size-1
        for x = 0:block_size-1
            for y = 0:block_size-1
                basis_functions(x+1, y+1, u+1, v+1) = ...
                    sqrt(2/block_size) * cos((2*x + 1) * u * pi / ...
                    (2 * block_size)) * cos((2*y + 1) * v * pi / (2 * block_size));
            end
        end
    end
end

% Display basis functions
figure;
colormap(gray);
for u = 0:block_size-1
    for v = 0:block_size-1
        subplot(block_size, block_size, u*block_size + v + 1);
        imagesc(squeeze(basis_functions(:, :, u+1, v+1)));
        axis off;
        title(sprintf('u=%d, v=%d', u, v));
    end
end
```

8.8.4 Huffman Coding

The following example illustrates generation of codewords using Huffman coding, given the list of symbols and their probabilities. The encoder generates the codewords from the symbols while the decoder reverts the codewords to their original symbols. The function "huffmandict" generates a dictionary of codewords from a set of given symbols and their probabilities, "huffmanenco" encodes a given signal containing the symbols into a compressed output using the dictionary and "huffmandeco" decodes the compressed output back to the original signal using the dictionary. The example finally compares whether the decoded output matches the original signal or not (Example 8.6).

EXAMPLE 8.6 HUFFMAN ENCODING AND DECODING

```
clear;
symbols = 1:6;
p = [.26 .25 .2 .15 .1 .04];
dict = huffmandict(symbols,p);
for i=1:6
    disp(dict{i,1})
    disp(dict{i,2})
end
sig = randsrc(100,1,[symbols; p]);
comp = huffmanenco(sig,dict);
dsig = huffmandeco(comp,dict);

isequal(sig,dsig)
```

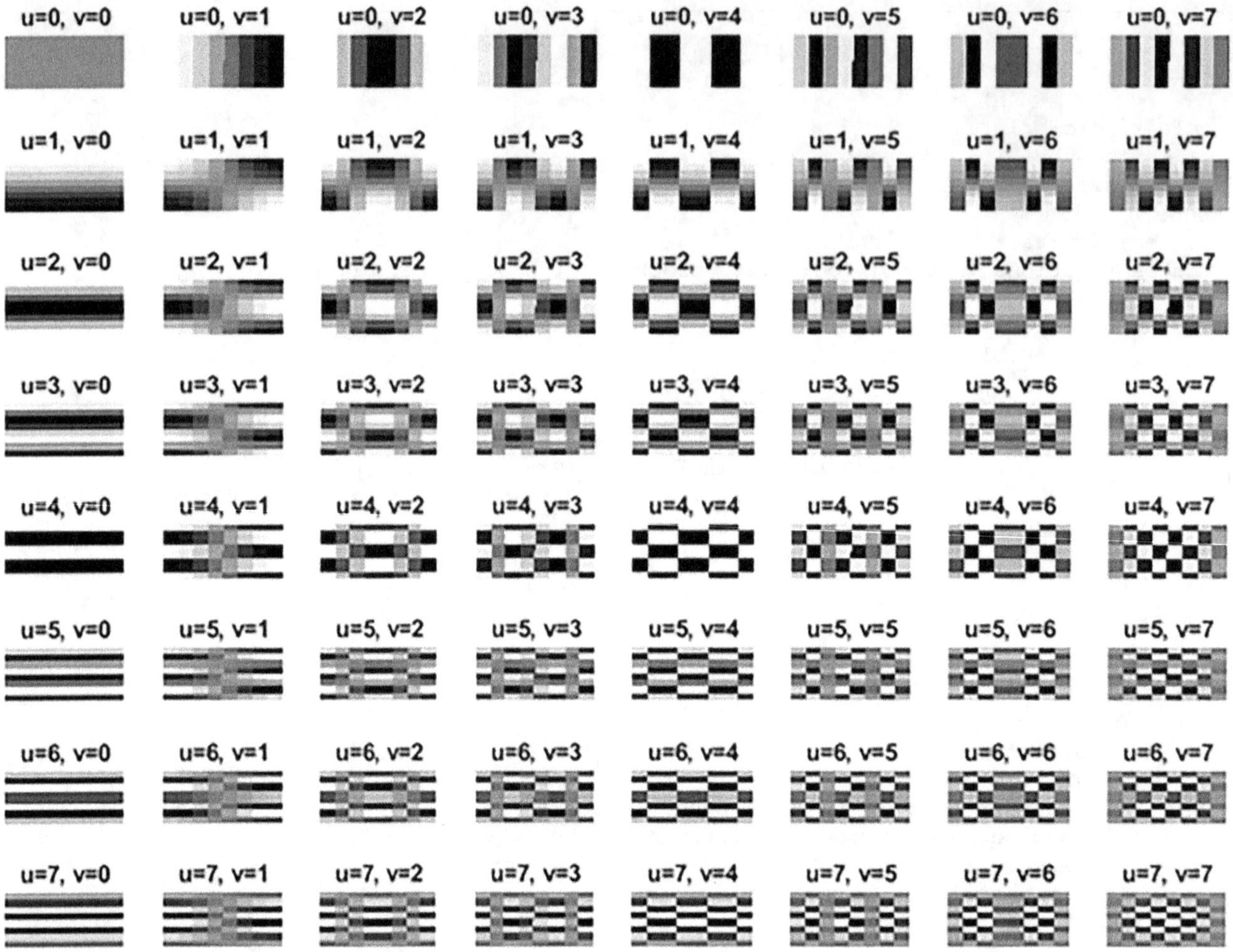

FIGURE 8.15
Output of Example 8.5.

8.8.5 DPCM

The following example 8.7 illustrates DPCM encoding and decoding using a sine wave. The function "dpcmenco" implements differential pulse code modulation to encode a signal. The "partition" vector specifies the endpoints of the partition vector and the "codebook" prescribes a value for each partition. The function "dpcmdeco" demodulates the encoded signal using the predictive error quantization codebook. Finally the mean square error between the original signal and the decoded signal is plotted (Figure 8.16). These two functions are part of the Communications Systems Toolbox (CST).

The following example 8.8 illustrates lossless predictive coding by calculation of prediction error subtracting each sample from its following sample. The predicted errors are displayed after the original signal (Example 8.8).

8.8.6 Quadtree Segmentation

The following example 8.9 illustrates quadtree segmentation of a graphical section. The function "qtdecomp" is used to implement quadtree decomposition and returns the QT structure S as a sparse matrix. If S(x,y) is non-zero, then (x,y) is the upper left corner of a block of size S(x,y). The function "disp" displays the

EXAMPLE 8.7 DPCM ENCODING AND DECODING

```
clear;
predictor = [0 1]; % y(k)=x(k-1)
partition = [-1:.1:.9];
codebook = [-1:.1:1];
t = [0:pi/50:2*pi];
x = sin(3*t); % Original signal
% Quantize x using DPCM.
encodedx = dpcmenco(x,codebook,partition,predictor);

% Recover x from the modulated signal.
decodedx = dpcmdeco(encodedx,codebook,predictor);
plot(t,x,t,decodedx,'--')
legend('Original signal','Decoded signal','Location','NorthOutside');
distor = sum((x-decodedx).^2)/length(x) % Mean square error
```

EXAMPLE 8.8 LOSSLESS PREDICTIVE CODING

```
clear;
x = [9,7,3,5; 1,2,3,4];
display(x);
b = x;

% prediction error
for i = 1:size(x,1)
    for j = 2:size(x,2)
        b(i,j) = b(i,j) - x(i,j-1);
    end
end
display(b);
```

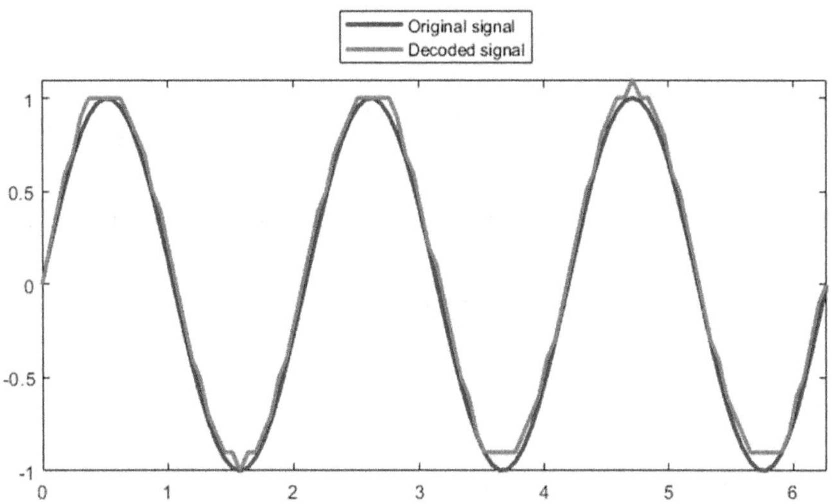

FIGURE 8.16
Output of Example 8.7.

quadtree structure in the sparse matrix S. The function "qtgetblk" returns all blocks of the specified dimension and their row, column locations. Starting out with a blank matrix J, the function "qtsetblk" arranges the blocks returned by the decomposition function and returns back the original matrix. The function "zeros" generates a blank matrix of the specified dimensions containing all zeros (Example 8.9).

EXAMPLE 8.9 QUAD-TREE SEGMENTATION

```
clear; clc;
I = [
         1     1     1     1     1     1     1     1
         1     1     1     1     1     1     1     1
         1     1     1     1     0     0     0     1
         1     1     1     1     0     0     1     1
         0     0     0     0     0     0     1     1
         0     0     0     0     0     0     1     1
         0     0     0     0     1     1     1     1
         0     0     0     0     1     1     1     0
      ];
S = qtdecomp(I); disp(full(S));

dim1 = 4; [blocks1, r, c] = qtgetblk(I, S, dim1)
dim2 = 2; [blocks2, r, c] = qtgetblk(I, S, dim2)
dim3 = 1; [blocks3, r, c] = qtgetblk(I, S, dim3)

J = zeros(8,8);
J = qtsetblk(J, S, dim1, blocks1);
J = qtsetblk(J, S, dim2, blocks2);
J = qtsetblk(J, S, dim3, blocks3);

subplot(121), imshow(I, []); title('I');
subplot(122), imshow(J, []); title('J');
```

The display function generates the quadtree structure which shows the upper-left corner of a homogeneous block containing the block size:

```
4     0     0     0     2     0     2     0
0     0     0     0     0     0     0     0
0     0     0     0     2     0     1     1
0     0     0     0     0     0     1     1
4     0     0     0     2     0     2     0
0     0     0     0     0     0     0     0
0     0     0     0     2     0     1     1
0     0     0     0     0     0     1     1
```

In the first case blocks of dimension 4 are displayed along with row and column numbers indicating their locations in the original matrix I:

```
#          blocks                row         column
--------------------------------------------------------------------
1          1     1     1         1           1          1
           1     1     1         1
           1     1     1         1
           1     1     1         1
2          0     0     0         0           5          1
           0     0     0         0
           0     0     0         0
           0     0     0         0
```

In the second case blocks of dimension 2 are displayed along with row and column numbers indicating their locations in the original matrix I:

Similarly in the third case eight matrices of size 1 are

```
#      blocks              row          column
-------------------------------------------
1      1     1              1            5
       1     1
2      0     0              3            5
       0     0
3      0     0              5            5
       0     0
4      1     1              7            5
       1     1
5      1     1              1            7
       1     1
6      1     1              5            7
       1     1
```

returned along with their positions. Finally starting out with a blank matrix J, all these blocks are inserted in their indicated locations to return back the original matrix I.

Review Questions

- Trace the historical evolution of compression technology highlighting landmark events.
- Explain with a block diagram concept of a CODEC.
- Distinguish between lossless and lossy compression.
- Explain how redundancies are exploited in compression schemes.
- What are the various metrics using which compression can be measured?
- Explain what is entropy along with its mathematical representation.
- Explain various types of differential coding schemes.
- What is RLE, and how can it be used for text and image compression?
- What is the LZ scheme, and how can it be used for text and image compression?
- Explain with examples how Huffman Coding method can be used for text compression.
- Explain in brief the encoding and decoding steps for JPEG image compression.
- What is quadtree segmentation, and how can it be used to compress graphical data?
- Discuss how iterated function systems can be used for fractal compression.
- Discuss popular schemes for lossless audio compression.
- Explain in brief the encoding and decoding steps for MP3 audio compression.
- Explain in brief the encoding and decoding steps for MPEG video compression.
- How does the M-JPEG differ from MPEG scheme?
- Distinguish between I, P and B frames.
- Distinguish between MPEG-1 Audio and MPEG-2 Audio.
- Distinguish between MPEG-1, MPEG-2 and MPEG-4 Video.

References

Falconer, K., *Fractal geometry: Mathematical foundations and applications*, John Wiley & Sons, 2003.

Liebchen, T., T. Moriya, N. Harada & Y. Kamamoto, The MPEG-4 ALS standard: Technology and applications, AES Convention, USA, 2005. http://elvera.nue.tu-berlin.de/files/0737Liebchen2005.pdf

Marpe, D., T. Wiegand & G.J. Sullivan, The H.264/MPEG-4 AVC standard and its applications, *IEEE Communications Magazine*, vol. 44, no. 10, pp. 134–143, 2005.

Puri, A. & A. Majumder, *Guide to video compression: From sgms to HEVC*, CRC Press, 2012.

Salomon, D., *Data compression*, Third edition. Springer, 2004.

Shannon, C.E., A mathematical theory of communication, *The Bell System Technical Journal*, vol. 27, pp. 379–423, 623–656, July, October, 1948.

Welch, T.A., A technique for high-performance data compression, *IEEE Computer*, vol. 17, no. 6, 1984.

Ziv, J., A. Lempel, A universal algorithm for sequential data compression, *IEEE Transactions on Information Theory*, vol. 23, no. 3, pp. 337–343, 1977.

Ziv, J., A. Lempel, Compression of individual sequences via variable rate coding, *IEEE Transactions on Information Theory*, vol. 24, no. 5, pp. 530–536, 1978.

Appendix

A-1: MATLAB® Function Summary

Function	Description
%	Comments
.	Element wise operation
:	Range of values or all current values
[]	Map current values to full range of values
'	Transpose of a vector or matrix
abs	Absolute value
acos / acosd	Calculate inverse cosine in radians / degrees
affine2d	2D affine geometric transformation
appcoef2	2D approximation coefficients
asin/asind	Calculates inverse sine in radians / degrees
atan	Calculates inverse tangent in radians
audioDevice Writer	Play to sound card
audioinfo	Information about audio files
audioread	Read audio files
audiorecorder	Create object for recording audio
audiowrite	Write audio files
axis	Set axis limits and aspect ratios
blockproc	Distinct block processing for image
bwarea	Area of objects in binary image
bwboundaries	Trace region boundaries in binary image,
bweuler	Euler number of binary image
bwmorph	Morphological operations on binary images
bwperim	Find perimeter of objects in binary image
cell	Create cell array
cell2mat	Convert cell array to ordinary array
checkerboard	Create checkerboard image
chirp	Generate signals with variable frequencies
clc	Clear command window of previous text
clear	Clear items from workspace memory
colormap	Color look-up table
compressor	Dynamic range compressor
contourf	Contour plot of a matrix
cos/cosd	Cosine of argument in radians / degrees
cross	Computes cross product of vectors
datetime	Display date and time
dct	Discrete cosine transform
dct2	2D discrete cosine transform
deg2rad	Convert degree values to radians
detcoef2	2D detail coefficients
diff	Differentiates symbolic expression
disp	Display value of variable
dot	Computes dot product of vectors
double	Convert to double precision data type
dpcmdeco	Implement a DPCM decoder
dpcmenco	Implement a DPCM encoder
dsp.AudioFile Reader	Stream from audio file
dsp.SineWave	Generate discrete sine wave
dsp.Spectrum Analyzer	Display frequency spectrum of time-domain signals
dwt2	Single level discrete 2D wavelet transform
edge	Find edges in intensity image
estimateFlow	Estimate optical flow
eval	Evaluates a symbolic expression
eye	Identity matrix
ezmesh	Creates a mesh of points
ezplot/ezplot3	Generate plots of symbolic variables in 2D/3D environments
fft, fft2	Fast Fourier transform, 2D fast Fourier transform
fftshift	Shift zero-frequency component to center of spectrum
figure	Create a figure window
fill	Fill 2D polygons
filter, filter2	1D digital filter, 2D digital filter
fimplicit3	Generate a 3D plot of an implicit function
fliplr	Flip matrix left to right
flipud	Flip matrix up to down
for ... end	Repeat statements specified number of times
format	Set display format in command window
fprintf	Prints out strings and values using formatting options
fspecial	Create predefined 2D filter
gca	Get current axis for modifying axes properties
getaudiodata	Return recorded audio from array
getFrame	Capture axes or figure as movie frame

Function	Description
graycomatrix	Create gray-level co-occurrence matrix from image
graycoprops	Properties of gray-level co-occurrence matrix
grid	Display grid lines in plot
hasFrame	Determine if frame is available to read
hex2dec	Convert hexadecimal to decimal
histeq	Enhance contrast using histogram equalization
hold	Hold the plot for additional inputs before displaying the results
huffmandeco	Implement a Huffman coding decoder
huffmandict	Create a dictionary for Huffman coding
huffmanenco	Implement a Huffman coding encoder
idct, idct2	1D and 2D inverse discrete cosine transform
idwt, idwt2	1D and 2D inverse discrete wavelet transform
ifft, ifft2	1D and 2D inverse DFT
im2bw	Convert image to binary
imabsdiff	Absolute difference of two images
imadd	Add two images or add constant to image
imadjust	Adjust image intensity values or colormap
imag	Imaginary part of complex number
image, imagesc	Display image, display scaled image from array
imbinarize	Convert grayscale image to binary image
imcomplement	Complement image
imcrop	Crop image
imdivide	Divide one image into another
imfilter	Multidimensional filtering of images
imfindcircles	Find circles using circular Hough transform
imfinfo	Display information about file
imhist	Histogram of image data
imlincomb	Linear combination of images
immultiply	Multiply two images
imnoise	Add noise to image
impixelregion	Pixel Region tool
implay	Play movies, videos, or image sequences
imread	Read image from file
imrect	Create draggable rectangle
imresize	Resize image
imrotate	Rotate image
imshow	Display image
imshowpair	Compare differences between images
imsubtract	Subtract one image from another
imtool	Open Image Viewer app
imtranslate	Translate image
imwarp	Apply geometric transformation to image
imwrite	Write image to file
input	Accept input from user
insertShape	Insert shape in image or video
insertText	Insert text in image or video
int	Integrate symbolic expression
inv	Compute inverse of a matrix
jet	Jet colormap
legend	Add legend to axes
line	Create line
linspace	Generate vector of evenly spaced values
load	Load variables from file into workspace
log	Natural logarithm
loudnessMeter	Standard-compliant loudness measurements
max	Maximum value
medfilt2	2D median filtering
mesh	Generates a 3D mesh
mesh	Generates a 3D mesh for plotting a function
meshgrid	Generates 2D grid coordinates
mididevice	Send and receive MIDI messages
mididevinfo	MIDI device information
midimsg	Create MIDI message
midisend	Send MIDI message to MIDI device
min	Minimum value
mmfileinfo	Information about multimedia file
msgbox	Creates a message dialog box to display textual messages
NaN	Not a number, undefined numerical value
Norm	Returns magnitude of a avector
ntsc2rgb	Convert NTSC values to RGB color space
num2str	Convert numbers to strings
numel	Number of array elements
ocr	Recognize text using optical character recognition
ones	Create array of all ones
opticalFlow Farneback	Estimate optical flow using Farneback method
opticalFlowHS	Estimate optical flow using Horn-Schunck method
patch	Generate filled polygons
play	Play audio

plot/plot3	2D line plot, 3D line plot
polyder	Differentiate polynomial expression
polyshape	Create a polygon defined by 2D vertices
polyval	Evaluate polynomial expression at a single point
projective2d	2D projective geometric transformation
projective2D	Create an projective transformation object
qtdecomp	Quadtree decomposition
qtgetblk	Get block values in quad-tree decomposition
qtsetblk	Set block values in quad-tree decomposition
quiver/quiver3	Arrow plot
readFrame	Read video frame from video file
real	Real part of complex number
recordblocking	Record audio holding control unitil recording completes
rectangle	Create rectangle with sharp or curved corners
regexprep	Replace text using regular expression
regionprops	Measure properties of image regions
release	Release resources
rgb2gray	RGB to grayscale
rgb2hsv	RGB to HSV color space
rgb2lab	RGB to L*a*b* color space
rgb2ntsc	RGB to NTSC color space
rgb2xyz	RGB to CIE 1931 XYZ color space
rgb2ycbcr	RGB to YCbCr color space
rng	Control random number generation
roifilt2	Filter region of interest (ROI) in image
roipoly	Specify polygonal region of interest (ROI)
roots	Find roots of polynomial equation
scatter, scatter3	2D scatter plot, 3D scatter plot
setdiff	Difference between first and second arguments
sign	Return sign of the argument as +1,0,-1
sin/sind	Sine of argument in radians / degrees
size	Return array size
sort	Sort array elements
sound	Convert matrix data to sound
spectrogram	Generate spectrogram
sqrt	Square root
strcat	Concatenate strings horizontally
strsplit	Splits strings using whitespace characters
subplot	Multiple plots in a single figure window
subs	Substitute symbolic variable with numerical values
syms	Declare symbolic variable name
tan/tand	Tangent of argument in radians / degrees
text	Insert text descriptions in graphical plots
title	Insert title in graphical plots
uint8	Unsigned integer 8-bit (0 to 255)
VideoReader	Read video files
VideoWriter	Write video files
view	Viewpoint specification in horizontal and vertical angles
viscircles	Create circle
vision.BlobAnalysis	Calculates statistics of connected regions in an image
vision.ForegroundDetector	Foreground detection using Gaussian mixture models
vision.HistogramBasedTracker	Histogram-based object tracking
vision.VideoFileReader	Read video frames from video file
vision.VideoPlayer	Play video
vpa	Provide variable precision arithmetic upto 32 bits
warp	Display image as texture-mapped surface
wavedec2	2D wavelet decomposition
whos	List variables in workspace, with sizes and types
window	Create a window function of specified type
writeVideo	Write data from an array to a video file
xlabel	Label x-axis
xyz2rgb	Convert CIE 1931 XYZ to RGB
ycbcr2rgb	Convert YCbCr values to RGB color space
ylabel	Label y-axis
zeros	Create array of all zeros
zlabel	Label z-axis

A-2: Abbreviations

AAC	Advanced Audio Coding
ADC	Analog to Digital Converter
ADPCM	Adaptive DPCM

AES Audio Engineering Society

AGP Accelerated Graphics Port

AI Artificial Intelligence

AIFF Audio Interchange File Format

ALAC Apple Lossless Audio Codec

AMOLED Active Matrix Organic Light-Emitting Diode

AMR Adaptive Multi Rate

API Application Programming Interface

AR Augmented Reality

ASCII American Standard Code for Information Interchange

ATSC Advanced Television Systems Committee

ATSC Advanced Television Systems Committee

BF Blending Function

BoVW Bag-of-Visual-Words

CAI Computer-Aided Instructions

CBSR Content Based Storage and Retrieval

CBT Computer-Based Training

CCD charge-coupled device

CCFL Cold Cathode Fluorescent Lamp

CCW Counter-clockwise

CDF Cumulative Distribution Frequency

CDN Content Delivery Network

CD-ROM Compact Disc-Read Only Memory

CIE Commission Internationale de l'Éclairage

CIF Common Intermediate Format

CLUT Color Look Up Table

CMM Color Management Module

CMOS Complementary metal-oxide-semiconductor

CMS Content Management System

CMYK Cyan Magenta Yellow Black

CNN Convolutional Neural Networks

CODEC Coder-Decoder

COI Center of Interest

COP Center of Projection

CP Control Point

CPU Central Processing Unit

CRT Cathode Ray Tube

CSMA/CD Carrier Sense Multiple Access with Collision Detection

CSS Cascading Style Sheets

CSV Comma-Separated Values

CW Clockwise

DAB Digital Audio Broadcasting

DAC Digital to Analog Converter

DAM Digital Asset Management

DASH Dynamic Adaptive Streaming over HTTP

DBMS Database Management System

DCT Discrete Cosine Transform

DFT Discrete Fourier Transform

DHTML Dynamic HTML

DICOM Digital Imaging and Communications in Medicine

DLS DownLoadable Sound

DMCA Digital Millennium Copyright Act

DoG Difference of Gaussian

DOM Document Object Model

DPCM Differential PCM

DPI Dots Per Inch

DRC Dynamic Range Compressor

DRM Digital Rights Management

DSLR Digital Single-Lens Reflex

DSP Digital Signal Processor

DVB Digital Video Broadcasting

DVI Digital Visual Interface

DWT Discrete Wavelet Transform

EBU European Broadcasting Union

ECMA European Computer Manufacturers Association

EPS Encapsulated PostScript

FIR Finite Impulse Response

FLAC Free Lossless Audio Codec

FOV Field of View

FTP File Transfer Protocol

GIF Graphics Interchange Format

GIMP GNU Image Manipulation Program

GIS Geographical Information Systems

GLCM Gray-Level Co-occurrence Matrix

GPL General Public License

GPS Global Positioning System

GPU Graphics Processing Unit

GUI Graphical User Interface

HCI Human Computer Interface

HD High-definition

HDD Hard Disk Drive

HDMI High Definition Multimedia Interface

HDR high dynamic range

HDTV high-definition television

HEVC High Efficiency Video Coding

HLS HTTP Live Streaming

HMD Head-Mounted Display

HOG Histogram of Oriented Gradients

HSV Hue, Saturation, Value

HTML Hyper Text Markup Language

HTTP Hypertext Transfer Protocol

HTTPS Hypertext Transfer Protocol Secure

ICC International Color Consortium

ICT Information and Communication Technology

IDCT Inverse DCT

IDFT Inverse DFT

IEC International Electro-Technical Commission
IEEE Institute of Electrical and Electronics Engineers
IETF Internet Engineering Task Force
IIR Infinite Impulse Response
IK Inverse Kinematics
IP Internet Protocol
ISO International Standards Organization
ITU International Telecommunication Union
JPEG Joint Photographic Experts Group
JS JavaScript
JSON JavaScript Object Notation
KV Knot Vector
LAN local area network
LCD Liquid Crystal Display
LDA Linear Discriminant Analysis
LED Light Emitting Diode
LoG Laplacian of Gaussian
LZW Lempel Ziv Welch
M4A MPEG-4 Audio
MATLAB MATrix LABoratory
MIDI Musical Instrument Digital Interface
MJPEG Motion JPEG
ML Machine Learning
MMA MIDI Manufacturers Association
MP3 MPEG-1 Audio Layer III
MPEG Moving Picture Experts Group
MR Mixed Reality
NAS Network Attached Storage
NLP Natural Language Processing
NTSC National Television Systems Committee
OAI Open Archives Initiative
OCR Optical Character Recognition
ODF Open Document Format
OIS optical image stabilization
OpenGL Open Graphics Library
PAL Phase Alternating Line
PCA Principal Component Analysis
PCI Peripheral Component Interconnect
PCM Pulse code modulation
PDF Portable Document Format
PDP Plasma Display Panel
PHP Hypertext Preprocessor
PNG Portable Network Graphics
POI Point of Inflection
PPI Pixels Per Inch
PRP Projection Reference Point
PS PostScript
PSF Point Spread Function
QoS Quality of Service
RCA Radio Corporation of America
R-CNN Region-based CNN
RGB Red Green Blue
RLE Run Length Encoding
RNN Recurrent Neural Network
ROI Region of Interest
RPN Region Proposal Networks
RTCP Real-Time Control Protocol
RTF Rich Text Format
RTMP Real-Time Messaging Protocol
RTP Real-Time Transport Protocol
S/PDIF Sony/Philips Digital Interface Format
SDI Serial Digital Interface
SHM Simple Harmonic Motion
SIFT Scale-Invariant Feature Transform
SMIL Synchronized Multimedia Integration Language
SMPTE Society of Motion Picture and Television Engineers
SNR Signal-to-Noise Ratio
sRGB Standard RGB
SSD Solid-State Drive
STFT Short-Time Fourier Transform
STT Speech-to-Text
SURF Speeded-Up Robust Features
SVG Scalable Vector Graphics
SVGA Super VGA
SVM Support Vector Machines
SXGA Super XGA
TCP Transmission Control Protocol
TFT Thin Film Transistor
TIFF Tagged-Image File Format
TRS Tip-Ring-Sleeve
TTML Timed Text Markup Language
TTS Text-to-Speech
UC Unicode Consortium
UCS Unicode Character Set
USB Universal Serial Bus
UTF Unicode Transformation Formats
UXGA Ultra XGA
VCP Video Cassette Player
VDU Visual Display Unit
VGA Video Graphics Array
VLC VideoLAN Client
VoIP Voice over Internet Protocol
VQ Vector Quantization
VR Virtual Reality
W3C World Wide Web Consortium
WAP Wireless Access Points
WebGL Web Graphics Library
WebP Web Picture
WebRTC Web Real-Time Communication
WebVR Web Virtual Reality
WebVTT Web Video Text Track
WebXR Web Extended Reality
WHATWG Web Hypertext Application Technology Working Group

WMA	Windows Media Audio
WMV	Windows Media Video
XGA	Extended Graphics Array
XMF	Extensible Music Format
XML	Extensible Markup Language

A-3: References

1. Adornato, A., *Mobile and social media journalism: A practical guide for multimedia journalism*, Routledge, 2021.
2. Akenine-Moller, T., E. Haines, N. Hoffman, *Real time rendering*, CRC Press, 2008.
3. Andina, T., T. Dreier (eds), *Digital ethics: the issue of images*, Nomos Publishers, 2022.
4. Armi, L., S. Fekri-Ershad, Texture image analysis and texture classification methods: A review, *International Online Journal of Image Processing and Pattern Recognition*, vol. 2, no. 1, pp. 1–29, 2019.
5. Assuncao, P.A., A. Gotchev, *3D visual content creation, coding and delivery*, Springer Nature Switzerland AG, 2019.
6. Bai, M., R. Urtasun, *Deep watershed transform for instance segmentation*, 2017.
7. Bansal, J.C., M.S. Uddin, *Computer vision and machine learning in agriculture*, Springer Singapore, 2022.
8. Bay, H., T. Tuytelaars, L.V. Gool, SURF: Speeded up robust features, *Computer Vision and Image Understanding*, vol. 110, no. 3, pp. 346–359, 2008
9. Bengio, Y., Learning deep architectures for AI, *Foundations and Trends in Machine Learning*, vol. 2, no. 1, pp. 1–127, 2009.
10. Berg, M., J. Boyar, L.M. Favrholdt, K.M. Larsen, "Online minimum spanning trees with weight predictions", in: Morin, P., Suri, S. (eds) *Algorithms and Data Structures*. WADS 2023. Lecture Notes in Computer Science, vol 14079, pp. 136–148, 2023.
11. Berners-Lee, T. & M. Fischetti, *Weaving the Web : The original design and ultimate destiny of the World Wide Web by its inventor*, Harper Collins, 1999 https://www.w3.org/People/Berners-Lee/Weaving/Overview.html
12. Boor, C., "Subroutine package for calculating with B-splines", Tech Rep. LA-4728-MS, Los Alamos Sci. Lab, Los Alamos, NM, pp. 109–121, 1971.
13. Boss, S., J.C. Teague, *The new Web typography*, CRC Press, 2017.
14. Bradski, G.R., Computer vision face tracking for use in a perceptual user interface, IEEE Workshop on Applications of Computer Vision, Princeton, NJ, pp. 214–219, 1998.
15. Breiman, L., Random forests, *Machine Learning*, vol. 45, no. 1, pp. 5–32, 2001.
16. Burger, W., M.J. Burge, *Principles of digital image processing: advanced methods*, Springer Verlag, 2013.
17. Burr, S.L., *Entertainment law in a nutshell*, West Group, 2004.
18. Cai, Z., N. Vasconcelos, "Cascade R-CNN: delving into high quality object detection", *IEEE Conference on Computer Vision and Pattern Recognition*, pp. 6154–6162, 2018.
19. Cardone, E.P., *The art and science of surround and stereo recording*, Springer Vienna, 2021.
20. Chakraborty, S., *Fundamentals of computer graphics*, Everest Publishing House, 2010.
21. Chaudhuri, B.B., *Digital document processing: major directions and recent advances*, Springer, 2007.
22. Chen, J.Y.C., G. Fragomeni (eds), Virtual, augmented and mixed reality: Design and interaction, *12th International Conference VAMR*, Springer, 2020.
23. Chen, L.-C., G. Papandreou, K. Murphy, A.L. Yuille, DeepLab: semantic image segmentation with deep convolutional nets, atrous convolution and fully connected CRFs, *IEEE Transactions on Pattern Analysis and Machine Intelligence*, vol. 40, pp. 834–848, 2016.
24. Chen, L.-C., G. Papandreou, K. Murphy & A. L. Yuille, *DeepLab: Semantic image segmentation with deep convolutional nets, atrous convolution and fully connected CRFs*, 2017. https://arxiv.org/abs/1606.00915
25. Chen, S.-C., M.-L. Shyu, *Multimedia data engineering: Applications and processing*, Idea Group US, 2013.
26. Christianini, N., J.C. Shawe-Taylor, *An introduction to support vector machines and other kernel based learning methods*, Cambridge University Press, 2000.
27. Clark, R.C., Mayer, R.E. (eds), *E-Learning and the science of instruction: Proven guidelines for consumers and designers of multimedia learning*, Wiley, 2016.
28. Cobussen, M., N. Nielsen, *Music and ethics*, Routledge, 2016.
29. Comaniciu, D., P. Meer, Mean Shift: A robust approach toward feature space analysis, *IEEE Transactions on Pattern Analysis and Machine Intelligence (PAMI)*, vol.24, no. 5, pp. 603–619, 2002.
30. Coppersmith,D.,S.J.Hong&J.R.M.Hosking,Partitioning nominal attributes in decision trees, *Data Mining and Knowledge Discovery*, vol. 3, pp. 197–217, 1999.
31. Crow, F., Summed up tables for texture mapping, *Proceedings of the . SIGGRAPH*, vol. 18, no. 3, pp. 207–212, 1984.
32. Csurka, G., C.R. Dance, L. Fan, J. Williamowski & C. Bray, Visual categorization with bags of key-points, Proc. of ECCV International Workshop on Statistical Learning in Computer Vision, 2004.
33. Cyganek, B., *Object detection and recognition in digital images*, Wiley, 2013.
34. Dalal, N. & B. Triggs. Histograms of oriented gradients for human detection, *IEEE Computer Society Conference on Computer Vision and Pattern Recognition*, vol. 1, pp. 886–893, 2005.
35. Danielsson, K., S. Selander, *Multimodal texts in disciplinary education: a comprehensive framework*, Springer Switzerland, 2021.
36. Das, R., *Content-based image classification*, CRC Press, 2020.
37. Dasiopoulou, S., et al., Knowledge-assisted semantic video object detection, *IEEE Transactions on Circuits and Systems for Video Technology* vol. 15, no. 10, pp. 1210–1224, 2005.
38. Davies, M.J., *Legal issues in the music industry*, BuzzGig LLC, 2009.

39. Deegan, M., K. Sutherland, *Text editing, print and the digital world*, Routledge, 2016.
40. Doerner, R., W. Broll, P. Grimm & B. Jung (eds), *Virtual and augmented reality (VR/AR)*, Springer Nature Switzerland, 2022.
41. Dryden, I.L., K.V. Mardia, *Statistical shape analysis*, Wiley, 2016.
42. Duckett, J., *"HTML and CSS: design and build websites"*, John Wiley & Sons, 2014.
43. Dutoit T, *An introduction to text to speech synthesis*, Springer Netherlands, 2013.
44. Eisenstein, J., *Introduction to natural language processing*, MIT Press, 2019.
45. Ester, M. et al. (eds.). "A density-based algorithm for discovering clusters in large spatial databases with noise". *Proceedings of the Second International Conference on Knowledge Discovery and Data Mining (KDD-96)*, AAAI Press. pp. 226–231, 1996.
46. Euler, L. *Introductio in analysin infinitorum*, Marcum-Michaelem Bousquet, vol. 1, pp. 1–320, 1748.
47. Falconer, K., *Fractal geometry: Mathematical foundations and applications*, John Wiley & Sons, 2003.
48. Farneback, G., Two-frame motion estimation based on polynomial expansion, *Proceedings of the 13th Scandinavian Conference on Image Analysis*, Gothenburg, 2003.
49. Flanagan, D., *JavaScript: the definitive guide*, O'Reilly Media, 2017.
50. Foley, J.D., A. van Dam & S.K. Feiner, et al. *Computer graphics: Principles and practice* Addison-Wesley Professional, 1990.
51. Fortner, B., T. E. Meyer, *Number by colors*, Springer, 1997.
52. Fourier, J.B.J., *Theorie analytique de la chaleur*, Chez Firmin Didot, 1822.
53. Frain, B., *Responsive Web design with HTML5 and CSS*, Packt Publishing Ltd., 2022.
54. Gadsden, D., M. Artz, *Preserving our planet: GIS for conservation*, ESRI Press, 2023.
55. Gazaway, D., *Introduction to game systems design*, Pearson Education (US), 2021.
56. Gillam, R., *Unicode demystified: A practical programmer's guide to the encoding standard*, Addison-Wesley Professional, 2003.
57. Girshick, R., J. Donahue, T. Darrell & J. Malik, Region based convolutional networks for accurate object detection and segmentation, *IEEE Transactions of Pattern Analysis and Machine Intelligence*, 2015. https://doi.org/10.1109/TPAMI.2015.2437384
58. Glassner, A.S., *Principles of digital image synthesis*, Morgan Kauffman Publishers, 1995.
59. Godse, A.P., D. A. Godse, *Multimedia technologies*, Technical Publications, 2020.
60. Godse, A.P., D. A. Godse, *Computer graphics and multimedia*, Technical Publications, 2021.
61. Gonzalez, R.C., R.E. Woods, *Digital image processing*, Prentice Hall, 2008.
62. Goodman, D., *Dynamic HTML – the definitive reference*, O'Reilly Media, 2007.
63. Gouraud, H., Continuous shading of curved surfaces, *IEEE Transactions on Computers*, vol. C-20, no. 6, pp. 623–629, 1971.
64. Guild, J., The colorimetric properties of the spectrum, *Pholosophical Transactions*, vol. 230, no. 685, pp. 149–187, 1931.
65. Gunturk, B.K., X. Li (eds), *Image restoration: fundamentals and advances*, CRC Press, 2018.
66. Haar, A., Zur Theorie der orthogonalen Funktionensysteme, *Mathematische Annalen*, vol. 69, pp. 331–371, 1910.
67. Haralick, R.M., K. Shanmugan & I. Dinstein, Textural features for image classification, *IEEE Transactions on Systems, Man, and Cybernetics*, vol. SMC-3, pp. 610–621, 1973.
68. Hastie, T., R. Tibshirani & J. Friedman, *The elements of statistical learning*", Second Edition. Springer, 2008.
69. Haykin, S., *Neural networks and learning machines*, Third Edition, Prentice Hall, 2009.
70. He, K., G. Gkioxari, P. Dollar & R. Girshick, Mask R-CNN, *IEEE International Conference on Computer Vision (ICCV), 2017*, pp. 2980–2988, 2018.
71. He, K., G. Gkioxari, P. Dollar & R. Girshick, *Mask R-CNN*, 2018. https://arxiv.org/abs/1703.06870
72. Hearn, D., M.P. Baker. *Computer graphics, C Version* Second Edition, Prentice Hall, 1996.
73. Hernandez, R.K., J. Rue, *Principles of multimedia journalism: Packaging digital news*, Routledge, 2015.
74. Horn, B.K.P. & B.G. Schunck, Determining optical flow, *Artificial Intelligence*, vol. 17, pp. 185–203, 1981.
75. Hua, X.-S., *"Online multimedia advertising" techniques and technologies*, IGI Global, 2010.
76. Huber, D. M., R. Runstein, *Modern recording techniques*, Routledge, 2017.
77. Hung, C.-C., E. Song, Y. Lan, *Image texture analysis: Foundations, models and algorithms*, Springer, 2019.
78. Hunt, R.W.G., D. Wright, in Luo, R (ed.), *Encyclopedia of color science and technology*, Springer, 2014.
79. Hunter, R., "Photoelectric color-difference meter", *Journal of Optical Society of America*, vol. 38, no. 7, p. 661, 1948.
80. Iglezakis, I., T.-E. Synodinou (eds), *E-publishing and digital libraries: Legal and organizational issues*, IGI Global, 2010.
81. Isaias, P., K. Blashki, *Human computer interfaces and interactivity*, Idea Group US, 2014.
82. Jackson, W., *Digital audio editing fundamentals*, APress, 2015.
83. Jain, A.K., *Fundamentals of digital image processing*, Prentice Hall, 1989.
84. Jong, T., L. Sarti (eds.), *Design and production of multimedia and simulation based learning material*, Springer, 2012.
85. Jurafsky, D., J.H. Martin, *Speech and language processing*, Pearson Education India, 2013.
86. Kallen, S.A., *Digital cameras and camcorders*, Lucent Books, 2014.
87. Kane, E.M., *Ethics: A graphic designer's field guide*, Simon & Schuster, 2010.
88. Kim, H., L. Remaggi, P. Jackson, A. Hilton, Immersive spatial audio reproduction for VR/AR using room acoustic modelling from 360° images, *IEEE Conference on Virtual Reality and 3D User Interfaces (VR)*, pp. 120–126, 2019.
89. Kriss, M. (ed), *Handbook of digital imaging*, Wiley, 2015.

90. Lancaric, S., A survey of shape analysis techniques, *Pattern Recognition*, vol. 31, no. 8, pp. 983–1001, 1998.
91. Leggett, E.R., *Digitization and digital archiving*, Rowman & Littlefield, 2020.
92. Lei, T, A.K. Nandi, *Image segmentation: principles techniques and applications*, Wiley, 2022.
93. Liebchen, T., T. Moriya, N. Harada & Y. Kamamoto, *The MPEG-4 ALS standard: Technology and applications*, AES Convention, 2005.
94. Liu, C.Z., S. Ramakrishnan, *Image recognition: progress trends and challenges*, Nova Science Publishers, 2020.
95. Liu, W., et al., SSD: Single shot multibox detector, in Leibe, B., Matas, J., Sebe, N. & Welling, M. (eds) *Computer Vision – ECCV 2016*. Lecture Notes in Computer Science, vol 9905, pp. 21–37, Springer, 2016.
96. Long J, E. Shelhamer, T. Darrell, "Fully convolutional networks for semantic segmentation", in *Proceedings IEEE conference on computer vision and pattern recognition (CVPR)*, pp. 3431–3440, 2015.
97. Lowe, D.G., Distinctive image features from scale-invariant key-points, *International Journal of Computer Vision*, vol. 60, no. 2, pp. 91–110, 2004.
98. Lucas, B.D. & T. Kanade, An iterative image registration technique with an application to stereo vision, *Proceedings of Imaging Understanding Workshop*, pp. 121–130, 1981.
99. Lucy, L.B., An iterative technique for the rectification of observed distributions, *Astronomical Journal*, vol. 79, no. 1, pp. 745–754, 1974.
100. MacQueen, J.B. Some methods for classification and analysis of multivariate observations, *Proceedings of 5th Berkeley Symposium on Mathematical Statistics and Probability*, vol. 1. University of California Press. pp. 281–297, 1967.
101. Mallat, S.G., A theory for multiresolution signal decomposition: The wavelet representation, *IEEE Transactions on Pattern Analysis and Machine Intelligence*. vol. 11, no. 7, pp. 674–693, 1989.
102. Mandelbrot, B.B., *The fractal geometry of Nature*, W H Freeman and Co., 1982.
103. Marpe, D., T. Wiegand & G.J. Sullivan, The H.264/MPEG-4 AVC standard and its applications, *IEEE Communications Magazine*, vol. 44, no. 10, pp. 134–143, 2005.
104. Marquis, O., B. Furht, *Content-based image and video retrieval*, Springer, 2012.
105. Marsh, D., *Applied geometry for computer graphics and CAD*, Springer, 2005.
106. Mathews, J.H., &C. D. Fink, *Numerical methods using MATLAB*, Prentice Hall, 2004.
107. Mehta, M., C. Gaie (eds.), *Recent advances in data and algorithms for e-Government*, Springer, 2023.
108. Mhiripiri, N.A., T. Chari, *Media law, ethics and policy in the digital age*, IGI Global, 2017.
109. Michael, W., *Color calibration techniques for true color measurement*, Lap Lambert Academic, 2015.
110. Milutinovic, V., *Infrastructure for electronic business on the Internet*, Springer, 2013.
111. Moreno, R., Optimising learning from animations by minimising cognitive load: Cognitive and affective consequences of signalling and segmentation methods, *Applied Cognitive Psychology*, vol. 21, no. 6, pp. 765–781, 2007.
112. Musburger, R.B., *Single-camera video production*, CRC Press, 2012.
113. Nunes, N., I. Oakley & V. Nisi (eds.), Interactive Storytelling, *10th International Conference on Interactive Digital Storytelling (ICIDS)*", Springer, 2017.
114. Nyquist, H., Certain topics in telegraph transmission theory, *Transactions of American Institute of Electrical Engineers (AIEE)*, vol. 47, no. 2, pp. 617–644, 1928.
115. O'Rourke, M., *Principles of three dimensional computer animation*, W. W. Norton & Company, 2003.
116. Olive, J., *Maths: A student's survival guide*, Cambridge University Press, 2003.
117. Olson H. F., *Acoustical engineering*, Van Nostrand, 1957.
118. Otsu, N., A threshold selection method from gray-level histograms, *IEEE Transactions on Systems, Man, and Cybernetics*, vol. 9, no. 1, pp. 62–66, 1979.
119. Phong, B.T., Illumination for computer generated pictures, *Communications of the. ACM*, vol. 18, no. 6, pp. 311–317, 1975.
120. Pirolli, B., *Travel journalism: Informing tourists in the digital age*, Routledge, 2018.
121. Pohlmann, K., *Principles of digital audio*, McGraw-Hill, 2010.
122. Poynton, C., A guided tour of color space, *Proceedings of the SMPTE Advanced Television and Electronic Imaging Conference*, pp. 167–180, 1995.
123. Poynton, C., *A technical introduction to digital video*, John Wiley & Sons Inc., p. 175, 1996.
124. Prettyman, S., *Learn PHP 7: object oriented modular programming using HTML5, CSS3, JavaScript, XML, JSON and MySQL*, Apress, 2016.
125. Puri, A. & Majumder, A., *Guide to video compression: From sgms to HEVC*, CRC Press, 2012.
126. Rajput, S.S., N.U. Khan, A.K. Singh & K.V. Arya (eds), *Digital image enhancement and reconstruction*, Elsevier Science, 2022.
127. Reed, C.S., *Copyright workflow for photographers*, Peachpit Press, 2015.
128. Richardson, W., Bayesian based iterative method of image restoration, *Journal of the Optical Society of America (JOSA)*, vol. 62, no. 1, pp. 55–59, 1972.
129. Robbins, J.N., *Learning Web design: a beginner's guide to HTML, CSS, JavScript and Web graphics*, O'Reilly Media, 2012.
130. Rossing, T., R. Moore & P. Wheeler, *Science of Sound*, Pearson, 2011.
131. Roth, S.D., Ray casting for modelling solids, *Computer Graphics and Image Processing*, Elsevier, vol. 18, no. 2, pp. 109–144, 1982.
132. Roussopoulos, N., S. Kelley & F.D.R. Vincent, Nearest neighbor queries, *Proceedings of 1995 ACMSIGMOD International Conference on Management of Data – SIGMOD '95*, p. 71, 1995.
133. Rovenski, V., *Modeling of Curves and Surfaces with MATLAB*. Springer, 2010.
134. Royds, A.B., K. Cagle & D Storey, *Using SVG with CSS3 and HTML5*, O'Reilly Media, 2018.

135. Rumsey, F., *Desktop audio technology: Digital audio and MIDI principles*, Routledge, 2003.
136. Salomon, D., *Data compression*, Third Edition. Springer, 2004.
137. Schutze, S., A. I. Schutze, *New realities in audio: a practical guide for VR, AR, MR and 360 video*, CRC Press, 2018.
138. Shannon, C.E., A mathematical theory of communication, *The Bell System Technical Journal*, vol. 27, pp. 379–423, 623–656, July, October, 1948.
139. Sharda, R., D. Delen & E. Turban, *Business intelligence and analytics: systems for decision support*, Pearson, 2018.
140. Shirley, P., R.K. Morley, *Realistic ray tracing*, A K Peters/CRC Press, 2/e, 2003.
141. Shirley, P., *Fundamentals of computer graphics*, AK Peters/CRC Press, 2002.
142. Sinha, P.K., *Image acquisition and preprocessing for machine vision systems*, SPIE, 2012.
143. Slater, J., *Modern television systems*, CRC Press, 1991.
144. Smith, J.O., *Introduction to digital filters: with audio applications*, Createspace Independent Publishers, 2006.
145. Solanki, A., S. Kumar, A. Nayyar, *Handbook of research on emerging trends and applications of machine learning*, IGI Global, 2019.
146. Somberg, G. (editor), *Game audio programming: principles and practices*, CRC Press, 2010.
147. Soydaner, D., *Attention mechanisms in neural networks: where it comes and where it goes*, 2022.
148. Steinkuehler, C., K. Squire, S. Barab, *Games, learning, and society: Learning and meaning in the digital age*, Cambridge University Press, 2012.
149. Steinmetz, R. & K. Nahrstedt, Multimedia computing: Prologue and overview, *Communications of the ACM*, vol. 38, no. 11, pp. 20–30, 1995.
150. Steinmetz, R. & K. Nahrstedt, *Multimedia fundamentals: Media coding and content processing*. Prentice Hall, 2004.
151. Strano, M., B.M. Colosimo, Logistic regression analysis for experimental determination of forming limit diagrams, *International Journal of Machine Tools and Manufacture*, vol. 46, no. 6, pp. 673–682, 2006.
152. Sundararajan, D., *Digital image processing: A signal processing and algorithmic approach*, Springer Nature Singapore, 2017.
153. Sutherland, Ivan E., *Sketchpad : A man-machine graphical communication system*, Technical Report UCAM-CL-TR-574, University of Cambridge, 1963 https://www.cl.cam.ac.uk/techreports/UCAM-CL-TR-574.html
154. Tan, M., R. Pang, Q. V. Le, EfficientDet: scalable and efficient object detection, *IEEE Conference on Computer Vision and Pattern Recognition (CVPR)*, pp. 10778–10787, 2020
155. Taskiran, M.N., F. Pinarbasi, *Multidisciplinary approaches to ethics in the digital era*, IGI Global, 2021.
156. Tatipamula, M., B. Khashnabish, *Multimedia communications networks: Technologies and services*, Artech Publishers, 1998.
157. Thomas, F., O. Johnston, The illusion of life: Disney animation, *Hyperion*, 1981, reprint 1997.
158. Toole F E, *Sound reproduction: The acoustics and psychoacoustics of loudspeakers and rooms*, Routledge, 2017.
159. Tyagi, A.K., A. Abraham & A. Kaklauskas (eds), *Intelligent interactive multimedia systems for e-healthcare applications*, Springer, 2021.
160. Valdez, G. *Multimedia in education: Designing complex systems for learning*, IGI Global, 2006.
161. Vatsky, S., *Interactive museum tours: a guide to in person and virtual experiences*, Rowman and Littlefield, 2023.
162. Vaughan, T. *Multimedia: making it work*, McGraw-Hill Education, 2014.
163. Viola, P., M.J. Jones, Rapid object detection using a boosted cascade of simple features, *Proceedings of the IEEE Computer Society Conference on Computer Vision and Pattern Recognition (CVPR)*, vol. 1, pp. 511–518, 2001.
164. Welch, T.A., A technique for high-performance data compression, *IEEE Computer*, vol. 17, no. 6, pp. 8–19, 1984.
165. Weynand, D., M. Weise, *How video works*, CRC Press, 2012.
166. White, B., *HTML and the art of authoring for the World Wide Web*, Springer, 2012.
167. Wiener, N., *Extrapolation interpolation and smoothing of stationary time series*, John Wiley & Sons Inc., 1949.
168. Wilkins, L., C. Painter, P. Patterson, *Media ethics: Issues and cases*, Rowman & Littlefield, 2021.
169. Wright, W.D., A re-determination of the trichromatic coefficients of the spectral colours, *Transactions of the Optical Society*, vol. 30, no. 4, pp. 141–164, 1929.
170. Xia, F., J. Liu, H. Nie, Y. Fu, L. Wan & X. Kong, *Random walks, a review of algorithms and applications*, 2020. https://arxiv.org/abs/2008.03639
171. Xia, F., J. Liu, H. Nie, Y. Fu, L. Wan & X. Kong, Random walks, a review of algorithms and applications, *IEEE Transactions on Emerging Topics in Computational Intelligence*, pp. 1–13, 2020.
172. Young, T, On the theory of light and colors, *Philosophical Transactions of the Royal Society of London*, vol. 92, pp. 12–48, 1802.
173. Zaramenskikh, E., A. Fedorova, *Digital transformation and new challenges*, Springer Nature Switzerland, 2020.
174. Zeman, N.B., *Essential skills for 3D modeling, rendering and animation*, CRC Press, 2015.
175. Zhang, S., Single shot refinement neural network for object detection, *Proceedings of the IEEE Conference on Computer Vision and Pattern Recognition (CVPR)*, pp. 4203–4212, 2018.
176. Zhou, Z., M. R. Siddiquee Md, N. Tajbakhsh, & J. Liang, *UNet++: A nested U-net architecture for medical image segmentation*, 2018. https://arxiv.org/abs/1807.10165
177. Zhou, Z., M.R. Siddiquee Md, N. Tajbakhsh & J. Liang, UNet++: S nested U-net architecture for medical image segmentation, *Lecture Notes in Computer Science*, vol. 11049, pp. 3–11, Springer Verlag, 2018.
178. Ziv, J., A. Lempel, A universal algorithm for sequential data compression, *IEEE Transactions on Information Theory*, vol. 23, no. 3, pp. 337–343, 1977.
179. Ziv, J., A. Lempel, "Compression of individual sequences via variable rate coding", *IEEE Transactions on Information Theory*, vol. 24, no. 5, pp. 530–536, 1978.

Index

www.ingramcontent.com/pod-product-compliance
Lightning Source LLC
LaVergne TN
LVHW080115011026
849160LV00013B/1114